A Companion to the Gilded Age and Progressive Era

WILEY BLACKWELL COMPANIONS TO AMERICAN HISTORY

This series provides essential and authoritative overviews of the scholarship that has shaped our present understanding of the American past. Edited by eminent historians, each volume tackles one of the major periods or themes of American history, with individual topics authored by key scholars who have spent considerable time in research on the questions and controversies that have sparked debate in their field of interest. The volumes are accessible for the non-specialist, while also engaging scholars seeking a reference to the historiography or future concerns.

PUBLISHED:

A Companion to the American Revolution
Edited by Jack P. Greene and J. R. Pole

A Companion to 19th-Century America
Edited by William L. Barney

A Companion to the American South
Edited by John B. Boles

A Companion to American Women's History
Edited by Nancy Hewitt

A Companion to American Indian History
Edited by Philip J. Deloria and Neal Salisbury

A Companion to Post-1945 America
Edited by Jean-Christophe Agnew and Roy Rosenzweig

A Companion to the Vietnam War
Edited by Marilyn Young and Robert Buzzanco

A Companion to Colonial America
Edited by Daniel Vickers

A Companion to American Foreign Relations
Edited by Robert Schulzinger

A Companion to 20th-Century America
Edited by Stephen J. Whitfield

A Companion to the American West
Edited by William Deverell

A Companion to the Civil War and Reconstruction
Edited by Lacy K. Ford

A Companion to American Technology
Edited by Carroll Pursell

A Companion to African-American History
Edited by Alton Hornsby

A Companion to American Immigration
Edited by Reed Ueda

A Companion to American Cultural History
Edited by Karen Halttunen

A Companion to California History
Edited by William Deverell and David Igler

A Companion to American Military History
Edited by James Bradford

A Companion to Los Angeles
Edited by William Deverell and Greg Hise

A Companion to American Environmental History
Edited by Douglas Cazaux Sackman

A Companion to Benjamin Franklin
Edited by David Waldstreicher

A Companion to World War Two (2 volumes)
Edited by Thomas W. Zeiler with Daniel M. DuBois

A Companion to American Legal History
Edited by Sally E. Hadden and Alfred L. Brophy

A Companion to the Gilded Age and Progressive Era
Edited by Christopher McKnight Nichols and Nancy C. Unger

A Companion to the Gilded Age and Progressive Era

Edited by

Christopher McKnight Nichols and Nancy C. Unger

WILEY Blackwell

This edition first published 2017
© 2017 John Wiley & Sons, Inc.

Registered Office
John Wiley & Sons Ltd, The Atrium, Southern Gate, Chichester, West Sussex, PO19 8SQ, UK

Editorial Offices
350 Main Street, Malden, MA 02148-5020, USA
9600 Garsington Road, Oxford, OX4 2DQ, UK
The Atrium, Southern Gate, Chichester, West Sussex, PO19 8SQ, UK

For details of our global editorial offices, for customer services, and for information about how to apply for permission to reuse the copyright material in this book please see our website at www.wiley.com/wiley-blackwell.

The right of Christopher McKnight Nichols and Nancy C. Unger to be identified as the authors of the editorial material in this work has been asserted in accordance with the UK Copyright, Designs and Patents Act 1988.

All rights reserved. No part of this publication may be reproduced, stored in a retrieval system, or transmitted, in any form or by any means, electronic, mechanical, photocopying, recording or otherwise, except as permitted by the UK Copyright, Designs and Patents Act 1988, without the prior permission of the publisher.

Wiley also publishes its books in a variety of electronic formats. Some content that appears in print may not be available in electronic books.

Designations used by companies to distinguish their products are often claimed as trademarks. All brand names and product names used in this book are trade names, service marks, trademarks or registered trademarks of their respective owners. The publisher is not associated with any product or vendor mentioned in this book.

Limit of Liability/Disclaimer of Warranty: While the publisher and authors have used their best efforts in preparing this book, they make no representations or warranties with respect to the accuracy or completeness of the contents of this book and specifically disclaim any implied warranties of merchantability or fitness for a particular purpose. It is sold on the understanding that the publisher is not engaged in rendering professional services and neither the publisher nor the author shall be liable for damages arising herefrom. If professional advice or other expert assistance is required, the services of a competent professional should be sought.

Library of Congress Cataloging-in-Publication data applied for

ISBN: 9781118913963 (hardback)
ISBN: 9781119775706 (paperback)

A catalogue record for this book is available from the British Library.

Cover image: From Library of Congress https://www.loc.gov/item/2004666561/

Set in 9.5/12pt Galliard by SPi Global, Pondicherry, India

SKY10034488_051922

Contents

Notes on Contributors

Omar H. Ali is Professor of Comparative African Diaspora History and Dean of Lloyd International Honors College at The University of North Carolina at Greensboro. A graduate of the London School of Economics and Political Science, he received his Ph.D. in History from Columbia University and is the author of *In the Balance of Power: Independent Black Politics and Third Party Movements in the United States and In the Lion's Mouth: Black Populism in the New South, 1886–1900.*

Lloyd E. Ambrosius is Emeritus Professor of History and Samuel Clark Waugh Distinguished Professor of International Relations at the University of Nebraska-Lincoln. He is the author of *Woodrow Wilson and the American Diplomatic Tradition* (1987), *Wilsonian Statecraft* (1990), *Wilsonianism* (2002), and *Woodrow Wilson and American Internationalism* (2017). He is past-president of the Society for Historians of the Gilded Age and Progressive Era.

James M. Beeby is dean of the College of Liberals Arts and professor of history at the University of Southern Indiana. He was previously professor of history and chair at Middle Tennessee State University from 2012–2016, and before that he taught at Indiana University Southeast and West Virginia Wesleyan College. He is the author of *Revolt of the Tar Heels: The North Carolina Populist Movement, 1890–1901* (2008) and *Populism in the South Revisited* (2012). Beeby has published several articles and essays on grassroots politics, populism, and race relations in the Gilded Age.

Matthew Bowman is the Howard W. Hunter Chair of Mormon Studies and associate professor of religion and history at Claremont Graduate University, and the author most recently of *Christian: the Politics of a Word in America* (Harvard University Press, 2018).

Kathleen Dalton is a specialist in US history, though she has also taught Chinese and transnational history, gender studies, and world history. She has written articles about Theodore Roosevelt and the Progressive Era, and in 2002 published *Theodore Roosevelt: A Strenuous Life*. As a public historian, she has consulted with the National Park Service and the Theodore Roosevelt Digital Library. After teaching at Philips Academy, Andover and Boston University, she is working on a book about Eleanor and Franklin Roosevelt and their World War I Era Dinner Club. She is especially grateful to E. Anthony Rotundo and Nancy Unger for reading and commenting on this essay.

Justus D. Doenecke is Emeritus Professor of History at New College of Florida. He has written extensively on the Gilded Age; American entry into World War I; the foreign policies of Herbert Hoover, Franklin D. Roosevelt, and Harry S Truman; and isolationism and pacifism from World War I through the early Cold War. Among his books is *The Presidencies of James A. Garfield and Chester A. Arthur* (1981). He is grateful to Irwin Gellman, John Belohlavek, and Alan Peskin for their reading of this essay.

Bruce J. Evensen is the Director of the Journalism Program at DePaul University in Chicago. For a decade he was a reporter and bureau chief in the American Midwest, in Washington, DC and in Jerusalem. He's written and edited several books on journalism history, including *Truman, Palestine, and the Press: Shaping Conventional Wisdom at the Beginning of the Cold War* (1992); *When Dempsey Fought Tunney: Heroes, Hokum and Storytelling in the Jazz Age* (1996); *God's Man for the Gilded Age: D. L. Moody and the Rise of Modern Mass Evangelism* (2003); *The Responsible Reporter: Journalism in the Information Age* (2008); and *The Encyclopedia of American Journalism History* (2007).

Maureen A. Flanagan is Professor of History in the department of humanities at Illinois Institute of Technology. She previously taught at Michigan State University. Flanagan is the author of several books and essays on the Gilded Age and Progressive Era, including *America Reformed: Progressives and Progressivisms, 1890s–1920s* and *Seeing with Their Hearts: Chicago Women and the Vision of the Good City, 1871–1933.* She is working on a manuscript on gender and the built environment of Chicago, Toronto, Dublin, and London from the 1870s to the 1940s.

Julie Greene is Professor of History at the University of Maryland at College Park and the author of several works on transnational labor, empire, and migration, including *The Canal Builders: Making America's Empire at the Panama Canal* (2009). Her most recent article is "Rethinking the Boundaries of Class: Labor History and Theories of Class and Capitalism," *Labor: Studies in Working-Class History* 18 (2), May 2021, 92–112. With Eileen Boris, Heidi Gottfried, and Joo Cheong Tham, Greene is co-editor of the forthcoming *Global Labor Migration: New Directions* (Illinois, 2022). She is completing a book entitled *Box 25: Archival Secrets and the Migratory World of the Panama Canal.*

Cristina Viviana Groeger is an Assistant Professor of History at Lake Forest College. Her research explores the history of work, labor markets, and education in the modern United States. Her first book, *The Education Trap: Schools and the Remaking of Inequality in Boston* (Harvard University Press, 2021) was awarded the Thomas J. Wilson Memorial Prize by Harvard University Press for best first book. Her research has been funded by the National Academy of Education / Spencer Foundation, and published in the *History of Education Quarterly, The Journal of Urban History*, and *The Journal of the Gilded Age and Progressive Era.*

Julia Guarneri is Associate Professor of American history at the University of Cambridge. Her book *Newsprint Metropolis: City Papers and the Making of Modern Americans* (University of Chicago Press, 2017) was awarded several prizes, including the Eugenia Palmegiano Prize from the American Historical Association. She continues to write on the history of media, while her new research focuses on twentieth-century consumer culture.

Kimberly A. Hamlin is the James and Beth Lewis Professor of History at Miami University and the author of two books: *Free Thinker: Sex, Suffrage, and the Extraordinary Life of Helen Hamilton Gardener* (2020) and *Free Thinker: Darwin, Science, and Women's Rights in Gilded Age America* (2014).

David C. Hammack is Haydn Professor of History Emeritus at Case Western Reserve University. His books include *Power and Society: Greater New York at the Turn of the Century* (1982), *Making the Nonprofit Sector in the United States: A Reader* (1998), with Helmut Anheier, *A Versatile American Institution: The Changing Ideals and Realities of Philanthropic Foundations* (2013), and with Steven R. Smith, *American Philanthropic Foundations: Regional Difference and Change* (2018). Hammack holds degrees from Harvard and Columbia universities and Reed College, has been a Guggenheim Fellow and a Visiting scholar at Yale and the Russell Sage Foundation. He received both the Distinguished Achievement and Leadership Award of the Association for Research on Nonprofit Organizations and Voluntary Action, and Case Western Reserve University's John S. Diekhoff Award for Distinguished Graduate Teaching.

Alexandra (Sasha) Harmon is professor emerita of American Indian Studies and History at the University of Washington in Seattle. She is the author of *Indians in the Making: Ethnic Relations and Indian Identities around Puget Sound* (1998); *Rich Indians: Native People and the Problem of Wealth in American History* (2010), and *Reclaiming the Reservation: Histories of Indian Sovereignty Suppressed and Renewed* (2019). She edited *The Power of Promises: Rethinking Indian Treaties in the Pacific Northwest* (2008).

David Huyssen is a Senior Lecturer in American History at the University of York (UK) and Visiting Scholar (2019–2022) at the J.F.K. Institute for North American Studies at the Freie Universität in Berlin. He specializes in the history of U.S. political economy and urban life, and is the author of *Progressive Inequality: Rich and Poor in New York, 1890–1920* (Harvard, 2014).

Brian M. Ingrassia is Assistant Professor of History at West Texas A&M University. He formerly taught at Middle Tennessee State University and Georgia State University. The author of *The Rise of Gridiron University: Higher Education's Uneasy Alliance with Big-Time Football* (2012), Ingrassia has published in *The Journal of the Gilded Age and Progressive Era.* He is currently writing a book on automobile racing, urban culture, and the good roads movement in the early 1900s.

Raised in the Midwest, **Thomas J. Jablonsky** returned to the region in 1995 as a member of Marquette University's History Department after several decades on the faculty at the University of Southern California. He is the Harry G. John Professor Emeritus of Urban Studies at MU. His scholarship has included books on Chicago and Milwaukee as well as on America's female anti-suffragists. His recent research focuses upon the biographies of nineteenth century mayors of Los Angeles.

Benjamin Johnson is Associate Professor of History at Loyola University Chicago. He is author of *Revolution in Texas: How a Forgotten Rebellion and Its Bloody Suppression Turned Mexicans into Americans* (2003), *Bordertown: The Odyssey of an American Place* (2008), a collaboration with photographer Jeffrey Gusky, and *Escaping the Dark, Gray City: Fear and Hope in Progressive Era Conservation* (2017).

He also serves as co-editor of the *Journal of the Gilded Age and Progressive Era*.

Robert D. Johnston is Professor of History and Director of the Teaching of History program at the University of Illinois at Chicago. He serves as co-editor of the *Journal of the Gilded Age and Progressive Era*. His book *The Radical Middle Class: Populist Democracy and the Question of Capitalism in Progressive Era Portland, Oregon* (2003) won the President's Book Award of the Social Science History Association. A multiple-award-winning teacher, Johnston works extensively with K-12 teachers in professional development programs.

Michael B. Kahan is the co-director of the Program on Urban Studies at Stanford University, and a Senior Lecturer in Sociology. His interest in the historical transformation of public space has led to publications on topics ranging from the integration of streetcars in the 1850s, to sanitation reform in the 1890s, to the geography of prostitution in the 1910s, to redevelopment in California in the 1990s. He holds a B.A. from Yale and a Ph.D. from the University of Pennsylvania.

Michael Kazin is a professor of history at Georgetown University and emeritus editor of *Dissent* magazine. He is the author of seven books, the latest of which is *What It Took to Win: A History of the Democratic Party*. His books on the Gilded Age and Progressive Era include *Barons of Labor: The San Francisco Building Trades* and *Union Power in the Progressive Era, A Godly Hero: The Life of William Jennings Bryan* and *War Against War: The American Fight for Peace,1914–1918*. He is at work on a biography of Samuel Gompers.

Alan Lessoff, University Professor of History, was editor of the *Journal of the Gilded Age and Progressive Era* from 2004 to 2014. Recent books *include Where Texas Meets the Sea: Corpus Christi and Its History* (2015) and *Fractured Modernity: America Confronts Modern Times, 1880s to 1940s*, edited with Thomas Welskopp (2012).

Allan E. S. Lumba is assistant professor of history at Virginia Tech. He is the author of *Monetary Authorities: Capitalism and Decolonization in the American Colonial Philippines* (2022). He writes on the entanglements of racial capitalism and colonialisms across the Pacific and Southeast Asia.

Christopher McKnight Nichols is Wayne Woodrow Hayes Chair in National Security Studies, Mershon Center for International Security Studies, and Professor of History, at The Ohio State University. Nichols previously was a professor at Oregon State University. An Andrew Carnegie Fellow and award-winning scholar and teacher, Nichols is the author or editor of six books, most notably *Promise and Peril: America at the Dawn of a Global Age* (2011, 2015) and *Rethinking American Grand Strategy* (2021). His next book is *Ideology in US Foreign Relations: New Histories* (2022).

Alan I Marcus is William L. Giles Distinguished Professor and Head, Department of History, Mississippi State University. He is the author or editor of some 22 books and journals and 35 essays covering a wide range of issues and periods. His *Malignant Growth: Creating the Modern Cancer Research Establishment, 1875–1915* (2018) and *Land of Milk and Money: Creation of the Southern Dairy Industry* (2021) are his most recent efforts. He is now turning to an agricultural scientist-centered history of agricultural science in America.

Noam Maggor is a Senior Lecturer in American History at Queen Mary University of London. He is the author of *Brahmin Capitalism: Frontiers of Wealth and Populism in America's First Gilded Age, published by* Harvard University Press in 2017 and "To Coddle and Caress These Great Capitalists: Eastern Money, Frontier Populism, and the Politics of Market-Making in the American West," published in the *American Historical Review*. Noam is currently at work on a project entitled *The United States as a Developing Nation: The Political Origins of the Second Great Divergence*.

Sidney M. Milkis is the White Burkett Miller Professor of the Department of Politics and Faculty Associate in the Miller Center at the University of Virginia. His books include: *The President and the Parties: The Transformation of the American Party System Since the New Deal* (1993); *Political Parties and Constitutional Government: Remaking American Democracy* (1999); *Presidential Greatness* (2000), coauthored with Marc Landy; *The American Presidency: Origins and Development, 1776–2014* (2015), 7th edition, coauthored with Michael Nelson; *Theodore Roosevelt, the Progressive Party, and the Transformation of American Democracy* (2009); and *The Politics of Major Policy Reform Since the Second World War*, co-edited with Jeffery Jenkins (2014). He is working on a project that examines the relationship between presidents and social movements.

Karen Pastorello is Emeritus Professor of History and Women and Gender Studies at Tompkins Cortland Community College (SUNY). She is the co-author with Susan Goodier of *Women Will Vote: Winning Suffrage in New York State* (2017). Her other works include *The Progressives: Activism and Reform in American Society, 1893–1917* (2014) and *A Power Among Them: Bessie Abramowitz Hillman and the Making of the Amalgamated Clothing Workers of America* (2008). She is working on a biography of Mary Elizabeth Pidgeon, suffragist and research director for the United States Department of Labor, Women's Bureau.

Heather Cox Richardson is Professor of History at Boston College. She is the author of a number of books about American politics and economics. Her work explores the Civil War, Reconstruction, the Gilded Age, and the American West, and stretches from the presidency of Abraham Lincoln to the present. In addition to her scholarly work, Richardson writes widely for popular audiences.

Logan Sawyer is the J. Alton Hosch Professor of Law at the University of Georgia and Director of Undergraduate Studies. His scholarship examines the connections between law and political institutions in the 19th and 20th centuries. He earned his JD and PhD in American History from the University of Virginia.

David G. Schuster is Associate Professor of History at Purdue University Fort Wayne, and has taught previously at the University of California, Santa Barbara, and Bahçeşehir University in Istanbul. His interests include the history of American health and culture and the development of a modern healthcare system. His is the author of *Neurasthenic Nation: America's Search for Health, Happiness, and Comfort, 1869–1920* (2011).

Anthony Sparacino is a graduate student at the University of Virginia in American Politics. He received his M. A. from the CUNY Graduate Center. His research focuses broadly on issues relating to American political development and American political thought. Of particular interest are the interplay of political parties and the state, the role of elections in political change, as well as the development of the modern conservative movement and conservative political thought.

Mark Wahlgren Summers is Professor of History at the University of Kentucky in Lexington. He has written ten books, including *Rum, Romanism, and Rebellion* (2000), *Party Games* (2004), *A Dangerous Stir* (2009), and *Ordeal of the Reunion* (2014), all published by the University of North Carolina Press. He is writing a biography of "Big Tim" Sullivan, a New York City boss. He teaches anything that he can get away with.

Ian Tyrrell is Emeritus Professor of History at the University of New South Wales, Sydney, Australia and was Harold Vyvyan Harmsworth Professor of American History at Oxford University in 2010–11. He is the author of *Reforming the World: The Creation of America's Moral Empire* (2010), and *Crisis of the Wasteful Nation: Empire and Conservation in Theodore Roosevelt's America* (2015), among other works.

Nancy C. Unger, President of the Society for Historians of the Gilded Age and Progressive Era 2021–2023, is Professor of History at Santa Clara University. She is the author of the prize-winning biographies *Fighting Bob La Follette: The Righteous Reformer* (2000; revised paperback 2008), and *Belle La Follette: Progressive Era Reformer* (2016). Her book *Beyond Nature's Housekeepers: American Women in Environmental History* (2012), was a California Book Award Finalist. She has published dozens of scholarly essays and articles, and served for eight years as book review editor for the *Journal of the Gilded Age and Progressive Era*. Her multi-media appearances include CNN.com, C-SPAN, NPR, TIME.com, and PBS. She is working on a book on the Diggs and Caminetti cases of 1913, which will examine progressive era efforts to employ the Mann Act to regulate American morals.

Katherine Unterman is Associate Professor of History at Texas A&M University. She is the author of *Uncle Sam's Policemen: The Pursuit of Fugitives across Borders* (2015) and numerous articles and essays about legal history and American foreign relations. Her next book project, which examines the long-term impact of the Insular Cases, has received support from the American Council of Learned Societies and the National Endowment for the Humanities.

Leigh Ann Wheeler is Professor of History at Binghamton University, former co-editor of the *Journal of Women's History*, and senior editor for the Oxford Research Encyclopedia on American History. Her books, *Against Obscenity: Reform and the Politics of Womanhood in America, 1873–1935* (2004) and *How Sex Became a Civil Liberty* (2013) examine how individuals and movements shaped sexual culture in the modern United States. Her next project examines twentieth-century episodes in the sexualization of women's bodies.

Amy Louise Wood is Professor of History at Illinois State University. She is the author of *Lynching and Spectacle: Witnessing Racial Violence in America, 1890–1940* (2009), which won the Lillian Smith Book Award and was a finalist for the *Los Angeles Times* Book Prize in History. Her current book project is entitled, "Sympathy for the Devil: The Criminal in the American Imagination, 1870–1940."

Introduction

Gilded Excesses, Multiple Progressivisms

Christopher McKnight Nichols and Nancy C. Unger

"In America nearly every man has his dream, his pet scheme, whereby he is to advance himself socially or pecuniarily. It is this all-pervading speculativeness which we have tried to illustrate in 'The Gilded Age'," wrote Mark Twain in the preface to the London Edition of the book which helped to establish the era's label (Twain and Warner 1873: 451–452). Twain emphasized the individualism, excess, and "shameful corruption" that had infected "every State and every Territory in the Union." He also held out "faith in a noble future for my country." Taken together, Twain's comments suggest some of the period's worst problems and injustices as well as the characteristic optimism that marked the myriad reforms that developed to address those issues.

By the end of World War I, which concluded the era often referred to by historians as the Gilded Age and Progressive Era (GAPE), the United States was thoroughly transformed domestically and with respect to its global status. A nation that just forty years before had been primarily rural and inward-looking, still recovering from a devastating civil war, emerged as an urban, industrial giant so convinced of its power and righteousness that it entered the Great War to, in the words of President Woodrow Wilson, "make the world safe for democracy." In the 1870s, roughly when the GAPE began, most Americans lived as farmers. By its end, most Americans lived in cities, where they worked for wages, purchased rather than raised their food, and depended on civic entities to ensure proper sanitation and a variety of services. This volume chronicles these and related changes and reveals the scholarly debates concerning both the nature of the transformations and their ongoing significance.

Perhaps no period in American history is as fraught with controversy and potential for misunderstanding as "The Gilded Age and Progressive Era." Even its title is confusing. Historians debate whether the Gilded Age and the Progressive Era should be studied as one long period, or two separate ones, with the Gilded Age (1870s–*c.* 1900) followed by the Progressive Era (*c.* 1900–1917), and the latter understood as a sort of antidote to the excesses of the former. This volume begins with a chapter by Heather Cox Richardson in which she explores the importance and substance of the controversy over periodization before presenting an original and intriguing alternative approach to identifying the era.

Generally speaking, however, this *Companion*, like most recent scholarship, approaches the GAPE as one long period. It examines "Gilded Age" excesses, such as political corruption, challenged by authors in this volume (including Justus Doenecke and Mark Wahlgren Summers), the rise of overcrowded slums (explored by Michael Kahan), and the exploitation of both workers (examined by David Huyssen) and the environment (addressed by Benjamin Johnson). Such extremes were constantly evolving, in part due to interactions with "Progressive Era" initiatives and intended solutions, such as election reform, health and safety regulations, and the conservation of natural resources (discussed particularly in chapters by Karen Pastorello, Sidney Milkis and Anthony Sparacino, and Kathleen Dalton).

The period spanned by the GAPE is one of the most fascinating, important, and instructive eras in American history. The nascent urban, industrial United States of Theodore Roosevelt and Woodrow Wilson serves as an historical and conceptual bridge between the rural, agrarian America of George Washington and Thomas Jefferson and the current global and technological America of Barack Obama and Hillary Clinton. Progressive giant Robert La Follette claimed that, in this period, "The supreme issue, involving all the others, is the encroachment of the powerful few upon the rights of the many" (La Follette 1913, 760). The progressives were the first ones in US history to tackle the then brand-new problems of the consolidation of power

A Companion to the Gilded Age and Progressive Era, First Edition. Edited by Christopher McKnight Nichols and Nancy C. Unger.
© 2017 John Wiley & Sons, Inc. Published 2017 by John Wiley & Sons, Inc.

and encroachments of an influential elite within an urban, industrial society—but they were far from the last. Much can be learned from their ideas, accomplishments, and failures, as well as those of their opponents.

The cutting-edge scholarly work that makes up this *Companion* was designed to establish the state of the field. These chapters strive to distill, consolidate, and make sense of past, present, and future directions and interpretive approaches to the Gilded Age and Progressive Era. This volume brings together scholars of law, race, religion, women's, gender, and sexuality studies; historians of capitalism, politics, ideas, culture, and urban life; US and world specialists, and many others to provide what is intended to be one of the most complete and up-to-date scholarly analyses of the era. The chapters both synthesize past work and also draw on pathbreaking recent and contemporary insights to provide considerable new depth, analytically and historiographically, and to shed new scholarly light on this vital period.

Given the current attention to the present era as a "new Gilded Age," it now seems all the more necessary to bring together some of the best scholars in the field to take stock of the burgeoning scholarly literature on the GAPE. This *Companion* is designed to appeal to scholars as well as to undergraduate and graduate students in history by incorporating a wide variety of disciplinary assessments of this period. It seeks to address the questions about the deeper meaning and legacy of this era that abound. For example, just how "gilded" was the Gilded Age component of the GAPE?

In *New Spirits: Americans in the "Gilded Age," 1865–1905* (2006), in attending to this and related questions, Rebecca Edwards rejects oversimplifications of the era. She argues for characterizing the period as one of many contradictions. Several notable chapters in this volume embrace that complexity in groundbreaking ways, including Julie Greene's explication of immigration and migration, Christina Groeger's analysis of conservatism and radicalism in the era, Mathew Bowman's exploration of patterns in religious and philosophical thought, and Alexandra Harmon's exploration of Indians in the period. The "who, what, where, and when" of the reform aspects of the GAPE, however, may be even harder to identify. Few scholars, however, have gone as far as Peter Filene, who in 1970 wrote "An Obituary for the Progressive Movement," in which he claimed that there was no unifying movement or even theme to the various attempts to bring order to this nearly chaotic society.

Most scholars agree that there was a progressive movement, but this consensus splits over the question of just how "progressive" it was. Progressivism is viewed by some as primarily a white urban middle-class operation designed as a kind of protection against being squeezed out of power by an ever-growing, increasingly diverse working class on the one hand and the expanding power of big business on the other. Others claim the main source of the movement to have been the workers themselves, while still others credit it to business leaders who were seeking to stabilize volatile conditions through regulation. Progressives have alternately been called altruistic reformers bent on improving the quality of American life (especially for the less advantaged, or so-called "unprotected") and selfish condescending meddlers aiming more for social control than social reform.

In a pioneering 1982 essay "In Search of Progressivism," Daniel Rodgers rejected simple definitions of progressivism, calling for a more plural understanding of progressive ideas set into action. Instead of wading in to find the "essence" of progressivism or to debate how progressive its efforts were, Rodgers emphasized multiple, sometimes overlapping "social languages" of progressivism. These "clusters of ideas," he argued, revolved around three core groupings: "social efficiency," the "rhetoric of antimonopolism," and an "emphasis on social bonds" (Rodgers 1982, 123). This model suggested the "active, dynamic aspect of [progressive] ideas" with shared senses of social ills and potential solutions, and yet progressivism "as an ideology is nowhere to be found." Many authors in this volume, including Robert Johnston in his chapter assessing patterns of historical interpretation, and most historians, follow elements of this analysis and no longer seek to depict the era in terms of a unitary framework of ideology or politics.

It is the plurality of perspectives and connections within the nation, and beyond it, that scholars now emphasize. The wide range of frequently competing progressive claims (national and international) have tended to be depicted by historians as a cacophony with at least one main focus: being aligned against the social language of the market. Yet this understanding, too, is in the process of revision by historians. Brian Balogh recently observed that consideration should be given to how such appeals and programs adapted to (rather than rejected) the powerful language of market choice in terms of extending the reach of the government into the lives of millions of Americans. At the heart of these developments related to new market conditions was a sprawling debate over the meaning and practices of democracy (Balogh 2015, 62–64, 237).

This *Companion* builds on such recent insights to delve into the meanings and impacts of the period, an era that seems to mirror—and illuminate—the present and suggests possibilities for the future. For example, was this *the* formative age for the history of capitalism? In what respects were the hugely successful businessmen of the GAPE (John D. Rockefeller, J.P. Morgan, and Andrew Carnegie) robber barons or industrial statesmen? How might their legacy shape questions today concerning vastly wealthy entrepreneurs like Bill Gates, Mark Zuckerberg, Warren Buffett, Larry Ellison, and Charles and David Koch? These and other pressing issues are topics adeptly addressed in the volume by Michael Kazin, David Hammack, and Noam Maggor.

Debates about the dynamics of race, gender, labor, and inequality also emerged in this era, preoccupying scholars, with clear contemporary relevance. For instance, questions about the progressive reformers at the turn of the last century also have application in the twenty-first. What are the stakes of the often binary critiques of the original (usually white) progressives as being either fairly or unfairly pilloried for their dismal record on racial justice? How should the limits of their reform sensibilities be understood?

Scholars increasingly recognize the individuals and groups who were able to remove some of the worst excesses plaguing American politics and society. Yet historians also emphasize the near-omnipresence of racism and sexism as well as an embrace of eugenics; many historians mount persuasive critiques of progressives as generally not going further to protect the rights of the many from the powerful few, or of deploying rhetoric that did not match up to their own lived reality. Others focus on the agency of various oppressed minorities and of women who applied progressive ideals to remedy their unequal status. This, after all, was the era in which the nation grappled with how to establish and protect racial equality after the Civil War, which descended into a regime of formal legal racial segregation that was profoundly resisted by people of color. It also was the period in which, after a multigenerational battle, woman suffrage finally became a reality. In view of the era's dramatic, sometimes contradictory changes at home and abroad, was this a period guided more by confidence in American exceptionalism, or by an appreciation of increasing globalization and exchange? In what ways did the era mark a period of integration, and in what ways is it best characterized as an age of fragmentation?

The thirty-four chapters in this *Companion* are organized into eight parts. The first, "Definitions, Precursors, and Geographies," begins with a provocative analysis of the challenge of defining the GAPE, followed by an examination of the precursors to GAPE reforms. The remaining four chapters in Part I reveal the importance of place in the era. These chapters present an unusual and dynamic mixture of geographies, integrating the West and the Midwest alongside urban America and attending to environmental issues. Although many early studies of the period focused almost exclusively on urban centers, particularly in the Northeast, more recent literature reveals the pervasive national and even international reach of the period's greatest changes and challenges.

Part II, "Sex, Race, and Gender," deepens the complexity of the GAPE by examining factors including race, ethnicity, and immigration as well as gender and sexuality. In an economy dependent upon unskilled labor in the factories as well as the fields, old-stock white Americans struggled to balance their ethnocentrism and racism with the desire for cheap labor. Recent immigrants, like the long-established populations of Indians and African Americans, sought, with varying degrees of success, to achieve acceptance, citizenship, and equality. Issues of gender as well as sexuality further complicated what it meant to be an American in a time of both rapid social change and stubborn traditionalism.

"Art, Thought, and Culture" form the subjects for the third part of the book. These chapters uncover the breadth and depth of the nation's transformation as reflected in its art and architecture, religion and philosophy, journalism, and popular culture. Overall the chapters in Part III argue for broad understanding of the profound intellectual and cultural changes sweeping the nation, as well as the impact of journalism and innovations in popular culture that changed the way Americans thought, received information, and spent their free time and discretionary income.

In the fourth part, "Economics, Science, and Technology," contributors examine the ways in which business and capitalism combined with science, technology, and medicine to turn the previously rural, agrarian America into an urban industrial nation. Investigations into resultant issues of labor and class as well as philanthropy demonstrate the challenges faced by the industrial labor force as well as the various private and public efforts to remedy extreme GAPE disparities in wealth.

"Political Leadership," the subject of Part V, focuses on GAPE political leaders, including the period's less celebrated presidents examined in a chapter that adds particular depth to the members of this group who have conventionally been dismissed as do-nothings. Chapters in this part are also devoted to the period's two most iconic chief executives, Theodore Roosevelt and Woodrow Wilson, and trace the cycles of critical response to their administrations. An additional chapter evaluates a variety of other leaders at the local, state, and national level, many of whom acquired power and wielded influence in non-traditional ways.

The sixth part of the book explores "Government, Politics, and the Law," with fresh interpretations of the political transformations of the era. It begins with a chapter on the pivotal national elections of the period—1876, 1896, 1912, and (to a lesser extent) 1920— and another on people and events in Congress. Together these chapters reveal how both major and seemingly minor political episodes combined to culminate in a new form of executive-centered partisanship, which continues to shape political parties and campaigns in the United States. As one of the chapters illuminates, the judiciary's understanding of liberty in the GAPE was shaped by free labor and equal-rights ideologies, extended and complicated by new questions about race, gender, religion, citizenship, and institutional developments, with important implications for the development of modern liberalism and conservatism. A final chapter caps Part VI by establishing that GAPE "radicalism" and "conservatism" must be understood in relation to each other. This chapter traces the foremost political and social movements that defined the outer limits of political possibility between Reconstruction and the 1920s.

In Part VII, three chapters open up new vistas onto the burgeoning and complicated landscape of the "US and the World." A cutting-edge historical approach to developing networks, connections, and exchanges helps to reveal the depth to which the US was embedded in what many in the era perceived as an integrated, transnational "global civilization." In turn, increasing international engagement propelled the US toward expansion, empire, and war, with unforeseen consequences. The United States assumed greater international police power (particularly within the Western hemisphere), became a force in international law, and eventually joined in World War I. This section follows the latest scholarly insights to characterize the GAPE as an age of globalization and greater interconnectedness, leading to new transnational social movements and dramatic changes in US foreign relations.

The final part of the book—on influences and relevance—comprises three succinct, discerning chapters exploring some of the most influential works of the era (novels, nonfiction, journalism, and more), some of the most influential historical works and interpretations about the era (historiography), and demonstrates the period's contemporary relevance.

The social, economic, political, intellectual, racial, religious, and diplomatic transformations from the end of the Civil War through World War I—the Gilded Age and Progressive Era—served to make America modern. These changes, in turn, shaped subsequent attempts to grapple with some of the most pressing issues related to equality and pluralism in a diverse, ever-changing, stratified, newly industrial society.

Much has happened that highlights the ongoing resonance of the Gilded Age and Progressive Era (GAPE) since this book's original publication. Following the election of Donald Trump, scandals and corruption at the highest levels of government and business increased, along with rising economic inequality. Many pundits declared a "new Gilded Age," a concept introduced early in the second decade of this century and evaluated in the book's final chapter by Michael Kazin.

The killing of George Floyd, a man of color, by a white police officer on May 25, 2020, starkly revealed one of the greatest failures of the GAPE and American society more broadly. Instead of incorporating racial justice more fully into progressive reform agendas, the GAPE is marked by the institutionalization and legalization of racism, dramatically revealed by the landmark *Plessy v. Ferguson* decision (1896) in which the U.S. Supreme Court upheld the constitutionality of racial segregation under the "separate but equal" doctrine. In the ensuing decades, despite valiant efforts by civil rights activists, Congress failed to pass anti-lynching legislation nearly 200 times, and the filibuster was increasingly used in the U.S. Senate as a means of blocking civil rights laws.

The rise of the Black Lives Matter movement also provides echoes of the GAPE. As Omar Ali points out in his chapter on African Americans, resistance to the nation's racism took a variety of important and innovative forms. He concludes his essay asking: "Does employing the concept of race help or hinder our understanding of people and their societies in the past?" Ongoing racial violence and the responses to it help to answer that question as they reveal the powerful legacies of race, racism, and assumptions about whiteness formalized in the GAPE.

The COVID-19 pandemic has eerily mirrored the 1918-19 influenza pandemic that killed an estimated 675,000 Americans, ravaging the U.S. and the world. Then, as now, pandemic crisis highlights fissures and fractures in society—regarding race and inequality, but also trust in government and experts, political polarization, and the willingness of leaders to make difficult decisions. The emerging conception of "community health," examined by David Schuster, was essential to pandemic responses, including "by-passing new regulatory legislation." Similar strategies were employed in 1918 and 2020, involving familiar non-pharmaceutical interventions such as closures, gathering limits, social distancing, quarantines, masking and hand hygiene. Unlike in the Progressive Era, pushback on interventions has become intensely politicized; as a partial result, the U.S. has suffered a staggering number of deaths (over 900,000 reported COVID deaths at the time of publication). The present population is far larger, but also enjoys a far better public health infrastructure as well as the benefits of modern medical knowledge. In 1918-19 people were eager for treatments and vaccines, but science and medicine came up with none; in 2020-21 vaccine skepticism, mis-information, disinformation, and unequal access, particularly worldwide, have stymied governments and societies. All of which hearkens back to one of the most compelling questions of the GAPE: how best to reform to build a better future? As Maureen Flanagan concludes, it is imperative that we continue to develop "new ideas about the nature of a good democratic society and the role that all individuals need to play in its construction."

References

Balogh, Brian. 2015. *The Associational State: American Governance in the Twentieth Century*. Philadelphia: University of Pennsylvania Press.

Edwards, Rebecca. 2006. *New Spirits: Americans in the "Gilded Age," 1865–1905*. New York: Oxford University Press.

Filene, Peter G. 1970. "An Obituary for the Progressive Movement." *American Quarterly* 22, 1: 20–34.

La Follette, Belle Case. 1913. "Segregation in the Civil Service." *La Follette's Magazine* 5, 50: 6.

Rodgers, Daniel T. 1982. "In Search of Progressivism." *Reviews in American History* 10: 113–132.

Twain, Mark (Samuel Clemens) and Charles Dudley Warner. 1873b. *The Gilded Age: A Novel*. Hartford: American Publishing Co.

Part I

Overview-Definitions, Precursors, and Geographies

Chapter One

Reconstructing the Gilded Age and Progressive Era

Heather Cox Richardson

No one today is quite sure what time period the Gilded Age and Progressive Era covers. It sprawls somewhere in the late nineteenth and early twentieth centuries, but few historians can agree on where its edges lie. Some argue for a period that begins in 1865 with the end of the Civil War, or in 1873, with economic overproduction, or in 1877, with the alleged death of Reconstruction (Schneirov 2006). The end of the era is even more problematic. Perhaps the period ended in 1898, when the Spanish–American War launched the nation into imperialism, or in 1901, with the ascension of Theodore Roosevelt to the White House, or in 1917 with the outbreak of World War I or in 1918, with its end. There is even a good argument that it might stretch all the way to the Stock Market Crash in October 1929 (Edwards 2009, 464). In trying to section off the late nineteenth century in America, there is also the problem of figuring out where the Gilded Age and Progressive Era overlaps with the period termed Reconstruction, which everyone agrees was also crucial to the rise of modern America.

Even the names Gilded Age and Progressive Era make historians chafe. Mark Twain and Charles Dudley Warner published *The Gilded Age: A Tale of Today* in 1873, but the name was not then applied to the era. It was only in the early twentieth century that critics trying to create what one called a usable past, men such as Van Wyck Brooks and Lewis Mumford, called the era from the 1870s to 1900 the Gilded Age. Their intent was to indict the post-Civil War materialism they despised, although Twain and Warner wrote their book to highlight the political corruption they insisted characterized the early 1870s. The twentieth-century part of the equation labeled the Progressive Era comes by its moniker more honestly, for contemporaries did, in fact, call themselves and their causes Progressive. But the label was hardly new to the twentieth century.

There was enough confusion over the terms that in 1988, when scholars interested in creating a society to study the late nineteenth and early twentieth century tried to find a name, only 49 of the 97 casting a ballot chose the Society for Historians of the Gilded Age and Progressive Era; the other options were Society for Historians of the Early Modern Era (1865–1917) or Society for Historians of Emerging Modern America (1865–1917) (Calhoun 2002).

And, again, where does Reconstruction fit? It overlaps significantly with the Gilded Age, and what whites and blacks sought to accomplish in that period certainly exemplified progressive policies.

This historical confusion is bad enough, but it is also missing a vital piece: How did people who lived through the time see their era? Surely, weighing their perspective is important to make sense of the period. And yet, nineteenth-century Americans did not see as epoch-making any of the dates commonly used to define those years. For them, some of the period's most crucial dates were ones that historians rarely use as benchmarks: 1870, when Georgia's senators and representatives were sworn into Congress, thus formally ending Reconstruction; 1883, when the Supreme Court handed down the Civil Rights Cases, overturning the 1875 Civil Rights Act; 1913, when a Democratic Congress passed and Woodrow Wilson signed a revenue act that shifted the weight of government funding from tariffs to taxes.

The ways scholars periodize the chaos of the late nineteenth and early twentieth centuries reflect what they consider its unifying theme. Over that, too, historians argue. Early attempts to come to grips with the history of the late nineteenth century occurred while it was going on, and so were embedded in contemporary culture and politics. The first major study of Reconstruction was written by a key player in the destruction of black rights: when Congressman

A Companion to the Gilded Age and Progressive Era, First Edition. Edited by Christopher McKnight Nichols and Nancy C. Unger.
© 2017 John Wiley & Sons, Inc. Published 2017 by John Wiley & Sons, Inc.

Hilary A. Herbert and his politician co-authors wrote *Why the Solid South?* (1890), they were justifying their suppression of the black vote by "proving" that African Americans had corrupted politics and driven the South into the ground. Herbert's "scholarly" construction shoehorned Reconstruction into dates that served his argument: 1865, when the Republican Congress began its own process of rebuilding the South, to 1877, when Democratic governments took over the last of the southern states. Those dates, chosen to justify the disfranchisement of black Americans, have perverted understanding of the era until the present, as historians studying Reconstruction have until recently been boxed into the frame dictated by the late nineteenth-century purveyors of a political travesty. Scholars either endorsed the Herbert thesis or excoriated it, but they accepted its boundaries as the significant ones for Reconstruction.

Setting Reconstruction off as its own unique period warped early studies of the rest of the late nineteenth and early twentieth centuries. When historians turned their attention to those years in the early twentieth century, they focused on issues of industrialization as separate from the racial questions of Reconstruction. They also tended to divide the Gilded Age from the Progressive Era, creating distinct periods, albeit ones with fuzzy edges. In this early formulation, the Gilded Age was an era in which unrestricted capitalism enabled wealthy industrialists to run amok, bending the government to their will and crushing workers. The Progressive Era was a reaction to this oligarchical corruption of America, a period in which reformers softened the edges of industrialization and took back the nation for democracy. Most notably outlining this distinction were two classic works: John R. Commons and his associates traced the rise of labor unions in their ten-volume *History of Labor in the United States*, published between 1918 and 1935; and Matthew Josephson's 1934 *The Robber Barons* traced the concentration of money and power in the hands of grasping capitalists in the late nineteenth century. The exception to this rule was Angie Debo's landmark *And Still the Waters Run*, which looked to the western prairies rather than the eastern cities to examine the contours of economic expansion. Her exploration of how legislation marginalized Indians focused on the racial issues that interested Reconstruction historians: she illustrated the way that America's allegedly color-blind government codified race into law. She wrote the book in 1936, but it was too controversial to be published until 1940.

The consensus historians who tried to explain American success after World War II did little to redefine the boundaries that had sprung up around three apparently distinct eras between the Civil War and World War I. Their concerns focused on how ideas translated into a distinct American identity, rendering questions of both race and economics to a subordinate status. Instead, consensus scholars like Louis Hartz and Richard Hofstadter tended to play down race and to dismiss the economic strife of the late nineteenth century, bundling all Americans and all eras into a single national narrative characterized by widely shared liberal values. While C. Vann Woodward's *The Strange Career of Jim Crow* (1955) did take on race, it suggested that it was law, rather than differences Americans developed organically, that created segregation.

Studies of the peculiar era of the turn of the century heated up again in the 1960s. In 1963, scholars launched a reexamination of the period from 1865 to 1900 with a collection of essays edited by H. Wayne Morgan. The studies of politics, labor, currency, and popular culture in *The Gilded Age: A Reappraisal* brought nuance to a period that had previously been characterized by cartoonish images of robber barons and radical workers. Scholars in this volume also reexamined the traditional periodization of the Gilded Age and Progressive Era. This collection of essays suggested that the era should start in 1865. Four years later, David Montgomery's *Beyond Equality: Labor and the Radical Republicans, 1862–1872* challenged scholars of Reconstruction by reading the major concerns of Gilded Age and Progressive Era scholars—concerns about labor and capitalism—into a study of Reconstruction.

But the impulse to erase the boundaries between eras would not last. At the same time scholars were rethinking the late nineteenth century, dynamic new scholarship about the black experience after the Civil War, notably Kenneth Stampp's *The Era of Reconstruction, 1865–1877*, published in 1965, set out to demolish Hilary Herbert's perversion of the era. In doing so, historians set off Reconstruction definitively as its own territory in which issues of race were paramount. This construction of the era as a distinct period in which black Americans and their white allies sought to redefine the nation would last for the next generation, culminating, most notably, in Eric Foner's 1988 *Reconstruction: America's Unfinished Revolution, 1863–1877*. This separation meant that new scholarship on the era maintained the division of Reconstruction from the rest of the period, even as scholars blended and redefined the Gilded Age and the Progressive Era.

That redefining took place immediately on the heels of the Morgan volume. In the mid-1960s, two key books insisted that historians focusing on the triumph of conservatism in the Gilded Age and progress in the Progressive Era had the story wrong. They erased the distinction between the two to create new interpretations of the late nineteenth and early twentieth centuries. Gabriel Kolko's 1965 *Railroads and Regulation, 1877–1916* argued that, far from marking the triumph of popular determination to rein in big business, railroad regulation in the Progressive Era resulted, at least in part, from the demands of the railroad barons themselves. This was a case study of the argument he had made two years before in *The Triumph of Conservatism: A Reinterpretation of American History, 1900–1916*, whose title summed up the argument that the Progressive Era, popularly interpreted as a victory for the people, was in fact characterized by the triumph of a cultural and economic system that reinforced capitalism. In 1967, Robert H. Wiebe's *The Search for Order, 1877–1920* also erased the boundary between the Gilded Age and the Progressive Era but shifted the focus away from the economic interpretations that had dominated previous studies. Wiebe argued that the period from 1877 to 1920 should be understood as one in which a forming middle class wrenched order out of the chaos of industrialization, transforming a country of isolated small towns into a nation of bureaucrats.

With barriers breaking down, historians of the late nineteenth century and early twentieth century banded together to reexamine the era. By 1988, scholars of the Gilded Age and Progressive Era had their own historical society, and in 1996, Charles W. Calhoun's edited volume, *The Gilded Age*, brought these new visions together in a set of essays that updated the Morgan volume of the previous generation.

This reexamination of the turn of the century has challenged the traditional understanding of the outlines of the era. Previous studies of labor, for example, had focused on class consciousness, an investigation that required eliding the racial divisions among workers and emphasized the different interests of workers and employers. When Eric Arnesen reintroduced the problem of race to labor studies with his *Waterfront Workers of New Orleans: Race, Class, and Politics, 1863–1923* (1991) he complicated the idea of a working-class consciousness by explaining how black workers and white workers cooperated—or not—depending on circumstances. Lawrence B. Glickman also pushed a new understanding of workers by examining how workers conceived of themselves as consumers. His *A Living Wage: American Workers and the Making of a Consumer Society* (1997) showed how workers shaped the market for their own benefit, and advocated a living wage not as a protest but as a positive adjustment to the modern era. Another crucial reworking of historical understanding of class in the era came from Glenda Elizabeth Gilmore, whose *Gender and Jim Crow: Women and the Politics of White Supremacy in North Carolina, 1896–1920* (1996) suggested that class lines could blur race lines in the fight for access to equality at the turn of the century.

A reexamination of the Progressive Era also produced a more complicated picture. Many studies followed Kolko in examining how reform exerted social and economic control over workers, especially workers of color, women, or immigrants. Lori D. Ginzberg's (1990) *Women and the Work of Benevolence*, for example, examined how a gender-based movement became a class-based one. But others emphasized that the era was more radical than conservative. Two notable biographies—Kathryn Kish Sklar's *Florence Kelley and the Nation's Work* (1995), and Joan Waugh's *Unsentimental Reformer* (1997), a biography of Josephine Shaw Lowell, interpreted their subjects as less interested in social control than in a fundamental reordering of industrial America.

Still, with a few notable exceptions, these studies tended to focus on the period after 1877 and, with the exception of studies of Populism—which have always been their own cottage industry—on the East. Reconstruction, with its emphasis on race, still largely stood apart from the Gilded Age and Progressive Era, which emphasized labor and capital. So, for the most part, did studies of the American West. Exceptions to this rule came from scholars who followed in the wake of the consensus historians to look at the origins of American liberalism and the creation of the American state. Richard Schneirov's 1998 *Labor and Urban Politics: Class Conflict and the Origins of Modern Liberalism in Chicago, 1864–97*, and Nancy Cohen's 2002 *The Reconstruction of American Liberalism, 1865–1914*, took a question of much interest to Progressive Era scholars—the origins of American liberalism—and found them not in the twentieth century, but in the immediate post-Civil War years. Interestingly, the gulf between Reconstruction and the Gilded Age persisted: despite Cohen's book title and the 1865 boundary the author set for her study, the publisher's description of the book explained that she found the origins of liberalism in the Gilded Age.

Scholars of state-making also tended to reach backward to the Civil War to explain the changes of the late nineteenth century. Three studies of the Civil War government found the roots of the American state not in the late nineteenth century, but in the war years. In 1997, my *Greatest Nation of the Earth: Republican Economic Policies During the Civil War* sought to explain the era of the robber barons by examining the years during which Republicans codified their economic ideology into law. Two years later, Scott Nelson's *Iron Confederacies: Southern Railways, Klan Violence, and Reconstruction* looked at the rise of capitalism and labor strife beginning during the Civil War. Most notably, Mark R. Wilson's powerful 2010 book, *The Business of Civil War: Military Mobilization and the State, 1861–1865* discovered the contours of the construction of the American state in wartime military contracting.

Other scholars have turned not to the war to understand the development of the state, but to the immediate postwar years. Recent scholars focusing on issues of gender and on the West have shaken ideas about the American state most dramatically. Rebecca Edward's *Angels in the Machinery: Gender in American Party Politics from the Civil War to the Progressive Era* (1997) persuasively argued that gender roles lay at the heart of the creation of the American state, as politicians sought to shore up the image of the traditional American family amid the dislocations of the late nineteenth century. Barbara Young Welke's 2001 *Recasting American Liberty* rounded up ideas about labor, capital, and gender to argue that the crucial concept in the creation of the state was the idea of liberty, in which individuals accepted a loss of autonomy in exchange for protection, protection usually dedicated to women.

As Gilded Age scholars were beginning to reach earlier in time, Reconstruction scholars were reaching later to challenge both the traditional temporal and geographic boundaries of their field of study. Several studies in the early 2000s broke the time barrier, building on Gaines Foster's remarkably prescient 1982 *Ghosts of the Confederacy: Defeat, the Lost Cause, and the Emergence of the New South, 1865–1913*, which argued that later myths of the Civil War enabled white southerners to obscure their own fondness for a modern economy. My own *The Death of Reconstruction: Race, Labor, and Politics in the Post-Civil War North, 1965–1901* (2001) sought to erase the boundaries established in 1890 by Hilary Herbert and to reexamine the late nineteenth century on its own terms. In 2003, Steven Hahn's *A Nation Under Our Feet: Black Political Struggles in the Rural South from Slavery to the Great Migration*, and Jane Turner Censer's *Reconstruction of Southern White Womanhood 1865–1895*, both found the patterns of the war and postwar years stretching far into the future.

The reexamination of the American state as period boundaries eroded gave Western historians, with their long tradition of examining state development, a newly powerful voice in Reconstruction history. In his *The West and Reconstruction* (1981), Eugene H. Berwanger had tried to tie the West to Reconstruction, but it took more than a decade for the idea to take off. Richard White's *It's Your Misfortune and None of My Own* (1991) sparked interest with its tight focus on the interrelationship of the West and the federal government. In 2003, T.J. Stiles's *Jesse James: Last Rebel of the Civil War* interpreted the western outlaw as a key player in the Reconstruction era's fight over the power of the federal government. In 2007, I explicitly tied Reconstruction to the West in *West From Appomattox: The Reconstruction of America After the Civil War*, which argued that the defining characteristic of the postwar years was the consolidation of an American middle-class ideology, made possible by the imagery of the American West. In 2009, Elliott West's *The Last Indian War: The Nez Perce Story* irrevocably intertwined the history of the West and Reconstruction when he reread the story of the Nez Perce as the final chapter of Civil War Era national redefinitions of citizenship.

Studies of the West also quite deliberately began to take on the issue of race after the traditional boundary of Reconstruction. In 2009, Peggy Pascoe's *What Comes Naturally: Miscegenation Law and the Making of Race in America* masterfully moved questions of race and Reconstruction to the West. In 2014, Stacey L. Smith examined how race and Reconstruction played out among the Chinese in California in *Freedom's Frontier: California and the Struggle over Unfree Labor, Emancipation, and Reconstruction*. Most recently, in 2015, the essays in Gregory Downs's and Kate Masur's edited collection *The World the Civil War Made* interpreted the post-Civil War American West as a reflection of the racial contours of Reconstruction.

From both sides of the divide between Reconstruction and the Gilded Age and Progressive Era, scholars since the mid-2000s have begun to recognize that questions of race and the state both demand the examination of the creation of citizenship. Hahn's *A Nation Under Our Feet* made the theme of African American citizenship the centerpiece of America in the years from the Civil War to the Great Migration; so much other scholarship had covered this idea that three years later I tied together recent books on race and the state in the years from the Civil War to 1900 and suggested that Reconstruction was being redefined as "the Era of Citizenship" (Richardson 2006, 69). Christopher Capozzola took the story through World War I in his *Uncle Sam Wants You: World War I and the Making of the Modern American Citizen* (2008), which examined how the demands of world war required Americans to define the lines between the rights of individuals and the lawful demands of the state. The next year, Sidney M. Milkis looked at conceptions of citizenship in the Progressive Era. His *Theodore Roosevelt, the Progressive Party, and the Transformation of American Democracy* (2009) examined the Progressive Party's conception of a new American state as its members redefined the rights and duties of citizens. Scholars from both sides of the historical divide have also looked at the limits of state control over citizens. In 2002, Gaines Foster's *Moral Reconstruction: Christian Lobbyists and the Federal Legislation of Morality, 1865–1920* (2002) examined the limits of state power on citizens as Americans rejected the efforts of postwar reformers to make America a Christian nation by law. Michael Willrich also examined the limits of state power on citizens in his 2011 *Pox: An American History*, which looked at the conflict over smallpox vaccinations at the turn of the century.

The recent churning of eras, regions, and periodization suggests that the time is ripe for a redefinition of the late nineteenth and early twentieth centuries. But how?

Redefining the Era

Grouping the years from the election of 1860 to the landslide election of November 1920 offers a new interpretation of this crucial period in American history. That new interpretation both draws from the new work that has so revolutionized American history since the 1960s and continues the process of breaking down the artificial walls separating Reconstruction, the Gilded Age, and the Progressive Era. This new periodization, reaching from one to another epoch-making election, incorporates Reconstruction historians' emphasis on race and citizenship with the emphasis of scholars of the Gilded Age and Progressive era on labor and capital, the construction of American liberalism, and the construction of the American state—all of which are inseparable.

Viewing the era from Lincoln to Harding identifies the crucial theme of late nineteenth-century America as a ferocious contest over the proper role of government in American society. In the years from the stunning victory of a fledgling political party pledged to use the government to promote economic opportunity for poor Americans to 1920, when voters overwhelmingly backed a government limited to promoting big business, Americans struggled over the nature of government, for that government defined the nation. This was the theme that contemporaries recognized as the most important one in the national consciousness. It is the one that made the most lasting impact on American history.

This contest, of course, was also over citizenship, for what the nation's government would become depended on who would have a say in it. From 1860 to 1920, a constant struggle waged over who would be permitted to vote and to exercise the rights of citizenship. While historians have focused on the racial dimension of political participation, race was hardly the only factor; gender, class, and ethnicity also played major roles. The Civil War had thrown a monkey wrench into the traditional American belief that a good voter must be a white man who owned property. Wealthy white men were the very people who had just spent four years trying to destroy the nation. In summer 1865, President Andrew Johnson's pardoning of the same Confederates who had attacked the government, thus readmitting them to political participation and threatening to reestablish the antebellum government, began several decades of debate over who should have a say in American government. This debate included every adult American.

Looking at the era from 1860 to 1920 as one of a contest over political participation and the nature of government does more than restore the themes that were central to the participants. It also offers two major new conceptual directions for historians. First, it promises to rejuvenate political history. Political history, the study of politicians and parties and policies, fell into neglect in the American academy with the dramatic growth of social history in the 1970s, and yet the nation itself is, and has always been, a political entity. Scholars recently have attempted to create a New Political History by integrating the study of politics with social history, focusing on the populace—African Americans, women, consumers, and other groups—to emphasize that political leaders depended on popular support. This examination of the concerns and organization of specific groups, however, means these studies downplay the overarching national political story through which all American individuals in the late nineteenth-century interpreted their own economic, racial, social, and cultural interests. It is *Hamlet* without the prince. Restoring the construction of the national government and its citizenry to centrality with the addition of the new, vastly expanded understanding of social forces in America offers a chance to redefine political history, seeing it as a space in which various voices contended for control over the emerging American government.

Even more profoundly, redefining this pivotal era as one of contest charts a way to reclaim narrative history for the profession in general. Since the 1970s, academic historians have rejected historical narrative because they believed it served an entrenched social order, privileging the voices that had always dominated American society and thus reinforcing their continued power. But recognizing the theme of the nineteenth century as one of contestation rather than the triumph of a specific historical development suggests that it will be possible to construct an inclusive narrative of American history. Americans argued, marched, sued, wrote, voted, and even killed to influence the development of government. As different groups hashed out the proper role of government, there were winners and losers, sometimes different ones at different times. Their results constructed the nation, citizenry, and ideology that formed modern America. Placing the thread of contest at the center of the era suggests that it is possible to write a new inclusive narrative of American history.

Writing a New Narrative

If a new narrative history emerged around the theme of political contest, what might it look like?

It would start with the notion that the struggle in 1860 was over two different concepts of the American government. Southern whites believed in a government that served a few rich men by focusing on the protection of property. Allowing them to amass huge amounts of capital, the argument went, would enable them to direct the labor of lesser men, thus producing a prosperous economy and a higher civilization. Northerners believed in a government that would protect equality of opportunity, thus allowing men at the lowest rungs of society to work their way up to prosperity, using their labor to produce capital that would, in turn, hire others.

During the war, the Republicans who controlled the country had turned the previously inactive national government into one of dramatic activism. They had fielded an army and navy that ultimately included more than 2 million men; invented a national system of taxes and tariffs to fund a war that cost more than $6 billion; put regular men on their own land and provided for their higher education; chartered a railroad corporation and funded immigration to develop the country; brought western Territories and States into the Union, dividing the West into political units that looked much like they do today; and, finally, freed the slaves and provided funding for destitute white and black southerners to transition to free labor. Their program reoriented the government from the protection of the wealthy to advancing the economic interests of regular men. The victory of the United States government over the Confederacy in 1865 dedicated the whole nation to a theory of political economy rooted in the idea that all men had a right to the fruits of their own labor.

But what would these changes mean for the postwar years? Was an active government just a product of the war?

Would the government continue to serve all men in the booming North, devastated South, and new West, or would it revert back to the prewar inaction that served the wealthy? That question would dominate the next fifty years of American history.

To answer it, American men and women from all races, ethnicities, and economic groups demanded a say in their government. African American men wanted to participate, of course, but so did northern women, who had given their husbands and sons to the cause of the Union, then worked in fields and factories to keep the northern economy booming, and had invested heavily in the US bonds that funded the war effort. White northern men simply assumed they would have a say, since they had fought and won the war. Southern white men also assumed they would be welcome participants, since they had always before been members of the body politic. Immigrants believed they, too, had an important role to play in the formation of the national government, as did the Mexican Americans who had become part of the nation when the Treaty of Guadalupe Hidalgo moved the national border from one side of them to the other. American Indians also took a stand on what the government could and could not do. And, finally, the people living in Puerto Rico, the Philippines, Guam, Samoa, and the other islands that America would absorb at the turn of the century also had a role to play in the creation of the United States.

The widespread demand for inclusion at this moment was fraught. Thanks to the Republicans' novel system of national taxation, every American citizen paid money to the treasury. This meant that, for the first time in American history, the government spent funds collected directly from taxpayers. The people literally owned the government. And the right to determine what the government did—the right to vote—became the right to spend other people's money.

This link between an active government that promoted equality of opportunity for all and taxation would dominate the national debate until voters definitively rejected the use of the government to promote equality in the landslide election of 1920. After 1860, Americans fought ideologically, politically, and, indeed, literally, over the proper nature of the American government.

The Universal Suffrage Years

The immediate postwar years saw Americans embracing universal suffrage and an activist government that answered to all citizens. They got there because President Andrew Johnson, who assumed sole control of the initial postwar reconstruction of the national government when Lincoln died during a congressional recess, hated the new concept of government. To restore the antebellum system, he offered generous amnesty to the white southerners who had taken up arms against the US government, pardoned high-ranking ex-Confederates, and backed the readmission of the eleven seceded states after they had abolished slavery, nullified the articles of secession, and repudiated Confederate debts. Southern legislatures followed this prescription—barely—then also passed the Black Codes that remanded ex-slaves to a situation as close to slavery as the legislators could construct. Nonetheless, when Congress reconvened in December 1865, Johnson announced that, once congressmen admitted the newly elected southern representatives and senators to their seats, the process of restoration of southern states to the Union would be complete. He had hurried the process, he explained, because leaving the military in the South would cost tax dollars and upset white southern Democrats.

This was an especially bitter pill for northerners because the upcoming 1870 census would count African Americans as full people, rather than three-fifths of a person. Southern leaders would have more power after the war than they had had before it. Northerners objected to Johnson's resurrection of the prewar body politic, and to protect black southerners while they tried to develop their own plan, congressmen passed a bill to protect civil rights and established federal courts that would hear black testimony. But Johnson vetoed these bills on the grounds that they would require taxation that fell largely on white men to pay for bureaucrats who helped African Americans. He claimed that the new concept of government that served the people was actually a redistribution of wealth. This linkage would hamstring efforts to use the government to help regular Americans from this time onward.

Johnson's attempt to restore the antebellum concept of government pushed Republicans to nudge southern states toward black suffrage—or at least to undercut the advantage southerners would gain with the 1870 census—with the Fourteenth Amendment to the Constitution, which threatened to trim congressional representation according to the numbers of men allowed to vote in a state. When southern states refused to ratify the amendment, Congress in 1867 passed the Military Reconstruction Act. By calling for black men to vote for delegates to state constitutional conventions, Republicans created a sea change in the nature of the American electorate. In 1868, the ratification of the Fourteenth Amendment established that anyone born in America was a citizen, and that any state abridging voting privileges for any reason other than crime would lose representation in Congress. Finally, the ratification of the Fifteenth Amendment in 1870 ostensibly guaranteed that the right of citizens to vote could not be denied on account of race or previous condition of servitude.

To those prospering in the nation's booming industries, it seemed the promise of free labor had now been engrafted onto the nation's political system, and the way was clear for every man to rise. In the wake of the war, industry boomed in the North. Immigrants came to America to try their luck; cities grew. In the West, ranching and mining took off and farmers poured onto the plains. The transcontinental railroads sparked economic development across the nation as they required the development of new financial tools as well as a new bureaucracy that created well-to-do middle managers. It seemed that postwar free-labor America would fulfill the Republicans' most hopeful predictions. Horatio Alger's 1868 bestseller *Ragged Dick* summed up the hope of the era when it promised that anyone, even an illiterate New York City bootblack, could make it in America, so long as he was willing to work hard.

But to others, the new structure seemed simply to emphasize their exclusion from the upward mobility of the free-labor vision. During the war, high employment and support for the war government had encouraged workers to look beyond the inflation that kept their real wages from rising. The war years had dramatically increased industrialization in the North as government contracts flowed to larger companies, and workers had lost ground as employers increased their hours without increasing their wages. After the war, workers dismayed by the financial inequities of the postwar economy demanded that Congress redress those inequalities. In 1866, the fledgling National Labor Union called for higher wages, better working conditions and for Congress to establish an eight-hour workday.

Workers were not the only ones left behind in postwar America. Notably missing from the guarantees of citizenship in the Fourteenth Amendment were "Indians not taxed": native peoples who either lived on reservations or roamed on their ancestral lands in what were now newly organized Territories. Far from offering these people economic opportunity, America's free labor system threatened their lands and resources. Plains Indians fought back against American interlopers. Warfare on the plains prompted the head of the army to transfer William Tecumseh Sherman from the South to the plains in summer 1865. Three years later, he would have to admit defeat at the hands of Lakota warrior Red Cloud.

But Red Cloud's victory would be short-lived. The Plains Indians' defense against free labor ideology could not survive. To move Indians out of the path of the transcontinental railroad, Sherman proposed pushing them onto two large reservations. The 1867 Treaty of Medicine Lodge and the 1868 Treaty of Fort Laramie did just that, forcing southern Indians into the land that is now Oklahoma and the northern Indians onto a large reservation that covered much of what is now South Dakota. Government commitments to protecting that land and providing for its inhabitants briefly promised peace, but the government's inability to keep settlers out of Indian lands would reignite warfare within a decade.

Also apparently unwelcome to have a say in government were American women. Women had agitated for the right to vote since the 1830s, but had been persuaded to defer their claims to equality in favor of those of American slaves. During the war, they had supported the US government with their labor, cash, and menfolk. If former Confederates and African American men were to have a say in their government, surely women should not be excluded. As women's rights leader Julia Ward Howe wrote: "The Civil War came to an end, leaving the slave not only emancipated, but endowed with the full dignity of citizenship. The women of the North had greatly helped to open the door which admitted him to freedom and its safeguard, the ballot. Was this door to be shut in their face?" (Howe 1900, 373).

Activist women were determined to have the right to shape the laws under which they lived. After Congress refused to include women in the Fourteenth Amendment, women in 1869 organized two suffrage associations: The National Women's Suffrage Association, which advocated a wide range of legislative reforms as well as suffrage, and, a few months later, the American Women's Suffrage Association, which advocated suffrage alone under the conviction that once women could vote, they could change other discriminatory laws under the normal electoral process. Their pressure worked. In 1869, Wyoming Territory accorded women the vote. The following year the Utah legislature followed suit.

When the Fifteenth Amendment did not protect women's suffrage, activists forced the issue in the election of 1872. Women demanded to vote under the Fourteenth Amendment's declaration that all persons born or naturalized in America were citizens, and thus had the right to vote. In Rochester, New York, Susan B. Anthony successfully cast a ballot, but was arrested, tried, and convicted for the crime of illegal voting. In Missouri, Virginia Minor didn't make it as far as Anthony did. The St. Louis County registrar Reese Happersett denied Minor the right to register to vote. She sued him on the grounds that her citizenship gave her that right.

As Minor's challenge worked its way through the courts, many Americans were reexamining the idea of universal suffrage. Anthony herself explained that her problem with political inequality was simply that it was applied against women: "An oligarchy of wealth, where the rich govern the poor; an oligarchy of learning, where the educated govern the ignorant; or even an oligarchy of race, where the Saxon rules the African, might be endured" (Harper 1898, 978).

Anthony's statement reflected that Americans served by the new economy were increasingly uncomfortable with the political demands coming from the newly enfranchised voices. Republicans based their free-labor theory on the idea that all Americans shared the same economic interests. What was good for workers was good for employers and vice versa, they thought, in a boundless system that enabled everyone to rise together. But this idea came from the rural antebellum world, a world increasingly obsolete in the industrial and urban growth of the postwar years. Encouraged by Democratic leaders eager to make inroads on the Republican majority, those at the bottom of the economic scale increasingly spoke of the economy and society as a class struggle for limited resources. The division of the nation into warring classes struck terror into the hearts of Republicans, not just because of the economic and social dangers it evoked, but also because the minute the government began to legislate in favor of one class over another, their concept of a harmony of economic interest would fall apart and would not be able to be resurrected.

The idea that classes struggled to control America emerged as a powerful concept in politics in 1866. In that year, the new National Labor Union declared: "There is [a] dividing line—that which separates mankind into two great classes, the class that labors and the class that lives by others' labor" (Richardson 2007, 65). In the same year, a crucial political shift exacerbated the growing rift between Republican leaders and workers. Johnson's attacks on Republican congressmen and his defense of the white southerners who rioted in Memphis and New Orleans in 1866 created a landslide for Republicans in the midterm elections of that year. This landslide swept moderate Democrats from power, leaving only the most extremist Democrats in ironclad districts to speak for the party. In 1867, they rallied Democratic workers to attack Republicans for catering to rich men by paying the interest on the national debt in gold, rather than in greenbacks. Devaluing the national debt would destroy the nation's credit, and threatened a very real attack on the stability of the government.

Farmers and entrepreneurs, too, especially in the Midwest, demanded government policies that would enable them to compete in the new economy. Most significantly, they wanted the nation to continue to use inflationary greenbacks as legal tender, a policy popular with borrowers and anathema to wealthy lenders, who wanted to return to a gold standard. Farmers also wanted government to regulate businesses. They were at the mercy of railroads and elevator operators that stored and transported their grain, and wanted the government to regulate the practices of those industries. In a series of laws known as the Granger Laws, after the Granger Movement that brought farmers together first socially and then politically, midwestern state legislatures curtailed the monopolies and discriminatory price scales of the industries on which farmers depended.

It was not just Democratic workers and farmers who seemed to want policies that would benefit them at the expense of others. With their newly acquired political voice, black Americans began to press for a government that protected their rights in the face of abuse from former masters. While Republicans tended to focus on light-skinned black leaders, who embraced the idea that men must work hard to accumulate wealth and rise, most former slaves saw former masters trying to cheat them of their hard-earned wages. To them, the idea of a harmony of economic interests seemed laughable. They began to strike for wages and better conditions, and to back political leaders who would curtail the power of the white landowners and employers.

Women, too, demanded government policies that mainstream white men did not necessarily see as promoting the general welfare. Most notably, men in the Utah state legislature had given women the vote with the expectation that they would throw Mormon leaders out of office. When women instead voted with their husbands and supported those leaders, mainstream white men worried that women would perhaps not advance American society after all.

Restricting the Suffrage

The Fifteenth Amendment was the high-water mark for the idea that every man should have a say in his own government. By 1870, the idea that universal suffrage was the key to a successful government was under attack as Republican men who controlled the government turned against the inclusion of new voices in the body politic and began to roll back the suffrage they had just expanded. Using the wedge Johnson had used against the activist government, these opponents complained that widespread suffrage meant poor men would devise policies paid for with money collected from richer men. They began their assault on universal suffrage by harnessing racism to their cause, attacking the voting rights of southern black men.

In the early 1870s, new southern state governments elected in part with black votes called for the reconstruction of the broken states. At the same time, the Democratic machine in New York City, run by Tammany Hall, garnered votes from workers in part by providing them with jobs on public works programs. In both cases, officials financed improvements to infrastructure through tax levies.

Democrats who loathed the Republican state governments in the South argued that black voters were electing representatives who cemented their votes by enacting policies that redistributed wealth. Black men were voting for governments that would rebuild the South after the devastating war, and the roads, bridges, schools, and hospitals would have to be funded through taxation. Those taxes, opponents wailed, came from the pockets of hardworking white men. When South Carolina seated a legislature that had a majority of black men, white Democrats immediately railed against the "crow-congress," the "monkey-show," that was prostituting the government to the interests of ex-slaves. African American voters were plundering white property owners, they insisted, overseeing "a proletariat Parliament… the like of which could not be produced under the widest suffrage in any part of the world save in some of these Southern States" (Richardson 2007, 103).

By 1871, members of a rising northern middle class were willing to listen to the idea that lazy men endangered the government. In March 1871, workers took over Paris in the wake of the Franco-Prussian War and established the Paris Commune. Americans looked on, horrified, at the violence that American newspapers attributed—incorrectly—only to the Communards. Communards' call for legislation based on economic classes sounded to Americans thriving in the postwar economy much like the language embraced by American workers. To men who believed that the genius of America depended the idea of economic harmony, workers' calls for apparent class-based legislation threatened the nation. Horatio Alger's *Ragged Dick* had extolled the virtues of success through hard work and warned against labor organization. Only three years later, though, that warning had turned apocalyptic. Famous urban reformer Charles Loring Brace worried that, "In the judgment of one who has been familiar with our 'dangerous classes' for twenty years, there are just the same explosive social elements beneath the surface of New York as of Paris" (Brace 1872, 29).

It also appeared that women did not necessarily contribute to a free-labor society. Reformers such as Elizabeth Cady Stanton and Susan B. Anthony wanted to rework the laws governing property, marriage, and divorce, challenging the very tenets of society. And, just as in the South, where observers looked at governments elected with the help of black votes and saw socialism, in the West, observers looked at Mormon leaders elected with the help of women's votes and saw social breakdown. Perhaps widespread suffrage was not, in fact, a way to guarantee a strong, progressive society.

Meanwhile, other Americans worried that the government had been corrupted by the influence of wealthy businessmen who had swung it in their favor. In 1872, Congress retired the income tax and placed the weight of the treasury on tariffs. These levies on imported goods kept the prices on consumer goods high, and people began to grumble that Congress was weighting laws to favor businessmen. Grant's opponents leveraged this fear in the 1872 election, attacking the president for his alleged corruption. They claimed the administration supported African Americans in the South solely to garner voters who would keep it in power so it could do the bidding of a minority of wealthy businessmen. It was this sentiment Twain and Warner inscribed into their 1873 political novel *The Gilded Age*.

As ideas about the proper role of government were shifting, the Panic of 1873 helped to increase Americans' sense that the nation's economy was not, in fact, harmonious, but rather characterized by class struggle. Voters agreed with Democrats that the cause of the panic was the Republicans' insistence on policies that protected big business at the expense of labor. Their main example was the tariff, which, at almost half a product's value, protected domestic business and enabled industrialists to collude to set prices, but that was not their only complaint. In a routine reworking of the currency in 1873, Congress demonetized silver, just as new silver mines would have created the inflation that workers and farmers craved. Angry at what seemed to be Republicans' use of the government to help wealthy businessmen, voters handed control of the House of Representatives to Democrats in the midterm elections of 1874.

Republicans and their business supporters pushed back against the voters' dictum. The problem with the economy was not their policies, they thought, but rather businessmen's fears that demands for government intervention in the economy on behalf of workers and farmers would come to pass. In 1875, the Secretary of the Treasury abandoned the inflationary greenbacks and resumed specie payments.

In the same year, the Supreme Court revised the idea that everyone should have a say in the American government. In *Minor v. Happersett*, the Court declared that women were citizens. But in a stunning conclusion, it also reworked the nature of government. Citizenship, the justices said, did not necessarily convey the right to vote.

Defining the Government

Once the Supreme Court had blessed suffrage restriction, the rest of the nineteenth century would be a battleground over whether the government should advance the interests of all Americans or support the businessmen who argued that their sector of the economy was central because it employed everyone else. In the service of that war, Americans enlisted politics, art, and culture, developing ideologies that would echo to the present. Each side sought to read the other out of the American tradition. And each side sought to disenfranchise its political opponents.

Republicans monopolized the national government, and they insisted that their legislation promoted the economic welfare of every American. Ironically, they illustrated that, in part, by continuing to back the spread of settlers into the Great Plains, sparking Indian wars that endangered farmers and miners, and ultimately devastated the tribes there. Leaders like Comanche Quanah, Apache Geronimo, and Lakotas Red Cloud, Sitting Bull, and Crazy Horse demanded the same right to their land American citizens claimed, only to be forced onto reservations too poor to support the free-labor economy the government tried to impose. Republicans also threw their weight behind tariffs, insisting that the protection of big business created a thriving economy that helped everyone. Those unable to thrive in that economy were, they argued, lazy or wasteful.

By the mid-1870s, opponents characterized Republican governance as a corruption of true American government. While historians tend to emphasize the issue of race in the South in the 1876 election, as paramilitary groups kept black men from voting, Democrats framed the central issue of the campaign as the corruption of the body politic by a special interest that wanted other people to subsidize the people it represented. In the South, that meant African Americans; in the North, for Democrats, it meant big businessmen. For all Americans, the concept that special interests were ruining the nation by perverting the government to their own ends made sense of the terrible economic and social turmoil of industrialization.

Democrats insisted that Republicans were the party of big business, and were deliberately monopolizing the government to keep themselves in power, in part by catering to lazy black voters in the South, offering them social services and jobs on government projects, paid for with taxpayers'—assumed to be white taxpayers—money. In the South, "Redeemers," led in South Carolina, for example, by Wade Hampton's Red Shirts, set out to take the state government out of the hands of the Republicans by keeping black voters from the polls. As a presidential candidate, Democrats ran New York reformer Samuel J. Tilden, who had gained popularity by busting New York City's Tweed Ring, which had stayed in power thanks to the votes of immigrants and workingmen who owed the ring their jobs.

When Democrats won the popular vote but lost the White House in what they believed was a corrupt bargain, they continued to fight to take government out of the hands of big businessmen and give it back to regular Americans. Only four months after Republican president Rutherford B. Hayes took office in March 1877, railroad workers in West Virginia sparked the nation's first general strike after the B & O cut their wages by 20%. Hayes called out federal troops to suppress the strike, convincing opponents that big business Republicans not only had stolen control of the government, but were also putting the muscle of the army behind business interests.

On the heels of the strike, voters pushed back to retake the government. As labor leader Samuel Gompers later remembered: "the railroad strike of 1877 was the tocsin that sounded a ringing message of hope to us all" (Richardson 2007, 178). The Supreme Court blessed government regulation of business in *Munn v. Illinois* (1877); the next year, Democrats in Congress passed the Posse Comitatus Act to prevent the president from using the US Army against civilians, a new Greenback Labor Party polled more than a million votes and elected fourteen congressmen, and voters gave control of the Congress to the Democrats. The Republicans eked out the 1880 presidential victory of James A. Garfield by less than 4000 votes after Garfield promised to restore the idea of universal suffrage and a government that responded to all Americans. Garfield followed through with his promises, undercutting big business Republicans in 1881 when he won a dramatic showdown with Senator Roscoe Conkling of New York to control the nation, but Garfield's subsequent assassination by a mentally ill follower of the Conkling wing of the party killed Americans' faith that the Republicans could operate for the good of everyone. In 1883, Congress passed civil service reform to try to keep government out of the hands of a corrupt political party. The following year, voters put a Democrat into the White House for the first time since 1856, electing Grover Cleveland, a reform Democrat who promised evenhanded government.

With Democrats now powerful enough to challenge Republicans for control of the White House, the struggle to define the nature of the government became white hot. Republicans fervently supported what they called a laissez faire government, which, to their way of thinking, promoted the good of everyone in America. That government inaction, though, was only rhetorical. In fact, both Republican financial policies and the tariffs to which Republicans were devoted disproportionately benefited big businessmen. While it was true that wealth was concentrated at the top of society, industrialist Andrew Carnegie explained in 1889 in *The Gospel of Wealth*, that concentration enabled the nation's leaders to exercise stewardship over the country's capital, investing it wisely for the good of all, rather than letting poorer individuals fritter it away. Republicans argued that Democrats' demands for the government to loosen the nation's money supply and lower the tariff—policies that would put more money in the pockets of working Americans—would, quite literally, destroy the nation. So Republican Party leaders did all they could to undercut their opponents and advance their own vision.

That undercutting took shape with a series of political machinations to strengthen Republicans' weakening popularity by shifting the electoral system. Republicans retook control of the government in 1888, putting Benjamin Harrison in the White House despite his loss to Cleveland by more than 100,000 votes. They promptly added six new western states to the Union to guarantee they could retain control of the Senate despite the growing Democratic majority. Then they tried—unsuccessfully—to manipulate the electorate by placing federal troops at the polls in the South and New York City, a system that would protect black Republicans in the South and cut down Democratic voting in the city on which control of the White House usually hinged. Their attempts to game the system were so egregious that even moderate Republicans finally rebelled, noting that it hardly seemed like proper American democracy when 105,000 people in the new states of Wyoming and Idaho would have four senators and two representatives while the 200,000 people in the first Congressional District of New York would have only one representative.

Insisting that workers and farmers who blamed high tariffs for their poverty were simply too lazy to work and wanted a handout, Republicans moved tariff rates higher, promising the 1890 McKinley tariff would make the economy boom. When it did not, and furious voters handed the House, Senate, and White House to the Democrats in 1892, Republicans howled that Democrats were communists or anarchists whose policies would amount to a wholesale redistribution of wealth. Anyone with money should take it out of the market immediately, they insisted, in a deliberate attempt to crash the economy and sabotage the Democrats. It worked. The economy tanked in 1893 and Republicans retook the House in 1894. Then businessmen entrenched their interests in the law. In 1895, the business-dominated Supreme Court declared the government was too weak to levy an income tax; within a month, with the *In re Debs* decision, it declared the government strong enough to issue an injunction against an individual to force him to obey the law (and, in this case, call off a railroad strike).

For their part, Democrats, backed by workers, farmers, and men on the make, argued that Republicans had perverted the government to make it serve big business. They tried to take the government back for regular American men. They turned on the Chinese workers they believed took western jobs, pressing for the passage of the Chinese Restriction Act in 1882, which kept Chinese workers out of the nation. In his 1884 campaign, Cleveland had promised to revise the tariffs downward, but once in office, could get nothing through the Republican Senate. Frustrated workers increasingly took to the streets, launching more than 23,000 strikes in the twenty years between 1880 and 1900. The Harrison administration's brazen championing of big business coincided with a horrific drought in the plains states, prompting farmers in 1890 to turn their longstanding protest of Republican governance into alliances led by people like Mary Elizabeth Lease, who told audiences: "Wall Street owns the country.... It is no longer a government of the people, by the people, and for the people, but a government of Wall Street, by Wall Street, and for Wall Street." She told farmers to "raise less corn and more hell" (Richardson 2007, 242). Members of the Alliance sought to make the government respond to the people again. When Republicans thumbed their noses at their opponents in 1890 by raising tariff rates, voters rebelled and Democrats took control of the government. Then, to combat the Republican-created depression, in 1894 Democrats imposed an income tax to make up for revenue lost when they lowered tariff rates slightly.

Just like Republicans, Democrats worked to manipulate the electorate so they could win control of the national government. Most dramatically, they worked to keep African Americans from voting in the South. When Republicans in 1890 pushed a Federal Elections Bill to protect black voting, southerners responded first with a dramatic increase in lynching, and then with a series of new state constitutions limiting voting by property, literacy, or even the voting status of a man's grandfather. In retaliation, Republicans pushed the Australian, or secret, ballot, regulating ballot colors and print, and requiring a man to vote in secret. While they argued that such a system would prevent employers or political bosses from pressuring men to vote a certain way, it also meant that voters had to be able to read. The electorate contracted as men of color, and poor and illiterate men, could no longer vote.

The late 1890s became a showdown between the two visions of government. The 1896 election pitted big business Republican William McKinley against Democrat and Populist William Jennings Bryan, who put the contest clearly:

> There are those who believe that, if you will only legislate to make the well-to-do prosperous, their prosperity will leak through on those below. The Democratic idea, however, has been that if you legislate to make the masses prosperous, their prosperity will find its way up through every class which rests upon them" *(Bryan 1896)*.

For their part, Republicans responded that Bryan and his supporters were communists and anarchists, and their rhetoric carried the day. Voters backed McKinley.

Reforming America

But the fight over the nature of the American government was not finished. If Republican policies had indeed made the nation the best on earth, men such as Theodore Roosevelt and Albert Beveridge asked, didn't that mean the nation had a responsibility to spread that system across the world? And if America was to be a beacon for other nations, shouldn't it make absolutely sure its own citizens were healthy and prosperous? From 1898 to 1920, progressive Americans sought to use the government to reform America and to launch it on an international crusade to spread American values. After an initial surge of success, voters crushed their vision in the landslide election of 1920, an election that reset America.

Progressive Republicans had begun to come together as young men during the election of 1884, when their party's championing of big business had seemed to them to cross the line into corruption. But they had not emerged as a powerful faction until the 1898 Spanish–American War. They saw throwing Spain out of Cuba as an opportunity to spread the American system overseas, to rejuvenate the American spirit, which had weakened under industrialization, and, not incidentally, to wrest power from party elders who were not making sufficient room for new blood in the party hierarchy. With the victorious conclusion of that "splendid little war," they turned their sights on America. They looked at the circumstances of urban workers, living and working in horrific conditions, and worried that they could never be properly educated or independent enough to become good citizens. Surely the government had a duty to protect the lives and opportunities of the people who made up its body politic.

While progressive Republicans' understanding of political economy as a web of harmonious interactions was very different than that of the class-conscious Democrats, the prescriptions of the two groups for improving society coincided. To silence the progressives, Republican Party leaders tried to bury the vocal Theodore Roosevelt in the vice presidency, only to have him ascend to the White House after the assassination of President McKinley. Once in power, Roosevelt found himself repeatedly thwarted by the party's Old Guard. Frustrated at every turn, he cultivated reporters who used his increasingly potent rhetoric to feed the popular interest in limiting the power of big business and returning the government to the service of Americans in general.

This progressive impulse dominated the 1912 election, in which all three major candidates— William Howard Taft, Woodrow Wilson, and Theodore Roosevelt—as well as Socialist candidate Eugene V. Debs embraced the idea that the government must regulate business and promote the good of all Americans. When Wilson won the White House and the Democrats control of Congress, the way was clear for a reworking of the government to make it responsive to the people. As soon as he was inaugurated, and before Congress was scheduled to meet, Wilson pushed Congress to cut the tariff and replace the funds lost with an income tax, now constitutional thanks to the Sixteenth Amendment, approved a month before Wilson took the oath of office. This shift, enacted in 1913, both actually and symbolically shifted the government away from the Republican theory that it must promote business. During these years, when progressives dominated the government, Congress weakened the power of financial leaders, regulated business activities, and began to protect workers and farmers.

But this shift in the government was not a pure reflection of the impulse toward universal suffrage that characterized the immediate post-Civil War years. Progressives achieved their triumph in large part by purging from the body politic those they deemed unworthy of government attention. African Americans, especially, suffered from lynchings, often held in public, to remove them from political influence. Japanese immigrants in the West could not vote because they were not free white persons; most Indians on reservations were not American citizens, either. More sweepingly, in the Insular Cases of 1901 to 1904, the Supreme Court had found that the Philippines, Puerto Rico, Guam, and other smaller islands, taken by the United States after the 1890 tariff required the powerful Sugar Trust to pay for the sugar they grew there, were "unincorporated territories." This meant that their lands were, as the Supreme Court put it, "foreign to the United States in a domestic sense." They were not fully American lands, but tariff laws against foreign products did not apply to them, so sugar could be imported without fees. Sugar was in, but what about the people who grew it? In 1904, in *Gonzalez v. Williams*, the Fuller Court decided that Puerto Ricans were not aliens, but they were not citizens, either. They were non-citizen nationals to whom neither immigration laws nor the perquisites of citizenship applied. They could not vote. The purging of the American electorate was important enough as a theme to warrant D.W. Griffith's attention in his 1915 film *The Birth of a Nation*, which was based in part on a history of Reconstruction written by a then-college professor, Woodrow Wilson.

While Americans took the suffrage from those they saw as special interests, they expanded it to the women, who appeared to support progressive ideals. In 1918, Congress passed the Nineteenth Amendment and sent it off to the states for ratification. Wilson finally threw his weight behind women's suffrage in part because he felt his support slipping and hoped that women would support the progressive cause, both at home and overseas. At home, women had turned their traditional domestic roles into powerful public ones as advocates for legislation to clean up the wretched cities and improve the lives of poor Americans and immigrants. They would, Wilson calculated, support the Democrats' program. But Wilson also needed their support to carry the American mission overseas when in 1917 the nation intervened in World War I.

That war, the Progressives' war, sent more than a million American men to fight in Europe and left more than 300,000 dead or wounded. It cost Americans more than $21 billion. Fought according to progressive ideals, the war enabled the government to impose order on the economy, but it did so in part by working closely with the businessmen whose industries produced material for the soldiers. The war also confirmed the staunch Americanism of progressives; attacks on immigrants intensified, especially on German immigrants and African Americans whose movement into war industries and northern cities convinced white workers they were being coddled by the government. When hardline Republican opponents persuaded voters that Democratic government meant Wilson would sell the nation out to communism in the negotiations over the Treaty of Versailles, Americans turned against Progressive government. They did so emphatically.

The election of 1920 marked a sea change in the nation. This change bracketed the era that had begun with the dramatic election of 1860. In 1920, a majority of Americans endorsed the hardline view of a government that looked much like the antebellum government had. In the first election in which women voted in all states, voters elected Warren G. Harding with a landslide 60.3% of the popular vote. The Republicans, who promised a government that worked for business and business alone, won one of the nation's rare supermajorities: they captured more than two-thirds of the seats in the House of Representatives and took 59 Senate seats to the Democrats' 37, the largest Senate majority in history. America's active contest over the nature of government and the electorate was over—at least for the moment.

Reconstructing America

Dubbing different portions of the era from 1865 to 1920 by three different names obscures that the periods called Reconstruction, the Gilded Age, and the Progressive Era all shared the same fundamental theme. The dates and monikers assigned to the first two are especially problematic, for political carpers invented them. The 1877 date that "ended" Reconstruction justified white control of southern state governments. The idea of a Gilded Age came from cultural critics of a later era who wanted to highlight their objections to the materialism of their own age.

The political reformers of the early twentieth century did, however, often call themselves Progressives. If taken at their word that they were a political movement, it becomes easier to clarify the dates of their national power: it began with Theodore Roosevelt's rise to the presidency in 1901, and ended with Harding's election in November 1920.

In the cases of each of these traditionally separated historical eras, the people living in them focused on government and suffrage. The very men who named and dated them chose their definitions to highlight these issues, revealing that they were the absorbing questions of their eras. So why should the period from 1860 to 1920, a period during which Americans contested the nature of the government, be divided into three artificial chunks that suggest fractured historical themes? Reinterpreting this era as one of contest over the nature of the government, and thus of American citizenship and even over America itself, reveals its larger themes. Examining struggles over suffrage also offers a way to include all voices in a new American narrative. The years from 1865 to the election of 1920 amounted to the creation of a new nation, a nation that had been reconstructed after the cataclysmic Civil War.

The era during which that took place seems properly to be called Reconstruction. Under this thematic umbrella fits racial change, gender issues, immigration, economics, legal studies, studies of the American West, literature and so on, to reveal how all Americans who lived between the Civil War and the Roaring Twenties contested the construction of a new nation. That name alone, though, currently bears a limited connotation of the immediate postwar years, making its adoption for the longer period seem to misrepresent the age by ignoring the Progressives. Until historians can rework the meaning of the word reconstruction to mean the reconstruction of the government and citizenship, then, they should simply drop "The Gilded Age," and call the era from 1865 to 1920 Reconstruction and the Progressive Era.

References

Arnesen, Eric. 1991. *Waterfront Workers of New Orleans: Race, Class, and Politics, 1863–1923*. Urbana: University of Illinois Press.

Berwanger, Eugene H. 1981. *The West and Reconstruction*. Urbana: University of Illinois Press.

Brace, Charles Loring. 1872. *The Dangerous Classes of New York and Twenty Years' Work Among Them*. New York: Wynkoop & Hallenbeck.

Brown, Thomas J. 2006. *Reconstructions: New Perspectives on Postbellum America*. New York: Oxford University Press.

Bryan, William Jennings. July 9, 1896, "Cross of Gold" Speech, at http://historymatters.gmu.edu/d/5354/Accessed July 12, 2016.

Calhoun, Charles W. 2002. "Making History: The Society for Historians of the Gilded Age and Progressive Era: A Retrospective View." *Journal of the Gilded Age and Progressive Era* 1: 12–24.

—, ed. 1996. *The Gilded Age: Essays on the Origins of Modern America*. Wilmington, DE: Scholarly Resources.

Capozzola, Christopher. 2008. *Uncle Sam Wants You: World War I and the Making of the Modern American Citizen*. New York: Oxford University Press.

Carnegie, Andrew. 1889. "The Gospel of Wealth." Originally published as "Wealth." *North American Review* 148: 653–665.

Censer, Jane Turner. 2003. *Reconstruction of Southern White Womanhood 1865–1895*. Baton Rouge: Louisiana State University Press.

Cohen, Nancy. 2002. *The Reconstruction of American Liberalism, 1865–1914*. Chapel Hill: University of North Carolina Press.

Commons, John R. et al. 1918–1935. *History of Labor in the United States*. New York: Macmillan.

Debo, Angie. 1940. *And Still the Waters Run: The Betrayal of the Five Civilized Tribes*. Princeton, NJ: Princeton University Press.

Downs, Gregory and Masure, Kate, eds. 2015. *The World the Civil War Made*. Chapel Hill: University of North Carolina Press.

Edwards, Rebecca. 1997. *Angels in the Machinery: Gender in American Party Politics from the Civil War to the Progressive Era*. New York: Oxford University Press.

—. 2009. "Politics, Social Movements, and the Periodization of U.S. History." *Journal of the Gilded Age and Progressive Era* 8: 463–473.

Foner, Eric. 1988. *Reconstruction: America's Unfinished Revolution, 1863–1977*. New York: Harper & Row.

Foster, Gaines. 1982. *Ghosts of the Confederacy: Defeat, the Lost Cause, and the Emergence of the New South, 1865–1913*. New York: Oxford University Press.

—. 2002. *Moral Reconstruction: Christian Lobbyists and the Federal Legislation of Morality, 1865–1920*. Chapel Hill: University of North Carolina Press.

Gilmore, Glenda Elizabeth. 1996. *Gender and Jim Crow: Women and the Politics of White Supremacy in North Carolina, 1896–1920*. Chapel Hill: University of North Carolina Press.

Ginzberg, Lori D. 1990. *Women and the Work of Benevolence: Morality, Politics, and Class in the Nineteenth-Century United States*. New Haven, CT: Yale University Press.

Glickman, Lawrence B. 1997. *A Living Wage: American Workers and the Making of a Consumer Society*. Ithaca, NY: Cornell University Press.

Hahn, Steven. 2003. *A Nation Under Our Feet: Black Political Struggles in the Rural South from Slavery to the Great Migration*. Cambridge, MA: Harvard University Press.

Harper, Ida Husted. 1898. *Life and Work of Susan B. Anthony*. Volume 2. Indianapolis: The Hollenbeck Press.

Herbert, Hilary A., et al. 1890. *Why the Solid South?* Baltimore, MD: R.H. Woodward & Company.

Howe, Julia Ward, 1900. *Reminiscences, 1819–1899*. Boston: Houghton, Mifflin.

Josephson, Matthew. 1934. *The Robber Barons: The Great American Capitalists, 1861–1901*. New York: Harcourt, Brace and Company.

Kolko, Gabriel. 1963. *The Triumph of Conservatism: A Reinterpretation of American History, 1900–1916*. New York: The Free Press of Glencoe.

—. 1965. *Railroads and Regulation, 1877–1916*. Princeton, NJ: Princeton University Press.

Milkis, Sidney M. 2009. *Theodore Roosevelt, the Progressive Party, and the Transformation of American Democracy*. Lawrence: University Press of Kansas.

Montgomery, David. 1967. *Beyond Equality: Labor and the Radical Republicans, 1862–1872*. Urbana: University of Illinois Press.

Morgan, H. Wayne, ed. 1963. *The Gilded Age: A Reappraisal*. Syracuse, NY Syracuse University Press.

Nelson, Scott. 1999. *Iron Confederacies: Southern Railways, Klan Violence, and Reconstruction*. Chapel Hill: University of North Carolina Press.

Pascoe, Peggy. 2009. *What Comes Naturally: Miscegenation Law and the Making of Race in America*. New York: Oxford University Press.

Richardson, Heather Cox. 1997. *Greatest Nation of the Earth: Republican Economic Policies During the Civil War*. Cambridge, MA: Harvard University Press.

—. 2001. *The Death of Reconstruction: Race, Labor, and Politics in the Post-Civil War North, 1965–1901*. Cambridge, MA: Harvard University Press.

—. 2006. "North and West of Reconstruction: Studies in Political Economy." In *Reconstructions: New Perspectives on Postbellum America*, ed. Thomas J. Brown, 66–90. New York: Oxford University Press.

—. 2007. *West From Appomattox: The Reconstruction of America After the Civil War*. New Haven, CT: Yale University press.

Schneirov, Richard. 1998. *Labor and Urban Politics: Class Conflict and the Origins of Modern Liberalism in Chicago, 1864–97*. Urbana: University of Illinois Press.

—. 2006. "Thoughts on Periodizing the Gilded Age: Capital Accumulation, Society, and Politics, 1873–1898." *Journal of the Gilded Age and Progressive Era* 5: 189–224.

Sklar, Kathryn Kish. 1995. *Florence Kelley and the Nation's Work: The Rise of Women's Political Culture, 1830–1900*. New Haven, CT: Yale University Press.

Smith, Stacey L. 2014. *Freedom's Frontier: California and the Struggle over Unfree Labor, Emancipation, and Reconstruction*. Chapel Hill: University of North Carolina Press.

Stampp, Kenneth. 1965. *The Era of Reconstruction, 1865–1877*. New York: Alfred A. Knopf.

Stiles, T. J. 2003. *Jesse James: Last Rebel of the Civil War*. New York: Vintage.

Twain, Mark and Charles Dudley Warner. 1873. *The Gilded Age: A Tale of Today*. San Francisco, CA: American Publishing Company.

Waugh, Joan. 1997. *Unsentimental Reformer: The Life of Josephine Shaw Lowell*. Cambridge, MA: Harvard University Press.

Welke, Barbara Young. 2001. *Recasting American Liberty: Gender, Race, Law, and the Railroad Revolution, 1865–1920*. New York and Cambridge: Cambridge University Press.

West, Elliott. 2009. *The Last Indian War: The Nez Perce Story*. New York: Oxford University Press.

White, Richard. 1991. *It's Your Misfortune and None of My Own: A New History of the American West*. Norman: University of Oklahoma Press.

Wiebe, Robert H. 1967. *The Search for Order, 1977–1920*. New York: Hill and Wang.

Willrich, Michael. 2011. *Pox: An American History*. New York: Penguin Press.

Wilson, Mark R. 2010. *The Business of Civil War: Military Mobilization and the State, 1861–1865*. Baltimore, MD: Johns Hopkins University Press.

Woodward, C. Vann. 1955. *The Strange Career of Jim Crow*. New York: Oxford University Press.

Chapter Two

Precursors to Gilded Age and Progressive Era Reforms

James M. Beeby and Brian M. Ingrassia

The debate over the precursors of the Gilded Age and Progressive Era reforms has long divided historians. In emphasizing the nature or scope of reforms, historians have focused on several key issues. Scholars argue over periodization, causation, and the consequences of reforms, among other things. These disagreements are not mere navel gazing; they are at the heart of the profession and the academy. Indeed, historians disagree; often quite heatedly it seems, over the contradictions within the Progressive Movement itself (some scholars ask if one can label progressivism a movement at all), and whether the influences came from one group or myriad groups and organizations. These debates have gone on for decades, sometimes ebbing and flowing, through a constant cascade of competing historiographical arguments, which show no signs of abating any time soon. This is not a bad thing.

The key historiographical differences over precursors to the reform period revolve around chronology, influence, how policy and laws are made, and the influence of disparate groups, movements, political organizations and parties, individuals, as well as debates over specific reforms and the reform agenda as a whole. For example, historians are divided over to what extent the Settlement House Movement influenced the reforms of the Progressive Era, or what role organized labor and agrarian reformers played in the political tumult of the period, and how politicians and interest groups were able to stymie or stimulate reform. There is even less agreement on the extent to which international issues and transatlantic relationships affected the ways in which reform evolved in the United States. Indeed, scholars ask, who were the Progressives and what did they believe? Therefore, how can sense be made of the seemingly contradictory elements of social justice and social control at the heart of the reform period? Perhaps, some scholars note, these elements are not so contradictory after all but a sign of the general fluidity and vitality of the reform era. It is useful, therefore to understand how the historiographical debate over the precursors of the Gilded Age and Progressive Era has developed since the 1920s. Having said that, this chapter can only touch on some of the key text and debates in the field; it is not meant to be exhaustive.

Although there is no clear consensus among historians regarding the precursors to the Progressive Era, since at least the 1960s scholars have tended to discuss several groups or movements as antecedents to the era's reforms. These include the Farmers' Alliances, Populists, Knights of Labor, Mugwumps, and the Nationalist Clubs. The Farmers' Alliance was first formed in the 1870s in central Texas. The group soon spread to other rural areas where farmers chafed against the authority of bankers and railroads, coalescing into regional associations in the Great Plains and South. By 1892, millions of members of these alliances came together to form the Populist movement, which promoted electoral reforms, national ownership of railroads, and the devaluation of money (beneficial to debtors and detrimental to creditors) through the "free" coinage of silver at a fixed ratio. While the Farmers' Alliances and Populists were rooted in rural, agricultural areas, the Knights of Labor were based in industrial cities. Founded in Philadelphia in 1869, under the leadership of "Grand Master Workman" Terence V. Powderly, the Knights hoped to educate workers and eventually assume control over the means of production. Farmers and industrial workers thus contributed to important precursor movements, but so did middle-class thinkers and reformers. A number of historians of the Gilded Age have discussed the "Mugwumps": urban, middle- and upper-middle-class reformers from the Northeast who, in the 1880s, hoped to eliminate corruption in government, especially through civil service reform and leadership by the "best men." The Mugwumps tended toward the functional.

A Companion to the Gilded Age and Progressive Era, First Edition. Edited by Christopher McKnight Nichols and Nancy C. Unger.
© 2017 John Wiley & Sons, Inc. Published 2017 by John Wiley & Sons, Inc.

On the more utopian side of things, Edward Bellamy's 1888 novel *Looking Backward, 2000–1887* prompted the formation of hundreds of so-called Nationalist Clubs throughout America (and even a few overseas). Members of these societies worked to make Bellamy's vision a reality, seeking socialist solutions for the widespread problems of modern American industrial society. Such movements—whether from rural or urban, middle- or working-class origins—presaged the wide variety of self-consciously "progressive" reforms that would sweep American society between the Depression of 1893 and the end of World War I.

An "Age of Reform": Mugwumps and Political Reformers

Several significant interpretations of the Progressive Era appeared in the decades following World War II. Franklin D. Roosevelt's New Deal had reshaped America's political landscape and historians sought the roots of American reform. In 1952, historian Eric Goldman published *Rendezvous with Destiny: A History of Modern American Reform*. Goldman acknowledged that he could have begun his study of twentieth-century liberalism with Jefferson or Jackson, or with Europeans who demanded representative rule in the 1600s. Instead, he saw modern American reform as a response to post-Civil War urbanization, industrialization, and western expansion. War and "pell-mell industrialization had shaken up the society, weakening if not shattering any crust of caste" (Goldman 1952, 7). Yet, Goldman argued that the progressive movement truly started in the 1890s, growing out of the Populist movement of the 1880s. Indeed, progressive reformers perpetuated many Populist traditions, insofar as they hoped to curtail "governmental interventions that benefited large-scale capital" and implement policies "that favored men of little or no capital." Many progressive reforms, in fact, came straight from Populism: direct election of Senators, anti-trust legislation, the federal income tax, the eight-hour work day, and the referendum. Goldman said that progressives also "took up new proposals for direct democracy," including primary elections, electoral recall, worker's compensation, and minimum-wage laws. Goldman noted that progressivism, though, was more urban than Populism and inclined to help all classes, including immigrants—not just farmers (Goldman 1952, 59–60).

Writing in a similar vein, influential Columbia University historian Richard Hofstadter saw the period from 1890 to the 1940s as an age of reform, a response to the "period of industrial and continental expansion and political conservatism" that dated from the end of the Civil War to the 1890s (Hofstadter 1955, 3). Hofstadter notoriously eschewed archival research in favor of synthesis and social theory. Nevertheless, his 1955 book *The Age of Reform* influenced a generation of scholars, with historian Alan Brinkley calling it "the most influential book ever published on the history of twentieth-century America" (quoted in Brown 2006, 99). Hofstadter argued for a clear connection between the Populists and progressives, with their legacies contributing directly to Roosevelt's New Deal reforms in the 1930s. Hofstadter wrote that Populism and progressivism were responses to the major social changes of the late 1800s, "during a rapid and sometimes turbulent transition from the conditions of an agrarian society to those of modern urban life" (Hofstadter 1955, 7). But instead of stressing the southern or western roots of progressivism, Hofstadter saw progressivism's origins in a Protestant "Yankee" tradition based in the countryside of rural New England and New York. After about 1880, the spread of industry and a decades-long period of mass immigration from southern and eastern Europe led to a reaction by these Protestant Yankees. Driven by status anxiety—fear that they would lose their privileged place in society—these old-stock Americans crafted a middle-class reform movement focused on public action. They sought clean government that transcended individual needs; they also "expressed a common feeling that government should be in good part an effort to moralize the lives of individuals while economic life should be intimately related to the stimulation and development of individual character" (Hofstadter 1955, 9).

Hofstadter tended to see the late-1800s Mugwump leaders of major Northeastern metropolises like Boston and New York—as well as Midwestern cities like Indianapolis and Chicago—as part of the progressive tradition of lashing out against municipal corruption and seeking economic reforms in order to reassert social status. Even those leaders who had not been born in New England, said Hofstadter, still looked to the region's literary and political traditions as well as its "moral idealism." Circumstances, though, pressured the Mugwumps into embracing the type of popular government that characterized the Progressive Era. As they experienced their ouster "by new men of the crudest sort," these transitional figures sought reforms that would reshape modern society without sinking to the level of demagoguery (Hofstadter 1955, 140). The rise of progressivism, argued Hofstadter, percolated from all classes of professional men, including the clergy. Sensing that their status had eroded in the new era, they looked for new ways to restore their power. After the economic turbulence of the mid-1890s, men with roots in old-line Yankee families turned from conservatism to progressivism in order to reassert control over religion, higher education, and the legal system. In this way, the professional classes restored their former prestige, or status (Hofstadter 1955). In the decade following publication of *Age of Reform*, discussion of "status anxiety" became *de rigueur*, spawning studies such as Joseph Gusfield's *Symbolic Crusade: Status Politics and the American Temperance Movement*, which stressed Protestant reformers' attempts to assert social control via anti-alcohol crusades (Gusfield 1963).

Hofstadter's emphasis on the Mugwumps foreshadowed several works on these late-1800s middle-class reformers. In 1968 John G. Sproat published *"The Best Men": Liberal Reformers in the Gilded Age*, in which he argued that post-Civil War liberal reformers were sympathetic neither to farmers nor laborers. Rather, they sought to establish a "good government" that would correct the problems of political and business corruption, high taxes, "and the general breakdown of order and morality in society." Rule by "good men," in short, would preserve America's "reputation as a stronghold of opportunity and individual freedom, a bulwark against despotism." Like Hofstadter, Sproat stressed the reformers' "moral code" based in Protestantism (Sproat 1968, 6–7). Later, Gerald W. MacFarland published *Mugwumps, Morals, and Politics, 1884–1920*, which focused on the political generation following the election of reform-minded Democrat Grover Cleveland in 1884. MacFarland blended realistic and idealistic views of the late-1800s political reformers, showing that "the Mugwump impulse is best understood as a blend of tradition and innovation." The Mugwumps, argued MacFarland, sought a thoroughly "professionalized" political and public sphere, trying "to bring greater order and efficiency to American politics through the civil service system and the secret ballot movement." Especially in the cities of New York and New England, this push led to tenement reforms, sanitation initiatives, settlement houses, and the development of parks and playgrounds (MacFarland 1975, 173–175).

"A Search for Order": Industrialization and its Consequences

While Mugwump historiography may have led to a focus on urban and state politics in the Northeast, the turbulent 1960s shifted the main focus of Progressive Era historiography. In 1967 Robert H. Wiebe published an influential interpretation of industrial-era America, *The Search for Order, 1877–1920*. Like Goldman and Hofstadter (the latter of whom he later acknowledged reading in graduate school), Wiebe's book was synthetic rather than focused on detailed primary source analysis. Unlike those other authors, Wiebe focused on a firm chronological period: he was characterizing the turn-of-the-century industrial era, rather than trying to unearth the roots of New Deal-era reforms. Wiebe stressed that the late 1800s in America was a time when disparate regions of the United States transformed themselves from a series of "island communities" into a single nation. Railroads, finance, and industry were instrumental in this process of cohesion, fueling the growth of cities both old and new—and also tying small towns and rural areas into national networks of communication, transportation, and finance. Apparently incorporating the lessons of historians such as Oscar Handlin and John Higham, Wiebe also noted that many Protestant Americans in the Progressive Era reacted to the massive waves of immigration that came along with the rise of large-scale industry (Wiebe 1967). With his emphasis upon Nativist backlash, Wiebe's account was somewhat less positive in this regard than the type of early-1950s cross-class consensus stressed in Goldman's *Rendezvous with Destiny*.

More explicitly than Goldman or Hofstadter, Wiebe enumerated progressivism's antecedents. He discussed three "mildly adhesive movements" that preoccupied "worried citizens" in the 1880s, just before the onset of the Progressive Era: various farmers' alliances, the Knights of Labor, and the "Nationalist" movement inspired by Edward Bellamy. All three groups, said Wiebe, sought to recreate the sense of community that had been lost or disrupted in post-Civil War America. With the possible exception of Bellamy's followers, however, none of these reform groups were led by the old-line Calvinists cited by Hofstadter—and they were not necessarily motivated by status anxiety. Rather, they were common people motivated by a wider range of self-interests (Wiebe 1967, 66).

The Knights of Labor, founded in 1869 and led by Philadelphia labor leader Terence V. Powderly, united workers into a national framework. The Knights "sought an ethical substitute for the capitalism they believed was destroying opportunity, equality, and brotherhood" (Wiebe 1967, 67). Although it thrived from the 1870s to the mid-1880s, with millions of members, the Knights organization ultimately collapsed in the late 1880s—later to be replaced by the more practically oriented American Federation of Labor. Like the Knights of Labor, with their utopian bent, the so-called Nationalist movement sought to reassert community via socialism. This group was prompted by Edward Bellamy's *Looking Backward, 1887–2000*, an 1888 novel that showed Americans in the year 2000 looking back on the corruption of the United States in the 1880s. Seeing Bellamy as a prophet, Nationalist Clubs sprouted up all over America, seeking to put his ideas into action. In the same spirit as the Knights and the Nationalists, the Farmers' Alliance movement sought to establish an agrarian community that would challenge the rising power of capitalism. Especially popular in the South and West, the farmers' alliances saw themselves in opposition to Northeastern financiers and "plutocrats." Like some other reform-minded groups of this time, a distinctive strain of Nativism ran through this movement. Wiebe noted that members of the farmers' alliances usually "visualized the new world as dry and white"—a vision that led them to support temperance and prohibition (Wiebe 1967, 71–72).

Social Justice and the Settlement House Movement

Wiebe's book gained traction and, like Hofstadter's, influenced a generation of Progressive Era historians. *The Search for Order* apparently solidified the view that the farmers' alliances and Knights of Labor were important progressive antecedents, even if its focus on Bellamy's Nationalist movement has not persisted in the historiography. In any case, by the mid-1960s American historians clearly saw the Progressive Era's antecedents in the 1880s, in the wide array of responses to industrialization and urbanization. Yet a greater level of nuance appeared as more historians examined specific progressive reforms. In particular, some historians—writing in an era of emergent globalization—started seeing progressivism's origins as extending beyond the boundaries of the United States. For example, in the same year that Wiebe's book appeared, Allen F. Davis published *Spearheads of Reform*, an important history of the social settlement movement. Davis kicked off his book with an account of the movement's origins that went back to 1880s England. Toynbee Hall, typically acknowledged as the first settlement house, was founded in London in 1884. Davis wrote that Toynbee Hall was "the culmination of a diverse reform movement, closely allied with Romanticism, [which] sought to preserve humanistic and spiritual values in a world dominated by materialism and urban industrialism." His book has some similarities to the work of earlier historians, such as Hofstadter, who stressed the role of professional men who were fighting back against the corruption of urban–industrial society. Toynbee Hall's founders were clergymen and professors influenced by Oxford professor John Ruskin, who hoped to use Christian ideals to shape the modern world (Davis 1967, 3).

Although Toynbee Hall had its critics, it also had numerous admirers, and it spawned imitators. American Stanton Coit visited in 1886 and subsequently started a similar organization on Manhattan's Lower East Side. This "Neighborhood Guild" attracted intrigued young reformers, including socialists. It disbanded when Coit moved back to England in 1887, but the settlement movement did not die with the passing of the Neighborhood Guild. Later that year, a group of Smith College alumnae gathered together near Boston and started the College Settlement Association, which opened its first settlement house in New York in 1889. The following week Jane Addams—a young woman from Rockford, Illinois, who possessed an abiding interest in social justice—established America's most famous settlement house in Chicago. Using money inherited from her father, Addams and Ellen Gates Starr, her friend and colleague, "moved into an old mansion on South Halsted Street" on the Windy City's west side. Addams and the other Hull-House settlement workers "believed that they were establishing an instrument for social, educational, humanitarian, and civic reform" (Davis 1967, 12).

The tendency of historians of the settlement house movement to stress international origins persisted, foreshadowing a larger trend in twenty-first-century historiography. In *Settlement Folk*, historian Mina Carson stressed the English predecessors of the settlement movement, arguing that settlements represented a transatlantic expression of humanitarianism: "an assertion of human brotherhood and spiritual equality." Social settlement proponents tried to use these institutions to reassemble American society into a new whole in face of the chaotic "fragmenting" of late-1800s society (Carson 1990, 7–8). Even historical studies focused on individual settlement reformers, such as Victoria Bissell Brown's *The Education of Jane Addams*, have stressed both domestic and international influence. Brown noted that "Addams introduced the British settlement scheme to Chicago labor activists, women reformers, and liberal clergy," all of whom "were hungry for practical, productive alternatives to the class alienation borne of laissez-faire capitalism and condescending charity." The founders of social settlements like Hull-House were among the urban leaders and reformers who were willing to challenge the industrial order that had dominated the nation ever since Union victory in 1865. Addams was just one of many "children of the Gilded Age" who sought to make a change and eliminate the greedy excesses of the 1870s and 1880s (Brown 2004, 3).

Jane Addams modeled her ideals after those of her Republican father, John Huy Addams, whom she idolized. Nevertheless, she was also influenced by her formal education. Rockford Female Seminary was not the elite New England women's college (such as Smith or Vassar) to which Jane had aspired, yet it was a place where she began to articulate the importance of women's role in reforming the public sphere (Brown 2004). As the story of Hull-House's founder demonstrates, higher education was an important factor in raising young women's progressive consciousness in the late 1800s. In *Beyond Separate Spheres: Intellectual Roots of Modern Feminism*, historian Rosalind Rosenberg showed how a generation of thinkers (both male and female) disproved the idea that women's bodies and minds were unsuited to education or other activities outside the home. Rejecting Victorian notions of domesticity and sex differences such as those advocated by physician Edward Clarke in the 1870s, scholars like Helen Thompson and Clelia Duel Mosher paved the way for women's increased participation in the public sphere (Rosenberg 1982). With the rise of such ideas, more and more women were attending college and becoming interested in progressive causes. Historian Lynn D. Gordon argued in *Gender and Higher Education in the Progressive Era* that by the 1890s young women "made up an important and growing percentage of undergraduates… and a much-discussed vanguard in the world beyond the campus gates." Subsequently, many of them took what they had learned in the universities and contributed to "the political and intellectual ferment of the Progressive Era" (Gordon 1990, 2–3).

In Search of Progressivism: The Kaleidoscope of Reform Traditions

By the 1980s, historians were exploring the many facets of progressivism, rather than simply treating it as a single entity. Indeed, it was during this decade that scholars started to argue that progressivism, rather than being a single movement, was actually a collection of movements. Prominent intellectual historian Daniel T. Rodgers promoted this stance in the influential journal article "In Search of Progressivism." By stressing the fragmentary nature of progressivism, Rodgers helped a new generation of historians circumvent the notion that the Progressive Era itself was dead as a concept simply because there was no coherent movement for scholars to isolate (Rodgers 1982). This realization opened up room for historians to interpret progressivism and the various avenues by which it had originated.

Around the same time that Rodgers's article appeared, cultural historian Robert Crunden published *Ministers of Reform: The Progressives' Achievement in American Civilization, 1889–1920.* Rather than seeing progressives as driven primarily by political or even social motivations, Crunden argued that progressivism "was a climate of creativity within which writers, artists, politicians, and thinkers functioned." Like earlier scholars such as Hofstadter, Crunden explicitly connected the roots of progressivism to the Civil War and mid-century Protestantism, especially Calvinism. He noted that the most of the progressives were born between 1854 and 1874, a time during which they "absorbed the severe, Protestant moral values of their parents"—values that they identified with the Civil War and the Union cause, especially Abraham Lincoln. Jane Addams, in particular, venerated Lincoln, who was her father's political hero. Rather than advancing a status anxiety argument, though, Crunden portrayed the progressives as seeking new ways to make a difference in both their own lives and in larger society. Turning away from the ministry, the new generation shifted to law, politics, higher education, social work, and journalism. In such professions, progressives "could become preachers urging moral reform on institutions as well as on individuals." Crunden even saw abolitionism as an important antecedent to Progressive Era reform, with the progressives seeking their own causes and leaders to continue the tradition established by mid-1800s firebrands. By the early 1900s, some Americans even compared progressive president Theodore Roosevelt to the martyred Lincoln (Crunden 1982, ix).

Cultural and intellectual historians such as Crunden were the most likely to imagine the Progressive Era's antecedents as stretching back to the antebellum era. Likewise, James Gilbert discussed the antebellum roots of progressivism in *Perfect Cities,* an analysis of the 1893 Chicago Columbian Exposition and the utopian experiments accompanying it. Gilbert noted that many of the men who remade Chicago in the 1890s—such as evangelist Dwight Moody, philanthropist Turlington Harvey, and industrialist George Pullman—were born in the 1830s either in New England or in western New York's so-called "Burned-Over District" near the Erie Canal. These reformers originated in farming or artisanal families such as the ones that pioneered a variety of noteworthy (and religiously influenced) antebellum social reforms. Gilbert implies that these men were trying not only to make money in Chicago, but also to reassert a certain Yankee vision in the bustling metropolis. They created the Columbian Exposition with its famous "White City," and also built utopian communities like the factory town of Pullman and the evangelical haven of Harvey. Although neither of these experiments outlasted the Progressive Era, Gilbert shows how both represented 1890s reform zeal. Gilbert's interpretation of Chicago reform was very different from Hofstadter's *Age of Reform* in its focus on culture instead of politics, yet it was similar insofar as it stressed progressivism's Calvinist, Yankee roots. Whereas Wiebe had moved the focus to workers and farmers in *The Search for Order* in the late 1960s, by the early 1990s Gilbert had turned the lens back to middle- and upper-class urban leaders (Gilbert 1991).

The Transnational Debate and Precursors to Reform

The late 1980s and early 1990s were a watershed time in Progressive Era historiography, especially because of a newfound focus on reform's transnational dimensions. Historians writing in the 1960s had acknowledged the international origins of the social settlement movement. By the end of the twentieth century, this transnational view of progressivism gained additional credence. Foreshadowing this new direction was James T. Kloppenberg's *Uncertain Victory: Social Democracy and Progressivism in European and American Thought, 1870–1920.* An intellectual historian, Kloppenberg showed how American and European thinkers crafted the "political theories of social democracy and progressivism" between 1870 and 1920. Rather than hewing strictly to socialism or "laissez-faire liberalism," scholars such as William James, John Dewey, Max Weber, and Richard T. Ely contributed to a progressive mindset that reshaped Euro-American society (Kloppenberg 1986, 3).

In 1998, Daniel Rodgers—the same historian who had stressed the multi-faceted nature of progressivism in 1982—published his influential volume *Atlantic Crossings: Social Politics in a Progressive Age.* Rodgers began this massive tome with the premise that American history has long been tied to political, commercial, and intellectual networks that stretch well beyond the nation-state. He echoed Goldman and Hofstadter by stressing the connections between the Progressive Era and New Deal, yet Rodgers deviated from those 1950s historians by situating the reforms of the 1890s to the 1930s in a distinctly transatlantic context. To understand the American liberal tradition, argued Rodgers, one had to know *fin de siècle* Paris or Berlin as well as late-1800s Boston or New York or Chicago. For progressive antecedents, Rodgers stressed the "social Protestantism" (or Social Gospel) of the North Atlantic region that fueled the settlement movement. Like Wiebe, he invoked socialism, but rather than starting with Edward Bellamy, he began with

London's Fabian Society, which inspired many American socialists. Transatlantic networks sustained a republic of letters that flowered in reform-minded American magazines like *McClure's* and *The New Republic* (Rodgers 1998).

In one chapter, Rodgers showed how the many Americans who trekked to Germany to study in its famous universities in the 1870s to the 1890s brought back with them reform ideas from that newly unified nation. In Berlin and Heidelberg, American students learned a new variety of economic thought that challenged laissez-faire, or what was then called on the continent "English economics." Although similar critics railed against unrestrained capitalism in France and England (including Arnold Toynbee, after whom Toynbee Hall was named), Prussian scholars were more influential because of the legions of young Americans—virtually all of them Protestant men who would have ended up as clergy in an earlier era—who studied in Germany before returning to work in government or teach in America's budding university system. Important educational institutions like Columbia University and the University of Pennsylvania's Wharton School of Finance and Economy were staffed by German-trained scholars such as Edmund J. James and Simon Patten. Such international antecedents were often unwelcome back on the other side of the pond, where they were seen as un-American. (German universities may have pre-dated industrial capitalism, but many of America's universities did not.) Over time, such international influences were forgotten via a type of conscious amnesia. For example, the influential University of Wisconsin economist Richard T. Ely responded to accusations of "un-Americanism" by making the disingenuous yet useful claim that the new ideas were a "pure, native product" that had originated in the pure soil and air of America's heartland (Rodgers 1998, 77).

By the 1990s and early 2000s, it was becoming more common for American historians to place their narratives in such a transnational context. Alan Dawley's *Changing the World: American Progressives in War and Revolution* explored the international interests of reformers, especially in the latter years of the Progressive Era (Dawley 2003). In 2005, Thomas Bender made the Progressive Era a part of his larger study of America's place in global history, *A Nation among Nations: America's Place in World History.* Bender noted that although Hofstadter and Wiebe were "scholars of cosmopolitan intellect," their accounts of American reform—written in the 1950s and 1960s—now "seem[ed] surprisingly... parochial, so deeply rooted... in the analysis of the particularities of American culture." While Hofstadter stressed peculiarly American characteristics such as "moralism, status anxiety, and the fear of failure among the old middle class," Wiebe focused upon "the dissolution of small-town life, the rise of a new middle class, and the emergence of bureaucracy." By contrast, Bender followed Rodgers, Kloppenberg, and Dawley in "emphasizing the transatlantic conversations about social policy, reform networks, and regulatory and welfare policies enacted" in Europe and the United States from the 1880s to the 1920s. For Bender, America's Progressive Era was part of a larger global reckoning with the dramatic transformations brought about by large-scale urbanization and industrialization. Reform movements drew on global precedents, not just local concerns and circumstances (Bender 2006, 247–248).

Leslie Butler continued in the same vein in *Critical Americans: Victorian Intellectuals and Transatlantic Liberal Reform*, which essentially reimagined Mugwump intellect for a new generation of American historians. While Rodgers saw the transatlantic intellectual antecedents of Progressivism in European economic theory generally and the German universities in particular, Butler envisioned those antecedents in a web of scholars who traveled and wrote from the 1850s to the 1890s. Butler showed how New England dons like Charles Eliot Norton, Thomas Wentworth Higginson, James Russell Lowell, and George William Curtis spent decades discussing and promoting democratic reform and cultural uplift. Like Crunden's *Ministers of Reform* a generation earlier, *Critical Americans* stressed the long-range impact of the Civil War on late-1800s thought. The sectional conflict "was the moment when [American thinkers] became 'liberal'"—and for decades they insisted on portraying the military victory as a victory for liberalism. The Civil War was also the crucible that forged transatlantic connections with "sympathetic Britons...who identified with the Union cause and connected it to their program of liberal reform." Unlike Rodgers, who in *Atlantic Crossings* saw a clear causal link between the German universities and American reform, Butler envisaged a more loosely knit community "rooted in friendship [and] mutual interests." It was "a network of print" rather than one of "specific institutions or organizations" (Butler 2007, 4).

Although a number of historians have articulated progressivism's international antecedents in recent decades, not all have jumped on this bandwagon. Steven J. Diner's *A Very Different Age: Americans of the Progressive Era* focused on the rich diversity of experiences among various Americans during the Progressive Era, yet somewhat conventionally stressed the fact that in the 1890s, "middle-class Americans began looking to government to do something about these wrenching changes in America's economy and culture." Like Hofstadter and Wiebe a generation earlier, Diner discussed progressive antecedents such as the Farmers' Alliance, the Knights of Labor, and the Mugwumps (the self-proclaimed "best men"). However, unlike Wiebe, Diner did not discuss Bellamy's utopian Nationalist Clubs. Furthermore, his account reflected the growth of scholarship on women and urban history by stressing the significance of the social settlement movement, especially Jane Addams and Hull-House (Diner 1998, 5).

In another synthetic account, *A Fierce Discontent: The Rise and Fall of the Progressive Movement in America*, Michael McGerr portrayed progressivism as a movement that sprang up organically around 1900 in response to late-1800s structural changes. McGerr wrote, "The relentless development of the industrial economy, the increasing spread of news in papers and magazines, and the unceasing political contests of a democracy all made the different classes constantly aware of one another and generated the many signs of friction in late-nineteenth-century America." Not only did McGerr de-emphasize international aspects, but he also chose not to stress any particular antecedents. Essentially, he portrayed organizations like the farmers' alliances less as groups that *influenced* progressivism and more as failed Gilded Age enterprises that were *superseded* by progressivism (McGerr 2003, 28).

McGerr's interpretation also diverged from that of some Progressive Era historians of the early twenty-first century who have tended to stress a long Progressive Era, dating from the 1860s to as late as 1930 (for example, Clarke 2007, 1). Leading this charge was historian Rebecca Edwards, who published *New Spirits: Americans in the "Gilded Age," 1865–1905*. In the revised edition of that book, Edwards argued that her goal was "to challenge historians' long-standing division between a corrupt, stagnant 'Gilded Age' and a laudable, optimistic 'Progressive Era.'" By contrast, Edwards envisioned the decades following the Civil War as an "Early Progressive Era." She argued that progressive attempts "to purify politics, regulate and restrict the extraordinary power of big business, and fight poverty and other social and economic injustices" were already going strong before the 1890s—and that many of the problems of the so-called "Gilded Age" lingered well after 1900 (Edwards 2011, 5–6). Edwards stressed the work of Henry George, the progressive economist whose 1879 *Progress and Poverty* first brought to many readers' attention the negative aspects of post-Civil War growth. She noted that the death of hundreds of thousands in the sectional conflict led to significant social ferment, citing the organization of the Women's Christian Temperance Union (1873) as a reaction against veterans' alcoholism. Edwards also echoed Nell Irvin Painter's 1987 synthesis, *Standing at Armageddon*, by stressing the role of Reconstruction and race in shaping the early Progressive Era (Edwards 2011).

The Labor Movement and the Era of Reform

In 2007, Maureen Flanagan published *America Reformed: Progressives and Progressivisms, 1890s–1920s*, a synthetic account that—like Rodgers's influential 1982 article—stressed the multifarious characteristics of the Progressive Era. Choosing not to emphasize a long Progressive Era, Flanagan began her account in 1893 at the Columbian Exposition (more commonly known as the Chicago World's Fair). Flanagan portrayed the Windy City, then becoming the nation's second-largest metropolis, as a good "place to start exploring why Americans began to change their ideas of what constituted a good society and government." There were many competing ideas and visions. Like Wiebe and others, Flanagan briefly noted that progressive-style reforms started to spring up in the 1880s. While the Mugwumps had tried to fix political corruption by placing the Best Men (especially themselves) in office, the Greenback Labor Party "focused on monetary reform as the path to a more democratic society." Meanwhile, the Knights of Labor proposed reforming society by creating cooperative agencies of producers. The farmers' alliances in the Midwest and South created a Populist Party "to defend the 'people' against the 'interests' of politicians and businessmen." The Populists wanted to place the power more firmly in the hands of the common people, and they influenced mainstream politics by merging with the Democratic Party in 1896, under the leadership of William Jennings Bryan (Flanagan 2007, 10). Even though the traditional trinity of Mugwumps, socialists, and farmers appeared in this synthetic account, Flanagan placed little emphasis on international antecedents of turn-of-the-century reforms. *America Reformed* did mention a few international organizations, but for the most part the book discussed internationalism in the context of anti-imperialist movements in the years between 1898 and 1917 (Flanagan 2007).

Labor historians were also less likely to stress progressivism's international aspects, instead choosing to see reform's roots in the agency of workers and labor unions. For instance, Shelton Stromquist stressed the role of labor in *Reinventing "The People": The Progressive Movement, the Class Problem, and the Origins of Modern Liberalism*. Like other historians, Stromquist traced progressive reforms back to the post-Civil War decades. He wrote that "years of economic expansion following the Civil War had produced new hierarchies of power and privilege that seemed to threaten the virtuous republican commonwealth." Capitalists—especially railroad barons and industrial tycoons—had taken over America's democracy. In turn, "producers" (workers) decided that they would take back power from these parasitic "nonproducers." Stromquist saw the Civil War as a catalyst—not just a starting point. Working people saw the sectional conflict as a moment when the federal government turned itself into a mechanism for confiscating ill-gotten property and "reconstructing a morally and economically bankrupt society." In turn, "[m]embers of the producing classes began to conceive a state that might acquire and operate railroads, telephones and telegraphs, coal mines, and even manufacturing monopolies, or that might construct and finance a vast network of cooperative warehouses and granaries." Subsequently, the Farmers' Alliance and Knights of Labor became vehicles by which "a generation of workers, farmers, and their reform allies" sought to reshape modern American society. Stromquist observed that although many workers looked to socialism, they also crafted a privilege based on "whiteness and masculinity." Workers in a wide array of industries excluded non-whites and women from their utopian vision. Despite labor's influence, middle-class progressives ultimately rejected the workers' cries and instead developed middle-of-the-road reforms, increasingly asserting "that class conflict could be transcended… and a classless citizenry—the people—made the agents of democratic renewal" (Stromquist 2006, 14–16). Historian Georg Leidenberger similarly argued in *Chicago's Progressive Alliance* that workers were agents of progressive change. Softening Stromquist's thesis somewhat, Leidenberger stressed the alliances between middle-class reformers and labor unions in Chicago's push for public streetcars (Leidenberger 2006). If the relationship between labor unions and middle-class reformers perplexed historians for decades and still provokes historiographical debate, then historians remain just as divided over the role of agrarians and the agrarian movement.

Agrarian Discontent and its Legacies

One key element in the major historiographical debate over the precursors to the Gilded Age and Progressive Era Reforms centers on the role of the agrarian movement, particularly the Populist Movement. Ever since the seminal work by John D. Hicks, *The Populist Revolt: A History of the Farmers' Alliance and the People's Party*, historians have grappled with central questions such as who were the Populist reformers, what was their agenda and what was their legacy. The main debate, for years, centered on the question of whether the Populists, and by extension agrarian reformers of all stripes, were forward thinking and innovative, or misguided nostalgists harking back to a time that never really existed, in much the same way as members of the United Kingdom Independence Party long for a return to the Golden Era of the 1950s. This debate raged for decades (Clanton 1969; Goodwyn 1976; Hicks 1931; Hofstadter 1955; Palmer 1980; Woodward 1951). Concomitant with arguments over the nature of the agrarian revolt was the debate by these same scholars over the precursors of the Progressive Era reform movement. Did agrarians, for example, push for government regulation, influence laws at the local, state, and national level in the period, and did agrarians influence the burgeoning middle-class and the associational culture at the heart of the Progressive Era? As long ago as the early 1930s, John D. Hicks argued that although the Populists were defeated as political party, much of what they advocated became law in the Progressive Era (Hicks 1931, 404–423). Several scholars agreed with Hicks, and noted that leading tenets of agrarian reform become central to the Progressive Era (electoral reform, economic policy and banking reforms, at least some government oversight of key industries, a postal service, and other areas). As early as 1963, Walter Nugent, in his superb book on Populism in Kansas, one of the most active and important hotbeds of the agrarian insurgency, completely undermined the argument promulgated by Richard Hofstadter and others that the Populists were anti-Semitic and anti-reform, and suffered from status anxiety. Rather, Nugent discerned, the Populists were in the vanguard of a movement for economic and social justice, and part of a long tradition of grassroots agrarian activism. Indeed, so significant is Nugent's work on Populism and agrarian reform, that in 2013 his *The Tolerant Populists* appeared again as a second edition, largely unchanged, except for an excellent preface that updated the state of the field of Populist historiography and agrarian reform. In the new preface, Nugent persuasively noted that although the Populists were defeated as a political party by 1900, "In the next twenty years, however, many of the Populists' specific proposals, and the overall thrust of using the government to benefit the people, were achieved." This central argument has largely found its supporters across the field of the Gilded Age and Progressive Era and remains a crucial strand in the historiography of precursors to the reform period (Nugent 2013, ix).

Another key book that shifted the historiographical plates was the magnum opus *Roots of Reform: Farmers, Workers, and the American State, 1877–1917*, in which Elizabeth Sanders takes Nugent's point and develops it to a whole new level of analysis. Sanders's work, which appeared in 1999, transformed the historical debate on the precursors of the Progressive Movement and reoriented historians' approaches to the role of agrarians and government policy in the Gilded Age. She deftly highlights the critical role of agrarians in writing and passing the federal legislation of the Progressive Era, and argues that "agrarian movements constituted the most important political force during the development of the American national state in the half century before World War I" (Sanders 1997, 1). Agrarian reformers were thus not only a precursor to, but also a vital player in progressive reforms at the national level. Indeed, Sanders discerned "the main contours of Progressive Era state expansion were direct results of the pressing of agrarian claims in the national legislature: the redefinition of trade policy, the creation of an income tax; a new, publicly controlled banking and currency system; antitrust policy; the regulation of agricultural marketing networks…, federal control of railroads…" (Sanders 1997, 7). In short, agrarian statism was pivotal to the reform period. Sanders book reoriented the historiographical debate over the precursors of Progressive Era reform. The 50th Anniversary edition of *The Tolerant Populists* noted that Sanders's work is crucial because it placed the People's Party "centrally in the historical development of agrarian politics and accurately describes what she (Sanders) calls 'the agrarian statist agenda'" (Nugent 2013, xv). Rebecca Edwards, in her beautifully written 2009 "Politics, Social Movements, and the Periodization of U.S. History" in the *Journal of the Gilded Age and Progressive Era*, also praised Sanders for her groundbreaking work. Edwards noted as well that scholars of Populism, including Charles Postel and Connie Lester, show that "progressivism strains" actually existed with agrarianism. Lester focused on the state of Tennessee, whereas Postel produced a narrative of national proportion and import (Edwards 2009, 470; Lester 2006; Postel 2007).

The article noted above by Rebecca Edwards is a crucial piece of historiographical writing that cemented her place as one of the scholars *par excellence* of the period. She also questioned, as many have in the past and probably will do in the future, the whole periodization of the Gilded Age and Progressive Era, and she made a plausible case for the "long Progressive Era." However, Edwards also sees continuity across the Gilded Age and Progressive Era. Thus the precursors are quite self-evident; muckrakers, agrarian reformers, the settlement-house movement, the women's movement and others. Indeed, as Edwards argued, "the breadth, complexity, and intensity of grassroots movements and ideas that arose before 1900 refutes the standard view that they were simply a prologue, and that the 'real' era of reform began after 1900" (Edwards 2009, 468). Thus, the debate over precursors, at least for Edwards, misses the point. What is more significant is that the Progressive Era reforms only make sense if one takes into account the entire post-Civil War period. In doing this, Edwards has aligned herself with the work of Hicks, Pollack, Nugent, Sanders, and others.

Such works are also influenced by the new generation of scholars of Populism and agrarian reform that emerged in the early to mid-1990s; scholars, who through exhaustive archival research, postulated that the agrarian movement all across the South, the West, and Midwest, from its nascent organizations in the 1870s to its pinnacle as the People's Party in the 1890s, was forward looking and transformative. Through various local studies, state histories, thematic monographs, and policy studies of the agrarian movement(s), the scholarship is all encompassing and strong. This new scholarship was capped by the superb, award-winning intellectual history of Populism by Charles Postel, *The Populist Vision*, which appeared in 2007. Building on the intellectual history of populism by scholars such as Gene Clanton and Norman Pollack, Postel was able to bring together all the latest work on the national Populist Movement and show that it was both a reforming and a forward-looking movement, not one stuck in the past. He noted that Populism involved a melding of rural reform with working-class organizations and urban middle-class activists, all of whom campaigned for a modern economy, with large-scale cooperative enterprises and state-centered regulation. Thus, for Postel, Populism was certainly a precursor of reform, though what followed the Populists was very different in terms of form and content (Postel 2007, 3–22; 269–289). In many ways, therefore, Postel agreed with the central arguments of Elizabeth Sanders. And, since 2007, most historians of agrarian reform tend to agree with their broad arguments (Ali 2010; Beeby 2008; Hild 2007). They conclude that the reform era only makes sense in the context of the agrarian reform movements, and that the agrarian movement was instrumental in the success of the reform period in general.

Conclusion: The Debate Continues

Even in the early twenty-first century, however, there is no clear consensus regarding the precursors of the Progressive Era. In a recent synthesis, *Rebirth of a Nation: The Making of Modern America, 1877–1920*, Jackson Lears continued the tradition of cultural and intellectual historians seeking progressivism's deep roots. He identified the force driving the Progressive Era as a post-Civil War longing for "regeneration," a deep-seated desire "rooted in Protestant patterns of conversion" that "also resonated with the American mythology of starting over, of reinventing the self." This analysis is reminiscent of Hofstadter's argument, but rather than basing progressivism in old-line Protestant "status anxiety," Lears focused on a genuine Protestant desire for rebirth that transcended a more secular desire for social power. In this way, he seemed to be reviving Crunden's early-1980s argument. As Lears noted, the end of the Civil War prompted many Americans to feel "that the Union had reaffirmed its very being through blood sacrifice," which in turn "promoted a postwar dream of national renewal through righteous war." This desire for rebirth fueled the effort to reunite and reform the nation, but it also prompted the late-1800s campaign for white supremacy, which manifested itself in notorious Jim Crow segregation laws. Lears focused on progressivism's domestic antecedents, rather than its international ones. For example, although he briefly discussed Jane Addams's trip to London when recounting Hull-House's founding in 1889, Lears stressed that "many settlement-house workers were affluent young women… seeking a moral purpose amid a life of aimless ease" (Lears 2009, 1–3).

While Lears has a lot to offer historians and scholars, and in the last two or three years others have added a plethora of local and case studies on the reform era, there is still no agreement on the precursors to the Gilded Age and Progressive Era reforms. This poses an exciting challenge. The stimulating intellectual debate and passionate arguments between historians and scholars have opened important seams for historians to mine. Scholars still need to flesh out the international scope of reform and they also need to complicate and explain the seemingly contradictory nature of reform itself. Rebecca Edwards's essay from 2009 still remains one of the most important assessments of the state of the field and on precursors to the reform period. She noted towards the end of her article, "Perhaps it would be useful to broaden our vision. Instead of looking for consistency inside Populism and progressivism, both of which were sprawling and protean movements (and probably, in the case of progressivism, not one coherent movement at all), we can look for themes and threads extending across the entire period." (Edwards 2009, 472). Only then will historians see how this jigsaw pieces together and better understand the precursors to the reform period and indeed, the reforms in their entirety.

References

Ali, Omar H. 2010. *In The Lion's Mouth: Black Populism in the New South, 1886–1900*. Jackson: University Press of Mississippi.

Beeby, James M. 2008. *Revolt of the Tar Heels: The North Carolina Populist Movement, 1890–1901*. Jackson: University Press of Mississippi.

—, ed. 2012. *Populism in the South Revisited: New Interpretations and New Departures*. Jackson: University Press of Mississippi.

Bender, Thomas. 2006. *A Nation among Nations: America's Place in World History*. New York: Hill & Wang.

Brown, David S. 2006. *Richard Hofstadter: An Intellectual Biography*. Chicago: University of Chicago Press.

Brown, Victoria Bissell. 2004. *The Education of Jane Addams*. Philadelphia: University of Pennsylvania Press.

Butler, Leslie. 2007. *Critical Americans: Victorian Intellectuals and Transatlantic Liberal Reform*. Chapel Hill: University of North Carolina Press.

Carson, Mina. 1990. *Settlement Folk: Social Thought and the American Settlement Movement, 1885–1930*. Chicago: University of Chicago Press.

Clanton, Gene. 1969. *Kansas Populism: Ideas and Men*. Lawrence: University Press of Kansas.

—. 1991. *Populism: The Humane Preference in America, 1890–1901*. Boston: Twayne.

Clarke, Michael Tavel. 2007. *These Days of Large Things: The Culture of Size in America, 1865–1930*. Ann Arbor: University of Michigan Press.

Creech, Joe. 2015. "The Tolerant Populists and the Legacy of Walter Nugent." *Journal of the Gilded Age and Progressive Era* 14, 2: 141–159.

Crunden, Robert M. 1984, 1992. *Ministers of Reform: The Progressives' Achievement in American Civilization, 1889–1920*. Urbana: University of Illinois Press.

Davis, Allen F. 1967. *Spearheads for Reform: The Social Settlements and the Progressive Movement, 1890–1914*. New York: Oxford University Press.

Dawley, Alan. 2003. *Changing the World: American Progressives in War and Revolution*. Princeton, NJ: Princeton University Press.

Diner, Steven J. 1998. *A Very Different Age: Americans of the Progressive Era*. New York: Hill & Wang.

Edwards, Rebecca. 2009. "Politics, Social Movements, and Periodization of U.S. History" *Journal of the Gilded Age and Progressive Era* 8, 4: 463–473.

—. 2011. *New Spirits: Americans in the "Gilded Age," 1865–1905*, 2nd ed. New York: Oxford University Press.

Flanagan, Maureen A. 2007. *America Reformed: Progressives and Progressivisms, 1890s–1920s*. New York: Oxford University Press.

Gilbert, James. 1991. *Perfect Cities: Chicago's Utopias of 1893*. Chicago: University of Chicago Press.

Goldman, Eric F. 1956, 1952. *Rendezvous with Destiny: A History of Modern American Reform*. New York: Vintage.

Goodwyn, Lawrence. 1976. *Democratic Promise: The Populist Moment in America*. New York: Oxford University Press.

Gordon, Lynn D. 1990. *Gender and Higher Education in the Progressive Era*. New Haven, CT: Yale University Press.

Gusfield, Joseph R. 1963. *Symbolic Crusade: Status Politics and the American Temperance Movement*. Urbana: University of Illinois Press.

Handlin, Oscar. 1941. *Boston's Immigrants, 1790–1880*. Cambridge, MA: Harvard University Press.

Hays, Samuel P. 1957. *The Response to Industrialism, 1885–1914*. Chicago: Chicago University Press.

Hicks, John D. 1931. *The Populist Revolt: A History of the Farmers' Alliance and the People's Party*. Minneapolis: University of Minnesota Press.

Higham, John. 1955. *Strangers in the Land: Patterns of American Nativism, 1860–1925*. New Brunswick, NJ Rutgers University Press.

Hild, Matthew. 2007. *Greenbackers, Knights of Labor, and Populists: Farmer—Labor Insurgency in the Late-Nineteenth Century South*. Athens: University of Georgia Press.

Hofstadter, Richard. 1955. *The Age of Reform: From Bryan to F.D.R.* New York: Vintage.

Kloppenberg, James T. 1986. *Uncertain Victory: Social Democracy and Progressivism in European and American Thought, 1870–1920*. New York: Oxford University Press.

Lears, Jackson. 2009. *Rebirth of a Nation: The Making of Modern America, 1877–1920*. New York: Harper.

Leidenberger, Georg. 2006. *Chicago's Progressive Alliance: Labor and the Bid for Public Streetcars*. DeKalb: Northern Illinois University Press.

Lester, Connie L. 2006. *Up From the Mudsills of Hell: The Farmers' Alliance, Populism, and Progressive Agriculture in Tennessee, 1870–1915*. Athens: University of Georgia Press.

MacFarland, Gerald W. 1975. *Mugwumps, Morals, and Politics, 1884–1920*. Amherst: University of Massachusetts Press.

McGerr, Michael. 2003. *A Fierce Discontent: The Rise and Fall of the Progressive Movement in America*. New York: Oxford University Press.

Nugent, Walter. 1963, 2013. *The Tolerant Populists: Kansas Populism and Nativism*. Chicago: University of Chicago Press.

Painter, Nell Irvin. 1987. *Standing at Armageddon:—A Grassroots History of the Progressive Era*. New York: Norton.

Palmer, Bruce. 1980. *"Man Over Money": The Southern Populist Critique of American Capitalism*. Chapel Hill: University of North Carolina Press.

Pollack, Norman. 1962. *The Populist Response to Industrial America*. Cambridge, MA: Harvard University Press.

Postel, Charles. 2007. *The Populist Vision*. New York: Oxford University Press.

Rodgers, Daniel T. 1982: "In Search of Progressivism," *Reviews in American History* 10, 4: 113–132.

—. 1998. *Atlantic Crossings: Social Politics in a Progressive Age*. Cambridge: Belknap/Harvard University Press.

Rosenberg, Rosalind. 1982. *Beyond Separate Spheres: Intellectual Roots of Modern Feminism*. New Haven, CT: Yale University Press.

Sanders, Elizabeth. 1999. *Roots of Reform: Farmers, Workers, and the American State, 1877–1917*. Chicago: University of Chicago Press.

Sproat, John G. 1968. *"The Best Men": Liberal Reformers in the Gilded Age*. New York: Oxford University Press.

Stromquist, Shelton. 2006. *Reinventing "The People": The Progressive Movement, the Class Problem, and the Origins of Modern Liberalism*. Urbana: University of Illinois Press.

Wiebe, Robert H. 1967: *The Search for Order, 1877–1920*. New York: Hill & Wang.

Woodward, C. Vann. 1951. *Origins of the New South, 1877–1913*. Baton Rouge: Louisiana State University Press.

Chapter Three

Urban America

Michael B. Kahan

The Long Gilded Age and Progressive Era was marked by an unprecedented growth in the nation's cities. In 1870, rural Americans outnumbered their urban compatriots by more than three to one, and no one in the United States lived in a city of a million inhabitants. By 1920, more Americans lived in cities than in rural areas, and more than 10 million people lived in the three American cities with a million or more inhabitants—Philadelphia, Chicago, and New York (*Historical Statistics of the United States* 1975).

This dramatic urban growth was driven by migration, both domestic and international. Some one-third of urban residents in 1910 were migrants from rural America; in that same year, between one-half and three-quarters of the population in the seven largest cities were either first- or second-generation immigrants (Katz 1996; Carpenter 1927).

For those who experienced it, the move to the cities was not merely a matter of numbers; it meant in many respects a qualitatively different existence. For many migrants, both domestic and international, city life entailed a transition from farm to factory. Indeed, the prospect of industrial work was a large part of the pull of the cities, and urban immigrant work forces were central to making America the world's dominant industrial power by the end of the nineteenth century. For the immigrants themselves, joining the industrial labor force meant a new relationship to work, time, money, family, home, nature— in short, to nearly everything in life. Days that formerly followed the cycle of the sun and moon were now ruled by the clock; families that had formerly grown their own food and produced or bartered many other necessities now obtained mass-produced goods in stores. Women went to work in factories or sweatshops and took in boarders or piecework, while children sought out their own opportunities to earn money on the streets or in shops and factories (Kleinberg 1989; Meyerowitz 1988; Nasaw 1985).

Of course, not every urban family struggled for economic survival. An emerging white-collar middle class built homes in new "streetcar suburbs" in places like West Philadelphia, Pennsylvania, and Roxbury and Dorchester, Massachusetts (Warner 1962). And in neighborhoods like New York's Fifth Avenue, Boston's Beacon Hill, and San Francisco's Nob Hill, the elite created their own enclaves.

The boom in urban population generated a host of expanded or wholly new institutions. City governments grew rapidly, trying to keep up with the need for services in areas such as sanitation and public health, paving, lighting, parks and playgrounds, policing, firefighting, and education. Their efforts were often remarkably successful, despite their reputation for machine-dominated corruption (Teaford 1984).

Non-governmental organizations also built institutions to ameliorate the conditions faced by the growing ranks of city dwellers. Private citizens formed a multitude of reform societies with aims ranging from the provision of charity to the prevention of cruelty to animals to the prohibition of alcohol. Many of these private reformers considered their work "Progressive," and that rubric gave the latter part of this era its name.

A third group of urban institutions arose from the efforts of profit-making corporations. Mass transit systems dominated by electric trolleys provided hundreds of millions of rides a year by the turn of the twentieth century (Cheape 1980). Newspapers sold similarly spectacular numbers of copies to masses of readers (Barth 1980). Grand department stores provided an opportunity to purchase, or at least to see and touch, luxury goods in a quasi-public setting. And dance halls, amusement parks, and vaudeville theaters provided mass, commercial entertainment for city crowds (Barth 1980; Peiss 1986).

Urban growth helped to spur the development of entire new professions, from social worker to traffic engineer to

A Companion to the Gilded Age and Progressive Era, First Edition. Edited by Christopher McKnight Nichols and Nancy C. Unger.
© 2017 John Wiley & Sons, Inc. Published 2017 by John Wiley & Sons, Inc.

playground supervisor. Among the professions that grew in tandem with the city were those that sought to explain urban growth itself, and what it meant for the nation. Sociologists, economists, statisticians, city planners, civil engineers, and muckraking journalists studied this emerging entity, and tried to explain its implications for society. Authors such as Carroll Wright (1889), Florence Kelley (1895), Adna Weber (1899), W.E.B. Du Bois (1899), and Jacob Riis (1906) published influential explanations of the city, attempting to account for these virtually unprecedented agglomerations of people.

A number of the most enduring of these early accounts of the industrial city emerged from the University of Chicago's department of sociology. The department's faculty and students, often referred to as the Chicago School of Urban Ecology or simply the Chicago School, took their home city as a model. In their writings, they described a city that functioned like a natural ecosystem. Founders Robert Park and Ernest Burgess and their disciples believed that various niches, arranged roughly in concentric circles, each provided a home to a different ethnic, racial, or economic population. New migrants arriving in the city settled near the center, pushing the previous occupants of that niche to move outward in a process of invasion and succession that led to frequent neighborhood change and constant urban growth (Burgess 1925).

Many of the Chicago School's ideas—its emphasis on upward social mobility, its assumption of urban growth, its concern with the processes of ethnic and economic segregation by neighborhood, and its interest in how social order could be maintained in such a dynamic environment—went on to play a large role in shaping the agenda of historians who studied the city. During the formative years of urban history as a field in the 1960s and 1970s, these issues, many of them first identified as subjects for academic study by the Chicago School urban ecologists, came to dominate much of the work in the field. Early scholars of the Gilded Age and Progressive Era city focused on issues of social mobility, ethnic neighborhoods, urban growth, and social control.

As the field evolved, the limits of the Chicago School's understanding of cities became more apparent. Its model of the city as an ecosystem, evolving according to a set of natural laws, omitted questions of power and culture. Its suggestion that urban populations, and cities themselves, followed a single, inexorable course of growth and development came to be seen as overly simplistic. Historians had always been a bit skeptical of these claims, and had placed more emphasis than sociologists on contingency and change over time. As the field evolved, historians' skepticism gathered more weight as they looked more closely at daily experience, and emphasized the role of human agency in shaping the city.

This chapter explores the urban history and historiography of the Gilded Age and Progressive Era city through the lens of the Chicago School in two senses. First, the Chicago School's typologies are used to organize the chapter, employing the famous schema drawn up by founder Ernest Burgess in his essay on "The Growth of the City" (1925). Despite its flaws and oversimplifications, this schematic conception of the city as a series of concentric rings remains a useful rubric for understanding the increasing segmentation of urban space during this time. Second, the major topics in urban history of the period are examined to show how writings on these issues have often evolved from models based on the Chicago School's ideas to new frameworks that reject or revise Chicago School thinking in significant ways.

Because there are separate chapters in this volume on the South (Chapter 4, by Amy Louise Wood) and the West (Chapter 5, by Tom Jablonsky), this chapter will primarily discuss the histories of cities in the Northeast and the upper Midwest, which together formed the industrial region that encompassed most major US cities at the time. The distinctive urban histories of the South and West are, however, considered briefly near the conclusion.

Finally, a note on periodization: This essay assigns the Gilded Age and Progressive Era to encompass the years roughly from 1877 to 1920. These years have significant resonance for urban history, beginning with the Great Railroad Strike that shook dozens of cities and towns, and ending with the federal census that showed a majority of Americans living in urban areas. The period was marked by dramatic changes but also significant continuities; it has been called both a Long Progressive Era (Edwards 2011) and a Long Gilded Age (Fink 2015). Whatever it is called, it seems fair to treat these years as a unit.

"The Loop": Urban Downtowns

If you had visited a city around the turn of the twentieth century, your visit would almost certainly have taken you to, or at the very least through, the city's Central Business District or "Downtown." This would have been the center of transportation networks, as well as the site of the city's major department stores, its city hall and other government offices, and the office buildings that were the worksite for increasing numbers of clerical workers.

To the Chicago School's adherents, the downtown or "Loop" (as it was called in Chicago) was part of the natural ecosystem of the city. Robert Fogelson's *Downtown* (2001) and Alison Isenberg's *Downtown America* (2004), however, both demonstrate the extent to which the downtown was a social and historical, rather than a "natural," phenomenon. It was shaped by the work of investors, policy-makers, planners, reformers, business owners, and others who shared an interest in how the downtown functioned economically, aesthetically, and socially. It also was molded by the experiences of the mass of urbanites who worked, shopped, and played there.

Nowhere was the role of human agency in shaping the downtown clearer than in the landmark buildings of the era: the skyscrapers. The term "skyscraper" came into use in the 1890s (shortly after "department store" and "downtown" itself), as technologies such as steel construction, elevators, and advances in fireproofing enabled buildings to rise to previously unimaginable heights. Technology and design alone did not create skyscrapers, however: investors who saw the buildings as reliable sources of rental income, and business owners such as F.W. Woolworth who saw them as spectacular urban entertainments and advertisements, were also instrumental (Willis 1995; Fenske 2008).

In addition to these monuments of finance, the downtown was home to temples of consumption: department stores. Flagship stores were not merely extremely large emporia; they were elaborately designed and furnished civic spaces, complete with lounges, restaurants, and concert organs. These retail palaces brought large numbers of women, both as customers and workers, to the center of the city. Like the skyscrapers, the department stores depended for their appeal in part on new technologies, such as elevators, plate glass, and telephones. And also like the skyscrapers, the department stores were both a cause and a result of the reorganization of urban space—specifically, the growing centralization of economic activity in the downtown. (Benson 1986; Hepp 2003).

Skyscrapers and department stores both required a concentration of large numbers of people, who were brought to their doors from all over the city and beyond. This urban density was possible because downtown was also the center of transit networks that tied together the city's diverse neighborhoods and its downtown, and that linked the city to its suburbs and more distant hinterlands. Cable cars, drawn by a cable beneath the street, were first introduced on a large scale in Chicago in 1883, but these were rapidly eclipsed by electric street railways, or trolleys, which were introduced in Richmond, Virginia, in 1887 (McShane 1994). While trolleys soon carried millions of passengers annually, horses remained a crucial source of locomotion and power (McShane and Tarr 2007). By the end of the period a few major cities, such as New York, Boston, and Chicago, enabled passengers to avoid street congestion with rapid transit provided by elevated trains or subways: Boston's underground opened in 1897, followed by New York City's in 1904 (Hood 1993).

These means of transportation brought people together, but also drove them apart. People of different classes, genders, and (outside the South) races mixed in the cars themselves and on the downtown streets where they alighted. But transit also made it easier for middle-class and wealthy urban residents to live in more economically exclusive neighborhoods and still travel on a regular basis to the center of town for work or shopping. Those who remained on foot, often the poor who could not afford car fare, faced a number of hazards to their safety. In the late nineteenth century steam railroads ran along many city streets, frequently causing injury and possibly contributing to the public resentment underlying the violent railroad strikes of 1877 (Stowell 1999). In the last decade of the century, bicyclists and sanitarians agitated for smooth asphalt pavements; this shift helped to (literally) pave the way for the widespread adoption of another hazardous technology, the internal combustion automobile, in the 1910s and 1920s (McShane 1994).

"Little Sicily," "Deutschland," and "Chinatown": Ethnicity and Immigration

While the downtown was, in many ways, the city's economic center, it was not central to the lives of all urban residents. The city's immigrants, in particular, led lives that were likely to be centered on homes, neighborhoods, workplaces, houses of worship, and communal institutions that were outside the "Loop" or downtown. The neighborhoods immigrants called home were believed by the Chicago School sociologists to be sites of disorganization and dysfunction, while subsequent generations of ethnic Americans have romanticized them as the sources of authentic food, close family, and meaningful identity (Burgess 1925; Diner 2000). In fact, however, immigrant life in the city was both more stable than the Chicago School sociologists believed, and more complicated than it appears through the haze of nostalgia. Both views mistake the neighborhood as an isolated and essentially unchanging enclave, whereas immigrant neighborhoods were dynamic urban environments that were not merely in, but of, America's increasingly cosmopolitan cities.

Above all, movement of immigrants into, out of, and within American cities ensured that immigrant neighborhoods underwent nearly constant change. Immigrants streamed into American cities throughout the period, but the major sources of this immigration shifted. Thus New York's population was 42% foreign-born in 1890, and 40% in 1910. But while this figure remained steady, the source of the immigration shifted dramatically, from countries of northern and western Europe to those of southern and eastern Europe. In the earlier year, Ireland and Germany together accounted for 63% of the city's immigrants, while Italy and Russia together made up only 14%. Two decades later, Irish and German immigrants made up only 27% of the city's foreign-born population, while those from Italy and Russia together accounted for 43% (Fink 2014, 136–137). The mobility that characterized immigrant neighborhoods was not only due to new arrivals. Once in the United States, immigrants displayed a high propensity for geographic mobility, with many moving to other neighborhoods or other cities in the United States in search of work or property ownership, while still others migrated back to their countries of origin (Bodnar 1985).

Many immigrant neighborhoods were the sites of dramatically harsh living conditions. Areas such as New York's

Lower East Side, San Francisco's Chinatown, and Chicago's Back of the Yards acquired reputations for crowding, poverty, and disease, as immigrants settled in poor housing and municipal services went disproportionately to more affluent sections of town (Riis 1906; Sinclair 1906).

Despite the harsh conditions, the immigrant neighborhoods offered their residents some advantages. Often work was the most important attraction. For unskilled laborers, low wages would have made a 10-cent round trip on the streetcars a hardship; therefore, it was important to live within walking distance of their employment. Many immigrant neighborhoods centered on a workplace, whether a meat-packing plant (Barrett 1987), a steel mill (Kleinberg 1989), or a network of work sites such as the clothing workshops of the Lower East Side (Howe and Libo 1976). For many immigrants, especially women and children in industries such as garment or cigar manufacturing, piecework meant that the workplace was the home. Even in these cases, it was important to work near suppliers and subcontractors, so clustering remained advantageous.

The workplace was not the only institution at the center of immigrant neighborhoods. These neighborhoods supported a dense network of communal institutions, such as newspapers, churches and synagogues, schools, burial societies, saloons, and theaters. Ethnically-based fraternal organizations such as the Sons of Italy or the Jewish *Landsmanshaftn* helped cement ethnic loyalties while performing practical functions such as providing mutual aid and insurance (Handlin 1973).

Yet, immigrant neighborhoods were not self-contained, isolated, monoethnic units. They were linked globally to co-ethnics in the home country and in other "diasporic" locations (Kobrin 2010), and locally to other ethnic groups whose settlement areas overlapped and interpenetrated with their own (Zunz 1982; Wild 2005). A settlement house worker in Philadelphia noted that the variety of ethnic groups visible every day on St. Mary's Street included "some stray Italians," as well as "the dark Hebrew women, or patient negroes, or stout Germans, who live out their story day after day before the eyes of the street" ("Philadelphia Settlement Report" 1894).

As this anonymous author suggested, much of life in immigrant neighborhoods was lived on the streets. With private space in very short supply, public space was turned to a variety of purposes: peddling, begging, playing, or simply socializing (Baldwin 1999). Streets took on additional significance when used for political protests or labor demonstrations, or for religious festivals (Keller 2009; Orsi 2010).

The very public life of immigrant neighborhoods repelled some among the native born, but also exercised a compelling attraction for many. Entrepreneurs, both immigrant and native-born, constructed exotic images of Chinatown, Little Italy, and other immigrant neighborhoods, bolstering their appeal as tourist attractions (Diner 2000; Blake 2006; Rast 2007). At the same time, many native-born reformers feared the crowded and (in their eyes) dirty streets as a source of disease as well as an embarrassment for a modern city (Shah 2001; Kahan 2013). Native-born fears of immigrants and immigrant neighborhoods could reach extreme heights, resulting in violence and restrictive legislation against the Chinese in the 1880s, and anti-German hysteria during World War I (Kazal 2004; Pfaelzer 2007). The Chicago School's assumption that immigrants inevitably assimilated as they moved further out from their initial zone of settlement has given way to historical analysis of the complex process by which immigrants from Asia, Latin America, and Europe were subsumed into America's racial hierarchies. Though the timing is subject to debate, historians agree that most European immigrants, or at least their children, were ultimately treated as white in essential ways, enabling their geographic and social mobility over time (Brodkin 1998; Guglielmo 2003).

The Black Belt: Race and the City

While immigrants and their children came to dominate many cities demographically during the Gilded Age and Progressive Era, African Americans and others considered not "White" by the census bureau remained a relatively small minority in cities outside of the South. In 1910, the census counted only 2.1% of New Yorkers and Chicagoans as non-white, along with 5.5% of Philadelphians. Blacks made up a significant percentage of urban populations only in the South: 15.3% of Baltimore's population was non-white, along with 26.4% in New Orleans and 28.6% of the population in Washington, DC (Carpenter 1927). Many Chicago School scholars assumed that African Americans in northern cities were the "last of the immigrants," and would follow European immigrants' trajectory of economic and geographic mobility. Historians, however, have more recently emphasized the distinctive disadvantages that racism imposed on black migrants.

In the decades leading up to 1920, racial discrimination in housing contributed to the formation of distinctly African American neighborhoods in northern cities. In neighborhoods such as New York's Harlem (Sacks 2006), Chicago's South Side (Philpott 1978), and Philadelphia's Seventh Ward (Du Bois and Eaton 1899), a combination of factors including discrimination, chain migration, employment patterns, and a desire for community led to the emergence of residential concentrations of African Americans. While these were still not the "hyper-segregated" neighborhoods of the post-World War II era, they contained what many historians have described as the origins of the urban black ghetto.

Like immigrant neighborhoods, African American enclaves were sites of appalling living conditions, vibrant community institutions, and complex social dynamics. W.E.B. Du Bois, whose 1899 study, *The Philadelphia Negro*, remains one of the most comprehensive portraits of black urban life during this period, found that blacks paid higher rents for worse housing than whites. Poor sanitation and "considerable overcrowding" led to high rates of mortality from tuberculosis and other diseases (Du Bois and Eaton 1899, 299).

Despite the widespread poverty of the Seventh Ward, Du Bois stressed that the neighborhood's African American residents were not a homogeneous mass, but included a broad economic and (in his eyes) "moral" range from a small "aristocracy" of professionals and entrepreneurs, to hard-working "representative" Negroes, to poor laborers, and finally to criminals and prostitutes. With white employers and unions making it nearly impossible to obtain factory jobs, the largest occupational category for black men and women was domestic and personal service. As Du Bois observed, many African Americans made ends meet by turning to prostitution and crime (Blair 2010; Gross 2006), although it is difficult in hindsight to separate the reality of these survival strategies from racist stereotypes and fears of black criminality (Muhammad 2010).

This heterogeneous population sustained a host of institutions, including secret and beneficial societies, co-operative businesses, homes for women and the aged, and newspapers. Churches were especially prominent and played a complex role in the black community. Through a rhetoric that stressed "uplift" and "respectability," black Methodist and Baptist churches critiqued white racism by showing that Blacks were deserving of respect. At the same time, they also exacerbated tensions between classes within the African-American community, with sometimes harsh and patronizing criticism of "lower-class" black behavior. These churches provided a space where women could achieve positions of communal leadership, challenging not only white domination of blacks in society, but also male subordination of women within the African American community (Higginbotham 1993).

The years leading up to 1910 thus found urban black communities socially divided but spatially concentrated. Both of these aspects were exacerbated by the Great Migration that occurred during and after World War I, in which some 1.5 million southern blacks moved to the cities of the North and Midwest in search of wartime employment as well as better living conditions, educational opportunities, and a chance to exercise their civil and political rights. Upon arrival in the city, the new migrants found much justification for their optimism, but also a sometimes chilly reception from more established black residents, and harsh discrimination by whites in housing, employment, and schooling (Grossman 1989). At its worst, this racism led to episodes such as the Chicago race riot of 1919, in which 23 blacks and 15 whites were killed following the drowning of a black teenager in Lake Michigan (Tuttle 1970; Fisher 2006).

The black urban ghettos that emerged by the end of the Gilded Age and Progressive Era were marked by a much more extreme and durable form of residential segregation than white immigrant neighborhoods (Zunz 1982; Grossman 1989). Some cities, notably Baltimore, even enacted ordinances mandating race-based residential segregation by block. When the US Supreme Court struck down such ordinances in 1917, segregationists turned to other mechanisms such as racially restrictive covenants, redlining, blockbusting, steering, and violence, setting the stage for the hypersegregation of the late twentieth century (Massey and Denton 1993; Nightingale 2012). Yet it would be a mistake to believe that members of different racial groups lived in isolation from one another. On the contrary, blacks and whites, as well as Asians and Latinos, met and mingled on playgrounds and street corners, in schools and missions, at nightclubs and dancehalls, in bedrooms and laundries, and occasionally in political coalitions organized by Socialists, Wobblies, and others (Mumford 1997; Lui 2005; Wild 2005). Ultimately, race during the Gilded Age and Progressive Era (as today) was not a biological given but a social relationship of power; and, unlike the neat concentric circles on the Chicago School's diagram, its urban boundaries were fluid and contested, shaping the lives of "whites" as well as people of color (Guglielmo 2003), and worked out in the workplace, the home, the street, and elsewhere.

The "Slum," the "Zone of Workingmen's Homes," and the "Commuter Zone": Class Divisions in the City

The Gilded Age was a time of growing inequalities in wealth and income, and these widening divides were manifest in the cities. Class status intersected with race and ethnicity to divide the population, and the space, of the Gilded Age and Progressive Era city. Zunz's (1982) careful analysis of Detroit shows that during the late nineteenth century, both whites and blacks lived in cross-class ethnic neighborhoods. In the early years of the twentieth century, residential experience diverged: for whites, class became as salient as ethnicity in determining residential location, as better-off residents sought out new middle-class neighborhoods and left poorer residents behind. For African Americans, however, segregation meant that race trumped class in determining residence, and even the relatively well-off continued to live in close proximity to the very poor.

While rich and poor may have grown increasingly distant spatially, like racial and ethnic groups they did not live in separate worlds. Class was a relation, and class relations during this period were often tense, played out in factories, but also in homes, schools, courtrooms, and streets. The stark inequalities of the Gilded Age and Progressive Era city contributed to labor disputes that often resulted in violence. The railroad strikes of 1877, the eight-hour movement of 1886, the Pullman strike and boycott of 1894, and the strike wave of 1919 were among the most notable episodes of labor action—and violence—in multiple cities

(Brecher 1972; Green 2006; Fink 2015a). The willingness of employers, in collaboration with the state, to break strikes with force compelled workers in most cases to compromise or concede their demands for higher wages and shorter hours. Nevertheless, a combination of union activity, protective legislation, and rationalization of production contributed to a gradual rise in pay and a decrease in overall hours of work—though this varied greatly depending on the industry, season, and even firm (Peiss 1986).

Class in the Gilded Age city affected life well beyond the factory floor. Outside of work, working-class urbanites fought to enjoy their leisure hours as they wished (Rosenzweig 1983). Parks, dancehalls, saloons, and streets became arenas in which men, women, and children sought to deploy their time and their bodies in ways often at odds with the more genteel expectations of the urban middle classes. Drinking, for instance, was an important part of many immigrant and working-class cultures, and saloons were a common sight in workers' neighborhoods. To temperance advocates, whose views were often influenced by nativism and racism, these saloons were a prime source of poverty, disease, political corruption, and broken families. To the working men who patronized these establishments, however, they were sites of labor union meetings, informal hiring halls, and even basic banking services (Duis 1983). Socially, they were a place for community building, where adult men, often sharing the same ethnicity and occupation, could build camaraderie and companionship through masculine rituals (Powers 1998).

While saloons were home to a strong working-class male homosocial culture, the Gilded Age and Progressive Era city also offered working-class residents an emerging assortment of heterosocial entertainments, in spaces such as dance halls, amusement parks, and movie theaters, particularly after the turn of the century. Cities attracted large numbers of young, unmarried men and women seeking work in department stores, restaurants, factories, and offices (Meyerowitz 1988; Bjelopera 2005). Free from the supervision of families and employers, often living with similarly situated young people in neighborhoods of rooming houses, these young people became the pioneers of a new culture of commercial amusements. Amusement parks and nickelodeon movie theaters challenged the dominance of genteel Victorian family entertainments and male-only recreations such as saloons and music halls. Despite some reformers' misgivings, the new commercial culture gained popularity not only among the working class, but among middle-class urbanites as well (Meyerowitz 1988).

Movies and amusement parks were part of a new culture of urban sexuality. Middle-class reformers were appalled by the overt sexuality of the dance halls, and the culture of "treating" in which a man paid for entertainment or consumer goods in exchange for a woman's sexual "favors" (Peiss 1986; Clement 2006). The rooming houses in which young clerks and factory workers tended to reside were sometimes used for prostitution and other sexual assignations, often by working women who engaged in prostitution as an occasional means of making financial ends meet (Meyerowitz 1988; Clement 2006; Kahan 2012).

The early twentieth century was a transformative moment in the urban geography of prostitution. In city after city, reformers created Vice Commissions and sought to shut down the red light districts where brothels had been tolerated by politicians and police. These campaigns often began as local initiatives, but during World War I they became a federal priority as the government sought to protect the moral fiber—and the sexual hygiene—of soldiers and sailors. Many of these crackdowns accelerated shifts that were already taking place. The spread of new technologies such as the automobile and the telephone, as well as the growth of apartment houses, office buildings, and commercial nightlife, led sex workers to shift away from brothels toward downtown streets, as well as toward tenements, cabarets, bars, and streets in more residential, working-class neighborhoods (Clement 2006; Blair 2010). In New York City, these neighborhoods and bars were also home to a culture of same-sex sexuality in which "trade," or working-class men who maintained a masculine persona, had sex with "fairies," men who adopted aspects of femininity such as feminine emotionality and dress (Chauncey 1994).

Like members of the working class, middle-class and elite urbanites carved out their own cultural spaces during the Gilded Age and Progressive Era; often these more exclusive spaces were in the suburbs. In the colonial era, suburbs had mostly been low-income areas on the outskirts of town; in the walking city, wealthy merchants and other elites wanted to live near the center (Jackson 1985). As railroads and streetcars emerged during the nineteenth century, this pattern turned inside-out: the wealthy found that they could relocate to exclusive neighborhoods far from the city's immigrant poor and still reach the city for work, shopping, and socializing. The wealthiest among them made their homes in railroad suburbs such as the Philadelphia Main Line (Fishman 1987). In their neighborhoods, workplaces, and associational lives, these elite urbanites created their own class cultures—often based on a shared opposition to the labor movement and a fear of the working class's growing influence (Beckert 2001).

Suburbs were not only for the middle and upper classes; some were industrial centers or company towns like Pullman, Illinois (Keating 2005). For those with moderate incomes, streetcar suburbs with easily built balloon frame houses made widespread home-ownership possible (Warner 1962; Jackson 1985). It was not simply technology that drove patterns of suburbanization, however. Investors, developers, builders, politicians, and bureaucrats played major roles, as did the ideologies and strategies of the residents themselves. Over the course of the Gilded Age and Progressive Era, those who could afford to own homes—which came to include many skilled or unionized members of the working class—began to look at them increasingly as a source of property values. This view of the house as investment, in turn, drove a desire for neighborhoods that were exclusive by class, race, and land use (Garb 2005; Lewinnek 2014).

Despite the increasing segmentation of the city, middle-class and working-class urbanites were not isolated from each other. Their relations, to be sure, were often patronizing or hostile. Wealthy urban residents led societies that investigated the poor to evaluate their worthiness, for instance, and received begging letters from poor strangers imploring them for assistance. Yet they also—in rare circumstances—collaborated with workers in genuine partnership, as in the Women's Trade Union League, which supported union activity in cities across the country, including most notably the New York shirtwaist strike of 1909 (Huyssen 2014).

In cities so marked by class differences, was mobility between classes possible? Urban historians of the 1960s and 1970s devoted much attention to this question, ultimately finding few simple answers (Thernstrom 1964; Kessner 1977). Geographical mobility was high, and property ownership became attainable for many, especially whites, often through strategies such as self-building, taking in boarders, or using the home as a site of production (Lewinnek 2014). There was limited occupational mobility for individuals, but intergenerational mobility was more common, especially for whites. As Michael Katz and Mark Stern have written, inequality in American history is paradoxically durable and fluid. Hierarchies have proven long-lasting, but within those hierarchies individuals and groups have moved up or down in surprisingly fluid ways (Katz and Stern 2006). As new immigrant groups entered the workforce, previous groups were often able to move up the occupational ladder, but urban society remained profoundly unequal: the ladder itself was unchanged.

Of course the ladder, like the Chicago School's concentric rings, is too simplistic a metaphor. Class, racial, and ethnic inequality was not simply a matter of sorting pre-established groups into urban zones or assigning them to rungs; urban life helped to create the categories themselves. These classifications assumed their specific meaning in the context of cities, where urban institutions and urban space determined how these relations shaped people's daily lives.

Progressivism, Women, and Urban Reform

Cities of the Gilded Age and Progressive Era, then, were highly divided by class, ethnicity, and race. It was in these divided cities that reformers of many stripes, often grouped under the banner of Progressivism, rose to prominence beginning in the 1890s. Many of them proclaimed that their goal was precisely to overcome these divisions: to create, or perhaps to restore, a sense of social unity and a striving for the common good. Historians continue to debate whether Progressives moved cities toward those goals, or in the opposite direction. Were the Progressives multiculturalists who embraced urban diversity and sought to build a pluralistic, cooperative democracy? Or were Progressives xenophobes who feared the growing numbers of immigrants, and sought to limit their political influence and control their behavior? The answers often seem to depend more on the circumstances at the time the historian is writing than on events of the Progressive Era itself. At the moment of this writing, a century after the peak of Progressivism, many believe Americans are living in a new Gilded Age. This has helped revive the reputation of the Progressives as crusaders against the excesses of the original Gilded Age.

One reason it is so difficult to come to a lasting consensus on the nature of urban Progressive reform is that it was such a diverse movement, or set of movements. It could include changes in political structure, improvements in street cleaning, the creation of playgrounds and juvenile courts, and the municipalization of streetcar companies. Indeed, Filene (1970) argued that the term "Progressivism" is so broad as to be meaningless. Yet these efforts shared certain general characteristics. They were based, fundamentally, on a belief in the possibility of individual and social progress. Progressive reformers believed that social problems could be corrected, and human nature could be improved, through improvements to the social and physical environment. These improvements, in turn, would stem from the proper application of scientific and social scientific expertise. Applying professional expertise to social questions, Progressives believed, would help a community, whether a neighborhood or a nation, to arrive at a shared, rational, orderly vision of the common good. Most Progressives also believed that the government should play a key role in helping to achieve that common good, and therefore they insisted that the state needed to expand its powers. Finally, most Progressives shared a Protestant religious faith, one that stressed the "social gospel's" ethic of serving others.

Cities proved fertile ground for applying this ideology to a wide range of issues. Progressive reformers were not successful in every change they attempted, but by 1920 they had transformed cities in sometimes dramatic ways. Their work helps illustrate the fallacy of the Chicago School's urban ecology. City neighborhoods are not natural areas; they are social creations that can be made and remade through human effort.

At the most basic level, Progressive reform had a noticeable impact on the physical maps of cities. Progressive reformers advocated the construction of parks, playgrounds, public baths, YWCAs, boarding houses, and other institutions (Spain 2001). Perhaps the most emblematic urban Progressive institution was the settlement house. Part community center, part school, part research institute, settlement houses were established first in England, then brought to New York in 1886, and shortly thereafter to Chicago, where Jane Addams founded Hull-House in 1889. Located in working-class immigrant neighborhoods, settlement houses were staffed largely by young, native-born, middle-class college graduates, many of them women for whom settlement houses represented one of the few socially acceptable ways to use the skills and ideals they had acquired through education. Settlement houses sought to help immigrants navigate life in America by teaching aspects of American culture, from art and literature to methods of cooking and child-rearing. Settlements hosted debating societies, vocational training, and painting classes for local residents. They also gathered data on their neighborhoods and used that information to advocate reforms such as improved sanitation and anti-sweatshop legislation. The settlement house movement has inspired debate between historians who have viewed it as a patronizing attempt to impose middle-class, Protestant values on poor immigrants (Shpaḳ-Lisaḳ 1989), and those who celebrate its democratic, multicultural aspects (Knight 2006; Westhoff 2007). Undoubtedly such a large, diverse movement contained many contradictory impulses. Recent writings on the movement's leading exponent, Jane Addams, have tended to vindicate her philosophy as a powerful and innovative effort to reconcile democratic ideals with the realities of urban industrial society (Knight 2006; Westhoff 2007). Ultimately, a full understanding of the role of the settlement houses, as well as other Progressive reforms, requires a closer look at neighborhood residents themselves. They had their own goals and interests, and sought to use institutions such as settlement houses, protective societies, charity organizations, police, and courts, to serve those goals. At the same time, given the imbalance of power between neighborhood residents and reformers, residents could not always determine the outcome of their interaction with these agencies (Gordon 1988; Hicks 2010).

Women played a prominent, and often a leading, role in the settlement house movement and other urban progressive reforms (Deutsch 2000; Spain 2001). Women reformers used the gendered roles associated with the domestic sphere to claim a special responsibility for maintaining the health, beauty, order, and welfare of their larger home, the city. This philosophy of municipal housekeeping was applied initially to local cleanup and beautification work, as when Jane Addams obtained an appointment as sanitary inspector for her neighborhood. But it came to be used in a much broader sense, providing a justification for women—usually middle-class, native-born, white women—to venture widely into public space, and to assume a leading role in improving health care, juvenile justice, education, and urban politics (Flanagan 2002).

As municipal housekeepers, women also helped to shape the city through one of the early movements in city planning. The City Beautiful movement drew its aesthetic from Haussmann's Paris, and from the Chicago World's Fair of 1893, where architect Daniel Burnham created a set of monumental, classically inspired buildings that were dubbed the White City. The buildings created such an impressive ensemble that many Americans left the fair inspired by the possibilities of creating rationally planned, aesthetically harmonious urban environments. City Beautiful advocates sought to replicate the look of the White City in cities across America. Although large-scale success was limited to a few cities—most notably Washington, DC—the City Beautiful movement shaped urban landscapes in smaller ways. In many cities, women's reform groups promoted policies such as public trash cans, placing utility wires underground, and limitations on billboards (Isenberg 2004).

Progressive reform also altered the political map of cities. During the Gilded Age, political scandals such as the Tweed Ring in New York City, together with the cozy relationship of many urban politicians with street railway entrepreneurs and brothel and saloon owners, gave American city governments a reputation for being, in the words of Lincoln Steffens, "Corrupt and Contented" (Steffens 1904). This picture, however, is misleading: through there was certainly corruption, urban governments during the Gilded Age were much more efficient and successful than usually believed, providing constituents with dramatic improvements in street paving, lighting, sewers, water, parks and playgrounds, and other infrastructures and services, while remaining fiscally sound (Teaford 1984). Machines—political organizations in which a single party headed by a boss maintained power over the distribution of government jobs, contracts, aid, and other benefits — held power in many wards, but rarely controlled an entire city's politics or policies (McDonald 1986). In many cities, upper middle-class businessmen, not machine politicians, controlled the executive branch, while professional experts, not party lackeys, controlled departments such as engineering, schools, and public health. Depending on the issue, these non-machine interests might work in opposition to, or in coalition with, a party machine or boss (Teaford 1984).

This arrangement effectively defined urban politics as a balance of competing interest groups. Yet many Progressives saw it as flawed, not only because it pointedly ignored many interest groups (such as women), but also because they felt that politics should be more than a balancing of competing interests; it should strive for a vision of the common good. Progressives with a moral streak, furthermore, saw this accommodation with machine-based ward politicians (and the liquor interests that generally supported them) as a bargain with the devil (Teaford 1984, 10), and many campaigned for revised city charters that would limit the power of the ward pols. To prevent public jobs from being filled by the boss's friends, Progressive reformers urged cities to adopt civil service regulations that awarded public employment on the basis of written examinations. Progressives also advocated at-large elections for city council to make it more difficult to elect politicians whose base of support lay in an ethnic neighborhood. Reformers moved power away from ward bosses by placing executive power in a non-partisan city manager position, or by strengthening the office of the mayor relative to the council. Progressive mayors, often businessmen by background such as Hazen Pingree of Detroit, Samuel "Golden Rule" Jones of Toledo, and James "Sunny Jim" Rolph of San Francisco, used their office to advance reforms such as municipal ownership of utilities and the creation of municipal parks and playgrounds. Together these approaches helped to reduce the power of political parties in local affairs, and helped bring an end to the raucous and broad participation typical of late nineteenth-century local politics (McGerr 1986). Ultimately, machine politics was both more resilient and less central to municipal politics than once believed. Civil service reform, strong mayor systems, and other changes often represented temporary setbacks that the machine could survive, and even turn to its advantage. At the same time, machines were far from all-powerful political monopolies; to hold power, they often had to compromise with taxpayers, businesses, reformers, professional experts, and officials in state, federal, and suburban governments.

Cities of the South and West

Cities of the West and South followed a distinctive trajectory from those of the Northeast and Midwest. The West was less urbanized than the nation's more industrial regions: only 39.9% of the West's population lived in cities in 1900, as compared with 66.1% of residents of the Northeast (Barrows 2007), and as late as 1920 only five of the 25 largest U.S cities (Los Angeles, San Francisco, Seattle, Portland, and Denver) were located in the West (Carpenter 1927). But the cities of the West were growing rapidly, and the region was urbanizing at a faster rate than the United States as a whole (Abbott 2008, 35).

Leading this rapid growth were "instant cities" such as San Francisco or Denver (Barth 1975), with explosive population growth originating in mining or oil booms. The rapid growth of these cities, combined with their dependence on extractive industries and their often arid locations, made their relationship to the natural environment especially fraught: while they projected an image of pristine natural beauty to attract settlers, investors, and tourists, their very existence often depended upon displacing the costs of their growth onto their surrounding region (Brechin 1999; Klingle 2007).

Tension between appearance and reality often marked racial and ethnic relations in these cities as well. Los Angeles, for example, marketed itself as the "white spot" of America, a city ostensibly free from the Northeast's corruption, pollution, and, by implication, its racial and ethnic diversity (Wild 2005). In reality, western cities were marked by their own racial and ethnic mixtures. In comparison with Northeastern or Midwestern cities, many cities of the West had a higher percentage of immigrants from Asia and from Mexico, and a larger proportion of Native Americans. The result of western cities' unique ethnic profiles could be vibrant cultural mixing (Wild 2005), or racial discrimination, exclusion, and violence. San Francisco's Chinatown, as Charlotte Brooks has argued, was "America's first segregated neighborhood" (Brooks 2009, 11).

A more notorious form of racial segregation became characteristic of southern cities. The South was the least urbanized region of the country; only 18% of the population lived in cities in 1900 (Barrows 2007), and by 1920 only 3 of the country's 25 largest cities (New Orleans, Baltimore, and Washington, DC) were in the South (Carpenter 1927). The ethnic mix of southern cities was distinctive, with smaller populations of immigrants and larger proportions of African Americans compared to western or northern cities; in 1900, nearly 43% of the South's urban population was black, compared to less than 2% in cities such as Chicago and New York (Katz 1996, 151).

This large population of urban African Americans lived under a formal, legal system of segregation known as Jim Crow. Most scholars agree that the legal codification of Jim Crow occurred primarily during the 1890s, but beyond that the origins of Jim Crow have been the object of much scholarly debate. An emerging consensus holds that there is no clear or simple answer, given the wide variety of communities, practices, and people involved (Brundage 2012). Southern historians have shifted their attention toward other questions about Jim Crow, such as its relationship to the creation of whiteness (Hale 1999), its connection to southern gender ideology (Gilmore 1996), and the persistent efforts of African Americans to resist its dictates (Lewis 1991; Hunter 1997; Kelley 2010).

The Jim Crow disfranchisement of African Americans in southern cities was part of a larger pattern of urban politics that characterized the region. Most southern cities were dominated by a coalition of civic elites that favored a low-tax, low-service approach to governance, and invested relatively little in education and public works (Brownell 1975; Hanchett 1998). Urban elite rule was bolstered most obviously by the exclusion of black voters, but also by apparently race-neutral governance "reforms" such as at-large elections and government by commission. Cities in the North and West adopted many of these reforms as well, reducing the influence of immigrant as well as black voters. Given the histories of racial exclusion and segregation in cities throughout the country, the distinctiveness of southern cities should not be overstated.

Future Directions

Understandings of the Gilded Age and Progressive Era city have evolved significantly since the sociologists of the Chicago School were writing in the early twentieth century. Nonetheless, the Chicago School, despite its oversimplifications and blind spots, foreshadowed many important innovations in the way that scholars have approached the topic of the city over the past century. For instance, the Chicago School understood cities as dynamic entities, constantly growing outward from the Loop to the Commuters' Zone; historians applied that insight to push the boundaries of urban history outward as well, incorporating the study of suburbs into urban history, and creating one of the most fruitful areas of scholarship in recent decades (Keating 2005; Lewinnek 2014).

But historians have begun to find that this boundary needs to be expanded even further: cities must be understood not just in a metropolitan context, but in a regional and global setting as well. William Cronon's influential *Nature's Metropolis* (1991) set Chicago in the context of the Great Plains, breaking down boundaries between urban and regional history, as well as between urban and environmental history. Cronon showed how Chicago-based industries such as meat, grain, and timber shaped the ecology of the midsection of America, converting species into commodities and transforming the landscape into a "second nature." His insight that "city and country have a common history" (xiv) has helped to inspire the growing sub-field of urban environmental history (Platt 2005; Rawson 2010; Melosi 2011). More studies are needed of how water, air, land, and nonhuman species were part of the history of cities in the Gilded Age and Progressive Era, and how different urban populations experienced the benefits and costs of environmental change.

Other historians have begun to push the boundaries of urban history by placing the history of American cities in a global context. Daniel Rodgers's *Atlantic Crossings* (1998) was a pioneer in this field. Rodgers showed that American and European reformers of the Progressive Era and New Deal periods shared ideas in a transatlantic world of research trips, reports, surveys, and conferences. American ideas for city planning, the municipalization of urban utilities, and many other reforms were heavily influenced by developments in Britain, Germany, Scandinavia, and elsewhere. Global history is a challenging undertaking, but this work is crucial for understanding the antecedents of the current global era. Rebecca Kobrin's (2010) work on the diaspora of emigrants from Bialystok is another excellent example of how global frameworks can be applied to the urban history of the Gilded Age and Progressive Era. More comparative histories, such as those by Keller (2009) and Platt (2005), will also help to put the American experience in global perspective.

Future research on the turn-of-the-century city must also continue to incorporate new techniques in digital humanities. The digitization of newspapers and other printed sources, as well as historical images, has made available vast new sets of sources for historical analysis, and new techniques such as topic mining can help to make sense of this large volume of material. Blevins (2014), for instance, employed a variety of "distant reading" techniques to understand how newspapers produced space for readers in turn-of-the-century Houston. Spatial analysis, enabled by Geographic Information Systems and other new technologies, is still in its infancy, and promises to shed new light on a wide range of questions, from how racial, gender, and ethnic inequalities were structured to how reforms shaped the urban landscape. In research on prostitution in Philadelphia, spatial analysis has identified three discrete zones where prostitution was concentrated in the 1910s (Kahan 2012).

While the study of the Gilded Age and Progressive Era should draw on the possibilities offered by new technologies, it should not neglect what remains valuable in old theories. Lately, the Chicago School is attracting new fans: Harvard sociologist Robert Sampson, for instance, has led the charge to bring back one of the Chicago School's favorite analytical lenses, the neighborhood, as a central concept in social analysis, and he has done it through an extensive study of the neighborhoods of Chicago itself (Sampson 2011). In this New Gilded Age, as inequalities of wealth and income reach levels not seen in nearly a century, study of the original Gilded Age and Progressive Era city promises to assume ever greater relevance and urgency.

References

Abbott, Carl. 2008. *How Cities Won the West: Four Centuries of Urban Change in Western North America.* Albuquerque: University of New Mexico Press.

Baldwin, Peter. 1999. *Domesticating the Street: The Reform of Public Space in Hartford, 1850–1930.* Columbus: Ohio State University Press.

Barrett, James. 1987. *Work and Community in the Jungle: Chicago's Packinghouse Workers, 1894–1922.* Urbana: University of Illinois Press.

Barrows, Robert G. 2007. "Urbanizing America." In *The Gilded Age: Perspectives on the Origins of Modern America*, 2nd ed., edited by Charles W. Calhoun, 101–118. Lanham, MD: Rowman and Littlefield.

Barth, Gunther Paul. 1975. *Instant Cities: Urbanization and the Rise of San Francisco and Denver.* New York: Oxford University Press.

—. 1980. *City People: The Rise of Modern City Culture in Nineteenth-century America.* New York: Oxford University Press.

Beckert, Sven. 2001. *The Monied Metropolis: New York City and the Consolidation of the American Bourgeoisie, 1850–1896.* Cambridge: Cambridge University Press.

Benson, Susan Porter. 1986. *Counter Cultures: Saleswomen, Managers, and Customers in American Department Stores, 1890–1940.* Urbana: University of Illinois Press.

Bjelopera, Jerome P. 2005. *City of Clerks: Office and Sales Workers in Philadelphia, 1870–1920.* Urbana: University of Illinois Press.

Blair, Cynthia M. 2010. *I've Got to Make My Livin': Black Women's Sex Work in Turn-of-the-Century Chicago.* Chicago: University of Chicago Press.

Blake, Angela M. 2006. *How New York Became American, 1890–1924.* Baltimore, MD: Johns Hopkins University Press.

Blevins, Cameron. 2014. "Space, Nation, and the Triumph of Region: A View of the World from Houston." *Journal of American History* 101: 122–147.

Bodnar, John E. 1985. *The Transplanted: A History of Immigrants in Urban America*. Bloomington: Indiana University Press.

Brecher, Jeremy. 1972. *Strike!* Boston: South End Press.

Brechin, Gray A. 1999. *Imperial San Francisco: Urban Power, Earthly Ruin*. Berkeley: University of California Press.

Brodkin, Karen. 1998. *How Jews Became White Folks and What That Says About Race in America*. New Brunswick, NJ: Rutgers University Press.

Brooks, Charlotte. 2009. *Alien Neighbors, Foreign Friends: Asian Americans, Housing, and the Transformation of Urban California*. Chicago: University of Chicago Press.

Brownell, Blaine A. 1975. *The Urban Ethos in the South, 1920–1930*. Baton Rouge: Louisiana State University Press.

Brundage, W. Fitzhugh. 2012. "Introduction." In *The Folly of Jim Crow: Rethinking the Segregated South*, edited by Stephanie Cole, Natalie J. Ring, and Peter Wallenstein, 1–16. College Station: University of Texas at Texas A&M University Press.

Burgess, Ernest W. 1925. "The Growth of the City: An Introduction to a Research Project." In *The City*, edited by Robert E. Park, Ernest W. Burgess, and Roderick D. McKenzie. Chicago: University of Chicago Press.

Carpenter, Niles. 1927. *Census Monographs VII: Immigrants and their Children*. Washington, DC: Government Printing Office.

Chauncey, George. 1994. *Gay New York: Gender, Urban Culture, and the Making of the Gay Male World, 1890–1940*. New York: Basic Books.

Cheape, Charles W. 1980. *Moving the Masses: Urban Public Transit in New York, Boston, and Philadelphia, 1880–1912*. Cambridge, MA: Harvard University Press.

Clement, Elizabeth Alice. 2006. *Love for Sale: Courting, Treating, and Prostitution in New York City, 1900–1945*. Chapel Hill: University of North Carolina Press.

Cronon, William. 1991. *Nature's Metropolis: Chicago and the Great West*. New York: W.W. Norton.

Deutsch, Sarah. 2000. *Women and the City: Gender, Space, and Power in Boston, 1870–1940*. Oxford: Oxford University Press.

Diner, Hasia R. 2000. *Lower East Side Memories: A Jewish Place in America*. Princeton, NJ: Princeton University Press.

Du Bois, W.E.B. and Isabel Eaton. 1899. *The Philadelphia Negro: A Social Study*. Philadelphia: Published for the University of Pennsylvania.

Duis, Perry. 1983. *The Saloon: Public Drinking in Chicago and Boston, 1880–1920*. Urbana: University of Illinois Press.

Edwards, Rebecca. 2011. *New Spirits: Americans in the "Gilded Age", 1865–1905*. 2nd ed. New York: Oxford University Press.

Fenske, Gail. 2008. *The Skyscraper and the City: The Woolworth Building and the Making of Modern New York*. Chicago: University of Chicago Press.

Filene, Peter. 1970. "An Obituary for the Progressive Movement." *American Quarterly* 22, 1: 20–34.

Fink, Leon. 2014. *Major Problems in the Gilded Age and the Progressive Era: Documents and Essays*. 3rd ed. Belmont, CA: Wadsworth.

—. 2015. *The Long Gilded Age: American Capitalism and the Lessons of a New World Order*. Philadelphia: University of Pennsylvania Press.

Fisher, C. 2006. "African Americans, Outdoor Recreation, and the 1919 Chicago Race Riot." In *"To Love the Wind and the Rain": African Americans and Environmental History*, edited by Dianne D. Glave and Mark Stoll. Pittsburgh, PA: University of Pittsburgh Press.

Fishman, Robert. 1987. *Bourgeois Utopias: The Rise and Fall of Suburbia*. New York: Basic Books.

Flanagan, Maureen A. 2002. *Seeing with Their Hearts: Chicago Women and the Vision of the Good City, 1871–1933*. Princeton, NJ: Princeton University Press.

Fogelson, Robert M. 2001. *Downtown: Its Rise and Fall, 1880–1950*. New Haven, CT: Yale University Press.

Garb, Margaret. 2005. *City of American Dreams: A History of Home Ownership and Housing Reform in Chicago, 1871–1919*. Chicago: University of Chicago Press.

Gilmore, Glenda Elizabeth. 1996. *Gender and Jim Crow: Women and the Politics of White Supremacy in North Carolina, 1896–1920*. Chapel Hill: University of North Carolina Press.

Gordon, Linda. 1988. *Heroes of Their Own Lives: The Politics and History of Family Violence: Boston, 1880–1960*. New York: Viking.

Green, James R. 2006. *Death in the Haymarket: A Story of Chicago, the First Labor Movement and the Bombing that Divided Gilded Age America*. New York: Pantheon Books.

Gross, Kali N. 2006. *Colored Amazons: Crime, Violence, and Black Women in the City of Brotherly Love, 1880–1910*. Durham, NC: Duke University Press.

Grossman, James R. 1989. *Land of Hope: Chicago, Black Southerners, and the Great Migration*. Chicago: University of Chicago Press.

Guglielmo, Thomas A. 2003. *White on Arrival: Italians, Race, Color, and Power in Chicago, 1890–1945*. Oxford: Oxford University Press.

Hale, Grace Elizabeth. 1998. *Making Whiteness: The Culture of Segregation in the South, 1890–1940*. New York: Pantheon Books.

Hanchett, Thomas W. 1998. *Sorting Out the New South City: Race, Class, and Urban Development in Charlotte, 1875–1975*. Chapel Hill: University of North Carolina Press.

Handlin, Oscar. 1973. *The Uprooted*. 2nd ed. enl. Boston: Little, Brown.

Hepp, John Henry. 2003. *The Middle-class City: Transforming Space and Time in Philadelphia, 1876–1926*. Philadelphia: University of Pennsylvania Press.

Hicks, Cheryl D. 2010. *Talk with You Like a Woman: African American Women, Justice, and Reform in New York, 1890–1935*. Chapel Hill: University of North Carolina Press.

Higginbotham, Evelyn Brooks. 1993. *Righteous Discontent: The Women's Movement in the Black Baptist Church, 1880–1920*. Cambridge, MA: Harvard University Press.

Historical Statistics of the United States: Colonial Times to 1970. 1975. Bicentennial ed. Washington, DC: U.S. Department of Commerce, Bureau of the Census.

Hood, Clifton. 1993. *722 Miles: The Building of the Subways and How They Transformed New York*. New York: Simon & Schuster.

Howe, Irving and Kenneth Libo. 1976. *World of Our Fathers*. 1st ed. New York: Harcourt Brace Jovanovich.

Hunter, Tera W. 1997. *To 'joy My Freedom: Southern Black Women's Lives and Labors After the Civil War*. Cambridge, MA: Harvard University Press.

Huyssen, David. 2014. *Progressive Inequality: Rich and Poor in New York, 1890–1920.* Cambridge, MA: Harvard University Press.

Isenberg, Alison. 2004. *Downtown America: A History of the Place and the People Who Made It.* Chicago: University of Chicago Press.

Jackson, Kenneth T. 1985. *Crabgrass Frontier: The Suburbanization of the United States.* New York: Oxford University Press.

Kahan, Michael B. 2012. "'There are Plenty of Women on the Street': The Landscape of Commercial Sex in Progressive-Era Philadelphia, 1910–1918." *Historical Geography* 40: 37–58.

—. 2013. "The Risk of Cholera and the Reform of Urban Space: Philadelphia, 1893." *Geographical Review* 103: 517–536.

Katz, Michael B. 1996. *In the Shadow of the Poorhouse: A Social History of Welfare in America.* 2nd ed. New York: Basic Books.

— and Mark J. Stern. 2006. *One Nation Divisible: What America Was and What it Is Becoming.* New York: Russell Sage Foundation.

Kazal, Russell A. 2004. *Becoming Old Stock: The Paradox of German-American Identity.* Princeton, NJ: Princeton University Press.

Keating, Ann Durkin. 2005. *Chicagoland: City and Suburbs in the Railroad Age.* Chicago: University of Chicago Press.

Keller, Lisa. 2009. *Triumph of Order: Democracy & Public Space in New York and London.* New York: Columbia University Press.

Kelley, Blair Murphy. 2010. *Right to Ride: Streetcar Boycotts and African American Citizenship in the Era of Plessy v.* Ferguson. Chapel Hill: University of North Carolina Press.

Kelley, Florence. 1895. "The Sweating System." In *Hull-House Maps and Papers, by Residents of Hull-House*, 27–48. Boston: Thomas Y. Crowell & Co.

Kessner, Thomas. 1977. *The Golden Door: Italian and Jewish Immigrant Mobility in New York City 1880–1915.* New York: Oxford University Press.

Kleinberg, S. J. 1989. *The Shadow of the Mills: Working-class Families in Pittsburgh, 1870–1907.* Pittsburgh, PA: University of Pittsburgh Press.

Klingle, Matthew W. 2007. *Emerald City: An Environmental History of Seattle.* New Haven, CT: Yale University Press.

Knight, Louise W. 2005. *Citizen: Jane Addams and the Struggle for Democracy.* Chicago: University of Chicago Press.

Kobrin, Rebecca. 2010. *Jewish Bialystok and Its Diaspora.* Bloomington: Indiana University Press.

Lewinnek, Elaine. 2014. *The Working Man's Reward: Chicago's Early Suburbs and the Roots of American Sprawl.* Oxford: Oxford University Press.

Lewis, Earl. 1990. *In Their Own Interests: Race, Class, and Power in Twentieth-century Norfolk, Virginia.* Berkeley: University of California Press.

Lui, Mary Ting Yi. 2005. *The Chinatown Trunk Mystery: Murder, Miscegenation, and Other Dangerous Encounters in Turn-of-the-century New York City.* Princeton, NJ: Princeton University Press.

Massey, Douglas S. and Nancy A. Denton. 1993. *American Apartheid: Segregation and the Making of the Underclass.* Cambridge, MA: Harvard University Press.

McDonald, Terrence J. 1986. *The Parameters of Urban Fiscal Policy: Socio-economic Change and Political Culture in San Francisco, 1860–1906.* Berkeley: University of California Press.

McGerr, Michael E. 1986. *The Decline of Popular Politics: The American North, 1865–1928.* New York: Oxford University Press.

McShane, Clay and Joel A. Tarr. 2007. *The Horse in the City: Living Machines in the Nineteenth Century.* Baltimore, MD: The Johns Hopkins University Press.

McShane, Clay. 1994. *Down the Asphalt Path: The Automobile and the American City.* New York: Columbia University Press.

Melosi, Martin V. 2011. *Precious Commodity: Providing Water for America's Cities.* Pittsburgh: University of Pittsburgh Press.

Meyerowitz, Joanne J. 1988. *Women Adrift: Independent Wage Earners in Chicago, 1880–1930.* Chicago: University of Chicago Press.

Muhammad, Khalil Gibran. 2011. *The Condemnation of Blackness: Race, Crime, and the Making of Modern Urban America.* 1st ed. Cambridge, MA: Harvard University Press.

Mumford, Kevin J. 1997. *Interzones: Black/White Sex Districts in Chicago and New York in the Early Twentieth Century.* New York: Columbia University Press.

Nasaw, David. 1985. *Children of the City: At Work and at Play.* Garden City, NY: Anchor Press/Doubleday.

Nightingale, Carl Husemoller. 2012. *Segregation: A Global History of Divided Cities.* Chicago: University of Chicago Press.

Orsi, Robert A. 2010. *The Madonna of 115th Street: Faith and Community in Italian Harlem, 1880–1950.* 3rd ed. New Haven, CT: Yale University Press.

Peiss, Kathy Lee. 1986. *Cheap Amusements: Working Women and Leisure in Turn-of-the-century New York.* Philadelphia: Temple University Press.

Pfaelzer, Jean. 2007. *Driven Out: The Forgotten War Against Chinese Americans.* New York: Random House.

"Philadelphia Settlement Report." 1894. In *Fourth Annual Report of the College Settlements Association.* Philadelphia: Avil Printing and Lithographing Co.

Philpott, Thomas Lee. 1978. *The Slum and the Ghetto: Neighborhood Deterioration and Middle-class Reform, Chicago, 1880–1930.* New York: Oxford University Press.

Platt, Harold L. 2005. *Shock Cities: The Environmental Transformation and Reform of Manchester and Chicago.* Chicago: The University of Chicago Press.

Powers, Madelon. 1998. *Faces Along the Bar: Lore and Order in the Workingman's Saloon, 1870–1920.* Chicago: The University of Chicago Press.

Rast, Raymond. 2007. "The Cultural Politics of Tourism in Chinatown, 1882–1917." *Pacific Historical Review* 76: 29–60.

Rawson, Michael. 2010. *Eden on the Charles: The Making of Boston.* Cambridge, MA: Harvard University Press.

Riis, Jacob A. 1906. *How the Other Half Lives: Studies Among the Tenements of New York.* New York: C. Scribner's Sons.

Rodgers, Daniel T. 1998. *Atlantic Crossings: Social Politics in a Progressive Age.* Cambridge, MA: Belknap Press/Harvard University Press.

Rosenzweig, Roy. 1983. *Eight Hours for What We Will: Workers and Leisure in an Industrial City, 1870–1920.* Cambridge: Cambridge University Press.

Sacks, Marcy S. 2006. *Before Harlem: The Black Experience in New York City before World War I.* Philadelphia: University of Pennsylvania Press.

Sampson, Robert J. 2011. *Great American City: Chicago and the Enduring Neighborhood Effect.* Chicago: University of Chicago Press.

Shah, Nayan. 2001. *Contagious Divides: Epidemics and Race in San Francisco's Chinatown.* Berkeley: University of California Press.

Shpaḳ-Lisaḳ, Rivḳah. 1989. *Pluralism & Progressives: Hull House and the New Immigrants, 1890–1919.* Chicago: University of Chicago Press.

Sinclair, Upton. 1906. *The Jungle.* New York: The Jungle Publishing Co.

Spain, Daphne. 2001. *How Women Saved the City.* Minneapolis: University of Minnesota Press.

Steffens, Lincoln. 1904. *The Shame of the Cities.* New York: McClure, Phillips & Co.

Stowell, David O. 1999. *Streets, Railroads, and the Great Strike of 1877.* Chicago: University of Chicago Press.

Teaford, Jon C. 1984. *The Unheralded Triumph, City Government in America, 1870–1900.* Baltimore: Johns Hopkins University Press.

Thernstrom, Stephan. 1964. *Poverty and Progress: Social Mobility in a Nineteenth Century City.* Cambridge: Harvard University Press.

Tuttle, William M. 1970. *Race Riot: Chicago in the Red Summer of 1919.* 1st ed. New York: Atheneum.

Warner, Sam Bass. 1962. *Streetcar Suburbs: The Process of Growth in Boston, 1870–1900.* Cambridge, MA: Harvard University Press.

Weber, Adna Ferrin. 1899. *The Growth of Cities in the Nineteenth Century: A Study in Statistics.* New York: Published for Columbia University by the Macmillan Co.

Westhoff, Laura M. 2007. *A Fatal Drifting Apart: Democratic Social Knowledge and Chicago Reform.* Columbus: Ohio State University Press.

Wild, Mark. 2005. *Street Meeting: Multiethnic Neighborhoods in Early Twentieth-century Los Angeles.* Berkeley: University of California Press.

Willis, Carol. 1995. *Form Follows Finance: Skyscrapers and Skylines in New York and Chicago.* New York: Princeton Architectural Press.

Wright, Carroll Davidson. 1889. *Working Women in Large Cities.* Washington, DC: Government Publishing Office.

Zunz, Olivier. 1982. *The Changing Face of Inequality: Urbanization, Industrial Development, and Immigrants in Detroit, 1880–1920.* Chicago: University of Chicago Press.

Further Reading

Addams, Jane. 1910. *Twenty Years at Hull-House: With Autobiographical Notes.* New York: The Macmillan Co.

Boyer, Paul S. 1978. *Urban Masses and Moral Order in America, 1820–1920.* Cambridge, MA: Harvard University Press.

Burnstein, Daniel Eli. 2006. *Next to Godliness: Confronting Dirt and Despair in Progressive Era New York City.* Urbana: University of Illinois Press.

Hickey, Georgina. 2003. *Hope and Danger in the New South City: Working-class Women and Urban Development in Atlanta, 1890–1940.* Athens: University of Georgia Press.

Kasson, John F. 1978. *Amusing the Million: Coney Island at the Turn of the Century.* New York: Hill & Wang.

Rabinowitz, Howard N. 1996. *Race Relations in the Urban South, 1865–1890.* [New ed.] Athens: University of Georgia Press.

Riordon, William L. and Terrence J McDonald. 1994. *Plunkitt of Tammany Hall: A Series of Very Plain Talks on Very Practical Politics.* Boston: Bedford Books of St. Martin's Press.

Schneider, Eric C. 1992. *In the Web of Class: Delinquents and Reformers in Boston, 1810s–1930s.* New York: New York University Press.

Soll, David. 2013. *Empire of Water: An Environmental and Political History of the New York City Water Supply.* Ithaca, NY: Cornell University Press.

Warner, Sam Bass. 1968. *The Private City: Philadelphia in Three Periods of Its Growth.* Philadelphia: University of Pennsylvania Press.

Welke, Barbara Young. 2001. *Recasting American Liberty: Gender, Race, Law, and the Railroad Revolution, 1865–1920.* Cambridge: Cambridge University Press.

Wood, Sharon E. 2005. *The Freedom of the Streets: Work, Citizenship, and Sexuality in a Gilded Age City.* Chapel Hill: University of North Carolina Press.

Chapter Four

The South

Amy Louise Wood

The South appears to stand outside the history of the Gilded Age and Progressive Era. While the rest of the nation was experiencing massive industrialization, urbanization, and economic growth, the former states of the Confederacy remained agrarian and impoverished. In 1900, only about 18% of the southern population lived in cities, compared to about 40% nationwide. Industrial manufacturing constituted only a small portion of the southern economy, less than it did before the Civil War. Per capita wealth in the southern states was about 25% of that in northeastern states. The South also did not experience the massive influx of foreign immigration that the North did. While the foreign-born population in the nation stood at around 14%, it constituted less than 5% of the southern population. White southerners remained, on the whole, suspicious of the centralization of state power and resistant to change. Progressive reforms in education, penal systems, and public health lagged behind the rest of the county. The national image of the South then, as it still often is now, was one of backwardness and ignorance. It is telling that southern historians do not call this period the Gilded Age or the Progressive Era, but "the New South" or "the Jim Crow era."

Nevertheless, historians have debated the degree to which the South was marginal to national developments. These debates have been entwined with questions about southern distinctiveness. For many, the South, with its entrenched racism and its political and economic conservatism, stood in opposition to American ideals of liberalism, inclusion, and innovation. Northerners, in this view, were individualistic and market-oriented, while Southerners remained loyal to traditional values rooted in localism and agrarianism. For C. Vann Woodward (1960), the South's history of racism, defeat, and poverty had not allowed southerners to embrace the illusion of innocence and moral righteousness that has marked American exceptionalism.

Many historians, though, have questioned the assumptions underlying notions of what has been called southern exceptionalism. As Michael O'Brien has pointed out (1973), Woodward's concept of southern distinctiveness rested on a consensus view of US history as a story of unremitting success and social cohesion. Similarly, the idea of southern marginality in the Gilded Age and Progressive Era presumes a Whiggish view of the period as an age of prosperity and progress from which the South was excluded. Historians have instead offered that the traits long associated with the south were national traits. Northerners, too, often resisted social change and clung to rural traditions and values. Northerners, too, had their own histories of racial prejudice and violence. Southern exceptionalism exists, it has been argued, but only as a political and cultural invention that allowed the rest of the nation to project its own deficiencies on the South (Lassiter and Crespino 2009). In allowing non-southerners to embrace a view of the nation as innocent and virtuous, southern exceptionalism helped sustain American exceptionalism.

For these reasons, recent scholarship on the South has sought to blur the Mason–Dixon line by drawing comparisons between regions or localities on either side of it, or by considering how the South as an idea operated ideologically to obscure what were national problems. Such work has been an important corrective to easy caricatures of the South and serves as a reminder that "the South" is foremost a construct, a myth. Geographically, there really is no "South," but rather many distinctive sub-regions each with their own cultures and histories: the south Atlantic, the piedmont, Appalachia, the Black Belt, the Delta, among others.

Yet, even as a myth, the South has had tremendous staying power. In the late nineteenth and early twentieth centuries, Americans, North and South, black and white, believed there was such a thing as "the South," and responded to it,

A Companion to the Gilded Age and Progressive Era, First Edition. Edited by Christopher McKnight Nichols and Nancy C. Unger.
© 2017 John Wiley & Sons, Inc. Published 2017 by John Wiley & Sons, Inc.

politically, ideologically, culturally, in ways that shaped social reality (Prince 2014). In challenging conceptions of southern distinctiveness, scholars risk obscuring the ways in which southern states and sub-regions faced common conflicts and conditions that set them apart from the rest of the nation, just as any locality or region has its own history, particularities, and trajectories. This chapter uses the term "the South" to examine these conflicts and conditions, not only because Americans at the time conceived of the region as a unified whole, but because historians have also presumed the existence of some kind of common regional experience—even those historians who take issue with the notion of southern exceptionalism.

To say the South was distinctive is not to say that it was marginal to rest of the nation. To question its marginality compels a reconsideration of national history, and, more specifically, the Gilded Age and Progressive Era. Indeed, the South should be anything but peripheral to the study of this period, for its history of racial segregation and violence, of reactionary politics, of evangelical religion, and more, shaped the history of the nation in ways that are still felt.

The history of the South in the late nineteenth and early twentieth centuries is rich and varied. This chapter cannot cover every aspect of this history. Instead, it focuses on three central areas about which there has been vigorous historical debate and that bear on questions of southern distinctiveness: the political economy of the postbellum South; the rise of Jim Crow segregation; and Progressive Era reform.

The Rise of the "New South"

In the late nineteenth century, business-minded civic leaders sought to pull the South out of the ashes of the Civil War and its reliance on plantation agriculture by remaking it into a modern industrial economy. With sectional pride, boosters, such as Atlanta journalist Henry Grady, claimed that a reinvigorated South could not only compete with, but best, the North. Grady coined the term "the New South" to denote the rupture from the past that southern modernization entailed. C. Vann Woodward in his opus, *The Origins of the New South* (1951), was the first to introduce the term into southern historiography. To Woodward and others that followed, the South in late nineteenth century bore little resemblance to the antebellum South. With the end of the Depression in 1879, northern and foreign capital flooded the region, railroads expanded, and new industries, such as textiles, lumber, turpentine, iron, and steel, emerged. Boosters like Grady championed a new creed that believed industry and capital would produce a moral and spiritual regeneration in the South. Many African Americans moved off plantations to take up work in these new industries and started populating the towns around them. Poor whites and struggling white yeomen families did the same to an even greater degree (Woodward 1951; Doyle 1990; Ayers 1992).

For decades after Woodward, southern historiography of this period centered on the degree to which this portrait of the New South held true, or, alternatively, whether social and political structures of the antebellum era persisted after the Civil War and into the new century. That is, historians debated whether this period saw more discontinuity or continuity. More recently, historians have appeared to abandon this debate, some claiming that it would never yield any satisfactory answers (Woodman 2001; Kolchin 2003). Yet, it remains significant because it serves as a stand-in for several important questions: what groups held power in this period and how? Why did the South remain relatively impoverished for so long after the Civil War? How and why were ex-slaves and their descendants denied the promise that war and Reconstruction once offered?

Before Woodward, few scholars had paid much attention to the political economy of the late nineteenth century, and those who did tended to emphasize continuity. Observers supposed that Redemption, when white Democrats re-ascended to power at the end of Reconstruction, had restored the political and economic hegemony of the planter elite. For traditionalists of the Dunning School, this was a triumphant return, a victory over the injustices of Reconstruction that restored class harmony and white supremacy after years of discord. For critics of the South, like W.J Cash (1941), it meant the persistence of a reactionary, violent mindset, what he called "the savage ideal."

Woodward's thesis that redemption did not restore the power of the planter elite was, therefore, a monumental revision. He argued that war and Emancipation had destroyed the wealth and influence of that elite. In their place, rose a new merchant class, men who held a capitalistic, bourgeois outlook that departed from aristocratic agrarianism. The "New South," in Woodward's view, held no promise or progress. He painted a grim picture of a region rent with geographical divisions and class conflicts that stymied real advancement. To ensure the solidity of Democratic rule and to maintain white supremacy, the new industrial bourgeoisie invoked the past, emphasizing tradition and racial order as a way to forge shaky alliances with low-country planters and up-country white yeoman. But once white, Democratic rule was secured, the seams that stitched these alliances together began to tear. Entrepreneurial leaders used their political power to shore up their interests and align them with northern industrial interests at the expense of small farmers and workers. Woodward's emphasis on class conflict was bold for its time, as it broke with the consensus school that downplayed class conflict as a central driver in US history, and harkened back to the Progressive-era historiography of Charles and Mary Beard (O'Brien 1973; Woodman 2001). To suppress this conflict, redeemers invoked white unity, often at the expense of their own economic self-interest. They practiced a policy of retrenchment, keeping taxes low, underfunding public services, rejecting federal aid, out of fear that any governmental growth would resurrect the specter of Reconstruction and provide a challenge to white supremacy.

Thus, while manufacturing increased and a new mercantile class arose, industry stalled, and the South remained agrarian and impoverished. Yet, even the rural landscape, Woodward argued, had changed. The planter elite adopted the same entrepreneurial outlook as the industrial bourgeoisie. Their plantations bore little resemblance to those of the antebellum South, as they became corporate enterprises, financed by banks and broken into shares. The consolidation of land into the hands of the wealthy spelled doom for small farmers. The crop-lien system, by which farmers mortgaged their anticipated crop for food and supplies, was, according to Woodward, the "new order," an evil "that may have worked more permanent injury to the South than the ancient evil"—slavery (Woodward 1951, 180). Unlike western farmers, southern yeomen could not mortgage their land, since it held little value, so they borrowed against their crops—a precarious gamble. They fell increasingly into debt to unscrupulous merchants. Many lost their farms altogether and were forced into tenancy or into industrial wage labor. External elements of the late-nineteenth century economy—declining cotton prices, restrictive tariffs, and the contraction of currency—exacerbated their plight and impeded the recovery of southern agriculture.

The southern economy was actually rising at the same rate as that of the North, but not enough to close the enormous gap that the Civil War had created (Wright, 1986). Historians who followed Woodward saw the cause of the region's persistent poverty in the spread of capitalist markets across the rural South, which destroyed the independence of the yeomanry and ensnared them into the crop-lien system and, eventually, tenancy. The war had devastated small farmers, but, in the late nineteenth century, business-minded landlords and merchants passed legislation restricting open grazing and hunting that made it even harder for yeoman to maintain self-supporting farms. These laws, coupled with the spread of railroads and markets effectively coerced yeomen into commercial cotton production, with disastrous results.

This view, as espoused by Steven Hahn (1983) and others, emphasizes discontinuity, but also argues that most white farmers remained rooted in the past and were drawn reluctantly into modernity (Daniel 1986a; Fields 1985). Ayers (1992), alternatively, posits that yeomen were not coerced into the market, but entered it gingerly on their own accord because they thought cash-crop farming would help them retain their independence and raise their standard of living. They might have lamented the effects of the market on their lives and certainly did not want it to jeopardize their independence, but historians should not mistake that for nostalgia or wholesale resistance to change. What the "discontinuity" historians agree upon is that the central conflicts of the era were not between business interests and agricultural interests, but between the powerful and the powerless: the agricultural and industrial elite against low-wage workers, small farmers, tenants, and sharecroppers (Woodman 1997).

Even boosters like Grady never repudiated the Old South even as they championed the New South. Instead, they represented themselves as continuing traditions of manufacturing that thrived in the Old South before slavery and the cotton economy came to dominate (Degler 1997). Such appeals may have served as a form of a jeremiad. White southerners had to look backward, cultivating plantation nostalgia and embracing Lost Cause ideology, in order to come to grips with their march forward. To do so was to cling to a sense of regional distinctiveness as northern capital and industry spread across their region. For if a New South was emerging, then the South began to look more like the rest of the nation. The centralization of economic production and distribution, a professionalized and specialized business class, the rise of monopoly power, and the use of government to support that power—these trends that Woodward identified with the southern postbellum economy also characterized northern industry (Degler 1997; Woodman 2001).

In the late 1960s, historians began to push back against Woodward's central claim that the political economy, if not the mentality, of the postwar south was marked by discontinuity. These historians did not deny that the Civil War and Emancipation had altered the southern economy and labor relations. But they also saw continuity between the antebellum and postbellum South, which, they argued, could explain the persistence of white supremacy, as well as why industrialization stalled and the rural economy remained relatively stagnant. According to this view, it was not until the New Deal or even World War II that the Southern economy underwent substantial transformation, when the intervention of federal programs helped mechanize southern farms, and the flood of defense contracts spurred southern industry (Daniel 1986b; Sosna 1987).

There were a number of objections to Woodward's thesis. First, it was problematically premised on the notion that if the New South outlook was capitalistic and market-driven, the antebellum South was not, that it was ruled by planter aristocrats who saw themselves as more feudal than modern. Historians of slavery have since debunked this view. Woodward may have also overstated the rise of southern industry and robustness of southern urbanization. According to Sheldon Hackney (1972), the share of the southern economy engaged in manufacturing remained static between 1877 and World War I. New cities arose in the postbellum era, such as Atlanta, Houston, San Antonio, and Birmingham, eclipsing in size the antebellum port cities like Charleston, New Orleans, and Mobile. Southerners, black and white, were migrating to cities at greater rates than Americans as a whole. Nevertheless, the South was still overwhelmingly rural, and the size of its largest cities paled in comparison to those in the North. Instead, the southern landscape in the late nineteenth century was scattered with small cities that reflected the localization of the cotton market. The rise of railroads allowed that market to bypass the antebellum port cities, which soon declined (Goldfield 1982). Southern cities were also tied to the rural economy in a way that northern cities were not, coming alive at when cotton and tobacco were harvested, and remaining sleepy the rest of the year. Cities remained commercial and administrative centers, rather than industrial centers, and they had neither the wealth nor the municipal services of northern cities. The South was therefore, according to David Goldfield (1982), still "an antebellum region", dependent on staple-crop agriculture and built on a legacy of white supremacy.

A group of social historians in the 1970s emphasized continuity in the rural economy. Civil War and Reconstruction had done little to transform the southern countryside. Rather, the plantation economy endured, and although, as sharecropping replaced slavery, the social relations of production had changed, planters largely retained their land, their wealth, and their political influence (Weiner 1978; Mandle 1978; Billings 1979). Planters used their power, both within and beyond the law, to bind ex-slaves and their descendants to their land, replicating the conditions of slavery and blocking black advancement.

Planters did work with merchants and industrialists as a means to strengthen their power, but, when their interests were threatened, they viewed them antagonistically (Billings 1979). Jonathan Wiener (1978) argued that Alabama planters used their political influence to limit the power of merchants in the Black-Belt regions, so that they, not merchants, could benefit from the crop-lien system. In the hill country, where the planter elite had little stake, they paid merchants little mind. Likewise, planters encouraged the building of textile mills to strengthen the local cotton economy, but opposed the development of industries like iron or coal mining since they threatened their control over their black labor force. When they could not stop industrialization, they used their political power to ensure that labor was non-unionized and low-wage to minimize the threat industry posed.

These historians likened regional economic development in the postbellum South to that of the nineteenth-century German empire, deeming it "the Prussian Road" to modernization. Economic growth did not entail increased industrialization and liberalism, but rather, a landed elite ruling over a repressive, closed society. According to this view, contra Woodward, planters did not embrace a bourgeois, capitalist approach to agricultural growth. They did not increase their profits through capital investment in technology to mechanize production or through division and specialization of labor, as northern industrialists were doing, nor did they increase labor productivity through encouraging a competitive labor market; rather, they increased productivity by coercing more work out of their bound labor force (Wiener 1978). However, this view, like Woodward's, assumes that antebellum planters were also precapitalist in their outlook. These historians, Marxist in approach, also tend to see racial oppression as an outcome of planters' economic desire for low-wage labor, rather than viewing white supremacy as driving force in and of itself that would lead planters to exploit their labor (see also Wright 1986). Such a view has not held up over time.

The "Prussian Road" thesis also does not hold up when southern planter power is viewed nationally. As Barbara Fields (1985) and Steven Hahn (2001) have indicated, although southern planters used their power in state legislatures to benefit their interests, they had little national political influence, especially compared to the sway they enjoyed before the Civil War. In the Prussian model, the landed aristocracy held the reins of the state, which allowed them to ensure compensation for the loss of their peasant workers and to gain bank credit to replace that labor with equipment. Southern landowners received no such assistance and instead relied upon the shaky crop-lien system for credit. They also found themselves politically at odds with northern industrial power; whatever alliances between big agriculture and big industry that Woodward saw happening within the South were not happening nationally.

Many historians have argued that, with modernization, the South took not the Prussian Road, but assumed a quasi-colonial status to the North. Southerners were largely consumers of manufactured goods, not producers, and the region's industries and agriculture were labor-intensive and extractive. Both industrialists and landowners relied on northern capital and credit and were at the mercy of northern-owned railroad companies. What is more, like a colonial society, cheap labor prevented the growth of a broad consumer base, and industrialists and planters had little incentive to boost productivity through innovation and technology (Woodward 1951; Hackney 1972; Cobb 1984; Ayers 1992; Daniel 1986b; Hahn 2001).

Since the 1990s, scholars have seemingly set aside this debate. Instead, they have turned to documenting the lived experience of yeoman, tenants, and sharecroppers, black and white, male and female, particularly as those groups moved out of the countryside and into growing urban centers and industries. Yet, even as scholars avoid taking up this debate explicitly, they do so implicitly. Some historians have emphasized a dramatic shift in the lives of farmers and farm laborers of both races in the face of encroaching markets and rising industries, while others note the migration of rural traditions and planter paternalism into those industries. Studies of convict leasing, with titles like *Worse than Slavery* and *Slavery by Another Name*, are explicit in their claim that, through the southern penal system, both the conditions of slavery and the power of planter elites persisted after Emancipation (Oshinsky 1997; Blackmon 2008). Questions of continuity and discontinuity continue to cast a shadow over the scholarship of the postbellum South.

Historians' approaches to the study of freedpeople's experiences in the rural economy are a case in point. Social historians in the 1970s emphasized continuity between the institutions of slavery and sharecropping, just as they argued that the planter elite retained its power after Reconstruction. To be sure, sharecropping signaled a sharp break from the gang-labor system of slavery. Nevertheless, former slaves had little choice but to return to the plantations of their former owners, where they were coerced into a cycle of dependency. In perpetual debt, sharecroppers were compelled to grow cotton exclusively rather than diversify their crops or engage in the self-sufficient farming that might have offered more avenues toward landownership (Ransom and Sutch 1977). Barbara Fields (1985), alternatively, argued that sharecropping left freedpeople powerless, but not because they retained the characteristics of slaves. Rather, former slaves were now members of an oppressed working class in a capitalist economy, an "agrarian proletariat," akin to wage workers (Fields 1985, 81).

More recent histories emphasize not the powerlessness of African Americans in the postbellum South, but the active strategies they took to carve out autonomy and develop their own communities (Hahn 2003; Holt 2003; Schultz 2006; Brown 2008; Glymph 2008). From the perspective of former slaves, there was nothing constant after Emancipation—it was revolutionary. They certainly resisted any restoration of antebellum social relations or dependency. Ownership of land was, arguably, the most important form of self-determination and remained the primary aspiration for many southern blacks. Although only a minority of African Americans owned their own land, black landownership across the South increased considerably in the early twentieth century, reaching a height of around 25% in 1910 (Ayers 1992). Most of these farms were small, yet, as Sharon Holt (2003) has argued, not necessarily because black farmers could not have acquired more; rather, black farmers remained cautious, unwilling to take on unnecessary financial risks. Black farms were often clustered together, connected by kin networks, forming enclaves that offered security and distance from their potentially hostile white neighbors (Hahn 2003).

Holt attributes the growth in black landownership not to the successes of sharecropping or tenancy, but to the successes of African Americans' household economies. Household production—the making and preserving of food and drink, game hunting, the manufacturing of clothing, shoes, furniture, and other household items—provided African Americans with income, whether through barter or sale. These goods opened up possibilities, as they could be pledged to gain credit or used to pay off debts or forestall foreclosures.

The work of these scholars stands as a counterpoint to "continuity" historians who see, in the postbellum narrative, only unremitting coercion and exploitation—for all intents and purposes, slavery in freedom. A similar dynamic between continuity and discontinuity, between oppression and resistance, exists in the scholarship on segregation and disenfranchisement.

The Rise of Jim Crow

In 1928, Ulrich Phillips posited as the South's "central theme" its adherence to white supremacy, the lens through which every southern social, political, and economic development could be understood. It stood as a hallmark of southern distinctiveness. As much as present-day historians have wanted to distance themselves from Phillips because of his apologetic stance toward slavery—and from the implication that white supremacy was not a national characteristic—white supremacy has held enormous explanatory power in southern historiography. After all, it came to define the period from the late nineteenth century to the 1950s: the Jim Crow era.

Between 1890 and 1915, white supremacy was codified into law, piece by piece, state by state, locality by locality, in waves of succession. Public schools had already been segregated when the first schools for African Americans were established during Reconstruction. The segregation of city streetcars, interstate railroad cars, and railway stations followed in the 1890s. Laws banning interracial marriage were reinstituted after Reconstruction rulings had lifted earlier bans. In 1883, the US Supreme Court had overturned the Reconstruction-era Civil Rights Act of 1875 that ensured African Americans equal access to places of public accommodation. And in 1896, *Plessy v. Ferguson* gave full force to state laws that maintained segregation in public facilities by affirming their constitutionality under the doctrine of "separate of equal." Laws governing the segregation of workers in places of employment were firmly in place by the 1910s, as were codes that segregated or excluded African Americans in places of entertainment, restaurants and hotels. Some towns passed laws excluding African Americans all together, while others used various legal means to keep black residents to certain districts.

Politically, southern states, beginning in Mississippi in 1890, passed constitutional amendments that systematically stripped African-American men of their constitutionally guaranteed right to vote through a variety of mechanisms: property ownership or residency requirements, poll taxes, literacy and other laws, etc. The number of black men eligible to vote declined dramatically in every state, constituting around 2% of the electorate in some states. If legal measures did not keep blacks from the polls, violence and intimidation did. Both segregation and disenfranchisement were maintained through a culture of terror that reigned across the South. The Jim Crow era was synonymous with the "lynching era," when over 3000 African Americans were killed at the hands of white mobs.

Jim Crow was, in this sense, a closed society that governed every aspect of life across the South. What could not be governed by law was governed by social custom. Rigid codes of behavior demanded black deference and subservience. Internalizing these codes was a matter of personal survival for African Americans. Southern whites also perceived them as a matter of personal survival, necessities to ensure the continued existence of white dominance and purity. They could not distinguish between political rights and economic equity for African Americans and the specter of complete social equality. They were thus quick to interpret black demands for civic rights as desires for interracial marriage and miscegenation, practices which, for them, spelled doom for the white race. In stripping away any one set of rights, they had to strip away all rights. These views found full expression in a fanatical strain of white supremacy, characterized by extreme racial animosity and "negrophobia," that escalated in the late nineteenth century and came to eclipse, or at least coexist with, traditions of white paternalistic superiority. In this view, emancipated from the civilizing shackles of slavery, African Americans were rapidly retrogressing into their natural state of savagery (Williamson 1984).

On this basic narrative, historians agree. What they have disagreed about is when these developments were set in motion and why. The historiography of Jim Crow begins, once again, with C. Vann Woodward, who in his landmark 1955 study, *The Strange Career of Jim Crow*, sought to challenge the common wisdom among southern whites that segregation was a long-standing and inevitable racial arrangement. In the wake of the 1954 *Brown v. Board of Education* decision, he wanted to denaturalize the practice, to show it had a history, with the implication that if segregation was constructed, it could be de-constructed. His main argument was that the introduction of Jim Crow laws in the 1890s did not codify existing practices, but rather represented a new form of race relations. Before the war, whites and blacks in the South mingled in close proximity, a proximity that was not threatening to whites because the hierarchy between the races was clearly demarcated through the institution of slavery. Reconstruction-era "black codes" served as a precursor to Jim Crow laws, but once overturned by Republican rule, the southern Democrats who "redeemed" their state governments after Reconstruction did not immediately reinstitute them. Instead, a degree of flexibility governed interactions between the end of Reconstruction and the beginning of Jim Crow—what Woodward called "an unstable interlude" (Woodward 1974, 32). This interlude was no golden era of race relations by any means, but African Americans continued to vote, and across the countryside, blacks and whites continued to mingle and live side by side. Several state studies soon followed that appeared to confirm Woodward's thesis (see Wynes 1961; Dittmer 1977).

But many historians took issue with Woodward's chronology, particularly his argument that the 1880s was a period of relative racial fluidity. State studies showed that rigid forms of de-facto segregation were established soon after Emancipation in both state institutions and places of public accommodation and amusement. The Jim Crow legislation that appeared in the 1890s simply codified these practices into law practices (Williamson 1968; Rabinowitz 1978; Cell 1982). Howard Rabinowitz (1978) argued that segregation was an invention of northern Republicans, who, during Reconstruction, established segregated institutions—schools, hospitals, asylums, etc.—as an alternative to complete exclusion. The de facto practice of "separate but equal" kept the Republican political coalition intact, as southern white and moderate Republicans would not have accepted complete integration. According to Joel Williamson (1968), legislation to ensure African Americans legal access to public facilities—including the Civil Rights Act of 1875—would not have been necessary if segregation was not already in practice. In terms of disenfranchisement, African Americans were already "depoliticized" before de jure suffrage restrictions were put into place, kept from the polls through fraud and intimidation or through their exclusion from voting in Democratic primaries (Williamson 1984). When southern Democrats came back to power, they simply ignored the 1875 Act and continued Reconstruction-era segregation practices. They did not move to immediately legalize these practices because they were already socially engrained (Williamson 1968).

Others countered Woodward's claim that segregation was a post-Civil War phenomenon by showing that patterns of segregation existed in antebellum cities, both North and South. In his 1974 revision of *Strange Career*, Woodward responded to these critics by conceding that segregation was practiced widely in the antebellum North and arguing that, although segregation did exist in some antebellum cities, it was not applied consistently or completely, nor was it always legally enforced. As for the claim that segregation began in Reconstruction, Woodward remained skeptical, as there was considerable variation between localities and states, and "too many cross currents and contradictions" existed (Woodward 1974, 25). African Americans were integrated into public life in unexpected ways, for instance—most notably, they exercised their political rights, served on juries, and held public office. The passage of Civil Rights acts, for Woodward, did not signal the solidity of Reconstruction-era segregation, but its weakness.

Ultimately, as Fitzhugh Brundage (2011, 5) has written, it is "folly to locate a single moment of creation for segregation." The development of Jim Crow took decades, involving a complex process of "experimentation and adaptation." Even the codification of segregation into law is difficult to pinpoint, as laws segregating various kinds of institutions were established at different times, and their establishment varied by state. Moreover, segregation itself is a not a uniform concept. All these various forms of segregation—whether in education or in public spaces or in prohibitions against interracial marriage—encompass different notions of rights and different conceptions of what constitutes full citizenship (Wallerstein 2011).

The more important question, then, might be not when segregation occurred, but *why* it occurred, or, more specifically, why it became legalized beginning only in the 1890s.

Woodward himself lamented that, because *Strange Career* began with the question of "when," that question came to dominate and even skew the debate (Woodward 1988). If Woodward and his critics disagreed on when and why segregation began, they agreed on where: in cities and places that heralded a changing social landscape (Woodward 1988). Modernization was a significant driving force. With the rise of towns and cities, whites were forced to interact with blacks in new ways—in railroad and streetcars, in the consumer marketplace, on the sidewalks, on job sites—as potential equals. Whites and blacks were also more likely to encounter each other as strangers, without the familiarity of longstanding relationships to guide their interactions. Jim Crow laws supplied clear racial hierarchies in places where relationships of power had become destabilized (Ayers 1992; Hale 1998). Indeed, as Mark Schultz (2006) has shown, the rural South, in contrast, retained a kind of "personalism," through which whites and blacks mingled together freely, and white supremacy was maintained not through law, but custom.

Gender and sexuality mattered as well. Public places where members of the opposite sex might interact—in particular where black men might interact with white women—became segregated, while, in homo-social spaces, boundaries remained more relaxed (Ayers 1992). It was precisely these kinds of demarcations that justified Jim Crow to whites, even moderate or northern whites who might otherwise object. Southern whites claimed that segregation was necessary to protect whites, particular white women, from the threat of black men, who were deemed dangerously violent and hypersexual. As Blair Kelley (2010) has pointed out, the exclusion of black women from white-only spaces—and the way they were often physically and violently removed from them—reveals the lie behind this justification. Segregation was not about protection, but power and humiliation. In fact, it was not even about physical distance as much as it was about creating social distance between the races, keeping African Americans "in their place" metaphorically. After all, whites did not want complete physical separation, as they depended on black labor in their worksites and in their homes (Ritterhouse 2006).

Woodward (1974) also rooted the origins of Jim Crow in class conflict, arguing that de-jure segregation and disenfranchisement resolved problems of class for elite whites. Elites remained conservative on issues of race, preferring the paternalism of informal associations between the races, largely because these associations did not challenge their social standing or power. It was poor whites who, by the 1890s, came to embrace a rabid form of racism and demanded more rigid form of segregation, especially because they saw African Americans as competition for jobs and wages. Elite whites began to foment this extreme racism as both a concession to poor whites and a means to control the threat of any interracial class alliances (Woodward 1951).

Rabinowitz (1978) challenged this "capitulation to racism" theory. Along with Williamson (1968), he saw the withdrawal of northern opposition as the most significant factor. As white northerners, Republicans in particular, abandoned their commitment to the advancement of black civil rights by the late nineteenth century, southern whites were free to set into law segregation and disenfranchisement practices. That alone, however, would not have prompted white southerners to act. In his epilogue, Rabinowitz argued that white southerners reacted against the activism of younger African Americans, who born in freedom, were unwilling to acquiesce to custom as their parents and grandparents had done. Scholars since have heeded Rabinowitz's call to see African Americans as "subjects" rather than "objects" of history (Rabinowitz 1978, 333), and have given much weight to the role of the "New Negro" in fomenting white backlash in the late nineteenth century. Younger blacks began to protest discrimination and refused to acquiesce to de-facto segregation. Their resistance prompted white legislatures to give permanence to segregation through the law. Jim Crow emerged in response to African Americans' assertions of power, as they participated in political life and sought equal access to urban spaces (Ayers 1992; Litwack 1998; Dailey 2000; Brown 2008). In this sense, Rabinowitz's emphasis on black agency undermined his own argument that there was no "unstable interlude" between Reconstruction and Jim Crow, since the arrival of the "New Negro" shows that in fact there was.

Recent studies have tended to downplay Jim Crow as a consequence of class conflict between whites. Earlier historians, however, followed Woodward in placing social class at the center of their analysis. Joel Williamson (1984) attributed the rise of the radical strain of racism that led to Jim Crow to the psychological frustrations of white farmers amidst the economic crises of the 1880s and early 1890s. When white men felt they could no longer maintain their independence or provide for their families, their core sense of manhood was threatened. Radical racism—and, in particular, the violence it generated in the form of lynching—offered these men "psychic compensation" for their sense of masculine and sexual inadequacy (Williamson 1984). Historians have critiqued Williamson for his armchair psychoanalysis, which was speculative at best. His treatment of racism as a kind of psychological disorder also elided the ways white supremacy operated as a social practice. And his focus on agrarian distress overlooked the urban origins of segregation.

Moreover, by attributing radical racism to the distress of poor whites, Williamson let elite and middle-class whites off the hook. They supported Jim Crow, he argued, but as a means to maintain social order, that is, to protect African Americans from the violence generated by this reactionary racial climate. Others have contended that the radical strains of white supremacy served the interests of planters and the bourgeoisie. This radicalism did not bubble up from below, nor did elites simply foment it or capitulate to it, as Woodward argued; rather, it was imposed from above. Conservative Democrats, particularly from the Black Belt regions, initiated disenfranchisement in order to thwart potential interracial challenges from upcountry Republicans and Populists. That poll taxes and literacy laws also disenfranchised poor whites, whose votes they could not control, further served their interests (Kousser 1974). In rising industrial centers, white supremacy—and segregation—benefitted the industrial bourgeoisie, as it divided the work force by race and bonded laboring whites to their employers against a threatening black enemy, while depressing white wages (Cell 1982). In these ways, white supremacy not only allowed whites to dominate African Americans, but elite whites to dominate poor whites (Fields 1982). These explanations differ from those of historians who argued that racism followed from planters' economic imperatives to maintain a low-wage, controlled labor force; rather, white supremacy existed as a discrete belief system that acted upon class relations.

These explanations also challenge the notion that class and race were competing categories of social interaction, that is, that racial identity always trumped class identity or vice versa. As Barbara Fields has argued (1982, 144), race and class cannot occupy the "same analytical space," since while class differences exist as an objective, material reality, albeit mediated by ideology, race exists only as a social construction. Unlike class, it does not emerge intrinsically from economic conditions, but rather it is a system of power imposed through politics and law (Cell 1982). Moreover, white supremacy was not a totalizing ideology so much as it was a political slogan that sought to unite superficially people with otherwise very different socioeconomic interests and circumstances (Fields, 1982). There was no triumph of racial unity in the South, as the cleavages between various white constituencies—tenants, yeomen, planters, industrial elites, middle-rank urbanites, industrial wage-laborers—remained, and class status shaped the tone and tenor of racist belief. In other words, racism is re-formed and fueled to serve particular social needs at particular points in time, and so its texture and meaning change to meet new sociopolitical conditions. This point is one that recent challenges to southern exceptionalism overlook, as they tend to emphasize the consistency and potency of American racism across time and place.

White supremacy was, therefore, a rather fragile and unstable system. Whiteness itself was a fluid category, as there was no uniform definition across states. Increased urbanization and mobility made establishing firm color lines difficult, since they opened up the possibility of racial passing. The notion that race might not be easily identifiable only intensified white attempts to fix the color line, to make it conspicuous, through Jim Crow laws (Wallenstein 2011). Historians in the 1990s and 2000s have taken to examining the ways in which white supremacy was a cultural and ideological project that once constructed, needed, through tremendous effort, to be continually replenished—through politics and public discourse, through consumer practices and popular culture, through the socialization of children in the home, and through violence (Hale 1998; Smith 2002; Ritterhouse 2006; Prince 2014; Wood 2009).

White supremacy relied on tropes of black savagery and white civilization that had national currency. And segregation, exclusion, and lynching were practiced across the country. Yet white Americans across various sub-regions saw what they called "the race problem" as specific to the South, an unresolved remnant of slavery and Reconstruction. White southerners believed that racial conflict was brewing in their region in a way that northerners could not fully understand, that friction between the races threatened to implode into an all-out race war at any time (Ring 2012). They positioned themselves as "race experts," claiming that they alone knew the burden of race and how to deal with it (Ring 2012; Prince 2014). White supremacy was not exclusive to the South by any means, but it defined and shaped southern society distinctively.

For these reasons, white southerners did not look to the North for comparisons to their racial state of affairs, but abroad. Recently, historians have turned their attention to the ways in which the postbellum South was integrated into global networks and discourses. A number of earlier historians had engaged in comparative studies between the South and other countries with racially stratified societies, such as South Africa and Brazil (Cell 1982; Fredrickson 1982; Hahn 1990; Kolchin 2003). That work broadened historians' view of the South and served as important reminders of the historically contingent nature of racial segregation. But, these studies did not take southerners out of the South. Scholars in the past ten years, on the other hand, have examined the various ways southerners in the Jim Crow era, black and white, looked to European and American imperial expansion in order to find models for their own circumstances. African American activists saw their struggle as a global one, drawing pointed comparisons between themselves and other colonized peoples. And black reformers such as Booker T. Washington and Mary Church Terrell sought to extend programs of racial uplift and education to other peoples of African descent in the Caribbean, South America, and Africa, often as a form of missionary work. (Zimmerman 2010; Ring 2012).

Global imperialism also became the framework through which white southerners conceptualized racial segregation and conflict (Ring 2012). New South entrepreneurs looked to European colonies in cotton-growing areas of Africa and India as "models of racialized capitalism" that could provide lessons on how to control a non-white labor force (Clune 2010). In turn, European imperialists traveled to the South for lessons on cotton-growing or the governance of non-white people (Ring 2012; Zimmerman 2010). The fact that white southerners positioned themselves as colonizers complicates historical understandings of the South as a colonial outpost to the North. These studies also undo any presumptions that the South remained provincial at the turn of the twentieth century, that it was marginal to wider events and currents. At the same time, this scholarship does not the discount the "southern-ness" of the South. Indeed, as Natalie Ring points out, foreign travelers in the South tended to see more differences than similarities between their imperial projects and conditions in the South (Ring 2012).

In addition to cultural and global turns, recent scholarship has brought fresh attention to black resistance under Jim Crow. Steven Hahn, in his monumental, *A Nation Under Our Feet* (2003), conceptualized rural blacks as "political actors" who remade themselves after slavery. As white southerners reestablished white rule after Reconstruction, black southerners embraced separatism, not simply in reaction against their exclusion from white institutions, as Rabinowitz (1978) and Williamson (1984) had argued, but as a political strategy. They built separate civic and associational organizations, such as schools, churches, farmers' alliances, and benevolent associations—even their own towns in some cases—as a means of self-determination. In these activities, Hahn saw a nascent black nationalism and the origins of the Civil Rights Movement. Echoing Hahn, Jacquelyn Dowd Hall (2005) in her 2004 Organization of American Historians presidential address on the "Long Civil Rights Movement," broadened the temporal boundaries of the movement to argue that it began before the 1950s and persisted long after the 1960s. Indeed, Jim Crow laws and black activism were birthed at the same time. Or, as Leslie Brown (2008, 24) has put it, "the part of the Jim Crow era called the nadir… was also the zenith of the black women's club movement, the black press, and black business." Southern workers formed and joined labor unions (Ortiz 2005). Blacks' newspapers began printing throughout the South, and journalists such as Ida B. Wells and John J. Mitchell, at great risk to themselves, spoke fiercely against segregation and lynching. African Americans picketed against segregation and organized boycotts of segregated streetcars and railways across the South. According to Blair Kelley (2010), between 1900 and 1907, protests were held in at least 25 southern cities. After 1909, the National Association for the Advancement of Colored People established branches throughout the region. And when peaceful protest failed, African Americans engaged in armed self-defense, especially in response to racist violence (Ortiz 2005).

This work challenges the claim made by Rabinowitz (1978) that this was an "age of accommodation." According to Rabinowitz, the fact that African Americans established separate organizations reflected their acceptance of segregation, especially as it represented an improvement over the exclusion from public institutions they experienced in slavery. Any protests demanding equal access to public facilities came from middle-class blacks who were not calling for broad-based rights or full integration into public life, but inclusion for themselves into white bourgeois society—an interracial class alliance. But, as Blair Kelley (2010) has shown, rather than allowing for acquiescence, black churches, clubs, and fraternities provided the basis and resources for organized resistance against Jim Crow that crossed class lines.

Scholars in the past twenty years have largely abandoned the debate over when and why Jim Crow came into being, just as they have set aside the debate over continuity or discontinuity in the postbellum political economy. These historians nevertheless implicitly take a stand. In the case of Jim Crow, recent work has vindicated Woodward, as it is predicated on the idea that segregation—as well as disenfranchisement and the increase in racialized lynching—represented something decidedly new in the late nineteenth century.

The Progressive Movement in the South

Despite the efforts of New South boosters, the national image of the South in the early twentieth century was of a region hopelessly backward and conservative, resistant to the progressive impulses seizing the rest of the country. Arthur Link was the first to challenge this perception in 1946 in a groundbreaking essay that identified a vibrant progressive movement in the South (Link 1946). Since then numerous scholars have turned their attention to detailing the nature and scope of southern progressivism across a wide range of intersecting reform movements and policies. Despite the fact that reformers, like those in the North, tended to be urban and middle class, their efforts did not mirror northern reform. Rather, historians tend to agree, southern reform emerged out of the particularities of regional economic and political structures, and reformers directed their attention to what they saw as distinctly southern problems (Woodward 1951). If reformers elsewhere sought to address the negative effects of massive urbanization and industrialization, southern reformers sought to solve the problem of rural poverty and underdevelopment. Southern rural education lagged far behind the North, as schools, black and white, were grossly underfunded and underattended. The rural south was also beset with high rates of typhoid and malaria, as well as diseases of malnutrition or poor sanitation like pellagra and hookworm. Progressivism in the South thus went hand in hand with the New South creed that the region could rehabilitate itself through a process of economic development and modernization (Grantham 1981; Link 1991).

Southern progressives in the Democratic party challenged monopoly power—of the railroads, insurance companies and oil conglomerates—and sought to regulate these industries as a means to resolve economic woes. In this way, as C. Vann Woodward and others have argued, Democrats coopted aspects of the agrarian radicalism that swept the South in the

1880s and 1890s. Indeed, many former Populist leaders found strong allies in southern Democrats, who came to accept their vision of an activist state. Like the Populists, these Democrats worked to abolish convict leasing and strengthen public schooling (Woodward 1951; Grantham 1981). Some scholars have challenged this continuity between southern Populists and progressives to argue that, although both groups shared common aims, there was little overlap between them (Hackney 1969; Link 1992). This might be a false dichotomy, as southern progressives were a diverse lot (Kirby 1972). Reformers included struggling farmers and small businessmen who adopted the Populists' democratic skepticism of big business, as well as urban professional and bureaucrats who came to dominate state governments in the late 1910s and 1920s—a strain George Tindall has called "business progressivism" (Tindall 1967). These reformers advocated industrialization to solve the region's problems and valued efficiency and innovation, in both the private and public sectors, as a means to improve things like infrastructure, schools, and public health. Southern progressives also embraced industrial reform, supporting safety and inspection legislation for factories and mines, as well as child labor laws. Perhaps the most successful of southern reform campaigns was prohibition, a cause that appealed to rural, town, and urban southerners alike. Georgia became the first southern state to outlaw alcohol in 1907, setting off a wave of prohibition laws across the region.

Historians have interpreted these developments and measured their success in very different ways. As William Link (1991) has posited, the historiography on southern progressivism has tended to divide between "optimists" who take seriously reformers' humanitarian intentions and desires for progress and "pessimists" who see reform as superficial at best, and anti-democratic, detrimental to real progress, at worst. Although Arthur Link (1946) recognized the deficiencies of southern reform, C. Vann Woodward (1951) was the first to emphasize the paradox of a progressivism that was "for whites only." A movement that did not disrupt racial segregation and violence could hardly be called progressive, nor did reformers address the economic injustices of the crop-lien system. As John Dittmer has argued (1977, 110), progressives were "at heart, conservative Democrats," who were more interested in "improving their own existence than uplifting the masses, black or white." Infrastructure improvements, such as paved roads, as well as public health and sanitation reforms, affected predominantly white areas.

White supremacy did not just limit southern progressivism; it actually made reform possible. As Kirby (1972, 4) has written, segregation and disenfranchisement were the "seminal" reforms of southern progressivism. Disenfranchisement was touted as a "good government" reform. Reformers advocated all-white primary elections and other means to restrict black voting in order to stop elite whites from buying or manipulating black votes (Dittmer 1977). The white yeomanry also supported these efforts as means to dilute the power of planter elites who were blocking their efforts to regulate the railroads and improve agricultural conditions (Kirby 1972). Once in place, disenfranchisement narrowed the electorate—keeping not only African Americans, but poor whites from the polls—which allowed reformers to gain a greater political foothold and keep undesirable voters out. It also helped to ensure the dominance of the Democratic Party, which then splintered into various factions; the reformist wing of the party gained influence over and against the patrician elites who had once dominated (Grantham 1981; 1983). Furthermore, southern Democrats were only willing to make government more responsive to its citizenry once the establishment of Jim Crow excluded African Americans from the public sphere and ensured that any government funding of public services would benefit whites only (Kousser 1974; Kirby 1972). For example, advocates for abolishing child labor focused their efforts on textile mills, where the labor force was largely all-white, while ignoring the needs of black children (Dittmer 1977).

Historians in the pessimist camp have furthermore viewed southern progressivism as a mechanism of class control. In his study of the uneven distribution of resources for public education in North Carolina, J. Morgan Kousser concluded that progressivism was not only "for whites only," but "for middle-class whites only" (Kousser 1980). Reformers working against child labor or advocating for increased support for public education acted more out of a desire for class stability and a disciplined labor force than humanitarian interest (Carlton 1982; Leloudis 1983). As Pippa Holloway (2006) has argued, through public health and welfare programs, progressives used state power to classify and regulate sexual deviance, which furthered the economic marginalization of poor whites and African Americans. Such a view explains why moral issues—most prominently prohibition—took such a firm hold in southern progressive politics.

Many scholars have seen more promise in southern progressivism than paradox. These historians portray southern reformers as conservative in spirit and recognize the ways in which white supremacy bolstered their power. But they also view them as committed to social uplift for the poor as means to further economic progress and create prosperity in the region (Tindall, 1967; Bailey 1969; Grantham 1983). The struggle for progressives, according to Grantham, was reconciling their longing for moderation and order with their desire for innovation and social change. Concerns for social justice were not incidental in this view. The social gospel was certainly weaker in the South than in the North, and southern churches were more involved in moral crusades than social justice, pushing state governments to legislate against vices such as gambling, drinking, and prostitution. But, southern Christians also adopted the New South creed and worked to improve social conditions through missionary work and church-based social service agencies (Grantham 1981; 1983; McDowell 1982).

White and black women forged alliances to work for social reform, for instance in the Women Christian Temperance Union or in public health campaigns. Social reform offered white women a public role and a degree of power that countered the image of helpless southern ladyhood and paved the path toward suffrage (Scott 1970). Black middle-class women, because they posed less of a political and social threat to whites, served, according to Glenda Gilmore (1996, xxi), as "diplomats" to the white community. Nevertheless, Gilmore argued, white and black women had different objectives, and their collaboration was often fraught with tension. White women welcomed black women's activism as a means to uplift the black community, but they did not view them as equals, nor would they have ever worked to dismantle segregation. Black women, on the other hand, adapted reform efforts to their own purposes of racial uplift, which cultivated and emphasized black dignity and industriousness, virtues through which they pushed for full social and political equality. They also built organizations to gain access to public services and welfare that white reformers would otherwise deny black communities. Without black women's activism, Gilmore writes, progressivism "would have been even more racist, more exclusive, and more oppressive..." (Gilmore 1996, 149).

Most studies of southern progressivism have focused on the intentions and activities of reformers. Other historians, though, have studied the wider social contexts that help explain the distinctive character of southern progressivism. William Link (1992) has examined the unfertile ground across the southern countryside in which reformers attempted to plant seeds of reform. Rural communities were "pre-bureaucratic" in the sense that government power was weak and decentralized, and southerners adhered to a culture of localism that prized self-reliance and was suspicious of both concentrated government power and outsiders. These values led them to reject the interventions of county and state officials, even if those interventions, as in the case of public health, would improve their lives. Rural southerners, for example, saw medicine as a private concern, which led them to resist reformers' immunization and disease-treatment campaigns. To solve social problems, reformers had to change cultural norms, and their democratic aims often required coercive tactics. For Link, who deemphasized race, this struggle between traditions of localism and reformers' paternalism stood as the primary conflict of progressivism, and explains why reform often stalled in the South.

The legacy of progressivism was that the growth of the bureaucratic state came to replace traditional forms of governance and community control. Although in the nineteenth century, the federal, or even state, governments rarely touched the lives of southerners, this was no longer true by the twentieth century, especially by the 1910s and 1920s when reform came to be shaped by national standards, and southern reformers looked to the federal government for solutions to local problems (Grantham 1981; Link 1992).

If Link looked at reform through the perspective of local communities, Natalie Ring (2011) has examined it in national and international contexts. The poverty and backwardness of the South was deemed not only a southern problem, but a national one, a hindrance to national economic development. Through their criticisms of the southern reactionary mindset and their pursuits for reform, southern liberals, such as Walter Hines Page and George Washington Cable, drew national attention from philanthropists, social scientists, and the federal government who sought a "rational intervention" to modernize the South. This intervention, Ring argues, happened against the backdrop of US imperialism, and reformers saw their efforts as part of a broader civilizing mission. The South in that context became a "colossal laboratory for social change," and progressive reform served as an experiment in nation-building (Ring 2011, 11). Ring's work highlights the ways in which southern distinctiveness existed as more than simply an idea, for the perceived backwardness of the South had real policy implications.

Conclusion: National Reconciliation

According to Ring, reformers believed that the rehabilitation of the South would unify the nation. There still existed well into the twentieth century a sense that the rifts of the Civil War had not healed and that the South remained outside the nation. If progressives sought to integrate the South back into the nation by eradicating what they considered the distinct, and damaging, features of the South, a parallel process of national reconciliation was occurring that encouraged the perpetuation of southern identity. A growing body of scholarship has been concerned with the cultural means—the rituals, performances, and images—through which the South came to be seen as once again part of the American nation after Reconstruction. This reconciliation, however, occurred on the South's terms and at the expense of African Americans (Silber 1993; Blight 2002; Blum 2007; Prince 2014). Civil War reunions and commemorations, for instance, obscured the role of slavery and emancipation in the War, and white northerners increasingly came to embrace Lost Cause ideology. Popular literature and plays, as well as national advertising, created a plantation ideal, through which northerners and southerners alike promoted a nostalgic vision of antebellum life and slavery. This cultural reconciliation was epitomized in the 1915 film, *The Birth of a Nation*, which literalizes the reunification of the nation through an inter-sectional romance, uniting two warring families, who come together to repel rampaging black forces who threaten white supremacy and purity. All of this stood in inverse to the New South creed. White southerners were eager to become more like the rest of the nation economically, as long as culturally their regional identity stood. Essentially after fighting a war that emancipated the slaves and instituting a Reconstruction to ensure freedpeople their civil rights, white northerners by the late nineteenth century had not only abandoned their interest in the cause of black freedom, but were actively opposing it.

These visions of national reconciliation may be overplayed, however. As Carolyn Janney has argued (2013), the political reunification that occurred after the War hardly entailed a cultural reconciliation. Janney contends that union veterans did not forget the causes of the war, but, rather, celebrated their role in keeping the union together and in emancipating the slaves. That white northerners were also white supremacists was not a new development, for they had long separated their antipathy for slavery from their ideas about race. Some one hundred years later, the existences of a distinctive South is still debated, a sign that national reunification has perhaps not yet been achieved.

References

Ayers, Edward L. 1992. *The Promise of the New South: Life after Reconstruction*. New York: Oxford University Press.

Bailey, Hugh C. 1969. *Liberalism in the New South: Southern Social Reformers and the Progressive Movement*. Coral Gables, FL: University of Miami Press.

Billings, Dwight B. 1979. *Planters and the Makings of a "New South": Class, Politics, and Development in North Carolina, 1865–1900*. Chapel Hill: University of North Carolina Press.

Blackmon, Douglas A. 2008. *Slavery by Another Name: The Re-Enslavement of Black Americans from the Civil War to World War II*. New York: Anchor Books.

Blight, David W. 2002. *Race and Reunion: The Civil War in American Memory*. Cambridge, MA: Belknap Press/Harvard University Press.

Blum, Edward J. 2007. *Reforging the White Republic: Race, Religion, and American Nationalism, 1865–1898*. Baton Rouge: Louisiana State University Press.

Brown, Leslie. 2008. *Upbuilding Black Durham: Gender, Class, and Black Community Development in the Jim Crow South*. Chapel Hill: University of North Carolina Press.

Brundage, W. Fitzhugh. 2011. "Introduction." In *The Folly of Jim Crow: Rethinking the Segregated South*, ed. Stephanie Cole and Natalie J. Ring, 1–16. Arlington: Texas A & M Press for The University of Texas at Arlington.

Carlton, David L. 1982. *Mill and Town in South Carolina, 1880–1920*. Baton Rouge: Louisiana State University Press.

Cash, W. J. 1941. *The Mind of the South*. New York: A.A. Knopf.

Cell, John Whitson. 1982. *The Highest Stage of White Supremacy: The Origins of Segregation in South Africa and the American South*. New York: Cambridge University Press.

Clune, Erin Elizabeth. 2010. "From Light Copper to the Blackest and Lowest Type: Daniel Tompkins and the Racial Order of the Global New South." *The Journal of Southern History* 76, 2: 275–314.

Cobb, James C. 1984. *Industrialization and Southern Society, 1877–1984*. Lexington: University Press of Kentucky.

Dailey, Jane. 2000. *Before Jim Crow: The Politics of Race in Postemancipation Virginia*. Chapel Hill: The University of North Carolina Press.

Daniel, Pete. 1986a. *Standing at the Crossroads: Southern Life Since 1900*. New York: Hill and Wang.

—. 1986b. *Breaking the Land: The Transformation of Cotton, Tobacco, and Rice Cultures since 1880*. Urbana: University of Illinois Press.

Degler, Carl N. 1997. *Place Over Time: The Continuity of Southern Distinctiveness*. Athens: University of Georgia Press.

Dittmer, John. 1977. *Black Georgia in the Progressive Era, 1900–1920*. Urbana: University of Illinois Press.

Doyle, Don Harrison. 1990. *New Men, New Cities, New South: Atlanta, Nashville, Charleston, Mobile, 1860–1910*. Chapel Hill: University of North Carolina Press.

Fields, Barbara Jean. 1982. "Ideology and Race in American History." In *Region, Race and Reconstruction: Essays in Honor of C. Vann Woodward*, ed. J. Morgan Kousser and James M. McPherson. New York: Oxford University Press.

—.1985. "The Advent of Capitalist Agriculture: The New South in a Bourgeois World." In *Essays on the Postbellum Southern Economy*, ed. Thavolia Glymph et al., 73–94. Arlington: Texas A & M Press for The University of Texas at Arlington.

Fredrickson, George M. 1982. *White Supremacy: A Comparative Study of American and South African History*. New York: Oxford University Press.

Gilmore, Glenda Elizabeth. 1996. *Gender and Jim Crow: Women and the Politics of White Supremacy in North Carolina, 1896–1920*. Chapel Hill: University of North Carolina Press.

Glymph, Thavolia. 2008. *Out of the House of Bondage: The Transformation of the Plantation Household*. New York: Cambridge University Press.

Goldfield, David R. 1982. *Cotton Fields and Skyscrapers: Southern City and Region, 1607–1980*. Baton Rouge: Louisiana State University Press.

Grantham, Dewey W. 1981. "The Contours of Southern Progressivism." *American Historical Review* 86, 5: 1035–1059.

—. 1983. *Southern Progressivism: The Reconciliation of Progress and Tradition*. Knoxville: University of Tennessee Press.

Hackney, Sheldon. 1972. "'Origins of the New South' in Retrospect." *Journal of Southern History* 38, 2: 191–216.

Hahn, Steven. 1983. *The Roots of Southern Populism: Yeoman Farmers and the Transformation of the Georgia Upcountry, 1850–1890*. New York: Oxford University Press.

—. 1990. "Class and State in Postemancipation Societies: Southern Planters in Comparative Perspective." *American Historical Review* 95, 1: 85–98.

—. 2003. *A Nation Under Our Feet: Black Political Struggles in the Rural South from Slavery to the Great Migration*. Cambridge, MA: Harvard University Press.

Hale, Grace Elizabeth. 1998. *Making Whiteness: The Culture of Segregation in the South, 1890–1940*. New York: Pantheon.

Hall, Jacquelyn Dowd. 2005. "The Long Civil Rights Movement and the Political Uses of the Past." *The Journal of American History* 91, 4: 1233–1263.

Holloway, Pippa. 2006. *Sexuality, Politics, and Social Control in Virginia, 1920–1945*. Chapel Hill: University of North Carolina Press.

Holt, Sharon Ann. 2003. *Making Freedom Pay: North Carolina Freedpeople Working for Themselves, 1865–1900*. Athens: University of Georgia Press.

Janney, Caroline E. 2013. *Remembering the Civil War: Reunion and the Limits of Reconciliation*. Chapel Hill: University of North Carolina Press.

Kelley, Blair L. M. 2010. *Right to Ride: Streetcar Boycotts and African American Citizenship in the Era of Plessy v. Ferguson*. Chapel Hill: University of North Carolina Press.

Kirby, Jack Temple. 1972. *Darkness at the Dawning: Race and Reform in the Progressive South*. Philadelphia: Lippincott.

Kolchin, Peter. 2003. *A Sphinx on the American Land: The Nineteenth-Century South in Comparative Perspective*. Baton Rouge: Louisiana State University Press.

Kousser, J. Morgan. 1974. *The Shaping of Southern Politics: Suffrage Restriction and the Establishment of the One-Party South, 1880–1910*. New Haven, CT: Yale University Press.

—. 1980. "Progressivism—for Middle Class Whites Only: North Carolina Education, 1880–1910." *Journal of Southern History* 46, 2: 169–94.

Lassiter, Matthew D. and Joseph Crespino, eds. 2009. *The Myth of Southern Exceptionalism*. New York: Oxford University Press.

Leloudis, James L. 1999. *Schooling the New South: Pedagogy, Self, and Society in North Carolina, 1880–1920*. Chapel Hill: University of North Carolina Press.

Link, Arthur S. 1946. "The Progressive Movement in the South, 1870–1914." *North Carolina Historical Review* 23: 172–95.

Link, William A. 1991. "The Social Context of Southern Progressivism, 1880–1930." In *The Wilson Era: Essays in Honor of Arthur S. Link*, ed. John Milton Cooper, Jr. and Charles Neu, 55–82. Arlington Heights, IL: Harlan Davidson, Inc.

—. 1992. *The Paradox of Southern Progressivism, 1880–1930*. Chapel Hill: University of North Carolina Press.

Litwack, Leon. 1998. *Trouble in Mind: Black Southerners in the Age of Jim Crow*. New York: Alfred A. Knopf.

Mandle, Jay R. 1978. *The Roots of Black Poverty: The Southern Plantation Economy after the Civil War*. Durham, NC: Duke University Press.

McDowell, John Patrick. 1982. *The Social Gospel in the South: The Women's Home Mission Movement in the Episcopal Church, South, 1886–1939*. Baton Rouge: Louisiana State University Press.

O'Brien, Michael. 1973. "C. Vann Woodward and the Burden of Southern Liberalism." *American Historical Review* 78, 3: 589–604.

Ortiz, Paul. 2005. *Emancipation Betrayed: The Hidden History of Black Organizing and White Violence in Florida from Reconstruction to the Bloody Election of 1920*. Berkeley: University of California Press.

Oshinsky, David. M. 1996. *"Worse Than Slavery": Parchman Farm and the Ordeal of Jim Crow Justice*. New York: Simon and Schuster.

Phillips, Ulrich B. 1928. "The Central Theme of Southern History." *American Historical Review* 34, 1: 30–43.

Prince, K. Stephen. 2014. *Stories of the South: Race and the Reconstruction of Southern Identity, 1865–1915*. Chapel Hill: The University of North Carolina Press.

Rabinowitz, Howard N. 1978. *Race Relations in the Urban South, 1865–1890*. New York: Oxford University Press.

—. 1988. "More Than the Woodward Thesis: Assessing the Strange Career of Jim Crow." *The Journal of American History* 75, 3: 842–856.

Ransom, Roger L. and Richard Sutch. 1977. *One Kind of Freedom: The Economic Consequences of Emancipation*. Cambridge: Cambridge University Press.

Ring, Natalie J. 2012. *The Problem South: Region, Empire, and the New Liberal State, 1880–1930*. Athens: University of Georgia Press.

Ritterhouse, Jennifer. 2006. *Growing Up Jim Crow: How Black and White Southern Children Learned Race*. Chapel Hill: University of North Carolina Press.

Schultz, Mark Roman. 2006. *The Rural Face of White Supremacy: Beyond Jim Crow*. Urbana: University of Illinois Press.

Scott, Ann Firor. 1970. *The Southern Lady: From Pedestal to Politics, 1830–1930*. Chicago: University of Chicago Press.

Silber, Nina. 1997. *The Romance of Reunion: Northerners and the South, 1865–1900*. Chapel Hill: The University of North Carolina Press.

Smith, Douglas J. 2002. *Managing White Supremacy: Race, Politics, and Citizenship in Jim Crow Virginia*. Chapel Hill: University of North Carolina Press.

Wallenstein, Peter. 2011. "Identity, Marriage, and Schools: Life Along the Color Line/s in the Era of Plessy v. Ferguson." In *The Folly of Jim Crow: Rethinking the Segregated South*, ed. Stephanie Cole and Natalie J. Ring, 17–53. Arlington: The University of Texas at Arlington.

Wiener, Jonathan M. 1978. *Social Origins of the New South: Alabama, 1860–1885*. Baton Rouge: Louisiana State University Press.

Williamson, Joel. 1968. *The Origins of Segregation*. Boston: D.C. Heath.

—. 1984. *The Crucible of Race: Black/white Relations in the American South since Emancipation*. New York: Oxford University Press.

Wood, Amy Louise. 2009. *Lynching and Spectacle: Witnessing Racial Violence in America, 1890–1940*. Chapel Hill: University of North Carolina Press.

Woodman, Harold D. 1987. "Economic Reconstruction and the Rise of the New South." In *Interpreting Southern History: Historiographical Essays in Honor of Sanford W. Higginbotham*, ed. John Boles and Evelyn Thomas Nolen, 254–307. Baton Rouge: Louisiana State University Press.

—. 1997. "Class, Race, Politics and the Modernization of the Postbellum South." *Journal of Southern History* 63, 1: 3–22.

—. 2001. "The Political Economy of the New South: Retrospects and Prospects." *Journal of Southern History* 67, 4: 789–810.

Woodward, C. Vann. *Origins of the New South, 1877–1913*. Baton Rouge: Louisiana State University Press, 1951.

—. 1955, rev. edn. 1974. *The Strange Career of Jim Crow*. New York: Oxford University Press.

—. 1960. *The Burden of Southern History*. Baton Rouge: Louisiana State University Press.

—. 1988. "Strange Career Critics: Long May They Persevere." *The Journal of American History*, 75, 3: 857–868.

Wright, Gavin. 1986. *Old South, New South: Revolutions in the Southern Economy since the Civil War*. New York: Basic Books.

Wynes, Charles E. 1961. *Race Relations in Virginia, 1870–1902*. Charlottesville: University of Virginia Press.

Zimmerman, Andrew. 2010. *Alabama in Africa: Booker T. Washington, the German Empire, and the Globalization of the New South*. Princeton: Princeton University Press.

Further Reading

Brundage, Fitzhugh W. 1993. *Lynching in the New South: Georgia and Virginia, 1880–1930*. Urbana: University of Illinois Press.

Dorr, Gregory Michael. 2008. *Segregation's Science: Eugenics and Society in Virginia*. Charlottesville: University of Virginia Press.

Gaston, Paul M. 1970. *The New South Creed: A Study in Southern Mythmaking*. New York: Alfred A Knopf, Inc.

Hall, Jacquelyn Dowd et al. 1987. *Like a Family: The Making of a Southern Cotton Mill World*. Chapel Hill: University of North Carolina Press.

Hunter, Tera. 1997. *To 'Joy My Freedom: Southern Black Women's Lives and Labors After the Civil War*. Cambridge: Harvard University Press.

Ingram, Tammy. 2014. *Dixie Highway: Road Building and the Making of the Modern South, 1900–1930*. Chapel Hill: University of North Carolina Press.

Kantrowitz. Stephen. *Ben Tillman and the Reconstruction of White Supremacy*. Chapel Hill: University of North Carolina Press.

Turner, Elizabeth Hayes. 1997. *Women, Culture, and Community: Religion and Reform in Galveston, 1880–1920*. New York: Oxford University Press.

Wilson, Charles Reagan. 1980. *Baptized in Blood: The Religion of the Lost Cause, 1865–1920*. Athens: University of Georgia Press.

Chapter Five

The Midwest and Far West during the Gilded Age and Progressive Era

Thomas J. Jablonsky

The Midwest

As Abraham Lincoln's funeral train carried his body home to Illinois in 1865, the well-developed portions of the Midwest had edged just beyond the Mississippi River. Yet the political foundations of the Midwest were securely in place. This section of the country had once been America's frontier. Now, to the far side of the Red and Missouri rivers, a "new" west awaited another generation of pioneers. In the "older" west, however, only three territories (Nebraska and the Dakotas) still anticipated elevation to statehood (achieved in 1867 and 1889 respectively). Unlike the Far West, the Midwest was politically primed for the postbellum regime and for the massive changes that the country would witness over the next half century. (For the purposes of this chapter, the Midwest of the Gilded Age and Progressive Era has been defined as Ohio west to Nebraska and north to the border with Canada. However, in Nebraska and the Dakotas, west of the 98th meridian is considered part of the Far West.)

Toward and then Beyond the Civil War

The Midwest's return to normalcy after the Civil War continued a pattern of development dating back to the area's original settlers. From the late eighteenth century, the regional economy had been built upon the family farm. This predilection carried forth into the Gilded Age. What began as subsistence living for the first settlers typically evolved over a generation or two into the production of surpluses, modest sums that increased with each passing decade (Faragher 1988). Surpluses suggested the possibility of profits, a phenomenon that relied upon functions provided by towns and later cities. Whether it was household supplies, farm implements, or outlets for harvested foodstuffs, settlements from 500 to 5,000 anchored the Midwest, even more so in the decades following the Union–Confederate conflict as the increasingly commercial nature of Midwest farming relied upon transportation routes, mortgage and credit options, commodity prices, and non-local customers, whether back East or overseas. Towns came to define both the landscape and the social–economic arrangements of late nineteenth-century midwesterners.

Throughout this region as well as elsewhere across the country, the Civil War wrenched apart many thousands of lives, but in the center of the country it also proved—unexpectedly—an economic boon. It turned out that Union armies needed everything that Midwestern farmers used or produced: from horses, hogs, and wagons to corn, wheat, and butter (Hurt 2013). Prices soared and incomes followed. This superheated wartime economy—the opposite of what was transpiring south of the Mason–Dixon line—brought wealth to some and well-being to more. And merchants and manufacturers who benefited the most from this overripe market rerouted wartime winnings into the "hottest" postwar investments, showcased in the grandest of manners by John R. Rockefeller. These new opportunities increasingly relied upon larger and larger population centers, from county seats and railheads to rapidly expanding urban locales situated strategically along the region's rivers and the Great Lakes. On the other hand, in the northern plains railroad companies guided settlement by choosing placements for water towers, grain elevators, and freight yards—but always with the expectation that permanent customers would follow, land would sell, and long-term profits, even if fairly modest at times, would be assured (Hudson 1985). Not every town site grew into a Kansas City, but eventually the trans-Mississippi Midwest became as anchored—economically, socially, and politically—by the presence of enduring towns and cities as lands east of the river.

A Companion to the Gilded Age and Progressive Era, First Edition. Edited by Christopher McKnight Nichols and Nancy C. Unger.
© 2017 John Wiley & Sons, Inc. Published 2017 by John Wiley & Sons, Inc.

In his study of town development in the Great Plains, historical geographer John C. Hudson opens by describing the process by which railroad companies chose their routes, depots, and switching yards, but deeper into his narrative he shifts the conversation to the area's social relations. In the end, human associations based upon sustainable institutions within compact settlements bound residents to one another. While geographical advantages may have provided the original attraction for any settlement, subsequent civic entanglements of economics, religion, education, transportation, recreation, and ancestry created conditions by which communities flourished or foundered. And out of a situational mixture of general stores, blacksmith shops, courthouses, saloons, hotels, churches, schools, and rail stations arose a commonly recognized, if not always uniformly accepted, set of beliefs about proper human behaviors. Small town values prevailed across vast stretches of the Gilded Age Midwest.

Even in off-the-grid corners of the region, such as the Northwoods of Wisconsin or the mining districts of Upper Michigan, this conversion of work-oriented outposts into institutional town life found root. The natural world's local distinctions—climate, forests, animals, and minerals—originally lured hearty folk to embrace dangerous occupations in godforsaken locales (Karamanski 1989; Lankton 1999; Hoagland 2010). But in many places, social relationships developed among workers, their families, and their neighbors, creating over a period of years a string of sawmill and mining towns and, even down the tracks, modest-sized cities. As with many mining sites in the Far West, these crossroad junctions and industrial camps often vanished in the time it took to extract the earth's riches, but others survived with such lasting vitality that a century later they still survive in the "frozen tundra" south and west of Lake Superior.

Linkages

Ultimately these everyday associations, especially after 1900, came under challenge by powerful, but seemingly advantageous, external forces. The influence in Indiana of the interurban train lines, for instance, or farmers' access to automobiles in central Illinois, or the arrival of electricity in southern Minnesota created consequential adjustments in every community's routines and behaviors.

No one depicted the nature of Midwestern town life with more visceral feeling than Lewis Atherton (1954) in *Main Street on the Middle Border*. With nuanced detail, he broke down the intricacies as to how a boy learned manly traits like spitting, swearing, boasting, rolling smokes, and the biological truths about animal mating by hanging around corrals, stables, and barnyards. Atherton also captured the episodic rhythms of holidays and holy days as well as the virtues and values imposed by a McGuffey Reader-based school system. Richard O. Davies (1998) took this storyline in a slightly different direction when he portrayed a single Ohio town from settlement through its glory days from 1900 to the 1920s. Other authors found similar patterns of success and well-being in the new century (Dunbar 1968; Meyer 2007). Into these homely routines, however, seeped gadgets and services that drew residents out of their small town worlds. Interurban rail lines, rural free delivery, catalogue stores, electricity, automobiles, radios, and even the first of two world wars expanded worldviews, creating subtle but complex dependencies—some regional in nature, others national and even international in scope.

Settlements of every size got caught up within these webs of commercial and financial dependencies. In *Nature's Metropolis*, William Cronon (1991) showed how hundreds of thousands of midwesterners became bound to urban juggernauts that controlled insurance, banking, transportation, and agricultural distribution systems. And along the Ohio, Mississippi, Missouri, and Red rivers as well as the Great Lakes, from Evansville to Grand Falls and Sandusky to Green Bay, urban centers fostered their own relationships between one another, in addition to each city's service relationships with its rural cousins. A system of cities solidified across the Midwest, ultimately uniting rural towns with urban America.

In *Cities of the Heartland* (1993), Jon Teaford showcased the consolidation of local specialties into finalized products by turning his attention, at one point, to the twentieth century's nascent automobile industry. Urban centers across the Midwest relied upon one another not only as locational stops along specific rail lines or as part of a string of Great Lakes ports, but as industrial dependencies whose specializations contributed to finished products such as a Nash (assembled in Kenosha) or a Studebaker (assembled in South Bend) or a Ford (assembled in Highland Park). Car frames from Milwaukee mixed with tires from Akron, ignition systems from Dayton, wood paneling from northern Wisconsin, and hog hair (for seats) from Chicago to create generations of vehicles driven in Peoria, Keokuk, Fargo, and every hamlet in between. And before the car frames could be metal-bent at Milwaukee's A.O. Smith plant, the steel cauldrons at Chicago's South Works or Gary's U.S. Steel plants had to create the base product. Similar mixtures of cooperation and competition arose in industries such as meatpacking, in which Kansas City and Omaha determinedly challenged the monster known as Chicago's Union Stockyards. Anheuser-Busch in St. Louis fought determinedly to convince Americans to drop their affections for distilled spirits and instead chose beer as their after-work refreshment of choice while, at the same time, competing against worthy challengers from Milwaukee in the form of the Pabst, Schlitz, Miller, and Blatz breweries. The Midwest became unified through its intraregional reliance upon one another's goods, whether from farms or factories.

Peopling

Town-building in the post-Civil War Midwest involved not only sites and situations, but also demographic patterns, most of which copied habits developed early in the nineteenth century. Migrations of pioneering midwesterners tended to be zonal, with folk paths originating in Virginia and Kentucky the further south one went in the Heartland, and from the North Atlantic the further north one moved. Although the Northwest Ordinance of 1787 disallowed slavery, Southern sympathies and cultural preferences prevailed in the southern portions of Ohio, Indiana, Illinois, and throughout Missouri. Across the hilly farmlands south of a line roughly connecting the state capitals of Columbus, Indianapolis, and Springfield, concentrations of Southern Baptists and Methodists shaped social behaviors and values. Rural hamlets and small cities as well as the area's coalmining districts sustained this sociocultural tradition throughout the Gilded Age and Progressive Era.

In contrast, population waves from New England and New York headed directly west along the south rim of the Great Lakes, creating farms and towns all along the northern halves of Ohio, Indiana, Illinois, and ultimately Michigan and Wisconsin. These former East Coast residents not only dominated the rural heartland of the Old Northwest into Iowa and Minnesota, but they also became the urban boosters who created Detroit, Chicago, Milwaukee, and Minneapolis. The urbanization of the northern half of the Old Northwest owed a great deal of its entrepreneurial energy to the real estate ambitions and commercial proclivities of young adventurers from New York and Massachusetts (Gray 1996; Sawyers 1991). In both rural and urban settings, these Yankee–Yorkers were supplemented by migrations of Germans—some Lutheran, some Anabaptist, some Roman Catholic, and some Jews. Joining them, typically, was the first of several Irish migrations, thereby enriching the religious culture of the Upper Midwest as the first half of the nineteenth century concluded.

During the Gilded Age, the territoriality of the Midwest not only advanced west and north, but the demographic complexity of the entire region deepened. From the Dutch farmers who made Holland, Michigan a picturesque stopping point along the eastern shore of Lake Michigan, to the Finns who leveled maple and pine forests or tunneled into the iron and copper mines of the Upper Peninsula of Michigan, to the earnest Norwegians and Swedes who conquered the prairie lands of western Minnesota and eastern North Dakota, peoples from across the European continent mixed among native born Americans throughout the Midwest. Concentrations of Swiss, Czechs, Poles, and Russians scattered across the region's rural outposts, providing a more cosmopolitan tone to the rural Midwest than is generally acknowledged.

Meanwhile midwestern cities attracted hundreds of thousands, eventually millions, of newcomers from every quadrant of Europe. By train, they made their way from Castle Garden or Ellis Island to unfamiliar destinations that housed family members or townsfolk or simply similarly spoken co-nationals from Greece or Slovakia. They gathered in identifiable clusters, creating at times fascinating patterns such as Minneapolis's Scandinavian Lutherans across the river from St. Paul's Irish Catholics.

Those who flocked to the northern rim of cities from Ohio to Nebraska provided the muscle that created steel cities, meatpacking capitals, and cereal centers such as Gary, Omaha, and Battle Creek. They were all linked by thousands of workers—some Italian, some Irish, some African American—who handled the tens of thousands of railcars that crisscrossed the region. European nationals made beer in St. Louis, plows in Moline, and turbines in West Allis, Wisconsin. By 1902, the industrial engines were cranking so fast in Milwaukee that no unused factory space was left in the city; four years later, the city's largest manufacturer faced an awful "burden": a two-year backlog of orders. The 1910 census revealed that in the entire country, only Detroit and Milwaukee had nearly six of ten laborers in their male workforces employed in manufacturing (Gurda 1999).

These greenhorns survived ten-hour workdays and went home to frame tenements situated on narrow lots amid countless saloons, grocery stores, butcher shops, saloons, bakeries, candy stores, churches, and saloons, each catering to a nationality and sometimes provincial subsections of Greece, Italy, or Poland. A cacophony of accents, cooking aromas, and prayerful chants created demographic kaleidoscopes that frightened some Americans, insuring that cities were seen as unsettling, alien, and hostile by their very nature. All this diversity helped define the Midwest, most notably in urban places but also within ethnic concentrations found in the region's rural patches. Amid eastern Wisconsin farm towns dominated by native-born Americans, for example, rested the sedate village of Belgium with the unlikely cluster in 1900 of two thousand settlers from Luxemburg. Ethnic diversity marked the rural as well as the urban Midwest by the second decade of the new century.

And soon this mixing, if not melting, became more complicated when the Great Migration introduced another wave of newcomers. At the turn of the century, black populations were noticeably small in most Midwestern states and far more urban than rural. As with black knickerbockers in Manhattan, urban-based African Americans in the Midwest prior to 1900 lived in scattered concentrations, seeking to remain as inconspicuous as possible. St. Louis, as part of the only former slave state in this construction of the Midwest, was an exception (Kusmer 1978; Spear 1967; Trotter 2006; Primm 2013). Initially, race relations tended to find a quiet routine, largely because the unthreatening number of African Americans in any given city failed to aggravate white citizens. Tensions mounted, however, in the early twentieth century as European immigrants threatened the status quo by cutting into the service sector jobs typically held by blacks: nannies, barbers, maids, janitors, and bootblacks.

More intense conflicts exploded when employers recruited African Americans as on-call, short-term strikebreakers used against American-born and foreign-born workers alike. Race became a tactical wedge, setting the stage for intense explosions, exemplified in East St. Louis in 1917 and across the country during the Red Summer of 1919 (Rudwick 1982; Tuttle 1996). Chicago's riot that year captured the complexity of racial tensions in the Midwest. The violence began among teenagers casually swimming at a segregated beach along Lake Michigan and eventually involved drive-by shootings and murderous mobs dragging black stockyard workers off streetcars. From leisure to labor, every Midwesterner, regardless of age, sex, nationality, or race, learned the regional rules about race relations.

In spite of these hatreds, the Great Migration flowed into the 1920s, with black populations in Chicago rising from 2% of the city's population in 1910 to 8% in 1940, from just over 1% in 1910 Detroit to more than 9% thirty years later, and in Cincinnati from 5.4% to more than 12%. Even smaller, blue-collar cities like Youngstown and Akron had increases of four and five times in that stretch of time (Teaford 1993). Residential segregation became spatially systematized, strengthened by the growing use of racial covenants. School boards in Milwaukee, St. Louis, and across the region perfected techniques whereby school policies reinforced residential separation. The Great Depression slowed the northward migration of African Americans—until, that is, America's "arsenals of democracy" were ultimately forced during World War II to accept workers regardless of skin color or nationality.

Politics

If significant change was afoot in the region's economic and social landscapes as the twentieth century arrived, the political structures that anchored civil society were also under refinement. The ethnic and occupational diversity of larger midwestern cities reinforced a proclivity for ward-based politics. Local aldermen—the sexist nature of the electoral system remained inviolate at the moment—ruled with a comfortable grip, commanding the timing and location of police and fire stations, street paving, sewer installations, and saloon licenses. The personal preferences of these elected officials—and their business/real estate allies—constituted "public" policy. In common councils, these powerbrokers rallied around self-serving ordinances in shifting factions, pairings that on occasion might be predicated upon nominal party affiliations. Urban politics during the Gilded Age and beyond was personal, from precinct captains who managed voters in more organized venues to the ubiquitous saloonkeepers who not infrequently served as ward committeemen and aldermen. Everyone knew who held the levers of power and who needed to be satisfied in order to arrange a light police presence for after-hours activities, ignore annoying notions like building codes, or close off the street for a church festival. While a few cities had better developed political organizations that sustained their time on the top, notably George Cox in Cincinnati and the Pendergast Brothers in Kansas City, integrated political machines were less entrenched than is sometimes portrayed (Miller 1968; Dorsett 1968). Chicago's Democratic machine, as a case in point, did not become operational until the Great Depression.

The personalized nature of urban politics in the late nineteenth and early twentieth centuries also explains a retinue of socialist mayors in cities such as Minneapolis, Rockford, Flint, and Dayton (Critchlow 1986). But nowhere did working-class sympathies among municipal chief executives achieve more or last longer than in Milwaukee. The local labor movement's political wing successfully promoted the 1910 election of Emil Seidel, a humble patternmaker. The new chief executive strove to improve living conditions for blue-collar Milwaukeeans through reasonable service fees, municipal ownership of the streetcar system, and an expanded park system. The fear of a socialist in charge of the Wisconsin's largest city prompted an immediate reaction within the state legislature. It abolished party designations on municipal and county ballots, aiming to vanquish the socialist party by taking away its presence on voting forms—as well as, admittedly, the presence of every other political party. This strategy worked for the next two terms during which a fusion candidate held office on behalf of the now collaborating Republican and Democratic parties. But in 1916, city attorney Daniel Hoan became the city's second socialist mayor, retaining this office through seven terms until 1940. Eight years later, yet another socialist succeeded Hoan, retaining his office until 1960 when he declined to run for a fourth term. Midwestern socialists favored "sewer socialism," an agenda that strove for affordable streetcar fares, equally shared city services, and police departments that did not serve as taxpayer-financed security guards for local manufacturers. All of this was accomplished through balanced budgets rather than an overthrow of the nation's economic order.

A survey of urban scholars has identified an alternative set of mayoral reformers who also sought a new moral order through fairness (Holli 1999). Hazen Pingree of Detroit, Samuel "Golden Rule" Jones of Toledo, and Tom Johnson of Cleveland all experienced hardships in their youth, but each settled into a very comfortable lifestyle during adulthood. Yet these two Republicans and one Democrat, respectively, rose above personal interests to manage mayoral administrations that promoted kindergartens, playgrounds, and public bathhouses during good times, and city gardens and job agencies during harsher stretches, programs that tentatively reached across the class divides that epitomized this age of industrialization.

At the state level, concern for the "general welfare" rather than special interests served the Badger State well, including legislation to regulate food safety and child labor, to revise the tax code, and, uniquely, to have the state's land grant university implement "The Wisconsin Idea," a visionary program that converted faculty research into service programs on behalf of industrial workers, farmers, and local government officials (Unger 2000). Reforms of this ilk across the region provided cutting-edge innovations such as workmen's compensation and the removal of economic inefficiencies within government bureaucracies. In Iowa, the Des Moines Plan, a midwestern version of the commission form of municipal government, epitomized a new approach to government motto: let impartial, trained professionals manage for the commonweal. As John Buenker noted in 1998, many midwesterner reformers (and, indeed, reformers across the United States) favored broad, systematic approaches to rectify the economic and political inequities produced during the Gilded Age. The region's "sewer socialists," with their attention toward quality of life matters, provided models for urban progressivism in the Midwest.

The aforementioned urban reforms followed on the heels of several decades of rural activism across the region. In the 1870s, the Patrons of Husbandry, the Grange, strove to alleviate the social and technological isolation of farmers while avoiding entanglements with politics per se. But in short order, a refined version of this public activism appeared, especially across the northern tier of the Midwest, when rural residents began to feel a desperation that demanded intervention by some governmental body. Whereas Jeffersonian agrarianism, housed within remnants of the region's Democratic Party, persisted with its small-government approach south of the capital line from Columbus to Springfield, to the north, among Yankee–Yorker or German and Norwegian farmers, state intervention became, at first, necessary and, then, expected.

The first ambitions of this rural unrest—railroad regulation—came about rather easily because, as noted by Andrew Cayton and Peter S. Onuf (1990), postbellum railroads had become non-local enterprises, harbingers of a new economic order. The corporatization of the nation's transportation system facilitated economic benefits for many Midwestern farmers, but did so by reducing them to the status of pawns in the unfettered accumulation of wealth by East Coast and European interests. As railroads consolidated in the post-Civil War decades, they became very different from the short-line roads before 1860. Unlike antebellum Wisconsin farmers who took out second mortgages in the 1850s to underwrite locally managed rail lines, their children twenty years later were determined to rein in the misuse of what was slowly being seen as public transportation corridors, not unlike canals and post roads.

So when agricultural activists became more assertive, insisting that interjurisdictional bodies such as state legislatures protect the citizenry from corporate exploitation, they turned to the largely Republican-based legislatures of Ohio, Illinois, Wisconsin, Minnesota, and Iowa to address farmers' vulnerabilities (Cayton and Onuf 1990). In these reforms, state governments came to be seen as public advocates who helped balance the economic scales against special interests.

Throughout the late nineteenth century, Midwesterners preferred to achieve these state-level reforms within the existing two-party system, rather than turning to third-party options (Nelson 1995). For example, James B. Weaver had lived in Iowa since childhood, but he failed to win his home state when he ran for President in 1880 on the Greenback Party ticket and when he was the 1892 People's Party candidate. In the latter case, the Hawkeye state preferred incumbent Hoosier, Benjamin Harrison. Working outside of the two-party system certainly occurred in the Midwest on occasion, most notably the farther west and north one went. South Dakota selected a Populist governor in 1896 and 1898, but even here significant improvements came later under Republican Peter Norbeck when child labor laws, a rural credit system, hail insurance, and a workmen's compensation program were enacted (Peirce 1973). Later still, the Non-Partisan League's aggressive approach in North Dakota in 1915 led to a state-controlled bank and grain elevators, and to fire, tornado, and hail insurance at reasonable costs. Minnesota followed its western neighbor in supporting a muscular farmer–labor party in the coming decades (Peirce 1973; Atkins 1988). But, by and large, most Midwesterners preferred change within the mainstream—usually a Republican mainstream—rather than through third-party alternatives.

This ambivalence toward who directed change was also evident in the region's labor activism during the Gilded Age. Daniel Nelson (1995) has noted the warmer sentiments that existed between Midwest coal miners and the Populist Party, for instance, than among any other types of industrial workers. The rural tilt of the People's Party played into the cultural comfort-zones of sons of the South whose labor dominated the region's coalfields in southern Ohio, Indiana, and Illinois. Labor conflicts were frequent enough in this most dangerous of industries, with at least 271 strikes in four Midwestern states between 1887 and 1894. The ebbs and flows in United Mine Workers membership reflected the union's irregular record of losses versus victories in these clashes. But, as demonstrated by John Laslett (1986), leftist activism remained vital to the area even after the Progressive Era.

Likewise the region's cities experienced violent clashes between employers and labor activists, also with various outcomes. The 1877 railroad strike may have started in Maryland, but Chicago's central position as the nation's rail hub brought matters to a head in the Midwest's largest city. Within days of the strike's outbreak back East, clashes between industrial security forces (and their municipal allies, the police) and rail workers in Chicago generated sympathetic support among laborers in the lumber and furniture industries. In this instance, unification crossed not only occupational types, but also nationalities, with Irish, Germans, Poles, and Czechs marching side by side on behalf of workers' rights. Unrest spread across the larger region with general strikes hitting other railheads such as St. Louis and Kansas City (Jentz and Schenirov 2012).

During the following decade, the Knights of Labor elevated this theme of unification a step further by merging labor interests not only across industries and ethnicities, but also across sexes and even races. The approach that the Knights took to labor organizing resonated among Midwesterners with, according to one estimate, as much as 40% of the Knight's local affiliates coming from this region (Nelson 1995). Social events among the members were particularly inviting because they bridged divisions that otherwise kept workers divided and generated camaraderie reminiscent of the Grange. This made an allegiance to the Knights something more valuable than endless union hall haggling over wage and hour demands. From Detroit to Dubuque, the union's victories on behalf of the Eight Hour movement in the early 1880s uplifted workers—until, as one might expect, the inevitable pushback. In 1885–86, the states of Ohio, Michigan, and Wisconsin sent militias to suppress strikes. In Michigan, the governor personally led the effort against mill workers and in Wisconsin, five strikers were killed at a Milwaukee iron mill strike, an event still honored with an annual re-enactment of the Bay View "Massacre." Police deaths in May 1886 in the Haymarket district of Chicago touched off a strong public reaction against the Knights, leading to a rapid decline in its membership. Tellingly, in December of the same year the American Federation of Labor was born in Columbus, Ohio. The new group signaled a less inclusive, less confrontational approach to union–management relations in the years to come. Nonetheless, labor conflicts continued unabated across the region as exemplified in the 1894 Pullman strike, and scattered mining and timber strikes throughout Minnesota's North Country during the new century's opening decades (Nelson 1995; Smith 1995; Atkins 1988). By the closing of the Progressive Era, measurable improvements to the economic well-being of workers were difficult to quantify.

Arguably, the most important force among these diversified campaigns for change came from a remarkable generation of female activists representing every class, age, and race. In the first years after the Civil War, their causes remained consistent with Victorian lifestyles, in line with stereotypical interests related to the health and safety of American families. Not surprisingly, the Women's Christian Temperance Union came out of Ohio in 1874. But broader and more consequential encounters with the Gilded Age's social evils derived from elements within the women's club movement during the 1890s. Some groups, understandably, remained insular, preferring travelogues about the pyramids or lectures on frost-resistant flowers. But so many other women—some married, others single, some college-educated, others barely out of elementary school, some descendants of Revolutionary War era families, others recent arrivals from Europe—steered their talents and resources toward addressing America's most pressing issues.

Their activism typically appeared, at first, as public expressions of maternal interests concerning entities such as kindergartens, infant welfare stations, and parks, but within a short time, greedy industrialists and self-serving political machines also came under scrutiny. In *Seeing with Their Hearts*, Maureen Flanagan (2002) captured the devotion, vision, and resourcefulness of these female activists in Chicago. Female allies, from Detroit to Davenport, rallied to local, regional, and national causes, whatever aroused their consciences and spurred each of them into the public arena. Ultimately one phalanx struck at the heart of public authority: the right to vote, the right to set policy, the right to manage governmental power. Throughout the Midwest, women and men alike grappled over updated definitions for the word "democracy" in an age in which divisions among peoples by income, nationality, race, and sex seemed so dramatic and conclusive. Could reason somehow build bridges to heal an increasingly divided America? (Westhoff 2007).

When they urged change, midwestern reformers clamored for "efficiency" whether their particular brand of progressivism favored social, economic, or political adjustments. Mordecai Lee (2008) brought this into sharp focus with his study of bureaus of efficiency. The intent of these progressives was not to revolutionize the governmental system, but to sharpen its operation through the recruitment of well-trained individuals guided by professional standards. Public and non-profit bureaus of efficiency alike appeared throughout the Midwest, in cities such as Des Moines, Detroit, Kansas City, Madison, Muskegon, Milwaukee, and Chicago. Investigations, evidence, and communications, progressives argued, would focus change-makers upon meaningful, equitable reforms. In the Midwest, some adjustments were as intimate as nursing stations and others as comprehensive as the regulation of interstate commerce. Every nook and cranny of economic and political life in the Midwest was open to review and reform as the rambunctious Gilded Age ran headlong into a flinty-eyed Progressive Era.

The Far West

For the purposes of this chapter, the Far West of the Gilded Age and Progressive Era has been defined as Kansas, the western portions of Nebraska and the Dakotas as well as the states to their west as far as the Pacific Ocean. Americans east of the 98th meridian in 1865—that is, those in established areas of the East Coast, South, and rapidly emerging Midwest—understood the "Far West" in an unformed and uninformed manner. Snippets of hearsay and fragments of unreliable journalistic accounts depicted terrains and circumstances that sounded like nothing more than tall tales. For those who did not live in the Far West, the Gilded Age and Progressive Era would clarify, in many ways, western facts from fiction. On the other hand, for those who actually resided in the Far West, everyday life was about seizing opportunities, whether by means of farms, orchards, mines, timber, shipping docks, or merchandizing. Their incomes, however, could come at some risk. Extraction industries, especially, involved laboring in remote slopes and valleys where everything went uphill or downhill, and where dynamite or hydraulic mining equipment or crosscut saws threatened to go awry at a moment's notice. In contrast, artisan, commercial, and real estate careers in Pacific Coast cities permitted East Coast skill sets to be applied in promising West Coast venues.

So many of these possibilities came wrapped, according to New Western historians, in a "conquering" motif, a campaign to overcome natural forces as well as the presence of interlopers (Native Americans, Hispanics). This re-creation of an Americanized society hundreds, even thousands of miles away from the original homelands of these latest occupiers eventually shaped, as Patricia Limerick (1987) posed several decades ago, both the conqueror and the conquered. William G. Robbins (1994) provided another set of insights into this process by taking measure of the new empire's capitalist components. Few westerners perceived their daily lives in such grandiose terms of course, but their dreams of hopeful tomorrows could be awfully captivating for any individual and so romantic when penning notes to kin back home.

The American Far West during the Gilded Age provided more vistas of what could be rather than what actually was. The size, magnificence, and potential of the region's landscapes could overwhelm residents and visitors alike. Greater distances had never been traversed in America. Higher mountains never encountered. Deadlier deserts never survived. Richer veins of gold, silver, and copper never obtained. Rivers never seemed to flow with such turbulence (except around Niagara Falls). Bioregions filled with unimaginable flora and fauna awaited this new generation of sojourners (Flores 2001). Frederick Jackson Turner may have been right when he spoke in terms of the West's exceptionalism—at least in terms of the region's natural bounties.

At the outset of the Gilded Age, the Midwest had once been America's edge whereas the Far West *was* a frontier of destinies for the remaining decades of the nineteenth century and beyond. Unlike the Midwest, which could embrace the Gilded Age with its resources—both natural and human—largely in hand, the Far West was blanketed with signs: "Under Development." When the Civil War concluded, the Far West remained a vague "out there," lacking even the thinnest of railroad links. In reality, the Far West was a *variety* of "theres" that, with the exception of San Francisco, was still considering how to take advantage of the gifts it had been bestowed.

The Federal Government

Unlike the rest of America (except, perhaps, sections of the South during Reconstruction), the federal government oversaw the blueprints for development of this "new" West. The "feds" owned nearly all of the land (and to this very day commands sizable portions of several states). The Departments of Agriculture, Interior, and War determined the disposition of property, resources, communications, transportation, and, in the case of Native Americans, the inhabitants themselves (Jackson 1995). Into the twentieth century, significant portions of the Far West remained subject to the capriciousness of elected members of Congress and of non-elected federal bureaucrats. No other corner of America during the Gilded Age and Progressive Era succumbed so completely to the authority of absentee landlords.

At the root of this condition was the fact that most of the West remained under territorial rule at the end of the Civil War. In 1864, only four states operated in the Far West: California, Oregon, Kansas, and Nevada. A dozen years later, Colorado joined the Union as a full partner. Another thirteen years passed before Montana and Washington advanced to statehood, followed in short order by Idaho, Wyoming, and Utah. New Mexico and Arizona (as well as Oklahoma) would wait until the new century for admission. Nearly a half-century unfolded before the entire "Far West" of the post-Civil War era came into political adulthood.

The federal government's influence during these decades touched every aspect of local life. In the beginning, military forts provided an irregular semblance of governmental authority among the region's dispersed settlers, from Nebraska north into the Dakotas and Montana as well as southwest into Utah, Nevada, and Arizona. When a reservation system was established in the immediate postwar period, the Indian Bureau provided a challenge to the Army's approach. Religious groups, most notably the Quakers, guided the Bureau during the early 1870s, representing an alternative face of the nation across the Great Plains, Rockies, and Great Basin. Nonetheless, the rifle-and-sword solution reasserted itself. Bloodshed resumed in America's centennial year with the Great Sioux War, followed the next year by the Nez Perce travail and ultimately the 1890 massacre at Wounded Knee (Yenne 2006). From the Supreme Court's 1870 decision granting Congress power to void treaties at its whim through various congressional actions leading to the Dawes Act of 1887, the federal government incrementally eliminated the spatial independence of Native Americans. Authorities in Washington turned over the futures of these many peoples to a free market economy under the premise of compelling Christianized conformity—not unlike their imperial counterparts in Africa and Asia (Hine and Faragher 2000).

For those along the furthest left edge of the Far West, the United States Navy supplemented the Army's broader footprint. The Navy's position became more vital as the nineteenth century closed with, first, the Spanish–American War and, then, the advent of an overseas empire. This responsibility expanded dramatically with the building of the Panama Canal. The West Coast's military agenda now became even more central to the Naval Department's vision of its global mission. Over decades, unprecedented investments in the ports at San Diego, San Francisco, and Oakland as well as in Puget Sound amplified the Navy's impact on the West Coast. For the first time, even a harbor in Los Angeles became a federal priority rather than just an item on the Chamber of Commerce's wish list.

At the local level, the federal government became the pied piper of the Far West during the last third of the nineteenth century through various land distributions, beginning with the Homestead Act of 1862. There were a host of legislative augmentations, some aimed at farming, some at herding, some at lumbering, and some at mining. While the government unabashedly promoted grazing, cultivating, and extracting, some of the richest properties in terms of fertility and resources came on the market through sales organized by railroads as they "flipped" the bountiful generosity of the federal government for tidy profits. In the forms of monetary grants, stock purchases, and land awards, taxpayers subsidized these privately owned enterprises. However, these same taxpayers—farmers, ranchers, miners, and developers—could, if they wished, reacquire these properties—while benefiting the railroad companies.

Interestingly, the federal government also interceded during the Gilded Age and Progressive Era to promote stewardship as well as exploitation. In 1872, the first national park, Yellowstone, became a test case for the national government's new role, even if it had to be achieved under the guise that these two million acres were capitalist deserts, worthless and unusable. As a sense of mission evolved for these public spaces, supplemental additions were gathered into the fold, including in 1890 a return of Yosemite Valley from state mismanagement to federal oversight. Greater expectations arose in 1916 with the creation of the National Park Service. Twenty-five years earlier amidst a major overhaul of federal land laws, forest reserves had been authorized, although with the continued purpose of exploitation, not preservation. The "wise use" approach advocated by Gifford Pinchot, who became chief of the Forest Service in 1898, evidenced a maturation in policy-making under the Progressive Era's fascination with "efficiency." Inevitably Pinchot's agency clashed with the nascent preservationist movement over a proposed dam in the Hetch Hetchy Valley of California, a structure intended to provide a great good for a great number in distant (200 miles) San Francisco (Hine and Faragher 2000).

This tussle over Hetch Hetchy foreshadowed the power of water as potentially the most critical resource in America's western empire. From the earliest infiltration of Americans into the Sacramento Valley during the gold rush until deep into the twentieth century, the escalating advancement of broadly enforceable water policies helped define the idea of government for many westerners (Kelley 1989). What began as hydrological issues to be handled by local authorities and later state governments became, by the Progressive Era, a federal matter. On top of the national government's long-time management of grasslands, forests, and minerals, the Newlands Reclamation Act in 1902 provided the framework, in Donald Worster's (1985, 166) phrasing, for the "federalization of water development." Through its control of dams, reservoirs, irrigation systems, and ultimately the subsidization of suburbanization, the federal government shaped the region's future (Vale 1995). By the twenty-first century, moisture and water became the West's greatest resource.

The open ranges of Montana, coal mines of Colorado, copper mines of Arizona, oil fields in California, and forests of Oregon and Washington came to be seen as natural riches available for any group's private gain, courtesy of the federal government's departments of distribution. A "new" West that was as forbidding as promising in 1865 transitioned over the next half-century into a bountiful provider of enriched opportunities. And alongside these dreams of fortunes and fame came the realization that local–federal relations dictated the security of these investments for individuals as well as corporations, from Weyerhauser to the Southern Pacific Railroad. In the end, it became clear that statehood rather than territorial status would provide greater standing in the halls of Congress and in the offices of federal agencies.

Settlement

The conquering of the West required, similarly to the Midwest, patterns of settlement. Historian Frederick Jackson Turner perceived the triumph of American democracy achieved across the nation's sequential "wests" at the tip of farmers' plows. In fact, when it came to drawing forth the earth's riches (whether through copper mining, tree-cutting, wheat farming, or cattle-rearing), these resources had to head somewhere else to earn their full monetary value. Westerners, it turned out, preferred urban places in greater percentages than anywhere else in the United States outside of New England and the Middle Atlantic states. Living in sizable settlements was a reasonable strategy for mastering lands west of the 98th meridian. The American empire in the Far West prospered through the functions of urban centers, large and small alike (Moehring 2004).

Salt Lake City, basically unknown to most Americans east of the 98th parallel, was home to over 118,000 people in 1920. At the same time, Denver, one of the West's "instant cities" in Gunther Barth's characterization, served as home for more than twice as many residents as Utah's capital. Though probably unappreciated by the nation at large in 1920, Colorado's capital had a larger population than Toledo or Louisville or St. Paul or Omaha—larger, in fact, than Providence, Albany, Syracuse, Hartford, Scranton, and Atlanta, and larger than *any* city in Texas at the end of the Progressive Era. And, yet, the coastal cities of Seattle and Portland with populations of 315,000 and 258,000 surpassed Denver in 1920. Meanwhile Los Angeles finally crossed the half-million mark as of 1920 on its way to more than a million within the next decade—a point at which it would join an elite band of New York, Chicago, Philadelphia, and Detroit.

Renowned urban historian Carl Abbott (2008) recognized this theme in his *How Cities Won the West*, a work that confirms Richard Wade's classic rebuttal to Frederick Jackson Turner: towns and cities probed the frontier and ultimately anchored the conquest of the West. In 1900, only four decades after the opening of the Civil War, 52% of Californians lived in urban places, 48% in Colorado, 41% in Washington, 38% in Utah, and 32% in Oregon. Add another twenty years and by 1920, when the US Census recognized that 50% of Americans lived in urban places, in the Far West these numbers had jumped to 68% for California, 55% in Washington, 48% in Utah, and 50% in Oregon while remaining the same in Colorado. West Coast cities dominated their hinterland's economy and culture, with Seattle, Portland, San Francisco, and Los Angeles playing the same roles that Boston, New York, and Philadelphia had performed in the eighteenth century, and Cincinnati, Chicago, and St. Louis in the nineteenth. On smaller scales, the same applied to Spokane, Boise, Butte, Fresno, and Tucson. And as Gunther Barth (1988) points out, a combination of technology and culture solidified this urban dominance.

Los Angeles, in contrast to its scholarly reputation as the prototype of post-World War II cities, actually offers an instructive lesson for Far West's urban experiences during the Gilded Age and Progressive Era. Founded as a Spanish pueblo purposed to feed California presidios, Los Angeles stumbled into the post-Civil War period having barely survived the opening of the 1860s because, like so much of the Far West, it rests in a semi-arid or arid zone. Following the election of Lincoln (an announcement received via the newest form of technology, the telegraph), this authentic Mexican village suffered devastating floods that swept away its adobe buildings and dirt streets, and then barely survived a multi-year drought that killed hundreds of thousands of cattle, the area's economic linchpin. Built on the extraction industries of agriculture and cattle raising, nature nearly wiped out LA before it could even be found on most American maps.

Over the next half century, the Americanization of Los Angeles meant not only a numerical conquest by American citizens, but also their ultimate domination of the economy, land ownership, and the culture of the area. This was new form of triumphalism. Racially, the population of Los Angeles County may have been as diverse as anywhere in the country. Native Americans, however, would vanish through disease and displacement, a process first started by the Spanish and now seemingly finished by the Americans. The original mixed-blood settlers from the Spanish–Mexican era had by 1890 been relegated to a barrio north of the city's plaza or to outlying towns such as Montebello and El Monte.

Chinese arrived in the area after Northern California's gold mines played out and railroad construction teams broke through the Tehachapi Mountains, before heading toward LA. Within short order, this largely male contingent of Chinese would also be squeezed into a residential slum adjacent to Sonoratown due to the rages of racism, most notably the mob action that killed nearly one of every ten Chinese residents on October 24, 1871 (Zesch 2012). In the opening decade of the twentieth century, Japanese migrants from Hawaii, gifted with superb agricultural skills, filtered into the area, choosing to avoid prevailing bigotries by decentralizing their presence in scattered settlements, such as Sawtelle or San Pedro. African Americans remained in modest numbers through the 1920s, integrated with low-income neighbors east and south of the city core.

White Americans came to control the area's key institutions: judicial system, law enforcement, school systems, banks, streetcar franchises, and the real estate market. By the twentieth century, Los Angeles had solidified its reputation as a tourist magnet, first as health mecca in the 1870s for those with pulmonary diseases and then in the 1890s when wealthy families from the East Coast and Midwest began to build winter havens in and around Pasadena. The Caucasianness of the region deepened in the opening decades of the new century as thousands of midwesterners flocked to both Los Angeles proper and its blue-collar suburbs (Nicolaides 2002). In a short time, Long Beach became known as the "Port of Iowa." And all the jobs that these transplants could ever need would be found in the rapidly developing oil, rubber, automotive, and movie industries.

San Francisco may have been more unionized than Los Angeles and certainly was more cultured in every sense of that word in 1900, but the earthquake in 1906 marked a moment when this longtime primary city of the West Coast surrendered urban supremacy to its cow-town cousin to the south. San Francisco rebuilt itself quickly (just as Chicago had done three decades earlier), in time to put itself on display at the 1915 Panama–Pacific International Exposition. But the continued growth of Portland and Seattle, as well as the new possibilities spilling out of Southern California, created relentless rivals for the Bay City. The ports along Puget Sound and at Portland never matched San Francisco and Oakland harbors in total tonnage, but they allowed their cities to become regional entrepôts, nourishing hinterlands that blossomed through lumbering and agricultural exports. Seattle and Portland continued the racial and ethnic diversity of West Coast cities with impactful Asian and Hispanic populations and, after 1900 especially, a more visible influx of European immigrants. For the Chinese residents, however, the periodic violence visited upon them in Los Angeles proved just as true for San Francisco, Seattle, and Tacoma.

Salt Lake City provided typical urban functions for the proposed state of Deseret. Mormons had remained withdrawn for decades, refusing to embrace gentiles—an appropriate reaction given their earlier experiences in the Midwest. The hardships of making a living in the Great Basin facilitated this detachment, keeping unwanted transplants at bay for many years. Yet with the arrival of rail lines and creative irrigation networks, Salt Lake City and the chain of smaller cities to its north and south developed a viable sub-regional economy (Winn 1993). In a similar manner, Denver delivered essential services as a vital distribution depot, serving its own population as well as those who made a living deeper in the Rockies.

When a traveler journeyed outside of the West's urban centers or beyond the lush grain and fruit fields of the Willamette Valley or California's San Gabriel Valley during the Gilded Age, rural life could appear intimidating, especially across the western Great Plains. Whereas in the Midwest, hamlets and towns anchored the move west with settlements positioned every few miles in most locales, the vastness of lands west of the 98th meridian led to isolation, and delayed access to advances in agricultural and residential technology.

In the post-Civil War era, sodbusters coped with limited timber supplies and less fertile topsoil than did fruit farmers in western Michigan. Nature's challenges presented themselves with greater intensity in the Great Plains than in the cornfields of Ohio. Clouds of grasshoppers and locusts, horizons filled with raging prairie fires, relentless periods of droughts, and seasonal onslaughts of blizzards, compounded by the distances between farmsteads, made everyday life that much more difficult in the ranges leading up to the Rockies. Mari Sandoz (2005), in reflecting upon the life of her father, Old Jules, captured the inherent stresses bred by survivalist conditions in western Nebraska. The toll that these nearly impossible lifestyles took on women in particular was both memorable and terrifying. In *The Children's Blizzard*, David Laskin (2004) captured the unpredictable violence that nature (a January 1888 low pressure system in this instance) could inflict with debilitating frequency, brushing aside human responses as inconsequential. His chapter, "God's Burning Finger," catches in a phrase the ferocity of this particular storm—and there were more to come each and every winter season. Tales of these hard lives that filtered outward served as disincentives to mass migrations from settled portions of the United States, with a notable exception of the exodusters, tens of thousands of African Americans who in the late 1870s sought options in the trying environs of Kansas and the Indian Territory. The topographical and hydrological conditions found in the Great Plains often required states to become creative in their public relations tactics when recruiting potential residents. Kansas distributed fliers lauding the Sunflower State's magnificent summers and inspiring springs and falls—inadvertently, it seems, omitting mention of winter.

Politics

The ruggedness of the terrain in so many areas of the Far West not only blunted the attractiveness of the region to prospective residents, but it also had an effect on those trying to make a living under these circumstances. Dangerous working conditions generated aggressive responses among poorly paid, poorly treated laborers, especially in the mining industry. The Western Federation of Miners (WFM), founded in 1893—the same year that the Sherman Silver Purchase's repeal cut into production and the year after seven miners lost their lives in a labor clash in Coeur d'Alene—mirrored the harshness of its membership's work environments with a confrontational attitude toward the mine owners and their armed allies—both hired guards and the state militia routinely available courtesy of friendly governors.

Members of the WFM, including Bill Haywood, enthusiastically attended the Chicago meeting in 1905 at which the Industrial Workers of the World, the Wobblies, was formed. Intended to be "one big industrial union" rather than be industry-specific, the IWW went national, with organizing successes in the West that included silver mines in Idaho as well as sawmills and logging camps in Washington. The outspoken goal of overturning America's economic system, with violence if necessary, tempered the overall allure of this organization, even though it maintained a presence across wide sectors of the Far West' labor force, including miners, foresters, longshoremen, and migrant harvesters (Hine and Faragher 2000). Endless clashes with state militia, legislative and judicial assaults on the IWW's legal standing, and convictions of IWW leadership made the group's successes in the Far West inherently unstable (McGerr 2003). The 1919 Seattle General Strike, as a case in point, failed to generate the tsunami of support that organizers had anticipated. Pushback from state governments and the formation of employer-unions by corporate leaders blunted labor's efforts in the diversified industries of the Far West. Then during World War I, the power of patriotism bore down upon labor's organizing efforts. This wartime reassertion of conservative politics took on a related form in the 1920s with the second coming of the Ku Klux Klan. This latest edition of the Klan developed a very strong presence throughout the West, especially in rural areas and small inland cities. Governments in several states, including Kansas and Oregon, fell under the sway of KKK members and sympathizers, not unlike Indiana further east (Malone and Peterson 1994).

Three decades earlier, Populism had established a strong presence in several plains states. As pointed out by Walter Nugent years ago, due to weaker economic conditions in a state such as Kansas and across other sections of the central and northern Great Plains, statist solutions to ongoing problems through a third party gained some traction (Creech 2015). This may explain the momentary success of James B. Weaver's effort in 1892 when the People's Party won electoral votes in Kansas, Colorado, Nevada, Idaho, North Dakota, and Oregon. Although Charles Postel (2007) has made a persuasive case for Populist activism as far west as California, shallower political traditions across most of the Far West limited the lure for third-party alternatives as early the 1890s. Thin populations and recent elevations to statehood left western citizens less interested in seeking solutions outside the newly institutionalized two-party system. Their political patience had not yet been tested, except in the face of corporate brutes such as the Great Northern or the Southern Pacific. In most parts of the West, agricultural economies were still under development (for example, the citrus orchards of the San Gabriel and Pomona valleys outside of Los Angeles) and had not reached the levels of crisis evident in Kansas or the Dakotas. In a similar manner, for brief moment Job Harriman nearly became Los Angeles' first and only socialist mayor in 1911, but again, as with the Midwest east of the Great Plains and the Far West west of Denver, a third-party alternative did not prove a winning option, let alone a political necessity.

However, Postel's depiction of the Populists as first-wave progressives carries with it important insights because the political continuity that he proposes between the end of the nineteenth century and opening decades of the twentieth century helps explain a generation of reform. In the Far West, with institutional systems still immature and evolving, change usually came at the state level. As Amy Bridges notes in her study of municipal reform in the Southwest, the area was "short of people and employers" (1997, 32). So a city such as Seattle could witness a campaign of coalition building between labor organizers and suffragists with the goal of rectifying both economic and political injustices (Putnam 2008). In Los Angeles, John Randolph Haynes, a physician whose philanthropic legacy lives on richly into this century, promoted direct democracy through a socialist organization, but realized his greatest successes working on behalf of the entire state in association with Hiram Johnson (Sitton 1992; Deverell and Sitton 1994). A similar success was the "Oregon System" with its emphasis upon the initiative, referendum, and recall—causes that resonated with reformers across the region and nation. As Robert D. Johnston (2003) points out, the country watched Oregon's experiment with direct democracy with interest, notably in Portland where between 1905 and 1913, the city's citizenry voted 129 times on municipal matters. Progressivism also had strong support coming out of California's capital of Sacramento, where crusaders such as Hiram Johnson promoted institutional reform aimed at preventing corruption as much as removing it.

Critical to the dynamism for reform in the West, as in the Midwest, was the presence of female activists. However in the Far West, these reformers attained greater influence because they were among the first to have the right to vote in local and state elections. In 1893, Colorado became the first state to enfranchise women through a referendum, followed shortly by Idaho. Earlier, Wyoming had granted women the vote in 1890 with its first state constitution, with Utah following its lead in 1896. After a brief spell of unsuccessful campaigns for the equal vote, Washington broke "the doldrums" with enfranchisement in 1910 and in the following year a California referendum granted enfranchisement. In every year but two from 1910 until 1919, at least one additional state granted partial or complete suffrage to women. If once the advice for a young man had been to "Go West," now the battle cry for women of all ages was to drive "East" toward the urbanized, industrialized sections of the country in order to complete the process of national enfranchisement (Jablonsky 1994).

Conclusion

The Gilded Age and Progressive Era represented a defining age for significant portions of the Far West. By the 1920s, glimpses of what directions the western half of the United States might take over the course of the rest of that century had been revealed. The city of Los Angeles would reach one million residents by 1930 and eventually become the country's second largest city. West coast ports would serve as embarkation points for hundreds of thousands of military service personnel on their way to faraway islands and Asian shores through three wars; upon their return, many found permanent homes in the Golden State and the Pacific Northwest. The minerals, forests, and hydrological riches of the West would become fully integrated —and exploited—while serving the nation's economy for the decades to come. And population diversity would thicken in time, with repeated migrations of African Americans and Hispanics, the epic Dust Bowl exodus of Okies and Arkies, and a renewed wave of newcomers from Asia in the aftermath of the 1965 Immigration Act.

The West with its host of sub-regional climates and entertainment potentials held the nation's fascination from the Grand Canyon to the Las Vegas strip to Lake Tahoe. Areas lightly touched by 1930, such as those in the Great Basin and Rocky Mountains, have been fully integrated into the national economy. Wyoming coal now fuels generating plants along the East Coast. Ski resorts across the West entertain hundreds of thousands from every corner of the globe. The nature of western urbanization (including suburbanization) helped redefine domestic American history during the post-World War II era. Construction of the interstate highway system bridged some of the vastness of the Far West, and if the Great American Desert can still seem tedious to contemporary travelers, at least the unending horizons are now measured in days, not months. By the twenty-first century, the West was not quite as "far," but just as resplendent with wonderment and promise.

References

Abbott, Carl. 2008. *How Cities Won the West*. Albuquerque: University of New Mexico Press.

Atherton, Lewis. 1954. *Main Street on the Middle Border*. Chicago: Quadrangle Books.

Atkins, Annette. 1988. "Minnesota." In *Heartland*, edited by James J. Madison, 9–31. Bloomington: Indiana University Press.

Barth, Gunther. 1988. *Instant Cities*. Albuquerque: University of New Mexico Press.

Bridges, Amy. 1997. *Morning Glories*. Princeton, NJ: Princeton University Press.

Buenker, John D. 1998. *The History of Wisconsin, Volume IV: The Progressive Era, 1893–1914*. Madison: Wisconsin Historical Society.

Cayton, Andrew R. L., and Peter S. Onuf. 1990. *The Midwest and the Nation*. Bloomington: Indiana University Press.

Critchlow, Donald T. 1986. *Socialism in the Heartland*. Notre Dame, IN: Notre Dame University Press.

Creech, Joe. 2015. "The Tolerant Populists and the Legacy of Walter Nugent." *Journal of the Gilded Age and Progressive Era* 14: 141–159. doi: 10.1017/S1537781414000760.

Cronon, William. 1991. *Nature's Metropolis*. New York: W.W. Norton.

Davies, Richard O. 1998. *Main Street Blues*. Columbus: Ohio University Press.

Deverell, William, and Tom Sitton. 1994. *California Progressivism Revisited*. Berkeley: University of California Press.

Dorsett, Lyle W. 1968. *The Pendergast Machine*. New York: Oxford University Press.

Dunbar, Willis Frederick. 1968. *How It Was in Hartford*. Grand Rapids, MI: Eerdmans.

Faragher, John Mack. 1988. *Sugar Creek*. New Haven, CT: Yale University Press.

Flanagan, Maureen A. 2002. *Seeing With their Hearts*. Princeton, NJ: Princeton University Press.

Flores, Dan. 2001. *The Natural West*. Norman: University of Oklahoma Press.

Gray, Susan E. 1996. *The Yankee West*. Chapel Hill: University of North Carolina Press.

Gurda, John. 1999. *The Making of Milwaukee*. Milwaukee: Milwaukee County Historical Society.

Hine, Robert V., and John Mack Faragher. 2000. *The American West: A New Interpretive History*. New Haven, CT: Yale University Press.

Hoagland, Alison K. 2010. *Mine Towns*. Minneapolis: University of Minnesota Press.

Holli, Melvin. 1999. *American Mayor*. University Park: Pennsylvania University Press.

Hudson, John C. 1985. *Plains Country Towns*. Minneapolis: University of Minnesota Press.

Hurt, R. Douglas. 2013. "The Agricultural Power of the Midwest during the Civil War." In *Union Heartland*, edited by Ginette Aley and J.L. Anderson, 68–96. Carbondale: Southern Illinois University Press.

Jackson, Richard H. 1995. "Federal Lands in the Mountainous West." In *The Mountainous West*, edited by William Wyckoff and Lary M. Dilsaver, 253–277. Lincoln: University of Nebraska Press.

Jablonsky, Thomas J. 1994. *Duty, Nature, and Stability*. Brooklyn: Carlson Publishing.

Jentz, John B., and Richard Schenirov. 2012. *Chicago in the Age of Capital*. Urbana: University of Illinois Press.

Johnston, Robert D. 2003. *The Radical Middle Class*. Princeton, NJ: Princeton University Press, 2003.

Karamanski, Theodore J. 1989. *Deep Woods Frontier*. Detroit: Wayne State University Press.

Kelley, Robert. 1989. *Battling the Inland Sea*. Berkeley: University of California Press.

Kusmer, Kenneth L. 1978. *A Ghetto Takes Shape*. Urbana: University of Illinois Press.

Lankton, Larry. 1999. *Beyond the Boundaries*. New York: Oxford University Press.

Laslett, John H.M. 1986. "Swan Song or New Social Movement?" In *Socialism in the Heartland*, edited by Donald T. Critchlow, 167–214. Notre Dame: Notre Dame University Press.

Lee, Mordecai. 2008. *Bureaus of Efficiency*. Milwaukee: Marquette University Press.

Laskin, David. 2004. *The Children's Blizzard*. New York: Harper Collins.

Limerick, Patricia Nelson. 1987. *The Legacy of Conquest*. New York: W.W. Norton.

McGerr, Michael. 2003. *A Fierce Discontent*. New York: Free Press.

Malone, Michael P., and F. Ross Peterson. 1994. "Politics and Protests." In *The Oxford History of the American West*, edited by Clyde A. Milner, Carol O'Connor, and Martha A. Sandweiss, 501–533. New York: Oxford University Press.

Meyer, Carrie A. 2007. *Days on the Family Farm*. Minneapolis: University of Minnesota Press.

Miller, Zane. 1968. *Boss Cox*. Columbus: Ohio State University Press.

Moehring, Eugene P. 2004. *Urbanism and Empire in the Far West*. Reno: University of Nevada Press.

Nelson, Daniel. 1995. *Farm and Factory*. Bloomington: Indiana University Press.

Nicolaides, Becky M. 2002. *My Blue Heaven*. Chicago: University of Chicago Press.

Peirce, Neil R. 1973. *The Great Plains States of America*. New York: W.W. Norton Press.

Primm, James Neal. 2013. *Lion of the Valley*. St. Louis: Missouri Historical Society Press.

Postel, Charles. 2007. *The Populist Vision*. New York: Oxford University Press.

Putnam, John C. 2008. *Class and Gender Politics in Progressive-Era Seattle*. Reno: University of Nevada Press.

Robbins, William G. 1994. *Colony and Empire*. Lawrence: University Press of Kansas.

Rudwick, Elliott. 1982. *Race Riot in East St. Louis*. Urbana: University of Illinois Press.

Sandoz, Mari. 2005. *Old Jules*. Lincoln: University of Nebraska Press.

Sawyers, June Skinner. 1991. *Chicago Portraits*. Chicago: Loyola University Press.

Sitton, Tom. 1992. *John Randolph Haynes*. Palo Alto, CA: Stanford University Press.

Smith, Carl. 1995. *Urban Disorder and the Shape of Belief*. Chicago: University of Chicago Press.

Spear, Alan. 1967. *Black Chicago*. Chicago: University of Chicago Press.

Teaford, Jon C. 1993. *Cities of the Heartland*. Bloomington: Indiana University Press.

Trotter, Joe William. 2006. *Black Milwaukee*. Urbana: University of Illinois Press.

Tuttle, William. 1996. *Race Riot*. Urbana: University of Illinois Press.

Unger, Nancy C. 2000. *Fighting Bob La Follette*. Chapel Hill: University of North Carolina Press.

Vale, Thomas R. 1995. "Mountains and Moisture in the West." In *The Mountainous West*, edited by William Wyckoff and Lary M. Dilsaver, 141–165. Lincoln: University of Nebraska Press.

Westhoff, Laura M. 2007. *A Fatal Drifting Apart*. Columbus: Ohio University Press.

Winn, Kenneth H. 1993. "The Mormon Region." In *Encyclopedia of American Social History*, edited by Mary K. Cayton and Elliot J. Gorn, 1089–1098. New York: Charles Scribner's Sons.

Worster, Donald. 1985. *Rivers of Empire*. New York: Pantheon Books.

Yenne, Bill. 2006. *Indian Wars*. Yardley, PA: Westholme Publishing.

Zesch, Scott. 2012. *The Chinatown War*. New York: Oxford University Press.

Chapter Six

Environment: Nature, Conservation, and the Progressive State

Benjamin Johnson

That the editors of this volume commissioned a chapter on the environment reflects the growing salience of the comparatively young field of environmental history. Questions of labor, class, monopoly, ethnicity, and reform have been central to the study of the United States of the late nineteenth and early twentieth century. These issues motivated the writers, activists, and political figures who provided the monikers "Gilded Age" (Mark Twain's formulation) and "Progressive Era" (itself a tribute to the influence of a host of social reforms). Environmental questions, in contrast, have not been central to historical examinations, if for no other reason than the fact that they have until recent decades been marginal to the historical profession as a whole. Even the rise of environmental history as an intellectually coherent sub-field, with journals, a disciplinary association, conferences, and job lines of its own, has until recently failed to make much of an impact on the ways that historians study the United States from 1880 to 1920. Synthetic treatments by Alan Dawley (2003), Rebecca Edwards (2006), Maureen Flanagan (2007), T.J. Jackson Lears (2009), Michael McGerr (2003), and Daniel Rodgers (1998) published in the last twenty years have paid only perfunctory attention to environmental matters.

Yet environmental history is an illuminating vantage from which to view the Gilded Age and Progressive Era. Moreover, recent work published under the rubrics of political, urban, women's, cultural, and environmental history present environmental questions as being much more central to the study of the period as a whole than they were in earlier accounts. This chapter endeavors to trace and explain the increasing mainstreaming of environmental questions in the study of the period. It also embraces this development and argues for ways in which historians can better show how questions about environmental matters speak to the era's other core issues. Environmental politics are the chapter's center of gravity, because they have been the subject of such sustained historical inquiry and because they are the most direct link between environmental matters and the larger history and historiography.

Scholars of the Gilded Age and Progressive Era, even those who do not define themselves primarily as environmental historians, should take environmental history seriously. It can be a revealing window onto the period and a midwife of compelling questions that in many cases return to the issues that have been at the heart of the study of the period for generations: the fate of democracy in the midst of an explosive economic transformation, struggles over control of new industrial workplaces, rapid urbanization, heavy immigration, the solidification of racial hierarchies, the rise of the professions, changes in and challenges to ideas of gender brought by corporate capitalism, the expansion of the powers of the state, and the emergence of a wide range of reform movements. Similarly, scholars of environmental history who do not necessarily reflexively think of themselves as Gilded Age or Progressive Era specialists can demonstrate the suppleness and reach of environmental history by making ambitious claims for the centrality of environmental questions to the fin-de-siècle United States.

The same socioeconomic transformations that moved Americans from the country to the city, drew millions of migrants from across the globe, fostered class conflict, and raised enduring questions about concentrated economic power and democracy, also dramatically altered the natural world, created new spaces such as trainline suburbs and industrial cities with their own distinctive environments, spawned new environmental hazards such as workplace toxins and urban smoke, and produced the conservation movement. Americans girded the continent with railroads, shot the Passenger Pigeon into oblivion, fouled countless rivers with industrial waste, created commodities and cities that

A Companion to the Gilded Age and Progressive Era, First Edition. Edited by Christopher McKnight Nichols and Nancy C. Unger.
© 2017 John Wiley & Sons, Inc. Published 2017 by John Wiley & Sons, Inc.

masked their continued connection to the non-human world, cut and burned down many of their forests, and rationalized an extermination campaign against wolves and other predators. They also created extensive city parks to provide a refuge for urbanites, turned to native plants and park designs that evoked wild nature, built extensive dams and irrigation networks to make gardens out of deserts, voraciously read stories of exploration and wildness, and created numerous private organizations and public bureaucracies to curtail environmental profligacy.

It is in the realm of this last issue—environmental politics—where environmental matters are most obviously implicated in the wider trajectories of the period. Scholars of the Gilded Age and Progressive Era (GAPE) should pay attention to environmental questions, if for no other reason than that many of their subjects did. Indeed, conservation politics and bureaucracies warrant consideration as one of the linchpins of national Progressivism. On the national level, Progressives were perhaps more successful in the realm of environmental management than in any of the other issues most important to them. By 1920, to pick a conventional ending point for the Progressive Era, a vigorous if often fractious conservation movement had brought into being an ambitious environmental state, one still with us nearly a century later. Specialized environmental organizations such as Audubon Societies and the Sierra Club joined with broader organizations such as the General Federation of Women's Clubs to pass national and state wildlife laws and create the National Park System and national forests. Countless cities established their own park and forest reserve systems. In the west, vast tracts of the American domain were now permanently managed by specialized federal agencies, either for the valuable economic benefits of such resources as timber and water, or for the spiritual and recreational attraction of wild nature. The United States Forest Service alone managed a domain of more than 150 million acres, or nearly twice the size of the nation of Germany. The younger National Park Service, charged with preserving wild and scenic nature, administered nineteen parks and twenty-four monuments, whose area comprised 8.1 million acres. The Reclamation Service, founded in 1902, estimated that its dams, reservoirs, and canals provided irrigation to over 2 million acres of farmland, with projects underway to water another 2 million (Johnson 2017, 131). Figures associated with environmental reform, such as Theodore Roosevelt, John Muir and Gifford Pinchot, achieved widespread recognition in their own time and have never ceased generating scholarly disputation.

In a sense, the recent convergence of environmental and Gilded Age Progressive Era scholarship is a return to the period itself. Many Progressive intellectuals saw environmental problems and proposals to address them as part of wider efforts to use scientific expertise and state power to solve problems of industrial life as diverse as monopoly, child labor, workplace injury, food and drug safety, and urban public health. William Temple Hornaday, a key figure in the preservation first of the bison and then of wildlife more generally, opened his seminal 1914 *Wild Life Conservation in Theory and Practice* on just this note: "The industrial development of the United States has wrought so many sweeping changes from conditions of the past that the American people are fairly compelled to adjust their minds in conformity with the new conditions." For Hornaday as for so many others, one of the most pressing "new conditions" was the extraordinary power of markets to decimate populations of wild animals. When the United States was still a rural and agrarian nation, an assumption that wildlife was indestructibly abundant made sense. Cataloguing the extinctions of the Passenger Pigeon, Great Auk, Labrador Duck, and other species, Hornaday urged that "it be remembered for all time" that "*no wild species of mammal or bird can withstand systematic slaughter for commercial purposes.*" In the face of this stark modern reality, the belief "that the resources of nature are inexhaustible" could only be pernicious because "it helps to salve the conscience of the man who commits high crimes against wild beasts and birds and forests" (Hornaday 1914, 6, 1, 7).

The insight that Hornaday applied to wildlife—that the unprecedented power of markets meant that humanity was now living in a new historical era that demanded a new environmental understanding—was applied by others to forest fires, the artificial and dangerous conditions of cities, deforestation, the unprecedented flooding of major waterways, and other environmental issues. It was the basis of a more material wing of conservation, epitomized by US Forest Service founder Gifford Pinchot, which sought to bring natural resources under the control of scientifically trained experts who would staff government agencies charged with preventing monopoly and fostering orderly economic development. Moreover, a similar sense informed more romantic and aesthetic reforms, such as Sierra Club founder John Muir's ecstatic vision of wilderness, or publisher J. Horace McFarland's proposals to beautify cities (Miller 2001; Worster 2010; Johnson 2017).

Not all important Progressive intellectuals were particularly invested in the concern for natural resources and splendor that animated conservationists, but contemporary commentators did recognize the deep affinities between conservation and Progressivism. In his 1915 *The Progressive Movement*, for example, political scientist Benjamin DeWitt noted that "[i]n so far as conservation of natural resources is considered, the progressive movement in the nation is of the utmost importance because of the aid which the national government, and it alone, can give." DeWitt saw conservation as one of the three most important issues requiring the intervention of the federal government, ranking along with taxation and "the protection of men, women, and children engaged in industrial work" (DeWitt 1915, 186, 163). Wisconsin economist Richard Ely, one of the most important Progressive intellectuals for providing an economic rationale for vigorous state action rather than laissez-faire, similarly saw conservation as part of his overall political stance. His 1917 *The Foundations of National Prosperity: Studies in the Conservation of Permanent National Resources* made the case that the rational, orderly use of natural resources under the supervision of such agencies as the Forest Service was a critical part of ensuring continued economic growth and equitable national prosperity (Ely 1917, 3, 11–12; Rodgers 1998, 77, 102).

A generation later, however, scholars of the Progressive Era paid much less attention to conservation and the environmental politics that prompted it. Richard Hofstadter's enormously influential *The Age of Reform* (1955) did not mention conservation. Hofstadter's argument that the "general theme" of Progressivism "was the effort to restore a type of economic individualism and political democracy that was widely believed to have existed earlier in America and to have been destroyed by the great corporation and the corrupt political machine" would have allowed for an exploration of natural resource politics. And his emphasis on the roles of middle-class reformers and professional expertise could certainly have been applied to urban environmental politics. But Hofstadter saw anti-monopoly and the regulation of the workplace as the fundamental features of Progressivism. He traced it to the 1890s creation of the Interstate Commerce Commission, the Sherman Act, and state working-hours legislation, altogether ignoring the creation of the federal forest service system and great expressions of concern about fires and timber shortages in the same decade (Hofstadter 1955, 5, 131, 149, 165).

Scholars of conservation, on the other hand, went to considerable lengths to locate its origins and ideology in the larger ferment of Progressivism. Writing in the *Mississippi Valley Historical Review* in 1957, J. Leonard Bates argued that conservation "was both a product of and a stimulant to the larger, so-called Progressive movement." Bates bemoaned the fact that "[h]istorians of modern reform have given scant attention to rationale of conservation or to conservation as a democratic movement." For him, the actions of such conservationists as Gifford Pinchot, explorer and anthropologist John Wesley Powell, and President Theodore Roosevelt, were, like the conservation movement itself, "both a product of and a stimulant to the larger, so-called Progressive movement," particularly in their opposition to monopoly, materialism, and the political power of organized wealth. Conservation in his rendering waxed and waned along with fortunes of Progressivism as a whole, through the tumult of the splitting of the Republican Party in 1912 and the nation's entry into World War I (Bates 1957, 29–30). Two years after Bates, in his enormously influential *Conservation and the Gospel of Efficiency* (1959), Samuel P. Hays portrayed conservation in very different terms, as the quest of professional elites to create an administrative state based on their expertise and authority. Foresters and engineers were the key actors in Hays's account, and their investment in efficiency and the orderly development and use of western lands were the linchpins of his understanding of conservation. He stressed "the vantage point of applied science, rather than of democratic protest," but like Bates's approach his argument also treated conservation as part and parcel of Progressivism. Environmental state-building was but one outlet for the quest for efficiency, a concept that provided a vantage onto the rest of the era as well. Environmental history *avant la lettre* was thus very much bound up with the central questions of the study of the period (Hays 1959, 2).

Bates and Hays wrote at a time when there was no such thing as environmental history. To be sure, environmental factors appeared in the study of US history before the emergence of environmental history as such. Frederick Jackson Turner's Frontier Thesis placed the comparative abundance of land and the incorporation of newly acquired territory at the heart of the American experience. A generation later, Walter Prescott Webb, writing in *The Great Plains* (1931), made a sustained argument for the impact of the arid mid-continent on settlement patterns, technology, and economic development. Moved by the rise of the environmental movement in the 1960s, Roderick Nash traced ideas of wilderness across the span of American history in *Wilderness and the American Mind* (1967). Perhaps most ambitiously, in *The Columbian Exchange: Biological and Cultural Consequences of 1492* (1973), Alfred Crosby showed the enormous role of the biological exchanges between the two hemispheres after Columbus's voyages.

Yet environmental history's emergence as a dynamic and self-conscious field ironically contributed to its marginalization within GAPE historiography. By the mid 1980s it was possible to speak of a coherent "environmental history:" Donald Worster's *Dust Bowl: The Southern Plains in the 1930s* (1978) and William Cronon's *Changes in the Land: Indians, Colonists, and the Ecology of New England* (1983) had won national awards and unexpectedly wide readership. Their central arguments both pointed to the power of capitalism, typically examined in terms of its social impact, to bring about equally dramatic environmental change. These arguments lent themselves to application across wide expanses of time and space, one of the reasons that the books enjoyed such wide readership. *Environmental Review*, founded in 1976, had become the field's central journal; in 1990, it was rechristened *Environmental History Review* (later simply *Environmental History*) and became the sponsored publication of the new American Society of Environmental History.

The young field drew much of its vitality from the social movement of environmentalism, just as labor history, women's history, African American history and other fields were animated by social movements (White 1985, 299). Yet much of the field's intellectual dynamism came from the broadening of inquiry away from the study of past environmental politics and thought (as in the work of Hays and

Nash) and to the larger questions of the reciprocal ties between social change and non-human nature. Making nature itself a historical actor led environmental historians to place a premium on ecological literacy. This reach across the disciplines allowed environmental historians to show that nature was not just a timeless backdrop for human history, or even a source of commodities or meanings over which people struggled, but rather that the non-human world responded in certain specific ways to such human actions as logging or trapping, or technologies such as the iron plow. Environmental history was thus a distinct methodology as well as a subject; it was not merely political, cultural, or intellectual history involving nature.

The turn to explaining reciprocal changes in the natural and human worlds was a tremendously fruitful one, allowing scholars over the next few decades to offer convincing explanations of a wide range of environmental developments of the late nineteenth and early twentieth centuries: the expansion of hay fever, the ironic consequences of state-sponsored forest fire suppression, the failings of professional forestry, the collapse of salmon fisheries, and the American Bison's narrow escape from extinction (Mittman 2008; Pyne 1982; Langston 1995; Taylor 1999; Flores 1991; West 1998; Isenberg 1999). Yet, ironically, environmental history's gain may have been GAPE historiography's loss. The turn to nature in environmental history was in a sense a turn away from the kind of political questions that had put the work of Hays and Bates in deep conversation with studies of Progressivism. As Richard White observed, "Ultimately environmental history as purely intellectual or political history must vanish back into the fields which gave it birth and on which it relies for explanations of its subject matter. Intellectual and political history may be environmental history's parents, but they are, by themselves, unable to nurture it" (White 1985, 317).

On the other hand, the way in which those historians who still examined environmental politics and thought approached their studies also served to limit their impact. Many of these scholars wrote with the assumption that their subjects were virtuous, and that their task was to trace the emergence and accomplishments of environmental virtue. Roderick Nash's Whig history of growing environmental enlightenment was often mirrored in studies of such figures as Gifford Pinchot and John Muir, of the establishment of national parks and other protected areas, and of organizations such as the Sierra Club and Save-the-Redwoods League. Yet just as often, these studies failed to replicate Nash's and Hays's situating of environmental dynamics in the context of larger developments such as the growth of the administrative state (White 1985, 300–301, 305–309; see, for example Cohen 1984; Fox 1981; Runte 1979; Searle 1977; Schrepfer 1983; Franklin and Schaeffer 1983). There was much for those readers convinced of the importance of these places, people, and institutions to profit from these works. But the insularity and lack of critical edge that characterized many of them ensured that they had little relevance to scholars of Progressivism, who since the 1950s had been much more critical of the motives and achievements of its subjects, even when they felt that Progressivism remained a generative political tradition (Hofstadter 1955; Kolko 1963; Weinstein 1968; for more critical work on environmental policy, see Pyne 1982 and Robbins 1982). Studies of Progressive Era environmental politics were not nearly as sophisticated as the general literature on Progressive Era politics.

The dynamic growth of environmental history soon changed this, laying the groundwork for scholars in this field to make arguments of sweeping importance for the period. William Cronon's second book, *Nature's Metropolis: Chicago and the Great West* (1991), another landmark work for environmental historians, examined the ways in which Chicago converted most of the American West into its hinterland. The Windy City made the most of its rail connections to become the key place in which corn and wheat, white pines and red pines, hogs and cattle, were converted into capital by silos, sawmills, meatpacking plants, and commodity exchanges. Chicago was his setting, but Cronon's real subject was the process of commodification, in which markets "accomplished the transmutation of one of humanity's oldest foods," corn or wheat, "obscuring its physical identity and displacing it into the symbolic world of capital." Marx and others had identified the surplus value of labor as the source of capital, and generations of historians had studied the ways in which labor conflicts and efforts to ameliorate or resolve them shaped American society between Reconstruction and the 1920s. Cronon nodded to this perspective but sought to place nature, not labor, at center stage. "By assembling shipments from fields, pastures, and forests into great accumulations of wealth," he wrote, "the city helped convert them into that mysterious thing called capital, what Karl Marx identified as 'self-expanding value.'" Wage labor may have distinguished industrial Chicago from the Native American societies it displaced and transformed, but the exploitation of nature lay at the heart of Gilded Age capitalism (Cronon 1991, 112, 148–150).

Wealth was not the only product of the processes of commodification that Cronon traced with such elegance. So was alienation. A new consciousness was fostered by the new exploitation of nature. An animal transformed into meat "also died a second death. Severed from the form in which it had lived, severed from the act that had killed it, it vanished from human memory as one of nature's creatures." Thus the "new corporate order, by linking and integrating the products of so many ecosystems and communities, obscured the very connections it helped create" (Cronon 1991, 256–257). Wilderness appreciation, Cronon argued several years later, was in a sense also a form of alienation. Rather than representing the acme of environmental enlightenment, as had Roderick Nash and others had argued, wilderness appreciation reflected a "dream of an unworked natural landscape" that "is very much the fantasy of people who have never themselves had to work the land to make a living—urban folk for whom food comes from a supermarket or a restaurant instead of a field." Wilderness was as much an impediment to environmental protection as a model for it, since "the romantic ideology of wilderness leaves precisely nowhere for human beings actually to make their living from the land" (Cronon 1995, 80).

These arguments about commodification and alienation positioned the late nineteenth century as the key period for the emergence of environmental modernity, drawing new attention to the trends of urbanization and corporate capitalism that had long been central questions of the study of the Gilded Age and Progressive Era. But in one important way, Cronon's account still stood at a distance from GAPE historiography: he minimized, to the point of denying, the relevance of politics and social division. Cronon's Chicago was the setting of Haymarket bombing, the Pullman Strike, and countless other labor conflicts. And its Midwestern and Great Plains hinterland saw the explosion of agrarian radicalism into electoral politics with the rise of the Populist Party in the 1890s. Yet none of this tumult, so central to political, labor, and social historians, really mattered for his arguments. "The settlement of the countryside, the growth of the city, and the expansion of the market that linked them, all rested on the basic premise that people could and should exploit the wealth of nature to the utmost. In the process, some people might gain more than others, certainly, but human gained over nonhuman most of all." Toward the end of *Nature's Metropolis,* Cronon discussed the deep rural resentments of Chicago and urban American as a whole that animated the Grange, Populism, and countless novels. But agrarian critiques of capitalism end up as a simplistic denial of the complicated webs re-created in *Nature's Metropolis.* Cronon's response to environmental modernity, in both his book and his critique of wilderness, was an implicit call for an enlightenment to puncture environmental alienation, a recognition of mutuality rather than the restoration or analysis of politics critical of modern capitalism. He thus preserved something of the traditional social holism of environmental history, in which humanity was treated as a whole unit and its connections to a nonhuman nature subjected to analysis (Cronon 1991, 150, 361; see also Robert Johnston's critique in Johnston 1998, 248–249).

Soon, other works focused precisely on the ways in which environmental dynamics interacted with social hierarchies and tension. This body of work played a critical role in the integration of environmental and GAPE studies. Studies of environmental politics, particularly Progressive Era conservation, led the way. In their examination of the thicket of laws and agencies created by the early twentieth century, these scholars returned to much of the same ground covered by Samuel Hays and Roderick Nash. But they did so in ways shaped by the larger turn to social history: instead of tracing the ideas of efficiency or validation of wildness that prompted such measures as hunting restrictions and the creation of forest reserves and national parks, they asked about the social consequence of these developments. In *The Hunter's Game: Poachers and Conservationists in Twentieth-Century America* (1997), Louis Warren showed that the clashes between wildlife conservationists and local hunters pitted ethnic groups and economic interests against one another. Game regulations were a huge burden for working-class hunters, and the destruction, confiscation, or selling of canoes, traps, and guns by state agents deprived these and other rural Americans of equipment necessary to engage in common subsistence activities (Warren 1997, 28–29). Native American peoples were even more disadvantaged. Many national forest and parks were carved from their territory, often in explicit violation of treaties, with conservation bureaucrats then curtailing native land uses or even removing them altogether. In Yellowstone National Park, managed by the Army in the 1880s, superintendents arrested Bannock and Shoshone hunters in order to preserve the Park's iconic elk herd. Blackfeet were similarly excluded from Glacier National Park. They responded by pressing their claims in court and routinely shooting at Park Rangers. The Yosemite, after whom California's park and its iconic valley was named, fared somewhat better. Their usefulness as a labor force for hotels and campgrounds, and their ability to serve as an alluring tourist attraction, helped to maintain their presence until restrictions put in place after World War II began to reduce their numbers (Spence 1999). Mark David Spence explained Indian removal from these and other national parks as a product of the interaction between wilderness thought and Indian policy. The idea that a true wilderness should contain no long-term inhabitants and should reflect minimal human impact, he argued, joined with the belief that Indian peoples should pressed to assimilate into mainstream culture, provided park managers the rationale for Indian removal.

Conservation was not always as authoritarian as the experiences of Italian American hunters and Yosemite Indians suggested. In *Common Lands, Common People: The Origins of Conservation in Northern New England* (1997), Richard Judd argued that efforts to protect woods, water, and fish in New England grew out of a longstanding popular belief in "democratic access to, and common stewardship of, the land; an aggressive approach to reshaping nature to serve human needs; and a pietistic, perfectionist vision of the balance of cultural and natural features." Judd framed Progressive game and fishing regulations and scientific forestry techniques as a retreat from "this magnificent democratic vision" rather than its culmination. These initiatives came "not from the farm districts but from the city" and were "predicated on recreational rather than utilitarian concepts of land use, and on Romantic visions of the wilderness. Unlike rural traditions," Progressive conservation "projected nature as immutable and separate from human activity."

But his was a story of negotiation and compromise, rather than dictation and submission. In New England, elite conservationists had to negotiate with a politically enfranchised white population that was able to preserve more of its own interests and values (Judd 1997, 7, 148, 197, 220, 247, 258, 264).

But perhaps this kind of negotiation was the exception rather than the rule. This was the suggestion of Karl Jacoby's *Crimes against Nature: Squatters, Poachers, Thieves, and the Hidden History of American Conservation* (2001). His examination of the social history of state conservation in the Adirondacks, Yellowstone, and Grand Canyon regions pointed to just how widespread conflicts over conservation were, and the extent to which they elicited an increasingly authoritarian state in the Progressive Era. Indeed, these conflicts were a principal concern of conservationists, who saw in backwoods resistance to their regulations not only the environmental profligacy of the ignorant, but also a kind of savagery and primitiveness that deserved to be crushed. As a Wisconsin forestry leader wrote in 1900, the "backwoodsman derive[s] his sustenance from the woods, but he d[oes] so by destroying them." He "has the poverty, the ignorance, the lack of civilized ways which we found in his predecessor, to an exaggerated degree." Nor did these conflicts always fall upon ethnoracial lines: the Havasupai Indians of the Grand Canyon were more thoroughly dispossessed and powerless in the face of restrictions on hunting, grazing, and gathering wood, but the experiences of the mostly native-born white inhabitants of the Adirondacks and Yellowstone country were quite similar. So were their reactions: in upstate New York, for example, where numerous private parks banned hunting, fishing, and foraging outright, locals cut fences, routinely shot at the guards of private estates, and set enough of the woods on fire to sometimes waft smoke all the way down to New York City (Jacoby 2001, 198, 42–43).

As in Richard Judd's work, Jacoby found that Progressive conservationists were not the only advocates or practitioners of environmental restraint. Instead, coining the term "moral ecology" as an adaptation of E.P. Thompson's notion of "moral economy," he pointed to the ways in which rural people often drew clear distinctions between legitimate and illegitimate uses of nature. Providing food or other essentials such as heat for one's self or one's family was a right that justified even trespass on private property. The killing of animals or harvesting of products for cash sale, on the other hand, was viewed with far greater suspicion, and was more likely to result in being turned in to the game warden or even in a kind of vigilante conservation. Rural people placed restrictions even on acceptable hunting. Most communities practiced some kind of "law of the woods," which in one rendering emphasized "Never kill anything you do not need." In environmental terms, the vigorous state of the Progressive Era did not so much replace profligacy with judicious use and restraint, but rather replaced one environmental ethos with another one more attuned to urban sensibilities and the market economy. As Jacoby noted, this outcome was parallel with the findings of histories of Progressivism, such as those by Robert Wiebe and Gabriel Kolko (Jacoby 2001, 3, 24, 169; Wiebe 1967; Kolko 1963).

As environmental historians expanded the range of actors that they examined, they also began to examine more kinds of spaces. Cities presented distinctive and pressing environmental issues, such as waste and its disposal, as Martin Melosi had examined at considerable length at an early stage of the development of environmental history (Melosi 1981). The industrial workplace could be examined as an environmental site as well as place of labor and production. This was the premise of Christopher Sellers' *Hazards of the Job: From Industrial Disease to Environmental Health Science* (1997), in which Sellers argued that the Progressive Era field of "industrial hygiene" later gave rise to the modern study of environmental health. "The origins of modern environmental health science," he concluded, "thus lead in an opposite direction from that usually taken by environmental historians: not toward the farm, the wilderness, the frontier, or even the urban park, but into a setting at the heart of industrializing America" (Sellers 1997, 203). Cities and efforts to reform them seemed to anticipate later environmentalism in other ways as well: David Stradling wrote a detailed examination of the problem of urban smoke pollution, showing the extent of Progressive efforts to combat it. As in other aspects of environmental reform, middle-class women and male professionals worked together but also clashed (Stradling 1999, 41). Harold Platt offered the most sustained analysis of the numerous challenges to health, cleanliness, and beauty presented by the new industrial "shock" cities such as Chicago and Manchester, England (Platt, 2005). Platt also sought to recover well-known urban reformers such as Jane Addams as part of a tradition of environmental as well as social reform; as he said of Addams's efforts against tenement housing, they "made explicit the links between bodies, neighborhoods, and the larger urban environment" (Platt 2005, 350). Urban environmental scholarship also moved beyond simple dichotomies of natural and artificial, healthy and hazardous. As Matthew Klingle wrote in his study of Seattle, newly-created cities were "hybrid landscapes, neither fully natural nor under human control" (Klingle 2007, 106). Indeed, urban environmental dynamics such as floods and landslides proved to be just as difficult to control as "natural" challenges of forests, fires, and wildlife populations, and just as fruitful to study (Klingle 2007; Orsi 2004).

Urban parks had not received anything like the kind of sustained attention paid to national forests or parks, but historians began to rectify this. There were no managed urban parks in 1850, but by century's end, of the 157 cities with more than 30,000 residents, all but one had a park (Young 2004, xi). Moreover, these parks were more evocative of wild nature than were their predecessors. As Robert Grese argues, in the 1910s, urban park design became more naturalistic, with designers aiming to evoke nearby ecosystems by choosing native plants in natural associations rather than relying on geometric forms, formally delineated playing spaces, and gymnastic and playground equipment. In many cases these design preferences came from the same conservationist commitments that prompted landscape architects to found organizations such as the Prairie Club or Friends of Our Native Landscape (Grese in Tishler 2000, 131; Johnson 2017, 123–7). Cities and networks of urban elites were also important if neglected factors in such developments as the preservation of forests. Ellen Stroud and Michael Rawson showed how leaders in Boston, New York, and Philadelphia spearheaded the establishment of eastern national forests (Rawson 2010, 249, 263; Stroud 2012, 46, 50, 73).

Increased attention to gender was another way in which accounts of Progressive Era environmental politics became more sophisticated and more explicitly linked with broader developments in the period. Gender analysis had had some presence in environmental history from its early years, as seen in the prominence of Carolyn Merchant's *The Death of Nature: Women, Ecology, and the Scientific Revolution* (1982) and *Ecological Revolutions: Nature, Gender and Science in New England* (1989), in which she closely identified patriarchy with reductionist scientific quests for mastery over nature in the early modern world (Merchant 1982 and 1989). In subsequent years, scholars paid more attention to the ways in which the environmental vision of classic figures such as Theodore Roosevelt was deeply colored by their gender ideology. Gail Bederman demonstrated that Roosevelt's brand of conservation was about preserving a virile masculinity as much as preserving nature itself. "In a perfectly peaceful and commercial civilization such as ours," wrote Roosevelt in the pages of *Harper's Weekly*, "there is always a danger of laying too little stress upon the more virile virtues—upon the virtues which go to make up a race of statesmen and soldiers, of pioneers and explorers." Since these virtues were "fostered by vigorous, manly, out-of-door sports, such as mountaineering, big-game hunting, riding, [and] shooting," conservation could help to preserve a robust American manhood (Bederman 1995, 186). Karl Jacoby extended Bederman's insights to men from different social classes, demonstrating that rural hunters marginalized by the conservation state enacted their own vision of masculinity, valorizing their outdoors prowess, ability to provide for their families, and independence from emasculating wage labor (Jacoby 2001, 128–129, 146).

Notions of femininity also deeply shaped conservation. Arguing that "women transformed the [conservation] crusade from an elite male enterprise into a widely based movement," Carolyn Merchant called attention to the ways in which the separate spheres ideology gave women a motive and rationale for environmental activism "as caretakers of the nation's home, husbands, and offspring" (Merchant 1984, 67, 73). Adam Rome and Nancy Unger profitably revisited the question of women's power in conservation. Arguing that politically active women in the Progressive Era "devoted more attention to environmental issues" than anything except (possibly) temperance and children's welfare, Rome joined Merchant in pointing to the ways in which male conservationists first embraced women's activism, but then marginalized women activists for fear of being dismissed as sentimental and soft. (John Muir, for example, was once lampooned by a cartoonist as a woman in a dress, apron and bonnet, trying frantically but quixotically to sweep back the waters of progress). This marginalization, he suggested, helps explain the relative quiescence of environmental reform from the 1920s to 1950s, as well as its reinvigoration in the 1960s with the rise of feminism (Rome 2006, 443, 440, 454–456). Similarly, Nancy Unger stressed the ways in which gender restrictions became "a credential rather than a handicap" for countless female conservationists, whose labors ranged from the intellectual (Mary Austin's celebration of deserts), to the scientific (industrial chemist Ellen Swallow Richards), to the lay activist (the hundreds of women's conservation organizations whose combined membership reached an estimated one million) (Unger 2012, 77–78, 84, 94).

Gender now seems essential to understanding conservation, but how it worked remains unclear and disputed. How important, for example, was masculinity to male conservationists, and how exclusive were men? There is no doubt that Roosevelt's focus on a strenuous masculinity was an important strain in wilderness and large-game protection efforts, but it was far from universal among male conservationists. Early Boy Scout practices, for example, incorporated a similar relish for the return to frontier conditions but soon came to critique the destructiveness and impulsiveness of masculine frontier culture (Jordan 2010). Sports hunting magazines such as *Field and Stream* and *Outdoor Life*, whose precocious advocacy of bird and game conservation dated to the 1870s, featured women hunters and writers in their columns, articles, advertisements, and cartoons. Perhaps most remarkably, some general interest articles such as Ruth Pepple's regular column on trapshooting in *Outdoor Life*, were written by women. As historian Andrea Smalley concludes, the prominence of women in sporting magazines helped their editors present readers "with an updated and upgraded image of hunting" consistent with their efforts to dissociate recreational hunting "from subsistence hunting, market hunting, and unproductive indolence" (Smalley 2005, 356–357).

Perhaps the most significant distinction between male and female conservationists was their very different relationship with scientific professions. As Samuel Hays had so effectively argued, engineers, foresters, and range scientists provided critical expertise and organizational support for conservation. The major national engineering societies, for example—the American Society of Civil Engineers, the

American Society of Mechanical Engineers, the American Institute of Electrical Engineers, and the American Institute of Mining Engineers—embraced the material side of conservation, publicizing conservation efforts and defending the federal conservation measures of the Roosevelt administration. In so doing they joined professional foresters, whose advocacy of long-term management and scientific analysis of timber resources had made them early proponents of federal conservation (Hays 1959, 123–124).

It went without saying that those doing this investigation were men. Most women had little access to scientific and technical professions given their exclusion from most colleges, and formal barriers to entrance into professional and graduate programs and societies. (The ranks of those who entered such professions included industrial chemist Ellen Swallow Richards, nature-study leader Anna Botsford Comstock, and toxicologist Alice Hamilton, whom Harvard offered a position with the understanding that she would not use the faculty club, was not entitled to football tickets, and would not participate in the commencement procession.) Women and men could both find places within an organized conservation movement, but they were in very different roles (Des Jardins 2010; Gottlieb 1993, 47–51, 216–217).

The burgeoning interest in gender led some scholars to conceptualize human bodies as part of the purview of environmental history. Bodies were tied to larger landscapes, whether rural or urban, and in miasmatic and germ theory understandings alike, these connections were believed to shape individual health and illness (Nash 2006; Maher 2010). Indeed, Progressives had articulated their own realization of these connections in their calls for agencies and departments of "child conservation" charged with improving the health and living conditions of children. Reformers pressing for aggressive care and rehabilitation for disabled soldiers returning from World War I similarly cast their efforts as, in the words of Harry Mock, "part of the great human conservation movement." By healing maimed soldiers, Mock and his compatriots believed that they were restoring to them their manhood (Lansing 2009, 35).

Some leaders thought of eugenics as part of this brand of conservation, a connection that has attracted recent historical scrutiny. Eugenics appealed to conservationists for parallel reasons as the state management of resources such as timber and water: the human body was another arena in which planning and scientific expertise could deliver social improvement. Madison Grant, who played a key role not only in American eugenics, but also in the push for immigration reduction and restriction policies in the 1920s, has attracted the most attention from scholars tracing the connections between conservation and eugenics. Much of the energies of his adult life were devoted to founding and running organizations devoted to natural history and conservation, including the Boone and Crockett Club, the American Bison Society, and more than a dozen others. Grant was particularly enamored with Redwood trees; in 1918, with fellow eugenicists John C. Merriam and Henry Fairfield Osborn, he helped to found the Save-the-Redwoods League. For Grant and his compatriots, the Redwoods were a singularly magnificent tree whose disappearance and replacement by lesser species would be a tragic degradation of the American landscape. Protecting superior trees from the encroachment of undesirable ones found direct analogy in American society. "A rigid system of selection through the elimination of those who are weak or unfit—in other words, social failures—would solve the whole question" of the disappearance of the "Great Race" just as it would "enable us to get rid of the undesirables who crowd our jails, hospitals, and insane asylums." As Grant once explained to his friend and collaborator Henry Fairfield Osborn, eugenics and conservation were both "attempts to save as much as possible of the old America" (Stern 2005, 121, 124; Spiro 2009, xiii, 391–392; Grant 1916, 50–51; Farmer 2013, 68–72).

Scholars dispute the meaning of the eugenics–conservation nexus. For Alexandra Stern and Jonathan Spiro, these connections demonstrated that notions of whiteness and racial supremacy were inseparable from conservation. Jared Farmer, Benjamin Johnson, and Ian Tyrrell offered more measured judgments: Johnson emphasized the different political ends to which hereditarianism was put. Other conservationists, he showed, explicitly rejected Grant's pronouncements as racist and anti-democratic, seeing in the greater importance of environment than birth another reason to make cities more beautiful and healthy. Tyrrell found that the conservationist concern with human bodies lead to comprehensive proposals about public health as well as to eugenics. Farmer noted that it was Redwood preservation in particular that generated enthusiasm among white supremacists such as Grant. Since many eugenicists displayed little interest in conservation, and so many conservationists little interest in eugenics, Farmer declined to make this nexus an important aspect of either movement (Farmer 2013, 68–72; Johnson 2017, 89–93; Tyrrell 2015, 184–185).

Collectively, these works on the social history of conservation, gender, and environmental reform, and eugenics and conservation reflected notable shifts in environmental history on two grounds: first, in methodological terms, it more fully joined social and environmental history than had been done before. The careful and detailed social history of the communities that Warren, Spence, Judd, and Jacoby examined made it clear that the control of nature was a critical question of material well-being and cultural identity. Environmental questions mattered greatly, and not just to a small elite of natural scientists and conservationists. Second, these books marked a new distance between environmental history and the traditional politics of environmentalism. Jacoby was particularly reflective about this distance. He offered neither a polemic on behalf of returning the federal domain to state or county control (as anti-conservationists had called for since the creation of the forest reserves in the 1890s) nor a dismissal of very real environmental damage such as deforestation, species extinction, and game scarcity. But his conclusion that "Americans have often pursued environmental quality at the expense of social justice" was at a considerable remove from the tone of warm adulation that had once typified the history of environmental politics (Jacoby 2001, 198). Environmental historians had come to embrace some of the political subtlety, complexity, and irony that had long marked scholars of Progressivism.

Very recent work on the environmental politics of the GAPE has placed conservation and its antecedents even more squarely in the heart of wider social developments. This body of work has generally taken seriously the insights of social history, but has also returned elites such as natural scientists and activists to the center of examination. Conservationists and other apostles of environmental virtue, it turned out, were interesting, complicated, and compelling in ways for which neither hagiography nor the emphasis on the victims of conservation had allowed. The assumption that only a small segment of American society gave environmental issues much consideration in the Progressive era marked both the older, celebratory and the newer, more critical scholarship, all of which seemed to assume that mass mobilizations on behalf of environmental causes did not happen until postwar environmentalism.

This distinction now seems overdrawn, perhaps even just wrong. Conservationists were overwhelmingly white and native-born, but like postwar environmentalists their ranks drew together large numbers of middle-class people. Efforts to preserve birds endangered by being hunted for plumage used on the ubiquitous women's hats of the period are a good example. As Carolyn Merchant and Jennifer Price demonstrate, the National Audubon Society grew quickly to encompass nineteen state chapters by 1905. Working with conservation committees of the enormous General Federation of Women's Clubs, Audubon Society chapters played critical roles in the passage of the 1900 Lacey Act, which banned the interstate transport of wildlife killed in violation of state laws; in the establishment of numerous federal bird preserves in the 1900s; in a 1913 tariff measure that forbad the import of wild bird feathers; and in a sustained campaign against adorning women's hats with bird feathers and heads. Women Audubon club members established traveling libraries on birds and the need to protect them; they gave school lectures in the hopes that children who answered the door when a woman with a bird on her hat called would say "Mama, there's a woman with a dead body on her hat who wants to see you" (Merchant 2010, 18; Price 1999, 64, 98–99). Kevin Armitage's examination of the Nature Study Movement similarly reveals a wide participation in home gardening, Bird Day (observed in more than half of the states by the 1910s), and in incorporating nature study into public school curricula (Armitage 2009, 4, 12, 93, 207). Benjamin Johnson traces extended discussions between Gifford Pinchot and Horace McFarland (head of the American Civic Association and one of the chief architects of the bill establishing the National Park Service) about forming a national conservation organization that would work on urban improvements, natural resource policy, and issues concerning federal wild-lands. Although the idea never came to fruition, it reflected the influence of other Progressive-era civic organizations such as the General Federation of Women's Clubs, and Progressive theorists who valued the national state as a catalyst for and coordinator of grassroots efforts, not simply a dictator of policy (Johnson 2017, 142–6). Ian Tyrrell similarly argues that the campaign led by Horace McFarland to preserve Niagara Falls brought an aesthetic critique of industrial development to wide swathes of the reading public. "Rather than popular grassroots conservation being merely a vehicle tacked on opportunistically to the spread the message of a scientific conservationist elite from Washington," he concluded, "civil society was an active force in the shaping of conservationist policies" (Tyrell 2015, 158–159). Johnson and Armitage joined Tyrrell in seeing strong links between conservation and the rest of progressivism in this mass constituency for conservation. Conservation resembled other Progressive reforms in the breadth of its supporters and its emphasis on cultural change as well as legal reform.

If the ranks of conservationists were wider than previously thought, so too were the concerns of GAPE environmental activists. Efficient production of natural resources and protection of a supposedly wild nature (whether treated admiringly or more critically) were, in these newer accounts, not so much the two poles of conservation as two of many environmental concerns, some of which made much more room for human landscapes and social concerns. Kevin Armitage argued that the gardens so dear to nature-study enthusiasts deserved greater attention: "Accessible to all, managed by people, yet also wild, the garden was wild nature rooted in domestic, day-to-day life, and it figured more prominently to Progressive-Era conservation … than has been commonly acknowledged" (Armitage 2009, 111). Aaron Sachs made a similar point about landscapes that were both human and natural in *Arcadian America: The Death and Life of an Environmental Tradition* (2013), an ambitious and wide-ranging argument for the capaciousness of the American environmental imagination after the Civil War. More of a sensibility than a philosophy, and not at all an organized movement like conservation, Arcadianism, in Sachs's loving re-creation, was at heart an appreciation for the blending of culture and nature. He argued that an arcadian sensibility undergirded some of the different ways in which "antebellum Americans established kinship with the land." This included park-like cemeteries that seemed to place human mortality in the larger cycles of nature's perpetual death and rebirth, actual parks such as the Boston Common or New York's Central Park where human creations were balanced with invocations of wilder nature, and in depictions by writers such as Hamlin Garland and Henry George of farmers as simultaneously altering, placating, and submitting to nature (Sachs 2013, 23, 333).

Some Americans were more concerned with urban environmental conditions, and with the well-being of urbanites, than the accounts of the 1990s and early 2000s had acknowledged. Extending some of the insights of Sellars and Platt to an earlier period and different urban conditions, Shen Hou convincingly argues that cities were the central concern of the most important environmental publication in the United States during the 1880s and 1890s. Running with the subtitle "A Journal of Horticulture, Landscape Art, and Forestry," the weekly magazine *Garden and Forest* was published out of New York from 1888 to the 1897 death of its editor, William Stiles. Much of its financial support and editorial guidance came from a group of Bostonians headed by Charles Sargent, the botanist director of Harvard's arboretum. The magazine's frequent contributors included Gifford Pinchot, Mira Lloyd Dock, agricultural reformer Liberty Hyde Bailey, and landscape architects Wilhelm Miller and Charles Eliot. Most of these figures, in Hou's words, "looked to government intervention at all levels, from local to federal, to manage more effectively the nation's cultural resources and treasures. Their major projects ranged from establishing federal forest reserves for efficient and wise use of endangered timber resources, setting up national parks to preserve primitive beauty, building urban parks to enhance the physical and moral environment of cities, and constructing and renovating sewer and water systems and cleaning the air in cities for the health of their residents" (Hou 2013, 17). Although Henry George did not write for *Garden and Forest*, the environmental aspects of his political economy have recently garnered more attention. George was a key figure in Aaron Sach's rehabilitation of Arcadianism, and Benjamin Johnson argues that his influence on urban environmental reform lasted decades after George's 1897 death. Although his apparent lack of concern with the exhaustion of resources set him apart from early conservationists, George's insistence that nature was a key part of the story of inequality marked subsequent environmental thought, inflecting conservation with an awareness of the power of markets, a deeply anti-monopolist strain, and a concern for the alienation of urbanites from the rhythms of the non-human world (Sachs 2013, 225–227, 279–281; Johnson 2017, 33–37; Tyrell 1999, 37–39).

Placing American developments in a transnational context is another way in which recent works have brought environmental studies closer to mainstream historiographical trends. The rise of a corporate, industrial economy in the late nineteenth-century United States was part of global processes of industrial development, capital accumulation, and resource extraction. Environmental historians have begun to explore the global entanglements of the United States, particularly the world circulation of ideas about nature and reform as well as how Americans transformed the non-human world outside of the territorial bounds of the United States.

Daniel Rodgers' *Atlantic Crossings: Social Politics in a Progressive Age* (1998) convincingly established the extent to which Progressivism in the United States was born out of deep contact between American reformers and academics and activists on the other side of the Atlantic. The "dramatic expansion of the social landscapes of industrial capitalism" and "new understanding of common histories" made municipal regulations, academic critiques of laissez-faire, experiments with social insurance, and other programs, especially in England and Germany, seem pressingly relevant for American conditions (Rodgers 1998, 33, 77, 133, 216). Rodgers had little to say about environmental politics, outside of the question of urban parks, but his demonstration of the transnational aspects of Progressivism and his emphasis on dealing with the consequences of industrial landscapes opened the way for transnational accounts of conservation.

Ian Tyrrell was a trailblazer in this field, showing by example how environmental historians could escape the prison of the nation-state. In *True Gardens of the Gods: California-Australian Environmental Reform, 1860 –1930* (1999), he argued that "Australians and Californians swapped ideas, plants, insects, personnel, technology, and dreams, and they created in the process an environmental exchange that transcended national boundaries of American or Australian history" (Tyrrell 1999, 6). Even apart from the ways in which it centered this exchange rather than the autochthonous development of environmental sensibilities, Tyrrell's analysis was important for the ways in which it captured the breadth and complexity of American environmental reform. He showed, for example, that irrigation agriculture reflected a "preference for a broader and more equitable distribution of wealth, for the shoring up of rural communities against the attractions of the city, and the defense of the Anglo-Saxon race against the threats of Asian and other 'servile' labor." This "popular crusade to create a middle-class utopia" gained deep appeal across wide portions of the Anglo world (Tyrrell 1999, 103).

Richard Tucker explored the material side of transnational US environmental history in his *Insatiable Appetite: The United States and the Ecological Degradation of the Tropical World* (2000). He analyzed the consequences of American consumption of such commodities as coffee, fruit, sugar, and beef from the 1890s to the 1960s, both in outright US possessions such as the Philippines and Hawaii, but also in the much larger informal empire of the dollar throughout Latin America and much of Malaysia and Indonesia. Tucker showed the connections between the more familiar story of US client states and dollar diplomacy with what he described as the "devastating" impacts of export monocultures on tropical environments. Moreover, this commodity production displaced small landholders, especially indigenous peasants. Social and environmental degradation went hand in hand. In *Banana Cultures: Agriculture, Consumption, and*

Environmental Change in Honduras and the United States (2005), John Soluri focused on the consumer side of this equation in his study of bananas, whose consumption exceeded an astonishing 20 pounds per capita by 1913. Soluri treated bananas as material objects whose production brought environmental consequences, but he also depicted them as cultural productions whose marketing served to encourage American tropical tourism along the very rail and steamship lines that brought bananas to the states.

If eating bananas connected Americans to other places, then so too in a different way did waging war. Edmund Russell shows how World War I was a catalyst for the development of insecticides and other agricultural chemicals that would remake agriculture in the decades ahead (Russell 2001). The United States became an empire in the GAPE, and together these studies suggest that this empire can be studied for its ecological as well as its cultural, economic, and military dimensions.

The transnational turn has prompted fruitful revisiting of classic figures in environmental politics of the GAPE. Donald Worster, one of the founders of environmental history as a self-conscious field, went to considerable lengths to place John Muir in a broad, rather than purely American context, in *A Passion for Nature: The Life of John Muir* (2008). Seeing beyond the encounter with North America's wilds and the American intellectual tradition of Transcendentalism, Worster argued that the "deepest cultural origins" of conservation "lie in the late 18th and early 19th century-revolution that introduced modern liberal democratic ideals, including the quest for human rights, personal liberty, and social equality." Where William Cronon saw the appreciation of wilderness as an inherently contradictory retreat from society, Worster framed it as a logical extension of liberal thought, writing that "the movement did not stop with the concept of social justice but continued on toward the rediscovery of nature, the appreciation of wildness, and the vision of a green society" (Worster 2008, 6).

Worster's book suggested some of the ways in which intellectual histories of American environmental thought might escape the trap of American exceptionalism. But in other ways his depiction of Muir perpetuated the isolation of environmental history from the wider study of the period. He was not above criticizing Muir, but he neither did he deign to discuss the impact of wildlands preservation on Indians or other rural people. Moreover, he insisted that conservation and Progressivism were quite distinct movements (Worster 2008, 344). In contrast, Ian Tyrrell placed conservation at the heart of a Progressivism very much bound up with global developments. In *Crisis of the Wasteful Nation: Empire and Conservation in Theodore Roosevelt's America* (2015), he argued that President Theodore Roosevelt's diverse conservation initiatives were born out of the global geopolitical situation at the turn of the century, in which the United States was a budding empire whose accesses to resources at home and abroad would be a factor in its struggle for world preeminence.

As Gifford Pinchot gushed of Philippine forests, "We are going to have in the islands one of the most productive forest regions of the globe, both for our own markets and for all of the markets of the east, all of it conserved by practical forestry" (quoted in Tyrrell 2015, 64). Tyrrell paid some attention to the transnational circulation of ideas about nature, parks, and conservation. As in Daniel Rodgers' work, some of this circulation was transatlantic, with European and American ornithological associations and foresters learning from one another, but Tyrrell also emphasized the importance of Australasian and British Indian experiments on US practices. Perhaps the most ambitious of Tyrrell's arguments was his insistence on seeing such developments as irrigation, the creation of the national forests, and concerns about the health and vigor of Americans as all being bound up with the question of US power on the world stage. Conceptualizing the mainland territory of the US as an "*inland empire* to complement the external one" in the Caribbean and Philippines, Tyrrell argued that "because the United States was a late-comer to the worldwide scramble for colonies, both preservation and wise use of internal resources through conservation policies became doubly important" (Tyrrell 2015, 14).

In a sense, the location of environmental history within the study of the Gilded Age and Progressive Era has come full circle, back to the ways in which Progressives themselves saw environmental matters, especially environmental politics, as deeply tied to overarching developments such as urbanization, the empowerment and exclusions of gender roles, robust social movements, the expanded powers of the national state, and the United States's empire. Authors penning synthetic treatments of the period as a whole are not likely to relegate environmental developments to the minor roles to which they have been confined in the last few decades. The sustained attention paid to environmental matters by such historians of the period in general as Ian Tyrrell, Brian Balogh, and Bruce Schulman suggests that this process of mainstreaming is well underway (Balogh 2002; Schulman 2005; Tyrrell 2015).

There is another sense in which recent scholarship is a return to the Progressive Era itself. Robert Johnston has argued for a recapturing of the democratic potential of Progressivism (Johnston 2002). The blend of critique and rehabilitation in recent work on GAPE environmental politics has gone a long way for doing this for environmental reform. Americans today can learn from both the shortcomings and accomplishments of this period of environmental reform.

References

Armitage, Kevin. 2010. *The Nature Study Movement: The Forgotten Popularizer of America's Conservation Ethic.* Lawrence: University Press of Kansas.

Balogh, Brian. 2002. "Scientific Forestry and the Roots of the American State: Gifford Pinchot's Path to Progressive Reform," *Environmental History* 7:198–225.

Bates, J. Leonard. 1957. "Fulfilling American Democracy: The Conservation Movement, 1907 to 1921," *Mississippi Valley Historical Review* 44: 29–57.

Bederman, Gail. 1995. *Manliness and Civilization: A Cultural History of Gender and Race in the United States, 1880–1917.* Chicago: University of Chicago Press.

Brechin, Gray. 1996. "Conserving the Race: Natural Aristocracies, Eugenics, and the Conservation Movement." *Antipode* 28: 229–245.

Cohen, Michael P. 1984. *The Pathless Way: John Muir and American Wilderness.* Madison: University of Wisconsin Press.

Cronon, William. 1983. *Changes in the Land: Indians, Colonists, and the Ecology of New England.* New York: Hill and Wang.

—. 1991. *Nature's Metropolis: Chicago and the Great West.* New York: W.W. Norton.

—. 1995. "The Trouble with Wilderness; or, Getting Back to the Wrong Nature," in *Uncommon Ground: Toward Reinventing Nature*, ed. William Cronon, 69–90. New York: W.W. Norton.

Crosby, Alfred. 1973. *The Columbian Exchange: Biological and Cultural Consequences of 1492.* Westport, CT: Greenwood.

Dawley, Alan. 2003. *Changing the World: American Progressives in War and Revolution.* Princeton, NJ: Princeton University Press.

Des Jardins, Julie. 2010. *The Madam Curie Complex: The Hidden History of Women in Science.* New York: City University Press.

Benjamin DeWitt, 1915. *The Progressive Movement: A Non-Partisan, Comprehensive Discussion of Current Tendencies in American Politics.* New York: Macmillan.

Edwards, Rebecca. 2006. *New Spirits: Americans in the Gilded Age: 1865–1905.* New York: Oxford University Press.

Richard Ely, et al. 1917. *The Foundations of National Prosperity: Studies in the Conservation of Permanent National Resources.* New York: MacMillan.

Farmer, Jared. 2013. *Trees in Paradise: A California History.* New York: W.W. Norton.

Flanagan, Maureen. 2007. *America Reformed: Progressives and Progressivism, 1890s–1920s.* New York: Oxford University Press.

Flores, Dan. 1991. "Bison ecology and bison diplomacy: The southern plains from 1800 to 1850," *Journal of American History* 78, 2: 465–485.

Fox, Stephen. 1981. *John Muir and His Legacy: The American Conservation Movement.* Boston: Little, Brown and Co.

Franklin, Kay and Norman Schaeffer, 1983. *Duel for the Dunes: Land Use Conflict on the Shores of Lake Michigan.* Urbana: University of Illinois Press.

Gottlieb, Robert. 1993. *Forcing the Spring: The Transformation of the American Environmental Movement.* Washington, DC: Island Press.

Grant, Madison. 1916. *The Passing of the Great Race; or, The Racial Basis of European History.* New York: Scribner's.

Grese, Robert. 2000. "Jens Jensen: the Landscape Architect as Conservationist." In *Midwestern Landscape Architecture*, ed. William H. Tishler, 117–141. Urbana: University of Illinois Press.

Hays, Samuel P. 1959. *Conservation and the Gospel of Efficiency.* Cambridge, MA: Harvard University Press.

Hofstadter, Richard. 1955. *The Age of Reform: From Bryan to F.D.R.* New York: Knopf.

Hornaday, William Temple. 1914. *Wild Life Conservation in Theory and Practice: Lectures Delivered Before the Forest School of Yale University.* New Haven, CT: Yale University Press.

Hou, Shen. 2013. *The City Natural: Garden and Forest Magazine and the Rise of American Environmentalism.* Pittsburgh, PA: University of Pittsburgh Press.

Isenberg, Andrew C. 1999. *The Destruction of the Bison: An Environmental History, 1750–1920.* Cambridge: Cambridge University Press.

Jacoby, Karl. 2001. *Crimes against Nature: Squatters, Poachers, Thieves, and the Hidden History of American Conservation.* Berkeley: University of California Press.

Johnson, Benjamin. 2017. *Escaping the Dark, Gray City: Fear and Hope in Progressive Era Conservation.* New Haven, CT: Yale University Press.

Johnston, Robert D. 1998. "Beyond 'The West': Regionalism, Liberalism, and the Evasion of Politics in the New Western History." *Rethinking History* 2: 239–277.

—. 2002. "Re-Democratizing the Progressive Era: The Politics of Progressive Era Political Historiography." *Journal of the Gilded Age and Progressive Era* 1: 68–92.

Jordan, Ben. 2010. "'Conservation of Boyhood': Boy Scouting's Modest Manliness and Natural Conservation, 1910–1930." *Environmental History* 15: 612–642.

Judd, Richard W. 1997. *Common Lands, Common People: The Origins of Conservation in Northern New England.* Cambridge, MA: Harvard University Press.

Klingle, Matthew W. 2007. *Emerald City: An Environmental History of Seattle.* New Haven, CT: Yale University Press.

Kolko, Gabriel. 1963. *The Triumph of Conservatism; a Re-interpretation of American History, 1900–1916.* New York: Free Press.

Langston, Nancy. 1995. *Forest Dreams, Forest Nightmares: The Paradox of Old Growth in the Inland West.* Seattle: University of Washington Press.

Lansing, Michael J. 2009. "'Salvaging the Man Power of America': Conservation, Manhood, and Disabled Veterans during World War I." *Environmental History* 14: 32–57.

Lears, T.J. Jackson. 2009. *Rebirth of a Nation: The Making of Modern America, 1877–1920.* New York: Harper Perennial.

Maher, Neil M. 2010. "Body Counts: Tracking the Human Body through Environmental History." In *A Companion to American Environmental History*, ed. Douglas Sackman, 163–179. Oxford: Wiley-Blackwell.

McGerr, Michael. 2003. *A Fierce Discontent: The Rise and Fall of the Progressive Movement in America, 1870–1920.* New York: Free Press.

Melosi, Martin V. 1981. *Garbage in the Cities: Refuse, Reform, and the Environment: 1880–1980.* College Station: Texas A & M Press.

Merchant, Carolyn. 1982. *The Death of Nature: Women, Ecology, and the Scientific Revolution.* San Francisco: Harper.

—. 1984. "Women of the Progressive Conservation Movement, 1900–1916." *Environmental Review* 8: 55–85.

—. 1989. *Ecological Revolutions: Nature, Gender, and Science in New England.* Chapel Hill: University of North Carolina Press.

—. 2010. "George Bird Grinnell's Audubon Society: Bridging the Gender Divide in Conservation." *Environmental History.* 15: 3–30.

Miller, Char. 2001. *Gifford Pinchot and the Making of Modern Environmentalism.* Washington, DC: Island Press.

Mitman, Greg. 2008. *Breathing Space: How Allergies Shape Our Lives and Landscapes.* New Haven, CT: Yale University Press.

Nash, Linda. 2006. *Inescapable Ecologies: A History of Environment, Disease, and Knowledge*. Berkeley: University of California Press.

Nash, Rod. 1967. *Wilderness and the American Mind*. New Haven, CT: Yale University Press.

Orsi, Jared. 2004. *Hazardous Metropolis:* Flooding and Urban Ecology in Los Angeles. Berkeley: University of California Press.

Platt, Harold. 2005. *Shock Cities: The Environmental Transformation and Reform of Manchester and Chicago*. Chicago: University of Chicago Press.

Price, Jennifer. 1999. *Flight Maps: Adventures with Nature in Modern America*. New York: Basic Books.

Pyne, Stephen J. 1982. *Fire in America: A Cultural History of Wildland and Rural Fire*. Princeton, NJ: Princeton University Press, 1982.

Rauchway, Eric. 2003. *Murdering McKinley: The Making of Theodore Roosevelt's America*. New York: Hill and Wang.

Rawson, Michael. 2010. *Eden on the Charles: The Making of Boston*. Cambridge, MA: Harvard University Press.

Rimby, Susan. 2005. "'Better Housekeeping Out of Doors': Myra Lloyd Dock, the State Federation of Pennsylvania Women, and Progressive Era Conservation." *Journal of Women's History* 17: 9–34.

—. 2012. *Mira Lloyd Dock and the Progressive Era Conservation Movement*. University Park: Pennsylvania State University Press.

Robbins, William G. 1982. *Lumberjacks and Legislators: Political Economy of the U.S. Lumber Industry, 1890–1941*. College Station: Texas A & M University Press.

Rodgers, Daniel. 1998. *Atlantic Crossings: Social Politics in a Progressive Age*. Cambridge, MA: Harvard University Press.

Rome, Adam. 2006. "'Political Hermaphrodites': Gender and Environmental Reform in Progressive America." *Environmental History* 11: 440–463.

Runte, Alfred. 1979. *National Parks: The American Experience*. Lincoln: University of Nebraska Press.

Russell, Edmund. 2001. *War and Nature: Fighting Humans and Insects with Chemicals from World War I to Silent Spring*. Cambridge: Cambridge University Press.

Sachs, Aaron. 2013. *Arcadian America: The Death and Life of an Environmental Tradition*. New Haven, CT: Yale University Press.

Schrepfer, Susan R. 1983. *The Fight to Save the Redwoods: A History of Environmental Reform, 1917–1978*. Madison: University of Wisconsin Press.

Schulman, Bruce. 2005. "Governing Nature, Nurturing Government: Resource Management and the Development of the American State, 1900–1912," *Journal of Policy History* 17, 4: 375–403.

Searle, R. Newall. 1977. *Saving Quetico–Superior: A Land Set Apart*. St. Paul: Minnesota Historical Society Press.

Sellers, Christopher. 1997. *Hazards of the Job: From Industrial Disease to Environmental Health Science*. Chapel Hill: University of North Carolina Press.

Smalley, Andrea. 2005. "'Our Lady Sportsmen': Gender, Class, and Conservation in Sport Hunting Magazines, 1873–1920." *Journal of the Gilded Age and Progressive Era* 4: 355–380.

Soluri, John. 2006. *Banana Cultures: Agriculture, Consumption, and Environmental Change in Honduras and the United States*. Austin: University of Texas Press.

Spence, Mark David. 1999. *Dispossessing the Wilderness: Indian Removal and the Making of the National Parks*. New York: Oxford University Press.

Spiro, Jonathan Peter. 2009. *Defending the Master Race: Conservation, Eugenics, and the Legacy of Madison Grant*. Burlington: University of Vermont Press.

Stradling, David. 1999. *Smokestacks and Progressives: Environmentalists, Engineers, and Air Quality in America, 1881—1951*. Baltimore, MD: Johns Hopkins University Press.

Stern, Alexandra. 2005. *Eugenic Nation: Faults and Frontiers of Better Breeding in Modern America*. Berkeley: University of California Press.

Stroud, Ellen. 2012. *Nature Next Door: Cities and Trees in the American Northeast*. Seattle: University of Washington Press.

Taylor, Joseph E., III. 1999. *Making Salmon: An Environmental History of the Northwest Fisheries Crisis*. Seattle: University of Washington Press.

Tucker, Richard P. 2000. *Insatiable Appetite: The United States and the Ecological Degradation of the Tropical World*. Berkeley: University of California Press.

Tyrrell, Ian. 1999. *True Gardens of the Gods: Californian–Australian Environmental Reform, 1860–1930*. Berkeley: University of California Press.

—. 2015. *Crisis of the Wasteful Nation: Empire and Conservation in Theodore Roosevelt's America*. Chicago: University of Chicago Press.

Unger, Nancy C. 2012. *Beyond Nature's Housekeepers: American Women in Environmental History*. New York: Oxford University Press.

Warren, Louis. 1997. *The Hunter's Game: Poachers and Conservationists in Twentieth-Century America*. New Haven, CT: Yale University Press.

Weinstein, James. 1968. *The Corporate Ideal in the Liberal State, 1900–1918*. Boston: Beacon.

Webb, Walter Prescott. 1931. *The Great Plains*. Boston: Ginn and Company.

West, Elliott. 1998. *The Contested Plains: Indians, Goldseekers, and the Rush to Colorado*. Lawrence: University of Kansas Press.

White, Richard. 1985. "American Environmental History: The Development of a New Historical Field." *Pacific Historical Review* 54: 297–335.

Wiebe, Robert. 1967. *The Search for Order, 1877–1920*. New York: Hill and Wang.

Worster, Donald. 1978. *Dust Bowl: The Southern Plains in the 1930s*. New York: Oxford University Press.

—. 2008. *A Passion for Nature: The Life of John Muir*. New York: Oxford University Press.

Young, Terence. 2004. *Building San Francisco's Parks, 1850–1930*. Baltimore, MD: Johns Hopkins University Press.

Further Reading

Isenberg, Andrew C. 2014. *The Oxford Handbook of Environmental History*. New York: Oxford University Press.

Sackman, Douglas Cazaux. 2010. *A Companion to American Environmental History*. Oxford: Wiley-Blackwell.

Scharff, Virginia, ed. 2003. *Seeing Nature through Gender*. Lawrence: University Press of Kansas.

Sutter, Paul, et al. 2013. "The World with Us: The State of American Environmental History." *Journal of American History* 100: 94–120.

Part II

Sex, Race, and Gender

Chapter Seven

Gender

Kimberly A. Hamlin

Popular Culture

If asked to select images to represent popular ideas about gender in the Gilded Age and Progressive Era (GAPE), many historians might suggest the attractive, sporty Gibson Girls and the macho Rough Rider ideal personified by Theodore Roosevelt. Named for their creator, Charles Dana Gibson, Gibson Girl illustrations appeared in countless periodicals and adorned many popular consumer products from the 1890s through the 1910s. Gibson Girls showed Americans what it meant to dress stylishly, go on co-ed excursions, and be "modern" (see Figure 7.1). By doing many of the same things that men did—climb mountains, ride bicycles, go to college—but in distinctly feminine ways, Gibson Girls provided a mainstream, politically non-threatening version of modern womanhood compared to that represented by suffragists and working women. The men epitomized by Roosevelt's Rough Rider military outdoorsman, on the other hand, combined a working man's virility with elite access to power in promotion of patriarchy in the home, nationally, and globally (see Figure 7.2). In many ways, these two gender ideals complemented each other: Gibson Girls could be fun companions to Roosevelt's strenuous men without challenging any of the underlying assumptions about race, class, or male privilege that constituted the Rough Rider ideal.

In the decades following the Civil War, women and men increasingly participated in similar activities, engaged with similar issues, and populated similar places. Historians celebrate women's entry into higher education, reform work, and the professions during the GAPE. Some even conclude, in the words of Rebecca Edwards, that after the Civil War "the idea of 'separate spheres' for men and women began to fade" (Edwards 2011, 4). The very busy Gibson Girls testify to the erosion of a separate sphere for women. Other GAPE scholars critique the separate spheres analogy, at least as it applied to the turn of the twentieth century, for failing to represent the real ways actual men and women lived their lives, generally together. As Elisabeth Israels Perry and others have persuasively argued, "women often functioned in the same sphere as men" (Perry 2002, 48). Indeed they did.

This chapter suggests, however, that a new regime of gender policing took the place of separate spheres during the GAPE. Yes, women did many things in the GAPE that were previously reserved for men (attending college, working outside the home, speaking in public), fundamentally disrupting the notion that there were separate spheres for men and women. But the ways in which women were allowed access to these new activities often served to bolster old ideas about the fundamental differences between men and women, to further entrench the gender binary, and to extend gendered standards to previously ungendered aspects of life. Activities that were previously all-male or gender-neutral—from leisure to education to labor—developed separate gendered standards for men and for women, just as the sexes were further polarized visually by the growing acceptance of makeup for women and the decreasing tolerance for women's facial and body hair. At the same time, people also began to accept the new idea that a strict gender binary mapped neatly onto a sexual one. Feminine women were, the thinking went, "naturally" attracted to masculine men, and vice versa.

To the two binary depictions of gender ideology epitomized by Gibson Girls and Rough Riders, the addition of a third, more nuanced visual illustrates how some of these gendered changes became normalized during the GAPE: the bearded woman. In 1877, a young woman named Viola M. confounded the medical community (see Figure 7.3). Despite the fact that she was a married mother of two whose character was "strictly womanly" and whose tastes were

A Companion to the Gilded Age and Progressive Era, First Edition. Edited by Christopher McKnight Nichols and Nancy C. Unger.
© 2017 John Wiley & Sons, Inc. Published 2017 by John Wiley & Sons, Inc.

Figure 7.1 "Picturesque America, anywhere in the mountains." Source: Charles Dana Gibson, 1900, Cabinet of American illustration, Prints and Photographs Division (LC-DIG-cai-2a12817).

Figure 7.2 Theodore Roosevelt in 1885. Source: Photo by George Grantham Bain, Library of Congress Prints and Photographs Division (LC-DIG-ppmsca-35995).

Figure 7.3 Portrait of Viola M., Frontispiece, "Case of a Bearded Woman". Source: by Louis A. Duhring, *Archives of Dermatology* 3 (1877).Copy residing at the Boston Medical Library in the Francis A. Countway Library of Medicine, Harvard Medical School.

"remarkably feminine and domestic," Viola's face and neck were covered in thick coarse hair. This visual conundrum fascinated doctors and medical students. Was she a woman? Could a real woman have a beard? Viola's quest for answers led her to leading dermatologist Dr. Louis Duhring, who published a lengthy case study about her (excerpts of which were included in medical textbooks for decades) called "The Case of a Bearded Woman." He also exhibited her to his dermatological students at the University of Pennsylvania Medical School. Duhring tentatively concluded that Viola M. was indeed a woman who suffered from "hypertrichosis," the devastating new disease of superfluous hair in women. Between the 1870s and the 1920s thousands of women across the nation with symptoms far milder than Viola's were treated for hypertrichosis.

At the same time that doctors pondered the significance of superfluous hair in women, men and women across the country flocked to see bearded ladies on display at the circus. Questions of sex and racial difference provided the appeal of the exhibits. Were bearded ladies women, or men in disguise? Could a man truly love a bearded lady? Countless jokes about bearded ladies appeared in newspapers from coast to coast, with punchlines suggesting that the bearded lady was really a man and that the husband had been duped, testifying to the close links between the histories of gender and sexuality. While most bearded ladies were women, part of their allure was that they blurred gender boundaries and presented viewers with the potential thrill of transgression and perhaps illicit sex. Likewise, while bearded white women were generally assumed to be human (but not necessarily female), bearded women of color were often described as troubling another boundary: the one supposedly separating humans from animals. The most popular bearded lady from the 1880s until her death in 1925 was Krao, who was first exhibited as "Darwin's Missing Link." Audiences claimed to marvel as they watched her progress from animal-like beginnings in her native Laos to cultured East Coast civilization (Hamlin 2011).

Women, obviously, did not suddenly sprout facial hair in the 1870s, but the meaning of facial hair on women changed markedly in the GAPE. Earlier in the nineteenth century, facial hair on women had been considered unfortunate but generally inevitable. *Godey's Lady's Book*, for example, advised readers to simply leave unwanted hair untouched. But after 1870, the gender binary hardened, leaving little tolerance for boundary-blurring or questionable cases. Bearded women offer some possible insight as to how and why the gender binary solidified and metastasized during the GAPE. As Viola M. and Krao demonstrate, one's looks became central to gender determination, and the emerging mass culture widely popularized acceptable appearances. Science rivaled popular culture in setting the standards for appropriate gender presentation and often classified these boundaries as "natural." At the same time, the varied responses to Viola M., Krao, and their bearded sisters delineate more precisely the ways in which race and class determined individual perceptions and performances of gender and the ways in which individuals resisted these new strict gender standards. The many nuances and boundary-blurring qualities of bearded women suggest new avenues and intersections for the already rich study of gender in the GAPE.

GAPE historians have modeled for the larger field of history how to analyze an era from the perspective of gender, especially masculinity. Indeed, scholars have established that the concept of "gender" as it is understood today was created during the GAPE. This chapter focuses on GAPE scholarship explicitly about gender, which sometimes includes scholarship on women and sometimes does not. It also suggests ways to better synthesize the histories of women, gender, and sexuality. Drawing on a wide variety of GAPE scholarship, it analyzes masculinity and femininity in concert; supports the contention that daily life became increasingly bifurcated according to gender during the GAPE by paying particular attention to work on politics, reform, labor, education, leisure, and beauty culture; and, drawing on the many unresolved issues presented by bearded women, suggests several areas for future research on gender in the GAPE.

Politics and Gender

Motivated by feminist concerns about the lack of inroads women's history had made toward transforming standard historical narratives, Joan Scott inaugurated the field of gender history in the late 1980s (Scott 1986, 1988). Then, an interesting thing happened throughout much of the 1990s: gender history initially focused on investigating masculinity (Carnes and Griffen 1990, to give just one example). In 1993, Anthony Rotundo helped cement this emphasis with the publication of *American Manhood: Transformations in Masculinity from the Revolution to the Modern Era*, which traces changing conceptions of masculinity using an innovative blend of private and public sources. In the nineteenth century, Rotundo persuasively argues, manhood underwent a transformation resulting from the growth of industrial capitalism and changing labor patterns. In the early republic, manhood was assessed according to one's standing in the community and one's personal probity. By the end of the nineteenth century being a man involved displaying outward signs of machismo, strength, and aggression.

Following this model, historians of gender debated to what extent ideas about gender were internalized and to what extent they were performative, as well as the extent to which gender ideologies were (and are) defined by race, class, and region. By providing close analysis of four leading GAPE figures—Ida B. Wells-Barnett, G. Stanley Hall, Charlotte Perkins Gilman, and Theodore Roosevelt—Gail Bederman's *Manliness and Civilization: A Cultural History of Gender and Race in the United States, 1880–1917* (1995) serves as a powerful reminder that ideas about gender have always been highly contingent on race. A sub-theme of Bederman's work is that mass media and popular culture, including *National Geographic* magazine, helped shape and spread these new masculine ideals.

The role of gender in US domestic politics has been the topic of much analysis by GAPE historians, though no consensus has emerged regarding either the definition of "gender" or the definition of "politics." Some use gender almost as a synonym for women, or for the fact that women and men both engaged in politics; others use gender as a "category of analysis," according to Joan Scott's classic formulation (Scott 1986). Michael Lewis Goldberg's *An Army of Women: Gender and Politics in Gilded Age Kansas* (1997) exemplifies the former method, providing an in-depth account of women's and populist activism in Kansas. Applying the gender-as-a-category-of-analysis method, Kevin P. Murphy's *Political Manhood: Red Bloods, Mollycoddles, & the Politics of Progressive Era Reform* (2008) analyzes the ways in which Roosevelt's strenuous version of political manhood triumphed over other expressions of manly activism. This book also models the rich analysis that can result from studying gender and sexuality in concert. As Murphy establishes, virile heterosexuality was a key component of being a "Red Blood," while charges of homosexuality were often lobbed at "mollycoddles."

Historical scholarship on Theodore Roosevelt demonstrates, among other things, the tension between gender history as the comparative study of men's and women's activities and gender history as probing the meanings of masculinity and femininity in relation to larger power structures and historical trends. In this volume, Kathleen Dalton (Chapter 23) encourages close attention to Roosevelt's actions in support of women's suffrage and his creation of a "Female Brain Trust." Other scholars, including Bederman and Sarah Watts (2006), focus their analysis on the hypermasculinity expressed through Roosevelt's highly crafted public persona and its implications for domestic and foreign policy.

Regardless of one's opinion on the manliness of Roosevelt, he clearly represents a "cult of masculinity" that powerfully shaped US domestic and foreign policy at the turn of the twentieth century. This line of analysis is best exemplified by Kristin Hoganson's pathbreaking *Fighting for American Manhood: How Gender Politics Provoked the Spanish–American and Philippine–American Wars* (1998). Laura Briggs builds on this with an examination of the role of gender in the US involvement in Puerto Rico (2002), and Sarah J. Moore explores how manliness was deployed in the service of US imperialism and exceptionalism at the 1915 Panama–Pacific Exposition (2013). In her fascinating study of Clemencia López, a Filipina activist, Laura Prieto details what it was like to be on the receiving end of this macho US imperialism and how resisters, too, deployed gender (Prieto 2013). Prieto contends that Americans who encountered López on her journey to the United States in support of Philippine independence were open to her message largely because, as she was a woman, they did not consider her message to be "political."

Historically, many GAPE scholars have taken a narrow definition of politics—often focusing on elections and elected officials— which tends to exclude women and their activities. Other scholars have maintained that this definition is inherently masculine and urged a reconsidered of "politics" to include social reform. Paula Baker's classic study "The Domestication of Politics: Women and American Political Society, 1780–1920" (1984) argued that two political cultures operated throughout the nineteenth century—a female system based on the continued expansion of domestic concerns into society through social policy and volunteerism, and a male one centered around electoral politics. She further contended that definitions of "politics" should include both formal and informal means of activism. Building on Baker, Anne Firor Scott suggested that women "invented Progressivism" through the women's club movement (Scott 1991). While these works permanently altered historical scholarship on the era, some scholars have questioned the extent to which Baker and Scott's articulation of the "municipal housekeeping" model of women's activism has limited historical understanding of women's contributions. As Elisabeth Israels Perry suggests, this critique is partly related to more recent historians' tendency to focus on Progressive reform efforts that used the language of "municipal housekeeping" over those that did not (e.g. moral reforms) and to conflate all female activism under the "municipal housekeeping" umbrella (Perry 2002).

Rebecca Edwards contends that, before 1890, she found "no evidence of a separate 'women's political culture' in the Gilded Age." Rather, she found "women who enlisted in a variety of political projects—even the most radical suffragists—repeatedly worked through party mechanisms and cooperated with male allies who shared their views." After 1890, however, Edwards concedes that such alliances broke down as a result of women's "disillusionment and exclusion" (Edwards 1997, 8). In part the debate about women's political culture also invokes the periodization question with which scholars of the GAPE have wrestled in the pages of the *Journal of the Gilded Age and Progressive Era* since the journal's inception in 2002. When did the Progressive Era begin, and when did it end? How one answers these questions impacts how one defines the era's politics and the role of gender within it.

Focusing on the years 1900 through 1920, Kathryn Kish Sklar has argued powerfully for the existence of two political cultures. In comparing the activities and priorities of the National Consumers League (NCL) led by Florence Kelley and the American Association for Labor Legislation (AALL) led by John Commons, Sklar found that "because they were differently situated in the polity, women and men reformers in the NCL and the AALL promoted social change in different ways" (Sklar 1995, 37).

State and regional studies also tend to support the thesis that if cross-gender reformist collaboration existed, it became increasingly fraught by 1900. Michael Lewis Goldberg's study of the women's and populist movements in Kansas supports Baker's original claim for two separate political cultures (Goldberg 1997). Likewise, John Putnam's *Class and Gender Politics in Progressive-Era Seattle* demonstrates how working-class women, through the Women's Card and Label League, "facilitated, if only temporarily, the formation of cross-class and cross-gender political alliances" (Putnam 2008, 2). By World War I, class conflict had soured relations between labor and middle-class feminists as middle-class women and men united against Communism and as labor activists became increasingly militant.

An influential subset of GAPE scholarship has addressed gender and the environmental movement. Again, as Perry persuasively argues, definitional questions frame the debate: what counts as the environmental movement? The efforts, led by men, to create the National Park system and preserve vast tracts of land in the West? What about the movement for clean water and urban parks, led mainly by women (Perry 2002)? Scholars also debate whether or not men and women worked together toward shared goals or along separate male–female tracks. Carolyn Merchant has suggested that men and women worked together in the Audubon Society (Merchant 2010). In *Beyond Nature's Housekeepers*, Nancy C. Unger disputes this claim, noting that "although men and women worked together between 1880 and 1905 to form Audubon societies and to pass legislation to preserve avifauna, this bridging of the gendered divide proved temporary." Moreover, Unger argues that the Audubon Society was an outlier within the environmental movement as a whole (Unger 2012). Similarly, Adam Rome has shown how charges of "effeminacy" broke down the male–female working relationship and limited the environmental agenda (Rome 2006). Regardless of the extent to which men and women worked together in support of individual environmental reforms, it is clear that ideas about masculinity and femininity influenced their relationships and, ultimately, shaped their efforts.

Perhaps the best example of the argument for a redefinition of GAPE "politics" and women's role within it is Glenda Gilmore's *Gender and Jim Crow: Women and the Politics of White Supremacy in North Carolina, 1896–1920* (1996), which rocked the historical profession by establishing the many vital ways that African American women in North Carolina participated in Progressive Era politics and precisely when (and why) white women did and did not work on behalf of white supremacy. Among many pathbreaking arguments, Gilmore established that the definitions of both gender and politics look different depending on race. Another more recent, exemplary study of black women's activism in this era is Lisa Materson's *For the Freedom of Her Race: Black Women and Electoral Politics in Illinois, 1877–1932* (2009).

Inspired by Kimberlé Crenshaw's theory of "intersectionality," GAPE historians have chronicled the ways in which ideas about gender and race inform each other, as well as the distinctive ways in which women and men experience gender according to their race and class. Gilmore, Evelyn Brooks Higginbotham, and others have analyzed the complex interplay between class and gender in the African American community, outlining how gender ideals of the middle class (or as Gilmore points out, "the better classes," was the term of choice) provided a means by which African Americans were judged by themselves and others. Politics, too, looks different from this vantage point. Higginbotham documents that during the age of disenfranchisement and Jim Crow, the African American church served as a counter-public sphere and that women's church-related and volunteer activities were very much "political" (Higginbotham 1993).

The intersections of gender, race/racism, and politics reach a crescendo in scholarship regarding woman suffrage (a category of Progressive Era reform that Perry rightly notes is still very under-studied). Led by Louise Michele Newman, some scholars contend that the racial ideology of white women activists tainted the entire movement by placing racism at the core of emerging feminist politics (1999). Others, including Michele Mitchell and Ann Douglas, argue that white suffrage activists, especially Elizabeth Cady Stanton, must be considered within their historical context (and that generally, in that context, they cannot be considered "racist") (Mitchell 2007; Douglas 2007). Faye Dudden's careful examination of the division between women's rights activists and abolitionists in debates over the Fourteenth and Fifteenth Amendments provides a crucial starting point for later GAPE discussions of gender, race, and racism within the women's movement (Dudden 2011). Scholarship on African American women activists who worked for suffrage makes painfully clear, however, the extent to which the larger suffrage movement excluded women of color and the baneful effects this had on long-term cross-racial collaboration among women (Painter 1996; Schechter 2001).

Whether or not one believes there were two political cultures separated by sex, it is hard to argue that GAPE political and reform work was not sex-segregated and gender-based, even if men and women often worked together on individual initiatives. Indeed, the very names of the largest reform groups, the Young Men's Christian Association (YMCA), the Young Women's Christian Association (YWCA), and the Woman's Christian Temperance Union (WCTU), emphasize how activists organized and conceptualized themselves according to sex. Scholars have debated the extent to which some of these groups, especially the WCTU, deployed a covert (perhaps even subconscious) feminist agenda. Nevertheless, their activities and public rhetoric stressed the increasing importance of adhering to gender binarism in the GAPE.

Overall, the earlier scholarly consensus that men and women had different reformist visions from the 1870s onward has given way to a more nuanced consensus that men and women worked together, at least occasionally, toward similar ends. Many such cross-gender collaborations fell apart by 1900, however, as reform work became gendered "female" and political activism/government employment "male," and as labor activism became more militant and less interested in social reform (Flanagan 2006). As Robin Muncy has shown, by the early 1900s, the only "manly" reform was "trustbusting," because this involved doing battle against powerful corporations and engaging in debates about what sort of man could best lead the nation (Muncy 1997). Likewise, by the early twentieth century, Theodore Roosevelt and his disciples chided men involved in all aspects of reform work as effeminate "mollycoddles" in contrast to "real" men who entered the manly arenas of politics and war (Murphy 2008). At the same time, women reformers were consigned to remain volunteers rather than employees of new Progressive Era government posts, as Jessica Pliley shows in her study of the short-lived experiment to hire female boarding inspectors at Ellis Island (Pliley 2013).

These and other groundbreaking works on gender and politics in the GAPE reveal that gendered rhetoric and practices undergirded America's two-party system as well as the many Progressive Era reforms; that the desire to foster virile, white, manly men informed America's decisions to enter into war with Spain and the Philippines; that ideas about femininity and masculinity are interconnected with and inseparable from ideas about race and class; and that individual men and women imbued ideas about gender from popular culture and used popular culture to fashion manlier and womanlier versions of themselves. Ideals of masculinity became both more inflexible and less attainable during the Gilded Age as a result of challenges to traditional male prerogatives such as financial autonomy and unquestioned familial authority. Some of the perceived threats to masculinity had to do with women's encroachment into previously male-only preserves. Threats also came from record economic uncertainty, rising immigration, the unmooring of the traditional extended family structure, and significant changes in labor patterns and opportunities.

Labor and Gender

In the GAPE, women entered labor and professional spheres formerly designated as male-only (the converse is not true; the era did not witness a flood of, say, male domestic servants). With women comprising 20% of the paid labor force by 1910, the number of women working for wages had almost tripled since 1870 (Woloch 2011, 216). The vast majority of them worked in exclusively feminine domains, as domestic servants, seamstresses, secretaries, nurses, and teachers. There were virtually no fields in which men and women worked side by side as equals or otherwise. In specialized professions such as law, science, or medicine, women's initial access (1860s–1880s) generally eroded by the end of the century (Drachman 1998; Morantz-Sanchez 2000; Rossiter 1984). Scholars have written volumes about how these fields came to be masculinized and about how difficult it was, and in some cases remains, for women to break into less feminized fields such as engineering, law, and business management. Women's paid labor was, from the start, conceptualized as temporary (before marriage) and/or auxiliary to male labor (providing help to more important male jobs—nurse to doctor, secretary to businessman, lab assistant to scientist), despite the fact that this was often not true in reality. Women seeking careers were most successful in areas deemed feminine because of associations with household issues and/or children, such as social work, domestic science, education, and nursing.

Even corporate practices and spaces were established to mirror the comfortable, idealized gender norms of the middle-class home. As Angel Kwolek- Folland demonstrates in *Engendering Business* (1994), the modern financial corporation attempted to graft separate-spheres ideology into its rapidly growing offices at the turn of the twentieth century. Male clerks gave way to female secretaries, who then became known as "office wives." In 1880 women represented only 5% of stenographers and typists; by 1900 this rose to 77% and by 1930 women held 96% of all stenographer and typist jobs (30). As the gender of the employee shifted, so too did job descriptions. While male clerks were in part apprentices who could imagine one day walking in the boss's shoes, female secretaries assumed an inherently subservient role with little room for promotion. Kwolek-Folland further shows that the financial industry was segregated by race, but that these gendered strictures on office work remained a constant. Women increasingly worked outside the home, but mainly doing womanly jobs in feminine ways.

At the same time, the idea that an essential part of being a successful businessman was being manly was impressed upon aspiring executives who subscribed to the new business periodicals and success manuals (Hilkey 1997). *System* magazine, for example, featured articles exhorting the importance of manliness in business and regularly ran a discomfiting ad for the American School of Correspondence asking, "How big a man are you?" (Kasson 2001). Indeed, as Jon Kasson has so vividly established, it was writing for such publications that inspired Edgar Rice Burroughs to leave the corporate world behind for the jungle in his creation of *Tarzan* (Kasson 2001). At least in the jungle a man could be autonomous. The very structure of the corporate office tower also served to remind observers that to be successful one had to be manly. Famed Chicago architect and creator of the modern skyscraper, Louis Sullivan, called for "manliness" in commercial design (Edwards 2010, 75–76).

Although during the GAPE women entered the professional labor force in record numbers, signaling the demise of separate spheres (if in fact these spheres ever existed), nearly everything about paid labor became increasingly gendered, from the task one did to the clothes one wore to the building in which one worked.

The gendering of labor was true of manual labor as well as the professions. Working- class women faced even stricter sex segregation and had fewer resources to fight unfair and dangerous policies than did middle-class women. Typically consigned to low-paying jobs men would not do (more women were employed as domestic servants than any other job), working-class women were generally excluded from unions, relegated to separate female auxiliaries, or not organized at all (Kessler-Harris 1982, 2003; Weiner 1985; Baron, ed. 1991; Vapnek 2009; Boris 1994). Many historians have claimed that the supposed manliness and physical strength required of working-class men helped to trigger a "crisis in masculinity" for middle-class men. African American women, especially those who resisted the social pressure to work as domestic servants for white families, were particularly vulnerable as non-unionized and disenfranchised workers in a segregated system. However, as Jacqueline Jones has established, black women workers regularly, and successfully, engaged in formal and informal acts of resistance, often cleverly using gender as a subterfuge (Jones 1985). In addition to excluding women from unions and barring them from most professions, male workers also employed more insidious discriminatory tactics such as sexual harassment, as Daniel Bender has shown (Bender 2004).

During the Progressive Era, many middle-class women reformers worked to ameliorate immigrant and working-class women's struggles but, as several historians have outlined, reformers' ideas about how to help working-class women were generally based more on middle-class gender ideology than on working women's actual needs [for an excellent illustration of this line of analysis see Peggy Pascoe's *Relations of Rescue* (1990)]. For example, women reformers led the charge for protective legislation for working women—often based on their own gendered ideals about what families should be like and without input from the working women themselves. Successful proposals for labor reforms set limits on the number of hours women could work, and sixteen states prohibited women from working at night (no such laws were passed regulating men's labor). Yet, no states passed legislation to provide high-quality, affordable childcare for workers. Alice Kessler-Harris has called this the "paradox" of labor reforms for women—reformers and lawmakers exhibited tremendous concern for women as potential mothers, but did little to help actual mothers, such as provide maternity leave or child-care (Kessler-Harris 1995, 339).

Debates about protective legislation offer a particularly vivid example of how Americans reconciled the new reality of women working with their ideas about appropriate gender roles. Reformers, labor leaders, and employers (who also often represented the views of mainstream Americans) delineated the bounds of acceptable female labor with the passage of numerous protective labor laws between the 1890s and the 1920s (Lehrer 1987; Woloch 2015; Kessler-Harris 2003). Initially, reformers and labor activists argued that it would be strategically wise to first push for protective laws for women workers (who could deny these?), and later use these victories as a "wedge" to insist on protections for all workers. Opponents argued that labor limits impinged upon individual workers' right to engage in contracts. After the 1908 Supreme Court decision in *Muller v. Oregon* affirmed that "sex is a valid basis for classification," the majority of states enacted protective labor laws for women (Woloch 2011, 240). What tipped the scales in the Court's landmark decision were arguments about mothers. Proponents argued that it was in the state's interest to protect female workers because it was in the state's interest that healthy children be born. The *Muller* decision embedded sex difference into constitutional law and declared that women were, by nature and immutably, dependent upon men. Protective legislation no doubt created safer environments for some women workers but also limited women's ability to form labor unions, precluded women from higher-paying jobs, and did not result in basic workplace safety laws that applied to both men and women. In terms of gender, such laws codified the idea that there was "men's" work and "women's" work, as well as masculine and feminine standards for performing work, and that women's work must be subordinated to women's defining role as mothers (Woloch 2011, 2015). Frustration over expanded options for female employment but constricted notions of gender came to a head in the 1920s in debates over the Equal Rights Amendment.

The overwhelming historical consensus that labor became increasingly gendered during the GAPE could leave the mistaken impression that this development was inevitable, when in fact it was highly constructed through corporate actions, legal decisions, and government policy. From denying women the right to work as immigration inspectors at Ellis Island to refusing to provide public teachers with pensions or workers with affordable child-care, government and industry repeatedly defined paid labor as male (Leroux 2009; Pliley 2013). Gendered conceptions of labor resulted in the passage of protective legislation for women, but not men, and persist in the legacy of New Deal legislation as well as in the persistent struggles working women face with what has come to be called "the second shift" of labor at home on top of full-time paid employment.

Education and Gender

The gendering of labor, both paid and unpaid, was made possible by and in turn fueled the gendering of education, both curricular and extra-curricular. As many historians have noted, women's entry into higher education in the 1870s was one of the most significant and controversial developments of the post-Civil War era. In 1870, women made up 21% of college students; by 1910 this had risen to 40% (Woloch 2011, 272). After the Civil War, the Morrell Act provided vast tracts of public land for the creation of universities in the West. Needing students to fill classrooms, these schools accepted women. At the same time, several prestigious women's colleges opened on the East Coast, most notably the "seven sisters," including Smith, Bryn Mawr, and Vassar, which offered women the standard male curriculum (Horowitz 1993; Hamilton 2004). These developments sparked intense public debate about the appropriateness of female intellectual activity. Doctors and public intellectuals worried that women's education would come at the expense of their reproductive capabilities. As with women's paid labor, a tenuous compromise was reached. It became acceptable for women to attend college as long as they studied feminine subjects, such as the new field of home economics, in feminine ways (Stage and Vincenti 1997; Elias 2008).

Indeed, many Americans came to believe that a key function of education should be the installation of binary gender thinking into young men and women. As the very influential G. Stanley Hall wrote in *Adolescence* (1904), "everything should be welcomed that makes men more manly and women more womanly" (quoted in Edwards 2011, 116). Rebecca Edwards describes how colleges followed Harvard's model and began to emphasize that they were not necessarily out to develop scholars or educated men, but manly men. It was at this same time that the term "masculine" came to be in vogue. Likewise, Daniel A. Clark demonstrates how a college degree, considered in the late nineteenth century to be antithetical to a successful career in business, was refashioned by popular magazines at the turn of the twentieth century as a prerequisite for success—largely by redefining ideal masculinity from self-made man to organization man (Clark 2010). The drive to develop masculine men also led to collegiate support for athletics, especially football. The brutality of today's football pales in comparison with football as practiced in the GAPE. In 1904, for example, twenty-four deaths were reported in college football games (Edwards 2011). Beyond college, the popular fascination with boxing and bodybuilding reinforced the belief that physical activity necessarily promoted masculinity, not health or fitness (Kasson 2001).

Women, too, wanted to participate in these new sporting crazes, especially in collegiate settings. In the 1870s students at Vassar demanded the right to play baseball, but their team was disbanded by end of the decade (Edwards 2011, 114). Instead, women were directed away from team sports and toward non-competitive athletics. Even women's bicycle riding was considered controversial, as doctors warned that sitting atop the seat on a bumpy road might stir a woman's sexual desires (Vertinsky 1994). Women who wanted to ride bicycles were instructed to do so in the "feminine" (and nearly impossible) way, by wearing a dress while riding. Such gendered nonsense was too much even for the otherwise traditional Frances Willard, the powerful president of the WCTU. In 1895, Willard published *A Wheel Within a Wheel: How I Learned to Ride the Bicycle*, to detail how she learned to master her bicycle and celebrate the freedom of movement that doing so gave her.

In keeping with the theme of more possibilities for women but a stricter gender binary, Andrea Smalley has found ample evidence of women in hunting and sporting periodicals including *Field and Stream*, the avatars of civilized masculinity, but these images generally served to make hunting acceptable to mainstream Americans by linking it to the emerging environmental movement. According to Smalley, women were a constant presence in hunting periodicals and sporting life but often "'our lady sportsmen' [provided readers] with an updated and upgraded image of hunting, thus linking the gender- and class-based politics of leisure to environmental policy and use" (Smalley 2005, 357).

At the same time, many new aspects of popular leisure—such as movie theaters, public beaches, amusement parks, and dance halls—opened up to both men and women, but women and men did not experience these developments in the same ways. Tremendous restrictions were placed on women's participation in these new activities—from the length of their bathing suits, to the type of sports in which they could engage, to the ways in which they could dance with men (Kasson 1978; Peiss 1986). Indeed, in the GAPE, public spaces and the built environment shaped, and were shaped by, gendered ideals (Spain, 2002; Deutsch, 2000). When on the streets, at the movies, or on the beach, a large part of how women and men were received depended upon their appearance, which was a seismic shift from earlier nineteenth-century formulations of identity based on virtue and character.

Physical Appearance

A hallmark of the new gendered norms for men and women were changes in beauty standards and, in particular, the growing acceptance of the idea that men should look as masculine as possible and women as feminine as possible. The simultaneous advents of popular culture, mass media, and mass advertising transformed public perceptions of gender as well as individual realities. Among the most significant of these changes were the standardization of beauty and the concomitant acceptance of the idea that one's appearance was one's most important attribute, especially when it came to securing a mate (Hamlin 2004, 2011; Banner 1983). For women, this meant the increased acceptance of makeup, concern regarding body shape, and worry about excessive body hair; for men, this meant visible muscles, boundless energy, and outward displays of strength.

In *Houdini, Tarzan, and the Perfect Man* (2001), Jon Kasson charted what the rise of these ideas meant for men. He demonstrated how the increasing importance of visual culture offered men new ways to construct identity, often through hypermasculinity, in an era in which industrial capitalism hindered individual autonomy. Kathy Peiss identified similar trends among women in her study of how cosmetics became normalized, required even, during the early years of the twentieth century. "Painting" one's face was once reserved for prostitutes and actresses (often considered the same category of women) but became a societal expectation for all women, and especially for middle-class women, by the 1930s (Peiss 1998).

These ideas about the importance of gendered appearance and, in particular, female beauty became so rooted in American culture that they provided one route to assimilation for immigrants and to middle-class respectability for working-class and African American women. As Peiss and others have shown, for immigrant women and women of color, personal appearance, including hairstyling and makeup practices, became important avenues of Americanization, ways to build self-esteem, and sources of intergenerational conflict (Ewen 1985; Peiss 1985, 1998). Even suffragists were not immune to the cultural imperative that women be pretty. At countless public events women's rights activists strategically deployed the lovely Inez Milholland, a lawyer, as the "most beautiful suffragist" (Nicholosi 2007).

The growing popularity of movies, mass culture, and national advertising in the 1920s heightened these trends which began in the 1880s, further cementing the idea that there were standardized ways to appear male or female and that conforming to those standards was very important. Another example of the standardization of appearance and the increasing importance placed on female beauty during the GAPE is the Miss America Pageant. Between the 1880s and 1920 numerous seaside towns, carnivals, and museums held photographic or in-person beauty contests, but these events were small-scale, local, and often frowned upon by the middle and upper classes. In 1921, the year after women attained the vote, the Miss America Pageant debuted in Atlantic City, New Jersey to national acclaim. The Pageant did not celebrate suffrage or "new women." Rather promoters, judges, and the press used the early pageants to promote "traditional" womanhood—"unpainted" and "unbobbed"—together with women's domestic role. The first winner, Margaret Gorman, age sixteen and barely five feet tall, remains the youngest and smallest Miss America on record. Gorman received tremendous acclaim for her lack of ambition as well as her good looks. In selecting one woman to represent the nation, pageant promoters also signaled the importance of appearance—especially for women—and the general consensus that beauty, too, had become standardized according to gendered, racialized, and class-based criteria (Hamlin 2004).

Gender Outliers

Just as popular culture and mass circulation magazines helped solidify the gender binary, mass culture also served as a site of resistance to dominant gender norms and gender binarism. In addition to the vast popularity and visibility of bearded ladies such as Krao, Julian Eltinge was a popular turn-of-the-twentieth-century performer whose fame rested on his ability to blur the lines between male and female. Known as "Mr. Lillian Russell," Eltinge fascinated audiences with his onstage transformation from manly man into feminine woman. But, as Jon Kasson establishes, Eltinge's female impersonating, while at first glance transgressive, ultimately reaffirmed the gender binary and linked it to heterosexual normativity (Kasson 2001). Similarly, George Chauncey's pathbreaking work on the emergence of gay male culture in the United States has shown how binary thinking with regard to gender went hand-in-hand with the growing consensus that all individuals were either heterosexual or homosexual—new identity categories in the early twentieth century (Chauncey 1994). Similarly, Lisa Duggan has chronicled the trial of Alice Mitchell, a young lesbian accused of murdering her lover. Duggan showed how, in its sensational coverage of the trial, the press wrote the script for "lesbian identity" and firmly rooted it in the gender binary. Media accounts accentuated the masculinity of Alice Mitchell and the attractive, feminine qualities of her lover, thereby dismissing alternative modes of gender and sexual expression for women and men (Duggan 1993).

Gender outliers can also be found in the realms of reform and politics. While men who championed certain reform efforts were accused of being feminine and women who demanded to be heard in the public were often criticized as being masculine, a few American reformers intentionally straddled the supposed gulf between male and female to challenge its very existence (Rome 2006; Behling 2001). Indeed, perhaps one way to assess the growing inflexibility of the gender binary is to measure the efforts of its most outspoken critic: Charlotte Perkins Gilman, the most prolific and well-known feminist thinker of the GAPE.

In Gilman's first book, *Women and Economics* (1898), she introduced her lifelong argument that women had become too "feminine." Specifically, she argued that women's oppression was fundamentally an economic problem, stemming from their lack of access to gainful employment and the mistaken societal assumption that paid labor was for men. Women's dependence upon men stood out to Gilman as peculiarly counter-evolutionary, a condition "unparalleled in the organic world." As she observed, "We are the only animal species in which the female depends upon the male for food, the only animal species in which the sex-relation is also an economic relation" (1898, 5). Of course women's meaningful entry into paid labor would require reforming domestic labor, and blurring the boundaries between male/female and public/private, changes that

Gilman also demanded. *Women and Economics* went into seven editions and was translated into seven languages. The *Nation* called it "the most significant utterance on the subject [of women] since Mill's *Subjection of Woman*." A generation of women grew up reading it (Degler 1991, xix).

Many of Gilman's subsequent books and articles further developed themes first articulated in *Women and Economics*, especially her rejection of gender essentialism in favor of a focus on "humanness." Throughout her life, she encouraged people to think of themselves as humans, rather than as males or females, and she resisted the label "feminist" in favor of "humanist." She decried her era's drive toward what she called "excessive sex distinction" and instead promoted gender neutrality. In her magazine the *Forerunner* and in several of her books, Gilman pointed out simple and complex alternatives to the gendering of daily life that she saw all around her. Why should not women wear sensible clothes—for example, pants with pockets—wondered Gilman? And why must women decorate themselves with silly hats and makeup? "We do not hear of 'a feminine paw' or 'a feminine hoof,'" Gilman observed. Once women rejected excessive sex distinction and realized their true power as humans, Gilman predicted "there will be nothing in the long period of their subservience upon which they will look back with more complete mortification than their hats" (1898, 45). Gilman presented the strongest challenge to the GAPE's push toward gender binarism. While she enjoyed tremendous readership and acclaim, her ideas did not gain sustained traction in her lifetime. As the wealth of scholarship on Gilman attests, however, they have continued to provoke both inspiration and frustration. Historians in particular continue to debate Gilman's ideas about race (Allen 2009 presents a thorough overview of this scholarship).

The Origins of Gender Ideology in the GAPE

One reason that scholars continue to find so much to debate in Gilman's work is that she both proposed solutions to society's most intractable gender issues and tried to understand what prompted America's gender norms in the first place. To Gilman, religion, anthropology, and science provided the main avenues for understanding gender ideology. Like many of her unorthodox colleagues, Gilman believed that the Genesis creation story based on Adam and Eve undergirded women's oppression and mandated excessive gender distinctions. In fact, she began *Women and Economics* with her own origins story, in which men and women were created equal. Compared to the "rib" version of creation, Gilman believed that evolutionary science, and to a lesser extent anthropology, offered a more convincing account of human origins and a better template for gender roles.

In the GAPE, evolutionary science powerfully disrupted traditional thinking about the "natural" differences between men and women, based on Adam and Eve, by suggesting that humans were part of the animal kingdom. In general, however, the turn to science often served to entrench binary thinking about gender in two distinct ways. First, a major element of the nineteenth-century scientific enterprise was to categorize all living things into coherent groups or taxonomies, an effort that appealed to and was popularized by many Progressive reformers. Sex differences between males and females and also between groups provided a key way to organize and differentiate between species and individuals, heightening the importance of sex as a way to understand physiology and popularizing the idea that there were only two possible ways to be sexed: male or female. Aiding and abetting this emphasis on the gender binary was the emerging science of sex difference, the cornerstone of which was the Darwinian idea that sex differentiation in a species signaled evolutionary progress (Russett 1989; Hamlin 2014).

This is not to say that religion offered a less binary approach to gender, or that religion and science were the only ways women and men in the GAPE understood sex difference. Indeed, even Jesus received a manly makeover in the 1880s (Morgan 1998). Gail Bederman and Clifford Putney, among others, have described late nineteenth-century calls for a "muscular Christianity" that was also highly masculine (Bederman 1989; Putney 2001). Nevertheless, religious and evolutionary, and to a lesser extent anthropological (Eller 2011), origin stories provided the templates for nineteenth-century thinking about the appropriate roles of men and women and for the cementing of binaristic thinking. Historians of gender and sexuality have long drawn on the insights of French theorist Michel Foucault, especially his multi-volume *History of Sexuality*, to puzzle through the structural and cultural shifts that prompted such a vast rethinking of gender and sexuality in the nineteenth century. Foucault highlights in particular the ways in which newly emerging specialties within science and medicine instigated, standardized, and sustained binary thinking about gender and sex while pathologizing outliers. During the GAPE, medicine sought to categorize and understand the human condition by turning all sorts of emotional states, appearances, and behaviors, previously considered along a spectrum of being, into recognizable diseases. Women who acted on unfeminine sexual urges were classified as nymphomaniacs, for example, and women who could not control their emotions were diagnosed with hysteria (Groneman 1994; Smith-Rosenberg 1985; Fleissner 2004). Many of these new nineteenth-century diseases, including hypertrichosis, stigmatized appearances and behaviors that blurred or transgressed the newly dominant gender binary.

Perhaps the best, or at least the most studied, example of the medicalization of the gender binary was the GAPE epidemic of neurasthenia. Women who were diagnosed with neurasthenia, famously including Charlotte Perkins Gilman, typically voiced a desire to do unfeminine things such as think, work, or write; as a remedy, they were often prescribed the "rest cure" which enforced upon them stereotypically feminine traits such as passivity and domesticity. Conversely, men diagnosed with neurasthenia typically displayed unmanly tendencies and were instructed to go west to partake in the "West Cure," following the example of cured neurasthenic Theodore Roosevelt, and participate in manly exploits like hunting (Gosling 1987; Lutz 1991; Schuster 2011). Overall, the professionalization and masculinization of science and medicine created and, in many ways, relied upon the structuring of the known world according to the related binaries of male/female and heterosexual/homosexual, trends that popularized the belief that human behavior and appearance should be polarized according to sex and that this was natural and inevitable (to say nothing of Freud or the medicalization of homosexuality and other sexual identities and practices that emerged).

Social progressives and those trained in the new fields of social science (often one and the same) rejected both biological determinism and religious fundamentalism as explanations for human behavior and sex difference. Instead, these scholars looked to cultural and environmental factors. By the end of the Progressive era, social scientists, led by Franz Boas at Columbia University and John Dewey at the University of Chicago, established that gender (and to some extent racial) differences were essentially cultural (Rosenberg 1982, 2004; Degler 1991). Such research challenged the idea that traits associated with masculinity and femininity were globally consistent, but these studies did not disrupt binary thinking as a whole. It was one thing to wage battle against biological determinists but quite another to take on popular culture and advertising, both of which, by the turn of the twentieth century, had vested lucrative interests in promoting gender binarism and gender totalism.

Suggestions for Further Research

Despite the explanatory appeal of science and medicine for gender history, a divide still persists between historians of science/medicine and generalists. Historians might continue to breach this impasse by doing more to incorporate science and medicine into introductory classes and research, just as gender is further incorporated into the history of science, technology, and medicine. For example, what might an introductory class look like that included selections from classics such as Cynthia Russett's *Sexual Science: The Victorian Construction of Womanhood* (1989), or more recent historical work on gender and science/medicine such as Carla Bittel's work on Dr. Mary Putnam Jacobi (2009) or Elizabeth Reiss's study of intersex individuals in the United States (2012)? Just as men and women did not inhabit separate spheres, neither did they inhabit disciplines. Scholars might also look more toward the relationship between gender and technology, and in particular those technologies that sought to alter or augment gender roles, as Carolyn Thomas de la Peña did so well in *The Body Electric: How Strange Machines Built the Modern American* (2005) or as Ruth Schwartz Cowan did in her classic *More Work for Mother: The Ironies of Household Technology from the Open Hearth to the Microwave* (1983).

Scholarship on gender and religion during the GAPE has tended to focus on Protestantism, as Kathleen Sprows Cummings attempts to correct with *New Women of the Old Faith* (2009); scholars might continue to explore non-Protestant religions and their prescriptions for gendered behavior. Some of the most interesting work on gender ideology during the GAPE has come from studies of non-mainstream religions, such as Beryl Satter's exploration of the New Thought movement, and much more work remains to be done with regard to gender and the Freethought movement (Satter 2001).

Thinking in terms of gender history is different than thinking in terms of women's history, and it leads to different conclusions about the GAPE. Since the emergence in the 1990s of gender history as a field, some historians have expressed concern that the focus on gender has obscured women's history, which was only beginning to make inroads into filling in the picture of women's lives in the GAPE (or any period for that matter). In her 2002 essay "Men are from the Gilded Age, Women are from the Progressive Era," Elisabeth Israels Perry laments that "despite a veritable boom" of scholarship on women in Progressive Era published in the 1990s, scholarship on the GAPE still tends to marginalize or oversimplify women's experiences and contributions. Nor, she contends, has "the larger vision of Progressive-era history" changed in light of (now) twenty-five years of scholarship on women (Perry 2002, 30, 34.) In part, this has to do with the sometimes fuzzy boundary between women's and gender history and some historians' tendency to conflate the two.

In 1996 the GAPE collection edited by Charles Calhoun contained a chapter on "Women in Industrialization" by Stacy Cordery; this 2017 collection includes a chapter on gender and one on sexuality, but not one on women. Has women's history been so fully incorporated into each individual chapter, and into the broader themes and periodization of the GAPE, that a separate chapter on women is no longer warranted? This has long been a goal of feminist historians and might be a useful topic of discussion. What might a future GAPE collection contain? Might the histories of men and women, gender, and sexuality begin to be addressed in concert? Such an approach might help move scholars away from binary thinking with regard to gender and toward the particulars of both gender articulation and individual action. Disrupting the standard historical narrative to place women more firmly in the center of the action might also lead to more precise thinking about how gender works across race and class lines. Likewise, scholarship that explores the histories of gender and sexuality in tandem will do much to reveal how these two supposed binaries developed in interconnected and interdependent ways.

Thanks to the groundbreaking work of GAPE scholars since the early 1990s, historians now rightly see gender everywhere, as a strong undercurrent structuring domestic and international policy; religious doctrine; political rhetoric and governmental priorities; labor practices; reform initiatives; personal opportunities; family relationships; scientific and medical research; and popular culture. Thanks to the theoretic work of legal scholar Kimberlé Crenshaw, among others, GAPE scholars also now use the concept of intersectionality to better understand the ways in which ideas about gender inform notions of race, and vice versa, as well as shape individual identities. The best gender histories, such as Glenda Gilmore's *Gender and Jim Crow* and Gail Bederman's *Manliness and Civilization*, pay careful attention to intersectionality and keep race as an essential element of gendered analysis. Another welcome development is the turn toward transnationalism and related efforts to situate the United States in a global context. GAPE scholars, including Kristin Hoganson, spearheaded this broader trend in US historical scholarship which is now resulting in fascinating, fruitful comparative scholarship such as Jonathan Zimmerman's *Too Hot to Handle: A Global History of Sex Education* (2015), the first chapter of which details the GAPE origins of sex education.

Future historical work on the GAPE will be enriched by critical examination of the supposed binary between men and women and to what extent historical scholarship affirms or problematizes it; scholars might also continue to analyze the origins of gender ideology, especially in terms of science, medicine, and religion; merge the history of gender more closely with that of sexuality; and foreground gendered analyses without neglecting the actual women and men whose words and actions comprise our shared history. Future scholarship might also continue to look closely at non-elite gender roles and pay more attention to the outliers, including those who actively challenged gender binarism within the Freethought, socialist, sex-reform movements. After all, it is the outliers who often best reveal both the construction of dominant gender ideology and its resistance. In the GAPE, there were perhaps no more poignant gender outliers than bearded women.

Conclusion

In their day, Viola M. became famous in medical circles, while Krao was a household name across the United States and Europe. What is their legacy? While the popularity of bearded ladies and the simultaneous epidemic of hypertrichosis could have served to challenge the emerging consensus that gender was a fixed binary (if most women had facial hair, how could it be a disease?), ultimately bearded women helped to entrench this binary and women's hair removal soon became a cultural norm (Herzig 2015). What made bearded women both so threatening and so appealing was that they blurred the supposed boundaries between male/female, human/animal, and nature/culture. For historians, bearded women help reveal how these very binaries were constructed. Likewise, their reception (both contemporary and historical) merges the histories of women, gender, and sexuality; just as their varied experiences and archives powerfully demonstrate the interrelatedness of race, class, gender, and sex, making them ideal figures to crystalize thinking about gender in the GAPE.

Bearded ladies vividly demonstrate how, between the 1870s and the early 1900s, separate spheres gave way to gendered lives. A variety of factors contributed to this change: The rise of mass-circulation magazines and national popular culture (and the standardized appearances and behaviors that they promoted); the popularization of scientific and, later, social-scientific ideas about sex difference; and a reluctant public's tenuous acceptance of women into formerly male-only realms. By the outbreak of World War I many facets of life that had once been all-male or gender-neutral now included distinct standards for men and for women. Could women play sports? Sure, as long as they wore long dresses and did not compete against each other. Go to college? Of course, as long as they stuck to feminine subjects and upheld strictly feminine behavior in and out of the classroom. In answer to the pressing question of whether or not women could enter previously male spheres, a gendered compromise developed in the GAPE that helps explain why today the United States has no Equal Rights Amendment, yet pink Lego sets for girls abound.

References

Allen, Judith A. 2009. *The Feminism of Charlotte Perkins Gilman: Sexualities, Histories, Progressivism.* Chicago: University of Chicago Press.

Baker, Paula. 1984. "The Domestication of Politics: Women and American Political Society, 1780–1920." *American Historical Review* 89: 620–647.

Banner, Lois. 1983. *American Beauty: A Social History…through Two Centuries…of the American Idea, Ideal and Image of the Beautiful Woman.* New York: Alfred Knopf.

Baron, Ava, ed. 1991. *Work Engendered: Toward a New History of American Labor.* Ithaca, NY: Cornell University Press.

Bederman, Gail. 1995. *Manliness and Civilization: A Cultural History of Gender and Race in the United States, 1880–1917.* Chicago: University of Chicago Press.

—. 1989. "'The Women Have Had Charge of the Church Work Long Enough': The Men and Religion Forward Movement of 1911–1912 and the Masculinization of Middle-Class Protestantism." *American Quarterly* 41, September: 432–465.

Behling, Laura L. 2001. *The Masculine Woman in America, 1890–1935.* Chicago: University of Illinois Press.

Bender, Daniel E. 2004. "Too Much of Distasteful Masculinity: Historicizing Sexual Harassment in the Garment Sweatshop and Factory." *Journal of Women's History* 15: 91–116.

Bittel, Carla. 2009. *Mary Putnam Jacobi and the Politics of Medicine in Nineteenth-Century America*. Chapel Hill: University of North Carolina Press.

Boris, Eileen. 1994. *Home to Work: Motherhood and the Politics of Industrial Homework in the United States*. Cambridge: Cambridge University Press.

Briggs, Laura. 2002. *Reproducing Empire: Race, Sex, Science, and U.S. Imperialism in Puerto Rico*. Berkeley: University of California Press.

Calhoun, Charles W., ed. *The Gilded Age: Perspectives on the Origins of Modern America*. Lanham, MD, Rowman & Littlefield.

Carnes, Mark C., and Clyde Griffen, eds. 1990. *Meanings for Manhood: Constructions of Masculinity in Victorian America*. Chicago: University of Chicago Press.

Clark, Daniel A. 2010. *Creating the College Man: American Mass Magazines and Middle-Class Manhood, 1890–1915*. Madison: University of Wisconsin Press.

Chauncey, George. 1994. *Gay New York: Gender, Urban Culture, and the Making of the Gay Male World, 1890–1940*. New York: Basic Books.

Cowan, Ruth Schwartz. 1983. *More Work for Mother: The Ironies of Household Technology from the Open Hearth to the Microwave*. New York: Basic Books.

de la Peña, Carolyn Thomas. 2005. *The Body Electric: How Strange Machines Built the Modern American*. Berkeley: University of California Press.

Degler, Carl N. 1991. *In Search of Human Nature: The Decline and Revival of Darwinism in American Social Thought*. New York: Oxford University Press.

Deutsch, Sarah. 2000. *Women and the City: Gender, Space, and Power in Boston, 1870–1940*. New York: Oxford University Press.

Douglas, Ann. 1998. *The Feminization of American Culture*. New York: Farrar, Straus and Giroux.

Drachman, Virginia G. 1998. *Sisters in Law: Women Lawyers in Modern American History*. Cambridge, MA: Harvard University Press.

Dudden, Faye. 2011. *Fighting Chance: The Struggle over Woman Suffrage and Black Suffrage in Reconstruction America*. New York: Oxford University Press.

Duggan, Lisa. 1993. "The Trials of Alice Mitchell: Sensationalism, Sexology, and the Lesbian Subject in Turn-of-the-Century America." *Signs* 18, Summer: 791–814.

Edwards, Rebecca. 1997. *Angels in the Machinery: Gender in American Party Politics from the Civil War to the Progressive Era*. New York: Oxford University Press.

—. 2010. *New Spirits: Americans in the "Gilded Age" 1865–1905*. 2nd edn. New York: Oxford University Press.

Elias, Megan J. 2008. *Stir it Up: Home Economics and American Culture*. Philadelphia: University of Pennsylvania Press.

Eller, Cynthia. 2011. *Gentlemen and Amazons: The Myth of Matriarchal Prehistory, 1861–1900*. Berkeley: University of California Press.

Ewen, Elizabeth. 1985. *Immigrant Women and the Land of Dollars: Life and Culture on the Lower East Side, 1890–1925*. New York: Monthly Review Press.

Flanagan, Maureen. 2006. *America Reformed: Progressives and Progressivism, 1890s–1920s*. New York: Oxford University Press.

Fleissner, Jennifer. 2004. *Women, Compulsion, Modernity: The Moment of American Naturalism*. Chicago: University of Chicago Press.

Gilman, Charlotte Perkins. (1898) 1966. *Women and Economics: A Study of the Economic Relation Between Men and Women as a Factor in Social Evolution*. Boston: Small, Maynard, & Co. Reprint, New York: Harper Torchbook. Citations refer to the Harper edition.

Gilmore, Glenda Elizabeth. 1996. *Gender and Jim Crow: Women and the Politics of White Supremacy in North Carolina, 1896–1920*. Chapel Hill: University of North Carolina Press.

Goldberg, Michael Lewis. 1997. *An Army of Women: Gender and Politics in Gilded Age Kansas*. Baltimore, MD: Johns Hopkins University Press.

Gosling, F.G. 1987. *Before Freud: Neurasthenia and the American Medical Community, 1870–1910*. Urbana: University of Illinois Press.

Groneman, Carol. 1994. "Nymphomania: The Historical Construction of Female Sexuality." *Signs* 19: 337–367.

Hamilton, Andrea. 2004. *A Vision for Girls: Gender, Education, and the Bryn Mawr School*. Baltimore, MD: Johns Hopkins University Press.

Hamlin, Kimberly A. 2004. "Bathing Suits and Backlash: The First Miss America Pageants, 1921–1927." In *"There She Is, Miss America": The Politics of Sex, Gender, and Race in America's Most Famous Pageant*, ed. Elwood Watson and Darcy Martin, 27–52. New York: Palgrave/St. Martin's.

—. 2014. *From Eve to Evolution: Darwin, Science, and Women's Rights in Gilded Age America*. Chicago: University of Chicago Press.

—. 2011. "'The Case of a Bearded Woman': Hypertrichosis and the Construction of Gender in the Age of Darwin." *American Quarterly* 63, December: 955–981.

Herzig, Rebecca. 2015. *Plucked: A History of Hair Removal*. New York: New York University Press.

Higginbotham, Evelyn Brooks. 1993. *Righteous Discontent: The Women's Movement in the Black Baptist Church: 1880–1920*. Cambridge, MA: Harvard University Press.

Hilkey, Judy. 1997. *Character Is Capital: Success Manuals and Manhood in Gilded Age*. Chapel Hill: University of North Carolina Press.

Hoganson, Kristin L. 1998. *Fighting for American Manhood: How Gender Politics Provoked the Spanish–American and Philippine–American Wars*. New Haven, CT: Yale University Press.

Horowitz, Helen Lefkowitz. 1984. *Alma Mater: Design and Experience in the Women's Colleges from Their Nineteenth Century Beginnings to the 1930s*. New York: Alfred A. Knopf.

Jones, Jacqueline. 1985. *Labor of Love, Labor of Sorrow: Black Women, Work, and the Family, from Slavery to the Present*. New York: Basic Books.

Kasson, John F. 1978. *Amusing the Million: Coney Island at the Turn of the Century*. New York: Hill & Wang.

—. 2001. *Houdini, Tarzan, and the Perfect Man: The White Male Body and the Challenge of Modernity in America*. New York: Hill & Wang.

Kessler-Harris, Alice. 1995. "The Paradox of Motherhood: Night Work Restrictions in the United States." In *Protecting Women: Labor Legislation in Europe, the United States, and Australia, 1880–1920*, ed. Ulla Wikander et al., 337–357. Chicago: University of Illinois Press.

—. 2003. *Out to Work: A History of Wage-Earning Women in the United States*, 20th anniversary edition. New York: Oxford University Press.

Kwolek-Folland, Angel. 1994. *Engendering Business: Men and Women in the Corporate Office, 1870–1930.* Baltimore, MD: Johns Hopkins University Press.

Lehrer, Susan. 1987. *Origins of Protective Labor Legislation for Women, 1905–1925.* Albany, NY: SUNY Press.

Leroux, Karen. 2009. "'Unpensioned Veterans': Women Teachers and the Politics of Public Service in Late Nineteenth Century United States." *Journal of Women's History* 21: 34–62.

Lutz, Tom. 1991. *American Nervousness, 1903: An Anecdotal History.* Ithaca, NY: Cornell University Press.

Materson, Lisa. 2009. *For the Freedom of Her Race: Black Women and Electoral Politics in Illinois, 1877–1932.* Chapel Hill: University of North Carolina Press.

Merchant, Carolyn. 2010. "George Bird Grinnell's Audubon Society: Bridging the Gender Divide in Conservation." *Environmental History* 15: 3–30.

Mitchell, Michele. "'Lower Orders,' Racial Hierarchies, and Rights Rhetoric: Evolutionary Echoes in Elizabeth Cady Stanton's Thought during the Late 1860s." In *Elizabeth Cady Stanton, Feminist as Thinker: A Reader in Documents and Essays*, ed. Ellen Carol DuBois and Richard Cándida Smith, 128–151. New York: New York University Press.

Moore, Sarah J. 2013. *Empire on Display: San Francisco's Panama-Pacific International Exposition of 1915.* Norman: University of Oklahoma Press.

Morantz-Sanchez, Regina Markell. 2000. *Sympathy & Science: Women Physicians in American Medicine.* Chapel Hill: University of North Carolina Press.

Morgan, David. 1998. *Visual Piety: A History and Theory of Popular Religious Images* Berkeley: University of California Press.

Muncy, Robin. 1997. "Trustbusting and White Manhood in America, 1898–1914." *American Studies* 38: 21–42.

Murphy, Kevin P. 2008. *Political Manhood: Red Bloods, Mollycoddles, & the Politics of Progressive Era Reform.* New York: Columbia University Press.

Newman, Louise Michele. 1999. *White Women's Rights: The Racial Origins of Feminism in the United States.* New York: Oxford University Press.

Nicholosi, Anne Marie. 2007. "'The Most Beautiful Suffragette:' Inez Milholland and the Political Currency of Beauty." *Journal of the Gilded Age and Progressive Era* 3, July: 287–309.

Painter, Nell Irvin. 1996. *Sojourner Truth: A Life, A Symbol.* New York: W.W. Norton.

Pascoe, Peggy. 1990. *Relations of Rescue: The Search for Female Moral Authority in the American West, 1874–1939.* New York: Oxford University Press.

Peiss, Kathy. 1986. *Cheap Amusements: Working Women and Leisure in Turn-of-the-Century New York.* Philadelphia: Temple University Press.

—. 1998. *Hope in a Jar: The Making of America's Beauty Culture.* New York: Metropolitan Books.

Perry, Elisabeth Israels. 2002. "Men are From the Gilded Age, Women Are from the Progressive Era." *Journal of the Gilded Age and Progressive Era* 1: 25–48.

Pliley, Jessica. 2013. "The Petticoat Inspectors: Women Boarding Inspectors and the Gendered Exercise of Federal Authority." *Journal of the Gilded Age and Progressive Era* 12: 95–125.

Prieto, Laura R. 2013. "A Delicate Subject: Clemencia Lopez, Civilized Womanhood, and the Politics of Anti-Imperialism." *Journal of the Gilded Age and Progressive Era* 12: 199–233.

Putnam, John C. 2008. *Class and Gender Politics in Progressive-Era Seattle.* Reno: University of Nevada Press.

Putney, Clifford. 2001. *Muscular Christianity: Manhood and Sports in Protestant America, 1880–1920.* Cambridge, MA: Harvard University Press.

Reiss, Elizabeth. 2012. *Bodies in Doubt: An American History of Intersex.* Baltimore, MD: Johns Hopkins University Press.

Rome, Adam. 2006. "'Political Hermaphrodites': Gender and Environmental Reform in Progressive America." *Environmental History* 11: 440–463.

Rosenberg, Rosalind. 1982. *Beyond Separate Spheres: Intellectual Roots of Modern Feminism.* New Haven, CT: Yale University Press.

—. 2004. *Changing the Subject: How the Women of Columbia Shaped the Way We Think About Sex and Politics.* New York: Columbia University Press.

Rossiter, Margaret. 1984. *Women Scientists in America: Struggles and Strategies to 1940.* Baltimore, MD: Johns Hopkins University Press.

Rotundo, E. Anthony. 1993. *American Manhood: Transformations in Masculinity from the Revolution to the Modern Era.* New York: Basic Books.

Russett, Cynthia Eagle. 1989. *Sexual Science: The Victorian Construction of Womanhood.* Cambridge, MA: Harvard University Press.

Satter, Beryl. 2001. *Each Mind a Kingdom: American Women, Sexual Purity, and the New Thought Movement, 1875–1920.* Berkeley: University of California Press.

Schechter, Patricia A. 2001. *Ida B. Wells-Barnett and American Reform, 1880–1930.* Chapel Hill: University of North Carolina Press.

Schuster, David G. 2011. *Neurasthenic Nation: America's Search for Health, Happiness, and Comfort, 1869–1920.* New Brunswick, NJ: Rutgers University Press.

Scott, Anne Firor. 1991. *Natural Allies: Women's Associations in American History.* Urbana: University of Illinois Press.

Scott, Joan. 1986. "Gender: A Useful Category of Analysis." *American Historical Review* 91, 5: 1053–1075.

—. 1998. *Gender and the Politics of History*, revised edn. New York: Columbia University Press.

Sklar, Kathryn Kish. 1995. "Two Political Cultures in the Progressive Era: The National Consumers League and the American Association for Labor Legislation." In *U.S. History as Women's History*, ed. Linda Kerber et al., 36–62. Chapel Hill: University of North Carolina Press.

Smalley, Andrea. 2005. "'Our Lady Sportsmen': Gender Class, and Conservation in Sport Hunting Magazines, 1873–1920." *Journal of the Gilded Age and Progressive Era* 4: 355–380.

Smith-Rosenberg, Carroll. 1985. *Disorderly Conduct: Visions of Gender in Victorian America.* New York: Alfred A. Knopf.

Spain, Daphne. 2001. *How Women Saved the City.* Minneapolis: University of Minnesota Press.

Sprows Cummings, Kathleen. 2009. *New Women of the Old Faith.* Chapel Hill: University of North Carolina Press.

Stage, Sarah and Virginia B. Vincenti, eds. 1997. *Rethinking Home Economics: Women and the History of a Profession.* Ithaca, NY: Cornell University Press.

Unger, Nancy C. 2012. *Beyond Nature's Housekeepers: American Women in Environmental History.* New York: Oxford University Press.

Vapnek, Lara. 2009. *Breadwinners: Working Women and Economic Independence, 1865–1920.* Urbana: University of Illinois Press.

Vertinsky, Patricia Anne. 1994. *The Eternally Wounded Woman: Women, Doctors, and Exercise in the Late Nineteenth Century.* Urbana: University of Illinois Press.

Watts, Sarah. 2006. *Rough Rider in the White House Rough Rider in the White House: Theodore Roosevelt and the Politics of Desire.* Chicago: University of Chicago Press.

Weiner, Lynn Y. 1985. *From Working Girl to Working Mother: The Female Labor Force in the United States, 1820–1980.* Chapel Hill: University of North Carolina Press.

Woloch, Nancy. 2015. *A Class by Herself: Protective Labor Laws for Women Workers, 1890s–1990s.* Princeton, NJ: Princeton University Press.

—. 2011. *Women and the American Experience*, 5th edn. New York: McGraw Hill.

Zimmerman, Jonathan. 2015. *Too Hot to Handle: A Global History of Sex Education.* Princeton, NJ: Princeton University Press.

Chapter Eight

Inventing Sexuality: Ideologies, Identities, and Practices in the Gilded Age and Progressive Era

Leigh Ann Wheeler

The Gilded Age—a moniker introduced by Mark Twain and Charles Dudley Warner in their 1873 novel by the same name—did not have sex. To be sure, *the Gilded Age* itself mentions "sex" frequently, but for Twain, Warner, and their contemporaries, sex referred only to the state of being male or female, a distinction that was crucial to how they organized their society, delineated the public and the private, and determined the workings of the economy, political system, religious institutions, and home life. Today, these might be considered issues of gender—or cultural derivatives of assumptions about biological differences between women and men. But neither gender nor sexuality, as they are known today, structured lives and identities in the Gilded Age. Does this mean that people did not think about, participate in, or legislate around behaviors that most Americans in the twenty-first-century would consider sexual? Not at all, but they did so in ways that demonstrate a very different understanding of matters that, on their face, might seem deceptively familiar.

In some respects, then, this chapter begins as an exercise in ahistoricism; it imposes on the Gilded Age a category of analysis, sexuality, that became an essential element of personal identification later, in the Progressive Era, with which the chapter ends. Nevertheless, historians of sexuality have written extensively about the Gilded Age using a wide range of approaches, sources, methods, and theories. Their work traces processes by which sexuality became a major element in the overarching system of gender differentiation in the United States. Indeed, this chapter argues that as various longstanding cultural, political, and economic differences between women and men collapsed, sexualization of girls and women became a strategy for maintaining gender difference.

Gilded Age Tensions and the Last Gasps of Victorianism: Keeping Sex Private and Spheres Separate

Gilded Age Americans lived in a society built around a fraying ideal of separate spheres, according to which women reigned in the private or domestic sphere where their "piety, purity, submissiveness, and domesticity" nurtured children, preserved virtue, and provided a haven for men; men ruled in the public realm where the competitive values of the market and politics held sway. Sex troubled the boundaries between these spheres even as it defined them. Marital sexual relations resided firmly in the private sphere, where chaste wives were expected to participate in reproductive sexual intercourse with their husbands. But the Gilded Age public sphere hosted a growing array of commercial sexual possibilities mainly for purchase by men, from prostitution to pornography.

This commercialization of sexuality incited the anti-vice activism of Anthony Comstock and many others. Today Comstock functions primarily as the butt of jokes and as shorthand for sexual repression and censorship, but at the end of the nineteenth century, he exercised great power and enjoyed considerable popularity. A devout New England Congregationalist and the younger brother of a soldier slain at Gettysburg, Comstock joined the Union Army, where he suffered harassment for resisting exhortations to gamble, chew tobacco, drink whiskey, look at dirty pictures, and cavort with prostitutes. Comstock joined forces with the Young Men's Christian Association (YMCA), an organization founded by merchants eager to shield their employees from the influences of urban vice. In 1865, the YMCA sponsored legislation that forbade the mailing of sexually explicit material to soldiers. In 1873, it helped Comstock

A Companion to the Gilded Age and Progressive Era, First Edition. Edited by Christopher McKnight Nichols and Nancy C. Unger.
© 2017 John Wiley & Sons, Inc. Published 2017 by John Wiley & Sons, Inc.

obtain a federal statute that expanded the law and extended it to the general population. As a special agent of the US Post Office and a full-time employee of the YMCA's New York Society for the Suppression of Vice (NYSSV), Comstock used postal regulations to apprehend and prosecute purveyors of obscenity.

Historians love to hate Comstock—and also to puzzle over what motivated him and other anti-vice reformers. Using the psychodynamic theories popular in their day, Oscar Handlin and Robert W. Haney speculated that Comstock was sexually repressed; indeed, Handlin suggested that repressed sexual energies inspired xenophobia and racism that led the Gilded Age middle class to try to control the sexual behavior of foreign others (Handlin 1948; Haney 1960). The social control thesis that held sway in the 1960s and 1970s shaped Paul Boyer's (2002) and David Pivar's (1973) characterizations of Comstock and other anti-vice activists as backward-looking elites who used censorship to defend their sense of order against the forces of urbanization and industrialization unleashed after the Civil War. Nicola Beisel's study developed similar themes, showing how values and practices associated with foreigners threatened not only the sexual purity of children but also a family's class status (Beisel 1997). Molly McGarry raised a different question, asking what led anti-vice crusaders to concentrate on printed material. She concluded that, in an age of rising literacy rates and increased circulation of ideas enabled by technological advances, printed matter seemed especially powerful. Reformers cared most about controlling behavior and bodies, but in the late nineteenth century, those concerns were "displaced onto the channels through which information travels" (McGarry 2008, 118).

Specialists in women's history introduced a new set of historiographical questions in the 1990s. They called attention to women and issues of gender even as they addressed contemporary debates central to the feminist "sex wars" in which some embraced pornography as sexually liberating while others condemned it as degrading. Charges of censorship inspired women's historians to reconsider Comstock and other anti-vice reformers. The first group to do so portrayed Comstock as interested less in social control, broadly construed, than in controlling women, especially strong-willed, independent women who rejected domesticity (Bates 1991; Brodie 1994; Hovey 1998). Alison M. Parker refocused the conversation on female anti-obscenity activists. Even if they did occasionally look backward and advocate repressive measures, these activists also developed progressive strategies for protecting children from obscene influences by creating wholesome alternatives to commercial amusements (Parker 1997). Amanda Frisken examines the role of race in determining which female bodies the press censored and which ones it sexualized. Her findings indicate that Comstock's activism helped to roll back exposure of the white female body in the 1870s but permitted the ongoing display of black women's legs and breasts. Racially specific sexualized depictions of female bodies helped to reinforce white supremacy by marking black women as sexually available (Frisken 2008).

Scholars who focus on censorship have challenged the notion that American society in the nineteenth century was prudish and repressed. Helen Lefkowitz Horowitz and Rochelle Gurstein depict a society saturated with sex and embattled over whether to suppress it. The Comstockian forces ultimately won not because of a Victorian consensus, according to Horowitz, but because no one offered a public, absolute defense of the right to produce, sell, or possess sexual material (Horowitz 2002). Rochelle Gurstein shows, however, that proponents of exposure demanded open exchange of ideas and information about sex, but advocates of reticence feared that in such a world, sex would become "desacralized, the public sphere polluted, and private life trivialized" (Gurstein 1996, 64). Commercial buying and selling of contraceptive devices violated that boundary, according to Andrea Tone, which is why Comstock and others considered birth control obscene; by contrast, reproductive control that remained fully private—abstinence, rhythm, and coitus interruptus, for example—posed no threat (Tone 2001). Alyssa Picard disputes the notion that Comstock aimed to preserve distinctions between the spheres, citing his concerns about the potential for vice to flourish in each. Her analysis fails to acknowledge, however, that Comstock consistently located the source of vice in the public sphere and endeavored to prevent its transmission into the private realm (Picard 2002).

Scholars have employed a wide range of sources to investigate the level of sexual repression in the Victorian era. Using medical documents and prescriptive literature, Ben Barker-Benfeld discovered a "spermatic economy" that prohibited masturbation in order to preserve men's semen, hence their "vigor," "power," and, ultimately, their sanity. Others discovered the coterminous rise of "drastic gynecology"—including ovariotomy and clitoridectomy—to curb women's masturbation and also "neurosis, insanity, abnormal menstruation and practically anything untoward in female behavior." These findings seemed to seal the deal on Victorians as sex-phobic, but not for long (Barker-Benfeld 1976, 47; 58–60; Smith-Rosenberg 1973; Walters 1974). Pioneers in women's history—concerned about women's agency and the nature of sexual liberation in their own time—challenged these conclusions. Among the first, Carl Degler anticipated Michel Foucault's rethinking of Victorian sexuality by turning the standard evidence on its head; he interpreted concerns about masturbation and heterosexual intercourse as proof not that Victorians feared sex but that they recognized its power. Moreover, using a survey conducted in the 1890s, he found that most middle-class women experienced orgasm and sexual desire (Degler 1974). Nancy Cott reinterpreted Victorian women's alleged passionlessness to show how it enhanced women's spiritual status and domestic authority even as it empowered women to resist marital sexual demands and limit pregnancies (Cott 1979). Advice might be one thing, experience another, and power yet another.

Victorian romance and passion absorbed the attention of a later generation of scholars who asked whether and how middle- and upper-class women and men found intimacy with each other in a culture that expected and groomed them to be so different. In groundbreaking studies of courtship and marriage, Ellen K. Rothman and Karen Lystra drew on love letters and diaries to unearth expressions of passionate attachment and sexual longing between Victorian couples. Romantic love and intimacy established common ground that helped spouses compensate for the stark differences in their roles and everyday lives (Rothman 1987; Lystra 1989).

Sharp gender differentiation also created unique opportunities for same-sex romance and eroticism. Carroll Smith-Rosenberg's classic 1975 study explained how Victorian restrictions on cross-gender relationships and emphasis on gender differences created homosocial worlds in which even married women often formed close, lifelong bonds and expressed their love for each other through romantic language and intimate physical contact. Smith-Rosenberg concluded that "the supposedly repressive and destructive Victorian sexual ethos may have been more flexible and responsive to the needs of particular individuals than those of mid-twentieth century" (Smith-Rosenberg 1975, 29). She and Lillian Faderman took care to note that "romantic friendships" preceded the creation of identities associated with sexual orientation, though modern readers readily imagine possibilities later associated with lesbianism (Faderman 1991). Smith-Rosenberg's groundbreaking article inspired a cottage industry of historical speculation about the possible sexual dimensions of nineteenth-century men's friendships, including famous Gilded Age personages such as Walt Whitman and Mark Twain. C.A. Tripp drew headlines when he presented evidence that Abraham Lincoln shared a bed and perhaps amorous encounters with other men (Reynolds 1995; Hoffman 1995; Stoneley 1996; Tripp 2005). Meanwhile, scholars documented romantic friendships across generations of men in the YMCA (Gustav-Wrathall 1998; Rotundo 1989). Together, this literature indicates that, whereas nineteenth-century homosocial spheres did not prevent marital intimacy, they may have fostered same-sex romance.

The question of whether the Victorian era was sexually repressive has been taken up more recently by historians of material culture and medicine. One argues that the open-crotch drawers worn by women until the early 1900s evoked eroticism and increased sexual access (Fields 2007). Another finds that Victorian-era physicians treated hysteria in women not only with gynecological surgery but also through genital massage to orgasm, a technique that seems not to have been considered sexual by its practitioners (Maines 1999). Late nineteenth-century physicians also apparently knew something Sigmund Freud would later deny—the importance of the clitoris to a healthy adult woman's sexual pleasure. Thus, they used clitoral surgery (especially clitoridectomy or removal of the clitoris) to curb masturbation, but they also used female circumcision (removal of the prepuce to expose the clitoris) even more frequently, to enhance a married woman's enjoyment of intercourse (Rodriguez 2014).

The Victorian masturbation taboo did result in sexual repression, but its most enduring impact may be on the countless American males who have undergone, and continue to undergo, circumcision. Gail Pat Parsons made this connection in a challenge to scholars who focused on the misogyny of Victorian medicine, arguing that "men as well as women suffered excruciating treatment at the hands of physicians whose limited knowledge reduced them to primitive, at times brutal, methods" (Parsons 1977, 57). More recently, David L. Gollaher and Robert Darby show that even as female sexual surgery declined in the late nineteenth century, male circumcision became standard practice by the twentieth, a routine procedure in US hospitals, and an aesthetic marker that distinguished white middle-class American men from the poor, immigrants, and African Americans. Only after fears of masturbation had subsided did physicians begin to rely on health-related justifications for male circumcision (Gollaher 2000; Darby 2003). Curiously, Thomas W. Laqueur does not even mention circumcision in his 500-page history of masturbation (Laqueur 2003).

Gilded Age Americans prohibited the "solitary vice" but tolerated the "social evil." Why so little tolerance for masturbation and so much for prostitution? An early article explained that Victorian ideals practically demanded prostitution, because they required a chaste wife but assumed a sexually voracious husband (Riegel 1968). Historians have also shown how prostitution in the West supported Victorian ideals by helping to set boundaries, define respectability, and develop civilization by advancing major social institutions, including the press, courts, and public health (Goldman 1981; Butler 1985; Shumsky 1986; Shah 2001). According to Timothy Gilfoyle, prostitution was integral to and integrated throughout New York City in the Gilded Age. Through it, commerce began to displace the church and family in determining appropriate sexual etiquette in the late nineteenth century (Gilfoyle 1992). Other historians have focused on middle-class female reformers who sought to eradicate and/or rescue women from prostitution. Writing in the shadow of the sex wars, several scholars associated late nineteenth-century anti-prostitution reformers with twentieth-century anti-pornography feminists, charging both groups with practicing a politics of morality and obtaining power at the expense of other women (DuBois and Gordon 1983; Pascoe 1990).

Recently, historians have taken up the challenge to treat prostitutes like workers. Sharon E. Wood includes prostitutes among the working women who helped to expand women's access to public life (Wood 2005). Cynthia Blair's investigation of turn-of-the-century Chicago traces demographic and geographic evolutions in the city's black sex districts, showing how black sex workers negotiated notions of respectability, individual self-respect, and economic self-reliance in a society that severely limited their options (Blair 2010). More recently, Stacey L. Smith incorporates Gilded Age prostitution into a study of unfree labor in late nineteenth-century California where the trafficking of captive indigenous women and bound Chinese prostitutes reveals a society uncertain about how to define freedom—and to whom to extend it—long after the Compromise of 1850 established the state's free status (Smith 2013).

Gilded Age prostitution flourished in a vibrant urban sexual underworld that offered a wide range of sexual possibilities. This world was especially well developed in Chicago's Levee and New York City's Bowery and Tenderloin districts, where it was segregated but not sealed off from respectable society. Indeed, Tera Hunter and Chad Heap show that affluent men and women went "slumming" for purposes of reform, voyeurism, and entertainment that included dining, drinking, dancing, and shopping (Hunter 1997; Heap 2008). Chauncey explains that the Gilded Age Bowery also provided a residential, recreational, and remunerative home for "gays"—a blanket term for prostitutes of both sexes, sexual "inverts," "fairies," and "queers." Here gay men were neither isolated from each other nor invisible to the broader culture. Indeed, middle-class men visited the gay world for adventure and sexual encounters with other men, all while maintaining their status as "normal men" (Chauncey 1994).

The relative fluidity and openness of the Gilded Age gay world began to give way to the rigid binaries of the modern era by the beginning of the twentieth century. The first historical scholarship on the origins of these binaries appeared soon after the American Psychiatric Association removed homosexuality from its list of psychiatric disorders in 1973—a change that raised questions about the historical impact of medicine on sexual identity. Many scholars argued that the medical profession had played a crucial role in creating and pathologizing the homosexual (Bullough 1975; Faderman 1978; Terry 1999; Hatheway 2003). George Chauncey, Jr. challenged this medical model of homosexuality by focusing on the agency of "sexual inverts"—men who defied gender conventions by wearing women's clothing, expressing attraction to other men, or engaging in activities associated with women—and their resistance to doctors' efforts to pathologize them (Chauncey 1994).

The US Supreme Court issued its own historical interpretation regarding homosexuality in 1986 when, in *Bowers v. Hardwick*, it upheld Georgia's statute on the grounds that sodomy had been outlawed since the founding of the nation. In response, historians produced a prodigious body of work that challenged *Bowers* by tracing dramatic changes in American legal approaches to sodomy. Nineteenth-century law defined sodomy broadly, using it as a catchall for non-procreative sexual behavior. Moreover, laws against sodomy were seldom enforced without some additional aggravating circumstance such as violence or coercion. For example, Chauncey and Stephen Robertson show that Victorian-era enforcement of sodomy laws targeted adult men who engaged in sexual conduct with children (Chauncey 1994; Robertson 2010). Legal scholar William Eskridge identifies a major turning point in sodomy law that invites further study: after 1880, most states revised their sodomy laws so that "fellatio—a crime nowhere in 1878—was a crime in almost all states outside the South by 1921." As a result, "women as well as men were now responsible actors in the theater of perverted sexuality" (Eskridge 2008, 52, 57). The history of sodomy, law was anything but static.

Surely it is an historical coincidence that even as fellatio became a crime, American women's fertility declined precipitously. In 1973, Daniel Scott Smith used quantitative methods to argue that women's increased power and autonomy within the home enabled them to persuade or coerce husbands to practice birth control. The first book-length study on the history of birth control, *Woman's Body, Woman's Right*, appeared a few years later and became a revered classic, but not before being savaged by established male historians who characterized it as "obtuse," "polemical"—a book directed only at "getting the goods on the chauvinists" (Kennedy 1970, 823; Lemons 1977, 1095; Shorter 1977, 271). Linda Gordon argued that for nineteenth-century women, "birth control" referred to a wide array of strategies for preventing conception—including abstinence and coitus interruptus. That suffragists, moral reformers, and free-love enthusiasts all advocated voluntary motherhood indicates the extent to which it reflected late Victorian sensibilities, highlights the importance of social movements to changing cultural assumptions, and shows how women used Victorian expectations to gain sexual autonomy (Gordon 1974). James Reed challenged Gordon and Smith by arguing that birth control transformed from a private vice into a public virtue not as a result of women's increasing power in the home or the demands of organized women, but out of "the desire of socially ambitious Americans to control their fertility" (Reed 2011, x). He, James Mohr, and Kristin Luker further showed that physicians supported laws against abortion and birth control in an effort to distance themselves from quacks and enhance their own professional status. Thus, unlike today, abortion and birth control politics in the late nineteenth century revolved around issues of social mobility, social control, and professionalization, not morality (Mohr 1978; Luker 1984).

Recently, scholarship has focused on the more quotidian—birth-control devices, abortion techniques, and the experiences of women who struggled to control their fertility in Gilded Age America. Janet Farrell Brodie portrays a culture that possessed a wide array of contraceptive options and abortion services but witnessed a decline in their quality and availability under the Comstock laws (Brodie 1994). Reagan and Andrea Tone argue that the existence of a sexual economy of birth control and abortion services indicates that Gilded Age law did not reflect popular morality. Leslie Reagan highlights the many nineteenth-century physicians who performed safe abortions in standard medical settings, while Tone demonstrates that contraceptive devices and chemicals escaped the law if they were marketed as disease preventatives (Reagan 1997; Tone 1996). Clearly, neither Comstockery nor Victorian reticence functioned as totalizing forces at the end of the nineteenth century. Women, men, doctors, and commercial entrepreneurs all found ways to limit fertility and bring about a precipitous decline in the nation's birthrate, despite living under the most restrictive laws against birth control and abortion the country had ever seen.

More radical sexual experimentation—from celibacy to group marriage—could be found in Gilded Age utopian communities, many of which disbanded by century's end. One scholar explained their demise as caused by their refusal to embrace marital monogamy, but others have argued that utopian communities failed because, even when they espoused ideals of equality, they operated according to patriarchal assumptions. For example, the Oneida Community's male leader demanded the right to sexual intercourse with all female virgins (Carden 1969; Muncy 1973; Kern 1981). Jason Vickers argued that Oneida folded when, by the late 1870s, an aging patriarch, generational turnover, and state opposition eroded the founders' spiritual inspiration, leaving in place only the regulatory apparatus of its sexual regime (Vickers 2013). Sexuality lay at the heart of many Gilded Age utopian visions and may, in addition, have brought about their downfall.

Advocates and practitioners of free love could be found in Gilded Age cities, small towns, and even farms in a movement made possible by the same burgeoning of literacy and print culture that disturbed Comstock and others. Free lovers and vice crusaders actually shared many concerns about the power of sexual impulses, importance of motherhood, and value of self-control, though they identified radically different solutions (Sears 1977). Using over three thousand letters written by women to sex-radical newspapers, most published in the Midwest, Joanne Passet argues that the same forces that gave rise to Populism—economic stress and a deep-rooted belief in individual sovereignty—also drew women to free love. Compared to men, they preferred sexual freedom to variety, reproductive autonomy to genetic improvement, and equality above all (Passet 2003). Jesse F. Battan shows that sex-radical periodicals exercised a transformative impact on their audience, freeing readers to seek sexual pleasure but also to resist unwanted sexual contact, including marital. Of necessity, free-love literature employed a strategy of exposure to highlight inconsistencies in Victorian ideals regarding sex and marriage, while challenging the idea that sex is shameful and should be secret (Battan 2004).

Victoria Woodhull—a prominent free lover whose flamboyance matched Anthony Comstock's—attracted renewed scholarly interest at the end of the twentieth century. The previous seventy years had seen the publication of only three biographies—all sensational accounts that failed to treat her as an historically significant political figure. In the 1990s, as Americans debated whether a sitting president should be required to testify about his sexual dalliances with a young intern, journalists and historians reconsidered Woodhull—a woman who more than a century earlier called the nation's attention to the sexual (mis)behavior of a highly placed man. Lois Beachy Underhill and Amanda Frisken reassessed Woodhull's historical importance by characterizing her run for president of the United States as the act, not of a deranged egotist, but a political idealist and suffragist. They also interpreted her exposure of Reverend Henry Ward Beecher's adultery as motivated not by personal animus or greed but to draw attention to the broader culture's hypocrisy about matters of sexuality. Frisken challenges those who blamed Woodhull for the decline in the women's rights movement, emphasizing that it survived an era that saw the death of other radical movements, notably free-love utopianism and Reconstruction (Underhill 1996; Frisken 2004). Journalist Myra MacPherson breaks new ground in a book that follows Woodhull to England in the 1880s. There Woodhull altered her name, endorsed eugenics, declared marriage a sacred institution, stalked a rich British man, threatened to sue him for damages if he did not marry her, married him, and until his death communicated such dependence and neediness that one searches her letters in vain for a glimmer of the legend (MacPherson 2014).

Woodhull's concept of free love included sexual autonomy; the ideal of Victorian womanhood required chastity; both demanded freedom from rape. Among the first historians of the nineteenth century to explore this topic, Elizabeth Pleck aimed to explain the tepid response of organized women to sexual assault. Were white women's rights activists afraid that calling men out on rape would compromise their bid for political rights? Did black suffragists refrain from discussing rape because it was so often an excuse for lynching black men? (Pleck 1983). Or was it, as Linda Gordon and Ellen DuBois suggested, that for Victorian women, "the norms of legal sexual intercourse were in themselves so objectionable that rape didn't seem that much worse!" (DuBois and Gordon 1983, 9). Later scholarship emphasized women's resistance to marital rape in particular by cataloging the frequency with which Victorian women's divorce applications cited and prescriptive literature lamented the sexual brutality of husbands (Smith-Rosenberg 1986; Pleck 1987; Battan 1999). Laws against seduction proliferated in the nineteenth century and, although historians have treated these as anti-prostitution strategies, Stephen Robertson demonstrates their use against rape (Robertson 2006).

Beginning in the 1880s, women did mobilize to raise the age at which a female could legally consent to sexual intercourse. That they organized from within a reform coalition that defeated state-regulated prostitution indicates how strongly they associated recruitment into prostitution with statutory rape. Mary Odem maintains that the age-of-consent movement's racialized rhetoric and focus on criminal law—long used against black men—alienated black women who turned instead to racial uplift. Odem's larger point, however, hews to an older social control model; reformers' success in raising the age of consent—from as low as ten years in some states to fourteen, sixteen, or eighteen in most—"did little to address the more common forms of sexual exploitation of working-class women and girls and, in fact, led to coercive and repressive measures against them" (Odem 1995, 185). Similarly, Sharon R. Ullman casts the age-of-consent laws as anti-immigrant rather than pro-woman, emphasizing that they fell hard on foreign-born men (Ullman 1997). Other scholars have contested social-control interpretations, arguing that the age-of-consent movement must be understood first and foremost as an anti-rape effort and one that initially attracted black women's support. Leslie Dunlap demonstrates that white and black women in the South worked together for age-of-consent laws until disfranchisement tore their alliance apart. For Dunlap, Robertson, and Jane Larson, women's rights activists did not ignore rape in the nineteenth century; they adhered to gender expectations by mobilizing to protect children rather than themselves, doing so in a world that claimed to believe in female passionlessness but readily assumed the licentiousness of women who charged men with rape. Thus, activists who worked to raise the age of consent aimed to protect young women using a strategy that addressed major cultural contradictions while preserving key cultural ideals (Larson 1997; Dunlap 1999; Robertson 2002).

The most recent research on rape in the Gilded Age examines the role of sexual violence in resurrecting racial hierarchies after emancipation and Reconstruction. This line of scholarly inquiry began in response to the 1970s feminist anti-rape movement and Susan Brownmiller's *Against Our Will: Men, Women, and Rape* (1975), a study that many criticized as insensitive to race. Jacquelyn Dowd Hall followed up with her own history of rape and racial violence in the post-Reconstruction South. "Rape is first and foremost a crime against women," she insisted, while maintaining that the history of rape is the history of lynching. Rape asserted white domination in the private sphere while lynching did the same in the public one. The myth of the black rapist defied the facts even as it reinforced white supremacy and bolstered the southern code of chivalry that protected white women in exchange for their subservience to white men (Hall 1983, 332).

By the 1990s, historians of rape in the post-Reconstruction South aimed to complicate racial categories by drawing attention to reproductive racial mixing and demonstrating that neither white nor black southerners behaved monolithically. Martha Hodes shows that until the end of the Civil War, interracial couplings were often tolerated, but after emancipation, white men created a new system of control based on the myth that black men wanted nothing more than to rape white women. This myth justified the lynching of black men, discouraged white women from pursuing sexual liaisons with them, and reestablished white men's control (Hodes 1997). Diane Sommerville situates the origins of the rape myth later in the nineteenth century and shows that a shared misogyny and prejudice against poor women sometimes led elite white men to defend black men accused of rape. Race did not always trump other loyalties; gender and class mattered too (Sommerville 2004). The question of how lynching affected southern women's politics and anti-rape reform lay behind Crystal Feimster's examination of a white southern woman who ceased to advocate lynching after she realized that violent white supremacy did not advance women's rights (Feimster 2009). Hannah Rosen argues that bodily integrity represented a crucial component of citizenship for black women and men, one denied by slavery and the vigilante violence that replaced it. White southern men used rape and the rape myth to shore up their own status and power by claiming to protect their families even as they prevented black men from doing the same (Rosen 2009). Questions about the relationship between sexual violence and citizenship also inform Estelle Freedman's recent work. She shows how the political empowerment of suffrage became linked to protection from sexual violence, but also how an emphasis on age of consent reinforced assumptions that only innocent females could be raped (Freedman 2013). Together, these books demonstrate the centrality of sex and violence to the political privileges of white men and reveal some of the ways that discourse, activism, and litigation around rape challenged even as it strengthened racial hierarchies and the Victorian ideal of separate spheres.

Progressive-Era Trade-offs and Modern Sexuality: Making Sex Public in an Era of Reform and Consumerism

If Gilded Age reformers have been associated with preserving separation between the spheres, their Progressive Era successors have been credited with collapsing them. The ideal, of course, never represented reality; nor was it sustainable. In Barbara Welter's memorable words, it contained the seeds of its own destruction; indeed, the very historical developments that gave rise to it brought it down (Welter 1966, 174). The growth of industrialization laid the groundwork for imagining separate spheres by removing production from the household, relocating it in the public realm, and remunerating it with cash. But ongoing industrial development further eroded the ideal; cities collapsed distinctions between public and private, attracted immigrants who brought diverse cultural practices and values, provided employment that took young women out of the home, developed a flourishing consumer culture, discouraged large families, and inspired middle-class women to take collective action on a wide range of issues. All of these changes would exercise a profound influence on American sexual culture, transitioning it, many would say, from Victorianism to modernity.

Scholars struggle to define sexual modernity. Some associate it with the emergence of sexual rights or the creation of heterosexual and homosexual identities. Others find it in the growing acceptance of pleasure as the purpose of sex or in the public display of sexualized and exposed (white) female bodies. Historians also credit the shaping of these developments to different agents, including Progressive reformers, women's rights activists, medical professionals, working-class youth, commercial entrepreneurs, bohemian radicals, and even middle-class slummers. Most agree, however, that the twentieth century opened a significant era of change in sexual ideology and behavior.

Unintended consequences have become a hallmark of Progressivism historiography generally, but especially with regard to prostitution. Here, scholars have tried to explain how the Victorian Era's necessary evil became, for Progressives, an eradicable social evil. John C. Burnham associated this shift with a sexual revolution launched by physicians in the social hygiene movement. Impelled by new scientific knowledge about venereal disease, they took aim at prostitution, the conspiracy of silence, and the Victorian double standard, using surveys, sex education, and other strategies that opened a "Pandora's box of sexual discussion" (Burnham 1973, 907). Ruth Rosen's classic study, inspired by the rise of a prostitutes' rights movement in the 1970s, portrayed Progressive reformers as paternalists who disregarded the individual rights of prostitutes. Rosen finds that female reformers may have been more likely to consider prostitutes innocent victims of male lust, while men saw them as threats to male health and morality. The results for prostitutes were the same; reformers drove them out of the protected female space of the brothel and into the danger of male-dominated streets. Timothy Gilfoyle's later work, by contrast, depicts the brothel less romantically and finds greater independence for prostitutes who worked in saloons and hotels (Rosen 1982; Gilfoyle 1992). More recent interpretations associate the decline in brothel prostitution with other forces and reform goals. Mara Keire argues that Progressives opposed prostitution less for its immorality than its association with corrupt commerce, while Elizabeth Alice Clements suggests that brothel prostitution succumbed to prostitutes' own choices and competition from sexually adventurous working-class girls (Keire 2010; Clements 2006). The Great Migration and racial segregation figure prominently in Cynthia Blair's work, which identifies an increase in black brothels in 1920s Chicago (Blair 2010). By contrast, racial politics ended the red-light district in late 1910s Storyville, Louisiana as the eroticized "octoroons" lost favor in a culture no longer comfortable with commercializing the sexual dynamics of the plantation (Landau 2013). Reformers alone did not bring about the demise of all red-light districts in the Progressive Era; moreover, broader cultural changes influenced the results of their eradication efforts.

Federal and state actors take center stage in another body of scholarship on Progressive-Era prostitution. Alan Brandt's social history of venereal disease demonstrates that moralists dominated Progressive-Era efforts to eradicate prostitution, though pragmatic medical professionals trumped them during World War I when the US military provided brothels for soldiers abroad (Brandt 1985). Similarly, Laura Briggs finds that US policymakers established a system of regulated prostitution in turn-of-the-century Puerto Rico, creating a modern colonial state that provided male occupiers with sexual access to healthy native women (Briggs 2002). Prostitution remained taboo stateside, and Mary Odem and Courtney Shah show how federal officials in the 1910s detained and imprisoned women suspected of it, often aided by female reformers and institutions designed to protect women (Odem 1995; Shah 2010). Similarly, Jessica Pliley discovers that the 1910 Mann—or White Slave Traffic—Act intended to protect women but actually contributed to the exponential growth of the new Federal Bureau of Investigation (FBI) which later expanded its reach to include women guilty of adultery and other forms of immorality (Pliley 2014). This new scholarship examines the role of race and sex in US state- and empire-building.

The juvenile justice system emerged in the Progressive Era and functioned, according to some scholars, as an agent of sexual counter-revolution. It reinforced the Victorian double standard by targeting sexually active girls but not boys, acting as "a rearguard defense against emerging modern views on the reality of female sexual desire" (Schlossman and Wallach 1978, 91). Many historians illuminate the class and ethnic biases, gendered perspectives, professional aspirations, and eugenic values of reformers and officials who operated juvenile reform institutions. Together they show the centrality of middle-class white women to the creation of the juvenile justice system, the ease with which sympathetic agencies of protection became punitive systems of control, and the ways that working-class and immigrant parents made use of a system that girls vigorously resisted (Alexander 1995; Odem 1995; Clapp 1999; Meis-Knupfer 2001; Rembis 2011).

Scholars who focused on the heterosocial world of working girls and young women debate their relative agency or victimization. Joanne Meyerowitz's work on women adrift explains that young white women participated in sexual encounters, sometimes out of personal choice, sometimes due to financial necessity, but always within narrow constraints (Meyerowitz, 1988). Kathy Peiss and Nan Enstad emphasize their agency, portraying young white women as pleasure-seekers who negotiated sexual encounters with men in a consumer culture of "treating" that was unequal—men had financial resources, women had only their bodies—but apparently "fun" (Peiss 1986; Enstad 1999). Black working women also sought out amusements in dance halls and juke joints where, Tera Hunter argues, sexual repartee, dancing, and touching provided renewal and recovery from the debasing work of domestic service and dehumanization of Jim Crow racism (Hunter 1997).

Elite black women saw things differently. Perceiving the reputations of all black women as precarious and black working women as especially vulnerable to assault and slander, they organized for "racial uplift." By embracing the ideal of chastity and employing a politics of respectability they aimed to elevate all black women. In addition, they offered the young wholesome amusements to distract them from harmful alternatives, and vocational training to help them escape the vices—including rape, sexual harassment, and dehumanizing treatment—of domestic service (Wolcott 1997; Hunter 1997; White 1999).

Not until the 1970s would sexual harassment emerge as a label for the flirtation, sexual pressure, and outright coercion that women have long experienced in the workplace. The first historians to study the topic in the Progressive Era showed how collaborations with middle-class women inspired industrial workers to resist sexual insults by employing strikes, collective self-help, and the language of ladyhood (Bularzik 1978; Siegel 2004; Bender 2004). More recently, Julie Berebitsky traces the emergence of the sexualized office alongside growing gender equality. In this context, female clerical workers became seductresses rather than victims of seduction, and fears about white slavery gave way to concerns about sexual blackmail. By the 1930s, states around the country began to overturn seduction laws designed to protect women from male sexual predators (McLaren 2002; Berebitsky 2012).

If the ideal Victorian woman was passionless, the "new woman" was sexually savvy, available, and potentially manipulative. Christine Stansell and Ellen Kay Trimberger trace the emergence of this new woman to the intellectual bohemians and radical communities of 1910s Greenwich Village. Here advocates of free love and opponents of traditional marriage continued the work of their utopian ancestors, leading unconventional sexual lives but failing to achieve gender equality. Through their own cultural products, however—novels, paintings, plays, stage performances, movies, court cases, fashion, and even comic strips—they exercised the sort of outsized influence that had escaped nineteenth-century utopians (Trimberger 1983; Ullman 1997; Rabinovitz 1998; Stansell 2000; Latham 2000; Glenn 2000; Lepore 2014; Wheeler 2014; Rabinovitch-Fox 2015).

These cultural products challenged older prohibitions against public sexual expression and inspired a new generation of anti-obscenity activism led by middle-class women who exercised influence through a politics of womanhood. Combining maternal moral authority with assumptions of female unity, women pressured local theater owners and city councils as well as motion-picture moguls who produced for a national market. But in the modern world, women voted and not as a bloc; new women expressed sexual desire and practiced seduction; and the politics of womanhood gave way to what Andrea Friedman identifies as democratic moral authority, the stuff of citizen juries and consumer demand (Parker 1997; Friedman 2000; Wheeler 2004).

Concerns about the impact of popular culture and urban amusements on youth, alongside the flourishing of sexology, led female anti-obscenity activists and other Progressive reformers to create sex-education programs and materials. Most scholars of sex education in the Progressive Era deem it a failure but, nevertheless, look to the past for lessons regarding ongoing controversies. Should sex education be abstinence-only or comprehensive? Focused on disease or health? Geared toward providing information or preventing experimentation? Historians have found that sex educators at the turn of the twentieth century were motivated by fears of pregnancy and disease, concentrated on danger, took an instrumentalist approach aimed at influencing adolescent behavior, and failed spectacularly. Their one crucial success—overcoming the Victorian ideal of reticence to establish sex education as a public obligation—has since been taken up by schools, the military, and other state agencies (Moran 2000; Jensen 2010; Lord 2010; Zimmerman 2015). Other scholars emphasize the darker side of Progressive-Era sex education, finding it deficient with regard to racial equality and gender inclusiveness but all-too effective at correlating heterosexual whiteness to normality (Carter 2007; Shah 2015).

Histories of the birth-control movement and its leaders also revolve around issues of success, failure, and race. The most critical biographical treatments of the movement's most prominent activist, Margaret Sanger, portray her as a racist who used birth control to advance eugenic visions of a white super-race, a megalomaniac who demanded submission from other birth-control activists, or an elitist who traded women's health for powerful alliances with the medical profession (Kennedy 1970; Gordon 1974; Rosen 2003; Frank 2005). Others emphasize how Sanger reflected her times, making pragmatic decisions that launched a veritable revolution in women's reproductive and sexual lives (Chesler 1992; McCann 1994; Baker 2011). Sanger takes a backseat to grassroots activists in a recent study of birth-control clinics between 1916 and 1939. Women who led these clinics did not simply follow the national movement or its leaders, but pursued practical strategies that responded to local needs (Hajo 2010). Birth controllers helped to expand the reach of the First Amendment as activists defended their right to free speech beginning in the 1910s. Birth control also mediated gender-related tensions for individuals who experimented with free-love marriages. By reducing the reproductive consequences of heterosexual promiscuity, it helped to level the playing field for women (Wheeler 2014).

Marriage has attracted a great deal of recent scholarly interest. New work on the topic ranges widely to show how Progressive-Era marital policies assisted in the colonization of Puerto Rico, strengthened white supremacy, established gender expectations, liberalized divorce and separation, and helped preserve the nation's reputation at the end of World War I (Findlay 1999; Cott 2000; Hartog 2000; Pascoe 2009; Zeiger 2010). Focusing less on policies and more on expectations of modern marriage, Elaine Tyler May and Christina Simmons find that, while men anticipated sexual satisfaction and domestic comfort, women sought economic security and happiness. Many worried that the rising divorce rate indicated disillusionment with marriage, but in fact it reflected greater hopes for fulfillment. Women remained disadvantaged, however, by a model of marriage that treated men's sexual desire and women's sexual deference as central to the relationship (May 1980; Simmons 2009).

Even as expectations for modern marriage defined gender roles along lines of biology, the biological sex of one's partner increasingly defined one's identity. George Chauncey cautions that as late as 1919, working-class men continued to operate under a much more complex system in which the gender with which one's sexual behavior was associated—inserter (male) or receiver (female)—rather than the sex of the partner determined one's status as "normal" or "perverted" (Chauncey 1994). John Wrathall and Peter Boag show, however, that the medical model of sexual binaries influenced the identities of men in the YMCA, while Kevin Murphy demonstrates how "cross-class brotherhood" presented a positive model of homosexuality (Gustav-Wrathall 1998; Boag 2003; Murphy 2008). Lesbian identity formation may have worked differently because, as Lillian Faderman points out, working-class women who loved women depended financially on marriage and could not create the sort of subcultures that allowed working-class men to develop their own identities. Medical morbidification of homosexuality helped to create a lesbian identity even as it made the Boston marriages middle-class women had enjoyed decreasingly viable (Faderman 1991; Rupp 1999). But lesbian identities did not derive only from medical pathology; Lisa Duggan identifies three contributors—newspapers that published stories about women's erotic relationships, sexologists who "reappropriated those stories as 'cases,'" and the "women themselves [who] reworked them as 'identities'" (Duggan 1996, 793). Even as some sexual identities solidified, others remained unstable. Indeed as Regina Kunzel argues, single-sex prisons exposed the situational dimensions of sexual desire and raised questions about acquired versus congenital homosexuality. Meanwhile, prison officials policed the emerging homo- heterosexual binary by segregating "true" homosexuals from other inmates (Kunzel 2008). Sexologists were the most visible creators of modern sexual identities, but clearly they did not work alone; nor did the binaries they developed prevent individuals from experimenting with a wide range of possibilities.

In the twenty-first century, the notion of sexual identity remains salient, if malleable, but another feature of sexual modernism—eugenics—has lost favor. In its day, the term eugenics held a variety of meanings along a spectrum that included prenatal care and better baby contests on one end, eugenic sterilization and euthanasia on the other (Pernick 1996; Selden 2005; Lombardo, ed. 2011). Even coercive surgical sterilization won support from the Progressive elite—Left and Right, black and white, male and female—including highly respected reformers, religious leaders, physicians, scholars, corporate philanthropies, and educated, middle-class folk. They embraced it as a scientific tool for improving "the race" variously defined, by sterilizing "the unfit," also variously defined, and were motivated by immigration and changing gender roles—especially the demise of the "true woman" and shrinking of the middle-class family (Pickens 1968; Kline 2001; Black 2003; Rosen 2004; Bruinius 2006).

Although eugenics is associated with the Progressive Era, its popularity extended well beyond. Recent research has focused on the South where, according to Edward Larson, eugenics came later due to the absence of a significant population of immigrants, lack of a fully developed delivery infrastructure, and, ironically, the presence of Jim Crow. Southern whites had established such effective racial control that they were able to direct eugenic policies primarily toward poor whites, especially sexually active women (Larson 1996). Gregory Michael Dorr shows how eugenic science helped Virginians "navigate between the extremes of New South 'modernism' and Old South 'traditionalism'" by equipping them with "progressive" devices—eugenics-inspired legislation and even settlement houses for black women—that attracted support from African American male leaders even as it shored up white supremacy and patriarchal control (Dorr 2008, 7).

Rape—real and imagined—did the same thing, solidifying white men's power in the Progressive Era as it had in the Gilded Age. Glenda Gilmore shows how white men in North Carolina used a black-on-white rape scare to destroy the Republican/Populist alliance that had trumped Democratic rule in 1896 (Gilmore 1996). After the disfranchisement of black men, southern black and white women's coalition against rape and for raising the age of consent crumbled. In place of it, white southern women transformed their attacks on white men's sexual behavior into tools for "gospel eugenics" and "race betterment" (Dunlap 1999). Charges of rape were leveled frequently at black men in Virginia, though, according to Lisa Lindquist Dorr, they did not go uncontested or lead automatically to lynchings or executions (Dorr 2004). As Freedman shows, however, the era that treated rape as the Negro crime also considered white men uniquely vulnerable to false charges of sexual assault. Despite the success of the movement to raise the legal age of consent, in practice, state institutions took a less protective and more punitive approach to girls and young women. In the early twentieth century, the white woman became subject to a dynamic with which the black woman was all too familiar—the sexualized female could not be trusted; she seduced men, falsely accused them of rape, and warranted punishment, not protection (Freedman 2013).

Conclusion

The Victorian-to-modern framework has come under attack, not only by those who identify countervailing trends, but also by scholars who call for abandoning it altogether. Catherine Cocks, for example, argues that the framework assumes a monolithic American sexual culture that ignores differences associated with race, class, region, and ethnicity (Cocks 2006). But clearly, as this chapter demonstrates, the framework remains useful precisely because it has inspired scholars to expose its mythical aspects while exploring the many possibilities for sexuality in the late nineteenth and early twentieth centuries. No longer understood as a totalizing system, Victorianism and modernism instead provide historians with a shorthand for periodizing the wide range of sexual ideologies and practices that underwent major changes between and across the Gilded Age and Progressive Era. While some would associate these changes with liberalization and growing sexual freedom, this chapter argues for a much more complicated understanding. The Victorian Era was not as hostile to sexuality as once thought, and sexual modernism brought a mixed bag of new laws, identities, assumptions, and expectations. For women, increasing equality with men came with growing sexualization of their bodies. Black and poor women were all too familiar with this phenomenon in a Victorian culture that denied them what it most prized—the ability to create stark gender differences—and imposed on them what it most scorned—sexualization. The modern world sexualized women of all races and classes, bringing new opportunities but also creating new vulnerabilities that undermined women's citizenship rights. The system of sexuality that emerged during the Progressive Era has proven surprisingly durable, extending throughout the twentieth and into the twenty-first century, across the continental United States, its territories, and around the world. Explaining that remains a major task for historians of sexuality.

References

Alexander, Ruth. 1995. *The Girl Problem: Female Sexual Delinquency in New York, 1900–1930*. Ithaca, NY: Cornell University Press.

Baker, Jean H. 2011. *Margaret Sanger: A Life of Passion*. New York: Hill & Wang.

Barker-Benfeld, Ben. 1976. *The Horrors of the Half-Known Life: Male Attitudes Toward Women and Sexuality in Nineteenth-Century America*. New York: Harper & Row.

Bates, Anna Louise. 1991. "Protective Custody: A Feminist Interpretation of Anthony Comstock's Life and Laws." Ph.D. diss., State University of New York.

Battan, Jesse F. 1999. "The 'Rights' of Husbands and the 'Duties' of Wives: Power and Desire in the American Bedroom, 1850–1910." *Journal of Family History* April: 165–186.

—. 2004. "'You Cannot Fix the Scarlet Letter on my Breast!': Women Reading, Writing, and Reshaping the Sexual Culture of Victorian America." *Journal of Social History* Spring: 601–624.

Beisel, Nicola. 1997. *Imperiled Innocents: Anthony Comstock and Family Reproduction in Victorian America*. Princeton, NJ: Princeton University Press.

Bender, Daniel E. 2004. "'Too Much of Distasteful Masculinity': Historicizing Sexual Harassment in the Garment Sweatshop and Factory." *Journal of Women's History* 15, 4: 91–116.

Berebitsky, Julie. 2012. *Sex and the Office*. New Haven, CT: Yale University Press.

Black, Edwin. 2003. *War Against the Weak: Eugenics and America's Campaign to Create a Master Race*. Washington, DC: Dialog Press.

Blair, Cynthia M. 2010. *I've got to Make My Livin': Black Women's Sex Work in Turn-of-the-Century Chicago*. Illinois: University of Chicago Press.

Boag, Peter, 2003. *Same-Sex Affairs: Constructing and Controlling Homosexuality in the Pacific Northwest*. Berkeley: University of California Press.

Boyer, Paul. 2002. *Purity in Print: Book Censorship in America from the Gilded Age to the Computer Age*. Madison: University of Wisconsin Press.

Brandt, Allan. 1985. *No Magic Bullet: A Social History of Venereal Disease in the United States Since 1880*. New York: Oxford University Press.

Briggs, Laura. 2003. *Reproducing Empire: Race, Sex, Science, and U.S. Imperialism in Puerto Rico*. Berkeley: University of California Press.

Brodie, Janet Farrell. 1994. *Contraception and Abortion in Nineteenth-Century America*. Ithaca, NY: Cornell University Press.

Brownmiller, Susan. 1975. *Against Our Will: Men, Women and Rape*. New York: Simon and Schuster.

Bruinius, Harry. 2006. *Better For All the World: The Secret History of Forced Sterilization and America's Quest for Racial Purity*. New York: Random House.

Bularzik, Mary. 1978. "Sexual Harassment at the Workplace: Historical Notes." *Radical America* 12: 25–43.

Bullough, Vern. 1975. "Sex and the Medical Model." *Journal of Sex Research* 11, 4: 291–303.

Burnham, John C. 1973. "The Progressive Era Revolution in American Attitudes toward Sex." *Journal of American History* 59, 4: 885–908.

Butler, Anne M. 1985. *Daughters of Joy, Sisters of Misery: Prostitutes in the American West, 1865–1890*. Urbana: University of Illinois Press.

Carden, Maren Lockwood. 1969. *Oneida: Utopian Community to Modern Corporation*. Baltimore: Johns Hopkins University Press.

Carter, Julian B. 2007. *The Heart of Whiteness: Normal Sexuality and Race in America, 1880–1940.* Durham, NC: Duke University Press.

Chauncey, George. 1994. *Gay New York: Gender, Urban Culture and the Making of the Gay Male World, 1890–1940.* New York: Basic Books.

Chesler, Ellen. 1992. *Woman of Valor: Margaret Sanger and the Birth Control Movement in America.* New York: Simon & Schuster.

Clapp, Elizabeth. 1999. *Mothers of All Children: Women Reformers and the Rise of Juvenile Courts in Progressive-Era America.* University Park: Penn State University Press.

Clements, Elizabeth Alice. 2006. *Love for Sale: Courting, Treating, and Prostitution in New York City, 1900–1945.* Chapel Hill: University of North Carolina Press.

Cocks, Catherine. 2006. "Rethinking Sexuality in the Progressive Era." *Journal of the Gilded Age and Progressive Era* 5, 2: 93–118.

Cott, Nancy. 1979. "Passionlessness: An Interpretation of Victorian Sexual Ideology, 1790–1850." In *A Heritage of Her Own: Toward a New Social History of American Women*, ed. Nancy F. Cott and Elizabeth H. Pleck, 162–181. New York: Simon & Schuster.

—. 2000. *Public Vows: A History of Marriage and the Nation.* Cambridge, MA: Harvard University Press.

Darby, Robert. 2003. "The Masturbation Taboo and the Rise of Routine Male Circumcision: A Review of the Historiography." *Journal of Social History* 36, 3: 737–757.

Degler, Carl. 1974. "What Ought To Be and What Was: Women's Sexuality in the Nineteenth Century." *American Historical Review* 79: 1467–90.

Dorr, Gregory Michael. 2008. *Segregation's Science: Eugenics and Society in Virginia.* Charlottesville: University of Virginia Press.

Dorr, Lisa Lindquiat. 2004. *White Women, Rape, and the Power of Race in Virginia, 1900–1960.* Chapel Hill: University of North Carolina Press.

DuBois, Ellen Carol and Gordon, Linda. 1983. "Seeking Ecstasy on the Battlefield: Danger and Pleasure in Nineteenth-Century Feminist Sexual Thought." *Feminist Studies* Spring 9, 1: 7–25.

Duggan, Lisa. 1996. "The Trials of Alice Mitchell: Sensationalism, Sexology, and the Lesbian Subject in the Turn-of-the-Century America." *Signs* 18, 4: 791–814.

Dunlap, Leslie K. 1999. "The Reform of Rape Law and the Problem of White Men: Age-of-Consent Campaigns in the South, 1885–1910." In *Sex, Love, Race: Crossing Boundaries in North American History*, ed. Martha Hodes, 352–372. New York: New York University Press.

Enstad, Nan. 1999. *Ladies of Labor, Girls of Adventure: Working Women, Popular Culture, and Labor Politics at the Turn of the Twentieth Century.* New York: Columbia University Press.

Eskridge, William, Jr. 2008. *Dishonorable Passions: Sodomy Laws in America, 1861–2003.* New York: Viking.

Faderman, Lillian. 1978. "The Morbidification of Love Between Women by 19th-Century Sexologists." *Journal of Homosexuality* 4: 73–90.

—. 1991. *Odd Girls and Twilight Lovers: A History of Lesbian Life in Twentieth-Century America.* New York: Penguin.

Feimster, Crystal N. 2009. *Southern Horrors: Women and the Politics of Rape and Lynching.* Cambridge, MA: Harvard University Press.

Fields, Jill. 2007. *An Intimate Affair: Women, Lingerie, and Sexuality.* Los Angeles: University of California Press.

Findlay, Eileen J. Suarez. 1999. *Imposing Decency: The Politics of Sexuality and Race in Puerto Rico, 1870–1920.* Durham, NC: Duke University Press.

Frank, Angela. 2005. *Margaret Sanger's Eugenic Legacy: The Control of Female Fertility.* Jefferson, NC: McFarland.

Freedman, Estelle. 2013. *Redefining Rape: Sexual Violence in the Era of Suffrage and Segregation.* Cambridge, MA: Harvard University Press.

Friedman, Andrea. 2000. *Prurient Interests: Gender, Democracy, and Obscenity in New York City, 1909–1945.* New York: Columbia University Press.

Frisken, Amanda. 2004. *Victoria Woodhull's Sexual Revolution: Political Theater and the Popular Press in Nineteenth-Century America.* Philadelphia: University of Pennsylvania Press.

—. 2008. "Obscenity, Free Speech, and 'Sporting News' in 1870s America." *Journal of American Studies* 42, 3: 537–577.

Gilfoyle, Timothy. 1992. *City of Eros: New York City, Prostitution, and the Commercialization of Sex, 1790–1920.* New York: W. W. Norton.

Gilmore, Glenda. 1996. *Gender & Jim Crow: Women and the Politics of White Supremacy in North Carolina, 1896–1920.* Chapel Hill: University of North Carolina Press.

Glenn, Susan A. 2000. *Female Spectacle: The Theatrical Roots of Modern Feminism.* Cambridge, MA: Harvard University Press.

Goldman, Marion S. 1981. *Gold Diggers and Silver Miners: Prostitution and Social Life on the Comstock Lode.* Ann Arbor: University of Michigan Press.

Gollaher, David L. 2000. *Circumcision: A History of the World's Most Controversial Surgery.* New York: Basic Books.

Gordon, Linda, ed. 1974. *Woman's Body, Woman's Right: Birth Control in America.* New York: Penguin.

Gurstein, Rochelle. 1996. *The Repeal of Reticence: A History of America's Legal and Cultural Struggles over Free Speech, Obscenity, Sexual Liberation, and Modern Art.* New York: Hill & Wang.

Gustav-Wrathall, John Donald. 1998. *Take the Young Stranger by the Hand: Same-Sex Relations and the YMCA.* Chicago: University of Chicago Press.

Hajo, Cathy Moran. 2010. *Birth Control on Main Street: Organizing Clinics in the United States, 1916–1939.* Urbana: University of Illinois Press.

Hall, Jacquelyn Dowd. 1983. "'The Mind that Burns in Each Body': Women, Rape, and Racial Violence." In *Powers of Desire: The Politics of Sexuality*, ed. Ann Snitow, Christine Stansell, and Sharon Thompson, 328–349. New York: Monthly Review Press.

Handlin, Oscar. 1948. *Race and Nationality in American Life.* Boston: Little, Brown.

Haney, Robert W. 1960. *Comstockery in America: Patterns of Censorship and Control.* Boston, MA: Beacon Press.

Hartog, Hendrik. 2000. *Man and Wife in America: A History.* Cambridge, MA: Harvard University Press.

Hatheway, Jay. 2003. *The Gilded Age Construction of Modern American Homophobia.* New York: Palgrave Macmillan.

Heap, Chad. 2008. *Slumming: Sexual and Racial Encounters in American Nightlife, 1885–1940.* Chicago: University of Chicago Press.

Hodes, Martha. 1997. *White Woman, Black Men: Illicit Sex in the Nineteenth-Century South*. New Haven, CT: Yale University Press.

Hoffman, Andrew J. 1995. "Mark Twain and Homosexuality." *Journal of American Literature* 67, 1: 23–49.

Horowitz, Helen Lefkowitz. 2002. *Rereading Sex: Battles over Sexual Knowledge and Suppression in Nineteenth-Century America*. New York: Alfred A. Knopf.

Hovey, Elizabeth Bainum. 1998. "Stamping out Smut: The Enforcement of Obscenity Laws, 1872–1915." PhD diss., Columbia University.

Hunter, Tera W. 1997. *To 'Joy My Freedom: Southern Black Women's Lives and Labors After the Civil War*. Cambridge, MA: Harvard University Press.

Jensen, Robin E. 2010. *Dirty Words: The Rhetoric of Public Sex Education, 1870–1924*. Champaign: University of Illinois Press.

Keire, Mara. 2010. *For Business and Pleasure: Red-Light Districts and the Regulation of Vice in the United States, 1890–1933*. Baltimore, MD: Johns Hopkins University Press.

Kennedy, David M. 1970. *Birth Control in America: The Career of Margaret Sanger*. New Haven, CT: Yale University Press.

Kern, Louis J. 1981. *An Ordered Love: Sex Roles and Sexuality in Victorian Utopias—the Shakers, the Mormons, and the Oneida Community*. Chapel Hill: University of North Carolina Press.

Kline, Wendy. 2001. *Building a Better Race: Gender, Sexuality, and Eugenics from the Turn of the Century to the Baby Boom*. Berkeley: University of California Press.

Kunzel, Regina. 2008. *Criminal Intimacy: Prison and the Uneven History of Modern American Sexuality*. Chicago: University of Chicago Press.

Landau, Emily Epstein. 2013. *Spectacular Wickedness: Sex, Race, and Memory in Storyville, New Orleans*. Baton Rouge: Louisiana State University Press.

Laqueur, Thomas. 2003. *Solitary Sex: A Cultural History of Masturbation*. New York: Zone Books.

Larson, Edward J. 1996. *Sex, Race, and Science: Eugenics in the Deep South*. Baltimore, MD: Johns Hopkins University Press.

Larson, Jane. 1997. "'Even a Worm Will Turn at Last': Rape Reform in Late Nineteenth Century America." *Yale Journal of Law and Humanities* 9, 1: 1–71.

Latham, Angela J. 2000. *Posing a Threat: Flappers, Chorus Girls, and Other Brazen Performers of the American 1920s*. Hanover, NH: University Press of New England.

Lemons, J. Stanley. 1977. Review of *Woman's Body, Woman's Right*. *American Historical Review* 82: 1095.

Lepore, Jill. 2014. *The Secret History of Wonder Woman*. New York: Alfred A. Knopf.

Lombardo, Paul A., ed. 2011. *A Century of Eugenics in America*. Bloomington: University of Indiana Press.

Lord, Alexandra M. 2010. *Condom Nation: The U.S. Government's Sex Education from World War I to the Internet*. Baltimore, MD: Johns Hopkins University Press.

Luker, Kristin. 1984. *Abortion and the Politics of Motherhood*. Berkeley: University of California Press.

Lystra, Karen. 1989. *Searching the Heart: Women, Men, and Romantic Love in Nineteenth-Century America*. New York: Oxford University Press.

MacPherson, Myra. 2014. *The Scarlet Sisters: Sex, Suffrage, and Scandal in the Gilded Age*. New York: Hachette.

Maines, Rachel P. 1999. *The Technology of Orgasm: "Hysteria," the Vibrator, and Women's Sexual Satisfaction*. Baltimore, MD: Johns Hopkins University Press.

May, Elaine Tyler. 1980. *Great Expectations: Marriage and Divorce in Post-Victorian America*. Chicago: University of Chicago Press.

McCann, Carole R. 1994. *Birth Control Politics in the United States, 1916–1945*. Ithaca, NY: Cornell University Press.

McGarry, Molly. 2008. *Ghosts of Futures Past: Spiritualism and the Cultural Politics of Nineteenth-Century America*. Berkeley: University of California Press.

McLaren, Angus. 2002. *Sexual Blackmail: A Modern History*. Cambridge, MA: Harvard University Press.

Meis-Knupfer, Anne. 2001. *Reform and Resistance: Gender Delinquency and America's First Juvenile Court*. New York: Routledge.

Meyerowitz, Joanne. 1988. *Women Adrift: Independent Wage Earners in Chicago, 1880–1930*. Chicago: University of Chicago Press.

Mohr, James C. 1978. *Abortion in America: The Origins and Evolution of National Policy, 1800–1900*. New York: Oxford University Press.

Moran, Jeffrey. 2000. *Teaching Sex: The Shaping of Adolescence in the Twentieth Century*. Cambridge, MA: Harvard University Press.

Muncy, Raymond Lee. 1973. *Sex and Marriage in Utopian Communities*. Bloomington: Indiana University Press.

Murphy, Kevin P. 2008. *Political Manhood: Red Bloods, Mollycoddles, and the Politics of Progressive Era Reform*. New York: Columbia University Press.

Odem, Mary E. 1995. *Delinquent Daughters: Protecting and Policing Adolescent Female Sexuality in the United States, 1885–1920*. Chapel Hill: University of North Carolina Press.

Parker, Alison. 1997. *Purifying America: Women, Cultural Reform, and Pro-Censorship Activism, 1873–1933*. Chicago: University of Illinois Press.

Parsons, Gail Pat, 1977. "Equal Treatment for All: American Medical Remedies for Male Sexual Problems: 1850–1900." *Journal of the History of Medicine* 32, 1: 55–71.

Passet, Joanne. 2003. *Sex Radicals and the Quest for Women's Equality*. Chicago: University of Illinois Press.

Pascoe, Peggy. 1990. *Relations of Rescue: The Search for Female Moral Authority in the American West, 1874–1939*. New York: Oxford University Press.

—. 2009. *What Comes Naturally: Miscegenation Law and the Making of Race in America*. New York: Oxford University Press.

Peiss, Kathy. 1986. *Cheap Amusements: Working Women and Leisure in Turn-of-the-Century New York*. Philadelphia, PA: Temple University Press.

Pernick, Martin S. 1996. *The Black Stork: Eugenics and the Death of "Defective" Babies in American Medicine and Motion Pictures Since 1915*. New York: Oxford University Press.

Picard, Alyssa. 2002. "'To Popularize the Nude in Art': Comstockery Reconsidered." *Journal of the Gilded Age and Progressive Era* 1, 3: 195–224.

Pickens, Donald. 1968. *Eugenics and the Progressives*. Nashville, TN: Vanderbilt University Press.

Pivar, David. 1973. *Purity Crusade: Sexual Morality and Social Control, 1868–1900*. Westport, CT: Greenwood Press.

Pleck, Elizabeth. 1983. "Feminist Responses to 'Crimes against Women.'" *Signs* 8, 3: 451–70.

—. 1987. *Domestic Tyranny: The Making of American Social Policy against Family Violence from Colonial Times to the Present.* New York: Oxford University Press.

Pliley, Jessica R. 2014. *Policing Sexuality: The Mann Act and the Making of the FBI.* Cambridge, MA: Harvard University Press.

Rabinovitch-Fox, Einav. 2015. "[Re]fashioning the New Woman: Women's Dress, the Oriental Style, and the Construction of American Feminist Imagery in the 1910s." *Journal of Women's History* 12, 2: 14–36.

Rabinovitz, Lauren. 1998. *For the Love of Pleasure: Women, Movies, and Culture in Turn-of-the-Century Chicago.* New Brunswick, NJ: Rutgers University Press.

Reagan, Leslie J. 1997. *When Abortion was a Crime: Women, Medicine, and Law in the United States, 1867–1973.* Berkeley: University of California Press.

Reed, James. 2011. *From Private Vice to Public Virtue: The Birth Control Movement and American Society Since 1830.* Princeton, NJ: Princeton University Press.

Rembis, Michael A. 2011. *Defining Deviance: Sex, Science, and Delinquent Girls, 1890–1960.* Urbana: University of Illinois Press.

Reynolds, David S. 1995. *Walt Whitman's America: A Cultural Biography.* New York: Alfred A. Knopf.

Riegel, Robert E. 1968. "Changing American Attitudes Toward Prostitution (1800–1920)." *Journal of the History of Ideas* 29, 3: 437–452.

Robertson, Stephen. 2002. "Age of Consent Law and the Making of Modern Childhood in New York City, 1886–1921." *Journal of Social History* 35, 4: 781–798.

—. 2006. "Sexual Violence and Marriage in New York City, 1886–1955." *Law and History Review* 24, 2: 331–373.

—. 2010. "Shifting the Scene of the Crime: Sodomy and the American History of Violence." *Journal of the History of Sexuality* 19, 2: 223–242.

Rodriguez, Sarah W. 2014. *Female Circumcision and Clitoridectomy in the United States.* New York: University of Rochester Press.

Rosen, Christine. 2004. *Preaching Eugenics: Religious Leaders and the American Eugenics Movement.* New York: Oxford University Press.

Rosen, Hannah. 2009. *Terror in the Heart of Freedom: Citizenship, Sexual Violence, and the Meaning of Race in the Postemancipation South.* Chapel Hill: University of North Carolina Press.

Rosen, Robyn L. 2003. *Reproductive Rights: Reformers and the Politics of Maternal Welfare, 1917–1940.* Columbus: Ohio State University Press.

Rosen, Ruth. 1982. *The Lost Sisterhood: Prostitution in America, 1900–1918.* Baltimore, MD: Johns Hopkins University Press.

Rothman, Ellen K. 1987. *Hands and Hearts: A History of Courtship in America.* Cambridge, MA: Harvard University Press.

Rotundo, E. Anthony. 1989. "Romantic Friendship: Male Intimacy and Middle-Class Youth in the Northern United States, 1800–1900." *Journal of Social History* 23, 1: 1–25.

Rupp, Leila J. 1999. *A Desired Past: A Short History of Same-Sex Love in America.* Chicago: University of Chicago Press.

Schlossman, Steven and Stephanie Wallach. 1978. "The Crime of Precocious Sexuality: Female Juvenile Delinquency in the Progressive Era." *Harvard Educational Review* 48, 1: 65–94.

Sears, Hal. 1977. *The Sex Radicals: Free Love in High Victorian America.* Lawrence: Regents Press of Kansas.

Selden, Steven. 2005. "Transforming Better Babies into Fitter Families: Archival Resources and the History of the American Eugenics Movement, 1908–1930." *Proceedings of the American Philosophical Society* 149, 2: 199–225.

Shah, Courtney Q. 2010. "'Against Their Own Weakness': Policing Sexuality and Women in San Antonio, Texas, during World War I." *Journal of the History of Sexuality* 19, 3: 458–482.

—. 2015. *Sex Ed, Segregated.* New York: University of Rochester Press.

Shah, Nayan. 2001. *Contagious Divides: Epidemics and Race in San Francisco's Chinatown.* Berkeley: University of California Press.

Shorter, Edward. 1977. Review of *Woman's Body, Woman's Right.* *Journal of Social History* 11, 2: 269–273.

Shumsky, Neil Larry. 1986. "Tacit Acceptance: Respectable Americans and Segregated Prostitution, 1870–1910." *Journal of Social History* 19, 4: 665–679.

Siegel, Reva B. 2004. "A Short History of Sexual Harassment." In *Directions in Sexual Harassment Law*, ed. Catharine A. MacKinnon and Reva B. Siegel, 1–39. New Haven, CT: Yale University Press.

Simmons, Christina. 2009. *Making Marriage Modern: Women's Sexuality from the Progressive Era to World War II.* New York: Oxford University Press.

Smith, Daniel Scott. 1973. "Family Limitation, Sexual Control, and Domestic Feminism in Victorian America." *Feminist Studies* 1, 3/4: 40–57.

Smith, Stacey L. 2013. *Freedom's Frontier: California and the Struggle over Unfree Labor, Emancipation, and Reconstruction.* Chapel Hill: University of North Carolina Press.

Smith-Rosenberg, Carroll. 1973. "The Female Animal: Medical and Biological Views of Woman and Her Role in Nineteenth-Century America." *Journal of American History* 60, 2: 332–356.

—. 1975. "The Female World of Love and Ritual." *Signs* 1: 1–29.

—. 1986. *Disorderly Conduct: Visions of Gender in Victorian America.* New York: Oxford University Press.

Sommerville, Diane Miller. 2004. *Rape and Race in the Nineteenth-Century South.* Chapel Hill: University of North Carolina Press.

Stansell, Christine. 2000. *American Moderns: Bohemian New York and the Creation of a New Century.* New York: Henry Holt.

Stoneley, Peter. 1996. "Rewriting the Gold Rush: Twain, Harte, and Homosociality." *Journal of American Studies* 30, 2: 189–209.

Terry, Jennifer. 1999. *An American Obsession: Science, Medicine, and Homosexuality in Modern Society.* Chicago: University of Chicago Press.

Tone, Andrea. 1996. *Devices & Desires: A History of Contraceptives in America.* New York: Hill & Wang.

Trimberger, Ellen Kay. 1983. "Feminism, Men, and Modern Love: Greenwich Village, 1900–1925." In *Powers of Desire: The Politics of Sexuality*, ed. Ann Snitow, Christine Stansell, and Sharon Thompson, 131–152. New York: Monthly Review Press.

Tripp, C. A. 2005. *The Intimate World of Abraham Lincoln.* New York: Free Press.

Ullman, Sharon R. 1997. *Sex Seen: The Emergence of Modern Sexuality in America.* Berkeley: University of California Press.

Underhill, Lois Beachy. 1996. *The Woman Who Ran for President: The Many Lives of Victoria Woodhull.* New York: Penguin.

Vickers, Jason. 2013. "'That Deep Kind of Discipline of Spirit': Freedom, Power, Family, Marriage, and Sexuality in the Story of John Humphrey Noyes and the Oneida Community." *American Nineteenth Century History* 14, 1: 1–26.

Walters, Ronald. 1974. *Primers for Prudery: Sexual Advice to Victorian America*. Englewood Cliffs, NJ: Prentice-Hall.

Welter, Barbara, 1966. "The Cult of True Womanhood: 1820–1860." *American Quarterly* 18, 2: 151–174.

Wheeler, Leigh Ann. 2004. *Against Obscenity: Reform and the Politics of Womanhood in America, 1873–1935*. Baltimore, MD: Johns Hopkins University Press.

—. 2013. *How Sex Became a Civil Liberty*. New York: Oxford University Press.

White, Deborah Grey. 1999. *Too Heavy a Load: Black Women in Defense of Themselves, 1894–1994*. New York: W. W. Norton.

Wolcott, Virginia W. 1997. "'Bible, Bath, and Broom': Nannie Helen Burroughs's National Training School and African-American Racial Uplift." *Journal of Women's History* 9: 88–110.

Wood, Sharon E. 2005. *The Freedom of the Streets: Work, Citizenship, and Sexuality in a Gilded Age City*. Chapel Hill: University of North Carolina Press.

Zeiger, Susan. 2010. *Entangling Alliances: Foreign War Brides and American Soldiers in the Twentieth Century*. New York: New York University Press.

Zimmerman, Jonathan. 2015. *Too Hot to Handle: A Global History of Sex Education*. Princeton, NJ: Princeton University Press

Further Reading

Berkman, Joyce. 2011. "The Fertility of Scholarship on the History of Reproductive Rights in the United States." *History Compass* 9/5: 433–447.

Brumberg, Joan Jacobs. 1997. *The Body Project: An Intimate History of American Girls*. New York: Vintage Books.

Carlson, Allan C. 2009. "Comstockery, Contraception, and the Family: The Remarkable Achievements of an Anti-Vice Crusader." *The Family in America* 23, 1.

Chauncey, George. 2004. "'What Gay Studies Taught the Court': The Historians' Amicus Brief in Lawrence v. Texas." *GLQ: A Journal of Lesbian and Gay Studies* 10, 3: 509–538.

Cullen, David. 2007. "Back to the Future: Eugenics—A Bibliographic Essay." *Public Historian* 29, 3: 163–175.

D'Emilio, John and Freedman, Estelle B. 1988. *Intimate Matters: A History of Sexuality in America*. Chicago: University of Chicago Press.

DuBois, Ellen Carol. 1982. "Beyond the Victorian Syndrome: Feminist Interpretations of the History of Sexuality." *Radical America* 16, 1/2: 149–153.

Epstein, Barbara. 1983. "Family, Sexual Morality, and Popular Movements in Turn-of-the-Century America." In *Powers of Desire: The Politics of Sexuality*, ed. Ann Snitow, Christine Stansell, and Sharon Thompson, 117–130. New York: Monthly Review Press.

Foster, Lawrence. 1981. "Free Love and Feminism: John Humphrey Noyes and the *Oneida* Community." *Journal of the Early Republic* 1, 2: 165–183.

Franks, Angela. 2005. *Margaret Sanger's Eugenic Legacy: The Control of Female Fertility*. Jefferson, NC: McFarland.

Freedman, Estelle. 2006. "When Historical Interpretation Meets Legal Advocacy: Abortion, Sodomy, and Same-Sex Marriage." In *Feminism, Sexuality & Politics*, ed. Estelle Freedman. Chapel Hill: University of North Carolina Press.

Garton, Stephen. 2004. *Histories of Sexuality: Antiquity to Sexual Revolution*. New York: Routledge.

Gilfoyle, Timothy. 1999. "Prostitutes in History: From Parables of Pornography to Metaphors of Modernity." *American Historical Review* 104, 1: 117–141.

Grossberg, Michael. 1985. *Governing the Hearth: Law and Family in Nineteenth Century America*. Chapel Hill: University of North Carolina Press.

Haller, John S. and Robin M. 1977. *The Physician and Sexuality in Victorian America*. New York: W. W. Norton.

Jackson, Charles. 1996. "Against the Grain: Writing the History of Sexual Variance in America." *Borderlines: Studies in American Culture*: 278–286.

Johnson, Richard Christian. 1973. "Anthony Comstock: Reform, Vice, and the American Way." Ph.D. diss., University of Wisconsin.

Neuman, R. P. 1976. "Masturbation, Madness and the Modern Concept of Childhood and Adolescence." *Journal of Social History* 9: 1–27.

Padgug, Robert A. 1979. "Sexual Matters: On Conceptualizing Sexuality in History." *Radical History Review* 20: 3–23.

White, Kevin. 2000. *Sexual Liberation of Sexual License? The American Revolt Against Victorianism*. Chicago: Ivan R. Dee.

Chapter Nine

African Americans

Omar H. Ali

As with other periods in American history, during the Gilded Age and Progressive Era African Americans have been described and analyzed in a range of ways by historians. Scholars of an earlier generation writing about the period from the collapse of Reconstruction through the turn of the twentieth century tended to present African Americans as passive victims of economic exploitation, political marginalization, and violence—a view that remained dominant among professional historians throughout much of the twentieth century. Over time, this perspective has changed, with new approaches presenting African Americans as active political agents, bringing forth the voices of black women, and better locating the experiences of African Americans within the global African Diaspora.

There were a number of self-taught historians in the nineteenth century writing about the history of African Americans, notably George Washington Williams—his *History of the Negro Race in America from 1619 to 1880* was published in 1882—and in the early twentieth century, John Henrik Clarke, based in Harlem. Among the first professionally trained historians were W.E.B. Du Bois and Carter G. Woodson. They were followed soon thereafter by John Hope Franklin and then by Benjamin Quarles and Charles H. Wesley. These black scholars were among the first to highlight African Americans in the history of the United States, including during the Gilded Age and Progressive Era. They and their works, however, were largely marginalized by the wider American historical profession until the mid-twentieth century (see Dagbovie 2010, 19–20).

Although some scholars, such as Du Bois, wrote about black political agency, the first wave of professional historical works on the Gilded Age and Progressive Era either ignored or downplayed the role of African Americans in shaping society. The historian Rayford Logan famously described the period of the late nineteenth century as "the Nadir" in terms of "race-relations" and racial discrimination towards African Americans (1954). Like other historians of his time, Logan's work emphasized the exploitative system of sharecropping and the disfranchisement of African Americans in the South through legal mechanisms such as grandfather clauses, white primaries, and literacy tests. However, as in both the antebellum period and throughout Reconstruction, violence—or the threat of violence—permeated the lives of African Americans in the decades following Emancipation (Recent studies on black disfranchisement during the late nineteenth century point to the full support of the US Supreme Court in reversing rights gained by African Americans in the Fourteenth and Fifteenth Amendments of 1868 and 1870, and the Civil Rights Act of 1875; see Goldstone 2011).

In addition to legal and extra-legal attacks on African Americans and their voting rights post-Emancipation, debt peonage ravaged rural communities in the South, where nearly 90% of African Americans lived during the closing decades of the nineteenth century and the opening of the twentieth. In describing this, Du Bois contrasts the richness of the land with the impoverishment of the people in *The Souls of Black Folk* (1903), noting the hierarchy into which rural African Americans were placed: "A pall of debt hangs over the beautiful land; the merchants are in debt to the wholesalers, the planters are in debt to the merchants, the tenants owe the planters, and laborers bow and bend beneath the burden of it all" (126). Du Bois not only paints a poignant picture of conditions in the South during the late nineteenth century but provides among the first analyses of black sharecroppers, agricultural workers, and townsfolk living under what came to be called Jim Crow—the legal disfranchisement and segregation of African Americans that kept poor and working-class southerners divided along racial lines.

A Companion to the Gilded Age and Progressive Era, First Edition. Edited by Christopher McKnight Nichols and Nancy C. Unger.
© 2017 John Wiley & Sons, Inc. Published 2017 by John Wiley & Sons, Inc.

While Du Bois largely looked at "race" through class, other historians of the twentieth century took "race" as the prism through which to understand class dynamics—Joel Williamson's *The Crucible of Race: Black–White Relations in the American South Since Emancipation* (1984) being among the most influential and representative of these works. But whether the analytic lens was one of class or race (the two concepts being inextricably linked in American history, starting with the codification of racial slavery in the second half of the seventeenth century), one response among rural southern African Americans to Jim Crow was to leave the countryside and head towards the towns and cities principally in search of employment; and from there to urban centers in the North and West. During the 1970s, the historian Nell Painter shed light on a prelude to what became the mass migration of African Americans out of the South starting in the final decade of the nineteenth century. Her study *Exodusters: Black Migration to Kansas After Reconstruction* (1977) details the migration of thousands of African Americans from Louisiana and Mississippi to Kansas in 1879, followed by thousands more individuals and families leaving Tennessee and Kentucky in the decade thereafter.

Since Painter's *Exodusters* there have been several studies on the flow of African Americans from rural areas to urban centers, and then outside of the South—collectively known as the Great Migration, spanning the late nineteenth through the mid-twentieth century. The most notable recent study, Isabel Wilkerson's *The Warmth of Other Suns: The Epic Story of America's Great Migration* (2011), threads the stories of three black migrants—a sharecropper's wife, an agricultural worker, and a physician—as part of the exodus out of the South. The stories of these individuals show the various paths, challenges, and outcomes of the multiple migration streams that started in the late nineteenth century. Ultimately, over six million African Americans left the South to go to the West, Midwest, and Northeast, settling in Chicago, New York, Philadelphia, St. Louis, Detroit, Los Angeles, and Oakland, among other cities. These migrations were as much expressions of desperation, fear, and frustration among African Americans as they were of their hopes and dreams about the prospects and possibilities that lay beyond the rural South.

While many African Americans chose to leave the region—voting with their feet against the injustices and brutality of Jim Crow—many others chose to stay and organize themselves politically. In this way the groundwork for the shift in academic works towards emphasizing black political agency during the late nineteenth and early twentieth centuries was not only prompted by the individual research of scholars such as Du Bois, but was fed by and done alongside the writings of other black journalists and activists—such as the early twentieth-century West Indian-born socialist Hubert Harrison and the outspoken Mississippi-born journalist Ida B. Wells. By the mid-twentieth century political and social pressures brought to bear by the Black Freedom movement as part of postwar changes across American society and culture created newfound legitimacy and understanding of African Americans as historical agents, not simply passive victims of racist attacks. Glenda Gilmore, for instance, traces some of this political pressure from a southern perspective in *Defying Dixie: The Radical Roots of Civil Rights, 1919–1950* (2008). Such changes could also be seen in graduate training and dissertation topics. For instance, Jack Abramowitz's Columbia University doctoral dissertation, "Accommodation and Militancy in Negro Life, 1876–1916" (1950), offered a new, distinctly activist-oriented perspective of African Americans in the late nineteenth and early twentieth centuries.

Movement-building and black-led political pressure, in conjunction with support among white historians with greater institutional location, created new and accepted ways of understanding American history and the role of African Americans in that history. In 1951, a year after Abramowitz completed his dissertation, C. Vann Woodward—the Johns Hopkins University (and later Yale University) professor best known for *The Strange Career of Jim Crow* (1955), which Martin Luther King, Jr. described in 1965 as the "historical Bible of the civil rights movement"—published *Origins of the New South, 1877–1913.* The most influential book on the history of the late nineteenth- and early twentieth-century South, *Origins* brought attention to the obstacles and struggles of African Americans during the period, serving as a signal moment in the historiography.

Woodward's work influenced several notable scholars of the second half of the twentieth century, including Lawrence Goodwyn, whose *Democratic Promise: The Populist Movement in America* (1976) began to look at the role of black organizers in the Populist movement of the late nineteenth century. Other works in the period delved further still into the role of African Americans in Populism, namely Gerald Gaither's *Blacks and the Populist Revolt: Ballots and Bigotry in the "New South"* (1977). Gaither's work, in turn, opened new pathways for a subsequent generation of scholars to explore, including Joseph Gerteis, whose *Class and the Color Line: Interracial Class Coalition in the Knights of Labor and the Populist Movement* (2007) drew attention to the "interracial" alliances of the period, and Omar H. Ali, whose *In the Lion's Mouth: Black Populism in the New South, 1886–1900* (2010) argued that Black Populism was an independent political movement separate from, although at times tactically joined in alliance with the white-led Populist movement. For both Gerteis and Ali networks created by the Knights of Labor, followed by the Colored Farmers Alliance, fueled Populism in the South with Populists, black and white, winning several key electoral victories through the People's Party in coalition with Republicans—that is, before the movement was violently destroyed (see Beeby 2012).

A new focus emerged among scholars of African American history starting in the 1990s that combined labor, social, and political history. Such studies were inspired by and manifested in the work of historians such as Robin D. G. Kelley, author of *Hammer and Hoe: Alabama Communists During the Great Depression* (1990), and Eric Arnerson, author of *Waterfront Workers of New Orleans: Race, Class, and Politics, 1863–1923* (1991). Scholars looked more carefully at all forms of black insurgency in the period between Reconstruction and the early twentieth century, producing additional studies that focused on black political action, broadly defined. Notably, and straddling the antebellum and post-emancipation periods, was Steven Hahn's sweeping study *A Nation Under Our Feet: Black Political Struggles in the Rural South* (2003). For historians writing in the late 1990s and early 2000s, the late nineteenth century was therefore not simply a 'nadir' for African Americans (in terms of racial segregation and other attacks on black people) but a period of ongoing movement-building among black farmers, sharecroppers, and workers—including agricultural, domestic, and waterfront workers.

In contrast to earlier academic views, this new understanding of African American history during the Gilded Age and Progressive era was one of persistent organization and mobilization by and among African Americans in the decades following the collapse of Reconstruction. As Hahn, among others, demonstrates, black churches, mutual aid societies, and fraternal organizations built on the progress made during Reconstruction. Such organizations served as vital leadership training grounds in African American communities. Black institutions and their networks became critical to efforts by African Americans—and their white allies—to challenge Jim Crow in the 1890s and into the twentieth century. However, and despite the shift in academic emphasis towards recognition and analyses of the political agency of African Americans, the particular roles of black women in these organizations and the movements they shaped remained either under-recognized or unknown.

The experiences of African American women, especially southern black women, which had been neglected by most historians, began to be carefully explored in the 1980s by revisiting sources and mining new ones. Jacqueline Jones's *Labor of Love, Labor of Sorrow: Black Women, Work, and the Family from Slavery to the Present* (1985) set a new standard by not only deftly synthesizing the available research but delving into new sources—including diaries, journals, and Works Progress Administration records. Building on Herbert Gutman's study from a decade earlier, *The Black Family in Slavery and Freedom, 1750–1925* (1976), Jones focused on the experiences and perspectives of black women. Three years after Jones's publication, Tera Hunter published another key study, *To 'Joy My Freedom: Southern Black Women's Lives and Labors after the Civil War* (1988), which detailed the working lives of southern African American women. Among other manifestations of black women's activism, Hunter described the washerwomen's strike of 1881, which mobilized upwards of 3000 women in Atlanta.

Since Jones's *Labor of Love, Labor of Sorrow* and Hunter's *To 'Joy My Freedom* a flurry of other works have been written looking at the ways in which black women were under attack and how they navigated their respective conditions. Among these, Hannah Rosen's *Terror in the Heart of Freedom: Citizenship, Sexual Violence, and the Meaning of Race in the Postemancipation South* (2009) and Crystal Feimster's *Southern Horrors: Women and the Politics of Rape and Lynching* (2009), have given wide-ranging expression to the ways in which black women were sexually assaulted and, like their male counterparts, exploited for their labor. As Feimster notes, between 1880 and 1930 over 200 black women were murdered by lynch mobs in the South, while countless other women were assaulted. Beyond documenting and better understanding the violent subjugation of black women, historians looked at the ways in which they resisted their oppression and sought ways of providing leadership.

African American women—notably Ida B. Wells, as the historians Paula Giddings and Mia Bay discuss in each of their respective biographies, *Ida: A Sword Among Lions* (2008) and *To Tell the Truth Freely* (2009)—spoke out with extraordinary courage against lynching, helping to draw public attention to these horrors via the press and her other forms of activism. In 1884, a year before the US Supreme Court ruled against the Civil Rights Act of 1875, banning racial discrimination in public accommodations, Wells was dragged off of the Memphis and Charleston Railroad after refusing to give up her seat. She sued and won. However, the railroad company appealed the case to the Tennessee Supreme Court, which reversed the lower court ruling, and she was forced to pay all court costs. Gaining attention by writing about the injustice, she continued to speak out against discrimination and violence against African Americans, using the press as her tool. Her pamphlet, "Southern Horrors: Lynch Law in All Its Phases," followed by other articles challenging the attacks and murders of African Americans, provoked a mob to burn the newspaper offices of the *Free Speech and Headlight* which published her articles. Wells was compelled to leave the state, going to New York, where she continued her political activism.

Although Ida B. Wells was an unusually talented and accomplished black female leader of the time with substantial primary sources to document her life, historians increasingly looked at the ways in which all black women—poor, working-class, and middle-class—either mobilized labor protest or used diplomacy to advance their interests. Glenda Elizabeth Gilmore focused on the diplomacy and activism of educated middle-class black women in North Carolina in *Gender and Jim Crow: Women and the Politics of White Supremacy in North Carolina, 1896–1920* (1996). Her study built on the work of earlier historians, notably Evelyn Brooks Higginbotham, who explored the "politics of respectability" in *Righteous Discontent: The Women's Movement in the Black Baptist Church, 1880–1920* (1993). As Higginbotham notes, "Between 1900 and 1920 … black Baptist women envisioned themselves as sorely needed missionaries to America … Their religious-political message was drawn from biblical teachings, the philosophy of racial self-help, Victorian ideology, and the democratic principles of the Constitution of the United States" (186). For these women in the early twentieth century, the uplift by black middle-class women meant the uplift of all—that is, notwithstanding their Victorian disdain towards the comportment of poor and working-class women.

Deepening analyses based on class and race, female scholars—from Jones and Higginbotham to Gilmore and Giddings—effectively made gender a category of analysis in African American history that was as important to consider as either class or race. Here black feminist writings by non-historians, from the poet Audre Lorde's womanism to the legal scholar Kimberlé Crenshaw's articulation of intersectionality (the intersection of gender, race, and class, among other related systems of oppression) pushed the boundaries, shaping new ways of looking at black women, historically. Black feminism challenged the narrower white, straight, and middle-class framing by white feminists by expanding the notion of "women" to include the narratives of African American women, especially poor, working-class, lesbian, and bisexual black women. Black feminist-inspired readings of the past therefore not only drew attention to black women but shaped the ways in which they were understood—that is, in their own words and on their own terms (see James and Sharpley-Whiting 2000).

Several reviews of African American historiography describe the shift in views and approaches. As early as 1988, Benjamin Quarles observed in *Black Mosaic: Essays in Afro-American History and Historiography*, "Among the topics which [have] received little scholarly attention is the role of black women …" (200). As Kevin Gaines explains in his chapter in *American History Now* (2011), "earlier narratives of antiblack oppression have given way to accounts of agency, resistance, grassroots organization, and mass activism" (407); and as Pero Gaglo Dagbovie notes in *African American History Reconsidered* (2010), "The foundations for the institutionalization of black women's history [are] rooted in the 1980s" (5). Continuing in the 1990s, those new narratives marked a shift from looking almost exclusively at black oppression toward accounts of resistance and local mobilization by and among African Americans, with greater attention on the lives of black women. As the new studies revealed, African American women—from washerwomen and domestic servants to "croppers" and "church mothers"—in helping to organize political resistance, also faced vicious counterattack.

Pushback to black insurgencies in the late nineteenth and early twentieth centuries as part of efforts to become or remain economically independent took violent forms. As David Fort Godshalk describes in *Veiled Visions: The 1906 Atlanta Race Riot and the Reshaping of American Race Relations* (2005), black communities sustained a series of attacks across the South during late nineteenth and early twentieth centuries. These included attacks in Leflore County, Mississippi in 1889, the infamous Wilmington Riot of 1898—which signaled the end of Black Populism in North Carolina—followed by an attack in Grimes County, East Texas, in 1900, and continuing over the years, culminating with the 1921 Tulsa, Oklahoma, "race riot"—a euphemism for violence perpetrated against African Americans—and an attack two years later in Rosewood, Florida, where surviving black residents fled their town after hiding in nearby swamps, a flashback to what African Americans in Leflore County were forced to do decades earlier.

Violence and the threat of violence against African Americans led some black leaders to pursue less militant actions and methods—a survival strategy under Jim Crow. Publicly eschewing either political action or migration out of the South, Booker T. Washington's accommodationist approach to "racial uplift" became a way for African Americans in the South to cope with their conditions. Building a network of support through his Tuskegee organization (funded in large part by northern white philanthropists), and appeasing white southerners opposed to black civil and political rights, Washington's autobiography *Up from Slavery* (1901) inspired many African Americans to focus on their own "uplift." Still others did not fit political or ideological categories in responding to Jim Crow. Some, as Shane White and Graham White write in *Stylin': African American Expressive Culture from its Beginnings to the Zoot Suit* (1998), defied white expectations of deference under Jim Crow through individual bodily displays (including dressing, walking, gesturing, and arranging one's hair in certain ways) or through collective public displays (such as parading). In these ways, defiance took the form of performances that were indirect and therefore ambiguous in their meaning.

While Jim Crow ruled the South, in the North—specifically in Harlem—a new movement formed in the 1910s around Marcus Garvey, the visionary Jamaican-born Black Nationalist leader who had been inspired by Washington's life. Garvey and his many followers formed chapters of the Universal Negro Improvement Association (UNIA) across the nation, including in the South—albeit largely clandestinely, as was the case in an earlier generation with the southern-wide Colored Farmers Alliance, among other black organizations. Claudrena Harold's *The Rise and Fall of the Garvey Movement in the Urban South, 1918–1942* (2007) and Colin Grant's *Negro with a Hat: The Rise and Fall of Marcus Garvey* (2008) serve as the latest scholarship on Garvey. Their research and analyses of Garvey and his movement build on the work of Robert Hill—his multi-volume edited collection of Garvey and UNIA documents

(2011)—as well as by historians of the black radical tradition in Harlem, notably Winston James. James's *Holding Aloft the Banner of Ethiopia: Caribbean Radicalism in Early Twentieth-Century America* (1998) details the cross-currents and contributions of West Indians (Hubert Harrison, Amy Jacques Garvey, Cyril Briggs, and Claude McKay, among others) in the Mecca of the "New Negro."

While Garvey popularized Black Nationalism through speeches, publications, and with parades that included thousands of proud, uniformed followers, the essential notion of "racial destiny" preceded him. Building on Kevin Gaines's *Uplifting the Race: Black Leadership, Politics, and Culture, in the Twentieth Century* (1996), the historian Michele Mitchell also argues in *Righteous Propagation: African Americans and the Politics of Racial Destiny after Reconstruction* (2004) that both the concept and practice of racial destiny in the late nineteenth and early twentieth centuries was profoundly gendered, privileging black men over black women. Also preceding Garvey was the metaphorical if not actual return of black people to Africa ("Back to Africa") for which he is perhaps best known, as Kenneth Barnes discusses in *Journey of Hope: The Back-to-Africa Movement in Arkansas in the Late 1800s* (2004).

Whether involving Black Nationalists and separatists (such as Garvey) or integrationists (such as Du Bois), or some other perspective, Harlem became the vibrant center for a range of political outlooks from across the African Diaspora. Streams of black southerners as well as West Indians joined the mix of people and perspectives converging on New York City, each vying for greater audiences from their soap boxes, podiums, and pulpits. Among the most radical of these voices was Hubert Harrison, who helped Garvey first gain public attention in Harlem, as detailed by Jeffrey Perry in *Hubert Harrison: The Voice of Harlem Radicalism, 1883–1918* (2009). The Great Migration, which created new tensions and conflicts in the North over, among other things, competition for jobs, therefore also created new political possibilities with increasing numbers of black migrants moving into the largest northern cities: Chicago, Philadelphia, and New York.

Despite poor relations between many black and white Americans at the turn of the twentieth century, in a few places, African Americans helped to create "interracial" alliances reminiscent of those forged during the Populist revolt. Peter Cole explores one of these in *Wobblies on the Waterfront: Interracial Unionism in Progressive-Era Philadelphia* (2007), in which African Americans and white immigrants formed the majority of Philadelphia's Local 8 of the Industrial Workers of the World. For a brief time, black and white workers successfully worked together in the face of multiple efforts to divide their ranks. But there were other reactions and responses to the inflow of black migrants into major northern cities.

Cynthia Blair's *I've Got to Make My Livin': Black Women's Sex Work in Turn-of-the-Century Chicago* (2010), Kate Masur's *An Example for all the Land: Emancipation and the Struggle over Equality in Washington, D.C.* (2010), and Jeanne Petit's *The Men and Women We Want: Gender, Race, and the Progressive Era Literacy Test Debate* (2010) each, in their own way, demonstrate the economic, social, and political challenges that African Americans faced trying to navigate and combat racial and sexual discrimination in various parts of the North. (As Petit argues, literacy tests targeting African Americans in the South were also used to discriminate against new immigrants coming from southern Italy and eastern Europe—that is, those of other so-called lower races.)

Underlying the struggles of African Americans during the final decades of the nineteenth century was the immediate legacy of American slavery, both ideologically and materially. Some African Americans sought financial redress not only for themselves but for all former enslaved African Americans and their descendants. Mary Frances Berry explored this reparations thread through the life of the ex-slave and washerwoman Callie House in *My Face is Black is True: Callie House and the Struggle for Ex-Slave Reparations* (2005). House's demand for reparations for unpaid work by enslaved African Americans—a demand that had its origins earlier in the nineteenth century—included repayment through the $68 million gained by the US Government from taxes on seized Confederate cotton during the Civil War.

In a number of ways, therefore, since the 1990s emphases on black agency, resistance to exploitation, and political mobilization have supplanted earlier accounts that largely viewed African Americans as passive victims of white supremacist violence and discriminatory laws and policies. Insurgent movements gained greater attention, as did the role of African American women as leaders in such movements or through individuated efforts, helping to transform the ways in which many historians would come to analyze and view African American history during the late nineteenth and early twentieth centuries.

Since the turn of the twenty-first century a number of new directions have begun to emerge in African American history covering the Gilded Age and Progressive Era. Among these developments are the work of scholars looking at perhaps even less visible elements: black maroons in the South still living in the forests and woods through the turn of the twentieth century—specifically, the work of Sylviane Diouf in *Slavery's Exiles: The Story of the American Maroons* (2014); the ways in which African Americans have wandered, philosophically and otherwise, as explored by Sarah Jane Cervenak in *Wandering: Philosophical Performances of Racial and Sexual Freedom* (2014); religious syncretism in black communities, as in the work of Jacob Dorman in *Chosen People: The Rise of American Black Israelite Religions* (2013); and "conjure," "root doctoring," and "hoodoo" in the South, as described by Jeffrey Anderson in *Conjure in African American Society* (2005) and Sylvester Johnson's broad study *African American Religions, 1500–2000: Colonialism, Democracy and Freedom* (2015).

Other areas of interest include African American ethnomusicology, namely the history of minstrelsy and "old time" music among black communities in the Carolinas—an area of work pioneered by Cecilia Conway in *African Banjo Echoes in Appalachia: A Study of Folk Traditions* (1995) but which has yet to be fully tapped. Additional research is also needed in terms of the history of the politics and impact of discrimination towards African Americans and the spread of diseases in urban black communities. Samuel K. Roberts's *Infectious Fear: Politics, Disease, and the Health Effects of Segregation* (2009) delves into the political economy of health, urban geography, and "race" between the late nineteenth century and the mid-twentieth centuries. This thread in African American history remains under-explored. Likewise, Quintard Taylor's *In Search of the Racial Frontier: African Americans in the American West* (1998) and, more recently, Tiya Miles's *Ties That Bind: The Story of an Afro-Cherokee Family in Slavery and Freedom* (2005), point to other important areas that could be further researched and incorporated into the many other strands of African American history: African Americans in the West and African American–Indian relations in the late nineteenth and early twentieth centuries.

Growing out of a global African Diasporic tradition championed by Joseph Harris starting in the late 1960s—*The African Presence in Asia* (1971), followed by his edited book *Global Dimensions of the African Diaspora* (1982)—is an emerging reconceptualization or shift in the field: to better understand, describe, and explore African American history as part of global African Diaspora histories that span the Atlantic, Mediterranean, and Indian Ocean worlds. More historians are beginning to use the term "African Diaspora" in their work. The term, first used by the historian George Shepperson, in an article (1966) which he presented on a panel organized by Harris at the International Congress of African History at the University of Dar es Salaam, in Tanzania, in 1968, has been increasingly used since the turn of the twenty-first century as a way of analyzing and describing particular topics, concepts, and people connected to prior and more geographically limited notions of African American history (namely, focused on North America). Brent Hayes Edwards delves into the concept of Black Internationalism (organized resistance to slavery, colonialism, and neocolonialism with regards to people of African descent), for instance, by building on the concept and practice of the African Diaspora in *The Practice of Diaspora: Literature, Translation, and the Rise of Black Internationalism* (2003). Concentrating on the African Diaspora in the Atlantic world, he looks at shared and divergent paths among black intellectuals across the United States, Africa, Europe, and the Caribbean. Meanwhile, Frank Guridy takes a more focused comparative analysis in *Forging Diaspora: Afro-Cubans and African Americans in a World of Empire and Jim Crow* (2010), which demonstrates the interconnectivity between Afro-Cubans and black Americans (including Washington and Garvey) and the ways in which they supported each other's political struggles, identifying themselves as part of a shared transcultural African Diaspora.

Harris, whose work first popularized the idea of an African Diaspora in Asia (including the Middle East, South Asia, and the Far East), has been followed by a number of critical studies tying African Americans to the African Diaspora in the Indian Ocean world. Among these are Nico Slate's *Colored Cosmopolitanism: The Shared Struggle for Freedom in the United States and India* (2011). Others have drawn out themes around concepts of the African Diaspora in the Indian Ocean world with relevance and applicability to African Americans—such as the notion and legacy of "creolization" in the work of Pier Larson, especially *Ocean of Letters: Language and Creolization in an Indian Ocean Diaspora* (2009).

In these ways, the work of pushing into the Indian Ocean world to gain a richer understanding of African Americans as part of the Black Atlantic, including Afro-Latin America—not to mention the African Diaspora in the Mediterranean world—are areas of work that are related to African American history by challenging certain assumed concepts of race, and slavery, cross-current and contributions in terms of ideas and movements, and the possibilities of upward mobility when taking a more global view of the African Diaspora. The recent exhibits "The African Diaspora in the Indian Ocean World" and "Africans in India: From Slaves to Generals and Rulers" at the Schomburg Center for Research in Black Culture of the New York Public Library, both the online and the traveling exhibit adopted by UNESCO, point to the interest and importance of understanding African Americans as part of the free and forced migrations of people of African descent across the world (see http://exhibitions.nypl.org/africansindianocean/index2.php).

A final critical area of historical investigation centers on the notion of "race." Karen Fields and Barbara Fields offer perhaps the most sophisticated critique of "race" and how it is repeatedly re-created in American history in their collected essays *Racecraft: The Soul of Inequality in American Life* (2012). Building on insights offered by the philosopher K. Anthony Appiah (*In My Father's House: Africa in the Philosophy of Culture* 1992, 13), they write:

> The term *race* stands for the conception or the doctrine that nature produced humankind in distinct groups, each defined by inborn traits that its member share and that differentiate them from the members of other distinct groups of the same kind but of unequal rank … *Racism* is first and foremost a social practice, which means that it is an action and a rationale for action, or both at once. *Racism* always takes for granted the objective reality of *race*, as just defined … The shorthand transforms *racism*, something an aggressor *does*, into *race*, something the target *is*, in a sleight of hand that is easy to miss (16–17).

Adding to such critiques is that of Dorothy Roberts, who looks at re-creations of "race" in more recent times in *Fatal Invention: How Science, Politics, and Big Business Re-Create Race in the Twenty-First Century* (2011). As she succinctly notes, "Race is not a biological category that is politically charged. It is a political category that has been disguised as a biological one" (1).

These and other critiques bring into question much of what has been written about African American history—including the designation of African American as distinct from other Americans. Does employing the concept of race help or hinder our understanding of people and their societies in the past? Are there ways of engaging the migration, struggles, contributions, and ordinary lives of people of African descent without relying on notions of race (even if understood to be social-political constructs)? Such questions raise new challenges and possibilities as scholars of African American history continue to expand, refine, and reconsider their methods and tools of analysis.

References

Abramowitz, Jack. 1950. "Accommodation and Militancy in Negro Life, 1876–1916." Ph.D. diss., Columbia University.

Ali, Omar H. 2010. *In the Lion's Mouth: Black Populism in the New South, 1886–1900*. Jackson: University Press of Mississippi.

Anderson, Jeffrey E. 2005. *Conjure in African American Society*. Baton Rouge: Louisiana State University Press.

Appiah, K. Anthony. 1992. *In My Father's House: Africa in the Philosophy of Culture*. New York: Oxford University Press.

Arnerson, Eric. 1991. *Waterfront Workers of New Orleans: Race, Class, and Politics, 1863–1923*. New York: Oxford University Press.

Barnes, Kenneth C. 2004. *Journey of Hope: The Back-to-Africa Movement in Arkansas in the Late 1800s*. Chapel Hill: University of North Carolina Press.

Bay, Mia. 2009. *To Tell the Truth Freely: The Life of Ida B. Wells*. New York: Hill & Wang.

Beeby, James M., ed. 2012. *Populism in the South Revisited: New Interpretations and New Departures*. Jackson: University Press of Mississippi.

Berry, Mary Frances. 2005. *My Face is Black is True: Callie House and the Struggle for Ex-Slave Reparations*. New York: Knopf.

Blair, Cynthia M. 2010. *I've Got to Make My Livin': Black Women's Sex Work in Turn-of-the-Century Chicago*. Chicago: University of Chicago Press.

Cervenak, Sarah Jane. 2014. *Wandering: Philosophical Performances of Racial and Sexual Freedom*. Durham, NC: Duke University Press.

Cole, Peter. 2007. *Wobblies on the Waterfront: Interracial Unionism in Progressive-Era Philadelphia*. Urbana: University of Illinois Press.

Conway, Cecilia. 1995. *African Banjo Echoes in Appalachia: A Study of Folk Traditions*. Knoxville: University of Tennessee Press.

Dagbovie, Pero Gaglo. 2010. *African American History Reconsidered*. Urbana: University of Illinois Press.

Diouf, Sylviane. 2014. *Slavery's Exiles: The Story of the American Maroons*. New York: New York University Press.

Dorman, Jacob S. 2013. *Chosen People: The Rise of American Black Israelite Religions*. New York: Oxford University Press.

Du Bois, W.E.B. 1903. *The Souls of Black Folk*. Chicago: A.C. McClure.

Edwards, Brent Hayes. 2003. *The Practice of Diaspora: Literature, Translation, and the Rise of Black Internationalism*. Cambridge, MA: Harvard University Press.

Feimster, Crystal. 2009. *Southern Horrors: Women and the Politics of Rape and Lynching*. Cambridge, MA: Harvard University Press.

Fields, Karen E., and Barbara J. Fields. 2012. *Racecraft: The Soul of Inequality in American Life*. London: Verso.

Foner, Eric and Lisa McGirr. 2011. *American History Now*. Philadelphia, PA: Temple University Press.

Gaines, Kevin. 1996. *Uplifting the Race: Black Leadership, Politics, and Culture, in the Twentieth Century*. Chapel Hill: University of North Carolina Press.

—. 2011. "African American History." In *American History Now*, ed. Eric Foner and Lisa McGirr. Philadelphia, PA: Temple University Press.

Gaither, Gerald H. 1977. *Blacks and the Populist Revolt: Ballots and Bigotry in the "New South."* Tuscaloosa: University of Alabama Press.

Gerteis, Joseph. 2007. *Class and the Color Line: Interracial Class Coalition in the Knights of Labor and the Populist Movement*. Durham, NC: Duke University Press.

Giddings, Paula J. 2008. *Ida: A Sword Among Lions: Ida B. Wells and the Campaign Against Lynching*. New York: Harper Collins.

Gilmore, Glenda Elizabeth. 1996. *Gender and Jim Crow: Women and the Politics of White Supremacy in North Carolina, 1896–1920*. Chapel Hill: University of North Carolina Press.

—. 2008. *Defying Dixie: The Radical Roots of Civil Rights, 1919–1950*. New York: W.W. Norton.

Godshalk, David Fort. 2005. *Veiled Visions: The 1906 Atlanta Race Riot and the Reshaping of American Race Relations*. Chapel Hill: University of North Carolina Press.

Goldstone, Lawrence. 2011. *Inherently Unequal: The Betrayal of Equal Rights by the Supreme Court, 1865–1903*. New York: Walker.

Goodwyn, Lawrence. 1976. *Democratic Promise: The Populist Movement in America*. New York: Oxford University Press.

Grant, Colin. 2008. *Negro with a Hat: The Rise and Fall of Marcus Garvey*. New York: Oxford University Press.

Guridy, Frank. 2010. *Forging Diaspora: Afro-Cubans and African Americans in a World of Empire and Jim Crow*. Chapel Hill: University of North Carolina Press.

Gutman, Herbert. 1976. *The Black Family in Slavery and Freedom, 1750–1925*. New York: Pantheon.

Hahn, Steven. 2003. *A Nation Under Our Feet: Black Political Struggles in the Rural South, from Slavery to the Great Migration*. Cambridge, MA: Belknap/Harvard University Press.

Harold, Claudrena N. 2007. *The Rise and Fall of the Garvey Movement in the Urban South, 1918–1942*. New York: Routledge.

Harris, Joseph E. 1971. *The African Presence in Asia*. Evanston, IL: Northwestern University Press.

—, ed. 1982. *Global Dimensions of the African Diaspora*. Washington, DC: Howard University Press.

Higginbotham, Evelyn Brooks. 1993. *Righteous Discontent: The Women's Movement in the Black Baptist Church, 1880–1920*. Cambridge, MA: Harvard University Press.

Hill, Robert A., ed. 2011. *Marcus Garvey and the Universal Negro Improvement Association Papers*. Durham, NC: Duke University Press.

Hunter, Tera W. 1988. *To 'Joy My Freedom: Southern Black Women's Lives and Labors after the Civil War*. Cambridge, MA: Harvard University Press.

James, Joy, and T. Denean Sharpley-Whiting, eds. 2000. *The Black Feminist Reader*. Oxford: Blackwell.

James, Winston. 1998. *Holding Aloft the Banner of Ethiopia: Caribbean Radicalism in Early Twentieth-Century America*. London: Verso.

Johnson, Sylvester A. 2015. *African American Religions, 1500–2000: Colonialism, Democracy and Freedom*. New York: Cambridge University Press.

Jones, Jacqueline. 1985. *Labor of Love, Labor of Sorrow: Black Women, Work, and the Family from Slavery to the Present*. New York: Basic Books.

Kelley, Robin D.G. 1990. *Hammer and Hoe: Alabama Communists During the Great Depression*. Chapel Hill: The University of North Carolina Press.

Larson, Pier M. 2009. *Ocean of Letters: Language and Creolization in an Indian Ocean Diaspora*. New York: Cambridge University Press.

Logan, Rayford W. 1954. *The Negro in American Life and Thought: The Nadir, 1877–1901*. New York: The Dial Press.

Masur, Kate. 2010. *An Example for all the Land: Emancipation and the Struggle over Equality in Washington*, D.C. Chapel Hill: University of North Carolina Press.

Miles, Tiya. 2005. *Ties That Bind: The Story of an Afro-Cherokee Family in Slavery and Freedom*. Berkeley: University of California Press.

Mitchell, Michele. 2004. *Righteous Propagation: African Americans and the Politics of Racial Destiny after Reconstruction*. Chapel Hill: University of North Carolina Pres.

Painter, Nell Irvin. 1977. *Exodusters: Black Migration to Kansas After Reconstruction*. New York: W.W. Norton.

Perry, Jeffrey B. 2009. *Hubert Harrison: The Voice of Harlem Radicalism, 1883–1918*. New York: Columbia University Press.

Petit, Jeanne D. 2010. *The Men and Women We Want: Gender, Race, and the Progressive Era Literacy Test Debate*. Rochester, NY: University of Rochester Press.

Quarles, Benjamin. 1988. *Black Mosaic: Essays in Afro-American History and Historiography*. Amherst: University of Massachusetts Press.

Roberts, Dorothy. 2011. *Fatal Invention: How Science, Politics, and Big Business Re-Create Race in the Twenty-First Century*. New York: New Press.

Roberts, Samuel K. 2009. *Infectious Fear: Politics, Disease, and the Health Effects of Segregation*. Chapel Hill: University of North Carolina Press.

Rosen, Hannah. 2009. *Terror in the Heart of Freedom: Citizenship, Sexual Violence, and the Meaning of Race in the Postemancipation South*. Chapel Hill: University of North Carolina Press.

Schomburg Center for Research in Black Culture, The New York Public Library. 2011. "The African Diaspora in the Indian Ocean World." http://exhibitions.nypl.org/africansindianocean/index2.php/Accessed October 3, 2016.

Shepperson, George. 1966. "The African Diaspora—or the African Abroad." *African Forum: A Quarterly Journal of African Affairs* 1, 2: 76–93.

Slate, Nico. 2011. *Colored Cosmopolitanism: The Shared Struggle for Freedom in the United States and India*. Cambridge, MA: Harvard University Press.

Taylor, Quintard. 1998. *In Search of the Racial Frontier: African Americans in the American West*. New York: W. W. Norton.

Washington, Booker T. 2002. *Up From Slavery by Booker to Washington with Related Documents*, ed. W. Fitzhugh Brundage, Boston, MA: Bedford St. Martin's Press.

White, Shane, and Graham White. 1998. *Stylin': African American Expressive Culture from its Beginnings to the Zoot Suit*. Ithaca, NY: Cornell University Press.

Wilkerson, Isabel. 2011. *The Warmth of Other Suns: The Epic Story of America's Great Migration*. New York: Vintage.

Williams, George Washington. 1882. *History of the Negro Race in America from 1619 to 1880*. New York: G.P. Putnam's Sons.

Williamson, Joel. 1984. *The Crucible of Race: Black–White Relations in the American South Since Emancipation*. New York: Oxford University Press.

Woodward, C. Vann. 1951. *Origins of the New South 1877–1913*. Baton Rouge: Louisiana State University Press.

—. 1955. *The Strange Career of Jim Crow*. New York: Oxford University Press.

Further Reading

Hine, Darlene Clark. 1989. *Black Women in White: Racial Conflict and Cooperation in the Nursing Profession, 1890–1950*. Bloomington: Indiana University Press.

Keita, Maghan. 2000. *Race and the Writing of History: Riddling the Sphinx*. New York: Oxford University Press.

Logan, Rayford W. 1997. *The Betrayal of the Negro, from Rutherford B. Hayes to Woodrow Wilson*. New York: Da Capo Press.

Muhammad, Khalil Gibran. 2010. *The Condemnation of Blackness: Race, Crime, and the Making of Modern Urban America*. Cambridge, MA: Harvard University Press.

Reid, Debra A. and Evan P. Bennett, eds. 2012. *Beyond Forty Acres and a Mule: African American Farm Families After Freedom*. Gainesville: University Press of Florida.

Schmidt, Peter. 2008. *Sitting in Darkness: New South Fiction, Education, and the Rise of Jim Crow Colonialism, 1865–1920*. Jackson: University Press of Mississippi.

Southern, David W. 2005. *The Progressive Era and Race: Reaction and Reform, 1900–1917*. Wheeling, WV: Harlan Davidson.

Wesley, Charles H. 1967. *Negro Labor in the United States, 1850–1925*. New York: Russell & Russell.

Yellin, Eric S. 2013. *Racism in the Nation's Service: Government Workers and the Color Line in Woodrow Wilson's America*. Chapel Hill: University of North Carolina Press.

Chapter Ten

From Dispossessed Wards to Citizen Activists: American Indians Survive the Assimilation Policy Era

Alexandra Harmon

When the World's Columbian Exposition opened in Chicago on May 1, 1893, half a million visitors streamed through the gates. Those who assembled for the inaugural ceremonies could see fifty American Indians, "in full war paint and feathers," stationed at the Administration Building. According to the *New York Times*, the eye-catching sentries stood "silent and unmovable" as they awaited "the coming of the great white chieftain." Everyone else watched not only for President Grover Cleveland but also for "the signal to shout the praises of Columbus, discoverer of 'the land of the free and home of the brave'" ("Opened by the President," May 2, 1893). The *Times* did not say whether "the free," "the brave," or Columbus's admirers included Indians, but at least one Indian wanted fairgoers to consider such questions. Simon Pokagon, chief of a Christian Potawatomi community, offered an alternative to the image of Indians as mute, apparently neutralized, pre-modern warriors.

Several times during the exposition's six-month run, Pokagon addressed large audiences. On Chicago Day, he mounted the rostrum accompanied by a man in moccasins, feather headdress, breech clout, and a "varied coat of paint," looking to a reporter like "a typical Indian on the warpath." Pokagon, however, was "in the dress of the white man," suitable for civilian pursuits in a modern city. After presenting the mayor with the 1833 treaty by which Potawatomis ceded land for the town of Chicago, Pokagon "stood beside the Columbian bell … and received the homage of thousands." He told the approving audience, "I shall cherish as long as I live the cheering words that have been spoken to me here by … friends of my race … ; I now realize the hand of the Great Spirit is open in our behalf," teaching Christian men and women that "the red man is your brother, and God is the father of all."

Yet Pokagon did not consistently bring a message of Indian amity and gratitude. He also wrote and sold throughout the fairgrounds a tract titled "The Red Man's Rebuke," forcefully denouncing Europeans' discovery and conquest of North America as a disaster that stripped Indians of their lands, resources, and power from coast to coast. ("Chicago's Day at the Fair," *New York Times*, October 10, 1893, 5; Pokagon 1893; Low 2011, 1; Maddox 2005, 1).

The hugely popular Columbian Exposition was a signal event—both showcase and stimulus for defining developments and preoccupations in the United States at a time of transition from the Gilded Age to the Progressive Era. As such, it is richly instructive for American history scholars, and that value extends to the subject of Indians. Indians' diverse roles and experiences at the fair exemplify several key themes in the history and historiography of Native Americans during the late nineteenth and early twentieth centuries—their subjugation and exploitation but also their resilience and resistance to erasure.

Indians participated in the exposition as exhibitors of aboriginal customs, living dioramas of "primitive life," exemplars of their race's educability, performers in open-air enactments of "Wild West" history, construction workers, and consumers of entertainment and educational exhibits. Some daringly made the fair a venue for practices that non-Indians were trying to suppress; others used it to show they had traded such practices for "civilized" ways. The inclusion of Indians in exhibits and ceremonies attests to their symbolic significance for non-Indians, both as overpowered, pre-modern foes of civilization's inevitable advance and as forgiving converts to superior white culture. Those contradictory representations of Indians also reflected ambivalence on both sides about increasing contact between the two "races." The fair dispensed with distances and territorial boundaries that separated most Indians from non-Indians, but the resulting encounters focused attention on remaining differences.

A Companion to the Gilded Age and Progressive Era, First Edition. Edited by Christopher McKnight Nichols and Nancy C. Unger.
© 2017 John Wiley & Sons, Inc. Published 2017 by John Wiley & Sons, Inc.

Other events of 1893 corroborate, elucidate, and supplement what the Chicago exposition exemplifies about Indians in that era. Congress made schooling compulsory for all Indian children, mandated that lands of the so-called Civilized Tribes be allotted as private property to tribe members despite Indian opposition, and opened Puyallup Reservation lands to non-Indian purchasers – all purportedly to serve the goal of assimilating Indians as US citizens. Newspapers carried stories of Indians who apparently wanted the benefits of Euro-American civilization – Indians prospering as farmers in Idaho and Washington State, Cherokees and Creeks profiting from land speculation, Northern Arapahos building themselves an Episcopal church. But reports of tribes "on the warpath" in several places and a "brutal" sun dance in Oklahoma generated other headlines evincing obdurate Indian savagery ("Rich Palouse Indian chief," *Los Angeles Times*, November 20, 4; Cherokee land speculators, *New York Times*, June 19, 6; "Sherman Coolidge reports church built for Arapaho," *New York Times,* March 24, 4; "Navajos on the warpath," *New York Times*, April 29, 5; "Yuma 'outbreak,'" *Los Angeles Times*, October 5, 4; "Arapahoes hold sun dance," *New York Times*, Aug. 19, 5).

It is also salient that San Francisco expelled its Chinese residents in 1893, US troops deposed Hawaii's queen, Osage Indians ejected "Negroes" from their reservation, and financial panic triggered a nationwide depression, exposing innocent workers' vulnerability to capitalists' bad bets ("Osages expel all Negroes," *Washington Post*, November 13, 7). Those events reflected forces at work in the United States—racism, imperial expansion, and unregulated speculation—whose effects Indians experienced, coped with, and sometimes furthered along with other Americans.

Thus, as the Gilded Age gave way to the Progressive Era, the culmination of Euro-Americans' three-century drive to dispossess and subjugate indigenous peoples presented Indians and non-Indians alike with difficult questions, chief among them whether Indians would be included in the political, economic, and cultural life of the United States and, if so, on what terms. Inconsistent non-Indian approaches to that "Indian problem" created great hardships but also opportunities for Indians, whose responses ranged from demoralization to daring defiance and selective adaptation, always with the hope of reconciling Indian identity and contemporary circumstances.

Indians on the Margins of History

More often than not, scholarship on Indians has cast their history as different in kind from that of other Americans. To be sure, Indians' descent from indigenous peoples does distinguish them significantly from everyone else who has taken part in North American history. Other differences, or decisions based on perceptions of deep-seated difference, account for additional uniquely Indian experiences. Some present-day scholars—many of them Native American—contend that histories of Indians should emphasize and exemplify their distinctiveness, attributed primarily to indigeneity (Mihesuah 1998). But the historical segregation of Indian-focused scholarship also has roots in a misguided non-Indian conception of indigenous Americans as people without and outside history. For lack of written annals and other familiar indices of human "advancement," Indian societies initially seemed static as well as primitive to heirs of European intellectual tradition.

A belief that such societies must yield to progressive civilization not only provided a rationale for colonial settlement and Indians' dispossession; it consigned Indians for more than a century to a limited role in Euro-American versions of US history. Indians were necessarily part of an American heritage, but merely as alien people who once presented obstacles to civilization's advance, thereby testing the mettle of Euro-American agents of progress (Berkhofer 1978). When Indians' final capitulation to United States rule seemed imminent in the 1870s, so did the end of their effect on history. Anachronisms, they would and should disappear, if not by dying off, then by forsaking their "Indianness."

Measures intended to hasten that disappearance subsequently provided the dominant story line for many accounts of Indians in the Gilded Age and Progressive Era. Those accounts depicted Indians at the nadir of their historical power and well-being, subordinated to a nation-state destined to eliminate them either as territory-holding peoples or as nonconforming cultures. That Indians consequently experienced irreparable loss of culture and autonomy seemed unquestionable.

Not until the late twentieth century, during a remarkable revitalization of Indian tribes and cultures, did historians produce a body of scholarship that tells the story differently. The recent studies show that indigenous culture loss was not universal, complete, or wholly involuntary and Indians were not entirely powerless, even at their weakest time (e.g., Bauer 2012; Bsumek 2008; Deloria 2004; Ellis 2003; Harmon 1998; Heaton 2005; Hosmer 1999; Hoxie 2001; LaPier and Beck 2015; Reid 2015; Warren 2015). It is incumbent on other historians as well to acknowledge and explain Indians' survival in the Gilded Age and Progressive Era. The explanation includes federal policy's ironic effects, but acknowledging Indian agency is also essential, above all by showing that Indians worked to define for themselves what being Indian would mean in the modern United States.

While persisting as distinct peoples, Indians were not insulated from developments affecting non-Indians. In contrast and occasional tension with scholars who assert the exceptional nature of Indian history, some historians deem it important to highlight shared and parallel experiences (e.g., Deloria 2004; Harmon 2003). During the late 1800s and early 1900s, for instance, Indians shared with newcomers from Eastern Europe and Asia the stresses of enforced Americanization or exclusion. Like black people, many felt the sting and practical damages of racism. Along with non-Indians, they witnessed, reacted to, and in some cases contributed to other national trends—economic, cultural, educational, political, and religious. Non-Indians who thought of Indians as isolated and radically different were apt to overlook experiences and challenges they had in common with Native Americans, but those commonalities are discernible to present-day scholars and deserve analysis by Gilded Age, Progressive Era, and Indian history specialists alike.

Nevertheless, as Sherry Smith observed in a 2010 issue of *The Journal of the Gilded Age and Progressive Era*, textbooks and other published surveys of US history have typically limited coverage of Indians in the late nineteenth century to three subjects—wars on the Great Plains, the movement for Indian schooling, and the Dawes Allotment Act of 1887—thereby relegating Indians to "a place at the margins" of history (Smith 2010, 504). Smith might have added that the same has been true of the journal where her comment appeared, introducing three articles. The nine-year-old journal had never featured an article on Indians until that issue, and five years passed before it did so again. That dearth of journal coverage corresponds to Indians' low visibility in monograph surveys of the Gilded Age and Progressive Era (GAPE). Long neglect is evident in Ray Ginger's *Age of Excess* (1965), which drew on scholarship from the three decades before 1965 but mentioned Indians in just seven scattered paragraphs (3–4, 114, 133–134). In four later notable books, the number of pages devoted to Indians ranged from one to ten (Painter 1987, 162–163; Cashman 1993, 293–301; McGerr 2003, 202–209; Lears 2009, 35–43).

Allocating more pages to Indians does not necessarily broaden subject coverage. Recent synthetic works have stuck to the topics Smith identified. An invariable subject - in some instances, the only subject—is the suppression of nomadic tribes' resistance to US expansion, particularly by Sioux bands. Also typical is a summary of subsequent government measures meant to transform Indians into sedentary, detribalized farmers. Accounts of Indian initiatives or tribes' persistence are nearly non-existent. Sean Cashman, for one, virtually wrote off the possibility of survival, asserting flatly, "Indians and bison were eliminated together …. What happened [to Native Americans] in the Gilded Age was a final catastrophe" (Cashman 1993, 293–294).

One likely reason for Indians' low profile in GAPE histories is their tiny share of the American population and their negligible political power in that period. Authors may understandably have assumed that vastly outnumbered, economically dependent, non-citizen Indians took minimal part in far-reaching developments. Few source materials from those years would prompt a contrary conclusion, generated as they were by people intent primarily on documenting civilization's triumph in North America. Indian societies, supposedly stalled at a low stage of social evolution and doomed to vanish, were a subject for antiquarians or ethnographers rather than historians (Conn 2004). Scarcely any professional historians studied Indian experiences for their own sake until the 1960s.

When historians did begin to specialize in Indians, their work was often methodologically distinctive. Aiming to correct the bias of existing literature and present history from Indian perspectives, they employed research techniques, sources, and theories from anthropology as well as the discipline of history. Much of the new Indian history thus became the province of ethnohistorians, who defined their work as the study of culture change in distinct ethnic or tribal groups.

Whether ethnohistory is or should remain a separate discipline has since been a subject of debate that overlaps with contention about Indian history exceptionalism (Meyer and Kline 1999). Meanwhile, general or thematic GAPE surveys have typically drawn their information on Indians not from ethnohistories but from books on US Indian policy and its administration—arguably the most common subject of scholarship concerning Indians in the late 1800s and early 1900s (e.g., Prucha 1984; Hoxie 1984; Holm 2005; Adams 1995). That emphasis on policy also reflects and perpetuates a preference for the nation-state as a framework of general American history narratives and Indian history specifically. Such a framework tends to obscure Indian perspectives and discourage thorough assessments of Indians' agency and significance.

Advocates of viewing the United States as a settler-colonial enterprise are gaining influence, contending that their analytical framework makes the actions and endurance of indigenous peoples mandatory subjects for historians of all periods (Sleeper-Smith et al. 2015, 259–272). But embracing the settler-colony paradigm is not a precondition of concluding that Indians merit more attention from GAPE historians. Nor should Indian history scholars' reliance on sources such as folklore, oral histories, linguistic data, and ethnological theory deter other historians from increasing the coverage of Indians. Although unique in several respects, Indians' history is also part of the larger American story. By tracing how it intersects with and diverges from non-Indian stories, scholars learn more about all the stories. As suggested in *Why You Can't Teach United States History without American Indians*, Native American experiences, whether unique or not, can inspire new and deeper analysis of subjects that mattered to all Americans in the GAPE, especially race, citizenship, opportunity, nation-building, and multiculturalism (Sleeper-Smith et al. 2015, 4).

Indians' Unique "Wardship"

In 1871, prompted by friction between the two houses of Congress and a belief in the army's ability to corral the last "wild" Indians, US lawmakers prohibited new treaties with Native American tribes. However, the legislation did not invalidate several hundred previously ratified treaties; nor did it end the federal practice of negotiating formal agreements with representatives of indigenous peoples. Prompt cessation of armed conflict with western tribes also proved elusive. Consequently, Indian societies' history of nationhood and nation-to-nation relations with the United States continued to differentiate them from other Americans through the next five decades (Wilkinson 1987, 64–66, 138; Banner 2012, 249–253). The bungled federal plan to eliminate that difference is an essential topic for a history of those decades, but that uniquely Indian history involves more than the oft-told stories of the last Indian wars, boarding-school curricula, and the privatization of tribal land.

By the 1870s, most Indians in the government's sights had no intention of fighting the United States. Instead, they pursued varying strategies for survival and coexistence with Euro-Americans, who had undeniable power to displace and impoverish them. In upstate New York, remnants of the formerly prosperous and powerful Iroquois nations maintained much poorer communities on scattered scraps of their ancestral territories (Snow 1994). Other descendants of indigenous people—some with African ancestry as well—lived less visibly in towns or rural recesses of New England and the Southeast (Mandell 2008; Lowery 2010). Indians of the Pacific Northwest, assured in treaties of access to off-reservation food sources, moved freely from reservations to fishing places and job sites (Harmon 1998). California Indians—their families and tribes shattered by disease, ecological change, enslavement, and genocidal raids—struggled simply to survive (Hurtado 1988). Meanwhile, in pueblos along the Rio Grande, life was little different than for generations of indigenous ancestors (Sando 1982).

The diversity of Indian cultures and circumstances was hardly unknown to US officials. Nevertheless, for them and for many other non-Indians, a few tribes' stubborn devotion to a bison-dependent nomadic life on the Great Plains defined "the Indian problem." A provisional alternative to waging war on the nomads—reserving portions of their territory for homes and farms – was so badly implemented that it proved objectionable to non-Indians and Indians alike. Reservations were therefore the federal government's preferred option for little more than a decade before Congress and the Indian Office embraced a program intended ultimately to dismantle reservations. In the 1880s, asserting what the Supreme Court eventually called "plenary" power over the now-dependent tribes and their members, Congress authorized the Indian Office to prepare Indians for citizenship by giving them private plots of reserved tribal land, holding their property in trust for twenty-five years, subjecting them individually to US law, and schooling their children in English, Christianity, patriotism, Victorian gender roles, and utilitarian skills (Hoxie 1984).

For the following five decades, assimilation remained the avowed aim of federal programs for Indians. Over time, however, non-Indian demands for access to reserved resources and doubt about many Indians' fitness for full citizenship prompted legislation and administrative measures at odds with that aim. On one hand, officials hastily relinquished responsibility for some Indians' welfare, thereby lowering barriers to non-Indian acquisition of Indian property. On the other hand, the government tightened control over the property and conduct of other Indians. In 1906, Congress allowed the Indian Office to extend indefinitely its guardianship of Indians who presumably needed protection from predatory whites. Thus, while non-Indians wrested millions of additional acres from Indian hands, reservations endured, and even Indians who once resented reservations came to cherish them as guaranteed homelands and concessions to aboriginal sovereignty (Prucha 1984; Hoxie 1984).

Ultimately, the programs that were supposed to end Indians' distinctive political-legal status worked to confirm it. For one thing, administrators had to identify persons entitled to tracts of reservation land or enrollment in federal Indian schools. In many cases, Indians' long and often intimate relations with non-Indians had blurred the once-clear marks of Indian identity, making eligibility for allotments hard to determine. Bureaucrats, courts, and councils of reservation residents were consequently drawn into a process of specifying what made someone an Indian, at least for legal purposes: was it ancestry, place of residence, kin ties, social affiliations, habits, or some combination of such factors? Codification of the answers ensured that people known as Indians would not vanish as predicted. They would live under federal laws and regulations that directed their personal lives, social relations, and economic options to a degree that no other Americans experienced (Spruhan 2006; Harmon 2001).

Incomplete and inconsistent execution partially explains the assimilation program's contrary consequences, but its failure to eradicate "Indianness" owes as much, if not more, to Indian responses and initiatives. Evidence abounds that Indians resisted and subverted the assault on their cultures and tribal relations in numerous ways—exploiting weaknesses in systems of rule, turning elements of the assimilation program to their own purposes, developing conceptions of indigenous life suited to modernity. Whether recasting forbidden gatherings as July Fourth celebrations, protesting injustices in letters and petitions to US officials, or defending Indian customs in speeches and publications meant for non-Indians, Indians identified what Philip J. Deloria calls "new grounds for struggle," and many found "ways to move within the institutions that did, in fact, constrain, dominate, and transform them" (2004, 229–230; Raibmon 2005; Hoxie 2001).

Indians' Significance for Non-Indians

Indian tribes' decisive dispossession and subjection to US rule – inevitable though it may have seemed to Congress in 1871—was not accomplished until at least 1890, the year a cavalry regiment slaughtered more than 200 noncombatant Lakotas at Wounded Knee, South Dakota. Then as now, the late nineteenth-century Indian wars had multifaceted significance. First and foremost, the tribes' fight for freedom was also a contest for territory and economic resources. By subduing indigenous owner-occupants of western lands, the United States appropriated immense wealth and made industrial agriculture possible across vast terrain. The costs of that acquisition—although arguably a bargain—were substantial, and some have been long-term. Indians exacted "payment" not only in military expenditures and deaths, but also in treaty concessions that have had enduring legal, political, and financial consequences for the United States.

The fact that Indians also contributed to US annexation of western territories, if often involuntarily or inadvertently, enabled Euro-Americans to construe the takeover as reasonable and ultimately benign. For every implacable Sioux, Cheyenne, or Apache opponent of non-Indian settler-colonization there were other Indians who grudgingly accepted the intruders' presence or welcomed them as sources of opportunity. Crow and Pawnee men, for example, provided active assistance for army campaigns against Sioux and Cheyenne bands whose aggressive territorial expansion they resented and feared more than American activity at the time (White 1978). In the Pacific Northwest, parts of California, New Mexico, and elsewhere, Indians supplied myriad services for non-Indians, from transportation to construction, farm work, childcare, and intimate companionship. In 1876, dependence on Indian harvesters forced Washington Territory hop ranchers to meet demands for a pay rate three times higher than Chinese workers accepted (Harmon 1998, 106).

Indian resistance and ultimate submission to US domination had particular significance for proponents of the imperialism that became federal policy by the turn of the century. Taking control of the West was precedent and practice for comparable American ventures abroad, particularly the Spanish–American War of 1898 and US rule of indigenous Pacific islanders. Imperialists themselves "underscored the continuity between Indian wars and war for empire," Jackson Lears noted, as when Theodore Roosevelt declared that the United States should no more return the Philippines to Filipinos than give Arizona back to Apaches (Lears 2009, 210–211). In the words of Matthew Frye Jacobson, "U.S. dealings with North American Indians … provided a template of sorts" for reforming other "savages" (Jacobson 2000, 51). However, unlike the separate "nation-building" attempted in the Philippines, the plan for American "savages" was to liquidate their polities, which the Supreme Court had styled "domestic dependent nations" (Suri 2011, ch. 3). Even so, some scholars cite the continuity of US imperialism in North America and overseas as one of several reasons for historians of foreign relations to pay Indians more mind (DeLay 2015; Rosier 2015).

By the 1890s, Indians may have lost importance to non-Indians as military threats or competitors for resources, but they continued to matter as symbols with considerable power in public and cultural affairs. Euro-Americans had long understood themselves and their nation partly in relation to Indians, and their ideas about Indians—even ideas with minimal basis in fact—could have material force. Conceptions of Indians served as rationales for government policy and action, models of desirable or undesirable social relations, and inspirations for artistic or intellectual endeavors, among other things (Dippie 1982). As Sherry Smith observed, government officials, intellectuals, artists, "low-brow" writers, and other non-Indians competed "for the right to construct identities for Indians" (Smith 2000, 5; Maddox 2005). The competition was particularly intense from the 1880s through the first decade or two of the 1900s as Americans debated the implications of the country's transition from an emerging nation with an Indian frontier to an urbanizing industrial powerhouse. The Columbian Exposition was but one of many places to see Indians' prominence as a topic in that discourse.

The meanings that non-Indians attributed to Indians were manifold and paradoxical. Depictions of pathetic Indians – images of dejected former fighters or articles labeling individuals the last of their tribes—served to explain Native peoples' losses and expected disappearance as poignant but unavoidable consequences of natural forces. The "wild" tribes' defeat could be a confirmation of American civilization's superiority—its moral merits and republican righteousness as well as its technological achievements and wealth. Non-Indians who viewed wars as character-building experiences could see in the painted faces of vanquished Indian warriors a reflection of the white victors' courage and heroism. Conversely, when Indians such as Simon Pokagon adopted the essential elements of civilized life—citizens' dress, Christianity, the English language, and economic individualism—they provided other evidence that Euro-American culture was desirable and righteous.

Indians could also seem to exemplify virtues or national ideals that civilized Americans were failing to honor. Imagining Indians as noble savages—brave, loyal, generous, freedom-loving people of nature—was a Euro-American tradition with deep historical and psychological roots. Once Indian wars were in the past, such romanticized conceptions of Indians regained appeal, particularly for people uneasy about industrialization, urbanization, or a perceived loss of the vigor it had taken to settle the West. Whites who showed interest in aboriginal traditions believed that such ethnographic information would go with aged Indians to their graves, but also that Indians held some admirable values. Hence the popularity of summer camps such as the one where Charles Eastman taught white youth the "Indian method" of learning about nature, as his Dakota grandparents had done for him (Wilson 1983, 151–152; Armitage 2007; Lears 2009, 35, 204; Smith 2000).

Indians recognized non-Indians' interest and image-making power as both a threat and a source of opportunities. To the self-identified "progressive" Indians that Lucy Maddox studied, whites' control over "the ability of Indian people to speak and act for themselves" created a "crisis" that called for educated Indians' participation in public discourse (9). Some saw the nostalgia-fueled popular fascination with Indians as a chance to steer discourse in a favorable direction, particularly by highlighting ideals that Indians and non-Indians shared. Other Indians saw openings to assert their identity in ways that missionaries and US officials disapproved. That was true of the masterful horsemen and onetime warriors who could play themselves in Wild West shows or movies as well as the Kwakwaka'wakw at the Chicago exposition who dared to perform a cannibal dance outlawed at home in British Columbia (Moses 1999; Deloria 2004; Raibmon 2005).

Non-Indian interest in Indians also brought economic opportunities. The Kwakwaka'wakw, for example, were paid well for appearing in Chicago, as were many of the Indian actors and dancers who toured the eastern United States and European capitals with Buffalo Bill Cody. Familiarity with aboriginal life enabled other Native people to earn money and apparent respect as public speakers and ethnographers' informants. English literacy could be an additional asset. By the early twentieth century, Simon Pokagon was not the only Indian who marketed his writings to non-Indians. Charles Eastman, Sioux musician and writer Zitkala-Ša (Gertrude Bonnin), and Seneca anthropologist Arthur Parker, among others, likewise put their Euro-American schooling to use in publications as well as speeches that catered to non-Indian interest while claiming for Indians a right to define themselves and their place in modern America (Deloria 2004).

Shared Economic History

In the four decades that bracketed the year 1900, being Indian could mean residing in a US government-supervised enclave for descendants of Native Americans, spending years in regimented boarding schools with other Indians, facing prosecution in a Court of Indian Offenses for engaging in pagan rites, and requiring bureaucrats' permission for transactions involving individually owned land or personal funds. Partly because Indians refused to be defined by the limited status and aspirations that non-Indians proposed for them, being Indian could also include living in a US city, managing a cattle ranch, hiring out as an itinerant farm laborer or logger, staking a homestead on the public domain, becoming a new US citizen, working as a US civil servant, being a Christian clergyman, or heading to a battlefield overseas as a soldier in the US Army. In other words, Indians could experience and do things that thousands of non-Indian Americans also did. Those common experiences are no less important to the history of GAPE Indians than the quintessentially "Indian" experiences of clashing with US troops on the Great Plains or struggling to make a living on a reservation.

Some broad, transformative economic developments of the time—escalating industrialization, the rise of corporations and industrial-commercial monopolies, the accumulation of extreme wealth by a small elite, the concomitant growth of an alienated factory labor force and workers' unions—involved few Indians directly; but Indians felt repercussions of those trends, especially Indian farmers.

Numerous indigenous people had farmed and/or raised stock of their own accord long before the 1880s. Many more responded to federal pressure and necessity by starting to farm once they had reservations or individual allotments (Hurt 1987). Proponents of the assimilation policy, clinging to an agrarian ideal as old as the republic, maintained that small family farms were Indians' assurance of a prosperous future. However, by the time US agents were meting out 80- or 160-acre parcels of reservation land to tribe members, that ideal had lessening basis in reality. The proportion of Americans who made a living as farmers was dropping rapidly, and commercial farms were increasing in scale (McGerr 2003, 21). While facing deterrents peculiar to Indian legal status, such as a prohibition on securing a loan with their land, would-be Indian farmers also suffered setbacks that drove non-Indians off the land or into the Populist movement—drought and other disastrous weather, unsuitable soil, plunging crop prices in times of surplus, and prohibitive equipment and transportation costs. When crop prices rose, as they did during World War I, Indians and non-Indians alike planted more acreage. When markets crashed, farmers of all races went broke (Lears 2009, 190; Lewis 1997; Heaton 2005).

Although no Indians joined the exclusive club of Gilded Age tycoons, some did acquire or generate substantial wealth in market transactions or profit-making enterprises. For Makahs in the Pacific Northwest who operated lucrative whaling and sealing fleets, the late nineteenth century was a period of notable prosperity (Reid 2015, ch. 5). Menominees took charge of commercial logging on their forested reservation in Wisconsin and managed the business profitably for the benefit of tribal community members (Hosmer 1999). Ambitious citizens of the Cherokee and Creek nations enclosed vast tracts of land for cattle ranching, drawing protests from fellow Indians and outsiders who called them monopolists or land barons and compared them to the speculators snapping up US public domain. By the 1920s, some Indians in Oklahoma gained renown for their fabulously high incomes, made possible by industry and consumer craving for the petroleum found under the land reserved for them (Harmon 2010, 133–208).

Meanwhile a majority of Indians, along with many non-Indians, sank to the low end of the country's increasingly skewed wealth distribution. For Indians, the causes of poverty included federal policies, laws, and actions that reduced the national total of reserved Indian lands by two-thirds before the Progressive Era was over (Meyer 1999; Banner 2007). Additionally, Indians' declared status as "wards" of the US government was the basis for regulations that could frustrate profitable use of their remaining acreage and limit their access to cash in the bank. But Indian poverty also had causes familiar to poor non-Indians, from lack of education and employers' racism to ill health and disabilities. While many non-Indians tried in vain to find or keep productive homestead land, numerous Indians never received hoped-for allotments; and much as debts, poor land, or lack of capital doomed many a white homesteader's efforts, penury prompted the sale of many an Indian allotment for a sum that financed no more than a few months of subsistence.

The odds against Indian prosperity increased as industrial development, government land-use plans, and non-Indian competition interfered with tribe members' accustomed access to other vital resources. In the Pacific Northwest, huge commercial fish wheels and intertidal traps scooped up salmon that would formerly have reached Indian nets, while dams and other damage to salmon habitat reduced the number of fish available for harvest (Harmon 1998). In southern Arizona, non-Indians devastated the healthy agricultural economy of the Gila River Reservation by diverting water that had irrigated the Indians' plentiful crops for countless generations (DeJong 2009). In northern Arizona, Havasupai food supplies dwindled as non-Indian ranchers took over water sources and wild animals' browsing areas (Jacoby 2001, 162).

Ironically, the emerging Progressive conservation movement, which aimed to stem heedless depletion of the nation's natural resources, was more harmful than helpful to Indians. The popular image of Indians who lived symbiotically with wilderness wildlife carried little weight when the federal government began creating national parks and forests. Managers of the new reserves insisted that Indians be barred to prevent ecological damage. As a result, according to Karl Jacoby, "It was Indians whose lives were most remade by the coming of conservation." In the case of the Havasupai, a key change was the "inescapable" need to rely on wage labor (Jacoby 2001, 151).

In fact, whether or not Indians hunted, fished, farmed, or raised some of their food in gardens, their economic activities often included a common way that other Americans supported themselves by the 1880s—selling their labor. Judging from published histories, Indian wage work in that era was either a well-kept secret or a matter of no interest to history scholars until the late twentieth century. Granted, the recent research has not uncovered evidence of numerous Indian workers in the urban factories where millions of non-Indians toiled. However, it does document northern California Indians' involvement in migrant farm labor (Bauer 2012), Pacific Northwest Indians' indispensability to annual hop harvests (Raibmon 2005), Northwest Indian women's work in salmon canneries (Harmon 1998), Southwest Indians' employment on railroad construction crews (Youngdahl 2011), Ottawa timber cutters in Michigan, and more (Littlefield and Knack 1996, 66–99). By 1889, Louis Warren found, "Paiutes had become a significant part of Nevada's working class" (Warren 2015, 148). Except in the most isolated areas of the largest reservations, Indians often supplemented traditional sources of subsistence with a variety of paid work, much of it seasonal, temporary, or part-time. On Sioux reservations, Indians could earn money hauling freight, chopping cordwood, or working for government overseers. Throughout Indian country, the federal Indian service was a source of income for men who could build fences or police reservation boundaries but also for men and women who had learned in federal or church schools to live by the clock and write English, make beds, play musical instruments, forge iron tools, or keep financial accounts. As early as 1900, Indians constituted a significant portion of Indian school employees (Ostler 2001; Cahill 2011).

Indians also earned money by participating in another general turn-of-the-century phenomenon—the commercialization of arts and culture. Plains Indians sold their intricate beadwork, Tlingits in southeast Alaska carved miniature totem poles and canoes for the tourist market, Indian women of many tribes adapted exquisite basketry skills to non-Indian buyers' tastes, and Navajos cultivated a national market for woven rugs and silver jewelry (Ostler 2001; Raibmon 2005; Bsumek 2008). Indians worked in a wide array of performing arts as well. By the late 1800s, according to Philip Deloria, a sizable "national cohort of Indian people" worked not only in Wild West shows but also in "circuses, traveling medicine shows, urban revues, lecture circuits, and sideshows." White audiences even created opportunities for musicians such as classically trained Tsianina Redfeather Blackstone, a Creek–Cherokee singer who performed "Indianist" compositions clad in buckskin dresses and beaded headbands. Perhaps the boldest Indians appearing in a new mass-entertainment medium were those who went to Hollywood and New York before World War I to work as movie extras or even lead actors, writers, and directors (Deloria 2004, 75, 210–218, 53–108).

Shared Cultural History

White Americans who purchased Indian art, crafts, or writings may have admired the workmanship, taken pleasure in collecting curiosities, or felt sympathy for Indians besieged by modernity. As the nation struggled to accommodate its growing cultural diversity, some non-Indians were also willing to make a place for other, inoffensive aspects of Indianness, particularly in the Progressive Era. Indians who no longer seemed like irredeemable enemies of civilization could exemplify an ongoing national unification process. Many were included for that purpose in public commemorations and celebrations. But how far could Indians' integration and empowerment go?

The devout Christian advocates of Indian policy reform in the 1880s maintained that race was no obstacle to Indians' advancement and absorption into US society. As children of God, Indians had the same potential for development and decency as whites; they needed only the incentive for self-improvement that came with individual property ownership, a proper education, and the guidance of law. This tenet of the assimilation policy, communicated with varying regularity and sincerity to young Indians, helped to motivate the educational accomplishments and cultural choices of many Native people who came of age in the late 1800s. However, it promised something most white Americans would not deliver: acceptance as equals.

By century's end, if not before, whites who held that race did not limit Indians' potential were likely a shrinking minority. A contrary ideology of race-determined destiny and inherent white superiority was ascendant in the United States, providing justification for Jim Crow in the South and congressionally sanctioned exclusion of Chinese immigrants. Whites with political and social power increasingly opted to regulate relations among racial and ethnic groups by segregating them (McGerr 2003, 182), and despite continuing federal lip service to assimilation, most Indians did remain segregated. Those whose Indianness was unmistakable were as apt as blacks, Asians, and Mexicans to meet with the institutionalized discrimination that maintained white Americans' hegemony.

US Indian service employees were not immune to racist thinking, especially regarding Indians who resisted wholesale culture change. Shortly after leaving office as Commissioner of Indian Affairs in 1909, Francis Leupp cited Indians' racial heritage as a reason that Indian schools should prepare the children for life on "the frontier," where they would "try to draw a living out of the soil" or "enter the general labor market as lumbermen, ditchers, miners, railroad hands or what not." Although Leupp professed to believe that some exceptional Indians could transcend their primitive heritage and thus gain full economic and political citizenship, he also wrote, "Nature has drawn her lines of race, which it is folly for us to try to obliterate along with the artificial barriers we throw down in the cause of civil equality. …In the course of merging this hardly-used race into our body politic, many individuals, unable to keep up the pace, will fall by the wayside and be trodden underfoot" (Leupp 1910, 45–46, 53, 60).

Gertrude Bonnin was an Indian school alumna who knew from experience that whites' prejudices and low expectations for people of color often applied to Indians. She wrote with patent bitterness about the condescending attitude of some boarding-school teachers and patrons she had encountered (Zitkala-Ša 1921, "Retrospection"). As an anthropologist, Arthur Parker was aware that the same attitude had legitimacy among his fellow intellectuals. He denounced the "school of race philosophy" that considered "the blonde Aryan or white man … the destined ruler and civilizer of the World" (Hoxie 2001, 122).

Yet Parker himself, like many Indians familiar with Euro-American thought on human differences, used language linking characteristics and dispositions to particular "races." In 1916, he wrote of "the Negro's" "natural servility and … imitativeness" (Hertzberg 1971, 158). The 1893 Osage expulsion of blacks is an additional example of Indians—their experiences embedded in the larger history of American race relations—who had internalized prevalent social constructs and had come to view other peoples in racialized, judgmental ways. Similarly, people with indigenous ancestry in Robeson County, North Carolina, founded their own Indian schools and allied politically with white segregationists in part because they hoped to avoid the cruelest consequences of being identified as "colored" (Lowery 2010).

Just as racist discrimination had targets besides Indians, so did the resocialization measures that Indians faced. The government-orchestrated assault on Indian culture paralleled Americanization efforts directed at immigrants from eastern and southern Europe who flooded into the United States concurrently, fueling the US population's cultural heterogeneity. The children of Sicilian fishermen, Russian peasants, and immigrant Jewish shopkeepers, no less than the children of Navajo shepherds or Ojibwe hunters, were expected to make their absorption into the nation possible by learning English, Victorian gender roles, a Protestant work ethic, and the established ideals of patriotic citizens.

Nevertheless some Indians, like some immigrants, detected in the discourse of Americanization a possible opening for the preservation and even celebration of selected indigenous traditions: they heard favorable talk of America as a cultural hybrid. While many Americans hoped for everyone's conformity to the English-rooted culture of the republic's founders, others liked a conception of the nation as a fusion of cultures, preferably embodying the best of each. The latter idea—dubbed the "melting pot" in the title of Israel Zangwill's 1908 play—inspired Eastman, Bonnin, and some contemporaries to assert that Indians had made and could make welcome additions to American culture. Reflecting in old age on his school experiences during the 1880s, Lakota author, educator, and actor Luther Standing Bear put it this way: "While the white people had much to teach us, we had much to teach them, and what a school could have been established upon that idea!" (Standing Bear 1978, 229–237).

Dreams of unqualified admission to US cultural and civic life did not inspire all Indians. A great many longed instead for fulfillment of promises that the United States had made to tribes. In the 1910s, Native people therefore established a number of regional and national organizations that lobbied Congress and pursued or supported tribal claims for judicial relief from government abuses and breaches of trust (Hoxie 2012, 254). Their organized resort to legal procedures was a notable example of adapting non-Indian culture to Indian quests for justice and self-determination.

Some Indians, hoping for protection from government suppression of Indian culture, also wanted legislation granting US citizenship to all Indians. Others feared that a condition of citizenship would be forfeiture of their rights as citizens of tribes. This became a hotter issue when male citizens faced conscription during World War I. Due to a hodgepodge of pertinent laws, some Indians of fighting age were citizens; others were not. Although Indians volunteered for military service at a higher rate than non-Indians and served in integrated units, a significant minority objected to the draft as an infringement on their tribes' sovereignty (Zissu 1995).

Thus, at a time when a massive influx of immigrants and US acquisition of overseas territories raised questions for Americans about the desirable reach and the meanings of citizenship, Indians confronted such questions as well. Congress finally resolved the Indian debate in 1924 by bestowing citizenship on Indians born within US borders while explicitly preserving their rights to tribal property (American Indian Citizenship Act 1924).

Indian Progressives

Leaders of the Indian campaign for citizenship came from a cohort of politically active, school-educated Indians who called themselves progressives. In 1911, just over one hundred of them launched the Society of American Indians (SAI), arguably the first modern national pan-Indian organization. The SAI set out "to promote and cooperate with all efforts looking to the advancement of the Indian in enlightenment which leave him free, as a man, to develop according to the natural laws of social evolution ...; to present in a just light the true history of the race, to preserve its records and to emulate its distinguishing virtues"; and "to promote citizenship among Indians and to obtain the rights thereof" (Hertzberg 1971, 80).

Like other self-identified progressives of the time, these Indians believed that government agencies, staffed by upstanding professionals and informed by scientific rationalism, could remedy social problems such as the class and race divides of the Gilded Age. During the SAI's dozen years of existence, members publicized US Indian Office corruption and malfeasance but quarreled about whether their ultimate goal should be the agency's reform or abolition. They also lobbied for legislation authorizing adjudication of tribal grievances against the United States. Education reform was another characteristically progressive SAI objective. SAI president Arthur Parker advocated a plan for improving Indian schools that Hazel Hertzberg termed "an Indian version of ... the most important educational reform ideas of the Progressive Era" (Hertzberg 1971, 131).

Ironically, "progressive" is also an apt term for the tenets of men who headed the Indian Office, so often the target of SAI condemnation. Early twentieth-century administrators of Indian affairs saw it as their duty to exert salutary influence on their Indian wards' conduct and social relations. In the name of the progressive creed that all people could be transformed for the better, and ethnocentrically confident that government managers knew what was "better," the Indian service remained sternly paternalistic through the 1920s. The effect on most Indians was to block rather than provide opportunities for the natural development that SAI envisioned.

The SAI progressives' impacts on history, particularly their relevance to twentieth-century tribal nationalism, is the subject of much historiographical debate, in part because they arguably had more in common with patronizing non-Indians than with fellow Indians. Largely educated in boarding schools and universities, working primarily in professions or the arts, and seldom living in their tribal communities, they were hardly representative of the American Indian population. Considering themselves more advanced than most Indians on the scale of human development, they aspired to be leaders of their "race."

But SAI members did not represent the only emerging model of Indian leadership. While SAI founder Carlos Montezuma advocated full US citizenship and integration as a solution to Indians' oppression, Indians on many reservations sought to exercise collective power through tribal councils of their own making or business councils convened by federal officials (Hoxie 2001, 92–96; Clow 1987). In an influential account of one such man's simultaneous commitment to some government-endorsed changes and some government-censured Native traditions, David Rich Lewis discredited a common assumption that Indians have been either progressive or "traditional." He urged historians instead to explore the ambivalence and complexity of Indians' motivations and strategies (Lewis 1991). Scholarship consistent with that advice has since produced enlightening portraits of Indians, including SAI activists, whose thinking about change and tradition was complex as that of any American in the GAPE.

Shared Religious Innovation and Fervor

The activists and intellectuals of SAI help to illustrate one more development that Indian societies experienced in tandem with the United States as a whole: increasing cultural heterogeneity. Long before the twentieth century, exposure to outsiders had contributed to cultural differentiation within tribes, inducing some members to take up practices or beliefs that others disdained. Due to contact with non-Indians, tribes had split into Christian and pagan factions or populations with individualist and communal economic cultures. By the Progressive Era, conditions promoting such diversification had intensified. Although the federal assimilation program's intended result was Indian cultural homogeneity on a Euro-American model, its uneven effectiveness contributed to the opposite effect. Individually as well as tribe by tribe, Indians accepted, rejected, or adapted the prescribed elements of "civilization" in differing combinations to differing degrees.

Government pressure for culture change and economic needs were not the only stimuli of diversification. Growth in the number of Indians who understood and read English opened new channels for "foreign" ideas to enter tribal communities. Automobiles and trains widened Indians' geographical and cultural horizons. Radio, movies, and other new forms of entertainment introduced additional influences, and an increase in Indians who visited or resided in the nation's booming cities compounded their effects (LaPier and Beck 2015). Consequently, by the 1920s, the word "Indian" denoted people who were diverse not only because they belonged to hundreds of aboriginally diverse tribes and shared the human propensity for creativity but also because they responded in varied ways to coexistence with an increasingly multicultural United States.

Indians' expanding cultural heterogeneity was manifest in religious practices as new spiritual movements sprang up and spread among Native peoples. When Jackson Lears identified widespread longing for spiritual regeneration as a characteristic of the GAPE, he could have cited numerous illustrations involving Indians. That longing probably accounts for many of the documented Indian conversions to Christianity during this period. Conversely, spiritual uneasiness eventually prompted Gertrude Bonnin to disavow the Christianity she was obliged to practice at Carlisle Indian School. In a magazine essay titled "Why I Am a Pagan," she announced her ensuing sense of renewal (Zitkala-Ša 1902).

A longing felt in more desperate circumstances ignited the "Ghost Dance" movement that swept through tribes from Nevada to the eastern Great Plains in 1889 and 1890, giving many Indians hope of regaining cherished indigenous lifeways and providing them in the meantime with "instructions for survival and good living" (Warren 2015, 143). Concurrently in the Pacific Northwest, a Squaxin man's apparent death and resurrection inspired a Christianity-influenced Indian mode of worship and moral code that endures today as the Indian Shaker Church (Harmon 1998). Other Indians participated in the far-reaching diffusion of an ancient Southwest Indian sacrament involving ingestion of hallucination-inducing cactus buttons. The practitioners, who included some Indian progressives, incorporated elements of Christianity and ultimately institutionalized their blended, pan-Indian religion as the Native American Church (Hoxie 2001, 20–21). Each of these religious innovations offered beleaguered Indians the satisfaction of joining with other Indians to seek ecstatic visions in a recognizably Indian way, but each also counseled believers to observe rules of conduct made necessary by changes that non-Indians had wrought in their world—work hard, be frugal, be peaceful, and send the children to school.

Conclusion

In "Rebuke of the Red Man," Simon Pokagon concluded his recital of Indian suffering at the hands of whites on a profoundly pessimistic note. The future, he predicted, would deal with his people "no better than in the past." "No rainbow of promise spans the dark cloud of our afflictions," he lamented. Although Pokagon's principal late-life activity—preparing legal claims against the United States—does not suggest a man devoid of hope, he wrote at a time when Indians did have cause for despair. Yet most did not "stand with folded arms" and wait for the "great ocean of civilization … to overwhelm them," as Pokagon foresaw (Pokagon 1893, 12). Instead, through complex combinations of resistance, adaptation, and innovation, they refuted Pokagon's prediction and defied the common expectation that Indians would soon vanish as distinctive peoples.

That collective survival came at great expense in lives, liberty, and well-being. As the United States deprived tribes of land, customary food sources, and autonomy, members' health suffered. Confinement on reservations, dependency on rations, coercive dispersion to allotments, and punishment for engaging in traditional practices had demoralizing effects on thousands of people. Later, US citizenship brought obligations without lifting the restrictions of government guardianship. Family relations and mutual support networks withered as children spent years in distant residential schools, forced to speak English and inculcated with an ethos of "intelligent selfishness." Many children did not learn the stories that had taught their ancestors who they were and how they must live.

Those hardships and losses, both tangible and intangible, are obligatory topics for any account of American Indians during the GAPE. Scholars will no doubt debate indefinitely how much emphasis the grievances warrant, but the rich record of Indian agency makes it unacceptable for historians simply to enumerate the losses and leave it at that. Depicting Indians solely as victims in a tale either of Euro-American misdeeds or of a modern society's inevitable development dehumanizes all the actors. It also implies, as US histories too often have, that Indians had a limited role in other people's history and did little or nothing to shape the terms of their survival or make history themselves.

Historians of American Indians, like the people they study, challenge common assumptions and oversimplified narratives about indigenous peoples' roles in history. Some do so as advocates of intensively Indian-centered ethnohistories that reveal the persistence of distinctive, though mutable, indigenous culture. Some argue for viewing Indians' history in larger frames such as settler-colonialism, even frames that encompass settler-colonial states and indigenous peoples elsewhere on the globe (Sleeper-Smith et al. 2015, 287–306). Much as intellectuals in the Society of American Indians struggled to reconcile their Indian identity with their education in the language and ethos of Euro-Americans, Indian history specialists also debate the importance and feasibility of purging their scholarship of colonial influences. And just as SAI members never resolved the disagreement about abolishing the Indian Office, differences in scholars' views on Indians' history will persist. But it should now be clear to all that analyses of Indians' significance to GAPE history must consider more Indians than those killed at Wounded Knee, exiled to reservations, or sent to boarding schools. They must take into account Indians who worked for wages, raised cattle, lectured to white audiences, preached Christianity, taught English to Indian children, sued the United States, and claimed a right to participate in vital national discourse, all without disavowing history, social relations, values, beliefs, or habits that distinguished them as American Indians.

References

Adams, David Wallace. 1995. *Education for Extinction: American Indians and the Boarding School Experience, 1875–1929.* Lawrence: University Press of Kansas.

American Indian Citizenship Act. 1924. 8 U.S. Code 1401 (b).

Armitage, Kevin C. 2007. "The Child Is Born a Naturalist: Nature Study, Woodcraft Indians, and the Theory of Recapitulation." *Journal of the Gilded Age and Progressive Era* 6: 43–70.

Banner, Stuart. 2007. *How the Indians Lost Their Land: Law and Power on the Frontier.* Cambridge, MA: Belknap Press.

Bauer, William. 2012. *We Were All Like Migrant Workers Here: Work, Community, and Memory on California's Round Valley Reservation, 1850–1941.* Chapel Hill: University of North Carolina Press.

Berkhofer, Robert F., Jr. 1978. *The White Man's Indian: Images of the American Indian from Columbus to the Present.* New York: Vintage Books.

Bsumek, Erika. 2008. *Indian Made: Navajo Culture in the Marketplace, 1868–1940.* Lawrence: University Press of Kansas.

Cahill, Cathleen D. 2011. *Federal Fathers and Mothers: A Social History of the United States Indian Service, 1869–1933.* Chapel Hill: University of North Carolina Press.

Cashman, Sean. 1993. *America in the Gilded Age.* New York: New York University Press.

Clow, Richmond L. 1987. "The Indian Reorganization Act and the Loss of Tribal Sovereignty: Constitutions on the Rosebud and Pine Ridge Reservations." *Great Plains Quarterly* 7: 125–134.

Conn, Stephen. 2004. *History's Shadow: Native Americans and Historical Consciousness in the Nineteenth Century.* Chicago, IL: University of Chicago Press.

DeJong, David. 2009. *Stealing the Gila: The Pima Agricultural Economy and Water Deprivation, 1848–1921.* Tucson: University of Arizona Press.

DeLay, Brian. 2015. "Indian Polities, Empire, and the History of American Foreign Relations." *Diplomatic History* 39: 927–942.

Deloria, Philip J. 2004. *Indians in Unexpected Places.* Lawrence: University Press of Kansas.

Dippie, Brian. 1982. *The Vanishing American: White Attitudes and Indian Policy.* Middletown, CT: Wesleyan University Press.

Ellis, Clyde. 2003. *A Dancing People: Powwow Culture on the Southern Plains.* Lawrence: University Press of Kansas.

Ginger, Ray. 1965. *Age of Excess: The United States from 1877 to 1914.* New York: Macmillan.

Harmon, Alexandra. 1998. *Indians in the Making: Ethnic Relations and Indian Identities around Puget Sound.* Berkeley: University of California Press.

—. 2001. "Tribal Enrollment Councils: Lessons on Law and Indian Identity." *Western Historical Quarterly* 32: 175–200.

—. 2003. "American Indians and Land Monopolies in the Gilded Age." *Journal of American History* 90: 106–133.

—. 2010. *Rich Indians: Native People and the Problem of Wealth in American History.* Chapel Hill: University of North Carolina Press.

Heaton, John. 2005. *The Shoshone-Bannocks: Culture and Commerce at Fort Hall, 1870–1940.* Lawrence: University of Press of Kansas.

Hertzberg, Hazel W. 1971. *The Search for an American Indian Identity: Modern Pan-Indian Movements.* Syracuse, NY: Syracuse University Press.

Holm, Tom. 2005. *The Great Confusion in Indian Affairs: Native Americans and Whites in the Progressive Era.* Austin: University of Texas Press.

Hosmer, Brian C. 1999. *American Indians in the Marketplace: Persistence and Innovation among the Menominees and Metlakatlans, 1870–1920.* Lawrence: University Press of Kansas.

Hoxie, Frederick E. 1984. *A Final Promise: The Campaign to Assimilate the Indians, 1880–1920.* Lincoln: University of Nebraska Press.

— ed. 2001. *Talking Back to Civilization: Indian Voices from the Progressive Era.* New York: Bedford/St. Martin's.

—. 2012. *This Indian Country: American Indian Activists and the Place They Made.* New York: Penguin.

Hurt, R. Douglas. 1987. *Indian Agriculture in America: Prehistory to the Present.* Lawrence: University Press of Kansas.

Hurtado, Albert. 1988. *Indian Survival on the California Frontier.* New Haven, CT: Yale University Press.

Jacobson, Matthew Frye. 2000. *Barbarian Virtues: The United States Encounters Foreign Peoples at Home and Abroad, 1876–1917.* New York: Hill & Wang.

Jacoby, Karl. 2001. *Crimes against Nature: Squatters, Poachers, Thieves, and the Hidden History of American Conservation.* Berkeley: University of California Press.

LaPier, Rosalyn R., and David R.M. Beck. 2015. *"Determining Our Own Destiny": American Indians in Chicago, 1893–1934.* Lincoln: University of Nebraska Press.

Lears, Jackson. 2009. *Rebirth of a Nation: The Making of Modern America, 1877–1920.* New York: HarperCollins.

Leupp, Francis E. 1910. *The Indian and His Problem.* New York: Scribners.

Lewis, David Rich. 1991. "Reservation Leadership and the Progressive-Traditional Dichotomy: William Wash and the Northern Utes, 1865–1928." *Ethnohistory* 18: 124–148.

—. 1997. *Neither Wolf nor Dog: American Indians, Environment, and Agrarian Change*. New York: Oxford University Press.

Littlefield, Alice, and Martha C. Knack. 1996. *Native Americans and Wage Labor: Ethnohistorical Perspectives*. Norman: University of Oklahoma Press.

Low, John N. 2011. "Chicago's First Urban Indians—the Potawatomi." Ph.D. diss., University of Michigan.

Lowery, Malinda Maynor. 2010. *Lumbee Indians in the Jim Crow South: Race, Identity, and the Making of a Nation*. Chapel Hill: University of North Carolina Press.

Maddox, Lucy. 2005. *Citizen Indians: Native Intellectuals, Race, and Representation*. Ithaca, NY: Cornell University Press.

Mandell, Daniel R. 2008. *Tribe, Race, History: Native Americans in Southern New England, 1780–1880*. Baltimore, MD: Johns Hopkins University Press.

McGerr, Michael. 2003. *A Fierce Discontent: The Rise and Fall of the Progressive Movement in America*. New York: Oxford University Press.

Meyer, Melissa L. 1999. *The White Earth Tragedy: Ethnicity and Dispossession at a Minnesota Anishinaabe Reservation, 1880–1920*. Lincoln: University of Nebraska Press.

Meyer, Melissa L, and Kerwin Lee Kline. 1999. "Native American Studies and the End of Ethnohistory." In *Studying Native America: Problems and Prospects*, ed. Russell Thornton, 182–216. Madison: University of Wisconsin Press.

Mihesuah, Devon A. 1998. *Natives and Academics: Researching and Writing about American Indians*. Lincoln: University of Nebraska Press.

Moses, L.G. 1999. *Wild West Shows and the Images of American Indians, 1882–1933*. Albuquerque: University of New Mexico Press.

Ostler, Jeffrey. 2001. "The Last Buffalo Hunt and Beyond: Plains Sioux Economic Strategies in the Early Reservation Period." *Great Plains Quarterly* 21: 115–130.

Painter, Nell Irvin. 1987. *Standing at Armageddon: The United States, 1888–1919*. New York: W.W. Norton.

Pokagon, Simon. 1893. *The Red Man's Rebuke*. Hartford, MI: C.H. Engle.

Prucha, Francis Paul. 1984. *The Great Father: The United States Government and the American Indian*. Lincoln: University of Nebraska Press.

Raibmon, Paige. 2005. *Authentic Indians: Episodes of Encounter from the Late Nineteenth Century Northwest Coast*. Durham, NC: Duke University Press.

Reid, Joshua L. 2015. *The Sea Is My Country: The Maritime World of the Makahs*. New Haven, CT: Yale University Press.

Rosier, Paul C. 2015. "Crossing New Boundaries: American Indians and Twentieth Century U.S. Foreign Policy." *Diplomatic History* 39: 955–966.

Sando, Joe S. 1982. *Nee Hemish: A History of Jemez Pueblo*. Albuquerque: University of New Mexico Press.

Sleeper-Smith, et al., ed. 2015. *Why You Can't Teach United States History without American Indians*. Chapel Hill: University of North Carolina Press.

Smith, Sherry. 2000. *Reimagining Indians: Native Americans through Anglo Eyes, 1880–1940*. New York: Oxford University Press.

—. 2010. "Comments: Native Americans and Indian Policy in the Progressive Era." *Journal of the Gilded Age and Progressive Era* 9: 503–507.

Snow, Dean R. 1994. *The Iroquois*. Cambridge: Blackwell.

Spruhan, Paul. 2006. "A Legal History of Blood Quantum in Federal Indian Law to 1935." *South Dakota Law Review* 51: 24–46.

Standing Bear, Luther. 1978 (1933). *Land of the Spotted Eagle*. Boston: Houghton Mifflin. Reprint, Lincoln: University of Nebraska Press. Citations refer to the University of Nebraska edition.

Suri, Jeremi. 2011. *Liberty's Surest Guardian: American Nation-Building from the Founders to Obama*. New York: Free Press/Simon & Schuster.

Warren, Louis S. 2015. "Wage Work in the Sacred Circle: The Ghost Dance as Modern Religion." *Western Historical Quarterly* 46: 141–68.

White, Richard. 1978. "The Winning of the West: The Expansion of the Western Sioux in the Eighteenth and Nineteenth Centuries." *Journal of American History* 65: 319–343.

Wilkinson, Charles F. 1987. *American Indians, Time, and the Law*. New Haven, CT: Yale University Press.

Wilson, Raymond. 1983. *Ohiyesa: Charles Eastman, Santee Sioux*. Urbana: University of Illinois Press.

Youngdahl, Jay. 2011. *Working on the Railroad, Walking in Beauty: Navajos, Hozho, and Track Work*. Logan: Utah State University Press.

Zissu, Erik M. 1995. "Conscription, Sovereignty, and Land: American Indian Resistance during World War I." *Pacific Historical Review* 64: 537–66.

Zitkala-Ša [Gertrude Simmons Bonnin]. 1902. "Why I Am a Pagan." *The Online Archive of Nineteenth-Century U.S. Women's Writings*, ed. Glynis Carr. Posted: Winter 1999, http://www.facstaff.bucknell.edu/gcarr/19cUSWW/ZS/WIAP.h/Accessed July 12, 2016.

—. 1921. *American Indian Stories*. Washington, DC: Hayworth.

Further Reading

Allen, Chadwick, et al. 2013. "The Society of American Indians and Its Legacies." *American Indian Quarterly* 37 and *Studies in American Indian Literatures* 26 (17 essays in joint special issues).

Britten, Thomas A. 1997. *American Indians in World War I: At Home and at War*. Albuquerque: University of New Mexico Press.

Eastman, Charles. (1916) 1977. *From the Deep Woods to Civilization*. Reprint. Lincoln: University of Nebraska Press.

Hosmer, Brian C., and Colleen M. O'Neill, ed. 2004. *Native Pathways: American Indian Culture and Economic Development in the Twentieth Century*. Boulder: University Press of Colorado.

Iverson, Peter. 1982. *Carlos Montezuma and the Changing World of American Indians*. Albuquerque: University of New Mexico Press.

Miner, Craig. 1976. *The Corporation and the Indian: Tribal Sovereignty and Industrial Civilization in Indian Territory, 1865–1907*. Norman: University of Oklahoma Press.

Ostler, Jeffrey. 2004. *The Plains Sioux and U.S. Colonialism from Lewis and Clark to Wounded Knee*. New York: Cambridge University Press.

Piatote, Beth H. 2013. *Domestic Subjects: Gender, Citizenship, and Law in Native American Literature*. New Haven, CT: Yale University Press.

Porter, Joy. 2014. "Progressivism and Native American Self-Expression in the Late Nineteenth and Early Twentieth Century." In *Native Diasporas: Indigenous Identities and Settler Colonialism in the Americas*, ed. Gregory D. Smithers and Brooke N. Newman, 273–295. Lincoln: University of Nebraska Press.

Rzeczkowski, Frank. 2012. *Uniting the Tribes: The Rise and Fall of Pan-Indian Community on the Crow Reservation*. Lawrence: University Press of Kansas.

Smoak, Gregory. 2008. *Ghost Dances and Identity: Prophetic Religion and American Indian Ethnogenesis in the Nineteenth Century*. Berkeley: University of California Press.

Troutman, John. 2009. *Indian Blues: American Indians and the Politics of Music, 1879–1934*. Norman: University of Oklahoma Press.

Vigil, Kiara M. 2015. *Indigenous Intellectuals: Sovereignty, Citizenship, and the American Imagination, 1880–1930*. New York: Cambridge University Press.

Chapter Eleven

Race, Immigration, and Ethnicity

Julie Greene

Race, Immigration, and Ethnicity

During the Gilded Age and Progressive Era, immigrants transformed the nation demographically, socially, politically, and culturally. They provided the labor that built industrial capitalism, they fueled debates about race, ethnicity, and national identity, they shaped the legal structure of the nation, they contributed, often unwillingly, to the global power of the United States, and they generated—and participated in—wide-reaching social reform efforts. The making of the modern United States is powerfully tied up with immigration and the issues of race and ethnicity so closely linked to it. Indeed, there is a stronger causal connection than that formulation suggests. Immigrants themselves, and immigration as a social and demographic force that caused consternation and anxiety, helped produce the racial and national categories that characterize the modern United States. This chapter considers the central transformations of the Gilded Age and Progressive Era—the rise of corporate capitalism, the transformation of the working class, the emergence of American global power, social and political reform, and the articulation of national identity—with an eye on the ways that immigration and immigrants contributed.

The immigrant experience during the Gilded Age and Progressive Era was remarkable in many ways, not least of which was simply its scale. Between 1870 and 1930, more than 30 million immigrants entered the United States. During the Gilded Age, from 1881 to 1900, 8.9 million immigrants came; during the Progressive Era, 1901 to 1920, another 14.5 million arrived. These newcomers entered a nation that numbered only 70 to 100 million people in the decades between 1890 and 1920, so they exerted a huge impact demographically, socially, culturally, and politically. This immigrant population was also very much in flux; at some moments, particularly during economic downturn, many people left the United States; some immigrants remained in the country only long enough to make some money and return home; others migrated in a circular fashion, timing their departures to harvest time at home; and once they had arrived immigrants often migrated onward beyond their first destination (Thistlethwaite 1964; Montgomery, 1987). Although their country of origin shifted over the decades from 1870 to the 1920s, with Germans and Irish dominating at the beginning of the Gilded Age, while Italians, Austro-Hungarians, and Russians overtook them by the 1890s, it is useful to remember that so-called “old immigrants” from northern and western Europe continued to come in large numbers throughout the period. For the decades between 1870 and 1930 the figures for the leading immigrant groups include:

Austria 4,123,000
Germany 3,564,000
Hungary 1,290,000
Ireland 2,176,000
Italy 4,579,000
Soviet Union 3,340,000
United Kingdom 2,832,000

In addition there were nearly 900,000 Asians, of which 270,000 were Chinese, nearly 700,000 Mexicans (almost all coming after 1900), and nearly 400,000 Caribbeans. These figures do not include groups such as Filipinos or Puerto Ricans, who were part of the foreign possessions acquired by the United States after the War of 1898, and whose movement was therefore characterized as insular migration rather than immigration (Department of Homeland Security 2003, Lucassen and Lucassen 1997).

Historians have developed a rich tradition of interpreting the immigrant experience and its impact on the United

A Companion to the Gilded Age and Progressive Era, First Edition. Edited by Christopher McKnight Nichols and Nancy C. Unger.
© 2017 John Wiley & Sons, Inc. Published 2017 by John Wiley & Sons, Inc.

States, but their approach to these issues has changed significantly over time. Oscar Handlin famously brought the study of immigrants to the forefront of the historical discipline in his 1951 *The Uprooted*. He began the book with a memorable observation, "Once I thought to write a history of the immigrants in America. Then I discovered that the immigrants *were* American history." His book brilliantly explored immigrants as key agents in the American experience, yet as his title suggests, he portrayed them as leaving a static world colored by dark pessimism. Peasant masses were uprooted and alienated from all they had known in Europe, facing a journey filled with "shattering shocks" and loneliness; they sought to create a wholly new, assimilated life for themselves in the United States. The difficulties they faced led them to a conservative acceptance of tradition and authority in their new home, Handlin concluded. In the 1960s and 1970s, the emergence of powerful new paradigms of historical methodology, particularly in labor and social history, generated new ways of interpreting the history of immigration. John Bodnar's *The Transplanted*, published in 1985, captured the shift of the historiography with a title that deliberately referenced and critiqued Handlin's earlier work. In Bodnar's view, immigrants were not static, premodern peasants, but were complex beings already enmeshed in capitalist social relations before leaving their home countries. Their culture in the United States blended old traditions and *mentalité* with new circumstances and ideas encountered upon arrival. Hardly victims of the transformations they confronted, immigrants actively shaped their own lives. By the late 1980s and early 1990s, scholars had added to Bodnar's account the notion of ethnicity's fluid, changing character. Rather than a primordial group identity, ethnicity in this view was an invented cultural construction, one requiring renegotiation over time. As Kathleen Conzen and her colleagues wrote in a pathbreaking article, "ethnicity is not a 'collective fiction,' but rather a process of construction or invention which incorporates, adapts, and amplifies preexisting communal solidarities, cultural attributes, and historical memories" (Conzen et al. 1992). Conzen and colleagues linked this process of invention to the broader history of American national identity; cultural constructions of "ethnicity" by Americans not only shaped their understandings of immigrants around them, but were also powerfully intertwined with emerging ideas of what it meant be an American citizen.

Despite the shifts in emphasis and interpretation, however, the above historians focused their attention on European immigrants and on one-way migration to the United States followed by assimilation—or what some call an "Ellis Island" model of immigration history. More recently the field has been transformed by a combination of Ethnic Studies scholars who focus more attention on race and on non-European immigrants, and by the impact of globalization and transnational methodologies (Sanchez 1996; Jacobson 2006; Azuma 2005). These influences have generated a striking reorientation of the basic narrative of US immigration history, with particular consequences for understandings of the Gilded Age and Progressive Era (Ngai and Gjerde, 2013). They have not only shifted attention to the important role played by non-European groups, but more broadly they highlight conditions in sending countries, continuing ties and solidarities held by immigrants to their country of origin, circular migrations, and the complexities of multidirectional flows of people, capital, cultures, and ideologies.

The "transnational turn" has reenergized many fields of US history, including the history of immigration, by exploring the connections between the United States and the world. Although the term "transnational" means different things to different people, most efforts to employ it as a methodology involve problematizing the boundaries of nation-state power (rather than seeing it as contained within its traditional territorial borders), focusing attention on the flow of people, commodities, capital, ideologies, and cultures across those borders (Bayly et al. 2006). And although historical approaches that examine movement across regions, nation-states and global dynamics are certainly not new, late twentieth- and early twenty-first century interest in the impact of globalization gave new impetus and energy to such approaches. As Michael Hanagan described the method, transnational history "follows processes across borders, but it is not 'borderless' history, it investigates the character of borders and how processes are affected by border crossings" (Hanagan 2004, 455–456). For the study of im/migration this historiographical development has meant that much more attention has been focused on the complex identities of immigrants, the continued influence exerted by their home country and culture, the conditions in sending countries, the impact of outmigration on those countries, and more generally, the connections between global dynamics and networks of migration and immigration (Foner 1997; Basch, Schiller, and Blanc, 1994).

Earlier approaches to immigration history structured the narrative around "old" versus "new" immigration—the former being northern and western Europeans who dominated numerically from the 1840s to 1880s, especially Germans, Irish, British, and Scandinavians, while the latter referred to southern and eastern Europeans from Italy, Austro-Hungary, and Russia. The "new" immigrants began to dominate numerically in the 1880s, and they continued in large numbers until the immigration restriction acts of 1921 and 1924 purposely cut off most immigration from southern and eastern Europe. Certainly the impact of millions of Italians, Russians, Austrians, and Hungarians arriving during the Gilded Age and Progressive Era cannot be underestimated. Much like the Irish and Germans when they first began arriving in the 1840s and 1850s, the new groups seemed to undermine native-born citizens' sense of national identity. Most of the new immigrants came from rural backgrounds, arriving often with few financial resources. Many worshiped in Catholic churches; others were Jewish immigrants from market towns across eastern Europe. In their large numbers and with cultures, religions, and languages native-born citizens had not previously encountered, the "new" immigrants generated vast and complex responses from American citizens, including the rise of social-reform efforts to help them acculturate and a nativist movement that would ultimately succeed in radically restricting the influx of immigrants from those countries.

Yet in many ways the emphasis on "old" versus "new" immigrants limits interpretations of the immigrant experience. It establishes a dichotomous structure to the narrative of immigration history that can diminish the ongoing importance of Irish, German, and British immigrants, for example, who continued to arrive in very large numbers throughout the decades at the turn of the century (Kazal 2004; Luebke 1974; Barrett 2013; Kenny 2000). But more importantly, this interpretative framework ignores the important role played by non-European immigrants—particularly Asian—as major catalysts in the rise of a bureaucratic regime of immigration surveillance and control, and in a transformed national identity around issues of naturalization, race, and ethnicity (Lee 2003; Salyer 1995; Motomura 2007).

The new insights regarding the role played by Asian immigrants—especially Chinese—constitute the most significant change in the historiography since the late 1990s. Chinese immigrants have shifted from a group that "mattered too," and should therefore be included in the history of immigration to now being, and recognized as a group whose impact far outweighed their relatively small numbers. Since the founding of the United States there had been some regulation of movement and migration, but this had been confined to state, county, or city regulations. The Chinese Exclusion Act of 1882 marked the first time a specific immigrant group was excluded by the federal government because of its race and class. It barred Chinese laborers from entering the United States for ten years, but allowed merchants, teachers, students, and diplomats. It also prohibited Chinese immigrants from becoming naturalized American citizens. A product of the virulent anti-Chinese movement, which brought white Westerners' racial and nativist views of Chinese together with white workers' economic anxieties, the Chinese Exclusion Act was renewed over the next decades and made permanent in 1902. It continued as the law of the land until 1943. In 1907 a Gentlemen's Agreement with Japan negotiated a diplomatic, voluntary restriction of Japanese immigration; the 1917 Immigration Act created an Asiatic Barred Zone that excluded most Asians; and the 1924 Immigration Act excluded all those deemed ineligible for citizenship, thereby expanding the nation's ability to bar Asians (Lee 2003, 2; Fairchild 2003, 10).

The Exclusion law not only transformed one immigrant group into an excluded pariah, it profoundly reoriented American jurisprudence, the federal bureaucracy, and political culture more generally. Implementation and enforcement of the Exclusion Act required the government to create mechanisms for tracking, surveying, detaining, and deporting immigrants. The United States became a "gatekeeper" nation, as Erika Lee (2003) has written, determining which immigrants were "fit" enough to be allowed entry as a result of their health, class, race, ethnicity, or gender. In the next decades the bureaucracy for regulating immigrants would grow and more laws gradually restricted entry to others. The Immigration Act of 1882 established the first head tax on immigrants (50 cents) to cover the cost of the emergent bureaucracy; it also barred entry to idiots, lunatics, and anyone likely to become a public charge. The Alien Contract Labor Law of 1885 barred foreigners coming into the country as contract laborers. In the 1890s a series of bills added to the list of people who would be excluded, created the Superintendent of Immigration's office within the Treasury Department, and required that Chinese immigrants carry permits, while banning them from serving as witnesses in trials. Meanwhile Ellis Island opened in 1892; in the next decade the regulatory machinery was significantly expanded via the creation of the Bureau of Immigration and Naturalization, and anarchists were added to those who would be excluded.

Several aspects of these historical processes are noteworthy. First, the role played by Chinese immigrants as the catalysts of an expanded regulatory regime highlights the powerful role played by race and racialization in this process. Chinese immigrants were not just foreigners and thus subject to nativist bias. They confronted virulent racism that equated them with barbaric savages, and such racist rhetoric became indispensable to the project of casting them as "unfit" to be allowed into the United States. Second, class anxieties and biases were extremely important in shaping the history of immigration law. Although the role of class is often neglected by scholars, the Chinese Exclusion Act specifically targeted laborers, as did the Alien Contract Labor Law of 1885, while the Immigration Act of 1882 focused attention on those likely to become a public charge. Thus central to immigration politics and policy in the GAPE were the key issues of labor and class. Expanding capitalism needed laborers, but workingmen and women were seen as the most problematic of all immigrants. Much immigration law evolved amidst concerns and anxieties regarding class status.

As important as Asian immigrants were, meanwhile, in generating reactions and political shifts that created new and more restrictionist approaches to immigration, there exists no simple, straight line connecting the Chinese Exclusion Act of 1882 to the larger project of restricting immigration. That project culminated in the Johnson–Reed Act of 1924, which specifically targeted southern and eastern Europeans for near-complete exclusion, in addition to people of African, Arab, or Asian descent. The 1924 Act set a 2% quota for the number of people who could enter the United States from any one nation, basing it on the number of people from that country already there in 1890—which in effect placed a racialized quota system at the heart of US immigration law for the next forty-one years. It resulted in a virtual shutdown of immigration from southern and eastern Europe, the Caribbean, Africa, and the Middle East. Italian immigration, for example, had involved some 200,000 people per year in the early twentieth century; the Johnson–Reed Act allowed only 5000 per year. Twenty-five thousand Germans, on the other hand, could still enter the nation each year, as well as some 65,000 immigrants from the United Kingdom. And ironically, although the desire to exclude or limit southern and eastern European migration inspired the Johnson–Reed Act, in the end it functioned, as Mae Ngai (2014) has argued, to construct "a white American race, in which persons of European descent shared a common whiteness distinct from those deemed to be not white" (24–25). The Johnson–Reed Act, in short, exemplifies the point made by Aristide Zolberg: immigration policy became a major instrument of US nation-building, and furthermore it "fostered the notion that the nation could be designed, stimulating the elevation of that belief into an article of national faith" (Zolberg 2006, 2).

Battles over Asian immigrants certainly shaped immigration politics by racializing the discussion and by introducing the idea that certain people were more or less fit for inclusion in the American community. But the influx of millions of Italians, Russians, and Austro-Hungarians also generated particular tensions and biases at the turn of the twentieth century. Anti-Catholicism and anti-Semitism were central to nativism towards the "new" immigrants, and both had deep roots in American history (Dinnerstein 1994, Nordstrom 2006). Anxieties that Catholics would be more loyal to the Pope than to the US government went back at least to the eighteenth century. In the mid-nineteenth century, as Irish Catholics entered the United States in large numbers, anti-Catholicism merged with xenophobia to erupt into the Know-Nothing political party. In the 1880s and 1890s, as Catholics from Italy began entering in large numbers and the power of the Catholic Church as an institution in the United States increased, anti-Catholicism surged forward again. As John Higham (1955) pointed out decades ago, the immigrants themselves were targeted now as much as were priests and Catholic institutions. Numerous secret societies emerged to oppose Catholicism and Catholics; the one that achieved greatest power—the American Protective Association (APA)—was also one of the most secretive. According to Higham, much of the APA's membership came from disillusioned members of the Knights of Labor and railroad unions, who feared competition from Irish workers. Anti-Semitism was less an organized force, yet riots against the hiring of Jews occurred in the 1890s, and throughout the Progressive Era Jews faced economic discrimination and general notions of them as lacking manners. Anti-Semitism was often intertwined with economic and class anxieties, as exemplified by the sad case of Leo Frank, the Georgia factory manager lynched by a mob in retribution for the (wrongful) accusation that he had murdered a female employee. Catholic and Jewish immigrants more generally became associated with evils attributed to the expanding industrialization of the United States, including impoverishment and urban congestion (Higham 1955, 58–63; MacLean 1991).

In the late nineteenth century such religious and ethnic antagonisms found reinforcement from the pseudo-science of Social Darwinism, which linked evolutionary theory to the notion that some races or ethnicities were more or less "fit" and able to survive. Those religious and scientific pillars of anti-immigrant prejudice left room for the idea that assimilation was possible. The discourse shifted in the early twentieth century. New ideas of biological determinism and racial immutability emerged: the eugenics movement stressed racial purity and saw any racial mixing as creating mongrel humans. Such ideas were popularized by books like Madison Grant's *The Passing of the Great Race* (1916). Grant stressed not only the unchanging biology of race, but the psychological and personality consequences as well. The Nordic race was vastly superior in Grant's eyes, and safeguarding it for the future required a strong eugenics program. The eugenics movement profoundly influenced immigration politics throughout the early twentieth century and beyond, directly shaping the Johnson–Reed Act and its predecessors. New security concerns during World War I, as well as anti-radicalism and anti-Communism, further shaped antipathy towards immigrants, particularly southern and Eastern Europeans (Grant 1916; Ngai 2014, 24–26; Higham 1955).

Throughout the Gilded Age and Progressive Era, the power of an expansive corporate capitalism and its concomitant industrialization constituted the central causal engine of the time, and it depended on and encouraged mass immigration. Industrialists' vast and desperate hunger for labor had fueled the economic rise of the United States across much of the nineteenth century. But in the aftermath of the Civil War, as industrialization sped up, the need for labor grew stronger as well. The construction of railroads, the expanding steel mills and textile factories, the sweatshops in cities like New York and Chicago, the sugar-cane fields of Louisiana, and the ports of Baltimore and New Orleans, all required more labor—the cheaper the better--and increasingly that labor came from across Europe.

But here was the crux of the problem: corporate leaders needed their laborers to be servile, cheap, easily disciplined and, when necessary, disposable. Yet the interests of the nation-state and its citizenry required respectable people who could assimilate and contribute to nation building. Immigration was very much tied up with, and productive of, national identity and nation building. So the goals of corporate leaders and those of the nation conflicted. In 1903 the Commissioner of Labor noted the contradiction, after scouring the globe for proper workers who might answer the needs of sugar planters in Hawaii: "nowhere was a people found combining the civic capacity to build up a state with the humility of ambition necessary for a contract laborer." This tension helps to explain why so much of immigration policy at the turn of the century specifically targeted laborers for restriction or exclusion. Their "humility of ambition," their lack of economic independence, their "unfreeness," in other words, was precisely what made certain laborers desirable to corporate leaders but problematic as members of the body politic or as future citizens ("Report of the Commissioner of Labor" 1903 698–99; Daniels 2004).

This also helps explain the hostility of native-born workers and their unions toward immigrants, as well as the zeal of social reformers to acculturate and "Americanize" them. Native-born workers, union leaders, and their middle-class supporters were influential opponents of immigrants and the policies that allowed them entry. Labor advocate Henry George was among the first to raise the threat Asians posed in a New York *Tribune* article in 1869. Workingmen in California played the leading role in the anti-Chinese movement, several of them building successful political careers around the issue. Labor activists were likewise leaders in the push for the Chinese Exclusion Act, their virulent—sometimes hysterical—language against Chinese profoundly shaping anti-immigrant sentiment. White workers dominated the murderous mobs who rioted against Chinese workers in towns like Rock Springs, Wyoming. In 1870 the National Labor Union changed its policy from one advocating equal rights for Chinese immigrants to the resolution that "the presence in our country of Chinese laborers in large numbers is an evil … and should be prevented by legislation." The official labor movement would remain anti-immigrant in its official policy until the late twentieth century, and successive labor leaders serving as Commissioners of Immigration forcefully advocated for discriminatory laws (Daniels 2004, 12, 16).

Even as labor leaders agitated, however, immigrants were entering factories across the United States and transforming the working class. Numerous scholars have examined the lives of Italian, Austro-Hungarian, and Russian immigrants at the turn of the twentieth century. Immigrants' flight from anti-Semitism or the grinding poverty of southern Italy, for example, led to their entry into jobs in Pennsylvania steel plants, New York City garment factories, and Colorado coal mines. There they introducded their cultures' emphasis on creating political and workplace activism and protest. From Herbert Gutman onward, scholars have explored such themes, demonstrating the interconnections between Gilded Age and Progressive Era labor historiography and the history of immigration (Gutman 1977; Bodnar 1977; Gabaccia 1988; Mormino and Pozzetta 1987).

One major contribution labor scholars have made to the study of immigration concerns the racial identity of European immigrants. In 1991 David Roediger brilliantly framed whiteness as an historical problem. Irish immigrants in effect became white, he argued, by differentiating themselves from African American slaves and freedmen. At that point Irish laborers' whiteness began to serve as a sort of psychological wage that compensated for their class oppression. Moving forward in time, Roediger and historian James Barrett argued that whiteness also shaped the worlds of new immigrants during the Gilded Age and Progressive Era. European immigrants arrived in the United States as "inbetween peoples," and had to struggle to become seen, over time, as white (Barrett and Roediger 1997; Roediger 2005). In 2003, historian Thomas Guglielmo forcefully challenged the Roediger/Barrett analysis. His study of Italian immigrants in Chicago argued that a distinction should be made between color and race. Italian immigrants were seen as "white on arrival" in terms of their color, and so fundamentally their whiteness was never in question. However, they were nonetheless perceived as racially suspect, as inferior "Dagoes," and as such they confronted widespread bias and discrimination. Thus as whites, Italian immigrants enjoyed privileges that were not available to African Americans and, in many cases, to Mexican Americans. They had access to jobs, could live in most any neighborhood, could marry whomever they desired, and so forth. Yet, Gugliemo argued, racial hierarchies were far more complex than a white versus black dichotomy might suggest; although perceived as white in color, the southern Italian race was marked as culturally and physically inferior and undesirable. Furthermore, he argues, Italian immigrants themselves embraced a racial identity as southern Italians for decades. Only gradually did they begin to identify more emphatically in terms of their color, stressing their whiteness to differentiate themselves from people of color and thus becoming prototypical "white ethnics" (T. Guglielmo 2003; J. Guglielmo 2012; Frank 2003).

Whiteness was also a key issue for Asian and Latino immigrants, albeit in different ways. Naturalization was limited to white or black immigrants throughout the Gilded Age and Progressive Era, and so most Asians were marked permanently as "ineligible for citizenship." Although in 1898 the Supreme Court ruled in *U.S. v. Wong Kim Ark* that birthright citizenship, as guaranteed in the Fourteenth Amendment, applied to Asians (again demonstrating the importance of Asians in shaping who could and would be seen as legitimate US citizens), naturalization remained a much more bounded category. In two Supreme Court cases in the early 1920s, two Asians petitioned for the right to naturalize. The decisions shed light on prevailing understandings of whiteness, at least according to Supreme Court justices. In *Ozawa v. U.S.*, in 1922, the Supreme Court held that Takao Ozawa, a Japanese man, was not a "free white person" as understood popularly or by scientific categories, and thus was ineligible for citizenship. In *Thind v. U.S.*, two years later, the Supreme Court again denied naturalization, this time to a South Asian who argued that as a high-caste Hindu he was by all scientific reckoning a free white person.

This time the Court rested its argument on popular understandings of race. Conceding that according to science a high-caste Indian was Caucasian and hence white, the decision nevertheless concluded that "the average man knows perfectly well that there are unmistakable and profound differences." Not until 1943, 1946, and 1952, respectively, did Chinese, Indians, and Japanese become eligible for naturalization (For *Bhagat Thind v. United States* see https://supreme.justia.com/cases/federal/us/261/204/case.html; for *Takao Ozawa v. United States* see https://supreme.justia.com/cases/federal/us/260/178/case.html). These landmark cases reinforced the sweeping exclusion of Asians codified in the 1924 Johnson–Reed Act. Even as the number of South Asians in the United States slowly grew, they would continue to be marked as non-white and as ineligible for citizenship (Haney-Lopez 1996; Ngai 2014; Bald 2013).

The number of Mexicans in the United States was much greater—some 250,000 entered the country between 1900 and 1920, and another 450,000 came in the following decade (as well as untold numbers who crossed the border unofficially), as unrest generated by the Mexican Revolution combined with economic opportunities in the United States. For Mexican immigrants racial identity was complex—they were arguably the quintessential "inbetween" group (Foley 1998; Pitti 2004). Until 1930, the US Census listed Mexican Americans as white. A federal court in Texas in 1897 had ruled that a Mexican immigrant, Ricardo Rodríguez, was eligible for naturalization; however, its ruling was based not on a judgment about his race but on treaty obligations. As Fernando Padilla has written, the decision treated Rodríguez "*as if* he were *white*, [but] the decision itself did not rule Mexicans to *be white*" (quoted in Foley 1998, 60). Thus in legal terms, Mexicans were white, but in practice, on social, cultural, and political terms, they confronted many of the same forms of discrimination as did African Americans. In Texas, for example, there existed no formal segregation of schools, but in practice Mexicans were educated in separate and inferior facilities. Suggesting once again the significance of class in determining an immigrant group's status, socioeconomic position was often used in Texas as a pretext for *de facto* segregation. In California, likewise, Mexican immigrants and Mexican Americans faced widespread discrimination and racial violence. As a result, becoming Mexican American often meant a struggle to become white as well. One might establish "whiteness" by learning English, achieving socioeconomic mobility, voting in elections, and other indicators of successful Americanization (Foley 1998, 2014; Sanchez 1994; Pitti 2004; Hernández 2014).

European immigrants—far more numerous than Asians or Latinos and facing much less legal and extra-legal discrimination—became central contributors to American political culture and workplace activism during the Gilded Age and Progressive Era. It is difficult to contemplate Gilded Age politics, for example, without consideration of the influence of German immigrants and German-Americans in building a radical political and labor movement. German trade unionists made Chicago into the nation's preeminent labor town. They, along with Irish workers, played key roles in the Great Upheaval of the 1880s, the eight-hour movement, the Knights of Labor, and the founding of the American Federation of Labor. They fueled anarchist and socialist politics in the 1880s and 1890s—the Haymarket incident of 1886 and the infamous trial that followed reflecting only the tip of a robust oppositional culture. They were central to major, defining strikes of the era such as the Homestead steel strike of 1892 (and they were defeated there in part because their union excluded the growing number of "new immigrants" employed by Carnegie and Frick). By the early twentieth century, they were seen as "old-stock" ethnic Americans, and presented themselves as pragmatic and "conservative" labor activists in contrast to unruly Italians or Hungarians. There is a fascinating transformation here that calls for more historical analysis (Nelson 1988; Schneirov 1998; Keil and Jentz, 1983; Kenny 1998).

During the Progressive Era, Italian and Jewish immigrants played the same sort of catalyzing, energetic role that Germans and Irish had decades earlier. In an historical moment when the major federation of labor unions in the United States devoted little energy to organizing immigrants, an alternative labor movement emerged—the so-called "New Unionism" launched predominantly by immigrants' workplace militancy. In strikes among New York City garment workers, steel workers in Pennsylvania, and textile workers in New Jersey and Massachusetts, male and female immigrant workers transformed the culture of the labor movement and paved the way for breakthroughs in the structure of trade unionism that would, by the 1930s, give rise to the Congress of Industrial Organizations (Montgomery 1974; Fraser, 1983). When the young garment worker Clara Lemlich rose at a meeting to speak about the working conditions she faced, and demanded that action be taken, she inspired a general strike. Her fellow workers took the traditional Yiddish oath upon invitation—"If I forget thee oh Jerusalem, may my right hand wither, may my tongue forget its speech" (with Jerusalem symbolizing the union movement), and launched 1909's Uprising of the 20,000. As historian Annelise Orleck noted, this moment demonstrated "how overwhelmingly Jewish this movement was and how closely linked Jewish imagery and their vision of unionism were" (Orleck 1995, 60). The remarkable militancy in the garment industry had Jewish and Italian female immigrants at its center, although they struggled often with the male leaders of their unions and they had to strategize carefully to build alliances with other groups such as the Women's Trade Union League and the Socialist Party. But along the way they demonstrated the assumptions that women and immigrants could not be organized were quite inaccurate, and they paved the way for the rise of industrial unionism decades later (Glenn 1991; Katz 2013; Greenwald 2005; Enstad 1999).

Many eastern and southern Europeans in the early twentieth century engaged in a robust radical subculture as well. Immigrant radicalism took many different forms, but anarchism provides the best example of a radical culture that was both homegrown and linked to vast transnational networks. Kenyon Zimmer's recent study, *Immigrants Against the State*, has shown that anarchism was popular not only among Italian immigrants but also Jews, Asians, Spaniards, and Mexicans. Since it is difficult to provide a quantitative sense of the anarchist subculture, Zimmer examined publications and demonstrated that nearly 120,000 people subscribed to anarchist newspapers at the movement's high point around 1907. Naturally the activism and culture of anarchism reached far beyond the number of subscribers, since newspapers would be passed around the family dinner table and shared with co-workers. Zimmer notes: "Anarchism was therefore not a miniscule sect but a substantial minority political movement within America's largest immigrant communities" (Zimmer 2015, 5).

Jennifer Guglielmo's recent study *Living the Revolution* explores with nuance the culture of those most neglected immigrant anarchists: the women. Examining Italian women and radicalism in New York City, Guglielmo demonstrates that oppressive conditions in the United States combined with a tradition of radical organizing in Italy to feed immigrants' political perspective and activism. Hundreds of different anarchist circles existed, and they followed several different strains of anarchist thought. Italian women were very involved in the anarchist movement, although they were often providing energy at the base rather than as leaders, Guglielmo argues, and they rejected the more violent strands of anarchism. These factors have made them less visible to scholars. Furthermore, Italian women have been neglected as labor activists because scholars have seen them as more traditional and less involved in strikes than their Jewish coworkers. Yet, relying heavily on the Italian-language press, Guglielmo demonstrates that Italian women were enthusiastic participants and that a feminist anarchism fueled their participation. Their anarchism Guglielmo characterizes as a sort of "feminism from the bottom up"; they saw their exploitation as tied to industrial capitalism, racism, imperialism, and patriarchy; their worldview included a philosophy of free love, dedication to fighting capitalism, and building industrial unionism. The latter project was made difficult because of Italian women's distrust of the male leadership of their garment unions, which led them to avoid membership in large numbers until the Depression era. The Industrial Workers of the World, on the other hand, became a major vehicle for their activism because it was more aligned with their anarchist philosophy (Guglielmo 2012, 139–199, especially 162; Gabaccia 2000; Tomchuk 2015).

The nation's cities were profoundly shaped by the politics of immigration and ethnicity in other ways as well. Historians have been intrigued by the political contributions of immigrants since Joseph Huthmacher (1962) and John Buenker (1978) developed the "urban liberalism" analysis. Noting that immigrants and their children constituted two-thirds or more of the population in the nation's major cities—and more than three-quarters of the population of New York, Chicago, and Boston, Buenker sought improved ways of understanding their political impact. He argued that a new breed of machine politicians built a base of support among these immigrants, and that in return they embraced a range of social reforms in order to provide their constituents with services. Machine politicians, in this view, were not conservatives beholden to business interests, but a vehicle through which immigrants contributed mightily to American politics—and in key respects, presaged the politics of the New Deal.

More recently historian James Connolly (1998) has critiqued the urban liberalism thesis and, in his study of Boston, demonstrated that the majority Irish population adapted Progressivism to its own ends. Connolly argues that politicians like James Curley generated strong support among the Irish Bostonians by portraying Yankees as an exploitative elite. This "ethnic progressivism" benefited from the antiparty, interest-group character of the Progressive Era and involved as much a stylistic or rhetorical triumph as anything else. It was, in other words, a broader and more complex creation than merely one of machine politics and politicians.

Yet political historians' analyses would benefit from engaging more fully with the vibrant world of labor and radical activism depicted so evocatively in the work of Elizabeth Ewen, Susan Glenn, Richard Greenwald, Annelise Orleck, and many others. Immigrants' contributions to political culture went well beyond the narrow channels of electoral politics, and this makes their influence difficult to measure by traditional means. The pioneering work of settlement-house women and men provides just one example of ways that native-born and middle-class people sought to transform the political order to improve life in immigrant communities. Or consider the impact of labor activism in New York City. Richard Greenwald has traced the emergence of industrial democracy as an ideal in Progressive-Era New York. Born of the activism of the mostly immigrant workforce in the garment industry, it peaked first with the 1909 Uprising of the 20,000. When that general strike failed to win full reform in the garment industry, it was followed by the tragedy of the Triangle Shirtwaist Company fire in 1911 that killed 146 people, most of them young Jewish and Italian women. The same coalition that had formed around the general strike came together again. The result was the New York State Factory Investigating Commission, with Robert Wagner as its chairman and Al Smith of Tammany Hall as vice-chairman. They investigated working and safety conditions in factories for four years;

their findings led to the passage of 38 laws regulating factory labor, giving New York state the most progressive code of labor laws in the United States. Linking these events was the notion that there should be democracy in US workplaces—a notion that owed its existence to the political culture and activism of immigrants (Greenwald 2005; Orleck 1995; Glenn 1991; Ewen 1985).

Meanwhile, many in the United States responded to mass immigration by seeking, in a variety of ways, to shape the newcomers' lives through education and training. Jeffrey E. Mirel (2010) has demonstrated the pervasiveness of Americanization efforts that encouraged immigrants to abandon their cultural traditions and assimilate to native-born ways. A contrasting strain in Progressive-Era thought celebrated the distinctive cultural traditions of immigrants and encouraged respect for them. The educator Horace Kallen, philosophers John Dewey and Randolph Bourne, and social reformer Jane Addams all embodied the latter, pluralist, approach. In 1902 Dewey, for example, noted unhappily that immigrants were losing their cultures and argued for educational policies that would help them adapt to the United States without losing their distinctive identities (Selig 2008). By the 1920s the cultural gifts movement emerged–inspired in part by these strains of Progressive era cultural pluralism, but emboldened by developments in the social sciences—which rejected the homogenizing impact of Americanization strategies and stressed appreciation for the distinctive cultural and social qualities of diverse immigrant groups. Diana Selig (2008) has shown that the cultural gifts movement became a pervasive influence on American education in the interwar decades.

During the late nineteenth and early twentieth centuries the United States also became a major power on the world stage, a development closely linked to but not entirely encompassed by its hothouse industrialization and related technological and scientific achievements. American corporate capitalism expanded globally in these decades, and simultaneously the US government launched its so-called "New Empire" with victory against Spain in the War of 1898. Acquiring an empire that stretched from Cuba and Puerto Rico to the Philippines, the United States aggressively positioned itself as a preeminent global power. In the following years the country fought a war to suppress the Filipino struggle for independence, established a colony there, annexed Hawaii, militarily intervened repeatedly in countries across Central America and the Caribbean, supported the coup that gave Panama independence from Colombia and acquired complete and permanent control over the Panama Canal Zone, "as if it were sovereign." This expansionist project generated new migratory flows and networks that reshaped the United States domestically while also creating a new relationship with large populations around the world (Kramer 2015; Greene 2015). Although the connections between immigration and empire were neglected by scholars for many years, they have recently become an area of serious exploration, along the way changing how the history of each is seen (Urban 2015; Chang 2012).

For expansionists like Theodore Roosevelt and Albert Beveridge, many of the same ideas of racial superiority that shaped understandings of immigrants also framed American global power as inevitable and beneficent. As Beveridge famously argued, the question facing the United States was indeed a racial one.

> God has not been preparing the English-speaking and Teutonic peoples for a thousand years for nothing but vain and idle self-contemplation and self-admiration. No! He has made us the master organizers of the world to establish system where chaos reigns. He has given us the spirit of progress to overwhelm the forces of reaction throughout the earth. He has made us adepts in government that we may administer government among savage and senile peoples (Beveridge 1999, 23–26).

Anxieties similar to those shaping reactions to Asian and southern European immigrants within the United States influenced anti-imperialists such as William Godkin, who complained the US empire would result in "the admission of alien, inferior, and mongrel races to our nationality." Likewise Henry Blackwell argued that annexing new "colored races is to add new elements of danger and discord" (McPherson 1995, 325–326). Answering such arguments, Beveridge himself took pains to point out that the newly conquered peoples would not come to the United States and compete with Americans for jobs: "No reward could beguile, no force compel, these children of indolence to leave their trifling lives for the fierce and fervid industry of high-wrought America" (Beveridge 1999, 23–26).

The combination of an expanding corporate capitalism and the "New Empire" of the American government remapped the relationship between the United States and the world, and historians are increasingly interested in probing the significant consequences this possessed for US immigration (and migration) history. Corporate leaders and government officials both relied heavily on labor migration to create easily managed and disciplined workforces, and the new imperial possessions themselves required a mass migration of soldiers, nurses, typists, colonial officials, politicians, lawyers, and more. US expansionism across the Caribbean and Central America intensified throughout the Gilded Age. Steamships carried American and Caribbean laborers to ports like Puerto Barrios in Guatemala to lay tracks or build roads. But by the early twentieth century, private US capital was forcefully remaking the Caribbean and Central America, modernizing plantations and processing plants, building roads, railroads, and canals. The Boston-based United Fruit Company, though founded only in 1899, soon emerged as the dominant economic engine in Central America. Historians have shown that it relied heavily on Afro-Caribbean migrants for its labor force, but added

Spanish-speaking Hispanics to create a labor force segmented and divided along racial lines. The often tense relations between the two groups, and the various efforts to build a labor movement that would make broad solidarities possible became an important theme in historical scholarship (Colby 2013; Opie 2009).

The US government's expansionism across the region was intertwined with the activities of corporate capitalists—particularly the emphasis on recruitment of migrant labor and reliance on racial and ethnic segregation to manage that labor. Isthmian Canal Commission officials embraced contract labor—despite its having been banned in the Alien Contract Labor Law of 1880—to recruit workers for the construction of the Panama Canal. That project epitomized the new relationship being forged between immigration policy and imperial ambitions. Building the Canal between 1904 and 1914 required immigration to the Canal Zone of more than 100,000 men and women. The US government rejected employing Panamanians to carry out the bulk of labor, hiring only a few thousand of them to work either at the lowliest jobs—clearing the jungle—or, in the case of elite Panamanians, as middle-level office workers. Instead of looking locally, US officials scanned the globe for ideal workers. When they were refused permission to import Chinese laborers, they settled instead on Afro-Caribbeans for the hardest labor, and looked to North Americans for skilled carpenters, machinists, and steam-shovel engineers. When the Caribbeans seemed not to be working hard enough, officials recruited Spaniards, Italians, and Greeks to compete and hopefully prod them toward more energetic efforts. The canal project was a highly regimented and authoritarian experiment in labor management, and relied on pervasive racial and ethnic segregation to maintain order and keep laborers working productively. And the canal operated like a vast magnet, drawing men and women from across the Caribbean to the Isthmus of Panama and then, when it was completed in 1914, the US government scrambled to find ways to send those tens of thousands of workers home or onward to other sites needing labor. Many returned to their home islands, others to banana plantations in Costa Rica or Honduras, or if they had saved enough money, onward to the United States (Greene 2009; Senior 2014).

Indeed, the origins of the Caribbean community in the United States lies with the diasporic movements generated by the Panama Canal and similar projects. Some canal workers headed straight to the United States from Panama; others traveled home to their original islands to save more money before boarding a ship for New York City. Nearly 125,000 migrated to the United States in the 1910s alone, most of that in the second half of the decade as the canal construction project wrapped up. Another 74,000 entered the United States in the 1920s, and almost all of those would have arrived before the 1924 Act took effect. This was a remarkable group of migrants—more worldly and cosmopolitan, and better educated, than typical immigrants of the era. In the United States they would contribute to the artistic, literary, radical and labor activist arenas far out of proportion to their numbers. Prominent West Indians included not only nationalists like Marcus Garvey but also communist activists Hubert Harrison and George Padmore; labor activists Ewart Guinier and Maida Springer Kemp, and also such eminent writers Claude McKay, Jamaica Kincaid, and Paule Marshall (Putnam 2013; James 1999).

As the US Empire mobilized and dislocated migrant labor for infrastructure projects like the Panama Canal, private capital did the same for the production of commodities. Meanwhile the territorial acquisitions acquired after the Spanish–American War generated imperial migrations of a different sort. The Philippines and Puerto Rico provide the best examples. US colonialism in the Philippines created a wide range of new connections between the two countries and if the power relations were unequal, there were spaces within the relationship for alliances that encouraged socio-economic as well as geographic mobility. The United States created new professions in the Philippines--such as nursing—and various opportunities for Filipinos to travel to the United States. The latter included the Pensionado Program that provided Filipino students full scholarships to attend American colleges or universities. The idea was to Americanize and educate these students so they could return home and serve efficiently in the colonial government. As a result students were among the first Filipinos to travel to the United States after 1898, but laborers heading for work in agriculture or canneries soon joined them (Choy, 2003; Hinnershitz 2015; Posadas 1999; Fujita-Rony 2002; Friday 1995). After the 1917 and 1924 Acts tightened the exclusion of all Asian immigrants, the Philippines would become a much more important source of labor. As subjects of the US Empire, Filipinos were free to come and go without restriction, and employers looking for labor recruited them energetically.

A similar situation existed with Puerto Rico. The United States acquired Puerto Rico from Spain as a result of the Spanish–American War, and the Foraker Act of 1900 established a government there but denied citizenship or constitutional protections to the island's residents. Like Filipinos, Puerto Ricans traveled to the United States not as immigrants but as subjects of the Empire. The US acquisition radically restructured the economy of the island, modernization, for example, displacing many laborers from their jobs on coffee plantations. Migration to the US mainland happened only gradually; in 1910 there were still only some 1500 Puerto Rican migrants in the mainland United States, for example; in 1920, only 12,000; by 1930 the number had grown to 53,000 (Gibson and Lennon, 1999). Until the Johnson–Reed Act of 1924 increased demand in the United States for Puerto Rican laborers, corporate officials recruited larger numbers to Hawaii, Cuba, the Dominican Republic, Ecuador, and Mexico. Puerto Ricans in the

United States meanwhile confronted an ambiguous status, as neither citizens nor immigrants. The Supreme Court in 1901 had held that Puerto Rico was a "non-incorporated territory." Puerto Ricans were merely "citizens of Porto Rico," placing them in a sort of legal limbo. In 1917 the Jones–Shafroth Act granted them US citizenship, but they lacked full rights. Their legal limbo continued, as did their ability to migrate freely to and from the mainland (Whalen 2005; Sanchez-Korrol 1994; Duany 2002).

In these diverse ways, then, immigration history intertwined with the rise of US global power. Although the stories Americans have historically told themselves about immigration considered it from only a domestic perspective, scholars are increasingly exploring the connections to global dynamics. The history of immigration has provided an important antecedent to newer, transnational methodologies, since the field has always explored movement across borders. Yet recent attention by scholars to the complexities of global history, and new efforts to examine the porous character of borders and the causal role movement across boundaries played, are together reshaping understandings of the immigrant experience (Gabaccia 2012; Kramer 2015; Jacobson 2000).

Conclusion

The field of immigration history has changed significantly in recent decades. Historians have moved away from a dichotomizing emphasis on "new" versus "old" European immigrants. They have not only explored in greater depth the experiences of immigrants from Asia, Latin America, and the Caribbean, but have shown decisively that those groups—particularly Asians—had a transformative impact on the laws and regulatory machinery of immigration. A growing interest in exploring the relationship between the United States and the world is combining with transnational methodologies to inspire new questions about circulatory networks of migration. Scholars' interest in human migration is being connected to analysis of the parallel flow of cultures, ideologies, identities, and commodities in ways that will further transform understandings of the immigrant experience. And while there has long been productive cross-fertilization between the fields of labor and immigration history, more work remains to be done to illuminate the political influence of working-class immigrants.

During the Gilded Age and Progressive Era, immigrants built the railroads and canals, sewed the shirts, and cleaned the houses. Along the way they also built modern America. Their experiences, and native-born American citizens' reactions to them, gave rise to a set of laws and a vast bureaucracy that regulated and tracked movement in and out of the United States while Supreme Court decisions articulated characteristics that would define eligibility for citizenship. All this shaped the ways American citizens and immigrants alike experienced national identity. Immigrants remade the demographic character of the working class, in particular, and contributed mightily to building a robust labor movement and a radical political subculture, and shaped American reform politics. Global matters influenced how, where, and when immigrants moved, and their continued ties to home countries shaped their identity and their ways of reacting to life in the United States. The rise of the United States to global power and the expansionist ambitions of corporations and the nation-state generated new networks of imperial migration. Rethinking the Gilded Age and Progressive Era with immigrants in mind provides a reminder of the pivotal role they played in the defining dynamics of the period.

References

Azuma, Eiichuro. 2005. *Between Two Empires: Race, History, and Transnationalism in Japanese America*. New York: Oxford University Press.

Bald, Vivek. 2013. *Bengali Harlem and the Lost Histories of South Asian America*. Cambridge, MA: Harvard University Press.

Barrett, James. 2013. *The Irish Way: Becoming American in the Multiethnic City*. New York: Penguin.

—, and David Roediger. 1997. "Inbetween Peoples: Race, Nationality and the 'New Immigrant' Working Class." *Journal of American Ethnic History* 16, Spring: 3–44.

Basch, Linda, Nina Glick Schiller, and Cristina Szanton Blanc. 1994. *Nations Unbound: Transnational Projects, Postcolonial Predicaments, and Deterritorialized Nation-States*. Newark: Gordon & Breach.

Bayly, C.A., et al. 2006. "AHR Conversation: On Transnational History." *American Historical Review* 111, 5: 1441–1464.

Beveridge, Albert J. 1999."Our Philippine Policy." Reprinted in Daniel B. Schirmer and Stephen Rosskamm Shalom, ed., *The Philippines Reader: A History of Colonialism, Neocolonialism, Dictatorship, and Resistance*. Boston, MA: South End Press.

Bodnar, John. 1977. *Immigrants and Industrialization: Ethnicity in an American Mill Town, 1870–1940*. Pittsburgh, PA: University of Pittsburgh Press.

—. 1985. *The Transplanted: A History of Immigrants in America*. Bloomington: University of Indiana Press.

Buenker, John D. 1978. *Urban Liberalism and Progressive Reform*. New York: W.W. Norton.

Chang, Kornel S. 2012. *Pacific Connections: The Making of the U.S.-Canadian Borderlands*. Berkeley: University of California Press.

Choy, Catherine Ceniza. 2003. *Empire of Care: Nursing and Migration in Filipino American History*. Durham, NC: Duke University Press.

Colby, Jason. 2013. *The Business of Empire: United Fruit, Race, and U.S. Expansion in Central America*. Ithaca, NY: Cornell University Press.

Connolly, James. 1998. *The Triumph of Ethnic Progressivism: Urban Political Culture in Boston, 1900–1925*. Boston, MA: Harvard University Press.

Conzen, Kathleen Neils et al. 1992. "The Invention of Ethnicity: A Perspective From the United States." *Journal of American Ethnic History* 12, 1: 4–41.

Daniels, Roger. 2004. *Guarding the Golden Door: American Immigration Policy and Immigrants Since 1882*. New York: Hill & Wang.

Department of Homeland Security. 2003. "Yearbook of Immigration Statistics: 2003 Immigrants, Table 2, 'Immigration by Region and Selected Country of Last Residence, 1820–2003'." http://www.dhs.gov/publication/yearbook-immigration-statistics-2003-immigrants/Accessed July 14, 2016.

Dinnerstein, Leonard. 1994. *Anti-Semitism in America*. New York: Oxford University Press.

Duany, Jorge. 2002. *The Puerto Rican Nation on the Move: Identities on the Island and in the United States*. Chapel Hill: University of North Carolina Press.

Enstad, Nan. 1999. *Ladies of Labor, Girls of Adventure: Working Women, Popular Culture, and Labor Politics at the Turn of the Twentieth Century*. New York: Colombia University Press.

Ewen, Elizabeth. 1985. *Immigrant Women in the Land of Dollars: Life and Culture on the Lower East Side, 1890–1925*. New York: Monthly Review Press.

Fairchild, Amy L. 2003. *Science at the Borders: Immigrant Medical Inspection and the Shaping of the Modern Industrial Labor Force*. Baltimore, MD: Johns Hopkins University Press.

Foley, Neil. 1998. "Becoming Hispanic: Mexican Americans and the Faustian Pact With Whiteness." In *Reflexiones*, ed. Neil Foley, 53–71. Austin: Center for Mexican American Studies, University of Texas at Austin.

—. 2014. *Mexicans in the Making of America*. Cambridge, MA: Harvard University Press.

Foner, Nancy. 1997. "What is New about Transnationalism: New York Immigrants Today and at the Turn of the Century." *Diaspora: A Journal of Transnational Studies* 6, 3: 355–375.

Fraser, Steve. 1983. "Dress Rehearsal for the New Deal: Shop Floor Insurgents, Political Elites, and Industrial Democracy in the Amalgamated Clothing Workers." In *Working-Class America: Essays on Labor, Community, and American Society*, ed. Michael Frisch and Daniel Walkowitz. Urbana: University of Illinois Press.

Friday, Chris. 1995. *Organizing Asian American Labor: The Pacific Coast Canned-Salmon Industry, 1870–1942*. Philadelphia, PA: Temple University Press.

Fujita-Rony, Dorothy. 2002. *American Workers, Colonial Power: Philippines Seattle and the Transpacific West, 1919–1941* Berkeley: University of California Press.

Gabaccia, Donna R. 1988. *Militants and Migrants: Rural Sicilians Become American Workers*. New Brunswick, NJ: Rutgers University Press.

—. 2000. *Italy's Many Diasporas*. Seattle: University of Washington Press.

— 2012. *Foreign Relations: American Immigration in Global Perspective*. Princeton, NJ: Princeton University Press.

—. Gibson, Campbell J., and Emily Lennon. 1999. "Nativity of the Population and Place of Birth of the Native Population, 1850–1990." *Historical Census Statistics on the Foreign-born Population of the United States: 1850–1990*. http://www.census.gov/population/www/documentation/twps0029/tab01.html/Accessed July 14, 2016.

Glenn, Susan. 1991. *Daughters of the Shtetl: Life and Labor in the Immigrant Generation*. Ithaca, NY: Cornell University Press.

Grant, Madison. 1916. *The Passing of the Great Race; or, The Racial Basis of European History*. New York: Scribner's.

Greene, Julie. 2009. *The Canal Builders: Making America's Empire at the Panama Canal*. New York: Penguin.

—. 2015. "The Wages of Empire: Capitalism, Expansionism, and Working-Class Formation." In *Making the Empire Work: Labor and United States Imperialism*, ed. Daniel E. Bender and Jana Lipman, 35–58. New York: New York University Press.

Greenwald, Richard A. 2005. *The Triangle Fire, the Protocols of Peace, and Industrial Democracy in Progressive Era New York*. Philadelphia, PA: Temple University Press.

Guglielmo, Jennifer. 2012. *Living the Revolution: Italian Women's Resistance and Radicalism in New York City, 1880–1945*. Chapel Hill: University of North Carolina Press.

Guglielmo, Thomas. 2003. *White on Arrival: Italians, Race, Color, and Power in Chicago, 1890–1945*. New York: Oxford University Press.

Gutman, Herbert. 1977. *Work, Culture, and Society in Industrializing America*. New York: Vintage.

Hanagan, Michael P. 2004. "An Agenda for Transnational Labor History." *International Review of Social History* 49: 455–474.

Handlin, Oscar. 1951. *The Uprooted: The Epic Story of the Great Migrations that Made the American People*. Boston, MA: Little, Brown.

Haney-Lopez, Ian. 1996. *White By Law: The Legal Construction of Race*. New York: New York University Press.

Hernández, Sonia. 2014. *Working Women into the Borderlands*. College Station: Texas A&M University Press.

Higham, John. 1955. *Strangers in the Land: Patterns of American Nativism 1860–1925*. New York: Atheneum.

Hinnershitz, Stephanie. 2015. *Race, Religion, and Civil Rights: Asian Students on the West Coast, 1900–1968*. New Brunswick, NJ: Rutgers University Press.

Huthmacher, J. Joseph. 1962. "Urban Liberalism and the Age of Reform." *Mississippi Valley Historical Review* 44: 231–241.

Jacobson, Matthew Frye. 2000. *Barbarian Virtues: The United States Encounters Foreign Peoples at Home and Abroad, 1876–1917*. New York: Hill & Wang.

—. 2006. "More 'Trans', Less 'National.'" *Journal of American Ethnic History* 25, 4: 74–84.

James, Winston. 1999. *Holding Aloft the Banner of Ethiopia: Caribbean Radicalism in Early Twentieth Century America*. New York: Verso.

Katz, Daniel. 2013. *All Together Different: Yiddish Socialists, Garment Workers, and the Labor Roots of Multiculturalism*. New York: New York University Press.

Kazal, Russell A. 2004. *Becoming Old Stock: The Paradox of German American Identity*. Princeton, NJ: Princeton University Press.

Keil, Hartmut and John B. Jentz, ed. 1983. *German Workers in Industrial Chicago, 1850–1910: A Comparative Perspective*. DeKalb: Northern Illinois University Press.

Kenny, Kevin. 1998. *Making Sense of the Molly Maguires*. New York: Oxford University Press.

—. 2000. *The American Irish: A History*. New York: Routledge.

Kramer, Paul. 2015. "Imperial Openings: Civilization, Exemption, and the Geopolitics of Mobility in the History of Chinese Exclusion, 1868–1910." *Journal of the Gilded Age and Progressive Era* 14: 317–347.

Lee, Erika. 2003. *At America's Gates: Chinese Immigration During the Exclusion Era, 1882–1943*. Chapel Hill: University of North Carolina Press.

Lucassen, Jan and Leo Lucassen, ed. 1997. *Migration, Migration History, History: Old Paradigms and New Perspectives.* New York: Peter Lang.

Luebke, Frederick C. 1974. *Bonds of Loyalty: German Americans and World War I.* DeKalb: Northern Illinois University Press.

MacLean, Nancy. 1991. "The Leo Frank Case Reconsidered: Gender and Sexual Politics in the Making of Reactionary Populism." *Journal of American History* 78, 3: 917–948.

McPherson, James M. 1995. *The Abolitionist Legacy: From Reconstruction to the NAACP.* Princeton, NJ: Princeton University Press.

Mirel, Jeffrey E. 2010. *Patriotic Pluralism: Americanization Education and European Immigrants.* Cambridge, MA: Harvard University Press.

Montgomery, David. 1974. "The 'New Unionism' and the Transformation of Workers' Consciousness in America, 1909–1922." *Journal of Social History* 7, 4: 509–529.

—. 1987. *The Fall of the House of Labor: The Workplace, the State, and American Labor Activism, 1865–1925.* New York: Cambridge University Press.

Mormino, Gary R. and George E. Pozzetta. 1987. *The Immigrant World of Ybor City: Italians and their Latin Neighbors in Tampa, 1885–1985.* Gainesville: University Press of Florida.

Motomura, Hiroshi. 2007. *Americans in Waiting. The Story of Immigration and Citizenship in the United States.* New York: Oxford University Press.

Nelson, Bruce C. 1998. *Beyond the Martyrs: A Social History of Chicago's Anarchists, 1870–1900.* New Brunswick, NJ: Rutgers University Press.

Ngai, Mae. 2014. *Impossible Subjects: Illegal Aliens and the Making of Modern America.* Princeton, NJ: Princeton University Press, updated edn.

—, and Jon Gjerde. 2013. *Major Problems in American Immigration History.* 2nd edn. Boston, MA: Wadsworth, Cengage Learning.

Nordstrom, Justin. 2006. *Danger on the Doorstep: Anti-Catholicism and American Print Culture in the Progressive Era.* South Bend, IN: University of Notre Dame Press.

Opie, Frederick Douglass. 2009. *Black Labor Migration in Caribbean Guatemala, 1882–1923.* Gainesville: University Press of Florida.

Orleck, Annelise. 1995. *Common Sense and a Little Fire: Women and Working-Class Politics in the United States, 1900–1965.* Chapel Hill: University of North Carolina Press.

Pitti, Stephen J. 2004. *The Devil in Silicon Valley: Northern California, Race, and Mexican Americans.* Princeton, NJ: Princeton University Press.

Posadas, Barbara. 1999. *The Filipino Americans.* Westport, CT: Greenwood Press.

Putnam, Lara. 2013. *Radical Moves: Caribbean Migrants and the Politics of Race in the Jazz Age.* Chapel Hill: University of North Carolina Press.

"Report of the Commissioner of Labor on Hawaii." 1903. *Bulletin of the United States Bureau of Labor* 8, 47.

—. 2005. *Working Toward Whiteness: How America's Immigrants Became White. The Strange Journey from Ellis Island to the Suburbs.* New York: Basic Books.

Salyer, Lucy. 1995. *Laws Harsh as Tigers: Chinese Immigrants and the Shaping of Modern Immigration Law.* Chapel Hill: University of North Carolina Press.

Sánchez, George J. 1993. *Becoming Mexican American: Ethnicity, Culture, and Identity in Chicano Los Angeles, 1900–1945.* New York: Oxford University Press.

—. 1999. "Race, Nation, and Culture in Recent Immigration Studies." *Journal of American Ethnic History* 18, 4: 66–84.

Sánchez Korrol, Virginia E. 1994. *From Colonia to Community: The History of Puerto Ricans in New York City.* Berkeley: University of California Press.

Schneirov, Richard. 1998. *Labor and Urban Politics: Class Conflict and the Origins of Modern Liberalism in Chicago, 1864–97.* Urbana: University of Illinois Press.

Selig, Diana. 2008. *Americans All: The Cultural Gifts Movement.* Cambridge, MA: Harvard University Press.

Senior, Olive. 2014. *Dying to Better Themselves: West Indians and the Building of the Panama Canal.* Jamaica: University of West Indies Press.

Thistlethwaite, Frank. 1964. "Migration from Europe Overseas in the Nineteenth and Twentieth Century." In *Population Movements in Modern European History*, ed. Herbert Moller. New York: Macmillan.

Tomchuk, Travis. 2015. *Transnational Radicals: Italian Anarchists in Canada and the U.S., 1915–1940.* Winnipeg: University of Manitoba Press.

Urban, Andrew T. 2015. "The Advantages of Empire: Chinese Servants and Conflicts over Settler Domesticity in the 'White Pacific,' 1870–1900." In *Making the Empire Work: Labor and United States Imperialism* ed. Daniel E. Bender and Jana Lipman, 185–207. New York: New York University Press.

Whalen, Carmen Teresa. 2005. "Colonialism, Citizenship, and the Making of the Puerto Rican Diaspora: An Introduction." In *The Puerto Rican Diaspora: Historical Perspectives*, ed. Carmen Theresa Whalen and Victor Vazquez-Hernandez. Philadelphia, PA: Temple University Press.

Zimmer, Kenyon. 2015. *Immigrants against the State: Yiddish and Italian Anarchism.* Urbana: University of Illinois Press.

Zolberg, Aristide. 2006. *A Nation by Design: Immigration Policy in the Fashioning of America.* New York: Russell Sage Foundation and Cambridge, MA: Harvard University Press.

Part III

Art, Thought, and Culture

Chapter Twelve

Art and Architecture

Alan Lessoff

This chapter concentrates on formal, professional art and architecture, rather than popular or vernacular arts. It therefore revolves around a distinction that is itself a contested legacy of the Gilded Age and Progressive Era. Textbook narratives of the era are demarcated by a series of insurgencies against academic-minded establishments and the genteel attitudes and formalist traditions that supported them. But realists and impressionists, naturalists and modernists shared with the establishments they assailed the assumption that high art improved people, while popular art entertained them.

By contrast, late twentieth-century modes of analysis—poststructuralism, deconstruction, hegemony theory—treated distinctions between high and low, refined and vulgar, and even good and bad art with suspicion, as rationalizations for authority and status. Overall, however, the postmodernist preoccupation with variety, ambiguity, and cross-fertilization has reinforced the efforts of cultural and intellectual historians to evoke the manifold transnational and domestic contexts that shaped American creative life after the Civil War. The resulting emphasis on depth and breadth undermined generations of teleological accounts that depicted artists and movements based mainly on their roles as precursors or obstacles to the international modernism that supposedly displaced provincial American styles and attitudes after the 1913 Armory Show. As the chapter stresses, gender analysis—an interest shared by recent historians, art scholars, and cultural critics—has proved an especially productive source of new perspectives on art and artists.

Within the history of architecture and urban planning, the rethinking of modernist narratives appeared with greater force and fewer qualifications. By the late twentieth century, scholars and the public commonly blamed modernist architecture and urban design for the dreary condition of American cities. No longer did many take seriously the modernists' equation of themselves with intellectual, aesthetic, and social progress. In city after city, movements for historic preservation, historic districts, New Urbanist design, and revitalization encouraged reassessment of Victorian and Beaux-Arts architects, structures, and places that had been neglected or deplored for much of the twentieth century. Idealization and nostalgia threatened to become more of a challenge than condescending dismissal of the past.

Nationalism, Transnationalism, and Hegemony

Suspicion of the distinction between high art and popular culture often leads to overemphasis on class and status as factors shaping the arts. Postmodernists hardly originated the tendency to perceive high art as an instrument of upper-class hegemony. Already in the late 1800s, skeptics suggested that insistence on setting high art apart and venerating it removed from scrutiny the agendas and preferences of the art world's capitalist paymasters. "Elite collectors and their advocates," runs one recent formulation, "staged patronage of the arts as a sensitive and versatile social instrument that could at once edify, rehabilitate, and placate industrial workers, forestall social revolution, promote the regional economy, and foster a unified and harmonious public culture" (Ott 2010, 257). Certainly rich, powerful people did use art collecting and arts philanthropy to build reputations for sophistication and civic-mindedness, abetted by artists, curators, and dealers. Still, this chapter emphasizes not such matters, but the nationalist agendas of American art, the professional aspirations of artists, evolving understandings of the modern, and the gendered character of art and the art world.

Among US historians, an influential formulation of the art-as-cultural-hegemony perspective appears in Lawrence

A Companion to the Gilded Age and Progressive Era, First Edition. Edited by Christopher McKnight Nichols and Nancy C. Unger.
© 2017 John Wiley & Sons, Inc. Published 2017 by John Wiley & Sons, Inc.

Levine's *Highbrow/Lowbrow* (1988). In music and theater as well as art, Levine depicts elitist intellectuals allied with wealthy patrons in the enterprise of "sacralizing" the arts, turning them into stifling vehicles for bourgeois values. The "tragedy" of cultural hierarchy, Levine concludes, arose from popular alienation from creators such as Shakespeare and Verdi, who once belonged to all classes, and also from the inability of self-styled highbrows to grasp what was "fresh, innovative, intellectually challenging, and highly imaginative" about blues, jazz, musical comedy, the movies, and other "new forms of expressive culture that were barred from high culture by the very fact of their accessibility to the masses" (Levine 1988, 232).

This case for an open-ended understanding of the relation between the popular and formal arts became conventional wisdom. Even so, historians of culture and the arts often express misgivings. Levine's cultural history hinges on versions of the authenticity argument, a perspective derided by theorists such as Lionel Trilling in *Sincerity and Authenticity* (1972). As Levine sees it, cultural innovation takes shape mainly bottom-up, sometimes in a feedback loop, rarely top-down. Culture loses vitality as folk arts become formalized, organized, or commercial or, alternately, as education and institutions interject themselves into people's appropriation of the formal arts for their purposes. A dubious enough view when applied to the twentieth century, this approach does violence to the Gilded Age and Progressive Era. For that era, a straightforward equation between class and status on one side and cultural hierarchy and sacralization of the arts on the other proves hard to maintain. The aesthetic sensibilities of the Gilded Age rich and their attitudes toward the educational, moral, and civic value of art differed little from those of most Americans. The rich had money and leisure to pursue widely shared aspirations.

Such arguments, moreover, treat the aesthetic, professional, and intellectual agendas of artists, critics, curators, educators, and dealers as adjuncts of the class interests of their patrons. While artists and arts professionals did proclaim art as useful for class uplift and ethnic acculturation, a more forcefully expressed motive for elevating the status of art and artists took as its starting point the country's cultural atmosphere vis-à-vis Europe and the international standing of American artists. In the pre-World War I decades, art counted as an international enterprise and profession that nonetheless defined itself in terms of national culture and nationalistic values. German, French, and British museums and arts education sought to balance art's national and international dimension by highlighting folk, regional, or high-culture traditions as the nation's contribution to the West's and the world's heritage. Euro-Americans, with their lingering sense of provincialism, perceived their traditions as weak and derivative. Only at the end of the period did white artists latch onto Native American arts (and African American arts later still) as sources of romance and inspiration. Accordingly, US museums and arts education sought to provide aspiring artists and the public with surveys of the arts and crafts of the West and the world. The world's heritage would provide raw material for an American art.

In the Gilded Age and Progressive Era, upper-class collectors and philanthropists probably served the purposes of artists and curators more than the reverse. Fortunes made in transportation, commodities, industry, and finance created pools of capital put to use by dealers such as Joseph Duveen, connoisseurs such as Bernard Berenson, and other specialists in the transatlantic traffic in European masterworks. Banker J.P. Morgan, the great patron of New York's Metropolitan Museum of Art, Charles Hutchinson, the commodities financier who oversaw the Art Institute of Chicago, and their counterparts in other cities pursued their satisfaction and prestige, to be sure. But also, the Gilded Age elite were furthering a patriotic enterprise, an achievement for which they intended to be recognized.

Across decades—and through stylistic revolutions from mid-century academicism to 1910s modernism—Americans' self-consciousness over their international stature endured. Events bookmarking the period underscored to contemporaries that Europe remained the source of depth and innovation. At the 1867 Paris Exposition, Europeans dismissed works by such acclaimed Americans as Albert Bierstadt and Frederic Church as empty virtuosity, "thereby proving our actual mediocrity," lamented critic James Jackson Jarves (Cohen-Solal 2001, 7). Generations of American artists took for granted that, if possible, they should study in Paris, Munich, or Rome, where they could absorb the swirl of European styles, techniques, and aesthetic debates. The county's apparent second-rateness drove a half-century of institutional development: museums, art schools, and professional organizations. Nevertheless, the 1913 Armory Show, which brought works by Cézanne, Picasso, Matisse, Duchamp, and Kandinsky to Manhattan and juxtaposed them to American realists and naturalists such as Robert Henri and George Luks, seemed to demonstrate that upgrades to infrastructure had so far failed to elevate the substance. Artist Jerome Myers rued that with the Armory Show, the United States reverted to "a colony; more than ever before, we had become provincials" (Shi 1995, 290–291).

As art scholar Sarah Burns (1996) demonstrates, artists used "modern" less to signify particular styles than to establish their legitimacy as professionals. A modern artist adopted mannerisms that were bohemian enough to satisfy expectations, but not so much as to compromise reputations as respectable, business-minded professionals. Like nearly all professional milieus in the Gilded Age, the network of organizations and social clubs that artists created remained determinedly male, which compelled women to carve out separate professional identities and networks.

As the careers of designer Louis Comfort Tiffany, landscape architect Frederick Law Olmsted, or architects as diverse as Henry Hobson Richardson, McKim, Mead, and White, Burnham and Root, and Adler and Sullivan suggest,

Americans attained a distinct, confident national identity earlier in design, architecture, and urban planning than in traditional fine arts. European architects and critics expressed ambivalence about the 1893 Columbian Exposition's fairgrounds, whose historicist, Beaux-Arts style seemed "imitative." They were fascinated, however, by the skyscrapers of Chicago's Loop, in their view an expression of a new type of civilization, "the very essence of the American genius" (Lewis 1997, 147, 184). Yet the concept of high art emphasized expression that transcended function or utility. Americans would not contribute fully to the world's artistic heritage until they nurtured impractical as well as practical arts.

Internal Contexts

Of the two most lauded American painters of the late 1800s, Thomas Eakins fits best within the narrative of art moving toward the modern and American art moving toward the world. Eakins never traveled abroad after his European studies in the late 1860s. Even so, he devoted himself to adapting European realism to American circumstances and values, and he sought to update the techniques and symbolism of Western painting for an era of cities, science, and photography.

Art scholars, by contrast, struggle to situate Winslow Homer within such a framework. Trained as a lithographer in Boston, prominent for his Civil War prints before establishing himself as a painter, Homer was already thirty when he first traveled to Paris at the time of the 1867 exposition. No direct evidence supports speculation that Homer picked up influence during that sojourn from impressionists Édouard Manet or Claude Monet, both then gaining notoriety. The influence of English landscape traditions is easier to document, even before Homer spent a year painting on the English coast in the early 1880s. Like his contemporary George Inness, who also had a background in engraving, Homer defied labels. Interpreters "bend over backwards," Sarah Burns remarks, to plug Homer "tightly into the mainstream of European modernism." When that fails, they go to the other extreme and make him into a crotchety Maine hermit, "an artist *sui generis*" who "operat[ed] in a near-vacuum," therefore requiring no explanatory context (Burns 1997, 626, 628). Homer becomes an equivalent of New York symbolist Albert Pinkham Ryder, also not the self-sufficient recluse often portrayed.

Homer and his friend Eastman Johnson (who did study abroad) were, Burns concludes, the standouts among "scores of other artist-illustrators," imbued with American genre and regional traditions and formed by New York's "industrial system" of magazine production (Burns 1997, 628). While a transatlantic outlook and a stance as modern did become central to artistic professionalism in the Gilded Age, certain key artists and trends are most comprehensible if one looks immediately around, rather than forward and abroad.

Sublime Land

The 1867 Paris Exposition marked an embarrassing repudiation for Hudson River-style landscape painting. English immigrant Thomas Cole had inspired companions such as Asher Durand and students such as Frederick Church to treat the American wilderness and the process of settlement as sublime material, equivalent to European ruins or pastoral scenes. Hudson River-style painters versed themselves in European traditions extending from English romantics John Constable and J.M.W. Turner back to Claude Lorrain and beyond. When turned to American subject matter, these elements would fuse into a new art for the New World. America, in this art, gained meaning from the land and the future, an attitude that supports analyses of mid-century landscape as an aesthetic expression of transcendentalism or Manifest Destiny. The results could be gorgeous and powerful, if grandiose and disturbing. Albert Bierstadt, a German immigrant with a flair for showmanship, raised in Massachusetts but trained in his native country, became master of what critic Robert Hughes labels "extravagant paeans to Manifest Destiny," such as his immense *Emigrants Crossing the Plains* (1867). Bierstadt was already coming to seem overwrought and provincial by the Paris Exposition when his *The Rocky Mountains, Lander's Peak*, along with Church's *Niagara*, struck reviewers as mistaking flourish for substance. Church retreated into the Orientalist fantasy he created at Olana, his house along the Hudson River. Bierstadt's "reputation was going the way of the buffalo," remarks Hughes, by the time judges for the 1889 Paris Exposition rejected *The Last of the Buffalo*, a nostalgic rather than future-oriented image (Hughes 1997, 196, 201).

Preoccupied with the sublime and the ideal, Hudson River-style painters manipulated scenes to heighten the spectacle. They filled paintings with allegorical, didactic content. This "sentimental dose of the ideal superimposed on the real," as art historian Barbara Novick puts it, is why scholars have often accepted the 1867 Paris dismissal of them as bombastic and provincial (Novak 1979, 117). By contrast, the Barbizon school, a realist-leaning movement then gaining notice in America as well as Europe, encouraged direct painting from nature and un-idealized depictions of rural life. Scholars attribute American realism mainly to such European sources, although partly also to American luminists such as John Frederick Kensett and Martin Johnson Heade, who similarly found meaning in quieter, less contrived landscapes.

The postmodern impulse to question narratives of progress and to validate particulars and genres against universals and mainstreams makes the Hudson River artists or Bierstadt seem less a dead end. Their influence and that of the mid-century engraver/artists endured in American regionalism, above all in the art of the American West, which, until the 1970s or 1980s, scholars and curators tended to dismiss as an unfortunate Colorado or Texas predilection. To cite the most significant example, Thomas Moran, an English native who grew up in Philadelphia, was yet another trained engraver who came to landscapes through Turner and the English romantics. Moran made his reputation when, along with photographer William Henry Jackson, he served as official artist on the US Geological Survey's 1871 Hayden Expedition to Wyoming. The photographer and the watercolorist created a visual record that appeared to depict the West rather than mythologize it. In 1873, Moran accompanied John Wesley Powell's expedition down the Colorado River. His *Chasm of the Colorado* (1873–1874) provided Americans with a dramatic introduction to the Grand Canyon.

Moran retained much of Bierstadt's penchant for presenting the West as a sublime spectacle. The context in which he worked, however, of scientific expeditions, reports on arid lands, and movements for national parks, made him an indicative figure in the emergence of an environmentalist-minded regionalism, a significant alternative to the placelessness of transatlantic modernism. Every portion of the US West developed a regionalist art engaged with specific places and peoples. Enhanced appreciation of such artists has made museums such as Fort Worth's Amon Carter Museum or the Oklahoma City's Gilcrease Museum enlightening experiences.

For the practice of regionalism, Moran's devotion to watercolor, a medium long considered suitable for studies but not a final product, proved as consequential as his grand, carefully worked oil paintings. The same was true of the western photography of Jackson, Carleton Watkins, or Eadweard Muybridge, who in 1872 photographed Bierstadt painting in Yosemite. Western museums also underscore the ongoing connection of regionalism to illustration and genre painting. For much of the twentieth century, Frederick Remington, a Yale-educated New York patrician, and Charles M. Russell, from a well-to-do St. Louis family, seemed purveyors of the frontier as Anglo male myth, more a part of cultural history than the trajectory of art. Yet such heroic genre art, imbued with nationalistic and ethnocentric lore, wove in and out of twentieth-century art, epitomized by Gutzon Borglum, who carved mountains in the spirit that Bierstadt painted them.

Narratives built around the trend toward modernism have found it easier to account for another genre of art that thrived through the Gilded Age: the still-lifes and *trompe-l'oeil* paintings of William Harnett or John Peto. Their half-hidden stories of memory and regret indeed prefigured modernist collage and later the found-object assemblies of Robert Rauschenberg and the box constructions of Joseph Cornell.

Renaissance Brought Home

"I want no more of America," proclaimed Kenyon Cox to his mother in 1877. Disenchanted after a year at the Pennsylvania Academy of Fine Arts, he implored his parents to support studies at the École des Beaux Arts. "The best in modern art," Cox insisted, "comes always to Paris" (Morgan 1986, 6). Son of Jacob D. Cox, the Union general, politician, and educator, Kenyon Cox returned to the United States to spend his career endeavoring to adapt the professionalism of Paris to American republican principles, which he allegorized in murals, mosaics, and stained glass. A prolific critic as well as artist, Cox became a steadfast proponent of academic methods and genteel sensibilities, the ***best*** in ***modern*** art in his view. His notorious attack in *Harper*'s on the Armory Show arose from his belief that Cézanne, Matisse, and their contemporaries solipsistically concentrated on their own perceptions and methods at the expense of the academic virtues of observation, beauty, and truth. In Paris, Cox studied with academician Jean-Léon Gérôme, whose students also included Thomas Eakins. Neither showed much interest their teacher's historical scenes and Orientalist fantasies; they sought out Gérôme for his meticulousness and self-discipline. Despite their vast differences, both Cox and Eakins saw such training as key to raising the standards and reputation of American art.

In the 1980s–1990s, H. Wayne Morgan, the historian of politics and foreign relations, published a biography of Cox, two volumes of his letters, and a book on Cox's circle of traditionalist critics. At first, Morgan's affinity with Cox seems anomalous. A major formulator of the historiographic model of the Gilded Age as a period of modernization, Morgan would seem more drawn to the insurgents than to the traditionalists. Cox's appeal to such a modernization-minded scholar makes sense if one highlights the transatlantic perspective and professional ambitions of artists. Artists such as Cox saw themselves as constructing an American Renaissance, a civilization elevated from vulgarity to refinement and from provincialism to significance. Tendencies as diverse as Gothic-revival, arts-and-crafts, and Beaux-Arts architecture shared the academicians' sense of mission. They drew upon diverse Western traditions in pursuit of a society defined by and infused with art.

Modernists of the following generation dismissed as retrograde the rigorous aesthetics of muralists such as Cox, Edwin Blashfield, and J. Carroll Beckwith, for whom rigor was progress. Female figures idealized into principles, Cox insisted in his art criticism, elevated a society in need of a higher level. Such attitudes, as art historian Bailey Van Hook (1996, 2003) explains, reinforced the tendency among professional artists to etherealize womanhood in a generic way at a time when women—including women artists—were pushing for a physical and individual presence.

Until disillusioned old age, Cox defined himself as a participant within a multidirectional present, not a voice against the degraded future. He spent decades teaching at the Art Students League. Founded in 1875 as an alternative to the rigid system followed at the National Academy of Design, the Art Students League embraced such diverse approaches as the academic Cox, the tonalist and aesthete Thomas

Dewing, impressionists J. Alden Weir and William Merritt Chase (whose own academy evolved into the Parsons School of Design), and eventually Robert Henri, Chase's protégé who became the personality behind Ashcan-style naturalism. With exception of the Munich-trained Chase, who developed deep Parisian connections, all these and many other teachers had spent time in Paris's sprawling system of art instruction. They had experienced Paris as a wave of directions and influences, and they meant to inject Paris's exacting standards and intellectual energy into US art instruction.

Cox came from the business/professional class background most associated with foreign study in the Gilded Age and with the Victorian ethic of personal and social improvement through culture. Yet Chase, Henri, and others discussed in this chapter managed to study overseas and establish a transatlantic professional life despite working-class or impecunious middle-class backgrounds. Artists from a range of backgrounds exhibited the sensibility, common to other forms of aspiring professionals in the era, that privileges afforded them by education and travel were tied to a responsibility to uplift society.

A Postwar Culture

As Cox's family story suggests, the Civil War formed the background for American Renaissance ideas about art's mission in society. Urban historians as well as biographers stress that while Frederick Law Olmsted's social-reform vision of landscape design derived from British and American romanticism, his activities in the Sectional Crisis and the war coalesced his outlook and approach. The war overturned a longstanding suspicion among Americans of public monuments as pretentious and unrepublican. The demand created by grieving families and communities gave rise to a domestic network of studios, foundries, and related enterprises. Artists such as Thomas Ball and Harriet Hosmer carried on the older connection of American sculpture to Italy. Beaux Arts-trained sculptors such as Augustus Saint-Gaudens, Laredo Taft, and Frederick MacMonnies imported French influence, while German and Austrian immigrants such as Karl Bitter drew on their own perspective. These foreign-educated sculptors—along with American-trained professionals such as J.Q.A. Ward and his student, Daniel Chester French—did not simply replicate European design principles in the myriad historical and allegorical monuments they produced. They updated what they had learned for what they perceived to be American conditions. The emergence in the South of a movement to memorialize the Lost Cause developed its own set of artists, who shared iconography if not outlook with their Unionist counterparts.

For people at the time, an outstanding example of the adaptation of European aesthetics to American history and principles appeared in the sculpture of Saint-Gaudens, an immigrant New Yorker who used night classes at Cooper Union as his route to Parisian study and then to numerous Civil War-themed monuments, most famously Boston's *Shaw Memorial* (1897). Working with architects on the level of Stanford White and Charles McKim, Saint-Gaudens applied to American cities European traditions of monuments as both expressions of civic values and as orienting points in urban space. Saint-Gaudens's *Adams Memorial* (1891)—the monument in Washington's Rock Creek Cemetery to Henry Adams's wife Marian Hooper, who committed suicide in 1885—exemplifies the expressive possibilities of an approach often misunderstood as formulaic and sentimental. Asked by Adams to evoke Buddhist ideas of transcendence and acceptance, the sculptor created a seated, hooded figure with no gender, mood, or message, in a peace outside time.

The American Renaissance adhered to the traditional Western view of public art—murals, stained glass, landscape, and architecture, as well as sculpture—as vocabularies that could, if widely learned, convey messages about civic identity and values. As art historians Michele Bogart and Kirk Savage detail, this meant that sculpture—freestanding and incorporated into pediments, friezes, and so on—absorbed and reflected the range of political currents and racial, ethnic, and cultural tensions raised by the Civil War, Reconstruction, industrial urbanization, corporate capitalism, and US territorial expansion.

Michele Bogart (1989) elaborates on how the sculpture programs of New York landmarks such as the New York Customs House, the New York Public Library, and the Metropolitan Museum of Art, developed by sculptors on the level of French and Bitter in collaboration with architects such as Cass Gilbert, McKim, Mead, and White, and Carrère and Hastings, projected visions intended to inspire and instruct a city riven by class and ethnic conflicts. Bogart goes on to explain that most segments of the city—not just political and economic establishments, as implied by sacralization models—shared this didactic understanding of public art. Political and ethnic groups used monuments to validate their presence and argue with one another. By the late 1800s, ethnic groups in New York and other cities promoted monuments to national heroes as "deliberate assertions of ethnic presence, pride, and political power" (Bogart 2006, 101). Popular groups seemed to hold more firmly to traditional styles than elites. A conventional, even predictable monument seemed to offer upstart groups the greatest legitimacy.

The American Renaissance, in sum, sought a vibrant engagement between present and past. A shortcoming of the concept of "antimodernism," which Jackson Lears (1981) made commonplace among cultural historians, is that it can distort this liveliness and imagination into a claustrophobic retreat from the present. Even so, Lears points to why artists and architects thought that historicist aesthetics might counteract the demoralizing effects of drab cities, vulgar materialism, and mass culture. Gothic revival architects such as Ralph Adams Cram and decorative artists such as John La Farge drew upon the notion that medieval Europe had been an organic society oriented around coherent principles and symbols, in contrast to the fragmentation and alienation of modernity. This understanding was then commonplace in history, social science, and cultural theory on both sides of the Atlantic.

Still Americans Abroad?

Of the thousands of American artists who studied in Europe, scores made careers in Paris, Munich, Rome, or London. Artists who stayed abroad mostly perceived themselves as participating in the cause of American art. Expatriate artists campaigned to ensure that their art did not face prohibitive tariffs and other obstacles when exported to the United States. Expatriates also pursued recognition, exhibition, and sales in host countries. Paris seemed particularly necessary to "the grand aim" of "a National Art for America," asserted the Paris Association of American Artists, founded in 1890 (Grant 1992, 7). France's policy of purchasing new works from official salons and other exhibitions underwrote Americans' quest for stature. James McNeil Whistler's *Arrangement in Grey and Black, No. 1*, better known as *Whistler's Mother*, was the most famed of dozens of paintings by Americans bought for Parisian or regional museums. France's purchase in 1897 of the *Resurrection of Lazarus* helped establish the era's most renowned African American artist, Henry Ossawa Tanner. Though Tanner acquired a devoted American following, he relished the mainstream acceptance he received in Paris and spent nearly all his career there.

Frank Duveneck, William Merritt Chase, and John Twachtman formed the core of an alternate American circle in Munich. The charismatic Duveneck mentored a generation of young Americans, often midwesterners with German backgrounds, in South German methods, bolder, more fluid, and less fussy than Paris's academic approach.

The two best-known expatriates, Whistler and John Singer Sargent, raise complex debates over whether an artist could become so international as to cease to be American. Despite attenuated connections to the country of their citizenship, both insisted on their Americanness and sought American patrons and collectors. Both used their status as permanent outsiders to cultivate controversial or ambiguous aesthetic, moral, and in Sargent's case, sexual identities.

A Gendered Profession

A third renowned expatriate, Mary Cassatt, underscores how gender shaped artists' experiences. Coming from a wealthy Pennsylvania family, Cassatt could afford to build a career in Paris while remaining connected to the United States. With women excluded from the École des Beaux Arts until 1897, Cassatt studied privately with Paris's famed teachers. Befriended by Edgar Degas and Camille Pissarro, among others, she became more identified than any American with the impressionist movement. Aware that impressionism had sensual connotations, Cassatt was "particularly vigilant" about respectability (Prieto 2001, 88). Intimate scenes of mothers and babies or images of fashionable young women in restaurants or theaters enabled her to experiment without compromising her reputation.

A commission for a mural on the theme, "Modern Woman," for the Woman's Building at the 1893 Columbian Exposition, designed by Sophia Hayden, the first female graduate of the Massachusetts Institute of Technology (MIT), enabled Cassatt to make a statement about women in art. Cassatt eschewed impressionism and domestic settings for symbolist depictions of young women pursuing fame, knowledge, and the arts. Critics found it jarring, given her previous work. "'Modern Woman' in the useless pursuit of fame," jested Florence Fenwick Miller, a British feminist writing for London's *Art Journal.* Critics contrasted Cassatt's mural to the "reverent," "dignified" use of domestic themes in the matching mural, *Primitive Woman*, by Mary Fairchild MacMonnies, wife of sculptor Frederick MacMonnies (Webster 2004, 122–123). Cassatt's rejection of reassuring themes for her mural and critical reaction to this dramatized tensions within the era's gender imagery.

The thriving women's history and gender analysis of the late twentieth century made untenable the older dismissal of the Gilded Age as feeble and arid *because* of its association with stereotyped feminine values: sentimentality, mannerism, and constraining propriety. A cloud of "feminization"—intertwined with the era's anxiety over neurasthenic males drained of virility by urban society—hung over artists. Sargent was unusual in his assimilation of gender ambiguities into his art and persona. Male artists sought to be associated with masculine qualities: professionalism, business, innovation, hard reality. John La Farge, who depended on commissions for decorative interiors, by definition an art associated with femininity, cultivated an image as a "fastidious and dignified intellectual," at odds with the warm but nervous and disorderly man whom friends knew (Burns 1996, 238). Among women artists, La Farge was notorious for condescending to and obstructing their ambitions.

In contrast to Paris, American art schools almost all admitted women. The expectation that cultured women would have artistic training enabled art schools to pay their bills. But, as historian Kirstin Swinth explains, male teachers and students feared that too many women would mark their schools as unserious. "We have endeavored," the Art Students League reported in 1886, "to keep in true balance the two opposing tendencies of high standard and popularity." By this, they meant that they allowed in enough women "to pay all [their] expenses and keep out of debt." Teachers treated manifestly talented women "with overt hostility and deliberate exclusion." Louise King Cox recalled that J. Carroll Beckwith, colleague and friend of her future husband Kenyon Cox, "never failed to give [women painters] a dig when the opportunity arose" (Swinth 2001, 25–26).

Professional organizations perpetuated such divisions. Groups such as the Woman's Art Club—founded in 1889, eventually evolving into the National Association of Women Painters and Sculptors—emerged in response to obstructive treatment by the National Academy of Design and the Society of American Artists. Male-dominated artist organizations accepted a few women members, but their exhibitions remained overwhelmingly male. The American Watercolor Society, representing a medium supposedly appropriate for woman, had four female members in 1882 and three in 1914. As the Watercolor Society became "a central player in the art market," it "self-consciously became more restrictive" (Swinth 2001, 76).

Some scholars posit that the outright sex segregation that confronted American women who studied overseas provided the unintended benefit of preparing them for a gendered profession. Integrated with male students in US schools, women struggled against the assumption of limited prospects. The "paradox of Paris," Swinth concludes, was that it compelled women to establish "a community of women artists who provided examples, inspiration, encouragement, and spurs to higher achievement" (Swinth 2001, 61).

Women chafed against even positive reviews that stressed gender qualities, for example a critics' pronouncement that portrait painter Cecilia Beaux represented a "union of womanly delicacy and refinement of feeling with a manly vigor in the painting" (Swinth 2001, 143). Female art critics, such as Mariana Griswold Van Rensselaer, often argued that women artists would benefit from having work evaluated according to male or at least non-gendered standards. Post-1970s feminist scholarship takes the opposite tack by stressing "recuperation of 'lost' or underestimated women artists," apart from male-defined narratives or standards. The goal is to compel "all art historical narratives to be rethought from the standpoint of how gender operates in shaping culture" (Langa 2004, 705–707). Until the 1970s–1980s, women who figured in standard narratives tended to have associations with male-defined movements and to have gained the respect and support of male art-world personalities, such as Degas in Cassatt's case, or Alfred Stieglitz in the case of photographer Frances Johnston and, memorably, Georgia O'Keefe.

Art for the People

Van Rensselaer was noted for her clear, sympathetic explanations of innovative figures such as Henry Hobson Richardson, Frederick Law Olmsted, and—despite the challenge his art and life posed to Victorian gentility—Thomas Eakins. Another Eakins defender, Frank Jewett Mather, Jr.—one of three critics, along with Kenyon Cox and Royal Cortissoz, whom H. Wayne Morgan identified as influential traditionalists—nonetheless put energy into making new artists and styles comprehensible. While deploring many new trends, Cox took to heart the task of explicating what he saw. Cortissoz, critic for the New York *Tribune*, remained a friend of modernist gallery owner and photographer Stieglitz, "though they often disagreed violently," Morgan notes. Even when dreading the direction that younger artists were taking, Cortissoz stressed that their "originality" and "ambition" were preferable "academic formulas … rich in mediocrity" (Morgan 1989, 77).

Probably the most significant aspect of such discussions is that they played out in newspapers and magazines commonplace in middle-class and many working-class homes. The critics' efforts to ensure that art was accessible was a corollary of the argument—identified with English writers John Ruskin and Matthew Arnold and their American ally Charles Eliot Norton—that a decent society required lives filled with art and culture. General-interest magazines provided access to these three essayists, along with William Morris and Gustav Stickley, whose Arts and Crafts movement similarly promoted a life infused with art and culture.

Numerous scholars have documented how gendered notions of culture encouraged women to form literary clubs and art associations and to give impetus to libraries and civic improvement leagues. Men tended to assert control of such activities as they grew into museums, planning commissions, and other formal institutions. But US women generally retained control of settlement houses, which made the arts available in immigrant, working-class neighborhoods through lectures, classes, performances, and exhibitions. Both genders embraced college extension programs and self-education movements, epitomized by the Chautauqua Literary and Scientific Circle and its copycat organizations, which together reached millions of people by the 1910s.

A commonplace manifestation of the popular yearning for art—the cheap color reproductions known as chromolithographs—sold by the millions; beyond sentimental or patriotic scenes produced by firms such as Currier & Ives, Americans mostly encountered artists such as Homer, Eastman Johnson, and the Morans through the humble, oft-satirized "chromo." This ubiquitous striving after culture underscores the wrongheadedness of historiographic models of high art as an elitist, hegemonic enterprise. The era saw much conflict over access to the arts. Ethnic and racial minorities, workers, and women desired that creators from their groups receive attention and respect. But labor activists, socialists and anarchists, African Americans, eastern and southern European immigrants, and virtually every other outsider group treated self-education in the arts as liberating, not oppressive. Indeed, middle-class and working-class lovers of the arts often expressed a sense that the upper classes did not take culture seriously enough, that for the decadent rich, the arts were about consumption and fashion, rather than personal and social improvement.

In a pointed critique of the sacralization–hegemony model, historian Daniel Borus recalls that the "Ruskin–Morris tradition of beauty as liberating" underpinned arguments of Jane Addams, W.E.B. Du Bois, and other social-reform progressives that universal arts education had "democratic possibilities." The blind spot in this position, in Borus's view, was not insidious bourgeois hegemony, but an inability to appreciate "the aesthetic virtues of new art forms" drawn from popular and commercial culture, such as musical theater and the movies. Progressive cultural reformers tended to dismiss commercialized culture as a shallow, manipulative distraction; like political freedom, cultural freedom required space outside the market. It is an error, Borus explains, closely to identify assertions of cultural hierarchy with "status conscious, politically conservative genteel custodians of culture," though that did sometimes happen (Borus 2001, 68).

In the 1960s, historian Neil Harris laid out a counterargument that subsequent research on urban cultural philanthropy mostly affirms. Organizers and underwriters of urban art museums certainly represented "social prestige and private fortune." But overall, they displayed little interest "in ostentation, prestige or elevating themselves above the brutish mass." Founders viewed museums as "highly rational attempt[s] to make the fine arts more popular, stimulate native art schools, and improve industrial design" (Harris 1962, 550, 562). That is to say, philanthropists defined their goal not as indoctrination through refinement but as upward leveling. "Nineteenth-century meliorism, the doctrine of Improvement," explains historian Daniel M. Fox, provided "museum philanthropists with justification and encouragement" (Fox 1963, 14).

Art and architecture do invariably raise class issues, if only because patrons and clients are almost entirely either wealthy individuals or businesses, institutions, and governments. As art museums spread across the Northeast and Midwest, starting in the 1870s with New York's Metropolitan Museum and the Boston Museum of Fine Arts, trustees tended to be, as Stephen Conn notes about the Metropolitan, "the richest and most exclusive 'club' in the city" (Conn 1998, 197). By imposing their names on galleries they paid for and collections they donated, rich people intended museums, remarks historian Thomas Adam, "not only as educational institutions but as memorials" to themselves (Adam 2009, 100).

Amid the era's raucous urban politics and relentless metropolitan press, philanthropists attuned to civic republican or progressive capitalist notions of responsible wealth tended to navigate the public sphere more easily than those who let their snobbishness or oligarchic streaks show. Scholars such as Levine highlight incidents when museum staffs treated working-class visitors brusquely or rudely on account of perceived or actual violations of middle-class standards. Such incidents created uproars precisely because they played into stereotypes of haughty elites. Until it relented in 1891, the Metropolitan Museum's refusal to open on Sundays, most workers' only day off, made it an irresistible target for critics of out-of-touch patricians. Levine highlights the arrogant actions and pronouncements of the Met's founding director, Louis di Cesnola, pompous son of an Italian count. But Cesnola's demeanor made him divisive among trustees. A faction of trustees sought to have Cesnola fired as a "deceptive, brusque, insulting" martinet who "does not fairly represent us" (Trask 2012, 46).

The quest by US art museums to gain acceptance as civic institutions in a democratic society led them to emphasize education and accessibility, often over aesthetics, scholarship, or regional and national heritage. A mission of popular education in turn justified quasi-public status. American museums typically took the institutional form of a philanthropic foundation located on public land, often housed in a publicly built and maintained building. An 1871 deal between Tammany Hall and the Met's merchant–patrician founders, along with a similar deal for the American Museum of Natural History across Central Park, set an influential precedent. The publicly supported, nonprofit foundation became more common than fully private museums, such as Cleveland's, or fully municipal ones, such as those of Detroit and St. Louis.

The main purpose of US art museums, as the secretary of the Pennsylvania Museum in Philadelphia reported in 1879, was to "benefit … the vast majority of our citizens, the artizans [*sic*] and mechanics" who could not readily encounter the arts (Conn 1998, 203). As recent scholars such as Steven Conn, Jeffrey Trask, and Ezra Shales trace, administrators, curators, and philanthropists disputed the substance of their benefit to the working classes and the urban public overall. One model addressed the public mainly as viewers of art, seekers after the educated mind and cultivated spirit that Arnold and Norton counseled. This perspective encouraged curators to ally with collectors and donors in pursuit of examples of as many varieties of Western and world art as possible. With every museum a survey, genteel culture would be available everywhere. The alternative perspective stressed the museum as promoter of improvement in the crafts, decorative arts, and industrial design. This perspective took London's South Kensington Museum—renamed the Victoria and Albert in 1899—as its archetype. Those espousing this model viewed collections as teaching tools. In addition to paintings, they filled museums with furniture, carpets, and textiles, ceramics, silver, and glass, and prints and lithography. They installed displays of plaster replicas of famous sculptures for students to work from. Fine-art advocates despised these replicas and likewise deplored applied arts programs at museum schools, as well as exhibitions of commercial art and industrial design.

Scholars admonish that one needs to recall the personal and psychological dimensions of collecting and philanthropy, as well as their civic and political goals. Pushed into finance by his commodities-dealer father, who ended up bankrupt and insane, the Art Institute of Chicago's Charles Hutchinson described himself as well as his city as hungry for purposes deeper than moneymaking. Railroad financier William Walters educated himself in art "with a remarkable zeal and seriousness of purpose," evident in the Baltimore museum that his son created (Johnson 1999, xiii). A one-time art-history student at Göttingen, J.P. Morgan seemed to recapture his youthful intellectual enthusiasm when amassing perhaps the largest art collection in history. The scale and scope on which Morgan and other industrial-era collectors operated made Americans "feared by [Europeans] whose condescension we formerly endured," as the *Nation* noted. European dread of American collectors prompted the first attempts at national art export restrictions. To art critic Mather, such all-encompassing acquisitiveness amounted to "an ideal, if at times ruthless, expression of our new capitalism." This "mania" benefited the country, but Mather admired smaller-scale expressions of "personal taste," such as Isabella Stewart Gardner displayed at her Fenway Court museum in Boston, opened in 1903 (McCarthy 1991, 155, 171).

Kathleen McCarthy uses Gardner's experience to examine the divergent approaches of men and women to art philanthropy. Gardner exhibited the same intensity, competitiveness, and ambition, which her agent, Bernard Berenson, "shamelessly fed." Her $4 million, inherited from her father and husband, gave her ample money, though a fraction of Morgan's or Henry Clay Frick's. She faced cash-flow constraints and gender-based allegations of poor financial sense. Her unconventional persona—a combination of Gilded Age aesthete and convention-defying New Woman—helped her assemble "an entourage of mentors, friends, and protégés" among male artists and scholars. Her unconventionality also gave her leeway to promote and run her museum at a time when women philanthropists usually maintained self-effacing profiles and when museums seemed a matter for male professionals (McCarthy 1991, 161, 176). Gardner foreshadowed such twentieth-century patrons as Gertrude Vanderbilt Whitney. The art rebellions of the twentieth century represented to such women an appealing cultural radicalism, as well as an opportunity to carve out a field of endeavor separate from male-run institutions.

Malleable Vocabularies

By the late 1800s, museums were well established as objects for philanthropy and civic activism. The museum as a building type, however, was fairly new, developing only after the Napoleonic Wars. American architects paid close attention to French and British debates about organization, style, lighting, and so on. James Renwick's Washington projects from the 1850s—the Smithsonian Castle and the Corcoran (later Renwick) Gallery, the country's first purpose-built art museum—reveal these transatlantic influences. The Castle's post-Reconstruction neighbor, the National Museum (later the Arts and Industries Building), was designed by Washington architect Adolf Cluss, a German 1848er who helped import the principles of Friedrich Schinkel, architect of Berlin's Altes Museum, and Gottfried Semper, designer of Dresden's Gemäldegalerie and a widely read architectural theorist. Cluss's eight DC schools connected Americans to transatlantic discussions of another building type for an age of cities and mass education.

Calvert Vaux, who with Frederick Law Olmsted designed Central Park, treated the Metropolitan Museum and the American Museum of Natural History as tolerable exceptions to their insistence on preserving the park from buildings. Working with architect Jacob Wrey Mould, Vaux devised matching Victorian Gothic structures for opposite sides of the park. As the Beaux-Arts notion spread that public buildings should be stately rather than picturesque or romantic, Vaux's museums, like the Washington museums or Frank Furness's Philadelphia buildings, came to seem undignified. The Metropolitan hid the Vaux–Mould building behind its imposing wing along Fifth Avenue, opened in 1902 and designed by Furness's one-time mentor, Richard Morris Hunt, the first American admitted to study architecture at the École des Beaux Arts.

For much of the twentieth century, architectural historians, preoccupied by the evolution of modernism, expressed little tolerance for either the romantic eclectics or the Beaux-Arts formalists. To the extent they leaned one way or the other, the modernists' heart was with the romantics. In *Sticks and Stones* (1924), a template for the modernist perspective, Lewis Mumford argued that few American romantics besides Olmsted and Richardson grasped the "social and economic implications" of John Ruskin or William Morris. Nevertheless, Mumford preferred the Victorians' "energy and vitality" and "belief in nature" to Beaux-Arts display and historicism, which in his view glorified plutocracy by associating it with monarchy and empire (Mumford 1955, 100, 119).

Mumford was constructing the familiar narrative that moves from Richardson—the second American to study architecture at the École—to the disillusioned Beaux-Arts dropout Louis Sullivan, and then to Sullivan's apprentice Frank Lloyd Wright. To some degree, the customary narrative makes sense; Beaux-Arts designers did deplore the Victorians and were, in turn, denounced by the modernists. Upon inspection, however, the story becomes less linear, with less clear sides drawn. At the time, Victorian eclecticism and Beaux-Arts formalism both seemed malleable vocabularies, capable of a range of civic and cultural messages. In the mid-1800s, romantic forms signaled democracy and fellowship, though medieval organicism could serve an antimodernist Anglo-Catholic like Ralph Adams Cram as readily as the modern-minded Richardson. Decades later, progressives and social democrats found their visions expressed in Beaux-Arts neoclassical and neo-Renaissance designs, though conservatives perceived their values in those styles as well. Starting in the 1920s, debates surrounding De Stijl or Bauhaus encouraged modernists to read backward equations between a building's appearance and its politics that were not so direct at the time.

Creators and Organizers

Also basic to the modernist narrative was the innovator as oppositional outsider, who pushed architecture forward against a timeserver establishment. Recent scholarship reveals the heroes as embedded within the structures and culture of the architecture profession.

Richardson's supposedly uncomprehending contemporaries made clear their admiration. A poll of architects in 1885, a year before his untimely death, named five of his buildings among the country's best ten, with Boston's Trinity Church coming in first, ahead of the US Capitol. The heroic stories of Sullivan and Wright to some degree reflected retrospective self-mythologizing. Until 1895, when his break with Dankmar Adler left Sullivan vulnerable to his own "alcoholism and erratic temperament," he operated as an outspoken insider among a generation of Chicago architects celebrated for organizational, technical, and design prowess (Woods 1999, 116). Like Daniel Burnham, William Holabird, and Martin Roche, Sullivan went from working for William LeBaron Jenney to ranking among the peers of that central figure in skyscraper development. Wright publicized his prairie houses through the respectable medium of the *Ladies' Home Journal.* Along middle-class boulevards throughout the Midwest, prairie-style houses, adapted by local architects and builders from standard plans acquired through Chicago mail-order firms, appeared alongside arts-and-crafts and mission-revival houses, also styles promoted as traditional, modern, and American at the same time. Wright thrived as a designer for the thoughtful middle class until 1909, when his abandoning of family for the wife of a client pushed him into the outsider's role.

Attentiveness to discussions among architects over business methods and building functions and technologies, as well as design, underscores that Sullivan and Wright initially defined their stances within and not against their profession. Critics and scholars took over the aging Sullivan's disparagement of Burnham as a retrograde designer and panderer to power, while downplaying Sullivan's observations of his former friend, with whom he had had wide-ranging youthful discussions, as "the only architect in Chicago" fully to understand the era's "tendencies toward bigness, organization, delegation, and intense commercialism." Dissolution of the Adler partnership caused Sullivan's practice and reputation to dissipate. Burnham's facility at overseeing a large office of architects, engineers, and draftsmen enabled him to thrive despite the early death of John Wellborn Root, reputed as the artist in their partnership. Without Root, Burnham oversaw commercial projects such as New York's Flatiron Building (1903), while branching into urban planning and public projects on the scale of Washington's Union Station (1908). Sullivan might have been the idol of modernist architects, but Burnham was their model, his office organization the "prototype for all great architectural firms" (Hines 2009, 24–25).

That generation of Chicago architects transformed the practice, technology, and content of architecture in ways that attracted worldwide attention. Still, they were so diverse in spirit, approach, and agenda that architectural historian Daniel Bluestone admonishes against perpetuating the notion that a "unified and definable 'Chicago School' of architecture actually existed." This notion gained currency through the writings of mid-twentieth-century scholars such as Carl Condit, who sought to establish Chicago's centrality in the evolution of modernism. In the 1960s–1970s, preservationists ratified and popularized the concept as justification for protecting the city's architectural heritage (Bluestone 2011, 165–166).

Architects, like artists, were attracted to the École des Beaux Arts as much for its rigorous professionalism as for any style associated with it. The first architecture programs at US universities appeared at MIT, Cornell, and the University of Illinois between 1868 and 1973. Until then, architects who were not immigrants either had backgrounds in the building trades or in engineering or trained in the offices of established practitioners. The rapid evolution of technologies, utilities, materials, and functions meant that much Victorian architecture emerged through trial and error. Some of the disdain that Beaux-Arts practitioners directed at Victorian eclecticism arose from their sense that the buildings themselves fell short in terms of durability and function, as well as design.

Beyond its prestige and rigor, foreign study in architecture was fairly affordable. By the late 1800s, 10–20 percent of newly admitted architecture students at the École came from the United States, with the total number of Americans at any time approaching a hundred. As with Paris's art students, architecture students worked closely with mentors in ateliers, while immersing themselves in design, building types, theory, and history. The École's use of high-pressure competitions for degree credit "prepared future professionals for fast-track competition work and for quick response to changes requested by a capricious client" (Gournay and Leconte 2013, 165). Beaux-Arts methods pervaded American training programs by World War I. Dexterity in drawing and design combined with a broad command of styles and expedients to enable an architect grounded in such methods consistently to produce durable, serviceable, attractive buildings.

Since the 1960s, the historic preservation and historic district movements have provided a powerful new context for perceiving and evaluating Victorian and Beaux-Arts buildings and urban places. An array of trends came together in these movements, but in New York, a signal event was the failure to save McKim, Mead, and White's Pennsylvania Station, demolished in 1963 in favor of the Madison Square Garden/Penn Station complex that epitomizes for New Yorkers modernism's drab oppressiveness. Some Beaux-Arts masterpieces of civic design, such as McKim, Mead, and White's Renaissance-style Boston Public Library never suffered rejection, even though critics at the time and since have wondered whether monumental effects in this library or Carrière and Hastings's New York Public Library—or the Smithmeyer and Pelz Library of Congress for that matter—came at the expense of their effectiveness as libraries.

A professional with habits different from those of his partner White, who was murdered in scandalous circumstances in 1906, McKim collaborated with Burnham in efforts to elevate the American Institute of Architects into an effective professional organization. Taking a similar French program as a model, the pair drew upon McKim's contacts among École alumni as well as their collaborators on the Columbian Exposition when developing the American Academy in Rome as an advanced training ground for architects, artists, and art scholars. The presence of Burnham and McKim—along with Frederick Law Olmsted, Jr. and Augustus St. Gaudens—on the US Senate commission that produced Washington's McMillan Plan of 1902 long acted as a red flag for those inclined to dismiss the City Beautiful approach that that plan represented. By the 1910s, proponents of the City Practical alternative, including by then Olmsted, Jr., distanced themselves from the City Beautiful as preoccupied with boulevards, civic centers, and other Beaux-Arts compositional effects at the expense of a city's environment and life. This criticism fed the overall critique of Beaux-Arts design as grand but superficial.

Social reform progressives certainly did challenge the City Beautiful approach as insufficiently concerned with housing, public health, social services, and working environments. Also, Burnham's planning had a boosterish appeal congenial to the civic-minded business figures with whom Burnham was accustomed to working. The Commercial Club of Chicago sponsored the *Plan of Chicago*, the 1909 masterwork of Burnham and his Beaux Arts-trained protégé, Edward Bennett. This plan helped set the precedent that endured until the mid-twentieth century of US city plans underwritten not by municipalities but by chambers of commerce or boards of trade, whose priorities planners tended to accommodate.

Still, as Jon Peterson, William Wilson, and other scholars have underscored, the City Beautiful approach, like the era's museums, represented a civic vision that transcended commercial agendas. City Beautiful planning won widespread support because it sought to give form to the Progressive Era goal of a humane, responsible urban community. A clean, healthy, beautiful city, Peterson elaborates, could be "uplifting, enobling, and purifying." City Beautiful planners projected boulevards or civic centers lined with majestic Beaux-Arts structures not because they imagined baroque or imperial forms would sacralize capitalist power and ensure class hegemony. Burnham's plans, like McKim's Boston Public Library or Cass Gilbert's courthouses and capitals, envisioned urban space transformed into a total art program that "powerfully evok[ed] civic values" (Peterson 2003, 146–147).

Revolts and Establishments

When a critic in the 1890s labeled Louis Sullivan "a great master of realism in architecture," he evoked themes of modern capitalism and the industrial city, professionalism in the arts, the United States' contribution to Western culture, but also masculine reality versus feminine sentimentality. In disputes over the arts, gender imagery was pervasive and went in many directions. Even though women critics and patrons frequently sided with artistic insurgents and outsiders of both genders, experimentation had the connotation of gritty, brave, and masculine, while feminine implied sentimental, respectable, and derivative. The insinuation of effeminacy that surrounded John Singer Sargent tied his alleged personal shortcomings to a supposed penchant for pandering and effect at the expense of manly depth, risk, and exploration. Modernist critics dismissed Daniel Burnham while lauding his partner John Wellborn Root, thereby endeavoring to separate the supposedly philistine, business-minded masculinity of the firm from the hearty, male creativity of Root's art. Root, for his part, made no such distinction. Skyscrapers, he insisted should express the "masculine" values of "modern business life—simplicity, stability, breadth, and dignity." Downtown office towers should provide honest, not "emasculated" homes for profit-seeking businesses (Shi 1995, 161–162).

Shifts in art's gender imagery paralleled shifts in notions of self and society. The City Beautiful movement's stately boulevards and formal compositions seemed outmoded to modernist-minded commentators in part because they expressed Victorian masculine virtues: self-control, character, and responsibility, not modernist virility. Fountains and pediments with idealized female figures conveyed femininity as ethereal rather than sensual. Realists, naturalists, and modernists shared with their romantic and American Renaissance predecessors a conviction that high art could serve high-minded purposes, but they defined that value in terms of confrontation with disturbing social and psychological realities, not in terms of refinement, uplift, and transcendence.

The cultural and historical analyses that thrived in the late twentieth century called into question the modernist narrative of progress through insurgency and disturbance, but without making room for older notions of transcendence through aesthetics, lives infused by art. The preoccupation in recent decades with deconstructing superannuated arguments—together with the embrace of popular culture at the expense of high culture—reinforced interpretations such as the sacralization–hegemony model, an obstacle to grasping how various groups in society experienced and used the arts before World War I. Intellectual and cultural historians from Neil Harris to Daniel Borus have admonished against drawing connections too quickly between privileged people's cultural philanthropy and the validation of privilege itself.

Intellectual and popular disenchantment with modernism and its products in recent decades can take an overwrought form that threatens a new round of destructive incomprehension, similar to what the modernists imposed on the Beaux Arts and the Victorians. But this attitude has brought useful scrutiny to the modernist history of American art and architecture, opening the way for broader comprehension of the manifold trends that exist in relation to one another in every era, from the most academic to the most avant-garde.

It makes sense that modernists structured their narrative around establishments and revolts. The transatlantic world of the arts predisposed Americans to perceiving cultural progress as taking place through periodic insurgency, since that dynamic governed the Parisian art disputes to which Americans looked. The National Academy of Design began in the 1820s as a revolt in the name of familiar goals: openness to new influences and people, an international level of training, artists' control of exhibitions. The rebels of the Gilded Age and Progressive Era targeted the National Academy. The impressionists behind the Ten American Painters exhibition of 1898—including Childe Hassam, John Twachtman, and William Merritt Chase—seceded from the National Academy over frustration that a "mere scattering of their paintings [were] accepted in the society's exhibition." As often happens, this revolution threw into relief the rebels' shortcomings. Critics then and since concluded that in gathering their works into one exhibition, the American impressionists proved mainly that they were "pale reflections of their French predecessors" (Weinberg, Bolger, and Curry 1994, 22).

Analogous assessments came to surround the exhibition of "The Eight" that Robert Henri organized in 1908 for his circle of realists and naturalists, whose deliberately unpolished manner and uncouth material eventually prompted the label "Ashcan School." John Sloan, Everett Shinn, George Luks, and William Glackens developed their skills, attitudes, and interests while working as illustrators for newspapers in Philadelphia, where they met Henri, who returned from Paris with the sense that like his heroes Homer and Eakins, he had "something great and serious to say" (Zurier, Snyder, and Mecklenburg 1995, 63). Ambition brought the group to New York, where they, along with George Bellows, not one of the original Eight, established urban working-class and outcast milieus as durable themes in American art. Their approach hinged on the naturalist notion—which has gender as well as political connotations—that a clear-eyed look at the ordinary, even the sordid, yielded a vision of beauty. Their work also drew upon and shaped New York's progressive politics, through, for example, Sloan's stint as art director of *The Masses* in the 1910s.

Like Eakins and other American artists across the nineteenth century, the Ten and the Eight defined their agenda in nationalist terms as adaptation of techniques drawn from France or Spain to "subjects that were specifically, self-consciously, intentionally American" (Weinberg, Bolger, and Curry 1994, 25). This opened both groups to a new round of charges of derivative provincialism. Arthur Davies, a restive member of the Eight who helped put together the 1913 Armory Show, came to dismiss his colleagues as "not of the slightest interest to any serious artist" (Crunden 1993, 360). The Association of American Painters and Sculptors, the insurgent coalition that sponsored the Armory Show, experienced intense disputes over whether American schools still counted as modern in the face of European expressionism and cubism. Americans contributed most of the works to the 1913 Armory Show, but they were vastly overshadowed by the uproar over Duchamp or Matisse. When critics praised American works in the show as relatively sane, that reinforced the conviction that Americans needed to see, as one favorable reviewer remarked, "what the rest of the advanced world is about" (Slavitsky, McCarthy, and Duncan 2013, 29).

Stieglitz, whose 291 Gallery preceded the Armory Show as a New York outlet for Matisse and Picasso, welcomed the modernist stance of subjectivity deplored by Cortissoz and Cox. But like the impressionists and naturalists he wrote off as "the dead" in a newspaper ad praising the show (Shi 1995, 290), Stieglitz, born in 1864, retained nineteenth-century notions of art's high-mindedness. To qualify as art, he insisted, a photograph could not be a mere commercial tool. The modernist photographer Edward Steichen repudiated his mentor's principles by turning much of his energy to advertising from the 1920s. In persisting in the belief that art must serve purposes beyond those of the mass-production/mass-communication society, Steiglitz shared more than some recent scholars concede with his alleged contrasting spirit in the formation of American photography, Lewis Hine. The documentary photographer's pursuit of a "straight" style—a true contrast to Stieglitz's aestheticism—connected Hine to the politically minded naturalism of the Ash Can School (Sampsell-Willman 2009, 238). Yet such earnest humanitarianism marked Hine as a provincial during the swirling aesthetic debates of the early 1910s, for reasons similar to those that caused Sloan and his friends to despair over the Armory Show.

With a century of perspective and after decades of reassessment, the trajectory of modernity seems less straightforward and irreversible than Sloan or the equally earnest and distressed Kenyon Cox feared. With luck, art scholars and cultural and intellectual historians will continue to elaborate on art's myriad manifestations and roles in society during the half-century after the Civil War and on the shifting, contested definitions of mainstream, modern, cosmopolitan, and American. Perhaps present-day scholars can also let their guard down in the face of Gilded Age and Progressive Era earnestness. The next decades may benefit from appreciating the hope, purpose, aspiration, and wonder that people then ascribed to the arts. These ought not be written off as merely subterfuges for status, power, and authority, though the arts do raise such issues.

While highlighting historical and cultural analyses that erode the narrative of modernism as progress, this chapter nonetheless identifies with the sense of wonder at their times that inspired the early modernists. Before the Manhattan skyline emerged in the 1920s as an aesthetic representation of modernity, the Brooklyn Bridge captivated writers, engravers, painters, and poets. Contemporaries perceived it as a Whitmanesque metaphor for urban vitality, civil engineering as the sublime of now. The doomed devotion attributed to the Roeblings and their crews heightened the bridge's modernist lore. Impressionist Childe Hassam, the Eight's Ernest Lawson—artists representing every urban-minded style attempted to convey it, the way that Monet became captivated by Paris and London train stations. After returning from European study in 1911–1912, two divergent early modernists, the abstract landscape artist John Marin and the futurist-inspired Joseph Stella, seized on the bridge as embodying, in Stella's words, "a new world" of "steel and electricity" (Trachtenberg 1979, 132–133).

The young Lewis Mumford also drew the bridge. He attempted to write a play about it in the same years that Hart Crane made it the subject of an epic poem. To Mumford, the bridge and the Roeblings represented the promise of modernity as technology in the service of humanity, in contrast to the perverse alliance of mechanization, the state, and corporate capitalism that his writings denounce. In his memoirs, he recounts a moment of "exaltation" as he walked across the bridge one March evening. "Here was my city," he wrote, "immense, overpowering, flooded with energy and light." He felt a vision crystalize, "the promise of a new day" (Mumford 1982, 130). This chapter has dwelled on the aesthetic spirit and hopes of transcendence that belonged to old days. One remembers that visions of new days are needed, too.

References

Adam, Thomas. 2009. *Buying Respectability: Philanthropy and Urban Society in Transnational Perspective*. Bloomington: Indiana University Press.

Bluestone, Daniel. 2011. *Buildings, Landscapes, and Memory: Case Studies in Historic Preservation*. New York: W.W. Norton.

Bogart, Michele H. 1989. *Public Sculpture and the Civic Ideal in New York City, 1890–1930*. Chicago, IL: University of Chicago Press.

—. 2006. *The Politics of Urban Beauty: New York and Its Art Commission*. Chicago, IL: University of Chicago Press.

Borus, Daniel H. 2001. "Cultural Hierarchy and Aesthetics Reconsidered." *Intellectual History Newsletter* 23: 61–70.

Burns, Sarah. 1996. *Inventing the Modern Artist: Art and Culture in Gilded Age America*. New Haven, CT: Yale University Press.

—. 1997. "Modernizing Winslow Homer." *American Quarterly* 49: 615–639.

Cohen-Solal, Annie. 2001. *Painting American: The Rise of American Artists, Paris 1867–New York, 1948*, trans. Laurie Hurwitz-Attias. New York: Knopf.

Conn, Steven. 1998. *Museums and American Intellectual Life, 1876–1926*. Chicago, IL: University of Chicago Press.

Crunden, Robert. 1993. *American Salons: Encounters with European Modernism, 1885–1917*. New York: Oxford University Press.

Fox, Daniel M. 1963. *Engines of Culture: Philanthropy and Art Museums*. Madison: State Historical Society of Wisconsin.

Gournay, Isabelle, and Marie-Laure Crosnier Leconte. 2013. "American Architecture Students in Belle Époque Paris: Scholastic Strategies and Achievements at the École des Beaux Arts." *Journal of the Gilded Age and Progressive Era* 12: 154–198.

Grant, Susan. 1992. "Whistler's Mother Was Not Alone: French Government Acquisitions of American Paintings, 1871–1900." *Archives of American Art Journal* 32: 2–15.

Harris, Neil. 1962. "The Gilded Age Revisited: Boston and the Museum Movement." *American Quarterly* 4: 545–566.

Hines, Thomas S. 2009. *Burnham of Chicago: Architect and Planner*, 2nd edn. Chicago, IL: University of Chicago Press.

Hughes, Robert. 1997. *American Visions: The Epic History of Art in America*. New York: Knopf.

Johnson, William R. 1999. *William and Henry Walters: The Reticent Collectors*. Baltimore, MD: Johns Hopkins University Press.

Langa, Helen. 2004. "Recent Feminist Art History: An American Sampler." *Feminist Studies* 30: 705–730.

Lears, Jackson. 1981. *No Place of Grace: Antimodernism and the Transformation of American Culture, 1880–1920*. New York: Pantheon.

Levine, Lawrence W. 1988. *Highbrow/Lowbrow: The Emergence of Cultural Hierarchy in the United States*. Cambridge, MA: Harvard University Press.

Lewis, Arnold. 1997. *An Early Encounter with Tomorrow: Europeans, Chicago's Loop, and the World's Columbian Exposition*. Urbana: University of Illinois Press.

McCarthy, Kathleen D. 1991. *Women's Culture: American Philanthropy and Art, 1830–1930*. Chicago, IL: University of Chicago Press.

Morgan, H. Wayne, ed. 1986. *An American Art Student in Paris: The Letters of Kenyon Cox, 1877–1882*. Kent, OH: Kent State University Press.

—. 1989. *Keepers of Culture: The Art-Thought of Kenyon Cox, Royal Cortissoz, and Frank Jewett Mather, Jr.* Kent, OH: Kent State University Press.

Mumford, Lewis. 1955. *Sticks and Stones: A Study of American Architecture and Civilization*, 2nd edn. New York: Dover.

—. 1982. *Sketches from Life: The Autobiography of Lewis Mumford*. New York: Dial Press.

Novak, Barbara. 1979. *American Painting of the Nineteenth Century: Realism, Idealism, and the American Experience.* 2nd edn. New York: Harper & Row.

Ott, John. 2010. "The Manufactured Patron: Staging Bourgeois Identity through Art Consumption in Postbellum America." In *The American Bourgeoisie: Distinction and Identity in the Nineteenth Century*, ed. Sven Beckert and Julia B. Rosenbaum, 257–276. New York: Palgrave Macmillan.

Peterson, Jon A. 2003. *The Birth of City Planning in the United States, 1840–1917.* Baltimore, MD: Johns Hopkins University Press.

Prieto, Laura. 2001. *At Home and in the Studio: The Professionalization of Women Artists in America.* Cambridge, MA: Harvard University Press.

Sampsell-Willman, Kate. 2009. *Lewis Hine as Social Critic.* Jackson: University Press of Mississippi.

Savage, Kirk. 1997. *Standing Soldiers, Kneeling Slaves: Race, War, and Monument in Nineteenth-Century America.* Princeton, NJ: Princeton University Press.

Shales, Ezra. 2010. *Made in Newark: Cultivating Industrial Arts and Civic Identity in the Progressive Era.* New Brunswick, NJ: Rutgers University Press.

Shi, David E. 1995. *Facing Facts: Realism in American Thought and Culture, 1850–1920.* New York: Oxford University Press.

Slavitsky, Gail, Laurette E. McCarthy, and Charles H. Duncan. 2013. *The New Spirit: American Art in the Armory Show, 1913.* Montclair, NJ: Montclair Art Museum.

Swinth, Kirsten. 2001. *Painting Professionals: Women Artists and the Development of Modern American Art, 1870–1930.* Chapel Hill: University of North Carolina Press.

Trachtenberg, Alan. 1979. *Brooklyn Bridge: Fact and Symbol.* 2nd edn. Chicago, IL: University of Chicago Press.

Trask, Jeffrey. 2012. *Things American: Art Museums and Civic Culture in the Progressive Era.* Philadelphia: University of Pennsylvania Press.

Trilling, Lionel. 1972. *Sincerity and Authenticity.* Cambridge, MA: Harvard University Press.

Van Hook, Bailey. 1996. *Angels of Art: Women and Art in American Society, 1876–1914.* University Park: Pennsylvania State University Press.

—. 2003. *The Virgin and the Dynamo: Public Murals in American Architecture.* Athens: Ohio University Press.

Webster, Sally. 2004. *Eve's Daughter/Modern Woman: A Mural by Mary Cassatt.* Urbana: University of Illinois Press.

Weinberg, H. Barbara, Doreen Bolger, and David Park Curry. 1994. *American Impressionism and Realism: The Painting of Modern Life, 1885–1915.* New York: Metropolitan Museum of Art.

Wilson, William H. 1989. *The City Beautiful Movement.* Baltimore, MD: Johns Hopkins University Press.

Woods, Mary N. 1999. *From Craft to Profession: The Practice of Architecture in Nineteenth-Century America.* Berkeley: University of California Press.

Zurier, Rebecca, Robert W. Snyder, and Virginia M. Mecklenburg. 1995. *Metropolitan Lives: The Ashcan Artists and Their New York.* New York: W.W. Norton.

Further Reading

Adams, Henry. 2005. *Eakins Revealed: The Secret Life of an American Artist.* New York: Oxford University Press.

Adler, Kathleen, Erica E. Hirshler, and H. Barbara Weinberg. 2006. *Americans in Paris, 1860–1900.* London: National Gallery.

Anderson, Nancy K. 1997. *Thomas Moran.* New Haven, CT: Yale University Press.

Boag, Peter. 1998. "Thomas Moran and Western Landscapes: An Inquiry into an Artist's Environmental Values." *Pacific Historical Review.* 67: 40–66.

Bogart, Michele. H. 1995. *Artists, Advertising, and the Borders of Art.* Chicago, IL: University of Chicago Press.

Braddock, Alan C. 2009. *Thomas Eakins and the Cultures of Modernity.* Berkeley: University of California Press.

Bryant, Keith L, Jr. 1991. *William Merritt Chase: A Genteel Bohemian.* Columbia: University of Missouri Press.

Capozzola, Christopher. 2000. "The Man Who Illuminated the Gilded Age?" *American Quarterly.* 52: 514–532.

Dabakis, Melissa. 2014. *A Sisterhood of Sculptors: American Artists in Nineteenth-Century Rome.* University Park: Penn State University Press.

Horowitz, Helen Lefkowitz. 1989 (1976). *Culture and the City: Cultural Philanthropy in Chicago from the 1880s to 1917.* Chicago, IL: University of Chicago Press.

Johns, Elizabeth. 2002. *Winslow Homer: The Nature of Observation.* Berkeley: University of California Press.

Johnston, Patricia. 1997. *Real Fantasies: Edward Steichen's Advertising Photography.* Berkeley: University of California Press, 1997.

Lessoff, Alan, and Christof Mauch, eds. 2005. *Adolf Cluss, Architect: From Germany to America.* New York: Berghahn Books.

Morgan, H. Wayne. 1994. *Kenyon Cox, 1856–1919: A Life in American Art.* Kent, OH: Kent State University Press.

O'Gorman, James F. 1991. *Three American Architects: Richardson, Sullivan, and Wright, 1865–1915.* Chicago, IL: University of Chicago Press.

Chapter Thirteen

Religion in the Gilded Age and Progressive Era

Matthew Bowman

When B.H. Roberts, a fiery young British autodidact and leading Mormon thinker, arrived to see Charles Carrol Bonney in Chicago in July of 1893, he was told he would have to wait, and he had never been a patient man. He had been sent by the leaders of his church to see Bonney, and as he made his way from the train station to Bonney's office, he likely passed the dozens of exhibitions of the Columbian Exposition, the 1893 World's Fair. But the reason Roberts had come was the event closest to Bonney's heart: the World's Parliament of Religions. Bonney, a follower of the eighteenth-century Christian mystic Emanuel Swedenborg, had joined the Fair to administer the Parliament, and upon reading press reports of the event in a newspaper, Roberts shared Bonney's passion. The Parliament appealed to both for similar reasons. Bonney and the men who surrounded him were representative of the respectable Protestant establishment of the late nineteenth century, secure, prosperous, and most inspired by the ethical and ecumenical aspects of their faith. They were convinced that the religious impulses of all humanity could be unified under the common conviction of "the fatherhood of God" and "the universal brotherhood of mankind." Bonney's committee had "affectionately invite[d]" some 200 representatives of various world religions to "show forth the moral and spiritual agencies which are at the root of human progress" (Barrows 1893, 1:10).

And yet, nobody from B.H. Roberts's church had received an invitation. He had persuaded his superiors to allow him to make a personal appeal, and from July to September he pursued Bonney and other leaders of the Parliament through letters, meetings, and the halls of the Exposition. When he met with Bonney he reported that he was told "great prejudice existed against the Mormons on account of the plural marriage system" and that allowing Mormons to speak "would doubtless prove to be a disturbing element in the Parliament." Roberts bristled. He pointed out that not only had the Mormons abandoned plural marriage, but the Parliament was slated to include members of several religious traditions, like Islam, which still sanctioned the practice. Bonney eventually relented and referred the matter to John Barrows, in charge of the Parliament's program. After some persuasion, Barrow scheduled Roberts to speak in Hall Three, a small venue far from the main hall where most representatives would give their primary address. In a huff, Roberts boycotted (Roberts 1899).

The Mormons were of course not the only religion excluded from the Parliament, even from the United States. Forty-one different religious traditions were invited—including Christians, Jews, Hindus, Buddhists, Muslims, Shinto, Confucians, and Zoroastrians, from China, India, and the Middle East, among other locations—but Christians were highly overrepresented, and only one Muslim, the American convert Alexander Russell Webb, participated. Native American religions were described by a Christian anthropologist.

Other religions marginal in the West received rapturous responses. A young charismatic advocate of Vedanta Hinduism and a master self-promoter, the Swami Vivekananda delivered a message which seemed to Barrows and Bonney a mirror of their own. He quoted Hindu scripture: "As the different streams having their sources in different places all mingle their water in the sea, so, O Lord, the different paths which men take, through different tendencies, various though they appear, crooked or straight, all lead to Thee!" Barrows noted that Vivekananda received overwhelming applause and remarked, "Why should Christians not be glad to learn what God has wrought through Buddha and Zoroaster?" In his closing address Barrows declared his faith in Jesus Christ, "who reconciles all contradictions, pacifies all antagonisms, and from the throne of his heavenly

A Companion to the Gilded Age and Progressive Era, First Edition. Edited by Christopher McKnight Nichols and Nancy C. Unger.
© 2017 John Wiley & Sons, Inc. Published 2017 by John Wiley & Sons, Inc.

kingdom directs the serene and unwearied omnipotence of redeeming love" (Barrows 1893, 1:102, 75, 184).

The paradoxes of the Parliament, its rejection of Roberts and embrace of both Vivekananda and Barrows's final invocation of Jesus Christ as the ultimate reconciler of difference are perhaps most neatly captured in Barrows's record of Webb's speech. Barrows reported that the Muslim's defense of polygamy was met with "hisses and cries of 'Shame!'" which only abated when he began describing the ethical teachings of Mohammed (Barrows 1893, 1:127) Historians of the Parliament, like R.H. Seager (1993) and John Burris (2001), have generally emphasized that it was representative of what William Hutchison (2007) has called the "inclusive" pluralism of the liberal Protestantism that rose to dominate the American establishment in the late nineteenth and early twentieth centuries. Inclusive pluralism combined a satisfied self-confidence with a genuine inquisitiveness into what, as Barrows put it, they might find God doing among other peoples. Its advocates were curious and open-minded, but also sure that their culture, religion, and civilization were the pinnacle of human development, and thus immediately and definitively suspicious of violations of their moral and ethical norms.

Religion in America in the Gilded Age and Progressive Era struggled with these paradoxes. In the forty years between 1877 and 1917 America rapidly became far more religiously diverse than it ever had been, and yet the Protestant establishment ended the period as powerful as when it began. The face of America in these years increasingly became urban, immigrant and non-Protestant; and yet, among the old stock of the Protestant establishment, interest in new religious movements rose to heights not seen since the Second Great Awakening. Americans looked to religion to alleviate new challenges posed by poverty, science, immigration, and imperialism. In many cases, Americans who vehemently disagreed with each other on these and other issues found religious support for their opposing positions.

This chapter explores religion in the American North, South, and West in the forty years after the end of Reconstruction, showing how the expanding diversity of American religion both strained and revitalized Americans' faith, equipping it to meet new problems which it itself sometimes created, and steering the nation closer to true religious pluralism.

Renewal and Reaction in the American South

Historians of Southern life and culture in the late nineteenth century have recently given increasing vitality to the old chestnut that the patriarchal white class which led the South into secession lost the war but won the peace. In the two decades after the end of Reconstruction, a group of Southerners called the Redeemers struggled to restore white dominance in Southern politics through a mixture of violence and law. Forced to legally accept Constitutional amendments guaranteeing African American voting rights and legal protection, Redeemers used paramilitary groups like the Red Shirts and Ku Klux Klan to harass and drive African Americans from the polls. Southern states passed a series of laws elaborately designed to bypass the Fourteenth and Fifteenth Amendments and bar African Americans from the public sphere. However, the revolution of the Redeemers was not simply political: it was cultural, and everything from holidays to statuary to religion was mobilized to reinstitute white supremacy in the South.

Charles Reagan Wilson most famously explored what he called "the religion of the Lost Cause" in his seminal *Baptized in Blood: The Religion of the Lost Cause* (1980, 2004), showing how the South developed a "religious nationalism" centered upon the memorialization of the Confederacy, the celebration of its values, and a sense of nostalgia for the South's lost state equaled by a sense of mission to preserve its aims and culture. Wilson draws on sociological notions of "civil religion" to link practices of worship and issues of ultimate concern to the state. White Southerners lined the paths of cemeteries on Decoration Day. Confederate veterans' organizations built statues to cultural heroes like Stonewall Jackson and, particularly, Robert E. Lee. They sang hymns to their defeated nation. In all these ways, they built a new religious culture dedicated to embodying a particular set of values based on an imagined antebellum South. Other scholars have followed Wilson. In particular, David Blight's work on the memory of the Confederacy shows how notions distasteful after the end of the war, like slavery or separatism, were carefully sifted until public memory in both the North and the South lionized Confederate nobility, gentility, and honor in another sort of public religion (Blight 2002).

By the 1890s, as Blight and other scholars like Gaines Foster (1988) and Karen Cox (2003) have shown, stewardship of the religion of the Lost Cause had largely passed into the hands of female organizations. Under their guidance it became increasingly ritualized, focused on monument building, holidays, and commemorating Civil War leaders. Consonant with traditional Victorian domestic values, women throughout the nineteenth century were viewed as the custodians of a community's spiritual values. The Lost Cause found its high priestesses in the South's Ladies' Memorial Associations and their eventual successor, the United Daughters of the Confederacy, founded in 1894. These associations organized the rituals of Confederate Memorial Day, first observed in 1866, and Decoration Day, which began two years later. They also raised funds and erected memorials. Perhaps the most famous of these was the Confederate Memorial at Arlington National Cemetery, for which the United Daughters of the Confederacy lobbied and raised funds from 1906 until its completion in 1914. The memorial and dedication encapsulate much of the ideals of the Lost Cause, blending biblical and Christian imagery with a sentimentalized vision of the antebellum South. Singing of hymns, speeches by Confederate veterans, wreath-laying, and an address by President Woodrow Wilson marked the dedication.

A final hymn and wreath-laying were disrupted by sudden rain. The Memorial itself combines biblical images evocative of peace—plows and pruning hooks—with wreaths of olives and laurels, classical symbols of victory. The figures on the memorial similarly illustrate the Lost Cause: faithful slaves serving Confederate soldiers and clergymen, and mothers celebrating the military. Every year to date the Memorial hosts a Confederate Memorial Day event.

Christianity was deeply interwoven into the triumph of the Lost Cause. The southern evangelical white denominations grew more powerful after the war, particularly the Southern Baptist Convention, the Methodist Episcopal Church, South, and the Presbyterian Church in the United States. As they had before the war, these churches preached a strict morality, promoting temperance and frowning on diversions like dancing. Organizations like the Ku Klux Klan embraced this ethos and made it a staple of the Southern honor the Lost Cause taught. Many Southern leaders proclaimed the coming of a "New South," urban and industrial, built around the expanding railroad, and indeed in Southern cities imposing Gothic churches began to rise, as was also the fashion in the urban North during the Gilded Age. Some of these Southern Christian churches embraced social activism; Southern Baptist churches, for instance, organized orphanages and schools, particularly targeting the poverty-stricken Ozark and Appalachian regions. But most southerners remained rural, dependent on an agricultural way of life. Long-established religious practices deeply entwined with the land persisted. Revivalists like Sam Jones, Mordecai Ham, and the "Yodeling Cowboy Evangelist" J.C. Bishop found their greatest success in the countryside during late summer and early fall, during breaks in the planting season when revivals served as major community events, and a capella hymn singing and baptism in the rivers of the Southern countryside remained constant.

Among the most dramatic developments in Southern religion during the late nineteenth century was the rise of Pentecostal and Holiness Christianity. As the work of Grant Wacker (2002), Balmer, Butler, and Wacker (2003), and Randall Balmer (2010) has shown, the Holiness movement developed from American Methodist churches in the late nineteenth century, as believers sought the gift of sanctification John Wesley had taught was possible for converted believers. Sanctification would fill believers with the Holy Spirit—called spirit baptism—and aid them as they led a sinless life. In 1901, a Holiness minister named Charles Fox Parham asked his students at a Kansas bible school to consider what other spiritual gifts might be given to those already baptized by the Spirit. Soon, speaking in tongues, faith healing, and ecstatic preaching, the gifts given in the Bible at Pentecost, were spreading across the nation: famously appearing at the Azusa Street Revival in Los Angeles in 1906, but taking especially deep root in the South and growing rapidly there throughout the early twentieth century. In 1914, the Assemblies of God, the largest Pentecostal denomination in the United States, was organized in Hot Springs, Arkansas.

Wacker emphasizes the intellectual paradoxes of the Pentecostal movement, showing how it was simultaneously nostalgic and modern, and the work of historians of faith-healing in nineteenth-century America ties its spiritual practices far closer to middle- and upper-class practitioners of nineteenth-century medicine than had been previously recognized (Curtis 2007). But many other historians, like Randall Stephens (2008) and Robert Mapes Anderson (1979), have viewed Pentecostalism's appeal in the South as a manifestation of the region's uneasy social divides. Stephens emphasizes that the movement was viewed by many southerners as a northern and western import, threatening to the South's established institutions. But it appealed to southerners who felt disenfranchised. The early Pentecostal movement was made up of African Americans and poor whites, and gave men and women equal access to the spiritual powers of heaven. For many years, until Pentecostal denominations began to emerge, worship was interracial and both men and women spoke at meetings. The movement's strong emphasis on the imminent second coming of Christ and on spiritual gifts empowered them to survive an environment which seemed, on the face of it, hostile to their well-being. The strength of Pentecostalism's faith provided an alternative world more appealing than that which lay before its followers.

The diversity of early Pentecostalism points to an important fact which the Lost Cause and the struggle of the Redeemers could never quite obscure: that practicing religion in the South, for most southerners, could not be separated from the diversity of the region. The work of Paul Harvey (1997, 2007) emphasizes the degree to which, for many southerners, even as law began to divide African and white Americans, religion was like much else of culture: inseparable from the entwined, if segregated, lives they led. As early Pentecostalism illustrated, their worship patterns and music were often formed in dynamic interaction and common worship, and lay Southern evangelicalism was often more deeply marked by racial interaction than the formal worship of more established churches.

Oftentimes, this interracialism was idealistic: sometimes heartbreakingly, and perhaps unsustainably so. Paul Harvey and Edward Blum (2007) tell the stories of postwar Northern missionaries to the South who sought to form common cause with African Americans and build a truly interracial society. Of course they failed: on the one hand, the hardening power of the Redeemers led to a gospel that emphasized racial hierarchy, distinction, and difference. But on the other hand, many African Americans also wanted the opportunity to organize their own churches. Often frustrated with the attempts of whites from either the North or

South to control black churches through national Baptist or Methodist organizations, these African Americans withdrew their churches from affiliation and began formulating their own Christian denominations: the National Baptist Convention, the Church of God in Christ (a Pentecostal organization), and the African Methodist Episcopal Church and African Methodist Episcopal Church Zion all either emerged or grew steadily during the late nineteenth century. These churches became central to the lives of the African Americans who worshiped in them, serving as community centers, schoolhouses, sites of political and social organization, and as the hub of insurance and farming cooperatives, with ministers often serving in all of these capacities as well as leading worship on Sundays. The African American churches, having emerged from the hiding into which many were forced during slavery, were beginning in many ways to professionalize: clergy were increasingly trained, often in the North, and their members, particularly in middle-class areas, were joining social improvement associations (Montgomery 1994; Hahn 2004). And yet, as W.E.B. Du Bois famously observed, traditional worship patterns often persisted: vocalization, active participation from the congregation, call and response, clapping, and swaying. African American Christianity remained distinct at its adherents' own insistence, and the black church remained one institution in the South fully supportive of social equality (Du Bois 1903). As with their counterparts in the United Daughters of the Confederacy or Pentecostalism, African American women found their faith a bridge to public activism that might have otherwise been suspect, or even, for African American men, impossible given the Jim Crow regime. African American women's church groups, however, frequently worked across racial lines with white women's groups to improve life in the South in many ways: erecting orphanages and schools, agencies to care for the indigent, and other such public works (Gilmore 1996).

The interplay between white and black Protestant southerners on its own is complex, but of course these were not the only groups in the South. As the nineteenth century progressed, the growing religious diversity in the United States touched the South as well, and provoked some negative reaction. Hostility toward Catholics grew in the late nineteenth-century South for two reasons: evangelical enthusiasm for temperance peaked in the early twentieth century, and the flood of Catholic immigrants coming to the United States touched the South as well as the North, fostering fears of immigration. Some Catholics resisted segregation: most famously, the Sisters of the Blessed Sacrament established a network of schools for African Americans. But many other Southern Catholics adopted the mores of segregation around them, despite the presence of some Roman Catholic African American converts, particularly in Louisiana, where Creole Catholics had long worshiped in integrated parishes. Some all-black parishes were established elsewhere in the South. Despite the degree of their assimilation, Catholics often faced persecution; mobs fearful of immigration and rumors of racial integration attacked Catholic churches throughout the South in the early twentieth century. In 1921 a Catholic priest in Birmingham was killed by a Methodist minister who accused the priest of marrying his daughter to a black man, who was actually a Puerto Rican Catholic immigrant (Davis 1995; Remillard 2007).

Judaism had a similarly long history in the South. Three of America's original six synagogues were in Southern cities: Richmond, Virginia; Savannah, Georgia; and Charleston, South Carolina. All of these congregations moved toward Reformed Judaism in the years after the Civil War, adapting traditional Jewish ritual and services to draw the faith into consonance with modern life. Southern Jews expressed a strong desire to assimilate. Jews had served in high posts in the Confederate government, and groups like the United Daughters of the Confederacy had counterparts such as the Hebrew Ladies' Memorial Association, which sought to integrate Jews into the Lost Cause. But at the same time, a wave of immigration from eastern Europe provoked hostility. Growing anti-Semitism in the 1890s, exacerbated by economic depression and growing Jim Crow laws, led the Redeemers to attack Jews as well as Roman Catholics. That decade saw the rise of social restrictions on Jews and growing attacks on Jewish politicians and community leaders. In 1913, Leo Frank, a Jewish factory supervisor in Marietta, Georgia, was accused, tried, and convicted of the murder of a teenage girl named Mary Phagan. He was released on appeal, only to be lynched in 1915, an act widely seen as an attack on Judaism. Tom Watson, the Georgia populist politician, labeled him a "filthy, perverted Jew." In the aftermath of Frank's lynching, many Jews fled Georgia (Ferris 2006; Dinnerstein 2008).

Urbanization and Diversity in the American North

The rise of the city impacted religion in the American North more than any other factor during the Gilded Age and Progressive Era. In 1860 one of every six Americans lived in a city; by 1920, the ratio was one-half. These vast concentrations of population, capital, and industry transformed the American cultural and religious landscape. The city, with its great poverty and wealth, new science and scholarship, posed challenges to religions of long standing in the United States. It also brought new religions to America. Roman Catholicism and Judaism, though present in the United States since the founding, were revitalized with new immigrants. Eastern religions began to make their presence felt. And American Christians began to rethink what Christianity might look like in the face of all of these challenges (Orsi 1999).

In 1850 Catholics made up only 5% of the American population; slightly over one million people. In 1906,

Roman Catholicism was the single largest religious denomination in the country. Catholics made up 17% of the American population, for a total of fourteen million people (Fisher 2008). Similarly, between 1880 and 1924, the total Jewish population in the United States increased from a quarter of a million people to 4.5 million. The great portion of these were immigrants from southern and eastern Europe: Polish, Italian, and German Roman Catholics, and Ashkenazi Jews from Poland, Russia, Romania, and the Austro-Hungarian Empire. Most ended up in the large cities of the American Northeast: New York, Boston, Baltimore, Philadelphia, Chicago, and Detroit. By 1924 half of American Jews lived in New York City. In these places immigrants continued to practice their faith, often building small ethnic communities that replicated those they had left behind in which the entire lives of migrants, from birth to marriage to death, could play out governed by the cultural and religious norms of the community (Orsi 1985; Soyer 1997).

Despite these efforts, it was also true that the United States provided a new context and culture within which these immigrant communities lived, and the influence of American disestablishment promoted religious experimentation and drift. For instance, German advocates of Reform Judaism had found the United States congenial territory for decades, but in the 1880s, under the pressures of a growing American Jewish immigrant population— many more orthodox than the multigeneration American reform movement—a division within American Judaism began to be formalized. In 1883, Hebrew Union College, a school for rabbis in Cincinnati dominated by the Reform element, graduated its first class. At the graduation banquet, shrimp was served. Many more conservative Jews, even those in the Reform movement, took the menu as a particularly flagrant violation of kosher law. In response to the controversy, a conference of more liberal Reform rabbis gathered in 1885 under the direction of Isaac Meyer Wise, head of Hebrew Union College, and produced the Pittsburgh Platform, setting forth Reform principles. Kosher and other Mosaic Law was given in the context of a particular time and place, and hence did not apply in the modern world. Rather, Reform Jews should seek to discover and emulate the great moral principles that lay behind that law, and hence produce a progressive morality for the modern age. In response, a group of rabbis in New York City banded around the new Jewish Theological Seminary, founded in 1902. By 1913 they sought to steer a middle path, calling themselves "Conservative" Jews. On the one hand, they rejected the totalizing modernization of the Reform movement. But on the other, they also could not accept the practices of the growing numbers of immigrant Orthodox Jews in the United States who strictly separated themselves from modern culture. Rather, Conservatives sought to observe the Mosaic code in ways harmonious with living in a modern Western nation (Silverstein 1994; Sarna 2004).

Roman Catholics in America faced similar challenges. The earliest waves of Roman Catholic immigration to the nineteenth-century United States were largely from Ireland. By the post-Civil War era, new groups of Catholics were arriving: French, Germans, Italians, Poles, and many others. Roman Catholic leaders in the United States had to grapple with how to formulate one church from such disparate groups, and often allowed the creation of national parishes, in which homilies would be given and hymns sung in native languages. This fostered the continuance of diverse types of Catholic piety, from Italian Catholics who strongly centered worship upon devotion to saints and upon the home, to Irish Catholics whose devotion centered upon the Church and the sacraments. Similarly, as the numbers of Roman Catholics in the United States rose, so did the parochial school system, long supported by Roman Catholic families who resented the fact that most American public schools taught a de facto Protestantism, using the King James version of the Bible and often voicing suspicion of Roman Catholicism. In New York, Boston, and other large cities dominated by Catholic immigrants, these parochial schools sometimes gained public funding. Finally, the growth of the American Catholic Church meant that the American clergy expanded; 6,000 American priests in 1880 became 17,000 by 1910 (Fisher 2008; McGreevy 2004).

As the Catholic Church and its leadership expanded, disputes on how best to adapt to the American setting emerged among their ranks. Edward McGlynn, a second-generation Irish Catholic priest at St. Stephen's Church in New York City, was excommunicated in 1887. He vocally opposed the parochial school system and involved himself in New York City politics, urging the church to participate more in American life. Similarly, other Catholic leaders promoted a more robust engagement with American culture and politics. John Ireland and James Gibbons, archbishops of Minneapolis and Baltimore, respectively, celebrated American religious diversity and political democracy, arguing that Catholicism would flourish best in a society with religious disestablishment. In 1899, Pope Leo XIII, influenced by European Catholic leaders suspicious of American democracy, issued an encyclical condemning what he named "Americanism," warning that the norms and doctrines of Roman Catholicism should not be altered to suit any particular context, condemning an excess of individualism, and denouncing what he called "natural virtue," or the notion that human beings were inherently good apart from the grace of God. Gibbons replied cordially, claiming that no Catholic leader in the United States was pursuing such aims, and the "Americanist" party in American Roman Catholicism proceeded apace (Appleby 1992).

Just as American Roman Catholics faced suspicion from European conservatives, they also faced suspicion from American democrats who thought their church was a spiritual tyranny making them unfit for American citizenship. Anti-Catholic and anti-Semitic movements gained power in late nineteenth- and early twentieth-century United States, and in some cases such conflict became physical. The expanding Catholic parochial school system and the occasional public support it gained in cities dominated by Catholic immigrants attracted criticism in national politics, as did Catholics generally for opposing Prohibition. For several presidential elections in the 1880s, the Democratic Party, which most immigrants joined, was denounced as an advocate of "Rum, Romanism, and Rebellion." In 1888, the Republican presidential candidate James Blaine ran on his advocacy of a Constitutional amendment barring any public support for "sectarian" schools. In 1887 the American Protective Association (APA) was organized, warning that Roman Catholics were beginning to subvert the US government, and declaring its mission to preserve the separation of Church and State (Higham 1955). The APA eventually claimed to have elected some two dozen members of Congress and recruited two million members (though that number is likely exaggerated).

In the face of the challenges of the city, from growing diversity to the apparent rising power of science, Protestants grew anxious. They dealt with that anxiety in a number of ways. One popular response was the revival, a longstanding evangelical religious practice. Revivals dated back to the First Great Awakening of the eighteenth century, and normally featured several days of meetings, hymn singing, and exhortation to sinners to repent and become Christian. For much of the seventeenth and early eighteenth centuries, the major American revivalists, from George Whitefield to Charles Finney, were controversial figures, their emotional tactics assailed as indecorous and degrading. By the late nineteenth century, however, the revival had become eminently civilized. The great revivalists of the late nineteenth-century American north were Dwight Moody and Wilbur Chapman, and both worked hard to ensure their religious mission affirmed and promoted the cultural norms of the urban Protestant middle class to whom they preached. Until recently, many historians interpreted these revivals as conservative reactions to the challenge of the city, seeing Moody and his fellows as fearful advocates of traditional Protestant values. In this reading, Moody extolled the virtues of American capitalism, urging his audience to work hard, embrace Victorian gender norms, and internalize moral self-discipline. As powerful as his sermons was his music; his song leader, Ira Sankey, popularized a large number of evangelical hymns that quickly gained lives of their own, and promoted a sentimental, decorous variety of Christianity. Moody was enormously popular, though historians have questioned how successful he was at reaching audiences beyond the already Protestant middle class who had lionized him from the beginning (McLoughlin 1955). More recently, historians have noted the extent to which revivalists like Moody were in fact full participants in the modernity they ostensibly feared, showing how they used mass media, industrial production, and corporate organizing techniques to their advantage (Evensen 2004).

Among Moody's greatest successes was the nurturing of a new international missionary movement at his Northfield, Massachusetts headquarters. Between its 1886 founding and 1891, the Student Volunteer Movement for Foreign Missions mobilized more than six thousand Protestant seminarians and college students to serve foreign missions, buttressing growing denominational missionary efforts, and making the late nineteenth century the golden age of Protestant missions. Many of these missionaries and their leaders were women, and many of their efforts expanded on the "social housekeeping" of female activism in the United States, opening and running hospitals and schools in Africa, Latin America, and Asia. To some extent, of course, these missionaries wittingly and unwittingly propagated cultural imperialism, carrying Western political, economic, and social values as well as Christianity (Hutchison 1997; Hill 1985).

Other Protestants, however, in particular academics and other educated elites, grew increasingly suspicious of traditional religious practices like revivals. They were coming to the same conclusions as Reformed Jewish leaders like Wise, and Catholic modernizers like Ireland or Gibbons: American Protestantism had to adapt. The reasons were many. Some Protestant intellectuals were beginning to grapple with the results of biblical scholarship Europeans had been producing for decades, and coming to the conclusion that traditional beliefs about the divine origin of the Bible and many of its supernatural claims were untenable. Buttressing these discoveries were the burgeoning sciences of geology and biology that threatened to render the creation accounts of the book of Genesis implausible, and led many Christians to wonder about the nature of humanity: were humans really beings with moral purpose, or was the universe a morally blind, purely mechanical system of atoms and electrical reactions? Finally, for many Americans, the petty partisan politics, political corruption, and growing economic inequality of the Gilded Age contrasted poorly with the moral fervor of the Civil War. In the mid-1870s, Henry Ward Beecher, the leading pastor of his day and one of the most famous men in America, was embroiled in a tawdry sex scandal that seemed to many an emblem of the moral vacuity of the age. Under all these blows, many educated Americans entered what one historian has called "the spiritual crisis of the Gilded Age." The famed agnostic Robert Ingersoll became a sensation on the lecture circuit, and a spiritual malaise settled over many educated Americans (Carter 1971; Fox 1999). The advancement of scientific ways of thinking about the universe, intersecting with growing concerns about the advancement of Roman Catholicism and Protestant moralizers, led to a golden age of free thought, or secularism, among many American intellectuals. Secularists like Ingersoll sought to lay out a coherent way of imagining what a secular society would look like, focused on the promotion of public schools, science, and the separation of Church and State (Jacoby 2004).

Many Protestants particularly bothered by such problems began to synthesize a new style of religiosity called "Protestant liberalism" or "modernism." They were often pastors or professors in divinity schools, anxious to preserve the spiritual value of Christianity, faith in Jesus's message, and the reality of a loving God. They began to argue that the essentials of Christianity lay not in the veracity of particular stories about miracles. Rather, the Bible was the record of an ancient people's encounter with the divine and as such should be read as a document produced by a less scientific civilization that nonetheless contained the essential message of Christianity. That message lay not in unprovable supernatural events, but in the book's representation of God's relationship with humanity, the ultimate equality of all human beings, and the moral imperatives of Jesus's life and message. Divisions within this group existed, however. William Hutchison (1976) labels this ideology the "modernist impulse," but other historians have drawn distinctions between "modernists," who tended to be academics more comfortable with shifting the claims of the Bible into metaphor, and "liberals," generally congregational leaders whose pastoral concerns made them more attuned to the spiritual lives of their congregations (Bowman 2014; Cauthen 1962).

Other liberal Protestants were less involved in the pulpit work of Christianity: they were sociologists, psychologists, and philosophers who began to consider the rudiments of what is today called "comparative religion." These thinkers, most famously the Harvard philosopher and psychologist William James, began to speculate that the religious impulse was a common human experience shared across all cultures and societies, and the particulars of any given person's religious life could be shaped by personality, circumstance, and upbringing. Though James was rather wary of over-optimism, other academics, like the psychologist George Coe, the philosopher Shailer Mathews, and the philosopher John Dewey, began to seek ways in which the human religious impulse could be steered in the direction of social progress. They began thinking about the relationships among science, emotion, and religion in new ways, attempting to apply science to filter out what they deemed the unproductive aspects of religion in order to emphasize instead the ethical and communal aspects of religious belief (Dorrien 2003; Taves 1999).

While academic and pastoral liberals were motivated by intellectual challenges to traditional Christianity, concerns shared by many, the primary motivation of a final group of liberal Protestants in what came to be called the social gospel movement was the poverty, abuses, and lifestyle suffered by workers in the modern industrial city. Many workers themselves drew on religion to combat their plight, often through the labor movement. The Knights of Labor, the largest labor union in the country through much of the 1880s, was primarily Roman Catholic in membership. While some Catholic leaders feared radicalism, through the efforts of Knights of Labor president Terence Powderly and Archbishop James Gibbons, in 1891 Pope Leo XIII issued *Rerum Novarum*, a papal encyclical condemning poverty and industrial abuses, and defending the rights of workers (Weir 2010). Similarly, Protestant workers drew on the ideas and motifs of Protestant Christianity to condemn the ills of industrial capitalism in language of good, evil, sin, and salvation (Carter 2015).

Many Protestant ministers joined in the crusade, arguing that Christianity properly understood was not simply a matter of individual ethics. Rather, the leaders of the social gospel movement, most prominently the ministers Washington Gladden and Walter Rauschenbusch, called upon Christians to understand that righteousness was a matter of mutual obligations, and that religion required them to pursue the alleviation of poverty and other social ills. Its most radical activists, like George Herron, even called for the elimination of capitalism itself in favor of a form of Christian socialism. While sometimes understood as simply an invocation of the Christian duty to aid the poor, historians more recently have come to describe the social gospel as a form of Protestant liberalism with its own theology, ritual, and devotional practices, as with its more academic counterparts adapting the practice of Christianity for a modern world. Advocates for the social gospel prompted the creation of many "institutional churches" in American cities, regular congregations that sponsored soup kitchens, shelters for the indigent, job-training programs, and other facilities designed to aid the urban poor (Hopkins and White 1976; Evans 2004).

Reformers involved in some aspect of the social gospel participated in a wide swath of what historians call the American progressive movement, and religious language and ideas underlay many of the reforms Americans pursued. Politicians and reformers like William Jennings Bryan brought explicitly religious language to their pursuit of progressive politics (Kazin 2006). Among the most successful and prominent of such leaders was Frances Willard, who helped to organize the Women's Christian Temperance Union (WCTU) in 1873 and led it from 1874 to her death in 1898. Behind Willard the WCTU certainly advocated for temperance among a vast range of other reforms, as she declared the slogan of the group to be "Do Everything." Under the banner of "protection of the home," which Victorian mores deemed to be the proper sphere of work for women, she led the WCTU into advocacy for women's suffrage, unions, aid to the poor, sanitation and health codes, and laws against rape and child abuse as well as prohibitions against alcohol. Like many evangelical Protestant feminists, Willard advanced a moral argument for women's suffrage, maintaining that female participation in politics would bring women's deeper sense of spirituality and moral insight into the public sphere, providing uplift and purification (Tyrrell 1991).

While Willard and the WCTU represented the evangelical Protestant intervention into politics, the Gilded Age and

Progressive Era also saw a great deal of religious inventiveness. Feminist groups more radical than Willard embraced less conventional religious ideas. Elizabeth Cady Stanton and other women's rights activists who rejected Willard's notion that women were naturally more spiritual than men produced, between 1895 and 1898, a controversial revision of the Bible entitled *The Women's Bible*, which challenged traditional Victorian notions about gender difference and separate spheres. Other women, like the activist Victoria Woodhull, who had received extensive publicity when she announced her bid for the presidency in 1872, rejected traditional Christianity entirely and pursued differing spiritual paths. In the 1870s and 1880s, Woodhull was likely the most prominent Spiritualist in the country, and the period from those decades through World War I was perhaps the golden age of American Spiritualism, the belief that certain people, called mediums, could contact the spirits of the dead and transmit their messages about the nature of existence, humanity, and the afterlife. During the Gilded Age, mediums toured the nation, delivering lectures and performing séances before audiences of thousands. In 1893, the National Spiritualists Association of America was founded, imitating a British society founded several years before, and supported by the famous mediums Leonore Piper and Cora Scott. Spiritualism made claims similar to the Protestant liberalism that underlay the Parliament of Religions and the liberal Protestant movement generally: all religions had within them the seeds of truth, but that truth had less to do with the dogmas of any particular faith and instead affirmed essential human goodness, the possibility of progress, and the ultimate harmony of science and religion (Moore 1977; Cox 2003). In 1894, a group of academics surrounding William James and the psychologist G. Stanley Hall founded the American Society for Psychical Research (ASPR), which began to formally investigate Spiritualist claims.

Though Spiritualism was the most prominent, other such movements gained ground in urban America in the Gilded Age, promising similar faith in human capacity to understand and shape the universe. The divine healing movement and New Thought each affirmed Spiritualism's faith that science and religion were simply two aspects of divine work in the world. Divine healers insisted that modern medicine needed to recognize that God continued to work miracles, and that traditional Calvinist quietism in the face of human suffering was unnecessary (Curtis 2007). Waldo Trine and other advocates of New Thought argued that dogmatic, organized religion constrained the power of the individual soul's connection with the universe, and argued for divine immanence, the cultivation of an authentic self, and humanity's ability to attract prosperity, health, and success through meditation and devotional practice (Schmidt 2005).

Other fin-de-siècle religious movements were more occult than New Thought or Christian healing, and representative of these was Theosophy, founded by Helena Blavatsky and Henry Steel Olcott in New York City in 1875. Raised in Russia, Blavatsky traveled widely in her youth, and claimed to have spent time studying Hinduism and Buddhism in Tibet. Arriving in the United States in 1873, she became a defender of Spiritualism with one caveat: according to Blavatsky, the spirits in question were not of the dead, but rather representatives of a vast hierarchical and spiritual cosmos of which humanity was largely unaware. According to Blavatsky, "Theosophy" (meaning "god-wisdom") was not a religion per se, but an organization promoting the investigation of secret knowledge of this spiritual realm, known in the ancient world but lost since the rise of Christianity. As with Spiritualists and liberal Protestants, Theosophists maintained an optimistic view of human nature, insisted upon the ultimate equality of humanity, and believed that spiritual progress would create a more just world. Blavatsky's books *Isis Unveiled* (1875) and *The Secret Doctrine* (1888), which laid out the occult nature of human spirituality, were widely publicized, and though Theosophy never grew large, it gained a great deal of attention among American intellectuals and popularized Eastern religious concepts in American culture (Campbell 1980; Cranston 1993; Prothero 1996).

Other Americans were less sympathetic to the spiritual exploration of Theosophists or Spiritualism, and instead insisted upon a strenuous reassertion of tradition. In response to academic criticism of the Bible, many Americans embraced new notions about how to read the sacred text. In the 1880s and 1890s, B.B. Warfield, a professor at Princeton, penned a series of articles and books defending what he called "inerrancy," the notion that the Bible as written by its original authors was without error. At the same time, other evangelicals began to explore the theology of "premillennial dispensationalism," which found in the Bible an emphasis on Jesus Christ's second coming and a series of global calamities that would precede it. Dispensationalists took seriously the notion of biblical inerrancy, and read the Bible as a road map for the future and a warning of God's impending judgment on a wicked people. Through a series of "prophecy conferences," these Protestants began to organize the nucleus of Protestant fundamentalism, a movement which took its name in the fires of World War I. Historians have found the essence of fundamentalism in different places. Matthew Avery Sutton (2014) followed Ernest Sandeen (1970) in emphasizing dispensationalism, while George Marsden (orig. 1980, 2008) saw fundamentalism as a broader response to modernity. However, all agree that unlike Protestant liberals and so many other religionists in the Gilded Age and Progressive Era, fundamentalists were deeply skeptical of the idea of human progress and discontented with the cultural developments of their age. Their pessimism and growing determination to prepare the world for the second coming presaged their powerful influence in politics later in the twentieth century.

Conquest and Resistance in the American West

The American West in the late nineteenth and early twentieth centuries was a region as diverse as the American north was becoming. As Protestants in the North used revivals and missions in an attempt to convert migrants in their cities to an ethical Protestant Christianity, and missions and military forces to transform the South, they similarly spent much of the late nineteenth and early twentieth centuries attempting to remake the West in their own image as well. Three major conflicts in the period deserve attention: the ongoing conflict with Native Americans in the Great Plains and the Southwest; the struggle over Mormon plural marriage and theocracy in Utah from the 1860s to the 1900s; and the growing presence of East Asian immigrants in California and the broader West.

In the years after the Civil War, the federal government focused its attention on what were deemed "hostile" tribes. The most powerful and populous Native American group in the Great Plains in the years after the Civil War were the loosely affiliated tribes known collectively as the Sioux. In a series of battles with the US army in the 1860s, the Sioux won control of much territory surrounding the Black Hills in the Dakotas. In 1876 and 1877, another series of conflicts led to Sioux defeat. A similar process occurred with regard to the other most powerful "hostile" tribe, the Apache of the far Southwest, who were in armed conflict with American military forces from 1863, when settlers began to encroach on Apache lands in search of gold, until 1875. Both Sioux and Apache were confined to a series of reservations on undesirable land. Along with cultural repression, these tribes endured hunger and lack of promised resources. American agents sought to eliminate as well their traditional religious practices, most prominently among the Sioux the Sun Dance, a ritual in which young Sioux men drove skewers through the flesh of their chests and danced around a ceremonial pole until they lost consciousness.

Messianic movements had been a common religious response to white imperialism among Native Americans since the seventeenth century, and the late nineteenth century saw perhaps the most prominent of these. In 1870 a Paiute from Nevada named Tavibo began preaching that if Native Americans danced a traditional circle dance and sang hymns revealed to him, the earth would swallow up white people and restore traditional Native lifestyles. Tavibo's movement lasted only a few years, but two decades later another Paiute named Wovoka revived the movement. In the midst of a trance during a solar eclipse in 1889, Wovoka claimed to have encountered the Supreme Being and the ghosts of all the dead and was given a new circle dance to perform and new hymns to sing. His "ghost dance" spread rapidly among Plains Indians, particularly the Sioux and Cheyenne. Many reported that while they danced and sang they saw visions of the dead. Many also began making "ghost shirts," marked with astral symbols which they believed would protect them from harm.

By the summer of 1890 excitement for the ghost dance had reached a peak, and government officials on Plains reservations were growing worried. In December of that year, the Seventh Calvary attempted to disarm Native Americans on the Pine Ridge reservation in South Dakota while some were performing the ghost dance. Fighting broke out. It was bitter hand-to-hand combat, and ended in the deaths of more than 150 Sioux, including women and children. Twenty-five soldiers died. The brutal fighting intensified the government's hostility for the ghost dance, and gradually the movement began to wane. Some scholars, like Gregory Smoak and Anthony Wallace, have called the dance a "revitalization movement," designed to reinvigorate certain aspects of Native culture against cultural change and crisis (Wallace, 1956; Smoak, 2006). Others, however, have emphasized the extent to which older readings of the ghost dance phenomenon relied upon romanticized and exotic narratives of the Native Americans as a doomed people. They rather stress the extent to which Native religious movement synthetized aspects of American Christianity (Holler 1995; DeMallie 1985).

At the same time the ghost dance seemed to challenge federal hegemony in the Midwest, the federal government's relationship with Mormons in Utah was also reaching a crisis point. After settling in the Great Basin after the murder of their founder Joseph Smith in the 1840s, the Mormons established a largely self-governing settlement. Though Utah was a federal territory and a myriad of appointed officials were sent from the East Coast to govern it, the longtime Mormon prophet Brigham Young largely ignored their jurisdiction and ran the Utah territory and his church in tandem until his death in 1877. As the nineteenth century wore on, frustration that the Mormons were ignoring federal authority blended with a growing Protestant outrage over plural marriage, a practice the Mormons had publicly confirmed in 1852, into a suspicion of Mormon theocracy. For several decades, the Mormons, geographically isolated from the rest of the nation, were largely left alone. They practiced polygamy with all the rectitude they could muster; they were, after all, Victorians, and the practice was strictly regulated by church leadership. Roughly 25% of Mormons were involved in a polygamous family, and most of those were wealthy and high leaders in the church. Mormon women suffered emotionally but also benefited publicly from the practice. It granted them a great deal of autonomy that other American women often lacked. The church's Relief Society, a women's organization, sponsored a powerful suffrage movement and benevolent efforts. Utah's legislature granted women suffrage in 1870, and the Relief Society opened a hospital, sent women to be educated in eastern universities, and published several periodicals. However, in 1869, the transcontinental railroad was completed near Brigham City, Utah, and increasingly Mormons were forced to deal with a growing non-Mormon population. Brigham Young, hoping to restore early Mormon economic communalism, frowned on economic interaction with non-Mormons and sought to create an independent, rather than nationally integrated economy in Utah. Tensions between Mormons and non-Mormon settlers rose precipitously (Daynes 2001; Arrington 1954).

In the 1860s, 1870s, and 1880s Congress passed a series of laws designed to force the Mormons into submission. In *Reynolds v. United States* in 1878, the Supreme Court affirmed that the First Amendment did not protect the practice of polygamy. Thus emboldened, Congress passed the Edmunds Act in 1882, followed in 1887 by the Edmunds-Tucker Act. These laws disincorporated the Church of Jesus Christ of Latter-day Saints as a legal entity, required Mormons to swear an oath renouncing polygamy in order to vote, and strengthened federal powers to prosecute polygamists. Through the 1880s, federal marshals swarmed over Utah, arresting polygamous Mormons and driving the leadership of the church underground. Finally, in 1890, Wilford Woodruff, president of the Church, announced that the Mormons would renounce polygamy and seek integration into the United States. Utah became a state in 1896, but integration was not simple. The practice of polygamy indeed waned after 1890, but it also went underground. When in 1903 the high Mormon leader Reed Smoot was elected to the US Senate, a national controversy broke out over the persistence of polygamy and worry whether an autocratic religion like Mormonism could indeed participate in American democracy. Polygamy persisted in more isolated Mormon settlements until 1904, when church leaders renounced the practice for good due in part to national attention. Still, it took three years of hearings and many avowals from Mormon leaders of their faithfulness to the Constitution before Smoot was finally seated (Flake 2003).

American Protestants were less successful in other areas of the country. Chinese immigration to the United States surged in the 1860s due to political and economic unrest in China and the perceived economic opportunity offered in the aftermath of the California gold rush. Nearly all young single men, most of these migrants, planned to make money in the United States and then return to China. Gradually, however, more and more Chinese immigrants stayed, mostly in California and other Western states, employed largely in manual labor. Like other immigrant groups, they sought to reproduce some element of their culture in the United States. Associations of immigrants, often structured around native regions in China, built Buddhist temples where they settled; the first was built in 1853. By 1875, San Francisco was home to eight, most in buildings owned by immigrant associations. By 1870, one-tenth of the population of California and Montana territory was Chinese, and there were Buddhist communities in most California cities and in Helena and Butte in Montana. This rapid growth alarmed many Americans, and in 1882 the federal government passed the Chinese Exclusion Act, slowing Chinese immigration to the United States to a trickle. However, by the 1880s Japanese migration began to pick up, and the Japanese took the lead in establishing a Buddhist presence in the United States. In 1898 Japanese Buddhist leaders established a Buddhist mission to the continental United States, and began sending trained and ordained Buddhist priests to run temples in California and other western settlements. By 1900 there were 400 Buddhist temples in America (Tweed 2000).

White Protestant Americans perceived all of these groups as a tandem threat to both true Christianity and American democracy. Mormons, Native Americans, Japanese, and Chinese were all understood to be deficient in one way or another, lacking an ethical spirituality of the sort liberal Protestants had come to value. They were deemed either unwilling or unable to exercise the independence of spirit and thought required both by Protestantism and democratic government, and perhaps most troublingly, lacking the capacity for these things (Chang 2010; Reeve 2014). Protestant missionaries visited Native American reservations, settled in Salt Lake City, and opened missions to Chinese and Japanese immigrants on the West Coast, where they frequently found themselves rebuffed. Often, as with Utah and the Sioux, the answer was the exertion of force, a strategy which began by the 1890s to frame how American Protestants perceived their responsibility overseas.

Epilogue: Christianity and Imperialism in Progressive-age America

When President William McKinley defended his decision to claim the Philippines as an American territory, he famously told a visitor to the Oval Office that "there was nothing left for us to do but to take them all, and to educate the Filipinos, and uplift and civilize and Christianize them, and by God's grace do the very best we could by them, as our fellow-men for whom Christ also died" (Rusling 1903). There were many reasons why the United States joined the European nations and became an imperial, colonialist power in the 1890s, but the rhetoric of American leaders places a desire to spread true Christianity among them. This was true for several reasons: many evangelical Americans sincerely believed that only their form of Christianity could bring salvation. At the same time, many Protestant Americans also believed that Protestant Christianity was a necessary predicate for democracy, because it fostered ethical behavior and a sense of spiritual independence. American intervention overseas frequently took on religious overtones.

Protestant missionaries, the sort inspired by Dwight Moody's revivals, took a deep interest in the territories where the United States expanded. American missionaries had been present in the independent Kingdom of Hawaii since the 1840s, and they consistently encouraged the Hawaiian monarch to embrace economic and political policies friendly to the United States. Many missionaries were themselves involved in the sugar trade that had come to dominate the Hawaiian economy, and organized the Missionary Party, which formally promoted these aims. When David Kalakaua became king of Hawaii in 1875, he began promoting traditional Hawaiian culture, angering the Missionary Party, which engineered a gradual coup, beginning with a new constitution in 1887, and culminating in the overthrow of the monarchy in 1893.

Similarly, advocates of the Spanish–American War of 1898 were motivated in part to combat the Roman Catholicism dominant in the Spanish colonies of Cuba and the Philippines. American journalists and politicians depicted Spanish Catholicism as corrupt, louche, and morally bankrupt, a tool of the authoritarian Spanish monarch abusing the helpless Cuban and Filipino people. In contrast, they portrayed American Protestantism as vigorous and virile, a robust and masculine alternative to sluggish and indolent Roman Catholicism. In this reading, Protestantism promoted virtue and self-government; Catholicism promoted laziness and dependence on government. Protestant advocates for the war, like Theodore Roosevelt, argued that war was actually the Christian act, because Christianity required vitality and effort on behalf of righteousness. Accordingly, by the end of the Spanish–American war, American Protestant missionaries flooded into Cuba and the Philippines, hoping to spread Protestantism hand in hand with the capacity for self-government. They were disappointed. Particularly in the Philippines, Filipinos who resisted the transfer of authority from Spain to the United States looked to Roman Catholicism as a symbol of Filipino cultural independence, and Protestant missionaries failed to make much headway (Hoganson 1998; Putney 2001).

If Roman Catholicism was the enemy in the Spanish–American War, by the time the United States intervened in World War I, the enemy was the corrupted Christianity of Germany, which American propaganda presented as an authoritarian nation whose ruling military class suppressed any pretense to free thought or inquiry. Germany had long been the home of the most advanced scholarship assailing traditional views of the Bible. Conservative American Protestants muttered that tyranny was the logical result of a nation that rejected scripture, while liberal American Protestants frowned at the fact that all churches in Germany were state agencies staffed by a ministry paid with taxes. Both sides found in German Christianity a symbol of failure, and both sides responded eagerly to Woodrow Wilson, the pious president, son of a pastor, when he called Americans to fight for the preservation of democracy (Sutton 2014; Jenkins 2014). American religionists' involvement in war in the late nineteenth and early twentieth centuries encapsulated many of the challenges that American religion faced in the period more generally. American Protestants were increasingly anxious, beset by new economic, social, and cultural norms which challenged their dominance, and they responded in a number of ways, from the adoption of new modes of thinking about their own faith to the mobilization of government and military power. Despite their assertions of authority, they were forced increasingly to accept the presence of religious diversity. Other groups of believers gained footholds in American public space during the Gilded Age and Progressive Era, and set the stage for what would come in the twentieth century: the negotiation of and slow movement toward true religious pluralism.

Recent scholarship has made ever more explicit the challenge posed of that ideal, broadening the mosaic of American belief to groups heretofore largely neglected, particularly Asian immigrants and freethinkers, as well as deepening our understanding of groups like African Americans and Native Americans. More, historians have uncovered new ways of approaching older topics like the social gospel movement, moving past the academic, educated theorists of the movement in divinity schools and universities and instead attempting to reach the experiences of urban workers, migrants, and religious leaders in the cities, blending intellectual and social history to produce new contributions to a school sometimes called "lived religion." There remains, though, work to be done on the intellectual and political leaders of the period, particularly with reference to international relations, where religion has often been relegated to a secondary motivation behind economic or political realism. In total, the revival of interest in religion in the Gilded Age and Progressive Era reveals the extent to which religious ideas and ideology contributed to how Americans imagined their lives and their nation in total, and changes in their religious lives contributed as much as changes in other spheres to the transformation of what it meant to be an American in the early twentieth century.

References

Anderson, Robert Mapes. 1979. *Vision of the Disinherited: The Making of American Pentecostalism*. New York: Oxford University Press.

Appleby, R. Scott. 1992. *Church and Age Unite: The Modernist Impulse in American Catholicism*. South Bend, IN: University of Notre Dame Press.

Arrington, Leonard. 1954. *Great Basin Kingdom: An Economic History of the Latter-day Saints, 1830–1890*. Cambridge, MA: Harvard University Press.

Balmer, Randall. 2010. *The Making of Evangelicalism: From Revivalism to Politics and Beyond*. Waco, TX: Baylor University Press.

Barrows, John H. 1893. *The World's Parliament of Religions: An Illustrated and Popular History of the World's Parliament of Religions, Held in Chicago in Connection with the World's Columbian Exposition*. Chicago, IL: Parliament Publishing.

Blight, David. 2002. *Race and Reunion: The Civil War in American Memory*. Cambridge, MA: Harvard University Press.

Blum, Edward. 2007. *Reforging the White Republic: Race, Religion and American Nationalism, 1865–1898*. Baton Rouge: Louisiana State University Press.

Bowman, Matthew. 2014. *The Urban Pulpit: New York City and the Fate of Liberal Evangelicalism*. New York: Oxford University Press.

Burris, John P. 2001. *Exhibiting Religion: Colonialism and Spectacle at International Expositions 1851–1893*. Charlottesville: University Press of Virginia.

Butler, Jon, Grant Wacker, and Randall Balmer. 2003. *Religion in American Life: A Short History*. New York: Oxford University Press.

Campbell, Bruce. 1980. *Ancient Wisdom Revived: A History of the Theosophical Movement*. Berkeley: University of California Press.

Carter, Heath. 2015. *Union Made: Working People and the Rise of Social Christianity in Chicago*. New York: Oxford University Press.

Carter, Paul L. 1971. *The Spiritual Crisis of the Gilded Age*. DeKalb: Northern Illinois University Press.

Cauthen, Kenneth. 1962. *The Impact of American Religious Liberalism*. Washington, DC: University Press of America.

Chang, Derek. 2010. *Citizens of a Christian Nation: Evangelical Missions and the Problem of Race in the Nineteenth Century*. Philadelphia: University of Pennsylvania Press.

Cox, Karen C. 2003. *Dixie's Daughters: The United Daughters of the Confederacy and the Preservation of Confederate Culture*. Tallahassee: University of Florida Press.

Cox, Robert. 2003. *Body and Soul: A Sympathetic History of American Spiritualism*. Charlottesville: University of Virginia Press.

Cranston, Sylvia. 1993. *HPB: The Extraordinary Life and Influence of Helena Blavatsky*. New York: Tarcher.

Curtis, Heather. 2007. *Faith in the Great Physician: Suffering and Divine Healing in American Culture, 1860–1900*. Baltimore, MD: Johns Hopkins University Press.

Davis, Cyprian. 1995. *The History of Black Catholics in the United States*. New York: Crossroads.

Daynes, Kathryn. 2001. *More Wives than One: The Transformation of the Mormon Marriage System, 1840–1910*. Urbana: University of Illinois Press.

DeMallie, Raymond. 1985. *The Sixth Grandfather: Black Elk's Teachings as Given to John G.* Neihardt. Lincoln: University of Nebraska Press.

Dinnerstein, Leonard. 2008. *The Leo Frank Case*. Athens: University of Georgia Press.

Dorrien, Gary. 2003. *The Making of American Liberal Theology: Idealism, Realism and Modernity*. Louisville, KY: Westminster/John Knox Press.

Du Bois, W.E.B. 1903. *The Souls of Black Folk*. Chicago: A.C. McClurg.

Evans, Christopher. 2004. *The Kingdom is Always But Coming: A Life of Walter Rauschenbusch*. Grand Rapids, MI: Eerdmans.

Evensen, Bruce. 2004. *God's Man for the Gilded Age: D.L. Moody and the Rise of Modern Mass Evangelicalism*. New York: Oxford University Press.

Ferris, Marcie Cohen, ed. 2006. *Jewish Roots in Southern Soil: A New History*. Providence, RI: Brandeis University Press.

Fisher, James. 2008. *Communion of Immigrants: A History of Catholics in America*. New York: Oxford University Press.

Flake, Kathleen. 2003. *The Politics of American Religious Identity: The Seating of Senator Reed Smoot, Mormon Apostle*. Chapel Hill: University of North Carolina Press.

Foster, Gaines. 1988. *Ghosts of the Confederacy: Defeat, the Lost Cause, and the Emergence of the New South*. New York: Oxford University Press.

Fox, Richard Wightman. 1999. *Trials of Intimacy: Love and Loss in the Beecher–Tilton Scandal*. Chicago: University of Chicago Press.

Gilmore, Glenda Elizabeth. 1996. *Gender and Jim Crow: Women and the Politics of White Supremacy in North Carolina, 1890–1920*. Chapel Hill: University of North Carolina Press.

Hahn, Steven. 2003. *A Nation under our Feet: Black Political Struggles in the Rural South from Slavery to the Great Migration*. Cambridge, MA: Harvard University Press.

Harvey, Paul. 1997. *Redeeming the South: Religious Cultures and Racial Identities Among Southern Baptists, 1865–1925*. Chapel Hill: University of North Carolina Press.

—. 2007. *Freedom's Coming: Religious Cultures and the Shaping of the South*. Chapel Hill: University of North Carolina Press.

Higham, John. 1955. *Strangers in the Land: Patterns of American Nativism*. New York: Harper.

Hill, Patricia. 1985. *The World their Household: The American Women's Foreign Mission Movement and Cultural Transformation, 1870–1920*. Ann Arbor: University of Michigan Press.

Hoganson, Kristin. 1998. *Fighting for American Manhood: How Gender Politics Provoked the Spanish–American and Philippine–American War*. New Haven, CT: Yale University Press.

Holler, Clyde. 1995. *Black Elk's Religion: The Sun Dance and Lakota Catholicism*. Syracuse, NY: Syracuse University Press.

Hopkins, C. Howard, and Ronald White. 1976. *The Social Gospel Movement in America*. New York: Harper & Row.

Hutchison, William. 1976. *The Modernist Impulse in American Protestantism*. Cambridge, MA: Harvard University Press.

—. 1987. *Errand to the World: American Protestant Thought and Foreign Missions*. Chicago: University of Chicago Press.

—. 2004. *Religious Pluralism in America: The Contentious History of a Founding Ideal*. New Haven, CT: Yale University Press.

Jacoby, Susan. *Freethinkers: A History of American Secularism*. 2004. New York: The Free Press.

Jenkins, Philip. 2014. *The Great and Holy War: How World War I Became a Religious Crusade*. New York: HarperCollins.

Kazin, Michael. 2006. *A Godly Hero: the Life of William Jennings Bryan*. New York: Knopf.

Marsden, George. 2008. *Fundamentalism and American Culture*. Revised ed. New York: Oxford University Press.

McGreevy, John. 2004. *Catholicism and American Freedom: A History*. New York: W.W. Norton.

McLoughlin, William.1955. *Modern Revivalism: From Charles Grandison Finney to Billy Graham*. New York: The Ronald Press.

Montgomery, William E. 1994. *Under their Own Vine and Fig Tree: The African American Church in the South, 1865–1900*. Baton Rouge: Louisiana State University Press.

Moore, R. Laurence. 1977. *In Search of White Crows: Spiritualism, Parapsychology, and American Culture*. New York: Oxford University Press.

Orsi, Robert A. 1985. *The Madonna of 115th Street: Faith and Community in Italian Harlem*. New Haven, CT: Yale University Press.

—. 1999. "Introduction: Crossing the City Line." In *Gods of the City: Religion and the American Urban Landscape*, ed. Robert A. Orsi. Indianapolis: Indiana University Press.

Prothero, Stephen. 1996. *The White Buddhist: The Asian Odyssey of Henry Steel Olcott*. Indianapolis: Indiana University Press.

Putney, Clifford. 2001. *Muscular Christianity: Manhood and Sports in Protestant America*. Cambridge, MA: Harvard University Press.

Reeve, W. Paul. 2015. *Religion of a Different Color: Race and the Mormon Struggle for Whiteness*. New York: Oxford University Press.

Remillard, Arthur. 2007. *Southern Civil Religions: Imagining the Good Society in the Post-Reconstruction Era*. Athens: University of Georgia Press.

Roberts, B.H. 1899. "The Church of Jesus Christ of Latter-day Saints at the Parliament of Religions: Preliminary Agitation." *Improvement Era* 2, 9: 671–677.

Rusling, James. 1903. "Interview with President William McKinley." *Christian Advocate* 22, January.

Sandeen, Ernest. 1970. *The Roots of Fundamentalism: British and American Millenarianism, 1800–1930*. Chicago, IL: University of Chicago Press.

Sarna, Jonathan. 2004. *American Judaism: A History*. New Haven, CT: Yale University Press.

Schmidt, Leigh Eric. 2005. *Restless Souls: The Making of American Spirituality*. Berkeley: University of California Press.

Seager, R.H. 1993. *The Dawn of Religious Pluralism: Voices from the World's Parliament of Religions, 1893*. La Salle, PA: Open Court.

Silverstein, Alan. 1994. *Alternatives to Assimilation: The Response of Reform Judaism to American Culture, 1840–1930*. Hanover, NH: University Press of New England.

Smoak, Gregory. 2006. *Ghost Dances and Identity: Prophetic Religion and American Indian Ethnogenesis in the Nineteenth Century*. Berkeley: University of California Press.

Soyer, Daniel. 1997. *Jewish Immigrant Associations and American Identity in New York, 1900–1939*. Cambridge, MA: Harvard University Press.

Stephens, Randall. 2008. *The Fire Spreads: Holiness and Pentecostalism in the American South*. Cambridge, MA: Harvard University Press.

Sutton, Matthew Avery. 2014. *American Apocalypse: A History of Modern American Evangelicalism*. Cambridge, MA: Harvard University Press.

Taves, Ann. 1999. *Fits, Trances and Vision: Experiencing Religion and Explaining Experience from Wesley to James*. Princeton, NJ: Princeton University Press.

Tweed, Thomas A. 2000. *The American Encounter with Buddhism, 1844–1912*. Chapel Hill: University of North Carolina Press.

Tyrrell, Ian. 1991. *Women's World/Women's Empire: The Women's Christian Temperance Union in International Perspective, 1880–1930*. Chapel Hill: University of North Carolina Press.

Wacker, Grant. 2002. *Heaven Below: Early Pentecostals and American Culture*. Cambridge, MA: Harvard University Press.

Wallace, Anthony F.C. 1956. "Revitalization Movements." *American Anthropologist* 58: 264–281.

Weir, Robert. 2010. *Beyond Labor's Veil: the Culture of the Knights of Labor*. University Park: Penn State University Press.

Wilson, Charles Reagan. 2009. *Baptized in Blood: The Religion of the Lost Cause*. Revised edn. Athens: University of Georgia Press.

Further Reading

Blair, William. 2004. *Cities of the Dead: Contesting the Memory of the Civil War in the South, 1865–1914*. Chapel Hill: University of North Carolina Press.

Goff, James. 1997. *Plain Folk of the South Revisited*. Baton Rouge: Louisiana State University Press.

Goodrick-Clarke, Nicholas. 2008. *The Western Esoteric Traditions: A Historical Introduction*. New York: Oxford University Press.

Hardy, B. Carmon. 1993. *Solemn Covenant: the Mormon Polygamous Passage*. Urbana: University of Illinois Press.

Janney, Caroline. 2013. *Remembering the Civil War: Reunion and the Limits of Reconciliation*. Chapel Hill: University of North Carolina Press.

Lindsey, William. 1997. *Shailer Mathews's Lives of Jesus: The Search for a Theological Foundation for the Social Gospel*. Albany: State University of New York Press.

Martinez, Anne. 2014. *Catholic Borderlands: Mapping Catholicism onto American Empire, 1905–1935*. Lincoln: University of Nebraska Press.

Minnix, Kathleen. 1993. *Laughter in the Amen Corner: The Life of Evangelist Sam Jones*. Athens: University of Georgia Press.

Stowell, Daniel. 2003. *Rebuilding Zion: The Religious Reconstruction of the South*. New York: Oxford University Press.

Chapter Fourteen

Journalism

Bruce J. Evensen

On September 25, 1932 Lincoln Steffens warned fellow muckraker Upton Sinclair of a forthcoming study of the Progressive Period by literary and social critic Edmund Wilson. "The fact that he lumps us is a bad sign," Steffens declared, suggesting playfully that they kill the critic and claim self-defense (Winter and Hicks 1938, 928).

More than 80 years have passed since scholars first began to get a better understanding of the extraordinary vitality and effectiveness of journalists in the Gilded Age and Progressive Era. During that time nearly every imaginable claim has been made about them. Faulkner (1931), Regier (1932), Goldman (1952), Grenier (1960), and Filler (1961), followed by Wilson (1970), Crunden (1982), Evensen (1989), and Applegate (1997), tended to see muckraking journalists as moral crusaders who helped transform America into a more civil society. Others, led by Hofstadter (1955), Wiebe (1962), Kolko (1963), and Hays (1964), saw muckrakers as reluctant upholders of the status quo. Chamberlain (1932) and McCormick (1981) argue that their proposed reforms did not go far enough. Schultz (1965), Miraldi (2000), Jensen (2000), and Serrin and Serrin (2002) charge that those reforms helped transform America. Thelen (1970) and Kates (1995) point out that Progressivism was a national movement as well as many local movements, appearing in newspapers and magazines, but also in arguments over land use, in city and park planning, in religion and temperance work, in fighting for the rights of women, labor, and minorities. This good work was carried on not only in English but in the language of every major constituent group in America. William Allen White, the nation's quintessential small-town editor, observed that what united many of these writers was an undiluted faith in "the moral purpose behind man's destiny" (White 1925, 23, 60, 87–88). Even Hofstadter freely admitted that muckraking was not only "a revolution in journalism"; it was also a "critical achievement of American Progressivism" (Hofstadter 1955, 186).

Some research cites May 10, 1883 as the date when the business of journalistic exposure began. It was on that day that Joseph Pulitzer arrived in New York to take over the *World*, an old gray lady who had exhausted herself trying to report financial news to a diminishing readership. Pulitzer self-consciously situated his paper on the side of those whom modernity was leaving behind—the foreign-born and working-class, as well as the old, the halt, the lame, the weak, the vulnerable, the under-resourced and under-represented. David Nord (1984), however, has demonstrated that this communitarian obligation was on display in Chicago and several other cities a decade earlier. Recent scholarship suggests this experimentation grew out of the intense competition among newspapers in Gilded Age America (Smythe 1980, Green 1989, Evensen 2008, Gentzkow 2012). Melville Stone, soon a leader in cooperative newsgathering through the Associated Press, described the news business in America's centennial year as "war in the mud and mud to the neck" (*Chicago Daily News*, December 20, 1876).

The late Gilded Age and Progressive Era witnessed a profound transformation of America and its press. Between the close of the Civil War and the start of U S participation in the World War I, the nation's population tripled to 100 million. Census data shows that there was one urban inhabitant for every three rural residents in 1870, with a population of only 2500 separating rural from urban. Using the same definition, there were two urban Americans for every three people living in rural America by 1900. The number of factory jobs during this period tripled. By 1890 manufacturing first exceeded agriculture as a source of American wealth. By 1900 American manufacturing eclipsed the combined output of France, Germany, and the United Kingdom, and fueled by average annual immigrations of 400,000,

A Companion to the Gilded Age and Progressive Era, First Edition. Edited by Christopher McKnight Nichols and Nancy C. Unger.
© 2017 John Wiley & Sons, Inc. Published 2017 by John Wiley & Sons, Inc.

industrial production continued growing. The research of Baldasty (1992), Rutenbeck (1995), Campbell (2006), and Erickson (2008) chronicles how journalism adapted to this new urban environment. These scholars found that political independence, and not partisanship, paid. The number of politically independent papers grew from one in ten to two in three during this period. Three of every four newspapers were without political affiliation by 1917. Americans were the most voracious newspaper readers in the world. In the early twentieth century half of all the world's newspapers were published for American readers. Many American adults read both a morning and an afternoon newspaper. That was how, for instance, Chicago's thirty-seven newspapers could have a combined circulation of 1.1 million in 1900, when the city's population was 1.1 million. Many cities showed the same pattern. Barely 200 newspapers and magazines existed when the penny press was founded in 1833. By 1910 the number had soared to 25,000 with an annual aggregate of eight billion pages.

"It was journalism that tracked us into the wilderness," Frances Willard remembered, growing up in rural Wisconsin. "It kept us company in our isolation, poured into our minds the brightest thoughts of the best speakers, and made us a family of rural cosmopolites. It was journalism that developed in us the passion of patriotism and the insight into politics. Upon our prairie farm, one mile from any neighbor and several miles from anywhere, the white wings of the press flew in, so broad and so free" (Willard 1889, 496). By the age of eleven, Frances, with her brother Oliver, was producing her own paper on white paper ruled off by their mother. Frances soon began publishing her pieces in Chicago's *Prairie Farmer*. Articles in *The Ladies Repository*, the *Chicago Tribune*, and the *Chicago Republican* soon followed. In 1857, at the age of eighteen, she relocated to Evanston, just outside Chicago, and helped edit the *Chicago Evening Post* with her brother. Her reform-minded prose aimed at re-moralizing America appeared in *Harper's*, *Century*, and the New York *Independent*, and later in *The Christian Union*, the *Sunday School Times*, and *The Forum*. She saw journalism as "progressive and humanitarian," with a capacity for "miraculous good" resting in its "inky power to take you into its fellowship" (Willard 1889, 513).

In 1871, at the age of thirty-two, Willard became the first dean of women at Northwestern University, where she intensified her advocacy of temperance and became an important ally to Susan B. Anthony and Elizabeth Cady Stanton in the women's suffrage movement. Her brother's death from alcoholism made her a lifelong enemy of the rum shop. She frequently referred to it as "a war to the knife and the knife to the hilt" (Gifford and Slagell 2007, 4). Willard sold the *Post* at auction to Victor Lawson and Melville Stone and the *Chicago Daily News*, appreciating the paper's communitarian concern and sabbatarianism. She was now free to found the Woman's Christian Temperance Union (WCTU) in 1874, becoming its president in 1879. Willard built its membership to a quarter-million, mobilizing her members through *The Union Signal*, in which she often argued, "this copy is as vital as the air you breathe" (Stewart 1906, 15). A prodigious speaking tour took her to every American town of 10,000 over the next decade. The WCTU's "home protection" plan, later pushed by the National Council of Women, of which Willard also served as president, included a national network of cooperating newspapers and magazines that advocated temperance, voting rights, equal pay for equal work, the eight-hour work day, and raising the legal age of sexual consent from ten to sixteen. Willard and her army demanded orphanages for homeless children; propelled reforms to care for inebriate women and those forced into prostitution. She won the right of every child to attend free kindergarten, and her organization placed thousands of water fountains in public parks across America. Congress later placed a statue to Willard in the Capitol as recognition for her importance in the passage of the Eighteenth and Nineteenth Amendments to the Constitution. She was the first woman so honored.

Willard often accompanied D. L. Moody from town to town in his extraordinary Gilded Age revival work. Moody headed a layman's movement, heavily dependent on a positive press, in the staging of citywide religious spectacles. "Crazy Moody" was barely in his twenties when he began antagonizing Chicago editors on the eve of the Civil War by barging into their offices demanding publicity for the local Young Men's Christian Association (YMCA). When they would not act, he did, producing several hundred thousand copies of *Everybody's Paper*. Moody made a name for himself in the English and Scottish revivals of 1873 and 1874 and returned home as "God's man for the Gilded Age." Moody saw publicity creating "a spirit of excitement among the people. It seems to me a good deal better to advertise than preach to empty pews" (Evensen 2008, 304). A cooperative press helped make Moody a spiritual celebrity and front-page news from Boston, Brooklyn, and New York, to Philadelphia and Chicago. Stenographers worked in waves to capture his every utterance. It helped produce, in the words of *Vanity Fair*, "the greatest multitudes ever gathered in this generation." At his death in 1899, editorial writers noted that no man had spoken to more men and women during his lifetime, nor better shown the power of the press as an engine of reform.

Many in the Gilded Age press praised Moody's layman's movement, but the institutional church did not receive comparable approbation. New York City's Trinity Church became a symbol of the indifference of Christ's army to the urban squalor about them. Trinity, one of America's wealthiest churches and greatest slumlords, became one of muckraking's longest-running targets. On June 23, 1883, barely a month after Pulitzer took possession of the *World*, the paper gave front-page attention to the death of Kate Sweeny, a young Irish girl who suffocated under the raw sewage that flooded her basement apartment. Pulitzer described it as a "home horror that is a pitiful sore in the heart of the great city." In a style out of Dickens, the *World* reported, "If you turn out of the Bowery on Mulberry Street and walk along the narrow thoroughfare for two or three blocks you will suddenly come upon a neighborhood" of chronic want. There one finds a horror zone "swarming with destitution, filth, wretchedness, and vice," of "tumble-down houses, where gin-soaked women sit wretchedly on the door-rails" and ragged children appear to play "oblivious of the stench."

Five years after this literary portrait of New York's notorious Five Points, America's first and greatest slum, Jacob Riis, a crime reporter for the *New York Tribune*, captured the area in a series of shocking flash photographs. The resulting book, *How the Other Half Lives*, eventually sold twenty-eight million copies worldwide, and helped lead to the break-up of the slums. Riis described these slums as "the hot-bed of epidemics that carry death to rich and poor alike; the nursery of pauperism and crime that fill our jails and police courts; that throw off a scum of forty thousand human wrecks to the island asylums and workhouses year by year; that turned out in the last eight years a round half million beggars to prey upon our charities; that maintain a standing army of ten thousand tramps with all that that implies; because, above all, they touch the family life with deadly moral contagion" (Riis 1890, 3).

Riis's agitation led New York City to pass legislation forcing tenement owners to build toilets inside rather than outside their apartments. The city surrendered to public pressure and began to build playgrounds for its public schools. Soon New York City Police Commissioner Theodore Roosevelt was walking the Five Points beat with Riis, later calling him "the most useful citizen of New York." In *McClure's Magazine*, the leading reform-minded publication of the period, Roosevelt wrote that Riis had shown him "the countless evils that lurk in the dark corners of our slums and have their permanent abode in the crowded tenement houses. They have met in Mr. Riis their most formidable opponent." Few men, Roosevelt wrote, had better exposed "the want and misery and foul crime which are bred in the crowded blocks of tenement rookeries." Roosevelt, whose presidency would soon see the Square Deal as central to a widened public appreciation of its communitarian obligations, believed Riis had "the great gift of making others see what he saw and feel what he felt" (Roosevelt 1901, 452–453).

The Attack on Trinity Church

The *New York Times* continued the pressure on Trinity Church one year later, calling its more than 700 holdings among "the worst tenements in New-York." The search by the *Times* of health department records found that on one church property at 83 Charlton Street, eight deaths had occurred in three years of children under the age of four. The church had ignored health-department orders to clean up the property. "It was with difficulty that our reporter groped his way up the dark and crooked stairs," the paper told its readers. "The walls were greasy and grimy to the touch. In a sudden turn in the hall the reporter stumbled against a door. There was no transom over the door, and it was almost impossible to see anything. From the other side of the door, curses, the sound of scuffling, and a variety of confused noises proceeded" (*New York Times*, December 24, 1894). Trinity's rector Morgan Dix released a statement defending the church against "sensational articles in the press." He decried the failure of the *Times* "to sift the material brought them by their reporters, leading to the grossest falsehoods placed before their readers" (Dix 1895, 3). Trinity claimed it did not own the property, but that a Mr. Peter E. Finegan did. The *Times* exposed the duplicity, finding the church paid taxes on the property. Supported by growing public opinion, the health department took Trinity to court, forcing it to "repair, alter, cleanse, and improve the premises" over Trinity's objections that the repairs would prove too costly and that pipes supplying water to the property might freeze, leading to "the great danger of injury to the property" (*Health Department of the City of New York v. The Rector, Church Wardens and Vestrymen of Trinity Church*).

Robert Miraldi has focused on the work of Iowa-born activist Charles Edward Russell in taking on Trinity. Russell had been the trusted editor of Joseph Pulitzer's *New York World* and William Randolph Hearst's competing *New York Journal* when he investigated 256 of Trinity's tenements in the late fall of 1907. His three investigative articles for *Hampton's New Broadway Magazine* and *Everybody's*, published between April and July 1908, made the case that no Iowa farmer would house hogs in the way Trinity abused its renters. "Whenever I saw a house that looked as if it were about to fall down, one that looked in every way rotten and weary and dirty and disreputable, I found that it was owned by Trinity." Its properties were "a prolific breeding place for the germs of tuberculosis." Russell wrote of "the loathsome contamination" that produced an "unspeakable terror in the eyes" of those forced to live in these "reeking and cheerless holes" (Miraldi 2003, 138–141). Ray Stannard Baker, a veteran of *McClure's* who was writing in the *American Magazine*, found "Trinity did not care for the people" who rented its tenements. Baker saw the "absurdity of taking from the people of the tenements and giving nothing back—except empty homilies." He argued that "the aristocratic, feudalistic system" under which Trinity operated needed to be replaced by a more democratic vision of public accountability. By 1910, the church agreed to take down 225 of its worst tenements. Some sold for $1 at auction. It ended two decades of Progressive Era agitation that Trinity live up to its "responsibility to the public" (Baker 1909, 15–16). The case established the precedent that no matter how powerful the organization and no matter how long it took, the best of Progressive Era journalism was in the business of fighting for social justice.

Going Undercover

Scholar Harry Stein (1991) has identified qualities that are common in reform-minded journalism at the turn of the century. Stein found that these writers start by revealing the hidden situation that needs remedy. They identify who is responsible for the injustice, and state what should be done to correct it. They attempt to incite a response by their readers by identifying who has been victimized. Most importantly, these writers described how alleviating this injustice leads to a better society. Each of these qualities can be seen in the work of Elizabeth Cochrane, who won worldwide fame as Nellie Bly. Mignon Rittenhouse (1956) and Brooke Kroeger (1994) portray Cochrane as a resolute twenty-three-year-old woman who arrived in Pulitzer's *New York World* office on September 22, 1887 determined to work at the paper. For her first assignment she went undercover, pretending to be insane, to reveal conditions at a lunatic asylum for women. Cochrane's findings first appeared in the *World* on October 9 under the pseudonym Nellie Bly. Her investigation concluded that sane, indigent, non-English speaking women were driven to insanity by their treatment at Blackwell's Island.

"My teeth chattered and my limbs were goose-fleshed and blue with cold," she wrote, remembering an ice cold bath in a tin tub. "Suddenly I got, one after the other, three buckets of cold water over my head—ice-cold water, too—into my eyes, my ears, my nose and my mouth. I think I experienced some of the same sensations as a drowning person as they dragged me, gasping, shivering and quaking, from the tub. For once I did look insane." Those patients who were seen as an annoyance were tied together with chains at the waist, like slaves. They were told to "shut up, or you'll get worse." The disobedient were beaten with broom handles and locked in closets. Bly wrote that patients prayed for death. "Take a perfectly sane and healthy woman," she wrote, "shut her up and make her sit from 6 a. m. to 8 p. m. on straight-backed benches, do not allow her to talk or move during these hours, give her no reading and let her know nothing of the world and its doings, and see how long it will take to make her insane." After Bly's exposé reached the public, $850,000 was appropriated from New York City's Department of Public Charities and Corrections to end the abuse (Bly 1887, 55).

The *World*'s circulation soared to a quarter-million as a result of Bly's series. Pulitzer and other publishers were finding that, properly publicized, reporting that took its social responsibility seriously was also good for business. The personal papers of Samuel Sidney McClure as well as his autobiography describe what happened next. "I'm having my usual nervous breakdown," McClure wrote his wife in March of 1903. In the event of his death, he told her, Ida Tarbell, the associate editor of *McClure's Magazine*, would take over his work. She understood his passion to rein in the "lawlessness" of major corporations and "to protect those who could not protect themselves" (Evensen 1989, 11–12). McClure's fears were misplaced. He lived until 1949 and the ripe old age of ninety-two, but his comments show Tarbell's importance to the Progressive movement and *McClure's*, the preeminent muckraking magazine of its period.

Like Cochrane, Tarbell was a determined woman from western Pennsylvania who recognized journalism as one of the few skilled professions open to women of talent and ability in the late Gilded Age. The scholarship of Mary Tomkins (1974) and Kathleen Brady (1984) shows how she took a personal interest in John D. Rockefeller and the Standard Oil Trust after it illegally and surreptitiously used the "Cleveland Plan" to put her father and other small oil producers out of business. The scheme gave Rockefeller special rates from the Erie and New York Central railroads, a criminal conspiracy that Tarbell and her research assistant John M. Siddall uncovered in a year's investigation. In her autobiography Tarbell wrote that she and Siddall worked "in a persistent fog of suspicion and doubt and fear" (Tarbell 1939, 207). Their first article, in November 1902, followed by two years of additional exposés, uncovered an elaborate system of kickbacks and oil conquests enabling Rockefeller to corner the oil business just as America was turning to the internal combustion engine to run its cars. Tarbell could not "submerge my contempt for their illegitimate practices. I never had an animus against their size and wealth. But they had never played fair, and that ruined their greatness for me" (Tarbell 1939, 230). McClure collected Tarbell's nineteen articles into a bestselling book, *The History of the Standard Oil Company*. It helped lead to the order of the US Supreme Court in May 1919 that Standard Oil was an illegal monopoly and had six months to dissolve itself.

Harold Wilson's research (1970) has rightly focused on McClure's group as a touchstone for Progressive-Era reporting. This is best demonstrated in the January 1903 issue of *McClure's Magazine*, where Tarbell's takedown of Standard Oil is joined by Lincoln Steffens's critique of municipal corruption in Minneapolis and Ray Stannard Baker's examination of a violent coal strike and the right to work. Samuel McClure's editorial for that edition framed their findings as demonstrating "the American contempt of law. Capitalists, workingmen, politicians, citizens—all breaking the law, or letting it be broken. Who is left to uphold it? There is no one left; none but all of us" (336). Steffens argued municipal graft relied on "good people" who let it happen. "Citizens work hard. They make money. They are sober, satisfied, busy with their own affairs. There isn't much time for public business" (228). In his autobiography, Steffens observed, "the law-abiding backbones of our society, in city after city, start out for moral reform, and turn back" (Steffens 1931, 525). His tawdry tales of municipal malfeasance in Minneapolis, St. Louis, Chicago, New York, Philadelphia, and Pittsburgh that he termed "the shame of the cities" led to the creation of municipal voter leagues, good-government groups, and citizens' associations aimed at curbing the power of big city machines. Baker's assignment to the coalfields of Wilkes-Barre, Pennsylvania exposed the brutality of the United Mine Workers against anthracite workers who refused to join their union. Charles Monie spoke for many men, terrorized by the union, but who refused to strike. "I claim that the individual," he told Baker, "has a right to work" (325). Baker's reporting helped generate bipartisan support for statewide initiatives banning union membership as a requirement to work.

Socialism and Journalism

Two Progressive Era socialists—Upton Sinclair and Abraham Cahan—used their platforms as journalists writing for a wider public to champion the right of workers to organize and strike for better pay and improved working conditions. Like Bly before him, Upton Sinclair went undercover to reveal working conditions in Chicago's stockyards. Between February 25 and November 4, 1905, his fact-based fiction was serialized in *Appeal to Reason*, a leading Socialist weekly with a circulation of a quarter-million. Harris (1975) shows the rhetorical strategies Sinclair employed in becoming one of the nation's best-known social critics, while Yoder (1975) emphasizes Sinclair's alienation from other social critics of his age. Bloodworth (1977) expands upon Sinclair's importance in social history. Bloom (2002), Arthur (2006), Mattson (2006), and Wiener (2008) each analyze how Sinclair's descriptive writing and the nation's anxiety over the purity of its food supply helped make *The Jungle* one of the most widely recognized stories of the early twentieth century. "There was never the least attention paid to what was cut up for sausage," Sinclair wrote in one of his most lurid passages. "There would be meat that had tumbled out on the floor, in the dirt and sawdust, where workers had trampled and spit uncounted billions of consumption germs. There would be meat stored in great piles in rooms; and the water from leaky roofs would drop over it, and thousands of rats would race about on it. It was too dark in these storage places to see well, but a man could run his hand over these piles of meat and sweep off handfuls of the dried dung of rats. These rats were nuisances, and the packers would put poisoned bread out for them; they would die and then rats, bread, and meat would go into the hoppers together" (Sinclair 1906,161–162). Sinclair had hoped to promote socialism as well as improve conditions for workers in the meatpacking industry. Instead, on June 30, 1906 the Pure Food and Drug Act became law with a mandate to protect the nation's food supply.

Abraham Cahan became a spokesman for the labor movement, and particularly the garment workers of New York City, as editor of the *Jewish Daily Forward*, a Yiddish-language newspaper that reached a nationwide readership of a quarter-million. Research by Sanders (1969) and Howe (1976) describes Cahan's importance to the Jewish community. Sorin (1985) and Lipsky (2013) analyze Cahan's significance as a radical politician. Rischin (1985) and Evensen (1992) point out that some of the strongest reform-minded journalism during the Progressive Period was not necessarily in English. Cahan developed as a writer while a member of Lincoln Steffens's staff at the *New York Commercial-Advertiser* between 1897 and 1902. This is where Cahan learned to humanize the problems of social injustice through the lived experiences of the people he wrote about. This made more real the struggles of the urban underclass. Cahan's reporting in the *Commercial-Advertiser* championed the hardships of 1500 pushcart operators "hardly earning more than $5 a week," who were forced to give fifty cents of it in protection money to city police (June 29, 1898). He reported on a butcher named Bauer who opened a candy store on Avenue C with the $150 he received for deliberately chopping off two of his fingers (July 8, 1899). He supported a 13-year-old raincoat-maker docked two cents for arriving to work ten minutes late. Cahan's memoir describes his determination to "realistically depict" working-class life as he saw it, a strategy that received its ultimate test in reporting the Triangle Shirtwaist Factory Fire (Cahan 1969, 404–405).

On November 24, 1909, 15,000 shirtwaist workers, many of them teenaged Jewish and Italian immigrant women, walked off their jobs in New York City's garment district, demanding better pay and safer working conditions. The next day, 5,000 more joined them. A six-day working week of 65 hours might make a young immigrant woman $10. Metal doors were locked while the women worked. They had to ask permission to go to the washroom. Exits were narrow, only one person wide, so that workers could be frisked to make sure they were not stealing thread or cloth. In March of 1910 the striking women returned to work, their demands for greater safety unmet. At 4:40 on the afternoon of March 25, 1911, a fire broke out on the eighth floor of the Asch Building at 23 Washington Place in Greenwich Village. A west-side staircase was blocked by a barrel of motor oil, trapping workers. That floor's water hose didn't work. A foreman who had the key to a ninth-floor exit fled. Fire and smoke quickly filled the elevator shaft. Outside the Asch Building, a disbelieving crowd gathered. Rescue ladders reached only the sixth floor. "Many hanging from windows let go," the *Jewish Daily Forward* reported, "when the fire reached their hands." Rescue nets were torn from the bleeding hands of first responders. Trapped against blackened windows, "some leaped out to their deaths. A young man and woman then appeared in a window. They kissed on an eighth floor ledge and sprang off, landing heavily on the sidewalk." One by one the victims jumped, "burning, smoking, flaming bodies with hair trailing upwards, burning like candles." The *Forward* reported that "the entire Jewish Quarter is in mourning. The morgue is full of our victims" (March 26, 1911). One hundred forty-six garment workers died that day in the greatest workplace disaster America had ever known.

The *Daily Forward* led demands to investigate safety-code violations of New York City workplaces. More than 200 of them were found in violation of minimum safety standards. Access and egress laws were passed in New York and many other American cities. Doors by law now had to open outward. Workplace fire extinguishers became mandatory. Hundreds of bills improving worker safety became a permanent part of state labor codes.

Child Labor

Most of those killed in the Triangle Factory Fire were teenagers. The youngest was an eleven-year-old girl. At the turn of the twentieth century, 1.7 million children under the age of fourteen labored in America's mills, mines, fields, and factories. More than 1300 laws had been passed in the previous seventy years limiting the exploitation of child labor, but were largely ignored. Stidger (1933) and Filler (1966) chronicle the committed work of Edwin Markham in ending the scourge of child labor. "Is it not a cruel civilization," Markham asked in *Cosmopolitan*, "that allows little hearts and little shoulders to strain under grown-up responsibilities, while in the same city, a pet cur is jeweled and pampered and aired on a fine lady's velvet lap on the beautiful boulevard?" (Markham 1907, 332–333). Markham partnered with the Child Labor Federation to raise public awareness of "the great American cancer" of child labor. Like a malignancy, "it eats at the body and it eats at the soul; it saddens today, and it damns tomorrow" (Markham, Lindsey, and Creel 1914, 297–298).

Others committing themselves to the cause of ending child labor include British-born socialist John Spargo, Marie and Bessie McGinnis Van Vorst (1903), Mary Alden Hopkins (1914), and from Chicago's Hull House, Florence Kelley, Robert Hunter, and William Hard. They endeavored to capture the lived detail that mobilized readers to demand action. Spargo biographer Markku Ruotsila (2006) notes that Spargo was a granite-cutter who stood in bread lines and shoveled snow to see how the other half lived, and became a passionate advocate of children's rights in the socialist monthly *The Comrade* and the bestselling *The Bitter Cry of the Children*. Spargo followed the work of twelve-year-old coal breakers, who "crouch over the chutes" for ten hours at sixty cents a day, picking out pieces of slate as the coal rushed past to the washers. "From the cramped position they have to assume, most of them become more or less deformed and bent-backed like old men," he reported. "Accidents to the hands, broken and crushed fingers are common. Sometimes a terrified shriek is heard, and a boy is mangled and torn in the machinery, or disappears in the chute to be picked out later, smothered and dead." For the living, "clouds of dust fill the breakers and are inhaled by the boys, laying the foundation for asthma and miners' consumption" (Spargo 1906, 163–164). Marie Van Vorst reported in a *Saturday Evening Post* series that underage South Carolina textile workers might earn forty cents for a sixteen-hour day. Her sister-in-law Bessie followed children into factories and mills from Maine to Alabama, finding "thousands and thousands of little children work, contrary to every principle of civilization and Christianity" (Van Vorst 1908, 10). Hopkins, writing in the *Child Labor Bulletin*, followed the lives of four-year-old Loretta, forced to panhandle violets from a high chair, the blind Rosie who sold gum on the steps of the elevated railway, and a frightened, nameless child burdened down by coats twice his size, yet trying to make a sale.

Florence Kelley, daughter of a US Congressman and aide to Illinois reform GovernorJohn Peter Altgeld, was drawn to the settlement work of Chicago's Hull House and its advocacy for children and the poor. She attacked the sweating system in *Child Labor Bulletin* and in *Survey Magazine* and created the National Consumers League that publicized its "white label" sewn into clothing by companies obeying minimum pay and maximum work hours for minors. As president of the Child Labor Committee, Robert Hunter drew readers' attention to the connection between child labor and poverty. In the magazine *World's Work* he deplored how an adolescent world of learning and play had been turned into prisons of mines, factories, and stores. "The poverty which oppresses childhood," he wrote in *Poverty*, "is a monstrous and unnatural thing, for it denies the child growth, development, and strength; it robs the child of the present and curses the man of the future. There are 10 million persons in this country underfed, underclothed, and badly housed, and the great majority are children" (Hunter 1904, 190–191). He added, "The tremendous struggle with poverty that the foreigner makes in order to survive means, in a great many cases, the sacrifice of the child, and the ruin of childhood" (288).

In 1908 the Child Labor Committee hired Lewis Hine to document child labor through photojournalism. Like Riis, his photographs were a sensation. Peter Seixas and Kate Sampsell-Willmann consider Hine's social documentary photography a crucial element in the fight against child labor (Seixas 1987; Sampsell-Willmann 2009). It depicted remarkable stories of breaker boys covered in coal dust in Pittstown, Pennsylvania and five-year-old newsboys in St. Louis who sold papers while jumping on and off moving trolley cars. William Hard, an editorial writer at the *Chicago Tribune* and confidante of Theodore Roosevelt, provided word pictures as he followed homeless children after hours. He found they "carried cocaine," shot craps, engaged in assaults, and were used as runners for organized crime (Hard 1908, 36). As a result of Progressive Era agitation, two-thirds of all states passed laws prohibiting child labor by 1907. Five years later, the US Children's Bureau, a federal agency, was tasked with the responsibility of preventing child exploitation. In 1916 and 1919, federal child labor laws were passed limiting the hours and ages of workers.

There were also many minors swept into prostitution. Weinberg and Bridges have emphasized the work of George Kibbe Turner (1907, 1909a, b) in challenging those who profited from prostitution (Weinberg and Weinberg 1961; Bridges 1984). In "The Daughters of the Poor" (1909b) Turner identified the East Side of New York City as "the chief recruiting ground for the so-called white slave trade in the United States, and probably in the world." At dance academies, "gangs of loafing boys look them over. These lonely and poverty-stricken girls, ignorant and dazed by the strange conditions of an unknown country, are very easily secured by promise of marriage, or even partnership." Cadets "with good political connections" do best in "obtaining control over simple and easily exploited creatures." The girls "are closely confined, see only their managers, and many do not talk English, and naturally do not know how to escape." Turner estimated that half of the nation's prostitutes were supplied through New York, as Tammany Hall and its affiliated slum lords made "a good profit in the wholesaling of bodies of the daughters of the poor." Turner found "the average life of women in this trade is not over five years, and supplies must be constantly replenished through tens of thousands of new and ignorant young girls" (Turner 1909b, 54–59). Turner reported that prostitution had expanded rapidly in Boston and New Orleans at fifty cents a transaction and was a $20 million business in Chicago. In each instance, corrupt city administrations were "retailers of women" through a network of ward bosses who protected prostitution and assured its profits (Turner 1909b, 120–121).

Turner's reporting revealed criminal conspiracies involving politicians, police, and compliant courts that used the profits from prostitution to finance the gambling and drug trades. His reporting led in 1910 to the creation of the Chicago Vice Commission, an initiative of civic reformers that soon became a Progressive Era model for Minneapolis, Portland, Hartford, and more than 300 American cities. In January of 1910 Turner was subpoenaed for two days of grand jury testimony probing the rise of organized crime in New York City. The publicity led to Congressional passage on June 25, 1910 of the Mann Act, making it a federal crime to engage in interstate or foreign commerce in the transport of any girl or woman for purposes of prostitution or for any other immoral purpose.

The spirit of reform was also captured in *La Follette's Weekly* (published today as *The Progressive*), founded in 1909 by Wisconsin Senator Robert La Follette. It soon surged to a circulation of 40,000, promising to "hit as hard as we can, giving and taking blows" in "the struggle between Special Privilege and Equal Rights" (*La Follette's Weekly*, January 9, 1909, 1). Emma Goldman and Alexander Berkman's *Mother Earth*, launched in March 1906, was a monthly dedicated to anarchist causes, but had a wider readership in its support of labor, early education, women's rights, and its opposition to war. Greenwich Village activists, led by editor Max Eastman, produced *The Masses*, beginning in the summer of 1912, to promote the culture, interests, and appetites of the Urban Left. Native American journalism in the Progressive Period reflects a similar determination to empower the marginalized. One of its most articulate spokesmen was Dr. Carlos Montezuma, a Mojave–Apache man who founded *Wassaja: Freedom's Signal for Indians* in 1916. In its pages he argued against paternalistic and demeaning federal Indian policies that made reservations little more than prisons for many Native Americans. He championed the abolition of the Bureau of Indian Affairs and the empowering of Native Americans to run their own internal affairs.

The Yellow Press

Biographers of Adolph S. Ochs, who bought the *New York Times* in August 1896, note that he positioned his paper as a "clean, dignified, and trustworthy" (August 19, 1896) antidote to the self-promoting press of Joseph Pulitzer and William Randolph Hearst and the moral outrage of the muckrakers. Ochs had little use for the circus makeup and banner headlines of the Yellow Press, a disapproving term used by the self-respecting journalistic establishment to criticize the hyperbolic and highly profitable papers of Pulitzer and Hearst. The term itself arose out of a quarrel the two men had over whose paper owned the rights to a highly popular comic strip called "The Yellow Kid." The invective spilled over into their news columns when each paper claimed circulation-stimulating "eye witness accounts" of supposed Spanish atrocities in Cuba on the run-up to America's war with Spain in 1898. The *World* reported the February 15, 1898 explosion aboard the US battleship *Maine* in Havana harbor, killing 260 sailors, "was caused by a bomb or torpedo" (February 17, 1898) and the *Journal*'s headlines were certain it "was the work of an enemy" (February 17, 1898). The *Times* was characteristically more cautious. "As yet the cause of the explosion is not apparent," it told its readers, "the wounded sailors of the *Maine* were unable to explain it" (February 16, 1898). The *Times* even quoted the Spanish minister, who said his country had nothing to do with it. On March 1, Ochs editorially excoriated "the epidemic flood of mendacity promoting the sale of extras" in the nation's rush to war. After Congress declared war on Spain on April 25, the New York *Evening Post* blamed the Yellow Press for the conflict. W. Joseph Campbell has shown Hearst's published comment, "How do you like the *Journal*'s war? (*New York Journal*, May 8, 9, 10, 1898) was a rebuke of his critics. And Campbell (2001) has found that Hearst's widely quoted comment to illustrator Frederic Remington that "you furnish the pictures, and I'll furnish the war" was simply the later invention of a former employee. Scholars of this period in press history warn it would be mistake to exaggerate the significance of the Yellow Press west of the Hudson River.

Trask (1981), Beede (1994), Pérez (1998), Bouvier (2001), Smythe (2003), and Schoonover (2003) are among recent historians demonstrating America's war with Spain was significantly more complicated than solely or even primarily the work of the Yellow Press. Their work on primary documents focusing on the ten-week war demonstrates that President William McKinley had a good deal more on his mind in steadfastly resisting public pressure to go to war with Spain. Trask, Beede, and Schoonover emphasize the global context in which the war took shape. Perez, through analysis of historical writings, is particularly good at deconstructing popular understandings of why the war occurred. McKinley was the last of the American presidents to have served in the Civil War and had no illusions about the deadly consequences of leading a nation into war. Furthermore, he had every reason to hope that Cuba's designation as an autonomous state on January 1, 1898 and the elevation of the moderate Praxedes Sagasta to the position of prime minister of Spain would allow a peaceful settlement of the crisis. This was a solution many in America's business community welcomed, if it stabilized Cuba as a reliable trading partner. McKinley's strategy was greatly complicated by the sinking of the *Maine* and the finding of a naval inquiry on March 28 that an external explosion had sunk the ship. It increasingly isolated McKinley and House Speaker Thomas Brackett Reed in their resistance to war. The April 19 Congressional resolution supporting Cuban independence, demanding Spanish withdrawal, and authorizing the use of military force quickly led to the very conflict McKinley could no longer politically resist.

Lynching and the Black Press

Ochs promised to print "all the news that's fit to print" (February 10, 1897), but like his white competitors, he paid little attention to the story of African American lynchings. Baker was one of the few white reporters to indict mob violence, which he did in the January and February 1905 issues of *McClure's Magazine*. He continued his series of articles in 1908 at the *American Magazine*, a publication he edited and partly owned. Baker noted that 1,678 African Americans were lynched between 1884 and 1900. Robert Sengstacke Abbott, founder of the nation's leading African American newspaper, the *Chicago Defender*, put the number at nearly twice that. His paper's front-page promise was, "If you see it in *The Defender* it's so." On January 9, 1915 Abbott noted, "Lynching is a form of punishment especially prepared for us," and he made it his job, and the job of the black press, to report the story. Ottley (1955), Hermans (1993), and Rice (2012) analyze Abbott's considerable influence inside and outside the black community.

Just as abolitionism was the cause that animated and united the black press in the mid-nineteenth century, the anti-lynching campaign united black newspapers later on in the century. Major studies of the black press during this period include Detwiler (1922), Dann (1971), Wolseley (1971), Bullock (1981), Daniel (1982), Suggs (1983, 1996). Detwiler's is the classic study. Dann examines the development of the black press in the context of American identity. Suggs provides regional studies of the black press in the South and Midwest. Leaders in the black press during this period include Chris J. Perry, who founded the *Philadelphia Tribune* in 1884, the oldest continuously published African American newspaper in the nation. Civil War veteran John H. Murphy launched the family-run *Afro-American* in Baltimore in 1892. The following year, Charles and Lilla Love established the *Texas Freeman*. It evolved into a voice for racial justice as the *Houston Informer*. George Stewart and Will Porter converted a two-page church bulletin in 1897 into the *Indianapolis Record*, where they were early supporters of the African American Council and its opposition to lynching.

Patricia Schechter has pointed out that Ida B. Wells's emphasis on faith and community made her a pre-eminent opponent of lynching during the Progressive Period (Schechter 2001). Later biographers (Davidson 2007; Giddings 2008; Bay 2009) have traced her birth as a Mississippi slave and the early loss of her parents and brother in a yellow fever epidemic. Wells supported five siblings by teaching school in Memphis, and writing on race for a black church weekly before starting her own paper, *Free Speech and Headlight*. The lynching of a friend by a white mob in 1889 launched her anti-lynching campaign. On May 27, 1892 a mob destroyed her offices after she published *Southern Horrors: Lynch Laws in All its Phases*, in which she insisted "a Winchester rifle should have a place of honor in every black home, and it should be used for that protection which the law refuses to give" (Wells and Duster 1892, 23–24). Wells received death threats, started packing a pistol, and continued publishing her pieces in the *New York Call* and the *Chicago Conservator*. She published her findings in *A Red Record* in 1895, co-founded the National Association of Colored Women the following year, and joined with W.E.B. Du Bois in 1909 to create the National Association for the Advancement of Colored People (NAACP). David Levering Lewis's updated 2009 biography of Du Bois carefully chronicles his use of journalism as a form of social activism. Du Bois edited the NAACP's monthly magazine, *The Crisis*. By the close of the Progressive Period in 1920, it had a circulation of 100,000 and pushed unsuccessfully for a federal ban on lynching. Lewis points out that Du Bois was not deterred and agitated his whole life through articles and speeches for the creation of a colorblind society.

On August 28, 1963, the day after Du Bois died, a quarter-million Americans marched to the Lincoln Memorial to hear the Rev. Martin Luther King, Jr.'s "I Have a Dream" speech. Before King spoke, a moment of silence was taken to honor the work of Du Bois. Du Bois was not the only

Progressive Era reformer who did not live to see the realization of his hopes for America. Writing to his friend Ray Stannard Baker on December 8, 1920, William Allen White looked back at the end of the Progressive Period with some disappointment. White and Baker had agitated for change in the belief that "righteousness exalted a nation," only to find the Great War had sapped the nation's appetite to continue the struggle against social injustice. "If anyone had told me ten years ago that our country would be what it is today," White wrote Baker, "I should have questioned his reason" (Johnson 1947, 213).

White's worry that progressive writers may not have done enough in the time available to bring about a more civil society should be balanced by what they did achieve. Theodore Roosevelt's Square Deal, Woodrow Wilson's New Freedom, Franklin Roosevelt's New Deal and Four Freedoms, John Kennedy's New Frontier, and Lyndon Johnson's Great Society all owed much to perhaps the greatest achievement of Progressive Era journalism. What came to be known as the "public square" and the "public interest" had been permanently widened to include a communitarian understanding that the country belonged to its people and journalism was in the business of assuring that government served to safeguard those rights. Theodore Roosevelt had seen as his lasting legacy his long partnership with John Muir, the nation's leading naturalist. Muir wrote more than 300 articles over several decades in *Century*, *Outlook*, *Atlantic Monthly*, *Harper's Weekly*, and other periodicals, advocating a wider recognition that the land belonged to the people and should be preserved as a national heirloom to successive generations. Like Frederick Olmsted before him, Muir insisted that urbanizing Americans desperately needed the transcendent and exultant to refresh their souls. He found in Roosevelt someone who shared his sensibility. Under Roosevelt, the Reclamation Act of 1902 doubled the number of national parks to ten, created eighteen national monuments, fifty-one federal bird sanctuaries, four national game refuges, and 230 million acres of national forests. Through the American Antiquities Act of 1906 Roosevelt and Muir were able to spare the Grand Canyon and Petrified Forest from commercial development. Over the next century, 378 wilderness areas were protected after designation that they belonged to the citizens of the United States in perpetuity.

When he laid the cornerstone of the Cannon House Office Building in Washington, DC on April 14, 1906, Theodore Roosevelt famously criticized those in the press who, like John Bunyan's Man with a Muck-rake in *Pilgrim's Progress*, seemed consumed with "the filth of the floor" instead of a "celestial crown." The name "muckraker" stuck, forever after a term implying venality and sensationalism in the press. Roosevelt later told his old friend Ray Stannard Baker what he had in mind were men like Hearst, who he thought portrayed themselves as reformers when they were instead self-promoters. In the same speech, the president celebrated the work of every writer involved in the "relentless exposure of and attack upon every evil man and every evil practice" that threatened the country and its people. Roosevelt saw "an urgent necessity for the sternest war" upon those threats to the public interest (Roosevelt 1910, 712–724). When he spoke at Osawatomie, Kansas on August 31, 1910, Roosevelt was out of office. In that speech he outlined a "New Nationalism" in remarks prepared by another old friend, William Allen White. This New Nationalism was rooted in a communitarian understanding by Progressive Era journalists that Roosevelt himself had labored to create. "Of all the questions that can come before this nation," Roosevelt told his listeners, "short of the actual preservation of its existence, there is none which compares in importance with the great central task of leaving this land even a better land for our descendants than it is for us, and training them into a better race to inhabit the land and pass it on." Our communitarian obligation to one another, Roosevelt insisted, was everyone's "patriotic duty of insuring the safety and continuance of the nation" (www.whitehouse.gov/blog/2011/12/06/archives-president-teddy-roosevelts-new-nationalism-speech).

That was an exercise in democratic purpose that Progressive Era journalists would have warmly approved. What united much of their best work was a widely shared certainty that society has obligations to serve the least of us, and that obligation sprang from a conviction that America's democratic experiment was rooted in the dignity of men and women as God-breathed creatures. Their role was to serve these citizens with the information needed to make democracy and self-governance more possible. McClure put it simply: journalism's job was "to fight for those unable to defend themselves" so that government might "protect those who cannot protect themselves" (Evensen 1989, 12). Put another way: it was the affirmative belief of Progressive Era journalists that citizens and governments would do their jobs when journalism did its own.

References

Applegate, Edd. 1997. *Journalistic Advocates and Muckrakers: Three Centuries of Crusading Writers*. Jefferson, NC: McFarland.

Arthur, Anthony. 2006. *Radical Innocent: Upton Sinclair*. New York: Random House.

Baker, Ray Stannard. 1903. "The Right to Work: The Story of the Non-striking Miners." *McClure's Magazine* 20: 323–335.

—. 1908. *Following the Color Line: An Account of Negro Citizenship in the American Democracy*. New York: Doubleday, Page.

—. 1909. "The Spiritual Unrest: The Case Against Trinity Church." *American Magazine* 68: 3–16.

Baldasty, Gerald E. 1992. *The Commercialization of News in the Nineteenth Century*. Madison: University of Wisconsin Press.

Bay, Mia. 2009. *To Tell the Truth Freely: The Life of Ida B. Wells*. New York: Hill & Wang.

Beede, Benjamin R. 1994. *The War of 1898 and U.S. Interventions, 1898–1934*. New York: Garland.

Bloodworth, William A., Jr. 1977. *Upton Sinclair*. Boston, MA: Twayne.

Bloom, Harold. 2002. *Upton Sinclair's The Jungle*. Philadelphia, PA: Chelsea House.

Bly, Nellie. 1887. *Ten Days in a Mad-house*. New York: Ian L. Munro.

Bouvier, Virginia Marie. 2001. *Whose America? The War of 1898 and the Battles to Define the Nation*. Westport, CT: Praeger.

Brady, Kathleen. 1984. *Ida Tarbell: Portrait of a Muckraker*. New York: Seaview/Putnam.

Bridges, Lamar W. 1984. "George Kibbe Turner of *McClure's Magazine*." *Journalism Quarterly* 61: 178–182.

Bullock, Penelope L. 1981. *The Afro-American Periodical Press, 1838–1909*. Baton Rouge: Louisiana State University Press.

Cahan, Abraham. 1969. *The Education of Abraham Cahan*. Philadelphia, PA: Jewish Publication Society of America.

Campbell, W. Joseph. 2006. *The Year That Defined American Journalism: 1897 and the Clash of Paradigms*. New York: Routledge.

Chamberlain, John. 1932. *Farewell to Reform: Being a History of the Rise, Life, and Decay of the Progressive Mind*. New York: Liveright.

Crunden, Robert M. 1982. *Ministers of Reform: The Progressive Achievement in American Civilization, 1889–1920*. New York: Basic Books.

Dann, Martin E. 1971. *The Black Press, 1827–1890: The Quest for National Identity*. New York: Putnam.

Davidson, James West. 2007. *"They Say": Ida B. Wells and the Reconstruction of Race*. New York: Oxford University Press.

Detwiler, Frederick G. 1922. *The Negro Press in the United States*. Chicago: University of Chicago Press.

Dix, Morgan. 1895. *Report as to the Sanitary Condition of the Tenements of Trinity Church and Other Documents*. New York: Evening Post Job Printing House.

Erickson, Emily. 2008. "The Press and a New America, 1865–1900." In *The Age of Mass Communication*, ed. David Sloan, 217–234. Northport, AL: Vision Press.

Evensen, Bruce J. 1989. "The Evangelical Origins of the Muckrakers." *American Journalism* 6: 5–29.

—. 2008. "Dwight Lyman Moody." In *Encyclopedia of American Journalism*, ed. Stephen L. Vaughn, Bruce J. Evensen, and James Landers, 304–305. New York: Routledge.

Faulkner, Harold Underwood. 1931. *The Quest for Social Justice, 1898–1914*. New York: Macmillan.

Filler, Louis. 1961. *Crusaders for American Liberalism*. Yellow Springs, OH: Antioch Press.

—. 1966. *The Unknown Edwin Markham: His Mystery and Significance*. Yellow Springs, OH: Antioch Press.

Gentzkow, Matthew, Jesse Shapiro, and Michael Sinkinson. 2012. *Competition and Ideological Diversity: Historical Evidence from U.S. Newspapers*. Cambridge, MA: National Bureau of Economic Research.

Giddings, Paula. 2008. *Ida, a Sword among Lions: Ida B. Wells and the Campaign against Lynching*. New York: Amistad.

Gifford, Carolyn DeSwarte and Amy R. Slagell, eds. 2007. *Let Something Good Be Said: Speeches and Writings of Frances E. Willard*. Urbana: University of Illinois.

Goldman, Eric. 1952. *Rendezvous with Destiny: A History of Modern American Reform*. New York: Knopf.

Green, Norma, Stephen Lacy, and Jean Folkerts. 1989. "Chicago Journalists at the Turn of the Century: Bohemians All?" *Journalism Quarterly* 66: 813–821.

Grenier, Judson. 1960. "Muckraking and Muckrakers: An Historical Definition." *Journalism Quarterly* 37: 552–558.

Hard, William. 1908. "De Kid Wot Works at Night." *Everybody's Magazine* 18: 25–37.

Harris, Leon. 1975. *Upton Sinclair, American Rebel*. New York: Thomas Y. Crowell.

Hays, Samuel P. 1964. "The Politics of Reform in Municipal Government in the Progressive Era." *Pacific Northwest Quarterly* 55: 157–169.

Health Department of the City of New York, Appellant, v. The Rector, Church Wardens and Vestrymen of Trinity Church, Argued January 15, 1895, Decided February 26, 1895, 145 N. Y. 32. New York Supplement. New York: West Publishing, 1895, 120.

Hermans, Tessa. 1993. "Robert Abbott's *Defender*: The Strongest Weapon." *Media History Digest* 13: 38–42, 64.

Hofstadter, Richard. 1955. *The Age of Reform: From Bryan to F.D.R.* New York: Knopf.

Hopkins, Mary Alden. 1914. "Some Working People." *Child Labor Bulletin* 3: 47–49.

Howe, Irving. 1976. *World of Our Fathers*. New York: Harcourt Brace Jovanovich.

Hunter, Robert. 1904. *Poverty*. New York: Macmillan.

Jensen, Carl. 2000. *Stories That Changed America: Muckrakers of the 20th Century*. New York: Seven Stories.

Johnson, Walter. 1947. *Selected Letters of William Allen White, 1899–1943*. New York: Henry Holt.

Kates, James. 1995. "A 'Square Deal' for a 'Primitive Rebel': Alfred E. Roese and the Battle of Cameron Dam, 1904–1910." *Wisconsin Magazine of History* 79: 83–108.

Kolko, Gabriel. 1963. *The Triumph of Conservatism: A Reinterpretation of American History, 1910–1916*. New York: Free Press of Glencoe.

Kroeger, Brooke. 1994. *Nellie Bly: Daredevil, Reporter, Feminist*. New York: Times Books.

Lipsky, Seth. 2013. *The Rise of Abraham Cahan*. New York: Nextbook/Schocken.

Markham, Edwin. 1907. "The Hoe-Man in the Making: The Sweat-Shop Inferno." *Cosmopolitan* 41: 327–333.

Markham, Edwin, Ben B. Lindsey, and George Creel. 1914. *Children in Bondage: A Complete and Careful Presentation of the Anxious Problem of Child Labor—its Causes, its Crimes, and its Cure*. New York: Hearst's International Library.

McCormick, Richard L. 1981. "The Discovery that Business Corrupts: A Reappraisal of the Origins of Progressivism." *American Historical Review* 86: 247–274.

Miraldi, Robert. 2000. *The Muckrakers: Evangelical Crusaders*. Westport, CT: Praeger.

—. 2003. *The Pen Is Mightier: The Muckraking Life of Charles Edward Russell*. New York: Palgrave Macmillan.

Nord, David Paul. 1984. "The Business Values of American Newspapers: The 19th Century Watershed in Chicago." *Journalism Quarterly* 61: 265–273.

Ottley, Roi. 1955. *The Lonely Warrior: The Life and Times of Robert S. Abbott*. Chicago: Henry Regnery.

Pérez, Louis A., Jr. 1998. *The War of 1898: The United States and Cuba in History and Historiography*. Chapel Hill: University of North Carolina Press.

Regier, Cornelius C. 1932. *The Era of the Muckrakers*. Chapel Hill: University of North Carolina Press.
Rice, Myiti Sengstacke. 2012. *Chicago Defender*. Charleston, SC: Arcadia Publishing.
Riis, Jacob. 1890. *How the Other Half Lives: Studies Among the Tenements of New York*. New York: Scribners.
Rischin, Moses. 1962. *The Promised City: New York Jews, 1870–1914*. Cambridge, MA: Harvard University Press.
—. 1985. *Grandma Never Lived in America: The New Journalism of Abraham Cahan*. Bloomington: Indiana University Press.
Rittenhouse, Mignon. 1956. *The Amazing Nellie Bly*. New York: Dutton.
Roosevelt, Theodore. 1901. "Reform Through Social Work: Some Forces That Tell for Decency in New York City." *McClure's Magazine* 16: 448–454.
—.1910. *Presidential Addresses and State Papers*. Vol. 5. New York: Review of Reviews.
Ruotsila, Markku. 2006. *John Spargo and American Socialism*. New York: Macmillan.
Rutenbeck, Jeffrey B. 1995. "Newspaper Trends in the 1870s: Proliferation, Popularization, and Political Independence." *Journalism & Mass Communication Quarterly* 72: 361–375.
Sampsell-Willman, Kate. 2009. *Lewis Hine as Social Critic*. Jackson: University Press of Mississippi.
Sanders, Ronald. 1969. *The Downtown Jews: Portrait of an Immigrant Generation*. New York: Harper & Row.
Schechter, Patricia A. 2001. *Ida B. Wells-Barnett and American Reform, 1880–1930*. Chapel Hill: University of North Carolina Press.
Schoonover, Thomas David. 2003. *Uncle Sam's War of 1898 and the Origins of Globalization*. Lexington: University Press of Kentucky.
Schultz, Stanley K. 1965. "The Morality of Politics: The Muckrakers' Vision of Democracy." *Journal of American History* 52: 527–547.
Serrin, Judith and William Serrin. 2002. *Muckraking! The Journalism That Changed America*. New York: New Press.
Sinclair, Upton. 1906. *The Jungle*. New York: Doubleday, Page.
Smythe, Ted Curtis. 1980. "The Reporter, 1880–1900: Working Conditions and Their Influence on the News." *Journalism History* 7: 1–10.
—. 2003. *The Gilded Age Press, 1865–1900*. Westport, CT: Praeger.
Sorin, Gerald. 1985. *The Prophetic Minority: American Jewish Immigration Radicals, 1880–1920*. Bloomington: Indiana University Press.
Spargo, John. 1906. *The Bitter Cry of the Children*. New York: Macmillan.
Steffens, Lincoln. 1903. "The Shame of Minneapolis: The Rescue and Redemption of a City That Was Sold Out." *McClure's Magazine* 20: 227–239.
—. 1931. *The Autobiography of Lincoln Steffens*. New York: Harcourt, Brace.
Stewart, Jane Agnes. 1906. *The Frances Willard Book*. Philadelphia, PA: Current Syndicate.
Stidger, William L. 1933. *Edwin Markham*. New York: Abingdon Press.
Suggs, Henry Lewis. 1983. *The Black Press in the South, 1865–1979*. Westport, CT: Greenwood Press.
—. 1996. *The Black Press in the Middle West, 1865–1985*. Westport, CT: Greenwood Press.
Tarbell, Ida. 1939. *All in the Day's Work*. New York: Macmillan.
Thelen, David P. 1970. "Social Tensions and the Origins of Progressivism." *Journal of American History* 56: 323–341.
Tomkins, Mary E. 1974. *Ida M. Tarbell*. New York: Twayne.
Trask, David F. 1981. *The War with Spain in 1898*. New York: Macmillan.
Turner, George Kibbe. 1907. "The City of Chicago: A Study of the Great Immoralities." *McClure's Magazine* 28: 575–592.
—. 1909a. "Tammany's Control of New York by Professional Criminals: A Study of a New Period of Decadence in the Popular Government of Great Cities." *McClure's Magazine* 33: 117–134.
—. 1909b. "The Daughters of the Poor: A Plain Story of the Development of New York City as a Leading Center of the White Slave Trade of the World Under Tammany Hall." *McClure's Magazine*, 34: 45–61.
Van Vorst, Bessie McGinnis. 1908. *The Cry of the Children: A Study of Child-Labor*. New York: Moffat, Yard.
—, and Marie Van Vorst. 1903. *The Woman Who Toils: Being the Experiences of Two Ladies as Factory Girls*. New York: Doubleday, Page.
Weinberg, Arthur and Lila Weinberg. 1961. *The Muckrakers: The Era in Journalism That Moved America to Reform*. New York: Simon & Schuster.
Wells, Ida. B. and Alfreda M. Duster. 1892. *Southern Horrors: Lynch Laws in All Its Phases*. New York: New York Age.
White, William Allen. 1925. *Some Cycles of Cathay*. Chapel Hill: University of North Carolina Press.
Wiebe, Robert H. 1962. *Businessmen and Reform: A Study of the Progressive Movement*. Cambridge, MA: Harvard University Press.
Wiener, Gary. 2008. *Workers' Rights in Upton Sinclair's The Jungle*. Detroit, MI: Greenhaven Press/Gale.
Willard, Frances. 1889. *Glimpses of Fifty Years: The Autobiography of an American Woman*. Chicago: H.J. Smith.
Wilson, Harold. 1970. *McClure's Magazine and the Muckrakers*. Princeton, NJ: Princeton University Press.
Winter, Ella and Granville Hicks, ed. 1938. *The Letters of Lincoln Steffens*. Vol. 2. New York: Harcourt, Brace.
Wolseley, Roland E. 1971. *The Black Press, U.S.A.* Ames: Iowa State University Press.
Yoder, Jon A. 1975. *Upton Sinclair*. New York: Frederick Ungar.

Further Reading

Baldasty, Gerald E. and Jeffrey Rutenbeck. 1988. "Money, Politics, and Newspapers: The Business Environment of Press Partisanship in the Late 19th Century." *Journalism History*, 15: 60–69.
Berger, Meyer. 1951. *The Story of the New York Times: The First Hundred Years, 1851–1951*. New York: Simon & Schuster.
Brewer, George D. 1910. *The Fighting Editor, or, Warren and the Appeal*. Girard, KS: George D. Brewer.
Campbell, W. Joseph. 2001. *Yellow Journalism: Puncturing the Myths, Defining the Legacies*. Westport, CT: Praeger.
Daniels, Walter. 1982. *Black Journals of the United States*. Westport, CT: Greenwood.
Davis, Elmer. 1921. *History of the New York Times, 1851–1921*. New York: New York Times.

Evensen, Bruce J. 1992. "Abraham Cahan." In *Literary Journalism: A Research Guide to an Emerging Genre*, ed. Thomas B. Connery, 91–100. Westport, CT: Greenwood Press.

—. 2008. "The Media and Reform, 1900–1917." In *The Age of Mass Communication*, ed. Wm. David Sloan, 317–328. Northport, AL: Vision Press.

—. 2005. "Progressivism, Muckraking, and Objectivity." In *Fair & Balanced: A History of Journalistic Objectivity*, ed. Steven R. Knowlton and Karen L. Freeman, 136–148. Northport, AL: Vision Press.

Faber, Doris. 1996. *Printer's Devil to Publisher: Adolph S. Ochs of the New York Times.* Hensonville, NY: Black Dome.

Fah, Alice. 2011. *Out on Assignment: Newspaper Women and the Making of Modern Public Space.* Chapel Hill: University of North Carolina Press.

Fishbein, Leslie. 1982. *Rebels in Bohemia: The Radicals of the Masses, 1911–1917.* Chapel Hill: University of North Carolina Press.

Glassgold, Peter, ed. 2001. *Anarchy! An Anthology of Emma Goldman's Mother Earth.* Washington, DC: Counterpoint.

Goodwin, Doris Kearns. 2013. *The Bully Pulpit: Theodore Roosevelt, William Howard Taft, and the Golden Age of Journalism.* New York: Simon & Schuster.

Johnson, Gerald W. 1946. *An Honorable Titan: A Biographical Study of Adolph S. Ochs.* New York: Harper.

La Forte, Robert S. 1966. "Theodore Roosevelt's Osawatomie Speech." *Kansas Historical Society* 32: 187–200.

Lewis, David Levering. 2009. *W.E.B. Du Bois: a Biography.* New York: Henry Holt.

Lyon, Peter. 1963. *Success Story: The Life and Times of S. S. McClure.* New York: Scribners.

McClure, S.S., and Willa Cather. 1914. *My Autobiography.* New York: Frederick A. Stokes.

Mattson, Kevin. 2006. *Upton Sinclair and the Other American Century.* New York: John Wiley& Sons.

Nord, David Paul. 1985. "The Public Community: The Urbanization of Journalism in Chicago." *Journal of Urban History*, 11: 411–442.

Seixas, Peter. 1987. "Lewis Hine: From 'Social' to 'Interpretative' Photographer." *American Quarterly Review*, 39: 381–409.

Stein, Harry H. 1991. "American Muckraking of Technology since 1900." *Journalism Quarterly*, 67: 401–409.

Stolberg, Benjamin. 1926. "The Man behind the Times." *Atlantic Monthly* 138: 721–730.

Tarbell, Ida. 1904. *The History of the Standard Oil Company.* New York: McClure, Phillips.

Thelen, David P. 1976. *Robert M. La Follette and the Insurgent Spirit.* Boston: Little, Brown.

Tifft, Susan E. and Alex S. Jones. 1999. *The Trust: The Private and Powerful Family behind the New York Times.* Boston: Little, Brown.

Wells, Ida B. 1970. *Crusade for Justice: The Autobiography of Ida B. Wells.* Chicago: University of Chicago.

Chapter Fifteen

Popular Culture

Julia Guarneri

In the late 1970s and the 1980s, when a critical mass of historians began taking popular culture seriously, they wrote prodigiously about the Gilded Age and Progressive Era. Thanks to Stuart Ewen's *Captains of Consciousness* (1976), Lawrence Levine's *Black Culture and Black Consciousness* (1977), John Kasson's *Amusing the Million* (1978), Lewis Erenberg's *Steppin' Out* (1981), Roy Rosenzweig's *Eight Hours for What We Will* (1983), Robert Rydell's *All the World's a Fair* (1984), Kathy Peiss's *Cheap Amusements* (1986), Elliott Gorn's *The Manly Art* (1986), and Michael Denning's *Mechanic Accents* (1987), studies of the Gilded Age and Progressive era dominated the field of popular culture. This chapter opens by investigating the reasons why historians suddenly took such an interest in popular culture, and in particular the popular culture of the late nineteenth and early twentieth centuries. The scholars of the 1970s and 1980s carved out pathways and precipitated debates that decisively shaped the field's future, and which influenced the study of the popular culture of other periods as well.

According to both European and American critics of the era following World War II, commercialization and mass production had corrupted—even ruined—culture. In its most harmless form, they said, mass culture flattened and cheapened experience. At its worst, it manipulated and deceived its audiences. They said that when mass culture adopted elements of high culture, as in the skilled draftsmanship of magazine cover illustrations, the result was not art but "kitsch," insipid and soulless. Whether historians and American Studies scholars encountered these attitudes in the writings of Theodore Adorno, Max Horkheimer, Herbert Marcuse, Clement Greenberg, or Dwight MacDonald, those interested in culture often steered clear of these discredited forms. The majority of midcentury cultural historians (mostly located in American Studies departments) focused almost exclusively on literature, and pieced together interpretations of American character with passages from Walt Whitman, Hamlin Garland, or Mark Twain.

When scholars of this generation considered popular sources, they tended to enlist them in stories of American ingenuity and distinctiveness. Henry Nash Smith (1950) cited Buffalo Bill's Wild West Show as one more example of how the westward "pull of open land" shaped the national character. David Potter (1954) integrated advertising into his study of the cultural impact of American "economic abundance." Daniel Boorstin, the midcentury scholar most immersed in and delighted by popular culture, used it to tell a triumphant national story of invention, prosperity, and growth in *The Americans: The Democratic Experience* (1973)—even as he expressed some ambivalence along the way.

Narratives of Manipulation and Resistance

The generation of scholars that followed refused to frame their studies in terms of any national project or narrative of progress. The trajectory of westward expansion and economic growth through consumption seemed, by the 1970s, to have led to an ugly, even shameful, place. Many historians who had witnessed or participated in the Civil Rights or antiwar movements abandoned the study of dominant values and instead tried to uncover the autonomy, wisdom, and beauty in working people's lives. In *Black Culture and Black Consciousness*, for example, Lawrence Levine treated the blues as a varied and subtle form that artfully communicated individual realities but also collective feeling. Historians took an interest in culture as a means through which people formed and expressed alternatives to the dominant values of their time. In *Eight Hours for What We Will*, Roy Rosenzweig looked at the saloons and Fourth of July

A Companion to the Gilded Age and Progressive Era, First Edition. Edited by Christopher McKnight Nichols and Nancy C. Unger.
© 2017 John Wiley & Sons, Inc. Published 2017 by John Wiley & Sons, Inc.

celebrations of Worcester, Massachusetts, and found that at night and on holidays, workers rebuilt the ethic of solidarity and mutuality that their workplaces broke down during the day. Many scholars also reacted against American Studies' 1950s and 1960s focus on "high" culture. Inspired in part by shifts taking place in England, between Raymond Williams declaring that "Culture is Ordinary" (1958) and E.P. Thompson celebrating *The Making of the English Working Class* (1963), US historians began writing about culture as something made, enjoyed, and used not just by poets and novelists, but by the uneducated and the poor.

It makes sense that these scholars, committed to recuperating the culture of the working class, focused on the Gilded Age and Progressive Era. They needed an age of dramatic distinctions between the powerless and the powerful, and the era of robber barons, sharecropping, and industrial labor fit the bill. The Gilded Age and Progressive Era also gave historians an opportunity to study the transition from what they saw as local, relatively autonomous cultures—what Robert Wiebe called "island communities" (1967)—to more commercialized forms. Levine, Rosenzweig, and also Francis Couvares, in *The Remaking of Pittsburgh* (1984), did not celebrate these patterns of commercialization, but they did insist that their subjects were not simply being manipulated by the new "mass" culture. Couvares and Rosenzweig both recognized that young immigrant women used amusement parks and theaters to escape from their paternalistic households for an afternoon. Rosenzweig and also Robert Sklar, in *Movie-Made America* (1977), characterized nickelodeons as spaces truly expressive of working-class culture, where audiences could come and go as they pleased, share snacks, shout at the screen, and celebrate movie heroes' triumphs with stomps and whistles. In his discussion of blues records, Levine commented, "We have become so accustomed to what appears to be the imposition of culture upon passive people by modern media that is it difficult to perceive variations in the pattern. In the case of blues at least … the imposition of tastes and standards was by no means a one-way process" (Rosenzweig 1985, 228). Even within a commercializing, homogenizing culture, these historians were determined to find agency and meaning.

Levine, Rosenzweig, and Couvares all shared sympathies with the social and labor historians of their generation, and their findings generally harmonized with those historians' narratives of struggle and resistance. As the 1980s progressed, though, cultural historians' research began to tell new kinds of stories. Several scholars found social and labor historians' focus on political and cultural resistance to be too doctrinaire, a wishful view of actual working-class lives. "I will state this baldly," wrote Elliott Gorn in the introduction to *The Manly Art*, his history of prizefighting. "Most workers did not spend their free time reading the *Rights of Man*, toasting Tom Paine, and struggling to resist oppression. Probably more hours were consumed at cockfights than at union meetings during the nineteenth century" (Gorn 1986: 13). Gorn studied leisure as a means of understanding working-class lives, but he was also determined to see every facet of that leisure—not just the parts that could be interpreted as resistance. He found boxing to be a method by which ethnic communities created their own heroes, but he also noticed that by the late nineteenth century, it had become white-collar workers' antidote to their docile, paper-pushing office jobs.

Kathy Peiss and Michael Denning, rather than telling stories of autonomous culture commercialized, made working-class commercial culture their central subject. Denning's study of the dime novels of the mid- and late-nineteenth century explained how "fiction factories" employed multiple authors to write stories about popular fictional characters such as Frank Merriwell, or even to write under fictional authors' names in a designated style. But Denning did not see this system as a reason to dismiss dime novels' content, and offered up subversive interpretations of their plots. Peiss, meanwhile, considered commercial leisure—fashion, dance halls, amusement parks—as a way for working women to define themselves outside of their families, to make their own choices and pursue their own pleasures.

A different set of scholars working at the same time—the late 1970s and 1980s—found almost nothing to celebrate in the popular culture they chose to study. To them popular culture seemed a means by which elite Americans articulated, packaged, and sold their ideology to the rest of the population. Stuart Ewen, in *Captains of Consciousness*, portrayed advertisers as expert psychological manipulators, intent on creating a dependable mass of consumers. Robert Rydell's *All the World's a Fair* described expositions designed to convince visitors that businessmen, manufacturers, and city planners could lead the nation to a dazzling future, one that depended on constant consumption and imperial expansion. Ewen and Rydell focused on the Gilded Age and Progressive Era for some of the same reasons that Rosenzweig and Levine did: it was a moment in which elites were consolidating their power, making it easy for historians to distinguish between mainstream and alternative, oppressors and oppressed. World's fair displays of colonized populations such as Filipinos or Native Americans could not have been more explicit about racial hierarchy and imperial might. Yet by focusing on elites' successful construction of a consumer economy and of an economic and political empire, Ewen and Rydell portrayed popular culture as nothing but a tool of the oppressors.

These historians did not butt heads with their popular culture-celebrating counterparts. After all, no one was making the counterargument that in fact world's fairs or cornflake advertisements expressed genuine working-class desires. Yet they did make up two different and almost-clashing schools of thought. Should popular culture be studied as a bastion of authenticity or a force of manipulation?

From American Exceptionalism to Transatlantic Modernity

A handful of scholars never took sides in this debate, since their interest in the popular culture of the Gilded Age and Progressive Era did not seem to stem from any dissection of power or struggle, but rather from questions about what it meant to be modern. Warren Susman, Gunther Barth, and John Kasson spoke explicitly about the questions that plagued them in the present day. "If the culture of abundance has become manipulative, coercive, vulgar, and intolerable in all the ways these critics would have it, why did this happen?" asked Susman in the introduction to his book of collected essays, *Culture as History*. "Were there alternatives?" (Susman 1985, xxix–xxx). In parallel, Kasson wondered whether popular and mass culture had begun to undermine democracy; Barth (1980) asked if the city was still a viable form of living. They then cast these questions backward in time, revisiting the moment when "the modern"—the cluster of behaviors and values ushered in by mechanization and urbanization—still held utopian promise. Although none of these writers mention it, it is worth noting that their books arrived right at the moment that scholars in English and Cultural Studies were defining and analyzing "postmodernism"—a word that had been floating around in architecture circles since the 1960s—as a term for defining their own era. The word raised an historical question that these scholars began to answer. If Americans were now living in the postmodern era, what characterized the modern era that came before? If modernity had an end, when was its beginning, and what did the beginning look like?

John Kasson's *Amusing the Million* grappled with these questions while acknowledging popular culture's ability to both liberate and manipulate. Kasson clearly shared 1970s social historians' desire to recover the experiences of ordinary people. In the front and end pieces of his book, he zoomed in on details of larger photographs of Coney Island crowds on the beach: a young woman leaning her elbow on her date's shoulder, a mother reclining in the sand with her child, an overdressed teenage boy squinting into the sun. Kasson seems to want his readers to recognize these people, to imagine what they were feeling in that moment. Yet he also concludes that for all of the joys Coney Island promised, it offered "fun" of a very managed, manufactured variety. "Dispensing standardized amusement," writes Kasson of Coney Island, "it demanded standardized responses. Beneath the air of liberation, its pressures were profoundly conformist, its means fundamentally manipulative" (Kasson 1978, 105).

Alan Trachtenberg, while interested in similar questions about the modern, seemed to tell a story not of fleeting promise and possibility, but of slow and inexorable defeat. He tracked the reshaping of "traditional culture" into more tightly organized, corporate-led spheres, from time zones to department stores. Where Kasson's questions about the modern led him to fuse the "democratic" and "domineering" interpretations of popular culture, Trachtenberg saw only domination. Yet his 1982 *The Incorporation of America* also provided one of the most wide-ranging and evocative portraits of the Gilded Age and Progressive Era in existence, and did it by engaging with questions that neo-Romantic and Weimar German writers had asked of early twentieth-century Europe. Writers such as Walter Benjamin, Siegfried Kracauer, and Georg Simmel had cemented certain qualities as "modern": the mediated nature of entertainment, the fraught presentation of self, the avalanche of stimuli on the city streets. Trachtenberg transposed and narrated these qualities into American history.

Trachtenberg's mirroring of European concerns points to a larger shift underway in these studies of the modern. Trachtenberg, Barth, Susman, and Kasson still told pointedly national stories. Yet they were not writing—as had the "myth and symbol" school—about what made Americans American. They wanted to see how Americans had made the transition to modernity, a transition that other peoples in other nations had clearly made as well. Because scholars such as Henry Nash Smith and Daniel Boorstin were so invested in narratives of national distinctiveness, partly for Cold War reasons, they turned instead to what seemed most distinctively American, whether that meant westward expansion or the Broadway musical. Only by the late 1970s and early 1980s did American Studies scholars prove ready to consider historical conditions—such as modernity—that the United States so obviously shared with other nations.

These books about "the modern" were already complicating the binary within the field between a popular culture that was truly "of the people" and a mass culture that only manipulated and cheated its consumers. A number of other developments in the study of popular culture—nearly all coming from scholars of the Gilded Age and Progressive Era—would combine to collapse that binary altogether by the early 1990s.

Ideology and Utopia in American Culture

Ideas from cultural studies began to filter into the US conversation. Fredric Jameson's "Reification and Utopia in Mass Culture" (1979) and Stuart Hall's essay "Notes on Deconstructing the Popular" (1981) together argued that popular culture did not solely exist to contain and control working people's lives, nor solely for those working people to resist domination. Instead, they saw traces of hierarchy *and* of utopian promise in all forms of popular culture. Trumpeted in US history circles by Michael Denning and Robin D.G. Kelley, Jameson's and Hall's ideas resonated among historians who had not wanted to choose between celebrating and critiquing popular culture. In 1985, T.J. Jackson Lears gave Antonio Gramsci's concept of cultural hegemony a formal debut in the *American Historical Review*. Though scholars would argue over exactly how accurately Lears had translated the spirit of the idea, Lears lent a name and a theory to the notion that the powerful people and dominant mores of any society exerted influence on even its most marginalized or resistant populations. A handful of Gilded Age and Progressive Era historians—mostly those rooted in social or labor history and looking for populist popular culture—were already articulating such ideas. Kathy Peiss had celebrated working women's self-expression in the spaces of popular culture, but was also frank about the fact that their modes of dancing and dating reproduced and reinforced many of the gender norms of their era. Elizabeth and Stuart Ewen (1982) found that silent movies both acknowledged the indignities and injustices of poverty, and taught their poor audiences to dream of joining—rather than rebelling against—the upper class.

A roundtable on popular culture in the 1992 *American Historical Review* dramatized the generational shift. Lawrence Levine, in the centerpiece article, described the skepticism he had encountered when using popular culture sources, and he made a case for their value. Yet he also argued that historians could treat commercial popular culture as what he called "folk" culture, culture that expressed the genuine emotions and desires of everyday people. The two Americanist respondents, T.J. Jackson Lears (1992) and Robin D.G. Kelley (1992), made it clear that they found Levine's logic and his language outmoded. They saw no need for Levine to defend his choice to study popular culture, for his books (alongside many others published in the 1970s and 1980s) had proven how rich and rewarding those sources could be. Yet, stated Lears and Kelley, it would be irresponsible to ignore the unequal power dynamic between producers and audience.

Even the very notion of "folk culture," Kelley argued, was misguided. Embedded in the term was the notion that the "folk"—be they working-class or poor, black or white—made culture in more authentic, spontaneous, and instinctive (and, implicitly, less sophisticated or self-aware) ways than other groups. This search for an authentic "folk," said Kelley, was destined for failure, since no group of people lay untouched by structures of power or uninfluenced by a dominant culture. In fact, many cultural products once taken as "authentic" came into being only through imitation, recycling, and carefully crafted self-presentation: the cakewalk, ragtime music, country western yodeling (Ross 1989, 68). Levine had not been alone in his use of the term "folk"; Elliott Gorn referred to early prizefighting as folk culture, and Alan Trachtenberg and Warren Susman used the phrase "traditional culture," which portrayed that culture as unauthored and timeless. But this 1992 exchange made it clear that for a rising generation of scholars of popular culture, there was no unsullied "folk culture," no timeless tradition. Ideology was everywhere.

At this juncture, the field of popular culture history, once so densely concentrated in the Gilded Age and Progressive Era, began to broaden. Allowing for the coexistence of ideology and utopia, historians found they could make meaning out of the popular culture of any era—not just the Gilded Age and Progressive Era in which, the old story went, "folk" culture gradually succumbed to "mass" culture, and in which all the promises of the modern flared up and flamed out. Scholars who had once looked for clear-cut "power" (world's fairs, advertisers) or "resistance" (rounds of whiskey at the saloon, ballads sung on the front porch) began to acknowledge that everyone could, and did, participate in systems of oppression. This set them free to dissect the entertainments of other eras. Labor-celebrating scholars of the 1970s had been hard-pressed to explain antebellum white workers' love of minstrelsy, for example, and mostly avoided the topic: by the 1990s scholars dissected minstrelsy's role in the construction of whiteness, blackness, and the working class with acuity (Saxton 1990; Roediger 1991; Lott 1993). When historians decided that mass culture could in fact be put to varied and meaningful uses by everyday people, they began studying the twentieth-century forms, such as television sitcoms, top-40 radio, and label-recorded popular music, which earlier scholars had found too manufactured.

Historians still turned out pathbreaking works on Gilded Age and Progressive Era culture, to be sure. And they benefited from the widespread acceptance of popular culture as a legitimate historical source, which rendered them freer to incorporate it into all kinds of studies. Gail Bederman's *Manliness and Civilization* (1995) wove the Tarzan novels, the Boy Scouts, and the Jim Jeffries/Jack Johnson boxing match in among intellectual and political studies of G. Stanley Hall, Ida B. Wells, and Charlotte Perkins Gilman. In *Gay New York* (1994), George Chauncey looked at cabarets and fashion alongside policing tactics and court decisions. In *To 'Joy My Freedom* (1998), Tera Hunter investigated Atlanta dance halls alongside washerwomen's strikes, mutual aid societies, and streetcar boycotts to show how Atlanta's black working women negotiated the terms of their work and insisted on maintaining the rights to their own bodies. It was a sign of the triumph of cultural history that popular culture sources started popping up everywhere.

Consumer Culture in the Gilded Age and Progressive Era

In a 1990 essay "The End of Mass Culture," Michael Denning summarized the new normal for scholars of popular culture. The ideas of Stuart Hall and of Frederic Jameson had become common currency among these scholars. Power and resistance, ideology and utopia—historians expected to find these in any form of cultural expression. Denning explained the quick absorption of these ideas using the puzzling events that scholars saw unfolding around them in the 1980s. Ronald Reagan seemed to be rigging the economy against the working class, yet millions of working-class voters adored him. Meanwhile, although feminists had revealed the sexism embedded in women's fashion, cosmetic advertisements, and mainstream film, all of these institutions continued to thrive. Only a theory of culture that recognized the attraction of Reagan's optimistic nationalism or the fantasy of a Maybelline ad could explain these phenomena, which otherwise looked like straight manipulation.

This theory proved equally useful in explaining the consumer culture of the turn of the century. There was an explosion of studies of advertising and consumer culture in the 1990s: Jackson Lears's *Fables of Abundance* (1994), William Leach's *Land of Desire* (1993), Jennifer Scanlon's *Inarticulate Longings* (1995), Richard Ohmann's *Selling Culture* (1996), Elizabeth Gruber Garvey's *The Adman in the Parlor* (1996), and Pamela Walker Laird's *Advertising Progress* (1998). The best of them captured the allure of this new culture even as they made clear how it fell far short of its promises. This body of work on consumer culture outlined a distinctive phenomenon of the Gilded Age and Progressive Era. For the first time, popular culture became a sphere in which businessmen—more than the church, the family, or the trade union—constructed appealing visions of the good life and won consumers over to their vision. Newly possessed of the ability to manufacture a seemingly bottomless supply of goods, merchants no longer tried merely to capture existing markets by making the best soap or the cheapest cloth available. Instead, they hired advertisers to create markets where none had existed before. As the *Thompson Red Book on Advertising* stated in 1901, "Advertising aims to teach people that they have wants, which they did not realize before, and where such wants can be best supplied. If the merchant were to wait nowadays for people to find out for themselves that they needed his wares he would have plenty of leisure and plenty of nothing else" (quoted in Ohmann 1996, 109).

Advertisers fit products into larger fantasies of romance, success, or family life—dreams made possible by new visual technologies. This era marks the invention of color standards, equivalents of the present-day Pantone, and of inks more brilliant than any naturally occurring color. Four-color presses turned out glossy magazines and Sunday newspapers, creating not only visual appeal but a new dimension of brand recognition, in which customers could simply remember the orange box. Lithography enabled sumptuous reproductions of illustrations; spotlights and floodlights turned display windows and fashion shows into dramatic stages. Large plate-glass windows and gleaming glass display counters let department stores artfully showcase their wares, surrounding them with luxurious materials and placing them in appealing tableaux. William Leach described advertisers' "strategies of enticement" as color, glass, and light—all, not coincidentally, borrowed from the church. These technologies allowed advertisers and retailers to attach products to feelings, to make a product much more than a physical object in customers' minds. Text advertisements of the nineteenth century had attested to the quality and utility of their goods, but turn-of-the-century illustrated ads could show viewers a person they wished to be and a world they longed to inhabit.

Magazines and newspapers, especially Sunday newspapers, became popular and effective vehicles for advertisements. Richard Ohmann argued that magazines such as *Cosmopolitan* and *The Century* existed solely to create harmonious surroundings for ads. Evidence from the publishing industry seemed to support his claim. "If bulk alone is considered, the title should be changed from 'news' paper to 'ad' paper," wrote circulation manager William Scott in 1915. "Laymen may assume that the Sunday newspaper has more space for advertising because it carries so much more news and feature reading. As a matter of fact, the extra news and special features really are carried because the paper has so much more advertising patronage and the displays must be sandwiched with reading matter" (Scott 1915, 36, 199). Integrating advertisements with the text, both in magazines and newspapers, forced readers to notice the ads, whether they wanted to or not. An annoyed Upton Sinclair described reading *The Saturday Evening Post* in 1919:

> You start an article or a story, and they give you one or two clean pages to lull your suspicions, and then at the bottom you read, "Continued on page 93." You turn to page 93, and biff—you are hit between the eyes by a powerful gentleman wearing a collar, or swat—you are slapped on the cheek by a lady in a union-suit. You stagger down this narrow column, as one who runs the gauntlet of a band of Indians with clubs; and then you read, "Continued on page 99." You turn to page ninety-nine, and somebody throws a handful of cigarettes into your face, or maybe a box of candy … before you get to the end of the article you have been tempted by every luxury from a diamond scarf-pin to a private yacht, and have spent in imagination more money than you will earn in the balance of your lifetime. (Sinclair 1919, 295–296)

Scholars have tended to see something democratic about the mass market and its advertisements, and they are right, of course. Advertisements subsidized the price of newspapers and magazines, so that a glossy color magazine cost an affordable ten cents. Mass-produced items allowed people living on modest incomes to own more clothing, to decorate their homes, to eat ice-cream—all privileges once reserved for the wealthy. William Leach, in *Land of Desire*, noticed that ads conveyed the idea that anybody could want anything—beauty, riches, glamour, romance—and called this a "democracy of desire." But the people who constructed this system were not concerned with democracy, nor with equality in any form. The "broker" class (as Leach dubbed them), made up of ad-agency men, interior designers, window dressers, and copywriters, was simply being paid to make products appeal to as many people as possible. Elizabeth Fogg Meade, advertising expert, wrote in 1901 that the successful merchant "must excite desire by appealing to imagination and emotion. Above all, he must make his goods familiar to every class in the community … We are not concerned, however, with the ability to pay," she said, "but with the ability to want and choose" (Fogg-Meade 1901, 221, 228, as quoted in Leach 1993, 37). The democratic nature of the pitch was a byproduct of mass marketing; democracy was never the goal.

Advertisers' appeals radically inverted the norms by which Americans had been taught to live, and this inversion is perhaps one of the great shifts in American culture of any era. For decades, ministers, politicians, and businessmen alike had framed work as character-building, a true end in itself. They saw thrift and saving as the morally righteous path, and believed that the men (and the nations) that produced the most would prosper the most. Yet expositions, advertisements, and department stores encouraged people to define themselves through consumption and leisure—the goods they bought, the games they played, the places they travelled. What had seemed wasteful under a producerist ethos seemed profitable under a consumerist one. The weekend, created by giving workers a half-day off on Saturday and by making entertainment options available on Sunday, became not a sign of a lazy and godless culture but a booming market for amusements. Consumer credit turned from a symbol of greed and irresponsibility into a means of greatly expanding the market for automobiles and appliances. The birth of consumer culture is by this point a well-told tale. But the Gilded Age and Progressive Era lays special claim to the ethos that became the basis of twentieth-century consumer culture and, by extension, the entire twentieth-century US economy.

Not surprisingly, the transition to a consumption-based economy led to an ever-faster churn of fashion and fads. Fashions for wealthy women had changed by the season for decades, but cheaper, mass-produced clothing allowed middle-class and working-class women and men to also buy and then retire their clothing according to the fashion calendar. "Narrow Shoulders, Tight Trousers and Plenty of Colors – He's 1915 Man," explained a cartoon in the *Milwaukee Free Press*, poking fun at the year's fashions (25 March 1915, 3). This was a new concept; fashion-wise, there had been no such thing as "1877 man." Songs that had once traveled via musicians now spread more quickly through sheet music and, eventually, phonograph records. Songwriters learned to treat their works like any other manufactured product, and to cultivate a taste for them by any possible means. David Suisman (2012) has described the elaborate ritual of pop music "plugging" born in the 1890s, in which songwriters or their agents paid performers to insert songs into their cabaret acts, and paid others to sit in the audience and applaud vigorously for those songs. Adman Truman DeWeese articulated the advertisers' project, by then well established, in 1915:

> Advertising must teach men new ways of shaving and dressing; it must teach women new ways of cleaning their teeth and preserving their complexions. Advertising must teach new ways of sweeping the carpet, new ways of furnishing the home, new ways of promoting cleanliness and health, new ways of enjoying life … (1915, 29)

It seemed no sphere of life was immune from fads: all tastes and habits were subject to change, if advertisers could only be persuasive enough.

"Plugging" and advertising cannot explain every fad, for not every fad made money. Sayings cycled in and out of Americans' vocabularies as they picked them up from their favorite newspaper columnist or comic strip. One hundred new dances swept across New York City's dance floors between 1912 and 1914 (Erenberg 1981, 150). What explains this churn? The phenomenon John Kasson noticed in Coney Island may apply here as well. "For Coney Island was necessarily an imperfect Feast of Fools," wrote Kasson, "an institutionalized bacchanal. It represented a festival that did not express joy *about* something, but offered 'fun' in a managed celebration for commercial ends" (Kasson 1978, 105). Tea dances did not celebrate any occasion or serve any obvious ritual purpose; instead patrons paid ten cents to enter a room of manufactured fun. Novelty became essential to luring them back.

Progressives and Popular Culture

The architects of consumer culture were the main, but not the only, population strategically constructing new modes of leisure in this era. Progressive reformers and civic leaders left their own stamp on popular culture, usually in an attempt to change the habits of the working class. Some of their efforts tried to conjure entirely new spaces and forms. Movements for city parks gained momentum from the middle of the nineteenth century onward. Although working-class city residents sometimes petitioned for public parks, the city commissioners who authorized them and the landscape architects who designed them usually lined up behind Frederick Law Olmsted's belief that parks would have a calming and civilizing effect on the working class (Rosenzweig 1982; Couvares 1984). The campaign for public libraries sought to get books—and the right sort of books—into working-class people's lives. In Pittsburgh, where the elaborate and extensive campaign was backed by Andrew Carnegie, reformers were so keen on readers taking away the right messages from their reading that they would send librarians to conduct book discussions in people's homes (Couvares 1984). Playground advocates envisioned spaces for young people to develop healthy bodies, to mix with children of other ethnicities, and to learn respect for the rules. The middle class did not entirely exempt their own children from these ideals; they signed them up for Boy Scouts or Camp Fire Girls, where they learned principles of fair play and good citizenship. The relatively new fields of child development and child psychology saw all children as harboring ancient instincts that could be productively channeled. Playground supervisors and Camp Fire Girls leaders alike taught children the "primitive" but supposedly enriching skills of basketry, storytelling, archery, and folk dancing.

Another strain of Progressive action simply sought to reshape, or shut down, the existing forms of working-class popular culture they found most objectionable. Temperance reformers, from the 1880s through Prohibition, consistently tried to revoke liquor licenses and to legislate how liquor was sold, bringing drinking out of homes and basements and into more commercial (easily regulated) spaces. Campaigns for a "Safe and Sane" Fourth turned the Fourth of July from a day of ethnic community celebrations full of alcohol and fireworks into centralized affairs with licensed vendors and businessmen speakers. In New York City, the police shut down all nickelodeons in 1908 and allowed them to reopen only when they submitted to police surveillance and agreed not to sell tickets to unaccompanied children. The New York City effort resulted in a broader movement to censor film, whether by the National Board of Review of Motion Pictures, formed in 1909, or by more piecemeal snipping out of objectionable scenes by local police (Sklar 1975, 30–32).

Jane Addams, writing in *The Spirit of Youth and the City Streets* (1904), shows the scope of Progressives' concerns about popular culture but also the limitations of their vision. Addams worried that the working-class and immigrant children in her Chicago neighborhood were absorbing the nickelodeons' stories of violence and revenge: "Is it not astounding that a city allows thousands of its youth to fill their impressionable minds with these absurdities which certainly will become the foundation for their working moral codes and the data from which they will judge the proprieties of life?" (Addams 1904, 79–80). She worried not only that children would pick up criminal habits, but that they would learn to want what they could not have, eventually coming to prefer life on the screen to the real thing. "To insist that young people shall forecast their rose-colored future only in a house of dreams," she wrote, "is to deprive the real world of that warmth and reassurance which it so sorely needs and to which it is justly entitled; furthermore, we are left outside with a sense of dreariness, in company with that shadow which already lurks only around the corner for most of us—a skepticism of life's value" (Addams 1904, 103).

As a substitute, Addams suggested gymnasiums; chaperoned dance parties; folk dances; theater, which would expand children's vocabularies and fulfill their desires for beauty and order; and baseball, both good exercise and conjurer of a "common mood" between classes. Addams was unusual for her time in acknowledging that ethnic culture had value, but she was also depoliticizing these children by conceiving of them as (or trying to turn them back into) "folk" rather than a working class. Her suggestions included no ideas for actually changing children's material circumstances; they demonstrate why Progressive attempts to create or reform popular culture did not tend to stick. Reformers tried to teach the working class to behave according to middle-class values and prerogatives, but they offered no clear reward. What would children get if they followed the rules laid out by the playground supervisor or read the books that the "library hour" volunteer told them to read? Approval, perhaps a small prize, but nothing more.

In contrast to Progressives' failure to offer their working-class neighbors (and especially working-class children and teenagers) anything more than points for good behavior, consumer culture and popular amusements proved both adaptable and rewarding. Some forms of commercialized popular culture in the Progressive Era created new forums for working-class kinds of sociability—the raucous, participatory culture of the nickelodeon transferred easily to the band pavilions, bowling alleys, and penny arcades of the same moment. Other forms catered to middle-class norms and incomes, yet remained hugely appealing to the working class. Adolph Zukor, eventual founder of Paramount Pictures, imported higher-brow films from Europe and even commissioned some himself; he catered to middle-class audiences beginning to frequent the tonier "movie palaces" of the 1910s. Yet the affordable luxury of these palaces appealed just as much to working-class audiences. Department stores, advertisements, and movie palaces all invited Americans, including working-class Americans, into a world of beauty and extravagance. It was this appeal, rather than reformers' moralizing ideas about the right ways to spend one's free time, that proved most beguiling and enduring.

Cultural Reach and Homogenization

Consumer culture became so deeply embedded during the twentieth century that it has taken hard work and careful research to piece together its prehistory. The same could be said about the homogenization of culture. Historians have looked to the popular culture of the Gilded Age and Progressive Era as the precursor to the mass culture of the mid twentieth-century United States, but have had to stay attentive to the piecemeal, uneven, and ongoing nature of cultural homogenization.

Several of the technologies that created mass audiences have been amply discussed and celebrated ever since their invention: the chromo-lithograph, the phonograph, celluloid film. Yet scholars of the last several decades have investigated the impacts of less glamorous, or just plain overlooked, technologies in the creation of these large audiences. The railroad enabled traveling performances of unprecedented size to make their way from town to town and country to country, eventually reaching millions of spectators. Buffalo Bill's Wild West show is the most well-studied of these traveling performances, but Janet Davis's *The Circus Age* (2002) shows that the circus reached just as far, and Cara Caddoo's *Envisioning Freedom* (2014) traces the paths of film exhibitors as they rode the rails from one southern black church to another. An older book of essays on American photographs in Europe serves as a reminder that stereograph images were wildly popular ways for late nineteenth-century Americans to see the world and for Europeans to see America (Nye and Gidley 1994).

Other technologies offered audiences secondhand, mediated experiences—again extending the reach of popular entertainments farther than ever. Alan Trachtenberg, Stephen Kern (1983), and Walter Benjamin before them, spent much time contemplating the meaning of such mediated experiences in broad terms, but historians of the 1990s and 2000s investigated them in detail. Michael Oriard (1993) rightfully noted that in 1900, football was a new animal in the American entertainment universe: more people had read about it than had either played or watched it in person. Oriard dissected the stories told about football in the daily press that ranged from tales of gentlemanly good sportsmanship, to allegories of military and imperial prowess, to jeremiads of moral degeneration and impending savagery. Where Trachtenberg had seen mediated entertainment as a distancing and dulling of immediate experience, Oriard—armed with the cultural turn's emphasis on narratives and discourses—treated the media's messages as every bit as important as the athletes' and spectators' own experiences. Also in the realm of sports, Theresa Runstedtler (2012) has thought carefully about the ways audiences experienced the Vitagraph silent films of boxing matches, and how the film viewings of the match between the reigning white champion Jim Jeffries and the ultimate black victor Jack Johnson became far more politically charged than the match had been in real time.

There may yet be more to say here. Newspapers and magazines, after all, reported on nearly every kind of urban entertainment, not just football. What experiences of theater, art exhibits, parades, and sports did these publications provide? Did the media act solely as curators of acceptable middlebrow entertainments in these cases, or did they use their reporting to tell larger stories? Perhaps the availability of second-hand entertainments gave rise to a new way of inhabiting the world, one which emphasized the importance of knowing all about "the latest" but placed relatively little value on participation and presence. Too ill to leave her house, a New York City resident wrote in 1911: "As it is not possible to visit art shows, theater, opera concert, or lecture, I am able to keep informed by the criticisms of pictures, the plots of the new plays, the actors who are to appear and the famous singers. Armed with the information gleaned from the newspapers, I am prepared to discuss any of these matters intelligently" ("The American Newspaper," 1911, 22).

One of the most surprising qualities of turn-of-the-century popular culture is how homogenous independently owned enterprises could be. Residents of most major cities could spend their Sundays in an amusement park at the end of the streetcar line, where they would find roller coasters, dance floors, Ferris wheels, and dazzling electric lights. Movie palaces of the 1910s nearly all shared the same opulent aesthetic made up of rococo decorations, plaster statuettes, and electric marquees welcoming audiences inside. No matter the name of their local department store, be it Filene's in Boston, Marshall Field's in Chicago, or The Emporium in San Francisco, customers encountered glamorous scenes in display windows, marble-and-mirror ground floors, revolving doors, escalators, and multistory atriums. Whether they read the *Denver Post* or the *Cleveland Plain Dealer*, Americans found their news divided into the same categories: local/national/international, sports, women, business, and real estate.

Why such sameness before the era of franchises and chains? The trade press explains it, in part. Movie theater owners read *Billboard* or *Movie Picture World*, department store managers read the *Dry Goods Economist*, and newspaper publishers read *Editor & Publisher* or *Printer's Ink*. The trade press told subscribers how to replicate the most eye-catching window displays or how their newspaper, too, could boost circulation with a Christmas charity drive. The sameness can also be explained by the growth of somewhat hidden, nationwide industries that served these new entertainments. Movie theater owners chose decorations themselves, but from mail-order catalogs (Bowser 1994, 127). Editors could select from menus of syndicated features to fill out their Sunday newspapers, and advertisers could buy pre-made "cuts"—etched illustrations of elegant hats, roast chickens, or whatever suited their needs. By the 1910s, the chain and franchise models had made inroads. Gimbels department stores had expanded through the East and Midwest, Paramount was "block booking" movie theaters, and workers were lunching at Horn & Hardart automats rather than at the corner saloon. But what the studies of the last several decades have shown is that the chainstore model was only a phase, appearing decades into a longer process of homogenizing leisure in the United States.

Even as, in the early twentieth century, popular culture appealed to masses as never before, the experiences of spectators and shoppers were still not as standardized as they would become in later eras. In nickelodeons, people watched nationally distributed short films accompanied by local pianists or narrated in Yiddish. They went to their church fundraiser to watch film footage rearranged by the exhibitor to tell a story or a lesson of the exhibitor's own invention. They arrived at Buffalo Bill's encampment before the show to meet a cowboy and step inside a tepee. They watched vaudeville programs made up of performers who traveled around the country, but which the theater owner had selected and ordered to suit his particular audience's tastes. They gazed at department-store displays created by the shopgirl inside, or perhaps suggested by her boss, but not dictated by national headquarters. Patterned but not quite homogenized popular culture—this is a hallmark of the Progressive Era.

Perhaps the most standardized and standardizing popular culture of this era was that which arrived in Americans' mailboxes one a week or once a month. Magazines offered a complete way of life, identical in every town where they were received. The *Ladies' Home Journal* told women to aspire to "the simple life" that was, paradoxically, stocked with newfangled products (Scanlon 1995). Magazine fiction set parameters for courtship while also becoming an allegory for shopping, in which women's most important skill was that of choosing the best item (Garvey 1996). Because these magazines aimed to appeal to a national audience, they traded in broadly defined, often identical "types" that readers could both recognize and aspire to: the Gibson Girl, the New Woman, the College Man (Kitch 2001; Clark 2010). Yet even in this most national and homogenous form of media, historians have managed to uncover ways that readers put magazines to their own uses. In *Writing with Scissors* (2012), Ellen Gruber Garvey finds readers assembling feminist histories or narratives of black accomplishment out of magazine and newspaper articles that, on their own, displayed no such politics.

The scholarship of the last several decades has qualified the language of "loosening" and "fluidity" that appeared in 1960s through 1980s studies of Gilded Age and particularly of Progressive Era popular culture (Higham 1965; Erenberg 1981). Popular culture at the turn of the century was often framed as an escape from constraints, but it nearly always removed people from one set of constraints and hierarchies and put them into another. Dance halls freed young women from family obligations but cast them in fairly rigid gender roles, with sexual obligations attached. Sports like football and boxing momentarily released men from expectations of restrained and "civilized" behavior, but set new standards of physical perfection and prowess. White couples doing black-inspired dances expressed their sexuality in new ways, but the notion of "going primitive" reinforced the status of blacks at the bottom of the civilizational hierarchy. Magazines and department stores seemed to offer an escape from local, provincial society but versed readers and shoppers in new, nationally understood class norms. Consumer credit freed working-class and middle-class people to buy items that they could not otherwise afford, but, as Lendol Calder (2001) has argued, the monthly bills turned them into more diligent workers than ever before.

Future Directions

The historical approach lobbying most energetically for itself at the moment is the history of capitalism. Historians of capitalism argue the importance of studying the institutions and individuals who gradually built up the financial system of credit and risk, personal data, and profit margins. They encourage histories from multiple perspectives; rather than focusing solely on workers or on firms, they advocate "history from below, all the way to the top" ("Interchange: The History of Capitalism," 2014). However, historians of Gilded Age and Progressive Era popular culture have been doing this for years. Robert Sklar opened his 1975 book *Movie-Made America* as follows:

> In the process of expanding my approach to movies I also began to redefine my ideas of culture, shifting my focus from artists and their creations to people and their lives. … That task has led me to examine, among other topics, the invention of motion-picture technology; the nature and evolution of the motion-picture audience; the organization and business tactics of the movie trade; the design and economics of theaters; the social and professional lives of movie workers; government policies toward movies, and the attitudes and strategies of censorship groups; and the cultural influence of movies at home and overseas. (Sklar 1975, v)

This certainly sounds like a multi-perspective history of capitalism. By the 1990s and 2000s, Gilded Age and Progressive Era scholars were producing sophisticated portraits of the economic engines and tools of popular culture, from ad agencies to the analysts, hired by circuses, who used crop yields and census reports to determine the most profitable towns for performances (Ohmann 1996; Scanlon 1995; Davis 2002). Perhaps because Theodor Adorno so emphatically inveighed against "the culture industry" in the 1940s, cultural historians have rarely separated the study of culture and industry.

A more surprising new direction is the study of heterogeneity within the "mass" and "modern" culture of this era. The fact that there is still so much diversity left to uncover shows how strong a stamp midcentury critics such as Dwight MacDonald and Clement Greenberg made on the field. Even for historians who put no faith whatsoever in the categories of "mass culture," "folk culture," and "kitsch," it has taken until the 2000s and 2010s to conceive of many cultural products apart from these words. Studies of southern music had, until recently, told a story of indigenous and isolated forms that were gradually incorporated into, and changed by, a mass market. Karl Hagstrom Miller (2010) has now argued that southern musicians were in fact steeped in commercial music coming from the North. They sang Broadway hits and Tin Pan Alley melodies alongside regional tunes. It was only because talent scouts and recording agents had no interest in southern renditions of pop songs that this more polyglot and omnivorous music-making has been forgotten. Steven J. Ross's *Working-Class Hollywood* (1998) tells a forgotten story of early films that communicated pro-worker, anti-capitalist sentiments and in some cases were made by labor organizations themselves. Historians first began to question the homogenizing and hegemonizing power of film by thinking creatively about how audiences may have interpreted film messages for themselves (Hansen 1994), in tandem with literary scholars interested in reception history. But only later, with Ross's work and also that of Jacqueline Najuma Stewart, in *Migrating to the Movies* (2005), did they also investigate film as a genre in which working-class and minority voices may have actually come through.

Miller, Ross, and Stewart are entering into a broader, ongoing conversation in the field about the modern—who participated in it, where it spread, and what it looked like. Because the combined Gilded Age and Progressive Era has been labeled (correctly) as America's great age of urbanization, historians of popular culture have looked to that era's cities almost by default. Yet a handful of scholars are calling into question the notion that modern entertainments spread from cities outwards. Janet Davis (2002) argues that circus performances, though crafted with small-town audiences in mind, forged a modern kind of entertainment, making a spectacle of the world's diversity. Cara Caddoo (2014) shows how African Americans created their own film entertainments in the rural South in the early twentieth century. To an earlier generation of historians, modern popular culture seemed synonymous with urban popular culture. But innovative research is turning up sophisticated popular culture in places—mining towns, circus tents, church fundraisers—where no one had previously thought to look.

On a different front, a new wave of historians has been investigating culture that was not intended to be political, but nonetheless made certain political changes possible. In a model cast decades ago by Lizabeth Cohen's *Making a New Deal* (1990), historians of the Gilded Age and Progressive Era are asking: how did popular culture realign populations, teach them new ideas, and enable changes beyond the realm of culture? In *Stories of the South* (2014), K. Stephen Prince looks to magazine fiction, travel writing, minstrelsy, and film to investigate the political and cultural retreat from Reconstruction. Narratives within popular culture cast the South as a distinctive region that had developed racial expertise; this helped to win consent among northerners for the southern system of Jim Crow. In *Staging Race* (2006), Karen Sotiropoulos finds black performers of the early twentieth century not only sending guarded messages of solidarity to black theater patrons relegated to the balconies; she also discovers them forming professional organizations to position themselves as leading "race men," although activists such as W.E.B. Du Bois did not necessarily want to call them that. Susan A. Glenn, in *Female Spectacle: The Theatrical Roots of Modern Feminism* (2000), is interested in the ways that popular culture performed or displayed modes of being female that overlapped with suffragist causes. While this kind of work has its frustrations—it can never be definitively proven that vaudeville made feminists or hastened women's suffrage—the resonances and parallels are important, and they help to explain both the momentum for political change and the potency of popular culture in its own day.

Two books published in 1999 wove popular culture and politics even more tightly together as they thought through the political meanings and uses of consumer culture among women of the early twentieth century. Margaret Finnegan's *Selling Suffrage* (1999) sees suffragists using consumer-culture strategies to pitch their cause to the American public and to portray themselves as modern, fun, likeable women. While the pitch worked, Finnegan argues that selling preserves, printing suffrage-sloganed aprons, and comparing the woman voter to the woman shopper actually weakened the feminist movement more broadly, for it continued to associate women with the domestic sphere. While Nan Enstad (1999) studies a different population, her premise contrasts sharply with Finnegan's. Imagining a labor movement among young urban immigrant women *without* consumer culture, writes Enstad, is to ignore the very sphere in which those women conceived of better lives. Enstad carefully reconstructs the meanings of flower-laden hats and French heels, and parses the plots of the dime novels and movies that working women enjoyed. She argues persuasively that consumer culture helps explain their political actions rather than serving as a distraction. There are many more possible ways that Gilded Age and Progressive Era scholars might investigate the political uses and meanings of consumer products, from the goods the Sears catalog offered to Populist rural families to the material worlds of W.E.B. DuBois's "talented tenth."

A final area just unfolding in this field is the global nature of Gilded Age and Progressive Era popular culture. The appearance and justification of empire in US popular culture may be the richest vein mined so far, with Robert Rydell and Gail Bederman now joined by Kristin Hoganson's *Consumers' Imperium* (2007). Hoganson examines the way that middle-class women participated in and enjoyed the United States' rising global power within their own homes, whether through lantern-slide travel, middle eastern-inspired living-room décor, or orientalist fashion by way of Europe. Somewhat less is known about what the United States was sending out into the world at this moment in time. American performers made remarkable careers for themselves abroad in this era; James Cook's forthcoming project, *Colored Men Heard 'Round the World: A Global History of Black Celebrity, 1770–1950*, promises to tell us more. Theresa Runstedtler's (2012) global history of Jack Johnson probes the meaning that different countries—Australia, France, England, South Africa—assigned to the boxer, depending on the racial hierarchies that governed their own societies.

Meanwhile, commodity history, which has so effectively knit together national histories in studies of the seventeenth and eighteenth centuries, has yet to really make inroads in the Gilded Age and Progressive Era. Robert Bruce Davies's (1976) global history of the Singer sewing machine tracks a phenomenally influential American invention around the world, and there is still more to be said about how that technology changed fashion, labor, and gender roles in other societies. A 1990s compilation on American photographs abroad began to investigate the way that the Kodak quickly created and then dominated the market for snapshot cameras; but again, there is much more to this story (Nye and Gidley 1994). Madame C.J. Walker had thousands of agents selling her beauty products around the world by 1916 (Baldwin 2008, 64), but as yet, little has been written about her global business. A glib observation by a London journalist in 1902 shows just how many possible avenues there are for such histories:

> The average citizen wakes in the morning at the sound of an American alarum clock; rises from his New England sheets, and shaves with his New York soap, and a Yankee safety razor. He pulls on a pair of Boston boots over his socks from West Carolina, fastens his Connecticut braces, slips his Waterbury watch into his pocket and sits down to breakfast. Then he congratulates his wife on the way her Illinois straight-front corset sets off her Massachusetts blouse, and begins to tackle his breakfast, at which he eats bread made from prairie flour (possibly doctored at the special establishment on the Lakes), tinned oysters from Baltimore and a little Kansas City bacon, while his wife plays with a slice of Chicago ox-tongue. The children are given Quaker oats. Concurrently he reads his morning paper, set up by American machines, printed with American ink, by American presses, on American paper, edited possibly by a smart journalist from New York City, and sub-edited with as close an approach to American brevity and verve as English pressmen can achieve …. (Mackenzie 1902, 142–143)

Every commodity here does not need its own book, but the categories are rich. Did American firms create fashions that they intended specifically for foreign markets, or did people around the world simply start dressing like Americans? Did an American-made conception of childhood and health sell Quaker Oats abroad, or did the company need new advertising strategies? What effect did multinational media conglomerates have on day-to-day news and entertainment?

In 1925, Stefan Zweig denounced "The Monotonization of the World" in the *Berliner-Börsen Courier*. He noticed that across the European and colonial world, people danced the same dances, sported the same hairstyles, wore the same dresses, and enjoyed the same formulaic movie styles. "What is the source of this terrible wave threatening to wash all the color, everything particular out of life?" he asked. "Everyone who has ever been there knows: America. … America is the source of that terrible wave of uniformity that gives everyone the same overalls on the skin, the same book in the hand, the same pen between the fingers, the same conversation on the lips, and the same automobile instead of feet" (Zweig 1925). Whatever scholars think of Zweig's judgments, surely this process must have been underway in the Progressive Era for him to declare it so complete by 1925. Historians of the Gilded Age and Progressive Era have their work cut out for them.

References

Addams, Jane. 1972 (1909). *The Spirit of Youth and the City Streets.* Chicago, IL: University of Chicago Press.

"The American Newspaper." 1911. *Collier's Weekly* 2, September: 22–23.

Baldwin, Davarian L. 2008. "From the Washtub to the World: Madam C. J. Walker and the 'Re-creation' of Race Womanhood, 1900–1935." In *The Modern Girl Around the World: Consumption, Modernity, and Globalization*, ed. Alice Eve Weinbaum et al. Durham: University of North Carolina Press.

Barth, Gunther Paul. 1980. *City People : the Rise of the Modern City Culture in Nineteenth-Century America.* New York: Oxford University Press.

Bederman, Gail. 1996. *Manliness and Civilization: A Cultural History of Gender and Race in the United States, 1880–1917.* Chicago, IL: University of Chicago Press.

Boorstin, Daniel. 1973. *The Americans: The Democratic Experience.* New York: Vintage Books.

Bowser, Eileen. 1994. *The Transformation of Cinema, 1907–1915.* Berkeley: University of California Press.

Caddoo, Cara. 2014. *Envisioning Freedom: Cinema and the Building of Modern Black Life.* Cambridge, MA: Harvard University Press.

Calder, Lendol. 2001. *Financing the American Dream: A Cultural History of Consumer Credit.* Princeton, NJ: Princeton University Press.

Chauncey, George. 1994. *Gay New York: Gender, Urban Culture, and the Making of the Gay Male World, 1890–1940.* New York: Basic Books.

Cohen, Lizabeth. 1990. *Making a New Deal: Industrial Workers in Chicago, 1919–1939.* New York: Cambridge University Press.

Clark, Daniel A. 2010.*Creating the College Man: American Mass Magazines and Middle-Class Manhood, 1890–1915.* Madison: University of Wisconsin Press.

Couvares, Frances G. 1984. *The Remaking of Pittsburgh: Class and Culture in an Industrializing City, 1877–1919.* Albany: State University of New York Press.

Davies, Robert Bruce. 1976. *Peacefully Working to Conquer the World: Singer Machines in Foreign Markets, 1854–1920.* New York: Arno Press.

Davis, Janet. 2002. *The Circus Age: Culture and Society under the American Big Top.* Chapel Hill: University of North Carolina Press.

Denning, Michael. 1987. *Mechanic Accents: Dime Novels and Working-Class Culture in Nineteenth-Century America.* New York: Verso.

—. 1990. "The End of Mass Culture." *International Labor and Working-Class History* 37: 4–18.

DeWeese, Truman A. 1915. *Keeping a Dollar at Work. Fifty "Talks" on Newspaper Advertising Written for the N.Y. Evening Post.* New York: New York Evening Post.

Enstad, Nan. 1999. *Ladies of Labor, Girls of Adventure: Working Women, Popular Culture and Labor Politics at the Turn of the Twentieth Century.* New York: Columbia University Press.

Erenberg, Lewis. 1981. *Steppin' Out: New York Nightlife and the Transformation of American Culture, 1890–1930.* Westport, CT: Greenwood Press.

Ewen, Elizabeth and Stuart Ewen. 1982. *Channels of Desire: Mass Images and the Shaping of American Consciousness.* New York: McGraw Hill.

Ewen, Stuart. 1976. *Captains of Consciousness: Advertising and the Social Roots of Consumer Culture.* New York: McGraw Hill.

Finnegan, Margaret. 1999. *Selling Suffrage: Consumer Culture and Votes for Women.* New York: Columbia University Press.

Fogg-Meade, Emily. 1901. "The Place of Advertising in Modern Life." *Journal of Political Economy* 5, 2: 218–242.

Garvey, Ellen Gruber. 1996. *The Adman in the Parlor: Magazines and the Gendering of Consumer Culture, 1880s to 1910s.* New York: Oxford University Press.

—. 2012. *Writing with Scissors: American Scrapbooks from the Civil War to the Harlem Renaissance.* New York: Oxford University Press.

Glenn, Susan A. 2000. *Female Spectacle: The Theatrical Roots of Modern Feminism.* Cambridge, MA: Harvard University Press.

Gorn, Elliott. 1986. *The Manly Art: Bare-Knuckle Prize Fighting in America.* Ithaca, NY: Cornell University Press.

Hall, Stuart. 1981. "Notes on Deconstructing 'The Popular.'" In *People's History and Socialist Theory*, ed. Raphael Samuel, 227–240. London: Routledge.

Hansen, Miriam. 1994. *Babel and Babylon: Spectatorship in American Silent Film.* Cambridge, MA: Harvard University Press.

Higham, John. 1965. "The Re-Orientation of American Culture in the 1890s" In *The Origins of Modern Consciousness*, ed. John Weiss, 25–48. Detroit, MI: Wayne State University Press.

Hoganson, Kristin L. 2007. *Consumers' Imperium: The Global Production of American Domesticity, 1865–1920.* Chapel Hill: University of North Carolina Press.

Hunter, Tera W. 1998. *To 'Joy My Freedom: Southern Black Women's Lives and Labors After the Civil War.* Cambridge, MA: Harvard University Press.

"Interchange: The History of Capitalism." 2014. *Journal of American History* 101, 2: 503–536.

Jameson, Fredric. 1979. "Reification and Utopia in Mass Culture." *Social Text* 1: 130–148.

Kasson, John F. 1978. *Amusing the Million: Coney Island at the Turn of the Century.* New York: Hill & Wang.

Kelley, Robin D. G. 1992. "Notes on Deconstructing 'The Folk.'" *American Historical Review* 97, 5: 1400–1408.

Kern, Stephen. 1983. *The Culture of Time and Space, 1880–1918.* Cambridge, MA: Harvard University Press.

Kitch, Carolyn. 2001. *The Girl on the Magazine Cover: The Origins of Visual Stereotypes in American Mass Media.* Chapel Hill: University of North Carolina Press.

Laird, Pamela Walker. 1998. *Advertising Progress: American Business and the Rise of Consumer Marketing.* Baltimore, MD: Johns Hopkins University Press.

Leach, William. 1993. *Land of Desire : Merchants, Power, and the Rise of a New American Culture.* New York: Pantheon Books.

Lears, T. J. Jackson. 1985. "The Concept of Cultural Hegemony: Problems and Possibilities." *The American Historical Review* 90, 3: 567–593.

—. 1992. "Making Fun of Popular Culture." *American Historical Review* 97, 5: 1417–1426.

—. 1994. *Fables of Abundance: A Cultural History of Advertising in America.* New York: Basic Books.

Levine, Lawrence W. 1977. *Black Culture and Black Consciousness: Afro-American Folk Thought from Slavery to Freedom.* New York: Oxford University Press.

—. 1992. "The Folklore of Industrial Society: Popular Culture and Its Audiences." *American Historical Review* 97, 5: 1369–1399.

Lott, Eric. 1993. *Love and Theft: Blackface Minstrelsy and the American Working Class.* New York: Oxford University Press.

Mackenzie, Fred. 1902. *The American Invaders.* London: Grant Richards.

Miller, Karl Hagstrom. 2010. *Segregating Sound: Inventing Folk and Pop Music in the Age of Jim Crow.* Durham, NC: Duke University Press.

Nye, David E. and Mick Gidley, eds. 1994. *American Photographs in Europe.* Amsterdam: VU Press.

Ohmann, Richard. 1996. *Selling Culture: Magazines, Markets, and the Class at the Turn of the Century.* New York: Verso.

Oriard, Michael. 1993. *Reading Football: How the Popular Press Created an American Spectacle.* Chapel Hill: University of North Carolina Press.

Peiss, Kathy Lee. 1986. *Cheap Amusements: Working Women and Leisure in Turn-of-the-Century New York.* Philadelphia, PA: Temple University Press.

Potter, David M. 1954. *People of Plenty: Economic Abundance and the American Character.* Chicago, IL: University of Chicago Press.

Prince, K. Stephen. 2014. *Stories of the South: Race and the Reconstruction of Southern Identity, 1865–1915.* Chapel Hill: University of North Carolina Press.

Roediger, David R. 1991. *Wages of Whiteness: Race and the Making of the American Working Class.* London: Verso.

Rosenzweig, Roy. 1985. *Eight Hours for What We Will: Workers and Leisure in an Industrial City, 1870–1920.* New York: Cambridge University Press.

Ross, Andrew. 1989. *No Respect: Intellectuals and Popular Culture.* London: Routledge.

Ross, Steven J. 1998. *Working-Class Hollywood: Silent Film and the Shaping of Class in America.* Princeton, NJ: Princeton University Press.

Runstedtler, Theresa. 2012. *Jack Johnson, Rebel Sojourner: Boxing in the Shadow of the Global Color Line.* Berkeley: University of California Press.

Rydell, Robert. 1984. *All the World's a Fair: Visions of Empire at American International Expositions.* Chicago, IL: University of Chicago Press.

Saxton, Alexander. 1990. *The Rise and Fall of the White Republic: Class Politics and Mass Culture in Nineteenth Century America.* London: Verso.

Scanlon, Jennifer. 1995. *Inarticulate Longings: The Ladies' Home Journal, Gender and the Promise of Consumer Culture.* New York: Routledge.

Scott, William R. 1915. *Scientific Circulation Management for Newspapers.* New York, NY: The Ronald Press Company.

Sinclair, Upton. 1919. *The Brass Check: A Study of American Journalism.* Pasadena, CA: Upton Sinclair.

Sklar, Robert. 1975. *Movie-Made America: A Cultural History of American Movies.* New York: Random House.

Smith, Henry Nash. 1950. *Virgin Land.* Cambridge, MA: Harvard University Press.

Sotiropoulos, Karen. 2006. *Staging Race: Black Performers in Turn of the Century America.* Cambridge, MA: Harvard University Press.

Stewart, Jacqueline Najuma. 2005. *Migrating to the Movies: Cinema and Black Urban Modernity.* Berkeley: University of California Press.

Suisman, David. 2012. *Selling Sounds: The Commercial Revolution in American Music.* Cambridge, MA: Harvard University Press.

Susman, Warren. 1985. *Culture as History: The Transformation of American Society in the Twentieth Century.* New York: Pantheon.

Thompson, E.P. 1963. *The Making of the English Working Class.* London: Victor Gollancz.

Trachtenberg, Alan. 1982. *The Incorporation of America: Culture and Society in the Gilded Age.* New York: Hill & Wang.

Wiebe, Robert. 1967. *The Search for Order, 1877–1920.* New York: Hill & Wang.

Williams, Raymond. 1989. (1958) "Culture is Ordinary." In *Resources of Hope: Culture, Democracy, Socialism,* 3–14. London: Verso.

Zweig, Stefan. 1925 (1944). "The Monotonization of the World." In *The Weimar Republic Sourcebook*, ed. Anton Kaes, Martin Jay, and Edward Dimendberg, 397–400. Berlin: Berliner Börsen-Courier. Trans. 1995, Berkeley: University of California Press. Citations refer to the University of California edition.

Further Reading

Allen, Robert C. 1991. *Horrible Prettiness: Burlesque and American Culture.* Chapel Hill: University of North Carolina Press.

Benson, Susan Porter. 1986. *Counter Cultures: Saleswomen, Managers, and Customers in American Department Stores, 1890–1940.* Urbana: University of Illinois Press.

Brooks, Daphne. 2006. *Bodies in Dissent: Spectacular Performances of Race and Freedom, 1850–1910.* Durham, NC: Duke University Press.

Brundage, Fitzhugh, ed. 2011. *Beyond Blackface: African Americans and the Creation of American Popular Culture, 1890–1930.* Chapel Hill: University of North Carolina Press.

Burgos, Adrian. 2007. *Playing America's Game: Baseball, Latinos, and the Color Line.* Berkeley: University of California Press.

Butsch, Richard, ed. 1990. *For Fun and Profit: The Transformation of Leisure into Consumption.* Philadelphia, PA: Temple University Press.

Cawelti, John G. 1965. *Apostles of the Self-Made Man.* Chicago, IL: University of Chicago Press.

Chudacoff, Howard P. 1999. *The Age of the Bachelor: Creating an American Subculture.* Princeton, NJ: Princeton University Press.

Cook, James W., Lawrence B. Glickman, and Michael O'Malley, ed. 2008. *The Cultural Turn in U.S. History: Past, Present, and Future.* Chicago, IL: University of Chicago Press.

DeLoria, Philip. 1998. *Playing Indian.* New Haven, CT: Yale University Press.

Douglas, Susan. 1987. *Inventing American Broadcasting, 1899–1922.* Baltimore, MD: Johns Hopkins University Press.

Gilbert, James. 1991. *Perfect Cities: Chicago's Utopias of 1893.* Chicago, IL: University of Chicago Press.

Hardy, Stephen. 1982. *How Boston Played: Sport, Recreation, and Community, 1856–1915.* Boston, MA: Northeastern University Press.

Hardy, Stephen, and Alan G. Ingham. 1983. "Games, Structures, and Agency: Historians on the American Play Movement," *Journal of Social History* 17, 2: 285–301.

Harris, Neil. 1990. *Cultural Excursions: Marketing Appetites and Cultural Tastes in Modern America.* Chicago: University of Chicago Press.

Hazzard-Gordon, Katrina. 1992. *Jookin': The Rise of Social Dance Formations in African-American Culture.* Philadelphia, PA: Temple University Press.

Heap, Chad. 2010. *Slumming: Sexual and Racial Encounters in American Nightlife, 1885–1940.* Chicago: University of Chicago Press.

Ingrassia, Brian. 2012. *The Rise of Gridiron University: Higher Education's Uneasy Alliance With Big-Time Football.* Lawrence: University Press of Kansas.

Jacobson, Lisa. 2005. *Raising Consumers: Children and the American Mass Market in the Early Twentieth Century.* New York: Columbia University Press.

Kammen, Michael. 1999. *American Culture, American Tastes: Social Change and the Twentieth Century.* New York: Knopf.

Kasson, John F. 2002. *Houdini, Tarzan, and the Perfect Man: The White Male Body and the Challenge of Modernity in America.* New York: Hill & Wang.

Kasson, Joy S. 2000. *Buffalo Bill's Wild West: Celebrity, Memory, and Popular History.* New York: Hill & Wang.

Kibler, Alison M. 1999. *Rank Ladies: Gender and Cultural Hierarchy in American Vaudeville.* Chapel Hill: University of North Carolina Press.

Levine, Lawrence W. 1988. *Highbrow/Lowbrow: The Emergence of Cultural Hierarchy in America.* Cambridge, MA: Harvard University Press.

May, Lary. 1980. *Screening Out the Past: The Birth of Mass Culture and the Motion Picture Industry.* Chicago, IL: University of Chicago Press.

McCrossen, Alexis. 2001. *Holy Day, Holiday: The American Sunday.* Ithaca, NY: Cornell University Press.

Moses, L. G. 1996. *Wild West Shows and the Images of American Indians, 1883–1933.* Albuquerque: University of New Mexico Press.

Musser, Charles. 1990. *The Emergence of Cinema: The American Screen to 1907.* Berkeley: University of California Press.

Nasaw, David. 1999. *Going Out: The Rise and Fall of Public Amusements.* Cambridge, MA: Harvard University Press.

Peiss, Kathy Lee. 2011. *Hope in a Jar: The Making of America's Beauty Culture.* Philadelphia: University of Pennsylvania Press.

Register, Woody. 2001. *The Kid of Coney Island: Fred Thompson and the Rise of American Amusements.* New York: Oxford University Press.

Riess, Steven A. 1980. *Professional Baseball and American Culture in the Progressive Era.* Champaign: University of Illinois Press.

—.1991. *City Games: The Evolution of American Urban Society and the Rise of Sports.* Champaign: University of Illinois Press.

Rydell, Robert W. and Rob Kroes. 2005. *Buffalo Bill in Bologna: The Americanization of the World, 1869–1922.* Chicago: University of Chicago Press.

Shaffer, Marguerite. 2001. *See America First: Tourism and National Identity, 1880–1940.* Washington: Smithsonian Institution.

Smith, Jacob. 2012. *The Thrill Makers: Celebrity, Masculinity, and Stunt Performance.* Berkeley: University of California Press.

Snyder, Robert W. 1989. *The Voice of the City: Vaudeville and Popular Culture in New York.* New York: Oxford University Press.

Strasser, Susan. 1989. *Satisfaction Guaranteed: The Making of an American Mass Market.* New York: Pantheon.

Thompson, Kristin. 1985. *Exporting Entertainment: America in the World Film Market, 1907–1934.* London: British Film Institute.

Part IV

Economics, Science, and Technology

Chapter Sixteen

American Capitalism: From the Atlantic Economy to Domestic Industrialization

Noam Maggor

The transformation of American capitalism has long provided the framing narrative for histories of the United States during the Gilded Age and Progressive Era. An overwhelmingly agrarian society of small communities, chroniclers of the period often explain, became gripped by the sweeping forces of industrialization, urbanization, and proletarianization. The rise of large industrial corporations in the decades after the Civil War superseded independent manufacturing establishments, prompting Americans to reconceive their political institutions and ideological assumptions. The goal of this chapter is to move capitalism from its conventional place as a structural backdrop and make it a topic of inquiry in its own right. Instead of fast-forwarding through a nearly autonomous economic transition and dashing to a contingent and mostly adaptive terrain of politics and culture, it seeks fruitful ways to unpack capitalism in historically-specific terms. It tackles the period's capitalist transformation as a contentious, uneven, and inherently political process, not "an external force to which Americans responded" but something Americans at the time "were doing" (Sklar 1988, 13).

The big interpretive obstacle to this task has been the resilient hegemony of a particular paradigm over the study of capitalism in this period, namely the theoretical apparatus derived from the work of Max Weber. William Novak recently lamented the "long and darkening shadow" that Weberian analytics have cast over the study of American political development, especially the association of modern institutions with the irresistible advance of a bureaucratically administered order (Novak 2015, 54). Novak's observations apply to research on political economy writ large. Indeed, much of the debate about American capitalism in the late nineteenth and early twentieth centuries, especially the conversation about economic change and state formation, has been a contentious conversation among three types of Weberians.

First and foremost, a group of "triumphalist Weberians" authored grand technology-driven narratives about the period, narratives that emphasized an overpowering thrust of centralization, bureaucratization, and professionalization (Chandler 1977, 1994; Galambos 1970; Haskell 1977; Wiebe 1967). Setting the tone for this scholarship, business historians such as Alfred D. Chandler cast American industrialization as synonymous with the rise of "managerial capitalism." Chandler emphasized the rapid expansion of the railroad network and the perfection of new capital-intensive methods of processing, fabricating, packing, distilling, and smelting in a variety of industries. The more critical development in his analysis, however, was the creation of large managerial bureaucracies within national corporations. New industrial leviathans like Carnegie Steel, Standard Oil, DuPont, and General Electric gained direct control over the entire industrial process, from the acquisition of raw materials down to the distribution of finished products. They developed intricate procedural and accounting methods that allowed them to coordinate complex operations across great distances. Most importantly, according to Chandler, these corporations invented a new type of businessman. No longer the owner of a proprietary enterprise, this modern businessman was a salaried middle manager who supervised a particular division within a firm and whose qualifications were primarily technical and administrative. These multidivisional firms facilitated the accelerated flow of unprecedented volumes of goods, realizing large economies of scale and making the relentless search for order into the organizing logic of American society.

A second milieu of "melancholy Weberians" echoed these triumphalist narratives with a similar emphasis on technology, consolidation, and rationalization (Cronon 1991; Maier 2014; Trachtenberg 1982). These scholars, however, have been emphatically less sanguine about the effects of

A Companion to the Gilded Age and Progressive Era, First Edition. Edited by Christopher McKnight Nichols and Nancy C. Unger.
© 2017 John Wiley & Sons, Inc. Published 2017 by John Wiley & Sons, Inc.

this transition and more attuned to its darker sides. William Cronon's magisterial *Nature's Metropolis*, perhaps the most influential account of the period's economic transformation, adopted the Chandlerian emphasis on technological breakthroughs. The book retained the focus on railroad and telegraph networks, even as it considered the role of more prosaic innovations such as grain elevators, refrigerated cars, barbed wire, and McCormick reapers in expanding and organizing economic activity. Like Chandler's managers, Cronon's businessmen "worship[ed] at the altar of efficiency" and made "war on waste" as they coordinated the seamless stream of livestock, lumber, and grain, from the countryside to Chicago and beyond (1991, 249). Cronon, however, associated the rise of these technocratic values, not with progress and abundance, but with a profound sense of loss. He lamented the erasure of individual autonomy, the degradation of the environment, and eradication of indigenous cultures. In his nineteenth-century America, the flow of commodities subsumed the independent farmer, butcher, lumberman, and shipper under impersonally administered commercial networks. True to Weber's own temperament, Cronon's account was layered with regret about the alienation from nature, disenchantment of the world, and the icy waters of modernity.

Finally, a third and longstanding tradition of "normative Weberians" widely diverged from the Weberian narrative even as it routinely referenced it more or less explicitly as an analytical baseline. Scholars in this vein have used the Weberian framework to identify the ways in which American modernization *fell short*. American industrialization was *not* led by industrial statesmen or efficiency-minded technocrats, Matthew Josephson famously argued, but by a set of crony capitalists. This notorious cohort of "Robber Barons" embodied values that were antithetical to Weberian Protestant capitalism—corruption, ambition, and greed. Railroad builders like Jay Gould and Collis P. Huntington did not strive to improve productivity and rationalize operations. Rather, their financial shenanigans nearly derailed the process of economic centralization. Instead of advancing industrial progress, they "retarded… the predestined consolidation of the whole American transportation system… at least forty years after it had become a logical necessity" (1934, 191).

Richard Hofstadter similarly made volatility and waste central themes in his treatment of America during the Gilded Age. In stark contrast to Weber's sober and impartial bureaucrats, the leading businessmen in Hofstadter's account were "shrewd, energetic, aggressive, rapacious, domineering, insatiable" (1948, 162). Similar normative assertions have been made about the American political system. Scholars like Stephen Skowronek and Theda Skocpol proposed that the development of centralized state capacity was undermined in the case of the United States by party patronage, traditional cultural mores, and an historically weak government bureaucracy (Skocpol 1980; Skowronek 1982). Modernization, according to this view, thus remained unfulfilled in ways that continued to haunt American society deep into the twentieth century.

Nothing has destabilized the familiar contours of the Weberian story in its different varieties more effectively than a recent wave of scholarship on American slavery. Whereas older historiography tended to discuss slavery as a feature of the precapitalist and regional economy of the South, new research paints a very different picture, underscoring slavery's dynamic expansion and its vitality as part of the Atlantic economy during the nineteenth century. Far from an outmoded and moribund institution, scholars now argue, American slavery was on the cutting-edge of modernity in its use of rationalized accounting practices, scientific agriculture, and labor-management methods, including the calibrated use of violence. Moreover, in making possible the mass cultivation of the United States' most important export commodity—cotton—American slavery provided the foundation for the economy of the United States and for industrial development in the Atlantic world as a whole (Baptist 2014; Beckert 2014; Beckert and Rockman 2016; Johnson 2013).

In tracing the origins of capitalism back to plantation slavery, this new work disrupts the familiar historical arc of modernization. If Southern agriculture was thoroughly commercial and enmeshed in transoceanic commodity chains prior to the Civil War, it cannot be easily bracketed out of the story of American economic development. Industrialization, therefore, did not mark a departure from some pastoral notion of traditional small-town society. This transition, rather, was a process of deep-seated economic reorientation, away from established involvement in Atlantic trade and toward an accelerated expansion of industrial production for a domestic market (Livingston 1994). This perspective brings to the fore questions about how the United States successfully pivoted from its origins as an exporter of agricultural commodities, most notably those produced by slave labor, toward a process of continental industrialization. The transition allowed the world's chief producer of raw cotton to emerge by century's end as the world's leading manufacturing nation. This was an unlikely shift, one that other postcolonial republics in the New World struggled to replicate in later decades for a variety of economic, political, and social reasons. Technological breakthroughs, however monumental, are clearly inadequate in accounting for such a transformation. It calls, instead, for a contextual explanation and analysis on several interpretive fronts.

This chapter explores this transition in three intimately-linked spheres, loosely labeled capital, geography, and politics and the state, where recent (and not so recent) historical work might identify the rough contours of a new synthetic narrative. These areas of research loosen the resilient hold of the Weberian templates and open up the conversation to a more historically grounded interpretation.

First, they engage categories and themes that previous scholarship tended to elide or treat as derivative rather than constitutive of a capitalist political economy. Second, whereas national frameworks have traditionally served as vessels of modernization narratives, these categories fruitfully treat the nation state (and particularly the formation of a national political economy) as an historical problem in need of explanation, rather than an obvious scale of analysis. Third, while it is tempting to counter overdetermined narratives with highly contingent and open-ended ones, these lines of inquiry consider larger structural imperatives, without which it would be impossible to explain the profound transformation of the era. Put together, these research avenues soften the explanatory power of technology and bureaucracy. They depart from the entrenched focus on the managerial firm and administrative state. Instead, they pay greater attention to the changing dynamics of capital accumulation, the remaking of economic geography, the formation of political institutions, and the moving contours of social conflict. They stress the malleability of economic change, the agency of grassroots movements, and the competing visions of industrial capitalism that were always in play.

Capital

Corporate-centered accounts of American industrialization have generally paid little attention to the role of finance in the restructuring of business, or, more broadly, to the mobilization of capital into new economic fields. Chandler relegated finance to an afterthought, maintaining that "the lack of a well-organized national capital market" was never a "constraint." His corporations remained self-propelled and largely self-contained agents of industrial efficiency, not vehicles for profit and accumulation (Chandler 1977, 93; John 2009; O'Sullivan 2010). Less optimistic accounts similarly upheld this separation between finance and industry. They treated finance not as an engine behind industrial change, but mostly as an external source of disruption and volatility (Josephson 1934). A finance-driven approach removes this artificial separation, embedding American industrialization in a longer history of investment and reinvestment. These "successive systemic cycles of accumulation" forged the malleable but nonetheless deeply structural connections between changes in production, management, and distribution and shifting patterns of wealth creation (Arrighi 1994, 6; Braudel 1982).

Prior to the Civil War, American wealth was decidedly bound up with the cotton economy and chattel slavery. On the eve of the war, cotton added up to more than half the value of all United States exports, allowing the young republic to gain a near-monopoly over the supply of this valuable staple to the industrializing United Kingdom. As a result, elites in the slave South were, on average, twice as wealthy as their northern counterparts. The South also boasted the twelve richest counties in the United States (Rothman 2005, 72). The economic centrality of cotton, however, was not confined to the South alone. It extended north of the Mason–Dixon line to the large port cities on the Atlantic coast. By far the wealthiest New Yorkers at the time were those merchants who became involved in the cotton trade. Gaining dominance over lucrative maritime shipping lanes, these men advanced credit to southern planters, acquired raw cotton, and transported the valuable staple to Liverpool, returning to New York with British manufactured goods. The gigantic volume of trade generated by the cotton kingdom became "the primary engine of profits" for New York's merchants, helping to propel the city to its national prominence (Beckert 2001, 20).

Like New York, Boston's fortunes had been entangled with the South ever since New England's leading businessmen turned to the industrial spinning and weaving of cotton textiles. After successful experiments in Waltham (1813) and Lowell (1822), affluent Bostonians financed a proliferation of cotton mills throughout the region. By the 1840s, cotton textiles had become the largest manufacturing industry in the United States, with more capital invested, more labor employed, and largest net value produced. This industry created what Senator Charles Sumner derisively called an "unholy union" between "the cotton-planters and flesh-mongers of Louisiana and Mississippi and the cotton-spinners and traffickers of New England—between the lords of the lash and the lords of the loom" (Dalzell 1987; Sumner 1870, 81; Ware 1931). Given these interregional alignments that created powerful bonds between business elites in the North and their Southern counterparts, it was hardly surprising that members of these elites fought tooth and nail to contain anti-slavery sentiment and avert the Civil War (Beckert 2001; Foner 1941; Maggor 2017a; O'Connor 1968).

The Civil War irreparably shattered the cotton economy, which had been the country's chief economic engine (North 1961). This might very well have been the beginning of American economic decline. Yet antebellum business elites, with the obvious exception of the planter class, showed a remarkable ability to respond to this crisis and redeploy their financial resources. Long beholden to Atlantic trade and King Cotton, businessmen in the north forged new avenues for profitable investment in the emerging industrial economy, most notably in the financing of American railroads. High-profile partnerships like Brown Brothers & Co. that had made their fortune financing Anglo-American trade and merchandising southern cotton in Liverpool, abandoned trade to focus exclusively on banking (Carosso 1970, 8–9; Killick 1977). August Belmont, the Rothschilds' agent in New York, had used his European connections to finance trade in slave-produced agricultural commodities. In the aftermath of the war, Belmont & Co. became a major player on the stock exchange and joined other Wall Street houses in floating railroad securities (Boodry 2016; Redlich 1951, 380, 383). German-Jewish cotton brokers like Henry

Lehman and his brothers, who had established business connections throughout the South, transitioned first to commerce in petroleum, then to railroad investment and industrial banking (Supple 1957, 152, 156). Altogether, New York's merchants supplied "more personnel to postbellum investment banking" than any other group. They also provided much of the leadership of railroad and other national corporations (Beckert 2001, 238; Berk 1994, 27). Transatlantic business networks that had facilitated trade now drew on European capital to bankroll American industrialization (Wilkins 1989).

The same transition occurred domestically as American savings were redirected into railroad and industrial development. Prior to the war, specialized houses that dealt with the securities of western railroads operated on the margins of Wall Street. In 1849 James F.D. Lanier "became convinced that capital could be safely invested in the securities of Western roads." He formed with Richard M. Winslow the first homegrown investment house that dealt specifically in these stocks and bonds, creating a near-monopoly on Wall Street in this line of business. It initially proved "pretty rough going" (Redlich 1951, 354–355). With Lanier and Winslow's support, Henry V. Poor launched the first American business journal devoted to railroad finance precisely to promote and advertise these ventures. One of his early editorials explained that New Yorkers had "too much [other] business constantly on hand [and have thus] remained in indifference to the importance of railroads" (Chandler 1956, 80). This situation changed dramatically after the war when a group of powerful investment firms and a proliferation of brokerage houses made railroad corporations into the nation's core economic sector. The New York Stock Exchange, listing nearly three hundred railroad corporations, rapidly expanded to accommodate this new magnitude of activity (Beckert 2001, 149).

Boston's business district similarly shed its former role as the hub of a textile-manufacturing region and turned emphatically to the financing of distant ventures. "One had not to look back far to see one or two brokers running about State Street and trying to get someone to buy or to sell a few shares of a cotton mill or one of the little New England railroads, and thus doing all the brokerage business that was offered," one Bostonian recalled. "But within a few years a new situation had developed. The lavish outpouring of bonds and stock by the new Western railroads… combined to make a stock exchange which would have dazed the old-time broker" (Morse 1920). As the manufacturing of cotton textiles lost its luster as an investment, the saved resources of Boston's financial sector moved into the financing of railroads and heavy industry out west (Gates 1951; Johnson and Supple 1967; Maggor 2017b).

The infusion of large-scale capital funded an enormous expansion of the railroad system. The railroad mileage of the United States jumped from just over 35,000 miles in 1865 to almost 167,000 in 1890, and to a peak of nearly 255,000 in 1916. Total capital investment soared from $300 million in 1850—much of it public money—to nearly $9 billion in 1890 and $20 billion in the 1910s (Carter and Sutch 2006). The United States drew in large amounts of European capital—German, Dutch, and primarily British—to finance this expansion. Between 1865 and 1914, the economy of the United States absorbed almost as much British capital as Argentina, Australia, and Canada combined. These large flows nevertheless represented a declining portion of overall investment as American industry increasingly relied on domestic savings, mobilized by investment houses in the United States (Davis and Gallman 2001, 9, 27).

The ever-improving ability to pool together and mobilize financial resources transformed American manufacturing. Prior to the war, banks and other financial institutions, primarily preoccupied with commerce, rarely extended credit to budding industrialists. The textile industry in New England was exceptional in using the corporate form for manufacturing enterprising and in drawing on large-scale financial resources. Other manufacturing industries, including important ones like clothing and shoemaking, drew on local credit networks or borrowed from wholesalers. Producers in these industries had little access to banking reserves and capital markets. In the war's aftermath, the former "handmaidens of international commerce" dramatically remade themselves into the close allies of "undercapitalized domestic industries" (Livingston 1994, 36). The financing of manufacturing became routine, giving American industries an entirely new scale. Among the beneficiaries were companies like Pabst Brewing, Carnegie Steel, Swift and Co., and Standard Oil whose growth was made possible by loans from banks and insurance companies.

Men like Andrew Carnegie, Gustavus Swift, and John D. Rockefeller owed much of their success to their ability to bring together a group of backers, or "friends,"—regionally at first, and then in the East—who provided their firms with plentiful and cheap credit. With these financial resources at their disposal, they introduced capital-intensive processes that revolutionized their respective industries (Davis 1958; 1960, 264; O'Sullivan 2010, 333–337; Porter and Livesay 1971, 127, 134–136). These patterns of "relationship lending" were formalized after the major breakthroughs in industrial processes had been made. In what historians called the "Great Merger Movement" around the turn of the century, investment bankers like J.P. Morgan leveraged the power of Wall Street to engineer a wave of corporate consolidations. These consolidations created enormous corporations like U.S. Steel, International Harvester, and General Electric and made "industrials" into stock market staples in the twentieth century (Lamoreaux 1985; Pak, 2013; Roy 1997).

The rise of large-scale industry did not displace or supersede American agriculture. The number of American farms continued to increase through the heyday of industrialization, more than tripling from two to six and a half million between 1860 and 1920 (Clark 2012, 13–15). Here, too, finance proved formative. Agricultural expansion was in large measure funded via farm mortgages, which became major items in the portfolios of large financial institutions, most notably insurance companies. Mortgage loans provided farmers with capital for the acquisition of land, machinery, and farm improvements. This growing debt burden, which covered almost 30% of all taxable farm acreage nationally, also pressed farmers and their household members to work harder and longer hours. Earlier in the century, American freehold farmers hedged their participation in the market by practicing "mixed farming." They met subsistence needs of their families and sold surpluses for a profit. Unlike slave plantations in the South, they did their best to avoid overreliance on a single cash crop. The permeation of capital into the countryside rendered this strategy obsolete in the postbellum decades. Landownership was widespread and family labor, not wage labor, remained the norm. Debt nevertheless imposed market discipline on farmers, impelling them to retreat from diversification and crop rotations. In a pattern typical of agricultural peripheries around the world, they instead devoted more and more of their land to single crops that brought "cash as soon as possible" (Bogue 1955, 1963; Levy 2012).

This pattern of single-crop farming proved to be strikingly complementary to urban growth. American producers found an expanding market for manufactured goods in the commercializing countryside, where items could no longer be produced within the household. Farmers, in turn, not only grew the food that sustained the booming population of cities, but also provided the raw materials for key industrial sectors like meatpacking, milling, and brewing. Agricultural goods flowing into markets from the countryside provided much of the freight traffic for the railroads, which of course also created demand for steel, coal, and lumber. These dynamics created potent links between city and countryside. They forged a veritable "agro-industrial complex" that became the core of an American continental market (Cronon 1992; Livingston 1994).

Geography

The flow of capital into new economic fields—railroads, large-scale industry, and freehold farms—did not merely signal massive financial infusions into a new set of economic sectors. It also, crucially, signaled the movement of capital across vast distances, primarily from urban centers like New York, Boston, and Philadelphia to the Midwest and beyond. This movement guided the integration of large continental hinterlands—abundant in fertile land and valuable minerals—ever more firmly into the orbit of the national economy. Always arduous, halting, and geographically uneven, it nevertheless gradually created a rapidly growing American domestic market.

The aggressive pursuit of ample and cheap supplies of minerals and agricultural commodities in this era was not unique to the United States. In what economists have called the "golden age of resource-based development," capitalists and statesmen the world over reached boldly into the deep interiors of all continents in search of natural resources and fertile land (Barbier 2011, 2; Hobsbawm 1989). Shifting from an earlier emphasis on tropical commodities in the world economy, international investment now went into continental hinterlands in temperate regions in the Americas, Australasia, and Russia. The Great Plains of the United States rose in tandem with the rapid growth in the Canadian prairies, the Argentine pampas, the South African veldt, the Central Asian steppes, and the Australian outback (Osterhammel 2014, 326). Primary products from all of these territories flowed on steamships and railroad cars into the core urban regions of the world economy, energizing a period of booming industrial development in Western Europe, Japan, and the United States.

While fully entwined with larger global process, the American case nevertheless stood out as distinctive among other frontiers of resource developments. The resource frontier of the United States was the most territorially extensive and capital intensive of all land expansions. Improved farmland in the American West increased more rapidly than anywhere else around the world, swelling in the Great Prairies alone from 78 million to over 250 million acres between 1870 and 1910. Fueled by access to credit, agriculture in these territories seamlessly assimilated farm improvements such as plows, threshers, harvesters, and fertilizers. By the early twentieth century, a long belt stretching from Iowa to eastern Nebraska produced nearly half of the nation's corn, and a vast frontier extending from southwestern Minnesota to the Dakotas, and west into the plains of Kansas, Nebraska, eastern Colorado, and the interior Pacific Northwest produced 65% of the nation's wheat (Barbier 2011, 395–397; White 1991, 244).

Alongside farming, cattle- and sheep-raising also expanded, leading to the growth of large-scale ranches that in many cases grazed their livestock on intensified irrigated pasturage. Texas maintained its position as the chief supplier of livestock from 1860 to 1920, its cattle population growing from 2.9 to 6.2 million, but it was joined by California, Colorado, Montana, Idaho, New Mexico, Oregon, and other western states, which together, by that year, raised over 10 million head of cattle and over 18 million sheep.

The lumber industry was yet another example of finance-driven western territorial expansion. Larger firms in Michigan and Wisconsin, employing thousands, made these states into the top lumber producers in the 1870s and 1880s. After the 1890s, the Pacific Coast—Washington, Oregon, and California—became another major source of lumber (Meyer 2001, 316, 320). With the influx of eastern capital, these western landscapes achieved a steady rise in productivity. They generated ever-growing portions of the overall American output of agricultural produce and natural resources.

Even more remarkable than farms, ranches, and forests, were American mines that yielded minerals and fossil fuels in larger quantities and faster rates than other global frontiers. This was not due to a better natural endowment, but a direct result of heavier investment—private and public—in the infrastructure of exploration, transportation, extraction, and refining (Barbier 2011, 402). The mining of coal, in established fields in Pennsylvania, West Virginia, and Ohio, but also in Colorado, Wyoming, and New Mexico, increased in productivity as miners used steam power to ventilate, pump water, and dig deeper shafts. Electric cutters also made coal extraction more efficient. With these capital-intensive methods, the annual output of coal in the United States climbed from 26 million to 562 million tons in the half century after the Civil War (Barbier 2011, 400; Meyer 2001, 321).

Bituminous coal, processed into coke, fired up the hot-blast furnaces of the iron and steel industry, which increasingly acquired its ore from rich deposits in Michigan and Minnesota. Massive investments in shipping facilities, high-capacity ore vessels, and lake and canal improvements made these mines readily accessible, leading to the formation of a steel belt that stretched between Cleveland and Pittsburgh (Meinig 2000, 233–234). Overall, territorial expansion made the United States into the world's leading producer of the era's most important fossil fuels and minerals, including coal, iron, copper, lead, petroleum, phosphate, silver, and zinc. More than in any other global periphery, the relentless exploitation of this "vertical frontier" created important linkages between extraction and processing (Barbier 2011, 401).

And yet, the shifting economic geography of the West was far from uniform, rational, or totalizing, something sweeping narratives have tended to downplay or ignore. The stage theory of development, made famous as Frederick Jackson Turner's "Frontier Thesis," has long been discredited. The West clearly did not develop in evolutionary fashion through a series of stages—subsistence farming, small towns and local industries, intensification of farming and industry, and finally specialization in export industries (Turner 1920). Export-based models similarly fail to capture the full complexity of the West's developmental arc. Long-distance commerce in high-volume commodities such as wheat, meat, and lumber provided only a partial impetus for the region's economic emergence. The manufacturing base of the West, and particularly what became the Midwest, had very diverse origins in the antebellum decades. It had always fostered homegrown manufacturing in a variety of sectors, including ones that were not directly related to the processing of agricultural commodities. This pattern only accelerated after the Civil War, despite rapid improvements in transportation that drastically lowered the costs of interregional commerce. Unlike other global peripheries in this period, the American West never became pure and simple an exporter of primary commodities to the industrializing East and a wide open market for Eastern manufactured goods (Meyer 1989, 287). The region successfully pushed back against "the Great Specialization" that sharply divided the world economy between supplier of foodstuffs and raw materials, on one hand, and urban-industrial cores on the other (Findlay and O'Rourke 2007).

In ways that have not been satisfactorily theorized or explained, the region did not become increasingly oriented exclusively toward cross-regional export sectors. Midwestern industries like apparel, furniture, printing and publishing, building materials, and fabricated metals which sold products in local and regional markets flourished and grew, despite competition from the East. They continued to employ large numbers of workers—by some measures the majority of workers (Meyer 1989, 30). The gravitational pull of large cities in the region also remained limited. Despite their prodigious growth, the major metropolises operated as part of a broader territorial production complex that included a dense network of small- and medium-sized cities that have been left out of many standard accounts. Chicago famously dominated the meatpacking industry but never monopolized it. Its meatpackers had rivals in St. Louis, Omaha, Kansas City, St. Joseph, and Sioux City, not to mention smaller centers like Cedar Rapids, Waterloo, Ottumwa, and Indianapolis. McCormick and Co., also of Chicago, became the best-known manufacturer of agricultural machinery, but it competed in a diversified industry with producers from Racine, Springfield, Peoria, Decatur, Rockford, and South Bend (Page and Walker 1991, 299–300). Overall, about half the industrial workforce of the Midwest was employed in smaller cities, the top eight industries cities—Chicago, Cincinnati, St. Louis, Cleveland, Milwaukee, Detroit, Louisville, and Indianapolis—in fact employing a steady, and perhaps even declining, percentage of the overall industrial labor force (Meyer 1989, 934). This multi-layered urban-industrial geography, irreducible to several monumental sectors, continued to grow into the twentieth century.

Politics and the State

None of the above trajectories can be explained without close attention to the development of American political institutions. The shift from the cotton economy to domestic industrialization, the expansion of railroads and manufacturing, the intensive exploitation of natural resources, and the commercialization of agriculture all rested in significant ways on state policy and government activism. The centrality of the American state in setting the terms of economic development at the end of the nineteenth century defies pervasive interpretations that have emphasized lack, if not absence, of government capacity (Novak 2008). Much of the literature casts the growth of government in the United States as a belated and often inadequate response to a fully realized process of industrialization. This scholarship rarely interrogated the power of political institutions to constitute economic change. It not only perpetuated the myth of a frail and ineffective American state, but also rendered immaterial, or at the very least incomprehensible, large swaths of policy questions and debates that animated American politics.

The American state was nevertheless at the forefront of American industrialization. Continental industrialization took off, not merely as an economic transition, but first and foremost as a political alternative to the further expansion of the Cotton Kingdom, which showed no sign of commercial decline prior to the Civil War. The war reversed the American government's commitment to free trade and the defense of slavery. It brought to the fore a new industrial program, championed by a hegemonic Republican Party. The continental scale of the Republican vision became clear during the summer of 1862 when Abraham Lincoln diverted Union troops from the Civil War effort to decimate the Sioux Indians in the Old Northwest (Hahn 2013). Congress followed up with measures that enacted high protectionist tariffs that nurtured industrial infrastructure and domestic industries (like iron and steel), distributed western land to farmers under the Homestead Act, and provided hefty government subsidies to transcontinental railroads (Livingston 1987; Bensel 1990; White 2011).

These policies inaugurated several decades of aggressive government action in support of national industrial development. Federal forces escalated violence against Indians in the trans-Mississippi West, opening it for extraction and cultivation. After two decades of violent conflict, they defeated the three most formidable Indian polities that had previously dominated large western territories: the Comanches of the southern plains, the Sioux of the central and northern plains, and, finally, the Apaches, who surrendered in 1886 (White 1991, 104–107; Hämäläinen 2008; DeLay 2008). Indian defeats shifted attention to ecological exploration, in a series of federally-funded surveys and expeditions that eventually led to the institutionalization of western exploration under the U.S. Geological Survey in 1879. These surveys of remote territories guided investors and settlers to mineral deposits, grazing lands, and sources of water. Private actors then seized the land in one of many manners by which the government distributed it. Under the provisions of the Homestead Act, for example, millions of acres of public land were privatized and turned into nearly 400,000 farms. Hundreds of millions of acres in land grants, 125 million between 1862 and 1872 alone, were handed over to railroad corporations to subsidize construction. Loggers, miners, and ranchers all harvested resources that were lavishly disbursed to them from public lands (White 1991, 132–135, 143, 145, 154). These government policies made industrial exploitation of western territories exceptionally intensive by international standards.

Equally significant were Federal policies that promoted the formation of a national market—the largest such free trade zone in the world—which was far from preordained or technologically necessary. A product of wartime emergency, a system of federally chartered and federally regulated national banks decisively displaced the decentralized, state-based banking system that characterized the antebellum years. This created for the first time a stable federal currency that was coextensive with the nation's territory. The country's highly controversial return to the gold standard in 1879 also stabilized currency and credit networks across space (Barreyre 2016). Crucial in this respect were a series of Supreme Court decisions that upheld the exclusive authority of the federal government over interstate commerce. Affirming the primacy of interregional commerce, the Court declared corporations to be legal persons and, therefore, free from state-level regulations that might impede "reasonable profits upon their invested capital." Federal authorities were concerned that if the states had been able to regulate commerce, the national market would be "balkanized" into small geographical units in ways that would derail industrial consolidation (Bensel 2000, 321–349).

The federal government's tenacious activism on behalf of the national market, however, was unthinkable without the robust efforts *to the contrary* on the part of a whole range of public authorities and political constituencies: workers, farmers, miners, local and regional merchants and producers, and many more. Monetary policy was a hotly contested political question throughout the period, facing a forceful heterodox challenge from the less urbanized and capital-poor regions of the country (Barreyre 2015; Sklansky forthcoming). State authorities in the Midwest insisted that railroads were public utilities and therefore subject to government regulation, including the regulation of shipping rates (Novak 2010; Miller 1971) An array of new western states like Colorado, Wyoming, Montana, Idaho, Washington joined the Union in the 1870s and 1880s with state constitutions that sanctioned railroad regulation, attenuated the property rights of financial investors, empowered workers to mobilize collectively without interference, and mandated government oversight over safety and labor conditions (Maggor 2017b, Bridges 2008). Paradoxically, within the structure of the American state, political and economic fragmentation accelerated in tandem with national unification. In ways that the Supreme Court could not hope to fully contain, the states passed hundreds if not thousands of statutes affecting every aspect of economic life (Novak 2010, Gerstle 2016). Any notion of a totalized "consolidation" of the political economy of the United States, therefore, both greatly simplifies and overstates the case. State formation produced, not a flat and noninterventionist platform for market actors, but a highly wrinkled regulatory landscape that survived deep into the twentieth century.

References

Arrighi, Giovanni. 2010. *The Long Twentieth Century: Money, Power, and the Origins of Our Times*, 2nd edn. New York: Verso.

Baptist, Edward E. 2014. *The Half Has Never Been Told: Slavery and the Making of American Capitalism*. New York: Basic Books.

Barbier, Edward. 2011. *Scarcity and Frontiers: How Economies Have Developed through Natural Resource Exploitation*. Cambridge: Cambridge University Press.

Barreyre, Nicolas. 2015. *Gold and Freedom: The Political Economy of Reconstruction*. Charlottesville: University of Virginia Press.

Beckert, Sven. 2001. *The Monied Metropolis: New York City and the Consolidation of the American Bourgeoisie, 1850–1896*. Cambridge: Cambridge University Press.

—. 2014. *Empire of Cotton : A Global History*. New York: Alfred A. Knopf.

—. and Seth Rockman, ed. 2016. *Slavery's Capitalism: A New History of American Economic Development*. Philadelphia: University of Pennsylvania Press.

Bensel, Richard Franklin. 1990. *Yankee Leviathan: The Origins of Central State Authority in America, 1859–1877*. Cambridge: Cambridge University Press.

—. 2000. *The Political Economy of American Industrialization, 1877–1900*. Cambridge: Cambridge University Press.

Berk, Gerald. 1994. *Alternative Tracks: The Constitution of American Industrial Order, 1865–1917*. Baltimore, MD: Johns Hopkins University Press.

Bogue, Allan G. 1955. *Money at Interest; the Farm Mortgage on the Middle Border*. Ithaca, NY: Cornell University Press.

—. 1963. *From Prairie to Corn Belt: Farming on the Illinois and Iowa Prairies in the 19th Century*. Chicago: Quadrangle Books.

Boodry, Kathryn. 2016. "August Belmont and the World the Slaves Made." In *Slavery's Capitalism: A New History of American Economic Development*, ed. Sven Beckert and Seth Rockman, 163–178. Philadelphia: University of Pennsylvania Press.

Braudel, Fernand. 1982. *The Wheels of Commerce*. New York: Harper & Row.

Bridges, Amy. 2008. "Managing the Periphery in the Gilded Age: Writing Constitutions for the Western States." *Studies in American Political Development* 22: 32–58.

Carosso, Vincent P. 1970. *Investment Banking in America, a History*. Cambridge, MA: Harvard University Press.

Carter, Susan B. and Richard Sutch, eds. 2006. *Historical Statistics of the United States*. Millennial edition. Cambridge: Cambridge University Press.

Chandler, Alfred D. 1956. *Henry Varnum Poor, Business Editor, Analyst, and Reformer*. Cambridge, MA: Harvard University Press.

—. 1977. *The Visible Hand: The Managerial Revolution in American Business*. Cambridge, MA: Belknap Press/Harvard University Press.

—. 1994. *Scale and Scope: The Dynamics of Industrial Capitalism*. Cambridge, MA: Belknap Press/Harvard University Press.

Clark, Christopher. 2012. "The Agrarian Context of American Capitalist Development." In *Capitalism Takes Command: The Social Transformation of Nineteenth-Century America*, ed. Michael Zakim and Gary J. Kornblith, 39–68. Chicago: University of Chicago Press. doi: 10.7208/chicago/9780226977997.001.0001.

Cronon, William. 1991. *Nature's Metropolis: Chicago and the Great West*. New York: W.W. Norton.

Dalzell, Robert F. 1987. *Enterprising Elite: The Boston Associates and the World They Made*. Cambridge, MA: Harvard University Press.

Davis, Lance. 1958. "Stock Ownership in the Early New England Textile Industry, A Case Study." *Business History Review* 32: 204–222.

— 1960. "The New England Textile Mills and the Capital Markets: A Study of Industrial Borrowing 1840–1860." *The Journal of Economic History* 20: 1–30.

—. and Robert E. Gallman. 2001. *Evolving Financial Markets and International Capital Flows: Britain, the Americas, and Australia, 1865–1914*. Cambridge: Cambridge University Press.

DeLay, Brian. 2008. *War of a Thousand Deserts: Indian Raids and the U.S.–Mexican War*. New Haven, CT: Yale University Press.

Findlay, Ronald and Kevin H. O'Rourke. 2007. *Power and Plenty: Trade, War, and the World Economy in the Second Millennium*. Princeton, NJ: Princeton University Press.

Foner, Philip Sheldon. 1941. *Business & Slavery: The New York Merchants & the Irrepressible Conflict*. Chapel Hill: University of North Carolina Press.

Galambos, Louis. 1970. "The Emerging Organizational Synthesis in Modern American History." *Business History Review* 44: 279–90. doi: 10.2307/3112614.

Gates, William Bryan. 1951. *Michigan Copper and Boston Dollars; an Economic History of the Michigan Copper Mining Industry*. Cambridge, MA: Harvard University Press.

Gerstle, Gary. 2015. *Liberty and Coercion: The Paradox of American Government from the Founding to the Present*. Princeton, NJ: Princeton University Press.

Hämäläinen, Pekka. 2008. *The Comanche Empire*. New Haven, CT: Yale University Press.

Hahn, Steven. 2013. "Slave Emancipation, Indian Peoples, and the Projects of a New American Nation-State." *Journal of the Civil War Era* 3: 307–330.

Haskell, Thomas L. 1977. *The Emergence of Professional Social Science: The American Social Science Association and the Nineteenth-Century Crisis of Authority*. Urbana: University of Illinois Press.

Hobsbawm, Eric J. 1989. *The Age of Empire, 1875–1914*. New York: Vintage.

Hofstadter, Richard. 1948. *The American Political Tradition and the Men Who Made It*. New York: Alfred A. Knopf.

John, Richard R. 2009. "Who Were the Gilders? And Other Seldom-Asked Questions about Business, Technology, and Political Economy in the United States, 1877–1900." *Journal of the Gilded Age and Progressive Era* 8: 474–80.

Johnson, Arthur M. and Barry E. Supple. 1967. *Boston Capitalists and Western Railroads; a Study in the Nineteenth-Century Railroad Investment Process*. Cambridge, MA: Harvard University Press.

Johnson, Walter. 2013. *River of Dark Dreams: Slavery and Empire in the Cotton Kingdom*. Cambridge, MA: Harvard University Press.

Josephson, Matthew. 1934. *The Robber Barons; the Great American Capitalists, 1861–1901*. New York: Harcourt.

Killick, John R. 1977. "The Cotton Operations of Alexander Brown and Sons in the Deep South, 1820–1860." *Journal of Southern History* 43: 169–194. doi:10.2307/2207344.

Lamoreaux, Naomi R. 1985. *The Great Merger Movement in American Business, 1895–1904.* Cambridge: Cambridge University Press.

Levy, Jonathan. 2012. "The Mortgage Worked the Hardest: The Fate of Landed Independence in Nineteenth-Century America." In *Capitalism Takes Command: The Social Transformation of Nineteenth-Century America*, ed. Michael Zakim and Gary J. Kornblith, 39–68. Chicago: University of Chicago Press. doi:10.7208/chicago/9780226977997.003.0003

Livingston, James. 1994. *Pragmatism and the Political Economy of Cultural Revolution, 1850–1940.* Chapel Hill: University of North Carolina Press.

Maggor, Noam. 2017a. *Brahmin Capitalism: Frontiers of Wealth and Populism in America's First Gilded Age.* Cambridge, MA: Harvard University Press.

—. 2017b. "To 'Coddle and Caress These Great Capitalists': Eastern Money, Frontier Populism, and the Politics of Market Integration in the American West." *American Historical Review* 122: 1.

Maier, Charles S. 2014. *Leviathan 2.0: Inventing Modern Statehood.* Cambridge, MA: Belknap/Harvard University Press.

Meinig, D. W. 2000. *The Shaping of America: A Geographical Perspective on 500 Years of History, Volume 3: Transcontinental America, 1850–1915.* New Haven, CT: Yale University Press.

Meyer, David R. 1989. "Midwestern Industrialization and the American Manufacturing Belt in the Nineteenth Century." *Journal of Economic History* 49: 921–937. doi: 10.1017/S0022050700009505.

—. 2001. "The National Integration of Regional Economies, 1860–1920." In *North America: The Historical Geography of a Changing Continent*, 2nd edn, ed. Thomas F. McIlwraith and Edward K. Muller, 307–332. Lanham, MD: Rowman & Littlefield.

Miller, George Hall. *Railroads and the Granger Laws.* Madison: University of Wisconsin Press, 1971.

Morse John T. 1920. "Memoir of Henry Lee Higginson." *Proceedings of the Massachusetts Historical Society*, 53: 105–127.

North, Douglass. 1961. *The Economic Growth of the United States, 1790–1860.* Englewood Cliffs, NJ: Prentice-Hall.

Novak, William J. 2008. "The Myth of the 'Weak' American State." *American Historical Review* 113: 752–772.

—. 2010. "Law and the Social Control of American Capitalism. *Emory Law Journal* 60: 377–405.

—. 2015. "Beyond Max Weber: The Need for a Democratic (not Aristocratic) Theory of the Modern State." *Tocqueville Review/La Revue Tocqueville* 36: 43–91.

O'Connor, Thomas H. 1968. *Lords of the Loom, the Cotton Whigs and the Coming of the Civil War.* New York: Scribner.

Osterhammel, Jürgen. 2014. *The Transformation of the World: A Global History of the Nineteenth Century.* Princeton, NJ: Princeton University Press.

O'Sullivan, Mary. 2010. "Finance Capital in Chandlerian Capitalism." *Industrial and Corporate Change* 19: 549–589. doi: 10.1093/icc/dtq016.

Page, Brian and Richard A. Walker. 1991. "From Settlement to Fordism : The Agro-Industrial Revolution in the American Midwest." *Economic Geography* 67: 281–315.

Pak, Susie. 2013. *Gentlemen Bankers: The World of J. P. Morgan.* Cambridge, MA: Harvard University Press.

Porter, Glenn and Harold C. Livesay. 1971. *Merchants and Manufacturers; Studies in the Changing Structure of Nineteenth-Century Marketing.* Baltimore, MD: Johns Hopkins Press.

Redlich, Fritz. 1951. *The Molding of American Banking: Men and Ideas.* New York: Hafner.

Rothman, Adam. 2005. "The "Slave Power" in the United States, 1783–1865." In *Ruling America: A History of Wealth and Power in a Democracy*, ed. Steve Fraser and Gary Gerstle, 64–91. Cambridge, MA: Harvard University Press.

Roy, William G. 1997. *Socializing Capital: The Rise of the Large Industrial Corporation in America.* Princeton, NJ: Princeton University Press.

Sklansky, Jeffrey P. Forthcoming. *Sovereign of the Market: The Money Question in Early America.* Chicago: University of Chicago Press.

Sklar, Martin J. 1998. *The Corporate Reconstruction of American Capitalism, 1890–1916: The Market, the Law, and Politics.* Cambridge: Cambridge University Press.

Skocpol, Theda. 1980. "Political Response to Capitalist Crisis: Neo-Marxist Theories of the State and the Case of the New Deal." *Politics and Society* 10: 155–201. doi: 10.1177/003232928001000202

Skowronek, Stephen. 1982. *Building a New American State : The Expansion of National Administrative Capacities, 1877–1920.* Cambridge: Cambridge University Press.

Sumner, Charles. 1870. *The Works of Charles Sumner.* Boston: Lee and Shepard.

Supple, Barry E. 1957. "A Business Elite: German–Jewish Financiers in Nineteenth-Century New York." *Business History Review* 31: 143–78. doi:10.2307/3111848.

Trachtenberg, Alan. 1982. *The Incorporation of America: Culture and Society in the Gilded Age.* New York: Hill & Wang.

Turner, Frederick Jackson. 1920. *The Frontier in American History.* Reprint. New York: Holt, Rinehart, and Winston.

Ware, Caroline F. 1931. *The Early New England Cotton Manufacture: A Study in Industrial Beginnings.* Boston: Houghton Mifflin.

White, Richard. 1991. *"It's Your Misfortune and None of My Own": A History of the American West.* Norman: University of Oklahoma Press.

—. 2011. *Railroaded: The Transcontinentals and the Making of Modern America.* W. W. Norton.

Wiebe, Robert H. 1967. *The Search for Order, 1877–1920.* New York: Hill & Wang.

Wilkins, Mira. 1989. *The History of Foreign Investment in the United States to 1914.* Cambridge, MA: Harvard University Press.

Further Reading

Andrews, Thomas G. 2008. *Killing for Coal: America's Deadliest Labor War.* Cambridge, MA: Harvard University Press.

Balogh, Brian. 1991. "Reorganizing the Organizational Synthesis: Federal–Professional Relations in Modern America." *Studies in American Political Development* 5: 119–72.

—. 2009. *A Government Out of Sight: The Mystery of National Authority in Nineteenth-Century America.* Cambridge: Cambridge University Press.

Cohen, Nancy. 2002. *The Reconstruction of American Liberalism, 1865–1914.* Chapel Hill: University of North Carolina Press.

Currarino, Rosanne. 2011. *The Labor Question in America: Economic Democracy in the Gilded Age.* Urbana: University of Illinois Press.

Davis, Lance E. 1963. "Capital Immobilities and Finance Capitalism: A Study of Economic Evolution in the United States, 1820–1920." *Explorations in Entrepreneurial History* 1: 88–105.

—. Lance. 1966. "The Capital Markets and Industrial Concentration: The U.S. and U.K., a Comparative Study." *Economic History Review* 19: 255–72.

—. and Robert J. Cull. 1994. *International Capital Markets and American Economic Growth, 1820–1914.* Cambridge: Cambridge University Press.

Fink, Leon. 2015. *The Long Gilded Age: American Capitalism and the Lessons of a New World Order.* Philadelphia: University of Pennsylvania Press.

Forbath, William E. 1991. *Law and the Shaping of the American Labor Movement.* Cambridge, MA: Harvard University Press.

Geyer, Michael and Charles Bright. 1995. "World History in a Global Age." *American Historical Review* 100: 1034–1060.

—. and Charles Bright. 2002. "Where in the World Is America? The History of the United State in the Global Age," in *Rethinking American History in a Global Age*, ed. Thomas Bender, 63–100. Berkeley: University of California Press.

Gourevitch, Alexander. 2015. *From Slavery to the Cooperative Commonwealth: Labor and Republican Liberty in the Nineteenth Century.* Cambridge: Cambridge University Press.

Gutman, Herbert George. 1977. *Work, Culture, and Society in Industrializing America: Essays in American Working-Class and Social History.* New York: Vintage Books.

Hahn, Steven. 1983. *The Roots of Southern Populism : Yeomen Farmers and the Transformation of the Georgia Upcountry, 1850–1890.* New York: Oxford University Press.

—. 2003. *A Nation under Our Feet: Black Political Struggles in the Rural South from Slavery to the Great Migration.* Cambridge, MA: Harvard University Press.

Hart, John M. 2002. *Empire and Revolution: The Americans in Mexico since the Civil War.* Berkeley: University of California Press.

Hunter, Tera W. 1997. *To "Joy My Freedom": Southern Black Women's Lives and Labors after the Civil War.* Cambridge, MA: Harvard University Press.

Jentz, John B. and Richard Schneirov. 2012. *Chicago in the Age of Capital: Class, Politics, and Democracy during the Civil War and Reconstruction.* Urbana: University of Illinois Press.

John, Richard R. 2010. *Network Nation: Inventing American Telecommunications.* Cambridge, MA: Harvard University Press.

Johnston, Robert D. 2003. *The Radical Middle Class: Populist Democracy and the Question of Capitalism in Progressive Era Portland, Oregon.* Princeton, NJ: Princeton University Press.

Leach, William. 1993. *Land of Desire: Merchants, Power, and the Rise of a New American Culture.* New York: Pantheon Books.

Lears, T. J. Jackson. 1994. *Fables of Abundance: A Cultural History of Advertising in America.* New York: Basic Books.

Levy, Jonathan. 2012. *Freaks of Fortune: The Emerging World of Capitalism and Risk in America.* Cambridge, MA: Harvard University Press.

Lewis, Robert D. 2004. *Manufacturing Suburbs: Building Work and Home on the Metropolitan Fringe.* Philadelphia: Temple University Press.

Licht, Walter. 1995. *Industrializing America: The Nineteenth Century.* American Moment. Baltimore, MD: John Hopkins University Press.

Livingston, James, 1986. *Origins of the Federal Reserve System: Money, Class, and Corporate Capitalism, 1890–1913.* Ithaca, NY: Cornell University Press.

—. 1987. "The Social Analysis of Economic History and Theory: Conjectures on Late Nineteenth-Century American Development." *American Historical Review* 92: 69–95.

Montgomery, David. 1979. *Workers' Control in America: Studies in the History of Work, Technology, and Labor Struggles.* Cambridge: Cambridge University Press.

—. 1987. *The Fall of the House of Labor: The Workplace, the State, and American Labor Activism, 1865–1925.* Cambridge: Cambridge University Press.

O'Sullivan, Mary. 2007. "The Expansion of the U.S. Stock Market, 1885–1930: Historical Facts and Theoretical Fashions." Enterprise & Society 8: 489–542. DOI: 10.1093/es/khm075.

Piketty, Thomas. 2014. *Capital in the Twenty-First Century.* Translated by Arthur Goldhammer. Cambridge, MA: Harvard University Press.

Postel, Charles. 2007. *The Populist Vision.* Oxford: Oxford University Press.

Sanders, Elizabeth. 1999. *Roots of Reform: Farmers, Workers, and the American State, 1877–1917.* Chicago: University of Chicago Press.

Scranton, Philip. 1989. *Endless Novelty: Specialty Production and American Industrialization, 1865–1925.* Princeton, NJ: Princeton University Press, 1997.

—. 1989. *Figured Tapestry: Production, Markets, and Power in Philadelphia Textiles, 1885–1941.* Cambridge: Cambridge University Press.

Sklansky, Jeffrey P. 2002. *The Soul's Economy: Market Society and Selfhood in American Thought, 1820–1920.* Chapel Hill: University of North Carolina Press.

Sklar, Martin J. 1992. *The United States as a Developing Country: Studies in U.S. History in the Progressive Era and the 1920s.* Cambridge: Cambridge University Press.

Chapter Seventeen

Nonprofit Organizations, Philanthropy, and Civil Society

David C. Hammack

American philanthropy supported both religious and secular ideals during the decades on either side of 1900. Often, the ideals conflicted. Through philanthropy, Americans reinforced and challenged divisions over religion, race, science, and national identity. Philanthropy did not directly confront poverty. Nor was philanthropy ever sufficient to support its cherished religious and nonprofit organizations; all relied on government support in the forms of tax exemption; many also relied on outright government subsidies and earned income. To persuade donors, volunteers, members, legislatures, courts, parishioners, students, patients, and others to support them, charitable organizations claimed they were simply "doing good." Because people deeply disagree as to what is "the good," charitable organizations and their donors reflected not only commitment to ideals but also disagreement and division. Increasingly, charities pursued religious aims that were more and more varied, as well as more and more purposes that were secular.

Under laws that have prevailed in the United States since the Revolution, "charity" is the legal term; it is also a term of praise. "Philanthropy," a related term of praise, has no legal meaning. To be accorded legal advantages as "charitable," a gift must not only go to a purpose legally accepted as "charitable": ordinarily it must also go to or through a legally established institution, normally a church or an incorporated nonprofit organization or trust. Purposes accepted as charitable include not only relieving physical need (for water, food, clothing, shelter, care in illness, attention in jail, ransom when captured, and burial after death), but also meeting the need for education and for moral and spiritual guidance (for legally charitable purposes, see Hammack and Anheier 2013). Charitable organizations of many kinds thus provide the structures that shape giving and volunteering, which define philanthropy. As Chief Justice John Marshall put it in the decision of the famous 1819 case of *Philadelphia Baptist Ass'n v. Hart's Executors*, a "bequest … intended for a society which was not… capable of taking it" because the society was not incorporated, was "void, and the property vests, if not otherwise disposed of by the will, in the next of kin."

Some definitions of "nonprofit" or "civil society" exclude religion by definition. For the United States, and certainly for the United States during the Gilded Age and Progressive Era, such an exclusion would make no sense. Americans obtained many of the basic services that sustained family and community life from their churches and religious associations, and from their religiously affiliated charitable private schools and colleges and libraries, clinics, child-placement agencies, orphanages, homes for the elderly, increasing numbers of nonprofit hospitals, and other charities. From the century's last decades, religious charities found themselves working side by side with secular colleges, universities, museums, research institutes, hospitals, and service organizations. These newer organizations fostered scientific and scholarly research and built the science-based professions that rapidly rose to dominate much of American life. Collectively, this charitable and philanthropic activity achieved many widely praised purposes. It enabled the United States to preserve religious and intellectual freedom and manage religious and cultural conflict. It also reinforced religious, racial, regional, and class distinctions. Historians disagree as to whether nonprofit, charitable, and philanthropic activity reinforced such distinctions more than it bridged them.

Before the Civil War, to judge from writings that used the word in the titles of books and articles, a "philanthropist" had been a person who disregarded his or her own safety to aid people who were vulnerable or scorned: a doctor who braved the risk of contracting a dread disease to stem an epidemic, an abolitionist who confronted militant defenders of slavery. As

A Companion to the Gilded Age and Progressive Era, First Edition. Edited by Christopher McKnight Nichols and Nancy C. Unger.
© 2017 John Wiley & Sons, Inc. Published 2017 by John Wiley & Sons, Inc.

the Gilded Age began, histories used the term "philanthropy" to describe the Protestant provision of medical and moral support for soldiers during the Civil War. An 1864 work described *The Philanthropic Results of the War in America*; four years later a *History of the United States Sanitary Commission* memorialized non-government, Protestant-led fundraising work for Union army hospitals. In a letter to the author of the *Annals of the United States Christian Commission*, which celebrated Protestant religious, moral, and material support for Union soldiers, historian George Bancroft praised the nation's wartime volunteerism: "[n]othing like the self-organized commissions for the relief of our armies ever was before" (Moss, 1868). The women who did a great deal of the work of actually raising funds to aid Union troops used similar language (Attie 1998; Giesberg 2000).

Since the mid-twentieth century, many historical accounts have dated the understanding of "philanthropy" as very large gifts for non-religious and "transformative" purposes, to the publication of "Wealth," Andrew Carnegie's 1889 essay in the *North American Review* on the proper uses of riches. But the term also continued to refer broadly to love for one's fellow human beings, and to embrace religious as well as secular giving. American courts sometimes added, as in the celebrated 1867 Massachusetts case of *Jackson v. Phillips*, that a gift intended to "change the laws" could not be held charitable under the law. But the decision did not set a clear standard as to which particular changes crossed the line: *Jackson v. Phillips* allowed a gift to challenge laws enforcing slavery and the subordination of African Americans even as it disqualified a gift to challenge the subordination of women.

From the Gilded Age on, the term "philanthropy" raised fundamental questions about the character of civil society in the United States. Carnegie singled out for praise very wealthy men who had made large gifts to secular institutions that, like Carnegie's two thousand libraries (and like Benjamin Franklin's bequests in aid of young tradesmen in Philadelphia and Boston), provided the means by which the aspiring might raise themselves. Carnegie wrote of Peter Cooper and Charles Pratt, who had endowed free technical schools in New York City and in Brooklyn. He wrote of Enoch Pratt of Baltimore, who had created a great library, freely open to all regardless of race. He added Leland Stanford and his wife, who had created a university in California and given it a large endowment. Other writers of the age preferred to celebrate the gifts and sacrifices of ordinary people. Mark Twain and Charles Dudley Warner (1873) used the word "philanthropist" to censure wealthy people who cheated and lied.

Historians have treated nonprofit and charitable organizations, and charity and philanthropy more broadly, in disparate ways (for a collection of essays reflecting recent perspectives, see Friedman and McGarvie 2003). Historians working within particular cultural and religious movements praise contributions that advance the movements they favor. Like Carnegie many historians emphasize secular giving and charitable organizations, seeing these as reflecting the "American character" (Schlesinger 1944; Curti 1958); as embodying "humanitarianism" and "reform" (Bremner 1988) or liberal progress (Zunz 2012); as products of fraternal or gender solidarity (Ferguson 1937; Scott 1991); or freedom (Handlin and Handlin 1961). Other historians have seen charitable organizations as constituting "parallel power structures" (McCarthy 2003), as reflections of structured and hierarchical pluralism (Hammack 1998), as devices for claiming social status (Adam 2009), or as instruments of patriarchy, matriarchy, or class or elite domination (Lindeman 1939; Arnove 1980; Ginzberg 1990; Hall 1992; Colwell 1993; Gordon 1995). Writers who have pointed to America's "government out of sight" (Balogh 2009) or to the "submerged state" (Mettler 2011) might deepen their arguments if they paid "charitable" organizations more attention.

Nonprofit Organizations

Described at the time as "charitable," "benevolent," or in legal parlance "eleemosynary" (having to do with alms), many late nineteenth-century organizations entirely met the definition of "nonprofit" that applies now, in the early decades of the twenty-first century (Hammack 1998; Hall 1992 argues that the term "nonprofit" applies only after 1969). Formally organized and formally separate from government, these organizations did not seek profit for their investors, and were governed by autonomous boards.

Discussions of "the charitable nonprofits" (notably Bremner 1988 and Bowen 1994), often emphasize donations and volunteers, but although religious organizations relied most heavily on private giving and raised the most money even they did not rely entirely on gifts. America's Protestant religious communities had long relied on creative fundraising techniques (Brackenridge 1999; Noll 2001; Hempton 2001); one of the most effective techniques was the sale of bibles and other religious works (Nord 2004; Wosh 1994). Like today's nonprofits, nineteenth-century nonprofits worked hard to assemble resources to advance a legally-accepted "public benefit" (Simon 1987; Salamon 1999). Colleges, schools, libraries, and arts nonprofits relied more on fees than on donations (as Burke 1982 shows for the antebellum years). For academies—usually secondary schools—"tuition fees" exceeded government funding at least until 1890 (Miller 1922). In many places governments gave more to orphanages, but a census report of 1910 revealed that private gifts still accounted for more than one-third of orphanage income, and that fees paid by parents (not a few orphanage residents were "half orphans" whose mothers worked and could not care for them) and other relatives added as much as 13%. Catholic orphanages got more than one-fifth of their income from their children's families (Hacsi 1997).

Government funds also underwrote, and imposed conditions on, much nonprofit activity. Substantial federal subsidies went to a few private colleges and universities including federal land grants to MIT and Cornell in the 1860s and 1870s and subsidies to Gallaudet University. In the century's last decades the federal government subsidized Protestant, and then also Catholic, schools and campaigns intended to change Native American cultures (Keller 1983; Prucha 1995). In many states, the bulk of the funds for orphanages and job-training charities came from local governments (Warner 1908; Hacsi 1997; Katz 1986). The federal, state, and city governments paid for some hospital care (Corwin 1946). America's first great museums appeared in New York, Brooklyn, Boston, Philadelphia, Chicago, Detroit, and Cleveland between the 1870s and the 1920s: in most cases local governments provided up to half of their land, buildings, and operating subsidies (Fox 1963).

Contrary to the oft-repeated notion that Americans have always been free to associate as they wish, state laws and practices have always imposed limits. Precisely because people disagree as to what is "good," states have limited access to legal status and have required nonprofit associations, nonprofit corporations, and trusts to follow very precise rules and to accept detailed restrictions (Clemens 1997; 2000). State governments withheld legal status to enforce religious, gender, racial, and in some cases class norms; they denied charters to disfavored people and limited the range of permissible charitable missions (Silber 2001; Diamond 2002). Because the courts defined "charity" as serving others, neither labor unions (Tomlins 1993) nor mutual benefit organizations nor chambers of commerce have had legal status as charitable.

The charitable nonprofits of the Gilded Age and Progressive Era differed from their twenty-first-century counterparts in three notable ways. They operated under closer direct control by state governments. More of them engaged closely with religious communities; few were committed to a universalistic, scientific ethos. And they were smaller, less numerous, far less wealthy.

"Benevolent" and religious organizations or "charities," and their cousins, voluntary mutual benefit associations, grew dramatically in the decades after the Civil War. Employment in churches and religious associations and publishing companies, in private, nonprofit schools and colleges, in libraries, hospitals, orphanages and old-age and veterans' homes, and in social welfare agencies, and the commitment of lives to convents rose strongly to about 1% of the non-farm labor force in 1900; it would grow more rapidly in the next decades (Hammack 2001; Burke 2001; for an overview and extensive data, see Hall 2006). Also much-discussed and often celebrated was the dramatic late nineteenth-century growth of membership in several mutual benefit organizations to 1% of the population, or more: the Grange, the Knights of Labor, several fraternal organizations, and the Red Cross surpassed 1% of the population in these years (Skocpol and Fiorina 1999; Skocpol, Ganz, and Munson 2000; Beito 2000; Gamm and Putnam 2001).

Religious Philanthropy as a Feature of the Gilded Age

Secular philanthropies and associations deserve close attention, but religious purposes dominated by far the largest number of organizations operating during the Gilded Age and the Progressive Era. The second half of the nineteenth century saw a dramatic increase in Americans' active engagement with religion. In 1850 just over one-third of the US population was actively affiliated with a religious community; by 1890 the proportion had risen to 45%, by the 1920s to 56% (Finke and Stark 2005). Several religious associations had joined the ranks of those whose members exceeded 1% of the entire population; these included the Young Men's Christian Association, the Women's Christian Temperance Union, the Methodists' Christian Endeavor, and the Catholic Knights of Columbus (Skocpol and Fiorina 1999). In 1850, 97% of all houses of worship had served Protestants, who divided themselves into a growing number of competing groups (Noll 2001; Harper 2008); over the next decades, churches became more numerous in relation to population (Burke 2001). Slaves had lacked the freedom to decide whether to affiliate; by the 1890s, African Americans were more likely to belong to a church than whites. Meanwhile the Catholic share of the total population more than doubled from 8% in 1860 to 17% in 1910 (Finke and Stark 2005).

In these years most gifts of money large and small, and most voluntary gifts of time and talent—that is to say, most philanthropy—went to churches and other religious organizations. Because religious communities were so diverse and so divided, these gifts went for a bewildering diversity of purposes. Making up about 11% of the US population, Methodists constituted the largest Protestant denomination through the Gilded Age, then saw their share decline a bit. The Baptist population share grew steadily from about 8% in 1865 until by the 1920s it had surpassed Methodists as the largest Protestant group. Immigration from northern Europe raised the Lutheran share to 3.4%, even as the other "mainline" Protestant denominations—Episcopalian, Presbyterian, Congregationalist, Quaker—saw stagnation or even decline from their early 2, 3 or 5% of the total US population. The Disciples of Christ, the Nazarenes, and other American groups also gained members (US Bureau of the Census 1929; Finke and Stark 2005; Harper 2008). Immigration from Eastern Europe and the Mediterranean added substantial new communities of Jews, whose numbers rose above 1% of the US population, and Eastern Orthodox Christians.

Because they depended on voluntary affiliation as well as voluntary giving, religious communities of all kinds in the United States experienced continuing change. Internal division added greatly to the complexity of America's religious map. Baptists, Presbyterians, and Methodists divided along North–South lines before the Civil War, and each division called forth new gifts of property, money, and voluntary labor, as well as the establishment of new seminaries, new funds for ministers, new missions, and new national offices. Baptists were so prone to division that they had created more than a dozen distinct groups by the end of the nineteenth century. Lutherans also maintained several distinct groups (On religious communities, see Finke and Stark 2005; Harper 2008; United States Bureau of the Census 1929). Catholics had to cope with the claims of immigrants who valued their native languages and the national role of the church in their home countries; Jews divided into a variety of Reform and Orthodox communities, and then into the Conservative movement created in the United States.

Houses of worship, schools, clergy, and teachers are essential to most religious communities, and these received the bulk of philanthropic giving during the Gilded Age and the Progressive Era. By the end of the century, several of the larger Protestant groups held multiple endowment, retirement, and mission funds, each worth more than $1 million (for one of the larger Presbyterian funds see Brackenridge 1999). Thousands of individual donors gave sums ranging from one dollar to more than one million dollars to pay for churches, theological seminaries, schools and colleges affiliated with a denomination, ministers, bibles and hymnbooks and Sunday school books, and weekly journals and tracts. The receipts of the Congregationalist American Missionary Association, which underwrote schools as colleges in the South and also in China, approached half a million dollars per year toward the end of the nineteenth century; Presbyterian "home missions" raised more. In 1912 Lutheran congregations found the resources to maintain nearly 5900 parochial schools (U.S. Office of Education 1914). Many individuals "gave their lives" to religious service, for a season, or for a lifetime: one good estimate has it that between 1870 and 1900 the number of Catholic priests rose from 3780 to 12,000, its women religious rose from 11,000 to 50,000 (Finke and Stark 2005; on Catholic giving more generally, see Oates 1995). By 1910, according to the church's report on its parochial schools to the US Commissioner of Education, there were nearly 5000 Catholic parochial schools, whose expenses, met by voluntary donations, exceeded $11 million a year (on Catholic schools in Chicago, see Sanders 1977). A report on Jewish religious education provided at the same time described efforts to raise money for a very substantial complex of Sunday Schools, religious schools, seminaries, and Jewish studies activities (US Office of Education 1914; Cohen 1999).

In building religious institutions, philanthropy combined with religion, race, and ethnicity to solidify divisions in American society. Some important divisions varied by region.

In the Northeastern and Great Lakes states, Protestants continued the antebellum practice of building and of giving money and volunteer time to private orphanages, academies, colleges, clinics, asylums, and hospitals. Some of these institutions operated under denominational sponsorship, some maintained less formal religious ties. When they were sufficiently concentrated, such institutions joined with churches to form more or less self-sufficient denominational worlds. Protestant church leaders and mostly-Protestant lay associations promoted the public schools and influenced the content of public schooling. Local governments not infrequently relied on Protestant child welfare agencies, academies, and hospitals to place and care for foundlings, orphans, poor scholars, and the sick poor. Immigration brought increasing numbers of Catholics and Jews to the Northeastern and Great Lakes states; by the 1890s Catholics constituted the largest share of the population in many of the most heavily urbanized of these states' counties. When government authorities assigned Catholic or Jewish children to Protestant-sponsored child placement agencies, foundling homes, orphanages, or schools, Catholics and Jews objected. Catholics also objected to the Protestant influence on public schools (Jorgenson 1987; McAfee 1998).

To care for their own and to maintain continuity within their communities, Catholics contributed gifts of money and of the lives of nuns and priests to Catholic schools, orphanages, and hospitals. By the 1860s state laws generally permitted these efforts (Carey 1987) and exempted Catholic facilities from taxes; anti-Catholic efforts to impose property taxes on church buildings during the 1870s failed (Diamond 2002). But Catholics could not cover the full costs of orphanages and hospitals, and when they sought government subsidies for their institutions, some Protestant associations and church leaders objected (Brown and McKeown 1997). In New York, Catholics and Protestants—and Jews—reached a settlement by the 1890s: the right of Catholics to maintain their own distinctive institutions, exempt from taxes, was confirmed; Catholic and Jewish as well as Protestant child welfare agencies would take custody of foundlings and orphans; state aid would go to welfare institutions, but not to Catholic or other schools under religious control (Pratt 1967). In New York City, and in Philadelphia, Boston, Cleveland, Chicago, the larger Jewish communities organized both for mutual aid along narrow lines of European background (Soyer 1997) and in more comprehensive ways to fight gentile discrimination and hostility through elite organizations and federations in New York City (Goren 1970). Within a few years, this pattern of diversity in houses of worship and religiously-affiliated welfare institutions was replicated in other Great Lakes and Northeastern cities (Elazar 1995; Ross 1989). In the spirit of this settlement, Protestant denominations, Catholics, and Jews in the larger cities of this region all built "community centers" and "settlement houses" intended to engage immigrants and poor people. Protestants supported the YMCA and YWCA; Catholics countered with the Catholic Youth Organization.

In the cities and states of the Northeast and the Great Lakes, in short, Protestant, Catholic, and Jewish philanthropy and volunteering combined with state policy and local subsidies to create separate networks of institutions. These institutions could constitute self-enclosed religious–social worlds. Because these worlds were voluntary, individuals could use many institutions for their own purposes, as Perlmann (1988) shows for young Catholics and Jews in Providence, Rhode Island. Turn-of-the-century religious–social worlds left many people out. They rarely embraced all who might be described as members of a community, and those who did not belong to the larger or wealthier religious communities often found themselves with greatly inferior access to clinics and hospitals, orphanages and old-age homes, schools and job training. Because many institutions explicitly excluded African Americans from their facilities while business practices and government policies denied them the resources to fund their own, these arrangements disadvantaged African Americans more than others.

In religion and in other configurations of philanthropy and civil society the Gilded Age South was another country, or two other countries, white and black (for an excellent set of essays on Southern religious history, see Schweiger and Mathews 2004). As Union armies secured control over territory in the border and Confederate states, northern Protestants sent in money and hundreds of volunteer missionaries and teachers to bring both white and black people into their denominational communities (McPherson 1975; Jones 1992). White Southern Baptists and Methodists acted to repel such overtures by their northern cousins. According to the leader of Southern Baptist missions, by the late 1880s "there was not a missionary to the white people of the South who did not bear a commission from either the Home Mission Board" of his denomination, "or one of our State Boards." Southern philanthropy met the gifts from the North: "[t]his could not be done without money" given to pay for more than 3400 Sunday schools, or without the voluntary or ill-paid service of 4500 missionaries who in a few years raised nearly $650,000 for houses of worship and engaged more than 110,000 churches (Tichenor 1901, quoted in Ammerman 1990, 38). African American withdrawal from the churches of the white ex-slaveowners confounded white church leaders, reinforcing their determination to control their own religious communities. Much more than before the Civil War, southerners organized their lives through churches and other private entities, often church-related, that worked outside government. Recent histories show that most of these communities celebrated the "Lost Cause" of the Confederacy and developed a "folk theology of segregation," although some did always engage in "racial interchange" about evangelical ideas and practices (Harvey 1997; Stowell 1998). White women helped rebuild and extend the reach of their Protestant churches and allied nonprofits (including cemeteries and other memorials to Confederate sacrifice) in the postbellum South; religious institutions in turn shaped and constrained women's lives (Friedman 1985; Edwards 1997; Sims 1997; Turner 1997).

A few—very few—racially integrated churches and schools continued to operate in the former Confederate states after the end of Reconstruction, although from 1877 states increasingly outlawed integration in schools. Emphasizing different religious thoughts and practices, Schweiger (2000) does find some Baptist and Methodist preachers diverging from a single white-supremacy script to express progressive views. Remillard (2011, 14) emphasizes disagreements among and between Baptists, Methodists, Presbyterians, Catholics, Jews, progressives, and the "many voices of the many souths." Wacker (2009) explores the origins of Pentecostalism and the development of its own denominational structures in Southern and Border states between 1885 and 1910. Yet Southern Baptists did come to dominate many counties in a way that had no counterpart in the northeastern parts of the nation.

Throughout the South, African Americans took advantage of freedom to build their own churches, seminaries, denominational structures, clergy, schools, and welfare arrangements. Starting with almost no material resources and working against violence, church burnings, and an often hostile legal environment, men and women alike worked with great determination and effectiveness. W.E.B. Du Bois celebrated the philanthropy of the first generation of freedmen, who gave "more in proportion to their means" than other Americans (Du Bois 1907, in Hammack 1998, 276); see among many others Montgomery 1993; Harvey 1997; Stowell 1998; and for African American women, Higginbotham 1993). Bennett (2005) shows that some African Americans preferred integration. Northern donors and volunteers offered assistance, but northerners insisted on their own approaches and accepted that they had to work within the segregated arrangements demanded by southern whites.

Throughout these decades (and after), religious institutions took on greater significance in the South than in the North. White southerners used private corporations and associations, including churches and Masonic associations, as private governments that allowed them to ignore federal military and civilian authorities during Reconstruction. Blacks responded with comparable uses of their own segregated organizations (Tripp 1997). Southern state governments granted few charters to independent nonprofit organizations, except for churches and fraternal organizations (Fox 2012). And the courts of southern states took the view (arguably contrary to the Supreme Court's famous decision in *Trustees of Dartmouth College v. Woodward*) that a legislature's power to grant corporate charters gave it the right to impose changing controls over their policies. States could insist, for example, that private nonprofit corporations impose racial segregation even after decades of integration, as Kentucky did in a 1906 case against long-integrated Berea College. With the approval of prominent northerners including the President of Harvard, in 1908 the US Supreme Court accepted the Kentucky courts' understanding of the state's authority (Nelson 1974; Rosen 1977). More generally, as southern states excluded African Americans from their electorates in the 1890s, they subordinated African Americans—together with their property and their churches, private schools, and charities—to the authority of white elected officials, judges, and juries (Dubois 1907). Political subordination meant an economic subordination that denied African American organizations the resources they needed despite extraordinary creativity, effort, and persistence. Southern states also placed severe restrictions on the right to join organizations that might challenge racial norms (Wisner 1970; Silber 2001). Southern reliance on church-affiliated charities' sponsorship persisted through the twentieth century (Burke 2001).

In the American West, settlers sought to maintain and increase their ties with the churches they had left in the eastern states and in Europe. Protestants engaged in conflict with Catholics in the Southwest and with Mormons in Utah, and continued to deny Native American religious traditions. As the United States consolidated control over the Southwest after the Civil War, the federal government encouraged leading Protestant denominations to set up missions and schools to engage and convert Hispano Catholics and Native Americans (Pascoe 1990; Yohn 1995). When Catholics protested their exclusion, federal officials worked with them as well (Beaver 1966; Keller 1983; Hoxie 1989; Prucha 1995). Missions and schools took varied approaches. Many simply offered primary or Sunday schools in connection with individual churches. Church-sponsored boarding schools working under federal contracts made particularly strong efforts to undermine the tribal worlds of the Native Americans, with often tragic results. To assure that their denominations had churches in every large town Protestants and Catholics subsidized new churches; to hold their communities together they built local denominational colleges and helped young westerners come to their colleges in the Midwest and the Northeast. Protestants also sent "orphan trains" to place children from Eastern cities with Protestant farm families in the West (Gordon 1999; DeRogatis 2003; Birk 2015).

These efforts rarely created self-sufficient denominational worlds of churches, schools, and other institutions in Western communities. On the ground, Protestants encountered competition as migrants from the South and Midwest maintained commitments to Southern Baptist and Methodist, Stone-Campbell, and Nazarene communities, as the Catholic Church retained influence with those of Mexican heritage and among many immigrants from Europe who formed significant communities in rapidly growing western cities, and as the West became a fertile ground for Fundamentalism and early Pentecostalism (Wacker 2009).

Not a few Americans retained the ambition of bringing their religious and moral standards—and, as many recent historians have argued, their preferences about class, race, and gender—to the entire nation. George Frederickson (1965) notably argued that the experience of total war pushed gentle transcendentalists (often more or less firmly associated with Congregationalist and Unitarian religious communities) toward tough-minded militancy. A number of northern Protestants moved on from the United States Christian Commission of the Civil War to the National Reform Association, the Young Men's and Young Women's Christian Associations, the Women Christian Temperance Union, the Anti-Saloon League, and other nonprofit associations to promote what they saw as specifically Protestant forms of education and morality. For decades they had only halting success in Congress (Foster 2002). Through such campaigns women played influential roles both in national politics and in arguments over the lines between respectable and not, "white" and not, "American" and ethnic. Indeed, historians disagree as to whether motives of religion, morality, gender, or class dominated the Protestant campaigns. These campaigns enjoyed considerable philanthropic support and attracted many volunteers, and when they formed large coalitions they won national legislation to ban the distribution of information about sex and reproduction from the 1870s into the 1950s (Broun and Leech 1927; Parker 1997; Beisel 1998; Horowitz 2002), and to prohibit the consumption of alcohol (Bordin 1981; Kerr 1985). Once past the water's edge, missionaries whose denominations competed sharply within the United States found ways to work together overseas, collaborating, for example, in building colleges in China (Lutz 1971).

Foreign missions constituted yet another fragmented and contentious field for American philanthropy during the Gilded Age and the Progressive Era. By the end of the 1890s, Protestants and their denominations had organized as many as ninety-six societies to support missions abroad. In a single year these organizations raised just under $6 million to support more than 4,500 Americans and 17,000 natives as workers in missions of many kinds (Dennis 1902). In China alone by 1906, Americans joined other Protestants in running 2500 schools enrolling 57,000 students, supported 300 doctors, underwrote a number of publishing houses and journals. Catholics had their own missions: altogether, "an impressive institutional foundation" (Bays 2011, 70). American Protestants supported a comparable set of institutions in the Middle East (Curti 1963). Historians have seen religious missions as constituting a philanthropically funded form of cultural imperialism; more recent historians are more inclined to see them as representing one of many aspects of global contact in an era of industrialized travel and exchange (Hill 1985; Hutchison 1989; Dunch 2002).

Edward J. Blum (2009) argues that moral reform organizations reflected an effective campaign to re-forge the United States as a Protestant white republic in the last decades of the nineteenth century (see also Fox 2012). But responses to such efforts often minimized attention to religion in the public schools. In the Southwest, Susan Yohn (1995) shows, the women teachers in Presbyterian missions subordinated religious conversion to meeting the more immediate needs of their students; teachers in overseas missions often did the same (Hill 1985; Hutchison 1987). Narrow campaigns for temperance and other reforms generally failed before 1910 (McAfee 1998).

If there was a Protestant establishment, it was a very divided establishment and much more effective in some states, and on some issues, than in Congress (Sehat 2010; Wheeler 2004). Among the best-funded and most effective national philanthropies, some sought to advance education for both whites and African Americans in the South. Others sought a white republic in the wake of the Civil War (Harlan 1958; Anderson 1988). But much of the educational philanthropy directed to the South reflected division, as it countered efforts of white Southerners, and their churches, to limit education for the freed people (Anderson and Moss 1999; Ascoli 2006). The large sums given to build thousands of small churches, to raise large and elaborate churches in the big cities, and to expand divinity schools, underwrote denominations that competed vigorously against one another.

Secular Philanthropy in the Progressive Era

Most late nineteenth-century American giving of money, time, and talent went to religious houses of worship and other activities closely associated with religion. Religious institutions dominated America's civil society, and directed the bulk of its philanthropy. At the beginning of the twentieth century, William R. Hutchison has argued, "Protestant churches felt responsible for America: for its moral structure, for the religious content of its national ideals, for the educative and welfare functions that governments would not (or, it was thought, should not) carry out." Hutchison adds, "Jews, Catholics, and others who considered themselves thoroughly accredited as custodians of American ideals found that stance at best disingenuous, at worst self-serving and outrageous; and today most mainline Protestants, along with nearly all secular commentators, would probably agree" (Hutchinson 1989, x). But Protestants disagreed among themselves over religious, national, and social ideals. To advance their own communities and ideals, Catholics and Jews advanced built their own educational and welfare institutions. Currents of thought outside religion were growing strongly, so that by the second decade of the new century, non-sectarian and secular initiatives defined America's fast-rising research universities and professions. Well aware of the challenges a nation of increasingly diverse religious affiliation posed for Protestants, and frustrated by Congressional opposition to a stronger national government, American nationalists sought to build up an array of "nongovernment" organizations to pursue the national interest at home and abroad. Smaller movements pushed for the rights of women and African Americans, for secular and cosmopolitan ideals, and for the causes of many nationalities.

Secular American philanthropy's most notable, enduring, and celebrated achievements after the Civil War involved the launching of world-class universities, professional schools, research institutions, libraries, and museums and other arts organizations. These and allied institutions played key roles in creating the modern, science-based professions, in developing consequential movements in public health, elementary and secondary education, the provision of public services, and in economic development and international relations.

Historians of higher education have preferred to disparage (Hofstadter 1955) or downplay (Rudolph 1962; Curti and Nash 1965) the religious commitments of nineteenth-century colleges. But those colleges often played wide and effective roles (Burke 1982; Sloan 1994; the essays in Geiger 2000). Religious communities, with their associated schools and colleges, constituted the environment in which secular philanthropy moved to advance the new science and professionalism. As late as the 1870s, as Thomas Haskell (1977) showed, men trained in religious seminaries still held authority in education, public health, social welfare, municipal affairs, and even science. By the beginning of the twentieth century, in most fields specialized experts were relying on peer review. This shift had been long in the making. Its origins can be found in intellectual movements, in the increasing diversification of the institutions of higher education and research in the United States, and in the importance of advances in chemical and other scientific knowledge for the development of industry in Europe as well as in the United States (Oleson and Voss 1979).

Secular institutions had already begun to appear early in the nineteenth century. Religious organizations generally enjoyed broad authority to govern themselves and to hold funds and to spend them for a wide range of purposes. But state law governed charities, and in New York, the South, and elsewhere legislatures and courts required non-church charities to limit their action to narrowly specified fields. Some states in New England and elsewhere allowed greater autonomy and flexibility. Boston's remarkable Lowell Institute, a trust committed broadly to science and education, dated from the 1830s; nineteenth-century Harvard evolved as a holding company for a wide range of educational, scientific, and even recreational facilities. Like the Lowell Institute, Philadelphia's Girard College, supported by a generously-defined trust dating from the 1830s, evolved into both an orphanage that barred clergy of any kind from interacting with the "white boys" in its charge—and a center for serious study of education. The few private technical institutes and engineering schools, many of which owed their origin to a large gift from a single philanthropist, operated independently from religious supervision: so, generally, did Cornell, Johns Hopkins, and Stanford. Until the 1910s, most of the best-endowed universities and colleges retained close ties to religious communities, yet in many ways they increasingly resembled general purpose foundations, obtaining large endowment gifts and using the income to support changing programs of education and scholarship, while expanding their collections of books, scientific instruments, gardens and park-like grounds, works of art, and athletic facilities (Rudolph 1962). When changes in New York state law allowed Andrew Carnegie, John D. Rockefeller, Margaret Olivia Sage, Elizabeth Milbank Anderson, several members of the Guggenheim family, and others to set up philanthropic foundations for increasingly broad purposes after the early 1890s, these famous philanthropists emulated the endowed universities (Hammack and Anheier 2013; on the legal change that allowed general purpose funds in New York, see Katz, Sullivan, and Beach 1985).

The outlines of the comprehensive modern research university, non-sectarian or secular and committed to scientific and medical research, had emerged by the second decade of the twentieth century. Intellectual changes and faculty initiatives pushed science forward (Veysey 1965), but big philanthropy, not government funding, student tuition, or subsidies from corporations provided a critical share of the needed means. Large gifts from a few hundred wealthy donors financed the expansion of research capabilities at existing universities and created new ones. Rockefeller, Carnegie, Guggenheim, Rosenwald, and other philanthropic funders provided critical support to university research in several fields (Geiger 1986). Andrew Carnegie's creation in 1905 of the Carnegie Teachers Pension Fund reinforced the shift away from religious control by providing pensions for faculty at institutions evaluated according to academic, rather than religious, criteria (Lagemann 1983). Carnegie, Rockefeller, and Rosenwald were among those who also underwrote the National Research Council, the National Bureau of Economic Research, and other institutions that coordinated expert peer review in the natural sciences, medicine, and the social sciences (Curti and Nash, 1965; Coben 1976; Kevles 1977; Bulmer 1984; Stocking 1985; Geiger, 1986; Lagemann 1989; Kohler, 1991).

In short, philanthropic funds set up by Carnegie, Rockefeller, the Harkness family, the Guggenheim family, Julius Rosenwald—and others in the first years of the twentieth century—gave to the modern American college and university, and to the non-sectarian and secular study of nature and society, an institutional framework comparable to that traditionally provided by religious institutions for religion, and by the national state for the military.

Philanthropic foundations also played a critical part in creating efforts to provide scientific knowledge, in a systematic, nationwide fashion, to many applied fields (Karl and Katz 1981 emphasize this national and applied quality of the foundations of the first decades of the twentieth century). An early model can be seen in the foundation-like New York City office set up by Andrew Carnegie, an office that eventually underwrote more than 2500 public libraries (Van Slyck 1995). The Carnegie Foundation for the Advancement of Teaching and the Rockefeller Foundation famously promoted the creation of the science-based medical school and the reform and elevation of the medical profession (Wheatley 1988). As science increasingly influenced medicine, philanthropy, often working with religious communities, did much to build modern hospitals (Stevens 1989; Rosner 1982). Rockefeller's General Education Board, the Milbank Memorial Fund, and others did much to promote the application of science to public health (Ettling 1981; Fox 2006). The Russell Sage Foundation, in a sense a capstone for the unusually sophisticated charity organization societies and Jewish federations of New York City, Philadelphia, Baltimore, and Chicago, undertook to put the analysis of social problems on a rigorous basis and to turn social work into a modern profession (Hammack and Wheeler 1994; Sealander 1997; Waugh 1998). The Carnegie, Rockefeller, Russell Sage, and other funds underwrote influential movements to coordinate secondary schools with colleges and to introduce age-grading and other standards for all children (Lagemann 1983). Many accounts view as characteristic of the progressive era exactly these applications of scientific, or scientific-sounding, standards to health, education, and welfare (Bremner 1988).

Secular philanthropy of the Progressive Era aimed to do more than advance science and the professions. The large topic of women, education, and social reform has attracted much attention and can serve as one example. In the view of Anne Firor Scott (1991), women worked with one another as natural allies in the pursuit of many secular purposes, Kathleen McCarthy (1990, 1) preferred the phrase "parallel power structure" to describe women's uses of nonprofit organizations. It is not clear that the structures women created were fully parallel, but they were significant. In higher education, for example, women leaders working with female as well as male donors created colleges whose graduates mastered curricula entirely equal to those of men's schools (Horowitz 1984; Gordon 1992). Mary Elizabeth Garrett's very large gift both allowed the Johns Hopkins University Medical School to launch its standard-setting career, and assured the admission of women students (Sander 2008); however Margaret Olivia Slocum Sage's very large gift to New York University, intended (though not in ironclad legal language) to create a women's college there, was used for a different purpose (Crocker 2000).

Women's schools and colleges—and religious missions—could provide platforms for critics of racism and ethnocentrism; examples include both the women teachers Susan Yohn (1995) found in Presbyterian missions in the

Southwest and such notable writers on immigrants as Emily Greene Balch (Wellesley College) and Mary Roberts Coolidge (Mills College). Hull-House, supported by the philanthropy of Jane Addams and others, gave critical aid to Florence Kelley and her associates (Sklar 1995); the Russell Sage Foundation gave a base to Mary Richmond, Mary Van Kleeck, and others (Crocker 2000). These women, together with Franz Boas (Columbia University), W.E.B. DuBois (Atlanta University), and Robert E. Park (Tuskegee Institute, University of Chicago), anticipated by decades the immigrant gifts movement that Diana Selig (2008) dates to the 1920s. Women employed by other charitable nonprofits also played prominent roles in social service and social reform (McCarthy 1990; Muncy 1994; Stivers 2000).

These efforts to advance universal, science-based standards proved complicated, controversial, and incomplete. The science-based professions aimed to provide services to all, but not to include women or people of color on an equal basis. Even as they gave work to female librarians, Carnegie's libraries imposed on women controls that they would not have imposed on men; and the libraries did not always provide desired service to immigrants, African Americans, or laborers. Jewish leaders and donors did much to establish the modern science-based medical research center, but because most hospitals refused to give admitting privileges to Jewish doctors, Jewish communities created their own. To advance their distinctive priorities, Catholics and several Protestant denominations also built their own hospitals. Influential Catholics denounced the Russell Sage Foundation as the charity trust; Protestant colleges denounced Carnegie's denial of annuities to their professors. New York City's American Museum of Natural History undertook scientific work, but also provided a base for the publication of works clearly recognized today as racist. Yet, each of these efforts created a community of professional practitioners that was quite distinct from the communities associated with the various traditions of faith, and that nurtured distinctive conversations.

Philanthropy also created America's most prominent secular institutions in the arts. Some of these dated to associations and donors at the end of the eighteenth century (Brown 1973; Harris 1966) and the early decades of the nineteenth century. In subsequent decades, the Boston Public Library and the Boston Atheneum, Hartford's Wadsworth Atheneum, and major arts organizations and private libraries in cities including New York City, Philadelphia, and Baltimore won many donations, including some very large ones. By the end of the nineteenth century, arts organizations were providing scope for many ambitious donors. Historians debate the relative importance of many motives: sheer enthusiasm for particular art forms and for civic education (Harris 1962, 1966; Horowitz 1976; Conn 1998); women's commitment to aesthetic ideals and civic advancement (Horowitz 1976; McCarthy 1982); celebration of many contributions to American life; the desire of some wealthy people to lay claim to social and cultural capital and prestige (DiMaggio 1986).

Donors to a number of the new non-sectarian or secular institutions intended to promote their own ideas of national unity—mostly, ideas of a national unity of white men. In some cases, as with the National Academy of Sciences (1863), the American Museum of Natural History (opened 1877), the Carnegie Institution of Washington (1904), the American Red Cross (1905), The National Education Association (1906), the American Academy of Arts and Letters (1914), and the Boy Scouts of America (1916), an organization's name proclaimed the ambition. In all of these cases, except for the American Museum of Natural History, a charter of nonprofit status from Congress rather than from a state added a sort of national authority. But none of these institutions enjoyed the exclusive relationship with the national government characteristic of their counterparts in London and Paris. Especially in the decades after the Civil War, Congress was as reluctant to charter national organizations as it was to endorse a national university or erect monuments to national unity. Until the 1890s, individual cities and states, churches and cemeteries, colleges and universities, and private memorial associations erected memorials that reinforced the North–South division. When efforts to reconcile northern and southern whites achieved sufficient success for the federal Government to create national memorial parks on several key Civil War battlefields, private donors provided many of the monuments, though these continued to celebrate sectional division.

Philanthropy and Civil Society in the Progressive Era

In the United States around the beginning of the twentieth century, philanthropy, in the sense both of large individual donations and of large numbers of smaller donations, played a key part in the creation of large institutions (universities, hospitals, research institutes, libraries, museums). Philanthropy, reinforcing other forces, also played a key part in the creation of entire *systems* of institutions and practices (scientific research, scientific medicine, public health, public education, public libraries, social work, and several of the most centrally organized religious communities). Historians praise this work for advancing particular causes, for advancing knowledge and welfare, for expanding opportunity. Historians also object that the new institutions and practices created new elites or reinforced the claims of old ones, undermined democracy, or undercut valued traditions (For discussions of the relevant historians, see Hammack 2002 and 2006a; Hammack and Anheier 2013).

What too often goes unacknowledged is the exceptional situation of these decades. It was not only that wealth was distributed in a highly unequal way, and that Carnegie and Rockefeller amassed fortunes of extraordinary size. It was also that many Americans lived at a standard not greatly above subsistence so that in real terms average family income was far lower than it is today. The professions engaged small numbers of people, and yielded low incomes to most of them, apart from a relatively few lawyers, doctors, and clergy. The federal government had very little at all to do with health, education, or welfare. Neither the federal, state, or local governments did anything to redistribute income, or to help ordinary people maintain living standards when they faced unemployment, disability, or old age. After World War II most of these factors changed. In the face of increasingly affluent consumers, wealthier and more strongly entrenched professions, and governments that controlled not 3 or 4% but more than 20% of national income, philanthropy lost its ability to make the major impact it had made at the beginning of the twentieth century. It is true that in the early twenty-first century wealth and incomes again became very unequal, perhaps to the level of the early twentieth century. But the basic standard of living remains far higher than it was one hundred years ago, the professions have expanded far beyond any imagination of that day, and government retains the relative size it had reached by 1980. Yet despite the real decline in its relative capabilities, big philanthropy's reputation for ability to do great things, for good or ill, persists to this day (Hammack and Anheier 2013).

The philanthropy and the nonprofit organizations of the Gilded Age and the Progressive Era had lasting consequences. Nineteenth-century practices in the relations of government and religion created a context in which private institutions, most often religious and supported in considerable part by philanthropy, provided a wide range of social and educational services. Religious institutions provided care and education within their own communities, reinforcing both in-group ties and separation from out-groups. The possibility of creating distinctive churches, schools, and care agencies may well have led many subordinated groups to build their own institutions rather than engage in bitter conflict over the control of government.

Because nonprofit providers of education and health and social care relied on gifts and charged fees, wealthier families could provide what they saw as the best for their children, their sick, and their elderly. The poor, and those who found themselves outside the religious communities and thus judged "unworthy," enjoyed little assistance. Despite the impression left by some accounts (Trattner 1974; Olasky 1992), voluntary giving went mostly to support religious and other nonprofit organizations. Gifts sometimes aided those identified as talented or deserving, but provided little aid to the poor in general. In 1913 private giving for the poor came at most to just over 0.2% of GNP—at a time when almost 30% of the US population was deeply impoverished (Patterson 1994, 25). Philanthropically supported nonprofit organizations did not work to reduce inequality by redistributing wealth.

Women did organize important nonprofits and by 1900 had reached the longstanding ratio of one woman's organization for every 4000 or so people in the United States (Burke, 2001). But despite the lifting of restrictions on those who were married, women continued to lack either the control over wealth or the legal standing to enforce their charitable preferences. African Americans, Hispanos, and members of other dispossessed racial communities could provide very little for the institutions that served them—and their institutions also stood at a legal disadvantage. The more affluent possessed the means to build the strongest organizations and to reinforce ties most effectively through schools, camps, conferences, institutes, and museums.

Historians often view these matters through the lens of overall economic inequality, or the inequalities associated with race and gender. The argument in this chapter is that increasing numbers of historians are paying attention to relation of philanthropy and nonprofit organizational structures to religion, science, the arts, culture in all forms high and low. Seen in this way, philanthropy and voluntary organizations give shape to the civil society of the United States. Voluntarily supported religious and secular organizations create many channels through which Americans can organize their lives and connect with one another. In some ways nineteenth-century Americans lived in geographically separated island communities. But rapidly growing associations, religious and not, often national in scope, embraced rising shares of the American population, supplementing links of family, commerce, and politics. Women, African Americans, and Catholics all made their own connections. Catholics, Jews, white southerners, many groups of Protestants, created institutions to serve their own purposes. Philanthropically supported nonprofit structures enabled scientists to build new communities outside religious control. Yet others enabled progressives, freethinkers, cosmopolitans, devotees of traditional and avant-garde arts, and advocates for women and other causes to create schools, colleges, and art institutes devoted to their ideals. The result was to multiply divisions and reinforce inequalities of race and gender as well as to advance opportunity and diversity—and more rarely to promote social integration and unity.

References

Adam, Thomas. 2009. *Buying Respectability: Philanthropy and Urban Society in Transnational Perspective, 1840s to 1930s.* Bloomington: Indiana University Press.

Ammerman, Nancy Tatom. 1990. *Baptist Battles: Social Change and Religious Conflict in the Southern Baptist Convention.* New Brunswick, NJ: Rutgers University Press.

Anderson, Eric A. and Moss, Alfred A. Jr. 1999. *Dangerous Donations: Northern Philanthropy and Southern Black Education, 1902–1930.* Columbia: University of Missouri Press.

Anderson, James. 1988. *The Education of Blacks in the South, 1860–1935.* Chapel Hill: University of North Carolina Press.

Arnove, Robert F., ed. 1980. *Philanthropy and Cultural Imperialism: The Foundations at Home and Abroad.* Boston: G.K. Hall.

Ascoli, Peter M. 2006. *Julius Rosenwald: The Man Who Built Sears, Roebuck and Advanced the Cause of Black Education in the American South*. Bloomington: Indiana University Press.

Attie, Jeanie. 1998. *Patriotic Toil: Northern Women and the American Civil War*. Ithaca, NY: Cornell University Press.

Balogh, Brian. 2009. *A Government Out of Sight: The Mystery of National Authority in Nineteenth-Century America*. Cambridge: Cambridge University Press.

Bays, Daniel H. 2011. *A New History of Christianity in China*. New York: John Wiley & Sons.

Beaver, R. Pierce. 1966. *Church, State, and the American Indians*. St. Louis: Concordia Publishing House.

Beisel, Nicola. 1998. *Imperiled Innocents: Anthony Comstock and Family Reproduction in Victorian America*. Princeton, NJ: Princeton University Press.

Beito, David T. 2000. *From Mutual Aid to the Welfare State: Fraternal Societies and Social Services, 1890–1967*. Chapel Hill: The University of North Carolina Press.

Bennett, James B. 2005. *Religion and the Rise of Jim Crow in New Orleans*. Princeton, NJ: Princeton University Press.

Birk, Megan. 2015. *Fostering on the Farm: Child Placement in the Rural Midwest*. Urbana: University of Illinois Press.

Blum, Edward J. 2009. *Reforging the White Republic: Race, Religion, and American Nationalism, 1865—1898*. Baton Rouge: Louisiana State University Press.

Bordin, Ruth. 1981. *Women and Temperance: The Quest for Power and Liberty, 1873–1900*. Philadelphia: Temple University Press.

Bowen, William G. 1994. *The Charitable Nonprofits: An Analysis of Institutional Dynamics and Characteristics*. San Francisco: Jossey-Bass Publishers.

Brackenridge, R. Douglas. 1999. *The Presbyterian Church (U.S.A.) Foundation: A Bicentennial History*. Louisville, KY: Geneva Press.

Bremner, Robert. 1988. *American Philanthropy*. 2nd edn. Chicago: University of Chicago Press.

Broun, Haywood, and Margaret Leech. 1927. *Anthony Comstock, Roundsman of the Lord*. New York: The Literary Guild of America.

Brown, Dorothy M., and McKeown, Elizabeth. 1997. *The Poor Belong to Us: Catholic Charities and American Welfare*. Cambridge, MA: Harvard University Press.

Brown, Richard D. 1973. "The Emergence of Voluntary Associations in Massachusetts, 1760–1830." *Journal of Voluntary Action Research* II: 64–73.

Bulmer, Martin. 1984. *The Chicago School of Sociology: Institutionalization, Diversity, and the Rise of Sociological Research*. Chicago: University of Chicago Press.

Burke, Colin B. 1982. *American Collegiate Populations: A Test of the Traditional View*. New York: New York University Press.

—. 2001. "Nonprofit History's New Numbers (and the Need for More)." *Nonprofit and Voluntary Sector Quarterly* 30, 2: 174–203.

Carey, Patrick W. 1987. *People, Priests, and Prelates: Ecclesiastical Democracy and the Tensions of Trusteeism*. Notre Dame, IN: Notre Dame University Press.

Clemens, Elizabeth. 1997. *The People's Lobby: Organizational Innovation and the Rise of Interest Group Politics in the United States, 1890–1925*. Chicago: University of Chicago Press.

—. 2000. "The Encounter of Civil Society and the States: Legislation, Law, and Association, 1900–1920." Paper presented at the annual meeting of the Social Science History Association, Chicago, Illinois.

Coben, Stanley. 1976. "Foundation Officials and Fellowships: Innovation in the Patronage of Science." *Minerva* 14, 2: 225–240.

Cohen, Naomi Wiener. 1999. *Jacob H. Schiff: A Study in American Jewish Leadership*. Hanover, NH: University Press of New England for Brandeis University Press.

Colwell, Mary Anna Culleton. 1993. *Private Foundations and Public Policy: The Political Role of Philanthropy*. New York: Garland.

Conn, Steven. 1998. *Museums and American Intellectual Life, 1876–1926*. Chicago: University of Chicago Press.

Corwin, Edward Henry Lewinski. 1946. *The American Hospital*. New York: Commonwealth Fund for the New York Academy of Medicine.

Crocker, Ruth. 2000. *Mrs. Russell Sage: Women's Activism and Philanthropy in Gilded Age and Progressive Era America*. Bloomington: Indiana University Press.

Curti, Merle. 1958. "American Philanthropy and the National Character." *American Quarterly* 10, Winter: 420–437.

—. 1963. *American Philanthropy Abroad: a History*. New Brunswick, NJ: Rutgers University Press.

Curti, Merle, and Roderick Nash. 1965. *Philanthropy in the Shaping of American Higher Education*. New Brunswick, NJ: Rutgers University Press.

Dennis, James S. 1902. *Centennial Survey of Foreign Missions*. New York: Fleming H. Revell Company.

DeRogatis, Amy. 2003. *Moral Geography: Maps, Missionaries, and the American Frontier*. New York: Columbia University Press.

Diamond, Stephen. 2002. "Efficiency and Benevolence: Philanthropic Tax Exemptions in 19th-Century America." In *Property-Tax Exemption for Charities: Mapping the Battlefield*, ed. Evelyn Brody. Washington, DC: The Urban Institute.

DiMaggio, Paul J. 1986. *Nonprofit Enterprise in the Arts: Studies in Mission and Constraint*. New York: Oxford University Press.

Du Bois, W.E.B. 1907. *Economic Co-Operation among Negro Americans*. Atlanta, GA: Atlanta University.

Dunch, Ryan. 2002. "Beyond Cultural Imperialism: Cultural Theory, Christian Missions, and Global Modernity," *History and Theory* 41, 3: 301–325.

Edwards, Laura F. 1997. *Gendered Strife and Confusion: The Political Culture of Reconstruction*. Urbana: University of Illinois Press.

Elazar, Daniel J. 1995. *Community and Polity: The Organizational Dynamics of American Jewry*. Revised ed. Philadelphia: Jewish Publication Society of America.

Ettling, John. 1981. *The Germ of Laziness: Rockefeller Philanthropy and Public Health in the New South*. Cambridge, MA: Harvard University Press.

Ferguson, Charles Wright. 1937. *Fifty Million Brothers: A Panorama of American Lodges and Clubs*. New York: Farrar & Rinehart.

Finke, Roger and Rodney Stark. 2005. *The Churching of America 1776–2005: Winners and Losers in our Religious Economy*. New Brunswick, NJ: Rutgers University Press.

Foster, Gaines M. 2002. *Moral Reconstruction, Christian Lobbyists and the Federal Legislation of Morality, 1865–1920*. Chapel Hill: University of North Carolina Press.

Fox, Cybelle. 2012. *Three Worlds of Relief: Race, Immigration, and the American Welfare State from the Progressive Era to the New Deal*. Princeton, NJ: Princeton University Press.

Fox, Daniel M. 1963. *Engines of Culture: Philanthropy and Art Museums* Madison: The State Historical Society of Wisconsin.

—. 2006. "The significance of the Milbank Memorial Fund for policy: an assessment at its centennial." *Milbank Quarterly* 84, 1: 5–36.

Frederickson, George. 1965. *The Inner Civil War*. New York: Harper & Row.

Friedman, Jean E. 1985. *The Enclosed Garden: Women and Community in the Evangelical South, 1830–1900*. Chapel Hill: University of North Carolina Press.

Friedman, Lawrence J. and Mark D. McGarvie, eds. 2003. *Charity, Philanthropy, and Civility in American History*. New York: Cambridge University Press.

Gamm, G., & Putnam, Robert D. 2001. "The Growth of Voluntary Associations in American, 1840–1940." In *Patterns of Social Capital: Stability and Change in Historical Perspective*, ed. R.I. Rotberg, 173–219. Cambridge, MA: Massachusetts Institute of Technology Press.

Geiger, Roger L. 1986. *To Advance Knowledge: The Growth of American Research Universities, 1900–1940*. New York: Oxford University Press.

—, ed. 2000. *The American College in the Nineteenth Century*. Nashville, TN: Vanderbilt University Press.

Giesberg, Judith Ann. 2000. *Civil War Sisterhood: The U.S. Sanitary Commission and Women's Politics in Transition*. Boston: Northeastern University Press.

Ginzberg, Lori. 1990. *Women and the Work of Benevolence: Morality, Politics, and Class in the Nineteenth-Century United States*. New Haven, CT: Yale University Press.

Gordon, Linda 1995. *Pitied But Not Entitled: Single Mothers and the History of Welfare, 1890–1935*. Cambridge, MA: Harvard University Press.

—. 1999. *The Great Arizona Orphan Abduction*. Cambridge, MA: Harvard University Press.

Gordon, Lynn D. 1992. *Gender and Higher Education in the Progressive Era*. New Haven, CT: Yale University Press.

Goren, Arthur. 1970. *New York Jews and the Quest for Community*. New York: Columbia University Press.

Hacsi, Timothy A. 1997. *Second Home: Orphan Asylums and Poor Families in America*. Cambridge, MA: Harvard University Press.

Hall, Peter Dobkin. 1992. *Inventing the Nonprofit Sector and Other Essays on Philanthropy, Voluntarism, and Nonprofit Organizations*. Baltimore, MD: The Johns Hopkins University Press.

—. 2006. "Nonprofit, Voluntary, and Religious Entities." In *Historical Statistics of the United States: Millennial Edition*, ed. S. B. Carter et al. New York: Cambridge University Press.

Hammack, David C. 1998. *Making the Nonprofit Sector in the United States: A Reader*. Bloomington: Indiana University Press.

—. 2001. "Growth, Transformation, and Quiet Revolution in the Nonprofit Sector over Two Centuries." *Nonprofit and Voluntary Sector Quarterly* June: 157–173.

—. 2002. "Nonprofit Organizations in American History: Research Opportunities and Sources" *The American Behavioral Scientist* 45, 11: 1638–1674.

—. 2006a. "American Debates on the Legitimacy of Foundations." In *The Legitimacy of Philanthropic Foundations: United States and European Perspectives*, ed. Kenneth Prewitt, Mattei Dogan, Steven Heydemann, and Stefan Toepler. New York: Russell Sage Foundation.

—, and Helmut K. Anheier. 2013. *A Versatile American Institution: The Changing Ideals and Realities of Philanthropic Foundations*. Washington, DC: The Brookings Institution Press.

—. and Stanton Wheeler. 1994. *Social Science in the Making: Essays on the Russell Sage Foundation, 1907–1947*. New York: Russell Sage Foundation.

Handlin, Oscar, and Mary F. Handlin. 1961. *The Dimensions of Liberty*. Cambridge: Belknap Press/Harvard University Press.

Harlan, Louis R. 1958. *Separate and Unequal: Public School Campaigns and Racism in the Southern Seaboard States, 1901–1915*. New York: Atheneum.

Harper, Keith. 2008. *American Denominational History: Perspectives on the Past, Prospects for the Future*. Tuscaloosa: University of Alabama Press.

Harris, Neil. 1962. "The Gilded Age Revisited: Boston and the Museum Movement." *American Quarterly* 14: 545–566.

—. 1966. *The Artist in American Society: The Formative Years, 1790–1860*. New York: George Braziller.

Harvey, Paul. 1997. *Redeeming the South: Religious Cultures and Racial Identities among Southern Baptists, 1865–1925*. Chapel Hill: University of North Carolina Press.

Haskell, Thomas. 1977. *The Emergence of Professional Social Science: The American Social Science Association and the Nineteenth-Century Crisis of Authority*. Urbana: The University of Illinois Press.

Hempton, David. 2001. "A Tale of Preachers and Beggars: Methodism and Money in the Great Age of Transatlantic Expansion, 1780–1830." In *God and Mammon: Protestants, Money, and the Market, 1790–1860*, ed. Mark A. Noll, 123–146. New York: Oxford University Press.

Higginbotham, Evelyn Brooks. 1993. *Righteous Discontent: The Women's Movement in the Black Baptist Church, 1880–1920*. Cambridge, MA: Harvard University Press.

Hill, Patricia. 1985. *The World Their Household: The American Woman's Foreign Mission Movement and Cultural Transformation, 1870–1920*. Ann Arbor: University of Michigan Press.

Hofstadter, Richard. 1955. *Academic Freedom in the Age of the College*. New York: Columbia University Press.

Horowitz, Helen Lefkowitz. 1976. *Cultural Philanthropy in Chicago*. Chicago: University of Chicago Press.

—. 1984. *Alma Mater: Design and Experience in the Women's Colleges from Their Nineteenth-century Beginnings to the 1930s*. Amherst: University of Massachusetts Press.

—. 2002. *Rereading Sex: Battles Over Sexual Knowledge and Suppression in Nineteenth-century America*. New York: Alfred A. Knopf.

Hoxie, Frederick E. 1989. *Final Promise: The Campaign to Assimilate the Indians, 1880-1920*. New York: Cambridge University Press.

Hutchison, William R. 1987. *Errand to the World: American Protestant Thought and Foreign Missions*. Chicago: University of Chicago Press.

—. 1989. *Between the Times: The Travail of the Protestant Establishment in America, 1900–1960*. New York: Cambridge University Press.

Jones, Jacqueline. 1992. *Soldiers of Light and Love: Northern Teachers and Georgia Blacks, 1865–1873*. Athens: University of Georgia Press.

Jorgenson, Lloyd P. 1987. *The State and the Non-Public School, 1825–1925*. Columbia: University of Missouri Press.

Karl, Barry D. and Stanley N. Katz. 1981. "The American Private Philanthropic Foundation and the Public Sphere 1890–1930." *Minerva: A Review of Science, Learning and Policy* 19: 236–70.

Katz, Michael. 1986. *In the Shadow of the Poorhouse: A History of Social Welfare in America*. New York: Basic Books.

Katz, Stanley N., Barry Sullivan, and C. Paul Beach. 1985. "Legal Change and Legal Autonomy: Charitable Trusts in New York, 1777–1893." *Law and History Review* 3: 51–89.

Keller, Robert H., Jr. 1983. *American Protestantism and United States Indian Policy*. Lincoln: University of Nebraska Press.

Kerr, K. Austin. 1985. *Organized for Prohibition: A New History of the Anti-Saloon League*. New Haven, CT: Yale University Press.

Kevles, Daniel J. 1977. *The Physicists: The History of a Scientific Community in Modern America*. New York: Vintage Books.

Kohler, Robert E. 1991. *Partners in Science: Foundations and Natural Scientists, 1900–1945*. Chicago: University of Chicago Press.

Lagemann, Ellen Condliffe. 1983. *Private Power For the Public Good: A History of the Carnegie Foundation for the Advancement of Teaching*. Middletown, CT: Wesleyan University Press.

—. 1989. *The Politics of Knowledge: The Carnegie Corporation, Philanthropy, and Public Policy*. Middletown, CT: Wesleyan University Press.

Lindeman, Eduard C. 1939. *Wealth and Culture*. New York: Harcourt, Brace, & Co.

Lutz, Jessie Gregory. 1971. *China and the Christian Colleges, 1850–1950*. Ithaca, NY: Cornell University Press.

McAfee, Ward. 1998. *Religion, Race, and Reconstruction: The Public School in the Politics of the 1870s*. Albany: State University of New York Press.

McCarthy, Kathleen D. 1982. *Noblesse Oblige: Charity & Cultural Philanthropy in Chicago, 1849–1929*. Chicago: University of Chicago Press.

—. 1990. *Lady Bountiful Revisited: Women, Philanthropy, and Power*. New Brunswick, NJ: Rutgers University Press.

—. 2003. *American Creed: Philanthropy and the Rise of Civil Society, 1700–1865*. Chicago: University of Chicago Press.

McPherson, James. 1975. *The Abolitionist Legacy: From Reconstruction to the NAACP*. Princeton, NJ: Princeton University Press.

Mettler, Suzanne. 2011. *The Submerged State: How Invisible Government Policies Undermine American Democracy*. Chicago: University of Chicago Press.

Miller, George Frederick. 1922. "The Academy System of the State of New York." Ph.D. diss., Columbia University.

Montgomery, William E. 1993. *Under Their Own Vine and Fig Tree: The African-American Church in the South, 1865–1900*. Baton Rouge: Louisiana State University Press.

Moss, Lemuel. 1868. *Annals of the United States Christian Commission*. Philadelphia: J. B. Lippincott & Company.

Muncy, Robyn. 1994. *Creating a Female Dominion in American Reform, 1890–1935*. New York: Oxford University Press.

Nelson, Paul David. 1974. "Experiment in Interracial Education at Berea College, 1858–1908." *The Journal of Negro History* 59, 1: 13–27.

Noll, Mark A. 2001. *God and Mammon: Protestants, Money, and the Market, 1790–1860: Protestants, Money, and the Market, 1790–1860*. New York: Oxford University Press.

Nord, David Paul. 2004. *Faith in Reading: Religious Publishing and the Birth of Mass Media in America*. New York: Oxford University Press.

Oates, Mary J. 1995. *The Catholic Philanthropic Tradition in America*. Bloomington: University of Indiana Press.

Olasky, Marvin. 1992. *The Tragedy of American Compassion*. Washington, DC: Regnery Publishing, Inc.

Oleson, Alexandra, and John Voss. 1979. *The Organization of Knowledge in Modern America, 1860–1920*. Baltimore, MD: Johns Hopkins University Press.

Parker, Alison M. 1997. *Purifying America: Women, Cultural Reform, and Pro-Censorship Activism, 1873–1933*. Urbana: University of Illinois Press.

Pascoe, Peggy. 1990. *Relations of Rescue: The Search for Female Moral Authority in the American West, 1874–1939*. New York: Oxford University Press.

Patterson, James T. 1994. *America's Struggle against Poverty, 1900–1994*. Cambridge, MA: Harvard University Press.

Perlmann, Joel 1988. *Ethnic Differences: Schooling and Social Structure Among the Irish, Italians, Jews, & Blacks in an American City, 1880–1935*. New York: Cambridge University Press.

Pratt, John Webb. 1967. *Religion, Politics, and Diversity: The Church–State Theme in New York History*. Ithaca, NY: Cornell University Press.

Prucha, Francis Paul. 1995. *The Great Father: The United States Government and the American Indians*. Lincoln: University of Nebraska Press.

Remillard, Arthur. 2011. *Southern Civil Religions: Imagining the Good Society in the Post-Reconstruction Era*. Athens: University of Georgia Press.

Rosen, F. Bruce. 1977. "The Influence of the Peabody Fund on Education in Reconstruction Florida." *The Florida Historical Quarterly* 55, 3: 310–320.

Rosner, David. 1982. *A Once Charitable Enterprise: Hospitals and Health Care in Brooklyn and New York, 1885–1915*. Princeton, NJ: Princeton University Press; selection in Hammack, *Making the Nonprofit Sector*, 1998.

Ross, Brian. 1989. "The New Philanthropy: The Reorganization of Charity in Turn of the Century Cleveland." Ph.D. diss., Case Western Reserve University.

Rudolph, Frederick. 1962. *The American College and University: A History*. New York: Alfred A. Knopf.

Salamon, Lester. 1999. *America's Nonprofit Sector: A Primer*. 2nd edn. New York: The Foundation Center.

Sander, Kathleen Waters. 2008. *Mary Elizabeth Garrett: Society and Philanthropy in the Gilded Age*. Baltimore, MD: Johns Hopkins University Press.

Sanders, James. 1977. *The Education of an Urban Minority: Catholics in Chicago, 1833–1965* New York: Oxford University Press.

Schlesinger, Arthur M. 1944. "Biography of a Nation of Joiners." *The American Historical Review*: 1–25.

Schweiger, Beth Barton and Donald G. Mathews. 2004. *Religion in the American South: Protestants and Others in History and Culture*. Chapel Hill: University of North Carolina Press.

Schweiger, Beth Barton. 2000. *The Gospel Working Up: Progress and the Pulpit in Nineteenth-Century Virginia*. New York: Oxford University Press.

Scott, Anne Firor. 1991. *Natural Allies: Women's Associations in American History.* Chicago: University of Illinois Press.

Sealander, Judith. 1997. *Private Wealth and Public Life: Foundation Philanthropy and the Reshaping of American Social Policy from the Progressive Era to the New Deal.* Baltimore, MD: Johns Hopkins University Press.

Sehat, David. 2010. *The Myth of American Religious Freedom.* New York: Oxford University Press.

Selig, Diana. 2008. *Americans All: The Cultural Gifts Movement.* Cambridge, MA: Harvard University Press.

Silber, Norman J. 2001. *A Corporate Form of Freedom: The Emergence of the Nonprofit Sector.* Boulder, CO: Westview.

Simon, John G. 1987. "The Tax Treatment of Nonprofit Organizations: A Review of Federal and State Policies." In *The Nonprofit Sector: A Research Handbook*, ed. Walter W. Powell, 67–98. New Haven, CT: Yale University Press.

Sims, Anastatia. 1997. *The Power of Femininity in the New South: Women's Organizations and Politics in North Carolina, 1880–1930.* Columbia: University of South Carolina Press.

Sklar, Katherine Kish. 1995. *Florence Kelley and the Nation's Work.* New Haven, CT: Yale University Press.

Skocpol, Theda, and Fiorina, Morris P. 1999. *Civic Engagement in American Democracy.* New York: Russell Sage Foundation for Brookings Institution Press.

Skocpol, Theda, M. Ganz, and Z. Munson. 2000. "A Nation of Organizers: The Institutional Origins of Civic Voluntarism in the United States." *American Political Science Review* 94, 3: 527–546.

Sloan, Douglas. 1994. *Faith and Knowledge: Mainline Protestantism and American Higher Education.* Louisville, KY: Westminster John Knox Press.

Soyer, Daniel. 1997. *Jewish Immigrant Associations and American Identity in New York, 1880–1939.* Cambridge, MA: Harvard University Press.

Stevens, Rosemary. 1989. *In Sickness and in Wealth: American Hospitals in the Twentieth Century.* New York: Basic Books.

Stivers, Camilla. 2000. *Bureau Men, Settlement Women: Constructing Public Administration in the Progressive Era.* Lawrence: University Press of Kansas.

Stocking Jr., George W. 1985. *Objects and Others.* Madison: University of Wisconsin Press.

Stowell, Daniel W. 1998. *Rebuilding Zion: The Religious Reconstruction of the South, 1863–1877.* New York: Oxford University Press.

Tichenor, I. T. 1901. "The Home Mission Board of the Southern Baptist Convention, in Albert Henry Newman." *A Century of Baptist Achievement.* Philadelphia: American Baptist Publication Society.

Tomlins, Christopher. 1993. *Law, Labor, and Ideology in the Early American Republic.* New York: Cambridge University Press.

Trattner, Walter I. 1974. *From Poor Law to Welfare State: A History of Social Welfare in America.* New York: The Free Press.

Tripp, Steven Elliott. 1997. *Yankee Town, Southern City: Race and Class Relations in Civil War Lynchburg.* New York: New York University Press.

Turner, Elizabeth Hayes. 1997. *Women, Culture and Community: Religion and Reform in Galveston 1880–1920.* New York: Oxford University Press.

Twain, Mark and Charles Dudley Warner. 1873. *The Gilded Age: A Novel.* Hartford, CT: American Publishing Co.

United States Bureau of the Census. 1929. *Census of Religious Bodies: 1926: Lutherans. Statistics, History, Doctrine and Organization.* Consolidated Report. Washington, DC: United States Government Printing Office.

United States Office of Education. 1914. *Annual Report of the Commissioner of Education* 1. Washington, DC: United States Government Printing Office.

Van Slyck, Abigail A. 1995. *Free to All: Carnegie Libraries & American Culture, 1890–1920.* Chicago: University of Chicago Press.

Veysey, Laurence R. 1965. *The Emergence of the American University.* Chicago: University of Chicago Press.

Wacker, Grant. 2009. *Heaven Below: Early Pentecostals and American Culture.* Cambridge, MA: Harvard University Press.

Warner, Amos Griswold. 1908. *American Charities: A Study in Philanthropy and Economics.* Revised by Mary R. Coolidge. New York: Thomas Y. Crowell & Co.

Waugh, Joan. 1998. *Unsentimental Reformer: The Life of Josephine Shaw Lowell.* Cambridge, MA: Harvard University Press.

Wheatley, Steven. 1988. *The Politics of Philanthropy: Abraham Flexner and Medical Education.* Madison: The University of Wisconsin Press.

Wheeler, Leigh Ann. 2004. *Against Obscenity: Reform and the Politics of Womanhood in America, 1873–1935.* Baltimore, MD: Johns Hopkins University Press.

Wisner, Elizabeth. 1970. *Social Welfare in the South from Colonial Times to World War I.* Baton Rouge: Louisiana State University Press.

Wosh, Peter J. 1994. *Spreading the Word: The Bible Business in Nineteenth-Century America.* Ithaca, NY: Cornell University Press.

Yohn, Susan Mitchell. 1995. *Contest of Faiths: Missionary Women and Pluralism in the American Southwest.* Ithaca, NY: Cornell University Press.

Zunz, Olivier 2012. *Philanthropy in America: A History.* Princeton, NJ: Princeton University Press, 2012.

Chapter Eighteen

Labor and Class in the GAPE: Fruitful Opposition and the Specter of the Middle Class

David Huyssen

The history of labor and class in the Gilded Age and Progressive Era (GAPE) may now be as robust and diverse a field as it has ever been, but the source of its vibrancy is not new. It continues to thrive on long-running but still-vigorous debates about how to characterize this period of labor and class history thematically. Do the swelling tide of workers' movements and the growth of corporate power and organization in the late nineteenth and early twentieth centuries make for a celebratory or cynical tale? Do early twentieth-century reform movements' efforts to demand state intervention in the economy describe a dramatic break with previous US history, or the logical outcome of continuously operating ideology and practice from the Revolutionary era and before?

The historiography of labor and class during the GAPE reads predominantly as a variation on these four distinct, sometimes interlocking themes, which appear as a set of opposed pairs: celebration versus cynicism, and transition versus continuity. "Celebration" should be self-explanatory, as should "transition" and "continuity"; "cynicism" is not. "Cynicism" here does not mean that the scholars in question see only ill in the period, nor that they lack hope for the future. It means only that their figurative account ledgers evaluating the period's progress tend to concentrate on the loss column, and that they rate those losses underappreciated.

The field has resided within this four-part framework since its inception during the GAPE, and the way scholars have positioned themselves has depended, in large part, on their chosen method of investigation. John R. Commons and his disciples in the Wisconsin school, long seen as having created the field of US labor and class history in the late 19th and early 20th centuries, leaned on statistical and institutional methods to understand skilled white male laborers' construction and jealous stewardship of a tightly defined working-class consciousness (ultimately resting within the AFL's craft unions), and the structures of state and legal power governing American working life (Commons 1905; 1918; Perlman 1928; Fink 1991). Taking the world of white male work in the industrial Northeast and industrializing Midwest as an index for the country, they painted a whiggish picture of labor and class in the GAPE that mirrored the normative view of their own time: gradual democratic progress and systematization through a de-facto partnership of moderate craft-union activists, sensible legislators, and pragmatic businessmen. This partnership would hold at bay the wild-eyed ideologues on both the left and right—from Socialists and industrial unionists to the Citizens Industrial Association of America and the National Association of Manufacturers' frothier members—while assimilating immigrants to the American order of free labor (Pearson 2015). With intellectuals and union leaders working hand in glove with employers and elected officials to guide laborers, a mutually productive era of labor–management peace could be at hand (Fink 1991). Theirs was a celebratory historical vision.

The standard historiographical narrative has the New Labor historians of the mid-twentieth century debunking this story, shifting the field away from prominent labor leaders and legislators by turning to ordinary workers' experience, revealing their writing, cultural practices, and community life—not to mention their workplace struggles—to be both far richer and less reassuring than the Wisconsin school had made out (Fink 1991). But innovative as Herbert Gutman, David Montgomery, and other radical New Labor and New Social historians were, they were not the first scholars to gaze upon labor and class in the GAPE with more dubious eyes.

W.E.B. Du Bois had investigated labor in the United States at the same time as the Wisconsin school but with strikingly different interests, methods, assumptions, and

A Companion to the Gilded Age and Progressive Era, First Edition. Edited by Christopher McKnight Nichols and Nancy C. Unger.
© 2017 John Wiley & Sons, Inc. Published 2017 by John Wiley & Sons, Inc.

thematic results. In a way, it was Du Bois who invented the field, not for his own day but as it would exist in a century's time. *The Souls of Black Folk* adds critical cultural and literary tools to the early social-science toolkit that Commons favored, while also conveying a keen apprehension of how race orders every aspect of life in the United States. Du Bois minces no words:

> For we must never forget that the economic system of the South to-day which has succeeded the old *régime* is not the same system as that of the old industrial North, of England, or of France, with their trades-unions, their restrictive laws, their written and unwritten commercial customs, and their long experience. It is, rather, a copy of that England of the early nineteenth century, before the factory acts,—the England that wrung pity from thinkers and fired the wrath of Carlyle (1990, 123).

Turning Commons and the Wisconsin school on their heads simply by recognizing black workers as full members of the American workforce (indeed, as fully human) and labor in the South as central to US labor history rather than a deviant peculiarity, Du Bois saw no justification for complacency or contentment in 1903. His view of labor and class in the GAPE, seen both through the lens of race and a more sophisticated methodology, was understandably cynical.

And Du Bois was not the only under-recognized trailblazer in critical assessments of labor and class history in the GAPE. As Jennifer Fronc recounts in *New York Undercover* (2009), women writers of the period—both "girl stunt reporters" such as Nellie Bly and trained social scientists such as Amy Tanner and Annie Marion MacLean—began pioneering participant-observer-style research by infiltrating and chronicling working-class women's jobs and workplaces. Perhaps MacLean, who exposed the punishing working experience of Chicago department store shopgirls in *The American Journal of Sociology* in 1899, held out more hope than Du Bois that conditions might improve through pragmatic application of knowledge, but her assessment of labor's then present was similarly discouraging (Fronc 2009, 13–17).

The fact that neither Du Bois nor MacLean was a practicing "labor historian" simply underscores the artificiality of that distinction (and its historically racist and sexist exclusions), in no way diminishing their accomplishments in offering clear, empirically rich alternatives to the Wisconsin school's relatively sunny vision of US labor and class history in the GAPE. Where Commons saw a transition worth celebrating, Du Bois and MacLean saw stubborn continuity in lasting forms of brutality and exploitation, as well as the urgent, unfulfilled need for transformation. The stark opposition of their interpretations laid the groundwork for the analytical vacillation that has described the field since.

Such vacillation, while arguably limiting, has not at all impeded fruitful inquiry. Women's, African American, environmental, transnational, and other trailblazing historians have thrived within its boundaries, providing substantive benefits to older narratives of industrialization, labor unrest, idealistic reform movements, and turbulent class relations—indeed, to US history as a whole—that neglected to take those insurgent fields' primary subjects into account. Today's histories of labor and class in the GAPE have never been more circumspect or inclusive, their subjects never understood as more consequential in shaping the contours of contemporary American life. In the exchange of force and pressure along the axes of celebration and cynicism, transition and continuity, what appear to be repetitive dialectics have created space and energy for new ideas while providing a continuing, easily comprehensible framework in which to fit them.

The following explorations into the framework's four elements—through hoary, standard-bearing authors; pivotal, field-shifting scholarship; and newer immanent critics—make no pretense at comprehensive or balanced coverage. Still, they should provide illuminating dips into both the history and historiographical development of labor and class in the GAPE. They also identify a few important historiographical trends worth discovering or revisiting (e.g., the transnational turn, renewed attention to violence, environmental labor histories, race and "contract" as formative in postbellum "free labor" regimes, and the "new history of capitalism"), and where their practitioners tend to fit within the oppositional framework.

The desire to engage these oppositions simply by picking a side and joining the fray, however, has serious dangers. No matter how frequently infused with innovative inflections, a repetitive framework risks interfering with a collective ability to pose new questions about basic categories or building blocks fundamental to practically *all* the histories of the period. Such categories—historical concepts such as "reform," "corporatization," or "progressivism"—can become part of the analytical furniture, specters haunting every corner of the thematic framework, but whose instrumental lexical usage often exempts them from critical scrutiny. Even something so basic as the received wisdom of labor history's origins can calcify through benign, or not so benign, neglect.

This observation leads to a concluding critical argument: that, given the current historical moment of intensifying inequality, and in light of Thomas Piketty's ample documentation that capitalism's default historical tendency over the past two centuries has been to aggravate divisions between the haves and have-nots, the time seems ripe for historians of labor and class in the GAPE to trouble perhaps the most elemental yet elusive of such specters haunting their field: the idea of the American "middle class" as a discrete and crucial historical actor of the period.

Celebration of "Middle-Class" Order

The centrality of the "middle class" to histories of the GAPE reflects the popular, celebratory understanding of the period's meaning, carved out in works such as Samuel Hays's

Response to Industrialism (1957), Robert Wiebe's *The Search for Order* (1967), and Alfred D. Chandler, Jr.'s *The Visible Hand* (1977). These accounts describe a stuttering, but ultimately clear transition from "The Great Barbecue" of unfettered postbellum capitalist rapacity and competition (the vision proffered in 1934 by Matthew Josephson's *The Robber Barons*) to a more moderate, even-keeled form of managed political economy. This middle-er ground allegedly blended basic principles of free enterprise with rational management techniques, interfirm cooperation, and reasonable government intervention in both trade and the labor market (Link and McCormick 1983; Dawley 1991; Diner 1998; McGerr 2003).

Some old and many new corporations, these scholars argue, began to rationalize production and distribution during the 1860s and 1870s, setting new standards of efficiency by adopting vertical integration and layered management systems (the "Managerial Revolution" of Chandler's subtitle). Concerned state officials, partly in response to public outcry over the increasingly monopolistic results of such corporate forms in industries from steel to sugar, began in turn to set limits on corporate power through legislation, most notably the Interstate Commerce Act in 1887 (aimed principally at controlling railroad cartelization) and the Sherman Anti-Trust act of 1890. These were hesitant steps toward more robust state action, such scholars aver, but they set the stage for Theodore Roosevelt's executive interventions during the Progressive Era, which he began sensationally by insisting on a managed solution to the 1902 anthracite coal strike in Pennsylvania. Both business and government in these accounts displayed a rejection of extremes and a turn to the managed middle.

Meanwhile, the process of bringing order out of chaos in the corporate world had an analogue in urban American life, where epidemics of disease—tuberculosis, diphtheria, typhoid, yellow and scarlet fevers—and their attendant social crises spurred major advances in public health, particularly for workers: for instance, the establishment of visiting nurse services, sanatorium construction, and housing codes requiring indoor plumbing (Davis 1967; Plunz, 1990; Sklar 1995; Gilmore 2002; Burnstein 2006). Exposure of urban squalor drew greater attention both to the graft-plagued urban political machines that mined poverty for power, and the industrial labor conditions that perpetuated want (Steffens 1906, 1931; Connolly 2005). Civil service reformers and commissions at every level of government—from New York's Bureau of Municipal Research and Factory Investigating Commission, to the federal government's Commission on Industrial Relations of 1912 to 1916—swung into action to root out political corruption and intervene in the most heinous forms of abuse (McCormick 1989; McGerr 2003). The publicity around such expert commissions and their findings prompted reorganizations of municipal politics and further legislative action to curb child labor (long since a target for reformers), establish or reinforce minimum workplace safety rules, limit hours (particularly for women), and expand or begin to offer workmen's compensation schemes (Bellamy 1997; Woloch 2015). As the story goes, all these initiatives and their ameliorative power for the nation bore the unmistakable stamp of the "middle-class" self-improvement ideal.

But it wasn't mere ideology. The material emergence and rapid expansion of an urban "middle class," or *Mittelstandt* of labor—business clerks, professionals, social workers, a civil service corps—occupies a privileged place as both the primary author of this story and one of its clearest consequences. Robert Wiebe saw the "ambition of the new middle class to fulfill its destiny through bureaucratic means" in their search for order as "the heart of progressivism" (1967, 166). Richard Hofstadter viewed its members' status anxiety in the face of urban industrial capitalist development as the major historical motor of the period (1955, 131–135). Hofstadter's signature sardonic detachment is much on display in his classic volume, *Age of Reform*, yet he yields an uncharacteristic moment of historical celebration when considering the Progressives' anti-trust legacy: "[S]ubsequent generations of Americans still owe a great debt to the anti-trust inheritance they hold from the Progressive era.… No doubt the immediate material achievement was quite small in proportion to all the noise; but there are many episodes in history in which intense struggle has to be waged to win modest gains, and this too must be remembered before we pass too severe a judgment on the great Progressive crusade against the trusts" (1955, 255–256). And whom does Hofstadter credit for this legacy? "The ferment of the Progressive era was urban, middle-class, and nationwide" (131).

Such generous interpretations of "middle-class" progressivism's legacy fell out of favor in the late 1970s and early 1980s, as historians influenced by early- and mid-century sociological literature of "social control" began to perceive darker motives in efforts toward order and efficiency (Boyer 1978; Gordon 1986). No longer did these historians identify in their middling protagonists a benevolent, meliorist desire to improve the lives of laborers (and hence the functioning of American democracy) through more regularized schooling, voluntarist and state support networks, and a smorgasbord of new workplace regulations. Instead, such scholars suspected them of harboring an essentially xenophobic, anti-modernist project aiming, as Paul Boyer put it, "to re-create in the city the moral homogeneity of the village" (1978, 292; Lears 1981). The "friendly-visitor" activities and organizational literature of S. Humphreys Gurteen's Charity Organization Society provided ample evidence for such scholarly skewerings, and still do (Boyer 1978; Huyssen 2014). Even settlement house founders such as Jane Addams and Lillian Wald, whose record of devotion to immigrants and the working class had won plaudits from historians (and condemnations from A. Mitchell Palmer as subversively radical), faced new allegations of "middle-class" condescension and moralizing (Boyer 1978; Pernick, 1996; Johnson

2006). These studies introduced an occasionally hamfisted but not unjustified critical perspective on "middle-class" primacy in the GAPE. Still very much in control of the era, "middle-class" progressives no longer appeared quite so benign or "progressive" in their intentions.

Yet these studies, despite their cynicism toward "middle-class" intentions, sometimes trafficked in, and certainly helped to stimulate, a different brand of celebratory analysis. Not infrequently, they devoted some of their pages to recovering various ways in which the working-class objects of reformers' dubious ministrations subverted those efforts to their own purposes, wresting power, material benefits, or a modicum of control from asymmetrical relationships (Katz 1986; Gordon 1988). Other historians of the period picked up on the trend and began writing histories of workers improvising on industrialization, colonizing and altering "middle-class" culture for the nation—laborizing American life (Painter 1987). The work of political scientist and anthropologist James C. Scott, especially *Weapons of the Weak* (1985), became a theoretical touchstone for many of these studies.

Women's labor, cultural, and African American historians such as Kathy Peiss, Nan Enstad, and Tera W. Hunter have provided particularly sharp insights into the ways many working women leveraged the new opportunities in employment—"opportunities," of course, that exposed them to all manner of indignity and abuse—to create new cultures of leisure and independence not only for themselves, but for "middle-class" women and men as well (Peiss 1986; Hunter 1997; Enstad 1999). Hunter's instant classic, *To 'Joy My Freedom*, does this particularly well, illuminating both sides of the "dialectic of repression and resistance" between African American women in Atlanta, their communities, and the city's white power structure from Reconstruction through 1920. Recovering histories of individual and collective resistance by black women within a regime that aimed to deny their womanhood and reduce them to perfectly pliable labor, Hunter celebrates the various ways—from pan-toting to nightclub-hopping, to the Atlanta washerwomen's strike of 1881—in which the perennially most disadvantaged workers in US history claimed joy for themselves and gave meaning to the Jubilee. She also attends to the community organization efforts of "middle-class" black women, capturing the tensions in their contributions, condescension toward their working-class sisters, and the way they reaped benefits from those laboring sisters' successes in creating space for new expressions of womanhood, politics, and labor in the South.

The celebration in such histories is bittersweet, of course. As Enstad notes in her conclusion, "[Working women's] dreams, no less than their material conditions, were inevitably rooted in and limited by the hierarchical structures of U.S. society" (1999, 206). Conceptions of gender, race, and politics for working women may have broadened nationally through the historical dynamics these scholars describe, but they did so unevenly. It was "middle-class" white women who would benefit most from the broadening of possibility. The transgressiveness and popularization of working-class female culture created spaces for them to question, as Peiss puts it, "the inviolability of women's traditional sphere." Such questioning would contribute to the attainment of women's suffrage, an achievement worth celebrating, but which white Americans made tragic by continuing to deny the vote's benefits to African American women and men for decades to come. Such denials, under new guises, continue to the time of this writing (Berman 2015).

Some historians, most notably Robert Johnston, have had enough of such qualified celebrations, and would like to see a judicious return to appreciating the democratic potential of the Progressive Era. Johnston has attempted to renew a sense that the "middle class" deserved the victories it enjoyed in the period, aiming not only to recover a bit of its members' dignity and genuinely democratic intentions, but also to argue for their radicalism. In doing so, he comes closer than any historian of labor and class in the period to mapping the contours of the "middle class," while also identifying the cynical strain in GAPE historiography quite explicitly.

In the inaugural issue of *The Journal of the Gilded Age and the Progressive Era*, he laments, "Far too many [historians] have simply abandoned hope in the democratic legacy of, and possibilities within, Progressive Era politics. In a cynical age, and given the leftist politics prevalent in the academy, it is easy to see that progressives did not address many of the age's fundamental issues of social justice," and indeed, "made many of them worse" (Johnston 2002, 70). Surveying the historiographical landscape, he observes, "The current wave of scholarship detailing the crimes of Progressivism is impressive, in fact seemingly unrelenting. Yet such work still falls far short of expunging the period's vigorous democratic impulses" (71). Johnston's aim is to see beyond his own "cynical age" to locate those democratic impulses and their legacy within the "middle classes." His book, *The Radical Middle Class* (2003), accordingly opens with three chapters under the heading "Rehabilitating the American Middle Class."

Johnston's rehabilitation campaign deserves scrutiny. But as a preliminary matter it is worth asking, why does the "middle-class" legacy require rehabilitation in the first place? Who are these "cynical," "leftist" killjoys, and what does their work actually look like?

Cynicism of the Margins

If considering the "middle-class" legacy of the Progressive Era causes even paragons of cynicism such as Hofstadter to make concessions to celebration, perhaps it is no accident that those historians who have most forcefully rejected this narrative of inexorable progress have often done so by turning their attention away from the middle, and toward either the top or the bottom. Such historians, in fact, have usually refrained from tangling with the idea of "the middle class" in any systematic way, even when the term peppers their prose. Their preferred focus on the wealthy or the workers, separately or simultaneously, has provided the most skeptical corner of the thematic framework for judging labor and class in the GAPE.

Those occupying this corner generally view Progressive-era "limits" on corporate dominance as an almost total sham; public health advances as the handmaiden of imperialism and, more often than not, constitutive of pseudo-scientific racism and patriarchal essentialism; and interventions to protect labor as either ineffective window-dressing, or lubricant for the full emergence of corporate welfare in the 1920s (Kolko 1963; Weinstein 1968; Livingston 1986; Bederman 1995). Fully on display in this body of scholarship are the ways in which nominal progressives undermined social justice for working people by exacerbating racism, sexism, classism, and imperialism, while continuing to countenance or accelerate the growth of material inequality (Jacobson 2000; Shah 2001; Bender 2009; Glotzer 2015). Hofstadter's chapters on Theodore Roosevelt and Woodrow Wilson in *The American Political Tradition* offer both an early representation of this viewpoint in political history, and a better instance of his ironic historical sensibility (1948). The main division within the cynical camp is between those who believe that legitimate hopes for democratic power and social justice among workers were dashed in this period, and those who suspect that such hopes never existed in any viable form.

No one typifies the latter stance more caustically than Gabriel Kolko, whose bilious 1963 book, *The Triumph of Conservatism*, still offers graduate students an object lesson in how to make a solidly researched argument against prevailing wisdom in a manner that consigns one's book to relative obscurity (or at least to the margins of consensus). *Triumph of Conservatism* was among the first works to examine the transactions of power among the Progressive Era's political and economic elite while eschewing the assumption that things turned out better at the end of the period. Kolko's key insight was to reject the assumption that those in power fought tooth-and-nail to obstruct any state intervention in the economy. One might say that Kolko—over a decade before neoliberalism began its hegemonic global ascent—saw neoliberalism's essential dynamics at work in the Progressive Era (Harvey 2005). As he put it, "Only if we mechanistically assume that government regulation of the economy is automatically progressive can we say that the federal regulation of the economy during 1900 to 1916 was progressive in the commonly understood sense of the term" (58). Hofstadter had observed businessmen's fingerprints on Progressive action, but had not made quite so much of it (1955, 252–254). Kolko saw such action—including Teddy Roosevelt's famed "trust-busting," the Federal Meat Inspection Act of 1906, the founding of the Federal Reserve in 1913, the Clayton Anti-Trust Act of 1914, and more—as fulfilling the express desire of big businessmen in both banking and industry (286). Hence the conservative triumph: big business and finance got exactly what they wanted, consolidating control with the assistance of the state.

Kolko's cynical dismissal of what he viewed as naïveté among his peers regarding progressivism ("[E]ven most of the critical historians have accepted the traditional view of progressivism as a whole") won him few explicit converts at the time of his book's publication. His strategy of reevaluating progressivism by examining the halls of power and privilege, however—and with it, some notion of an active, successful upper-class struggle for control of American life through the Gilded Age and Progressive Era—has arguably caught on, and is finally receiving its due. Sven Beckert's *Monied Metropolis* revived the practice in 2001, charting the rise and self-definition of a unified American bourgeoisie in nineteenth-century New York, and carrying his analysis of growing bourgeois dominance through the Gilded Age to conclude in the early Progressive Era.

Beckert's geographical frame is narrower than Kolko's, his theoretical approach and periodization broader. Kolko's exclusive focus on high politics and business machinations at the national level over sixteen years carries a whiff of teleological inevitability, while Beckert, more attuned to Bourdieuian expressions of class power, describes the decades-long formation of an urban elite whose consolidation was not necessarily assured, and whose influence asserted itself on the street and in the opera house as well as in the legislature and at the workplaces its members managed (in fairness to Kolko, Bourdieu had only begun researching *Distinction* in the year Kolko published his book). Yet the two authors' common focus on the most powerful segment of society seems to unite them in cynicism toward both optimistic accounts of "middle-class" values forging a path of progress through the period, or the usefulness of histories that lavish attention on embattled laborers. Taking a swipe at the cultural turn (and hitting New Labor and New Social historians' legacy in the process), Beckert writes that "many social historians desired to uncover the once-hidden history of the 'common people' and to de-emphasize those who for so long had dominated historical narratives." The fruit of this, he concludes, was that "they neglected the most powerful social group in the nineteenth-century United States—the bourgeoisie" (10). This critique has animated a sizeable faction of the "new history of capitalism" phenomenon, of which Beckert is the most visible champion (Scheussler 2013; Sklansky 2014). Much of this emerging field has focused on antebellum or post-World War I US history, but a few works have also ventured into the GAPE (Ott 2011; Pak 2013; Glotzer 2015).

Beckert refrains from adopting Kolko's unapologetic socialism, but he has usefully reinvigorated Kolko's perspective, seeing the long-run dynamics of labor and class in the GAPE (not entirely unlike Matthew Josephson, or Charles and Mary Beard for that matter) as a function of upper-class power and its steady consolidation. Because Beckert ends his narrative a few years before Kolko's begins, the epilogue to *Monied Metropolis* reads almost like a prequel-style set-up for Kolko's analysis in *Triumph of Conservatism*:

> Trying to secure legitimacy as well as more favorable conditions for accumulation, bourgeois New Yorkers formulated new political preferences, preferences rooted in an awareness of the systemic nature of the crisis… [they] retained enormous influence in shaping the precise outcomes of these turn-of-the-century reforms. They did so because they had forged social, cultural, and economic institutions that enabled them to act collectively (Beckert 2001, 325–326).

In more recent years, as Beckert has been the beating the drum for the "new history of capitalism," several practitioners in this field have continued to home in on bourgeois—and in particular, bankers'—influence over the period. Julia Ott's *When Wall Street Met Main Street* (2011) demonstrates how Progressive Era bankers deliberately transformed Wall Street's public image from a bacchanalian den of besuited thieves into more of what it is today: the institution most identified with the health of the national economy, the repository of many ordinary Americans' hopes for long-term financial security, and a close ally of the federal government. Susie J. Pak's *Gentlemen Bankers* (2013) explores the social and cultural implications of, as her subtitle has it, "The World of J.P. Morgan," concluding much as Beckert does that bourgeois class power neither stems from nor expresses itself primarily through extraordinary individuals bestriding the earth as colossi, but from and through networks forged in common rituals and shared ideological formation.

There is an implication, both in Beckert's critique and in some of this subsequent work, that historians who focus on the "common people" misunderstand where power lies—or worse, that they allow their politics to guide their methodology, thus romanticizing and exaggerating the importance or historical influence of the non-bourgeoisie simply through disproportionate attention. Perhaps. Such historians have, however, shown greater care than scholars of the bourgeoisie in attending to paths not taken and movements snuffed out—in other words, to the contingency of history—that played such a crucial role in eliciting and indirectly shaping the exertions of bourgeois power that Beckert & Co. deem more historically consequential. This has also made them more attentive to the dialectical dimensions of class as an historical process. Where the "new history of capitalism" often seems to understand (bourgeois) class as *sui generis*, historians of labor could indulge no such illusions or oversights.

Yet ultimately, these are two sides of the same story, so it is no accident that when the time comes to evaluate the era's outcomes for labor, Beckert finds himself in the same gloomy corner as the New Labor and New Social historians (and their methodological descendants) who examine strikes, radical movements, and working-class life in the GAPE. The difference is that these earlier historians represent the other strand of cynicism—the one whose advocates allow themselves to see possibility in the hopes of the rebels before recounting the rebellion's demise. Lawrence Goodwyn's 1976 doorstop history of Populism, *Democratic Promise*, provides an early example, analyzing the era's most dramatic revolt of working people. Goodwyn sought to recover and celebrate the "movement culture" of the Texas Farmer's Alliance, and the threat of Charles Macune's Sub-Treasury proposal, as the period's most viable, democratic alternative to capitalism in the United States. Yet his analysis ends under a shroud of defeat and despair. Concluding his abridged version of the book, he writes, "By 1889… the Alliance dream of a national federation of regional cooperatives was untenable, because of the power and hostility of the American financial community" (1978: 330).

Likewise, though sounding notes of hope for the survival and renewal of workers' solidarity, David Montgomery's magisterial *Fall of the House of Labor* (1987)—the crowning achievement of New Labor history methods even as it distinguished itself from that school's general aversion to high politics—presages its conclusion in its title. Montgomery's keen sensitivity to the day-to-day heroism of the working class, as its members struggled to overcome divisions of race and gender to form bonds of mutualism and workplace cultures that could withstand the capitalist juggernaut, hardly leads him to conclusions so distant from Beckert's. "By the mid-1920s," Montgomery writes, "the designs of corporate management had clearly prevailed over those of its rivals" (464).

Historians of labor using race, gender, environmental, transnational, and even more old-fashioned political approaches—from Jacqueline Jones to Priscilla Murolo, Julie Greene to Leon Fink—often paint a similarly bleak portrait of worker empowerment over the GAPE's course, both within and without US borders (Jones 1985; Murolo 1997; Greene 2006; Fink 2011). The new hope for autonomy after emancipation and the hard-won victories described in Tera Hunter's work do not eclipse Jones's demonstration that the reality of labor for African American women nationwide remained overwhelmingly restricted to backbreaking agricultural and domestic employment on which their families depended, even as the consolidation of Jim Crow and the expansion of carceral labor systems baldly reimagined the constraints of slavery for a world of "free labor" (Jones 1985; Montgomery 1993; Alexander 2010; LeFlouria 2015; Haley 2016). Murolo shows how attempts to forge lasting alliances across class lines on the basis of shared womanhood reshaped, but failed to overcome (and in certain ways reinforced) hierarchies of both class and gender (Murolo 1997). Greene exposes AFL leaders such as Samuel Gompers—the heroes of the Wisconsin School's labor history—as infighting, backstabbing hypocrites willing to abandon principle and sacrifice their working-class constituents to protect any meager influence in the political and corporate realms they believed they possessed (Greene 2006). Greene and Leon Fink, the most prominent contributors to a rich and still-developing transnational historiography of labor and class in the GAPE, both reckon with the way systems of racial and xenophobic ordering conditioned international worksites such as the Panama Canal or ocean-going merchant vessels, confounding attempts, or even inclinations to build interethnic, cross-border labor solidarity in a globalizing world (Greene 2009; Fink 2011).

These are not celebratory tales of inexorable liberation, but catalogues of suffering and obstructions to liberty, or at best grim appreciations of resilience under varying degrees of subjection. Sometimes the stories become even darker: for example, when the focus turns to the western labor movement's eager complicity in anti-Chinese legislation, and their campaigns to enforce white supremacy in the workplace, sometimes through terrorism and lynching (Jacobson 2000; Lee 2003). Suffice it to say there is ample extant literature proving that to write about the working class in the GAPE need hardly require romanticizing workers, nor ignoring where power disproportionately subsists under capitalism.

Historians who study either the bourgeois or the working class broadly agree that the history of labor and class in the GAPE is best understood as an extended class war eventually won by the rich. A spate of recent work that looks simultaneously at the wealthy and workers in the period bolsters this conclusion, while also recovering the violence and viciousness of that war. Thomas G. Andrews's *Killing for Coal* (2008) investigates the Colorado mining industry through a deeply—geologically, in fact—contextualized history of the Ludlow Massacre, treating coal baron William Jackson Palmer's patriarchal visions of "coal-fired benevolence" and the daily lives of mining workers as subjects equally worthy of historical investigation. He adds a valuable dimension to the field by understanding the class war in literal terms as a war over control of land and its natural resources, demonstrating how deeply invested were the dreams of both miners and managers in the black gold they devoted their lives to extracting from the Colorado hillsides. Richard White set a standard for grace and economy in this mode of environmental labor history with *The Organic Machine* (1995), and Andrews is one of many who have since produced rich examples or considerations of it (Henderson 1999; Peck 2006). The fact that Andrews recovers an environmentally situated appreciation for the Ludlow Massacre as more "War" than "Massacre" does not, however, change the outcome of the conflict. As he writes, "the Rockefellers held to a vision of Western industrialism that left workers no real place on the land" (286).

In *The Day Wall Street Exploded* (2009), Beverly Gage weaves the rollicking tale of violent anarchist and labor resistance to corporate and state power in the GAPE. She traces a clearly and loudly articulated radical politics of destruction across the period: Johann Most's terrorist fulminations in favor of *Attentat*, or "propaganda-by-deed," before the Haymarket bombing of 1886; Alexander Berkman's failed attempt in 1892 to kill Carnegie Steel manager Henry Clay Frick (in revenge for Frick's having ordered the Pinkerton assault on strikers at Homestead); Leon Czolgosz's assassination of William McKinley in 1901; the IWW leader Bill Haywood's acquittal for his likely 1905 dynamite murder of Idaho governor Frank Steunenberg; the 1910 *Los Angeles Times* explosion and the Ironworkers' union leaders' confession to having arranged it; Tom Mooney's conviction for the 1916 Preparedness Day bombing in San Francisco; all culminating in the deadly TNT-packed horse-and-buggy outside J.P. Morgan's offices on Wall and Broad Streets in 1920. Gage neither romanticizes the workers' various campaigns of deadly violence, nor neglects to point out either the ruthlessness of the conditions against which they were rebelling or the nearly uniform (and wildly disproportionate) state response in defense of bourgeois property and political conservatism. She attends to legislation repressing speech; military assistance to break strikes; and, ultimately, the establishment of clandestine police services aimed at infiltrating and subverting radical political activists.

It all ends, however, in the same place as Goodwyn, Montgomery, and Andrews, or for that matter Beckert and Kolko: "To the men and women who had… sought to create a unified movement of reformers and revolutionaries," Gage writes, "the 1920s were a period as bleak as any they had ever known" (319). Even those like Gage who do not perceive the wealthy as the age's Machiavellian puppeteers tend to recognize their dominance at the end of it. Which raises another central question for students of labor and class in the GAPE: from this era so legendary in the popular imagination for the way it placed state-enforced limits on the raw power of capitalism, how did the wealthy emerge with their mastery intact? What really changed?

Transition and Continuity

Well, a lot, of course, not least what that mastery consisted of, the avenues for its exertion, and how it affected the texture of labor and class.

Between 1865 and 1920, the extent of wealth's command over the United States grew in all directions. Railroad, coal, and telegraph companies—with crucial assistance from all levels of state power—transformed the physical and temporal space of the country, creating previously unimaginable high-speed transportation, energy production, and communication networks that helped stimulate or accelerate wild, uneven cycles of boom-and-bust development. As Richard White demonstrates in *Railroaded* (2011) and Andrew B. Arnold shows in *Fueling the Gilded Age* (2014), this process was anything but rational, efficient, or productive of responsible government. In fact, its stubborn irrationality, inefficiency, and continuous output of failing enterprises careening toward bankruptcy (that nevertheless yielded great fortunes for a few men) encouraged byzantine forms of political and financial corruption. This marriage of corporations to the state served the profit motives of would-be industrialists and financiers far more effectively than it did the wishes of American citizen-workers or consumers. Yet for all the differences between White's and Chandler's—not to mention Wiebe's or Alan Trachtenberg's—accounts of Gilded Age incorporation, all agree that corporate power became the dominant feature of American life, and that this constituted the major transition of the age (Trachtenberg 1982; Klein 2007).

Historians who privilege the voices of the working class in their research have different ways of describing the same transition. The process of achieving corporate dominance produced giant, sprawling, hierarchically managed operations that systematically eroded traditions of control over work processes and craft skill in long-established working-class positions. It also undermined local and regional trading patterns, and demanded ever-increasing quantities of "unskilled" labor met by the continuous arrival of immigrants and accelerating entry of women into the industrial workforce. Steve Fraser's *Age of Acquiescence* (2015) is only the most recent of many rich, provocative works arguing that the advent of industrial de-skilling, layered management, automation, and Taylorist techniques of production elicited both despair and revolt from an American working class whose members—regardless of color, sex, national origin, or region, it often seems—had previously experienced both their productive and reproductive labor in more intimate terms (Kessler-Harris 1982; Lamphere 1987; Laurie 1989; Sellers 1991; Fraser 2015).

The "cannibalist" system of late-nineteenth-century capitalism, as Fraser calls it, ripped from their lives forever a "precapitalist and preindustrial" world of the antebellum period "in which wage labor and market relations were limited, one in which household economies, handicraft production, and self-sufficient agriculture remained deeply rooted" (84). In its place, American workers faced a bewildering system in which unfeeling corporate ciphers determined the price of their labor or its output with a vicious caprice unrelated to either how hard they worked or how much they produced. Native-born workers found themselves competing with more and different people for jobs that commanded less autonomy, social respect, and not infrequently pay, than they had previously known. In its basic outline, this history reflects the testimony of many workers who lived through it: sharecroppers, steel puddlers, garment stitchers, slaughterhouse operators, and coalminers alike, as well as would-be working-class spokespeople such as Henry George (O'Donnell 2015).

Yet for many historians of the GAPE, corporatization and denigration of labor are not the only, or even most lasting transitions of the period. They identify a linchpin in the emerging relationship between wealthy and worker in America that also represented a fundamental transition: new, or vastly multiplied and restructured forms of professional employment. Lawyers, clerks, traders, account managers, and other office workers multiplied faster than the rate of compound interest. Generations of historians, observing the differences between these rapidly expanding forms of labor and more traditional, producerist working-class labor, have described this process as the expansion of the American "middle class." They have attributed to that new "middle class" the reformist instincts that drove and ultimately defined the era. This, they concluded, was the most important transition: the arrival of a defined, self-aware "middle class" whose members would spearhead the great moral and legislative reforms that brought Gilded Age capitalists, corrupt politicians, and unruly workers to heel.

This all constitutes plentiful evidence for transition across the entire spectrum of labor and class in the GAPE. It would seem difficult in the face of such evidence to mount an argument for continuity. But to be a historian is to be a contrarian, so perhaps it was also inevitable. In any case, none who argue for continuity attempt to make the case that nothing changed in the period. Instead, scholars working with such diverse approaches as Fraser, Rebecca Edwards, and Amy Dru Stanley take the implicit position that disproportionate attention to the era's various dramatic changes has tended to mask the entrenched characteristics of culture, ideology, and material life that drove those changes (Dru Stanley 1992; Edwards 2006; Fraser 2015). In other words, they believe that the field focuses too much on effects and not enough on causes. This allows them, somewhat paradoxically, to argue for continuity by describing continuous transitions.

The argument for continuity internal to the period is straightforward: it rejects the received wisdom of a putative transition between the Gilded Age and the Progressive Era that resulted in the two periods' having separate names. The narratives of transition outlined above do not significantly challenge this criticism, because they describe transformations—the consolidation of bourgeois dominance, erosion of worker control, and the growth of "middle-class" professional labor—that developed with relative steadiness between 1865 and the 1920s. The transitional argument more difficult to overcome for partisans of internal continuity is that of "middle class" reformers' advent as a seismic shift that divides the era.

Fraser evades this difficulty by defining the entire period as an "Era of Anticapitalism" whose animating spirit of emancipatory politics drew strength from a tradition of resistance stretching back to the early nineteenth-century abolitionists. He traces this spirit from the Great Strike of 1877 to the U.S. Steel strike of 1919 and beyond, making a persuasive case for its continuity throughout the age. Of course, he devotes scant attention to the "middle-class" reformers that have so long personified what arguably made the Progressive Era so different from the Gilded Age, but one suspects that Fraser would see such actors as the equivalent of confused diplomats wandering onto an active battlefield. The real action for him would remain with the two major armies—capital and labor—and any concessions to diplomacy would prove strategic gambits rather than genuine efforts at peace or conflict-altering interventions. In fact, if anyone could claim true credit for reform, it would be anti-capitalist worker collectives that created both the political will and sense of urgency driving these "middle-class" reformers, or the capitalist and political chieftains bending that reform to their own programs.

Rebecca Edwards takes a different approach in her fine synthesis of the entire period, *New Spirits*. Rather than proposing, as Fraser does, that the dynamics traditionally ascribed to the Gilded Age (e.g., unchecked corporate avarice, ruthless degradation of labor, and potentially revolutionary collective action) extend to 1929, she reads robust assertions of state power and efforts at moral and social reform back as far as Reconstruction, offering a "long Progressive Era" (Edwards 2006, 7). This version of the internal continuity argument, at least superficially, has a greater capacity than Fraser's to accommodate a "middle class" element. Elizabeth Sanders's and Charles Postel's respective analyses of Populism jibe nicely with Edwards's argument, if one understands Populism broadly as a modernizing reform movement. Populism's tendrils emerged well before what usually counts as the Progressive Era; whatever its membership, its major leaders were publishers and petit bourgeois landholders (indeed, Postel offers an interesting discussion of whether historians should approach Populists in class terms at all, though he mischaracterizes Hofstadter's position in the process); and, its primary legislative and political accomplishments came to fruition only during the (short) Progressive Era or afterward (Hofstadter 1955, 61–64; Sanders 1999; Postel 2007, 223–234).

The most contrarian argument—the one for extended continuity—is that the history of labor and class in the GAPE lies squarely within traditions that defined those phenomena both before and after the period. The two most obvious objections to such a position are fairly compelling: one, that the shape of labor in the United States before the Civil War included slavery, and afterward did not; and two, that the Progressive Era saw the rise of a "middle class" that hadn't properly existed before. These would seem to be firm grounds on which to reject any proposal to revise the broadly accepted understanding that the GAPE altered the essential terms of both labor and class in the United States.

Yet that understanding depends, as some scholars have pointed out, on a question of emphasis. Despite emancipation, the postbellum history of "free labor" bears more than just a tincture of bondage's legacy. Historians of African American labor and class in the South between 1865 and 1920, even those such as Hunter who find hope in the darkness, might be forgiven a healthy measure of incredulity, even outrage, at a popular historical narrative that identifies the freedom to work and the advent of the reforming "middle class" as the most important features of labor and class in the era. Du Bois captured the contrary experience of African Americans in the title and content of the penultimate chapter in his still searing 1935 *Black Reconstruction*: "Back Toward Slavery" (1998 edition, 670–710). Generations of scholars studying black labor in the GAPE have expanded on Du Bois's insights—from Manning Marable to Jacqueline Jones, Douglas Blackmon to Sarah Haley—demonstrating time and again how over that decades-long span, Southern legislatures enforced debt peonage and carceral work through a concerted campaign of judicial fraud, pillage, terror, and murder (Marable 1983; Jones 1985; Blackmon 2008; Haley 2016). The New South, as much as the Old, laid its foundations on conscripted black labor, using that cornerstone, as ever, to build the concepts of race, gender, and class that pervaded everyday life.

Although the passage of the Civil Rights Act in 1866 and the 14th Amendment's ratification in 1868 rendered the earliest iterations of the Black Codes unconstitutional, the use of contract law and language to paint a thin veneer of freedom atop what in essence remained bondage augured ill for notions of "free labor" beyond Dixie. Among their many constraints on black freedom, the Black Codes threatened the criminal prosecution of any black worker without a labor contract in the first month of the year. As Amy Dru Stanley and David Montgomery each show, "contract" widely became a euphemism for regimes of nominally at-will labor that rested on state-enforced coercion in the form of "tramp laws" and vagrancy statutes. Montgomery writes, "In place of master-and-servant law… the principle of employment at will was now supplemented by laws requiring the free worker to have *some* employer" (Montgomery 1993: 88).

Dru Stanley makes the connection between emancipation and "free-labor" compulsion even more explicit: "The endeavor of reconstructing the southern labor system and installing contract practices recast conceptions of dependency, obligation, and labor compulsion. Just as the ideal of free labor was transported south, so its coercive aspects—articulated in rules governing the freed people—were carried back north" (1992, 1288). This process, with its clear antebellum roots, had implications for emerging national understandings of class, dependency, and a racial order of labor across the globe that helped stitch together the ideological justifications of American empire in the century to come (Jacobson 2000; Renda 2001; Bender 2009). At home, it fed an increasingly ideological antipathy among bourgeois Americans toward collective efforts by workers to improve their circumstances—justified by specious appeals to individual freedom, independence, and rights—that persists to this day. This is continuity indeed.

That Fuzzy "Middle Class"

Individualism, independence, rights: those "middle-class" values allegedly defined the age, and so once again raise the problem of the "middle class." At every turn—celebration, cynicism, transition, or continuity—this specter haunts the history of labor and class in the GAPE. What is this category, and whom does it actually comprise?

Proliferating urban professionals in the East? No doubt, but small entrepreneurs in the West—certainly members of a putative "middle class"—viewed such office men (not always unreasonably) as ciphers for the great monopolies. Undoubtedly the small landowning farmers resisting the railroads must count. But what of their sometime nemeses, the small-town store owners who supplied them with seed and equipment on credit, and bilked them after harvest? Surely this latter group, struggling to survive in their own right as independent "middling folk," cannot be considered proper capitalists in the era of Rockefeller, Harriman, and Carnegie? And the complications do not end there: for landowners, no matter how small, often scraped their margins off the labor of sharecroppers. Does simultaneously occupying a position of capital *and* labor, debtor and creditor in a local economy make someone "middle class," or does it mean that they occupy an awkward juncture in the gears of a fundamentally dialectical political economy?

What of those supposedly pervasive "middle-class" values: self-improvement and the urge toward moral, educational, and economic reform? Who are the most prominent exemplars? To be sure, the black bourgeoisie of the GAPE personified and advocated such values in transactions with black workers. But do the brutal white supremacist politics of reunion and Jim Crow leave room to describe its members as "middle class" with any interpretive clarity? What does the analysis of labor and class gain by doing so? What would it sacrifice by abandoning the label, replacing it with less categorical descriptors such as "aspirational" or "professional," or more historically specific references to philosophies of "respectable" race progress advocated by figures such as Booker T. Washington or organizations such as the NAACP?

No one exemplified the "middle-class" values more iconically than the rising generation of Progressive women activists, from Josephine Shaw Lowell to Florence Kelley, and Jane Addams to Lillian Wald. Yet all these women could lay claim to solidly bourgeois roots: Lowell, the daughter and widow of Boston Brahmin families; Kelley, the daughter of a Congressman with substantial West Philadelphia real estate holdings; Addams, daughter of an Illinois bank president and industrialist; Wald, the daughter of a successful optician and niece of textile factory owners in Rochester (Daniels 1989; Waugh 1997; Sklar 1995; Knight 2005). Combing the lists of donors and allies to these women's Progressive, "middle-class" value-driven enterprises yields primarily the names of bankers, industrialists, and prominent politicians, with a "Mrs." often preceding them. Does it make sense to describe such enterprises or their creators as "middle-class" if they depended much more centrally for their existence and operations on the charitable indulgence of the wealthy and a healthy dose of gendered solidarity?

The existence of an historical entity that serves such chameleonic purposes depending on the methodological or analytical inclinations of its interpreter deserves serious questioning. The truth is, no one can really define the "middle class" in the GAPE, or describe who was in it, without confronting imminent contradiction, yet everyone is intent on asserting what it represents, what it did, or that its material and ideological consolidation was a signal consequence of the era. Not only its existence, but its ubiquity has long been accepted: at one point or another it has occupied every corner of the thematic framework delimiting the scholarship on labor and class in the GAPE. Louis Hartz cynically mocked its self-conception as radical, asserting its ideological continuity within a much longer liberal tradition of "Americanism" (1955, 228–255). Wiebe celebrated its ambitions as new, and strove to demonstrate the fundamental transitions those ambitions wrought (1967). Boyer and Linda Gordon agreed that its ambitions were new, but viewed them cynically as efforts not to transform and unite, but to control and repress (Boyer 1978; Gordon 1988). Robert Johnston's more recent bid to rehabilitate the GAPE's "middle class" by rescuing its members from such derision and slander continues to struggle with the more pressing problem: to make the "middle class" coherent as a political-economic position that, while capacious, remains recognizably discrete from that of either workers or the bourgeoisie.

Examining Johnston a bit more closely here is instructive, for he, more than any historian of the GAPE before him, courageously attempts to grapple with the use of the term rather than simply using it. After opening his *Radical Middle Class* with an impressively thorough review of the sociological and historical literature on the "middle class," he sensibly points out that it is impossible to "formulate a satisfactory a priori theoretical definition that a scholar can use to examine the middle class with any chronological depth—if at all" (2003, 12). By acknowledging that "class" is a moving target, he clears away the ahistorical, social scientific cobwebs that impede much scholarly thinking about that category.

This wouldn't necessarily preclude his identifying the historically specific "middle class" whose radicalism he means to celebrate; indeed, the singular form of "Middle Class" in his book's title suggests that he will. Instead, he opts for an "antidefinition" that recognizes the existence of multiple, overlapping, and sometimes contradictory "middle classes." This allows him to continue using the term without, strictly speaking, defining it. He defends this definitional evasion by claiming E.P. Thompson as his theoretical lodestar, citing Thompson's famous dictum, "Class is defined by men as they live their own history, and, in the end this is its only definition." This, to Johnston, means that "class," in some final sense, exists only in the minds and experiences of each individual as a creation of his or her own "agency." Urging that scholars "take Thompson to his logical conclusion," Johnston declares, "We need to see that if people are genuinely making their own history, they are making *their own classes* as well" (13). In light of this interpretation, it is enough that the "middle class" calls itself "middle-class" to justify the category's existence.

But Johnston's admirable democratic optimism has colored his reading of Thompson. The latter's phrase, "Class is defined by men as they live their own history," has far less affinity with Johnston's, "classes have the agency to actually make themselves," than it does with Marx's, "men make their own history, but they do not make it just as they please" (Johnston 2013, 13; Marx 1963, 15). Living history transitively, as Thompson understood, is not reducible to "agency," and nor is the process by which people "make" their class. Both are dialectical processes in which choices and self-imaginings face the stubborn, often insurmountable obstacles of historically specific conditions, which include material structures of political economy and—within those structures—people who have a say in how the lives and classes of others are lived and created.

In fairness, Johnston would seem to acknowledge this by subsequently pointing out, "*politics*... is central to the way people in any society construct their classes," but in this instance he seems not to trace *his* argument to its logical conclusion (14). As Jeffrey Sklansky points out in *Reviews in American History* (2004), "Johnston follows the sociologist Richard F. Hamilton and others in drawing the great divide in modern America down the middle of the middle class itself, finding radical potential not in the upper echelon of management and the professions, but in the lower middle class of 'small-scale merchants and manufacturers, clerical workers, and lower-level professionals'" (60). In other words, when faced with the necessity of mapping those politics so central to the construction of class, Johnston finds a single rough division: the "lower middle class" allies itself with the interests of workers; the "upper echelon of management and the professions" with the bourgeoisie. Yet both cohorts claim membership in the American "middle class." When Johnston proclaims, "[B]y calling my subjects middle class... I validate their political and cultural claims to being not just part of the middle class, but 'the middle class' itself," can he really be providing a tent large enough to accommodate people on both sides of his dividing line? How could he, and still be imputing analytical coherence to the term?

Lewis Corey (whom Johnston spurns as a supercilious Marxist) long ago recognized similar attributes of the "middle class" in the *ancien régime*, noting,

> The middle class ideal was one of independent property, assuring independent means of earning one's livelihood, and this ideal was threatened by political privileges and monopoly. Where the big bourgeoisie urged the rights of property in general, the middle class emphasized small property and direct ownership, one's own independent enterprise, initiative, thrift and simplicity (1992 c.1935, 46).

Likewise, Corey recognized the impetus to radical, anti-bourgeois politics that such an ideal could create: "While the petty-bourgeois ideals and struggle created and invigorated many elements of the capitalist spirit, they were directed as much against the big bourgeoisie as against the aristocracy" (46–47). Johnston agrees, and wishes to locate democratic potential in such opposition of a petty bourgeoisie to its bigger brethren in a later historical moment. Again, he is in harmony with Corey, who writes of the petty bourgeoisie, "It was the struggles of the middle class, rallying the dispossessed plebian elements, which enlarged democratic rights in capitalist society" (49).

Corey, however, also observes the rub:

> There was a fatal contradiction in the [middle-class] ideal. Small property breeds big property. The rights of property include the right to amass property on a large scale. Out of the middle class itself arose enterprisers who, more aggressive or more fortunate, piled up great riches and trampled upon the small property of their former brethren (47).

It is on the rock of this paradox that Johnston's radical, democratic, "middle-class" ship runs aground. Johnston attempts to preempt such arguments by providing demographic evidence that the proportion of smallholders in the United States did not decline significantly, even into the 1950s. Setting his data against Thomas Piketty's, however, suggests that although the number of such "middle-class" actors may have remained relatively steady through mid-century, this was primarily a function of global restraints on capital (total war and its aftermath) that created historically specific space for such actors to subsist (Piketty, 2014). With those restraints now largely removed, that demographic layer is shrinking fast in most developed nations, including the United States.

In any case, Corey recognized how this contradiction played out in the GAPE beyond demography, in the ideological relationship between smallholders and labor:

> As the middle class waged its struggle against concentration and trustification, in defense of independent small enterprise, it sought the support of the wage-workers—but on a middle class program which generalized its interests as the people's interests, and always strictly within the limits of the capitalist order. That was the essential character of American populism and progressivism. The underlying tendency was to discourage and repress the independent action of labor (245).

Many millions of Americans have called, and do call themselves, "middle class," and Johnston is correct, as far as it goes, that this "represents not a contradiction, or false consciousness, but rather a genuine attempt by the mass of Americans to explain their distinctive middling social situation" (2003, 258). But explanations, no matter how genuinely attempted, sometimes fall short in empirical or persuasive terms. Whatever the particular ideological or material attributes such "middle class" Americans might claim, their historical actions at any given moment tend to align them with either the interests of capital or labor. Johnston has performed a valuable historiographical service by recognizing how often during the Progressive Era his self-described "middle-class" subjects aimed to align themselves with the interests of the working class rather than with the bourgeoisie, in Portland and beyond. There is, as he insists, democratic hope to be drawn from such alliances. But there are also cautionary lessons to be drawn about structural inequality, which Corey saw more clearly. No less laudable was Corey's recognition that those subjects, attempting in good faith to align themselves with labor, often unwittingly served the interests of capital.

The term "middle class," then, fails to provide a useful third category for understanding the long-run historical dimensions of capitalist power, either in material or political terms. Thomas Piketty's *Capital in the Twenty-First Century* (2014), in fact, suggests that parsing the "middle class" may simply obscure those dimensions. By providing a vast, multi-national body of evidence demonstrating fluctuations in income and wealth distribution over two centuries, Piketty confirms Corey's hypothesis that "small property breeds big property": that the tendency of a capitalist political economy, unchecked or exacerbated by state intervention, is to redistribute wealth to the owners of capital; and, moreover, that the historical practice of capitalists has been to repurpose any such state intervention—regardless how democratic in original conception—to the end of further capital accumulation. As Johnston so vividly demonstrates, this does not preclude the owners of capital, large or small, from choosing to act politically in the service of interests other than their own enrichment. It does, however, mean that to call such actors "middle-class" is to separate histories of individual and local choice from those of national and global political economy.

"Middle class" has long been and continues to be a term that many Americans (and others) self-apply to excuse themselves from grappling with the precise contours of their role in a capitalist political economy. This need not be a conscious evasion: there are often solid material and cultural grounds on which to demur from identifying as either "working-class" or "bourgeois." But if, as Johnston points out, "Class should help tell us, most fundamentally, how society organizes power and inequality in the economic sphere, but with spillover effects to other areas of life," then the term "middle class" does not qualify. It does not clarify, but rather muddies the lines of dialectical power and inequality within historical systems of capitalist political economy.

In the context of the GAPE, the "middle class" reformers who play such pivotal roles in extant histories of labor and class fall into two categories: aspirational workers committed to private property and the fond dream of reconciling capital and labor under a democratic flag; or, bourgeois men and women who have at least partially recognized and wish to reduce the exploitative quality of capitalist growth's relationship to labor, and their class's—or their own, individual—complicity in it. The history of the 20th century to the present day describes the tragic failure of both dreams, no less than their continuing appeal.

References

Alexander, Michelle. 2010. *The New Jim Crow: Mass Incarceration in the Age of Colorblindness.* New York: The New Press.

Andrews, Thomas G. 2008. *Killing for Coal: America's Deadliest Labor War.* Cambridge, MA: Harvard University Press.

Arnold, Andrew B. 2014. *Fueling the Gilded Age: Railroads, Miners, and Disorder in Pennsylvania Coal Country.* New York: New York University Press.

Beckert, Sven. 2001. *The Monied Metropolis: New York City and the Consolidation of the American Bourgeoisie, 1850–1896.* Cambridge: Cambridge University Press.

Bederman, Gail. 1995. *Manliness & Civilization: A Cultural History of Gender and Race in the United States, 1880–1917.* Chicago: University of Chicago Press.

Bellamy, Paul B. 1997. *A History of Workmen's Compensation, 1898–1915: From Courtroom to Boardroom.* New York: Garland Publishing.

Bender, Daniel E. 2009. *American Abyss: Savagery and Civilization in the Age of Industry.* Ithaca: Cornell University Press.

Berman, Ari. 2015. "Alabama, Birthplace of the Voting Rights Act, Is Once Again Gutting Voting Rights." *The Nation*, October 1. http://www.thenation.com/article/alabama-birthplace-of-voting-rights-act-once-again-gutting-voting-rights/Accessed July 21, 2016.

Blackmon, Douglas A. 2008. *Slavery by Another Name: The Re-Enslavement of Black Americans from the Civil War to World War II.* New York: Doubleday.

Bourdieu, Pierre. 1979. *La distinction: critique sociale du jugement.* Paris: Éditions de Minuit.

Boyer, Paul. 1978. *Urban Masses and Moral Order in America, 1820–1920.* Cambridge, MA: Harvard University Press.

Burnstein, Daniel Eli. 2006. *Next to Godliness: Confronting Dirt and Despair in Progressive Era New York City.* Urbana: University of Illinois Press.

Chandler, Alfred D., Jr. 1977. *The Visible Hand: The Managerial Revolution in American Business.* Cambridge: Belknap Press/Harvard University Press.

Commons, John R., ed. 1905. *Trade Unionism and Labor Problems.* Boston: Ginn.

—. 1918. *History of Labour in the United States, Vol. I & II.* New York: Macmillan Company.

Connolly, James J. 2005. "The Public Good and the Problem of Pluralism in Lincoln Steffens's Civic Imagination." *The Journal of the Gilded Age and Progressive Era* 4, 2: 125–147.

Corey, Lewis. 1992 c.1935. *The Crisis of the Middle Class.* New York: Columbia University Press.

Daniels, Doris Groshen. 1989. *Always a Sister: The Feminism of Lillian D. Wald.* New York: Feminist Press at the City University of New York.

Davis, Allen F. 1967. *Spearheads for Reform: The Social Settlements and the Progressive Movement, 1890–1914.* New York: Oxford University Press.

Dawley, Alan. 1991. *Struggles for Justice: Social Responsibility and the Liberal State.* Cambridge: Belknap Press/Harvard University Press.

Diner, Steven J. 1998. *A Very Different Age: Americans of the Progressive Era.* New York: Hill & Wang.

Dru Stanley, Amy. 1992. "Beggars Can't Be Choosers: Compulsion and Contract in Postbellum America." *Journal of American History* 78, 4.

Du Bois, W.E.B. (1903) 1990. *The Souls of Black Folk.* New York: Vintage. Reprint, Des Moines: The Library of America. Citations refer to the Library edition.

—. (1935) 1998. *Black Reconstruction in America, 1860–1880.* New York: Free Press. Reprint, New York: Free Press. Citations refer to the 1998 edition.

Edwards, Rebecca. 2006. *New Spirits: Americans in the Gilded Age, 1865–1905.* New York: Oxford University Press.

Enstad, Nan. 1999. *Ladies of Labor, Girls of Adventure: Working Women, Popular Culture, and Labor Politics at the Turn of the Twentieth Century.* New York: Columbia University Press.

Fink, Leon. 1991. "'Intellectuals' versus 'Workers': Academic Requirements and the Creation of Labor History." *American Historical Review* 96, 2: 395–421.

—. 2011. *Sweatshops at Sea: Merchant Seamen in the World's First Globalized Industry, from 1812 to the Present.* Chapel Hill: University of North Carolina Press.

Fraser, Steve. 2015. *Age of Acquiescence: The Life and Death of American Resistance to Organized Wealth and Power.* New York: Little, Brown and Company.

Fronc, Jennifer. 2009. *New York Undercover: Private Surveillance in the Progressive Era.* Chicago: University of Chicago Press.

Gage, Beverly. 2009. *The Day Wall Street Exploded.* New York: Oxford University Press.

Gilmore, Glenda Elizabeth, ed. 2002. *Who Were the Progressives?* Boston: Bedford, St. Martin's.

Glotzer, Paige. 2015. "Exclusion in Arcadia: How Suburban Developers Circulated Ideas about Discrimination, 1890–1950." *Journal of Urban History* 41, 3: 479–494.

Goodwyn, Lawrence. 1978. *The Populist Moment: A Short History of the Agrarian Revolt in America.* New York: Oxford University Press.

Gordon, Linda. 1986. "Family Violence, Feminism, and Social Control." *Feminist Studies* 12, 3: 452–478.

—. 1988. *Heroes of Their Own Lives: The Politics and History of Family Violence.* New York: Viking.

Greene, Julie. 2006. *Pure and Simple Politics: The American Federation of Labor and Political Activism, 1885–1917.* Cambridge: Cambridge University Press.

—. 2009. *The Canal Builders: Making America's Empire at the Panama Canal.* New York: Penguin.

Haley, Sarah. 2016. *No Mercy Here: Gender, Punishment, and the Making of Jim Crow Modernity.* Chapel Hill: University of North Carolina Press.

Hartz, Louis. 1955. *The Liberal Tradition in America: An Interpretation of American Political Thought since the Revolution.* New YorkHarcourt, Brace, and Company.

Harvey, David. 2005. *A Brief History of Neoliberalism.* Oxford: Oxford University Press.

Hays, Samuel P. 1957. *Response to Industrialism, 1885–1914.* Chicago: University of Chicago Press.

Henderson, George L. 1999. *California and the Fictions of Capital.* New York: Oxford University Press.

Hofstadter, Richard. 1948. *American Political Tradition and the Men Who Made It.* New York: Alfred A. Knopf.

—. 1955. *Age of Reform: From Bryan to F.D.R.* New York: Vintage.

Hunter, Tera W. 1997. *To 'Joy My Freedom: Southern Black Women's Lives and Labors After the Civil War.* Cambridge, MA: Harvard University Press.

Huyssen, David. 2014. *Progressive Inequality: Rich and Poor in New York, 1890–1920.* Cambridge, MA: Harvard University Press.

Jacobson, Matthew Frye. 2000. *Barbarian Virtues: The United States Encounters Foreign Peoples At Home and Abroad, 1876–1917.* New York: Hill & Wang.

Johnson, Val. 2006. "'The Moral Aspects of Complex Problems': New York City Electoral Campaigns against Vice and the Incorporation of Immigrants, 1890–1901." *Journal of American Ethnic History* 25, 2/3: 74–106.

Johnston, Robert. 2002. "Re-Democratizing the Progressive Era: The Politics of Progressive Era Political Historiography." *Journal of the Gilded Age and Progressive Era* 1, 1: 68–92.

—. 2003. *The Radical Middle Class: Populist Democracy and the Question of Capitalism in Progressive Era Portland, Oregon.* Princeton, NJ: Princeton University Press.

Jones, Jacqueline. 1985. *Labor of Love, Labor of Sorrow: Black Women, Work and the Family, From Slavery to the Present.* New York: Vintage.

Katz, Michael B. 1996. *In The Shadow of the Poorhouse: A Social History of Welfare in America.* New York: Basic Books.

Kessler-Harris, Alice. 1982. *Out to Work: A History of Wage-Earning Women in the United States.* New York: Oxford University Press.

Klein, Maury. 2007. *The Genesis of Industrial America, 1870–1920.* Cambridge: Cambridge University Press.

Knight, Louise W. 2005. *Citizen: Jane Addams and the Struggle for Democracy.* Chicago: University of Chicago Press.

Kolko, Gabriel. 1963. *The Triumph of Conservatism: A Reinterpretation of American History, 1900–1916.* New York: The Free Press.

Lamphere, Louise. 1987. *From Working Daughters to Working Mothers: Immigrant Women in a New England Industrial Community.* Ithaca, NY: Cornell University Press.

Laurie, Bruce. 1989. *Artisans into Workers: Labor in Nineteenth-Century America.* New York: Hill and Wang.

Lears, T.J. Jackson. 1981. *No Place of Grace: Antimodernism and the Transformation of American Culture, 1880–1920.* New York: Pantheon Books.

Lee, Erika. 2003. *At America's Gates: The Exclusion Era, 1882–1943.* Chapel Hill: University of North Carolina Press.

LeFlouria, Talitha L. 2015. *Chained in Silence: Black Women and Convict Labor in the New South.* Chapel Hill: University of North Carolina Press.

Link, Arthur and Richard L. McCormick. 1983. *Progressivism.* Arlington Heights, IL: Harlan Davidson, Inc.

Livingston, James. 1986. *Origins of the Federal Reserve System: Money, Class, and Corporate Capitalism, 1890–1913.* Ithaca, NY: Cornell University Press.

Marable, Manning. 1983. *How Capitalism Underdeveloped Black America: Problems in Race, Political Economy, and Society*. Cambridge, MA: South End Press.

Marx, Karl. 1963. *The Eighteenth Brumaire of Louis Bonaparte*. New York: International Publishers.

McCormick, Richard L. 1989. *The Party Period and Public Policy: American Politics from the Age of Jackson to the Progressive Era*. New York: Oxford University Press.

McGerr, Michael. 2003. *A Fierce Discontent: The Rise and Fall of the Progressive Movement in America, 1870–1920*. New York: Free Press.

Montgomery, David. 1987. *The Fall of the House of Labor: the Workplace, the State, and American Labor Activism, 1865–1925*. Cambridge: Cambridge University Press.

—. 1993. *Citizen Worker: The Experience of Workers in the United States with Democracy and the Free Market During the Nineteenth Century*. Cambridge: Cambridge University Press.

Murolo, Priscilla. 1997. *Common Ground of Womanhood: Class, Gender, and Working-Girls' Clubs, 1884–1928*. Urbana: University of Illinois Press.

O'Donnell, Edward. 2015. *Henry George and the Crisis of Inequality: Progress and Poverty in the Gilded Age*. New York: Columbia University.

Ott, Julia. 2011. *When Wall Street Met Main Street: The Quest for an Investors' Democracy*. Cambridge, MA: Harvard University Press.

Painter, Nell Irvin. 1987. *Standing at Armageddon: The United States, 1877–1919*. New York: W.W. Norton & Company.

Pak, Susie J. 2013. *Gentlemen Bankers: The World of J.P. Morgan*. Cambridge, MA: Harvard University Press.

Pearson, Chad. 2015. *Reform or Repression: Organizing America's Anti-Union Movement*. Philadelphia: University of Pennsylvania Press.

Peck, Gunther. 2006. "The Nature of Labor: Fault Lines and Common Ground in Environmental and Labor History." *Environmental History* 11, 2: 212–238.

Peiss, Kathy. 1986. *Cheap Amusements: Working Women and Leisure in Turn-of-the-Century New York*. Philadelphia: Temple University Press.

Perlman, Selig. 1928. *A Theory of the Labor Movement*. New York: Macmillan.

Pernick, Martin S. 1996. *The Black Stork: Eugenics and the Death of "Defective" Babies in American Medicine and Motion Pictures Since 1915*. New York: Oxford University Press.

Piketty, Thomas. 2014. *Capital in the Twenty-First Century*. Cambridge: Belknap Press/Harvard University Press.

Plunz, Richard. 1990. *A History of Housing in New York City*. New York: Columbia University Press.

Postel, Charles. 2007. *The Populist Vision*. New York: Oxford University Press.

Renda, Mary. 2001. *Taking Haiti: Military Occupation and the Culture of U.S. Imperialism, 1915–1940*. Chapel Hill: University of North Carolina Press.

Sanders, Elizabeth. 1999. *Roots of Reform: Farmers, Workers, and the American State, 1877–1917*. Chicago: University of Chicago Press.

Scheussler, Jennifer. 2015. "In History Departments, It's Up With Capitalism." *New York Times*, April 6.

Scott, James C. 1985. *Weapons of the Weak: Everyday Forms of Peasant Resistance*. New Haven, CT: Yale University Press.

Sellers, Charles. 1991. *The Market Revolution: Jacksonian America, 1815–1846*. New York: Oxford University Press.

Shah, Nayan. 2001. *Contagious Divides: Epidemics and Race in San Francisco's Chinatown*. Berkeley: University of California Press.

Sklansky, Jeffrey. 2004. "Progress and Populism." *Reviews in American History* 32, 1.

—. 2014. "Labor, Money, and the Financial Turn in the History of Capitalism." *Labor: Studies in Working-Class Histories of the Americas* 11, 1: 23–46.

Sklar, Kathryn Kish. 1995. *Florence Kelley and the Nation's Work: The Rise of Women's Political Culture, 1830–1900*. New Haven, CT: Yale University Press.

Steffens, Lincoln. 1906. *Struggle for Self-Government: Being an attempt to trace American political corruption to its sources in six states of the United States, with a dedication to the czar*. New York: McClure, Phillips & Co.

—. 1931. *Autobiography of Lincoln Steffens*. New York: Harcourt, Brace, and Company.

Trachtenberg, Alan. 1982. *The Incorporation of America: Culture and Society in the Gilded Age*. New York: Hill & Wang.

Waugh, Joan. 1997. *Unsentimental Reformer: The Life of Josephine Shaw Lowell*. Cambridge, MA: Harvard University Press.

Weinstein, James. 1968. *The Corporate Ideal in the Liberal State, 1900–1918*. Boston: Beacon Press.

White, Richard. 1995. *The Organic Machine: The Remaking of the Columbia River*. New York: Hill & Wang.

—. 2011. *Railroaded: The Transcontinentals and the Making of Modern America*. New York, W.W. Norton.

Wiebe, Robert. 1967. *The Search for Order, 1877–1920*. New York: Hill & Wang.

Woloch, Nancy. 2015. *A Class by Herself: Protective Laws for Women Workers*. Princeton, NJ: Princeton University Press.

Further Reading

Arnesen, Eric, Julie Greene and Bruce Laurie, eds. 1998. *Labor Histories: Class, Politics, and the Working-Class Experience*. Urbana: University of Illinois Press.

Bender, Daniel E. and Richard A. Greenwald, eds. 2003. *Sweatshop USA: the American Sweatshop in Historical and Global Perspective*. New York: Routledge.

Currarino, Roseanne. 2011. *The Labor Question in America: Economic Democracy in the Gilded Age*. Urbana : University of Illinois Press.

Dru Stanley, Amy. 1998. *From Bondage to Contract: Wage Labor, Marriage, and the Market in the Age of Slave Emancipation*. Cambridge: Cambridge University Press.

Frankel, Noralee and Nancy S. Dye, eds. 1991. *Gender, Class, Race, and Reform in the Progressive Era*. Lexington: University Press of Kentucky.

Gilmore, Glenda Elizabeth and Thomas J. Sugrue. 2015. *These United States: A Nation in the Making, 1890 to the Present*. New York: W.W. Norton.

Roll, Jared. 2010. *Spirit of Rebellion: Labor and Religion in the New Cotton South*. Urbana: University of Illinois Press.

Rosenow, Michael K. 2015. *Death and Dying in the Working Class, 1865–1920*. Urbana: University of Illinois Press.

Sklar, Martin. 1988. *The Corporate Reconstruction of American Capitalism, 1890–1916: The Market, the Law, and Politics*. Cambridge: Cambridge University Press.

Zimmerman, Andrew. 2012. *Alabama in Africa: Booker T. Washington, the German Empire, and the Globalization of the New South*. Princeton, NJ: Princeton University Press.

Chapter Nineteen

Science and Technology

Alan I Marcus

American historians have long acknowledged aspects of technology and science when writing about the Gilded Age and Progressive Era (GAPE). Railroads, electric traction, and automobiles transported people at speeds and to places never before encountered. Steam and then electricity generated motive force. Electricity turned night into day, powered communication devices such as the telegraph and telephone, and factories. The late nineteenth and early twentieth centuries also witnessed the creation of new scientific/professional and other knowledge-based organizations and ushered in an unprecedented involvement of federal government in social, cultural, and economic affairs.

Older generations of American historians wielded the holy trinity of industrialization, urbanization, and immigration as cause and as explanation for those events. They saw the application of science and technology in terms of creating order from what had become an increasingly chaotic situation. To these scholars, science and technology served as mechanisms to reestablish an old order or, most commonly, to form a new one. Science and technology each functioned as forces and means to rationalize the present and to establish a more certain, less wasteful future. Historical debates, such as they were, primarily revolved around the success of specific sciences and technologies in achieving those ends.

Historians of science and technology have never bought into that framework. They have chafed at the idea of attempting to analyze what went on during GAPE; they find what has been in essence a political and economic history designation antithetical to their notions of how science and technology happened and happen. To these men and women, science and technology cannot be shoehorned into discrete political eras but rather have their own timetables, their own rhymes and reasons. These scholars reject outright attempts to localize or nationalize science and, to a lesser extent, technology. Their mantra has been that science has no bounds. It is and has always been an international enterprise, not the province of any geopolitical unit. Their focus has long been upon the developmental process. Historians of technology have traced things from preindustrial to industrial to postindustrial. Historians of science have identified communities of persons engaged in the same intellectual inquiry. They observed these practitioners adopt successive paradigms and move from preprofessional to professional. Finally, they see professions descend into specialization. The approach of historians of technology and of science has been ruthlessly scientific. Both sets of scholars have passionately endeavored to create patterns—rules and laws—with which to categorize things not known previously without respect to place or time. In this enterprise, context plays an exclusively negative role. Its sole purpose is as a corrective to justify why the universal pattern constructed by historians of science and technology fails to accommodate snugly every historical fact. It is nothing more than what used to be called a fudge factor.

To be sure, a certain hagiography persists among historians of science and technology. Billington and Billington (2006) honor their heroes collectively, sanctify them with the glorious appellation "engineers" and maintain that were responsible for the making of the twentieth century. While an earlier generation and the Billingtons reasoned that without heroes and their seminal moments there would not be laws and no material accomplishments, more modern scholars use the hero in a different way. For better and for worse, it resolves for them the existential dilemma. Celebrating the heroes of science and technology serves as a reminder that an individual, even among communities and within disciplines reasoned to be communitarian, can make a difference. More recent historians of American science and technology have carried it to yet another level. They find

A Companion to the Gilded Age and Progressive Era, First Edition. Edited by Christopher McKnight Nichols and Nancy C. Unger.
© 2017 John Wiley & Sons, Inc. Published 2017 by John Wiley & Sons, Inc.

that major figures may be as likely to be villains as heroes and perhaps both at the same time.

Three technologies of the Gilded Age and Progressive Era—electricity, railroads, and automobiles—dominate this new heroic historiography just as they had the earlier incarnations. Edison remains the preeminent symbol of the electric revolution. He is acknowledged for his inspiration and perspicacity—one author argues that his efforts led to the creation of the modern metropolis (Wasik 2006)—but the recent literature asserts his desire for profits exceeded his commitment to the public weal. Edison's vocal and unrelenting support of alternating current for electric chair use was, according to Essig (2003), to convince the public of the danger of that variety of electricity and to prop up his inferior direct current generating system.

In the case of railroads, the long debate persists over whether to declare magnates robber barons or captains of industry—heroes or villains. White (2011) has added much-needed nuance. He claims that an ex post facto rendition of the virtues of the railroads to modernity is beside the point. Railroads and their architect/financiers, including Charles Francis Adams and James J. Hill, must be evaluated within their time. There he finds their acts deeply flawed. They overbuilt, underperformed, delivered commodities no one needed, and went bankrupt at an appalling rate. While they enabled farmers to get goods to market and manufacturers to get their wares to consumers, they also absorbed and destroyed massive quantities of capital at a time of great capital expansion.

Automotive heroes are a bit more problematic. To be sure, Henry Ford remains the heroic focus of an impressive number of studies as scholars seek to determine whether he was a visionary, a racist, a conservative, or an innovator. His early career as a racer and marine engine repairman—two activities often used to suggest rugged individualism or a Horatio Alger story fit for late nineteenth-century America—have given way to considerations of his sociological department, labor-busting activities, and assembly line machinations (Casey 2008; Loizides 2015). Other GAPE-era automobilers are rarely explored in such depth but are not forgotten. Theirs are the names of the major product lines of contemporary automotive manufactures. Chevrolet, Chrysler, Dodge, Pontiac, Buick and others reflect back to what seemed a more transparent time (Hyde 2005; Gustin 2008).

The changing perspective of the heroes of science and technology results not from new information about the heroes themselves but from those who study and analyze them. As Carl Becker noted over 80 years ago, each generation must write its own history (Becker, 1932). Each generation asks the questions of the past that it wants answered. In that sense, the past becomes what the present brings to it. It has no fruitful or usable integrity of its own.

For probably the past 40 years, historians have brought this usable understanding to their labors, often en passant. It has been much more obvious among historians of America than their history of science and technology counterparts. Indeed, the goals of the two groups have often been quite different. Many recent historians of the United States embed this understanding in their work, and it manifests itself most clearly in vocabulary. In this parlance, text matters little, pretext a bit more, but subtext reigns nearly supreme. Events and occurrences must be de-privileged and intellectual constellations unpacked and interrogated. Explanations require complication. Individuals heretofore ignored now demonstrate voice and maybe agency, and sometimes even emerge empowered. Projects become problematic; analyses reveal nuance, and conflicting interests undergo mediation through negotiation. Once, in a spate of mischievousness, I tried to introduce the profession to "suture," a Frankensteinian metaphor of epic proportions (Marcus 2004, 2007). It failed, at least in part, not because the word suggested unnatural imagery but because it sought to combine rather than to differentiate or make separate. My next playful attempt was to trumpet the word "cleave" (Marcus and Bix 2007, 280–291). Its deliciously contrary meanings—to separate and to adhere closely—promised just the kind of ersatz clarity I sought. It, too, failed to engage the profession.

These words—these ideas—lead to tangible products. This postmodernist understanding among American historians has made science and technology generally historically accessible. A slew of investigators who would have found a science- or technology-dependent understanding of the relationship among those two variables and society and culture an insurmountable barrier now rush pell-mell to these issues. By raising subtext above pretext or context and all far beyond text, the postmodernist ethos has opened the historical study of science and technology to many American historians by reducing the science and technology involved in most processes to virtual insignificance, a mere trifle. That profound reductionism alleviates the need to learn the intricacies of the science and technology of whatever topic is studied. In a very real sense, the text—the scientific principles and technology artifacts—has been abandoned as irrelevant as American historians look for their true underpinnings. They usually find them in race, class, or gender.

Scholars of postmodernism and deconstruction would recognize aspects of the characterization above. Few historians of science and technology examining the GAPE years would go beyond it into the ultra-postmodernist world of cute and clever. Most would even deny that anything they did had the slightest whiff of postmodernity. Despite their indignant protests and their sincere distain for many, if not most, of the elements of the postmodern project, a postmodernist paradigm has ruled the day even among historians of science and technology. This is perhaps an exaggeration but historians of science and technology have moved hard away from examining the actual sciences or technologies. Investigators stress two not dissimilar phenomena.

They accentuate who practiced science and technology and how they practiced it, and/or whom these historical creatures practiced it on or subjected to it.

An analysis of the science and technology history written about the United States during the last decade that concerned itself at least in part with GAPE shows just how deeply this postmodernist system of thought has penetrated the practice of American history and history of science and technology. Historians have devoted considerable attention to the biological explanations for differences among groups that came to the fore in the late nineteenth and early twentieth centuries. People defined as having black, red, yellow, or white skin have all been scrutinized, as have any number of what are now called ethnic or cultural groups. In some instances, the idea has been to show how the science has been misapplied. Notions of inferiority and various other bigotries are overthrown. For instance, in the case of skin color, forgotten black inventors (Fouche 2003) and black social and other scientists (Hersey 2011; Williams 2006; Brooks 2004; Farland 2006) have all been resuscitated. This retrospective remembrance undercuts stereotyping and shows how these historical figures overcame serious bias and other obstacles. Recounting the demonstration of agency by these historical figures engenders a sense of empowerment within those who read them. Historians of science and technology have also extended the analysis to groups not based on skin color, geography, or ethnicity. Categorizations that emerged and were applied ruthlessly in the late nineteenth and early twentieth centuries, such as feeble-minded, poor, and criminal—usually explained during those years as the consequence of weak or bad biology—found common expression in what has become known as the eugenics movement. These conditions are now exposed as the product of disease (Patterson 2009; Dorr 2006), unfortunate surroundings and influences (Caron 2008; Rembis 2011; Dorr 2008; Lombardo 2008), or blatant prejudice (Mezzano 2005; Carson 2007).

Historians have examined the American eugenics movement in considerable detail. They have debated the identity of its founders and what those founders and proponents hoped to achieve. For example, Rosen (2004) found "progressive" Protestant, Catholic and Jewish leaders supported eugenics, and argues that embracing that new science marked those leaders and their institutions as modern at a time when religion generally was suspect; retaining power was their subtext. Others have examined eugenics to see if it was truly a cultural movement (Coates 2006), a mass public display (Parezo and Fowler, 2007), or if it only penetrated a handful of broad, national institutions (Bender 2009; Regal 2002). In short, they wish to know if it were an elitist project with elitist goals. To that end, they also considered the consequences and attempted consequences of the policies of the American eugenicists. What laws did they cause to be effected, what policies did they introduce, and what procedures were employed to achieve eugenical ends (Largent 2008; Juzda 2009)? Emergence of new professional groups, especially those created to study differences in human biology (Spiro 2009; Baker 2010; Gilkeson 2010; Sokal 2010; Young 2009), also followed from the stark assessment of the racial basis of difference.

The biology as cause argument also extended to gender (Ha 2011; Deluzio 2007) and sometimes sexual orientation (Hathaway 2004) and class. Historians have recounted the perceived biological basis for the female gender and for homosexuality as a means to explain the creation of particular institutions during GAPE as well as the absence of some other ones. They have noted that GAPE reformers recognized that differential biology resulted in different abilities, which manifested itself in different occupational statuses (Levin 2005). Bound by their racial heritage, the analysis went, immigrant women, especially from Italy and Russia, were suited only for menial activities, such as scullery maid. But even among these defectives, GAPE scientists and technologists labored to maximize their innate abilities, no matter how limited. Many historians have focused on the role of women in the home and attempts to enhance their performance. In that sphere, women applied the rules derived by their academic compatriots to have the head guide the hands. Women's inherent biology also relegated them to the less taxing natural sciences where women—as in home economics—devoted themselves to gathering and ordering rather than the increasingly mathematically dependent physical and laboratory sciences. As men in science shrilly demanded federal and corporate support for investigation of nature's laws, women concentrated on the applications of their domestic and natural science. Not only did the science (the rules) of home economics save labor and money for families but the application of that science in the home also kept females mentally acute and engaged, an important factor in maintaining the family (Biltekoff 2013).

Women had a stranglehold on home economics but their centrality to museum science and nature study work proved nearly as pronounced. To be sure, museum science and nature study were soft sciences; they were about ordering and describing, not calculating. But there was more. Organizing nature so as to teach the public, especially those long divorced from nature, of the inalterable pattern of the natural world held critical cultural applications. Museum work targeted everyone (Madsen-Brooks 2009, 2013; Kohlstedt 2013), but nature study took children as its object (Kohlstedt 2005; 2010). Children were the future, the ultimate subject of the eugenic crusade. This crusade was an attempt to maximize whatever potential—no matter how limited the racial biology—these progenitors held. Living an urban existence was mitigated by application of both endeavors (Schuster 2011; Hickman 2004).

Scientists, especially women scientists, frequently took children as their mission. Conservation of that potential became the inspiration for and goal of various child development and social science programs (Smuts 2006; Apple

2006; Kohlstedt 2008; Paris 2008) as well as various educational reforms (Gelber 2011; Turner 2011, Kremer 2011). Conservation was not limited to children. During the past two decades, historians, especially those who have insisted that the environment—or at least nature—become a full-fledged actor in every historical drama, have increasingly written about conservation in nature in a multitude of ways. Here women of the Gilded Age and Progressive Era figure much less prominently. Scholars have portrayed the conservation science ethos as a response to modernity (Kohler 2006; Grusin 2004; Bankoff 2009), a practical means to ensure future business success—a latter day gospel of efficiency especially in the agricultural and forestry sectors (Hersey 2006, 2011; Mickulas, 2007; Armitage 2009; Giesen 2011; Spear 2005; Keiner 2009; Lockwood 2004)—and as a nostalgic remnant of times long past (Punke 2007; Alter 2005; Mitman 2003; Andrei 2005, Worster 2008; Berger 2011; Pauly, 2008; Fiege 2012).

Just as recent historians labor to complicate the past by adding nature and a much greater number of sub-populations than their predecessors, they also seek to expand the sensory and emotional horizons of scholarship (Van Campen 2008). Smells, tastes, sentimentalities, sounds and the like (Brown 2005; Kemp 2007; Oliver 2007; Rose 2012) have joined rationality and the written and spoken word as part of the historical panoply. Noxious effluvia, smoke, bird cries, and a passion for the natural now account for historical action as investigators delve into areas previously unexplored—and unrecognized.

Setting up the past in this way begs for examinations of how various entities got themselves entrenched. Nowhere has the explanation been more intense than among the learned professions. Scholars steeped in the sociology of science and elsewhere have erected and applied various theories of boundaries and margins and what those rhetorical creations have meant to the emergence of new professional groups. Simply put, they find outgroups, especially GAPE women (Ristaino 2008; Bittel 2005; Tracy 2005; Kohlstedt 2011; Benjamin and Baker 2003) and persons lacking the newly recognized and mandated credentials, carving out their own social space from space otherwise unoccupied—itself a sensory designation—and operating rigidly within it (Vetter 2008, 2012; Rafferty 2003; Kohler 2008). A desire to create indigenously American professions often accompanied the pursuit. Mickulas (2007) recounts the attempts of Nathaniel Britton to create a scientific and American taxonomical botany. Britton rejected the work of Europeans, attempted to fashion an American nomenclature, and declared a 'botanical Monroe Doctrine' to raise the profession in the Western Hemisphere. Others point to new social problems as the progenitor of new professional groups. The scenario goes this way: The new realities of the late nineteenth and early twentieth century created new social needs; unappreciated groups rose up to seize those heretofore unanticipated chores (Williams 2006; Morin 2011; Ziegler 2012; Noll 2011; Strom 2009; Goldstein 2008). Their clarion call to service, their identification with that particular task, enabled these "new professions" to achieve a designated and permanent position within American society. The new social circumstance enabled them to achieve cultural authority, even hegemony in a discrete arena (Recchiuti 2007; Jewett 2012; Herron 2010; Kimmelman 2006; Cassedy 2009; Kingsland, 2005; Thurtle 2007; Endersby 2013; Herzig 2006; Shulman 2003).

At the center of these frameworks lies a series of critical questions. Each focuses on professionalism and professionalization. How do professions arise and when do they do so? Are there things in common, or does the term "professionalism" simply disguise the various facets of any cohort by incorporating multiple phenomena under a single banner? Is the emphasis on objectification as opposed to subjectification in the professions a characteristic of professionalism or of the later nineteenth century generally?

These are all approaches and questions generated by the conclusions of historians interested in the sciences. Historians who write about technology may also celebrate heroes (Middleton and Middleton 2009; Smil 2005; LeCain 2009; Gertner 2012; Harwood and Fogel 2012; Wasik 2006; Billington and Billington 2006) or the environment (Arnold 2014; Peterson 2003; Simon 2004; Black 2006; Fenske 2008); they may ask some similar questions about agency (Kline 2003; Solnit 2003) and about persons of color and of difference (Bix 2014; Fouche 2006). But a far greater number attack the history of technology question from far different premises. Their studies are more frequently intertwined with economics. Structures—bridges, buildings and roads (Haw 2005; Zink 2011; Holley 2008); modes of transportation—automobiles, trains and street cars (Orsi 2005; Casey 2008; Rees, 2013; Greene 2009; Missal 2008; Churella 2012); modes of communication—telegraph, telephone and motion pictures (John 2010; Hochfelder 2012; Morton 2004); and modes of power—steam, electric and gasoline (Essig 2003; Baldwin 2012; Hirt 2012)—are privileged for their economic implications. That factor grounds histories of technology, providing them with a dimension that most histories of science lack; however, there are a few history of science exceptions (Olmstead and Rhode 2008; Pettit 2013). But economic privileging also circumscribes the analysis in a rather superficial way. Many histories of technology devolve into de-facto paeans to technoeconomic determinism or slightly more sophisticated economic histories (O'Neill 2006; Thiesen 2006).

These two economic-centric analyses have profound consequence. They often treat technology as a distinct phenomenon, as a neatly drawn entity with a clearly defined and universally agreed upon government—rules, boundaries, requirements and more (Adas 2006). Indeed, historians of technology devote an amazing amount of time and energy attempting to fashion a failsafe definition of technology so as to make it universal, an effort that eschews any serious attempt to employ culture as a discriminant. Historians often push their technology as concrete category further, sometimes even anthropomorphizing technology. They treat it as if a willful human (or superhuman) force that intervenes in all varieties of human affairs. Equally significantly, the economic lens of historians tends to identify commodities or things that can be commoditized as technologies and the results of technologies; the staunch economic focus privileges commodities over other possible forms of technology (Plotnick 2012; Corn 2011; Hahn 2011; Kevles 2007; Wilder 2010). Fenske (2008), for instance, reduces skyscrapers to little more than "cathedrals of commerce," extant simply to serve the ambitions of capitalist masters. Even more to the point, technologies themselves are reduced to commodities. Technologies become things to be bought and sold for opportunity of profit, really little more. In this characterization, a technology is a raw material, whether material or not—a technique, a device, a quantity, or an idea. Technologies that could be explained or considered in any number of ways become primarily—almost exclusively—considered within the realm of economics. Relations to culture are derivative at best—usually of economic considerations—more often downplayed or even ignored (Bennett and Abbott, 2014).

Mechanical refrigeration, for example, made cold a truly marketable commodity, salable for huge profits. It enabled industries to rise far from population centers as refrigerator cars carried perishable goods to quite distant markets. A dependable source of cold in individual residences required a power source to manufacture cold and a device that contains/constrains the cold. Large enterprises arose to stock cold products to provide supplies for individual use. Rees calls this the "cold chain" and maintains that it incorporates "creating the cold," "managing the cold," "controlling temperature with precision," and "the expansion and extension of volume and reach" (Rees 2013, 5, 6).

Electricity is treated quite similarly. Purchasing electricity and all the accoutrements that went with it allowed night to become day. Electricity in its permutations permitted expansion of working hours for some and leisure hours for many, and spawned industries and opportunities for both (Baldwin 2012). It also became a means of motive power, mobile enough to be employed virtually anywhere. It could and did power street cars, individual motors, arc lights, and the electric chair, and proved the basis for a new industry in each case. Electricity in the guise of the telegraph was commodified in the later nineteenth century into the "printing telegraph" (stock ticker), "speaking telegraph" (telephone), and "talking telegraph recorder" (phonograph). Each developed into an important money-making sector. Hochfelder's (2012) assessment is more profound. The telegraph's power to disseminate information almost instantaneously makes it the engine of modern capitalism.

Photography—motion pictures—was commodified from its inception and not just because Edison and others developed the kinescope to tap an amazed public. As Brown (2005) notes, corporations immediately recognized photography's possibilities to reinvent labor and to make industry an efficient, rational enterprise. Interviews were filmed to detect undesirables, identified as those with certain habits or skin tones. Photography entered factories where the actions and movements of each worker were recorded. Viewing these movies enabled experts to determine what were each laborer's essential working strokes. This compendium of indispensable movements was codified as the laws of industrial efficiency. The rest was dismissed as waste. The task-by-task determinations became the basis for speed of assembly lines, rates paid for piecework and times permitted for breaks.

Manufacturers used photography in yet other ways. They recorded employees collectively, especially during their break periods. Those motion pictures enabled industrial experts to "understand" the psyche of industrial workers and through personnel departments to manipulate them in a way more favorable to the corporate agency. In addition to enabling persons to devise mechanisms to rationalize labor and heighten productivity, photography also targeted consumers. Still photography became corporate illustration and galvanized the modern advertising industry.

Technologies far less glamorous than photography were transformed into commodities. Purveyors of barbed wire created poems, posters, trade cards, broadsides, and almanacs to push their product. There they argued that barbed wire protected its users from bands of marauders, hostile Indians, and emancipated slaves. In short, these barbed wire capitalists sold terror. Advertisers maintained that barbed wire was an essential commodity in sparsely populated places. It domesticated landscapes, ordered and controlled livestock, and enabled users to protect and rationalize their lives (Bennett and Scott, 2014).

This tight connection of technology and economics, especially during GAPE, serves historians in the same way that postmodern assessment does science histories. It opens the subject to numerous persons not savvy about the parameters and dynamics of the actual technology by essentially eliminating these aspects as a relevant or significant analytical event. This, of course, is ironic. Historians ignore the physical or manifestation of physicality in the history of technology—something relentlessly physical—opting instead for the centrality of commodification in the creation or application of the technology. The metaphysics of invention and discovery have almost disappeared from the history of technology. Even more to the point, economic determinist-like analyses conflate functionalist sociology with culture. Emergent economies and critical sectors are pinpointed as this version of modernization theory moves from agrarian society through market revolution to industrial economy and finally relatively sophisticated modernist capitalist state. Walt Rostow could not have said it better (Rostow 1960).

This is the skeletal system of contemporary work in history of technology. Studies undertaken serve as little more than flesh. To be sure, sometimes practitioners differ over the position of a vertebra but the essential framework remains tall. Cultural context often receives a perfunctory nod as rational choice, social class and other economic-dependent variables masquerade as cultural context but are derivative of some such overarching economic model—mercantilism, domestic production, market revolution, or capitalism—and applied as causation. Each stands as a kind of postmodern subtext (Ellenberg 2007; Heinrich and Batchelor 2004; Lucier 2012).

Here historians of technology join American historians studying the same period. Both remain irredeemably economic reductionist in explication. This clever, simple model amuses but does not satisfy. Put baldly, the past is never simple. It is people making judgments, seeking solace and opportunity wherever those two objectives can be found and whenever people deem it essential to find them. Humans are not a mass of amoebae predictably behaving according to a stimulus–response model that extends only so far as their means of production. The past is the result of millions and millions of individual decisions, desires, wants. In late nineteenth-century America, it is about a sense of the past, a sense of the present, a sense of the future and the relationships among them. It is about the aftermath of a calamitous war and the scars that never heal. These things and many, many more are not necessarily exclusively rooted in economics.

Equally significantly, these economically exclusive American historians of the late nineteenth and early twentieth centuries solemnly apply terms that are much less circumscribed or precise than their models and analyses demand they should be. "Rise to dominance of capitalism" (Schneirov 2006, 203) means exactly what? What constitutes dominance? "Great aggregations of wealth" mark the Gilded Age. But just how is that differentiated from "moderate aggregations of wealth?" Is there a trigger, a tipping point? Can it be quantified? Were there greater accumulations of wealth in the 1890s than there had been in the early 1870s? Sure. But that does not mean it was significant or that it provided some sort of driving force. As used by historians, great accumulations of wealth were the means, the engine of the transformation, not its ends. What has happened, in effect, is that an ersatz economic rationality, complete with the "winners"— accumulators of great wealth who serve in this model as anthropomorphized force—highlighted as causative agents and directors of the process, has been erected as a central means to understand the late nineteenth and early twentieth century (Schneirov 2006). In terms of historians of technology, great inventions—the electric light, telephone, railroads—and great captains of industry/robber barons/moguls—Carnegie, Rockefeller, Vanderbilt—reign supreme and confirm the wisdom of the historians' *a priori* assumption. Lucier (2012, 527) put it more generally: the virtually limitless possibilities for commercializing and commodifying scientific knowledge "bespoke the inseparable relations of science and capitalism in the Gilded Age."

The objections to this approach within the literature are not what they should be. Few, if any, dispute the fundamental assumptions of economic essentiality but rather what the essential economics were. Is there a national economy, regional economies, a dominant Boston–New York economy that drives everything else (Edwards 2006; Klein 2007; Delfino and Gillespie 2008)? As America marches relentlessly to a capitalist economy, is the offshoot a new notion of freedom, a new relationship to humanity and the economic order? Can that be reduced to Americans trading classical notions of freedom for self-expression, or is that sentiment merely applying the troubles of the present to a different past (Sklansky 2002; Levy 2012)?

Identity and self-definition remain important factors in late nineteenth- and twentieth-century American life. But the matter proves to be much broader. Categorization extended far beyond human identity. Americans of the late nineteenth and early twentieth century categorized virtually everything in their everyday lives. Creating categories, types, deciding what units are "real" and sacrosanct, and exactly what makes each grouping unique proved an American way of life. But it was the manner in which these categories were conceived that makes them unique to the period. Americans reckoned that these units were discrete, inviolable entities. Each had integrity and a reality of its own. Each was separate and separable. Each could be defined in a precise and constant way no matter what other elements were introduced. Indeed, it was no accident that words and concepts such as standardization and systematization played such a critical factor during GAPE. Both were crucial formulations. Both extended far beyond economics.

In the case of standardization, for example, Americans debated such grossly different things as how to categorize animals in zoos and the discrete units of urban space. They considered the fundamental constituents of fertilizers, of factories, and of skyscrapers. They identified the "true" parts of such diverse things as the rooms of houses, curricula for each grade of school, and what appliances should be in each indoor bathroom. The list is endless but the point is clear. Americans of the late nineteenth and early twentieth century had an almost unquenchable passion to taxonomize and categorize things. When those designations were found wanting—when some members of a group lacked the precise character that typified that group—contemporaries labored to find or devise some mechanism to overcome that deficiency.

Standardization spoke directly to the classification mania. It indicated just how important it was to make each category consistent. Imprecise or inaccurate collections rendered the groups themselves asunder. Americans created a slew of institutions and redefined others—schools, unions, professions, clubs, for instance—and adopted an equally impressive number of new techniques—manufacture of interchangeable parts, dairying, the assembly line, standard building designs, fire codes, corn-seed selection, file cabinets, codification of state laws—to establish, maintain or enforce standardization in those cases where standardization was not considered the product of biology or some such inherent property.

Systematization made standardization essential. Systematization meant "a place for everything and everything in its place." Implicit in that statement was the idea that each standardized thing differed from every other standardized thing. If these disparate categories were to be combined for some purpose, that purpose and/or the intrinsic stereotypical property or character of the entity was paramount. This essential definition pointed to the place in the system where the specific standardized unit rested. And since these standardized categories were fixed, inviolable, and fundamentally dissimilar, the positions among them within any system were necessarily unequal; systems were hierarchically based. Categories did not and could not bleed into each other. None of these units received definition from others in the system. It was the system that mattered, a system where the whole was exactly the sum of its discrete constituent parts. And it mattered where the parts were positioned. Systems worked optimally when each part achieved its appropriate place and discrete function.

Two metaphors found extensive use in the late nineteenth and early twentieth centuries. Contemporaries often likened various systems to machines. They understood that the parts of these devices were distinct—there was power generation, angular translation, power delivery, crown gearing, subordinate gearing, and more. They also recognized that each of those different, unequal categories of the machine must function in its proper role for system success. They knew, for example, that without power generation, there could be no system. But they also recognized that a system retained considerable function if a smaller gear in a subordinate position broke a tooth. Operation would be further impeded if a line shaft belting slipped regularly and delivered power sporadically.

A similarly hierarchical framework guided the second model: that of a living being. There the brains, legs, heart, and arms each had a particularistic job and position. The being would survive at reduced efficiency if it lost its appendix or even an arm. Loss of the brain or heart caused total system collapse.

Commentators repeatedly noted that the twin Corliss steam engines that powered the entire array of machines in Machinery Hall at the Centennial Exhibition in Philadelphia were the exposition's heart. They pumped power—often referred to as life blood—through metal arteries and leather capillaries to every other machine in the hall. Underground and overhead pulleys and line shafting carried the power throughout the arena. Each display—each machine—tapped into this hierarchically-defined system of power delivery and did its work as if it was a hand or a foot. A distinct set of gearing brought the power from the lines to each machine—sometimes referred to as the nerves—to complete the complex, well-articulated system.

Systematization focused exclusively on how things worked. It coordinated, directed, and managed the hierarchal relationships among the various parts. The point of the late nineteenth and early twentieth century was to construct things that would work and in a manner consistent with contemporary notions; it was to take "real" things and juxtapose them in the sequence that would employ them to best advantage. Factory design provided a potent model. Operators needed to deduce which activities in their factory were concrete, identifiable activities. They then employed machines to fulfill those tasks and placed those machines in such an order as to simulate the manufacturing process. In the factory, and in all other actions, there was nothing remotely like consensus on what were true and actual categories and in what orders they ought to be joined together. It was the process and goal that mattered. Those tasks permeated and then dominated GAPE thought and, through that thought, action. They constituted the era's guts, its fundamental thrust and promise.

The history of technology viewed from this perspective turns the impact of technology on society and economics question on its head and reveals a series of questions rarely asked. The impact of late nineteenth century notions of standardization and systematization on technology becomes paramount. It places the focus squarely on invention, discovery, design, structure, process, and procedure—the technology—all fundamental to the history of technology but woefully under-studied. It helps explain why some technologies, such as wires for overhead trolleys and high-resistance electric lighting, were accepted and profitable, while others, including third-rail electric traction and low-resistance electric lighting, disappeared with little trace. It treats technology as a cultural product, not simply as an economic byproduct. A fundamental reinterpretation of technology-based institutions also flows from this approach. Professional organizations, licensure laws, reform of technological education, relation of technology to business, design of office space, and myriad more become fair game for exploration.

With standardization and systematization—not just organization but coordination and coherence—serving as touchstones, concepts such as efficiency took on particularistic meaning. Efficiency dealt with the structure of the system; it asked if the appropriate parts were in place and if they were properly ordered for peak function. Garbage collection, wastewater treatment, and water delivery—each was subjected to those strictures. Only when the twin objectives of standardization and systematization had been achieved was the system operating at maximum efficiency. Application of that rigorous template, in an age in which the nature and properties of the categories remained subject to much debate, generated any number of contentious moments and public disputes.

Application of GAPE notions of standardization and systematization to the history of science has no less profound scholarly implications. At the heart was how to pursue science. What did it require? What made it scientific? What were its fundamental activities and how were they to be conducted? What were disciplines? Did disciplines differ from each other? How were disciplines arranged? What were the goals of science? The rise of the laboratory as a rigidly controlled and defined space in which experts practiced their unique techniques and specialties, the objectification and mathematization of science, the professional revolution joining public and private, and drafting codes of ethics, all fall comfortably within this revamped vision. So, too, do attempts to distinguish applied science from other kinds of science. How scientific investigators in numerous facilities all working on a similar problem but achieving different results achieve certainty and uniformity is also a consequence of late nineteenth-century intellectual frameworks and desires, as is the introduction within the national government of responsibility and regular funding for some kinds of scientific enterprises. The late nineteenth- and early twentieth-century creation of a series of scientific bureaus in the United States Department of Agriculture—animal industry, plant industry, chemistry, entomology and more—testify to the latter point. Creation of business–science partnerships, especially the idea of knowledge-for-knowledge's-sake industrial research laboratories, is also derivative of this mode of thought.

Standardization and systematization as predominant thrusts revive exploration into the nuts and bolts of technologies and sciences. But that does not necessarily diminish other forms of exploration. Eugenics still would draw interest but would not possess the exclusivity it has achieved during recent decades. Chemistry and, to a lesser extent, physics, two branches of science long in decline among historians, might be resurrected. Chemistry may well have been the quintessential Gilded Age and Progressive Era science, essential to agriculture in soil composition, nutrition in dietary factors, and manufacture in industrial chemical processes. Explosives, dyes for fabrics, pharmaceuticals to relieve pain and heal the sick, and regulation in all these areas were chemical concomitants of GAPE science, yet they have been virtually ignored during the past several decades. Just as importantly, scholars might choose to examine activities in slightly different ways. Utilization of the telegraph—rather than the impact of the telegraph—restores process to history, while standardization of railroad cars, engines, time and time zones, and especially tracks, helps explain the parameters of a nationwide rail system and why those activities were such an important part of late nineteenth-century life. Even economics can be incorporated into the standardization and systematization scheme. Double-entry bookkeeping, farm accounts, the rise of the office, creation of a secretary as an office employee—not an apprentice businessman—and introduction of office machines speak to attempt to rationalize the recording and operation of business practice.

By freeing technology from economic exclusivity and science from postmodern clutches, new vistas open wide. The actual technology and science reemerge. Emphasis is redirected from the tedious dissection into categories to the uncovering of inherent inequalities among the categories. Weight is now placed squarely on the reasons that categories were posited as categories, and on the mechanisms that bound them together. History again becomes about the text, not the subtext. It is about how things worked or were supposed to work rather than why or how they did not. The history of science and technology in the Gilded Age and Progressive Era becomes less about the present day and more about the Gilded Age and Progressive Era.

References

Adas, Michael. 2006. *Dominance By Design: Technological Imperatives and America's Civilizing Mission.* Cambridge, MA: Belknap Press/Harvard University Press.

Alter, Stephen G. 2005. *William Dwight Whitney and the Science of Language.* Baltimore, MD: Johns Hopkins University Press.

Andrei, Mary Anne. 2005. "The Accidental Conservationist: William T. Hornaday, the Smithsonian Bison Expeditions and the US National Zoo." *Endeavor* 29, 3: 109–113.

Apple, Rima D. 2006. *Perfect Motherhood: Science and Childbearing in America*, New Brunswick, NJ: Rutgers University Press.

Armitage, Kevin C. 2009. *The Nature Study Movement: The Forgotten Popularizer of America's Conservation Ethic.* Lawrence: University Press of Kansas.

Arnold, Andrew B. 2014. *Fueling the Gilded Age: Railroads, Miners, and Disorder in Pennsylvania Coal Country.* New York: New York University Press.

Baker, Lee D. 2010. *Anthropology and the Racial Politics of Culture.* Durham, NC: Duke University Press.

Baldwin, Peter C. 2012. *In the Watches of the Night: Life in the Nocturnal City, 1820–1930.* Chicago: University of Chicago Press.

Bankoff, Greg. 2009. "First Impressions: Diarists, Scientists, Imperialists and the Management of the Environment in the American Pacific, 1899–1902." *Journal of Pacific History* 44, 3: 261–280.

Becker, Carl. 1932. "Everyman His Own Historian." Annual address of the president of the American Historical Association, Minneapolis, MN. December 29, 1931. *American Historical Review* 37, 2: 221–236.

Bender, Daniel E. 2009. *The American Abyss: Savagery and Civilization in the Age of Industry.* Ithaca, NY: Cornell University Press.

Benjamin, Jr., Ludy T. and David B. Baker. 2003. *From Séance to Science: A History of the Profession of Psychology in America.* Belmont, CA: Thomson-Wadsworth.

Bennett, Lyn Ellen and Scott Abbott. 2014. "Barbed and Dangerous: Constructing the Meaning of Barbed Wire in Late Nineteenth-Century America." *Agricultural History* 88, 4: 566–590.

Berger, Molly W. 2011. *Hotel Dreams: Luxury, Technology, and Urban Ambition in America, 1829–1929.* Baltimore, MD: Johns Hopkins University Press.

Billington, David P. and David P. Billington, Jr., 2006. *Power, Speed and Form. Engineers and the Making of the Twentieth Century.* Princeton, NJ: Princeton University Press.

Biltekoff, Charlotte. 2013. *Eating Right in America: The Cultural Politics of Food and Health*, Durham, NC: Duke University Press.

Bittel, Carla Jean. 2005. "Science, Suffrage, and Experimentation: Mary Putnam Jacobi and the Controversy over Vivisection in Late Nineteenth-Century America." *Bulletin of the History of Medicine* 79, 4: 664–694.

Bix, Amy Sue. 2014. *Girls Coming to Tech! A History of American Engineering Education for Women.* Cambridge, MA: Massachusetts Institute of Technology Press.

Black, Brian. 2006. *Nature and the Environment in 20th Century American Life.* Westport, CT: Greenwood Press.

Brooks, Tim. 2004. *Lost Sounds: Blacks and the Birth of the Recording Industry, 1890–1919.* Champaign: University of Illinois Press.

Brown, Elspeth H. 2005. *The Corporate Eye: Photography and the Rationalization of American Commercial Culture, 1884–1929.* Baltimore, MD: Johns Hopkins University Press.

Caron, Simone M. 2008. *Who Choses? American Reproductive History since 1830.* Gainesville: University of Florida Press.

Carson, John. 2007. *The Measure of Merit: Talents, Intelligence, and Inequality in the French and American Republics, 1750–1940.* Princeton, NJ: Princeton University Press.

Casey, Robert. 2008. *The Model T: A Centennial History.* Baltimore, MD: Johns Hopkins University Press.

Cassedy, James H. 2009. *John Shaw Billings: Science and Medicine in the Gilded Age.* Philadelphia: Xlibris Corporation.

Churella, Albert J. 2012. *The Pennsylvania Railroad. Volume 1: Building an Empire, 1846–1917.* Philadelphia: University of Pennsylvania Press.

Coates, Peter. 2006. *American Perceptions of Immigrant and Invasive Species.* Strangers on the Land. Berkeley: University of California Press.

Corn, Joseph J. 2011. *User Unfriendly: Consumer Struggles with Personal Technologies, from Clocks and Sewing Machines to Cars and Computers.* Baltimore, MD: Johns Hopkins University Press.

Delfino, Dusanna and Michele Gillespie, eds. 2008. *Technology, Innovation and Southern Industrialization: From the Antebellum Era to the Computer Age.* Columbia: University of Missouri Press.

Deluzio, Crista. 2007. *Female Adolescence in American Scientific Thought, 1830–1920.* Baltimore, MD: Johns Hopkins University Press.

Dorr, Gregory Michael. 2006. "Defective or Disabled?: Race, Medicine, and Eugenics in Progressive Era Virginia and Alabama." *Journal of the Gilded Age and Progressive Era* 5, 4: 359–392.

—. 2008. *Segregation's Science: Eugenics and Society in Virginia.* Charlottesville: University of Virginia.

Edwards, Rebecca. 2006. *New Spirits: Americans in the Gilded Age, 1865–1905.* New York: Oxford University Press.

Ellenberg, George B. 2007. *Mule South to Tractor South: Mules, Machines, and the Transformation of the Cotton South.* Tuscaloosa: University of Alabama Press.

Endersby, Jim. 2013. "Mutant Utopias. Evening Primroses and Imagined Futures in Early America." *ISIS* 104: 471–503.

Essig, Mark. 2003. *Edison and the Electric Chair.* A Story of Light and Death. New York: Walker Publishing Co.

Farland, Maria. 2006. "W.E.B. DuBois, Anthropometric Science, and the Limits of Racial Uplift." *American Quarterly* 58, 4: 1017–1044.

Fenske, Gail. 2008. *The Skyscraper and the City: The Woolworth Building and the Making of Modern New York.* Chicago: University of Chicago Press.

Fiege, Mark. 2012. *The Republic of Nature: An Environmental History of the United States.* Seattle: University of Washington Press.

Fouche, Rayvon. 2003. *Black Inventors in the Age of Segregation.* Baltimore, MD: Johns Hopkins University Press.

—. 2006. "Say It Loud, I'm Black and I'm Proud: African Americans, American Artifactual Culture, and Black Vernacular Technological Creativity." *American Quarterly* 58, 3: 639–661.

Gelber, Scott M. 2011. *The University and the People: Envisioning American Higher Education in the Era of Populist Protest.* Madison: University of Wisconsin.

Gertner, John. 2012. *The Idea Factory. Bell Labs and the Great Age of American Innovation.* New York: Penguin Press.

Giesen, James C. 2011. *Boll Weevil Blues: Cotton, Myth, and Power in the American South.* Chicago: University of Chicago Press.

Gilkeson, John S. 2010. *Anthropologists and the Rediscovery of America, 1886–1965.* New York: Cambridge University Press.

Goldstein, Daniel. 2008. "Outposts of Science. The Knowledge Trade and the Expansion of Scientific Community in Post-Civil War America." *ISIS* 99: 518–546.

Greene, Julie. 2009. *The Canal Builders: Making America's Empire at the Panama Canal.* New York: Penguin Press.

Grusin, Richard. 2004. *Culture, Technology, and the Creation of America's National Parks.* New York: Cambridge University Press.

Gustin, Lawrence R. 2008. *Billy Durant: Creator of General Motors.* Ann Arbor: University of Michigan Regional Press.

Ha, Nathan Q. 2011. "The Riddle of Sex: Biological Theories of Sexual Difference in the Early Twentieth-Century." *Journal of the History of Biology* 44: 505–546.

Hahn, Barbara. 2011. *Making Tobacco Bright: Creating an American Commodity, 1617–1937.* Baltimore, MD: Johns Hopkins University Prcss.

Harwood, Craig S. and Gary B. Fogel. 2012. *Quest for Flight: John J. Montgomery and the Dawn of Aviation in the West.* Norman: University of Oklahoma Press.

Hathaway, Jay. 2004. *The Gilded Age Construction of Modern American Homophobia.* Basingstoke, UK: PalgraveMacmillan.

Haw, Richard. 2005. *The Brooklyn Bridge: A Cultural History.* New Brunswick, NJ: Rutgers University Press.

Heinrich, Thomas and Bob Batchelor. 2004. *Kotex, Kleenex, and Huggies: Kimberly-Clark and the Consumer Revolution.* Columbus: Ohio State University Press.

Herron, John P. 2010. *Science and the Social Good: Nature, Culture, and Community, 1865–1965.* New York: Oxford University Press.

Hersey, Mark D. 2006. "Hints and Suggestions to Farmers: George Washington Carver and Rural Conservation in the South." *Environmental History* 11, April: 239–268.

—. 2011a. *My Work Is That of Conservation: An Environmental Biography of George Washington Carver.* Athens: University of Georgia Press.

—. 2011b. "'What We Need is a Crop Ecologist': Ecology and Agricultural Science in Progressive-Era America." *Agricultural History* 85, 3: 297–321.

Herzig, Rebecca. 2006. *Suffering for Science: Reason and Sacrifice in Modern America*. New Brunswick, NJ: Rutgers University Press.

Hickman, Timothy A. 2004. "'Mania Americana': Narcotic Addiction and Modernity in the United States, 1870–1920." *Journal of American History* 90, 4: 1269–1294.

Hirt, Paul W. 2012. *The Wired Northwest: The History of Electric Power, 1870–1920*. Lawrence: University Press of Kansas.

Hochfelder, David. 2012. *The Telegraph in America, 1832–1920*. Baltimore, MD: Johns Hopkins University Press.

Holley, I. B., Jr. 2008. *The Highway Revolution, 1895–1925: How the United States Got Out of the Mud*. Durham, NC: Carolina Academic Press.

Hyde, Charles K. 2005. *The Dodge Brothers: The Men, the Motor Cars, and the Legacy*. Detroit, MI. Wayne State University Press

Jewett, Andrew. 2012. *Science, Democracy, and the American University: From the Civil War to the Cold War*. New York: Cambridge University Press.

John, Richard R. 2010. *Network Nation: Inventing American Telecommunications*. Cambridge, MA: Belknap/Harvard University Press.

Juzda, Elisa. 2009. "Skulls, Science, and the Spoils of War: Craniological Studies at the United States Army Medical Museum, 1868–1900." *Studies in History and Philosophy of Biomedical Sciences* 40: 156–167.

Keiner, Christine. 2009. *The Oyster Question: Scientists, Watermen, and the Maryland Chesapeake Bay since 1880*. Athens: University of Georgia Press.

Kemp, Kathryn W. 2007. "'The Dictograph Hears All': An Example of Surveillance Technology in the Progressive Era." *Journal of the Gilded Age and Progressive Era* 6, 4: 209–230.

Kevles, Daniel J. 2007. "Patents, Protections, and Privileges: The Establishment of Intellectual Property in Animals and Plants." *ISIS* 98: 323–331.

Kimmelman, Barbara A. 2006. "Mr. Blakeslee Builds His Dream House: Agricultural Institutions, Genetics, and Careers 1900–1915." *Journal of the History of Biology* 39: 241–280.

Kingsland, Sharon E. 2005. *The Evolution of American Ecology, 1890–2000*. Baltimore, MD: Johns Hopkins University Press.

Klein, Maury. 2007. *The Genesis of Industrial America: 1870–1920*. New York: Cambridge University Press.

Kline, Ronald R. 2003. *Consumers in the Country: Technology and Social Change in Rural America*. Baltimore, MD: Johns Hopkins University Press.

Kohler, Robert E. 2006. *All Creatures: Naturalists, Collectors, and Biodiversity, 1850–1950*. Princeton, NJ: Princeton University Press.

—. 2008. "From Farm and Family to Career Naturalist: The Apprenticeship of Vernon Bailey." *ISIS* 99: 28–56.

Kohlstedt, Sally Gregory. 2005. "Nature, Not Books. Scientists and the Origins of the Nature-Study Movement in the 1890s." *ISIS* 96: 324–352.

—. 2008. "'A Better Crop of Boys and Girls': The School Gardening Movement, 1890–1920." *History of Education Quarterly* 48, 1: 58–93.

—. 2010. *Teaching Children Science. Hands-On Nature Study in North America, 1890–1930*. Chicago: University of Chicago Press.

—. 2011. "Place and Museum Space: The Smithsonian Institution, National Identity, and the American West, 1846–1896." In *Geographies of Nineteenth-Century Science*, edited by David N. Livingstone and Charles W. J. Withers. Chicago: University of Chicago Press.

—. 2013. "Innovative Niche Scientists: Women's Role in Reframing North American Museums, 1880–1930." *Centaurus* 55: 153–174.

Kremer, Richard L. 2011. "Reforming American Physics Pedagogy in the 1880s: Introducing 'Learning By Doing' Via Student Laboratory Exercises." In *Learning By Doing. Experiments and Instruments in the History of Science Teaching*, edited by Peter Heering and Roland Wittje, 243–280. Stuttgart: Franz Steiner Verlag.

Largent, Mark A. 2008. *Breeding Contempt: The History of Coerced Sterilization in the United States*. New Brunswick, NJ: Rutgers University Press.

LeCain, Timothy J. 2009. *Mass Destruction: The Men and Great Mines That Wired America and Scarred the Planet*. New Brunswick, NJ: Rutgers University Press.

Levin, Miriam R. 2005. *Defining Women's Scientific Enterprise: Mount Holyoke Faculty and the Rise of American Science*. Hanover, NH: University Press of New England.

Levy, Jonathan. 2012. *Freaks of Fortune: The Emerging World of Capitalism and Risk in America*. Cambridge, MA: Harvard University Press.

Lockwood, Jeffrey A. 2004. *Locust: The Devastating Rise and Mysterious Disappearance of the Insect that Shaped the American Frontier*. New York: Basic Books.

Loizides, Georgios P. 2015. *Henry Ford's Project in Human Engineering: The Sociological Department of the Ford Motor Company (1913–1941)*. Lewiston, NY: Edwin Mellen.

Lombardo, Paul A. 2008. *Three Generations. No Imbeciles. Eugenics, the Supreme Court, and Buck v. Bell*. Baltimore, MD: Johns Hopkins University Press.

Lucier, Paul. 2009. "The Professional and the Scientist in Nineteenth-Century America." *ISIS* 100: 699–732.

—.2012. "The Origins of Pure and Applied Science in Gilded Age America." *ISIS* 103: 527–536.

Madsen-Brooks, Leslie. 2009. "Challenging Science as Usual: Women's Participation in American Natural History Museum Work, 1870–1950." *Journal of Women's History* 21, 2: 11–38.

—. 2013. "A Synthesis of Expertise and Expectations: Women Museum Scientists, Club Women and Populist Natural Science in the United States, 1890–1950." *Gender and History* 25, 1: 27–46.

Marcus, Alan I. 2004. "Manufacturing Government: Total Quality Management, the National Performance Review, and the Bridge to the Twenty-First Century." Annual Meeting of the American Historical Association, January 8. Washington, DC.

—. 2007. "Reagan, Bush, and Clinton: The Rise and Fall of American Technology Policy." Annual Meeting of the American Historical Association, January 4. Atlanta, GA.

—. and Amy Sue Bix. 2007. *Science and Technology Policy in America since 1950*. New York: Prometheus Books.

Mezzano, Michael. 2005. "The Progressive Origins of Eugenics Critics: Raymond Pearl, Herbert J. Jennings, and the Defense of Scientific Inquiry." *Journal of the Gilded Age and Progressive Era* 4, 1: 83–97.

Mickulas, Peter. 2007. *Britton's Botanical Empire: The New York Botanical Garden and American Botany, 1888–1929*. Bronx, NY: New York Botanical Garden Press.

Middleton, William D. and William D. Middleton III. 2009. *Frank Julian Sprague: Electrical Inventor and Engineer.* Bloomington: Indiana University Press.

Missal, Alexander. 2008. *Seaway to Future: American Social Visions and the Construction of the Panama Canal.* Madison: University of Wisconsin Press.

Mitman, Greg. 2003. "Hay Fever Holiday: Health, Leisure, and Place in Gilded-Age America." *Bulletin of the History of Medicine* 77, 3: 600–635.

Morin, Karen M. 2011. *Civic Discipline: Geography in America, 1860–1890.* Burlington: Ashgate Press.

Morton, David L., Jr. 2004. *Sound Recording: The Life Story of a Technology.* Baltimore: Johns Hopkins University Press.

Noll, Richard. 2011. *American Madness: The Rise and Fall of Dementia Praecox.* Cambridge, MA: Harvard University Press.

O'Neill, Karen M. 2006. *Rivers by Design: State Power and the Origins of U.S. Flood Control.* Durham, NC: Duke University Press.

Oliver, M. 2007. "George Eastman's Modern Stone-Age Family: Snapshot Photography and the Brownie." *Technology and Culture* 48, 1: 1–19.

Olmstead, Alan L. and Paul W. Rhode. 2008. *Creating Abundance: Biological Innovation and American Agricultural Development.* New York: Cambridge University Press.

Orsi, Richard J. 2005. *The Southern Pacific Railroad and the Development of the American West, 1850–1930.* Berkeley: University of California Press.

Parezo, Nancy J. and Don D. Fowler. 2007. *Anthropology Goes to the Fair: The 1904 Louisiana Purchase Exposition.* Lincoln: University of Nebraska Press.

Paris, Leslie. 2008. *Children's Nature: The Rise of the American Summer Camp.* New York: New York University Press.

Patterson, Andrea. 2009. "Germs and Jim Crow: The Impact of Microbiology on Public Health Policies in Progressive Era American South." *Journal of the History of Biology* 42: 529–559.

Pauly, Philip J. 2008. *Fruits and Plains: The Horticultural Transformation of America.* Cambridge, MA: Harvard University Press.

Peterson, Jon A. 2003. *The Birth of City Planning in the United States, 1840–1917.* Baltimore, MD: Johns Hopkins University Press.

Pettit, Michael. 2013. *The Science of Deception: Psychology and Commerce in America.* Chicago: University of Chicago Press.

Plotnick, Rachel. 2012. "At the Interface: The Case of the Electric Push Button, 1880–1923." *Technology and Culture* 53, 4: 815–845.

Punke, Michael. 2007. *Last Stand. George Bird Grinnell, the Battle to Save the Buffalo, and the Birth of the New West.* Washington, DC: Smithsonian Books.

Rafferty, Edward C. 2003. *Apostle of Human Progress. Lester Frank Ward and American Political Thought, 1841–1913.* New York: Rowan and Littlefield.

Recchiuti, John Louis. 2007. *Civic Engagement: Social Science and Progressive-Era Reform in New York City.* Philadelphia: University of Pennsylvania Press.

Rees, Jonathan. 2013. *Refrigeration Nation: A History of Ice, Appliances, and Enterprise in America.* Baltimore, MD: Johns Hopkins University Press.

Regal, Brian. 2002. *Henry Fairfield Osborn: Race and the Search for the Origins of Man.* Burlington, VT: Ashgate.

Rembis, Michael A. 2011. *Defining Deviance: Sex, Science, and Delinquent Girls, 1890–1960.* Urbana: University of Illinois Press.

Ristaino, Jean Beagle ed. 2008. *Pioneering Women in Plant Pathology.* St. Paul, MN: APS Press.

Rose, Anne C. 2012. "An American Science of Feeling: Harvard's Psychology of Emotion During the world War I Era." *Journal of the History of Ideas* 73, 3: 485–506.

Rosen, Christine. 2004. *Preaching Eugenics: Religious Leaders and the American Eugenics Movement.* New York: Oxford University Press.

Rostow, Walt Whitman. 1960. *The Stages of Economic Growth: A Non-Communist Manifesto.* New York: Cambridge University Press.

Schneirov, Richard. 2006. "Thoughts on Periodizing the Gilded Age: Capital Accumulation, Society, and Politics, 1873–1898." *Journal of the Gilded Age and the Progressive Era* 5, 3: 189–224.

Schuster, David G. 2011. *Neurasthenic Nation: America's Search for Health, Happiness, and Comfort, 1869–1920.* New Brunswick, NJ: Rutgers University Press.

Shulman, Peter A. 2003. "'Science Can Never Demobilize': The United States Navy and Petroleum Geology, 1898–1924." *History and Technology* 19, 4: 365–385.

Simon, Linda. 2004. *Dark Light: Electricity and Anxiety from the Telegraph to the X-Ray.* San Diego, CA: Harcourt Brace Jovanovich.

Sklansky, Jeffrey. 2002. *The Soul's Economy. Market Society and Selfhood in American Thought, 1820–1920.* Chapel Hill: University of North Carolina Press.

Smil, Vaclav. 2005. *Creating the Twentieth Century: Technical Innovations of 1867–1914 and Their Lasting Impact.* New York: Oxford University Press.

Smuts, Alice Boardman. 2006. *Seen and Heard: The Scientific Study of Children. Science in the Service of Children, 1893–1935.* New Haven, CT: Yale University Press.

Sokal, Michael K. 2010. "Scientific Biography, Cognitive Deficits, and Laboratory Practice. James McKeen Cattell and Early American Experimental Psychology, 1880–1904." *ISIS* 101: 531–554.

Solnit, Rebecca. 2003. *River of Shadows. Eadweard Muybridge and the Technological Wild West.* New York: Penguin Press.

Spear, Robert J. 2005. *The Great Gypsy Moth War: The History of the First Campaign in Massachusetts to Eradicate the Gypsy Moth, 1890–1901.* Boston: University of Massachusetts Press.

Spiro, Jonathan. 2009. *Defending the Master Race: Conservation, Eugenics, and the Legacy of Madison Grant.* Lebanon, NH: University of Vermont Press.

Strom, Claire. 2009. *Making Catfish Bait Out of Government Boys: The Fight against Cattle Ticks and the Transformation of the Yeoman South.* Athens: University of Georgia Press.

Thiesen, William H. *Industrializing American Shipbuilding: The Transformation of Ship Design and Construction, 1820–1920.* Gainesville: University Press of Florida.

Thurtle, Phillip. 2007. *The Emergence of Genetic Rationality.* Seattle: University of Washington Press.

Tracy, Sarah W. 2005. *Alcoholism in America: From Reconstruction to Prohibition.* Baltimore, MD: Johns Hopkins University Press.

Turner, Steven. 2011. "Changing Images of the Inclined Plane, 1880–1920: A Case Study of a Revolution in American Scientific Education." In *Learning By Doing. Experiments and Instruments in the History of Science Teaching*, edited by Peter Heering and Roland Wittje, 207–242. Stuttgart: Franz Steiner Verlag.

Van Campen, Cretien. 2008. *The Hidden Sense. Synesthesia in Art and Science.* Cambridge, MA: Massachusetts Institute of Technology Press.

Vetter, Jeremy. 2008. "Field Science in the Railroad Era: The Tools of Knowledge Empire in the American West, 1869–1916." *Historia, Ciencias, Saude-Manguinhos* 15, 3: 597–613.

—. 2012. "Labs in the Field? Rocky Mountain Biological Stations in the Early Twentieth Century." *Journal of the History of Biology* 45: 587–611.

Wasik, John F. 2006. *The Merchant of Power. Sam Insull, Thomas Edison, and the Creation of the Modern Metropolis.* Basingstoke, UK: PalgraveMacmillan.

White, Richard. 2011. *Railroaded: The Transcontinentals and the Making of Modern America.* New York: W.W. Norton.

Wilder, Gordon M. 2012. *The American Reaper: Harvesting Networks and Technology, 1830–1910.* Burlington, VT: Ashgate.

Williams, Jr., Vernon J. 2006. *The Social Sciences and Theories of Race.* Urbana: University of Illinois Press.

Wilson, Francille Rusan. 2006. *The Segregated Scholars: Black Social Scientists and the Creation of Black Labor Studies, 1890–1950.* Charlottesville: University of Virginia Press.

Worster, Donald. 2008. *A Passion for Nature: The Life of John Muir.* New York: Oxford University Press.

Young, Cristobal. 2009. "The Emergence of Sociology From Political Economy in the United States: 1890–1940." *Journal of the History of the Behavioral Sciences* 45, 2: 91–116.

Ziegler, Edith M. 2012. "The Burdens and the Narrow Life of Farm Women." *Agricultural History.* 86, 3: 77–103.

Zink, Clifford W. 2011. *The Roebling Legacy.* Princeton, NJ: Landmark Publications.

Further Reading

Allen, Garland. 2013. "'Culling the Herd': Eugenics and the Conservation Movement in the United States, 1900–1940." *Journal of the History of Biology* 46: 31–72.

Alrich, Mark. 2006. "From Forest Conservation to Market Preservation. Invention and Diffusion of Wood-Preserving Technology, 1880–1939," *Technology and Culture* 47, 2 (April): 311–340.

Anderson, John D. 2004. *Inventing Flight: The Wright Brothers and Their Predecessors.* Baltimore, MD: Johns Hopkins University Press.

Dalzell, Frederick. 2010. *Engineering Invention: Frank J. Sprague and the U.S. Electrical Industry.* Cambridge, MA: MIT Press.

Farber, Paul L. 2010. *Mixing Races: From Scientific Racism to Modern Evolutionary Ideas.* Baltimore, MD: Johns Hopkins University Press.

Geiger, Andrea. 2011. *Subverting Exclusion: Transpacific Encounters With Race, Caste, and Borders, 1885–1928.* New Haven, CT: Yale University Press.

Kinney, Thomas A. 2004. *The Carriage Trade: Making Horse-Drawn Vehicles in America.* Baltimore, MD: Johns Hopkins University Press.

Lavine, Matthew. 2013. *The First Atomic Age: Scientists, Radiations, and the American Public, 1895–1945.* New York: Palgrave Macmillan.

Marcus, Alan I ed. 2015. *Science as Service. Establishing and Reformulating American Land-Grant Universities, 1865–1930.* Tuscaloosa: University of Alabama Press.

Nadis, Fred. 2005. *Wonder Shows: Preforming Science, Magic, and Religion in America.* New Brunswick, NJ: Rutgers University Press.

Newfield, Christopher. 2003. *Ivy and Industry: Business and the Making of the American University, 1880–1980.* Durham, NC: Duke University Press.

Stross, Randall E. 2007. *The Wizard of Menlo Park: How Thomas Edison Invented the Modern World.* New York: Crown Books.

Sturchio, Jeffrey L. and Louis Galambos, 2011. "The German Connection: Merck and the Flow of Knowledge from Germany to the United States, 1880–1930," *Business and Economic History On-Line*, 9: 1–14.

Swibold, Dennis L. 2006. *Copper Chorus: Mining, Politics, and the Montana Press, 1889–1959.* Helena: Montana Historical Society.

Watts, Trent A. 2010. *One Homogeneous People: Narratives of White Southern Identity, 1890–1920.* Knoxville: University of Tennessee Press.

Chapter Twenty

The Rise of a Modern Concept of "Health"

David G. Schuster

In 1869, Philadelphia physician S. Weir Mitchell was concerned for the health of his fellow Americans. "The cruel competition for the dollar, the new and exacting habits of business, the over-education and the overstraining of our young people," he explained to readers of *Lippincott's Magazine*, "have brought about some great and growing evils." In Mitchell's mind, Americans, in their drive for progress, had over the years built around them a way of life that was exhausting, an existence that wore people out as if they were calibrated tools being abused by clumsy workers. Mitchell saw the trajectory of American development as being towards urbanization and business, and believed that it was against human biology to live in densely packed environments—"teeming city hives," in his words—and to work high-pressure jobs that burdened people with excessive anxiety. Mitchell's message was not without hope. He advised Americans to fortify themselves by making improvements "in education, in dress, and in diet and habits of daily life" (Mitchell 1869, 493). At its core, his message was simple: modern America needed to invest more heavily in its health.

The basics of American development added weight to Mitchell's argument. From 1870 to 1920, the nation's population rose from just under 40 million to over 105 million, a remarkable 260% increase in just two generations. The bulk of this growth occurred in urban areas, where people—many of whom were immigrants—wrestled with life in overcrowded cities, threatened by epidemics and without proper housing or sanitation (Foner and Garraty 1991). Urbanization also underscored the changing nature of work in America, as pastoral jobs on farms increasingly gave way to hectic work in factories and business that took their toll on people's minds and bodies. The economy grew unevenly but prodigiously, with average urban wages increasing over 50% in real value from 1870 to 1900, thereby helping to establish a general prosperity that allotted more and more Americans the disposable income to spend on healthcare (Wiebe 1967).

Indeed, in as much as *life* was part of the national triumvirate of values including *liberty* and the *pursuit of happiness*, improving one's life was a sanctioned, if not encouraged, act. It served as the basis of an expansive health-care movement that took shape during the late nineteenth century and grew into the twentieth century. The development of American medicine was heavily influenced by a larger *progressive* impulse around the turn of the twentieth century that motivated people to look to experts abroad and at home in the hopes of finding solutions to modern problems (Rodgers 1998).

In the history of American medicine, the progressive impulse manifested itself in four fundamental ways. The first area of analysis centers on the professionalization of medicine and the rise of medical doctors as America's foremost health-care experts. The second explores public health and the evolution of community-based healthcare in the United States. Third is the influence of the pharmaceutical industry, a key player in American healthcare. The fourth area of analysis is popular culture and how Americans began seeing healthcare as a regular part of daily life. In short, at the start of the long Gilded Age and Progressive Era, the concept of *health* increased in importance; it became an organizing principle that shaped the development of professional medicine, public health, the pharmaceutical industry, and popular culture, giving rise to America's modern health-care marketplace.

Professional Medicine

Much to the chagrin of American physicians, the public did not hold the medical profession in particularly high esteem at the beginning of the twentieth century. "I dare say that if

A Companion to the Gilded Age and Progressive Era, First Edition. Edited by Christopher McKnight Nichols and Nancy C. Unger.
© 2017 John Wiley & Sons, Inc. Published 2017 by John Wiley & Sons, Inc.

any question of public importance were to be propounded for solution," Dr. Alexander Rovinsky of New York observed at a meeting of the Eastern Medical Society in 1901, "the one offered by the physician would very likely carry the least weight and importance" (Rovinsky 1901, 692). For years, the medical profession was dogged by circumstances that sapped the public's confidence in its ability to offer healthcare. Doctors had notorious reputations for administering heroic treatments that kept many potential patients at bay, including bloodletting and prescribing harsh purgatives such as mercury-based calomel. State deregulation of the medical profession during the Jacksonian period had led to the proliferation of quacks. The public had difficulty discerning properly trained physicians from masquerading opportunists, further eroding the reputation of doctors (Starr 1982). Eager to build public trust and increase the flow of patients to well-educated physicians, progressive reformers in professional medicine sought to transform their industry by developing new specialties, prescribing amenable treatments, and strengthening medical education.

The idea of *scientific medicine* stood at the philosophical center of the Gilded Age and Progressive Era transformation of the medical profession. Growing out of the enlightenment and European rational thought, scientific medicine stressed the importance of experimentation and sought to incorporate the study of chemistry and physiology into the practice of medicine. American physicians who studied in Europe (especially France, starting in the 1840s, and Germany by the 1870s) brought the principles of scientific medicine back with them. The concept spread through American medical schools and professional organizations (Warner 2003). Advocates claimed that scientific medicine allowed for greater innovation in theory and treatment than did previous approaches to medicine faulted for being dogmatic systems of thought, such as Galen's legacy of balancing the humors. In a larger sense, scientific medicine represents what historian Robert Wiebe has called the "search for order" that guided the development of American professionalism near the turn of the century (Wiebe 1967). It helped make sense of the confusing nature of sickness and health, established physicians as recognized experts in medicine, and is emblematic of a progressive movement that embraced expertise in many fields, including sociology, public policy, and business. Scientific medicine could not escape the dogma of social and cultural prejudice during the period, however (Russett 1989). Harvard professor of medicine Edward H. Clarke, for instance, used scientific medicine to ostensibly prove that boys were more intellectually capable students than were girls in his influential 1873 book *Sex in Education; or, a Fair Chance for Girls.* Scientific medicine also helped New York neurologist George M. Beard conclude in his widely read 1881 *American Nervousness, Its Causes and Consequences* that Anglo Americans enjoyed superior cognitive capacities compared to those of Asian, American Indian, and African descent.

Despite reinforcing some commonly held prejudices, scientific medicine led to a host of new innovations and the formation of medical specialties. The development of the speculum during the mid-nineteenth century, for instance, helped further the study of gynecology and increased focus on women's health. When it came to surgery, dentist William T. G. Morton's public demonstration of ether as a general anesthetic at the Massachusetts General Hospital in 1846 combined with successful antisepsis studies published in 1867 by Englishman Joseph Lister removed some of the trepidation with which patients and physicians alike approached the scalpel. By the turn of the twentieth century, surgery had emerged as one of the most prestigious medical specialties. Scientific research continued to inform the development of specialties, with German physicist Wilhelm Rontgen's 1895 experiments with x-rays leading to advancements in radiology. Studies on hormones published in 1905 by British physiologists William M. Bayliss and Ernst H. Starling helped to establish endocrinology. Neurology also accelerated as a specialty after the Civil War, as Thomas Edison's experiments with electricity helped inspire a new paradigm of health, the supposed existence of vital *nervous energy*. This innovation allowed physicians to develop new diagnoses such as *neurasthenia* that medicalized many of life's common displeasures, such as mood swings, weight fluctuation, lack of concentration, insomnia, chronic pain, headaches, indigestion, hair loss, and sexual dysfunction. Treatments for neurasthenic ailments proliferated as doctors and patients devised ways to restore the body's reputed supply of *nervous energy* through exercise, diet, rest, clothing reform, electrostimulation, and engaging in relaxing hobbies (Schuster 2011).

As the theory of nervous energy faded in the twentieth century, a *psychosomatic* understanding of health began to take its place (Shorter 1993). For years, medical doctors had kept a wary eye on the rise of Christian Science, a therapeutic religion akin to the late nineteenth-century New Thought movement and descended from Transcendentalism and the Second Great Awakening of the first part of the century. Mary Baker Eddy founded Christian Science in 1876. Within a decade the religion had positioned itself as a spiritual alternative to professional medical care. According to Eddy, the physical body was a manifestation of one's mind and spirit, and, as such, one's mind and spirit ultimately possessed the ability to heal the body through thought and prayer (Albanese 2007). Christian Science techniques proved remarkably effective, especially when treating people suffering from chronic symptoms typified by the *neurasthenia* diagnosis. Professional physicians took note and worked to develop an alternative, more scientific explanation for why Christian Science healing worked. In 1895 Harvard neurologist James Jackson Putnam claimed to an audience of physicians that it was the psychological power of *suggestion* that gave Christian Science its ability to heal. The process of spiritual healing sowed "seeds of hopefulness and confidence" that compelled people to feel better (Putnam 1895, 505). Supporting Putnam's basic premise was his university colleague William James, whose books *Principles of Psychology* (1890) and *Varieties of Religious Experience* (1902) sought to reconcile religion and science through a system of thought associated with *pragmatism* (Menand 2002). Their research helped prime America for the 1909 arrival of Austrian neurologist Sigmund Freud, whose theories of psychoanalysis would support the development of psychosomatic-based talk therapy and the field of mental health well into the late twentieth century (Lunbeck 1996).

New specialties and treatments might have led to the expansion of medical services, but the profession still needed to convince the public that these services could be trusted. To this end, organizations such as the American Medical Association (AMA) sought to build an aura of infallibility around scientific medicine by generating the outward impression of consensus within the profession (Starr 1982). Bylaws were enacted by the AMA to prevent members from publicly criticizing colleagues' medical opinions. Some of these regulations went counter to the conventions of a number of alternative medical sects, such as homeopaths and eclectics, who had a tradition of public rivalry with competing physicians. Homeopathy had arisen out of Germany during the first part of the nineteenth century and found its way to the United States via immigration and physicians who studied abroad. Based loosely on the idea that "like cures like," homeopathy relied on mild herbal remedies to relieve symptoms rather than heroic medicine and the harsh drug compounds upon which regular physicians had long relied. Eclectics were medical professionals who cast a wide net when it came to treatment, borrowing from American Indian traditions and herbal folk remedies (Whorton 2002). Like homeopaths, they positioned themselves as genial professional alternatives to the regular medical establishment. By the end of the nineteenth century, outward consensus within the AMA came at the cost of professional diversity within the organization itself, as homeopaths and eclectics found themselves being squeezed out of the ranks of American medicine.

At the turn of the twentieth century the AMA began a reorganization process that would serve as a watershed moment in the organization's ability to regulate the practice of medicine in the United States. Founded in 1847, the AMA had been a loose confederation of doctors and regional medical groups that sought to create a nation-wide umbrella organization for American physicians. Its influence was limited by small numbers—in 1900 it had 8,000 members out of the more than 100,000 physicians nationwide—and a lack of cohesion. That began to change in 1901 when the AMA established the House of Delegates (modeled after the US House of Representatives) composed of representatives from county and state medical organizations to serve as a formal, reform-minded legislative body. The AMA also restructured membership so as to dedicate more resources to pressing issues, establishing the Council on Medical Education (1904) and the Council on Pharmacy and Chemistry (1905). It also empowered state-level organizations to more actively regulate the profession in accordance with AMA guidelines (Starr 1982). Left out of the reform agenda was racial equality. Although the AMA had diversified membership to allow women since 1876, it enforced Jim Crow. The barring of African Americans led in turn to the 1895 formation of the National Medical Association, the organizational alternative to the AMA established by black doctors (Byrd and Clayton 2000).

Of all reforms advocated by the newly reorganized AMA, educational reform was one of the most urgent. Deregulation of medical licensing during the Jacksonian period led to the establishment of numerous proprietary medical schools that reformers blamed for lowering the overall quality of American medicine. These for-profit schools typically offered medical degrees for the price of tuition and the completion of an unambitious curriculum that included as little as two six-week terms. Prerequisites for study were kept notoriously low, prompting Dr. Frederick Henry Gerrish, president of the American Academy of Medicine, to dryly observe in 1888 that the only people not routinely earning medical degrees were "females, children, the moneyless, and negroes" (Gerrish 1889, 466). Leading the cause of medical education reform was Harvard University president Charles W. Eliot, who personally oversaw, beginning in 1869, what he called "a complete revolution of the system of medical education" (Starr 1982: 114). He moved Harvard away from the proprietary model by placing faculty on salaries and insulating them from the business of tuition and financing. He lengthened the academic year from four to nine months, the number of years of study from two to three, and required laboratory courses such as chemistry and physiology of all medical students. The founding of Johns Hopkins Hospital in 1889 and the Johns Hopkins Medical School in 1893 represents a further maturation of American medical school reform. Bachelor degrees were required as prerequisites for all medical students, women were allowed entry on equal status as men, and the length of study was extended to four years. What is more, Johns Hopkins Medical School operated in close conjunction with its affiliate hospital so that students could experience hands-on training (Ludmerer 1996).

The 1910 Flexner Report followed the efforts of the AMA to help make the Johns Hopkins Medical School the gold standard in medical education. The report itself was funded by the Carnegie Foundation, an educational philanthropic organization endowed by steel magnate Andrew Carnegie, who hired Dr. Abraham Flexner to oversee a comprehensive review of medical schools in America and issue recommendations for their reform. The report found that the United States had a surplus of schools and that many of them had embarrassingly low standards for admission and graduation. It recommended consolidating the number of medical schools, which had reached a high-water mark of 162 in 1906, so as to eliminate those with antiquated facilities or thin faculty, and encourage the development of programs following the Johns Hopkins model. State legislatures used the report in conjunction with closely aligned AMA guidelines to establish standards governing medical schools (Beck 2004). Newly established philanthropic organizations, such as the Carnegie Institute and Rockefeller Foundation, used the report to determine which medical schools to support with grants.

Not all of the changes sparked by the Flexner Report and AMA were progressive. The consolidation of education led to a reversal of gains made by women in the medical profession and spelled the ultimate demise of homeopathy and eclectic medicine as respected alternatives to regular medicine. Following Elizabeth Blackwell's 1849 graduation from Geneva Medical College, opportunities for women to earn their MD had slowly increased within the United States. Thirty-seven out of 105 regular schools accepted women by 1893, and by 1899 women composed approximately 5% of all medical students (Morantz-Sanchez 1985). While some of these schools were top-tiered co-educational programs such as Johns Hopkins, many more were smaller programs or women's-only schools. Without the resources to meet the new standards, the latter schools and programs were eventually forced to close their doors. In addition, a number of coeducational schools that otherwise passed muster under the Flexner Report ended up succumbing to pressure from alumni who thought the presence of women lessened a school's prestige. They called for enrollment limits or outright bans on female students. The impact was marked: by the end of 1910 women composed less than 3% of the total medical school population and would generally remain below 5% for the next fifty years. The report also prioritized regular medicine over alternative traditions, thereby pushing homeopathic and eclectic physicians further to the margins and eventually leading the last medical school dedicated to homeopathy to close in 1920 and the last eclectic school to close in 1939 (Morantz-Sanchez, 1985).

The medical profession's relationship with women has been a topic of historical debate. In the early 1970s historians of women began heavily critiquing the male-dominated Gilded Age and Progressive Era medical profession for using medicine as a tool of social control. According to Barbara Ehrenreich and Deirdre English (1973), doctors encouraged a "cult of invalidism" among women that equated femininity with sickly helplessness. They argued that much of the medical care administered by men for women was essentially a series of gimmicks designed to make women respect male authority and act submissively. Ann Douglas Wood's research (1973) further emphasized the victimization of women as she singled out S. Weir Mitchell as a brutal patriarch who designed his popular rest cure to bully grown women into accepting submissiveness as their lot in life. Not by chance are Mitchell and the Gilded Age medical profession the object of scorn for many scholars. After treating writer and economist Charlotte Perkins Gilman for neurasthenia in 1887, Mitchell reportedly instructed her to devote her attention to her family and never again write. This drove Gilman to the brink of insanity and provided the impetus for her 1893 work "The Yellow Wallpaper," a semi-autobiographical short story of a woman's slide into madness as a result of her medical treatment.

Other scholars have faulted such social control interpretations as lacking contextualization and have identified ways woman have exerted agency within professional medicine. Regina Morantz-Sanchez (1985), for instance, has emphasized that the patriarchy amongst physicians was not much different from the patriarchy found elsewhere in American society at the time, and that criticism of it should be shared by the nation as a whole, not just the medical profession. She notes that women doctors themselves were divided on the question of the essential similarities and differences between men and women, and that women physicians, as well as men, performed the radical hysterectomies and ovariectomies frowned upon by feminist scholars. According to Morantz-Sanchez (2000), research into the doctor-patient relationship demonstrates that women were not all passive victims but could be adroit at "negotiating with power" in their interactions with physicians. Nancy Theriot's research (1993) supports similar conclusions: the sterilization operations that feminist scholars point to as evidence of patriarchy, for instance, were sometimes performed at the request of the patient to prevent unwanted pregnancies.

Public Health

Challenging professional medicine's concept of individual health was a public health movement that was coalescing around the concept of community health. Momentum for this movement traces back to the Civil War and the establishment of the US Sanitary Commission, a private–public organization that worked to keep healthy the hundreds of thousands of men and women hastily assembled for war (Martin 2012). Doctor Stephen Smith organized the American Public Health Association in 1872 and many physicians participated in the public health movement. Tensions grew between public health advocates and professional physicians who feared that effective public health efforts would steal away private practice patients (Starr 1982). Public health nonetheless grew to become a major component of America healthcare, gaining in importance throughout the Gilded Age and Progressive Era. The movement developed in three phases. The first phase focused on organizational development and the formation of groups of experts to help guide public health policy into the twentieth century. The second phase involved renewed efforts to tackle the threats posed by infectious diseases that had long plagued society. The third phase took place after the turn of the twentieth century when the government revamped its regulatory system so as to more effectively protect the health of Americans.

Among the most important institutional developments in public health were the settlement houses. Begun by Jane Addams in 1889, the settlement house movement brought the efforts of American women to bear upon the plight of America's poor, largely immigrant urban populations. By 1900 nearly every major American city had at least one settlement house. The movement began to define the charitable heart of progressivism. Women who staffed the houses often taught classes in pre- and post-natal care to new mothers and stayed current in the latest medical news. Many settlement houses contained medical dispensaries to distribute medical advice and medication (Rosen 1985). Importantly, settlement houses also served as centers of social research. Activists used access to poor neighborhoods to establish an incontrovertible link between poverty and public health. The publication of *Hull-House Maps and Papers* in 1895 and the work of Florence Kelley, for instance, provided a block-by-block analysis of the livelihoods of the urban poor and threats to health posed by criminal activities such as assault and prostitution as well as substandard housing and child labor. Alice Hamilton, a Hull-House alumna, became a pioneer in the study of occupational health as she drew attention to workplace safety. In 1908 Hamilton became a chief investigator for the Illinois Occupational Disease Commission before becoming the first female professor at Harvard University in 1919, accepting a position in the newly formed Department of Industrial Medicine.

Growing in conjunction with the settlement house movement were American nursing programs. Given that men dominated the doctoring profession, women interested in careers in healthcare often entered nursing, especially during the years following the Civil War, a bloody event in which many women served as nurses. Between 1880 and 1900, the number of nurses in the United States grew from 15,600 to 120,000, an increase that also saw the number of nursing schools grow from three in 1873 to 432 in 1900, a remarkable increase that reflects the rising influence of nursing in American healthcare (Morantz-Sanchez 1985). Beginning in 1893, health reformer Lillian Wald championed the role of the "public health nurse." She encouraged nurses to operate out of whatever systems would give them access to those in need of healthcare, including settlement houses, trade unions, and public schools (the latter of which allowed a coordinated effort to treat childhood afflictions such as scabies, ringworm, lice, and dermatitis). Wald, working with peers such as Mary Brewster, also helped establish the Visiting Nurses' Association of New York, an organization that quickly became a model for incorporating nurses into home healthcare (Kalisch and Kalisch 2004).

Despite the efforts of progressives such as Wald and Addams, many people in America lacked appropriate healthcare during the period, including southern blacks and immigrant factory workers. Southern blacks carried with them healthcare traditions from Africa, as Cotton Mather discovered back in 1722 when he learned from slaves of an efficacious strategy of inoculating against smallpox (Mather 1722). During slavery, slave owners had an economic incentive to allow at least minimal levels of healthcare so as to keep workers in the fields and performing domestic duties. After the Civil War, however, the health of southern blacks fell precipitously, as dislocation and poverty cast a long shadow over their care. The efforts of the Freedmen's Bureau during Reconstruction did little to help, and black codes and later Jim Crow laws kept southern blacks isolated from the white-dominated medical profession. As historians W. Michael Byrd and Linda A. Clayton have pointed out, southern blacks did not see an uptick in healthcare until the progressive impulse made its way to their populations on the eve of the First World War. This delayed incorporation into America's larger healthcare system came as result of racial, gender, and class prejudice that continued to stymie southern black healthcare through the twentieth century (Byrd and Clayton 2000). Poor immigrants to the United States also faced healthcare challenges. While some immigrant communities were able to retain traditional healthcare methods, including folk medicine and midwifery, many others lack proper healthcare. In particular were the large numbers of immigrants who ended up working in factories, displaced from their traditional Old World communities. For these immigrant workers, labor organizations such as the Knights of Labor and other fraternal groups sought to provide access to medical care and sometimes offered financial relief for on-the-job injuries. Employer-based workers' compensation did not become common in the United States until well into the twentieth century (Rodgers 1978).

Professional physicians' contribution to public health typically came in the form of dispensaries and hospitals. Dispensaries traced their roots back to the eighteenth century and by the late nineteenth century could be found operating in association with settlement houses, medical schools, and hospitals (Rosenberg 1985). These were places where the indigent could consult with a physician or a nurse and receive medicine, sometimes at a discount. The dispensary operating in conjunction with the Cooper Medical School of San Francisco for instance, supported seven clinics (eye and ear; medical; surgical; neurological; gynecological; genitourinary; and children) and served over 13,300 patients in 1893 alone, giving medical students plenty of opportunity to practice their trade. Serious cases that required overnight care were generally relegated to hospitals, which, during the late nineteenth century, were in the process of transforming from primarily charity organizations on the margins of medicine to centers of scientific medicine and treatment. From 178 hospitals active in 1872 to more than 4,000 in business by 1910, hospitals became destinations for more capital-intensive medical equipment such as X-ray machines and surgical units, investments that placed hospitals on the cutting edge of innovation but also increased healthcare costs as well as hospitals' reliance on managing administrators (Starr 1982). Dispensaries largely disappeared from the healthcare landscape by the 1920s, as reforms forced the closure of many medical schools, and hospitals began incorporating increasingly sophisticated outpatient programs.

A strengthened public health infrastructure and the growing influence of the germ theory lead to a sustained campaign against infectious diseases in the late nineteenth century. Bouts with epidemic diseases were nothing new to the United States. Indeed, America had wrestled with disease epidemics since the colonial era, with smallpox, yellow fever, and cholera still existing as feared killers going into the long Gilded Age and Progressive Era. Such diseases traditionally afflicted communities in waves and, given that there were no readily effective treatments available, public health officials relied heavily on quarantine (of individual homes as well as entire cities) to stop a disease's spread. In reaction to an 1878 yellow fever epidemic in the Caribbean, the federal government passed the National Quarantine Act designed to protect New Orleans by banning the entry of immigrants who might be carrying fever. Fear over contagious disease lead to backlashes against immigrants and heightened nativist sentiment (Schrag 2011). The work on germ theory by Louis Pasteur in France and Robert Koch in Germany lead to new ideas on how to combat infectious diseases, especially after Koch's 1884 discovery of *Vibrio cholera*, the waterborne microbe that caused cholera. Reforming the nation's sewage and public water systems became a public health imperative by the turn of the twentieth century, and chlorination—a cheap, effective disinfectant process that conveniently leaves a residue to encourage water purity—came into general use in the first part of the twentieth century to ward against waterborne diseases such as cholera and typhoid (Duffin 1999).

In addition to promoting public works to clean up sewage and drinking water supplies, public health advocates fought against disease through a series of educational and vaccination programs. In 1882 Koch identified *Mycobacterium tuberculosis*, the bacterium largely responsible for tuberculosis, the most lethal infectious disease in human history. At that time tuberculosis, or consumption, as it was often called, was responsible for approximately one death out of five in American cities. Linking transmission of the disease to a germ associated with the respiratory system, rather than inherited through parentage, as many had assumed, was a boon to public health advocates who hoped that they might be able to reduce the tuberculosis death rate through public education campaigns (Rothman 1995). Organizations such as the American Lung Association (originally founded in 1904 as the National Association for the Study and Prevention of Tuberculosis) printed and distributed posters to schools, settlement houses, and hospitals. These visual aids reminded citizens of the communicability of tuberculosis and encouraged them to cover their coughs and not spit in public. Concomitantly, cities such as New York were employing plain-clothes officers to patrol rail lines, ferries, and other modes of public transportation to enforce anti-expectorate laws. Beginning in the 1890s aggressive vaccination and antitoxin programs also went into effect aimed at stymieing the spread of epidemics such as smallpox (cases in New York City fell from 1,200 in 1878 to a mere six in 1909), diphtheria (antitoxin was developed in 1890 and by 1907 its death rate had dropped to one-fifth of the pretreatment rate), and typhoid (the entire US military was vaccinated against the illness by 1911) (Engs 2003). Vaccination programs were not always embraced by the populations they were intended to help. In Montreal in 1885, a smallpox epidemic that killed more than three thousand people caused a riot when rumors spread that mandatory vaccinations would cause the disease rather than protect against it (Duffin 1999). In 1901 the *New York Times* reported on the "widespread popular distrust of vaccine virus and antitoxin serums" (Anonymous 1901b, 6) that arose with rumors of unhygienic preparations and carried stories with headlines such as "Doctors Make Raid… Infected Children Torn from Shrieking Mothers" (Anonymous 1901a, 10).

The most deadly epidemic in American history, the "Spanish flu," afflicted communities from 1918 through 1919. Despite its name, the influenza epidemic almost certainly did not begin in Spain, but its origin has been the topic of historical debate, with northern India, Kansas, and France all being suggested as possibilities (Killingray et al 2011). Soldiers brought the disease home with them from European battlefields, spreading it to big cities and small town around much of the world. This influenza H1N1 pandemic killed between 50 and 100 million people worldwide (3–6% of the earth's population) and infected about a quarter of all Americans in two brutal waves, resulting in 500,000 to 600,000 deaths nationwide. Most flu deaths in America occurred within just a 9-month period and quickly overwhelmed the nation's public health infrastructure, forcing the establishment of emergency hospitals and morgues. Despite the flu's deadly impact, public memory of the epidemic faded at a surprisingly quick rate. Within a generation it was largely forgotten. Possible explanations include: the epidemic being overshadowed by the war; the epidemic being short-lived; and previous waves of epidemics had conditioned American communities to expect death by disease (Crosby 2003). More recently, however, memory of the Spanish flu and its devastation has spurred public health initiatives, such as the 1976 campaign to vaccinate 50 million Americans against swine flu, and public education campaigns during the 1990s and 2000s to teach people how to hygienically cough and wash their hands.

By the time of the 1918 influenza epidemic, the United States government was strengthening its dedication to public health by passing new regulatory legislation and eliminating overly restrictive laws. Influenced by muckrakers such as Samuel Hopkins Adams, whose *Great American*

Fraud (1905) cast doubt on America's drug manufacturers, and Upton Sinclair, whose *The Jungle* (1906) exposed the unsanitary conditions in Chicago's meat packing industry, congress passed the Pure Food and Drug Act in 1906 to provide regulatory oversight to the nation's food and drug supply. The progressive impulse at the start of the twentieth century also led states to enact labor legislation to protect women and children from unhealthy exploitation in factories and sweatshops. The Supreme Court endorsed those laws in *Muller v. Oregon* (1908), which held that America's success as a nation was inextricably linked to the health of future mothers (Kessler-Harris 2001). Birth control advocate Margaret Sanger stressed the link between women's health and the health of the nation as well in her pamphlet "Family Limitation" (1914) and through the family planning movement she spearheaded. Since 1873 Comstock laws, originally passed to fight obscenity, had made it illegal to distribute information and devices related to birth control. In 1916 Sanger established her Brooklyn birth control clinic and although she was arrested, her efforts lead to the unraveling of Comstock laws, the legalization of birth control, and the 1921 founding of the American Birth Control League (renamed Planned Parenthood in 1942) (Engelman 2011).

Eugenics represents one of the more notorious legacies of the public health movement. As initially proposed by Englishman Sir Francis Galton, eugenics sought to strengthen human evolution through sexual selection and was the product of the progressive impulse to improve society combined with scientists' fascination with genetics, heightened with the "rediscovery" of Gregor Mendel's research in 1900 and Thomas Hunt Morgan's 1915 chromosome theory of inheritance. Prompted by Anglo-Saxon racism and fears among the nation's dominant white population that the post-1890 influx of new immigrants would genetically weaken the United States, eugenicists sought to limit the ability of "undesirable" people to have children (Kevles 1985). Biologist Charles B. Davenport founded the Eugenics Record Office in Cold Springs Harbor in 1911 thanks to large grants from corporate philanthropic organizations such as Carnegie Institute and the Rockefeller Foundation. It soon became the national clearinghouse for eugenics information and public policy ideas. Advocates encouraged Americans to consider biology when choosing prospective husbands and wives, and even promoted "healthy family" and "healthy baby" competitions at state fairs to reward those deemed the most perfect specimens of humanity. Eugenicists also promoted immigration restrictions, culminating in the 1924 National Origins Act to keep out people from eastern and southern Europe deemed inferior to America's dominant Anglo-Saxon population (Kevles 1985). They advocated the forced sterilization of undesirable members of the population, including criminals, the insane, and the destitute—especially immigrants and non-whites. The Supreme Court gave its approval to eugenics sterilization for "the protection of the health of the state" in *Buck v. Bell* (1927) and laws targeting criminals and those with mental disorders spread rapidly in the United States. The enormity of the Nazi eugenics program turned public opinion in the United States against eugenics following World War II, but sterilization laws largely remained on the books and were enforced to various degrees going into the late twentieth century (Pernick 1996).

The Pharmaceutical Industry

Competing with professional physicians for the patronage of sick Americans were the nation's pharmaceutical manufacturers, who produced a wide variety of drugs designed to soothe the symptoms of suffering. Drugs had long been part of a physician's trade, but by the late nineteenth century professional physicians were seeking to distance themselves from their traditional reliance on heroic medicine. "I firmly believe that if the whole *materia medica*, as now used, could be sunk to the bottom of the sea," Dr. Oliver Wendell Holmes told a group of colleagues in 1860, "it would be all the better for mankind—and all the worse for the fishes" (Holmes 1860, 39). Pharmaceutical companies had many powerful drugs at their disposal (including alcohol, opium, cocaine, marijuana, and bromides) and marketed their products directly to the American consumer. What emerged in the Gilded Age was a thriving drug market that owed much of its success to a strategy of getting Americans to self-diagnose and self-medicate (Young 1974). By 1904 the AMA estimated that the American pharmaceutical industry was capitalized at $250 million and earned $74.5 million in yearly profits, an amount that exceeded the total value of the nation's production of chocolate, flavoring extracts, axle grease, beet sugar, glue, castor oil, lard, kindling wood, cosmetics, and gun finishing.

American drug companies rooted their success in advertising, which grew tremendously during second half of the nineteenth century. Much of this growth traces back to the Civil War, when Americans were reading newspapers in record numbers in their search for information about the battlefront. After the war the American habit of reading remained strong. Pharmaceutical advertisers invested heavily in print media to cultivate consumer markets for their products. An adman during the 1880s estimated that it took at least $50,000 in advertising to create a market for a new medicine in the United States, a price that could dwarf other business expenses, including product manufacturing, bottling, and shipping (Cantley 1898). Given their reliance on print advertising, some drug companies more closely resembled publishing firms than pharmaceutical laboratories. For instance, the Doctor Miles Medical Company of Elkhart, Indiana—purveyor of fine tinctures such as its patented Nervine—owned its own printing press and bindery, employed more typesetters than chemists, and in 1889 alone distributed more than 100,000 sixteen-page booklets in the hopes of making their company a household name (Cray 1984). The drug firm Dr. D. Jayne and Sons targeted immigrant populations with its line of "Family Medicines," printing brochures in twelve languages. The 1897 *Sears, Roebuck & Co. Catalogue* dedicated twenty pages to advertising over 400 different medicines (Israel 1897). In 1905 the *New York Times* estimated that, as a percentage of the industry's total worth, American pharmaceutical companies were spending more on advertising than any other commercial interest on earth.

The goal of such advertising was to get the American consumer to bypass physicians and reach directly for the medicine bottle. Marketers' brochures often imitated useful family almanacs, listing common symptoms, illnesses supposedly associated with symptoms, and names of medicines the company recommended for relief. For instance, *Warner's Safe Cure Almanac, 1892* claimed that "headache, palpitation and insomnia, neuralgia, sick headache, etc.," could be the result of "nervous prostration," an illness that the Warner drug company claimed was best treated with the combined use of two products: its flagship medicine Warner's Safe Cure and its nervous-system fortifying partner Warner's Safe Nervine (Warner 1891, 36). For those who lacked the wherewithal to self-diagnose, drug companies such as Doctor Miles Medical offered "treatment by mail" programs that encouraged sick Americans to submit letters containing biographical information (including age, sex, occupation, and home town) and a list of their symptoms. Each letter was reportedly reviewed by a company doctor, who, in turn, mailed back seemingly tailor-made prescriptions from the company's catalog (Schuster 2011). The overall impact of such advertising was the increased medicalization of American life. Common experiences such as headaches and insomnia that might have been seen as normal, albeit unpleasant, aspects of life a generation earlier were being recast by the turn of the twentieth century as symptoms of illness treatable through medicine for purchase.

By the turn of the twentieth century, the pharmaceutical industry attracted the attention of progressive journalists and regulators concerned that drug firms were making ill-gotten profits from addictive and dangerous medications. In 1905 medical journalist Samuel Hopkins Adams published in *Collier's Weekly* his ground-breaking series "The Great American Fraud," a deep investigation into pharmaceuticals. Adams concluded that the industry was "founded on fraud and poison" (Adams 1906, 3). Documenting numerous deaths and debilitating addictions reportedly caused by some of the nation's most popular medicines, Adams derided as reckless the prioritizing of profit over health found in the industry's efforts to get Americans to self-diagnose and self-medicate. A year later, the AMA, which saw the pharmaceutical firms as ruthless turn-of-the-century competitors, dedicated funds to reprint and widely distribute Adams's series as a book so as to further mobilize public opinion against the industry. In addition to waging a publicity campaign against drug companies, the AMA also established the Council on Pharmacy and Chemistry to review medicines marketed by drug manufacturers. The AMA passed bylaws to mitigate abusive drug advertising within affiliate medical journals (Boyle 2013).

With popular opinion turning against drug companies and the AMA taking the lead in curbing the industry's influence, government participation soon followed. This was not simply about the court of public opinion. Within the judicial system, drug companies found their questionable public reputations to be a dangerous liability. For instance, in 1906 the landmark case *Miles Medical Company v. May Drug Company* centered on whether the May Drug Company had the legal right to discount the Miles Medical products they put on their shelves. Judge James R. Macfarlane ruled that although Miles Medical had won its legal argument, he could not rule in the medicine company's favor because its "treatment by mail" marketing scheme represented a "serious menace" to the "health and lives of the public" and its strategy of having people self-diagnose and self-medicate was the "height of folly" and "contrary to public policy" (Anonymous 1906a, 177; 1906b, 1459; Cray 1984). In what would become a hallmark of twentieth-century progressive government, the federal government relied on regulation to curb the dangerous behavior of drug companies. The Pure Food and Drug Act of 1906 and subsequent founding of the Food and Drug Administration (FDA) created the regulatory infrastructure to act as a counter weight to aggressive pharmaceutical marketing. Although loopholes in the law initially prevented the FDA from exerting much influence over drug companies other than insisting on listing ingredients on labels, by 1912 amendments allowed the FDA to crack down on fraudulent claims of effectiveness made by drug advertisers. Shortly thereafter, state legislatures began passing an advertising law known as the Model Statute that made it illegal to make any false "assertion, representation or statement of fact" about a product (Hess 1922). Within a generation, by the end of the 1930s, what evolved within the United States was a drug system that designated more powerful pharmaceuticals as "prescription" drugs unmarketable directly to consumers and sold only with a physician's authorization. Less-powerful, "over-the-counter" drugs could be advertised directly to consumers and did not need a physician's prescription (Boyle 2013).

While the AMA and medical doctors emerged from the progressive era as gatekeepers of American pharmaceutics, the Harrison Narcotics Tax Act of 1914 established a federal policy of banning altogether certain drugs—opiates and cocaine—deemed too dangerous for public use. America's addiction to narcotics grew out of the Civil War, when many soldiers developed morphine addictions while seeking pain relief from injuries. The use of opiates grew in the wake of America's importation of Chinese labor to work on the railroads. By 1914 narcotic use, as seen through the nation's anti-Asian nativist eyes, was associated with the shiftless and the foreign. Cocaine, once widely used as treatment for hay fever and to cure alcoholism and morphine addiction, had gained a notorious reputation by 1914 as a drug that would drive people to rape and murder, placing it alongside opiates as forbidden. By 1924 heroin—a medicine originally created by Bayer pharmaceutical to help people kick their morphine addictions—was added to the Harrison Act's list of banned substances. With the passage of the 1937 Marijuana Tax Act, the foundation for what would become America's late-twentieth-century "war on drugs" had been established (Musto 1999).

Health and Popular Culture

As professional physicians, public health advocates, and the pharmaceutical industry jostled for position within the nation's healthcare system, individual American citizens took keener interest in their own health. Beginning in the late nineteenth century and accelerating into the next, articles and stories that connected health to issues of the day appeared in the nation's books, magazines, and newspapers. Leading a strenuous life and making the most out of growing leisure time became facets of personal health for Americans as they sought to adjust their lives to meet the new demands of a modernizing nation. Gender roles complicated those adjustments.

For many people by the turn of the century, the traditional role of women in society seemed antiquated. Since 1848 the women's movement led by Elizabeth Cady Stanton and Susan B. Anthony had used the idea of political equality to advocate the expansion of women's rights. In her 1898 book *Women and Economics*, feminist economist Charlotte Perkins Gilman offered additional justification: individual and national health. Commonly held prejudice against women's abilities kept them chained to domestic labor, Gilman argued, and thereby robbed the nation of women's productive potential. What is more, not all women were suited for domestic labor, Gilman pointed out. Forcing them to perform housework in lieu of other careers took a toll on women's psychological, emotional, and physical wellbeing, a theme she expanded on in her 1916 essay "The Nervous Breakdown of Women." The path to improved women's health, according to Gilman (who suffered breakdowns herself), was to shrug off traditional expectations and encourage women to follow their natural strengths and interests and share with men the responsibility for life in the public sphere (Bederman 1995; Gilman 1916). Settlement house leader Jane Addams echoed Gilman's sentiment. In an 1892 lecture entitled "The Subjective Necessity for Settle Houses," Addams explained that in addition to helping their nations, women who dedicate themselves to working in settlement houses help themselves by avoiding the prostration and despondency that can grow when they feel trapped at home, unable to use their talents to improve the community at large. "There is nothing after disease, indigence, and a sense of guilt," Addams explained, "so fatal to health and to life itself as the want of a proper outlet for active faculties" (Addams 1912).

Men's health was hampered by traditional sex roles as well, as the pressure of being the head of the family and financially and socially successful proved more than many men could bear (Filene 1998). Theodore Dreiser, for instance, suffered a profound breakdown when publishers snubbed his first novel, *Sister Carrie*, and he felt as if he were a failure as a writer as well as a failure as a husband. Numerous male patients at the Cooper Dispensary in late-nineteenth century San Francisco also exhibited paralyzing despondency, symptoms that attending physicians often attributed to the demoralizing effect of unemployment and the inability to live up to personal and social expectations. The healthy solution was for men to psychologically divest from their careers and invest more heavily in their relationships with family and friends. This process was multi-generational. "I used to worry about the career of my boy," a lawyer recovering from a breakdown wrote in 1910, "now I believe I should be glad if he were to decide to become a farmer. I dread the dangers of his striving for success; I want him instead to keep healthy and happy" (Schuster 2011).

If how to remain healthy and happy was the question, then Americans found their answer in physical exercise and activity. Theodore Roosevelt recognized as much in his 1899 speech "The Strenuous Life" that warned Americans about becoming complacent in their comfortable cities and homes. Bicycling, considerably less expensive and more convenient than horseback riding, became a popular activity starting in the 1890s, giving men and women the opportunity to exercise in the open air and enjoy freedom of movement, especially in paved urban areas. Physical education became part of public school curriculums starting in the late nineteenth century as educators sought to balance mental and physical activities. They feared that stimulating young minds without also building young bodies would become a "menace to the future health of the community" as boys grew into weak men and girls grew into barren women. The nation's colleges and universities also began heavily promoting men and women's athletics during the late nineteenth century with the proliferation of rowing, track and field, baseball, and football programs. The last proved to be so brutally violent as to warrant the 1906 founding of the National College Athletics Association in the hopes of reducing gridiron injuries and deaths (Schuster 2011). For those not in school or college, community centers such as the Young Men's Christian Association (YMCA) and Young Women's Christian Association (YWCA) sprang up in cities during the late nineteenth century to help Americans remain active and healthy. New sports such as basketball and volleyball were created within the YMCA/YWCA system during the 1890s to provide indoor sporting opportunities—and to enhance fitness and vitality—for men and women during the doldrums of winter (Putney 2001).

From the perspective of many Americans, the rapid rate of urbanization was a health crisis in itself that warranted a concerted effort to reintegrate the natural environment into everyday life. During the second half of the nineteenth century, cities began incorporating major park projects, such as New York's Central Park (1857) and San Francisco's Golden Gate Park (1870), as a way of providing healthy havens for urban populations. Camping also became a popular healthy activity. Traditionally, camping was prescribed for cases of consumption with the understanding that fresh air would provide a cure. By the 1870s doctors also began prescribing camping to men suffering from frayed nerves, a condition supposedly cured by the healing powers of nature and the fortifying act of living primitively. Within a generation, women, too, would be prescribed the camp cure (Mitchell 1888). Naturalist John Muir also directed attention to the restorative aspects of nature when he founded the Sierra Club in 1892 and led a national campaign to get Americans out of the city and back to the land "where nature may heal and give strength to body and soul" (Muir 1912). By the time historian Frederick Jackson Turner presented his celebrated "frontier thesis" in 1893, the United States was well on its way to preserving wilderness that would serve as a surrogate frontier to keep alive the hardy rough-and-ready spirit of America. The federal government had already established Yellowstone National Park (1872) and Yosemite National Park (1890), and would follow with the establishment of the National Forest Service (1905) and National Park Service (1916).

Leisure presented another way for people to fortify their health. Leisure has had a complicated place in the lives of Americans, a population that valorized hard work and discouraged sloth within a cultural tradition that sociologist Max Weber called the "Protestant work ethic" (Weber 1930). During the late nineteenth century, however, more and more Americans began seeing leisure as an energizing counterweight to the depleting character of modern life. Hobbies such as painting, writing, music, and woodworking—anything that could generation "wholesale amusement," in the words of one doctor—became sanctioned ways for people to take time off from their regular workplace and family duties and focus on repairing their mind and body (Holbrook 1878). Out of this emerged occupational therapy shortly after the turn of the century (Anthony 2005). Health tourism also gained momentum going into the twentieth century. John Harvey Kellogg's Battle Creek Sanitarium, for instance, sought to cultivate healthy habits by encouraging well-heeled patrons to experiment with vegetarian diets and practice various exercise routines. California's Loma Linda Sanitarium, founded in 1900, promised ideal weather and landscape to create an "ethereal trust for the purpose of comforting the weary, the lonely, the sick and distressed" (Anonymous 1900a). Railroads also encouraged health tourism in a bid to increase traffic, with the Kansas Pacific railway printing brochures encouraging the "pleasure-seeker, tourist and invalid" to patronize Colorado's resorts and attractions, and California's Southern Pacific Railroad promoting the Golden State to the "invalid, tourist, capitalist, and homeseeker" (Anonymous 1892). Out of the push for health tourism would emerge the conventional two-week vacation, a hallmark of middle-class life during the first part of the twentieth century that allowed the nation's weary population to take a break from work to rest and recuperate (Aron 1999).

Conclusion

Doctor Mitchell's 1869 warning that the demands of daily life would increase "wear and tear" on the minds and bodies of Americans was prescient. The Gilded Age and Progressive Era was a time of rapid development in American medicine, as the concept of *health* gained currency and began exerting considerable influence within the United States. The nation as a whole was undergoing a remarkable period of development that could be destabilizing as people wrestled with how to best deal with the impact of urbanization, immigration, and the maturation of competitive capitalism. Medical doctors coalesced around the concept of *medical science* to guide research and education, and in the process forged a powerful professional identity in the American Medical Association. Public health advocates saw health as a community matter connected to socioeconomic issues warranting broad-based action by institutions such as settlement houses and the government to curb problems associated with poverty and disease. The pharmaceutical industry reaped profits by convincing people to question their personal health, self-diagnose sickness, and self-medicate. A popular culture took shape by the turn of the century in which Americans paid greater attention to healthy habits and developing healthy lifestyles.

Even today, the degree to which the healthcare reforms of the Gilded Age and Progressive Era have contributed to the good health of Americans remains unclear and hotly contested by scholars. British physician Thomas McKeown suggested in 1979 that, in general, a population's health has had more to do with socioeconomic developments than advances in medical science. Historian Gerald Grob (2002) agrees that this was indeed the case of the United States during the late nineteenth and early twentieth centuries. Life-spans expanded proportionately with income, Grob noted, as poor people suffered from the unhealthy effects of poverty while the wealthy enjoyed the longevity that comes with a proper diet, safety, and comfort. Not until the antibiotic era of the mid-twentieth century, according to Grob, could medicine genuinely claim to have improved the lives of Americans beyond what socioeconomic improvement might bring.

Recent trends within the historical study of medicine include breaking away from the traditional concept of *medicine* and moving towards a broader understanding of *health*. Much of this has to do with rethinking developments during the Gilded Age and Progressive Era that tied the meaning of *medicine* to the professional development of medical doctors and medical science and, as a result, the term risks being too exclusive. Christian Scientists, for instance, would not claim to practice medicine despite helping people live happier, healthier lives. The same could be said for psychologists, settlement house workers, and outdoor enthusiasts who strive for mental and physical improvement. Also, historians such as Michel Foucault (1994) have pointed out that the concept of *medicine* carries with it considerable intellectual baggage, including scientific hubris and the doctor–patient relationship that historically have led to the abuse of power. *Health*, on the other hand, allows for historical studies on wellness that are not wedded to the more strictly defined medical perspective. It enabled Elizabeth Lunbeck (1996) to explore psychiatry as an expression of early-twentieth century popular culture, for instance, and for Nancy Tomes (1999) to trace the impact of germ theory on the daily lives of Americans.

References

Adams, Samuel Hopkins. 1906. *The Great American Fraud: Articles on the Nostrum Evil and Quacks, in Two Series, Reprinted from Collier's Weekly*. New York: P. F. Collier and Son.

Addams, Jane. 1912. *Twenty Years at Hull House with Autobiographical Notes*. New York: The Macmillan Company.

Albanese, Catherine L. 2007. *A Republic of Mind & Spirit: A Cultural History of American Metaphysical Religion*. New Haven, CT: Yale University Press.

Anonymous. 1892. "California: Its Attractions for the Invalid, Tourist, Capitalist, and Homeseeker." San Francisco: Southern Pacific Rail Road Company.

Anonymous. 1900. "Loma Linda California for Health and Pleasure." Loma Linda, CA: Loma Linda Sanitarium.

Anonymous. 1900. "Secret Nostrums and the Journal." *Journal of the American Medical Association* 34, June 2: 1420.

Anonymous. 1901a. "Doctors Make Raid." *New York Times* February 2, 10.

Anonymous. 1901b. "Vaccine and Antitoxin." *New York Times* December 8, 6.

Anonymous. 1902. "Protection Against Public Nuisances." *Medical News* 80: 463.

Anonymous. 1905. "Doctors Assail Patent Medicine Advertising." *New York Times* October 19, 6.

Anonymous. 1906a. "Miles Loses Suit in Equity." *American Druggist and Pharmaceutical Record* 48, January–June: 177.

Anonymous. 1906b. "Dr. Miles Medical Company vs. the May Drug Company." *Journal of the American Medical Association* 46, May 12: 1459–1460.

Anthony, Susan Hall. 2005. "Dr. Herbert J. Hall: Originator of Honest Work for Occupational Therapy, 1904–1923 (parts 1 and 2)." *Occupational Therapy in Health Care: A Journal of Contemporary Practice* 19: 3–32.

Aron, Cindy S. 1999. *Working at Play: A History of Vacations in the United States*. New York: Oxford University Press.

Beard, George M. 1881. *American Nervousness: Its Causes and Consequences*. New York: G. P. Putnam's Sons.

Beck, Andrew H. 2004. "The Flexner Report and the Standardization of American Medical Education." *The Journal of the American Medical Association* 291, May: 2139–2140.

Bederman, Gail. 1995. *Manliness & Civilization: A Cultural History of Gender and Race in the United States, 1880–1917*. Chicago: University of Chicago Press.

Boyle, Eric W. 2013. *Quack Medicine: A History of Combating Health Fraud in Twentieth-Century America*. Santa Barbara, CA: Praeger.

Byrd, W. Michael and Linda A. Clayton. 2000. *An American Health Dilemma: A Medical History of African Americans and the Problems of Race: Beginnings to 1900*. New York: Routledge.

Cantley, A. C. 1898. "Some Facts about Making Patent Medicines." *The Chautauquan: A Weekly Newsmagazine* 27, July: 389.

Clarke, Edward H. 1873. *Sex in Education; or, a Fair Chance for Girls*. Boston: J. R. Osgood and Co.

Cray, William C. 1984. *Miles 1884–1984: A Centennial History*. Englewood Cliffs, NJ: Prentice Hall.

Crosby, Alfred W. 2003. *America's Forgotten Pandemic: The Influenza of 1918*. New York: Cambridge University Press.

Duffin, Jacalyn. 1999. *History of Medicine: A Scandalously Short Introduction*. Toronto: University of Toronto Press.

Engelman, Peter C. 2011. *A History of the Birth Control Movement in America*. Santa Barbara, CA: Praeger Press.

Engs, Ruth Clifford. 2003. *The Progressive Era's Health Reform Movement*. Westport, CT: Praeger Press.

Ehrenreich, Barbara and Deirdre English. 1973. *Complaints and Disorders: The Sexual Politics of Sickness*. New York: The Feminist Press.

Filene, Peter G. 1998. *Him/Her/Self: Gender Identities in Modern America*. 3rd ed. Baltimore, MD: Johns Hopkins Press.

Foner, Eric and John A. Garraty, eds. 1991. *The Reader's Companion to American History*. Boston: Houghton Mifflin Company.

Foucault, Michel. 1994. *The Birth of the Clinic: An Archaeology of Medical Perspective*, trans. A. M. Sheridan Smith. New York: Vintage Books.

Gerrish, Frederic Henry. 1889. "The Special Function of the American Academy of Medicine." *Philadelphia Medical Times* 19, April: 465–476.

Gilman, Charlotte Perkins. 1898. *Women and Economics: A Study of the Economic Relation of Men and Women as a Factor in Social Evolution*. Boston: Small, Maynard & Company.

—. 1892 (1973). "The Yellow Wallpaper." *New England Magazine* 11, 5: 647—657. Reprint, New York: The Feminist Press. Citations refer to the Feminist edition.

—. 1916. "The Nervous Breakdown of Women." *Forerunner* 7, August: 202—206.

Grob, Gerald N. 2002.*The Deadly Truth: A History of Disease in America*. Cambridge, MA: Harvard University Press.

Hess, Herbert W. 1922. "History and Present Status of the 'Truth-in-Advertising' Movement." *Annals of the American Academy of Political and Social Science* 101 May: 214.

Holbrook, M.L. 1878. *Hygiene of the Brain and Nerves and the Cure of Nervousness. With Twenty-Eight Original Letters From*

Leading Thinkers and Writers Concerning Their Physical and Intellectual Habits. New York: M. L. Holbrook.

Holmes, Oliver Wendell. 1860. "Currents and Counter-Currents in Medical Science: An Address Delivered before the Massachusetts Medical Society and the Annual Meeting, May 30, 1860." Boston: Ticknor and Fields.

Israel, Fred L., ed. 1897. *Sears, Roebuck Catalogue.* Chicago: Sears, Roebuck and Co.

Kalisch, P. and Kalisch, B. J. 2004. *American Nursing: A History.* 4th ed. Philadelphia: Lippincott, Williams, and Wilkins.

Kessler-Harris, Alice. 2001. *In Pursuit of Equity: Women, Men, and the Quest for Economic Citizenship in 20th-Century America.* New York: Oxford University Press.

Kevles, Daniel J. 1985. *In the name of Eugenics: Genetics and the Uses of Human Heredity.* Berkeley: University of California Press.

Killingray, David, et al. 2011. *The Spanish Influenza Pandemic of 1918–1919: New Perspectives.* New York: Routledge.

Laird, Pamela Walker. 1998. *Advertising Progress: American Business and the Rise of Consumer Marketing.* Baltimore, MD: Johns Hopkins University Press.

Lears, Jackson. 1994. *Fables of Abundance: A Cultural History of Advertising in America.* New York: Basic Books.

Le Page du Pratz, Antoine Simon. 1758 (1763). *The History of Louisiana, or the Western Parts of Virginia and Carolina.* Translation, London: T. Becket and P. A. De Hondt.

Ludmerer, Kenneth M. 1996. *Learning to Heal: The Development of American Medical Education.* Baltimore, MD: Johns Hopkins University Press.

Lunbeck, Elizabeth. 1996. *The Psychiatric Persuasion: Knowledge, Gender, and Power in Modern America.* Princeton, NJ: Princeton University Press.

Martin, Justin. 2012. *Genius of Place: The Life of Frederick Law Olmsted.* Cambridge, MA: Da Capo Press.

Mather, Cotton. 1722. *An Account of the Method and Success of Inoculating the Small-Pox, in Boston in New-England.* London: J. Pells.

Menand, Louis. 2002. *The Metaphysical Club: A Story of Ideas in America.* New York: Farrar, Straus and Giroux.

McKeown, Thomas. 1979. *The Role of Medicine: Dream, Mirage, or Nemesis.* Princeton, NJ: Princeton University Press.

Mitchell, S. Weir. 1869. "Wear and Tear." *Lippincott's Magazine of Literature, Science and Education* 4: 493–502.

—. 1888. *Doctor and Patient.* Philadelphia: J. B. Lippincott.

Morantz-Sanchez, Regina Markell. 1985. *Sympathy & Science: Women Physicians in American Medicine.* New York: Oxford University Press.

—. 1999. *Conduct Unbecoming a Woman: Medicine on Trial in Turn-of-the-Century Brooklyn.* New York: Oxford University Press.

—. 2000. "Negotiating Power at the Bedside: Historical Perspectives on Nineteenth-Century Patients and their Gynecologists." *Feminist Studies* 26, Summer: 287–309.

Muir, John. 1912. *The Yosemite.* New York: The Century.

Musto, David F. 1999. *The American Disease: Origins of Narcotic Control.* 3rd edn. New York: Oxford University Press.

Pernick, Martin S. 1996. *The Black Stork: Eugenics and the Death of "Defective" Babies in American Medicine and Motion Pictures since 1915.* New York: Oxford University Press.

Putnam, James Jackson. 1895. "Remarks on the Psychical Treatment of Neurasthenia." *Boston Medical and Surgical Journal* 132, May: 505–508.

Putney, Clifford. 2001. *Muscular Christianity: Manhood and Sports in Protestant America, 1880–1920.* Cambridge, MA: Harvard University Press.

Rodgers, Daniel T. 1978. *The Work Ethic in Industrial America, 1850–1920.* Chicago: University of Chicago Press.

—. 1998. *Atlantic Crossings: Social Politics in a Progressive Age.* Cambridge, MA: Harvard University Press.

Rosen, George. 1985. "The First Neighborhood Health Center Movement: Its Rise and Fall." In *Sickness & Health in America: Readings in the History of Medicine and Public Health,* ed.Judith Walzer Leavitt and Ronald Numbers, 475–489. Madison: University of Wisconsin Press.

Rosenberg, Charles E. 1985. "Social Class and Medical Care in 19th-Century America: The Rise and Fall of the Dispensary." In *Sickness & Health in America: Readings in the History of Medicine and Public Health,* ed. Judith Walzer Leavitt and Ronald Numbers, 273–286. Madison: University of Wisconsin Press.

Rothman, Sheila M. 1995. *Living in the Shadow of Death: Tuberculosis and the Social Experience of Illness in American History.* Baltimore, MD: Johns Hopkins University Press.

Rovinsky, Alexander. 1901. "The Physician as a Social Factor." *Medical News* 79, November: 692.

Russett, Cynthia Eagle. 1989. *Sexual Science: The Victorian Construction of Womanhood.* Cambridge, MA: Harvard University Press.

Schrag, Peter. 2011. *Not Fit for Our Society: Immigration and Nativism in America.* Berkeley: University of California Press.

Schuster, David G. 2011. *Neurasthenic Nation: America's Search for Health, Happiness, and Comfort, 1869–1920.* New Brunswick, NJ: Rutgers University Press.

Shorter, Edward. 1993. *From Paralysis to Fatigue: A History of Psychosomatic Illness in the Modern Era.* New York: Free Press.

Sinclair, Upton. 1906. *The Jungle.* New York: Doubleday, Page.

Starr, Paul. 1982. *The Social Transformation of American Medicine.* New York: Basic Books.

Theriot, Nancy. 1993. "Women's Voices in Nineteenth-Century Medical Discourse: A Step Toward Deconstructing Science." *Signs* 19: 1–31.

Tomes, Nancy. 1999. *The Gospel of Germs: Men, Women, and the Microbe in American Life.* Cambridge, MA: Harvard University Press.

—. 2005. "The Great Medicine Show Revisited." *Bulletin of the History of Medicine,* 79, Winter: 627–663.

Warner, H.H. 1891. *Warner's Safe Cure Almanac 1892.* Rochester, NY: H. H. Warner.

Warner, John Harley. 2003. *Against the Spirit of System: The French Impulse in Nineteenth-Century American Medicine.* Baltimore, MD: Johns Hopkins University Press.

Weber, Max. 1930. *The Protestant Ethic and the Spirit of Capitalism,* trans. Talcott Parsons. London: G. Allen and Unwin.

Whorton, James C. 2002. *Nature Cures: A History of Alternative Medicine in America.* New York: Oxford University Press.

Wiebe, Robert H. 1967. *The Search for Order, 1877–1920.* New York: Hill & Wang.

Wood, Ann Douglas. 1973. "'The Fashionable Diseases': Women's Complaints and Their Treatment in Nineteenth-Century America." *The Journal of Interdisciplinary History* 4: 36–44.

Young, James Harvey. 1961. *The Toadstool Millionaires: A Social History of Patent Medicines in America before Federal Regulation*. Princeton, NJ: Princeton University Press.

—. 1974. *American Self-Dosage Medicines: An Historical Perspective*. Lawrence, TX: Coronado Press.

Further Reading

Bliss, Michael. 2011. *The Making of Modern Medicine: Turning Points in the Tradition of Disease*. Chicago: University of Chicago Press.

Brandt, Allan M. 1987. *No Magic Bullet: A Social History of Venereal Disease in the United States since 1880*. New York: Oxford University Press.

Burnham, John C. 1987. *How Superstition Won and Science Lost: Popularizing Science and Health in the United States*. New Brunswick, NJ: Rutgers University Press.

Caplan, Eric. 1998. *Mind Games: American Culture and the Birth of Psychotherapy*. Berkeley: University of California Press.

Curtis, Heather D. 2007. *Faith in the Great Physician: Suffering and Divine Healing in American Culture, 1860–1900*. Baltimore, MD: Johns Hopkins University Press.

Gosling, F. G. 1987. *Before Freud: Neurasthenia and the American Medical Community, 1870–1910*. Chicago: University of Illinois Press.

Hale, Nathan G. 1971. *Freud and the Americans: The Beginnings of Psychoanalysis in the United States, 1876–1917*. New York: Oxford University Press.

Haller, John S. 1994. *Medical Protestants: The Eclectics in American Medicine, 1825–1939*. Carbondale: Southern Illinois University Press.

Harrington, Anne. 2008. *The Cure Within: A History of Mind–Body Medicine*. New York: W. W. Norton & Company.

Kraut, Allen M. 1995. *Silent Travelers: Germs, Genes, and the Immigrant Menace*. Baltimore, MD: Johns Hopkins Press.

Lutz, Thomas. 1991. *American Nervousness, 1903: An Anecdotal History*. Ithaca, NY: Cornell University Press.

Micale, Mark. 2008. *Hysterical Men: The Hidden History of Male Nervous Illness*. Cambridge, MA: Harvard University Press.

Nye, Robert. 1997. "Medicine and Science as Masculine 'Fields of Honor.'" *OSIRIS* 12: 60–79.

Pernick, Martin S. 1985. *A Calculus of Suffering: Pain, Professionalism, and Anesthesia in Nineteenth-Century America*. New York: Columbia University Press.

Reiser, Stanley Joel. 2009. *Technological Medicine: The Changing World of Doctors and Patients*. New York: Cambridge University Press.

Rosen, George. 1993. *A History of Public Health, Expanded Edition*. Baltimore, MD: Johns Hopkins Press.

Rosenberg, Charles E., ed. 2003. *Right Living: An Anglo-American Tradition of Self-Help Medicine and Hygiene*. Baltimore, MD: Johns Hopkins University Press.

Rothstein, William G. 1987. *American Medical Schools and the Practice of Medicine: A History*. New York: Oxford University Press.

Sappol, Michael. 2002. *A Traffic in Dead Bodies: Anatomy and Embodied Social Identity in Nineteenth-Century America*. Princeton, NJ: Princeton University Press.

Sicherman, Barbara. 1977. "The Uses of a Diagnosis: Doctors, Patients, and Neurasthenia." *Journal of the History of Medicine* (January): 33–54.

Smith-Rosenberg, Carroll and Charles Rosenberg, "The Female Animal: Medical and Biological Views of Woman and Her Role in Nineteenth-Century America." *Journal of American History* 60 (September): 332–356.

Walzer-Leavitt, Judith. 1986. *Brought to Bed: Childbearing in America, 1750–1950*. New York: Oxford University Press.

Warner, John Harley. 1986. *The Therapeutic Perspective: Medical Practice, Knowledge, and Identity in America, 1820–1885*. Cambridge, MA: Harvard University Press.

Whorton, James. 1984. *Crusaders of Fitness: The History of American Health Reformers*. Princeton, NJ: Princeton University Press.

Vogel, Morris J. and Charles E. Rosenberg. 1979. *The Therapeutic Revolution: Essays in the Social History of American Medicine*. Philadelphia, University of Pennsylvania Press.

Zaretsky, Eli. 2005. *Secrets of the Soul: A Social and Cultural History of Psychoanalysis in America*. New York: Vintage.

Part V

Political Leadership

Chapter Twenty-One

Gilded Age Presidents

Justus D. Doenecke

Historians have often found the Gilded Age an embarrassment, an unfortunate hiatus between the noble crusades embodied in the War for the Union and the progressive movement. Indeed, as Vincent P. De Santis notes, writers "seemed to have competed with one another to find suitably disparaging phrases to censure the politics of the age for its barrenness, dreariness, and monotony" (De Santis 1975 75). Charles W. Calhoun depicts the era from 1877 to 1900 as "the most disparaged period in the political history of the United States" (Calhoun 2007 239).

For decades the presidents of this period have been neglected, patronized, and occasionally vilified. Usually portrayed as weak, isolated, ineffectual men of portly bearing and drab countenance, they were more often subject to quips than analysis. In 1935, novelist Thomas Wolfe wrote of these chief executives as "the lost Americans: their gravely vacant and bewhiskered faces mixed, melted, swam together… Which had the whiskers, which the burnsides: which was which?" (Wolfe 1935, 121). Matthew Josephson's highly influential *The Politicos* (1938) offered a Marxian–Beardian interpretation of America's leaders. Comparing this book to his still more famous *The Robber Barons* (1934), he began: "In a preceding work, I wrote of men who spoke little and did much. In the present work … I write of men who, in effect, did as little as possible and spoke all too much" (Josephson 1938, v). In his classic *American Political Tradition and the Men Who Made It* (1948), the usually perceptive Richard Hofstadter wrote that Rutherford B. Hayes and Benjamin Harrison were "as innocent of distinction as they were of corruption," "famous in American minds chiefly for their obscurity." Hofstadter patronized James A. Garfield as "essentially an honest and worthy soul" (Hofstadter 1948 170) and dismissed Chester A. Arthur as a reformed spoilsman. Grover Cleveland, a "dogmatic, obtuse, and insensitive" man, "turned his back on distress more acute than any other president would have the sang-froid to ignore" (182). In short, leadership was portrayed as uninspired, the presidents unequal to the tasks confronting them.

Hayes Administration

A major breakthrough came in 1969 with the appearance of H. Wayne Morgan's *From Hayes to McKinley: National Party Politics, 1877–1896*, which showed that politicians dealt with significant issues. A further step was taken in the 1970s when the University Press of Kansas launched its American Presidency series, a breakthrough significant enough for Calhoun to write, "Nothing has done more than this series to spur a reconsideration of the Gilded Age presidency." Presidents who were seen as "ciphers at worst or mere office mongers at best now appear to be active, hard-working administrators," men who had clear notions of public policy and sought to steer Congress towards their goals (Calhoun 2002, 229). In the first decade of the twenty-first century, Arthur M. Schlesinger, Jr. launched the "American Presidents" series, which offered much briefer but equally appreciative accounts. The *Journal of the Gilded Age and Progressive Era*, published by the Society for Historians of the Gilded Age and Progressive Era in collaboration with Cambridge University Press, in many ways a sequel to the *Hayes Historical Journal*, also offers responsible treatment of such chief executives.

Little substantial scholarship on Rutherford B. Hayes was produced until the appearance of Kenneth E. Davison's study (1972), which renders strong praise of his subject. "He was not brilliant or colorful, but he was kind, high-principled, public-spirited, unaffected, loyal, and singularly decent and honest, a man without pretense, without

A Companion to the Gilded Age and Progressive Era, First Edition. Edited by Christopher McKnight Nichols and Nancy C. Unger.
© 2017 John Wiley & Sons, Inc. Published 2017 by John Wiley & Sons, Inc.

egoism." "Of the five Republican Presidents from 1869 to 1893," Hayes "deserved most to be reelected," in part because he created "the ablest presidential term between the end of the Civil War and the twentieth century" (Davison 1972, 235, 237). Hayes recovered the authority of the presidential office, in shambles after the impeachment of Andrew Johnson and the scandals of Ulysses Grant. He resisted the Senate oligarchy in choosing cabinet members, reformed the New York Customhouse (a major source of patronage), vetoed badly needed appropriation bills because of destructive riders, and withstood Democratic efforts to reopen the contentious 1876 election.

In covering the controversial Hayes–Tilden race, Davison concurs with Paul L. Haworth's pioneering study (1906) in claiming that highly contested Florida belonged to Hayes, which would have given him a legitimate victory. (Davison later said that Hayes would have won a fair election easily [Davison 1978, 111].) Essentially a conciliator, Hayes ably expedited America's transition from sectional antagonism to national harmony. Drawing heavily upon the research of Vincent P. De Santis (1959), Davison defends Hayes's removal of federal troops from the last two outposts in the South, Louisiana and South Carolina. The president really had no choice: the Grant administration had already ended military occupation; public opinion opposed further Reconstruction; the carpetbag governments lacked national respect; and the army was not strong enough to enforce federal policy in the South. Hayes greatly underestimated the obstacles to black equality, though he wholeheartedly supported the Fourteenth and Fifteenth amendments.

Davison concedes certain mistakes, noting Hayes bestowed government posts on undeserving Democrats to gain political support and to members of the controversial Louisiana Returning Board, a body that had helped make him president. He finds Hayes playing a mixed role during the Great Railroad Strike of 1877, exercising considerable restraint under great pressure but engaging in strike-breaking to restore normal service. He calls the removal of the Ponca Indian tribe from its reserve in southeastern Dakota to Indian Territory (Oklahoma) a tragic error.

Ari Hoogenboom has contributed two definitive works on the nineteenth president: *The Presidency of Rutherford B. Hayes* (1988) and *Rutherford B. Hayes: Warrior and President* (1995). Like Davison, Hoogenboom challenges the stereotype of ineptitude and inefficiency; rather, Hayes was "both a good man and an able president" (Hoogenboom 1988: 223), who enhanced the power and prestige of his office and was in fact a precursor of the progressive movement. Far from being incompetent, "he was an astute political analyst who often masked his calculated political moves with a cloak of principle" (Hoogenboom 1995, 3).

Hayes, Hoogenboom observes, was probably legally entitled to be president, though one could not determine the legitimate winner in Florida. He defends Hayes against the accusations made by a number of historians—W.E.B. Du Bois (1935), William Gillette (1979), and Eric Foner (1988)—that he appeased white-supremacist Democrats. Continuing a "bayonet policy" in the South would have impossible in the best of times and absolutely hopeless given a hostile Congress, apathetic public, and severe economic depression. Conservative white Democrats had already gained control of all but two southern states before Hayes took the oath of office. Though the Louisiana and South Carolina Democrats soon broke promises to Hayes that they would respect the civil rights of black and white Republicans, the president lacked any leverage in the matter: "nothing was given up that had not already been lost" (Hoogenboom 1995, 2). Hayes merely ordered small contingents of troops from Baton Rouge and Columbia back to their barracks, withdrawing support from Republican regimes that were already untenable. The choice was never whether to pull out the troops but simply when. During his presidency he issued ringing vetoes of Democratic efforts to cripple civil rights legislation. Once he saw that further federal action was unattainable, he worked ceaselessly, even after leaving office, to foster education for blacks. Hoogenboom is more critical of Hayes's Indian policy, specifically for the severalty policy the president endorsed, which focused on individual—not tribal—ownership of land, for it meant "the annihilation of the Native Americans' way of life" (Hoogenboom 1988, 165).

Hoogenboom defends Hayes's conduct in the Great Railroad Strike, as the president neither did the bidding of the railroad managers nor broke the walkout. Ordering federal troops only when exhausted local or state authorities requested them, he specifically instructed the army not to quell the strikers or operate the trains but simply to protect public property. Admittedly his commitment to maintaining industrial peace and one's right to work benefited management more than labor. Although Hayes never learned how to control capitalists, he was no tool of big business, much less a Social Darwinist, for he distrusted plutocrats and monopolists and endorsed railroad regulation.

Hayes's most serious mistake, argues Hoogenboom, lay in his failure to seek reelection. Knowing the president had no political leverage, Congress had little reason to do his bidding. The biographer finds Hayes ambivalent towards civil service reform; he cleansed the Interior Department but not the more significant Treasury Department. Reluctance to fire able civil servants marks Hayes as the least partisan chief executive between John Quincy Adams and Theodore Roosevelt. Such initial moves helped lay the foundation for the modern governmental bureaucracy, a serious step towards establishing the modern presidency.

Hans L. Trefousse's *Rutherford B. Hayes* (2002) compares the president favorably to another leader who assumed office after a contested election, George W. Bush. Unlike his twenty-first-century counterpart, Hayes sought to conciliate various factions within the nation. Finding Hayes one of the best-educated men to occupy the White House,

Trefousse portrays him as honest, evenhanded, and humane. In covering the Hayes–Tilden election, Trefousse sees so much intimidation of blacks in the disputed states that Hayes was rightfully chosen president. Though Hayes abandoned the Republican governors of Louisiana and South Carolina, he sought adherence to the Reconstruction amendments. Certainly, Hayes was naive in accepting southern pledges at full value, but he had no option. He did not capitulate to extremist demands for war against Mexico during a time of border tension. He vetoed an immigrant exclusion bill that would have violated the Burlingame Treaty of 1868 made with the Chinese empire.

Rethinking the Garfield Years

Theodore Clarke Smith's *Life and Letters* (1925) was the first major biography of James A. Garfield. It benefited from extensive use of manuscript sources, including Garfield's journals, turned over to Smith by the president's widow. Because of the richness of these sources, the book, pedantic in tone, reads in part like an autobiography, in part like a source book, though quotations are too often garbled. At times offering what seems like a sanitized exercise in hagiography, Smith doubts the often-repeated charge that the president was the instrument of James G. Blaine, Garfield's secretary of state and leader of the Half- Breeds, a Republican faction that emphasized a high tariff.

Allan Peskin's definitive biography *Garfield* (1978) stresses the brevity of his stormy presidency. "His accomplishments were neither bold nor heroic," Peskin writes, but the age itself did not call for heroism. Far from being the self-made man portrayed by Horatio Alger in his biography *From Canal Boy to President* (1881), Garfield embodied one contradiction after another: "a pacifist turned soldier, an educator turned politician, a preacher turned economist, a man of essentially literary tastes cast in the role of party chieftain, a husband who, at length, fell in love with his wife, a man racked by self-doubts who was, at the same time, convinced of his higher destiny." His career centered on a major contradiction: "a misplaced intellectual thrown onto the stage of public life, moving restlessly between the worlds of action and introspection, drawing strength from both but at home in neither" (Peskin 1978, 64; 612). The twentieth president was no calculating "trimmer" but a moderate by instinct.

Peskin presents the Stalwarts, the Republican wing stressing a harsh southern policy, as uncompromising. Its leaders, such as Senator Roscoe Conkling of New York, should have been satisfied with their share of Garfield's cabinet appointments, but they wanted all or nothing. The biographer implies that as president Garfield would not have been Blaine's tool but very much his own man. Broadly perceived, the early fights of his administration reveal the president's desire to redress governmental balance by curbing the increasing power of the Senate. Certainly Garfield was not a quintessential civil service reformer, having no quarrel with the spoils system in principle, but the Blaine–Conkling rivalry involved far more than a patronage struggle. Conking spoke only for a faction and a state; "Blaine looked to the future, to the problems of an industrialized America with the trials of the Civil War behind it" (Peskin 1978, 557).

In presenting his account, Peskin eliminates certain stereotypes. Garfield only worked on canals for six weeks, was not an outstanding college student, always tempered his ambition with fatalism, and helped to modernize both the presidency and the Republican party.

Justus D. Doenecke's *The Presidencies of James A. Garfield and Chester A. Arthur* (1981) notes that as a man Garfield was extremely intelligent, sensitive, and alert. Decades before Woodrow Wilson made his mark, the Ohio politician was "the scholar in politics." Indeed, his knowledge of governmental workings was unmatched. Obviously his advocacy of education as the solution to the tragic plight of African Americans was simplistic, but Doenecke sees it as an essential first step in their advancement. Garfield's flirted with the Virginia Readjusters, an insurgent movement within the Democratic Party headed by Governor William Mahone and centering on his state's antebellum debt. His activity here revealed a needed flexibility, one that aided both his party and a segment of the defeated South.

Yet Doenecke finds the Garfield record an ambivalent one. The president lacked judgment on crucial points, as seen by his replacement of General Edwin A. Merritt, the reformist collector of the port of New York, by Half-Breed politico William H. Robertson. Whether he could have really recovered after the bloody Robertson fight, which he won, remains problematic, as he was assassinated within two months. Doenecke doubts whether Garfield would have curbed the power of his secretary of state, whose influence extended far beyond matters of diplomacy. As Garfield rigidly adhered to laissez faire and hard money, his ability to cope with a declining economy remains in doubt. To grow in office, the president needed greater distance from the Half-Breeds.

Doenecke sees Blaine's diplomacy as particularly embarrassing, taking issue with such pro-Blaine historians as Milton Plesur (1971) and Edward P. Crapol (1973) to back such critics as David M. Pletcher (1962), upon whom Doenecke draws heavily, John A. Garraty (1968), and Charles C. Campbell (1976). He finds the secretary continually blundering. In a dispute between Mexico and Guatemala in 1881, Blaine misled Guatemalan dictator Justo Rufino Barrios, thereby delaying the very settlement he sought. During the war between Peru and Chile the same year, called the War of the Pacific, the secretary failed to watch his emissaries closely, foolishly stiffened Peru's intransigence, rigidly adhered to an impossible status quo, and sought to saddle Garfield's successor with extremely risky policies. In attempting to terminate the Clayton–Bulwer treaty of 1850, giving the United States and Britain joint control over any canal built across the isthmus of Panama, Blaine used crude arguments and sophistic logic; his efforts failed.

In 1978, Margaret Leech and Harry J. Brown published *The Garfield Orbit: The Life of James A. Garfield*. Leech died in 1974, having finished eight chapters. Brown, coeditor of the Garfield diary (1967–81), added the half dealing with Garfield's congressional life and presidency. The work captures the president's need for approval, negative physical reaction to stress, and moody, self-indulgent personality. It treats with respect his religious searching, omnivorous reading habits, and wide grasp of public affairs. Brown sees the showdown between Garfield and Conkling as inevitable, but claims that the chief executive could have been more courteous, telling the Stalwart boss just what he intended concerning the New York collectorship and why. Surely, given the impact on the unbalanced mind of assassin Charles Guiteau, "the victory was not worth the price" (Leech and Brown 1978, 234).

Ira Rutkow, a professor of medicine, devotes almost half of his *James A. Garfield* (2006) to the assassination and its aftermath. As Garfield's presidency was brief, he had few accomplishments, something that reduced his leadership to a tantalizing "what if." Clumsy in controlling his party's factions and indecisive by nature, he lacked natural leadership, failing to dominate men or events.

The Surprising Presidency of Chester A. Arthur

George Frederick Howe's *Chester A. Arthur: A Quarter Century of Machine Politics* (1934) marks the president's first biography by a professional historian. Based on a Harvard doctoral thesis, Howe maintains that Arthur filled "a place of power and responsibility far above his aspirations, bravely and adequately, if not with greatness." Though Arthur was a practical reformer, not a doctrinaire one, he advanced the cause of civil service reform, honestly prosecuted a mail scandal known as the Star Route cases, vetoed a "pork barrel" river-and-harbors bill, and began modernizing the American navy.

In 1975 Thomas C. Reeves published his definitive *Gentleman Boss: The Life of Chester A. Arthur*. Based largely on recently discovered manuscript collections, some stored in wooden fruit boxes, Reeves demolishes old stereotypes in portraying his subject as an able, sensitive, and humane figure. Just as important, Reeves revealed that during his last two years in the White House, Arthur lived with the knowledge that he was a dying man, suffering from incurable Bright's disease. Reeves thereby contradicts John A. Garraty, who claimed that Arthur's "positive accomplishments had been negligible" (Garraty 1968, 281) or with a 1970s textbook that contends that aside from the Pendleton Civil Service Act, "it was doubtful whether even he could remember having done anything in particular" (McDonald, Decker, and Govan 1972, 561).

Reeves stresses his subject's achievements. In addition to his positive naval and civil service policies, Arthur usually made sound appointments and appointed an able tariff commission. If his terminal illness often made him lethargic and depressed, he still appears more decisive and straightforward than his vacillating predecessor, Garfield. All told, Arthur is portrayed as a good president, a man who overcame his shady reputation as Stalwart sycophant to command the respect of his fellow citizens. Reeves refers to "the abrupt but nonetheless genuine transformation from a spoils-hungry, no-holds-barred Conkling henchman into a restrained, dignified Chief Executive who commanded the admiration of the American people" (Reeves 1975, 420).

To Reeves, Arthur was a deeply emotional, even romantic person. Arthur possessed an extraordinary sensitivity to death. The loss of his wife Ellen was partially responsible for "the tragic gloom that would haunt his presidency." Knowing of his fatal illness, Arthur kept his name in the 1884 race while secretly telling his lieutenants not to seek his nomination. To withdraw, Arthur believed, would only cast doubt upon his competence, raise suspicions concerning his health, and imply that he was a coward. Reeves disputes Stanley Hirshson's claim (1962) that Arthur's administration was unconcerned about southern blacks. On the contrary, the president personally protested against the Supreme Court's decision in the Civil Rights Case of 1883 and was often praised by the African American press.

Doenecke finds Arthur one of the nation's great political surprises, for few expected such a limited man to do a commendable job. Despite his poor health and dubious reputation, Doenecke writes that he governed competently, succeeding to a degree never acknowledged by the press, fellow politicians, the great mass of the citizenry—and, most of all, historians. Arthur could be vindictive, as when he deposed reformer Silas Burt, naval officer to the New York Customhouse. Equally true, his laissez-faire ideology equaled that of Garfield; hence, he was unable to deal with a failing economy. But some appointments were superior. Secretary of State Frederick Theodore Frelinghuysen, in particular, revealed a genuine grasp of America's economic problems and offered a positive program, based upon reciprocal trade, to meet them. Arthur showed genuine courage in vetoing a flawed steamship safety bill (passed again once necessary revisions were made), a pork-barrel rivers-and-harbors bill, and, most important of all, a racist Chinese Exclusion Act of 1882. Similar resolution is found in the endorsement of his tariff commission, in so doing bucking strong protectionist sentiment. Doenecke echoes Howe and Reeves concerning the Pendleton Act, the Star Route affair, and naval reform. Arthur was somewhat insensitive to the condition of African Americans, yet his southern strategy, which centered on Republican alliances with white independents, won substantial black endorsement. His stress on Indian severalty, in retrospect, inadvertently led to further degradation, but leading reformers sincerely considered this policy the best alternative. His state papers were often far-sighted, showing a grasp of such matters as consular reform, commercial agreements, currency policy, and presidential disability.

Arthur, Doenecke concedes, initiated little new legislation and was assuredly not proactive, but he conducted the office with dignity and restraint. By twentieth-century standards, he would be evaluated as a weak president. Doenecke finds this judgment unfair, for Arthur seldom had to confront directly the massive problems created by the burgeoning technological revolution. By the standards of his time, which stressed administrative competence, Arthur was most adequate. If as an institution, the presidency did not gain much power, it did not lose much either.

Zachary Karabell's *Chester Alan Arthur* (2004) finds his subject a cipher, one whose rather large footprint has been "trampled on and all but erased." Yet this circumstance was quite understandable, for Arthur was "an unexpected president during a time when no one expected much from the presidency, and in an age of low expectations he was more than satisfactory." Turning away from such "troubling intractables" as freedom, democracy, and equality, he sought refuge in order, stability, and prosperity. To Karabell, Arthur's greatest achievement lay in his signing of the Pendleton Act, legislation that created the modern bureaucratic state, a professional civil service being necessary to democracy and good government. The president was also "a vital element" in asserting United States primacy in South and Central America. Above all, "Arthur managed to be a decent man and a decent president in an era when decency was in short supply" (Karabell 2004, 2, 5, 139, 141, 143).

More Than Two Nonconsecutive Terms: Competing Interpretations of Grover Cleveland

In 1923 Robert McElroy published the first scholarly life of Grover Cleveland (*Grover Cleveland, the Man and the Statesman*). In a two-volume work totaling close to 800 pages, McElroy pursued thousands of handwritten documents, some almost illegible and often reproduced verbatim. The tone of the work is set by statesman Elihu Root, who wrote in the introduction that Cleveland applied "old and simple tests of morality" to everything he did. McElroy seldom faults his subject, be the matter government appointments, civil service policy, the Pullman strike, financial negotiations with J.P. Morgan, or the Samoan and Venezuelan crises. Only in the case of Hawaiian annexation did the president make "many minor mistakes" (McElroy 1923, 73).

In 1933, Allan Nevins's equally massive *Grover Cleveland: A Study in Courage* was published; it devotes three-fourths of its 766 pages to Cleveland's two presidencies. During the same year, Nevins published an edition of the Cleveland papers (Nevins 1933b). Often a paean to its subject, Nevins writes: "He left to subsequent generations an example of the courage that never yields an inch in the cause of truth" nor "surrenders an iota of principle to expediency." Whether preserving presidential power against congressional onslaughts, defying Tammany, crusading for a low tariff, furthering the modernization of the navy, supporting the new Interstate Commerce Commission, opposing the annexation of Hawaii, or ignoring jingoes who sought to exploit the Cuban rebellion, the president took the wise course. His preservation of the gold standard kept the nation from "heavy loss and perhaps economic chaos," although he tore the Democratic Party apart in the process. Calling Cleveland a reformer, not a progressive, Nevins claims that in his day "the hour of progressivism had not yet struck, but the need for more efficiency and earnestness in government was great" (Nevins 1933a, 766, 215).

Nevins is not totally positive. Cleveland recklessly risked war during the Venezuela crisis of 1895–96, encouraging irresponsible imperialist sentiment in the process, though the president deserves praise for ultimately resolving the matter. Often, though, Nevins lays negative aspects of Cleveland's presidencies at the hands of others. He blames the ordering of federal troops to repress the Pullman strike in 1894 upon the impetuous and bellicose Attorney General Richard Olney, who led the president sadly astray at several points. Similarly, Olney hindered anti-trust initiatives that Cleveland sorely desired. The Supreme Court deserves the blame for declaring the income tax unconstitutional (*Pollock v. Farmers' Loan and Trust Company*, 1893); Cleveland favored the measure.

In a brief account, *Bourbon Leader: Grover Cleveland and the Democratic Party* (1957), Horace Samuel Merrill portrays Cleveland as being unable to take the presidency in his stride, lacking "the broad view that stimulates public leaders to great success." At times "politically awkward, inconsistent, uncertain and obtuse, … his knowledge and understanding left much to be desired." He was a spokesman for business interests who sought to limit government regulation and prevent domination by farmers, wage-earners, and incompetent and corrupt officeholders. In sum, he was "much more successful as a defender of the *status quo* than as a crusader for change" (Merrill 1957, 91; 134; 190).

In his *Presidencies of Grover Cleveland* (1988), Richard E. Welch, Jr. finds Nevins's portrayal of the president simplistic, as it suggests that the Gilded Age so suffered from a lack of courageous politicians that Cleveland appears as an "overweight George Washington." In reality, the chief executive was "a man of little charisma, less eloquence, and limited imaginative and intellectual powers." Furthermore, he contained "a tangle of self-contradictions: humble and ambitious, courageous and cautious, practical and moralistic, irritable and kindly, aggressive and sensitive" (Welch 1988, 213–14, 17).

Welch finds Cleveland strengthening the presidency, giving the executive branch a vigor and morale it had not seen in twenty years, even if his conception of the office was "vaguely monarchical." If he was not a candidate for Mount Rushmore, he was not an ideological reactionary or tool of plutocrats. Though his accomplishments did not radically transform America, they were substantial. The president protected many western lands from railroad and timber corporations, doubled the size of the National Forest Reserve, and fought railroads on behalf of homesteaders. He signed the Interstate Commerce Act even as he harbored reservations concerning the constitutional soundness of "government by commission." He denounced protectionist lobbyists, warned against the dangers of monopoly, and sought voluntary arbitration of labor disputes. Though Cleveland neither modernized the federal government nor changed the institutional structure of his office, his electorate made no demands he do so. "He advocated the reform of personal behavior, not the reform of governmental structure" (Welch 1957, 215, 213–14, 222).

In some ways, Welch concedes, Cleveland was weak or inept. Though the president was undoubtedly correct in opposing the free and unlimited coinage of silver, he offered farmers no solution for their increasing debt. Efforts at tariff reform were terribly artless, too cautious in rationale and too unsuccessful in result to create needed dialogue over economic development and consumer welfare. In dealing with the Pullman strike, he failed to consult with state and local officials, did not supervise Olney, and allowed the federal government to be used in a one-sided manner. An anti-Cuban bias marred his dream of mediating between insurgents and their Spanish rulers. Believing African Americans inferior, he was far more concerned with retaining the Democratic allegiances of the South than protecting blacks from intimidation. He did not object to Jim Crow ordinances or segregated education. Because he abdicated his role as party leader, he inadvertently fostered the fatal split of the Democrats in 1896.

Welch contests many textbook stereotypes. Cleveland's 1884 victory over James G. Blaine was less attributable to disaffected Mugwumps, a group of upper-class patrician reformers, than to Conkling's refusal to forget party rivalries. Similarly, the triumph of Benjamin Harrison in 1888 should not be ascribed to the Murchison letter, in which the British minister ineptly endorsed the incumbent president, or to Indiana's "floaters," paid by Republican national treasurer W.W. Dudley to vote against Cleveland. Instead, Cleveland failed to supply needed direction to his inept campaign. Cleveland's famous 1887 veto of a bill providing free seed for drought-stricken Texas farmers was motivated less by callousness as by an effort to preserve a Jacksonian tradition wherein individual effort, private charity, and local assistance should alleviate poverty.

The book challenges certain historians in particular. Welch sees Merrill's portrait of Cleveland as "Bourbon leader" simplistic at best. He finds Cleveland neither a reactionary nor proponent of rule by a self-chosen elite. Contradicting H. Wayne Morgan (1969) and John G. Sproat (1968), Welch affirms that Cleveland was not hypocritical concerning civil service reform. Though partisan considerations dominated many of his appointments in his second term, Cleveland brought a larger percentage of the federal bureaucracy under the Pendleton Act than has any other president. Welch doubts the arguments of Tom E. Terrill (1973) and Walter La Feber (1963), as he denies that Cleveland's low-tariff policies were rooted in a strategy of economic imperialism. Siding with Paul S. Holbo (1970), Welch sees the president focusing on lowering domestic prices, in fact showing less interest in reciprocity than Chester Arthur. Welch also differs with R. Hal Williams (1972), who views Cleveland's Hawaiian diplomacy as marked by "a mixture of admirable principle and blundering naiveté" (Welch 1988, 192); instead, Cleveland effectively postponed the march towards empire.

Alyn Brodsky's *Grover Cleveland: A Study in Character* (2000), the first full-scale biography in close to seventy years, is strongly eulogistic. On almost every issue, including government appointments, silver policy, or the bargain with J.P. Morgan, Brodsky sees Cleveland acting responsibly. He does, however, fault the president on several matters. During the Venezuela boundary dispute, Cleveland first yielded to the irascible temper of Secretary of State Richard Olney, drafting a belligerent war message that fostered such jingoistic sentiment that it risked a shooting war. His fight over tariff reform was counterproductive, for he unnecessarily made enemies when he needed all the congressional support he could find. In dealing with Native Americans, Cleveland's approach was commendable in such matters as civilization, citizenship, and assimilation but foolish in insisting that English be the sole medium of instruction in government schools.

In a brief account titled *Grover Cleveland* (2002), Henry F. Graff notes that his subject made no effort to help the freedman, lacked the tact needed to reconcile North and South, adopted a destructive "antistatist Jeffersonianism," and ran a lifeless campaign in 1888. On the other hand, Graff defends the 1894 "gold deal" with Morgan, since allowing the United States to go on a silver standard would have shaken financial confidence at home and abroad.

Revisionism Can Only Go So Far: The Presidency of Benjamin Harrison

In 1968, when Harry J. Sievers published the third volume of his massive study (subtitled *The White House and After)*, Benjamin Harrison finally had a biographer. For eighteen years, historian Albert T. Volwiler held exclusive access to the Harrison papers, but was only able to edit the president's correspondence with James G. Blaine (Volwiler 1940). In 1950 the Arthur Jordan Foundation of Indianapolis, which financed Harrison research, shifted its support to Sievers, who had written his doctoral thesis at Georgetown University on the chief executive's early career (Spetter 1993).

Siever's volume is long on narrative of Harrison's personal life, short on interpretation of policy. Over half the work covers Harrison's first year in office. Before Sievers, historians had rated Harrison at best only an "average" president, as humdrum as his era. Sievers concedes that Harrison "seems to emerge greater as a man than as a president," but presents him as one possessing an "active intellect firmly backed by moral courage." He finds his subject compiling "a strong record of constitutional government which enabled the country to approach the threshold of world power with prudence and caution" (Sievers 1968, 277, 4). He backs Harrison's hard money stance, citing Gresham's Law that cheap currency drives out the dearer. Sievers is uncritical concerning Hawaiian annexation and minimizes the vigorous naval expansion advanced by Navy Secretary Benjamin F. Tracy. Such topics as Indian policy, Senator Henry W. Blair's education bill, and the Sherman Anti-Trust Act are totally neglected.

Homer E. Socolofsky and Allan B. Spetter's *The Presidency of Benjamin Harrison* (1987) is far more analytical. Socolofsky focused on domestic policy, Spetter on foreign affairs. The authors challenge the popular stereotype that depicts their subject as at best a figurehead, at worst a nonentity. Certainly, there was far more to his presidency than apocryphal stories concerning his "corrupt" campaign or his feuds with House Speaker Thomas Reed of Maine and Senators Matthew Quay of Pennsylvania and Thomas Platt of New York. A surprisingly strong president, Harrison had no qualms about expanding executive power, in this sense serving as a role model for William McKinley. His first two years in office—which produced such landmark legislation as the McKinley tariff, the Sherman Anti-Trust Act, and the Sherman Silver Purchase Act—compare in impact to Lincoln's and Wilson's initial two years; Congress was one of the most productive in all American history, having a record for constructive legislation not equaled for decades. Support for African Americans, as shown by his support of Senator Henry Blair's education bill and Senator Henry Cabot Lodge's misnamed "Force Bill," embodied "the most courageous stand by any president of his era in favor of black Americans" (Socolofsky and Spetter 1987, 207).

Some myths are destroyed: like Richard E. Welch, Jr., Socolofsky and Spetter discount Dudley's role in the 1888 campaign, claiming that the tariff played the crucial role. Because of the frequent illness of Secretary of State James G. Blaine, Harrison often directed foreign policy, deserving credit for fostering the new navy, a Samoan protectorate, the first Pan-American Conference, and commercial reciprocity. "Clearly, the president stimulated the national self-assertion that led the United States inevitably toward the dramatic events of 1898" (Socolofsky and Spetter 1987, 126).

In Harrison's case revisionism can only go so far. Socolofsky and Spetter acknowledge Harrison's lack of imagination and reserved and cold manner, possessing "all the attractiveness of a dripping cave." In many cases, he tactlessly alienated party leaders, driving "the Republican elephant alone." The president was "ever the Whig at heart," supporting but not initiating legislation (Socolofsky and Spetter 1987, 34, 77, 47). By backing the McKinley tariff, Harrison committed a first-class political blunder, for the public blamed high prices on legislation yet untested. Though Harrison endorsed the Sherman Anti-Trust Act, he never attempted to enforce the law, much less explore regulatory options created by the bill. He remained oblivious to labor unrest and the plight of the farmer.

Charles W. Calhoun's *Benjamin Harrison* reiterates many of the conclusions made by Socolofsky and Spetter. Harrison, Calhoun maintains, was no caretaker but "a legislative president far more than most other nineteenth-century chief executives" (Calhoun 2005, 3). Ironically, his activist agenda, evidenced by the strong legislative record of the fifty-first Congress, frightened many conservative voters in 1890, handing the House to the Democrats. As with previous historians, Calhoun downplays Dudley's effort to buy Indiana votes in 1888, arguing that southern intimidation of black voters was far more important. He agrees with Robert Beisner (1975) in finding Harrison helping to usher in a "new paradigm" in foreign policy, one that focused on a diplomacy acting less in response to other powers than in engaging in a more purposeful and coordinated effort.

A Turning-Point Presidency: William McKinley and the Rise of Modern America

Scholarly studies on McKinley's presidency begin with publisher Charles S. Olcott's two volume *Life of William McKinley* (1916). Olcott drew from the diaries of three people close to the president: George B. Cortelyou, his aide and literary executioner; William R. Day, secretary of state; and Charles G. Dawes, controller of the currency. Because the study reproduces many documents, letters, and speeches, at times it resembles an anthology.

For years historians and textbooks have dismissed McKinley as "spineless,""a postage-stamp President," "a good, dull man," "a tool of vested interests," a person who, in Theodore Roosevelt's words, possessed "no more backbone than a chocolate éclair." In contrast, Olcott is eulogistic, presenting an almost Lincoln-like figure. McKinley's gold position was "unmistakably sound." By 1897 he had "completely overthrown the spoils system" (1: 342). McKinley wanted war with Spain "to end a situation that had become insufferable" (2: 25). Olcott justifies McKinley's suppression of the Philippine insurrection, portraying rebel leader Emilio Aguinaldo as a reckless dictator. The president "was no Levite to pass by on the other side when he saw a man stripped and beaten and left half dead by robbers" (Olcott 1916, 1: 342, 2: 25, 188). After China's Boxer

Rebellion, McKinley's light indemnity prevented dismemberment while keeping the Open Door open.

It took close to thirty-five years before McKinley was again the subject of serious work. In her *In the Days of McKinley* (1959), Margaret Leech presents an almost encyclopedic tome, such a beautifully written book that reviewer John Morton Blum called it "a first-rate study of a second-rate president" (Blum 1959, 1). Yet, despite its title, the work lacks a certain proportion. For example, she devotes lengthy chapters to the infirmities, fits, and seizures of the president's wife Ida, and to the triumphal return of naval hero Admiral George Dewey, but says little on the underlying economic and intellectual developments of the era, much less pays attention to voices of protest. Like Olcott, she relies heavily on Cortelyou's diary and Dawes's journal. This sympathetic intimate study does ably capture the core of her subject's identity: "In brains and heart, he was himself the average middle-class American, abounding in optimism, proud of the national efficiency and enterprise; respectful of self-made success, and pious in devotion the past" (Leech 1959, 35).

Of necessity, Leech engages in much demythologizing. The claim was often made that a prominent Ohio industrialist so dominated the president that, to cite a poem of Vachel Lindsay, he was "Mark Hanna's McKinley, His slave, his echo, his suit of clothes" (poem "Bryan, Bryan, Bryan, Bryan" in Lindsay 1925, 96–105). In reality, McKinley was the dominant figure, Hanna treating him with conspicuous deference.

Though she is generally sympathetic to her subject, on some matters Leech is quite critical. She finds McKinley's much touted support of bimetallism full of "threadbare arguments," denying "the legitimate public demand for enlightenment" (Leech 1959, 78). The chief executive erred in making John Sherman secretary of state and choosing Russell A. Alger to head the war department; Sherman was growing increasingly senile, Alger a disastrously bad manager of men and materiel. In 1900, McKinley sacrificed himself to political expediency by reversing his position on a tariff for newly conquered Puerto Rico. In the same year, he attacked trusts in general, but did not propose concrete legislation to curb their power.

In regard to the Spanish–American War, Leech argues that even when the *Maine* was sunk, McKinley did not expect diplomacy to fail. During the crucial last week of March 1898, when the nation needed a bold assertion of leadership, McKinley remained silent and uncommitted. Instead of breaking diplomatic relations with Spain, the president should have permitted Prime Minister Praxedes Sagasta, who was attempting to meet American demands, more time to resolve the Cuban crisis. Though he "remained the captive of caution and indirection," even a more cautious president could not have prevented war. Finding himself forced to act, McKinley "rightly refused to abdicate his function as Commander in Chief, and leave nation, as well as party, divided and rudderless in a time of crisis" (Leech 1959, 185).

Though commander in chief, McKinley took no action to resolve a clash between Admirals William T. Sampson and Winfield Scott Schley. Nor did he remedy the chaos found in the army of General William Rufus Shafter. Once the war ended, Leech argues, McKinley's reaction to revelations of logistical incompetence were belated. Neglecting journalists' reports of the Philippine insurrection, McKinley gave far too much authority to the inept General Elwell S. Otis. More important, McKinley stubbornly maintained that most Filipinos sought to live under American sovereignty, even as they were waging massive guerilla warfare to secure total independence.

Four years later, H. Wayne Morgan became the first professional historian to examine McKinley's leadership. In *William McKinley and His America* (1963), the author presents a highly favorable portrait. McKinley restored prosperity, unified North and South, and preserved the nation's credit. He sought eminence, not riches, possessed an admirable caution, and offered a vision of economic nationalism. Had he lived out his second term, this friend of labor would have cracked down on trusts and advanced commercial reciprocity.

Morgan concedes that McKinley lacked "creative vigor" and surely did not rank among the "great" presidents. By his conciliatory skills, however, he paved the way for more activist successors. In restoring unity within his party, "he brought many skills, born of patience, experience and calmness of temper, fortified by his belief in the national system that party unity and public trust could construct." His greatest contribution lay in foreign policy, for he sought international cooperation and insisted that reluctant Americans accept "the burdens of greatness in world affairs." In domestic policy, he possessed less vision, facing "issues with old ideas simply because no precedent guided him, and it was difficult to tell how far he could go and still retain the authority of public support" (Morgan 1963, 528–529).

In his treatment of the Spanish–American War, Morgan stresses that McKinley's "deep sense of humanitarianism made him look with horror upon the savage events in Cuba" (Morgan 1963, 335). Concurring with Leech, the biographer finds McKinley's silence after the *Maine*'s sinking inexplicable. The president's diplomacy exhibited both consistency and courage but lacked a needed imagination, for he could not posit any alternative to eventual intervention. McKinley might have called an international meeting where, at the very least, a settlement could have been proposed.

Overall, Morgan presents McKinley as a courageous statesman guiding America's colonial expansion with firmness and humanity. He argues that from the first McKinley desired to retain the Philippines, his apparent hesitation being merely a "long search of support for that position" (Morgan 1963, 388). The chief executive should not be faulted for the Platt Amendment, which turned Cuba into a quasi-protectorate, as only later was it used in ways he could not conceive.

In an article published in 1966 in the *Review of Politics*, Morgan suggests that in the long run McKinley's foreign policy might have been more profound than Theodore Roosevelt's. While TR's internationalism was simply "an old-fashioned exercise of national power in a world setting," McKinley's more genuine brand reflected a focus on world trade (Morgan 1966, 431). If McKinley's stress on peaceful indirect cooperation with other nations was far less colorful than White Fleets and revolutions in Panama, it would have bade better for the future.

Lewis L. Gould's *Presidency of William McKinley* (1980) might be even more appreciative of its subject. The book begins with the statement "William McKinley was the first modern president," a claim that sets the tone for the entire work. Building upon Leech and Morgan, it has the added advantage of using not just Cortelyou's diary but his papers as well. Gould rhapsodizes that McKinley "transformed the presidential office from its late-nineteenth-century weakness to a recognizable prototype of its present-day form" (Gould 1980, vii; 152). Evidence includes having regular press briefings, maintaining an alertness to public opinion, drawing upon the expertise of professionals, and directing strategies in the Spanish–American War and Philippine insurrection. In making peace with Spain, he unobtrusively functioned as chief diplomat. During the Boxer Rebellion, he sent troops to China without congressional approval. He governed new territories through presidential commissions, giving Congress only a subsidiary role. Similar activism can be found in McKinley's policies concerning currency, banking, the trusts, and using the civil service to enhance his power in Congress. The eventual selection of John Hay and Elihu Root to the State and War departments brought great credit, while the caliber of his civilian colonial appointments was superior. Irrespective of their subsequent application, the Open Door notes displayed much tactical skill, particularly as the United States lacked the military leverage to attain commercial equality in China. His manner and bearing alone served as a prototype for later decades. McKinley's contribution is particularly significant as his predecessor Cleveland, by one inept policy after another, had left the presidency in shambles.

McKinley's 1896 victory, Gould posits, was not as crucial as the congressional races two years earlier. The election of 1894, which the Republicans won handily, remade national politics, ending twenty years of tight races. Except for the election of Woodrow Wilson in 1912 (and reelection in 1916), the Democrats were condemned to minority status until the Great Depression and the New Deal. The 1896 presidential election, stereotyped as "the hick" (William Jennings Bryan) against "the hack" (McKinley), did not depend on bought votes, Democratic errors, the coercing of workers, or "Dollar Mark" Hanna's political acumen. Rather McKinley was genuinely the more attractive candidate, his defense of a high tariff and the gold standard drawing far more support than it lost. Not since Grant's 1872 victory had the margin of popular votes been so great. The result: a president who dominated the politics of his time just as Franklin Roosevelt did during the 1930s.

Crucial to Gould's claims concerning the modern presidency is McKinley's role in the Spanish–American War and its aftermath. The author denies that the president caved in to a hysterical press or an overheated public. Such publishers as Joseph Pulitzer and William Randolph Hearst reflected popular sentiment far more than they created it; they represented only a minority of the business community. Gould takes issue with Walter La Feber's *The New Empire: An Interpretation of American Expansion, 1860–1898* (1963), which argues that McKinley responded to a business community increasingly fearful that instability in Cuba would thwart America's ongoing recovery from the depression. Unlike Leech and Morgan, Gould argues that after the *Maine* sinking McKinley could not have tempered the nation's belligerent sentiment. Ultimately, neither the Spanish government nor the Cuban rebels would have accepted a mere truce.

Once hostilities between the United States and Spain broke out, McKinley, so Gould observes, oversaw the war day by day, sometimes hour by hour. The author praises the much-maligned General Shafter, a man whose administrative weaknesses were "balanced by his good sense, his determination, and his ability to make a decision." There was no embalmed beef scandal, the assertions of General Nelson A. Miles notwithstanding. McKinley's postwar speaking tour has usually been depicted as instrumental in convincing the hesitant president that an imperialist-minded public favored Philippine annexation. In reality, McKinley molded popular sentiment with his constant stress on "duty" and "destiny." Gould finds American atrocities in the Philippines greatly exaggerated, though he concedes that "the conduct of the United States Army fell below the highest standards of the rules of war" (Gould 1980, 109, 188). He sees McKinley misguided in underestimating Filipino support of rebel leader Emilio Aguinaldo, but portrays the chief executive as a genuine friend of the indigenous population.

Gould concedes that such revisionism has its limits. In domestic policy, McKinley often adhered to the conventional wisdom of his time: tariff protection and reciprocity, government fostering of business, and a "trickle down" belief that saw benefits to labor coming strictly through full employment and corporate profits. Serious McKinley errors include the appointments of Sherman and Alger, an expediential shift concerning a tariff for Puerto Rico, and apathy towards the ever-worsening plight of African Americans.

Political commentator Kevin Phillips offers the most eulogistic treatment of all. In his *William McKinley* (2003), Phillips challenges stereotypes of Hanna's domination, Spain's conciliatory posture, and McKinley's innate conservatism. Rather the president was "arguably ahead of his time," one whose second term "would have basked in a brightening ideological sun, encouraging his Lincolnian streak on subjects ranging from tax fairness to attempts to reduce trusts and monopolies, especially those nurtured by special-interest tariff provisions." McKinley's series of "interrelated successes—a new period of economic prosperity, including the entrenchment of the protective tariff framework in 1897 and the gold standard in 1900—ended a quarter-century of bitter acrimony over currency, money supply, and tariffs with a clear decision in favor of manufacturing, global commerce, and a sound currency *with* mild inflation" (Phillips 2003, 126, 109–210; emphasis Phillips).

One forgets, writes Phillips, that in 1896 Theodore Roosevelt was far more conservative than McKinley, who outpaced TR on women's suffrage, direct election of senators, and black voting in the South. In reality, it was McKinley who launched the progressive era, putting in place the political organization, anti-machine spirit, critical party alignment, and firm commitment to popular and economic democracy that marked Roosevelt's leadership. In many ways, Roosevelt's first administration was McKinley's second.

In an article in the *Journal of the Gilded Age and Progressive Era* (2005), Eric Rauchway challenges Gould and to a greater degree Phillips. Rauchway differs with Gould's arguments of a Republican ascendency, noting the Democratic control of the House in 1913 and the success of the Wilson administration in passing the bulk of the most important progressive legislation of the early twentieth century, laws that foreshadowed the New Deal coalition.

Differing with Phillips concerning economic prosperity, Rauchway maintains that protective tariffs cannot be considered as particularly favorable to global commerce, at least not in comparison with free trade or lower tariffs. Rauchway cites Milton Friedman and Anna Jacobson Schwartz's *A Monetary History of the United States* (1963) to assert that the inflation of 1897–1914 was not particularly mild, and Friedman's *Money Mischief: Episodes in Monetary History* (1994) to claim that this inflation was triggered by increases in the world supply of gold, not by McKinley's policies. McKinley, Rauchway posits, did nothing to end the acrimony over currency and tariffs, with rancor over currency persisting until the Federal Reserve Act of 1913. Anger over trade raged through the creation of the General Agreement on Tariffs and Trade in 1947 and the World Trade Organization in 1995, continuing to this very day. If McKinley was a proto-progressive, there is something wrong with the definition, for this "bloodless, scholar's progressivism" was "assuredly unrecognizable to the voters of the early 1900s. These progressives do no standing at Armageddon, they harbor no fierce discontent, they make not the slightest reference to other people's money; though they may be moral people, they evince no moral passion." Using data supplied by David R. Mayhew (2002), Rauchway sees limits to McKinley revisionism; the president was "an almost perfectly conservative President who presided over a very few institutional changes in the Presidency during a period when global trends well out of his or anyone's control favored the American economy" (Rauchway 1994, 244–245).

Thanks to the labors of skilled biographers, writing for the most part over the past half-century, Gilded Age presidents are accurately shown as able men, possessing vision and integrity and eager to recover the power and prerogatives of the institution. Admittedly biographers in general can overidentify with their subjects, and those of late nineteenth-century "politicos" may not be an exception. The era did not lack its seamy side and some muckraking was indeed necessary. But if, as Charles W. Calhoun argues, some politicians were corrupt and took bribes, it is unlikely the percentage was higher in the Gilded Age than during most other periods in American history. Despite the many obstacles they faced, they were able to transform the presidency once more into the center of America's political system (Calhoun 2007, 259). Robert W. Cherny (1997) and Calhoun (2010) offer syntheses that present a far more sophisticated and balanced view of the period.

The presidential biographers have played a major part in revealing genuine differences between the two major parties. No longer can one see these contrasts as sham battles between Tweedledum and Tweedledee. As Calhoun writes, "What leaders said mattered to voters, and what they did affected the well-being of the nation" (Calhoun 2007, 240). The northern- and western-based Republicans espoused nationalism and governmental activism, stressing industrial development and government aid to business. Hence their focus on a high tariff and such social legislation as prohibition and Sabbath laws. In contrast, the agrarian, southern-based Democrats adhered to states-rights localism and minimal government, which explains their low-tariff stance (Calhoun 1988, 141; Calhoun 2007, 244).

If the Gilded Age presidents were not successful activists, able to transform the nation in the way that some of their twentieth-century successors did, it was for good reason. Americans in general opposed government regulation of the economy as unnecessary, unjust, perhaps immoral. To the late nineteenth-century American, "good government," as Calhoun writes, "meant limited government," its main purpose being to maintain order and protect persons and property (Calhoun 2007, 241). The frequent accusations of corruption led not to positive programs but to further retrenchment. When, in 1890, the Harrison administration passed such significant laws as the Sherman Anti-Trust Act and the McKinley Tariff, it was punished, not rewarded, at the polls.

Presidents often confronted a divided Congress, which retarded much legislation. During most of the Gilded Age, the Democrats held the House and Republicans the Senate. Presidential elections depended on certain swing states, Indiana, Ohio, and New York. Although the Republicans won three of the five presidential elections from 1876 to 1892, they failed to carry a majority of the popular vote in any one of them. Only in 1880 did they receive a plurality, although less than one-tenth of one percent. With outcomes in doubt, candidates often bucked their own party. For example, though the Republican Party as a party stood for the gold standard, some within its ranks flirted with free silver.

The presidents, as Allan Peskin observes, were forced to devote much time to appointments, but not because they were impervious to more pressing national demands. Rather, in the absence of a comprehensive civil service system, they needed the party structure to fill over 100,000 posts (Peskin 1980, 37). At the same time, as Calhoun notes, the spoils system had its own logic, for one could argue that a president's policies would best be executed by employees drawn from his own party (Calhoun 2007, 248).

Proportionately more people went to the polls in presidential elections than had ever done so before or would do so again, no mean accomplishment in light of the usually successful efforts to keep blacks from voting. In the national elections of the 1880s, for example, 80 percent of the electorate voted. Richard Jensen shows how "the electorate followed political developments, recognized politicians, and understood the issues" (Jensen 1971, 58). They could sit through hours of speeches without a break, absorbing minor details concerning the tariff, currency, and industrial policy.

Such matters were not inconsequential. Presidential policy concerning gold, silver, and greenbacks show an implicit recognition that government must play a role in determining money supply and therefore the level of economic activity. Because the tariff touched people across class lines, it lay at the core of a debate over governmental responsibility for economic prosperity. Efforts to deal with the corporation, increasingly the linchpin of Western industrialization, were halting and spasmodic, but involved a recognition that laissez faire was at best counter-productive. As the problems they faced were of unprecedented scope, centering on the most radical transformation any peacetime nation ever experienced, in retrospect it is remarkable how much, not how little, the Gilded Age presidents were able to accomplish.

Certain matters deserve further study. Candice Millard's best-selling *Destiny of the Republic: A Tale of Madness, Medicine and the Murder of a President* (2011) skillfully details Garfield's assassination while Eric Rauchway's *Murdering McKinley: The Making of Theodore Roosevelt's America* (2003) offers a perceptive account of McKinley's death. Needed now is an account of popular reaction to these events so as to discern the meaning Americans found in these tragedies. Obviously neither president achieved the canonization as martyr and redeemer that Lincoln did, a phenomena so skillfully described in Allen E. Guelzo's *Abraham Lincoln: Martyred President* (1999), but obviously more was expressed than simple grief. Here one must work in the realm of images, anxieties, symbols, ways of thinking, and resonant words and concepts.

More could be done with the ideologies of Gilded Age presidents. Both David Herbert Donald (rev. ed. 2001) and Guelzo (1999) stress that Lincoln's political philosophy was rooted in Whig ideology, a stance based on an activist state dedicated to centralized economic development combined with a restrained view of the presidential office. (Lincoln's broad use of his office was based on the war powers of the chief executive.) To what degree did Lincoln's Republican successors either maintain or break with such this stance? Robert Kelley's *Transatlantic Persuasion: The Liberal-Democratic Mind in the Age of Gladstone* (1969) perceptively draws parallels between Grover Cleveland on the one hand and British liberal William E. Gladstone and Canadian liberals George Brown and Alexander Mackenzie on the other. Similar comparisons might well be made for other presidents. Psychological approaches can play a role in explaining political behavior, though scholars may not want to go as far did Robert Irving Cottom, Jr. in his study of Garfield's early life (1975). If, as Robert C. Hilderbrand (1981) notes, McKinley was the first president to make the White House the source of presidential news, how did earlier Gilded Age presidents relate to "the third estate"?

Today, well over a century later, as Americans anguish over such matters as race, globalization, living standards, corporate power, labor unrest, an American mission, and national budgets, they can only empathize with those presidents, for their problems have a surprising relevance. The task, therefore, does not lie in writing more exhaustive studies of the Gilded Age presidents, piling even more detail upon detail. Since the 1950s, we have had more than our share of distinguished biographies and detailed analyses of presidential administrations. The goal now is to show the pertinence of the issues these leaders confronted to people of a very different century. Such efforts have borne surprising fruit in earlier periods, as witnessed by the rich scholarship synthesized by such authors as David Hackett Fischer on the colonial period (1989), Gordon S. Wood on the early national era (2009), Daniel Walker Howe on the Jacksonian age (2007), James McPherson on the Civil War epoch (1988), and Jackson Lears on the Progressive generation (2009). It is time that Thomas Wolfe's "lost Americans" were given their due.

The author is grateful to John Belohlavek, Irwin F.Gellman, and Allan Peskin for their careful reading of this article.

References

Alger, Horatio. 1881. *From Canal Boy to President.* Boston: DeWolfe, Fiske.

Beisner, Robert. 1975. *From the Old Diplomacy to the New, 1865–1890.* Arlington Heights: AHM Publishing.

Blum, John Morton. 1959. Review of Leech, *New York Review of Books*, November 1: 1.

Brodsky, Alyn. 2000. *Grover Cleveland: A Study in Character.* New York: St. Martin's Press.

Brown, Harry James and Frederick D. Williams. 1967–81. *The Diary of James A. Garfield*. East Lansing: Michigan State University Press.

Caldwell, Robert Granville. 1931. *James A. Garfield, Party Chieftain*. New York: Dodd, Mead.

Calhoun, Charles W. 1988. "Benjamin Harrison, Centennial President: A Review Essay." *Indiana Magazine of History* 84: 134–160.

Calhoun, Charles W. 2002. "Reimagining the 'Lost Men' of the Gilded Age: Perspectives on the Late Nineteenth Century." *Journal of the Gilded Age and Progressive Era* 1: 225–257.

—. 2005. *Benjamin Harrison*. New York: Henry Holt.

—. 2007. "The Political Culture: Public Life and the Conduct of Politics." In *The Gilded Age: Perspectives on the Origins of Modern America*, ed. C.W. Calhoun. 2nd edition. Lanham, MD: Rowman & Littlefield.

—. 2010. *From Bloody Shirt to Full Dinner Pail: The Transformation of Politics and Governance in the Gilded Age*. New York: Hill & Wang.

Campbell, Charles C. 1976. *The Transformation of American Foreign Relations, 1865–1900*. New York: Harper and Row.

Cherny, Robert W. 1997. *American Politics in the Gilded Age, 1868–1900*. Wheeling, IL: Harlan Davidson.

Cottom, Robert Irving, Jr. 1975. "To Be Among the First: The Early Career of James A. Garfield, 1831–1868." PhD diss., Johns Hopkins University.

Crapol, Edward P. 1973. *America for Americans: Economic Nationalism and Anglophobia in the Late Nineteenth Century*. Westport, CT: Greenwood.

De Santis, Vincent P. 1959. *Republicans Face the Southern Question: The New Departure Years*. Baltimore, MD: Johns Hopkins Press.

—. 1975. "The Political Life of the Gilded Age: A Review of the Recent Literature." *History Teacher* 9: 73–106.

Davison, Kenneth E. 1972. *Presidency of Rutherford B. Hayes*. Westport, CT: Greenwood.

—. 1978. "The Search for the Hayes Administration." *Hayes Historical Journal* 2: 107–118.

Doenecke, Justus D. 1981. *The Presidencies of James A. Garfield & Chester A. Arthur*. Lawrence: University Press of Kansas.

Donald, David Herbert. 2001. *Lincoln Reconsidered: Essays on the Civil War Era*. Revised edition. New York: Vintage.

Du Bois, W.E.B. 1935. *Black Reconstruction in America*. New York: Harcourt, Brace.

Fischer, David Hackett 1989. *Albion's Seed: Four British Folkways in America*. New York: Oxford University Press.

Foner, Eric. 1988. *Reconstruction: America's Unfinished Revolution, 1863–1877*. New York: Harper and Row.

Friedman, Milton. 1994. *Money Mischief: Episodes in Monetary History*. San Diego, CA: Mariner Books.

Friedman, Milton and Anna Jacobson Schwartz. 1963. *A Monetary History of the United States*. Princeton, NJ: Princeton University Press.

Gillette, William. 1979. *Retreat from Reconstruction: 1869–1879*. Baton Rouge: Louisiana State University Press.

Gould, Lewis L. 1980. *The Presidency of William McKinley*. Lawrence: Regents Press of Kansas.

Graff, Henry F. 2002. *Grover Cleveland*. New York: Times Books.

Guelzo, Allen E. 1999. *Abraham Lincoln: Martyred President*. Grand Rapids, MI: Eerdmans.

Haworth, Paul L. 1906. *Hayes–Tilden Disputed Election of 1876*. Cleveland, OH: Burrows Bros.

Hilderbrand, Robert C. 1981. *Power and the People: Executive Management of Public Opinion in Foreign Affairs, 1897–1921*. Chapel Hill: University of North Carolina Press.

Hirshson, Stanley. 1962. *Farewell to the Bloody Shirt: Northern Republicans and the Southern Negro, 1877–1893*. Bloomington: Indiana University Press.

Hofstadter, Richard. 1948. *The American Political Tradition and the Men Who Made It*. New York: Knopf.

Holbo, Paul S. 1970. "Economics, Emotion, and Expansion: An Emerging Foreign Policy." In *The Gilded Age: A Reappraisal*, ed. H. Wayne Morgan. Revised edition. Syracuse, NY: Syracuse University Press.

Hoogenboom, Ari. 1988. *The Presidency of Rutherford B. Hayes*. Lawrence: University Press of Kansas.

—. 1995. *Rutherford B. Hayes: Warrior and President*. Lawrence: University Press of Kansas.

Howe, Daniel Walker. 2007. *What Hath God Wrought: The Transformation of America, 1815–1848*. New York: Oxford University Press.

Jensen, Richard. 1971. *The Winning of the Midwest: A Social Analysis of Midwestern Politics, 1880–1896*. New York: Oxford University Press.

Josephson, Matthew. 1934. *The Robber Barons*. New York: Harcourt, Brace.

—. 1938. *The Politicos, 1865–1896*. New York: Harcourt, Brace.

Kelley, Robert. 1969. *The Transatlantic Persuasion: The Liberal-Democratic Mind in the Age of Gladstone*. New York: Knopf.

La Feber, Walter. 1963. *The New Empire: An Interpretation of American Expansion, 1860–1898*. Ithaca, NY: Cornell University Press.

Lears, Jackson. 2009. *Rebirth of a Nation: The Making of Modern America, 1877–1920*. New York: Harper Collins.

Leech, Margaret. 1959. *In the Days of McKinley*. New York: Harper & Brothers.

Leech, Margaret and Harry J. Brown 1978. *The Garfield Orbit: The Life of James A. Garfield*. New York: Harper and Row.

Lindsay, Vachel. 1925. *Collected Poems*. New York: Macmillan.

Mayhew, David R. 2002. *Electoral Realignments: A Critique of an American Genre*. New Haven, CT: Yale University Press.

McDonald, Forrest, Leslie E. Decker, and Thomas P. Govan. 1972. *The Last Best Hope: A History of the United States*. Reading, PA: Addison-Wesley.

McElroy, Robert. 1923. *Grover Cleveland, the Man and the Statesman*. New York: Harper and Brothers.

McPherson, James M. 1988. *Battle Cry of Freedom: The Civil War Era*. New York: Oxford University Press.

Merrill, Horace Samuel. 1957. *Bourbon Leader: Grover Cleveland and the Democratic Party*. Boston: Little Brown.

Millard, Candice. 2011. *Destiny of the Republic: A Tale of Madness, Medicine and the Murder of a President*. New York: Doubleday.

Morgan, H. Wayne. 1963. *William McKinley and His America*. Syracuse, NY: Syracuse University Press.

Morgan, H. Wayne. 1966. "McKinley as Political Leader." *Review of Politics* 28: 417–432.

Nevins, Allan. 1933a. *Grover Cleveland: A Study in Courage*. New York: Dodd, Mead.

Nevins, Allan ed. 1933b. *Letters of Grover Cleveland, 1850–1908*. Boston: Houghton Mifflin.

Olcott, Charles S. 1916. *The Life of William McKinley*. 2 volumes. Boston: Houghton Mifflin.

Peskin, Allan. 1978. *Garfield*. Kent, OH: Kent State University Press.

—. 1980. "President Garfield Reconsidered." *Hayes Historical Journal* 3: 35–40.

Phillips, Kevin 2003. *William McKinley*. New York: Times Books.

Plesur, Milton 1971. *America's Outward Thrust: Approaches to Foreign Affairs, 1865–1890*. De Kalb: Northern Illinois University Press.

Pletcher, David M. 1962. *The Awkward Years: American Foreign Relations under Garfield and Arthur*. Columbia: University of Missouri Press.

Rauchway, Eric. 2003. *Murdering McKinley: The Making of Theodore Roosevelt's America*. New York: Hill & Wang.

—. 2005. "William McKinley and Us." *Journal of the Gilded Age and Progressive Era* 2: 235–253.

Rutkow, Ira. 2006. *James A. Garfield*. New York: Times Books.

Sievers, Harry J. 1968. *Benjamin Harrison, Hoosier President: Volume 3, The White House and After*. Indianapolis: Bobbs Merrill.

Smith, Theodore Clarke. 1925. *The Life and Letters of James Abram Garfield*. 2 volumes. New Haven: Yale University Press.

Socolofsky, Homer E. and Allan B. Spetter. 1987. *Presidency of Benjamin Harrison*. Lawrence: University Press of Kansas.

Spetter, Allan. 1993. "Rev. Harry J. Sievers, S.J., the Arthur Jordan Foundation and the Biography of President Benjamin Harrison." *Presidential Studies Quarterly* 23: 555–565.

Sproat, John G. 1968. *"The Best Men": Liberal Reformers in the Gilded Age*. New York: Oxford University Press.

Terrill, Tom E. 1973. *The Tariff, Politics, and American Foreign Policy, 1874–1901*. Westport, CT: Greenwood.

Trefousse, Hans L. 2002. *Rutherford B. Hayes*. New York: Times Books.

Volwiler, Albert T. 1940. *The Correspondence between Benjamin Harrison and James G. Blaine*. Philadelphia: American Philosophical Society.

Welch, Richard E., Jr. 1988. *The Presidencies of Grover Cleveland*. Lawrence: University Press of Kansas.

Williams, R. Hal. 1972. *The Democratic Party and California Politics, 1880–1896*. Palo Alto, CA: Stanford University Press.

Wolfe, Thomas. 1935. *From Death to Morning*. New York: C. Scribner's Sons.

Wood, Gordon S. 2009. *Empire of Liberty: A History of the Early Republic, 1789–1815*. New York: Oxford University Press.

Chapter Twenty-Two

Political Movers and Shakers

Karen Pastorello

In 1873 Mark Twain and Charles Dudley Warner published *The Gilded Age*, a best-selling satire that portrayed the final decades of the nineteenth century as a time when the promise of new found wealth obscured the darkness and corruption that lay just beneath the glittering surface. The novel provided both a moniker for the era and an interpretation of post-Civil War America that lasted through the next century. Thanks to recent analysis by political scientists, biographers, and historians however, the Gilded Age, and the politics associated with it, is no longer perceived as a stagnant era dominated by fraudulent politicians or elite Robber Barons out to serve corporate interests by touting meaningless issues to a subdued public. Instead, the Gilded Age political scene has been more accurately depicted as a period marked by passionate partisan fervor and unprecedented voter turnout.

Americans, the majority of who still farmed for a living, initiated the rise of several vibrant political movements that responded to the adverse effects of unchecked industrialization including poverty, exploitation of workers, child labor, unsafe living and working conditions. What began as local issues burgeoned into problems of epic proportion that required national solutions during the long Gilded Age and Progressive Era. Political "Movers and Shakers" clamored for government intervention on behalf of both the nation's rural residents and urban populace to mitigate the intrusion of corporate capitalism into all aspects of American life. Reformers, and eventually the state, began to heed the cries for reform.

Over time historians have attempted to explain the origins and the nature of political activity in the Gilded Age and Progressive Era. Recently historians have expanded their definition of the progressive movement to include reformers outside the formal political arena. Farmers, women, African Americans and Native Americans as well as those who spoke and acted on behalf of the marginalized have earned their place among the multitude of individuals and coalitions that comprised the progressive movement. Reformers attacked the existing political and economic systems at the turn of the century but they did not stop there. They devised solutions to the issues associated with industrialization, urbanization, and immigration. They demanded that the government enact those solutions.

Populism's origins lay in the South and West. Populist leaders, very few of whom were farmers, made it their mission to defend agrarian interests against modernity. The search for progressive reform brought together diverse coalitions to effect change. Only in recent decades however, have historians begun to recognize that not all progressives were white urban men. Glenda Gilmore embarked on a seminal study by asking "Who Were the Progressives?" (2002). Elizabeth Sanders is one of a number of scholars, beginning with John Hicks, who has traced the roots of progressivism to the 1890s farmers' revolt (Sanders 1999; Hicks 1931). While early historians of the populist movement like Hicks maintained that Populist demands were so conservative that they were readily adopted by the major parties, Sanders sees the Populists in a more radical light. She recognizes the irony of reformers who, perhaps because of their Protestant upbringings, were hostile to bureaucracy yet ultimately encouraged the formation of a benevolent bureaucratic state.

The Politics of Populism

In the wake of the Civil War, Populism spread across the country like wildfire. Arguably one of the most intense mass democratic movements in American history, Populism traces its roots back to the Grange and Alliance movements in the

A Companion to the Gilded Age and Progressive Era, First Edition. Edited by Christopher McKnight Nichols and Nancy C. Unger.
© 2017 John Wiley & Sons, Inc. Published 2017 by John Wiley & Sons, Inc.

rural reaches of the West and South. Populist leaders, too, emanated from the nation's heartland. Populism's appeal lay in the homage it paid to those who tilled the soil. In the last half of the nineteenth century, many farmers felt the consequences of unstable markets, rising railroad rates, escalating mortgage interest, the high costs of mechanization, plagues of locusts, boll weevils, and drought, making it very difficult for them to sustain their livelihoods. While earlier movements failed to convince politicians to support the economic and political reforms necessary to ameliorate the problems of debt-ridden agrarians, the populist politicians heard the farmers' pleas and offered the promise of a collective voice in the political arena.

By the early 1890s, in the midst of the nation's most severe financial crisis to date, the Populists (or the People's Party as it became known) had evolved into an official political entity. The Populists and their allies resembled a coalition of reform groups rather than a single cohesive party. In *The Populist Vision*, Charles Postel characterizes the Populists as a broad coalition of farmers, wage earners, and middle-class activists with enough confidence to challenge the rising corporate power contained within the ethos of modernity (Postel 2007). As the country industrialized, Populism sought to unite diverse social classes, to bridge the urban–rural divide, and to more equitably distribute the wealth.

Women helped to swell Populist ranks. Rural women made many sacrifices but reaped few rewards in the world outside their homes. They were attracted to Populism's reform agenda and the educational, political, and economic opportunities they imagined that a more modern rural life might offer. Farmers' wives wanted a way out of their daily drudgery for themselves and their children. They wanted more equitable partnerships with their husbands. Many rural women, especially those previously associated with the Women's Christian Temperance Union or the Grange or Alliance movements, demanded voting rights and abolition of the liquor trade. Nancy Grey Osterud traces rural women's struggles for temperance and equality to farm organizations, and Donald B. Marti examines women's advocacy in Granges (Osterud 1991, 255–256; Marti 1991, 107). Complicating factors include Grange's uneven history with regard to issues of gender equality.

In 1892, Frances Willard, the leader of the largest female reform organization in the country, the Women's Christian Temperance Union, served as a delegate to the Populist Party's founding convention in St. Louis. She hoped that the new party would endorse female suffrage and support the demand for a prohibition plank. However, some of the Populist leaders felt that the inclusion of a suffrage platform might split the voters so they deferred woman's suffrage to the states. While most rank-and-file Populists favored prohibition, national party leaders rejected the idea of prohibition because they feared the backlash from urban labor.

Roused by Willard's example, Mary Elizabeth Lease, the child of impoverished Irish immigrants, toured the country as a stump speaker for the Populist Party. Lease was one of several Populist women who rose to prominence out of the labor and anti-monopoly movements that foreshadowed Populism (Edwards 1997, 102; Baker 1991, 46). Ironically, like Lease, these women were not necessarily wives of farmers. Lease and her husband had farmed in Texas until the depression of 1873. After their farm failed, the Leases moved with their four children to Wichita where Charles Lease worked as a pharmacist and Mary continued her activism as an organizer for the Knights of Labor and the suffrage movement. She became the first woman to pass the Kansas bar exam. Celebrated for her suggestion that farmers should "raise less corn and more hell," a line she later admitted that she borrowed from a local newspaper reporter, Lease became an advocate for what she began to refer to as "the People's Party," serving as a Kansas delegate at Populist conventions. However, thoroughly disappointed by the Populist refusal to support prohibition and by Bryan's noncommital stance on suffrage, Lease's enthusiasm faded.

Most Populist supporters, however, stayed the course. And for them what had started as an agrarian protest movement quickly became a major political force or, in the words of John Hicks, "a revolt" (Hicks 1931). What helped distinguish Populism from the major parties was its positive attitude toward the state. The Peoples' Party called for the direct election of US Senators, the initiative and the referendum, a graduated income tax, and an eight-hour day. Ohio-born James Weaver won the presidential candidacy at the Omaha nominating convention in July 1892. The Omaha platform, which emphasized a distinction between the producers and the corporations, contained a strong radical element. Running under the People's Party banner, Weaver garnered over a million votes; but Populism's apex came with William Jennings Bryan's candidacy in 1896.

William Jennings Bryan

William Jennings Bryan is synonymous with Populism. The future presidential contender earned an early reputation as a "righteous reformer" who envisioned a civil government that would act as a positive agent in improving the welfare of the farming and laboring classes. Bryan's father, Silas, was a lawyer, a circuit court judge, a gentleman farmer of Irish stock, and an ardent Democrat. Because his father's farm was the largest in the county, Bryan's family enjoyed a level of prosperity that most rural families did not. Bryan grew up in a household that valued education, hard work, and piety.

Biographer Robert Cherny emphasizes the importance of the world in which Bryan, born in 1860, came of age (Cherny 1994). He describes it as a place laden with interdependent social and economic networks which emphasized responsibility to family and community. William Jennings Bryan received a hearty dose of morality reinforced through his *McGuffey Reader*, his church, and his family. Bryan never smoked, gambled, danced, or swore. He signed the temperance pledge before he knew what temperance meant. Yet the values and lifestyle of urban industrial America gradually made inroads into rural homes like the Bryans' through interaction with the outside world. The intrusion sometimes came through publications like *Atlantic Monthly* and *Harper's Weekly*. Even residents in remote areas could not escape the ethos of modernity.

Bryan modeled his political career as a "Christian Statesman" on the Bible and the political principles of Jefferson rooted in self-government but a minimal government. Influenced by his father, he aligned tightly with the Democratic Party to oppose concentrated wealth. With his previously callused hands now smooth, Bryan came to believe that responsive political parties could help to resolve farmers' problems. In 1890, Bryan won a position as a Congressman from Nebraska only to lose the Senate race several years later. By 1895, he had honed his oratorical skills to the point that his magnetic voice had become a powerful instrument responsible for winning a precarious hold on the Democratic Party in Nebraska. By the following year, at the age of thirty-six, ran as the Democratic candidate for the presidency.

Populists in the South and West viewed Eastern money interests as a threat. By 1895 the question of free silver had become a major issue. In the farmers' minds, the return of silver-backed currency that had been dropped by Congress in 1873 translated to a more abundant supply of money and easy credit. After winning the Democratic nomination and the endorsement of the People's Party by inciting a "joyous riot" in support of free silver with his "Cross of Gold" speech, Bryan embarked on a crusade-like cross-country speaking tour in 1896 while the Republican presidential candidate, William McKinley, stayed home in Canton, Ohio. In campaigning for McKinley Republicans championed honest money and national honor. They pointed to the depression and pushed for prosperity while promising "a full dinner pail" for all. McKinley avoided alienating ethnic groups by rejecting the prohibition that Bryan advocated.

Financier J.P. Morgan, John D. Rockefeller's Standard Oil, and the railroad corporations gave big money to McKinley. Bryan's appeals to the public garnered support from publishing magnate William Randolph Hearst, mining interests, labor leaders, and the nativist American Protective Association. However, Bryan's attacks on Wall Street, banks, and railroads alienated many. He failed to overcome the gulf between rural farmers and urban immigrant workers. In the election of 1896, four of five eligible voters went to the polls, ushering in McKinley. The victory initiated a generation of Republican dominance in national politics.

Despite his defeat, Bryan drew on his inner strength to remain optimistic and politically active. The Democrats nominated him for presidency again in 1900 and 1908. Relying on the theme "Shall the people rule?" Bryan called for the regulation of corporations, tariff reform, an insurance fund for bank depositors, income tax, direct election of senators, publication of campaign contributions, and independence for the Philippines. Political scientist Elizabeth Sanders (1999) recognizes that Bryan may have been defeated but the components of his platform that survived, impacted the national political agenda for years to come. The demands of the Populists proved to be the first step in the transition to the modern interventionist state. Populism, in the words of Charles Postel, "proved far more successful dead than alive" (2007, 271).

Emma Goldman

Disillusioned with the Populists' lack of commitment to the issues she held dear, Mary Elizabeth Lease packed her belongings and, with her four children in tow, left her husband behind and moved to New York. When Lease arrived in 1896 she found a city that was just beginning to recover from the severe depression that began in 1893. The rapidly improving economic circumstances made it possible for her to find work as a writer for Joseph Pulitzer's sensationalist paper the *New York World*.

Perhaps it was no coincidence that Emma Goldman had left her husband behind in search of her political self a few years earlier. Nellie Bly, another writer for the *New York World*, interviewed Goldman whose "girlish" appearance, including her light brown hair, turned-up nose, and very expressive blue-gray eyes, seemed typical. Bly's innocuous 1893 description of the five-foot high Goldman made it seem virtually impossible that by 1917, US Attorney General Francis Caffey called Goldman "exceedingly dangerous" (Falk 1995, 15).

Emma Goldman's politics did not take shape on the prairies of the American Midwest but were conceived in the *shtetls* of Eastern Europe where the quest for social justice was so tightly intertwined with Judaism it was difficult to separate religious practice from political activity. Goldman spent her childhood in a dichotomous world where orthodox acts of charity were commonplace, yet radicalized anarchy seemed like a plausible solution to life's insurmountable problems. Although Jews like the Goldman family were in the majority in Lithuania in the final decades of the nineteenth century, anti-Semitic discrimination, including hostile civil disturbances known as *pogroms*, increasingly disrupted their lives. In addition to the violence Jews experienced during the *pogroms*, families like the Goldmans were plagued by economic hardship. Tired of being pressured by her father to marry so that she could assume the subservient place of a traditional Jewish wife, Emma Goldman emigrated to the United States in 1885 at the age of fifteen. She moved in with her married sister in Rochester, New York and within a year her parents followed her. Although it took some getting used to, her family supported Emma's controversial endeavors for the rest of their lives.

Finding work in a local tailor shop did not bring Goldman happiness or financial independence. Days spent at her sewing machine brought little satisfaction at the end of the long weeks. Despite the harsh realities that threatened to dash her hopes for a better life in her new country, Goldman soon attracted the attention of a handsome young Russian immigrant seated close to her. Jacob Kershner and Emma Goldman brought a shared fascination with radical politics into what soon became a tumultuous marriage.

In 1889, both to escape her unhappy marriage and, as the result of her reaction to the Haymarket executions, Goldman relocated to New York City. Buoyed by an almost immediate sense of belonging, Goldman immersed herself into a new political world that differed drastically from the uninspired socialist meetings through which she had suffered in Rochester. On July 19, 1908 in Union Square, she passionately articulated a set of anarchist ideals which did not openly promote the destruction of the government but made reference to the abolition of capitalism, disdain for militarism, and disillusionment with established marriage practices. She advocated for complete and absolute freedom that included freedom of expression, free love, birth control, total equality for women, radical education, the right of unions to organize workers, and workers' rights.

Goldman's personal life often contradicted her publically espoused ideals. Regularly expounding on the need for women to achieve complete independence from men, Emma's two longest affairs rendered her emotionally helpless. The day she arrived in New York, Goldman met and became forever tied to Alexander Berkman. The mutual attraction that fueled the fiery relationship between "Sasha" Berkman and Goldman, first as lovers and later as committed anarchist comrades, resulted in Goldman being linked to Berkman's botched assassination attempt on Homestead manager Henry Clay Frick. Because Frick had acted as Andrew Carnegie's right-hand man during the 1892 Homestead Strike, Berkman held him accountable for the deaths of ten workers and a ten-year-old boy.

In 1901, a twenty-eight-year-old son of Polish immigrants, Leon Czolgosz, assassinated President William McKinley in Buffalo. Although Goldman had met Czolgosz only once in passing, newspaper headlines claimed that she incited the assassination. She spent a few months in jail. When the assassin refused to implicate Goldman in the crime, she was released and decided to live anonymously in New York as Miss E.G. Smith.

In 1902, "Red Emma" emerged to found a platform for expression of her anarchist beliefs in *Mother Earth* which she published until 1917. She printed contentious articles in her magazine and spoke frequently on behalf of the No-Conscription League about her opposition to the draft. Goldman and Berkman soon found themselves behind bars on charges of conspiring to "induce persons not to register." After a brief stint of freedom while the courts determined the constitutionality of the draft, federal officers rearrested Goldman under the Alien Immigration Act of 1917 and the Anti-Anarchist Act of 1918 (Falk 1999, 159, 176).

The Justice Department's infamous J. Edgar Hoover ordered the deportation of both Berkman and Goldman. Exile came quickly but not before Goldman appeared on the speaker's platform to give a series of farewell speeches. Prior to her joining the other 248 political exiles being shipped out of Ellis Island in December 1919, Goldman's one request to her former lover and fellow anarchist, Ben Reitman, was to keep her memory alive. Lenin's Russia disappointed the fifty-year-old Goldman, who drifted for the rest of her life. She always hoped to come back to the United States but authorities never permitted her to do so, with the exception of a brief speaking tour in the 1930s. By that time, anarchism seemed a relic of the past.

Eugene Debs

Whereas the strife in Emma Goldman's early life in tsarist Russia may have predisposed her to radicalism, the Eugene Debs that Goldman met while on a speaking tour in 1898 was not born a radical. As noted in Nick Salvatore's *Eugene V. Debs: Citizen and Socialist* (2007), Debs's workplace experiences explained his conversion to socialism. In the span of a few short years, Debs moved from a provincial view of corporate America, where he believed the assertion of individual rights was of primary importance, to a way of thinking that dissented from the mainstream and where collective action reigned paramount.

The first-born son of French immigrant grocery store owners, Debs personified the small-town Protestant work ethic that encompassed industry, frugality, sobriety, and benevolence. Young Debs harbored dreams of rising to the top of the nascent corporate world that he naively admired for its productivity and efficiency. When he was twenty years old, he joined the Brotherhood of Locomotive Firemen and became a union officer. Debs later took a job as a warehouse worker but his heart stayed with the railroad workers and the others who he had helped to organize.

Running as a Democrat in 1884, Eugene Debs won a seat in the Illinois State Assembly. From this vantage point, Debs began to observe the effects of concentrated industrial power on workers and citizens. He resented the way in which unmitigated corporate power undermined the individual's connection to democracy and community. Debs detested the fact that corporations could buy votes and nothing could stop them. In Debs's mind, according to Nick Salvatore, not only were citizens victims of corporate abuses but entire governments served the interests of the corporations.

In 1894 the Pullman Strike crushed whatever hopes Debs held for the promise of corporate America. Pullman Palace

Car Company owner George Pullman built a multi-million dollar business manufacturing luxury passenger cars in Pullman, Illinois. Pullman workers rented their houses from George Pullman in the company town that he built. Rents were more expensive than in neighboring Chicago so when Pullman decided to cut wages by almost 20% without cutting any expenses, the workers struck in protest. As the president of the American Railway Workers' Union, Debs led the Pullman employees. George Pullman attached mail cars to the trains pulling Pullman passenger cars leaving the plant. Pullman then convinced President Grover Cleveland to call out federal troops to break the power of the strikers who the railroad magnate accused of interfering with the delivery of the US mail.

The Pullman Strike was the last in a series of three late-nineteenth-century labor conflicts in which the authorities were called out on the side of the employers. In the aftermath of the 1886 Haymarket bombing, many Americans began to associate workers' strikes with anarchy. In the 1892 Homestead Strike, Henry Clay Frick's orders resulted in the deaths of workers to little public reaction. Debs's refusal to honor a federal injunction to halt the 1894 Pullman Strike earned a six-month jail sentence for contempt of court. Socialist newspaper editor Victor Berger visited Debs and left him a copy of Karl Marx's *Das Kapital.* Upon his release from Woodstock Prison in 1895, Debs delivered what many consider the most profound speech of his career to a crowd of about 100,000 in Chicago's Central Music Hall. His "Liberty" speech drew a connection between the American Revolutionaries of 1776 and the cause of labor. It would be at least a decade, however, before organized labor recovered from its losses, with Debs playing a leading part in the resurgence.

Debs's experiences as a union man confronting the railroad companies' labor practices and subsequent jail stay furnished abrupt lessons in the necessity of working-class solidarity. The protection of individual rights could best be achieved not in isolation but with the mutual dependence characterized by brotherhoods or unions. Debs believed that trusts and corporations posed a threat to the working class and, by extension, of the American republic. Debs maintained that his imprisonment violated the Constitution and in 1897 he openly declared himself a socialist. Hoping to reaffirm the value of democracy for Americans experiencing the tumultuous transition to an industrial power, he worked to the point of exhaustion

In 1901, Debs helped to establish the Socialist Party of America and lent his support to the Industrial Workers of the World (IWW), an organization for workers who advocated fighting for justice directly against employers. This new party was not the first socialist party in the United States but it was the first one did not consist primarily of immigrants. Until the birth of the Socialist Party there were few opportunities for collective action on the part of the workers. The American Federation of Labor (AFL) had existed since 1886 but it represented only skilled trade unionists. AFL president Samuel Gompers made his interests clear when he refused to call a sympathy strike to support workers during the Pullman Strike.

Debs's rendition of socialism had a uniquely American cast. Debs differed from European socialists in that he wanted to reform American society through traditional political channels by finding ways to coexist with the new industrial capitalism. Debs tried to create a viable program for the United States that resonated beyond the working class. He attempted to draw support from the Knights of Labor, the IWW, the Populists, and Communists. At times "the Prophet to Workers," as some called Debs, seemed to, in the words of Emma Goldman, "lack political clarity" (Goldman 1977, 221). For many, his strength was in his ability to relate socialism through workers' own experiences. His rhetoric interspersed Biblical references and masculine imagery. In an effort to attract the broadest following possible, he coached listeners not to follow him but to reach their own level of commitment to the common good.

Turn-of-the-century politics were far from business as usual. While Populism had managed to push some rural conservatives to the middle, Socialism moved a number of moderate urbanites to the left. Between 1900 and 1912, membership in the Socialist Party grew from 10,000 to over 150,000. It proved especially influential in American cities in the 1910 elections, when 56 cities, including Milwaukee, Berkeley, and Schenectady, elected Socialist mayors. Victor Berger won election to Congress. If the United States was ripe for a socialist conversion Debs would lead the charge. He offered himself up for the presidency on five separate occasions. The last time Debs ran for election in 1920, he did what no person before or since has done—he ran from his prison cell. Before he was pardoned for violating the Espionage Act for speaking out against World War I, Debs earned 3% of the votes and had piqued even President Harding's curiosity.

In the nation's cities several reform mayors used their positions of authority to begin to reshape local government in the best interests of the citizens. Republican mayor of Detroit Hazen Pingree initiated the city's first public relief program during the depression of 1893. He also demanded that the city's cable, streetcar, and utility companies lower their rates.

Progressivism

As the Democrats began to more readily consider unconventional demands, another movement that also radiated from the nation's middle gained popularity. Progressives differed from Populists in that progressive reformers focused primarily on the industrial cities and sprang from a different kind of intellectual foundation. Progressivism surfaced in urban areas just as the hard economic times from the 1893 to 1897 depression receded. The strongest push for reform emanated from Chicago, the centrifugal home to radical activity, and where a number of groups coalesced around the common goal of improving life for immigrant workers and their families.

Adherents to what eventually became a more formalized movement and ultimately a political party, the progressive label encompassed a diverse and sometimes seemingly disparate range of individuals. Progressive ranks included muckrakers, radicals, populists, educators, clubwomen, settlement house residents, labor leaders, politicians, civic officials, suffragists, temperance workers, members of the clergy, and even some businessmen. Those who were college-educated and lived what at the time was considered a middle-class lifestyle were especially drawn toward the ideological tenets of progressivism. Virtually all progressives recognized the necessity of government intervention to confront the country's mounting problems.

Restricted from entering the exclusively male political world, women, through their work in urban neighborhoods first as clubwomen and charity workers, and later as social workers based in settlement houses, devised a grassroots approach toward reform. Women like Hull-House's Jane Addams and Florence Kelley systematically identified, analyzed, and proposed solutions to their neighbors' problems. Chicago's Near Westside became an urban laboratory for such studies. The University of Chicago provided both the academic research facilities necessary for sociological studies and the pragmatic philosophy to energize the activists.

Florence Kelley

Florence Kelley has been described by her biographer, Kathryn Kish Sklar as "a colossus" for the part she played in shaping the modern welfare policies of the United States in the first thirty years of the twentieth century. Kelley's compulsion for change led her away from the charity model of Gilded Age clubwomen to devote her life's work to initiating a more proactive process through which, in the words of Supreme Court Justice Felix Frankfurter, "social legislation is promoted and eventually gets on the statute books"(Sklar 2001, 467). Kelley's work concentrated on prompting the government to protect workers from the abuses and exploitations inherent in the industrial workplace.

Florence Kelley was the child of two dedicated Philadelphia abolitionists, Caroline and William Kelley. Kelley's mother suffered throughout Florence's childhood from severe depression due to the deaths of five of her eight children. Her father served in Congress from 1860 to 1890 where he helped to draft the Fifteenth Amendment guaranteeing the rights of freedmen. William Kelley became a political and educational mentor to his daughter. Florence Kelley also grew close to her great aunt, Sarah Pugh, who counted Lucretia Mott among her best friends. Pugh, head of the Philadelphia Female Antislavery Society, exemplified a woman who devoted her life to activism. Florence Kelley's privileged childhood enabled her to pursue study in history and social science at Cornell University. After completing her honors thesis concerning the legal status of children, becoming in 1882 one of the early women graduates of Cornell, Kelley began to write about how college-educated women could help their wage-earning sisters.

Kelley accompanied her brother overseas where she decided to continue her public policy studies at the University of Zurich, the only European university that granted graduate degrees to women. Kelley's European experiences changed the trajectory of her life. She converted to socialism and became a leader in the German Social Democratic Party. She gave up her formal studies to devote her time to translating Friedrich Engel's *The Conditions of the Working Class in England* into English. In 1884, she married a fellow socialist, a Russian Jewish medical student Lazare Wishchnewetzky and gave birth the next year.

Shortly after the growing family relocated to New York in 1886, Kelley's criticism of the German Socialists' distance from the American working class in the preface of her translated work led to her expulsion from the Socialist Labor Party. Kelley redirected her interests toward what she perceived as a pressing issue—child labor. Through her writing, Kelley began to earn a reputation as a critic of the state's inattention to the plight of working children. Kelley had two more children while her husband grew frustrated over the failure of his medical practice. Unable to endure her husband's violent rage which had turned physical, Kelley fled with her children to Chicago where she took refuge at Hull-House. Its founder, Jane Addams, and the other residents welcomed Kelley into the settlement. Once she had found a place for her children at the home of the journalist Henry Demarest Lloyd, Kelley's reform career began in earnest.

Immersion in the extraordinary political culture of the activist women at Hull-House afforded Kelley the luxury of completing a law degree at Northwestern University. She also developed a vision for public policy toward women and children that would require the government to assume the responsibility for its neediest citizens. Sklar explains that Kelley's "understanding of the material basis of class conflict and her familiarity with American political institutions, combined with her spirited personality, placed her in the vanguard of a generation of reformers who sought to make American government responsive to what they saw as the needs of the working people"(Sklar 2001, 462). Jane Addams helped Kelley to secure employment with the Illinois Bureau of Labor Statistics so that she could support herself and her children. The bureau hired Kelley to investigate the "sweating" system in the garment industry.

Florence Kelley's work was so impressive that in 1892 the US Department of Labor Commissioner, Carroll Wright, asked her to coordinate a systematic survey of the occupations and ethnicities in Chicago's Nineteenth Ward. Kelley's findings were published in *Hull-House Maps and Papers* (1895), one of her best known works. In 1893 Governor John Peter Altgeld appointed Kelley chief factory inspector for Illinois where she worked to enforce the only eight-hour law for women wage-earners in the country and to prevent the employment of children under the age of fourteen. When the Illinois Supreme Court rendered the eight-hour law unconstitutional in 1895, Kelley decided to work against the power of state courts to overturn protective labor legislation for women. She reached beyond Hull-House for support and enlisted Ellen Henrotin, the wife of a prominent Chicago banker. Henrotin encouraged Kelley to serve as the Secretary of the newly established National Consumers' League, a position she would hold for over thirty years, until her death in 1932.

Moving to New York to lead the League in 1899, Kelley took up residence at a nurses' settlement, Henry Street, headed by Lillian Wald. Kelley devoted her life to shaping the National Consumers' League into an activist agency that promoted protective labor legislation for women and children. Founding league branches in virtually every large city outside the South by 1904, Kelley helped educate her constituency by enacting a white label campaign to identify goods made under fair labor conditions for purchase. Kelley soon turned her attention to enacting protective legislation through the judicial process. Kelley's efforts helped to win court recognition of medical and sociological evidence to convince state courts to limit work hours and require a minimum wage for women. In 1907 Kelley and her research director, Josephine Goldmark, enlisted the help of Goldmark's brother-in-law, prominent Boston attorney Louis D. Brandeis, to successfully argue in *Muller v. Oregon* that the state had the authority to regulate working hours for women in non-hazardous occupations. Eventually the League would also move to defend hours legislation for men as well as for women. Kelley's strategy rested on the controversial premise of using "gender-driven legislation as a surrogate remedy for class exploitation" (Sklar 1995, 259). She reasoned that once women gained benefits like maximum hours laws that the same protections would also be extended to men. Some feminists viewed this approach as an obstacle to gender equality (Woloch, 2015).

Kelley did not let the criticism directed at her, both for her support of protective legislation for women and her anti-militaristic stance during World War I, deter her from her work. She considered the 1921 passage of the Sheppard–Towner Maternity and Infant Protection Act, which provided federal funds to prevent maternal and infant mortality, her most important accomplishment. The act set a precedent in that it provided the first federal health care funds. Although Kelley held out great hope that the act marked the inception of a national health care program, by 1926 Congress refused to fund the program. The responsibility for the health of mothers and their young children reverted to the state and county level. While Kelley did not accomplish all her goals in her lifetime, in 1935 the federal government created a social security program that began to care for dependent children, the elderly, and the disabled. Three years later, Franklin Roosevelt's Secretary of Labor Frances Perkins drafted the Fair Labor Standards Act that incorporated minimum wage and maximum hour provisions and child labor regulations for the first time in the nation's history.

Robert Marion La Follette

At the state level, Republican politician Robert Marion La Follette, Sr. represented a prime example of a reform-minded political leader. Like many other early reformers, his roots were in the Midwest. Born in Primrose, Wisconsin to a prominent farming family in 1855, La Follette's mother, Mary, groomed him to always do what was right to honor the memory of his politically active father who died when Bob was not yet a year old. Out of respect for his parents, La Follette held himself to high standards. By the time he reached his mid-twenties, he had graduated from college and law school at the University of Wisconsin. After practicing law and serving as district attorney of Dane County for four years, La Follette was elected in 1885 to the US House of Representatives where he amassed a record as a moderate liberal until his reelection bid failed in 1890.

Months after La Follette left Congress, a Republican Party leader offered him a bribe to fix a court case against several state officials. Incensed, La Follette rejected the offer and launched a crusade to prevent such corrupt use of money and influence and in essence, to make government more democratic, earning him the nickname of "Fighting Bob." La Follette's biographer, Nancy C. Unger asserts that he "dedicated his life to returning power to the people" (Unger 2008, 1). La Follette's struggle yielded political rewards. While serving as governor from 1901 to 1906, he began to formulate a progressive agenda. The main premise of what became known as the "Wisconsin Idea" revolved around the government acting in the public interest. La Follette relied on faculty members from his alma mater to help him draft and develop legislation that resulted in innovative public policies.

Governor La Follette passed a civil service law that dictated the system be based on merit rather than on political favors, broke up monopolies, and reined in railroads with a tax based on the value of the land that they owned and by establishing a commission to regulate railroad rates. La Follette backed environmental laws to protect forests, laws to uphold the rights of small farmers, supported workers' rights, and increased funding for education. He supported measures that would help regulate lobbying efforts to end patronage politics. La Follette also oversaw the creation of an electoral system whereby Wisconsin became the first state in the nation to require that all candidates for public office be subject to the direct vote of the people, which proved particularly significant because it meant that gubernatorial candidates were elected rather than chosen. In 1911 Wisconsin also became the first state in the nation to pass a workers' compensation law.

La Follette resigned from his post as the top state official in 1906 to carry his progressive platform to the federal level. By the time he joined the Senate, had earned recognition as a national figure. He served as a US Senator leading the Senate's progressive forces until his death in 1925. Senator La Follette helped pass bills to increase taxes on corporations, require physical evaluation of railroads, and helped to protect the rights of seamen. Although he failed to secure multiple presidential bids, throughout his life he remained self-righteous to a fault. He refused to stand behind legislation that he considered imperfect and, in part because of his uncompromising principles, he failed to maintain close working relationships with either Theodore Roosevelt or Woodrow Wilson.

All of his life, Robert La Follette fought against the encroachments of the powerful few upon the rights of many. He spoke for the marginalized. In an 1889 Congressional address he argued that southern whites would benefit as much as blacks from ending racial discrimination. He championed woman's suffrage as an extension of democracy. He consistently encouraged women to advance into leadership positions. He called for a woman factory inspector in Wisconsin and women appointees to the Board of the State University and the Normal School Board of Regents. La Follette demonstrated his support of women's rights on a personal level in his relationship with his wife, Belle. In his autobiography he publically acknowledged her help and they co-published *La Follette's Weekly Magazine*. For Belle La Follette, her husband's devotion meant that she felt comfortable speaking her mind. She urged privileged women to renounce their "parasitic" existence and devote themselves to the betterment of the country. Alice Paul referred to Belle La Follette as "the most consistent supporter of equal rights of all the women of her time" (Unger 2016, 2).

Carrie Chapman Catt

Carrie Lane Chapman Catt proved to be one of the most brilliant political strategists of the twentieth century. Born in 1859 she spent her earliest years on a farm in Ripon, Wisconsin. Although she would later describe herself as "an ordinary child in an ordinary family on an ordinary farm," young Carrie Clinton Lane acquired a love of reading and feminist aspirations from her mother, Maria who had attended Oread Collegiate Institute in Worcester, Massachusetts, a center of feminist activity (Van Voris 1987, 5). Oread's founder, Eli Thayer, believed that women needed to be afforded the same intellectual opportunities as men.

In a move that involved careful planning at the end of the Civil War, the Lane family relocated to a farm outside of Charles City, Iowa. Carrie attended a one-room schoolhouse where the essence of her determined and curious personality began to show. At the impressionable age of thirteen, Catt became indignant when she realized her mother would not be allowed to vote in the 1872 presidential election while her father and the Catts' hired man could cast their ballots. Catt's biographer Jaqueline Van Voris asserts that Catt had "discovered feminism before she knew the word." The popular and ambitious Catt graduated at the top of her college class of twenty-seven students in 1880 with a degree in the General Science Course for Women. She also had "definite ideas of how the world should be ordered" and possessed enough self-confidence to believe that she numbered among those who would help to set it right (Van Voris 1987, 9). Shortly after graduating, Catt published an article in the *Iowa Homestead* condemning the drudgery of housework and suggesting that educating women in basic chemistry and physiology would promote nutrition and hygiene and elevate the housewife's status. Hoping to take advantage of a profession newly opened to women, Catt became a clerk in the office of a Charles City lawyer. While clerking, she enthusiastically accepted an offer to teach high school in the booming prairie town of Mason City. She immediately proved to be a talented teacher. Before the end of her second year, in 1883, the Mason City superintendent resigned and Catt replaced him thanks to a unanimous petition drawn up by the students. Her experience in education and reading the law helped her to enhance the organizational skills that she later found so useful.

While serving as superintendent, Catt married Leo Chapman, the owner and publisher of the *Mason City Republican*. By all accounts Carrie Catt had found her soulmate in Chapman. However, due to the prohibition barring married women from teaching, Catt was forced to resign. The blow would be softened by her husband's offer of a coediting position at his newspaper. A fervent proponent of woman's suffrage, Chapman encouraged his young wife's column, "Woman's World," which provided a forum for woman's issues. Catt articulated her belief that the struggle for women's rights would not progress without organization.

Leo Chapman's dispute with a conservative local politician played out publicly in the *Mason City Republican* and Chapman soon found himself the defendant in a libel suit. Forced to sell the paper, Chapman went to San Francisco in search of work but died there of typhoid fever a few days before his twenty-seven-year-old wife arrived. Devastated, Catt stayed for a year at the San Francisco home of her aunt, earning her keep as the city's first woman news reporter. While in California, Catt attended a number of lectures that inspired her to think more deeply about feminist concerns. Returning to Charles City in August 1887, she joined the Women's Christian Temperance Union and also began to actively fight for suffrage. Suffrage women were divided between those who saw victory in gradual steps, winning on a state-to-state basis, and those who wanted to follow the

African American suffrage route with a federal constitutional amendment. Catt's work with the suffragists, who were on the brink of reconciliation after twenty years, afforded an inside view of the divisive results of infighting on an organization. By 1890, she had become a professional writer and lecturer for the Iowa Woman's Suffrage Association.

In June 1890, Catt married a wealthy fellow Iowa State alumnus, George Catt, who encouraged his wife's suffrage work. The Catts moved to New York where George headquartered his work as a structural engineer. Calling the largest city in the country home, Catt continued her suffrage advocacy. Her relentless work in the South Dakota campaign and her speech at the 1890 National Woman's Suffrage Association's (NAWSA) annual convention in Washington, DC impressed the national suffrage leaders. Aged NAWSA president Susan B. Anthony dissolved the executive committee and replaced it with a business committee chaired by Catt, who now became responsible for recruiting what would become a network of lecturing organizers.

In 1892, Susan B. Anthony surprised Catt by requesting that she be the first in a contingent of women to address Congress on the suffrage amendment. Catt resolved that the women's efforts would no longer be placed at the bottom of the pile of ignored legislative work. She reconsidered every aspect of the campaign. She realized how detrimental negative publicity was to the suffragists. Older leaders, like Anthony, were drawn wearing ill-fitting clothes and wielding unfashionable umbrellas. Catt criticized the cartoonists who consistently depicted suffragists in such an insulting light. After 1893, at Catt's insistence, depictions of suffragists began to improve.

By 1893, the charismatic Catt, with a voice that could "be heard in out of door meetings" campaigned hard in Colorado speaking before Chautauqua Assemblies, Populists, Knights of Labor, Republican and Democratic clubs (Van Voris 1987, 35). Twenty-six of the twenty-nine counties in which Catt spoke voted for suffrage, making Colorado the second state after Wyoming to pass woman's suffrage. The West seemed to offer the best chances for suffrage success. Before the turn of the century, suffrage passed in Utah and Idaho but failed in California where the suffragists waged a substantial campaign. There would not be another state victory for the suffragists for more than a decade.

When Susan B. Anthony celebrated her eightieth birthday in 1900, she reluctantly began to look to the younger NAWSA leaders for a new president. Anthony considered three potential candidates. Reverend Anna Howard Shaw seemed an obvious choice, but although she was a brilliant speaker she did not have independent financial means. Writer and journalist Lilly Deveraux Blake was also an effective speaker and very witty but lacked a seminal vision. Carrie Chapman Catt possessed all the attributes of a born leader. She was creative, practical, an organizational genius, an inspirational speaker and, most of all, resilient in the face of defeat. Catt triumphed but not without some dissention in the leadership ranks.

For the next four years, Catt concentrated on waging a counteroffensive against the anti-suffrage forces. Later she would recall with resentment how these "certain combines of interests" led by the liquor manufacturers delayed suffrage for years (Catt and Shuler 1926, Chapter X). Catt resigned from NAWSA to care for her ailing husband in 1904. Distraught from his death the following year and from the death of Susan B. Anthony in 1906, Catt heeded the advice of her doctor and her friends and traveled to Europe where she continued to work with the International Woman's Suffrage Association, an organization that she had helped found in 1902. She spent the next several years traveling abroad before helping to create the Woman's Suffrage Party to begin organizing women along New York City precinct lines in October 1909. She wanted to unite all the various women's clubs and organizations that had championed the suffrage cause for years and turn this coalition into an organization rivalling a political machine. By 1914, the New York State Woman Suffrage Association and its affiliate Woman's Suffrage Party claimed 450 branches and an estimated membership of 350,000.

With the coming of war in Europe, Catt returned to the United States permanently in 1915 where she found NAWSA tensely divided under the leadership of Reverend Anna Howard Shaw. Catt became president of the national association once again and in 1916 she unveiled her "Winning Plan," promising the passage of the woman's suffrage amendment within six years. Frustrated by countless public appeals designed to convince apathetic uneducated male voters to support woman's suffrage, Catt redirected the campaign toward aggressive nonpartisan lobbying on Capitol Hill. Taking a risk that ultimately paid off, Catt persuaded the political elites to side with the suffragists. In the meantime NAWSA recruited two million women and conducted a massive educational campaign of its organizers. Catt believed, as did other reformers, that education was the key to a solid organizational foundation. She revitalized the entire movement to the point that it could no longer be ignored and pushed it on to victory with the passage of the Nineteenth Amendment in 1920.

Helen Hunt Jackson

Women finally attained political rights, but other minorities were not as fortunate. While some have cast dispersions on progressives for failing Native Americans and, particularly in the South, African Americans, a number of reformers did recognize that these groups continued to experience widespread prejudice and discrimination. As noted in Kate Phillips's 2003 biography, *Helen Hunt Jackson: A Literary Life*, Helen Hunt Jackson, childhood friend of Emily Dickinson, turned to writing for solace following the death of her husband, achieving wide acclaim for her poems, prose, and travel sketches. Often writing under the pseudonym H.H., Jackson geared her writing toward a growing market of female readers tied to their homes and their children. Her writings drew on her own experiences including an 1872 transcontinental railroad trip that took her from New York to San Francisco.

Jackson's transformation to the cause of Indian justice came when she visited Boston in 1879. After attending a reception for Indian leaders who were touring the country protesting the confiscation of their land by the US government, Jackson set out to publicize their plight. In 1881, she published an expose of Indian mistreatment, *A Century of Dishonor*. Several years later, she wrote *Ramona*, about a romance novel about a half-breed girl raised by an affluent Spanish family and an Indian forced off his tribal land. Jackson died shortly after the publication of *Ramona*; however, her work brought the plight of Native Americans to the attention of those in power and inspired other reformers to continue to champion her cause. Ironically the goal of most reformers working on behalf of Native American rights aimed to integrate them into mainstream American culture. They supported the Dawes Severalty Act which sanctioned government reallocation of Indian land. Under the 1887 act, community-held tribal lands were sectioned into 160 acre parcels and distributed to individual Natives who agreed to become farmers.

Robert La Follette also championed the rights of Indians when in 1909 and 1910 he led a commission to investigate the living conditions of Wisconsin Indians following the passage of the Dawes Severalty Act. The results not only reaffirmed the dismal state of affairs of Indians living on various reservations but they were a testament to the cultural devastation of the tribes who by 1910 had lost over 174,000 acres of tribal land in Wisconsin alone. Confiscation of tribal lands would not be halted, however, until 1934 with the passage of the Indian New Deal.

W.E.B. Du Bois

Although some have criticized progressive reformers for their seeming lack of concern regarding minorities, African Americans did advance under the auspices a biracial group of reformers who founded what eventually became the nation's largest civil rights organization, the National Association for the Advancement of Colored People (NAACP) in 1910. Scholar W.E.B. Du Bois, whose life has been extensively chronicled by David Levering Lewis (1994), led the charge to ensure political, educational, economic, and social equality for black Americans. His efforts were assisted by a number of white reformers including settlement workers Florence Kelley, Jane Addams, and Lillian Wald, as well as by Mary White Ovington and Oswald Garrison Villard, both descendants of abolitionists.

The NAACP formally organized following a conference called to address the horrific practice of lynching and in reaction by both blacks and whites to the 1908 race riot in Abraham Lincoln's hometown of Springfield, Illinois. Headquartered in New York City, the organization quickly established branches in other large cities. A few years earlier, Du Bois had launched the Niagara Movement to advocate for the civil and political rights of African Americans. Although the militant movement responded to the growing segregation and escalating racial violence against blacks, it ultimately failed, due to white racism as well as the opposition of the more conservative Booker T. Washington and his allies, and from lack of funding. The spirit of the Niagara Movement that refused to succumb to whites' assimilationist demands was echoed in the NAACP.

Hailing from the small Massachusetts town of Great Barrington, W.E.B. Du Bois was the son of Mary Silvina Burghardt, a domestic worker, and Alfred Du Bois, a barber and itinerant laborer who deserted his family when his son was two years old. An excellent student, William Edward Burghardt Du Bois was one of the first beneficiaries of Massachusetts's racially integrated school system. He began to publish newspaper articles while still in high school, continuing his studies in the classics at Fisk University in Nashville. While at Fisk, Du Bois was exposed to the overt racism of the Jim Crow south. Eventually enrolling as a junior at Harvard, he completed his doctoral thesis, "The Suppression of the African Slave Trade to the United States of America, 1638–1870," in 1896. That same year he married Nina Gomer, a student at Wilberforce University where he was teaching.

Du Bois's sociological writing was among the first to examine racial issues from an intellectual perspective. Rather than subscribing to the white accommodationist solutions, Du Bois defended black identity and culture. He studied the social and economic conditions of urban residents in *The Philadelphia Negro* (1899) as well as the cultural and institutional lives of southern blacks in *The Negroes of Farmville, Virginia* (1898), later revised as *The Souls of Black Folk* (1903). Du Bois explored the so-called Negro Problem and sought to develop appropriate responses. In essence, he demanded full racial equality. Atlanta University hired Du Bois to teach sociology and empirical studies, and he left Atlanta in 1910 to assume the position of director of research and publications for the NAACP. The journal he edited, *The Crisis*, became the voice for the organization and the nation's largest forum for the representation of black intellectual and cultural life. In a controversial 1918 *Crisis* editorial, Du Bois urged support for the war effort. He also advocated equal treatment for black troops. With his work interrupted by World War I, Du Bois turned to Pan-Africanism and Marxism to combat racial prejudice.

Progressivism's Hiatus

The entry of the United States into World War I derailed the momentum of progressive reformers, as Robert La Follette had predicted it would. Some, like W.E.B. Du Bois and Carrie Catt, refused to let the war impede their work. Although politically diverse, Eugene Debs, Carrie Catt, and Robert La Follette were among the many who believed that international disputes should be resolved peacefully. Settlement women, including Florence Kelley, founded the Women's International League for Peace and Freedom to voice their abhorrence of war. William Jennings Bryan's opposition was so intense that he resigned his position of Secretary of State in protest of the US military involvement. Emma Goldman considered her anti-war activism "her best and most important work" (Chalberg 2008, 133). From the moment war broke out in Europe, Goldman opposed both the war and US participation in it, rationally arguing that only American financiers stood to benefit from the "War Mania." With all eyes turned toward Europe, domestic reform slowed. Once the war ended, the conservative Republicans leading the county paid little attention to the drive for reform. The prohibition and suffrage amendments squeaked through Congress but other Progressive measures would be taken up by the Democrats only after the 1920s roared by.

In the two opening decades of the twentieth century, the reformers had a good run. Political victories even at the federal level were calculable. Protective labor legislation for women and children advanced. Minimum wage, maximum hours, and workers' compensation laws began to pass in select states. By 1910, even the federal government had begun to take action. The Seventeenth Amendment under the Taft administration answered the Populists' call for the direct election of senators. Congress also created the Children's Bureau in the Department of Labor and legislated an eight-hour day for federal workers. American workers hoped that the US Commission on Industrial Relations created by William Howard Taft as he left office in 1912 would lead to new laws mandating workplace improvements. The horrific Triangle Shirtwaist Fire headlines shook every American to the core and stimulated workplace safety laws at the state level across most of the country.

Acting on their principles, the movers and shakers who came of age around the turn of the century tried to create a more benevolent world replete with genuine concern for others. As the base of the political landscape shifted from the countryside to the urban areas, the reform leaders concentrated on restructuring the political system to ensure a more just America for all. The meaning of democracy changed along with the composition of the country. America was no longer defined and directed entirely by white men. The participation of women in particular led to a more caring and humane version of democracy. Women's political activism meant that the issues that most affected them and their communities could be identified, articulated, and acted upon. Blacks and select whites, including descendants of abolitionists, tried to end racial discrimination and lynching. Radical political theorists' ideas, many of which originated in Europe, reached across the Atlantic. Alternative forms of government such as socialism demanded that American politicians pay attention to the working and living conditions of the working class. Reformers passed this responsibility on to the state. The confluence of diverse and formerly marginalized groups led to a unique transition—progressivism and its predecessor, populism—marking the gestation of the modern welfare state. For the first time in its history, the United States government began to assume the responsibility for the well-being of its citizens.

References

Baker, Paula. 1991. *The Moral Frameworks of Public Life: Gender, Politics, and the State in Rural New York, 1870–1930*. New York: Oxford University Press.

Catt, Carrie Chapman and Nettie Rogers Schuler. 1926. *Woman Suffrage and Politics: The Inner Story of the Suffrage Movement*. New York: Scribner and Sons.

Chalberg, John C. 2008. *Emma Goldman: American Individualist*. New York: Pearson.

Cherny, Ronald. 1994. *A Righteous Cause: The Life of William Jennings Bryan*. Norman: University of Oklahoma Press.

Edwards, Rebecca. 1997. *Angels in the Machinery: Gender in American Party Politics from the Civil War to the Progressive Era*. New York: Oxford University Press.

Falk, Candace. 1990. *Love, Anarchy, and Emma Goldman*. New Brunswick, NJ: Rutgers University Press.

— ed. 1995. *Emma Goldman: A Guide to her Life and Documentary Sources*. Cambridge: Chadwyck-Healey.

Gilmore, Glenda Elizabeth. 2002. *Who Were the Progressives?* New York: Bedford/St. Martin's.

Goldman, Emma. 1977. *Living My Life*. New York: New American Library.

Hicks, John. 1931. *The Populist Revolt*. Minneapolis: The University of Minnesota Press.

Lewis, David Levering. 1994. *W.E.B. Du Bois: Biography of a Race, 1868–1919*. New York: Henry Holt and Company.

Marti, Donald B. 1991. *Women of the Grange: Mutuality and Sisterhood in Rural America, 1866–1920*. New York: Greenwood Press.

Osterud, Nancy Grey. 1991. *Bonds of Community: The Lives of Farm Women in Nineteenth-Century New York*. Ithaca, NY: Cornell University Press.

Phillips, Kate. 2003. *Helen Hunt Jackson: A Literary Life*. Berkeley: University of California Press.

Postel, Charles. 2007. *The Populist Vision*. New York: Oxford University Press.

Salvatore, Nick. 1982. *Eugene Debs: Citizen and Socialist*. Urbana: University of Illinois Press.

Sanders, Elizabeth. 1999. *Roots of Reform: Farmers, Workers, and the American State, 1877–1917*. Chicago: University of Chicago.

Sklar, Kathryn Kish. 2001. "Florence Kelley." In *Women Building Chicago: A Biographical Dictionary, 1790–1990*, ed. Rima Lunin Schultz and Adele Hast. Bloomington: University of Indiana Press.

—. 1997. *Florence Kelley and the Nation's Work: The Rise of Women's Political Culture, 1830–1900*. New Haven, CT: Yale University Press.

Unger, Nancy C. 2016. *Belle La Follette: Progressive Era Reformer*. New York: Routledge.

—. 2008. *Fighting Bob La Follette: The Righteous Reformer*. Second edition. Madison: Wisconsin Historical Society Press.

Van Voris, Jacqueline. 1987. *Carrie Chapman Catt: A Public Life*. New York: The Feminist Press.

Woloch, Nancy. 2015. *A Class by Herself: Protective Laws for Women Workers, 1890s–1990s*. Princeton, NJ: Princeton University Press.

Further Reading

Addams, Jane. 1912. *Twenty Years at Hull-House*. New York: Macmillan.

Baker, Jean H. 2005. *Sisters: The Lives of America's Suffragists*. New York: Hill & Wang.

Beeby, James M. 2002. *Populism in the South Revisited: New Interpretations and New Departures*. Jackson: University of Mississippi Press.

Bensel, Richard F. 2008. *Passions and Preferences: William Jennings Bryan and the 1896 Democratic Convention*. New York: Cambridge University Press.

Bordin, Ruth. 1986. *Frances Willard: A Biography*. Chapel Hill: University of North Carolina Press.

Brown, Victoria Bissell. 2003. *The Education of Jane Addams: Politics and Culture in Modern America*. Philadelphia: University of Pennsylvania Press.

Chester, Eric T. 2014. *The Wobblies in their Heyday: The Rise and Destruction of the Industrial Workers of the World during the World War I Era*. Santa Barbara, CA: Praeger.

Davis, Allen F. 1973. *American Heroine: The Life and Legend of Jane Addams*. New York: Oxford University Press.

Davis, Allen F. 1967. *The Social Settlement and the Progressive Movement, 1890–1914*. New York: Oxford University Press, 1967.

Dawley, Alan. 2003. *Changing the World: American Progressives in War and Revolution*. Princeton, NJ: Princeton University Press.

Diner, Steven. 1998. *A Very Different Age: Americans of the Progressive Era*. New York: Hill & Wang.

Drake, Richard. 2013. *The Education of an Anti-Imperialist: Robert La Follette and U.S. Expansion*. Madison: University of Wisconsin Press.

Dubofsky, Melvyn and Joseph A. McCartin. A. 2000. *We Shall be All: A History of the Industrial Workers of the World*. Urbana: University of Illinois Press.

Falk, Candace. 2008. *Emma Goldman: A Documentary History of the American Years:* Volume 1 *Made for America, 1890–1901*. Volume 2 *Making Speech Free, 1902–1909*. Urbana: University of Illinois Press.

Feld, Marjorie. N. 2008. *Lillian Wald: A Biography*. Chapel Hill: University of North Carolina Press.

Fischer, Marilyn, Nackenoff, Carol, and Wendy Chmielewski, ed., 2009. *Jane Addams and the Practice of Democracy: Multidisciplinary Perspectives on Theory and Practice*. Urbana: University of Illinois Press.

Fowler, Robert B. 1986. *Carrie Catt, Feminist Politician*. Boston: Northeastern University Press, 1986.

Franzen, Trisha. 2014. *Anna Howard Shaw: The Work of Woman Suffrage*. Urbana: University of Illinois Press.

Freeberg, Ernest. 2008. *Democracy's Prisoner: Eugene V. Debs, the Great War, and the Right to Dissent*. Cambridge, MA: Harvard University Press.

Goodwin, Doris Kearns. 2013. *The Bully Pulpit: Theodore Roosevelt, William Howard Taft and the Golden Age of Journalism*. New York: Simon and Schuster.

Goodwyn, Lawrence. 1976. *Democratic Promise: The Populist Movement in America*. New York: Oxford University Press.

Hofstadter, Richard. 1955. *Age of Reform: From Bryan to FDR*. New York: Vintage Books.

Kaplan, Richard L. 2002. *Politics and the American Press: The Rise of Objectivity, 1865–1920*. Cambridge: Cambridge University Press.

Knight, Louise. 2005. *Citizen: Jane Addams and the Struggle for Democracy*. Chicago: University of Chicago Press.

Link, Arthur and Richard McCormick. *Progressivism*. Wheeling, IL: Harlan Davidson.

Marable, Manning. 1986. *W.E.B. Du Bois: Black Radical and Democrat*. Boulder, CO: Paradigm Publishers.

McGerr, Michael. 2003. *A Fierce Discontent: The Rise and Fall of the Progressive Movement in America, 1870–1920*. New York: Free Press.

McMath, Robert. 1993. *American Populism: A Social History*. New York: Hill & Wang.

Mitchell, Robert B. 2008. *Skirmisher: The Life, Times, and Political Career of James B. Weaver*. Roseville: Edinborough Press.

Nugent, Walter. 2013. *The Tolerant Populists, Second Edition: Kansas Populism and Nativism*. Chicago: University of Chicago Press.

Orr, Brooke Speer. 2014. *The "People's Joan of Arc": Mary Elizabeth Lease, Gendered Politics and Populist Party Politics in the Gilded Age*. New York: Peter Lang.

Papke, David Ray. 1999. *The Pullman Case: The Clash of Labor and Capital in Industrial America*. Lawrence: University of Kansas Press.

Pastorello, Karen. 2014. *The Progressives: Activism and Reform in American Society*. Chichester: John Wiley and Sons.

Peck, Mary G. 1944. *Carrie Chapman Catt: A Biography*. New York: H.W. Wilson.

Rodgers, Daniel T. 1998. *Atlantic Crossings: Social Politics in a Progressive Age*. Cambridge, MA: Harvard University Press.

Willrich, Michael. 2003. *City of Courts: Socializing Justice in Progressive Era Chicago*. Cambridge: Cambridge University Press.

Williams, Chad L. *Torchbearers of Democracy: African American Soldiers in the World War I Era*. Chapel Hill: University of North Carolina Press.

Williams, R. Hal. 2010. *Realigning America: McKinley, Bryan, and the Remarkable Election of 1896*. Lawrence: University Press of Kansas.

Chapter Twenty-Three

Changing Interpretations of Theodore Roosevelt and the Progressive Era

Kathleen Dalton

The Heroic Period of Historical Interpretation of Theodore Roosevelt

Theodore Roosevelt remains a vital subject of study because of his colorful personality and historic significance. Youthful president, cowboy, writer, trust buster, big game hunter, family man, conservationist, and a loud voice urging Americans to lead a more strenuous and moral life, he still draws cheers and boos from audiences. He argued fiercely for the United States to make its way out of its third-rate military power status to become an international leader, and in his third party Bull Moose run for the presidency in 1912 he spoke up for the creation of a social safety net of unemployment and health insurance, old age pensions, and the right to organize unions which would make his country a better place to live for the average worker. He invented the modern presidency and built a stronger federal government. His bold pronouncements and daring deeds coupled with his flair for self-dramatization have appealed to numerous later fans and to scholarly observers who have used him as a place of origin for the story of the rise of America to world power—or the start of a misguided American imperial hegemony and a national security state (McCoy 2009). Others pin him to the wall like a butterfly specimen to represent the evolution of more favorable attitudes toward labor or America's transition from a weak state to a modern strong nation. In one book he appears as a bloodthirsty racist and another as a farsighted leader. Whether seen as a chauvinistic buffoon or a statesman–savant, he stands out as an historic figure of consequence scholars need to understand. His fate in the judgment of historians is still linked to debates over what progressivism was and to debates over how well or badly America has used its foreign policy leadership. Theodore Roosevelt has been persistently useful to historians and fans alike, but the story of TR's posthumous fate among historians and popular interpreters reveals a path of Balkanized, contradictory interpreters, and a trail of still-unanswered questions.

Early interpreters of Theodore Roosevelt's life put heroism at the center of their stories. The "Great Man" theory of individual agency and power that Thomas Carlyle posited in the aftermath of Napoleon shaped the heroic tales of the brave Theodore. As early as 1902 popular writers such as Robert C.V. Meyers told TR's ongoing life as "The True Story of an Ideal American," replete with dramatic scenes of charges up San Juan Hill and the cowboy TR catching boat thieves and lassoing varmints out West. Meyers declared that TR was "the most prominent figure in the Western hemisphere," "the typical American of strong manly attributes," and "one of the foremost worthies that ever shaped a nation's destiny" (Meyers 1902, 5–7). TR's close friend Jacob Riis further stoked the fires of hero worship in newspaper and magazine articles before he published *Theodore Roosevelt, The Citizen* in 1904, leaving no doubt that Riis believed his hero had molded his times. With chapters called "A Young Men's Hero," Riis regaled readers with stories of Roosevelt racing down Cooper's Bluff at Sagamore Hill with young sons Archie and Kermit. Telling of TR's eggs and bacon for breakfast and his talk around the Roosevelt family dinner table, Riis evoked a familiar TR to build bonds between his hero and his readers, and he wrote that such stories "brings us all so much nearer together, which is where we ought to be" (Riis 395, 332). Cartoonists further immortalized his presidency with images of TR knocking out the oil, beef, and railroad trusts as a formidable cowboy with a big stick. In *Puck* J.S. Pughe dramatized TR's fight for railroad regulation, showing him sword in hand about to decapitate the hydra-headed senators under the control of railroads. Whether portrayed as Hercules fighting with Rockefeller or as a hunter killing off bad trusts, TR in

A Companion to the Gilded Age and Progressive Era, First Edition. Edited by Christopher McKnight Nichols and Nancy C. Unger.
© 2017 John Wiley & Sons, Inc. Published 2017 by John Wiley & Sons, Inc.

cartoons often provided a reassuring image of the federal government's ability to tame emerging corporate bullies. Cartoons of a colossal TR, the world leader digging a Panama Canal ditch to unite the Atlantic and Pacific oceans, made the United States appear to be an all-powerful unifier of worlds: pulling great oceans together in the interest of peace and world commerce. TR the mighty captain appeared steering the ship of state, encouraging the public to believe that the federal government should be driven by an activist president who controlled economic forces and institutions and mastered world problems. In this heroic version TR mastered corporations by busting a few trusts and gave labor a Square Deal by intervening in the Anthracite Coal Strike. TR, a political Galahad, master of his universe, made a good story and fit within the early narrative of progressive reform as a movement that significantly improved the nation (Lorant 1959; Gros 1910; McCutcheon 1910; Shaw 1910; Valaik 1993; Dalton 1981).

Writers inclined to praise TR only had to peruse the travel accounts and histories he had written, with himself as the star. In Africa he wrote about his own bravery as he shouldered a gun against charging elephants and lions and triumphed, and in Cuba he led his men into battle and victory without a pang of doubt or fear. As an explorer he faced death and great odds traversing an unknown and god-forsaken Amazon tributary and came out alive to tell the tale (Dalton 2002, Millard 2005). His autobiography places him and his moral courage at the head of his nation; it argues that his political enemies were wrong and he was right and so he emerged victorious. When he urged Americans to "strive after great things" and to "lead clean, vigorous, healthy lives" and as a nation "to play a great part in the world" and to live "the life of strenuous endeavor," he, like Winston Churchill wrote to inspire citizens to live larger lives and to be willing to sacrifice for the love of their country. And like Churchill, TR found he could guarantee himself a better place in history if he penned the history himself (Roosevelt 1896 in *Works*).

The Deflation of Theodore Roosevelt's Reputation

His reputation had reached such an apex that TR's death in January 1919 sparked a sizable memorial movement with religious overtones. Memorial organizations, the Roosevelt Memorial Association and the Women's Roosevelt Memorial Association, celebrated his birthday and used their grassroots organizations and political clout to sponsor educational programs about TR all over the country. During a special Roosevelt Memorial Week in 1919 public schools across the country required their students to sing "Onward Christian Soldiers," one of TR's favorite hymns, to honor the values he represented. That week an estimated 110 million people participated in Roosevelt memorial celebrations. Eleanor Roosevelt, TR's favorite niece, served on the board of the Women's Roosevelt Memorial Association and in the District of Columbia's fund drive to refurnish TR's childhood home and open it as a house museum to honor TR (Lancos 1992). The men's Roosevelt Memorial Association made movies to perpetuate the memory of TR, including "Theodore Roosevelt: Fighter for Social Justice," and built shrines to TR. Historic sites dedicated to remembering TR proliferated over the years and now include twenty-one National Park Service sites. Beloved by the public, honored as a revered national hero, TR was voted the most admired man in America. Despite this adulation his reputation would not remain elevated for long after his death (Dalton 1981, 1992).

Historians early in the twentieth century rarely approached TR as memorializers did, but they accepted his version of events often and saw him favorably. Though TR as a writer of history and as President of the American Historical Association celebrated blood and guts, man-on-horseback action history, Progressive historians in his lifetime began to explore how much trends shaped individuals and they looked more often in history for the workings of gigantic forces upon average people. W.E.B. Du Bois and Charles Beard wrote innovatively about racial and economic forces, while others explored environmental history, Western history, immigration history, and other aspects of social history. In questioning Carlyle's focus on the impact of great men on their times and drawing more focus upon social and economic forces, they planted seeds that would germinate slowly (Higham 1965; Fitzpatrick 2002; Hofstadter 1968). Vernon L. Parrington spoke of the progressive "democratic renaissance" in words reminiscent of TR's New Nationalism speech and his later Bull Moose campaign rhetoric: "The problem confronting liberalism was the problem of the subjection of property to social justice." To Parrington TR's presidency and the muckraking journalists who exposed corruption heralded a constructive generation of "brisk housecleaning" in American politics (Parrington 1963 reprint, orig. 1930, 406, 409).

Though the Progressive historians were not unanimous in the way they saw TR and progressive reform, the intellectual climate of the Progressive Era opened up a vigorous debate about progress in history and underlying economic motivations that provided a fruitful foundation for later generations (Hofstadter 1968). These advances in historical analysis, however, had little effect on the early major studies of TR and his times. In 1919 William Roscoe Thayer, for example, ignored Progressive historians' emphasis on forces and instead published a Great Man theory biography of TR in which he judged the ex-president to be "the incarnation of Americanism" and a fierce fighter for righteousness who "sacrificed his life for patriotism" (Thayer 1919, 435, viii).

The Progressive Era zeppelin-size image of TR as a great man astride history was ripe for deflation. He had loudly promoted US involvement in World War I, and then, after his death, historians and the American public sharply revised their view of that war. As the public slowly came to understand how cynically European nations had grabbed land and how soldiers suffered during the Great War, suddenly the Great Adventure TR had promoted was tarnished. In the irreverent aftermath of World War I, H.L. Mencken derided cheering crowds and the charismatic leaders who moved them and called TR "a charlatan of the highest skill," a "mob master," and pronounced that TR's "gifts as a mountebank amounted to downright genius." Mencken also was reminded of TR's raucous followers when legions of KKK members marched down Pennsylvania Avenue in the 1920s, hardly a flattering comparison (Mencken 58, 53, 82). In the same belittling spirit John Chamberlain in his book about progressivism termed TR "an economic moron" (Chamberlain 1932, 272). Newspaper exposes and widely-read books by Harry Elmer Barnes and others questioned whether the United States should have involved itself in World War I at all; unneutral Wilson, biased advisors, Wilson's Anglophilia, decisions influenced by munitions-makers, all these factors pushed America, they claimed, into an unnecessary war. Great War debunkers wrote books that taught readers to question whether TR, their World War I Galahad, had been so noble and wise after all (Cohen 1968).

When the journalist Henry Pringle approached TR's widow, Edith Roosevelt, asking her to give him access to family papers and restricted archives, he evidently reassured her that he admired her husband and would write a positive biography. She was hesitant, but, cajoled by Herman Hagedorn, the director of the Roosevelt Memorial Association, she agreed to share archives with Pringle. Pringle, however, had misrepresented his intentions. He produced a negative portrayal of TR and ridiculed the ex-president's accomplishments, dismissing TR as "the most adolescent of men" and his eagerness to fight in the war in Cuba in 1898 as "ludicrous" (Pringle 1931, 4, 128). Pringle emphasized that TR's hour of military bravery charging up Kettle Hill had only been against inaccurately aimed bullets, and his motives were simply vainglory and ambition. Pringle's biography won a Pulitzer Prize and shifted the prevailing interpretation of TR.

Greatly influenced by Pringle, Richard Hofstadter, in his classic 1948 essay "Theodore Roosevelt: the Conservative as Progressive," judged the late president as an unwilling and hypocritical reformer, an overcompensating invalid whose "penchant for violence" spilled into his aggressive foreign policy views, a combative moralist whose brain held only "the intellectual fiber of a muscular and combative Polonius" (Hofstadter 1948, 228–229). Hofstadter's lively style and colorful portrayal of TR amused readers for generations and left them with the impression that, while progressive reform may have been real and even somewhat effective, TR joined hands only briefly with progressives for reasons of political expediency. In the same book Hofstadter also mocked FDR, TR's fifth cousin and nephew-by-marriage, as a president who preserved capitalism largely to serve the rich. The criteria by which Hofstadter marked the Roosevelts as rather worthless presidents was their failure to make permanent and deep changes in the class structure, the distribution of wealth and power, and the capitalist system. In Hofstadter's version, TR went through life driven by no worthwhile ideas, just irrational acts. Plagued by deep insecurity, fraught with anxiety, TR, in Hofstadter's eyes, showed a "persistent desire to impose himself upon others," all of which resulted in his imperialism and the "unnecessary" Spanish War (Hofstadter 1948, 211). Glib as his psychology was and high as his standards were for what constituted a true reformer, Hofstadter raised pertinent questions about how much TR had risked as president to gain reform and how wise his foreign policy views were. His effect on TR's reputation was immense and magnified Pringle's view that TR had been rather mad. Together, Pringle and Hofstadter put forth the Crazy Teddy theory which became historical gospel: a great many historians after 1948 believed, as Thomas Bailey put it, that TR suffered from "almost pathological bellicosity" (Bailey 1966, 307).

Though the Pringle–Hofstadter Crazy Teddy Theory made a lasting mark on public and historians' views, TR's colorful personality occasionally moved off center stage for a few exceptional writers who wanted to understand TR as a creature of his progressive times. As early as 1952 William Leuchtenburg foreshadowed future generations' inquiries into the relationship between imperial and progressive attitudes, and looked past the personal quirks of TR to ask why Progressives were so often exuberant imperialists. He still assumed that Progressives, i.e. supporters of the National Progressive Party or Bull Moosers, could be conflated with progressives, i.e. a wide variety of progressive reformers unconnected with the 1912 campaign. He also looked at progressivism as a coherent, Protestant, and male-only movement, assumptions which later historians would challenge. But Leuchtenburg asked key questions that could have revolutionized the study of TR and his times. Though he was writing in an era that was supposedly a moment of bland consensus history, Leuchtenburg saw Progressives' nationalism and disdain for other races as the key link between their foreign policy and domestic views. Because Leuchtenburg did not make a very clear distinction between early progressives who favored a wide variety of contradictory reforms in the early years of the twentieth century and the specific group of Progressives who supported TR and the Bull Moose Party in 1912, the Progressives he studied are not representative of progressive reform as it is understood today (Leuchtenburg 1952). But Leuchtenburg spotted the spirit of uplift and moral condescension that imperialists and some progressives had in common, and he asked an often-neglected central question about the simultaneity and overlap of imperialism and progressivism. In doing so, he invited further exploration of race, reform, and imperialism as a way to interpret TR and progressivism. His pleas had to await a later generation of historians to gain the hearing they deserved.

Despite the influence of the Crazy Teddy theory, new information came to light in the 1950s about TR and his times, and serious scholars followed their data rather than the most entertaining interpretive story. Deep scholarly research advanced because of the work of Elting Morison and John Blum in editing and publishing TR's letters (Morison and Blum 1951–1954). Monographs and biographies revised the Hofstadter–Pringle Crazy Teddy theory somewhat. Blum's 1954 book *The Republican Roosevelt*, though critical, paid TR respect as a rational and skilled political operator. Hofstadter also changed his views of TR by the time he wrote his important *Age of Reform*. According to Hofstadter: "the first major political leader to understand this need of the public for faith in the complete neutrality of the powerful state was Theodore Roosevelt, whose intuitive sense of the importance of this motive, as well as his genuine personal sympathy with it, explains much of his popularity" (Hofstadter 1955, 235). In the eyes of scholars such as Michael Cullinane, whose forthcoming study will go into much greater detail and depth than this chapter, the Morison volumes of the 1950s changed everything for scholars (Cullinane forthcoming; Gable 1992). The Morison edition of TR's letters prompted a generation of historians to study TR with a new level of scholarly respect. George Mowry in a book written in 1946 relied on Pringle: "The bald fact was that Roosevelt liked war—its noise, its smoke, its action were a part of his soul" (Mowry 1946, 313). By 1958 Mowry had been influenced by the Morison letters and Blum's book, so he told a story of TR as a cagey and complicated politician, more socially conscious than war-loving (Mowry 1958). The Crazy Teddy theory remained popular, but Blum and Mowry had made a solid case for TR's political sanity.

Similarly, as historians' views of TR broadened and gained nuance, progressivism came in for its first gender adjustment. In the 1960s Allen Davis stepped ahead of his generation in *Spearheads for Reform: The Social Settlements and the Progressive Movement 1890–1914* which showed how important settlement houses were in labor, civic reform, social justice, and anti-boss progressive campaigns and pointed the way toward placing women activists closer to the center of the story of progressive reform (Davis 1967). His study looked beyond the middle-class white males who preoccupied the political historians of the 1950s, and he noted that TR worked with Florence Kelley and Jane Addams. But Davis's and Leuchtenburg's post-World War II generation did not fully embrace race or gender as central issues, and so they did not pursue TR's link to women reformers any further (Davis 1964, 1967, 1973).

The best of the post-World War II studies of Theodore Roosevelt and his times arrived in the early 1960s written by William Harbaugh, a World War II veteran who had studied with the Wilson scholar Arthur Link. Though Harbaugh allowed himself to use a few colorful Pringle-isms in his fine biography of TR, he kept his balance in reminding his readers that TR avoided new wars as president and favored moderate reform late in his presidency and certainly during his 1912 Bull Moose third party venture. For Harbaugh, as for most statist liberals of the 1960s, the story of the rise of America's welfare state was a heroic story in which a selfish, materialistic, and unequal nation embraced justice and fairness in a time of emergency, led by a strong president. For Harbaugh, who understood the Great Depression first-hand and who had fought the Nazis in France, TR deserved a place in the history of the rise of the good federal government and a necessarily stronger state that could defeat fascism and militarism. Among Greatest Generation historians, it was Harbaugh, not the more celebrated Hofstadter, who had the deepest understanding of TR. Furthermore, it was Harbaugh who placed TR as a major actor in his generation's story of the rise of liberalism, i.e. TR as the first of the great activist presidents who built the strong and good American nation-state.

Historians' Understanding of Theodore Roosevelt and Progressivism from the 1960s Onward

Nonetheless, when the mid-1960s arrived, it was Hofstadter and not Harbaugh who provided an ideological bridge between the Old Left critics of capitalism and the New Left, because they shared a suspicion that American government would usually do the bidding of the wealthy and powerful while still calling it reform. In the 1960s the Great Man theory of history seemed long dead, archaic, a relic of your grandfather's day, and young academic turks, not unlike the Progressive historians such as Turner and Beard, called for their readers to ignore the men on horseback and to look instead at the underlying forces. In the 1960s Gabriel Kolko and Robert Wiebe dealt with TR's era not to do character studies but to explore instead the social and economic forces which loomed large—the rise of corporations and their talent for getting the political outcomes they wanted. Kolko, in *Railroads and Regulation*, looked at the legislative response to farm protest against unfair railroad practices and found it wanting, and Wiebe documented businessmen's favorable attitudes toward progressive reforms that they could easily turn to their own ends. Wiebe even went on to argue that TR's presidential mediation of the Anthracite Coal Strike was overpraised as a gain for labor because it had not won recognition for the mineworkers' union (Kolko 1965; Wiebe 1962, 1961). The popular story of TR as a tamer of corporate power became the new 1960s story of TR as a servant of corporate power. Though subsequent generations may argue that TR set regulatory precedents that were used more effectively later, most professional historians today do concede that TR's prosecution of corporations achieved only modest gains in curbing the growth of corporate power. Corporate power looked to many historians under better control in the 1950s than it does in the post-Reagan era. Was TR a tool of the wealthy or merely one of the first presidents who tried quixotically to set limits on rising corporate power? Later Wiebe, in his influential *The Search for Order,* moved even farther away from a TR-centered Great Man theory interpretation of the Progressive Era. Wiebe portrayed the rising generation of educated progressive professionals as modernizers obeying social and economic forces, creatures destined to seek order through cleaning up cities and other kinds of reform no matter who was in the White House. Wiebe and his use of modernization theory swept to the sidelines the Crazy Teddy Theory and Harbaugh as well. His book revived the spirit if not the politics of the Progressive historians. Forces, not people, made history.

The political upheavals of the 1960s left young scholars asking hard questions about the narrowness of the history they had studied, and Vietnam and Watergate challenged the explanatory power of the World War II generation's narrative about the good executive leading a benign nation-state. Liberal intellectuals, i.e. Johnson–Kennedy statist liberals who defended the New Frontier and the Good Society, were attacked by New Left radicals who questioned how deeply or sincerely the liberal establishment embraced true justice, a schism which exploded on the pages of the *New York Review of Books* and other journals. The peaceful Civil Rights movement, followed by riots, police brutality, student demonstrations, the rise of Black power advocates, the killings of activists, and assassinations, sparked a variety of conservative backlashes. America polarized in the 1960s, becoming a battleground of unfulfilled promises and reactionary hatred. Within academia, a sea change became noticeable by the early 1970s. The rising social history generation, influenced by trends in French history, looked at their discipline as it had been practiced in the recent past and asked "Where are the voices of the poor, women, blacks, the many whose actions and beliefs shaped history?" Questioning the good government narrative, shocked by injustices at home and war abroad, and fueled by generational anger, young historians criticized the mainstream narratives that marginalized African American experience and ignored the long persistence of slavery and racism. After the second wave feminist movement encouraged women to seek graduate degrees, more women entered the history profession, and women's history drew more practitioners, though not necessarily commensurate jobs or tenure rates. Social science knowledge including quantitative, demographic, and psychological perspectives, shifted the kinds of questions asked by the newer generation of scholars.

By the 1970s, progressivism and Theodore Roosevelt were ripe for new interpretations, and in the intellectual ferment of the early 1970s the old image of TR as the man on horseback leading legions of a coherent reform movement faltered. Peter Filene questioned whether, in fact, there had ever been anything as coherent as a progressive movement (Filene 1970). Disorganized, filled with people at odds with each other, progressivism was demoted by Filene to a diffuse reform impulse. If progressives were not the white, male, middle-class Protestant who sang "Onward Christian Soldiers" at the Bull Moose convention in 1912, then who were they and what did TR have to do with all these non-Bull Moose reformers, all of them newly discovered people? The floodgates of research were opened (Gable 1978).

TR sat on the sidelines awaiting rediscovery while New Left historians and the social history generation came to prominence in the 1970s and started to look at groups long absent from the central political narratives. While once the progressive movement was defined as white, male, urban, middle-class reformers, historians found urban workers and farmers closer to the forefront of electoral change (Buenker 1973). Women, blacks, immigrants, the poor, Native Americans, and a much wider variety of ethnic voices burst the seams of old narratives. When the Organization of American Historians finally announced race, class, gender, and ethnicity were on the table for research, teaching, and conversation, older political, military, and foreign policy historians felt shunted aside and called for a revival of political history and for the state to be brought back into the discipline's research agenda (Leuchtenburg 1986). However, the social history era produced new insights for TR and Progressive Era history that illustrated the value of that generation's critique, and their new interpretations of progressivism affected how TR was judged (Dalton 2002).

The Effects of the Social History Revolution on Understandings of Progressivism and Theodore Roosevelt

The social history revolution changed forever perceptions of progressive reform and also transformed understandings of Theodore Roosevelt: today, progressive reform looks like part of an international trend, but also a reform spirit that was untidy, contradictory, coeducational, and not always nice. How did the research on Progressive Era women change the way TR looks to historians? Social historians discovered that women influenced policy-making even before most women got the vote. In local activism, settlement houses, churches, women's clubs, through lobbying, research, writing, and even party politics, women waged political war on a variety of problems like drunk husbands, poor garbage pick-up, corrupt bosses, and tuberculosis spread by impure milk. After Karen Blair put club women on the progressive map as key activists, Paula Baker and Ann Scott traced the formation of a women's political culture built upon volunteer networks (Baker 1984; Blair 1980; Scott 1991). Kathryn Sklar showed how much women's contribution to progressive reform made American reform culture different from the social democratic movements in other industrial nations (Sklar 1993, 1995). Ellen Fitzpatrick uncovered the vital links between TR and Women's Trade

Union League activists Frances Kellor, Margaret Robbins, and Mary Dreier, and she showed how women activists influenced progressivism, the Progressive Party, and TR (Fitzpatrick 1990; Payne 1988; Salem 1990). All of a sudden, progressivism at large, the Bull Moose Party, and TR's circle of advisors looked coeducational. After finding new manuscript and published evidence that Josephine Goldmark and other women activists wrote parts of TR's speeches and planned fact-finding trips for him, my own scholarship told the expanded story of TR's Female Brain Trust. For TR and other elected officials open to reform ideas, settlement houses and the new generation of university-trained women social scientists offered the think tank/policy research center they needed. TR welcomed the counsel of advisors like Jane Addams, Florence Kelley, and Maud Nathan, who worked with him on the state minimum wage and suffrage campaigns. Women turned TR into a suffragist and pulled him closer to accepting European welfare state ideas. My biography of TR, though closer to a non-heroic "warts and all" treatment, provided abundant evidence that, despite his political caginess and ambivalence about reform, TR deserves to be understood as a sincere and committed social justice reformer and advocate of the modern welfare state by 1905. His conversion story, however, is incomplete without his partnerships with women reformers (Dalton 2002).

Women progressives, including TR's sister Corinne Roosevelt Robinson, who was active in the National Consumers' League, helped to move TR towards social democratic ideas in the same way that Gifford Pinchot encouraged TR's nascent commitment to conservation. Furthermore, in her biography of Frances Perkins, Kirstin Downey found that TR had recommended Perkins for the Factory Investigating Commission that made legislative history in New York after the Triangle Shirtwaist Fire. Though historians already understood Perkins' progressive roots in settlement house culture and the women's reform network, Downey's work solidifies the link between progressive activism, TR, and Perkins, the mother of the important Social Security system (Downey 2009). The story of progressivism has broadened far beyond the Bull Moose Party membership to include NAACP activists, African American church women, labor activists, club women pure food and drug advocates, and many other groups. Biographies that return to the all-male story of TR's reform career or claim that he was never alive to reform ideas are sadly out of date; it is time for textbooks to recognize that progressives were women, too. (Goodwin 1999; Koven and Michel 1993; Ladd-Taylor 1994; Muncy 1991, 1999; Dye 1980; Nugent 2010).

In remapping progressivism to include the agency of women, blacks, local reformers, queers, outsiders, and new immigrants, the social history generation explored gender with innovative perspectives and their work altered the meanings of progressivism and TR's role as a leader. The gendering of progressive history began with Peter G. Filene's book about what he then called "sex roles," and TR proved to be a convenient figure to discuss ways that the meaning of gender had changed over time. When E. Anthony Rotundo wrote his pioneering book *American Manhood: Transformations in Masculinity from the Revolution to the Modern Era*, TR became not merely a reflection of changing roles for men from Victorian to modern roles, but also a change agent who helped to redefine masculinity for other men. Since that time TR has appeared again and again as a specimen of exaggerated concern with masculinity, and historians have interpreted the gendered meaning of many of his writings. Was his call for men to live a manlier and more strenuous life a central part of the appeal of his leadership? (Rotundo 1993; Testi 1995).

Following in the wake of the social history revolution the next generation of historians asked new questions because they were steeped in poststructural cultural and critical theory. Foucault, Lacan, Derrida, and Bourdieu were only the beginning. The theoretical turn in the history profession highlighted hegemony and situated knowledge. Like their social history and New Left predecessors, the new cultural historians shared a suspicion of government and concentrated power and wrote from a left-wing viewpoint. The cultural turn produced Gail Bederman's bold *Manliness and Civilization: A Cultural History of Gender and Race in the United States, 1880–1917* which argued that in TR's time "middle-class men were casting about for new ways to explain the sources and nature of male power and authority" (Bederman 1995). In this view, Roosevelt and other men sought to remasculinize their culture and restore their political authority over women and blacks, and they promoted the ideology of "civilization" to link white supremacy to male power by showing that the civilized men who led western society deserved the right to uplift the less civilized. Racist imperialists argued that progress would result from the assertion of white male leadership around the world: "God… made us adepts in government that we may administer government among savage and senile peoples," according to progressive Senator Albert Beveridge. Out of Bederman's interpretation, TR rises as the embodied virility of his generation as he combined "civilized manliness and primitive masculinity" to represent and reassert the fictions of racial and male superiority for the new century (Bederman 1995, 22).

Finally, a historian had found a way to bring together the progressives' reformism and its acceptance of imperialism. In placing cultural fictions at the center of her story, Bederman was not going to please everyone. Was this a reborn version of the old Marxist view that hegemonic economic and political power depends on the perpetuation of false consciousness? Many historians find Bederman's view of TR persuasive, yet her view of TR is as one-dimensional as Pringle's and Hofstadter's. However, Hofstadter assumed that TR's preoccupation with manhood was TR's alone, a quirk of personality, while Bederman places it in the context of a well-documented national crisis of manhood. Bederman's view of TR is also intersectional, that is, it does not see race, class, or gender in separate categories but combines them in her analysis (for a different view of TR and manhood see Dalton 2002, and of TR and race, Dyer 1980).

Other scholars have also examined Theodore Roosevelt from new critical perspectives. Sarah Watts, for example, employs critical theory to explore the aggressive impulses in TR's actions and his ability to give voice to the anxieties and desires of his generation. Watts discovered that TR's fear of "unhealthy softness" in men reflected his perception of the danger of national downfall, so she explored "why Roosevelt thought white men's bodies represented the fate of the nation and why he focused so obsessively on sexuality as the source of social breakdown" (Watts 2003, 9–10). Perhaps the most gratifying section of the Watts book is her discussion of TR's fondness for the naughty transgressions of his Rough Riders, a revealing piece of textual analysis that shows how much TR admired men behaving badly.

Using another intersectional analysis of race and gender to reexamine racial politics, Amy Kaplan in "Black and Blue on San Juan Hill" examines how the stories TR and Richard Harding Davis told about the Battle of San Juan Hill served to represent "a monumental frieze" of black and white troops mixing in the chaos of battle. Then, Roosevelt's assertion of white racial command of black soldiers "reestablishes the reassuring order of the domestic color line in a foreign terrain" (Kaplan 1993, 222). Though Cubans had been fighting a war for independence for years against Spain, Stephen Crane and other reporters' erasure of Cuban soldiers and their condescension toward them tells Kaplan that Americans saw their Cuban allies through a racial lens as unmanly, unwhite, and unworthy of freedom (Kaplan 1993, 224–226; see also Perez 1998). Though African American soldiers told a story of the Battle of San Juan Hill that affirmed that they had gone up the hill before TR and saved the Rough Riders from a surprise Spanish attack, it was TR's version of events that prevailed and finally slowed down the appointment of black officers. By reexamining often-repeated stories, the cultural turn historians have up-ended old "facts," and they have brought the discipline to focus on how accepted truths and categories came into being (Glickman 2011).

Like gender, race became a much more central question for historical analysis by the 1990s. Historians discovered that race had shaped ideas about citizenship and nationality, whiteness, and it made for differences in life expectancy, residential patterns, life chances, and education. Race molded domestic policy and foreign policy. Race moved from the periphery to the center of historical conversation, notably in new surveys of the era such as Nell Painter's survey in which Anglo-Saxonism and racism feature in the rise of imperialism, the US–Philippines War, segregation and disenfranchisement, Asian exclusion laws, and the exterminationist Plains Wars. Glenda Gilmore's book about disenfranchisement examines the deep background of party friction in TR's time (Painter 1987; Gilmore 1996). Gary Gerstle sees TR's racial nationalism as much more flexible than pure Anglo-Saxonism but nonetheless unwelcoming to blacks, Asians, and non-whites. Gerstle's TR attempts to reconcile racial nationalism with a more open civic nationalism, but at his core is an aggressive Americanizer who signed immigration restriction laws and expected the public schools to wash away old country customs and beliefs from immigrants. Race remains a central issue for understanding Theodore Roosevelt—from Booker T. Washington and Brownsville to the evening TR stood with W.E.B. Du Bois during World War I (Gossett 1965; Horsman 1991; Knupfer 1996; Lasch-Quinn 1993; Neverdon-Morton 1989; Salem. 1990; Shaw 1991; Gerstle 2001).

Revisionists who see TR primarily as a jingo and false reformer often skip over his commitment to protecting nature. Debates still rage about Hetch Hetchy and TR's preference for conservation rather than pure preservationism, but Char Miller's work on Gifford Pinchot shows that TR played on both teams in his private letters (Miller 2001). TR and Pinchot, as I argued in my biography of TR, were desperate for allies in their battle for conservation, and the woman-founded Pennsylvania Forestry Association, and women prominent in the Audubon Society and the Sierra Club, were much more likely to lobby on behalf of their conservation bills than the mainstream of TR's own party. Douglas Brinkley's detailed book about Theodore Roosevelt's campaigns to save wildlife and natural habitats also provides a great deal of new insight into TR's active work as a conservationist (Dalton 2002; Brinkley 2009; Unger 2012).

At the same time that historians have looked at TR and progressivism with new questions about race, gender, and the environment, the narrowness of the old definitions of what constituted political activity and who was a real progressive have also inspired new research. Historians used to explain progressive reform as middle-class, white, male Protestants' response to the corruption of boss-ridden politics and the human suffering brought about by rapid urbanization and industrialization. Historians have since proven that Catholic progressives deserve a place in the progressive story. Catholic women such as Lucy Burns fought for the vote alongside Alice Paul, the radical Quaker suffrage leader, and the Catholic Church itself, after women won the vote, encouraged Catholic women to vote. TR scholars have documented his pre-presidential courtship of Catholic journalists and voters, but the discovery of extensive Catholic involvement in progressive era charities and emerging welfare systems helps provide a fuller context for the debates by TR's advisors over the Protestant-preferred mother's pensions or Catholic-favored unemployment benefits. TR often sided with the Protestants, but he worked with the American Anti-Saloon League leader, Archbishop John Ireland, Father John J. Curran famous for his work among the poor and a supporter of the Total Abstinence Society, and the Campaign against Child Labor's Cardinal Gibbons. TR may have used these bonds to grasp at Catholic votes, but he also may have been seeking out alternative models of aiding the poor (Skok 2008; Dalton 2002).

Another of the central interpretive challenges in studying the Progressive Era and Theodore Roosevelt is finding a way to comprehend the role that moral reform played in stirring progressives to action. To understand TR it is worthwhile to look again at the company he kept and the moral reform causes about which he preached from his "bully pulpit." In the days when Mowry wrote as if women did not exist, and as if the really important reforms were largely direct democracy or railroad regulation, most scholars dismissed the white slave trade crusaders as irrelevant, hysterical cranks. Newspaper accounts of 60,000 girls drugged and kidnapped into prostitution shocked moral reformers including James Mann to stop the white slave trade in interstate transportation cases, a reform which TR supported. Today, during the resurgence of sex trafficking, moral reform has to be taken seriously.

TR agreed with moral reformers that the American family was in crisis. Deep in his heart TR was never a fan of temperance or prohibition, but he made common cause with the Women's Christian Temperance Union and other purity reformers on censorship. He was so friendly with the anti-cigarette crusade that the Anti-Cigarette League offices kept his picture on the wall. New ways to understand the differences between TR and Wilson may be found by comparing their relationships with moral reform movements and their willingness to call for the nation-state to protect the poor to stop them from becoming immoral. Underexplored aspects of Progressive Era historiography include book censorship, pure milk and anti-tuberculosis campaigns, positive and negative eugenics, opposition to prize-fighting movies, homes for unwed mothers, captive prostitution, fraudulent employment agencies, pure food and drug reformers other than Harvey Wiley, divorce regulations, birth control, wife-beating, temperance and prohibition workers, and many, many more crusades.

In my biography of TR I placed moral reform at the center of his progressivism, but his moralism pulled him in several directions at once. When TR chose reforms he imagined the nation-state as the agent of protective manhood guarding sacred, domestic motherhood, which convinced him to support women and child-protecting policies. When Molly Ladd-Taylor wrote that "motherhood was a central organizing principle of Progressive era politics … inextricably tied to state-building and public policy," she helps explain why TR joined hands with some moral reform groups and not others. Lillian Wald, Maud Nathan, Florence Kelly, and Jane Addams found that TR's chivalry urged him toward reforms that protected women and children (Dalton 2002; Fitzpatrick 1990; Ladd-Taylor 1994). TR, as my biography shows, had a lot to say about moral issues: "race suicide," divorce, selfishness, and immorality and moral outrage accelerated his political journey toward support of welfare state reforms.

The effect of the social history revolution and the later cultural turn on the historiography of the Progressive Era cannot yet be fully assessed, but even now the definition of what is basic to know about progressivism and TR's times has changed. Historians Rebecca Edwards and Maureen Flanagan have questioned the traditional periodization and boundaries of what constitutes progressivism, and scholars who try to place Theodore Roosevelt within the context of his times will have to deal with the possibility that agrarian, Catholic, female, queer, and non-white voices may very well have to be a part of the story of TR and his times (Edwards 2009; Flanagan 2007; Murphy 2008).

Comparative or international studies of race, imperialism, migration, environmentalism, and the development of welfare states have been fruitful new areas of research so far for TR scholars and students of the Progressive Era (Frederickson 1981; Jacobson 1999, 2000; Sklar 1993, 1995; Koven and Michel, 1990, 1993; Tyrrell 1999, 2007). Roosevelt's nationalistic uses of muscular Christianity for popularizing his state-building efforts reveal that he behaved like many of his international counterparts. TR met Fabian Socialists Beatrice and Sidney Webb through Lillian Wald, and took a keen interest in Britain's social insurance schemes and Lloyd George's ideas. His social justice and settlement house worker allies kept him in touch with advanced European programs to provide old-age pensions. By 1910 TR and many other progressives knew enough to compare limited US programs with what workers received in Germany and England (Dalton 2002; Guarneri 2007).

Historiographical Debates about Theodore Roosevelt and US Foreign Policy

In the realm of foreign policy Theodore Roosevelt has been interpreted primarily by two groups of scholars, the Open Door group who sees him as a prime advocate for imperialism motivated by a search for markets and a wish to dominate peoples he sees as weaker. Open Door scholars usually see TR as an imperialist who pushed McKinley into war in 1898 and then as a president who started America's ugly interventions in Panama, Haiti, and other western hemisphere sites. TR's influence, they say, led to the later overextension of America's business and military might in the twentieth century. Work by Pringle and Hofstadter have influenced Open Door interpreters such as Foster Rhea Dulles, who judged that TR, unlike ideological and strategically-motivated imperialists Henry Cabot Lodge and Alfred Thayer Mahan, developed his foreign policies from "his own propensity for martial activity and exciting adventure" (Dulles 1964, 39). In a classic Open Door interpretation William Appleman Williams argued that TR's "concern for economic expansion was complemented by an urge to extend Anglo-Saxon ideas, practices, and virtues throughout the world....the inherent requirements of economic expansion coincided with such religious, racist, and reformist drives to remake the world" (Williams 1962, 57). The creation of a world market for American goods underlay American outreach to the rest of the world, but the expansionist worldview of elites including TR meant that ideology and prejudice worked alongside economics. Later, Walter LaFeber argued that "the conservative Roosevelt played a role in creating a revolutionary, war-wracked world, instead of creating a balance-of-power complex that maintained a healthy, gradually evolving international system" (LaFeber 1993, 184–185).

A second group of foreign policy scholars who study TR, called the Realist school, follow in the wake of Howard K. Beale's *Theodore Roosevelt and the Rise of America to World Power* (Beale 1956). Realists argue that industrial productivity, military success in the Spanish–American War, a growing navy, and increased contact with the rest of the world because of expanded transportation and travel did not automatically turn the United States into a respected world power. Realists credit TR with making the United States a more respected nation around the world, and, for the first time, a major diplomatic player. As president he expanded and supported the education of the frightfully small and inadequate diplomatic corps, and he made the army and navy stronger and more efficient tools to intervene in world affairs. Hoping to advance the interests of more technologically advanced powers or "civilization," TR used personal diplomacy to make his country more respected around the world and to resolve international conflicts in the Russo-Japanese War and the Moroccan Crisis. However, Realists concede that TR's colonial administration of the Philippines, Puerto Rico, and even Cuba, and his conduct during the crisis with Japan that followed San Francisco's anti-Asian segregation of its schools, reveal a pattern of racial condescension. Frederick Marks and Richard Collin are notable as defenders of TR's diplomatic policies (Marks 1979; Collin 1985). Tilchin, like Beale, traced TR's careful building of a special relationship with Great Britain, and H.W. Brands also gives TR credit for skilled diplomacy. The Realists prefer to downplay TR's loud imperialism in 1898 and instead look at his career as a successful diplomat: bringing a peaceful end to the Russo-Japanese War, possibly averting war between France and Germany in the Moroccan Crisis, and proposing arbitration and international cooperation to prevent war (Widenor 1980; Tilchin 1997, 2014; Brands 1997; Gould 1991).

Not all foreign policy experts fall neatly into Realists and the Open Door camps. For instance, Frank Ninkovich rejected economic motivation and analyzed TR's foreign policy as one guided by a belief that civilized nations (i.e. more economically developed and more advanced by the cultural evolutionary theory measures of the day) needed to intervene in less-civilized nations' affairs to uplift them. Ninkovich saw TR as ideologically rather than economically motivated to intervene in other nations. But he objects to Gail Bederman's use of his framework and the most schematic of the Open Door interpreters of TR's imperialism who see racism and aggression as central to TR's imperialism. Where TR failed, in Ninkovich's view, was that he was a half-formed internationalist, i.e. he was so stuck in the romantic nationalism of the nineteenth century that he could not imagine that civilization as an idea could be adapted to serve the purposes of peace-making in an interdependent international world, by providing "an international collective conscience or superego, an effective world opinion, which would serve as counterpart and antidote to the structural dangers generated by growing interdependence" (Ninkovich 1994, 1999).

Outside the Open Door/Realist split, Pacificist scholars charge that too much time has been focused on European affairs and Atlantic stratagems. They argue instead for a new history that looks at the Pacific Rim. Among them, Bruce Cumings praises TR as "the first president to have a clear sense of the United States as both an Atlantic and a Pacific power." Cumings adds that in pushing Open Door goals in China TR was inventing "a new conception of global leadership" to replace the old imperialistic rivalries. Cumings' primary intention is not to praise TR but to question the post-FDR American trend toward "unilateralism and easy recourse to the use of force in Asia" (Cumings 2009, 138–139, xv). Similarly, other scholars outside the usual boxes ask: what if TR the imperialist changed over time and emerged as one of the forefathers of modern human rights diplomacy? In examining TR's advocacy of an international organization to prevent war, especially in Europe, and in exploring his use of emergency relief when disasters hit other nations, I have added to the foreign policy debates among those who see TR as an imperialist who was also much more than an imperialist (Dalton 2001, 2002). Other new studies find TR as ex-president unusually receptive to defending human rights around the world, and they use as evidence TR's passionate championing of the Armenians when the Turks were exterminating them (Bass 2008).

Historians also debate the racial or Anglo-Saxon roots of the U.S. drive toward empire at the end of the nineteenth century. In 1898 was TR motivated by economics, nationalism, racialism, Social Darwinism, or war-hunger? Reginald Horsman put race and Anglo-Saxonism above economics or diplomatic strategy in TR and other imperialists' drive to fight Spain and gain new territories (Horsman 1981). However, America's biggest racists opposed expansionism because building an empire would incorporate new races into the American sphere. Younger scholars have called for another look at TR's evolutionary views that posited gradual improvement of less technologically advanced people as the goal of expansionism (Chin 2007). Gender as an explanatory lens for foreign policy decision-making should have shaken up the field, but so far has met resistance. Kristin Hoganson in her pathbreaking book about the role that gender played in the decision to go to war in 1898 unearthed impressive research in records of congressional debates and memoirs that illustrate how much concerns about manhood influenced foreign policy decision-making (Hoganson 1998). However, reviews of the Roosevelt literature give it short shrift (Ricard 2014).

Conclusion

In the years when social and cultural history were ascendant in the profession and when foreign policy specialists were deeply divided about TR's worth as a foreign policy leader, his rating among historians nevertheless rose. While critical analysis of Roosevelt mushroomed in academia the public has rediscovered him as a colorful and entertaining remnant of Americana and lively personality. How did he win a second honeymoon with the reading and television watching public? The answer cannot be simple. Public history and a new public hunger for stories about the past blossomed at the same time that the academy delved into deeper theory and criticism. Though both the public in general and the history profession were shaken by the upheavals of the 1960s and 1970s, the history profession embraced research questions about neglected and powerless groups while the public sought entertainment in public history and biography, and embraced a sunnier view of the past.

Celebrationists with a flair for literary history, David McCullough and Edmund Morris, saw in TR a romantic and appealing figure, and, for the most part, were happier to skip the "warts and all" style of biography popular when Pringle wielded his pen like a knife. McCullough's romantic story of TR's family circle appealed to readers. Morris's talent for putting TR back in the man on horseback pose made for a bestseller. A friend of Ronald Reagan and his revolution, Morris did not see TR's imperialism as much of a problem. Historians have taken McCullough to task for a variety of flaws, but as McCullough began hosting PBS' *American Experience* and narrating Ken Burns' documentary films, he became the fatherly voice of American history for millions of Americans. TR appeared on stage, once more interesting and heroic, and deep in the recesses of the authors' and readers' minds TR stood for a better time, far from Vietnam, Watergate, culture wars, polarized politics, and fears of American decline. As audiences rediscovered TR and his era, Pringle and Hofstadter made a surprising comeback. Piles of scholarly research discrediting the Crazy Teddy theory were swept off the table. The recent Ken Burns series *The Roosevelts: An Intimate History* brought the Pringle–Hofstadter Crazy Teddy back onto to the stage for an encore with George F. Will, Evan Thomas, and Clay Jenkinson agreeing that to understand TR you have to remember he loved war and was a pretty bloodthirsty guy (McCullough 1981; Morris 1979; Burns 2014). Although some entertaining stories never die, reducing Roosevelt to well-worn stereotypes, no matter how colorful or amusing, flies in the face of the ever-growing historiography of Theodore Roosevelt that embraces the complexity of its subject and his era.

References

Bailey, Thomas A. 1966. *Presidential Greatness: The Image and the Man from George Washington to the Present.* New York: Appleton-Century.

Baker, Paula. 1984. "The Domestication of Politics: Women and American Political Society, 1780–1920" *American Historical Review* 89, June: 620–647.

Bass, Gary J. 2008. *Freedom's Battle: the Origins of Humanitarian Intervention.* New York: Alfred A. Knopf.

Beale, Howard K. 1956. *Theodore Roosevelt and the Rise of America to World Power.* Baltimore, MD: Johns Hopkins University Press.

Bederman, Gail. 1995. *Manliness & Civilization: a Cultural History of Gender and Race in the United States, 1880–1917.* Chicago: University of Chicago Press.

Blair, Karen J. 1980. *Clubwoman as Feminist True Womanhood Redefined, 1868–1914.* New York: Holmes and Meier.

Blum, John Morton. 1954. *The Republican Roosevelt.* Cambridge, MA: Harvard University Press.

Brands, H. W. 1997. *T.R.: The Last Romantic.* New York: Basic Books.

Brinkley, Douglas. 2009. *The Wilderness Warrior: Theodore Roosevelt and the Crusade for America.* New York: Harper Collins.

Buenker, John D. 1973. *Urban Liberalism and Progressive Reform.* New York: Scribner.

—, John C. Burnham, and Robert M. Crunden. 1977. *Progressivism.* Cambridge, MA: Shenkman.

Burns, Ken. 2014. *The Roosevelts: An Intimate History.* PBS Documentary.

Chamberlain, John. 1965. *Farewell to Reform: The Rise, Life and Decay of the Progressive Mind in America.* Chicago: Quadrangle Books.

Chin, Carol C. 2007. "'Uplifting the Barbarian.'" In *A Companion to Theodore Roosevelt*, ed. by Serge Ricard. Oxford: Wiley-Blackwell.

Cohen, Warren I. 1968. *The American Revisionists: The Lessons of Intervention in World War I.* Chicago: University of Chicago Press.

Collin, Richard H. 1985. *Theodore Roosevelt, Culture, Diplomacy, and Expansion: A New View of American Imperialism.* Baton Rouge: Louisiana State University Press.

Cullinane, Michael Patrick. Forthcoming. *Theodore Roosevelt's Ghost: The History of an American Icon.*

Cumings, Bruce. 2009. *Dominion from Sea to Sea: Pacific Ascendancy and American Power.* New Haven, CT: Yale University Press.

Dalton, Kathleen. 1981. "Why America Loved Teddy Roosevelt: Or Charisma is in the Eyes of the Beholders." In *OurSelves/Our Past: Psychological Approaches to American History*, ed. Robert J. Brugger. Baltimore, MD: Johns Hopkins University Press.

—. 1992. "The Bully Prophet: Theodore Roosevelt and American Memory." In *Theodore Roosevelt: Many-Sided American*, ed. Natalie A. Naylor, Douglas Brinkley, and John Allen Gable. Interlaken, NY: Heart of the Lakes Publishing/Hofstra University.

—. 2001. "Between the Diplomacy of Imperialism and the Achievement of World Order by Supranational Mediation: Ethnocentrism and Theodore Roosevelt's Changing Views of World Order." In *Ethnocentrism et diplomatie: l'Amerique et le monde au XXe siècle*, ed. Pierre Melandri and Serge Ricard. Paris: Editions L'Harmattan.

—. 2002. *Theodore Roosevelt: A Strenuous Life*. New York: Alfred A. Knopf.

Davis, Allen F. 1964. "The Social Workers and the Progressive Party 1912–1916." *American Historical Review* 69, April: 671–688.

—.1967. *Spearheads for Reform: The Social Settlements and the Progressive Movement, 1890–1914*. New York: Oxford University Press.

Downey, Kirstin. 2009. *The Woman behind the New Deal: the Life of Frances Perkins, FDR's Secretary of Labor and his Moral Conscience*. New York: Nan A. Talese/Doubleday.

Dye, Nancy Schrom. 1980. *As Equals and Sisters: Feminism, the Labor Movement, and the Women's Trade Union League of New York*. Columbia: University of Missouri Press.

Dyer, Thomas G. 1980. *Theodore Roosevelt and the Idea of Race*. Baton Rouge: Louisiana State University Press.

Edwards, Rebecca. 2009. "Politics, Social Movements, and the Periodization of U. S. History." *The Journal of the Gilded Age and Progressive Era* 8, 4: 463–473.

Filene, Peter G. 1970. "An Obituary for 'The Progressive Movement.'" *American Quarterly* 22, Spring: 30.

Fitzpatrick, Ellen. 1990. *Endless Crusade: Women Social Scientists and Progressive Reform*. New York: Oxford University Press.

—. 2002. *History's Memory: Writing America's Past 1880–1980*. Cambridge, MA: Harvard University Press.

Flanagan, Maureen A. 2007. *America Reformed: Progressives and Progressivisms, 1890s–1920s*. New York: Oxford University Press.

Fredrickson, George M. 1997. *The Comparative Imagination: on the History of Racism, Nationalism, and Social Movements*. Berkeley: University of California Press.

Gable, John. 1978. *The Bull Moose Years: Theodore Roosevelt and the Progressive Party*. New York: Kennikat.

—. 1992. "The Historiography of Theodore Roosevelt." In *Theodore Roosevelt: Many-Sided American*. Interlaken, NY: Heart of the Lakes Publishing/Hofstra University.

Gerstle, Gary. 2001. *American Crucible: Race and Nation in the Twentieth Century*. Princeton, NJ: Princeton University Press.

Gilmore, Glenda Elizabeth. 1996. *Gender and Jim Crow: Women and the Politics of White Supremacy in North Carolina, 1896–1920*. Chapel Hill: University of North Carolina Press.

—. 2002. *Who Were the Progressives?* Boston: Bedford/St. Martin's.

Glickman, Lawrence B. 2011. "The 'Cultural Turn.'" In *American History Now*, ed. Eric Foner and Lisa McGirr. Philadelphia: Temple University Press.

Goodwin, Lorine Swainston. 1999. *The Pure Food, Drink, and Drug Crusaders, 1879–1914*. Jefferson, NC: McFarland.

Gossett, Thomas F. 1965. *Race: The History of an Idea in America*. New York: Schocken Press.

Gould, Lewis L. 1991. *The Presidency of Theodore Roosevelt*. Lawrence: University Press of Kansas.

Gros, Raymond. 1910. *T.R. in Cartoon*. New York: Saalfield.

Guarneri, Carl. 2007. *America in the World: United States History in World Context*. New York: McGraw-Hill.

Harbaugh, William H. 1997. *Power and Responsibility: The Life and Times of Theodore Roosevelt*. Reprint. Newtown, CT: American Political Biography Press.

Herring, George C. 2008. *From Colony to Superpower: U.S. Foreign Relations since 1776*. New York: Oxford University Press.

Higham, John, with Leonard Krieger and Felix Gilbert. 1965. *History: Professional Scholarship in America*. New York: Prentice-Hall.

Hofstadter, Richard. 1948. *The American Political Tradition and the Men Who Made It*. New York: Alfred A. Knopf.

—. 1955. *The Age of Reform: From Bryan to F.D.R.* New York: Vintage Books.

—. 1968. *The Progressive Historians: Turner, Beard, Parrington*. New York: Knopf.

Hoganson, Kristin L. 1998. *Fighting for American Manhood: How Gender Politics Provoked the Spanish–American and Philippine–American Wars*. New Haven, CT: Yale University Press.

Horsman, Reginald. 1981. *Race and Manifest Destiny: The Origins of American Racial Anglo-Saxonism*. Cambridge, MA: Harvard University Press.

Jacobson, Matthew Frye. 2000. *Barbarian Virtues: the United States Encounters Foreign Peoples at Home and Abroad, 1876–1917*. New York: Hill & Wang.

Kaplan, Amy and Donald Pease, eds. 1993. *Cultures of Imperialism*. Durham, NC: Duke University Press.

Knupfer, Anne Meis. 1996. *Toward a Tenderer Humanity and a Nobler Womanhood: African American Women's Clubs in Turn-of-the-Century Chicago*. New York: New York University Press.

Kolko, Gabriel. 1965. *Railroads and Regulation, 1877–1916*. Westport, CT: Greenwood Press.

Koven, Seth and Sonya Michel. 1993. *Mothers of a New World: Maternalist Politics and the Origins of Welfare States*. New York: Routledge.

Ladd-Taylor, Molly. 1994. *Mother-Work: Women, Child Welfare, and the State, 1890–1930*. Chicago: University of Chicago Press.

LaFeber, Walter. 1993. *The Cambridge History of American Foreign Relations: Volume II, The American Search for Opportunity, 1865–1913*, ed. Warren I. Cohen. New York: Cambridge University Press.

Lancos, John R. 1992. "Theodore Roosevelt Birthplace: Study in Americanism." In *Theodore Roosevelt: Many-Sided American*, ed. Douglas Brinkley. Interlaken, NY: Heart of the Lakes Publishing.

Lasch-Quinn, Elisabeth. 1993. *Black Neighbors: Race and the Limits of Reform in the American Settlement House Movement, 1890–1945*. Chapel Hill: University of North Carolina Press.

Leuchtenburg, William E. 1952. "Progressivism and Imperialism: The Progressive Movement and American Foreign Policy, 1898–1916." *The Mississippi Valley Historical Review* 39, 3: 483–504.

—. 1986. "The Pertinence of Political History: Reflections on the Significance of the State in America." *The Journal of American History* 73, 3: 585–600.

Link, Arthur S. and Richard L. McCormick, 1983. *Progressivism*. Arlington Heights, IL: Harlan Davidson.

Lorant, Stefan. 1959. *The Life and Times of Theodore Roosevelt*. New York: Doubleday & Co.

McCoy, Alfred W. 2009. *Policing America's Empire: The United States, the Philippines, and the Rise of the Surveillance State*. Madison: University of Wisconsin Press.

McCullough, David. *Mornings on Horseback*. New York: Simon and Schuster, 1981.

McCutcheon, John T. 1910. *T.R. in Cartoons*. Chicago: A. C. McClurg.

Marks, Frederick W., III. 1979. *Velvet on Iron: The Diplomacy of Theodore Roosevelt*. Lincoln: University of Nebraska Press.

Mencken, H.L. 1920 (1967) "Roosevelt I." Reprinted in *Theodore Roosevelt: A Profile*, ed. by Morton Keller. New York: Hill & Wang. Citations refer to the Hill edition.

Meyers, Robert C.V. 1902. *Theodore Roosevelt: Patriot and Statesman. The True Story of an Ideal American*. Chicago: P.W. Ziegler.

Millard, Candice. 2005. *The River of Doubt: Theodore Roosevelt's Darkest Journey*. New York: Doubleday.

Miller, Char. 2001. *Gifford Pinchot and the Making of Modern Environmentalism*. Washington, DC: Island Press.

Morison, Elting E., John Morton Blum, and Alfred Chandler, ed. 1951–1954. *The Letters of Theodore Roosevelt*. Cambridge, MA: Harvard University Press.

Morris, Edmund. 1979. *The Rise of Theodore Roosevelt*. New York: Coward, McCann & Geohagan.

Mowry, George E. 1946. *Theodore Roosevelt and the Progressive Movement*. New York: Hill & Wang.

—. 1958. *Era of Theodore Roosevelt and the Birth of Modern America 1900–1912*. New York: Harper Torchbooks.

Muncy, Robyn. 1991. *Creating a Female Dominion in American Reform*. New York: Oxford University Press.

—. 1999. "The Ambiguous Legacies of Women's Progressivism." *OAH Magazine of History* 13, 3: 15–19.

Murphy, Kevin P. 2008. *Political Manhood: Red Bloods, Mollycoddles, and the Politics of Progressive Era Reform*. New York: Columbia University Press.

Ninkovich, Frank. 1986. "Theodore Roosevelt: Civilization as Ideology." *Diplomatic History*, 10, 3: 221–245.

—. 2006. "The United States and Imperialism." In *A Companion to American Foreign Relations*, ed. Robert D. Schulzinger. Oxford: Wiley-Blackwell.

Ninkovich, Frank A. 1994. *Modernity and Power: A History of the Domino Theory in the Twentieth Century*. Chicago: University of Chicago Press.

Neverdon-Morton, Cynthia. 1989. *Afro-American Women of the South and the Advancement of the Race, 1895–1925*. Knoxville: University of Tennessee Press.

Nugent, Walter. 2010. *Progressivism: A Very Short Introduction*. New York: Oxford University Press.

Painter, Nell Irvin. 1987. *Standing at Armageddon: The United States, 1877–1919*. New York: W.W. Norton.

Parrington, Vernon L. 1963. "The Progressive Era: A Liberal Renaissance." Reprinted in *The Progressive Era: Liberal Renaissance or Liberal Failure?* ed. by Arthur Mann. New York: Holt, Rinehart and Winston.

Payne, Elizabeth. 1988. *Reform, Labor, and Feminism: Margaret Dreier Robins and the Women's Trade Union League*. Chicago: University of Illinois Press.

Perez, Louis A. Jr. 1998. *The War of 1898: The United States and Cuba in History and Historiography*. Chapel Hill: University of North Carolina Press.

Pringle, Henry F. 1931. *Theodore Roosevelt: A Biography*. New York: Harcourt Brace.

Ricard, Serge. 2014. "The State of Theodore Roosevelt Studies." *H-Diplo*. October 24. http://tiny.cc/E116 Accessed July 30, 2016.

Riis, Jacob A. 1904. *Theodore Roosevelt, the Citizen*. New York: Outlook.

Roosevelt, Theodore. 1919–1926. *The Works of Theodore Roosevelt*. Memorial Edition. New York: Charles Scribner's Sons.

Rotundo, E. Anthony. 1993. *American Manhood: Transformations in Masculinity from the Revolution to the Modern Era*. New York: Basic Books.

Salem, Dorothy. 1990. *To Better Our World: Black Women in Organized Reform, 1890–1920*. Brooklyn: Carlson.

Shaw, Albert. 1910. *A Cartoon History of Roosevelt's Career*. New York: The Review of Reviews.

Scott, Anne Firor. 1991. *Natural Allies: Women's Associations in American History*. Urbana: University of Illinois Press.

Sklar, Kathryn Kish. 1993. "The Historical Foundations of Women's Power in the Creation of the American Welfare State, 1830–1930." In *Mothers of a New World: Maternalist Politics and the Origins of Welfare States*, ed. Seth Koven and Sonya Michel, 43–93. New York: Routledge.

—. 1995. *Florence Kelley and the Nation's Work: The Rise of Women's Political Culture, 1830–1900*. New Haven, CT: Yale University Press.

Skok, Deborah A. 2008. "The Historiography of Catholic Laywomen and Progressive Era Reform." *U.S. Catholic Historian* 26, 1: 1–22.

Testi, Arnaldo. 1995. "The Gender of Reform Politics: Theodore Roosevelt and the Culture of Masculinity." *Journal of American History* 81, March: 1509–1533.

Tilchin, William N. 1997. *Theodore Roosevelt and the British Empire: A Study in Presidential Statecraft*. New York: St. Martin's Press.

—. 2014. "Then and Since: The Remarkable and Enduring Foreign Policy of Theodore Roosevelt." *Theodore Roosevelt Association Journal* Winter–Spring: 45–51.

Tyrrell, Ian. 2007. *Transnational Nation: United States History in Global Perspective since 1789*. Basingstoke: Palgrave Macmillan.

Unger, Nancy C. 2012. *Beyond Nature's Housekeepers: American Women in Environmental History*. New York: Oxford University Press.

Valaik, J. David. 1993. *Theodore Roosevelt, an American Hero in Caricature*. Buffalo: Western New York Heritage Institute of Canisius College.

Watts, Sarah Lyons. 2003. *Rough Rider in the White House: Theodore Roosevelt and the Politics of Desire*. Chicago: University of Chicago Press.

Widenor, William C. 1980. *Henry Cabot Lodge and the Search for an American Foreign Policy*. Berkeley: University of California Press.

Wiebe, Robert H. 1961. "The Anthracite Strike of 1902: A Record of Confusion." *Mississippi Valley Historical Review* 48.

—. 1962. *Businessmen and Reform: a Study of the Progressive Movement*. Cambridge, MA: Harvard University Press.

—.1967. *The Search for Order, 1877–1920*. New York: Hill & Wang.

Williams, William Appleman. 1962. *The Tragedy of American Diplomacy*. New York: Dell.

Chapter Twenty-Four

Woodrow Wilson

Lloyd E. Ambrosius

Among historians and other scholars as well as the American public, Woodrow Wilson has enjoyed a generally good reputation. He has typically ranked among the top ten US presidents. But he has also had his critics. In *Reconsidering Woodrow Wilson*, John Milton Cooper, Jr. noted that *The Atlantic Monthly* had recently ranked the former president tenth on its list of "The 100 Most Influential Americans of All Time." Only four other presidents–Abraham Lincoln, George Washington, Thomas Jefferson, and Franklin D. Roosevelt–outranked him. Yet, as Cooper observed, "Wilson has not become a figure of warm, generalized adulation. Rather, nine decades after his death, he still draws sharply conflicting estimates of his accomplishments and legacies; people still admire and revile him" (Cooper 2008, 1). Thus, Wilson's place in history depends on the memory or perspective of those who determine the rankings or evaluate his life and presidency.

Arthur S. Link, author of a five-volume biography of *Wilson* (Link 1947–1965) from his birth to 1917, and editor of sixty-nine volumes of *The Papers of Woodrow Wilson* (Wilson 1966–1994), offered a mostly favorable evaluation of the president. Although not uncritical, Link adopted Wilson's own progressive American worldview as the framework for assessing his academic and political career and his statecraft. As the preeminent authority on Wilson, Link profoundly influenced historical scholarship for more than a generation. Most writers embraced Link's positive perspective in their biographies and historical studies. For example, August Heckscher substantially agreed with Link in his comprehensive biography of *Woodrow Wilson* (Heckscher 1991). Only a few dissented from this pro-Wilson consensus. They too benefited from Link's monumental achievement as editor. In recent years, historians have increasingly highlighted Wilson's flaws or limits, emphasizing his responsibility for the failures of his presidency rather than blaming others for not following his so-called higher realism or prophetic leadership. Among others, John A. Thompson offered a less admiring assessment in his biography, *Woodrow Wilson* (Thompson 2002). Ross A. Kennedy also gave a more balanced evaluation of the president's strategy to protect American security during and restore peace after World War I in *The Will to Believe* (Kennedy 2009). But some, such as John Milton Cooper, Jr. in his biography, *Woodrow Wilson* (Cooper 2009), still mostly adhered to Link's legacy.

Early Life

Thomas Woodrow Wilson was born in Staunton, Virginia, on December 28, 1856. From his parents, the Reverend Joseph Ruggles Wilson and Janet Woodrow Wilson, he inherited his personal identity from their Scots-Irish and English ancestry, Christian religious faith, and traditional southern values. His father was pastor of the town's First Presbyterian Church and director of its women's college, the Augusta Female Seminary. His mother cared for the family at home.

Tommy, as he was known then, experienced the Civil War and Reconstruction as a boy in the South. In 1858, Rev. Wilson had moved the family to Augusta, Georgia, where he accepted the First Presbyterian Church's call to become its pastor. He defended slavery in his sermons. Black slaves served the family in the manse. In 1861, he hosted the organizational meeting of the General Assembly of the Southern Presbyterian Church, and continued as its clerk for the next thirty-seven years. His church became a temporary hospital for Confederate soldiers. In 1870, the family moved to Columbia, South Carolina, where Rev. Wilson joined the Columbia Theological Seminary faculty and served as the First Presbyterian Church's pastor. In 1873,

A Companion to the Gilded Age and Progressive Era, First Edition. Edited by Christopher McKnight Nichols and Nancy C. Unger.
© 2017 John Wiley & Sons, Inc. Published 2017 by John Wiley & Sons, Inc.

the adolescent boy became a member of his father's church. Henceforth his Christian faith sustained him during times of trial. In the Calvinist theological tradition, he believed that God guided human history toward its millennial end—a providential guarantee of historical progress toward that predestined culmination. The boy absorbed his parents' religious faith.

Wilson witnessed the Civil War's devastation of the South and the postwar turmoil of Reconstruction. This experience provided an important part of his early education. He attended Presbyterian colleges. In 1873, he entered Davidson College in western North Carolina. However, before the academic year ended, he returned to his parents' home in Wilmington, North Carolina. The family had moved there for his father's latest pastorate at the city's First Presbyterian Church. During the next year, under his father's tutelage, Wilson read about such topics as modern British liberalism. He greatly admired British Liberal statesman William Gladstone. In 1875, Wilson resumed his formal education at the College of New Jersey in Princeton, where several other southern Presbyterian students also matriculated. In *Woodrow Wilson and the Roots of Modern Liberalism*, Ronald J. Pestritto traced the British origins of Wilson's political thought and his subsequent intellectual development that would later shape his statecraft (Pestritto 2005).

Wilson thrived as a student at Princeton. History and politics were his favorite subjects, given his desire to learn more about government. As an active member of the prestigious Whig Society, he learned the art of political persuasion. He organized the Liberal Debating Club, drafting a constitution for it. Inspired by the British parliamentary tradition, Wilson began to think of himself as a future American statesman. He found the political theories of Edmund Burke and Walter Bagehot especially appealing. While still an undergraduate, he wrote his first published article, "Cabinet Government in the United States," for an 1879 issue of *International Review*. Ironically, Henry Cabot Lodge, the editor who accepted it, would later become his chief nemesis. Wilson's interests were varied, as seen in his election as editor of the *Princetonian* and as secretary of the Football Association. For recreation he played baseball. Wilson graduated in the class of '79.

Like other young men who wanted to become statesmen, Wilson hoped to qualify for a career in both law and politics. He enrolled at the University of Virginia to study law. He joined the Jefferson Society, a debating and literary club at the university that Thomas Jefferson had founded in Charlottesville. Debating in 1880, he affirmed a pro-Union, nationalist interpretation of the Civil War. He endorsed John Bright's liberal British critique of the southern Confederacy. Although himself a white southerner, he believed that the South's independence had been a futile dream and that its reunion with the North was the South's best hope for future prosperity. This interpretation of the Civil War prepared Wilson later to contribute to national reconciliation between white southerners and northerners. Complaining of poor health, he left Virginia early in 1881 and again returned home.

Wilson continued to study law and passed the bar exam in 1882. He set up a law practice in Atlanta, Georgia, with his law partner Edward Renick, but they did not benefit from the city's thriving economy during this era of the New South: they attracted very few clients. Having little else to do, Wilson testified before a federal commission in favor of tariff reduction, advocating tariff reform as the way to promote international trade and peace. His stance on this issue in 1882 anticipated his later position as president. In 1883, Wilson's mother gave him some legal work regarding a family inheritance, which took him to Rome, Georgia. There he met and quickly fell in love with Ellen Louise Axson, the town's Presbyterian pastor's daughter.

Recognizing that he could not afford a family, but yearning for marriage, Wilson decided to change careers. Abandoning law, he enrolled, in 1883, as a graduate student at the Johns Hopkins University in Baltimore, Maryland. Modeled on German higher education, this new university offered the Ph.D. degree. Professor Herbert Baxter Adams, who had earned his own doctorate at Heidelberg University in Germany, taught Wilson the germ theory of history, which emphasized Anglo-Saxon contributions to American political institutions. Wilson also studied political economy with Professor Richard T. Ely, who rejected laissez-faire economics. Later, as a professor at the University of Wisconsin, Ely collaborated with Governor Robert M. La Follette on progressive reforms in the state. Wilson's subsequent academic and political career revealed that he had fully comprehended his professors' lessons about the nation's Anglo-Saxon heritage and its changing political economy.

Wilson did not abandon his ambition for political leadership. He found German-style research in historical documents, as taught by Adams, exceedingly tedious. He revealed to Ellen Axson that, given his keen interest in public affairs, he wanted to become a statesman, using his powers of oratory. He was not content with devoting himself to a solitary life of scholarship. Rather than commit himself to the kind of archival research he found boring, he read what he enjoyed and relied more on his own imagination and experience. He wrote *Congressional Government* (1885), his first book. Emulating Bagehot's approach to British politics and expressing his negative reaction to postwar Reconstruction in the South, Wilson contrasted how the US Constitution actually worked with how the founding fathers had theorized it should operate, as they had expressed in the *Federalist Papers*.

Wilson argued that the Civil War and Reconstruction had fundamentally altered the American system of government under the Constitution. The northern Union's victory over the southern Confederacy had ended the historic tradition of federalism in the relationship between the national and state governments. Moreover, the checks-and-balances of the three branches of government had collapsed during the postwar years, when Republican-controlled congressional committees dominated the legislative process behind closed doors at the expense of both public discourse and presidential leadership. Despite President Andrew Johnson's resistance, Congress had imposed radical, interracial governments on the South. In Wilson's view, this undesirable imposition on southern states demonstrated that the traditional balances under the Constitution no longer functioned as its framers had intended. Unhappy about this outcome, he could only hope that the federal courts would intervene to restore a better balance. In 1886, Professor Adams and his colleagues approved Wilson's book as a doctoral dissertation. Johns Hopkins awarded him the Ph.D. in history, making him the first and, so far only, US president with an earned doctorate.

Wilson began his academic career teaching history and political science at Bryn Mawr, a Quaker college for women near Philadelphia. This job promised steady income, which enabled him to marry Ellen Axson on June 24, 1885. The new couple soon welcomed three daughters into their family with the birth of Margaret in 1886, Jessie in 1887, and Eleanor in 1889. In their traditional marriage, Wilson pursued his career while his wife devoted her time to the family. She also helped him with research for his next book.

In *The State* (1889), a textbook on the origins of governments in Western Europe and the United States, Wilson affirmed his Social Darwinian belief in the racial and political superiority of the West. "In order to trace the lineage of the European and American governments which have constituted the order of social life for those stronger and nobler races which have made the most notable progress in civilization," he wrote,

> it is essential to know the political history of the Greeks, the Latins, the Teutons, and the Celts principally, if not only, and the original political habits and ideas of the Aryan and Semitic races alone. The existing governments of Europe and America furnish the dominating types of today. To know other systems that are defeated or dead would aid only indirectly towards an understanding of those which are alive and triumphant, as the survived fittest (Wilson 1889, 2).

In accordance with the germ theory, Wilson saw the West's historical progress from ancient Greece to modern America as the product of its racial or ethnic heritage. The West had triumphed over the rest of the world, making the history of other peoples or civilizations essentially irrelevant. History seemed to move along a unidirectional path, which culminated in the West, even more in the United States than in modern Europe.

Wilson thrived in his academic career, although he was unhappy teaching women. He preferred to shape the minds of young men, who would serve as the nation's future leaders. In 1888, he welcomed the opportunity to depart Bryn Mawr and move to Wesleyan University in Middletown, Connecticut. Then, in 1890, he returned to Princeton as professor of jurisprudence and political economy at the College of New Jersey. His popularity as a teacher and productivity as a scholar now gave him an increasingly national as well as local reputation.

During his years on Princeton's faculty, Wilson published several books and articles. In *Division and Reunion, 1829–1889* (1893), he interpreted the Civil War and Reconstruction from a pro-Union and pro-white perspective. He criticized white southerners for attempting to create an independent Confederacy, but not their resistance to northern-imposed Reconstruction. Notwithstanding his racial bias, Wilson no longer affirmed the germ theory in this book. Now he offered his own frontier thesis to explain American history. From historian Frederick Jackson Turner, he had gained a greater appreciation of the American West and of the western frontier's impact on the American character. They had engaged in extensive conversations when Wilson returned to Johns Hopkins to give a series of lectures and Turner was a graduate student there. Wilson now credited the nation's experience of westward expansion, more than its Anglo-Saxon heritage, for the historic rise of free and democratic institutions in the United States.

In his writings and lectures, Wilson emphasized the themes of freedom and democracy and the importance of liberal education. He thought that Princeton University, renamed in 1896, should contribute to the nation's service. His books not only enhanced his scholarly reputation but also provided extra income for his growing family and their new house. He published for profit, which required him to write popular books such as *George Washington* (1896) and *A History of the American People* (5 volumes, 1902).

Princeton's trustees selected Wilson as the university's new president in 1902. They wanted his national stature and potential leadership to raise its reputation. He also possessed strong Presbyterian credentials, although he was the university's first president without formal theological education. Wilson espoused liberal Christianity, unlike some clergy who rejected modern science and embraced fundamentalist religious beliefs. He identified with his uncle, James Woodrow, who had taught Darwinian science at Columbia Theological Seminary and consequently faced a trial for heresy in 1888 before the General Assembly of the Southern Presbyterian Church. Like his uncle, who quit the seminary but not his views, Wilson saw no contradiction between modern science and religion.

As Princeton's president, Wilson sought to reform the university to improve its academic standing. Emphasizing scholarship, he established new departments and hired new faculty. With the trustees' approval in 1905, he recruited young faculty as tutors or preceptors. To stimulate intellectual activity among undergraduate students, he attacked their exclusive eating clubs and proposed a residential quadrangle. Students as well as alumni resisted these reforms.

Wilson also encountered opposition from the graduate dean, Andrew Fleming West, who pressed ahead with his own plans for a residential graduate college. Facing overwhelming foes, Wilson failed to replace the undergraduate eating clubs with a residential quadrangle. Moreover, contrary to his advice, Princeton trustees decided in 1909 to accept a generous bequest that West had secured for the graduate college. Wilson denounced this decision as a violation of both educational and democratic values, further alienating the trustees, who welcomed his resignation in 1910.

Wilson shifted from an academic career to politics, running for governor of New Jersey in 1910. Democratic political bosses in the state enabled him to win their party's nomination and the gubernatorial election. Once elected, however, he distanced himself from them, presenting himself as the people's advocate against special interests. He further enhanced his reputation as a progressive governor by convincing the legislature to enact laws guaranteeing an open political process, if only for white men, with direct nomination of candidates and honest elections. His other reforms, which sought to limit the worst abuses of corporate capitalism, established workmen's compensation, regulated public utilities, and improved labor conditions for women and children. New Jersey continued, however, as a haven for corporations. Wilson did not fundamentally challenge the political economy of capitalism.

Progressive Presidency

Governor Wilson soon focused his ambition on the American presidency. He nurtured a new relationship with William Jennings Bryan, despite his earlier criticism of the Democratic Party's losing candidate in the presidential elections in 1896, 1900, and 1908. He now acknowledged that Bryan had transformed the Democratic Party into a more progressive institution. In his Jackson Day address on January 8, 1912, Wilson praised Bryan for steadfastly advocating democratic principles. Although he had denounced Bryan's agrarian radicalism, he now emphasized their areas of agreement. They both advocated self-government by the people, a theme that Wilson had articulated long before he entered politics or praised Bryan. Their common Presbyterian faith inspired their calls for progressive reform. "Let no man suppose that progress can be divorced from religion or that there is any other platform for the ministers of reform than the platform written in the utterances of our Lord and Saviour," Wilson affirmed in 1911. Moreover, he believed the United States epitomized Christianity. "America was born a Christian nation," he proclaimed. "America was born to exemplify that devotion to the elements of righteousness which are derived from the revelations of Holy Scripture" (Wilson 1977, 23: 12–20). Wilson, like Bryan, combined his Christian religion with American patriotism to justify progressive reform.

Wilson's progressive reputation as New Jersey's governor improved his prospects for winning the 1912 Democratic presidential nomination. Colonel Edward M. House of Texas, who became a close friend after they first met in 1911, encouraged him to run, as did other Democrats throughout the country. Wilson increasingly attracted nationwide support. At the Democratic Party's national convention in Baltimore in June 1912, neither he nor any other candidate commanded the two-thirds majority required for the nomination. His campaign strategists, including William Gibbs McAdoo, hoped delegates would switch to him after their first choices fell short. Indiana's delegation, led by Governor Thomas R. Marshall, was one of the first to shift. Marshall was later selected to run for the vice presidency. Bryan, who initially supported James Beauchamp "Champ" Clark of Missouri, also changed to Wilson. As prospects faded for Clark and Oscar Underwood of Alabama, other delegates followed Bryan's example, eventually giving the nomination to New Jersey's governor.

In the 1912 presidential election, Wilson faced a divided field. After the Republicans nominated President William Howard Taft for a second term, his rival for the nomination, former president Theodore Roosevelt, changed parties and ran as the Progressive candidate. Eugene V. Debs offered a more radical alternative as the perennial Socialist contender. The Republican split between Taft and Roosevelt created a real chance for Democrats to capture the White House. During the campaign, Wilson presented himself as the people's champion within the Bryan progressive tradition. His concept of democracy was limited, however. As his brother-in-law Stockton Axson observed,

> His instinct for democracy involved the idea that, because a democracy is free, it is the more necessary that it be led. His faith in the people has never been a faith in the supreme wisdom of the people, but rather in the capacity of the people to be led right by those whom they elect and constitute their leaders (Axson 1993, 231).

Wilson left many on the margins. He did not favor voting rights for women, nor did he challenge Jim Crow segregation that excluded African Americans from political participation and barred them from educational and economic opportunities, nor did he expect Native Americans to assimilate into the nation as citizens. Although advocating democracy, Wilson did not seek freedom and equality for all Americans.

Both leading candidates, Wilson and Roosevelt, claimed to offer progressive agendas but presented different solutions for the nation's industrial and agricultural problems. Wilson's New Freedom and Roosevelt's New Nationalism embraced democratic capitalism, differing over how best to preserve both efficiency and equality of opportunity in America's modern corporate society. Wilson wanted to keep the free market open to fair competition for new entrepreneurs. Roosevelt, less distrustful of large-scale organizations, preferred more government regulation of monopolistic trusts, rather than breaking them up, so that the country could benefit from their efficient productivity. They agreed, in contrast to Taft, on the need for reforms to preserve the capitalist political economy and protect it against Debs's radical alternative of socialism. In the election on November 4, 1912, Wilson won only 42% of the popular vote but, more importantly, captured 435 electoral votes to Roosevelt's 88 and Taft's 8. Aided by the Republican split, the solidly Democratic South triumphed with the election of its first native son to the presidency since the Civil War.

Inaugurated on March 4, 1913, Wilson began to implement his ideas of New Freedom. He employed a new concept of the presidency to win approval for his reforms. In *Congressional Government*, he had regarded Congress as the dominant branch of government, while the president was a mere administrator. After observing Roosevelt's use of executive power, however, Wilson saw new opportunities for the American presidency. In *Constitutional Government in the United States* (1908), he had offered a positive view of presidential leadership; now he could put his ideas into practice. He wanted to establish a direct link to the American people. He thought the president, as their spokesman, should be the preeminent leader of the democratic nation. Long convinced that British parliamentary government was better than the American constitutional system, he exerted personal influence on the legislative branch in unprecedented ways. Rejecting the traditional republican understanding of the separation of powers among the branches of government as an old Whig or Newtonian theory, he endeavored to establish executive control over both domestic and foreign affairs. The first president to hold regular press conferences, he sought to manage the news and shape public opinion from the White House. Moreover, he delivered messages in person to Congress, reviving a practice that George Washington and John Adams had used on a few occasions. From Jefferson through Taft, other US presidents had submitted only written messages. By speaking before Congress, Wilson hoped to mold public opinion with his rhetoric and thereby persuade senators and representatives to vote as he desired. He successfully used these techniques of presidential leadership to win approval for his New Freedom agenda.

Modern liberalism characterized Wilson's progressivism, which had emerged from transnational connections in the late nineteenth and early twentieth centuries. Ideas about reform passed back and forth across the Atlantic between the United States and Europe. Daniel T. Rodgers explored these exchanges in social politics during the Progressive Era in *Atlantic Crossings* (Rodgers 1998). Alan Dawley placed Wilson, the preeminent American progressive, in the global framework of war and revolution in *Changing the World* (Dawley 2003). Ian Tyrrell, in *Reforming the World*, examined the creation of America's moral empire at the turn of the century in a transnational context, which "influenced the United States as much as it did the colonial and quasi-colonial peoples that Americans touched and shaped the architecture of American dealings with the larger world of empires through to the era of Woodrow Wilson" (Tyrrell 2010, 6). These and other historians recognized that Wilson and other American progressives derived their ideas from abroad as much as they hoped to spread them to foreign countries. Modern British liberalism profoundly influenced his progressivism but some of his ideas came from Germany and elsewhere in Europe as well as the United States.

Wilson advocated three major reforms in the American political economy, beginning with the tariff. He wanted to promote international trade by reducing protective tariffs on imports. He saw no reason for excessive barriers against foreign competition, especially now that the United States had become the world's leading industrial nation. A lower tariff would encourage greater efficiency in American factories and undermine the monopolistic trusts. Stimulating international trade, he believed, would also contribute to world peace. Wilson appeared before a joint session of Congress on April 8, 1913, to make his case. On his behalf, Oscar Underwood, chairman of the House Ways and Means Committee, introduced a tariff bill. It included a new income tax, which the recently ratified Sixteenth Amendment to the Constitution authorized, to replace the anticipated loss of tariff revenue. The House quickly approved the bill. The Senate took longer. Wilson worked with the Democratic caucus to exert pressure on senators, and finally succeeded. The Underwood Tariff Act, which he signed on October 3, 1913, lowered duties on imports by about one-fourth and added many items to the free list.

Reforming the banking system became Wilson's next priority. The Panic of 1907 had convinced almost all bankers, businessmen, and farmers that the nation needed a more modern arrangement to manage its banks and currency. They disagreed, however, about what it should be. Republicans preferred a privately controlled central bank, while progressive Democrats such as Bryan, now serving as secretary of state, advocated a regional banking system along with government control of the nation's currency. Working with Bryan and McAdoo, his treasury secretary, and with Carter Glass and Robert L. Owen, the chairmen of the House and Senate banking committees, Wilson urged them to reconcile conflicting plans for a new Federal Reserve System that could regulate the money supply for the nation's expanding economy. Their compromise provided for regional banks under a single Federal Reserve Board which would control the issuance of currency. Wilson appeared before Congress again on June 23, 1913, to appeal for support. Both the House and Senate eventually enacted his banking and currency reform, which the president signed into law as the Federal Reserve Act on December 23, 1913.

Finally, Wilson turned to antitrust reform. Appearing before Congress on January 20, 1914, he called for authority to impose more sanctions against monopolies for the purpose of preserving the free market for new entrepreneurs. Samuel Gompers, who led the American Federation of Labor, urged him to exempt labor unions from anti-trust injunctions. As Wilson wrestled with the complexities of enforcing a new anti-trust law against industrial corporations and labor unions, he shifted his thinking more toward Roosevelt's New Nationalism. He signed the Federal Trade Commission Act on September 26, 1914, which Congress had passed to create a new regulatory commission. He subsequently signed the Clayton Anti-Trust Act on October 15, 1914, which revised the Sherman Anti-Trust Act to prohibit the restraint of trade and to provide penalties and remedies for violations. This anti-trust legislation further defined the distinction between legitimate and illegal corporate practices and partially exempted labor unions from injunctions.

Wilson's New Freedom focused on the political economy. He sought to preserve entrepreneurial opportunities in a free and competitive marketplace for a new generation of Americans by reforming the tariff, banking, and anti-trust laws. These reforms did not address the issues of race or gender. The president's progressive vision for the nation left women as well as racial minorities on the margins. He criticized the woman suffrage movement, authorized racial segregation in federal executive departments, condoned discrimination against Asian immigrants, and enabled an increase in the number of American Indians to lose their land to white owners.

The president particularly disappointed people of color. W.E.B. Du Bois and William Monroe Trotter, two prominent African Americans who had supported him in 1912, became quickly disillusioned. On November 12, 1914, Trotter led a delegation of African Americans to the White House. Wilson told them that racial segregation, which his administration had begun to implement in the federal bureaucracy, benefited black as well as white Americans. When Trotter challenged this view, the president angrily ordered the delegation out of his office. There were limits to his New Freedom and his underlying concept of democracy.

Wilson drew a sharp color line despite his apparently universal liberal rhetoric. During his presidency, the racial segregation of the Jim Crow South became the common practice in the federal government. In 1915, he watched the racist film *The Birth of a Nation* at the White House as a favor to his Johns Hopkins classmate and friend, Thomas Dixon, Jr., who had joined David W. Griffith to make this movie about the Civil War and Reconstruction. They included quotations from Wilson's *A History of the American People* in this silent film to give credibility to their historical interpretation of the "war between the states" and postwar Reconstruction. They used his words to exonerate the Ku Klux Klan, which had inflicted violence and terror against African Americans and their white allies to overturn the new interracial Republican governments of the Reconstruction era and restore exclusively white rule in a solidly Democratic South. All viewers of this most popular silent movie ever produced, when they read the film's quotations from Wilson's book at the theater, would have identified him with it. The audience knew that the president had seen it and had not criticized its virulently racist message. Thus, although he never publicly praised it, Wilson implicitly endorsed the film's glorification of the KKK and white supremacy. Even when asked, he refused to express any criticism of the film. Despite his universal liberal rhetoric about democratic government, his New Freedom excluded and marginalized African Americans (Ambrosius 2007).

During the early White House years, Wilson experienced both joy and grief in his family. Two daughters left home after their marriages, Jessie to Francis B. Sayre in 1913 and Eleanor to William McAdoo in 1914, and the third, Margaret, to pursue her musical career. The death of his wife Ellen, on August 6, 1914, was the president's greatest sorrow. She had given him constant love and support during triumphs and failures in his academic career and consoled him in times of hardship in the family. During his recurrent health problems, especially since 1896, she had nurtured him. She encouraged him to take vacations in Great Britain and Bermuda. She also tolerated his close friendship with Mrs. Mary Allen Hulbert Peck, a socialite whom he met in Bermuda in 1906. Mrs. Peck's divorce in 1912 during the presidential campaign had generated rumors about their relationship, but he steadfastly denied any impropriety.

Soon after Ellen's death, the lonely president met Edith Bolling Galt, a wealthy widow who resided in Washington, DC. They married on December 18, 1915, despite concerns among some of the president's closest advisers that a marriage so soon after his wife's death might hurt his chances for reelection. Wilson's second wife, also a southerner, from Virginia, furnished the emotional warmth he needed. She became not only his closest friend but also his occasional consultant on public issues throughout the remainder of his presidency and life. Phyllis Lee Levin, in *Edith and Woodrow*, underscored the importance of this second marriage for Wilson's wartime and postwar presidency, especially after he suffered a stroke in 1919 (Levin 2001).

Fortunately for Wilson, the 1916 presidential election came at an opportune time during the Great War that began in Europe two years earlier. He had struggled to keep the United States out of the war, while defending its neutral rights. The election occurred before Imperial Germany created another submarine crisis that would shatter the hope that the United States could remain at peace without sacrificing maritime and commercial rights. At the June 1916 Democratic convention in St. Louis and during the subsequent campaign, Wilson profited from this false expectation. Republicans, having healed the split between the conservative and progressive wings of their party, united behind Charles Evans Hughes. Roosevelt endorsed him, hoping to defeat Wilson. The endorsement was problematic, however, because Roosevelt had openly identified with the Allies, particularly the British and French, since the beginning of the Great War. This suggested that Hughes, if elected, might lead the United States into the European war.

Before the 1916 election, Wilson expanded his political appeal to progressives. He nominated Boston attorney Louis Brandeis, a trusted adviser who had helped define the New Freedom, to the Supreme Court. Confirmed by the Senate on June 1, 1916, Brandeis became the first Jew on the nation's highest court. Wilson now advocated reforms that the Progressive Party had championed in 1912, hoping to attract Roosevelt's former voters to the Democratic Party. Going beyond his original New Freedom agenda, Wilson supported laws to benefit agricultural and labor constituencies. On July 17, 1916, he signed the Federal Farm Loan Act, which provided credits to farmers; on September 3, 1916, he approved the Adamson Act, which guaranteed the eight-hour day to railway workers. Wilson's record of peace and progressivism enabled him to win the presidential election on November 7, 1916, by a narrow margin of 277 electoral votes to Hughes's 254, although with slightly less than half the popular vote. Despite losing several states in the East and Midwest that had supported him in 1912, Wilson won again by carrying all of the South and most of the West.

International Relations

Wilson derived his orientation in international relations from his understanding of the history and political culture of the United States as the preeminent Western nation in the modern world. At home and abroad, he believed that democracy required progressive order. He preferred reform to revolution. He wanted to manage change rather than suffer uncontrollable chaos or anarchy. After Europe plunged into war in 1914, he applied to the Old World the vision of America's role in foreign affairs that he first offered to the Western Hemisphere. The rise of the United States in the global political economy and the collapse of Europe's balance of power, which the war clearly revealed, provided the conditions for his redefinition of America's mission worldwide.

Beginning with a new Latin American policy in 1913, Wilson urged "the development of constitutional liberty in the world" (Wilson 1978, 28: 448–452). Edward House encouraged him to negotiate a Pan-American treaty of nonaggression and political cooperation, starting with Argentina, Brazil, and Chile. Wilson's idea of Pan-Americanism affirmed the Monroe Doctrine's guarantee of territorial integrity and republican political institutions for nations in the Western Hemisphere. At the Pan-American Scientific Congress on January 6, 1916, he called for "the ordered progress of society" from Mexico to South America (Wilson 1980, 35: 439–446). For nations of this region, he said, the proposed treaty would protect them against the threats of both external aggression and internal revolution. Latin Americans, however, saw the danger of US hegemony in Wilson's Pan-Americanism, as Mark T. Gilderhus noted in *Pan American Visions* (Gilderhus 1986). Although the president eventually dropped the treaty in early 1917, this failure did not prevent him from proposing the same idea of collective security through a new League of Nations for the entire world after the Great War.

While promoting Pan-Americanism, Wilson used military force unilaterally in the Caribbean. Its strategic importance for the United States had increased in 1914 when the Panama Canal opened and the Great War began in Europe. Despite having denounced Taft's Dollar Diplomacy, Wilson vigilantly protected American economic interests. Fostering friendly governments, he sought to exclude European influence and establish American control in the region. He used military occupation of Haiti in 1915 and the Dominican Republic in 1916 to impose new governments on these nations and compel them to meet their financial obligations. Military intervention consolidated US hegemony in the Caribbean. However, although Wilson promised constitutional liberty, the United States could not export its democratic political culture to these island nations. In *Taking Haiti*, Mary A. Renda revealed the Wilson administration's "culture of U.S. imperialism" as seen in its lackluster attempt and colossal failure to bring democracy to Haiti during the military occupation of the nation (Renda 2001).

Wilson encountered more difficulty with Mexico than any other country in the Western Hemisphere. US rivalry with Europe in Latin America became most intense during the Mexican Revolution, as Great Britain and Germany sought to protect their interests. Early in 1913, General Victoriano Huerta captured Mexico City, ousting Francisco Madero's revolutionary government. Madero was murdered during this counter-revolutionary coup. Refusing to recognize Huerta's new government, Wilson sought an acceptable alternative. Huerta turned to Europe to counter Wilson's plan to replace him through a democratic election. Failing to shape Mexico's politics by peaceful methods, Wilson resorted to military intervention. The occupation of Veracruz in April 1914, although timed to prevent the landing of a German ship with munitions and justified by the brief detention of US sailors in Tampico, revealed his determination to remove Huerta from office. Yet he could not control the Mexican Revolution. Unexpected Mexican resistance and US casualties led Wilson to accept mediation by Argentina, Brazil, and Chile to end the crisis. As Mark Benbow demonstrated in *Leading Them to the Promised Land*, Wilson had attempted to apply his Calvinist religious beliefs, particularly his understanding of covenant theology, to the Mexican Revolution but this formulation of US foreign policy led to misunderstanding and failure (Benbow 2010).

After Venustiano Carranza replaced Huerta as Mexico's president, Wilson recognized his government in October 1915. Yet Carranza, too, resisted American paternalism. The Mexican president perceived General John J. Pershing's punitive expedition into Mexico in March 1916, which Wilson had ordered to capture Francisco "Pancho" Villa who had raided Columbus, New Mexico, as a threat to national sovereignty. Pershing's soldiers clashed with Mexican army troops as well as Villa's. Carranza turned to Germany for military assistance and, in January 1917, hoping to divert the United States from Europe by embroiling it in a war with Mexico, German foreign secretary Arthur Zimmermann proposed a possible alliance against the United States. This ill-conceived German plan failed. British intelligence intercepted the Zimmermann telegram and gave it to Wilson. As the United Stated moved toward war against Germany in 1917, Wilson released the telegram to the press, and ordered Pershing's withdrawal from Mexico. This episode left a legacy of distrust, however, in Mexico's relationship with the United States.

Although Wilson had sought to keep the United States out of the European war, his efforts failed by early 1917. Long before the Zimmermann telegram, America's relations with Germany had been deteriorating. From the beginning, the Great War had threatened to entangle the United States in Europe despite Wilson's pursuit of neutrality, which he proclaimed on August 4, 1914. He wanted to remain aloof from the world war that pitted the British, French, and Russian empires against the German, Austro-Hungarian, and Ottoman empires. He did not want to align with either the Allies or the Central Powers.

Wilson recognized, however, that the war might threaten American interests, especially on the high seas. Before this occurred, he hoped to arrange a compromise peace. He offered US mediation and sent *Colonel House*, who had been in Europe at the early stages of the July 1914 crisis, back to resume his efforts at peacemaking. House returned to Europe in February 1915 to seek a settlement between the Allies and the Central Powers and thereby protect neutral rights. Germany's decision to use its submarines against Allied shipping, in retaliation against the British offshore blockade of German ports, underscored the urgency of House's task. Yet, by April, it was obvious that he had failed to overcome the irreconcilable differences between the two sets of belligerents. He returned home.

After the sinking of the British passenger liner *Lusitania* by a German submarine on May 7, 1915, Wilson vigorously protested Germany's violation of the rights of the 128 American passengers who had lost their lives. He refused to make a comparable protest against British maritime practices, which led Bryan to resign as secretary of state, believing that the president was no longer impartial. Yet Wilson still intended to avoid war, proclaiming that Americans were "too proud to fight." Robert Lansing, Bryan's successor, also wanted to maintain US neutrality, despite his belief that Imperial Germany, under Kaiser William II, threatened all democracies.

Wilson was endeavoring not only to keep the United States out of the European war but also to protect its maritime and commercial rights. The contradiction between these goals reappeared when another German submarine sank the British ship *Arabic* on August 19, 1915, injuring two Americans. Both House and Lansing now favored a diplomatic break with Germany, but Wilson hesitated. His vigorous protest convinced Germany to resolve the crisis by pledging not to use submarines against passenger liners. In pursuit of neutrality, the president also pressed the British to modify their maritime system. On October 21, 1915, he denounced their off-shore blockade and broad definition of contraband. He was still seeking to protect American rights and interests on the high seas, yet keep the United States out of war.

Hoping to end the war before German submarines forced the United States into it, Wilson sent House back to Europe in early 1916 in search of peace. The British and French, no less than the Germans, resisted House's vague proposals. Neither side welcomed American meddling in Europe's affairs, although they received him graciously because they did not want to offend the president of the world's potentially most powerful nation. British foreign secretary Edward Grey encouraged House to focus on future guarantees of world peace. Nevertheless, on February 22, 1916, he approved the House–Grey memorandum, which provided for the possibility that the president might convene a peace conference if requested by the Allies. House believed this agreement was significant, but the Allies never intended to implement it. They did not plan to invite Wilson to call a conference to settle the conditions of peace as House expected. Charles E. Neu, in his biography of *Colonel House*, rendered a devastating criticism of his incompetence. "House's curious performance in Paris revealed once again his uneven skills as a diplomat. He had exaggerated his own accomplishments, misunderstood French leaders, and conveyed to Wilson an inaccurate assessment of the possibilities for peace." When House returned to London, he once more showed his inability to comprehend European international relations. "Instead," Neu concluded, "he continued to pursue his illusion of peace" (Neu 2015, 232, 235). This damning critique of House raises the question as to why Wilson persisted in relying on House's judgment, giving him important diplomatic assignments until 1919, when the president finally lost confidence in his close friend during the peace conference.

A new submarine crisis encouraged Wilson to continue searching for peace. On March 24, 1916, a German torpedo struck the English Channel steamer *Sussex*, injuring some Americans. He denounced this violation of the *Arabic* pledge and demanded an unequivocal German promise to follow the cruiser warfare rules of international law. Rather than risk a diplomatic break at this time,

Germany capitulated, pledging on May 4, 1916, to abide by these rules. In the midst of this crisis, Wilson pursued the idea of a future League of Nations, which Grey had encouraged. The president announced his vision of postwar peace-keeping in an address to the League to Enforce Peace on May 27, 1916. In place of traditional alliances and rivalries, he called for a new global community of democratic nations to preserve world peace and protect universal human rights.

The *Sussex* pledge effectively stopped Germany from using its submarines. Under these conditions, the United States experienced more difficulty with British maritime practices, which restricted American access to the ports and markets of the Central Powers. On July 26, 1916, Wilson protested this British discrimination against American trade. The British largely ignored the protest. Still, he seemed to have asserted the nation's rights while keeping it out of war. This apparent achievement aided him in his bid for re-election.

After winning the election, Wilson made another attempt to stop the Great War. In a peace note on December 18, 1916, he asked the belligerents to state their war aims. Minimizing differences between the Allies and the Central Powers, he urged them to negotiate a compromise and then join the United States in a new international system of universal collective security. Both sides, however, shunned Wilson's peace initiative. They continued fighting for victory.

Persevering in his search for peace, Wilson developed his idea of a new world order. In his "peace without victory" address to the Senate on January 22, 1917, he proclaimed that "the nations should with one accord adopt the doctrine of President [James] Monroe as the doctrine of the world: that no nation should seek to extend its polity over any other nation or people." Wilson wanted a new League of Nations, which would extend the Monroe Doctrine around the globe, to replace the Old World's discredited system of international relations. "There must be, not a balance of power, but a community of power; not organized rivalries, but an organized common peace." The president offered his vision of a new "covenant" among democratic nations (Wilson 1982, 40: 533–539).

Germany's decision to begin unrestricted submarine warfare in February 1917 finally forced the United States to abandon neutrality. The president immediately broke diplomatic relations, but still hoped to avoid war with Germany. In a desperate attempt to win the war, Kaiser William II had approved the new submarine policy on January 9. Earlier, in the *Arabic* and *Sussex* pledges, the German government had promised to restrict submarine warfare so as to avoid a confrontation with the United States. Now, however, it chose to violate these pledges: German submarines sank three US ships in mid-March 1917. These sinkings forced Wilson to make a choice. No longer able both to protect the nation's maritime and commercial rights and to keep it out of war, he chose war with Germany.

At the beginning of his second term, Wilson led the United States into the European war. Calling a special session of the new Congress on April 2, 1917, he denounced Germany's submarine attacks and called for war to liberate all nations, even the German people. As his rationale for America's entry into the war, he proclaimed that "the world must be made safe for democracy" (Wilson 1983, 41: 519–427). Four days later, after both branches of Congress voted overwhelmingly in favor, the president declared war against Germany. As Robert W. Tucker emphasized in *Woodrow Wilson and the Great War*, the president fundamentally shifted the rationale for his foreign policy from protecting US neutral rights to making the world safe for democracy (Tucker 2007).

Wilson mobilized the nation for war, appointing General Pershing to command the American Expeditionary Force (AEF) in Europe. The War and Navy departments, under Newton D. Baker and Josephus Daniels, created the AEF and prepared to transport it to France. The United States had planned for a defensive war against Germany, but not for fighting in Europe. Only after the declaration of war did Congress pass and Wilson sign the Selective Service Act on May 18, 1917, to draft young men into the nation's armed forces. The AEF required more than a year to organize and train before it could make a significant contribution to the war's outcome.

On the home front, Wilson exerted vigorous leadership. He established the Committee on Public Information under George Creel's direction to disseminate official propaganda. With the Lever Act of August 10, 1917, he mobilized the economy by creating the Food Administration under Herbert Hoover and the Fuel Administration under Harry Garfield. He named McAdoo to manage the Railroad Administration, in addition to the Treasury, in order to resolve transportation problems. He appointed former president Taft and labor lawyer Frank P. Walsh to direct the National War Labor Board, which mediated labor–management disputes to prevent strikes. In March 1918, he placed Bernard Baruch in charge of the War Industries Board to harness key industries for wartime production. Congress granted Wilson more executive power under the Espionage Act of June 15, 1917, the Trading with the Enemy Act of October 6, 1917, and the Sedition Act of May 16, 1918. Using this authority aggressively, the president silenced his radical critics, such as Eugene Debs and other Socialists. These wartime measures gave the Wilson administration unprecedented powers over the American society and economy, which it used to mobilize the nation for war but also to violate the civil liberties of its citizens. In *Uncle Sam Wants You*, Christopher Capozolla examined these pressures toward wartime conformity that Americans experienced in the name of patriotism as defined by the government (Capozolla 2008).

The 1917 Russian Revolution seemed at first to justify Wilson's wartime crusade for democracy. He recognized the provisional government, which replaced the czarist regime in March and promised a new constitutional republic in Russia, as a fit partner for the United States. But, after the Bolsheviks seized power in November, he opposed the radical socialist government of Vladimir I. Lenin. Rejecting its appeal for peace and revolution, Wilson outlined his liberal vision of a new world order in his Fourteen Points address to Congress on January 8, 1918. He called for open diplomacy and unimpeded international trade and navigation, for disarmament and self-determination of nations, and for a postwar League of Nations. The Fourteen Points outlined a better alternative, in Wilson's view, than Lenin's socialism or Communism. Expecting the Russian people to reject Bolshevism and remain in the war as one of the Allies associated with the United States, he approved American and Allied military intervention in northern Russia and Siberia in the summer of 1918 to help them against their common German and Bolshevik enemies. Wilson wanted democracy in Russia, but here, as in Mexico, he could not control the revolution. Among others, David S. Fogelsong examined this limitation in *America's Secret War against Bolshevism* (Fogelsong 1998).

On March 3, 1918, Lenin's government concluded a separate peace with Germany by acquiescing to the harsh terms of the Treaty of Brest-Litovsk, which ended fighting on the Eastern Front and shifted the military balance on the Western Front. The Central Powers threatened to defeat the Allies in 1918 before the United States could provide much assistance. British and French forces absorbed the brunt of Germany's spring offensive before Pershing's AEF contributed decisively to the Allied victory. In October 1918, finally facing military defeat, Germany appealed to Wilson for peace on the basis of his Fourteen Points. He sent Edward House to Europe to commit the Allies as well as Germany to these terms. On this basis, with reservations, the victorious and defeated enemies concluded the armistice on November 11, 1918, ending the Great War.

Wilson participated personally in the Paris Peace Conference of 1919. The United States and Japan joined the United Kingdom, France, and Italy as the five great powers in the negotiations. Russia was conspicuously absent. Delegates from Germany's new Weimar Republic, which had replaced the government of Kaiser William II, arrived only after American and Allied leaders prepared the peace treaty. Poland and Czechoslovakia were welcomed, but other new nations were not. In *Paris 1919*, Margaret Macmillan depicted the dramatic six months of the peace conference as it sought to settle conflicts among established and aspiring states around the world (Macmillan 2002). Wilson applied the principle of national self-determination with caution only to the defeated enemies. He did not call for universal decolonization. Just as he had kept the Philippines as a US colony under the Jones Act of 1916, which had only promised Philippine independence sometime in the future, he accepted continuing British rule in Ireland, Egypt, and India, and French rule in Indochina. He recognized only some new nations that emerged from the breakup of the empires of the Central Powers. He did not expect peoples of color in Africa and Asia to apply his principle of national self-determination to themselves against colonial empires. Despite his rhetoric, he was not ready for anti-colonial nationalist uprisings, as Erez Manela demonstrated in *The Wilsonian Moment* (Manela 2006).

At the heart of Wilson's peace program was the new League of Nations. His top priority was drafting the Covenant, the founding document for this new international organization. It was central to his quest for a new world order, as Thomas J. Knock stressed in *To End All Wars* (Knock 1992). He insisted on making the League an integral part of the peace treaty. Both he and British prime minister David Lloyd George anticipated Germany's eventual membership. Wanting an anti-German alliance instead, French premier Georges Clemenceau sought to restore Europe's balance of power. In collaboration with the British, Wilson succeeded in drafting the Covenant as he desired. Article 10 offered a mutual guarantee of territorial integrity and political independence for member-states in the new League, yet Article 19 anticipated future revision of the peace settlement. The Covenant thus embodied Wilson's vision of progressive order in international relations. He presented it to a plenary session of the peace conference on February 14, 1919, stressing that "throughout this instrument we are depending primarily and chiefly upon one great force, and that is the moral force of the public opinion of the world." The president realized, however, that military force might be needed "if the moral force of the world will not suffice" (Wilson 1986, 55: 164–178). He viewed the League as a practical way to reform the Old World on an ongoing basis as well as maintain its peace, thus achieving progressive order.

On other issues, Wilson compromised with the Allies to win their support for the League. He approved Clemenceau's request for at least fifteen more years of American and Allied military occupation of the Rhineland. He and Lloyd George also offered separate guarantees of French security, promising to defend France against future German aggression. They agreed to disarm Germany, force it to relinquish some European territory and all its colonies, and require it to pay an unspecified amount of reparations. The Covenant disappointed the Japanese because it did not affirm racial equality, a principle they had sought to add by amending the Anglo-American draft of the document. Drawing a global color line, the British and American delegates rejected the Japanese amendment. To ensure Japan's approval of the Covenant, however, Wilson joined the Allies to approve the transfer of Germany's rights in the Shandong province of China to Japan.

Almost all Germans denounced the peace treaty, which the German delegates received on May 7, 1919. They claimed that it violated the Fourteen Points. Wilson and the Allied leaders made only a few concessions, deciding instead to compel Germany to sign the treaty on June 28, 1919, at the Palace of Versailles. They denied Germany the peace settlement that its government and people had expected, as Klaus Schwabe emphasized in *Woodrow Wilson, Revolutionary Germany, and Peacemaking, 1918–1919* (Schwabe 1985).

Returning home, Wilson presented the Versailles Treaty to the Senate. "We entered the war as the disinterested champions of right, and we interested ourselves in the terms of the peace in no other capacity," he asserted on July 10, 1919. He affirmed that the treaty embodied his Fourteen Points, although "it was not easy to graft the new order of ideas on the old." Defending the Covenant, he claimed that "the League of Nations was not merely an instrument to adjust and remedy old wrongs under a new treaty of peace. It was the only hope for mankind." He saw the treaty as fulfilling America's God-given destiny in world history. "It has come about by no plan of our conceiving, but by the hand of God who led us into this way. We cannot turn back" (Wilson 1989, 61: 426–436). The influence of Wilson's religious beliefs on his foreign policy, as revealed in his affirmation of America's God-given mission to ratify the Versailles Treaty and enter the League of Nations, was once largely ignored by historians. More recently, however, scholars such as Lloyd E. Ambrosius in *Woodrow Wilson and the American Diplomatic Tradition* (Ambrosius 1987), Jan Willem Schulte Nordholdt in *Woodrow Wilson* (Schulte Nordholdt 1991), and Malcolm D. Magee in *What the World Should Be* (Magee 2008), have focused on the religious factor in Wilson's foreign policy.

Once Wilson identified the Versailles Treaty not only with his Fourteen Points but also God's will, he refused to compromise. He rejected all efforts by Republican senators, and even some Democrats, to amend or attach reservations to the treaty, and particularly their desire to limit US obligations in the postwar League under Article 10 of the Covenant. Wilson's great foe in the treaty fight was Massachusetts senator Henry Cabot Lodge, the Republican majority leader and chairman of the Senate Foreign Relations Committee. It soon became apparent that the Senate would not approve the treaty without attaching at least reservations, if not amendments, to the resolution of ratification. Wilson decided to appeal over the senators' heads to the American people. In September 1919, he went on a speaking tour of western states. During this tour, he advocated American membership in the League to enable it to guarantee world peace and contain the spread of Bolshevism. Exaggerating the danger of radical revolution, Wilson contributed to the postwar Red Scare but failed to mobilize public opinion against the Republican-controlled Senate.

Wilson's health collapsed during the western tour. Returning to the White House, he suffered a massive stroke on October 2, 1919. With Edith Wilson's assistance, the president managed to finish his term but could give only minimal leadership during the seventeen remaining months. His cabinet secretaries ran their departments without much presidential direction. He focused primarily on the treaty fight. After the stroke, Wilson rigidly adhered to his position on the Versailles Treaty. On his behalf, Nebraska senator Gilbert M. Hitchcock, the Democratic minority leader, stopped Democratic senators from joining Republicans to provide a two-thirds majority for the treaty with Lodge's reservations, thus ensuring its defeat. The Senate rejected the treaty on November 19, 1919, and again on March 19, 1920, thereby preventing the United States from joining the League of Nations. When the ailing president perceived that the cabinet was apparently too independent, he forced Lansing's resignation as secretary of state on February 12, 1920, replacing him with Bainbridge Colby, who faithfully maintained Wilson's uncompromising stance.

Wilson's techniques of presidential leadership no longer worked. After the war, he faced a strong backlash against his wartime use of executive powers. In the 1918 elections, Democrats had lost their majority in both the House and Senate. Postwar deregulation of production, prices, and wages resulted in high inflation and labor strikes in 1919, and then a recession in 1920. Striking workers became scapegoats for postwar anxiety and frustration. Corporate executives exploited their opportunities to gain advantages over the alleged radicals. Wilson's rhetoric inflamed the Red Scare, and demobilization of Pershing's AEF added to social unrest as veterans rapidly returned to civilian life. Race riots and lynchings throughout the nation inflicted violence on African Americans. Given Wilson's own racial and class biases and his neglect of postwar reconstruction at home, he must bear some responsibility for these reactionary postwar developments. Just as colonial peoples, who aspired to the national self-determination that they thought Wilson had promised during World War I, had learned that he excluded them from "the Wilsonian moment" during the peacemaking, African Americans and American Indians, despite their wartime loyalty and service, discovered that Wilson left people of color on the margins in the United States (Britten 1997; Ellis 2001; Lentz-Smith 2009). American workers also continued to experience marginal status, a consequence of a president who privileged capital over labor. Unlike Debs and other Socialists, he did not embrace industrial democracy in his vision of a new world order, although he helped create the new International Labor Organization (McKillen 2013). As Jeanette Keith showed in *Rich Man's War, Poor Man's Fight* (Keith 2004), the hierarchies of race and class persisted during World War I. Wilson did not lower the barriers to racial or class equality in the United States during the war and even reinforced them during the postwar Red Scare.

American voters rejected Wilson's leadership and priorities in the 1920 presidential election. He had considered running for a third term to make it a referendum on the League of Nations, but his closest associates eventually forced him to abandon this fantasy. The Nineteenth Amendment to the Constitution, which had just been ratified, extended voting rights to women in 1920. Although

Wilson had finally, in 1918, endorsed woman suffrage as an essential wartime reform in his global crusade for democracy, this expansion of the American electorate did not help him. On November 2, 1920, Republican senator Warren G. Harding won a landslide victory over Democratic nominee James Cox, who had attempted to defend Wilson's legacy. The American people wanted less government at home and less entanglement abroad, opting for a new era of Harding's "normalcy."

Woodrow and Edith Wilson retired to their new home in Washington, DC, on March 4, 1921. He lived there in relative obscurity. He reaffirmed his most basic beliefs in an article in *Atlantic Monthly* (1923). To protect "modern civilization" against Communist revolution, he urged Americans to draw upon "the spiritual life" to reform capitalism and preserve democracy. He wanted to save "Christian civilization" in the United States by infusing it with "the spirit of Christ." He thought this nation, as "the greatest of democracies," should keep the world "safe for democracy" (Wilson 1993, 68: 393–395). Although the US Senate and American voters had rejected his League of Nations and repudiated his style of progressivism, the former president remained faithful to his vision of the nation's God-given global mission. He died at home on February 3, 1924.

Legacy and Reputation

President Woodrow Wilson left an enduring legacy, which enhanced his lasting reputation. Although the Republicans triumphed over the Democrats in the 1920 elections, they did not overturn all the progressive reforms of his New Freedom, nor did they succeed in killing his vision of America's mission in international relations. With Republicans in charge of the White House and Congress during the 1920s, the nation turned away from Wilson's style of presidential leadership and his progressive policies. But that reversal ended with the Great Depression and the Second World War. These new crises in the 1930s and 1940s created the context for President Franklin D. Roosevelt to revive and expand Wilson's agenda at home and abroad.

In its continuously revised forms, Wilson's legacy influenced American and world history for the next century. In the late 1940s and 1950s, most Americans embraced modern liberalism in the tradition that he had championed and that now characterized the Cold War consensus. By the 1960s, a new conservatism challenged the persisting progressive dominance in American politics. As the terms "liberalism" and "conservatism" acquired new meanings in this era of the civil rights movement, greater ideological conflict over America's national character and its role in the world replaced the Cold War liberal consensus. The new conservatism questioned some, but certainly not all, of Wilson's progressive legacy. In the aftermath of the Cold War and of 9/11, Americans reaffirmed many of his beliefs about the nation's global mission. The tenets of Wilsonianism, the ideas that he had articulated during the Great War, continued to define US foreign policies in the contemporary world. His legacy endured.

Historians have offered various assessments of Woodrow Wilson. John Milton Cooper, Jr. acknowledged some of his flaws. He was not "a perfect president," Cooper conceded in *Woodrow Wilson*. "Two things will always mar his place in history: race and civil liberties. He turned a stone face and deaf ear to the struggles and tribulations of African Americans … During the war, Wilson presided over an administration that committed egregious violations of civil liberties." Even so, Cooper's biography presented an otherwise generally positive account of Wilson's life. Contrary to a significant trend in historiography that highlighted the importance of religion in his statecraft, Cooper argued that "Wilson practiced a severe separation not only between church and state but also between religion and society." He rejected the idea that Wilson was "a secular messiah or a naïve, wooly-headed idealist." Instead, Cooper saw him as "one of the most careful, hardheaded, and sophisticated idealists of his time." Accordingly, the president led the United States into the Great War as a shrewd statesman, not as a crusader for democracy. "Wilson spoke the language of exalted idealism, but he did it in a humble, circumspect way… He did not say that Americans must make the world safe for democracy; he did not believe that they could. They could only do their part, join with other like-minded nations, and take steps toward that promised land" (Cooper 2009, 4–5, 10–11, 397).

In fundamental disagreement with Cooper, A. Scott Berg emphasized the centrality of Wilson's Christian faith in all aspects of his life. He used religious terms for all the chapter titles in *Wilson*. In this biography Berg observed that

> the Wilson Cabinet of 1913 was a ten-way mirror, each panel of which reflected a different aspect of the man at the center. This was mostly a team of Rebels–lawyers from the South who had pursued other professions and never shed their Confederate biases, Anglo-Saxon Protestants all, mostly newcomers to Washington, if not politics altogether… For the most part, the President would delegate power to his Secretaries… to run their own departments, as he seldom found reason to countermand any of them. Every decision from this administration, noted one close observer, would contain a moral component, inspired by "the breath of God."

After the United States entered the Great War, moreover, Wilson hoped "to carry the 'Gospel of Americanism' to every corner of the globe" (Berg 2013, 266–267, 449).

Richard Striner as well rejected Cooper's interpretation in his sharply critical account, *Woodrow Wilson and World War I*. By the time of the armistice, for example, Wilson had alienated the Republicans to such an extent that there was no prospect for bipartisan peacemaking. "With Wilson being the stubborn and delusional man he had become by the final months of 1918," Striner concluded, "what good would the presence of leading Republicans in the American delegation have done? Wilson, being Wilson, was his own worst enemy in ways that were far beyond retrieval. Any blunders he committed were the latest missteps in a very long series that were leading him, his country, and the world to disaster" (Striner 2014, 171). Unlike Cooper's Wilson, who was leading the United States toward the promised land of a world safe for democracy, Striner's Wilson was heading it toward global disaster.

Thus, in recent scholarship, Wilson remains controversial. *A Companion to Woodrow Wilson*, ed. Ross A. Kennedy, examined this contested historiography in an excellent selection of essays on all aspects of the president's life (Kennedy 2013). Despite his enduring legacy and fairly positive reputation, Wilson still has his critics as well as admirers.

References

Ambrosius, Lloyd E. 1987. *Woodrow Wilson and the American Diplomatic Tradition: The Treaty Fight in Perspective.* Cambridge: Cambridge University Press.

—. 2007. "Woodrow Wilson and *The Birth of a Nation*: American Democracy and International Relations," *Diplomacy and Statecraft* 18: 689–718.

Axson, Stockton. 1993. *"Brother Woodrow": A Memoir of Woodrow Wilson.* Princeton, NJ: Princeton University Press.

Benbow, Mark E. 2010. *Leading Them to the Promised Land: Woodrow Wilson, Covenant Theology, and the Mexican Revolution, 1913–1915.* Kent, OH: Kent State University Press.

Berg, A. Scott. 2013. *Wilson.* New York: G. P. Putnam's Sons.

Britten, Thomas A. 1997. *American Indians in World War I: At War and at Home.* Albuquerque: University of New Mexico Press.

Capozolla, Christopher. 2008. *Uncle Sam Wants You: World War I and the Meaning of the Modern American Citizen.* New York: Oxford University Press.

Cooper, John Milton, Jr., ed. 2008. *Reconsidering Woodrow Wilson: Progressivism, Internationalism, War, and Peace.* Washington, DC: Woodrow Wilson Center Press.

—. 2009. *Woodrow Wilson: A Biography.* New York: Alfred A. Knopf.

Dawley, Alan. 2003. *Changing the World: American Progressives in War and Revolution.* Princeton, NJ: Princeton University Press.

Ellis, Mark. 2001. *Race, War, and Surveillance: African Americans and the United States Government during World War I.* Bloomington: Indiana University Press.

Fogelsong, David S. 1998. *America's Secret War against Bolshevism: U.S. Intervention in the Russian Civil War, 1917–1920.* Chapel Hill: University of North Carolina Press.

Gilderhus, Mark T. 1986. *Pan American Visions: Woodrow Wilson in the Western Hemisphere, 1913–1921.* Tucson: University of Arizona Press.

Heckscher, August. 1991. *Woodrow Wilson.* New York: Charles Scribner's Sons.

Keith, Jeanette. 2004. *Rich Man's War, Poor Man's Fight: Race, Class, and Power in the Rural South during the First World War.* Chapel Hill: University of North Carolina Press.

Kennedy, Ross A. 2009. *The Will to Believe: Woodrow Wilson, World War I, and America's Strategy for Peace and Security.* Kent, OH: Kent State University Press.

—, ed. 2013. *A Companion to Woodrow Wilson.* Oxford: Wiley-Blackwell.

Knock, Thomas J. 1992. *To End All Wars: Woodrow Wilson and the Quest for a New World Order.* New York: Oxford University Press.

Lentz-Smith, Adriane. 2009. *Freedom Struggles: African Americans and World War I.* Cambridge, MA: Harvard University Press.

Levin, Phyllis Lee. 2001. *Edith and Woodrow: The Wilson White House.* New York: Scribner.

Link, Arthur S. 1947–1965. *Wilson.* Princeton, NJ: Princeton University Press.

Macmillan, Margaret. 2002. *Paris 1919: Six Months That Changed the World.* New York: Random House.

Magee, Malcolm D. 2008. *What the World Should Be: Woodrow Wilson and the Crafting of a Faith-Based Foreign Policy.* Waco, TX: Baylor University Press.

Manela, Erez. 2007. *The Wilsonian Moment: Self-Determination and the International Origins of Anticolonial Nationalism.* New York: Oxford University Press.

McKillen, Elizabeth. 2013. *Making the World Safe for Workers: Labor, the Left, and Wilsonian Internationalism.* Urbana: University of Illinois Press.

Neu, Charles E. 2015. *Colonel House: A Biography of Woodrow Wilson's Silent Partner.* New York: Oxford University Press.

Pestritto, Ronald J. 2005. *Woodrow Wilson and the Roots of Modern Liberalism.* Lanham, MD: Rowman & Littlefield.

Renda, Mary A. 2001. *Taking Haiti: Military Occupation and the Culture of U.S. Imperialism.* Chapel Hill: University of North Carolina Press.

Rodgers, Daniel T. 1998. *Atlantic Crossings: Social Politics in a Progressive Era.* Cambridge, MA: Harvard University Press.

Schulte Nordholdt, Jan Willem. 1991. *Woodrow Wilson: A Life for World Peace.* Berkeley: University of California Press.

Schwabe, Klaus. 1985. *Woodrow Wilson, Revolutionary Germany, and Peacemaking, 1918–1919: Missionary Diplomacy and the Realities of Power.* Chapel Hill: University of North Carolina Press.

Striner, Richard. 2014. *Woodrow Wilson and World War I: A Burden Too Great to Bear.* Lanham, MD: Rowman & Littlefield.

Thompson, John A. 2002. *Woodrow Wilson.* London: Longman.

Tucker, Robert W. 2007. *Woodrow Wilson and the Great War: Reconsidering America's Neutrality, 1914–1917.* Charlottesville: University of Virginia Press.

Tyrrell, Ian. 2010. *Reforming the World: The Creation of America's Moral Empire.* Princeton, NJ: Princeton University Press.

Wilson, Woodrow. 1889. *The State: Elements of Historical and Practical Politics.* Boston: D. C. Heath & Co., Publishers.

—. 1966–1994. *The Papers of Woodrow Wilson.* Ed. Arthur S. Link. Princeton: Princeton University Press.

Part VI

Government, Politics, and Law

Chapter Twenty-Five

Pivotal Elections

Sidney M. Milkis and Anthony Sparacino

Historians and political scientists have long considered elections a mainspring of American politics. As Walter Dean Burnham has emphasized, however, "American electoral politics is not all of a piece" (Burnham 1970, 1). Some elections appear to confirm Alexis de Tocqueville's refrain that American democracy was swarming with "small parties" that, lacking "political faith" and dominated by "material interests," were animated by professional politicians jockeying for power (Tocqueville 2000, 166–170). Yet, the major periods of American political development such as the Gilded Age and the Progressive Era arouse conflict, not only over interests but also over riveting issues pertaining to race, the political economy, and war. The elections of 1876, 1896, and 1912, especially, stand out as pivotal during the period covered in this volume. These contests played an enormous role in shaping the traumatic efforts to reconstruct the South in the wake of the Civil War; the profound challenge of coming to terms with the emergence of giant corporations—trusts—that threatened the "fair race of life" that Lincoln identified as the major objective of the Union's struggle; and the first efforts to forge a national state by Progressive reformers in an era when most Americans seemed to shun centralized administration.

Viewing this period from the perspective of Burnham's realignment theory, most scholars have identified the 1896 contest, which appeared to confirm the triumph of industrial capitalism, as the critical election of this era. Without question this contest between William McKinley and the "Great Commoner" William Jennings Bryan was a major episode in the emerging struggle between champions of the Industrial Revolution and those reformers who sought to tame its excesses. But an investigation of the 1896 contest alone cannot adequately capture the major political developments of the late nineteenth and early twentieth century. As Karen Orren and Stephen Skowronek point out, realignment theory is but a variation of Louis Hartz's "liberal consensus theory" that stresses the "arrested development" of constitutional government in the United States (Orren and Skowronek, 2004, 62–65). Critical realigning elections, Burnham argues, episodically arouse but do not spur the development of American political ideas and institutions. In contrast, this chapter views the pivotal elections of 1876, 1896, and 1912 as contests that began to transform political life in the United States from the state and local, patronage-based parties that dominated most of the nineteenth century to the national and candidate-centered partisanship that has roiled American democracy since the Progressive Era. The 1912 election, especially, recast partisanship as a contest between progressives and conservatives for the services of the emerging national state, a change that presupposed the demise of localized parties and the "spoils system" that sustained them. Moreover, these elections chronicle the beginnings of a shift from the sectional politics of the post-Civil War era to more centralized yet fractious politics that reverberate through the present time.

Gilded Age and Progressive Era Politics

Reformers indicted the political economy of the late nineteenth century as the "Gilded Age," a term Mark Twain and Charles Dudley Warner coined in their novel *The Gilded Age: A Story of Today*, which was published in 1873. For the first time, the country had to grapple with the troubling question of how to curb the excesses of big business amid socioeconomic conditions that seemed excessively opulent and held little promise for industrial workers and small farmers. Moreover, many believed that great business interests had captured and corrupted the men and methods of government for their own profit. Party leaders—both Democrats

A Companion to the Gilded Age and Progressive Era, First Edition. Edited by Christopher McKnight Nichols and Nancy C. Unger.
© 2017 John Wiley & Sons, Inc. Published 2017 by John Wiley & Sons, Inc.

and Republicans—were seen as irresponsible bosses who did the bidding of special interests.

Although fraught with economic conflict, the political contests of the Gilded Age at the end of the nineteenth century and the Progressive Era at the beginning of the twentieth century defied a purely class-based dimension of conflict. Economic conflict was intertwined with and influenced by other significant developments tied to regionalism, race and ethnicity, partisan strategy, and the cult of personality. While space prevents the presentation of an exhaustive list of the factors that marked these developments, this chapter highlights four that shaped the most important electoral contests of this period: the transformation of the sectional divide after the Civil War; the emergence of the American state, which altered the relationship between the people and government; the attack on what Stephen Skowronek has called the "state of courts and parties"—the anchor of the decentralized republic that dominated most of the nineteenth century (Skowronek 1982); and the rise of more candidate-centered presidential campaigns—the origins of executive-centered partisanship.

These four factors highlight the importance of elections during the Gilded Age and Progressive Era in remaking American democracy. The major candidates during the 1876, 1896, and 1912 contests were all responding in part to a transformed political setting, even as they framed the choices about how to confront challenges posed by an industrial economy and fractious society.

Sectionalism and the Transformation of Political Competition

Sectional divides were in place throughout the period between 1876 and 1912. The literature on this topic is vast; scholars have stressed two themes. The first is the role of the South in political competition. Painted broadly, though there was some variation across states, the South became a one-party region, which would have immense significance for partisan competition and development (Key 1949; Ware 2006). The disenfranchisement of African Americans in the region gave conservative whites a prominent place within the Democratic Party until the 1960s. The second sectional divide reflected tension between the East and West. The West would be an area in which both parties would compete for votes, but the constituencies sought after would shift between 1876 and 1912 as progressive ideas became more prominent in national discourse.

North and South: The Enduring Divide

The victory of the North in the Civil War, while preserving the Union, did not put an end to sectional cleavages in American society. This was true in two senses. First, there would remain a bad taste in the mouths of many Southerners who resented the destruction that resulted from the pillaging of the region as the North edged closer to victory in the Civil War; this resentment would have enduring electoral consequences. Bensel notes that even before the war, "Southerners viewed the growing strength of the Republican Party as a threat to the interests of both slavery and the plantation system generally" (1990, 19–20). This animosity toward the party of Lincoln, aggravated by the GOP's waving the bloody shirt, would continue through the 1880s and beyond.

The resistance to Reconstruction politics only sharpened the divide between the GOP and southern whites. From a political standpoint, many of the state-level officials who came to power in the South during Reconstruction were carpetbaggers from the North whose financial interests often dictated their behavior in office. Eric Foner has illustrated that while many carpetbaggers hoped to improve the conditions of the freedmen, many also bought plantations in order to profit from the cotton industry (2014). Union veteran and Mississippi Governor Albert Ames, for instance, who was seen as an honest carpetbagger, was unable to maintain peace in his state towards the end of his tenure and ultimately contributed to a schism between black and lily-white Republicans (Lemann 2006). The actions of the GOP in Congress also contributed to racial antagonism, perhaps most notably in the Force Acts (1870) and the Ku-Klux-Klan Act (1871), which provided legal justification for the federal government to continue to uphold the constitutional protections of African Americans, often by bringing charges against southern whites. These enforcement statutes notwithstanding, Republicans began to lose their grip on power in the region at the state level and northern support for an activist presence in the region waned, especially among moderate northern Republicans. Ultimately, the judicial system would step in and greatly reduce the federal government's military rule in the Reconstruction South by declaring large portions of these laws unconstitutional (Howard 1999).

Elections in the South at the state, congressional, and presidential levels, provided the principal means by which power shifted away from the Republican Party and contributed to the region's reformulation of political participation. These electoral developments were fully realized with the controversial 1876 election. The 1876 contest was the last presidential election in which a Republican presidential candidate would carry the electoral votes of a Southern state until 1920. Indeed, all three of the states carried by the Republican presidential nominee, Rutherford B. Hayes, were contested. The resolution of these contests, roiled by competing factions over Reconstruction policy, greatly exacerbated the tension between the North and South at a moment when there was some hope that the schism was moving towards some sort of rapprochement. After sixteen years of Republican rule, a Democratic victory seemed certain. The Democratic candidate, Samuel J. Tilden, who won the praise of the reform-minded Mugwumps for exposing the efforts of Boss Tweed and various political rings to corrupt New York state's canal system, initially appeared to have won the presidential election. Hayes himself told reporters on election night, "Democrats have carried the country and elected Tilden" (Ellis 2012, 41). But the contested electoral votes of the three southern states still under military rule—Louisiana, Florida, and South Carolina—as well as those of Oregon, were in doubt. Without them, Tilden had only 184 electoral votes. If Hayes carried all of the disputed states, he would have 185 votes and win the election.

The partisan machinations began when all four states sent two sets of electoral votes to Washington. Congress responded by creating a fifteen-member commission to arbitrate the dispute: five Republican members of Congress, five Democratic members, and four Supreme Court justices who were charged with naming a fifth from among their ranks. The Justices chose a Grant appointee, Joseph Bradley. On March 2, 1877, the electoral commission, by a strict party vote, rejected the Democratic returns from the doubtful states and declared Hayes the winner by a margin of one electoral vote.

Still, Congress had to declare the election official before the Commission's recommendations could take effect and the Democratic-controlled House threatened not to meet. At this point, a deal—the so-called Compromise of 1877—was struck between Republicans and southern Democratic leaders. In return for the Democrats acquiescing to Hayes's selection, the Republicans promised to remove the remaining occupying military forces from the South. Both sides lived up to their ends of the bargain. Hayes removed federal troops from the South, putting an end to virtually all attempts to enforce the Fourteenth Amendment's guarantees of civil rights to every citizen, including former slaves. Nor, thereafter, was any serious effort made to uphold the Fifteenth Amendment, which since 1870 had affirmed the right of citizens to vote regardless of "race, color, or previous condition of servitude."

It is hardly shocking that race played large in these partisan maneuvers. Mayhew points to the lack of enforcement of the Civil Rights Act of 1875 and the failed passage of the 1890 Federal Election Rights Bill as the historical bookends that reveal how race "intruded into elections, party strategies, and policy making in this phase of American history" (Mayhew 2002, 158–159). The emergence of the Ku Klux Klan and the spread of Jim Crow throughout the region highlight the cultural barriers that prevented the injustices of the legacy of slavery and the reformation of the plantation system from being resolved.

The plummeting of African American voter turnout in the South in the aftermath of 1876 had significant consequences for party campaign strategies for the next century. Heersink and Jenkins show that "Southern delegates in several election years represented the deciding votes in ballots selecting the presidential and vice-presidential candidates for the Republican ticket;" yet in the aftermath of the Compromise of 1877, the South decidedly became a one-party region (Heersink and Jenkins 2015, 69). The Southern Republican Party not only became a Potemkin's Village in presidential contests; the GOP also lost control of congressional seats and state government positions. By the 1878 midterm elections, the only potential threat to the Democrats in the region came from the third-party Greenbacks, whose anti-monopoly message appealed to an emerging economic populism in the South, not from the Republicans who did not control a single congressional district in the Old Confederacy. African Americans would remain loyal to the party of Lincoln until the advent of the New Deal but, thereafter, their votes, squelched in the South, would never again be a prominent factor in Republican electoral success.

As important as it was in motivating the unsavory bargain of 1877, the issue of race was inextricably tied to the question of federalism and the desire of southern whites to regain control of their home turf. In tandem with the establishment of a new form of racial hierarchy in the South came a doctrine of non-interference on the part of the federal government in the local affairs of the southern states. In truth, the resolution of the 1876 election was sealed in protracted negotiations that revealed the Republican Party's reluctance to continue a system of centralized military control that offended the constitutional sensibilities of North and South alike. The negotiations between Democrats and Republicans that led to the 1877 agreement had stretched over several months. Prompted by the Democrats regaining control of the House in 1874, and the waning power of the military occupation, Grant maintained a benevolent neutrality during the last three months of his administration that enabled the so-called Redeemers of South Carolina and Louisiana to take de-facto control of the two remaining Republican governments in the South (Woodward 1951, 4–9, 10; Holt 2008, 246–247).

Although both parties were complicit in the Compromise of 1877, the notorious bargain and its aftermath led to serious recriminations. As Roy Morris Jr. scathingly notes, by formally acquiescing to "a legalized fraud," leaders of both parties in Congress "heedlessly fostered an atmosphere of mutual suspicion, antagonism, and hatred that lingered over the political landscape for the better part of a century" (Morris 2003, 3). Regional economic competition contributed significantly to this virulent sectionalism. C. Vann Woodward has famously argued that an emerging Southern economic elite was eager, not just to preserve racial hierarchy but also to rebuild the South economically (1951). However, as Peskin has revealed, a number of the promises made to southerners in the deal were not kept, such as the promise to build a railroad line through Texas (1973).

In the end, the 1877 bargain both revitalized national electoral politics and rooted partisan competition in an intractable sectionalism that severely circumscribed the legacy of the Civil War. As Michael Holt aptly expresses the upshot of this pivotal election:

> Democrats' astounding remobilization of previously apathetic white voters both in the North and especially in the South in 1876, along with Republicans' miraculous comeback after the 1874 debacle in most northern states, brought Democrats and Republicans to a competitive equilibrium that had not existed since the 1850s and would continue until the 1890s. That political achievement of the elections of 1876 constitutes their major historical significance, not the fact that Hayes was counted in and Tilden was not (2008, 248).

The West: Up For Grabs

The stalemate between North and South focused both parties' attention on the West, where Republicans and Democrats energetically competed for electoral support during the Gilded Age and Progressive Era. Westward expansion aroused conflict over matters such as how to regulate currency and expand the railroad, issues that not only divided East and West, but also stirred fractious intraparty battles and spirited third-party competition. The West—mainly rural—was mobilized by insurgent agricultural organizations; the politics of the East and its burgeoning cities operated under the spell of finance and industry. Financial titans like John Rockefeller, J.P. Morgan, Cornelius Vanderbilt, Andrew Mellon, and Andrew Carnegie were not just building personal fortunes; they also were developing an industrial form of capitalism that would fundamentally transform the economic landscape of the country. This was the era in which the metropolis in America began to take its modern form. The West, however, lagged behind in terms of economic growth and technological modernization.

Beyond the economic disparities were stark cultural differences. Richard Jensen argues that in the Gilded Age "religion was the fundamental source of political conflict in the Midwest, shaping "the issues and the rhetoric of politics, and played the critical role in determining party alignments of the voters" (Jensen 1971, 58). In particular, "the two polar theological positions, pietistic and liturgical, expressed themselves through the Republican and Democratic parties, respectively" (Jensen 1971, 58). In New York City, for instance, Irish Catholics became a base of support for Tammany Hall and the Democratic Party while Anglo-Saxon Protestants typically supported Republicans. Westward migration brought individuals of varying religious denominations to new territories and their religious affiliations correlated highly with their ballots. Especially during the early part of the Gilded Age, the parties would rely on religious rhetoric and symbolism that led to dramatic swings in electoral votes and congressional representation in this competitive region.

Partisan combat over currency, which reached a climax in 1896, best illustrated how economic interests were not separate from, but rather polarized by moral piety. In 1876, the parties had not yet clearly divided on the issue. John Gerring classifies the Democratic Party during the Jeffersonian Epoch (1828–1892) as "more anxious about the health of the republic than about the health of the economy." He thus paints the quintessential Democrat of the period as a yeoman farmer who steadfastly embraced the concept of limited government and agrarian social norms (Gerring 1998, 176–177). Still, language over specie payments became a stumbling block at the Democratic Convention of 1876 (Holt 2008, 112–113). This struggle over the gold standard would be a nettlesome issue for Democrats—one that plagued them through the two terms of Grover Cleveland (1884–1888, 1892–1896), the first Democrat to be elected to the presidency since the Civil War. Cleveland's ascent to the White House demonstrated the significant influence of the so-called Gold Democrats, who were sensitive to business interests and their reliance on a sound currency. Cleveland led a crusade to repeal the Sherman Silver Purchase Act in 1893, but at the cost of dividing his party between the Democrats from the East and the older industrializing Midwestern states, who tended to support the gold standard, and those from the South and West whose constituencies were firmly behind free silver (Sundquist 1983, 147). So divisive was the conflict over currency that Gold Democrats, consisting mainly of Cleveland and his political allies, would establish the National Democratic Party in opposition to William Jennings Bryan's 1896 silver crusade.

Bryan's moralistic campaign repudiated the Democrats' first president since the Civil War as well as the alliances that Cleveland and his New York allies had formed with purveyors of economic orthodoxy and finance. As Jensen notes, Bryan, envisioning a grassroots uprising of the producer class—farmers, laborers, and small businesses, championed silver with evangelical fervor. His famous Cross of Gold speech at the 1896 Democratic Convention, delivered in the midst of a platform fight over currency, likened the battle for the free coinage of silver to the crucifixion of Christ. "You shall not press down upon the brow of labor this crown of thorns," he told the excited gathering, his fingers running over his temple in agony. Then, spreading his arms far apart, he shouted, "You shall not crucify mankind upon a cross of Gold" (Jensen 1971, 276–277).

Gerring points to the dramatic election of 1896 as a transformative contest for the Democratic Party—a time when Populism, previously championed by an insurgent third-party movement, became its core commitment. He argues that "William Jennings Bryan is the rightful father of the Progressive–New Deal Democratic Party, bringing to it a regulatory style and redistributive purpose found hitherto only outside the mainstream of American party politics" (Gerring 1998, 189). Gerring might overstate his case; Bryan's platform, calling for the coining of 16 ounces of silver for every one ounce of gold, was a compromised version of Populism. In 1892, the insurgent Populist Party candidate James B. Weaver had called for a graduated income tax as well as public ownership of railroads, telegraphs, and telephones. Dominated by a Jeffersonian hatred of monopoly, which the Democratic candidate expressed in evangelical terms, Bryan's campaign is better viewed as a last hurrah for the decentralized republic of the nineteenth century than as a precursor to the economic reform programs of the Progressive Era and New Deal. Indeed, his campaign framed the 1896 contest as a decisive battle between the industrial North and rural South and West. As Bryan described this apocalyptic conflict in his Cross of Gold speech:

> "You come to us and tell us that the great cities are in favor of the gold standard. I tell you that the great cities rest upon these broad and fertile prairies. Burn down your cities and leave our farms, and your cities will spring up again as if by magic. But destroy our farms and the grass will grow in the streets of every city in the country" (Bryan 1896).

Cleveland's conservatism severely damaged his second term. But city dwellers' suspicion of Bryan was equally damaging to his evangelical campaign. McKinley won a sold victory against Bryan by capturing the industrial states of the Northeast and Midwest. Like Burnham, Sundquist views the Republican triumph in the 1896 contest as a realigning election that broke the partisan stalemate wrought by the 1876 election and established the GOP and its program dedicated to industrial capitalism as the dominant force in American politics for the next four decades. (Sundquist 1983, 36). The shift within the Democratic Party was a critical prelude to this contest. Cleveland had been a staunch supporter of gold. However, with the base of Democratic support now firmly entrenched in the South, and silver becoming a viable political issue in the Midwest and West, Bryan was able to win the nomination. But his free silver platform, although it resonated widely in rural America, meant little to the industrializing regions of the country. Most important, the rising urban laborer, attracted to McKinley's promise of business prosperity and the "full dinner pail"—one Republican newspaper dubbed him the "Advanced Agent of Prosperity"—abandoned the Democratic Party in the Midwestern states that decided the election (Jensen 1971, 287).

The Republicans were also divided on the issue of specie. During the debate over the Specie Resumption Act of 1875, for instance, many Republicans advocated silver bullion, while northerners "of both major parties condemned inflation of the money supply as the ultimate evil" (Holt 2008, 39). R. Hal Williams describes the strategy of McKinley and Hanna during the 1896 Republican Convention as "a waiting game, letting sentiment gather among Republicans for an unequivocal plank, a strategy designed to build consensus and avoid bitter divisiveness within a party that contained members favoring gold, silver or both" (Williams 2010, 60). Forging consensus within the party in support of the gold standard was seen as key to constructing a platform that would project the GOP as a bulwark of economic responsibility after the issue had caused significant ruptures in both parties over the last two decades.

The McKinley and Hanna savvy embrace of the gold standard and the protective tariff—the pillars of the GOP prosperity platform—were the key ingredients of the Republican victory. Past elections had seen numerous third parties arise, often complicating the major parties' abilities to win a plurality in the Midwest and the West. Partisan insurgency was especially prevalent in the several new states that were added to the Union during the Gilded Age. Between 1888 and 1892, Washington, the Dakotas, Montana, and Idaho were granted votes in the Electoral College. Although McKinley would lose most of these silver states in 1896, his conquest of the Northeast, Midwest, and California established a new regional alignment that left Republicans in command of the fastest-growing areas of the country.

These regional divisions would become an enduring feature of American politics. Power in the Democratic Party shifted decisively to the South; as Burnham points out, excluding the special case of 1912, 84.5 per cent of the total electoral vote for Democratic presidential candidates between 1896 and 1924 was cast in the Southern and Border States (Burnham 1967, 300). Even the progressive Democrat Woodrow Wilson, whose two terms marked an important interregnum in the GOP's control over the White House and Congress, would find his strongest base of support in the Solid South—a harbinger of his retrograde positions and policies on civil rights. Just as surely, sectionalism circumscribed the critical election of 1896. Although the GOP was clearly the dominant party between 1876 and 1912, having ceded control of African American rights to southern Democrats, it never was able to become a truly national party. From this perspective, the 1896 campaign was the culmination of political changes that began in the regional battles of 1876. The Midwest and North, although typically areas of Republican strength, were more competitive than was the South. This proved a burden to the party of Lincoln, as it had to protect a majority that was regionally based and sensitive to recurrent battle over industrial capitalism, especially the mammoth corporations this revolution of the political economy spawned.

Elections and the Growth of the American State

By modern standards, the American state during the Gilded Age may seem trivial. As Skowronek points out, "the United States was born in a war that rejected the organizational qualities of the state as they had been evolving in Europe over the eighteenth century" (1982, 19). In contrast, American party politicians, empowered by a highly mobilized, highly competitive, and locally oriented democracy, had the commanding voice in late nineteenth-century American politics and government. The federal judiciary, which proscribed the national government's authority to regulate the economic and social conditions, molded the political character of the decentralized republic into a formal legal tradition (Skowronek 1982, 41; see also Keller 2007, Chapter 8). Yet scholars have pointed to the Radical Republicans' pursuit a more nationalistic agenda, one that would not simply grow government but consolidate it at the federal level (Bensel 2000 and Skowronek 1982). As Scott James has argued, moreover, the pivotal elections of the Gilded Age and Progressive Era suggest that the period's incipient state-building efforts were tied closely to electoral competition and partisan strategy (James 2000).

War, Constituencies, and Nation

The end of the Civil War, the bloodiest conflict in American history, and the Reconstruction Era that followed on from it, created a new constituency in American politics, namely veterans of the Union Army. Skocpol illustrates that "from the 1880s through the 1910s, federal veterans' pensions became the keystone of an entire edifice of honorable income supplements and institutional provision for many northern Americans who were longstanding citizens" (Skocpol 1992, 8). These men had served the Union by the millions and could justifiably claim the title of hero. Even in 1912, President Taft, in accepting his nomination said:

> [T]he passage of time has brought the burdens and helplessness of old age to many of those veterans of the Civil War who exposed their lives in the supreme struggle to save the Nation, and, recognizing this, Congress has added to previous provision which patriotic gratitude had prompted, a substantial allowance, which may properly be characterized as an old man's pension (Taft 1912).

Taft's encomium illustrates how Civil War veterans had natural ties to the Republican Party. The pension system was "run by a tightly interlocked group of Republican politicos and the Grand Army of the Republic, the chief spokesman for veterans and a wholly owned subsidiary of the GOP" (Keller 2007, 155). Although Democrats would be vilified for attempting to scale back the benefits program, the political potency of veterans' pensions was limited as a result of its inextricable ties to a national crisis and partisan patronage. To be sure, the Republican Party gained an important constituency, one that gave it strong support in the North, Midwest, and West for much of the second half the nineteenth century. Indeed, the GOP ran a number of Union veterans in presidential elections during this period, including Hayes and McKinley. But the "precocious social spending state," as Skocpol dubs it, although it contributed significantly to Republican partisan strategy during the late nineteenth and early twentieth century, did not establish an electoral coalition that supported an enduring expansion of the national government's authority. The passing of the Civil War generation—McKinley was the last president who had fought in the Union army—and the pension system's inextricable connection to party patronage led to the fading of social provision. Not until the New Deal would the federal government enact an enduring social security program.

Robert Saldin (2011) suggests that the Spanish–American War, fought in the wake of the Republican triumph of 1896, rather than the Civil War, gave birth to a significant change in the national government's authority. The hostilities were so brief, the American victory so complete, and, most important, the acquisition of Spanish territory in the Caribbean and Pacific so considerable, that no postwar reaction against federal power occurred, as it had after the Civil War. In the short term, the "splendid little war," as John Hay, McKinley's secretary of state, famously characterized the brief conquest, greatly benefitted the Republican Party, which gained victories in the 1898 and 1900 elections in campaigns that were framed by the governing party's victory over Spain. Without denying the importance of the 1896 election as a pivotal contest in confirming the GOP's pro-business policies, Saldin argues persuasively that the 1898 midterm campaign and 1900 presidential contest demonstrated how long-term Republican electoral success also was owed to "a war-spurred set of issues and to the GOP's success in prosecuting the war." The political realignment of the 1890s thus brought foreign affairs—and a partisan contestation over America's place in the world—to the forefront of US politics (Saldin 2011, 47–64).

At the same time, the acquisition of the Philippines and the greater influence over Cuba that accompanied the Spanish–American War established a new imperial role for the United States that subdued partisan differences and prompted efforts to strengthen national administration. For example, McKinley undertook the first efforts to establish a professional army that would eventually replace the decentralized, state-run militia system. Consequently, the Republican electoral successes at the twilight of the nineteenth century abetted the rising antagonism towards the state of courts and parties that would become a conspicuous feature of electoral politics during the Progressive Era. As McKinley said to his personal secretary, "I can no longer be called the President of a party. I am now the President of the whole people" (Olcott 1916, vol. 2, 296).

Industry, Constituencies, and Centralization

The rise of an industrial class also affected in important ways the emergence of a more centralized state authority. Republicans viewed federal revenues as a means to maintain and enforce Reconstruction policies through 1876. This would change as industrial interests began to look westward and internationally for increased economic opportunities.

Beyond the gold standard, the industrial class rallied behind the protective tariff. McKinley's first inaugural address noted this shift in distinguishing internal and external taxes:

> The country is clearly opposed to any needless additions to the subject of internal taxation, and is committed by its latest popular utterance to the system of tariff taxation. There can be no misunderstanding, either, about the principle upon which this tariff taxation shall be levied. Nothing has ever been made plainer at a general election than that the controlling principle in the raising of revenue from duties on imports is zealous care for American interests and American labor (McKinley 1897).

Like the Spanish–American War, the tariff issue provided a rationale for Republican leadership to cast the party in a nationalistic light. America's industrial output could now compete with that of Britain and continental Europe. A high tariff both filled the coffers of the national treasury, which would remain in Republican control until 1912, and protected industrial interests in the growing metropolitan areas of the Northeast and Midwest. As Lewis Gould argues, "in the aftermath of the Civil War the tariff became 'the sacred temple of the Republican Party.' For several generations a test of Republican orthodoxy was devotion to the tariff and the ideology of nationalistic government that it represented" (Gould 2014, 69).

The tariff issue became more than a means by which the GOP could fuel Treasury surpluses in the period. McKinley's tariff speech illustrates that presidential campaign rhetoric was careful to point out potential benefits to the burgeoning urban working class, even though many of them worked in factories with horrendous safety conditions, poor salaries, and excessively long hours. Given the absence of a strong labor movement, the Republican promise that protective tariffs would provide a "full dinner pail" trumped the Populist idea of free silver. This is not to say that labor politics did not intrude on the Gilded Age. The Homestead and Pullman strikes of 1892 and 1894 were only the two most dramatic demonstrations of deep animosity between industry and labor. These violent demonstrations did not, however, enable the Democratic Party to win the support of workers in the Northeast or Midwest. Part of this failure to build the farmer–worker alliance that Bryan envisioned was due to the economic crisis of 1893, which affected not only Cleveland's but also the Democrats' political fortunes. More broadly, however, the labor movement was hindered by cultural animosities that obscured class conflict. Racial and ethnic tensions helped justify the view of Republicans and Democrats alike that union syndicalism was motivated by socialist values that were wholeheartedly un-American. The campaigns of Eugene Debs, from 1904 to 1920, failed to inspire the working poor in large enough numbers to secure a strong social democratic party. Even the self-styled progressive reformers Roosevelt and Wilson refused to look outside the American political tradition in their views on labor issues. Working-class Americans in the North remained part of the Republican coalition until Al Smith's campaign of 1928, an important precursor to the alliance between unions and the New Deal (Key 1955).

Railroad regulation was another issue that illustrated the emergence of a business-friendly state. James illustrates that "railroad regulation was the federal government's first attempt to exert systematic oversight of the daily decision making of a critical sector of the emerging industrial economy" (James 2000, 42). Of critical importance to the eventual form of railroad regulation were Mugwump Republicans, a swing constituency that helped to elect Grover Cleveland to the presidency in 1884. Characterizing this group, James claims that "they placed their faith in the creation of new governmental authorities, insulated from partisan political pressures and staffed by experts" such as those who would head the Interstate Commerce Commission, which was created in 1887 (James 2000, 43). As Gerring argues, "National Republicans looked to parties, legislatures, bureaucracies, and courts to provide the political leadership necessary to conduct the affairs of government in a rational and considered manner" (Gerring 1998, 87). Ultimately, the railroad issue propelled national economic growth but it also created an incentive for state laws to be overridden in favor of a more transcontinental system. The result was a more activist government tied to commercial interests in the industrial centers of the Northeast.

The centralization of these interests into powerful trusts was the most important issue in shaping party competition during the Progressive Era. Although strong progressive wings formed in both the Democratic and Republican parties, philosophical and policy differences animated conflict over the political economy. Bryan, as noted, approached the money and politics question from an agrarian perspective. But in the pivotal 1912 election, former president Theodore Roosevelt—who led many progressive Republicans out of the GOP Convention and ran as the standard bearer of the insurgent Progressive Party—championed a New Nationalism that favored a comprehensive system of industrial reform. "Our aim," Roosevelt argued, "should be to make [the United States] as far as may be not merely a political, but an industrial democracy" (Roosevelt, 1912a). The Progressives' vision of industrial democracy included a commitment to a full-blown welfare state. The platform of the Progressive Party, which won 27.4% of the popular vote—the best showing of a third party in a presidential campaign in US history—was an important prelude to the triumph of FDR and the New Deal in the 1936 election. In words that Theodore Roosevelt drafted, it called for "the protection of the home life against the hazards of the sickness, irregular employment and old age through a system of social insurance adopted to American use" (Progressive Party Draft Platform, 1912).

Still, the important shift in regime norms and practices that progressive reformers advocated did not envisage a straightforward evolution from partisan to administrative politics. The Progressive Party was seriously crippled by fundamental disagreements among its supporters over issues that betrayed an acute sensitivity, if not attachment, to the commitment to local self-government. The party was deeply divided over civil rights, leading to struggles at the convention over delegate selection rules and the platform, struggles that turned on whether the party should confront the shame of Jim Crow. In the end it did not, accepting the right of states and localities to resolve the matter of race relations. Moreover, Progressive delegates waged a fractious struggle at the party convention over whether an interstate trade commission with considerable administrative discretion or a militant anti-trust policy was the appropriate method to tame the trusts. Militant New Nationalists, led by Roosevelt, prevailed, pledging the party to regulate, rather than dismantle, corporate power. An industrial power, they insisted, must accept, and try to regulate, big business. But this disagreement carried over to the general election. The Democratic Party, under the guidance of their candidate for president, Woodrow Wilson, and his advisor, Louis Brandeis, embraced a New Freedom version of progressivism, which prescribed anti-trust measures and tariff reform as an alternative to the expansion of national administrative power. Anticipating the debate of the present time about whether corporations can grow too big to fail, Wilson and Brandeis argued that the American people would not accept the aggrandizement of national administrative power that would be required to control immense trusts.

No less than New Nationalism, however, Wilson's New Freedom envisioned an expansion of the national government's responsibility to regulate markets. Elected with large Democratic majorities in the House and Senate, Wilson pushed through Congress the Underwood Tariff Act in October 1913, the first major reform of the protectionist system since before the Civil War. Moreover, poaching from the Progressives' platform, he reversed the emblematic stand of his own party on business regulation and pressed for the creation of a Federal Trade Commission with broad discretion in moving against unfair practices. Similarly, Wilson persuaded the Democratic Congress to accept a Federal Reserve Act that established a board to oversee the national banking and currency system. In each case, Wilson overcame the Democratic Party's traditional antipathy to national administrative power, suggesting that with the advance of progressive reform, party leaders in Congress were induced to sacrifice partisan principles to win the White House (James 2000). The 1912 election thus reconfigured partisanship in a contest between progressives and conservatives for control of an emerging national state—a development that accelerated the decline of the decentralized patronage parties.

Political Parties, Corruption, and Progressive Reform

Most scholarship on parties and elections during the Gilded Age and Progressive Era has emphasized how reforms led to the decline of the decentralized, patronage based organizations that dominated most of the nineteenth century (Rusk 1970). Recent research, however, has suggested not the decline but the transformation of parties. Indeed, Daniel Klinghard argues provocatively that presidents and national party leaders "looked to the method of reformers… and saw a means of revitalizing party democracy." The 1896 election marked the critical moment, he argues, in the "nationalization of American politics" (Klinghard 2010, 16–17). Although the development of a more presidency-centered and national politics crested in 1912, Klinghard shows that this transformation began at the end of the nineteenth century as reformers, sometimes with the complicity of party leaders, undertook an assault on what was considered the corrupt and antediluvian character of the state of courts and parties.

The 1876 election abetted this indictment. It was the first presidential contest since the Civil War that a Democratic candidate had a real shot at winning—a possibility that promised a renewal of a revitalized two-party system. Indeed, both parties had nominated candidates known for their personal integrity. The Republican Hayes was a war veteran and reform-minded governor. The Democrat, Tilden, was a former Governor of New York who his party saw "as a welcome contrast to the scandals of the Grant administration" (Rehnquist 2004, 78). And yet, despite the quality of the candidates, the 1876 contest proved to be the most controversial election of the century.

Ballot returns became the subject of scrutiny in three Southern states: Louisiana, South Carolina and Florida. The disputed states would submit competing slates of electors to the Electoral College, putting Congress in an unprecedented situation of arbitrating a bitter sectional and partisan scandal. Democrats could point to the voiding of entire counties' Election Day returns as evidence of fraud. Republicans scorned the violence against African Americans in the South as violations of the democratic process. Both parties could point to suspicious returns from numerous precincts in all three states. Although the Constitution grants the House of Representatives the power to choose the President if the Electoral College does not produce a winner, Congress's formation of an ad-hoc commission to resolve the competing partisan claims marked the first time in American history an extra-constitutional settlement decided a national election (Mayhew 2002, 56).

The party machinations that led up to this settlement made the Compromise of 1877 all the more controversial. Had it not been for former Republican Congressman and Spanish envoy Daniel Sickles's late night telegrams to Republican leadership in the contested states, urging them to hold out for a GOP victory, the election may very well have gone to Tilden. Sickles's midnight maneuver, approved by the patronage king, Chester A. Arthur, encouraged the Republican press not to concede defeat. "A doubtful election" was the title of a *New York Times* editorial in the early morning on November 8 (Holt 2008, 173). The *New York Herald* headline expressed this uncertainty more histrionically: "The Result—What is it? Something that no fellow can understand. Impossible to name our next President. The returns too meager" (Harmon 1987, 37). Party leaders and the partisan press did more than simply prop up their favored candidates and launch attacks on the opposition; they created doubts among the public that could hardly be assuaged by the tainted final rapprochement.

The narrative that developed from the centennial crisis of 1876 dramatically confirmed the Mugwumps' disdain for partisan politics. Forgotten amid the fraudulent resolution of the election was that both Hayes and Tilden had promised to institute civil service reform that would limit the power of local party organizations by reducing the number of government jobs that could be provided in reward for services to the party. In his inaugural address, Hayes proclaimed

> "the President of the United States of necessity owes his election to office to the suffrage and zealous labors of a political party, the members of which cherish with ardor and regard as of essential importance the principles of their party organization; but he should strive to be always mindful of the fact that he serves his party best who serves the country best" (Hayes 1877).

This was more than rhetorical flourish; soon after he became president Hayes would launch an assault of the federal Custom Houses in New York, San Francisco, and New Orleans, and several other port cities. These outposts, which were under the control of local party machines, had fallen into outrageous patterns of corruption in the course of collective federal revenues. The New York Custom House, which collected more than two-thirds of the custom revenues and provided the federal government with about half its income, was an especially notorious servant of patronage politics. The commission Hayes authorized to investigate its practices found that employees were expected to contribute a percentage of their salary to the Republican Party. After a protracted and bitter skirmish with New York Senator Roscoe Conkling, Hayes managed to replace the head of the Custom House, Chester A. Arthur—who ironically had played a key part in securing Hayes's controversial elevation to the White House—with General E.A. Merritt.

In his letter of congratulations to Merritt, Hayes established the principles for the complete overhaul of the New York Custom House's personnel system. Besides insisting that Merritt conduct the office "on strictly business principles," the president required the new collector to confine patronage to the narrowest possible bounds. "Let no man be put out merely because he is a friend of the late collector," he wrote, "and no man be put in merely because he is our friend" (Hayes 1879). Although Hayes was not able to pursue comprehensive reform during his one compromised term as president, the assassination of his successor, James A. Garfield, by a disappointed office-seeker added further fuel to the fire that had begun to consume the patronage state. That the deposed patronage-hound Arthur, who had been named Garfield's running mate to bandage party wounds over the Hayes–Conking dispute, now sat in the White House amplified the attack on spoils. The savvy former Custom House director, hoping to strengthen his political position, surprised reformers and his political patron Conkling in supporting the Pendleton Act, which Congress enacted in 1883. The civil service reform bill contained measures such as competitive examinations for federal jobs and a ban on political assessments.

Although the Pendleton Act's original impact was limited to a small part of the federal workforce, the reform legislation, as Leonard D. White has written, "was a fundamental turning point in the history of the federal administrative system" (White 1958, 346). A few decades later, Progressive reformers would begin to realize the full potential of this organic statute. As Martha Derthick and John Dinan have written, "scholars would probably concur that the Progressives' expansion of the civil service at the federal and municipal levels and their promotion generally of professional expertise in government became a force for centralization as professional leaders found positions in large scale governments" (1999, 97).

The assault on patronage was but one key ingredient of a broader reform program to undermine the party organizations of the Gilded Age. The direct election of senators and the institution of referenda and recall provisions in certain states offered voters a more direct role in the political process. Institutional changes to the ballot itself provided a devastating blow to local party organizations' hold on their constituencies' voting habits. Rusk illustrates that the adoption of an Australian secret ballot during the 1880s and 1890s, opened voters' opportunities to vote their personal preferences for candidates rather than follow the instructions of local party bosses (Rusk 1970). Voters no longer had to specifically request non-party-line ballots. All of the candidate options were given to them and their ballots would be turned over to new election boards, free of the partisan overseers that drove the military style campaigns of the post-Reconstruction era. Whereas Rusk argues that the ballot reforms, combined with voter registration requirements, emancipated the voter from the corrupt and provincial influence of machine politics, Burnham views these institutional changes as integral to an anti-democratic movement that reached fruition with McKinley's conquest of Bryan in 1896 (Burnham 1974, 1016). The weakening of parties and the triumph of the pro-business Republicans, Burnham argues, led "to the complete insulation of elites from attacks by the victims of the industrializing process, and a corresponding reinforcement of political conditions favoring an exclusively private exploitation of the political economy" (Burnham 1967, 301). Robert Wiebe probably comes closest to the truth. Echoing Burnham's lament that lower-class men were disenfranchised, he views this development as a unintentional consequence of reform efforts:

> "Voting, once a loyalty affirming public action, became an individualized private act. Instead of crowding to the polls and waving the party's ballot as they went to vote, lower class men, one by one, ran the gauntlet of election officials, perhaps only to discover that they could not decipher the procedures" (Wiebe 1995, 137).

Voters were thus freed from the manipulation of parties, but at the cost of weakening partisan ties that drew individuals into the political process. Turnout reached a peak at the national level during the contested election of 1876, with 82.6% of the eligible electorate voting (McDonald 2014). Political participation remained high through the 1880s and 1890s, averaging over three-quarters of the voting-eligible population in the elections that brought Grover Cleveland, Benjamin Harrison, and William McKinley to the Oval Office. But turnout declined thereafter, falling below 50% of the eligible electorate by the end of the Progressive Era. Midterm election turnout also fell during this period from 65% in 1874 to less than 40% in 1918.

The decline in voting might also have been influenced by the shift of influence from state and local to national organizations. As Klinghard reveals, "national party leaders reconfigured the conduct of national campaigns to reach voters directly with nationally printed material and with direct presidential campaigning" (2010, 1). The Republicans' 1896 campaign, orchestrated by Mark Hanna, marked a development that made national party committees, rather than state and local organizations, the principal site of campaign strategy. These strengthened committees forged ties with clubs and organizations that enabled them to circumvent the traditional party apparatus and orchestrate campaigns that "abandoned the republican values of communal appeals, compromise, localism, and mobilization" and "emphasized instead substantive appeals that were national in scope, appealed to voters' interests and questioned traditional partisan lines" (Klinghard 2010, 104).

The transformation of party organizations at the height of the Gilded Age showed that party leaders could adapt to the growing demand for reforms, but they constructed nationalized and programmatic parties that operated at a greater distance from the immediate concerns of the voters. Moreover, the nationalization of party activity went hand in hand with a decline of partisan competition that reinforced political demobilization (Burnham, 1974). In effect, the regionalism that became a staple of American politics with the 1876 election was institutionalized by party reforms and the realignment of partisan support in 1896. Bryan's votes came primarily from twenty-six states and territories, most of them in the sparsely populated Rocky Mountain, Great Plain, and Deep South regions. African American political participation vanished in the South, and despite some glimmers of hope for a regional resurgence in some pockets, most notably Louisiana, a lily-white southern Democratic Party became the anchor of what was a decidedly minority coalition until the New Deal. McKinley's sweep of the Midwest and the Northeast secured Republican dominance in the urban and industrial regions of the country (Williams 2008, Chapter 8). Republicans would maintain control of the presidency and both houses of Congress until 1912, when the Progressive Party challenged the national, regionally based partisanship that seemed to have disenfranchised or rendered indifferent a large part of the American electorate. Wilson captured the White House and Democrats assumed power in Congress, not because they had captured a majority of voters but because the dispute between Theodore Roosevelt and William Howard Taft led the celebrated former president to bolt from his party and divide it deeply between progressive and conservative wings. Wilson thus won the presidency with just 42% of the popular vote, but this Democratic interregnum came to an end in 1920.

Roosevelt's 1912 Progressive Party campaign illustrated how third parties played an important part in challenging the two-party system and providing impetus for a transformation of partisanship. Rosenstone, Behr, and Lazarus note that "periods of third party strength indicate that the major parties are not representing citizens' political demands" (1996, 4). Third parties paved the way for Silverites to send a message to the national political establishment in 1896. The Progressive Party pushed the Democrats and Republicans to accept industrial reforms. Just as important, Roosevelt's Bull Moose campaign championed political reforms that marked the most systematic attack on the traditional parties and brought into full relief the executive-centered partisanship that would be the most enduring political legacy of the Progressive Era.

Presidency-Centered Parties

Although the 1876 election began as a contest between two upright candidates, pledged to challenge traditional partisan drills, the individual merits of Hayes and Tilden were overshadowed by the organizational politics that resolved the Electoral College dispute. The 1896 election marked the first clear advance of the candidate-centered campaign. Prior to 1896, party brokers dominated the quadrennial nomination conventions. Delegates were selected to represent the interests of the local parties at the convention and, outside of periods of serious political upheaval, these provincial representatives brought local, or sectional, interests with them. The passionate conflict at the Democratic Convention between Goldbugs and Silverites, Bensel argues, threw open the doors and window of the "smoke-filled room," and transformed the Chicago gathering into a "public sphere"

(2008, 2–8). Bryan's Cross of Gold speech raised the contentious deliberations to a fever pitch; it "all but openly invited his listeners to create a riotous uproar that was entirely forbidden by the ritual formalities of the moment" (203). Bryan's very appearance at the convention symbolized a new relationship between candidates and parties. In the past, party nominees had stayed away from the convention, waiting to be officially notified of their nomination; a presidential candidate was expected to demur as a sign of respect for the party's collective purpose. Bryan's presence at the Chicago Coliseum showed that he was not considered a major candidate for the nomination—his unexpected nomination the day after his stirring Cross of Gold speech represented a major advance in the development of the candidate-centered campaign.

Bryan's general election campaign also broke new ground. Abandoned by many powerful Democrats because of his defense of free silver, and yet confident of his oratorical prowess, Bryan became the first presidential candidate to tour the country and appeal directly to the voters. Blessed with a powerful voice and boundless energy, the Great Commoner visited twenty-seven states and gave more than 800 speeches. As the historian Gil Troy has described Bryan's ground-breaking campaign, "Consuming up to six meals per day, sleeping in snatches, and taking periodic alcohol rubdowns to preserve his strength—though never imbibing—Bryan sang his silvery song. So many people crowded his train that he spoke from the rear platform of the last car, and a campaign tradition was born"—the whistle stop campaign through strings of small-town railway stations (Troy 1996, 104).

Although the GOP candidate, McKinley, displayed far more allegiance to conventional party practices, his campaign also revealed the growing importance of candidate-centered campaigns. Building on an approach that Benjamin Harrison had employed on a small scale in 1888, McKinley and his master political strategist, Hanna, mobilized the national Republican Party for a front porch campaign in which the candidate greeted delegations of voters at his home in Canton, Ohio. From mid-June through November, McKinley spoke to more than 300 crowds totaling 750,000 visitors from thirty states. No less than Bryan's silver crusade, McKinley's front porch speeches exalted the 1896 campaign as the most important contest since the Civil War: "then it was a struggle to preserve the government of the United States"; now "it was a struggle to preserve the financial honor of the government" (McKinley 1896, 14). Beyond these broad strokes, each event was carefully planned, so as to cultivate a direct, personal bond between the presidential candidate and the voters. Shortly before a delegation arrived, a telegram would reach Canton with information about the group's members, political attachments, and community. By the time the visitors arrived, McKinley was able to greet some of them by name, mention absent family members, and refer to matters of interest in the visitors' hometowns (Crenson and Ginsberg 2007, 114–120).

Like Bryan's whistle stop tour, McKinley's carefully orchestrated front porch campaign foretold the prominence of candidate- rather than party-centered campaigns. Subsequent campaigns displayed additional halting steps toward the modern candidate centered campaign. Not until the 1912 election, however, did the ingredients that were transforming American politics from party- to candidate-centered campaigns come into full view. Although they engaged in practices that departed from traditional partisan norms, neither Bryan nor McKinley directly attacked party organizations or the critical role these associations played in American elections and government. Nor did Roosevelt, when he was elected in his own right in 1904, publicly challenge traditional party drills. Although Roosevelt was very active behind the scenes—appointing the officers of the Republican Convention, dictating the platform, and actively courting funds—he did not attend the convention or actively campaign. Similarly, the 1908 election, pitting Bryan, running for the third time, against Taft, advanced the form of the candidate-centered campaign—for the first time, both major party candidates stumped actively and openly—but neither campaign challenged the critical function that parties played in nominating and electing candidates (Troy 1997, 112–125).

In contrast, Roosevelt's challenge to Taft for the Republican nomination and his campaign as the standard bearer of the Progressive Party elaborated the innovations that had begun to transform the relationship between the presidency and the voters into a comprehensive program of political reform (Milkis 2009). Although more enthusiastic about state-building than Wilson and his New Freedom colleagues, Roosevelt and other supporters of New Nationalism conceded that the construction of a regulatory and welfare state had to go hand in hand with "more direct action by the people in their own affairs" (Roosevelt 1910). The direct primary, Roosevelt said in his famous 1910 New Nationalism speech at Osawatomie, Kansas, was a step in this direction. In 1912, Roosevelt engaged the incumbent president, William Howard Taft, in the first presidential primary campaign, a landmark in the development of presidential elections. Political reforms had established the popular selection of candidates as a fixture of local, state, and congressional elections during the first decade of the twentieth century; however, the 1912 campaign was the first time that direct primaries played a significant role in a presidential election. Prior to Roosevelt's campaign, six states had scheduled primaries for 1912: North Dakota, California, New Jersey, Wisconsin, Minnesota and Nebraska. All of the states, save New Jersey—which enacted a direct primary law as part of Governor Woodrow Wilson's reform program—were in the Midwest and West, where progressive reforms had to this point made the greatest impact. As a consequence of Roosevelt making the direct primary a cause cèlèbre, many northern states fought fiercely over whether to hold popular contests. In the end, six additional states scheduled popular contests: Massachusetts, Pennsylvania, Illinois, Maryland,

Ohio and South Dakota. "With the six states in which the system was already in operation," George Mowry wrote, "this made a sizable block of normal Republican states from which a popular referendum could be obtained" (Mowry 1946, 228). Roosevelt carried nine of these states, accumulating 278 delegates to Taft's 48 and Wisconsin Senator Robert La Follette's 36. Roosevelt even won Taft's home state of Ohio by an almost 3–2 margin. But two-thirds of the convention delegates were still selected at gatherings dominated by state party leaders, who much preferred Taft's stolidity to Roosevelt's militant progressivism. With good reason, they perceived that Roosevelt's celebration of the popular primary presupposed a direct relationship between candidates and public opinion that portended a fundamental challenge to the essential role that party organizations had played in American politics since these institutions had become critical intermediaries in politics and government.

When it became clear at the Republican convention that Roosevelt would not be chosen, he and his followers walked out, reconvening in Chicago on August 5 under the banner of the Progressive Party. The Progressive Party was more than a personal vehicle for Roosevelt, but his control of it was extraordinary. The Progressive campaign advanced a development initially foretold by the 1896 Bryan–McKinley contest: the coming of presidential elections conducted less by parties than by individual candidates. Roosevelt's speech to the Progressive Party Convention was the first in history by a major presidential candidate, and it elicited a 52-minute standing ovation that echoed the passionate aftermath of the Bryan's Cross of Gold. His closing words—"We stand at Armageddon, and we battle for the Lord"—roused the delegates to such an emotional state that could only be subdued by a reverential singing of the "Battle Hymn of the Republic" (Roosevelt 1912b; Proceeding of the First National Convention of the Progressive Party 1912).

The delegates' reverence went beyond devotion to their candidate, however; it expressed their collective identity. Drawing on the Social Gospel movement, whose members viewed the Progressive party as a political expression of their commitment to promote Christian social action, Roosevelt and his fellow Bull Moosers most clearly defined the Lord's cause as a new idea and practice of democracy. The Progressive covenant with the people championed, not just measures to strengthen representative government, such as the right of women to vote and the direct election of Senators, but also reforms dedicated to what Roosevelt called pure democracy, that is, democracy purged of the impure influence of special interests and emancipated from court rulings that obstructed government efforts to curb "unfair money getting" (Roosevelt 1910). Beyond the universal use of the direct primary, these measure included the initiative; the recall of public officials; popular referenda on laws that the state courts declared unconstitutional; and an easier method to amend the Constitution.

This program was highly controversial—especially its planks calling for popular referenda on court decisions and giving a more majoritarian bent to the Constitutional amendment process. But Roosevelt's campaign was even more controversial than the Progressive platform; it championed an unvarnished majoritarianism. Toward the end of September, he announced in a speech at Phoenix, Arizona that "he would go even further than the Progressive party platform [in promoting the recall of public officials]; he would apply the recall to everybody, including the President." Roosevelt "stands upon the bold doctrine of unrestricted majority rule," the *Nation* warned. "But it is just against the dangers threatened, by such majority rule, in those crises that try the temper of nations, that the safeguard of constitutional government as the outgrowth of the ages of experience has erected" (*Nation* 1912). Even the Great Commoner blushed; plebiscitary measures such as the recall and referendum, William Jennings Bryan, who supported Wilson, insisted, should be confined to the states.

Like many third parties, the Progressive Party itself would have a brief life—when Roosevelt refused to run again in 1916, he doomed it to the dustbin of history. Consequently, scholars of parties and elections have tended to discount, as Paul Allen Beck writes, "the result of a split within the ranks of the majority party over personalities rather than over policies" (Beck 1979, 138). According to Burnham, it featured a "major-party bolt," but not the kind of protest movement that signals a transformation of American democracy (Burnham 1970, 27–28). Roosevelt was a party bolter, and personality conflicts played a big part in fracturing the Republican Party. Just as surely, Roosevelt's disaffection from Taft and Republican Party leaders was the result of his important disagreements with received party wisdom. He led an army of crusading reformers—insurgent Republican office-holders, disaffected Democrats, muckraking journalists, academics, settlement house workers, and other activists—aiming at social and industrial justice and a new form of democracy. Indeed, Roosevelt's insurgency brought to national prominence and bestowed considerable legitimacy on reforms developments that had been under way since the beginning of the 1890s.

The 1912 presidential election was a triumph for the progressive movement but it sent Wilson, not Roosevelt to the White House. Although Wilson polled much less than a majority of the national popular vote, he won the election easily. The final tally awarded 6.3 million popular votes and 435 electoral votes to Wilson, 4.1 million popular votes and 88 electoral votes to Roosevelt (the most ever won by a third-party presidential candidate before or since), and 3.5 million votes and eight electoral votes to Taft. Eugene V. Debs collected 900,000 popular votes, the highest total ever for a Socialist Party candidate, but no electoral votes. Above all, the 1912 election was a decisive rejection of traditional party politics, most strongly defended by Taft and the Republican Old Guard. Taft carried only Vermont and

Utah. The combined popular vote won by Wilson, Roosevelt, and Debs, each an advocate of Progressive politics and policies in one form or another, exceeded 75% (Mowry 1971, 3: 2163–2165). The results enabled Wilson to reap the benefits of a reform movement that was cresting just as he entered the White House.

Wilson poached from the Progressives' program of social and industrial justice during his presidency; he also borrowed from the third party's proposals for political reform. Impressed by the excitement that Roosevelt's Bull Moose campaign had aroused, Wilson vowed to advance the presidency-centered democracy that the Progressive Party had championed. No sooner had he been elected than Wilson disavowed the Democratic Party's platform that called for a constitutional amendment to limit presidents to a single term. As he lamented to A. Mitchell Palmer of Pennsylvania in February 1913, progressive Democrats "are seeking in every way to extend the power of the people, but in the matter of the Presidency, we fear and distrust the people, and seek to bind them hand and foot by rigid constitutional provision" (Wilson 1913). Hoping to deflate support for one-term presidency, Wilson resolved to make the executive office more democratic rather than try to diminish its powers. Most famously, he revived the practice, abandoned by Thomas Jefferson, of appearing before Congress to deliver important messages, including the State of the Union Address (Tulis 1987; Ceaser 1987, Chapter 4). Wilson's innovation displayed subtle differences with Roosevelt and the Progressive insurgents. Rather than arouse public opinion directly, the new president seemed intent on strengthening, rather than denigrating, partisanship by remodeling the presidency somewhat after the pattern of a prime minister. Still, Wilson appreciated the position of New Nationalists, put most forcefully by the prominent Progressive intellectual Herbert Croly, that the executive depended on public opinion "for his weapons" (Croly 1914, 348). With the rise of the mass media, Wilson believed, such occasions as the State of the Union would help concentrate public attention on the actions of the president and Congress (Cornwell 1965, 46). Overcoming the resistance of Democrats who still revered Jefferson as the patron saint of their party, Wilson addressed Congress frequently, beginning with an important address on tariff reform, a central issue of his presidential campaign. Well received by most members of Congress and the press, the president's precedent-shattering speech, delivered on April 8, 1913, launched the successful campaign for serious tariff reform that marked the signature achievement of his first term. Assessing Wilson's revolutionary approach to congressional relations, his close associate Ray Stannard Baker wrote, "These vigorous innovations occasioned an enormous amount of publicity. The country at large was vastly interested, amused, impressed" (Baker 1932, 4; 109).

For all the excitement, active campaigning, and high stakes that marked the 1912 election, however, the cresting of Progressive democracy did not reverse the decline of turnout that followed the 1896 election. As Gould points out, the measures to bar blacks from voting in the South, which the Progressive Party did not challenge, accounted for part of the reduction (Gould 2008, 181, 182). But so did the ongoing assault on party organizations that culminated with the Progressive Party's promotion of "pure democracy." Roosevelt's crusade championed a direct relationship between candidates and voters that made for good theater but helped to "undercut the ability of parties to act as agents of mass mobilization" (Kornbluh 2000, Chapter 5).

Conclusion: Partisanship Beyond the Parties

Although the pivotal elections during the Gilded Age and the Progressive Era brought about important changes in American politics, the powerful sectional cleavages that instigated the Civil War endured; indeed, these fissures were reinforced in important ways by the 1876 and 1896 campaigns. The South became a Democratic bastion while the North and Midwest were regions of Republican strength. For a time, the Compromise of 1877 seemed to establish a modus operandi between the parties that obscured economic, ethnic and racial conflicts. As Morton Keller has written of the unsavory bargain between Democratic and Republican leaders that signaled the failure of Reconstruction: "The retreat from the purposive, ideological politics of the Civil War could not have been more complete" (Keller 1977, 258). Yet developments were under way in the country that would pose challenges to the weak national state and the decentralized, patronage-based parties that handicapped it. Massive social and economic changes were increasing the scale and complexity of American life, producing jarring dislocations and intense political conflicts. In the face of these changes, pressures mounted for a more expansive national government and more systematic administration of public policy. Populists, Progressives, and Conservatives responded to these challenges not just with policy proposals but also with new understandings of the social contract that envisioned a reconfiguring the relationship between state and society.

The reimagining of American democracy came into full view with the 1912 campaign. It brought to fruition developments that began in the 1890s that would transform the character of American democracy from a politics shaped by localized, patronage-based parties to one driven by nationalized, presidency-centered partisanship. Committed to "pure democracy," many turn-of-the-century reformers hoped to sweep away intermediary organizations like political parties. As Eldon Eisenach has argued, Progressives championed "new parastates," such as labor unions, civic associations, settlement houses, crusading newspapers and magazines, and universities, that might enlarge provincial and partisan loyalties into "enlightened opinion" (Eisenach

1994, 134–135). In their disdain for partisan politics and their enthusiasm for good government, they sought to fashion the Progressive Party as a party to end parties. The Progressive campaign of 1912, Barry Karl observed, "was as much an attack on the whole concept of political parties as it was an effort to create a single party whose doctrinal clarity and moral purity would represent the true interest of the nation as a whole" (Karl 1983, 234–235). Yet, the hope that Progressive leaders could rise above factions to articulate public opinion, synthesize the public's interests, and anchor programmatic reform in a unified sense of national purpose has proven an elusive dream. Roosevelt's battle with Taft drove a wedge between progressivism and conservatism that would only grow wider over time. Although not always expressed through formal party channels, this ideological struggle has confounded the Progressive Party aspiration to transcend partisanship and represent the whole people. Instead, the ongoing battle between progressives and conservatives has fostered an executive-centered partisanship that reverberates through to today.

`The important developments advanced by these pivotal elections call for a reconsideration of realignment theory, which has long been the dominant framework for making sense of the booming, buzzing confusion of America's electoral history. As even the harshest critic of this paradigm, David Mayhew, grants, "The study of realignments has been one of the most creative, engaging, and influential intellectual enterprise ever undertaken by political scientists" (Mayhew 2002, 1). Yet to focus on 1896 as one of the critical cyclical events in the history of elections deflects attention from how campaigns and parties were undergoing major developments from the 1870s to the 1920s. The rise of the modern state and candidate-centered campaigns—the birth of a presidency-centered partisanship—suggests that the pivotal contests of the Gilded Age and Progressive Era deserve scrutiny as episodes that began to change fundamentally the meaning of partisanship. Even the conservative Republicans elected in the 1920s felt compelled to go directly to the public to ensure support for themselves and their programs. The landslide election that brought Warren Harding to the office (he won 60% of the popular vote, 40% below the Mason–Dixon line) was fought on the issues of World War I and the League of Nations. But in rejecting the League, so closely identified with Wilson and his aspirations for national and international reform, voters were expressing their general desire for quieter times after two decades of far-reaching political change. Still, even though Harding's defeat of the Democratic nominee, Ohio Governor James Cox, marked the end of the Progressive Era, "the stature of executive office in the eyes of the public, which had been growing since [the late 1890s] …at least held its own if it did not actually continue to grow after 1920" (Cornwell 1965, 60). Indeed, Harding and his two Republican successors, Calvin Coolidge and Herbert Hoover, tended to bestow bipartisan legitimacy on the executive-centered party that had begun to take form during Wilson's Democratic administration.

The celebrated theme of Harding's triumphant campaign—"return to normalcy"—captured the nation's longing for a moratorium on the major changes advanced by Wilson's domestic and wartime leadership. Yet the Republican landslide was abetted by new marketing techniques that showcased Harding "as a folksy, hardworking small town American who preferred Main Street to Pennsylvania Avenue" (Morello 2001, 50). Even as Republicans reprised the "front porch campaign," which had worked so well for McKinley, Albert Lasker, the pioneering advertising executive who played a critical role in formulating the Republicans' election strategy, did a masterful job of using innovative sales techniques to seal the deal with the American people. He not only flooded the country with campaign literature but also utilized new media such as movie newsreels and sound recordings to amplify the effects of Harding's warm and engaging personality.

Having served as the editor and publisher of the of the *Marion Star* in Ohio before entering politics, Harding took naturally to the public relations techniques that Lasker brought to the campaign. During the election season, he had a three-room cottage built near his home in Marion to accommodate the press. There, Harding would meet with reporters daily to discuss political developments in frank, off-the-record sessions. He continued to court the journalistic fraternity during the post-election transition period as he waited to be inaugurated. He was the first president to recognize the press could be courted in casual as well as formal encounters, even to the extent of playing golf with certain correspondents (Cornwell 1965, 63). Lest Harding be identified too closely with the game of golf, which was considered at the time as an elitist sport, Lasker arranged to have the presidential candidate play in an exhibition baseball game between his hometown Kerrigan Tailors, a minor league team, and the Chicago Cubs. Filmed participating in a sport most Americans followed, Harding preached the importance of "team play" to criticize Wilson's "go it alone" posture during the League of Nations fight (Morello 2001, 56–59).

Neither Harding nor his Vice President, the taciturn Coolidge, who became president in the tragic aftermath of scandal and the incumbent's mysterious death, aspired to be a tribune of the people in the manner embraced by Roosevelt and Wilson; however, each found that they could not advance the conservative economic policies they preferred without deploying the arsenal of presidential techniques for leading public opinion. As Coolidge acknowledged, after his masterful use of the radio helped overcome the opposition of Republican regulars to his nomination in 1924, the president, not the parties or Congress, had become the "sole repository of partisan responsibility" (Coolidge 1929).

Joined to social movements and interest groups, the presidential politics forged on the crucible of the pivotal elections during the Gilded Age and Progressive Era established the conditions for a partisanship beyond parties that has become the leading character of contemporary American politics. In the final analysis, these contests resulted in a major political realignment but one that advanced a new concept and practice of democracy whereby candidates and public officials would form more direct ties with the public. For all the important differences between contemporary Republicans and Democrats—conservatives and liberals—both champion the president as the steward of the public welfare, and both claim that executive power must be used in the name of the whole people. Yet, the development of a presidency-centered democracy has weakened political organizations that nurtured a sense of collective responsibility and political participation among individual men and women. Can the president of a vast and fractious nation, even with the tools of mass communication, function as a truly democratic institution with meaningful links to the public? This is the dilemma that the fascinating and troubling politics of the Gilded Age and Progressive Era has bequeathed to us.

References

Baker, Ray Stennard. 1932. *Woodrow Wilson: Life and Letters*. 8 volumes. London: Heinemann.

Beck, Paul Allen. 1979. "The Electoral Cycle and Patterns of American Politics." *British Journal of Political Science* 9: 129–156.

Bensel, Richard Franklin. 1990. *Yankee Leviathan: The Origins of Central State Authority in America, 1859–1877*. Cambridge: Cambridge University Press.

—. 2000. *The Political Economy of American Industrialization: 1877–1900*. Cambridge: Cambridge University Press.

—. 2008. *Passion and Preferences: William Jennings Bryan and the 1896 Democratic Nominating Convention*. Cambridge: Cambridge University Press.

Bryan, William Jennings. 1996. Cross of Gold Speech: http://historymatters.gmu.edu/d/5354/Accessed August 2, 2016.

Burnham, Walter Dean. 1967. "Party Systems and the Political Process." In *The American Party Systems: Stages of Development*, ed. Burnham and William Chambers, 277–307. New York: Oxford University Press.

Burnham, Walter Dean. 1970. *Critical Elections and the Mainspring of American Politics*. New York: W. W. Norton and Company.

—. 1974. "Theory and Voting Research: Some Reflections on Converse's 'Change in the American Electorate.'" *The American Political Science Review* 68, 3: 1002–1023.

Ceaser, James. 1979. *Presidential Selection: Theory and Development*. Princeton, NJ: Princeton University Press.

Coolidge, Calvin. 1929. *The Autobiography of Calvin Coolidge*. New York: Cosmopolitan.

Cornwell, Elmer. 1965. *Presidential Leadership of Public Opinion*. Bloomington: Indiana University Press.

Croly, Herbert. 1914. *Progressive Democracy*. New York: Macmillan.

Crenson, Matthew and Benjamin Ginsberg. 2007. *Presidential Power: Unchecked and Unbalanced*. New York: W.W. Norton.

Derthick, Martha and John Dinan. 1999. "Progressivism and Federalism." In *Progressivism and the New Democracy*, ed. Sidney M. Milkis and Jerome M. Mileur. Amherst: University of Massachusetts Press.

Eisenach, Eldon J. 1994. *The Lost Promise of Progressivism*. Lawrence: University Press of Kansas.

Ellis, Richard. 2012. *The Development of the American Presidency*. New York: Routledge.

Foner, Eric. 2014. *Reconstruction: America's Unfinished Revolution, 1863–1877*. Updated Edition. New York: Harper Perennial Modern Classics.

Gerring, John. 1998. *Party Ideologies in America: 1828–1996*. Cambridge: Cambridge University Press.

Gould, Lewis. 2008. *Four Hats in the Ring: The 1912 Election and the Birth of American Politics*. Lawrence: University Press of Kansas.

—. 2014. *The Republicans: A History of the Grand Old Party*. Oxford: Oxford University Press.

Harmon, Mark D. 1987. "The New York Times and the Theft of the 1876 Presidential Election." *Journal of American Culture* 10, 2: 35–41.

Haworth, Paul Leland. 1906. *The Hayes–Tilden Disputed Presidential Election of 1876*. Cleveland, OH: The Burrows Brothers Company.

Heersink, Boris and Jeffery A. Jenkins. 2015. "Southern Delegates and Republican National Convention Politics, 1880–1928." *Studies in American Political Development* 29: 68–88.

Hofstadter, Richard. 1948. *The American Political Tradition and the Men Who Made It*. New York: Vintage Books.

Holt, Michael. 2008. *By One Vote: The Disputed Presidential Election of 1876*. Lawrence: University Press of Kansas.

Howard, John R. 1999. *The Shifting Wind: The Supreme Court and Civil Rights from Reconstruction to Brown*. Albany: State University of New York Press.

James, Scott C. 2000. *Presidents, Parties, and the State: A Party System Perspective on Democratic Regulatory Choice, 1884–1936*. Cambridge: Cambridge University Press.

Jensen, Richard. 1971. *The Winning of the Midwest: Social and Political Conflict, 1888–1896*. Chicago: University of Chicago Press.

Karl, Barry.1983. *The Uneasy State: The United States from 1915–1945*. Chicago: University of Chicago Press.

Keller, Morton. 1977. *Affairs of State: Public Life in Late-Nineteenth Century America*. Cambridge, MA: Harvard University Press.

—. 2007. *America's Three Regimes: A New Political History*. New York: Oxford University Press.

Key Jr., V. O. 1955. "A Theory of Critical Elections." *Journal of Politics* 17, 1: 3–18.

—. 1984. *Southern Politics in State and Nation*. New edition. Knoxville: University of Tennessee Press.

Klinghard, Daniel. *The Nationalization of American Political Parties, 1880–1896*. New York: Cambridge University Press.

Kornbluh, Mark. 2000. *Why America Stopped Voting: The Decline of Participatory Voting and the Emergence of Modern American Politics*. New York: New York University Press.

Lemann, Nicholas. 2006. *Redemption: The Last Battle of the Civil War*. New York: Farrar, Straus & Giroux.

Mayhew, David. 2002. *Electoral Realignments: A Critique of an American Genre*. New Haven: Yale University Press.

McDonald, Michael. "National VEP Turnout Rates, 1789–Present." United States Elections Project. Last modified June 11, 2014. http://www.electproject.org/home/voter-turnout/voter-turnout-data Accessed August 2, 2016.

McKinley, William. "First Inaugural Address." March 4, 1897.

—. "Campaign Speech." July 11, 1896. In 1896. *The Presidential Candidates and Platforms, Candidates and Nominating Speeches*. University of Michigan Library.

Milkis, Sidney. 2009. *Theodore Roosevelt, the Progressive Party and the Transformation of American Democracy*. Lawrence: Kansas University Press.

Morello, John A. 2001. *Selling the President: Albert D. Lasker, Advertising, and the Election of Warren G. Harding*. Westport, CT: Praeger.

Morris, Roy, Jr. 2003. *Fraud of the Century: Rutherford B. Hayes, Samuel Tilden, and the Stolen Election of 1876*. New York: Simon and Shuster.

Mowry, George. 1946. *Theodore Roosevelt and the Progressive Movement*. Madison: University of Wisconsin Press.

—. 1971. "The Election of 1912." In *History of American Presidential Elections, 1789–1968*. 4 volumes. New York: Chelsea.

Nation. 1912. "Let the People Rule." *Nation*. September 26.

Olcott, Charles S. 1916. *William McKinley*. 2 volumes. Boston: Houghton Mifflin.

Orren, Karen and Stephen Skowronek. 2004. *The Search for American Political Development*. New York: Cambridge University Press.

Peskin, Allen. 1973. "Was There a Compromise of 1877?" *The Journal of American History* 60, 1: 63–75.

Proceedings of the First National Convention of the Progressive Party. 1912. August 5–7. Progressive Party Archives, Theodore Roosevelt Collection, Houghton Library, Harvard University.

Progressive Party. 1912. Platform, August 7. http://teachingamericanhistory.org/library/document/progressive-platform-of-1912/Accessed August 2, 2016.

Prescott, Lawrence F. 1896. *1896: The Great Campaign or Political Struggles of Parties, Leaders and Issues*. Peoria, IL: Loyal Publishing Company.

Rehnquist, William. 2004. *Centennial Crisis: The Disputed Election of 1876*. New York: Alfred A. Knopf.

Roosevelt, Theodore. 1910, 1926. *Roosevelt: The Works of Theodore Roosevelt*. Volumes 17 and 20. New York: Scribner's.

—. 1912. "The Case against the Reactionaries." June 17. http://www.theodore-roosevelt.com/images/research/speeches/trreactionairies.pdf Accessed August 2, 2016.

—. 1912a. "A Charter for Democracy." Address before the Ohio Constitutional Convention at Columbus, Ohio. February 21. Roosevelt Collection, Houghton Library, Harvard University.

—. 1912b. "Confession of Faith." In *Roosevelt: The Works of Theodore Roosevelt, volume 17*, 219. New York: Scribner's.

Rosenstone, Steven J., Roy L. Behr, and Edward H. Lazarus. 1996. *Third Parties in America: Citizen Response to Major Party Failure*. Princeton, NJ: Princeton University Press.

Rusk, Jerrold G. 1970. "The Effect of the Australian Ballot Reform on Split Ticket Voting: 1876–1908." *The American Political Science Review* 64, 4: 1220–1238.

Saldin, Robert F. 2011. *War, the American State and Politics Since 1898*. New York: Cambridge University Press.

Skocpol, Theda. 1992. *Protecting Soldiers and Mothers: The Political Origins of Social Policy in the United States*. Cambridge, MA: Belknap/Harvard University Press.

Skowronek, Stephen. 1982. *Building a New American State: The Expansion of National Administrative Capacities: 1877–1920*. Cambridge: Cambridge University Press.

Sundquist, James L. 1983. *Dynamics of the Party System: Alignment and Realignment of Political Parties in the United States*. Revised edn. Washington, DC: The Brookings Institution.

Taft, William Howard. "Acceptance Address." August 1, 1912.

Tocqueville, Alexis de. 2000. *Democracy in America*. Ed. Harvey C. Mansfield and Delba Winthrop. Chicago: University of Chicago Press.

Troy, Gil. 1997. "Money and Politics: The Oldest Connection." *The Wilson Quarterly* 21, 3: 14–32.

Tulis, Jeffrey. 1987. *The Rhetorical Presidency*. Princeton, NJ Princeton University Press.

Ware, Alan. 2006. *The Democratic Party Heads North: 1877–1962*. Cambridge: Cambridge University Press.

Warner, Charles Dudley and Mark Twain. 1923. *The Gilded Age: A Tale of Today*. Chicago: American Publishing Company.

Wiebe, Robert. 1995. *Self Rule: A Cultural History of American Democracy*. Chicago: University of Chicago Press.

Williams, R. Hal. 2010. *Realigning America: McKinley, Bryan, and the Remarkable Election of 1896*. Lawrence: University of Kansas Press.

Wilson, Woodrow. 1885. *Congressional Government: A Study in American Politics*. Boston: Houghton Mifflin Company.

—. 1913. "Wilson to Alexander Mitchell Palmer, February 5." In *The Papers of Woodrow Wilson*, ed. Arthur S. Link. 69 volumes. Princeton, NJ: Princeton University Press.

Woodward, C. Vann. 1951. *Reunion and Reaction: The Compromise of 1877 and the End of Reconstruction*. Boston: Oxford University Press.

Further Reading

Cooper, John Milton, Jr. 2009. *Woodrow Wilson: A Biography*. New York: Vintage Books.

Durden. Robert F. 1965. *The Climax of Populism: The Election of 1896*. Knoxville, University of Kentucky Press.

Gould, Lewis L. *The Presidency of Theodore Roosevelt*. New York: Oxford University Press, 2012.

—. *The William Howard Taft Presidency*. Lawrence: University Press of Kansas, 2009.

Guenther, Karen. 1983. "Potter Committee Investigation of the Disputed Election of 1876." *The Florida Historical Quarterly* 61.3: 281–295.

Harpine, William D. 2000. "Playing to the Press in McKinley's Front Porch Campaign: The Early Weeks of a Nineteenth-century Pseudo Event." *Rhetoric Society Quarterly* 30.3: 73–90.

Hoogenboom, Ari. *Rutherford B. Hayes: Warrior and President*. 1995. Lawrence: University of Kansas Press.

Kelly, Patricia J. 2003. "The Election of 1896 and the Restructuring of Civil War Memory." *Civil War History* 49.3: 254–280.

Morgan, Howard Wayne. *William McKinley and His America*. Kent, OH: Kent State University Press, 2003.

Oldaker, Nikki and John Bigelow. 2006. *Samuel Tilden: The Real 19th President*. Branford, CT: Show Biz East Productions

Polsky, Andrew. J. 2012. "Partisan Regimes in American Politics." *Polity* 44.1: 51–80.

Prescott, Lawrence F. 1896. 1896: *The Great Campaign or Political Struggles of Parties, Leaders and Issues*. Loyal Publishing Company.

Shefter, Martin. 1994. *Political Parties and the State: The American Historical Experience*. Princeton, NJ: Princeton University Press.

Springen, Donald K. 1991. *William Jennings Bryan: Orator of Small-Town America*. New York: Greenwood Press.

Tunnell Jr., T. B. 1966. "The Negro, the Republican Party, and the Election on 1876 in Louisiana." *Louisiana History: The Journal of the Louisiana Historical Association* 7.2: 101–16.

Chapter Twenty-Six

Congress in the Gilded Age and Progressive Era

Mark Wahlgren Summers

As America came of age, Congress grew up. More states meant more congressmen than ever before, and as the population swelled, each of them represented more people and became less able to make themselves known to their constituents personally. Sessions lengthened; more and more often, the country's business could not wait until the usual December assembling in an odd-numbered year. Turnover lessened from one election to the next, first in the increasingly one-party South, and then in the Republican-dominated North (Abram and Cooper 1968; Fiorina, Rhode, and Wissel, 1975). Gerrymanders and partisan redistrictings, first regulated and then shrugged away by courts determined to make districts equal in population even at the expense of doing fairness to the proportionate strength of parties, made uncertain seats sure (Argersinger 2012). In the House, lawmakers who had been virtually sojourners became fixed points in a changing age. Where serving two terms was once relatively unusual, three odd, and more terms than that uncanny, legislators made their service into a lifetime career, ended only by death, executive appointment, or translation into the Senate (Kernell 1977). A collective memory developed, helped along by the growth and professionalization of the press gallery. Foolish was the congressman who did not take advantage of his connections with reporters to build up at home a personal base, separate from party fealty. This skill became all the more necessary after 1872, since party-designed ballots made any splitting of tickets a challenge, and Congress applied increasing pressure to have state and national elections fall on the same day (James 2007; Engstrom and Kernell 2005; McDonagh 1989; 1993). Constituents might not follow the intricacies of copyright protection legislation, but a network of other, more individual favors from Capitol Hill made them beholden to their congressman: private pensions to veterans or their dependents, free packets of seeds from the Agriculture Department, services performed to expedite claims or disentangle complications before the bureaus on which both the regulatory and distributive functions of government relied (Skocpol 1992; Sanders 1980). The more independent agencies and separate bureaucracies there were, the more necessary became a representative with the influence to negotiate, cajole, or simply be a nuisance. All politics may not have been local, but General Winfield Scott Hancock's gaffe in calling the tariff a local issue was not half as simple-minded as scoffers made out. Duties on wool and woolens, salt and steel, each had its own discrete constituencies. Ironmongers in West Virginia hated duty-free Nova Scotia coal as passionately as those in New England doted on it, while fuel-hungry industries on the west coast found no salvation closer than the Antipodes. Every river and harbor improvement bill was comprehensive only in satisfying as many run-of-the-mill rivulets in as many districts as it could—and none more generously than those represented on the Commerce Committee (Wilson 1986; Current 1950).

Committees proliferated to handle, modify, and murder the tremendous quantity of proposed legislation that had grown from a trickle to a torrent since the 1850s. Not until after the Civil War did committees take on a permanent membership; the Senate started choosing members for an entire Congress and not just a session only in 1886 (Alexander 1916; Polsby 1968; Wander 1972; Canon, Nelson and Stewart 2002; Aldrich and Rohde 2005). With the long turn of the century both branches came to privilege seniority in their selection of committee chairmanships and positions of influence (Abram and Cooper 1968; Polsby, Gallaher and Rundquist 1969; Hinckley 1971). In the House, the power to filibuster was diminished, then broken, as the machinery at the Speaker's control permitted the effective silencing of obstructive minorities. Justly or not (and a few recent articles have suggested the latter, that

A Companion to the Gilded Age and Progressive Era, First Edition. Edited by Christopher McKnight Nichols and Nancy C. Unger.
© 2017 John Wiley & Sons, Inc. Published 2017 by John Wiley & Sons, Inc.

party caucuses and not gavel-wielding dictators directed the House) (Cox and McCubbins 2002; Jones 1968; Krehbiel and Wiseman 2001), the presiding officer was proclaimed a czar, able to stack the committees as he pleased and put the "outs" in their place—quite literally, in some cases, by barring the doors so that they could not escape a quorum call (Robinson 1930; Grant 2011; Peters 1997). Channeling and stemming the flow of inconvenient legislation, the House Rules Committee became a necessary stopgap for conservatism fearful of too much regulation.

With heavier workloads and greater demands for action came the spread of congressional staffs and the recourse to more professional expertise in the drafting of legislation. This also included the rise and advancing sophistication of the "third house" of outsiders seeking to influence Congress in particular directions. Lobbyists and petitioners had nudged members for years, but now their operations were more sophisticated. Corporations put down permanent beachheads in the capital, discovering the possibilities of public opinion made to order or grass-roots movements not simply fertilized but seeded on hitherto barren ground (Thompson 1985; Wood 1985; Jacob 2009). A growing cadre of congressmen-turned-lobbyists or corporate clienteles-turned-statesmen clustered in Washington. Ministers delivered their sermons against Sunday mail delivery and nationally distributed lottery advertisements. The professionalization of doctors, lawyers, social workers, scientists, accountants, and scholars, among others, and the associations they formed, forged another force that could press for change from state and national government (Wiebe 1967; Miranti 1986). If sugar barons helped congressmen see the light on bounties and duties, farmers organized into the Grange or Farmers' Alliance were at hand to make congressmen feel the heat on matters of concern to them, whether the unfair advantage of oleomargarine over butter, or the positive benefits of rural free delivery (Sanders 1999). Long before Congress enacted a rural credits bill, those who worked the fields knew that their success depended (at least in part) on those who worked the cloakrooms. Until late in the Progressive Era, Congress was a men's club, and voting east of the Mississippi River just as exclusively male. No lawmaker, however, had to be reminded that women's opinions held sway with their husbands, fathers, and friends, and that pressure helped change political discourse away from the old war issues and towards those involving family, morality, and the market-basket. It also shifted the main theme of tariff tinkering from meeting the desires of producers to catering to the demand of consumers (Edwards 1997).

Mingled with all these forces were other pressures transforming the influences on elected officials. Politicking as a business grew all the more because partisan loyalties weakened. Candidates had to sell their own good qualities to voters less certain to walk the straight party line, especially after the ascendancy of the Australian secret ballot in the 1890s. But salesmanship cost more than before. As the old personal style of politics gave way to the advertised and packaged varieties, and as civil service reform edged out the parties' ability to provide the means on which a campaign could be run, candidates needed to have built-in constituencies: special interests, economic and moral, with their own particular agendas and contributors, some of them corporate, with plethoric bank-accounts ready for a healthy bleeding. That shift may itself have spurred on the impulse to legislate, and not just for buncombe. The old vindicationist campaigns, where Civil War veterans would vote as they shot or elect a one-armed mediocrity to send a message to the Rebels or blue-bellies in Congress, gave way to something more substantial. Most groups paying out expected value for money, veterans included (Skocpol 1992).

Traditional accounts have seen the Gilded Age as a period when Congress did nothing in particular and did it pretty badly (Bryce 1891; Wilson 1900; Caro 2002). According to competing and complementary legends, the period after Reconstruction was the era of laissez-faire, where every measure for laborers' or farmers' benefit met a chorus of objections that it violated the sacred precepts of liberal economics and stood in the way of progress, where the fittest alone deserved to survive (Josephson 1938). It was also the age when business had its way in compelling every favor that an activist government could grant (Beatty 2007). All but one of the five major transcontinental railroad lines was built with subsidies or public land grants. A Homestead Act helped populate the west, while the loopholes in the Timber and Stone Act and the Desert Act allowed corporations to grab valuable coal and timber deposits for pennies. Every Congress considered and most of them revised in some ways the tariff, and every wholesale change—those of 1883, 1888, 1890, 1894, 1897, and 1913—brought an ill-tempered scramble among the needy, the greedy, and the seedy. The primacy of gold in the nation's money supply owed itself to Congress's passage of the "Crime of '73," long blamed on corruption and equally long upheld as enlightened statesmanship. But the whole financial system shook or solidified (sometimes both, at the same time) depending on what Congress did. Its legislation set the terms for the issuance of banknotes or their distribution among the states, for the chartering of national banks, for the limited coinage of silver in 1878, for the government purchase of silver bullion in 1890 and the repeal of the same act in 1893, and, finally, in 1900, for the passage of an official gold standard (Bensel 2000; Calhoun 1996).

By contrast, the Progressive Era saw a host of legislation regulating the marketplace on behalf of the public good and mandating morality. The Elkins Act, the Hepburn Act, and the Mann–Elkins Act turned railroads from robber barons into wailing supplicants who claimed to be struggling to break even. If Americans ate safer food or no longer relied on Liquizone to cure cancer, catarrh, and every other ailment but credulity, the Pure Food and Drug Act and Meat Inspection Act deserved some credit (Wood 1985; High and

Coppin 1988). The first national mine-safety legislation; the first child-labor law; a slight and, four years later, a steep downward revision of the tariff; the creation of a Federal Reserve Board and a Federal Trade Commission; an eight-hour day for railroad workers, and a fresh anti-trust act: historians trying to list them all lead a strenuous life of almost Rooseveltian proportions. If Americans stopped drinking (legally, anyhow) or started paying income tax, voted regardless of gender, or had national parks to visit, if San Franciscans paid less for their electricity thanks to a lake flooding one of Yosemite's most beautiful valleys, if cotton farmers in the Southwest fed off federally funded irrigation projects initiated under the Carey and Newlands Acts, if immigrants had to pass a literacy test, and if the Chinese found themselves barred permanently, regardless of their educational attainments, they owed blessings or maledictions to a Congress ever up and doing (Gold 2012; Gyory 1998).

The traditional account never worked very well. Historians have questioned the sharp dividing line in 1901 between the two eras. In fact, a mischief-maker might describe the entire Gilded Age as a Progressive Era on depressants, and the Progressive Era as simply a Gilded Age on stimulants. It was entirely true that for much of the earlier era, legislation found a harder path to passage than in the later, but the reasons had less to do with an underlying philosophy and more with political dynamics. From 1875 to 1897, the same party controlled House, Senate and Presidency for only six years: 1881–83, 1889–91, and 1893–95. Between 1883 and 1889, Democrats ran the House, Republicans the Senate; between 1895 and 1897, it was the other way around. On a strongly contested issue like how far the tariff should protect American enterprise, divisions within the parties, sectional, ideological, and economic, made mustering a majority in either chamber very much a struggle (Barfield 1970). A dishwater compromise like that of 1883 could pass largely because it did things that the Democratic minority liked in cutting internal revenue taxes on whiskey and tobacco. A southern-oriented reduction in duties like the Mills bill sailed through the House in 1888 with Democratic supporters expecting (and some even hoping) that the Republican senate would stifle it—as proved the case. Procedural barriers only slowed action further. No majority of senators could stop a filibuster until 1917 when a two-thirds rule was adopted after "a little group of willful men" talked to death the bill arming merchant seamen against the German U-boat threat. In the House, Democrats did not need to slay majority action with their jawbones. They could simply refuse to answer their names on quorum calls (Reed 1889a, b). Republican majorities found themselves helpless, at least until Speaker Thomas Brackett Reed changed the rules in 1890 by ordering a count of everyone present. It was an action intended, as one scholar has recently noted, to help Republicans carry through their challengers to southern seats out of which they had been cheated fair and square, and to create a majority large enough to push through a Federal Elections bill guaranteeing a free and honest count across a South where government by the consent of the governed had become a fading memory (Dion 1997; Forgette 1997; Jenkins 2004; 2007; Valelly 2009).

When the same party commanded both ends of Pennsylvania Avenue, legislation had a better chance. Reed's "Billion-Dollar Congress" carried more substantive measures than any since the early 1870s: the Sherman Anti-Trust Act, the Sherman Silver-Purchase Act, the McKinley Tariff, a Dependent Pension Law, and subsidies for the merchant marine. By no accident, it was the least filibuster-prone chamber that passed that Federal Elections Bill; by no chance, it was in the Senate that it perished, as well as the last comprehensive measure aiding education, Henry W. Blair's bill to support black schools in the South (Upchurch 2004; Morgan 1969). Slimmer Democratic margins accomplished less in 1893–94, but the Sherman Silver-Purchase Act repeal, the Wilson–Gorman Tariff, and the repeal of the Enforcement Acts giving government oversight over national elections, suggested how much majorities could do, for good or ill (James and Lawson, 1999). Only after 1897, when Republicans had staggeringly large margins in both houses, and defections from their ranks could not affect the result, did the pace of legislation quicken (Brady 1972; 1973; Brady and Althoff 1974). It quickened still further, and in a progressive direction, as Democrats regained their share of seats after 1908; especially from the South and West. The minority party sent hosts of members ready to join hands with Republican insurgents. Given encouragement from the White House, this coalescence of forces could speed on many of the legislative initiatives associated with the Progressive Era (Barfield 1965; Sarasohn 1989; Harrison 2010; Brady, Brody and Epstein 1989; Balch 1972; Green 2002).

The dividing line between Age and Era never worked as well as political scientists have mapped out: a general and continuous evolution from one great war to the next in the professionalization of Congress and an increase in legislation. Never had so much legislation been offered as after the Civil War, nor so much of it passed. Nowhere has so much gone unsaid (but nonetheless printed) as in the *Congressional Record*; researchers, looking at the tens of thousands of pages of published prose for each session, must feel like paraphrasing the belittling words aimed at Edward Gibbon: "What, another d—d fat book? Gabble, gabble, gabble, eh, Mr. Congressman?" (Keller 1977). At the same time, the very need of lawmakers to go on record or to express their constituencies' (and contributors') views before a national audience showed how vital it had become for them to look as if they really were trying to do things.

In terms of the *kinds* of things that Congress did, that line between Age and Era has a particularly arbitrary quality. The first national regulatory agency, the Interstate Commerce Commission, was created in 1887, and the 1913 income tax amendment was only made necessary because the Supreme Court had killed the tax that lawmakers had enacted in 1894. Those historians who mark the earlier period as a time when most legislation was "distributive"—that is, handed out favors, pensions, jobs, and benefits to everybody—rather than regulatory, now are seen to have overshot the mark (McCormick 1986; John 2004; 2006; Brock 1984). Legislation was always heavily distributive; private bills always heavily outnumbered those of general utility, and congressional majorities had always been willing to regulate and control where the subject was one that they did not feel would be better handled at the local or state level. That respect for federalism diminished through the nineteenth century. With the ascendancy of William Jennings Bryan and the Democrats either agreeing with or coopting much of the Populist agenda, it lost a great deal of the support it had enjoyed in the South since before the Civil War—except, of course, on issues of race and civil rights. Congress never had a qualm about using the law to shut out the Chinese, first for ten-year periods, and then permanently (Gold, 2012). If anything, legal theory gave a wider scope to lawmakers' use of the police power in the 1870s than it would a generation later, and that power could do everything from banning the shipment of liquor through the mails to outlawing "bucket shops" and various forms of stock speculation.

Year by year, Congress met more, spoke more, did more. But somehow it did not seem to matter more. Quite the contrary, in fact. Its reputation, never high, dropped. The drama of debate rarely could match the daily din of disorder. It was easy enough to have the feeling that Woodrow Wilson voiced in another context, that nothing had ever been done so systematically as nothing was being done now. A press gallery reported every failure and foible, the drunken spectacle lawmakers performed on closing night of the session, the pell-mell rush of bills without attention and sometimes without adequate punctuation in the final minutes before adjournment (Ritchie, 1992). Senators trading insults made good copy, those trading blows even better. The constant clack of debate, the desultory pace of the simplest procedures, the regular quorum calls and the vast array of empty seats, robbed the House of a dignity to which the Senate, simply by its lesser numbers, just barely could aspire. If legislators could not bear to stick around for their colleagues' addresses, why should anyone? Contemporaries readily agreed that the Senate by 1900 was not what it was, and, the more historically minded added, never had been. A canny crafter of legislation from a conservative point of view, Wisconsin's John Coit Spooner could never rank with Daniel Webster. Only his ability to read, write, and spell made him superior to his colleague, lumberman Philetus Sawyer (Current 1950). The Empire State once sent William Marcy and William Henry Seward to Washington; only a cynic would have tried comparing them to New York's duo in 1905, "Easy Boss" Thomas Platt and New York Central executive Chauncey Depew, most known for his after-dinner speeches, every gem fashioned of the very best paste.

Around the Capitol, too, a smog of scandal settled, a general sense that Congress's most valued players were worth their weight in gold to those who had that gold (Thompson 1985). Long before muckraker David Graham Phillips wrote *The Treason of the Senate* (Phillips 1964), the "Millionaires' Club" had a reputation for housing members who had bought their seats or sold their services. Some moonlighted as corporate attorneys and defended their clients not just in the courtroom but on the floor. Others came from the business world, but never seemed to leave it. The senator from Standard Oil could parse legal language any day with the senator from the Southern Pacific Railroad, with his colleague the Comstock Lode bonanza king chiming in. Any reporter could name a dozen House members whose "barrel" of money bought their nomination or guaranteed their election. From the rotten boroughs of the ex-Confederate South came members whose electorate was as precious as rubies, and for the same reason: its scarcity. Election laws and "bulldozing" had whittled out nearly anyone with the inconvenient habit of voting Republican. Proofs enough exist to characterize some lawmakers as one was described in an Ambrose Bierce parable: "The gentleman's connection with commerce is close and intimate. He is a commodity." (Bierce 1970, 69–70). Those assumptions and the belief, always erroneous, that senators owed their selection to the party machine at worst and the whims of state lawmakers at best, helped speed on a constitutional amendment transferring the power to elect senators from the state legislature to the people (Bernhard and Sala 2006; Schiller, 2006; Schiller and Stewart 2014). In some places, progressives shifted the nominating process for House and Senate from conventions to direct primaries.

Reputation and reality were not, of course, the same thing. In terms of general capacity, senators and congressmen probably matched those in the so-called "Golden Age" before the Civil War. Those holding themselves up to Webster's ethical standards set the bar very low indeed. Longer service, indeed, may have made the typical member of the House better versed in its parliamentary procedures and far more influential in meeting constituents' needs than his antebellum predecessors. In every era, the Charles Sumners, orotund, bookish, high-minded, and exasperatingly righteous, were exotics, though Robert La Follette came close to the ideal—unpopularity with colleagues included (Thelen 1976; Unger 2000). Standing rigidly on principle made a figure fit for a pedestal, but it was the worst possible way to make legislation advance. For all the partisan confines in which members of either party voted, both houses worked best when the most hands were stretched across the aisle. That cooperation, collusion, and comity, understudied but constant, allowed a level of good will on the floor and in the back rooms to keep measures moving, even if it was no more than the shared taste for that jug of whiskey in the Judiciary Committee room that the ranking members from either party, Allen G. Thurman and George F. Edmunds, shared in the late 1870s (Rothman 1969; Krehbiel and Wiseman 2005). An atmosphere of mutual respect overcame all the passions on the floor. Insurgent Republican George Norris of Nebraska, for example, did more than anyone to trim Speaker Joe Cannon's power. But when they met two years later, Cannon heading into what proved a temporary retirement and Norris into the upper house, the felled "Czar" took him aside to express satisfaction that he, of all his gang, should end up in the Senate (Lowitt 1963; Norris 1945).

Yet it is unquestionable that the more active and productive Congress grew, the less its relative power in Washington became. That was through no fault of personal character, despite Mark Twain's quip that there was no distinctly American criminal class except Congress. Rather, it stemmed from the essential nature of an institution of some 400 competing voices and inspired silences. The other two branches were simply outpacing the legislative, both in their initiatives and in their public prominence.

Since Andrew Johnson's time, presidents had found themselves hemmed in by Congressional authority (White 1958). All the same, they had tugged against the restraints from the first, loosening the bonds upon them. Repeal of the Tenure of Office Act eliminated the last formal limits on the executive's power to remove. The spread of the merit system placed an increasing number of offices beyond congressional pressure to be filled with favorites or emptied of enemies. As one study has made clear, the first tentative steps in the nineteenth century only whittled away the spoils system, while the number of jobs open to political appointment actually grew (Skowronek 1982). In the twentieth century, the move towards professionalization accelerated, and with it lawmakers' ability to reward their friends. A bureaucracy beholden to the president or to an apolitical standard of excellence became the norm, from the Treasury building to the fourth-class post offices in the Aleutian Islands.

The presidential office itself was growing. Administrative staff increased. Discovering the uses of office as a bully pulpit, embracing the idea that congressmen spoke for their constituents while the President alone spoke for the whole country, chief executives began cultivating the press. A separate pressroom was added to the White House under Theodore Roosevelt. By 1917, White House briefings and interviews on and off the record had become the norm, not the exception. One might lose track of what Chester Alan Arthur was doing for weeks at a time; a day without Woodrow Wilson on the front page in some capacity was one worth remembering. No presiding officer over the House could speak with such authority on a wide range of issues, even if he belonged to a separate party from that of the president, which, after 1897, he rarely did. The simple immediacy of action that captured public attention was within any president's power—far more dramatic in getting anything done than the sluggish, slogging deliberative process of a legislative body. Newspaper cartoons caught the shift (Marschall 2011). Where in the 1880s, a few dozen senators and a handful of congressmen appeared regularly and, indeed, almost as frequently as the president, Roosevelt and Wilson dominated the pictures of the early twentieth century. Even the foremost congressmen appeared with a diminishing frequency as individuals. In their place, a stock image represented Congress: tellingly, an overfed hayseed with chin-whiskers, rural, parochial, and out of date.

Nor could Congress compete for attention or influence where foreign affairs were concerned. War and the prospect of war gave the president a role that Congress was ill-equipped to match. It could carry the country into a conflict, as it did in 1898 and 1917, but the commander in chief took the star turn in whatever followed. Where America's relations to the world fell short of fighting, the State Department and the White House got all the glory and most of the headlines. From the late 1890s on, foreign policy no longer appeared as an occasional diversion in the paper but as a regular, steady bit of news. It was as if, by besting Spain's decaying empire, the United States had discovered the world. And in that discovery, the point-men were diplomats, soldiers, and dignitaries, all of them carrying out the will of the president. Significantly, it was in matters relating to war and America's ability to flex its muscle abroad that the pace of modernizing the government machinery sped the fastest, and in just about every case, the only role left to Congress was to second-guess, investigate, or respond to how the executive branch was using its authority (Skowronek 1982). Only in tariff policy could Congress play more than a supporting role, and even there the clauses encouraging reciprocity on duty reduction between nations gave wide discretion to that man in the White House.

In domestic affairs as well, the initiative fell away from the Congress throughout the Gilded Age and into the Progressive Era. For a president to propose a policy of his own was treated as outlandish in the late 1860s; for him to campaign for office, particularly for his own, was considered in the worst possible taste. A Ulysses S. Grant might offer a special message with recommendations in an emergency, and gentle requests in his annual State of the Union address, but he would not insist. When Congress gutted his civil service commission, he let it perish without a murmur. Only in 1913 did a president break the precedent set in George Washington's day and address Congress in person. Only in Theodore Roosevelt's time did it become the custom for a State of the Union message to include a wish-list of legislation desired for the public good. Gradually, incrementally, presidents became more public and more energetic in their lobbying of lawmakers for measures that they found good and in doling out disfavor to the uncooperative.

Presidential power was just one part of the tapering of Congressional authority. Independent authorities proliferated: among them, the Interstate Commerce Commission, the Federal Trade Commission, the Federal Reserve Board. Cabinet offices multiplied: a full-blown Justice Department in 1870, a Bureau of Labor Statistics in 1884, an Agriculture Department in 1888, a Commerce Department in 1903, and a Labor Department in 1914. Each of them employed staff, enforcing existing laws, promulgating and interpreting regulations. By 1914, the lacerating edge of railroad regulation was not wielded by Congress, but by the Interstate Commerce Commissioners (Martin 1971; Kolko 1965). A regulatory state affected most Americans far more immediately and far more steadily than acts of Congress could do, and, to some extent, the fault lay with a Congress to which passing the buck to an independent agency came easier than working out the intricacies of complicated legislative Thou-Shalt-Nots (Harrison 2010).

At the same time, Congress found itself checked ever more severely by a Supreme Court determined to make itself a co-equal branch of government. Before the Civil War, the judges had overturned just two national laws. They passed judgment on hundreds thereafter. A new view of its police power allowed the Court to limit the scope of economic regulation. A fresh reading of the Fourteenth Amendment permitted conservative justices to give corporations the privileges of individuals, and the evolving doctrine of substantive due process only made the passage of legislation on consumers or workers' behalf that much trickier. Court decisions modified anti-trust laws' scope and wiped out the income tax for a generation, defined the permissible limits of railroad regulation and of controls on pooling, and, by defining what states could not do, generated the pressure that led to Congress creating the Interstate Commerce Commission in the first place. Progressive measures that carried Congress, notably the first child labor law, were overturned by the Supreme Court judgment; as was a successor measure using the taxing power to accomplish the same end.

Hemmed in and confined, outshone and outclassed, it was a wonder that Congress accomplished what it did. It is equally a wonder how little any scholars have done to answer the question, "How did Congress do?" with the counter-question, "Compared to what?" No studies have examined how, in terms of personal integrity, special interest control, growth of professionalism and decline of membership turnover, or just in success at handling its growing workload, Congress compared with state legislatures. Anyone familiar with the "Oil Room" that greased through railroad legislation in Nebraska or the "bell-ringers" of Albany, skilled at offering bills to alarm special interests and make them come running, cash in hand, to arrange for the measures' smothering, might suspect that the national legislature may have deserved its reputation as the greatest deliberative body in the world. Nor do studies exist to compare competence, effectiveness, and the relative freedom of members with that in other parliaments and chambers of deputies elsewhere. What were turnover rates like? How much, how more disorderly, were proceedings in Berlin, in Paris, or in Rome? And what was the trade-off between firmer control at the top and the ability to get things done?

In their evident effort to make Congress as uninteresting to the general reader as possible, political scientists have performed wonders. Historians, by contrast, commit sins of omission, not commission. Well aware that political history does not sell and that the discipline has found worlds elsewhere to embrace, they have steered away from the state studies and purely political accounts that half a century ago loaded up library shelves. Even the in-depth studies of economic measures (railroads particularly) to prove or disprove that regulatory reforms were the very best that money could buy, have vanished (Kolko 1965; Martin 1971). As presidential authority has increased and the clamor and glamour focuses on the occupant of the White House, what national political history exists has found itself tugged ever more into examining presidents and their role. The presidential lens skews and astigmatizes. Looking from Woodrow Wilson's or Theodore Roosevelt's spectacles, Congress appears in the distance. It is no initiating force—simply a reactive one, responding to the presidential program and either meeting or failing to meet his aspirations for America. Where, in biographers' treatment of the Square Deal, is Congress more than either a helpmeet or a hobbler, and in either case, far less enlightened than that man in the White House? For historians of the Gilded Age and Progressive Era, as any glance at purely historical scholarly journals show, Congress has become the neglected foundling, perhaps on the assumption that to hardly know it is to know it well. There are marvelous exceptions, of course: Martin Gold's examination of the making of Chinese exclusion policy and Robert Harrison's study of three disparate progressive reform agendas in the period between 1905 and 1911 (Gold 2012; Harrison 2010). But they enjoy too lonely an eminence. A voluminous but nowhere close to comprehensive list could be made of all the articles and books never written, about things in the Gilded Age that happened and statesmen who stood and delivered.

Amidst the mountains of research, so much is left undone. With a few honorable exceptions, scholars in recent years have left biography to journalists, grinding axes and ransacking professionals' work, without dipping more than a toe into the ocean of primary sources available. Presidents make good trade-book copy: the recent biographies of Grover Cleveland, either just plain travesties or else pale imitations of Allan Nevins's labor of love and Horace Samuel Merrill's edged critique, show clearly that among Gilded Age presidents, he is loved not so much for the enemies he made as for those the biographers wish he would make today (Nevins 1932; Merrill 1957; Walters 2012; Pafford 2013; Jeffers 2000; Lachman 2013; Brodsky 2000). Just lifting all the biographies of Theodore Roosevelt would give reviewers a strenuous life, and among them are best-selling heavyweights from Douglas Brinkley, Doris Kearns Goodwin,

David McCullough and Edmund Morris (Morris 1979, 2001, 2010; Brands 1997; Brinkley 2009; McCullough 1981; Goodwin 2013; Millard 2005). Together, they have given him far more than a square deal; there is even a worshipful collection of political cartoons, no less than what all that zest, zeal, teeth and temperament deserves (Marschall 2014). Woodrow Wilson gets pilloried by right-wing commentators deluding themselves into thinking they can author books or, on rare occasions, perhaps, even write them; fortunately, as he also is handled astutely and sympathetically by professionals like Arthur S. Link and John Milton Cooper (Napolitano 2012; Brands 2003; Berg 2013; Cooper 1983, 2009; Link 1947–65). The prospect of his neglect will never break the heart of the profession. But where on Capitol Hill shall the like be found?

The outliers, rare in their own time, and speaking to a less white-male-oriented age, have received some attention: among the last black congressmen in a Jim Crow America, scholars have honored Robert Smalls of South Carolina (Miller 1995) and North Carolina's George Henry White (Justesen 2001). Jeannette Rankin, the first congresswoman, is enshrined as well (Josephson 1974). In a class all by itself, Anderson's study of the "black Second" District of North Carolina (Anderson 1981), tells more about the dynamics of getting, keeping, and losing political power than anyone has done for any other congressional district anywhere; would that the same had been done for the "Shoestring" district in Mississippi, or, for that matter, for the dozen-plus districts where African American votes occasionally helped white candidates to a majority too firm to cheat them out of!

Mark Twain once joked about two boys, one of whom ran off to sea and the other of whom became vice president—and neither one was heard of again. To judge from the biographies, he could have said the same about most Speakers of the House, Thomas Brackett Reed excepted (Grant 2011; Hazard 2004; Robinson 1930). Not since the 1930s have biographers taken on Speakers John G. Carlisle (Barnes 1931), James G. Blaine (Muzzey 1934; Russell 1931), nor since the early 1950s "Uncle Joe" Cannon (Bolles 1951; Busbey 1927; Roger 1998). As for the rest, they rank among the great and not-so-great unknowns. The world will little note Michael C. Kerr, Joseph Warren Keifer (Pope 2002), David Henderson (Hoing 1957), and Charles Crisp (Malone 1962; Martin 1954), perhaps, but there is a far greater loss in the failure to cover the careers of Champ Clark and Samuel J. Randall (House 1934), who, whether wielding the gavel or leading the Democratic minority, proved among the ablest parliamentary practitioners.

Senators, particularly progressives, fare better: Hiram Johnson (Lower 1993; Weatherson 1995), William Borah (McKenna 1961), Albert Beveridge (Bowers 1932; Braeman 1971), Jonathan P. Dolliver (Ross 1958), George Norris (Lowitt 1963, 1971; Budig 2013), all have their chroniclers, and the most progressive, Robert La Follette, is far more than merely a Wisconsin ideal (Margulies 1976; Weisberger 1994; Unger 2000; Thelen 1976). Strident white supremacists like James K. Vardaman, Tom Watson, and Ben Tillman made too lively a stir in their own time to rest unattended since. (Holmes 1970; Woodward 1938; Simkins 1944; Kantrowitz 2000). Once upon a time, the foremost standpatters like William Boyd Allison (Sage 1956) and Henry Cabot Lodge (Garraty 1953; Widenor 1980) had a biographers prepared to rehabilitate their faded reputations. But how much they could use company! The only thing more monumental than Senator John Sherman's half-century career is his papers—rivaling those that Randall kept—but it is his military brother who gets all the attention, with a line of biographies long enough to march from Atlanta to the sea: proof that war is not just hell but a best-seller. Only in imagination does the rough, rotten history of Pennsylvania politics get its due with a modern biography of Boies Penrose, perhaps because only a Rabelais could do him justice. The constructive contrary-mindedness of George F. Edmunds will never find an immortalizer, even among his fellow-Vermonters, and Texas is not big enough to find anyone to examine the mixture of white supremacy and classical liberalism that made Roger Q. Mills a notable figure in both House and Senate. The wiles of Nelson J. Dingley, the verbal pyrotechnics of John Sharp Williams, the occasional statesmanship and common oratorical thunders of Daniel W. Voorhees, "Tall Sycamore of the Wabash," go unexamined. So, too, do the productive careers of William S. Holman and William D. "Pig-Iron" Kelley, two of the record-holders for House service in their day, heads of Appropriations and Ways and Means Committees, whose involvement in politics began in the 1850s and lasted into the 1890s. From any of the last five, an effective study could be made of how, exactly, legislation worked or stopped cold in the long Gilded Age and Progressive Era.

Rare were the Randalls and many the one-shots and mediocrities, but it may be from them—from all of them—that a real understanding might come of how, from day to day, session to session, the Congress ran, of what it took to be elected or reelected, of the vagaries of personality and constituency service that marked, made, or ended the careers of the nonentities crying out for no biography at all, the Amos Cummingses and Buck Kilgores. What history needs (though of course it will never get it) is a vast, money-losing volume, based on the present-day biennial mainstay, Michael J. Barone's *Almanac of American Politics: A Wayfaring Stranger's Guide to the Political Galaxy* for 1886, 1894, 1910, or 1914. Such a tome might condense into a few thousand pages of minuscule type the voting records and political ups and downs of members of the House and Senate in a time when re-election was far from certain and turnover the fact of life. All it would require to write and publish one would be a donor accustomed to throwing away millions of dollars on forlorn hopes—as, in fact, most donors to political campaigns already do.

References

Abram, Michael and Joseph Cooper. 1968. "The Rise of Seniority in the House of Representatives." *Polity* 1, 1: 52–85.

Aldrich, John H., and David W. Rohde. 2005. "Congressional Committees in a Partisan Era." In *Congress Reconsidered*, ed. Lawrence C. Dodd and Bruce I. Oppenheimer. 8th edn. Washington, DC: Congressional Quarterly Press.

Alexander, De Alva. 1916. *History and Procedure of the House of Representatives.* Boston: Houghton Mifflin.

Anderson, Eric. 1981. *Race and Politics in North Carolina, 1872–1901: The Black Second.* Baton Rouge: Louisiana State University.

Argersinger, Peter. 2012. *Representation and Inequality in Late Nineteenth-Century America: The Politics of Apportionment.* Cambridge: Cambridge University Press.

Balch, Stephen. 1972. "Party Government in the United States House of Representatives, 1911–1919." PhD diss., University of California at Berkeley.

Barfield, Claude E. 1965. "The Democratic Party in Congress, 1909–1913," PhD diss., Northwestern University.

—. 1970. "'Our Share of the Booty': The Democratic Party, Cannonism, and the Payne–Aldrich Tariff." *Journal of American History* 57, 2: 308–323.

Barnes, James A. 1931. *John G. Carlisle: Financial Statesman.* New York: Dodd, Mead.

Beatty, Jack. 2007. *Age of Betrayal: The Triumph of Money in America, 1865–1900.* New York: Knopf.

Bensel, Richard F. 2000. *The Political Economy of American Industrialization, 1877–1900.* Cambridge: Cambridge University Press.

Berg, Andrew Scott. 2013. *Wilson.* New York: G. P. Putnam's.

Bernhard, William and Brian Sala. 2006. "The Remaking of an American Senate: The 17th Amendment and Ideological Responsiveness." *Journal of Politics* 68, 2: 345–357.

Bierce, Ambrose. 1970. *Fantastic Fables.* New York: Dover.

Bolles, Blair. 1951. *Tyrant from Illinois: Uncle Joe Cannon's Experiment with Personal Power.* New York: W.W. Norton.

Bowers, Claude G. 1932. *Beveridge and the Progressive Era.* Boston: Houghton Mifflin.

Brady, David W. 1972. "Congressional Leadership and Party Voting in the McKinley Era: A Comparison to the Modern House." *Midwest Journal of Politics* 6, 2: 439–459.

—. 1973. *Congressional Voting in a Partisan Era.* Lawrence: University of Kansas Press.

— and Philip Althoff. 1974. "Party Voting in the U.S. House of Representatives, 1890–1910: Elements of a Responsible Party System." *Journal of Politics* 36, 3: 753–775.

— and David Epstein. 1997. "Intraparty Preferences, Heterogeneity, and the Origins of the Modern Congress: Progressive Reformers in the House and Senate, 1890–1920." *Journal of Law, Economics, and Organization* 13, 1: 26–49.

—, Richard Brody, and David Epstein. 1989. "Heterogeneous Parties and Political Organization: The U.S. Senate, 1880–1920." *Legislative Studies Quarterly* 14 2: 205–223.

Braeman, John. 1971. *Albert J. Beveridge: American Nationalist.* Chicago: University of Chicago Press.

Brands, Henry W. 1997. *T. R.: The Last Romantic.* New York: Basic Books.

—. 2003. *Woodrow Wilson.* New York: Times Books.

Brinkley, Douglas. 2009. *The Wilderness Warrior: Theodore Roosevelt and the Crusade for America.* New York: HarperCollins.

Brock, William R. 1984. *Investigation and Responsibility: Public Responsibility in the United States.* Cambridge: Cambridge University Press.

Brodsky, Alyn. 2000. *Grover Cleveland: A Study in Character.* New York: St. Martin's Press.

Bryce, James. 1891. *The American Commonwealth.* 2 volumes. New York: Macmillan.

Budig, Gene A. 2013. *George Norris, Going Home: Reflections of a Progressive Statesman.* Lincoln: University of Nebraska Press.

Busbey, L. White. 1927. *Uncle Joe Cannon: the Story of a Pioneer American.* New York: H. Holt and Company.

Calhoun, Charles W. 1996. "Political Economy in the Gilded Age: The Republican Party's Industrial Policy." *Journal of Policy History* 8, 3: 291–309.

Canon, David. T., Garrison Nelson, and Charles Stewart III. 2002. *Committees in the U.S. Congress, 1789–1946.* 4 volumes. Washington, DC: Congressional Quarterly Press.

Caro, Robert. 2002. *The Years of Lyndon Johnson: Master of the Senate.* New York: Knopf.

Cooper, John M. 1983. *The Warrior and the Priest: Woodrow Wilson and Theodore Roosevelt.* Cambridge: Belknap Press/Harvard University Press.

—. 2009. *Woodrow Wilson: A Biography.* New York: Knopf.

Cox, Gary W. and Matthew D. McCubbins. 2002. "Agenda Power in the U.S. House of Representatives, 1877 to 1986." In *Party, Process, and Political Change in Congress*, ed. David W. Brady and Matthew D. McCubbins. Palo Alto: Stanford University Press.

Current, Richard N. 1950. *Pine Logs and Politics: A Life of Philetus Sawyer, 1816–1900.* Madison: State Historical Society of Wisconsin.

Dion, Douglas. 1997. *Turning the Legislative Thumbscrew: Minority Rights and Procedural Change in Congress.* Ann Arbor: University of Michigan Press.

Edwards, Rebecca. 1997. *Angels in the Machinery: Gender in American Party Politics from the Civil War to the Progressive Era.* New York: Oxford University Press.

Engstrom, Erik J., and Samuel Kernell. 2005 "Manufactured Responsiveness: The Impact of State Electoral Laws on Unified Party Control of the Presidency and House of Representatives, 1840–1940." *American Journal of Political Science* 49, 3: 531–549.

Fiorina, Morris P., David W. Rohde, and Peter Wissel. 1975. "Historical Change in House Turnover." In *Congress in Change: Evolution and Reform*, ed. Norman J. Ornstein. New York: Praeger.

Forgette, Richard G. 1997. "Reed's Rules and the Partisan Theory of Legislative Organization." *Polity* 29, 3: 382–384.

Garraty, John A. 1953. *Henry Cabot Lodge: A Biography.* New York: Knopf.

Gold, Martin B. 2012. *Forbidden Citizens: Chinese Exclusion and the U.S. Congress: A Legislative History.* Washington, DC: TheCapitolNet.

Goodwin, Doris K. 2013. *The Bully Pulpit: Theodore Roosevelt, William Howard Taft, and the Golden Age of Journalism.* New York: Simon and Schuster.

Grant, James. 2011. *Mr. Speaker! The Life and Times of Thomas B. Reed, The Man Who Broke the Filibuster.* New York: Simon and Schuster.

Green, Matthew N. 2002. "Institutional Change, Party Discipline and the House Democratic Caucus, 1911–1919." *Legislative Studies Quarterly* 27, 4: 601–633.

Gyory, Andrew. 1998. *Closing the Gate: Politics and the Chinese Exclusion Act.* Chapel Hill: University of North Carolina Press.

Harrison, Robert. 2010. *Congress, Progressive Reform and the New American State.* Cambridge: Cambridge University Press.

Hazard, Wendy. 2004. "Thomas Brackett Reed, Civil Rights, and the Fight for Fair Elections." *Maine History* 42, 1: 1–23.

High, Jack and Clayton A. Coppin. 1988. "Wiley and the Whiskey Industry: Strategic Behavior in the Passage of the Pure Food Act." *Business History Review* 62, 2: 286–309.

Hinckley, Barbara. 1971. *The Seniority System in Congress.* Bloomington: Indiana University Press.

Hoing, Willard L. 1957. "David B. Henderson: Speaker of the House." *Iowa Journal of History* 55, 1: 1–34.

Holmes, William F. 1970. *White Chief: James Kimble Vardaman.* Baton Rouge: Louisiana State University Press.

House, Albert V. 1934. "The Political Career of Samuel Jackson Randall." PhD diss., University of Wisconsin.

Jacob, Kathryn A. 2009. *King of the Lobby: The Life and Times of Sam Ward, Man About Washington in the Gilded Age.* Baltimore: Johns Hopkins University Press.

James, Scott C. 2007. "Timing and Sequence in Congressional Elections: Interstate Contagion and America's Nineteenth-Century Scheduling Regime." *Studies in American Political Development* 21, 2: 181–202.

James, Scott C., and Brian L. Lawson. 1999. "The Political Economy of Voting Rights Enforcement in America's Gilded Age: Electoral College Competition, Partisan Commitment, and the Federal Election Law." *American Political Science Review* 93, 1: 115–131.

Jeffers, Harry P. 2000. *An Honest President: The Life and Presidencies of Grover Cleveland.* New York: W. Morrow.

Jenkins, Jeffery A. 2004. "Partisanship and Contested Election Cases in the House of Representatives, 1789–2002." *Studies in American Political Development* 18, 1: 113–135.

—. 2007. "The First 'Southern Strategy': The Republican Party and Contested-Election Cases in the Late 19th-Century House." In *Party, Process, and Political Change in Congress. Volume 2: Further New Perspectives on the History of Congress,* ed. David W. Brady and Matthew D. McCubbins. Palo Alto: Stanford University Press.

John, Richard R. 2004. "Farewell to the 'Party Period': Political Economy in Nineteenth-Century America." *Journal of Policy History* 16, 2: 117–125.

—. 2006. "Ruling Passions, Political Economy in Nineteenth-Century America." *Journal of Policy History* 18, 1: 1–20.

Jones, Charles O. 1968. "Joseph G. Cannon and Howard W. Smith: An Essay on the Limits of Leadership in the House of Representatives." *Journal of Politics* 30, 3: 617–646.

Josephson, Hannah. 1974. *Jeanette Rankin, First Lady in Congress: A Biography.* Indianapolis, IN: Bobbs-Merrill.

Josephson, Matthew. 1938. *The Politicos.* San Diego: Harcourt, Brace.

Justesen, Benjamin R. 2001: *George Henry. White: An Even Chance in the Race of Life.* Baton Rouge: Louisiana State University Press.

Kantrowitz, Stephen. 2000. *Ben Tillman and the Reconstruction of White Supremacy.* Chapel Hill: University of North Carolina Press.

Keller, Morton. 1977. *Affairs of State: Public Life in Late-Nineteenth-Century America.* Cambridge: Belknap Press/ Harvard University Press.

Kernell, Samuel. 1977. "Toward Understanding Nineteenth Century Congressional Careers: Ambition, Competition, and Rotation." *American Journal of Political Science* 21, 4: 669–693.

Koko, Gabriel S. 1965. *Railroads and Regulation, 1877–1916.* Princeton, NJ: Princeton University Press.

Krehbiel, Keith. 2005. "Joe Cannon and the Minority Party: Tyranny or Bipartisanship?" *Legislative Studies Quarterly* 30, 4: 479–505.

— and Alan E. Wiseman. 2001. "Joseph G. Cannon: Majoritarian from Illinois." *Legislative Studies Quarterly* 26, 3: 357–389.

Lachman, Charles. 2013. *A Secret Life: The Lies and Scandals of President Grover Cleveland.* New York: Skyhorse Publishing.

Link, Arthur S. 1947–1965. *Wilson.* 5 volumes. Princeton, NJ: Princeton University Press.

Lower, Richard C. 1993. *A Bloc of One: The Political Career of Hiram W. Johnson.* Palo Alto: Stanford University Press.

Lowitt, Richard. 1963. *George W. Norris: The Making of a Progressive.* Syracuse, NY: Syracuse University Press.

—. 1971. *George W. Norris: The Persistence of a Progressive, 1913–1933.* Urbana: University of Illinois Press.

McCormick, Richard L. 1986. *The Party Period and Public Policy: American Politics from the Age of Jackson to the Progressive Era.* New York: Oxford University Press.

McCullough, David. 1981. *Mornings on Horseback.* New York: Simon and Schuster.

McDonagh, Eileen L. 1989. "Issues and Constituencies in the Progressive Era: House Roll Call Voting on the Nineteenth Amendment, 1913–1919." *Journal of Politics* 51, 1: 119–136.

—. 1993. "Constituency Influence on House Roll-Call Votes in the Progressive Era, 1913–1915." *Legislative Studies Quarterly* 18, 2: 185–210.

McKenna, Marion C. 1961. *Borah.* Ann Arbor: University of Michigan Press.

Malone, Preston S. C. 1962. "The Political Career of Charles Frederick Crisp." PhD diss., University of Georgia.

Margulies, Herbert F. 1976. "Robert M. La Follette Goes to the Senate, 1905." *Wisconsin Magazine of History and Biography* 59, 3: 214–225.

Marschall, Rick. 2011. *Bully! The Life and Times of Theodore Roosevelt Illustrated with More Than 250 Vintage Political Cartoons.* New York: Regnery History.

Martin, Albro S. 1971. *Enterprise Denied: Origins of the Decline of American Railroads, 1897–1917.* New York: Columbia University Press.

Martin, S. Walter. 1954. "Charles F. Crisp: Speaker of the House." *Georgia Review* 8, 2: 164–177.

Merrill, Horace S. 1957. *Bourbon Leader Grover Cleveland and the Democratic Party.* Boston: Little, Brown.

Millard, Candice. 2005. *The River of Doubt: Theodore Roosevelt's Darkest Journey*. New York: Doubleday.

Miller, Edward A., Jr. 1995. *Gullah Statesman: Robert Smalls from Slavery to Congress, 1839–1915*. Columbia: University of South Carolina.

Miranti, Paul J. 1986. "Associationalism, Statism and Professional Regulation: Public Accountants and the Reform of Financial Markets, 1896–1940." *Business History Review* 60, 3: 438–468.

Morgan, H. Wayne. 1969. *From Hayes to McKinley: National Party Politics, 1877–1896*. Syracuse: Syracuse University Press.

Morris, Edmund. 1979. *The Rise of Theodore Roosevelt*. New York: Coward, McCann, and Geoghan.

—. 2001. *Theodore Rex*. New York: Random House.

—. 2010. *Colonel Roosevelt*. New York: Random House.

Muzzey, David S. 1934. *James G. Blaine: A Political Idol of Other Days*. New York: Dodd, Mead.

Napolitano, Andrew P. 2012. *Theodore and Woodrow: How Two American Presidents Destroyed Constitutional Freedom*. Nashville, TN: Thomas Nelson.

Nevins, Allan. 1932. *Grover Cleveland: A Study in Courage*. New York: Dodd, Mead.

Norris, George W. 1945. *Fighting Liberal*. New York: Macmillan.

Pafford, John M. 2013. *The Forgotten Conservative: Rediscovering Grover Cleveland*. New York: Regnery.

Peters, Ronald M., Jr. 1997. *The American Speakership: The Office in Historical Perspective*, 2nd edn. Baltimore, MD: Johns Hopkins University Press.

Phillips, David G. 1964. *The Treason of the Senate*. Chicago: Quadrangle Books.

Polsby, Nelson W. 1968. "The Institutionalization of the U.S. House of Representatives." American Political Science Review 62, 1: 144–168.

Polsby, Nelson W., Miriam Gallaher, and Barry S. Rundquist. 1969. "The Growth of the Seniority System in the U.S. House of Representatives." *American Political Science Review* 63, 3: 787–807.

Pope, Thomas E. 2002. *The Weary Boys: Colonel J. Warren Keifer and the 110th Ohio Volunteer Infantry*. Kent, OH: Kent State University Press.

Reed, Thomas B. 1889a. "Rules of the House of Representatives." *Century Magazine* 37: 792–795.

—. 1889b. "Obstruction in the National House." *North American Review* 149: 431–428.

Ritchie, Donald A. 1992. *Press Gallery: Congress and the Washington Correspondents*. Cambridge, MA: Harvard University Press.

Robinson, William A. 1930. *Thomas B. Reed: Parliamentarian*. New York: Dodd and Mead.

Roger, Scott W. 1998. "Uncle Joe Cannon: The Brakeman of the House of Representatives, 1903–1911." In *Masters of the House: Congressional Leadership over Two Centuries*, ed. Raymond W. Smock and Susan W. Hammond. Boulder, CO: Westview Press.

Ross, Thomas R. 1958. *Jonathan Prentiss Dolliver: A Study in Political Integrity and Independence*. Iowa City: State Historical Society of Iowa.

Rothman, David J. 1966. *Politics and Power: The United States Senate, 1869–1901*. Cambridge, MA: Harvard University Press.

Russell, Charles E. 1931. *Blaine of Maine*. New York: Cosmopolitan Book Corporation.

Sage, Leland. 1956. *William Boyd Allison: A Study in Practical Politics*. Iowa City: State Historical Society of Iowa.

Sanders, Elizabeth. 1999. *Roots of Reform: Farmers, Workers, and the American State, 1877–1917*. Chicago: University of Chicago Press.

Sanders, Haywood T. 1980. "Paying for the 'Bloody Shirt': the Politics of Civil War Pensions." In *Political Benefits*, ed. Barry S. Rundquist. Lexington: D.C. Heath and Co.

Sarasohn, David. 1989. *The Party of Reform: Democrats in the Progressive Era*. Jackson: University Press of Mississippi.

Schiller, Wendy J. 2006. "Building Careers and Courting Constituents: U.S. Senate Representation 1889–1924." *Studies in American Political Development* 20, 2: 185–197.

—, and Charles Stewart III. 2014. *Electing the Senate: Indirect Democracy before the Seventeenth Amendment*. Princeton, NJ: Princeton University Press.

Simkins, Francis B. 1944. *Pitchfork Ben Tillman, South Carolinian*. Baton Rouge: Lousiana State University Press.

Skocpol, Theda. 1992. *Protecting Soldiers and Mothers: The Political Origins of Social Policy in the United States*. Cambridge: Belknap Press/Harvard University Press.

Skowronek, Stephen. 1982. *Building a New American State: The Expansion of National Administrative Capacities, 1877–1920*. Cambridge: Cambridge University Press.

Thelen, David P. 1976. *Robert La Follette and the Insurgent Spirit*. Boston: Little, Brown.

Thompson, Margaret S. 1985. *The "Spider Web": Congress and Lobbying in the Age of Grant*. Ithaca, NY: Cornell University Press.

Unger, Nancy. 2000. *Fighting Bob La Follette: The Righteous Reformer*. Chapel Hill: University of North Carolina Press.

Upchurch, Thomas A. 2004. *Legislating Racism: The Billion Dollar Congress and the Birth of Jim Crow*. Lexington: University Press of Kentucky.

Valelly, Richard. M. 2009. "The Reed Rules and Republican Party Building: A New Look." *Studies in American Political Development* 23, 2: 115–142.

Walters, Ryan S. 2012. *The Last Jeffersonian: Grover Cleveland and the Path to Restoring the Republic*. Nashville, TN: Westbow.

Wander, W. Thomas. 1972. "Patterns of Change in the Congressional Budget Process, 1865–1974." *Congress and the Presidency* 9, 4: 501–527.

Weatherson, Michael A. 1995. *Hiram Johnson: Political Revivalist*. Lanham, MD: University Press of America.

Weisberger, Bernard A. 1994. *The La Follettes of Wisconsin: Love and Politics in Progressive America*. Madison: University of Wisconsin Press.

White, Leonard D. 1958. *The Republican Era, 1869–1901: A Study in Administrative History*. New York: Macmillan.

Widenor, William C. 1980. *Henry Cabot Lodge and the Search for an American Foreign Policy*. Berkeley: University of California.

Wiebe, Robert H. 1967. *The Search for Order, 1877–1920*. New York: Hill & Wang.

Wilson, Rick K. 1986. "What Was It Worth to Be on a Committee in the U.S. House, 1889 to 1913?" *Legislative Studies Quarterly* 11, 1: 47–63.

Wilson, Woodrow. 1900 *Congressional Government: A Study in American Politics*. Boston: Houghton Mifflin.

Wood, Donna J. 1985. "The Strategic Use of Public Policy: Business Support for the 1906 Food and Drug Act." *Business History Review* 59, 3: 403–32.

Woodward, C. Vann. 1938. *Tom Watson, Agrarian Rebel*. New York: Macmillan.

Further Reading

Aldrich, John H., David W. Rohde, and Michael W. Tofias. 2007. "One D is not Enough: Measuring Conditional Party Government, 1887–2002." In *Party, Process, and Political Change in Congress. Volume 2: Further New Perspectives on the History of Congress*, ed. David W. Brady and Matthew D. McCubbins. Palo Alto: Stanford University Press.

Bensel, Richard F. 1990. *Yankee Leviathan: The Origins of Central State Authority in America, 1859–1877.* Cambridge: Cambridge University Press.

Binder, Sarah. 1997. *Minority Rights, Majority Rule: Partisanship and the Development of Congress.* Cambridge: Cambridge University Press.

Brady, David W. and Mark A. Morgan. 1987. "Reforming the Structure of the House Appropriations Process: The Effects of the 1885 and 1919–20 Reforms on Money Decisions." In *Congress: Structure and Policy*, ed. Matthew McCubbins and Terry Sullivan. Cambridge: Cambridge University Press.

Brady, David W., Richard Brody, and David Epstein. 1989. "Heterogeneous Parties and Political Organization: The U.S. Senate, 1880–1920." *Legislative Studies Quarterly* 14, 2: 205–223.

Brady, David W., Kara Buckley, and Douglas Rivers. 1999. "The Roots of Careerism in the U.S. House of Representatives." *Legislative Studies Quarterly* 24, 4: 489–510.

Brady, David W. and Joseph Stewart. 1982. "Congressional Party Realignment and Transformations of Public Policy in Three Realignment Eras." *American Journal of Political Science* 26, 2: 333–360.

Campbell, Andrea C., Gary W. Cox, and Matthew D. McCubbins. 2002. "Agenda Power in the U.S. Senate, 1877–1986." In *Party, Process, and Political Change in Congress, ed.* David W. Brady and Matthew D. McCubbins. Palo Alto: Stanford University Press.

Cooper, Joseph and Cheryl D. Young. 1989. "Bill Introduction in the Nineteenth Century: A Study of Institutional Change." *Legislative Studies Quarterly* 14, 1: 67–105.

Finocchiaro, Charles J., and David W. Rohde. 2007. "Speaker David Henderson and the Partisan Era of the U.S. House." In *Party, Process, and Political Change in Congress, Volume 2: Further New Perspectives on the History of Congress*, ed. David W. Brady and Matthew D. McCubbins. Palo Alto: Stanford University Press.

Hurley, Patricia and Rick K. Wilson. 1989. "Partisan Voting Patterns in the U.S. Senate, 1877–1986." *Legislative Studies Quarterly* 14, 2: 225–250.

Jenkins, Jeffery A. and Timothy P. Nokken. 2008. "Legislative Shirking in the Pre-Twentieth Amendment Era: Presidential Influence, Party Power, and Lame-Duck Sessions of Congress, 1877–1933." *Studies in American Political Development* 22, 1: 111–140.

Jenkins, Jeffery A. and Charles Stewart III. 2013. *Fighting for the Speakership: The House and the Rise of Party Government.* Princeton, NJ: Princeton University Press.

Johnson, Kimberly S. 2011. "Racial Orders, Congress, and the Agricultural Welfare State, 1865–1940." *Studies in American Political Development* 25, 2: 143–161.

Jonathan, N. Katz and R. Sala Brian. 1996. "Careerism, Committee Assignments, and the Electoral Connection." *American Political Science Review* 90, 1: 21–33.

Kolko, Gabriel S. 1963. *The Triumph of Conservatism: A Reinterpretation of American History, 1900–1916.* New York: Free Press of Glencoe.

Stewart III, C., and Barry R. Weingast. 1992. "Stacking the Senate, Changing the Nation: Republican Rotten Boroughs, Statehood Politics, and American Political Development." *Studies in American Political Development* 6, 2: 223–271.

Swenson, Peter. 1982. "The Influence of Recruitment on the Structure of Power in the U.S. House, 1870–1940." *Legislative Studies Quarterly* 7, 1: 7–36.

Usselman, Steven W., and Richard R. John. 2006. "Patent Politics: Intellectual Property, the Railroad Industry, and the Problem of Monopoly." *Journal of Policy History* 18, 1: 96–125.

Wolf, Thomas W. 1981. "Congressional Sea Change: Conflict and Organizational Accommodation in the House of Representatives, 1878–1921." Ph. D. dissertation, MIT.

Chapter Twenty-Seven

Revising Constitutional History

Logan E. Sawyer III

Through the 1970s, the standard account of the Gilded and Progressive Era legal history was a remarkably potent brew of progressive historiography's emphasis on class conflict and legal realism's doubts about the causal role of legal reasoning. That progressive synthesis asked why the Supreme Court before the New Deal was so willing to frustrate efforts to use state authority to solve the problems of industrial capitalism. The answer it offered was that the Court used abstract legal categories to camouflage its campaign to protect a Darwinian, laissez-faire economic order that placed the interests of capitalists over the interests of workers, farmers, consumers, and even children.

By the 1980s, a new standard account had emerged that offered a very different answer to the same core question. That revisionist account looked beyond the progressive emphasis on interests and argued instead that ideas best explained the judiciary's opposition to the expansion of state authority. It first noted that the Supreme Court approved significantly more economic regulation than the progressive synthesis recognized, then argued that the Court frustrated some efforts to address the problems of industrial capitalism but not others because it was influenced by entrenched Jacksonian equal rights and free labor ideologies; an honest, if misguided, faith in the efficacy and importance of local authority; and a particular affinity for categorical and abstract styles of reasoning. In the revisionist account, the Court was no handmaiden of business interests. It was instead engaged in a misguided, perhaps even tragic, effort to protect nineteenth-century visions of liberty with the tools of nineteenth-century legal thought in a world that industrialization had changed forever.

The 1990s, however, saw the field fracture. The legal history of the Gilded Age and Progressive Era, like the rest of American history, was extended into new areas by scholars raising new questions. Historians inspired by the techniques of social history investigated the role of women, minorities, and other historically disadvantaged groups. Others complicated the original revisionist focus on ideas by looking beyond formalism, free labor, and equal rights. Some examined the role of race, gender, and citizenship; others the influence of religion and alternative forms of legal thought. Of similar importance were scholars who pushed beyond ideas to ask about the role of institutional arrangements, especially the institutions of state authority. These new questions and approaches did not reject the revisionist narrative. They used it as a base to extend the boundaries of legal history far beyond revisionism's original focus while simultaneously enriching understandings of core revisionist claims.

More recently, however, some scholars have sharpened these extensions into outright challenges to revisionism's central claims. A neoprogressive account challenges revisionism's focus on ideas and resurrects the progressive synthesis's focus on class. Some question whether formalism was a characteristic of the period's legal thought. A third challenge rejects the core question asked by both progressives and revisionists. Rather than asking why the judiciary limited the authority of the state, this third challenge argues the field should work to explain how the judiciary worked in tandem with the legislature and the administrative state to shape society and the economy. Together with the extensions and complications of the original revisionist account, these unresolved challenges make the legal history of the Gilded Age and Progressive Era a capacious and exciting field.

A Companion to the Gilded Age and Progressive Era, First Edition. Edited by Christopher McKnight Nichols and Nancy C. Unger.
© 2017 John Wiley & Sons, Inc. Published 2017 by John Wiley & Sons, Inc.

Framing Gilded and Progressive Era Legal History: The Progressive Synthesis

Since nearly the Progressive Era itself, issues raised by the progressive synthesis have framed the legal history of the decades surrounding the turn of the twentieth century. In the shadow of conflict over the New Deal, historians asked why the judiciary so firmly resisted efforts to use state power to solve the problems of industrial capitalism. The progressive synthesis answered that question by combining progressive historiography's emphasis on class conflict with legal realism's doubts about the causal importance of legal categories into a powerful and lasting indictment of the Court. The judiciary, it claimed, manipulated legal categories in order to advance a Darwinian, laissez-faire economic order that placed the interests of rapacious capitalists above those of workers, farmers, consumers, and even children (Paul 1960; Twiss 1942; McCloskey 1960; Jackson 1941; Corwin 1941).

More than a handful of high-profile decisions support those claims. During the Gilded Age and Progressive Era the Court limited the state's authority to set railroad and other rates, break up monopolies, regulate the hours and conditions of work, and institute a progressive income tax. Simultaneously, it restricted the tactics labor unions could employ and undermined their ability to organize.

Many of those decisions rested on the Fourteenth Amendment's due process clause. No state, that clause reads, shall deprive any person of life, liberty, or property without due process of law. Perhaps the most famous interpretation of the clause was *Lochner v. New York*, a decision that often provides the title for the era. There, the Court invalidated a New York state maximum hour law for bakers on the grounds that the Fourteenth Amendment's protection of liberty extended to a laborer's "liberty of contract." Liberty of contract, the Court explained, allowed the state to interfere with a worker's right to sell his own labor only when the state was exercising its police power—the vaguely defined authority to protect the health, morals, and welfare of the community. The New York statute, the Court found by a one vote majority, was not a health measure, but was instead an unconstitutional interference with the bakers' liberty of contract. Justice Holmes's famous dissent saw the decision as an example of the court's commitment to social Darwinism.

Liberty of contract doctrine not only restricted the ability of laborers to call on the government to limit hours of work, it also restricted their efforts to use government to advance labor organizing. In *Adair v. United States* and *Coppage v. Kansas*, the Court held that liberty of contract would not allow the state to outlaw "yellow dog" contracts—employment contracts that prohibited workers from joining a labor union. What seemed clear to many laborers at the time, and to the progressive historians later, was that liberty of contract really protected the ability of employers to keep wages low and working conditions poor.

The progressive synthesis also drew support from cases interpreting the Fourteenth Amendment's protection of property. In 1877, *Munn v. Illinois* recognized that the Fourteenth Amendment allowed the state to regulate rates for any business "affected with a public interest," which included both common carriers like railroads, and, the Court held, the grain elevators that farmers needed to access railroads and national markets. But despite *Munn*'s suggestion that the category of business affected with a public interest would be capacious, the Court instead followed the lead of Justice Stephen Field's *Munn* dissent. Between *Munn* and *Wolff Packing Co. v. Court of Industrial Relations* in 1923, the category of businesses affected with a public interest—and thus the state's authority to regulate rates—saw almost no expansion. The Court also kept a watchful eye on the rates set for railroads and other industries that did qualify as businesses affected with a public interest. In *Smyth v. Ames*, for example, the Court held that the Constitution prohibited rates so low they would deny railroad investors a fair return on their investment. The Court protected property rights in other ways as well. The first income tax, which applied only to the top 2% of earners, was invalidated in *Pollock v. Farmers Loan & Trust Co.* on the basis of an obscure prohibition on "direct taxes."

Some of the Court's best known federalism decisions offered further support for the progressive synthesis. Most importantly, concern with the division of authority between the state and federal governments allowed the continued growth of the trusts—those businesses of nationwide scope that were one of the chief concerns of public policy. In *United States v. E.C. Knight* the Court appeared to gut the landmark Sherman Antitrust Act when it ruled that a business combination in control of 98% of the nation's sugar refining capacity was beyond the reach of the law because the Constitution only gave Congress authority to regulate "commerce among the states." Sugar refining, the Court held, was manufacturing, not commerce, and thus could be regulated only by the states. Critics noted that it was the states' failure to address the trust problem that had prompted the Sherman Act in the first place. In later cases, the government found some success prosecuting the trusts, including railroads like J.P. Morgan's Northern Securities Company in 1903, and the American Tobacco and Standard Oil companies in 1911. But in upholding the prosecutions of loose business combinations, and in adopting the "rule of reason" interpretation of the Sherman Act—which permitted "reasonable" restrictions on trade—the Court effectively encouraged the growth of integrated corporations of nationwide scope. Lawyers were quick to see these doctrines made integrated corporations less vulnerable to antitrust prosecutions than loose combinations.

The Court's federalism doctrines protected business in other ways, too. In 1918, the Court's decision in *Hammer v. Dagenhart* struck down an attempt to use federal power over commerce to attack the problem of child labor. Though the statute operated by prohibiting the interstate shipment of goods produced by factories that employed children, the Court held that the law was not, for constitutional purposes, a regulation of interstate commerce. It was instead an attempt to regulate employment, which was properly the province of state regulation. Again, critics noted, it was the states' failure to act that had made the federal law necessary. Congress's second attempt to limit child labor was based on its power to tax, but it met a similar fate in *Bailey v. Drexel Furniture*.

The progressive synthesis also noted that while the Court's federalism doctrines limited the national government's authority to break up trusts and stop child labor, it did not stop the Court from upholding the use of the Sherman Act against labor unions. Coordinated boycotts by labor unions, the Court held in *Loewe v. Lawlor* in 1908, fell within the Act's prohibition of conspiracies in restraint of trade. Nor did concerns with federalism stop the Court from approving the use of federal injunctions to help end the strikes, including the Pullman Strike in *In Re Debs* in 1894.

The progressive synthesis had heroes as well as villains. Among the prominent heroes was future Justice Louis Brandeis, who as a lawyer brought important cases that made inroads into the Court's laissez faire doctrine. His "Brandeis Brief" and ultimate victory in *Muller v. Oregon*, which upheld a maximum-hour law for women, was one example. But above all, it was Justice Oliver Wendell Holmes who was lionized. Holmes' pithy dissent in *Lochner v. New York* crystalized the progressive synthesis's critique of the Court. The 14th Amendment, Holmes quipped, did not enact the social Darwinism of "Mr. Herbert Spenser's Social Statics." Holmes's dissents, Brandeis's litigation, and the critiques of leading progressive academics helped reveal the Court's commitment to laissez-faire. But, in the progressive synthesis, ultimate credit for ending the laissez faire era went to Franklin Roosevelt. His appointments to the Court combined with the political pressure applied through his Court Packing Plan to put laissez-faire constitutionalism into a well-deserved grave.

Revisionism Emerges

Revisionism's response to the progressive synthesis asked the same core question: How ought the Court's resistance to the use of government be understood, especially its opposition to the use of national authority to address the problems of industrial capitalism? But while the progressive synthesis adopted the behavioralist assumptions of legal realism and focused on the importance of interests, a group of revisionist scholars in the 1970s drew on ongoing intellectual developments, a new historiography of Reconstruction, and a deeper evidentiary base to emphasize the importance of ideas.

Early revisionists, including Alan Jones, Michael Les Benedict, and Charles McCurdy agreed that the Court's regime of laissez-faire formalism limited the state's ability to address the problems of industrial capitalism. But they saw a more complex pattern of decisions than the progressives, and offered a new kind of explanation (Jones 1967; Benedict 1985; McCurdy 1975). They built their explanations on the recognition, first emphasized by Charles Warren in 1913, that the Court in the Gilded Age and Progressive Era upheld far more economic regulations than it struck down. By Warren's count, the "*Lochner* Court" considered 560 due process challenges to state legislation or state action but struck down only three, *Lochner* included (Warren 1913). State Courts proved similarly accepting of much of the core progressive agenda, found Mel Urofsky. They upheld restrictions on child labor and the establishment of workers' compensation systems, validated employers' liability laws, and approved both hours and wage regulation for men in dangerous or unhealthy occupations, and women in any occupation (Urofsky 1985).

To explain this more complex picture, the revisionists turned away from the behavioralist assumptions of legal realism and drew strength from the structuralist and poststructuralist perspectives that helped generate the critical legal studies movement (Kennedy 1975), although their perspective remained separate (McCurdy 1984). "Law," wrote Benedict, "does not develop in isolation from the perceptions and ideas of the general community" (Benedict 1985, 296). Revisionists also drew heavily on Reconstruction scholarship's increasing emphasis on the conflicting goals of the Republican Party. That work produced new perspectives on the drafters of the Fourteenth Amendment and thus supported a new understanding of the Court's behavior through the Gilded Age and Progressive Era (Nelson 1988; Benedict 1978).

The revisionists' core claim was that the line the Court drew between the public sphere—where government regulation was appropriate—and a private sphere—where it was not—was determined by the free labor and Jacksonian equal rights ideologies that shaped the judiciary's understanding of liberty (Siegel 2002). It was neither Herbert Spencer's Social Statics, nor an alliance with business interests that drove the Court's decisions. The Court was instead protecting a concept of liberty drawn from a well-established Jacksonian ideology of equal rights—which emphasized that government power could not be legitimately used to benefit one group at the expense of another—and an associated free labor ideology—which defined liberty in opposition in chattel slavery as the ability to sell one's labor for whatever compensation one thought best and which the Civil War had hardened into a bedrock principle of American law and politics.

Alan Jones, for example, challenged claims that Thomas Cooley's famous nineteenth-century treatise, *Constitutional Limitations* was inspired by laissez-faire economics (Cooley 1868). Cooley, Jones noted, was not an outright opponent of government authority. He had a broad perspective on the states' tax, eminent domain, and police powers. His focus on economic liberty, said Jones, grew from his concern that the state would arbitrarily deprive some of rights others could freely exercise, and his paradigmatic example was the freedmen in the post-war South (Jones 1967). Charles McCurdy performed a similar reconstruction of Justice Stephen Field. Field's decisions striking down economic regulations, McCurdy argued, needed to be integrated with his decisions upholding exercises of the state's tax and eminent domain powers. Doing so, McCurdy wrote, revealed a consistent doctrinal system that drew bright, formal lines between public and private spheres in service of Field's Jacksonian and free labor concern with allowing individuals to pursue their callings on equal terms with others (McCurdy 1975).

McCurdy's reinterpretation of Field emphasized political ideas, but he also noted a pronounced affinity for abstract, categorical reasoning that other scholars identified in virtually every area of law, both public and private. That attraction to formalism became a major theme of revisionism (Gordon 1983; Horwitz 1992; Grey 1983; White 1980; Nelson 1974). Doctrinal tests that differentiated between "direct" and "indirect" effects, between "businesses affected with a public interest" and "ordinary trades," between "rights" and "remedies," "supervening" and "intervening" causes, "taxes" and "takings" were enough to convince Morton Horwitz that "[n]othing captures the essential difference between the typical legal minds of the nineteenth- and twentieth-century American quite as well as their attitudes towards categories" (Horwitz 1992, 17).

The Court's decision in *E.C. Knight* was emblematic. As the Court invalidated the anti-trust prosecution of a combination that controlled 98% of the nation's sugar refining capacity, it drew a bright line between "commerce," which Congress could regulate with its authority to "regulate commerce among the several states," and "manufacturing," which it could not. "No distinction," wrote Chief Justice Fuller, "is more popular to the common mind, or more clearly expressed in economic and political literature, than that between manufacture and commerce. Manufacture is transformation—the fashioning of raw materials into a change of form for use. The functions of commerce are different. The buying and selling and the transportation incidental thereto constitute commerce..." (*E.C. Knight* 14). That formalistic approach, the revisionists argued, combined with the values of free labor and Jacksonian equal rights ideology to produce the distinctive pattern of decisions and justifications that characterized law in the Gilded Age and Progressive Era.

Revisionism Elaborated

Over the ensuing decades, these insights were elaborated into a new account of the legal history of the Gilded Age and Progressive Era. Scholars reconceptualized the Court's most notorious doctrines, including liberty of contract. William Nelson, Howard Gillman, and others reexamined the *Lochner* decision and found significant similarities between that decision and the themes the early revisionists had identified (Gillman 1993; Nelson 1988; McCurdy 1998). Liberty of contract doctrine, argued Gillman, had significant support in long-established American political traditions. It was an expression of a well-established "principle of neutrality" that he traced from James Madison, through Jacksonianism, into the twentieth century. For Gillman, *Lochner* itself, and doctrines associated with it, were an effort to differentiate between legitimate, public-regarding regulation and illegitimate "class legislation," which used government power to arbitrarily favor one group over another (Gillman, 1993).

McCurdy's reconsideration of *E.C. Knight* put the decision in the context of assumptions about the structure of federalism, changes in the economic structure of corporations, and developments in corporate law. Fuller's decision, he showed, was based in part on a recognition that states had the formal authority to address the problems of monopolies as well as a failure to recognize that interstate competition for industry destroyed their incentive to do so (McCurdy 1979).

Barry Cushman built on McCurdy's insights to identify much more coherence in the Court's commerce clause doctrine than previous scholars had seen. When the limits the Court placed on Congress's commerce power were seen in conjunction with the limits the Court's dormant commerce clause placed on the authority of states to interfere with interstate commerce, the result was not incoherence, a "twilight zone" vacuum of regulatory authority, or camouflage for anti-labor activism. Instead, those doctrines were an effort to ensure free trade among the states while simultaneously preserving the authority of states and localities to regulate business (Cushman 2000).

Another elaboration of core revisionist insights was inspired by critical legal studies. By combining the insights of revisionism and the critical tradition, William Forbath constructed a new explanation for the relative conservatism of the American labor movement. The Supreme Court's labor law decisions not only created practical hurdles for the labor movement to overcome, he argued. Those decisions also had crucial ideological consequences: they imposed a particular interpretation of free labor ideology on the American labor movement. By the turn of the twentieth century, the radical goals of the American labor movement had been transformed and Samuel Gompers could proclaim that the labor movement's "whole gospel... is summed up in one phrase... freedom of contract" (Forbath 1991, 131; Tomlins 1985).

Though many scholars continued to see the Court's behavior as the result of a reprehensible lack of sympathy for the less powerful, or willful blindness to their concerns, by the 1990s these and other elaborations of revisionist themes had been synthesized in a new standard account with a valence quite different from the progressive account (Fiss 1993; Wiecek 1998). In that revisionist account, the Court's decisions were no longer condemned as expressions of class bias or as opposition to any sort of economic regulation. Instead, revisionism often portrayed the Court, implicitly or explicitly, as making misguided or even tragic efforts to protect conceptions of liberty and local authority that were dysfunctional in a world that industrialization had changed forever (Gillman 1993; McCurdy 1975).

Scholars also extended these insights to explain the decline of the legal doctrines whose rise revisionism had reinterpreted. The important debates over how, why, and when the Supreme Court abandoned what some call laissez-faire formalism in the years surrounding the New Deal lie outside the time period addressed by this chapter (Cushman 1998; Leuchtenburg 1995; White 2000; Kalman 2005). But much of that work built on the revisionist framework to emphasize how lawyers, judges, and progressive academics expanded the scope of economic regulation though step-by-step expansions of the limiting categories of laissez-faire formalism, including the police power and businesses affected with a public interest doctrines (Urofsky 1985; Tomlins 2008; Welke 2001). Barry Cushman's rethinking of the constitutional transformation that occurred following the New Deal, for example, described how lawyers extended the scope of the government's authority to regulate wages and prices by slowly expanding the category of "businesses affected with a public interest" (Cushman 1998, 78). Others showed similar processes at play in the undermining of *Lochner*'s restriction on the authority of the state to regulate hours, first by the efforts of Louis Brandeis and Florence Kelley in *Muller v. Oregon*, and later by future Supreme Court Justice Felix Frankfurter in *Bunting v. Oregon* in 1917 (Batlan 2010).

Scholars also examined how these doctrinal changes were associated with challenges to the formalist and free labor ideology that supported laissez-faire constitutionalism (Witt 2004; Menand 2001). Barbara Fried's appreciative biography of Robert Hale, for example, describes how he undermined the conception of liberty on which laissez-faire formalism rested. Both liberty and property, Hale argued, should be defined functionally. Liberty did not mean freedom from government regulation, as laissez-faire formalism assumed. Defined functionally, it was simply the absence of constraints on choices. Given that such constraints exist in every transaction, no matter how "private," removing government regulation did nothing to "increase" liberty. In fact, the goal of "increasing" liberty was a chimera. The goal of public policy for Hale was to distribute constraints in a way that maximized the right values (Fried 1998).

The themes of revisionism were also applied to the legal history of race during the Gilded Age and Progressive Era. The same Court that was willing to step in to protect the economic liberties of American citizens did not extend the same sympathy to what came to be called civil rights. In a series of decisions the Court seemed to drain the 14th Amendment of its potential to help the new freedmen. In upholding a municipally created butchers' monopoly, the *Slaughterhouse Cases* defined the privileges and immunities clause of the 14th Amendment so narrowly that it offered no meaningful protections to the freedmen or their descendants. *Plessey v. Ferguson*'s separate but equal doctrine undermined the potential of the equal protection clause to address state-sponsored segregation. The potential of the 14th Amendment was further eroded by *United States v. Cruickshank*, which limited the reach of the 14th Amendment's due process and equal protection clauses to the state and its officers by establishing the state action doctrine. In the *Civil Rights Cases*, the Court struck down the 1875 Civil Rights Act by limiting the rights guaranteed by Thirteenth Amendment. The Act's attempt to prohibit discrimination in places of public accommodation, the Court held, was unconstitutional because the Thirteenth Amendment's prohibition of slavery did not allow Congress to prohibit private racial discrimination.

Though no one denied that racism and a lack of concern for the plight of racial minorities was characteristic of period or important to these decisions, some of the same historians who revised the history of the Court's treatment of economic regulation drew on similar themes to paint a more complex picture of the Court's treatment of race (Benedict 1978). William Nelson, for example, argued that the Court's application of the Fourteenth Amendment to racial issues largely mirrored its treatment of economic regulations. Nelson supported the revisionist claims that the Court gave broad deference to legislative judgments about economic regulations and stepped in only when the government was clearly disadvantaging one class of people without advancing the public good. He also saw the Court applying a similar approach to the regulation of race. The Court's decision in the *Civil Rights Cases*, *United States v. Cruickshank*, and *Plessey v. Ferguson* were consistent, he believed, with the Court's understanding that the Fourteenth Amendment left the authority to protect private rights to the States. Decisions like *Strauder v. West Virginia* and *Yick Wo v. Hopkins*, he argued, were evidence that the Court would invalidate egregious violations of equal treatment under the Fourteenth Amendment's due process and equal protection clauses. *Strauder* overturned the conviction of an African American defendant because state law barred African Americans from the jury. *Yick Wo* invalidated a racially neutral law purportedly passed to reduce the risk of fires from San Francisco laundries on the grounds that it was applied with the intent to discriminate against Chinese immigrants (Nelson 1988).

Revisionism Extended

While revisionism was being elaborated into a new synthesis, scholars drew on developments in other fields and disciplines to push beyond revisionism's emphasis on the role of ideas and its focus on economic regulation. The emergence of social history not only recaptured the agency of women, immigrants, and other under-studied groups, but also deepened the field's understanding of the sources and development of core revisionist themes (Welke 2010). The work of scholars inspired by social scientists to investigate the development and influence of the structure of the state was similarly enriching. These scholars added an emphasis on institutions to the revisionist emphasis on ideas and the progressive emphasis on interests (Ernst 1998). Revisionism itself also continued to develop. It kept its focus on the role of ideas, especially free labor ideology, but it also identified other important influences, emphasized the instability of both legal and political ideas, and recovered significant contingency in the period's legal history (Ernst 1993; White 1993).

The emergence of social history led scholars to a new emphasis on the myriad ways that women were excluded from the full measure of liberty, but Linda Kerber, Linda Gordon, Barbara Welke, and others also showed that ideas of gender and women themselves were critical to the legal history of the period (Kerber 1998). They showed that the very ideas of liberty that underlay the revisionist account were inextricably linked to conceptions of gender (Dubber 2005; Stanley 1998), and they demonstrated that women reformers, lawyers, litigants, and writers were critical to the transformation of Gilded Age and Progressive Era constitutionalism. The lawsuits, briefs, arguments, and organizations of these women, for example, made important contributions to the expansion of the public sphere that occurred as progressives sought to address the problems of industrial capitalism (Sklar 1995; Batlan 2015). And when these arguments succeeded, it was often by leveraging maternalist ideas or other gendered categories (Gordon 1990; Woloch 1996; Kessler-Harris 2001).

Both women as litigants and assumptions about gender play a central role, for example, in Barbara Welke's study of how the railroad and streetcar transformed Americans' understanding of liberty. Tort law, Welke argued, was transformed by women and ideas of gender. The law of injury in the nineteenth century emphasized letting losses lie where they fell and drew strength from a vision of liberty that emphasized the individualized autonomy of free men. Injured women litigants, however, were able to use their perceived vulnerability to argue for legal rules that were more favorable to injured parties. The changes their arguments produced radiated out from decisions about women to include men, and ultimately produced a new twentieth-century vision of ordered liberty that approved of the use of state authority as a means to protect the vulnerable (Welke 2001).

Studies of immigration showed how other groups that were excluded from full citizenship nevertheless made critical contributions to the transformation of law and the state. The foundation of modern immigration law was set during the Gilded Age and Progressive Era and was produced, as Lucy Salyer and others have shown, by the complicated interaction of law, nativism, and racial assumptions (Lee 2003; Salyer 1995). Salyer's study sought to explain the broad discretion immigration officials acquired during the Gilded Age and Progressive Era. The limited judicial oversight those officials face even today was a paradoxical result, she argued, of the success Chinese immigrants had using habeas corpus proceedings to resist deportation in late-nineteenth-century San Francisco. Their legal victories created a backlash that produced a series of increasingly stringent immigration laws, which included the 1882 Chinese Exclusion Act. The Supreme Court, influenced by racism and nativism as well as existing precedent, upheld those laws as well as future restrictions on immigration that culminated with the racial categories of the 1924 Immigration Act. Immigrants later won some victories in court and in Congress, but their efforts largely produced more legalistic and bureaucratic procedures without threatening the broad authority of immigration officials (Salyer 1995).

An emerging area of interest is the study of the new American Empire that emerged in the late nineteenth century, and what the Court's treatment of the resulting issues reveals about constitutional development and the American state (Erman 2014; Burnett and Marshall 2001). Bartholomew Sparrow, for example, examined the Court's decision in the Insular Cases to allow "unincorporated territories" like Puerto Rico and the Philippines to be subject to United States authority without the prospect of statehood, and to deny the inhabitants of those territories full rights of citizenship. The Constitution, as a result, would not follow the flag. Those decisions, he argued, resulted from a combination of the nation's economic interest and racial assumptions, and the Court's concern with economic liberties (Sparrow 2006).

The study of law and race in the period began to ask new questions as well. Since C. Vann Woodward's work in the 1950s, a central question of the period's legal history has been how legal and social change influenced one another, specifically whether legal change ratified social change or played a significant causal role itself. Woodward argued the law was an important force. He claimed segregation laws enacted in the early twentieth century helped end a system of race relations that was much more fluid and allowed significant interracial interaction (Woodward 1974). Later scholars doubted law's ability to alter racial attitudes. The segregation laws of the early twentieth century, they argued, were ratifications of established practices (Rabinowitz 1988). That discussion remains important, but new questions about how black men and women responded to segregation, and how race, class, and gender identities responded to and shaped the law have become increasingly important (Mack 1999).

A second important extension of revisionism was the shift from asking why the judiciary limited the reach of state power to understanding how the state exercised the authority it did have, how it extended its authority, and how changing institutional arrangements interacted with those processes. Central to this interest in state-building has been the work of historically minded political scientists and sociologists like Stephen Skowronek and Theda Skocpol (Skowronek 1982; Skocpol 1992). By emphasizing the important role the judiciary played in exercising governing authority in some areas, but not others, Skowronek's description of a "state of courts and parties," fit neatly with revisionism's focus on understanding how the judiciary drew the line between public and private activity (Skowronek 1982, 24). But, as Dan Ernst discussed, their focus on institutions both raised new questions and provided new insights on older issues (Ernst 1998).

The Gilded Age and Progressive Era saw the beginnings of the shift from Skowronek's state of courts and parties to the modern administrative state, in which bureaucrats had both the capacity and political independence to play a central role in the regulation of business and society (Carpenter 2001). Much of the modern administrative state was created during the New Deal, but it emerged as an important force well before then. State railroad commissions were important antecedents for the Interstate Commerce Commission, whose creation in 1887 was a key marker. And developments continued into the early twentieth century. The forerunners of the Food and Drug Administration and Federal Reserve emerged then, as did the Federal Trade Commission (Keller 1977; 1990).

Explaining these changes is a fertile area of research. Nicholas Parrillo's investigation of the development of "salarization," is an example. He traces a profound shift in how Americans paid their government officials, from the eighteenth century when government officials often drew significant income from what today would be called bribes, to the 1940s, when salaries were the only proper way to pay government officials. Pay-for-service models of compensation—such as payment for the issuance of a permit—were undermined by the need to ensure equal treatment from the government and the need to enforce compromises over access to limited resources made by mass interest groups. Payment by bounty—such as paying port inspectors a percentage of the illegal goods seized—was discarded when it produced enforcement so zealous it undermined cooperation and became counter-productive. Salaries solved both these problems and thus contributed to the growing authority of the administrative state (Parrillo 2014).

Other important work includes Jerry Mashaw's recovery of the history of administrative law, which describes administrative law's development from the founding era (Mashaw 2010), and Ajay Mehrotra's study of the development of a powerful system of federal taxation. Mehrotra shows how elite lawyers in the Department of the Treasury built state capacity, helped develop the positive rights associated with a new understanding of American liberalism, and simultaneously limited opportunities for radical reform to the American economic system (Mehrotra 2013). Studies of governance at the state and local level have also investigated the process of state-building. Michael Willrich, for example, shows how new conceptions of crime, citizenship, and personal responsibility were institutionalized in Chicago's municipal court system (Willrich 2003). Each of these studies show how questions about institutional developments could both chart new territory and cast informative light on established revisionist themes.

Revisionism Complicated

The interest in institutions, identity, and a plethora of new actors did not, however, push the revisionist narrative out of the field. In fact, scholars continue to produce important research on core revisionist themes. This research retains the revisionist concern with formalism, equal rights principles, and free labor ideology, and has kept the judiciary's resistance to state authority near its core. But it has also identified other ideas that played an important role, emphasized the instability of both legal and political categories, and thus recovered significant amounts of contingency in legal development of the period (Ernst 1993; White 1993).

One set of complications finds other intellectual supports for the constitutional law of the period. Herbert Hovenkamp agreed with the revisionists that ideas, not just interests, drove the Court's decisions. But he put at the center the ideas of classical economics, which were independent from but consistent with the free labor and equal rights ideologies the revisionists emphasized. A core question, for example, of the court's substantive due process doctrine since *Slaughterhouse* was whether a business was, like common carriers, part of the public sphere or, like grocers, an a "ordinary trade" in the private sphere. That issue, Hovenkamp argued, was determined not by free labor ideology, but by the understanding of free markets advanced by classical economics (Hovenkamp 1991). The decline of those doctrines, Hovenkamp has argued recently, was due to the gradual displacement of classical economics by neoclassical, marginalist economic theory (Hovenkamp 2014).

Other scholars have argued religion was an important support for the Court's doctrines (Bailey 2004). Justice David Brewer's concern with protecting individual liberty from state interference, and thus his support of liberty of contract in cases like *Lochner* and *Adair*, was associated with his religious conviction that individuals needed to make their own moral choices in order to pursue salvation, argued Gordon Hylton (Hylton 1998). Stephen Siegel similarly identified religion as a core concern of important Gilded Age treatise writers, including Joel Bishop and Francis Wharton (Siegel 1995; 2004).

Siegel has also joined David Rabban in arguing that history played an important role in the period's legal thought

(Grossman 2002; Siegel 1990). Rabban's meticulous reconstruction of historicist jurisprudence of the writers of central nineteenth-century treaties, including Christopher Tiedman, James Coolidge Carter, Thomas Cooley, and others shows how American legal thinkers in the decades following the Civil War drew on German models to generate historically based understandings of legal development that were very open to change over time and the law's social context (Rabban 2013).

David Bernstein has questioned the connection between equal rights ideology and freedom of contract. Liberty of contract doctrine, he argued, was more closely associated with the free labor, natural rights tradition that he argued also produced early-twentieth-century decisions that protected religious and associational liberties. The strongest defenders of freedom of contract, Bernstein noted, were also some of the strongest defenders of freedom of conscience. Justice McReynolds, for example, defended liberty of contract though the New Deal, but he also used the same reasoning to strike down nativist laws that prohibited teaching elementary students in any language other than English, and anti-Catholic laws that required elementary students attend public schools *Pierce v. Society of Sisters* (1924); *Meyer v. Nebraska* (1923); (Bernstein 2011).

Other scholars emphasized contingency in the relationship between free labor and equal rights ideology, formalism, and judicial doctrine (White 1993). William Forbath emphasized the centrality of free labor ideology to debates over the proper relationships between government, workers, and employers. But that free labor ideology, he showed, could be used as a resource by workers seeking to justify further state involvement as well as by employers who sought to limit the rights of laborers. While courts were using free labor ideas to justify their claims that liberty of contract protected the freedom of workers, many of the workers themselves drew on a similar heritage to argue that being forced by the necessity of earning a living to sell their labor was not freedom, but "wage slavery" (Forbath 1985). Amy Dru Stanley demonstrated the central role that the concept of contract played in discussions about a remarkable variety of issues. It framed debates over the regulation of employment by making the ability of workers to negotiate their own terms of employment the badge of freedom. It similarly framed debates over the treatment of beggars and women. But Stanley also showed how ambiguous the analogy to contract could be. Again and again she showed how both sides in the debate found analogies to contract that supported their position (Stanley 1998).

John Fabian Witt's explanation of changes to the law of industrial accidents also emphasized the importance and ambiguity of free labor ideology in explaining the development of the law of industrial accidents. He saw, with most scholars, an important transition from a late-nineteenth-century system of compensation for industrial accidents that was based on common law principles of negligence, to a twentieth-century system of workers' compensation. But unlike previous scholars, Witt argued that free labor ideology framed the debate over whether to retain the highly individualized and fault-based system of negligence or adopt an alternative, and emphasized that the shift to the class-based system of workers' compensation was not an inevitable result of those new approaches' ability to lower costs for employers (Witt 2004). Work on core revisionist subjects like freedom of contract and federalism also reflects this more complex revisionist perspective (McCurdy 1998; Sawyer 2012; Cushman 2013; Sawyer 2013).

Revisionism Challenged

The roles formalism, federalism, and free labor and equal rights ideologies play in the legal history of the Gilded Age and Progressive Era have declined as a result of these complications of revisionism, new questions about race, gender, immigration, and empire, and the new emphasis on institutions. But as that scholarship pushed beyond revisionism's boundaries and complicated its claims, it did not reject the account's core themes. More recently, however, some scholars have built on those developments to mount just such a challenge.

One challenge rejects the revisionist claim that formalism was an important characteristic of Gilded Age and Progressive Era judging. While previous scholars questioned the bright lines between formalism and instrumental approaches to law (Duxbury 1995), Brian Tamahana urges the field to abandon the concept of formalism altogether. Those labeled formalist, he argues, recognized that judges "made" law, that deductive reasoning alone could not determine the outcome of cases, that a judge's politics shaped his decisions, and that the law responded to social and economic changes. These judges, in other words, were not formalists at all, but "balanced realists," just like the so-called "realists" who followed them. There was, claimed Tamanaha, no meaningful jurisprudential break between the Gilded Age and the Realist period that followed it (Tamanaha 2010).

A second challenge rejects the revisionist focus on Jacksonian equal rights principles and free labor ideology. With echoes of the progressive synthesis, these scholars argue that constitutional doctrine in the Gilded Age and Progressive Era had been driven by class interests all along (Cachan 2002). Paul Kens, for example, has challenged the revisionist characterization of Stephen Field as a champion of equal rights and free labor ideology. He agreed Field played a central role in translating the political ideas of free labor and Jacksonian equal rights into the doctrines of the Gilded and Progressive Era constitutional law. But he denied those ideals drove the decisions of Field and his allies. Instead, Field and other conservative jurists abandoned the true heritage of the ideals they supposedly championed and used them as rhetorical justification for a class-based opposition to democratic government (Kens 1997).

A third challenge rejects the core question of the revisionist project by extending the insights of scholars who have investigated state-building and the role of institutions. The field should, William Novak argued, shift its attention from the reasons the judiciary limited the authority of the state for the simple reason that the judiciary did no such thing. There was, Novak argued, no weak American state, and, as a result, the field should focus its attention on explaining the rise of the nation's remarkably effective legal, political, and economic systems. His claims draw strength from his own *The People's Welfare*, which pointed out the myriad issues regulated by state and local governments in the nineteenth century (Novak 1996), from the work of political historians like Brian Balogh who have emphasized all the work the federal government accomplished during the period (Balogh 2009), and from the work of legal historians who extended the revisionist account into examinations of the role law played in shaping putatively private economic and social relationships (Witt 2010). Backed by this evidence, Novak argued that the history of the Gilded Age and Progressive Era should focus on explaining how the nineteenth-century American state was able to project power so effectively when it did not correspond to a Weberian model of a centralized, hierarchical, bureaucratic state (Novak 2008).

Whether these new challenges offer a more accurate or useful picture of the past than the current extended, elaborated, and complicated version of revisionism is an issue of ongoing debate. One or more of these challenges might undermine the central pillars of the revisionist account, or they may ultimately be understood as important reminders that the categories historian need to chart the past can also become so reified that they distort rather than clarify understanding.

Tamanaha's challenge to formalism, for example, might ultimately be understood as a helpful reminder that Gilded Age and Progressive Era judges should not be dismissed as jurisprudential automata whose decisions were independent of politics, economic development, and social change. A cartoonish version of formalism, in which judges resolved cases by unthinkingly applying abstract verbal formulations, refused to consider the effects of their decisions, and denied that either politics or changing economic and social conditions affected the law, cannot survive Tamanaha's argument. But there are reasons to doubt that the nineteenth and twentieth centuries should be considered a unified period of "balanced realism." The guiding assumptions of Gilded Age and Progressive Era judges, and the emphasis they placed on categorical reasoning and abstract principles, may still differentiate them from their successors (White 2000).

It is also not clear that the cartoonish version of formalism holds much purchase in the extended and complicated revisionism of today (Brophy 2013). Even from its start, the revisionist project sought to explain how the assumptions of nineteenth-century political ideology and political economy supported the constitutional law of the Gilded and Progressive Era. Charles's McCurdy's early revision of the ur-formalist decision in *E.C. Knight*, for example, emphasized the critical role played by Justice Fuller's assumptions about the potential of state corporate law to solve the problem of the trusts (McCurdy 1979). Barry Cushman's description of the period's commerce clause doctrine was similarly attentive to such "realist" issues, as the title to his article attests (Cushman 2000).

Similarly, the reemphasis Kens and others put on class and economic thought might successfully displace the revisionist emphasis on political ideology. But that work might also ultimately be understood as a reminder that legal decisions are not just about political philosophy or styles of reasoning, they are also, and perhaps most importantly, about power. They produced winners and losers, and it is important to recall how often state authority has been used to hurt rather than help the disadvantaged. Yet the revisionist emphasis on free labor and equal rights ideologies has not prevented Barbara Welke, William Forbath, and others from eloquently criticizing such abuses (Welke 2001; Forbath 1991). It is also unclear that dismissing political ideology as camouflage is more true to the evidence than the extended and complicated version of revisionism that resulted from the contributions of Hovenkamp, Siegel, Ernst, and others (Ernst 1995; Hovenkamp 2014; Siegel 2004).

Novak's bracing challenge has the potential to revolutionize the field. Yet, scholars continue to point out that the historical record is replete with evidence of courts protecting the rights of property, limiting the responsibility of employers to injured workers, curbing the power of the state to regulate working conditions, and allowing private parties to contract around many of the rules that were implemented. And those decisions were supported by a liberal ideology heavily invested in distinctions between private and public authority (Schiller 1997). Recently, Mary Furner provided a powerful response to Novak's challenge. She has argued that though the judiciary became more accepting of government regulation of business and labor in the early twentieth century, it did, in the late nineteenth century, regularly interfere with attempts to regulate the conditions of labor and stoutly protect competition among formally equal businesses within a sphere of private economic activity. Combining those decisions with the widely shared belief of late-nineteenth-century intellectuals that they were living through a laissez-faire era is enough, Furner argued, to reject Novak's depiction of at least the last decades of the nineteenth century (Furner forthcoming). If she is right, the field should retain a core interest in explaining the Court's opposition to state authority and Novak's challenge should be understood as an important reminder that the power of the state often can be exercised most effectively by mechanisms other than the hierarchical structure of its bureaucratic entities.

Conclusion

What, then, is left of the original revisionist synthesis? Its emphasis on ideas has been fortified by research into the role of institutions and identity. Its focus on law and economic regulation has been expanded to include questions about women, gender, immigration, and empire. And its central claims have been complicated. Jacksonian equal rights and free labor ideologies have been shown to be only one source of Gilded Age and Progressive Era constitutional law, the connections between political ideology and legal doctrine have been loosened, and abstract, categorical analysis has been shown to be but one part of the period's legal thought. Scholars now see more complexity, more ambiguity, and more contingency in the legal history of the Gilded Age and Progressive Era. But, though the elaboration, extension, and complication of the revisionist program has led some to question whether the revisionist narrative and its main themes remain central to the field. Those themes are far from the only game in town. But they still provide a set of concepts that help organize the field. Resolving the recent challenges to revisionism will help determine whether they will continue to do so.

References

Bailey, Mark Warren. 2004. *Guardians of the Moral Order: The Legal Philosophy of the Supreme Court, 1860–1910.* Dekalb: Northern Illinois University Press.

Balogh, Brian. 2009. *A Government Out of Sight: The Mystery of National Authority in Nineteenth-Century America.* Cambridge: Cambridge University Press.

Batlan, Felice. 2010. "Notes from the Margins: Florence Kelley and the Making of Sociological Jurisprudence." In *Transformations in American Legal History, II: Essays in Honor of Professor Morton J. Horwitz*, ed. Daniel W. Hamilton and Alfred L. Brophy, 239–253. Cambridge, MA: Harvard University Press.

—. 2015. *Women and Justice for the Poor: A History of Legal Aid, 1863–1945.* Cambridge: Cambridge University Press.

Benedict, Michael Les. 1978. "Preserving Federalism: Reconstruction and the Waite Court." *Supreme Court Review*: 39–79.

—. 1985. "Laissez-Faire and Liberty: A Re-Evaluation of the Meaning and Origins of Laissez-Faire Constitutionalism." *Law and History Review* 3, 2: 293–331.

Bernstein, David E. 2011. *Rehabilitating Lochner: Defending Individual Rights against Progressive Reform.* Chicago: The University of Chicago Press.

Brophy, Alfred L. 2013. "Did Formalism Never Exist?" Review of *Beyond the Formalist Realist Divide: the Role of Politics in Judging*, by Brian Z. Tamanaha. *University of Texas Law Review* 92, 2: 383–412.

Burnett, Christina Duffy, and Burke Marshall, eds. 2001. *Foreign in a Domestic Sense: Puerto Rico, American Expansion, and the Constitution.* Durham, NC: Duke University Press.

Cachan, Manuel. 2002. "Justice Stephen Field and 'Free Soil, Free Labor Constitutionalism': Reconsidering Revisionism." *Law and History Review* 20, 3: 541–576.

Carpenter, Daniel P. 2001. *The Forging of Bureaucratic Autonomy: Reputations, Networks, and Policy Innovation in Executive Agencies, 1862–1928.* Princeton, NJ: Princeton University Press.

Cooley, Thomas M. 1868. *A Treatise on the Constitutional Limitations Which Rest Upon the Legislative Power of the States of the American Union.* Boston: Little, Brown.

Corwin, Edward S. 1941. *Constitutional Revolution, Ltd.* Claremont, CA: Claremont Colleges.

Cushman, Barry. 1998. *Rethinking the New Deal Court: The Structure of a Constitutional Revolution.* Oxford: Oxford University Press.

—. 2000. "Formalism and Realism in Commerce Clause Jurisprudence." *University of Chicago Law Review* 67, 4: 1089–1150.

—. 2013. "Carolene Products and Constitutional Structure." *Supreme Court Review* 2012, 1: 321–377.

Dubber, Markus Dirk. 2005. *The Police Power: Patriarchy and the Foundations of American Government.* New York: Columbia University Press.

Duxbury, Neil. 1995. *Patterns of American Jurisprudence.* Oxford: Oxford University Press.

Erman, Sam. 2014. "Citizens of Empire: Puerto Rico, Status, and Constitutional Change." *California Law Review* 102, 5: 1181–1242.

Ernst, Daniel R. 1993. "The Critical Tradition in the Writing of American Legal History." Review of *Transformation of American Law 1870–1960: Crisis of Legal Orthodoxy*, by Morton J. Horwitz. *The Yale Law Journal* 102, 4: 1019–76.

—. 1995. *Lawyers Against Labor: From Individual Rights to Corporate Liberalism.* Urbana: University of Illinois Press.

—. 1998. "Law and American Political Development, 1877–1938." *Reviews in American History* 26, 1: 205–19.

Fiss, Owen M. 1993. *Troubled Beginnings of the Modern State 1888–1910.* New York: Macmillan.

Forbath, William E. 1985. "The Ambiguities of Free Labor: Labor and the Law in the Gilded Age." *Wisconsin Law Review* 1985, 4: 767–817.

—. 1991. *Law and the Shaping of the American Labor Movement.* Cambridge, MA: Harvard University Press.

Fried, Barbara H. 1998. *The Progressive Assault on Laissez Faire: Robert Hale and the First Law and Economics Movement.* Cambridge, MA: Harvard University Press.

Furner, Mary. Forthcoming. "The U.S. Laissez Faire Era: From *In re Jacobs* and *E. C. Knight* to *Northern Securities* and *Muller v. Oregon*."

Gillman, Howard. 1993. *The Constitution Besieged: The Rise and Demise of Lochner Era Police Powers Jurisprudence.* Durham, NC: Duke University Press.

Gordon, Linda, ed. 1990. *Women, the State, and Welfare.* Madison: University of Wisconsin Press.

Gordon, Robert. 1983. "Legal Thought and Legal Practice in the Age of American Enterprise." In *Professions and Professional Ideologies in America.* In *Professions and Professional Ideologies in America*, ed. Gerald L. Geison, 70–110. Chapel Hill: University of North Carolina Press.

Grey, Thomas. 1983. "Langdell's Orthodoxy." *University of Pittsburgh Law Review* 45, 1: 1–53.

Grossman, Lewis A. 2002. "James Coolidge Carter and Mugwump Jurisprudence." *Law and History Review* 20, 3: 577–629.

Horwitz, Morton J. 1992. *The Transformation of American Law, 1870–1960: The Crisis of Legal Orthodoxy.* Oxford: Oxford University Press.

Hovenkamp, Herbert. 1991. *Enterprise and American Law, 1836–1937.* Cambridge, MA: Harvard University Press.

—. 2014. *The Opening of American Law: Neoclassical Legal Thought, 1870–1970.* Oxford: Oxford University Press.

Hylton, Gordon. 1998. "David Josiah Brewer and the Christian Constitution." *Marquette Law Review* 81, 2: 417–26.

Jackson, Robert H. 1941. *The Struggle for Judicial Supremacy; A Study of a Crisis in American Power Politics.* New York: A.A. Knopf.

Jones, Alan. 1967. "Thomas M. Cooley and 'Laissez-Faire Constitutionalism': A Reconsideration." *The Journal of American History* 53, 4: 751–71.

Kalman, Laura. 2005. "The Constitution, the Supreme Court, and the New Deal." *American Historical Review* 110, 4: 1052–80.

Keller, Morton. 1977. *Affairs of State: Public Life in Late Nineteenth Century America.* Cambridge, MA: Harvard University Press.

—. 1990. *Regulating a New Economy: Public Policy and Economic Change in America, 1900–1933.* Cambridge, MA: Harvard University Press.

Kennedy, Duncan. 1975. *The Rise and Fall of Classical Legal Thought.* Washington, DC: Beard Books.

Kens, Paul. 1997. *Justice Stephen Field: Shaping Liberty from the Gold Rush to the Gilded Age.* Lawrence: University Press of Kansas.

Kerber, Linda K. 1998. *No Constitutional Right to Be Ladies: Women and the Obligations of Citizenship.* New York: Hill & Wang.

Kessler-Harris, Alice. 2001. *In Pursuit of Equity: Women, Men, and the Quest for Economic Citizenship in 20th Century America.* Oxford: Oxford University Press.

Lee, Erika. 2003. *At America's Gates: Chinese Immigration During the Exclusion Era, 1882–1943.* Chapel Hill: University of North Carolina Press.

Leuchtenburg, William E. 1995. *The Supreme Court Reborn: The Constitutional Revolution in the Age of Roosevelt.* Oxford: Oxford University Press.

Mack, Kenneth W. 1999. "Law, Society, Identity, and the Making of the Jim Crow South: Travel and Segregation on Tennessee Railroads, 1875–1905." *Law & Social Inquiry* 24, 2: 377–409.

Mashaw, Jerry L. 2010. "Federal Administration and Administrative Law in the Gilded Age." *The Yale Law Journal* 119, 7: 1362–1472.

McCloskey, Robert G. 1960. *The American Supreme Court.* Chicago: University of Chicago Press.

McCurdy, Charles W. 1975. "Justice Field and the Jurisprudence of Government–Business Relations: Some Parameters of Laissez-Faire Constitutionalism, 1863–1897." *The Journal of American History* 61, 4: 970–1005.

—. 1979. "The Knight Sugar Decision of 1895 and the Modernization of American Corporation Law, 1869–1903." *The Business History Review* 53, 3: 304–42.

—. 1984. "Roots of Liberty of Contract Reconsidered: Major Premises in the Law of Employment, 1867–1937." In *Yearbook of the Supreme Court Historical Society.* Washington, DC: Supreme Court Historical Society.

—. 1998. "The 'Liberty of Contract' Regime in American Law." In *The State and Freedom of Contract*, ed. Harry N. Scheiber, 161–197. Palo Alto, CA: Stanford University Press.

Mehrotra, Ajay K. 2013. *Making the Modern American Fiscal State: Law, Politics, and the Rise of Progressive Taxation, 1877–1929.* New York: Cambridge University Press.

Menand, Louis. 2001. *The Metaphysical Club.* New York: Farrar, Straus, and Giroux.

Nelson, William E. 1974. "The Impact of the Antislavery Movement upon Styles of Judicial Reasoning in Nineteenth Century America." *Harvard Law Review* 87, 3: 513—566.

—. 1988. *The Fourteenth Amendment: From Political Principle to Judicial Doctrine.* Cambridge, MA: Harvard University Press.

Novak, William J. 1996. *The People's Welfare: Law and Regulation in Nineteenth-Century America.* Chapel Hill: University of North Carolina Press.

—. 2008. "The Myth of the 'Weak' American State." *The American Historical Review* 113, 3: 752–72. Oxford: Oxford University Press.

Parrillo, Nicholas R. 2014. *Against the Profit Motive: The Salary Revolution in American Government, 1780–1940.* New Haven, CT: Yale University Press.

Paul, Arnold M. 1960. *Conservative Crisis and the Rule of Law: Attitudes of Bar and Bench, 1887–1895.* Ithaca, NY: Cornell University Press.

Rabban, David M. 2013. *Law's History: American Legal Thought and the Transatlantic Turn to History.* Cambridge: Cambridge University Press.

Rabinowitz, Howard N. 1988. "More than the Woodward Thesis: Assessing the Strange Career of Jim Crow." *Journal of American History* 75, 3: 842–56.

Salyer, Lucy E. 1995. *Laws Harsh as Tigers: Chinese Immigrants and the Shaping of Modern Immigration Law.* Chapel Hill: University of North Carolina Press.

Sawyer, Laura Phillips. 2013. "Contested Meanings of Freedom: Workingmen's Wages, the Company Store System, and the Godcharles v. Wigeman Decision." *Journal of the Gilded Age and Progressive Era* 12, 3: 285–319.

Sawyer, Logan E. 2012. "Creating Hammer v. Dagenhart." *William & Mary Bill of Rights Journal* 21, 1: 62–127.

Schiller, Reuel E. 1997. "Regulation's Hidden History." Review of *The People's Welfare: Law and Regulation in Nineteenth-Century America*, by William Novak. *Reviews in American History* 25, 3: 416–21.

Siegel, Stephen A. 1990. "Historism in Late Nineteenth Century Constitutional Thought." *Wisconsin Law Review* 6: 1431–1547.

—. 1995. "Joel Bishop's Orthodoxy." *Law and History Review* 13, 2: 215–59.

—. 2002. "The Revision Thickens." *Law and History Review* 20, 3: 631–37.

—. 2004. "Francis Wharton's Orthodoxy: God, Historical Jurisprudence, and Classical Legal Thought." *The American Journal of Legal History* 46, 4: 422–46.

Sklar, Kathryn Kish. 1995. *Florence Kelley and the Nation's Work: The Rise of Women's Political Culture, 1830–1900.* New Haven, CT: Yale University Press.

Skocpol, Theda. 1992. *Protecting Soldiers and Mothers: The Political Origins of Social Policy in the United States.* Cambridge, MA: Belknap Press/Harvard University Press.

Skowronek, Stephen. 1982. *Building a New American State: The Expansion of National Administrative Capacities, 1877–1920.* Cambridge: Cambridge University Press.

Sparrow, Bartholomew H. 2006. *The Insular Cases and the Emergence of American Empire.* Lawrence: University Press of Kansas.

Stanley, Amy Dru. 1998. *From Bondage to Contract: Wage Labor, Marriage, and the Market in the Age of Slave Emancipation.* Cambridge: Cambridge University Press.

Tamanaha, Brian Z. 2010. *Beyond the Formalist–Realist Divide: The Role of Politics in Judging.* Princeton, NJ: Princeton University Press.

Tomlins, Christopher L. 1985. *The State and the Unions: Labor Relations, Law, and the Organized Labor Movement in America, 1880–1960.* Cambridge: Cambridge University Press.

—. 2008. "Necessities of State: Police, Sovereignty, and the Constitution." *Journal of Policy History* 20, 1: 47–63.

Twiss, Benjamin R. 1942. *Lawyers and the Constitution; How Laissez Faire Came to the Supreme Court.* London: H. Milford, Oxford University Press.

Urofsky, Melvin I. 1985. "State Courts and Protective Legislation During the Progressive Era: A Reevaluation." *The Journal of American History* 72, 1: 63–91.

Warren, Charles. 1913. "The Progressiveness of the United States Supreme Court." *Columbia Law Review* 13, 4: 294–313.

Welke, Barbara Young. 2001. *Recasting American Liberty: Gender, Race, Law, and the Railroad Revolution, 1865–1920.* Cambridge: Cambridge University Press.

—. 2010. *Law and the Borders of Belonging in the Long Nineteenth Century United States.* New York: Cambridge University Press.

White, G. Edward. 1980. *Tort Law in America: An Intellectual History.* Oxford: Oxford University Press.

—. 1993. "Transforming History in the Postmodern Era." Review of *Transformation of American Law: The Crisis of Legal Orthodoxy*, by Morton Horwitz. *Michigan Law Review* 91, 6: 1315–1352.

—. 2000. *The Constitution and the New Deal.* Cambridge, MA: Harvard University Press.

Wiecek, William M. 1998. *The Lost World of Classical Legal Thought: Law and Ideology in America, 1886–1937.* Oxford: Oxford University Press.

Willrich, Michael. 2003. *City of Courts: Socializing Justice in Progressive Era Chicago.* Cambridge: Cambridge University Press.

Witt, John Fabian. 2004. *The Accidental Republic: Crippled Workingmen, Destitute Widows, and the Remaking of American Law.* Cambridge: Harvard University Press.

—. 2010. "Law and War in American History." Review of *Myth of the "Weak" American State*, by William J. Novak. *American Historical Review* 115, 3: 768–778.

Woloch, Nancy. 1996. *Muller v. Oregon: A Brief History with Documents.* Boston: Bedford Books of St. Martin's Press.

Woodward, C. Vann. 1974. *The Strange Career of Jim Crow.* 3rd edn. Oxford: Oxford University Press.

Cases Cited

Adair v. United States, 208 U.S. 161 (1908).
Bailey v. Drexel Furniture, 259 U.S. 20 (1922).
Bunting v. Oregon, 243 U.S. 426 (1917).
Civil Rights Cases, 109 U.S. 3 (1883).
Coppage v. Kansas, 236 U.S. 1 (1915).
United States v. E.C. Knight Co., 156 U.S. 1 (1895).
Hammer v. Dagenhart, 247 U.S. 251 (1918).
In Re Debs, 158 U.S. 564 (1895).
Lochner v. New York, 198 U.S 45 (1905).
Loewe v. Lawlor, 208 U.S. 274 (1908).
Meyer v. Nebraska, 262 U.S. 390 (1923).
Muller v. Oregon, 208 U.S. 412 (1908).
Munn v. Illinois, 94 U.S. 113 (1876).
Pierce v. Society of Sisters, 268 U.S. 510 (1925).
Plessey v. Ferguson, 163 U.S. 537 (1896).
Pollock v. Farmers' Loan & Trust Co., 157 U.S. 429 (1895).
Slaughterhouse Cases, 83 U.S. 36 (1872).
Smyth v. Ames, 171 U.S. 316 (1898).
Strauder v. West Virginia, 100 U.S. 303 (1880).
United States v. Cruickshank, 92 U.S. 542 (1875).
Wolff Packing Co. v. Court of Industrial Relations, 262 U.S. 522 (1923)
Yick Wo v. Hopkins, 118 U.S. 356 (1886).

Chapter Twenty-Eight

Radicalism and Conservatism

Cristina V. Groeger

Introduction

One era's radicals may seem conservative or even reactionary to later generations; one era's conservatives might appear quixotic after the passage of sweeping social reform. The political landscape of the Gilded Age and Progressive Era does not neatly prefigure the political map of the twenty-first century. Modern liberalism emerged out of the New Deal, modern conservatism took shape in response to it. Only in the 1940s did Consensus school historians discover a "conservative" tradition in the United States as such. They distinguished between moderate conservatives and a "radical right" dating from the Federalists through the agrarian populists to William F. Buckley. Both a radical right and radical left stood outside of "a vital center" (Schlesinger 1949). New Left historians rejected the notion of such a center, instead stressing contestation and conflict among diverse groups. New Left historians contributed to a growing historiography of the radical ideas and tactics of primarily leftist dissidents. Since the 1980s, the history of conservatism has become a burgeoning sub-field, and while the latter half of the twentieth century has received most attention, more scholars are tracing the roots of the modern political right back to the nineteenth century.

This scholarship continues to unsettle easy definitions of radicals and conservatives. Increased attention to race, gender, and class has made radical heroes of the left appear to be as much predecessors of twentieth-century conservatism as liberalism. Social histories of non-elites, including recent studies of the Ku Klux Klan, have demonstrated that supposedly "radical" movements were in fact quite mainstream. These insights indicate that it is necessary to specify the particular ways in which individuals and groups were radical, and understand their radicalism in relation to a changing political common sense and balance of social power.

This chapter focuses on political and social movements that defined the outer limits of political possibility between Reconstruction and the mid-1920s. Some individuals and groups entered electoral politics directly; others organized outside the formal political process. All helped shape the political landscape that defined this era. The first section, focusing on the period between 1877 and 1896, explores the politics of national reunion after the Civil War. As the radical Reconstruction agenda was abandoned, a politically powerful economic elite was consolidated. The agrarian insurgency in the South and West, labor insurgency across the North, confrontations with Native Americans, and the growing participation of women in public life, among other major developments, shaped this process.

The second section focuses on the years between 1890 and 1914, and explores the politics of the varied movements that made up progressive reform in the Northeast, West, and the "New South." A new, educated middle class championed reforms that used the power of the state to humanize the effects of industrial capitalism and reform society along rational, scientific lines. These reformers were driven by a missionary zeal to realize social harmony and America's unique destiny at home and abroad. At the same time, progressive reforms were often premised upon the perpetuation of white supremacy, imperialist ventures, and immigration restriction. These aspects were resisted by a variety of pacifists, anti-imperialists, socialists, and anti-racist activists.

The third section, focused on the years between 1914 and 1927, explores the politics of state power leading up to and following World War I. The progressive agenda of a more aggressive state apparatus laid the foundation of the modern American welfare state. However, World War I and the failure of Wilson's internationalist vision abroad fractured the progressive movement and revealed its dark side: severe state repression of socialists, anarchists, feminists, pacifists,

A Companion to the Gilded Age and Progressive Era, First Edition. Edited by Christopher McKnight Nichols and Nancy C. Unger.
© 2017 John Wiley & Sons, Inc. Published 2017 by John Wiley & Sons, Inc.

and those deemed "un-American." Centralized state repression drew on long traditions of violence toward African Americans, Native Americans, immigrants, and political dissenters. New attention to state repression in the 1920s would fuel the movement for civil liberties and shape modern forms of liberalism and conservatism in the mid-twentieth century.

1877–1896: The Long Shadow of the Civil War

Since the 1960s, most historians no longer believe the myth of "black reconstruction" in which northern carpetbaggers, ignorant freedmen, and white southern scalawags took over the South, later "redeemed" by Southern Democrats. The revisionist interpretation, synthesized by Eric Foner and still the paradigm in which historians of Reconstruction operate, stressed the period's real gains in political and economic equality (Foner 1988). Over time, increased southern resistance, racist terrorism, and a shift in national attention to labor conflict eased relations between northern Republican capitalists and southern Democratic landholders. Laissez-faire liberalism and Social Darwinism shaped their worldview, not incompatible with a stress on philanthropy and stewardship of the poor. Radical Republicans retreated from the national project of enforcing the freedmen's newly acquired rights. But exactly how, when, and what factors were the most important in this retreat are still debated.

Many historians continue to emphasize the role of class. As Heather Cox Richardson (2001) argues, northern elites increasingly associated blacks with dangerous forms of worker radicalism. If Republicans were initially willing to protect the political rights of blacks, they stopped when faced with demands for full economic justice on behalf of both poor whites and blacks. The largest upwelling of insurgency focused on economic inequality in the late nineteenth century was the Populist movement. In response to declining agricultural prices and rising debt, farmers and sharecroppers in the South and West formed networks such as the fraternal Grange and Farmers' Alliance as alternative cooperative systems to finance and market their crops. Moving into politics by 1892 as the Populist or People's Party, they condemned the monopolistic power of corporations—especially the railroads—and sought to counter this power through state regulation and administration. In addition to the free coinage of silver, they called for a graduated income tax, a national currency, and the nationalization of an array of public goods: railroads, the telegraph and telephone, postal savings bank, and land for settlers. To avoid the corruption of an expanded government power, they also called for civil service regulations and the limitation of government expenses.

These agrarian populists have been perceived as provincial, backward agrarians (Hofstadter 1955), as the vanguard of a radical "movement culture" (Goodwyn 1978, Argersinger 1995, Sanders 1999), as evangelists (Creech 2006), to fully modern progressives (Postel 2007). The debate continues over the ways this amorphous, multi-faceted movement was radical, and the ways it was conservative.

The role of race in the populist movement brings out this ambivalence. The Farmers' Alliance was an amalgam of multiple regional alliances. The predominantly white Northern Alliance of the Midwest and plain states and the exclusively white Southern Alliance in Texas, Louisiana and Arkansas have received the bulk of historians' attention. Omar Ali's *In the Lion's Mouth: Black Populism in the New South, 1886–1900* (2010) is to date the most comprehensive work on black populism. Ali (2010) argues that Black Populism should be understood as its own, autonomous movement, rather than a biracial offshoot of white populism. The Colored Farmers' Alliance—at its height reaching 1.2 million affiliates across the South—consolidated multiple networks of black farmers and agrarian workers who demanded higher wages, better working conditions, better prices for crops, and better access to land and credit. As the populist movement transitioned from agrarian organizing in the 1880s to electoral politics in the 1890s, it opened up possibilities for interracial political alliances at the state and local level. Some of the earliest studies of populism explored these interracial alliances: C. Vann Woodward's dissertation and first book *Tom Watson: Agrarian Rebel* (1938) examines the life of a Georgia Democrat turned Populist who championed political equality for African Americans. However, after electoral failures in the 1890s, a frustrated Watson turned to racism and anti-Semitism. Deborah Beckel (2010) traces a longer history of "fusionist" politics in North Carolina, leading to successful Republican and Populist state governments in the 1890s. Joseph Gerteis (2007) examines short-lived biracial cooperation in Georgia and Virginia populism. These studies also reveal the movement's limitations, as the racism of many white Republican and Populist leaders repeatedly threatened to overcome strategic political alliances. The People's Party effective merger with the Democratic Party in 1896 undercut populism as a force against white supremacy. Some historians reject the notion that populism ever held out the possibility of a truly biracial egalitarian movement. As Stephen Hahn (2005) argues, the limits of biracial politics in the South led many African Americans to embrace nationalist and emigrationist alternatives.

In addition to freed blacks and white agrarians, Native Americans also played an important role in shaping the course of nation building after the Civil War. Heather Cox Richardson (2007) and Eliot West (2009) have sought to shift the historiography of this era away from an exclusively North–South axis, to one that encompasses federal policy and the struggle over citizenship in the West. Eliot West uses the Nez Perce War of 1877 to explore what he calls the "Greater Reconstruction," or the contestation over the federal government's attempts to incorporate multiple nations and peoples into one nation. The broader framework of nation-building and the subjugation of colonial subjects holds out promising possibilities for further comparative studies that situate the United States in a global context (Chang 2011).

One of the most dramatic opposition movements to emerge among Native Americans in this era was the Ghost Dance movement. The movement was inspired by Wovoka, described by his followers as a Christ-like Indian prophet who preached a moral code and a renewed world in which Indians would be forever free. Gregory E. Smoak (2008) argues that this movement was central to the process of "ethnogenesis," or pan-Indian identity formation. Smoak traces its roots to earlier traditions of native shamanism as well as Christianity spread by missionaries, and shows how it became a form of resistance to assimilation and forced adaptation to reservation life. He ends his story with the more commonly known 1890 Ghost Dance movement of the Lakota Sioux. Heather Cox Richardson (2011) describes the national party politics that ultimately led to aggressive federal suppression of this movement. Republicans, seeking to secure more votes through expanding statehood in the West, broke up the Great Sioux Reservation to encourage more white settlers. This social upheaval helped fuel the Ghost Dance movement. When South Dakotan white settlers turned to populism in 1890, President William Harrison believed that suppression of the Ghost Dance would win him electoral favors. In December of 1890, 400 federal troops massacred a band of Sioux Indians at Wounded Knee, South Dakota, killing or injuring between 200 and 300. Faced with overwhelming state violence, the Ghost Dance movement went into decline.

While farmers, tenants, and sharecroppers mobilized through the Populist movement, urban workers faced different challenges. Organized labor has long received the bulk of attention of labor historians. The Knights of Labor, founded as a secret society of Philadelphia garment workers in 1869, grew into the largest labor organization in 1886, peaking at over 750,000 members. While the Knights positioned themselves against revolutionary modes of social change and divisive labor tactics like strikes, they sought to counter the "alarming development and aggression of aggregated wealth, which, unless checked, will invariably lead to the pauperization and hopeless degradation of the toiling masses" (Knights of Labor 1878). This trend could only be checked if all laborers, across divisions of skill, trade, gender, and race, acted in unison, to secure "the toilers a proper share of the wealth that they create" and realize a "cooperative commonwealth" (Knights of Labor 1878). Towards this end the Knights advocated an eight-hour workday, workplace safety laws, a ban on child and convict labor, gender equity in wages, land reserved for public use, cooperative institutions, and the establishment of bureaus of Labor Statistics (Fink 1983; Weir 2000). As shown by John Jentz and Richard Schneirov's study of Chicago (2012), the Knights played an important role in forging cross-class alliances that shaped late nineteenth-century municipal reform associated with the Progressive Era. At the national level, they briefly succeeded in joining forces with the agrarian populists as the People's Party.

While nominally embracing workers regardless of race or sex, the Knights did not always live up to this standard of inclusiveness. Theresa Ann Case (2010) explores instances of successful biracial alliances forged in Texas, Arkansas, Missouri, and Illinois, but this alliance was premised on shared antipathy to Chinese workers and convict labor. Some of the most powerful female organizers started with the Knights of Labor, prominent among them Mary "Mother" Jones, the subject of Elliot J. Gorn's biography (2001). Jones, an Irish Catholic immigrant, later led strikes for the United Mine Workers. Many wives, sisters, and daughters of labor unionists played an important role in labor organizing. However, females made up a small number of the organized workers themselves, and their demands reflected the dominant gendered division of labor. Most, including Mother Jones, advocated for a family wage for working men that would allow wives to stay home and care for their children. Like many Catholic women, Jones ascribed to conservative gender roles, and she opposed women's suffrage on the grounds that it was an unnecessary distraction from more important labor reform and from women's duty as mothers.

In addition to female labor activism, the female-led political movements of women's suffrage and temperance also came to be allied with the People's Party, and recent scholarship has teased apart both their radical and conservative aspects. The white women leaders of the female suffrage movement emerged out of the radicalism of abolitionism, but their alliance with African Americans was broken during Reconstruction and the failure to cover women in the Fifteenth Amendment. Some of these first-generation suffragists sought to reconcile these two movements. In 1872 Victoria Woodhull ran as a presidential candidate for the Equal Rights Party, encompassing both women suffragists and African American activists. She also advocated a range of radical cultural and feminist reforms, and was involved with the free thought and spiritualism movements that, as Ann Braude (2001) shows, forged a powerful critique of patriarchal political and religious institutions. A proponent of free love, Woodhull was arrested for violation of the 1873 federal Comstock Law banning pornography and the circulation of information about contraception and birth control.

Most women were not this radical on issues of gender, sexual morality, and race. But many participated in politics, and defied traditional gender norms by entering the public sphere in new ways. Rebecca Edwards (1997) challenges the standard chronology of women entering the public sphere, long seen as an early twentieth-century phenomenon, by documenting how women participated in earlier party politics and third-party movements like the Prohibition Party and Populist Party. Frances Willard embodied some of the radical as well as conservative tendencies of these movements. President of the Women's Christian Temperance Union (WCTU) from 1879 to 1899, she pioneered an agenda that went well beyond banning liquor to advocate for women's suffrage, labor reform, federal aid to education, boards of health, prison reform, and the moral reform of prostitutes. While helping to carve out a new field of political activism for women, the widespread support for the movement relied upon arguments that tended to reinforce traditional gender norms. For the WCTU, female suffrage was premised upon "home protection," a rationale that allowed women to enter the public sphere in order to protect their proper domestic sphere from drunken men. As Louise Newman (1999) argues, these gendered rationales for women's political roles also took on a strong racial dimension, especially in the South, as they cast black men as responsible for corrupting politics and the home, which white women were uniquely qualified to purify. The racial dimension of women's political reform continues to be a fruitful area of historical scholarship.

Along with the populists and labor organizations, the People's party brought together the followers of a variety of socialist visions. It drew in adherents of Henry George, whose bestseller *Progress and Poverty* (1879) promoted a single tax on land to challenge the stranglehold of land monopoly, which George believed to be enriching non-producers at the expense of workers and manufacturers. It also drew in members of hundreds of Nationalist Clubs, inspired by Edward Bellamy's equally popular *Looking Backward, 2000–1887* (1888), which imagined a utopian future in which state ownership and regulation harnessed the abundance made possible by industrial capitalism to realize a harmonious, disciplined social order. The People's Party also channeled the religious energies of the popular Social Gospel movement, articulated by theologians such as Baptist pastor Walter Rauschenbusch, who reframed the dire social consequences of capitalism as social sins that compelled Christians to work to realize the Kingdom of God on earth.

The climax of the People's Party in 1896 marked the end of its most radical elements. The People's Party joined the Democratic Party to nominate William Jennings Bryan as their presidential candidate. While Bryan employed the fiery rhetoric of the populist insurgency, his famous Cross of Gold speech narrowly focused on the free coinage of silver at the expense of the wide array of pro-labor policies adopted in the People's Party platform. Additionally, as historians of the South have stressed, the alliance of the Populists and the Democratic Party fragmented local populist and Republic an "fusionist" parties, facilitating the consolidation of Jim Crow in the South.

This turning point also marked an important shift in the labor movement. The radically inclusive vision of the general unionism of the Knights of Labor was replaced by an exclusive, craft unionism of the American Federation of Labor (AFL) in the next decades. The Knight's broad political agenda was replaced with a tighter focus on wages and working hours. However, some radical labor organizations and political parties were important exceptions to this trend, and, as we will see, bridged the nineteenth-century labor movement with the radical industrial unionism that emerged in the wake of the Great Depression.

Finally, this moment marked a transition for women's political movements. As Rebecca Edwards has argued, by the end of the century, both the Democratic and Republican parties had taken a conservative, masculine turn that pushed women out of direct engagement in party politics. Far from a decline in women's political activity, however, their activism shifted to other sites. In particular, women's leadership in non-partisan organizations became one of the defining features of the Progressive Era.

1890–1914: Progressive Reform

The progressive movement drew support from a new middle class that sought to use the power of the state to eliminate the worst abuses of capitalism and to restructure society on a more rational, scientific basis. Progressives drew on many of the same reform traditions of populists and labor unions, such as a producerist tradition of labor republicanism and an evangelical social gospel. But they also adopted new practices and institutions. They embraced the administrative capacities of corporations and the state while seeking to place them on more efficient and ethical grounds. They filled the ranks of new research universities that facilitated technological innovation and promised new scientific solutions to social problems. Women educated in newly founded women's colleges flocked to social settlements to address social ills directly, and led non-partisan associations to advocate for reforms in child labor, public health, city governance, public morality, and education.

Were progressives conservative or radical? This question continues to be debated by historians, and has been the ground on which, as Robert D. Johnston (2002) observed, historians are in effect debating the meaning of American democracy. Historians of the Progressive Era like Charles Beard and V. L. Parrington celebrated reformers defending the "people" against the "special interests." Consensus-era historians such as Richard Hofstadter and Louis Hartz (1955) focused on progressives' efforts to minimize class conflict and class consciousness, and portrayed them as solidly middle class. The fiercest critique came from New Left historians such as Gabriel Kolko (1963) and Samuel Weinstein (1968), who portrayed progressives as allies of a triumphant "political capitalism" or "corporate liberalism." Some recent works have continued to stress the ways progressives perpetuated class-based inequality (Stromquist 2006; Huyssen 2014). But later historians also attempted to reclaim some of progressives' democratic credentials. Intellectual historians like James T. Kloppenberg (1986) saw progressives as navigating a "via media" between liberalism and socialism, and Douglas Rossinow (2008) placed progressives squarely alongside left radicals in a broad democratic tradition. Theda Skocpol (1992) traced the emergence of the "maternalistic welfare state" leading a generation of historians to study the role of women in the progressive movement and shifting the debate from the axis of class to gender. Increasing attention to race, empire, as well as gender and class, have continued to expose both radical and conservative elements of this era.

One site to look for radicalism in the Progressive Era is in states and municipalities that were "laboratories of democracy." As detailed in Nancy C. Unger's biography (2000), Wisconsin governor, senator, and presidential candidate Robert La Follette, Sr., became one of the strongest advocates of political reforms to make the state more responsive to citizens' needs and to challenge monopolies and trusts. These reforms included direct legislation, workmen's compensation for injuries, progressive taxation, and the regulation of railroads. La Follette believed that the state university system had an important role to play in developing public policy, a concept that became known as the Wisconsin Idea. Municipalities were similar laboratories during this era. A number of turn-of-the-century mayors—Samuel "Golden Rule" Jones of Toledo, Hazen S. Pingree of Detroit, and Tom Johnson of Cleveland—saw corporate greed as the root of government corruption, and sought to increase mechanisms of popular democracy (through the referendum, initiative, and recall) and expanded a wide range of public services (public utilities, evening schools, kindergartens, public baths, parks, and playgrounds). Robert D. Johnston (2003) shows how this same strain of anti-corporate populism in Portland drew support from the working class and, crucial to its success, a broad middle class. At the same time, many structural political reforms of this era—such as civil service reform, the city commission system, and the city manager system—drew on a technocratic strain of progressive reform that had the effect of sharply decreasing voter participation.

As the Wisconsin Idea indicates, new institutions—universities foremost among them—also shaped progressive politics. Universities were the sites in which intellectuals and social reformers developed new philosophical paradigms and new sciences of human society. Richard T. Ely, founder of the American Economic Association and professor at the University of Wisconsin-Madison, developed the school of "ethical economics" which posited the ethical problems of poverty and labor conflict as crucial objects of scientific analysis, and suggested broad economic and political reforms to address them. Andrew Jewett (2012) traces this democratic understanding of science that dominated the early human sciences, and examines the political process through which that understanding was forced out of universities and replaced by supposedly "value-free" sciences by mid-century.

Alongside radical traditions, universities also lent scientific credence to conservative disciplinary innovations. One of the most reactionary movements was eugenics. Although it had earlier precedents in statistics and agricultural and animal breeding, biologist Charles Davenport became one of the primary promoters of policies to improve the genetic pool of the human species. His Eugenics Record Office, founded in 1910, collected the medical histories of thousands of Americans and published studies purportedly demonstrating the hereditary unfitness of lower-class immigrants. Scientific racism, a corresponding movement that emerged out of the discipline of anthropology, sought to establish the scientific basis of a hierarchy of races. Scientific racism and eugenics were popularized in the writings of Madison Grant, whose *The Passing of the Great Race* (1916) advocated eugenic policies to promote Nordic superiority. Trained as a lawyer, Grant did not have professional credentials as a scientist, but as Jonathan Spiro's biography of Grant (2009) demonstrates, Grant inhabited a still-fluid position between nineteenth-century gentleman naturalist and professional scientist, and he sought to fix the criteria of authority on racial superiority rather than on academic credentials. Eugenic ideas were widely popular, accepted by feminists like Charlotte Perkins Gilman and Margaret Sanger, and even African American rights activist (and first African American to earn a PhD from Harvard), W.E.B. Du Bois. Organizations like the Immigration Restriction League and American Breeders Association lobbied for eugenic policies across the nation. Over 30 states adopted forced sterilization legislation, leading to the sterilization of 60,000 people by mid-century.

Other disciplinary developments had both reformist and conservative elements. Richard T. Ely, for example, sought to apply science to society by helping to found the Harvard Graduate School of Business Administration in 1908. Business schools aimed to both elevate business into a subject of scientific research and inculcate a service ethic into professional managers. However, the new fields of scientific and personnel management at best humanized some of the most obvious forms of labor exploitation, and at worst turned the exploitation of human labor into a science (Nelson 1992). As women increasingly entered the ranks of universities, they played a leading role in developing the disciplines of domestic science and home economics. Ellen Swallow Richards, a founder of home economics, was the first woman admitted to the Massachusetts Institute of Technology in the field of chemistry and was appointed as an instructor in a newly founded MIT laboratory of sanitation. On the one hand, these were some of the first venues for women to enter fields of scientific research, and as these fields became ubiquitous in public high schools, they also provided thousands of women with teaching positions. On the other hand, these new disciplines reinforced a gender division of labor in both education and the workplace.

Educational institutions of a variety of types came to embody the environmentalist reform vision of many Progressives. The institutional form with the widest reach was the public school. The most ubiquitous of public services funded as part of the progressive political agenda, public school systems not only included new high schools and common schools, but also evening schools, vocational schools, commercial schools, nursery schools, kindergartens, health centers, gymnasiums, and free school lunch programs. These reforms were inspired by the ideas of progressive educators, none more prominent than philosopher and social reformer John Dewey. Dewey challenged the distinction between the liberal education of the historically leisured class and the vocational education of the working class. Instead, he argued that the criteria of educational value was the reconstruction of experience that allowed individuals to intelligently direct that experience. He imagined his Laboratory school in Chicago, in which students would collectively solve problems across a wide range of activities and vocations, to be an experiment in industrial democracy that would liberate human intelligence and sympathy. This holistic education, Dewey hoped, would transform labor relations and make possible the realization of an ethical social democracy.

In practice, however, a new stress on practical education within a rapidly expanding school system did less to reshape the economy than respond to its demands. The vast expansion of schooling in the early twentieth century replaced alternative forms of on-the-job training, but largely reflected the class-based, racial, and gendered norms of the labor market. By providing women with vocationally appropriate education, public schools reinforced the gendered division of labor. In the South, as James Anderson (1988) documents, northern philanthropists funded industrial education and teacher-training normal schools like the Hampton Institute and Tuskegee Institute. Philanthropists worked closely with figures like Booker T. Washington, who saw practical education and economic uplift as a better strategy to racial equality than classical academic education or the more confrontational demands for political enfranchisement and civil rights championed by activists such as W.E.B. Du Bois. On the one hand, these industrial normal schools marked a vast improvement over the alternative dearth of educational opportunities for African Americans, as many southern whites sought to keep public education in rudimentary stages through the mid-twentieth century (Kantrowitz 2000). Furthermore, it provided education to many African Americans who would become leaders in the fight for racial equality. At the same time, it circumscribed educational opportunities for African Americans, reinforced segregation, and was unable to challenge employment discrimination.

The middle-class women who led a variety of progressive movements grew up in the new educational institutions of the Progressive Era. Teaching, a feminized profession since the mid-nineteenth century, was a rapidly expanding occupation for women at the turn of the century, and played a crucial role in expanding higher education for women (Clifford 2014). Taking advantage of new educational opportunities, women entered a wide range of professions and helped develop new professions like social work and public health. These educated women, who led campaigns for labor laws, civil service reform, temperance, and public services, saw their activities as a means of social salvation. They often had their start in particular urban "redemptive places" (Spain 2001) such as social settlements, pioneered in the United States by Jane Addams in Chicago. As shown in Louise Knight's biography of Addams (2008), settlement houses served as communities that brought together middle-class women, like Addams herself, and poor and working-class immigrants. They offered a range of social services and activities shaped by the local needs of members. For Addams, these settlements, like the public school, served in practice as microcosms of radical democracy—across divisions of class, race, ethnicity, and gender.

But as an increasing number of historians have demonstrated, much of women's reform activity embraced conservative elements that sharpened these divisions. On gender, as seen with the women's suffrage campaign, the most politically successful non-partisan activities of women claimed to bring the domestic, nurturing role of women to politics. The most successful welfare services they championed were also premised on a male breadwinner model of the family. As Linda Gordon (1994) describes, white female reformers who assumed the death of a wage-earning husband was the primary source of insecurity for women successfully won widows' pensions and mothers' aid in states across the country by 1930. However, their efforts helped shape a bifurcated welfare state consisting of a privileged social insurance program for participants in economic sectors dominated by white men, and inferior welfare programs for others. Female-led moral reform efforts to "save" delinquent children, fallen women, and "white slaves" fueled the expansion of an intrusive and discriminatory system of state surveillance. Mary Odem (1995) describes the use of state regulation by these reformers to impose their own standards of gender and sexuality on working class, immigrant, and African American girls and their families. Brian Donovan (2005) examines the ways the panic over "white slavery," or forced female prostitution, and anti-vice activism in Chicago constructed and perpetuated racial and gender hierarchies.

The racially conservative dimensions of women's political activity are seen especially in new scholarship on women in the South. Francesca Morgan (2006) looks at the political role of both white and black female organizations. She details how the African American National Association of Colored Women, the mixed race Women's Relief Corps, and the white nationalist Daughters of the American Revolution and the United Daughters of the Confederacy all shared assumptions of the moral and cultural superiority of women, while each constructed distinctive gendered and racial definitions of patriotism and citizenship. A number of scholars have also explored the particular shape of the southern women's suffrage movement. As Elna C. Green (1997) demonstrates, the arguments of white female federal suffragists, state suffragists, and anti-suffragists alike were premised on black disenfranchisement. As the new biography of anti-lynching activist Ida B. Wells (Giddings 2008) details, Wells dramatically and publically criticized suffragists like Frances Willard in the 1890s for contributing to racial arguments that gave ammunition to white supremacists in the South.

Historians have used gender as a lens to further enrich the broader political history of the Jim Crow South. As Bruce Baker (2008) describes, the 1890s witnessed a dramatic spike in lynching by reactionary vigilante groups like the Ku Klux Klan, building on a long tradition of mob violence. Many African Americans decided to leave segregation, the threat of lynching, and scarce job opportunities in the South and move north in the Great Migration. Those who remained navigated the transformations of the New South. Glenda Gilmore (1996) argues that as black men were disenfranchised, new spaces opened for the political activity of black women. Communities of faith played a crucial role. Within churches and voluntary associations—including the Women's Christian Temperance Union, the YWCA, and the National American Women's Suffrage Association (NAWSA)—a "better class" of black women sought strategic alliances with white women progressives to gain from the expanding welfare state. Their class-based strategies of respectability, uplift, hard work, education, and moral behavior were used to subvert a racially exclusive reformist agenda, as demonstrated by Evelyn Brooks Higginbotham (1993) and Stephanie Shaw (1996). Maggie Lena Walker represents one such woman. Walker was born to slave parents in Richmond, Virginia, and grew up within the black community of the First African Baptist Church. After graduating from a black normal school and teaching for several years, she married, but did not cease working outside the home. She is most well-known for becoming president of the St. Luke Penny Saving Bank in 1903, making her the first black woman bank president (Marlowe 2003). As Elsa Barkley Brown (1989) notes, Walker championed universal suffrage and a "womanist" vision of Black Nationalism based on the crucial role of women in African-American economic and political empowerment.

These strategies were innovated in response to the terror and violence of the Jim Crow South. Leon F. Litwack (1998) shows how the first generation of African Americans born in freedom, less inclined to show deference to whites, helped to provoke the most violent period of American race relations. In his bleak portrait, the achievements of middle-class blacks did not create a way out of this cycle, but only generated more antipathy among whites who perceived them to be threatening competitors. While Gilmore (2008) highlights the few instances of interracial cooperation and the political activists who laid the groundwork for the Civil Rights Movement, Litwack gives voice to countless black southerners who privately upheld dignity in the face of everyday brutality. The stranglehold of white domination helps explain the continuous appeal of separatist rather than integrationist strategies. Like Hahn's nationalism lens, Michele Mitchell (2004) argues that the notion of a common fate shaped post-emancipation African American politics, and traces separatist and emigration movements from "Liberia fever" to Garveyism. She also shows the ways in which gender and sexuality—often in conservative forms—were central to these reform discourses. 1870s emigrationists argued colonization would improve masculinity, fecundity, and protect black women; Garveyites emphasized black motherhood and the control of black women's sexuality in the realization of an idealized, racially pure nation.

African Americans not only confronted racial exclusion by white political and economic elites, but also within the very organizations aimed to challenge those elites: labor unions. The labor question emerged as the central concern of many progressives. Most supported organized labor as an important means of challenging corporate power and realizing "industrial democracy." Labor organizations, however, existed on a spectrum of more or less radical visions and tactics. The AFL emerged as the dominant labor organization of the Progressive Era, and focused on "bread and butter" gains for a skilled aristocracy of labor. The AFL did play an important role in politics, as Julie Greene (1998) argues. However, it did not reimagine workplace governance along democratic lines or challenge wage labor itself, and also tended to exclude women, immigrants, and African Americans.

Women did carve out important new spaces, including new feminists' spaces, in the labor movement. Annelise Orleck (1995) focuses on female labor leaders who emerged out of the 1909 "Uprising of 20,000," or the mass spontaneous strike of Jewish, Polish, and Italian female garment workers in New York that grew the ranks of the International Ladies Garment Workers Union (ILGWU). While many women involved in the labor movement still held to traditional gender norms, a new group of "industrial feminists" also advocated for feminist causes. For example, Rose Schneiderman, a Jewish immigrant who had grown up in the sewing trades, became an organizer for ILGWU as well as a prominent member of the class-bridging Women's Trade Union League (WTUL) and an active member of NAWSA. As Lara Vapnek (2009) discusses, Schneiderman, along with Clara Lemlich, the ILGWU organizer who led the 1909 strike, and Leonora O'Reilly, founding member and organizer of the WTUL, formed the Wage Earner's Suffrage League in 1911. This league, which emerged out of disagreements within the predominantly middle-class dominated NAWSA and over the role of women's suffrage within the Socialist

Party, aimed to give a political voice to working women, directly linking economic independence with political rights.

While most progressives tended to shy away from the word "socialism" and favored incremental reformist strategies, a variety of more radical social reformers gained momentum during this period. The most popular third party was the Socialist Party, led by Eugene V. Debs, which won 6% of the popular vote in 1912. As Nick Salvatore's biography of Debs (2007) describes, after Debs was jailed for his leading role in the Pullman Strike in 1894 as president of the American Railway Union, he helped found the Socialist Democratic Party in 1898, which became the Socialist Party in 1901. Drawing on traditions of labor republicanism, populism, the Social Gospel, Bellamy's nationalism, and Marxism, Debs accused capitalism of reducing workers to slaves, and advocated worker control of the state to realize true political and industrial democracy. While his ultimate goal of abolishing the capitalist system was more radical than the aspirations of even the most democratic progressives, the immediate program of the Socialist Party, including public ownership of banks and railroads, unemployment aid, stricter labor laws, and a graduate income tax, was substantively similar to that of many progressives.

While the Socialist Party included women, immigrants, and African Americans, a critique of gender norms and racial inequity was not central to its program. Sally Miller (1993) details the life of one of the most popular female socialist orators, Kate Richards O'Hare, a Kansas native who lectured to audiences across the plains states. While preaching socialist reform as a married mother of four, she believed that the "Woman Question" was subsumed within the "Social Question," and she reassured a southern audience that socialism would not mean full social equality with blacks. The most prominent black socialist, Hubert Harrison, was drawn to socialism as a radical alternative to Booker T. Washington's accommodationist strategy of economic uplift (Perry 2008). However, he became disillusioned by the party's lack of unified action on race and its tolerance of segregated local branches in the South, and became a leader of the New Negro movement.

The Industrial Workers of the World (IWW) presented a more radically inclusive vision. David Brundage (1994) traces the emergence of the IWW out of many reform currents: Irish nationalism, republicanism, populism, prohibition, the general unionism of the Knights of Labor, and the militancy of the Western Federation of Miners. Other interpretations stress the crucial role of foreign immigrants and their anarchist and syndicalist roots. Undoubtedly, when it was founded in 1905, the IWW drew together a wide range of workers, labor organizers, and socialists who were frustrated with the limited craft unionism of the AFL. The IWW instead presented an inclusive vision of worker solidarity to regain full control of their workplace and the fruits of their labor. While the IWW's call for "one big union" evoked the Knights of Labor, it was based on an updated analysis of labor relations. As their 1905 Manifesto stated, new machines and technological innovations continuously wiped out entire trades and threw workers "upon the scrap pile" to sink into the "uniform mass of wage slaves" (IWW 1905). Rather than unite to challenge this system, workers were being manipulated by employers and exclusive unions that promoted differences of skill, trade, race, and gender to turn workers against each other. The IWW ridiculed progressive institutions of business–labor collaboration—such as the National Civil Federation, of which AFL President Samuel Gompers was a member—as instruments to mislead workers and better carry out the wealthy's war upon labor. Against this united front, workers needed to overcome their differences and form a broad industrial organization that could use the most powerful tool available to workers: the general strike. As articulated by IWW leader William D. "Big Bill" Haywood, the general strike was more powerful than the ballot: it "prevents the capitalist from disenfranchising the worker; it gives the vote to women, it re-enfranchises the black man and places the ballot in the hands of every boy and girl employed in a shop" (Haywood 1911). A fully organized workforce deploying the general strike would allow workers to take control of the industries in which they worked, realizing the true meaning of industrial democracy.

The IWW led some of the few successful organizing campaigns for women, immigrant, and African American workers—dockworkers, agricultural workers, textile workers, and mining workers—in the early decades of the twentieth century. They were involved in over 100 strikes. They also championed free speech and free assembly, and opposed laws banning street meetings that were a primary mode of labor organizing. But while the organization made new inroads into organizing the "unorganizable," the IWW's own tactics made the consolidation of its significant, if not revolutionary, victories difficult. Based on the philosophy of constant labor agitation that was extremely challenging to maintain in practice, the IWW's refusal to negotiate contracts led to the rapid loss of any concessions won from employers during strikes, as occurred after the 1912 Lawrence textile strike and 1913 Patterson silk strike. It was this "industrial anarchy" that led to Eugene Debs, a founding member of the IWW, to break with the organization (Salvatore 2007).

Historians of U.S. labor have long noted the particular violence of labor conflict in the Progressive Era. This was dramatically apparent in the battles between one of the most aggressively anti-union employers' associations, the National Erectors' Association, and the Ironworkers' Union, which funded a dynamite campaign to bomb iron and steel buildings, employers and contractors. In what became known as the "crime of the century," union members John J. and James B. McNamara were tried for bombing the Los Angeles Times building, leading to the death of 21 employees. As Sidney Fine (1995) argues, explanations for these violent tactics must be attentive to particular workplace cultures and worldview. In this case, violent tactics had developed among largely Irish ironworkers, the least skilled of the construction trades, who inhabited a more aggressive working-class culture and drew on traditions of Fenianism and Darwinism. Anti-union campaigns have also been the subject of recent works tracing the longer history of conservatism back to the early twentieth century (Millikan 2001; Gage 2009).

Other historians have similarly looked away from the leadership of unions to the workers themselves to find evidence of radicalism in the labor movement. As Howard Kimeldorf argues (1999) in his study of Philadelphia dock workers and New York hotel and restaurant employees, workers' strategic choices to organize with the AFL or IWW were determined less by ideological commitments than the nature of their particular workplace environment. Kimeldorf finds continuous evidence of syndicalist, radical tendencies of workers seeking to control their own workplaces, challenging interpretations of workers as conservative. Racial inclusion and class solidarity made possible the IWW-affiliated, predominantly African American, Marine Transport Workers Union Local 8 in Philadelphia in 1913. When this union dissolved, the strategies of racial and class solidarity and direct action were carried into the subsequent unions under AFL leadership. But these cases remained on the fringe of the labor movement. As documented by Bruce Nelson (2001) and Robert Zieger (2007), African Americans would only become integrated into the mainstream labor movement in the 1930s.

Much labor radicalism in the early twentieth century was dominated by immigrants, who inhabited the lowest rungs of the economic ladder and brought revolutionary European traditions with them. Feminist activist Emma Goldman emigrated from the Russian Empire and became involved in New York City's subculture of anarchists in the late 1880s. As detailed in Vivian Gornick's biography (2011), in the midst of the Homestead Strike in 1892, Goldman and co-conspirator Alexander Berkman planned to assassinate Henry Frick, the factory manager of the Homestead plant, in the hopes of inciting a wider workers' revolt. Goldman was arrested and subsequently detained dozens of times for seditious statements, but she tirelessly spoke to audiences around the country about anarchism, women's rights, birth control, homosexuality, and the freedom to be able to discuss all these matters openly.

Despite the reputation of anarchism as a destructive and violent movement, Emma Goldman defended anarchism as fundamentally opposed to violence. According to Goldman, anarchism was premised on the theory that violence was at the foundation of all forms of government, which anarchism rejected in defense of the "freest possible expression of all the latent powers of the individual" (Goldman 1911, 293). Rather than a purely individualistic notion of freedom, however, anarchism reconciled the individual and society, as it would eliminate the pernicious economic, political, and religious influences that hindered this unity. Like socialism, anarchism held that "a perfect personality, then, is only possible in a state of society where man is free to choose the mode of work" (Goldman 1911, 293). And far from a foreign or anti-American philosophy, Goldman repeatedly invoked transcendentalists Ralph Waldo Emerson and Henry David Thoreau, calling the latter the "greatest American Anarchist" (Goldman 1911, 294). The willingness of anarchists to openly resist the law, she argued, had a long American tradition, including the activism that led to American independence, the emancipation of slavery, universal suffrage, and the achievements of the labor movement.

While most immigrants were not anarchists, the stereotype of immigrant radicalism gave fodder to widespread anti-immigrant sentiment during the Progressive Era. A rash of anarchist violence, including the assassination of President William McKinley in 1901, led to the passage of the 1903 Immigration Act, or the Anarchist Exclusion Act. The relationship between anarchism and immigration policy in the United States continues to frame contemporary historiography. As Mary Barton (2015) has recently argued, while European nations pursued collective multilateral action against anarchism, the United States tended to opt for unilateral anti-immigration policies.

American anti-foreign sentiment has a long historiographical tradition dating back to John Higham's classic study, *Strangers in the Land: Patterns of American Nativism, 1860–1925* (1955). Aristide Zolberg (2006) takes a broad interpretation of immigration—including slavery and internal migration—in a sweeping survey of American state policy as an instrument of nation building. Jeane Petit (2010) focuses more narrowly on the literacy test as a means of immigration restriction, originating in the 1890s and passed into law in 1917. Some organizations like the Immigration Restriction League, founded in 1894 by three Harvard alumni, championed the literacy test to make sure genetically inferior southern and eastern Europeans would not degrade and emasculate the Anglo-Saxon race. Other groups like the American Association of Foreign Language Newspapers opposed the literacy test, but on a different set of racial and gendered assumptions: they claimed that southern and eastern Europeans (although not non-Europeans) would reinvigorate an effete American stock through inter-breeding.

The "barbarian virtues" of manliness, vitality, and vigor, in Theodore Roosevelt's terms, linked immigration to imperialism in the minds of many Americans. They have also provided a conceptual framework for historians to link American domestic and foreign policy. Matthew Frye Jacobson (2000) posits immigration and empire as two sides of the same coin. White man's civilizing mission provided the justifications for both the Americanization of immigrants at home as well as imperialism abroad. As millions of immigrants entered the country and the United States acquired new territories, however, Jacobsen argues that both immigrants and colonial dependents threatened racialized conceptions of citizenship, provoking extensive debate over the meaning of American nationalism.

Along with ethnic and racial assumptions shaping foreign policy, numerous studies of American foreign policy explore the gendered dimensions of empire. Kristin L. Hoganson (1998) argues that specific scripts of masculinity directly informed foreign policy to determine the place of the United States in an emerging world order. In the wake of an economic depression that threatened the male wage-earner, Hoganson argues that men pursued empire as an arena in which to enact martial virtues, and elevate their stature with these territorial possessions. Mary Renda (2001) uses "paternalism" as the central lens through which to explore the military occupation of Haiti from 1915 to 1934. Renda reveals how, through the encounter with an exotic other, the United States was in turn shaped by the cultural legacies of the occupation.

Despite the powerful cultural, racial, and gendered ideologies that supported American imperialism, there were many Americans opposed to these military ventures. Michael Patrick Cullinane (2012) roots anti-imperialist sentiment in earlier critiques of American expansion within a transnational network of anti-imperialist activism. William James, member of the Anti-Imperialist League formed in 1898, articulated the moral repugnance some Americans felt at the brutality of U.S. activities in the Philippines. To the *Boston Evening Transcript* in 1899 he wrote: "Could there be a more damning indictment of that whole bloated idol termed 'modern civilization' than this amounts to? Civilization is, then, the big, hollow, resounding, corrupting, sophisticating, confusing torrent of mere brutal momentum and irrationality that brings forth fruits like this!" (James 1899). Trygve Throntveit (2014) interprets James' opposition to imperialism as a central component of his broader ethical philosophy. While a proponent of martial virtues, James observed how quickly a sense of philanthropic duty could be undercut by moral superiority and chauvinism. Not all anti-imperialist arguments were driven by the same democratic ideals, however. Christopher Nichols (2011) places 1890s anti-imperialism at the root of an isolationist ideology, premised on soft-power forms of economic international engagement rather than formal imperialism. Other anti-imperialist arguments derived from the same racist premises that drove anti-immigration efforts. As Eric Tyrone Lowery Love (2004) describes, it was a defense of a republicanism premised on a racial conception of citizenship that led many to oppose the incorporation of foreign people through empire.

1914–1927: World War I, State Repression, and the Birth of Civil Liberties

The U.S. entrance into World War I was an important turning point in progressive reform and the history of radicalism and conservatism in this era. But there are many narratives about how and why the war was a turning point. One common narrative focuses on the climax and decline of progressive internationalism. According to Alan Dawley (2003), many progressives who supported entry into the war, including John Dewey and W.E.B. Du Bois, were lured by Wilson's vision of internationalism and self-determination. However, Wilson's failure to convince his own nation to join the League of Nations is often taken as the decisive blow to the heady idealism of the war to end all wars.

Another narrative in which World War I was a turning point focuses on anti-war activism and state repression. While many progressives were persuaded by Wilson's vision, the majority of Americans had been opposed to U.S. entry, and the war remained unpopular even after 1917. Opposition to the war fueled a broad pacifist movement. Joseph Kosek (2011) uses the history of the United States Fellowship of Reconciliation (FOR USA) founded in 1915 to demonstrate how pacifists shaped the primary modes of non-violent political action crucial to subsequent social justice movements. Many women—including prominent progressive social reformers—became leaders of the peace movement. The Women's Peace Party (WPP), to which Jane Addams, a co-founder of FOR USA, was elected first president, was also founded in 1915 and made use of public demonstrations to advocate against militarism and for women's suffrage. The WPP also helped organize an international gathering of female peace activists, the International Congress of Women, held in The Hague in 1915. This international organization became the Women's International League for Peace and Freedom (WILPF) in 1921, with Emily Balch and Jane Addams as central leaders (Gwinn 2010; Nichols 2011). Joyce Blackwell (2004) and Melinda Plastas (2011) look at the role of black women in the WILPF, who, while combatting racial prejudice within the organization, helped expand its agenda to address racist violence in the United States and fight racism around the world.

As a testament to the war's unpopularity, multiple state measures were used to repress dissent. President Wilson enlisted progressive muckraker George Creel to lead the War Committee on Public Information, deploying all the latest techniques of modern advertising to sell the war to the public. For those not convinced, a heavier hand was used. Under the broad umbrella of the Espionage and Sedition Acts, passed between 1917 and 1918, many anti-war activists were targeted. In June of 1918, while making an anti-war speech in Ohio, Eugene V. Debs was arrested under the Espionage Act and sentenced to 10 years imprisonment. The Supreme Court upheld the legality of the Espionage Act in *Debs v. United States.* It followed the logic Oliver Wendell Holmes had used in an earlier anti-war case, *Schenk v. United States,* limiting First Amendment rights when posing a "clear and present danger." Extra-legal measures were also deployed. William Thomas Jr. (2008) used the declassified files of the Bureau of Investigation to recount the wide variety of targets of federal repressions: socialists, pacifists, immigrants, labor organizers, teachers, students, and Roman Catholic and Lutheran clergy.

The Russian revolution, the founding of the Communist Party of the USA, a wave of labor strikes, and an anarchist bombing campaign in the year 1919 led to the continued repression of radicals, especially immigrant labor radicals. After several anarchist bombings aimed at prominent government officials, Attorney General Mitchell Palmer orchestrated the deportation of hundreds of immigrants, including Emma Goldman, to the Soviet Union. In 1921, Italian anarchists Sacco and Vanzetti were convicted on flimsy evidence of killing two people during an armed robbery of a shoe company in Boston. While their cause drew international attention and sparked protests around the world, they were executed in 1927. The classic text by William Preston, Jr., *Aliens and Dissenters: Federal Suppression of Radicals, 1903–1933* (1963), presents the Red Scare within a nativist tradition as the logical consequence of decades-long attempts by the federal government to repress alien radicals. Preston uses the Bureau of Immigration records to detail federal policies that targeted the IWW, colluding with powerful interests at the state level as well as the more conservative wing of the labor movement. Scholars have pointed out the limits of anti-foreign sentiment as an explanatory device, drawing attention to the federal repression of other racial groups including Native Americans, African Americans, Chinese, and Japanese. Along these lines, more recent studies such as Theodore Kornweibel, Jr.'s *Seeing Red: Federal Campaigns Against Black Militancy, 1919–1925* (1998) and Regin Schmidt's *Red Scare: FBI and the Origins of Anticommunism in the United States, 1919–1943* (2000) have broadened the scope and the legacy of federal surveillance and repression during this period.

One of the most important legacies of state repression was the new salience of free speech. Debs turned his trial into a platform to defend First Amendment rights. Addressing the court, he recalled famous dissenters now considered patriotic heroes: "Washington, Jefferson, Franklin, Paine and their compeers were the rebels of their day" (Debs 1918). Rather than breaking the law, he and other rebels were in fact the ones upholding the Constitution of the United States. Ernest Freeberg (2008) argues that the amnesty movement to liberate anti-war and leftist dissenters after World War I provoked a much larger debate over the meaning of civil liberties. The American Civil Liberties Union, founded in 1920, drew together both progressives and peace activists like Jane Addams as well as IWW organizers and Communist Party activists like Elizabeth Gurley Flynn (Camp 1995; Vapnek 2015).

Historians have increasingly traced the roots of the free speech movement to earlier radical dissent movements. David Rabban (1999) describes a long tradition of free speech activism by both labor radicals and feminists. The 1873 federal Comstock Law and other anti-obscenity laws were the primary targets of free-speech feminists. The Bohemian circle of anarchists, cultural modernists, and feminists in New York's Greenwich Village became the center of free-speech activism before and after WWI. Christine Stansell (2000) describes the activism of New Women like Emma Goldman and Margaret Sanger, who popularized the term "birth control," and who both championed free speech on behalf of women's rights, health, and safety. For Stansell, sexual expression and the politics of free speech were at the heart of American modernism. This milieu of anarchism and cultural radicalism was also foundational to the origins of gay rights prior to 1917, as Terence Kissack (2008) describes.

The religious fundamentalist movement of the 1920s can also be understood as a reaction to labor radicalism, feminism, anti-racism, cultural modernism, as well as theological divisions among American Protestants. While drawing on some of the same evangelical traditions that had animated populist and progressive era reform, religious fundamentalists moved solidly to the far right of the American political spectrum in the 1920s. George Marsden (1980) explores the roots and development of fundamentalism as first and foremost a religious movement, while seeking to place it within its broader cultural and political context. Janette Hassey (1986) traces the shift from "evangelical feminism" at the turn of the century to 1920s fundamentalism that severely circumscribed women's ministries. While most studies have focused on the North as the central site of struggle between fundamentalism and theological liberalism, William Glass (2001) explores the complex denominational terrain of the South, and William Trollinger (1990) uses the life of popular evangelist William Bell Riley to tell the history of fundamentalism in the Midwest. Understanding the relationship between religious beliefs, practice, and political activity in the United States remains an important area of further research.

The turning point of World War I also saw the realization of women's suffrage, which gained momentum as a patriotic reform at the onset of the war and was ratified as the Nineteenth Amendment in 1920. A new generation of radical feminists was active in the final push for women's suffrage. Alice Paul, a settlement house worker and sociologist, used militant tactics in the UK women's suffrage movement before playing a key role in the corresponding movement in the U.S. (Zahniser and Fry 2014; Lunardini 2013). But suffragists continued to rely on conservative arguments to make women's suffrage politically palatable. Other women were not convinced at all, and joined an active anti-suffragist movement. These women are central players in Kim Nielson's study of anti-radical, anti-feminist women (2001). As Nielson describes, after the Nineteenth Amendment was passed, the network of women involved in the anti-suffrage movement mobilized against other radical and progressive causes: socialism, pacifism, birth control, a federal education bureau, welfare legislation, and protective labor legislation. Anti-feminists saw this progressive agenda as a subversive socialist conspiracy that would undermine male authority and degrade the nation.

The turning point of World War I also looked different from an African American perspective. The war witnessed the height of the first wave of the Great Migration, as African Americans moved to cities in the North and West to take advantage of wartime job opportunities. Many African Americans also went to war to fight in the name of democracy. When they returned, they demanded their rights as citizens. However, with renewed postwar job competition and the conflation of Soviet Bolshevism with demands for racial and economic equality, newly emboldened African Americans were subject to a wave of brutal attacks. During the "Red Summer" of 1919, there were at least 38 separate race riots across the nation in which 43 blacks were lynched and eight were burned at the stake. The Ku Klux Klan also experienced a revival during the 1920s, the subject of many recent works (Blee 1991; MacLean 1994; Pegram 2011). These studies have debunked notions that the "New Era Klan" was a marginal extremist organization. Rather, they portray it as a popular organization among native-born white Protestant men and women, standing for a wide range of causes adaptable to local conditions: moral policing on prohibition and prostitution, local control of community affairs, the cultural authority of religion, anti-political corruption, and even promoting popular public services. At its height, the new Klan reached a membership of approximately 4 to 5 million. Just how "mainstream" this organization was, and what the answer to that question implies about other social groups and movements, should provide a rich line of inquiry for continued historical research.

The violence and betrayal experienced by African Americans after the war led many to support the separatist movement of Marcus Garvey. Inspired by Booker T. Washington's ideas of economic uplift and Pan-African nationalism, the Jamaican native founded the Universal Negro Improvement Association in 1914. By the early 1920s Garveyism had become the largest black activist organization in the history of the United States. Most scholarly attention has focused on Garveyism in the North, but there is increasing scholarly attention to Garvey's appeal in the South (Harold 2007; Rolinson 2007). Like Stephen Hahn, Rolinson argues that Garveyism gained a large southern constituency, drawing on southern traditions of racial uplift, separatism, and religious redemption. In addition, scholars have explored Garveyism with a broader transnational network. Winston James (1998) details the distinct ways in which Caribbean immigrants contributed to new waves of African American radicalism in the United States.

One of these immigrants was Hugh Harrison, the aforementioned socialist activist who went on to embody the widest range of twentieth-century economic and political radicalism. After his disillusionment with the Socialist Party, he led the New Negro movement and embraced a "race first" approach to social change that stressed black leadership of black organizations. Dubbed the "father of Harlem radicalism," he founded the Liberty League as a radical alternative to the NAACP, advocating for federal anti-lynching laws, enforcement of the Fourteenth and Fifteenth Amendments, labor organizing, and anti-imperialism abroad. Harrison strongly influenced both Marcus Garvey and labor leader A. Philip Randolph, and his biographer presents Harrison as the key link between the Black Nationalist trend associated with Malcolm X, and the labor and civil rights trend associated with Martin Luther King, Jr. (Perry 2009).

Glenda Gilmore (2008) traces a different radical path to the Civil Rights Movement. Hers follows the labor activism of the Communist Party in the South. Her central actors include activists such as Lovett Fort-Whiteman, a graduate of Tuskegee Institute who spent time in Mexico before joining the circle of Harlem radicals where he became editor of the political and literary journal *The Messenger*. He became a Communist Party activist in 1919 and after attending a Comintern training school in the Soviet Union helped found the American Negro Labor Congress in 1925 that brought together black workers, labor leaders, and community organizers in a central black Communist organization. Activists like Fort-Whiteman were the earliest examples of Communist organizing among African Americans, which reached a height in the 1930s and laid important groundwork for the black labor and civil rights tradition.

Conclusion: Tracing Radicalism and Conservatism Backwards

The many paths from the radicalism and conservatism of the late nineteenth century to the twentieth and early twenty-first century will continue to be a fruitful agenda for historical research. While traditions of left radicalism have received the most attention from historians, the history of conservatism is catching up. In 2011 Leo Ribuffo criticized the current "rediscovery" of conservatism for failing to look to events before 1950 and ignoring the works of earlier scholars of conservatism such as Richard Hofstadter (1965), Daniel Bell (1963), and Seymour Martin Lipset (1970). However, historians have begun to trace the roots of modern conservatism back to the Gilded Age and Progressive Era, exploring anti-union battles (Millikan 2001; Gage 2009), anti-feminist women (Goodier 2013; Nielson 2001), nativism and racism (MacLean 1994; Pegram 2011), and religious fundamentalism (Glass 2001; Hart 2002). Julia Ott (2011) explores the popularization of a free-market ideology in the early twentieth century through the sale of stocks and bonds to a broad public. Lisa McGirr (2015) places Prohibition at the center of the development of the modern penal state. These studies have revealed the many ways in which some "conservative" ideas had widespread public appeal. As Ribuffo also points out, studies of these rank-and-file political actors promise to aid understanding of the ways in which the United States "may be in some sense a conservative country" (Ribuffo 2011). Because the political landscape has changed dramatically, further studies would continue to reveal unexpected lineages and relationships and deepen our understanding of these political contours.

This chapter is a sketch of what a synthetic narrative of radicalism and conservatism in the United States might look like. Although they would not be consolidated until the Great Depression and New Deal, the major political fault lines of modern liberalism and conservatism emerged by the mid-1920s. The new civil liberties tradition that grew in the aftermath of World War I, coupled with a populist and progressive reform agenda, defined the modern political left. However, strains of radical populism and progressivism had deeply conservative elements woven into their history. The modern political right, defined by a new anti-statist, white conservatism that emerged in opposition to the New Deal, also drew on populist traditions of political dissent, white supremacy, religious traditionalism, and moralistic reform. Radicals and conservatives defined and redefined themselves in relation to one another, and a historical understanding of their interconnectedness reveals both the stark disjunctures as well as deep continuities between the current age and theirs.

References

Ali, Omar H. 2010. *In the Lion's Mouth: Black Populism in the New South, 1886–1900.* Jackson: University Press of Mississippi.

Anderson, James D. 1988. *The Education of Blacks in the South, 1860–1935.* Chapel Hill: University of North Carolina Press.

Argersinger, Peter H. 1995. *The Limits of Agrarian Radicalism: Western Populism and American Politics.* Lawrence: University Press of Kansas.

Baker, Bruce E. 2008. *This Mob Will Surely Take My Life: Lynchings in the Carolinas, 1871–1947.* London: Continuum.

Barton, Mary S. 2015. "The Global War on Anarchism: The United States and International Anarchist Terrorism, 1898–1904." *Diplomatic History* 39, 2: 303–30.

Beckel, Deborah. 2010. *Radical Reform: Interracial Politics in Post-Emancipation North Carolina.* Charlottesville: University of Virginia Press.

Bell, Daniel. 1963. *The Radical Right : The New American Right Expanded and Updated.* Garden City, NY: Doubleday.

Bellamy, Edward. 1888. *Looking Backward, 2000–1887.* Boston: Ticknor and Company.

Blackwell, Joyce. 2004. *No Peace Without Freedom: Race and the Women's International League for Peace and Freedom, 1915–1975.* Carbondale: Southern Illinois University Press.

Blee, Kathleen M. 1991. *Women of the Klan: Racism and Gender in the 1920s.* Berkeley: University of California Press.

Braude, Ann. 1989. *Radical Spirits: Spiritualism and Women's Rights in Nineteenth-Century America.* Boston: Beacon Press.

Brown, Elsa Barkley. 1989. "Womanist Consciousness: Maggie Lena Walker and the Independent Order of Saint Luke." *Signs* 14, 3: 610–33.

Brundage, David Thomas. 1994. *The Making of Western Labor Radicalism: Denver's Organized Workers, 1878–1905.* Urbana: University of Illinois Press.

Camp, Helen C. 1995. *Iron in Her Soul: Elizabeth Gurley Flynn and the American Left.* Pullman: Washington State University Press.

Case, Theresa Ann. 2010. *The Great Southwest Railroad Strike and Free Labor.* College Station: Texas A&M University Press.

Chang, David A. 2011. "Enclosures of Land and Sovereignty: The Allotment of American Indian Lands." *Radical History Review* 109: 108–19.

Clifford, Geraldine. 2014. *Those Good Gertrudes: A Social History of Women Teachers in America.* Baltimore, MD: Johns Hopkins University Press.

Creech, Joe. 2006. *Righteous Indignation: Religion and the Populist Revolution.* Urbana: University of Illinois Press.

Cullinane, Michael Patrick. 2012. *Liberty and American Anti-Imperialism: 1898–1909.* Basingstoke: Palgrave Macmillan.

Dawley, Alan. 2003. *Changing the World: American Progressives in War and Revolution.* Princeton, NJ: Princeton University Press.

Debs, Eugene. 1918 (2003). "Address to the Jury." In *The Radical Reader: A Documentary History of the American Radical Tradition*, ed. Timothy Patrick McCarthy and John Campbell McMillian, 285–287. Reprint. New York: The New Press.

Donovan, Brian. 2005. *White Slave Crusades: Race, Gender, and Anti-Vice Activism, 1887–1917.* Urbana: University of Illinois Press.

Edwards, Rebecca. 1997. *Angels in the Machinery : Gender in American Party Politics from the Civil War to the Progressive Era.* New York: Oxford University Press.

Fine, Sidney. 1995. *Without Blare of Trumpets: Walter Drew, the National Erectors' Association, and the Open Shop Movement, 1903–57.* Ann Arbor: University of Michigan Press.

Fink, Leon. 1983. *Workingmen's Democracy: The Knights of Labor and American Politics.* Urbana: University of Illinois Press.

Foner, Eric. 1988. *Reconstruction : America's Unfinished Revolution, 1863–1877.* Updated edition. New York: Harper & Row.

Freeberg, Ernest. 2008. *Democracy's Prisoner: Eugene V. Debs, the Great War, and the Right to Dissent.* Cambridge, MA: Harvard University Press.

Gage, Beverly. 2009. *The Day Wall Street Exploded: A Story of America in Its First Age of Terror.* New York: Oxford University Press.

George, Henry. 1879. *Progress and Poverty: An Inquiry into the Cause of Industrial Depressions and of Increase of Want with Increase of Wealth; the Remedy.* National Single Tax League.

Gerteis, Joseph. 2007. *Class and the Color Line: Interracial Class Coalition in the Knights of Labor and the Populist Movement.* Durham, NC: Duke University Press.

Giddings, Paula J. 2008. *Ida: A Sword Among Lions: Ida B. Wells and the Campaign Against Lynching.* New York: Amistad.

Gilmore, Glenda Elizabeth. 1996. *Gender and Jim Crow: Women and the Politics of White Supremacy in North Carolina, 1896–1920.* Chapel Hill: University of North Carolina Press.

—. 2008. *Defying Dixie: The Radical Roots of Civil Rights, 1919–1950.* New York: W.W. Norton.

Glass, William Robert. 2001. *Strangers in Zion: Fundamentalists in the South, 1900–1950.* Macon, GA: Mercer University Press.

Goldman, Emma. 1911 (2003). "Anarchism: What it Really Stands For" In *The Radical Reader: A Documentary History of the American Radical Tradition*, ed. Timothy Patrick McCarthy and John Campbell McMillian, 288–295. New York: The New Press.

Goodier, Susan. 2013. *No Votes for Women: The New York State Anti-Suffrage Movement*. Women in American History. Urbana: University of Illinois Press.

Goodwyn, Lawrence. 1978. *The Populist Moment : A Short History of the Agrarian Revolt in America: A Short History of the Agrarian Revolt in America*. New York: Oxford University Press.

Gordon, Linda. 1994. *Pitied But Not Entitled: Single Mothers and the History of Welfare, 1890–1935*. New York: Free Press.

Gorn, Elliott J. 2001. *Mother Jones: The Most Dangerous Woman in America*. New York: Hill & Wang.

Gornick, Vivian. 2011. *Emma Goldman: Revolution as a Way of Life*. New Haven, CT: Yale University Press.

Grant, Madison. 1916. *The Passing of the Great Race: Or, The Racial Basis of European History*. New York: C. Scribner.

Greene, Julie. 1998. *Pure and Simple Politics: The American Federation of Labor and Political Activism, 1881–1917*. Cambridge: Cambridge University Press.

Green, Elna C. 1997. *Southern Strategies: Southern Women and the Woman Suffrage Question*. Chapel Hill: University of North Carolina Press.

Gwinn, Kristen E. 2010. *Emily Greene Balch: The Long Road to Internationalism*. Urbana: University of Illinois Press.

Hahn, Steven. 2003. *A Nation Under Our Feet: Black Political Struggles in the Rural South, from Slavery to the Great Migration*. Cambridge, MA: Belknap Press/Harvard University Press.

Harold, Claudrena N. 2007. *The Rise and Fall of the Garvey Movement in the Urban South, 1918–1942*. New York: Routledge.

Hart, D. G. 2002. *That Old-Time Religion in Modern America : Evangelical Protestantism in the Twentieth Century*. Chicago: Ivan R. Dee.

Hartz, Louis. 1955. *The Liberal Tradition in America: An Interpretation of American Political Thought Since the Revolution*. New York: Harcourt, Brace.

Hassey, Janette. 1986. *No Time for Silence: Evangelical Women in Public Ministry at the Turn of the Century*. Grand Rapids, MI: Academie Books.

Haywood, William. 1911 (2003). "The General Strike." In *The Radical Reader: A Documentary History of the American Radical Tradition*, ed. Timothy Patrick McCarthy and John Campbell McMillian, 285–287. New York: The New Press.

Higginbotham, Evelyn Brooks. 1993. *Righteous Discontent: The Women's Movement in the Black Baptist Church, 1880–1920*. Cambridge, MA: Harvard University Press.

Higham, John. 1955. *Strangers in the Land: Patterns of American Nativism, 1860–1925*. New Brunswick, NJ: Rutgers University Press.

Hofstadter, Richard. 1955. *The Age of Reform: From Bryan to F.D.R.* New York: Vintage Books.

—. 1965. *The Paranoid Style in American Politics: And Other Essays*. 1st edition. New York: Knopf.

Hoganson, Kristin L. 1998. *Fighting for American Manhood: How Gender Politics Provoked the Spanish–American and Philippine–American Wars*. New Haven, CT: Yale University Press.

Huyssen, David. 2014. *Progressive Inequality: Rich and Poor in New York, 1890–1920*. Cambridge, MA: Harvard University Press.

IWW (Industrial Workers of the World, The). 1905 (2003) "Manifesto and Preamble." In *The Radical Reader: A Documentary History of the American Radical Tradition*, ed. Timothy Patrick McCarthy and John Campbell McMillian, 281–284. New York: The New Press.

Jacobson, Matthew Frye. 2000. *Barbarian Virtues: The United States Encounters Foreign Peoples at Home and Abroad, 1876–1917*. New York: Hill & Wang.

James, William. 1899. "The Philippine Tangle." *Boston Evening Transcript*, March 1.

James, Winston. 1998. *Holding Aloft the Banner of Ethiopia: Caribbean Radicalism in Early Twentieth-Century America*. New York: Verso.

Jentz, John B., and Richard Schneirov. 2012. *Chicago in the Age of Capital: Class, Politics, and Democracy during the Civil War and Reconstruction*. Urbana: University of Illinois Press.

Jewett, Andrew. 2012. *Science, Democracy, and the American University: From the Civil War to the Cold War*. Cambridge: Cambridge University Press.

Johnston, Robert D. 2002. "Re-Democratizing the Progressive Era: The Politics of Progressive Era Political Historiography." *The Journal of the Gilded Age and Progressive Era* 1, 1: 68–92.

—. 2003. *The Radical Middle Class: Populist Democracy and the Question of Capitalism in Progressive Era Portland, Oregon*. Princeton, NJ: Princeton University Press.

Kantrowitz, Stephen David. 2000. *Ben Tillman & the Reconstruction of White Supremacy*. Chapel Hill: University of North Carolina Press.

Kimeldorf, Howard. 1999. *Battling for American Labor: Wobblies, Craft Workers, and the Making of the Union Movement*. Berkeley: University of California Press.

Kissack, Terence S. 2008. *Free Comrades: Anarchism and Homosexuality in the United States, 1895–1917*. Edinburgh: AK Press.

Kloppenberg, James T. 1986. *Uncertain Victory: Social Democracy and Progressivism in European and American Thought, 1870–1920*. New York: Oxford University Press.

Knight, Louise W. 2005. *Citizen: Jane Addams and the Struggle for Democracy*. Chicago: University of Chicago Press.

Knights of Labor. 1878 (2003). "Preamble." In *The Radical Reader: A Documentary History of the American Radical Tradition*, ed. Timothy Patrick McCarthy and John Campbell McMillian, 243–245. New York: The New Press.

Kolko, Gabriel. 1963. *The Triumph of Conservatism: A Reinterpretation of American History, 1900–1918*. Chicago: Quadrangle Books.

Kornweibel, Theodore. 1998. *Seeing Red: Federal Campaigns Against Black Militancy, 1919–1925*. Bloomington: Indiana University Press.

Kosek, Joseph Kip. 2009. *Acts of Conscience: Christian Nonviolence and Modern American Democracy*. New York: Columbia University Press.

Lipset, Seymour Martin. 1970. *The Politics of Unreason: Right Wing Extremism in America, 1790–1970*. New York: Harper & Row.

Litwack, Leon F. 1998. *Trouble in Mind: Black Southerners in the Age of Jim Crow*. New York: Knopf.

Love, Eric Tyrone Lowery. 2004. *Race Over Empire: Racism and U.S. Imperialism, 1865–1900.* Chapel Hill: University of North Carolina Press.

Lunardini, Christine A. 2013. *Alice Paul: Equality for Women.* Lives of American Women. Boulder, CO: Westview Press.

MacLean, Nancy. 1994. *Behind the Mask of Chivalry : The Making of the Second Ku Klux Klan.* New York: Oxford University Press.

Marlowe, Gertrude Woodruff. 2003. *A Right Worthy Grand Mission: Maggie Lena Walker and the Quest for Black Economic Empowerment.* Washington, DC: Howard University Press.

Marsden, George M. 1980. *Fundamentalism and American Culture.* New York: Oxford University Press.

McGirr, Lisa. 2015. *The War on Alcohol: Prohibition and the Rise of the American State.* New York: W.W. Norton.

Miller, Sally M. 1993. *From Prairie to Prison: The Life of Social Activist Kate Richards O'Hare.* Columbia: University of Missouri Press.

Millikan, William. 2001. *A Union Against Unions: The Minneapolis Citizens Alliance and Its Fight Against Organized Labor, 1903–1947.* St. Paul: Minnesota Historical Society Press.

Mitchell, Michele. 2004. *Righteous Propagation: African Americans and the Politics of Racial Destiny After Reconstruction.* Chapel Hill: University of North Carolina Press.

Morgan, Francesca. 2006. *Women and Patriotism in Jim Crow America.* Chapel Hill: University of North Carolina Press.

Nelson, Bruce. 2001. *Divided We Stand: American Workers and the Struggle for Black Equality.* Princeton, NJ: Princeton University Press.

Nelson, Daniel. 1992. *A Mental Revolution: Scientific Management Since Taylor.* Columbus: Ohio State University Press.

Newman, Louise Michele. 1999. *White Women's Rights: The Racial Origins of Feminism in the United States.* New York: Oxford University Press.

Nichols, Christopher McKnight. 2011. *Promise and Peril : America at the Dawn of a Global Age.* Cambridge, MA: Harvard University Press.

Nielsen, Kim E. 2001. *Un-American Womanhood: Antiradicalism, Antifeminism, and the First Red Scare.* Columbus: Ohio State University Press.

Odem, Mary E. 1995. *Delinquent Daughters: Protecting and Policing Adolescent Female Sexuality in the United States, 1885–1920.* Chapel Hill: University of North Carolina Press.

Orleck, Annelise. 1995. *Common Sense & a Little Fire: Women and Working-Class Politics in the United States, 1900–1965.* Chapel Hill: University of North Carolina Press.

Ott, Julia C. 2011. *When Wall Street Met Main Street: The Quest for an Investors' Democracy.* Cambridge, MA: Harvard University Press.

Pegram, Thomas R. 2011. *One Hundred Percent American: The Rebirth and Decline of the Ku Klux Klan in the 1920s.* Chicago: Ivan R. Dee.

Perry, Jeffrey Babcock. 2009. *Hubert Harrison: The Voice of Harlem Radicalism, 1883–1918.* New York: Columbia University Press.

Petit, Jeanne D. 2010. *The Men and Women We Want: Gender, Race, and the Progressive Era Literacy Test Debate.* Rochester, NY: University of Rochester Press.

Plastas, Melinda. 2011. *A Band of Noble Women: Racial Politics in the Women's Peace Movement.* Syracuse, NY: Syracuse University Press.

Postel, Charles. 2007. *The Populist Vision.* New York: Oxford University Press.

Preston, William. 1963. *Aliens and Dissenters; Federal Suppression of Radicals, 1903–1933.* Cambridge, MA: Harvard University Press.

Rabban, David M. 1997. *Free Speech in Its Forgotten Years, 1870–1920.* Cambridge: Cambridge University Press.

Renda, Mary A. 2001. *Taking Haiti: Military Occupation and the Culture of U.S. Imperialism, 1915–1940.* Chapel Hill: University of North Carolina Press.

Ribuffo, Leo P. 2011. "Twenty Suggestions for Studying the Right Now That Studying the Right Is Trendy." *Historically Speaking* 12, 1: 2–6.

Richardson, Heather Cox. 2001. *The Death of Reconstruction.* Cambridge, MA: Harvard University Press.

—. 2007. *West from Appomattox: The Reconstruction of America After the Civil War.* New Haven, CT: Yale University Press.

—. 2011. *Wounded Knee: Party Politics and the Road to an American Massacre.* New York: Basic Books.

Rolinson, Mary G. 2007. *Grassroots Garveyism: The Universal Negro Improvement Association in the Rural South, 1920–1927.* Chapel Hill: University of North Carolina Press.

Rossinow, Douglas Charles. 2008. *Visions of Progress: The Left-Liberal Tradition in America.* Philadelphia: University of Pennsylvania Press.

Salvatore, Nick. 2007. *Eugene V. Debs: Citizen and Socialist.* Urbana: University of Illinois Press.

Sanders, Elizabeth. 1999. *Roots of Reform: Farmers, Workers, and the American State, 1877–1917.* Chicago: University of Chicago Press.

Schlesinger, Jr., Arthur M. 1949. *The Vital Center: The Politics of Freedom.* Boston: Houghton Mifflin.

Schmidt, Regin. 2000. *Red Scare: FBI and the Origins of Anticommunism in the United States, 1919–1943.* Copenhagen: Museum Tusculanum Press.

Shaw, Stephanie J. 1996. *What a Woman Ought to Be and to Do: Black Professional Women Workers during the Jim Crow Era.* Chicago: University of Chicago Press.

Skocpol, Theda. 1995. *Protecting Soldiers and Mothers.* Cambridge, MA: Harvard University Press.

Smoak, Gregory E. 2006. *Ghost Dances and Identity: Prophetic Religion and American Indian Ethnogenesis in the Nineteenth Century.* Berkeley: University of California Press.

Spain, Daphne. 2001. *How Women Saved the City.* Minneapolis: University of Minnesota Press.

Spiro, Jonathan Peter. 2009. *Defending the Master Race: Conservation, Eugenics, and the Legacy of Madison Grant.* Burlington: University of Vermont Press.

Stansell, Christine. 2000. *American Moderns: Bohemian New York and the Creation of a New Century.* New York: Metropolitan Books.

Stromquist, Shelton. 2006. *Reinventing The People: The Progressive Movement, the Class Problem, and the Origins of Modern Liberalism.* Urbana: University of Illinois Press.

Thomas, William H. 2009. *Unsafe for Democracy: World War I and the U.S. Justice Department's Covert Campaign to Suppress Dissent.* Madison: University of Wisconsin Press.

Throntveit, Trygve. 2014. *William James and the Quest for an Ethical Republic*. Basingstoke: Palgrave Macmillan.

Trollinger, William Vance. 1990. *God's Empire : William Bell Riley and Midwestern Fundamentalism*. Madison: University of Wisconsin Press.

Unger, Nancy C. 2000. *Fighting Bob La Follette: The Righteous Reformer*. Chapel Hill: University of North Carolina Press.

Vapnek, Lara. 2009. *Breadwinners: Working Women and Economic Independence, 1865–1920*. Urbana: University of Illinois Press.

—. 2015. *Elizabeth Gurley Flynn: Modern American Revolutionary*. Boulder, CO: Westview Press.

Weinstein, James. 1968. *The Corporate Ideal in the Liberal State, 1900–1918*. Boston: Beacon Press.

Weir, Robert. 2000. *Knights Unhorsed: Internal Conflict in a Gilded Age Social Movement*. Detroit, MI: Wayne State University Press.

West, Elliott. 2009. *The Last Indian War : The Nez Perce Story*. New York: Oxford University Press.

Woodward, C. Vann. 1938. *Tom Watson: Agrarian Rebel*. New York: Oxford University Press.

Zahniser, Jill Diane and Amelia R. Fry. 2014. *Alice Paul: Claiming Power*. New York: Oxford University Press, 2014.

Zieger, Robert H. 2007. *For Jobs and Freedom: Race and Labor in America Since 1865*. Lexington: University Press of Kentucky.

Zolberg, Aristide R. 2006. *A Nation by Design: Immigration Policy in the Fashioning of America*. Cambridge, MA: Harvard University Press.

Further Reading

Ali, Omar H. 2008. *In the Balance of Power: Independent Black Politics and Third-Party Movements in the United States*. Athens: Ohio University Press.

Brinkley, Alan. 1994. "The Problem of American Conservatism." *The American Historical Review* 99, 2: 409–29.

Foner, Eric. 1998. *The Story of American Freedom*. New York: W.W. Norton.

Horowitz, David A. 1997. *Beyond Left & Right: Insurgency and the Establishment*. Urbana: University of Illinois Press.

Kazin, Michael. 1995. *The Populist Persuasion: An American History*. New York: Basic Books.

Lichtman, Allan J. 2008. *White Protestant Nation : The Rise of the American Conservative Movement*. New York: Atlantic Monthly Press.

McCarthy, Timothy Patrick, and John Campbell McMillian. 2003. *The Radical Reader: A Documentary History of the American Radical Tradition*. New York: The New Press.

Phillips-Fein, Kim. 2011. "Conservatism: A State of the Field." *Journal of American History* 98, 3: 723–43.

Ribuffo, Leo P. 1992. *Right Center Left: Essays in American History*. New Brunswick, NJ: Rutgers University Press.

—. 2003. "The Discovery and Rediscovery of American Conservatism Broadly Conceived." *OAH Magazine of History* 17, 2: 5–10.

Voss-Hubbard, Mark. 1999. "The 'Third Party Tradition' Reconsidered: Third Parties and American Public Life, 1830–1900." *The Journal of American History* 86, 1: 121.

Part VII

The United States and the World

Chapter Twenty-Nine

Connections, Networks, and the Beginnings of a Global America in the Gilded Age and Progressive Era

Ian Tyrrell

The Gilded Age, from the 1870s to the 1890s, was long considered one of the most inward-looking periods of American history. Economic growth accelerated, large corporations came to dominate and rationalize expanding domestic markets amid labor and farmer protests, and a class of super-rich emerged to exert power through their great financial influence, and through politics. The Progressive Era that followed (*c.*1900–1917) is typically seen as a time in which the built-up dynamism of the previous two decades burst forth and produced energetic "expansion" of American power and culture abroad. At the same time, the Progressive Era at home reputedly brought political reform of the economic excesses that had come before.

These views, bequeathed by the Progressive historians who flourished in the early to mid-twentieth century, continued to shape US historiography on the Gilded Age and the Progressive Era, arguably through the 1950s if not beyond (Parrington 1930; Beard and Beard 1927; Josephson 1938; DeSantis 1988). But in more recent scholarship, the boundaries between the two periods have blurred. Reform movements before 1900 are now considered to have anticipated the later so-called Progressive reform (Edwards 2009; Sanders 1999; Nugent 2013; Postel 2007; Flanagan 2007).

The internal focus of earlier research has also come into question. Transnational history has, particularly since the 1990s, enhanced knowledge of the close relations between domestic American developments and international ones across the entire time frame from the 1870s to 1917, thus blurring distinctions between the conventionally conceived demarcations. This chapter builds upon this newer scholarship, concentrating on cross-national connections of the nongovernmental kind, and examines both continuity and discontinuity between the Gilded Age and the Progressive Era. While both comparative and transnational studies on the North Atlantic world are considered, Pacific world contacts and those covering the global British Empire were key parts of the developing US global outlook. The rise of American formal imperialism from 1898 forced a stronger nation-state presence in US relations with the wider world, yet this state activity was founded on expanding nongovernmental contacts before 1898 that went far beyond nation-state actions. Pre-1898 action only episodically involved extensive US political or economic coercion abroad. Thereafter, political and military intervention in the Caribbean and economic penetration of Latin America intensified, but these Progressive Era changes were part of the emerging shift toward global rather than merely regional power (Tucker 2000; Tyrrell 2015a).

What follows focuses on the origins and consequences of this informal, non-state expansion stimulated by economic globalization of the late nineteenth century, rather than US foreign policy and diplomacy. A key point in the greater interest of Americans in the world outside was changing technology and communications. This is not a question of isolated technological change, but a synergetic cluster of changes linking the United States to a global economy in the making. This chapter does not profess international engagement as a reflexive and technologically determined process. The timing of the new global connectivity was not sudden, but a series of spurts both temporally and spatially, from the uneven and protracted spread of the telegraph cable system beginning in the early 1870s through to the newfangled radiotelegraphy by the time of World War I. This unevenness accentuates the importance of human aspirations (and exasperation) as central in the exploitation and deployment of technological change. Non-state actors

A Companion to the Gilded Age and Progressive Era, First Edition. Edited by Christopher McKnight Nichols and Nancy C. Unger.
© 2017 John Wiley & Sons, Inc. Published 2017 by John Wiley & Sons, Inc.

and governments interacted in this process, and perceptions of opportunities abroad were as important as material changes in shaping actions.

The New Communications Networks

A striking shift in historiographical outlook revolves around the emphasis upon the "shrinking" of time and space (Rosenberg 2012). That is to say, global contacts became denser, more extensive, and speedier in ways that made for a new spatial and temporal understanding of the world and its opportunities for Americans. Communications infrastructure was central to this new outlook from the 1870s, but the process accelerated in the 1880s and beyond. The world was becoming networked, and the United States was a part of these networks. These connections centered on the telegraph, steamships, railroads, and, after 1900, the early radiotelegraphy and telephone system (though the latter was almost entirely within the nation and, indeed, restricted to local areas). The building of the Suez and Panama Canals, opened in 1869 and 1914, respectively, was another part of this interlocking system, integral to the creation of global communications, especially for reducing sailing time for steamships engaged in international commerce.

These communications changes coincided with a shift in American perceptions of geographic space and geopolitics. Africa, an old area of US interest, because of the suppression of the slave trade and the introduction of American missions to Liberia, did not disappear from calculation, nor did the Caribbean or South America. Europe was the site of a perceived though sometimes exaggerated inundation of US-manufactured goods at the end of the nineteenth century. Yet the biggest proportional growth in American trade from 1860 to 1905 was with Japan, and cultural and economic involvement from 1870 to 1920 surged most in East and South Asia and the Pacific. The global networking of telegraphs, steamship services, the Suez Canal, and railroads facilitated greater American interest in and contact with these distant regions, even as the building of facilities such as cable lines and the Panama Canal was shaped by geopolitical aspirations (Tyrrell 2007b; Hughes 1987, 365, 368).

While the domestic aspect of a communications revolution is increasingly well covered in American historiography, the integration of the United States with international communications is almost virgin territory, so far as major historical writing is concerned. The best introduction to the growth of American "telecommunications" in the nineteenth century and after is in Richard John's *Network Nation*, but, like others, his work concerns how the telegraph and telephone contributed to a national economy. At the same time, the original, antebellum purpose of creating what John calls "a vast transnational arc" of communications in the interests of the global cotton trade remained important internationally as well as to the nation. Only small if revealing glimmers of global communication influences can be found in the existing literature (John 2010, 11). Certainly the impact of the telegraph on diplomacy is beginning to be understood in terms of public opinion's role in conditioning short-term events, such as occurred before the Spanish–American War, in creating a climate for foreign policy interventions, and in the conduct of war. As David Paull Nickles points out in *Under the Wire: How the Telegraph Changed Diplomacy*, a telegram room was set up in the White House in 1898 to receive news of the Spanish–American War (Nickles 2003, 92). Nickles suggests that the telegram increased the speed of diplomatic exchange in periods of crisis and hastened decision-making. His account makes clear that winning the information war in times of military conflict meant not only speed of communications but also denial of the same to the enemy. Cutting the cables of belligerents was an important military consideration. During the Spanish–American War, the cables off Cuba became a priority, and were, with great difficulty, severed and respliced to give American access, but not Spanish (Nickles 2003, 85, 91, 155, 27–36).

Similarly neglected in American historiography is the rise of international steamship travel. Cable was important for the metaphor of shrinking global space and hence portended cultural change, but steamships (along with railroads) carried much of the burden of practical application of speed where the bulk of communication was concerned. Steamships began to ply the Atlantic from the late 1830s, though the major expansion of steam came post-1865. By 1900 a dense network of (cheaper and faster) international steamship communications had been established, with the costs of transatlantic travel falling fast. This was an innovation of importance to the flow of immigrants to the United States, to tourists going to Europe and elsewhere, and to commerce more generally. A mid-century journey of three weeks had been reduced to less than one by the speedy ocean liners of 1900 (Knoblock 2014, 303). Yet the literature on this topic remains antiquarian. The failure of the United States to maintain its native shipping industry for international trade (a major feature of the Gilded Age political economy, where railroads flourished instead) is noted by some, but little is known of how and why this allocation of priorities occurred and with what effect (see Plowman 2010; Matthews 1987; Kemble 1950). The United States relied to a considerable degree on British shipping and insurance for external commercial expansion.

The problem was that railroads had been given land grants, whereas steamships required direct subsidies. At a time when graft had distinguished these grants and the companies founded upon them, Congress was, once the railroad scandals became public, averse to subsidies for steamships, though some were given for postal services (Sexton 2014, 404–405; McDowell and Gibb 1954, 250–253). The extension of steamship lines to Hawaii and Japan from 1867 has been especially neglected, despite the links between this route and the growth of the west-coast sugar trade. The economic colonization of the Hawaiian Islands was spurred by the vertical integration of plantations with rail and sea transportation through the business interests of the German–American Claus Spreckels, whose influence extended across the Pacific (Teisch 2010, 21; Adler 1960). Spreckels' Ocean Steamship Company "octopus" in the South Pacific, fueled by British and American capital, snared Antipodean mail subsidies to complement the American ones. This case aside, there is no major scholarship even though the mail subsidies, as for the Pacific mails and in the Caribbean, open issues of political patronage and graft that would be familiar to historians of the Gilded Age (Steel 2013; McLean 1990; Tate 1986; Kemble 1950; Sexton 2014).

Railroads are better treated in the historiography, because they were more important to American internal development and the integration of the great national markets that powered the economy to its increasingly important position in world commerce in the 1880s and 1890s. Topics such as the place of individual railroads and entrepreneurs, as well as labor relations, have been prominent (Licht 1983). But rarely have major studies of US railroads for the late nineteenth century addressed their international linkages. American railroad entrepreneurs were not limited to these geographically contiguous spaces, or to railroads alone. Nowhere was this point more important that the involvement of entrepreneurially minded individuals in Latin American railroad expansion in the 1870s and 1880s, for example through the work of Henry Meiggs, who helped to build lines in Peru and Bolivia, often with British capital. Such speculative ventures bear resemblance to those in the US railroads of the Gilded Age, but cross-national comparisons of these entrepreneurs are mostly lacking (Stewart 1946).

One study that does encompass international and domestic economic history is Michael Malone's biography of James J. Hill, *Empire Builder*. Malone shows the very structure of the Canadian confederation and its economic development to be closely tied to the building of railroads in which Hill played a prominent role, and in which the integration of Canadian transport with that of the United States was a serious issue (Malone 1996, 64–80). But such sensitivity to the North American rather than the specifically US industry is rare. The extension of US railroad connections with Mexico (reaching Mexico City in 1884) was important to American investment and the growth of mining for copper and other minerals. The US mining industry that expanded into northern Mexico from the 1870s depended on regionally linked railroad systems, as did the California farmers and fruit growers, who began to draw upon Mexican labor after the 1890s. Even Richard White's magisterial study of Gilded Age railroads has surprisingly little to say on Canadian and Mexican railroads and their impact. White focuses on issues of corporations, finances, and speculation. Yet, as Samuel Truett indicates, American investment in railroads was a key part of the environmental transformation of the borderland landscapes (Gutiérrez 1995, 44–45; White 2011, 51–55; 215–16; Truett 2006, 82-83; 108–109).

The failure to produce a North American history of railroads (and of other communications) reflects a reality of nineteenth-century politics. The role of Congress in allocating public land for both agriculture and railroad construction is well known as part of the vast historiography of US land policy. Despite the relentless growth of communications, political decision-making influenced both the United States and foreign countries in the pace, scope, and direction of development, especially railroads. Growing economic nationalism in Canada, for example, interfered with a purely rationalized capitalist development of a marketplace in North America. Canadian politicians strove to tie the western provinces to the newly founded (1867) Dominion of Canada rather than allow branch lines to the United States to siphon off the potential fruits of the Dominion's prairie agriculture to shippers and merchants in Chicago and in St. Paul, Minnesota in the 1880s. Nevertheless, Hill retained interests in the Manitoba railroad linked to his own Great Northern Railroad that ran to St. Paul (Malone 1996). This topic cuts across political and business history, and shows how the intervention of national legislative priorities could influence the purely technological development of cross-national communications.

Coming at the question from a global angle, there are many studies that consider the role of communications in world history from the 1870s to the 1910s, and beyond. These studies offer insights otherwise lacking in an American-focused study. They point to the importance of seeing changes in sea and land communications, and the different modes of communication—telegraph, steamships, and railroads—as interrelated. Available studies also suggest putting communications in the same frame of reference as the shifting political geography of late nineteenth-century European imperialism in which the United States was to play a part. They stress the links between technological advance and political and cultural change. Since the 1980s, the role of communications in changing American and Western culture in the late nineteenth century has received treatment in the historiography, but this work has been in global history. Daniel Headrick's *The Tools of Empire* considered the global surge and political implications of the telegraph and other technological innovations for world history. Stephen Kern's *The Culture of Time and Space, 1880–1918*, is a transcultural history that covers almost the exact period that is said to constitute the Gilded Age and Progressive Era. While Kern gives little space to specifically American developments, he tackles the big questions of space and time, including the cultural reception of ideas of shrinking space (Headrick 1981; Kern 2003). This is not to say that, in a deterministic fashion, communications enmeshed the United States in global relationships. Networks advanced, but, as historian Patricia Sinn argues for Chinese migration and trade, "network" can be a vague word that too often "projects a static image" (Sinn 2014). As Ballantyne and

Burton demonstrate, technologies "were not free-floating and their use was directed and determined by human choice and agency" (2012, 351).

The cultural context of these new networks must be recognized. Emily Rosenberg (2012) documents the importance of the human contacts that developed in these spaces of connectivity. She shows international non-state actors working in international associations, congresses, and exhibitions. Thereby she explains not only how improved international communication spread global exchanges, but also how international organizations themselves changed thinking about cooperative action across national boundaries. Arguably the late nineteenth century was an age of Victorian internationalism as well as imperialism, in which the United States participated, for example through the Lake Mohonk Peace Conferences, and through the legal profession's contribution to international law. Established in 1907, the *American Journal of International Law* featured the work of US legal scholars such as Simeon Baldwin and Paul Reinsch, who studied international treaties and organizations. Moreover, the United States aided substantially in the creation of a system of international arbitration through the Permanent Court of Arbitration at The Hague set up as a result of the First Hague Peace Conference in 1899. Internationalism was championed in a variety of moral and social reform movements, too. US presidents Theodore Roosevelt, William Howard Taft, and Woodrow Wilson all supported the strengthening of international institutions of a nongovernmental kind, and understood that the assertion of a stronger American role in informal international cultural and scientific as well as legal and political exchange was necessary for the international state system to prosper (Ninkovich 2014; Baldwin 1907; Kuehl 1969, 38–41; Reinsch 1907).

One can certainly agree that the shrinking of the world was a *perception* of the times, yet its American dimensions, in what might be termed an "emotional history," remain to be sketched regarding the creation of a global outlook. In *The Global Republic*, Frank Ninkovich examines a small, highly literate elite who wrote for or read magazines such as *Nation* and *North American Review* and promoted a more cosmopolitan worldview. In the response to globalizing pressures that Ninkovich identifies with the spread of "civilization," he locates the foundations for American liberal internationalism. The point should not be to assert the commonplace that "we have always been global," at least in the same way, and with the same implications. To be sure, a key technological change of the era was the telegraphic "cable," and Ninkovich finds its cultural importance to be far-reaching in creating the notion of the interconnected world during the Gilded Age. Communications were perceived in ways producing changes in the mental world of American leaders and opinion makers, thus contributing substantially to what Ninkovich calls the "global dawn" of American internationalism (Ninkovich 2014, 326).

Yet the use of a word such as "cable," associated with the modern-day methods of data transfer, should not imply equivalence. The telegraph mostly reached readers through newspaper reports of cable information and was thus filtered through other media. In the case of great events, public announcements and rituals created a specifically *public* discourse through the shared nature of the diverse facilities for disseminating the accelerated volume of information available. In contrast to this public context, modern fiber-optic cable is different in impact: not only is it faster and more reliable; it supports the privatization of knowledge (and therefore of culture and politics), especially through the delivery of information and entertainment directly to homes and businesses, on demand.

The uneven global response to these changes is revealed in the adoption of uniform time zones. Increased trade and travel made agreement on a standard meridian desirable for business. Because the accurate and standard measurement of time was a pressing issue for rail connections, the railroads pushed through a de facto standardization of time zones for the United States in 1883. Internationally, it was likewise in the interests of commerce and travelers that standardized zones and a fixed and universally accepted meridian be agreed upon. The United States took a leading part in the holding of the International Meridian Conference of 1884, where Greenwich Mean Time was set as the global standard. But, as with other aspects of the new global technologies, the actual implementation of international time zones was protracted and uneven. Differences between countries and regions revealed different perceptions and experiences of time, particularly outside the Euro-American world (Ogle 2013; Bartky 2010, 154).

The idea of the shrinking of time and space was not unknown in the cultural history of the late nineteenth-century United States. As Richard John indicates for the telegraph and telephone, the idea became, in fact, a cliché, and even a misleading one in the latter case during the Gilded Age and Progressive Era. From its early use in the 1840s, the telegraph embodied the hopes, expectations, and even demands of Americans (Howe 2007, 2–6). But the announcements that a brave new world was arriving continued, and became more shrill and expansive as the realities of the technological changes and its shortcomings were manifest not only in the United States but also abroad. Enunciations of the new connectedness were commonplace from the 1860s to well after 1900. Contemporary observers waxed lyrical at the penetration of the new technology. In *Exploits of the Signal Corps in the War with Spain*, Howard A. Giddings gushed: "cities are honeycombed, as it were, by telephone lines, penetrating even to the very separate rooms and desks in our great buildings; States … are enmeshed in intricate webs of telegraph and telephone lines" (1900, 9).

While this analysis was hyperbolic, the cable's reception reflected new emotional *expectations* of connectivity. Giddings noted that "instant communications" was the "insistent *demand*" of the late nineteenth century, thus making the emphasis upon expectation clear (1900, 17). When William Henry Seward went on his round-the-world trip in 1870–1871 after eight years as US Secretary of State, he pined during a long stay in China (where the telegraph did not then extend) for greater access to news from the outside world. In arriving at Singapore from China, Seward's first thought was getting up-to-date news from home. He "eagerly" inquired "whether the telegraph-cable (had) been laid from Point de Galles," in present day Sri Lanka, through to Singapore. Finding the answer to be affirmative, he rejoiced at being put back into immediate contact with the "civilized" world (Seward 1873, 272; Paolini 1973; Stahr 2012, 165; 393–394).

China was connected to the international telegraph system the following year but cable's availability and use remained globally and socially unequal for much longer. It was tied for most of the late nineteenth century to business activity and to the movements of the rich. A cable message even within the United States in 1866 cost an average of $1, at a time when common laborers and seamstresses often struggled to earn that, or less, a day. The cable did facilitate commercial transactions and allow the wealthy to travel with better organization and greater certainty of their movements and expenditures (Hochfelder 2012, 56). In the 1880s, sending a cable message to the other side of the world was still expensive, with international (submarine) cable costs averaging $1.3 dollars per message, three times that for domestic messages. To compensate, ingenious cable codes that cut the cost per word were devised, but limitations remained, especially for private individuals (Hartfield 1896; Fernandes 2009, 9). Moreover, the flow of information was not quite the almost instantaneous one that the writer Simon Winchester gushingly asserts for the reporting of the gigantic Krakatoa volcanic explosion of 1883: "Thanks to the transmission of the news of the occurrence around the world *within mere minutes*, it helped with the origins of the globally connected village of today" (Winchester 2014). For 1910, such an analysis would be plausible, but not for 1883. Moreover, the information conveyed was restrictive at first. After his initial euphoria in Singapore, Seward found the cable's news in 1871 to be "meagre" in detail. The technology's potential seemed gratifying and emotionally important to him, but at the same time he was frustrated that it provided only cryptic accounts of the momentous events of the Franco-Prussian War (Seward 1873, 272).

This response raises the commonplace of the glass half-full. The glass half-empty would suggest that communications to the other side of the world still took a day in 1871, but a six-week gap in news from home received in Beijing (beyond the reach of cable in 1871) became 24 hours in Singapore as Seward's party moved south. A more sanguine analysis would therefore note that the time lag had already been cut to about 2.3% of the previous gap, a huge change in the *experience* of users. By the time the United States entered the Spanish–American War in 1898, technological progress looked even rosier. Commercial messages could reach Singapore from New York in less than half an hour, and twelve parallel submarine cables crossed the Atlantic, as opposed to one in 1867 when Seward was Secretary of State (Giddings 1900).

The cable thus opened business and diplomatic opportunities, but the implications remained quite mixed. A decade after Seward circumnavigated the globe, it still took about two days for important news to arrive from one corner of the world to its Antipodean extremity and be published in newspapers in the 1880s, as reports of the assassination of President James Garfield in 1881 recorded in Melbourne, Australia, showed. What had increased considerably was the volume of timely information that could be communicated and published with three or four days. As Mike Sewell remarks of the emotional reception in Britain to the news of Garfield's wounding and eventual death, "By the time of Garfield's death, news travelled much faster than the diplomatic bag, and mass circulation dailies carried it far and wide" (Sewell 1991, 672). This news was not skimpy and perfunctory but profuse, providing a blow-by-blow account of the changes in Garfield's condition over the eleven weeks to his death.

The cultural infrastructure in which the new technology was embedded both shaped and extended its influence. A heightened sense of "immediacy concerning distant events" allowed, in the case of the reception in Britain of Garfield's assassination, "simultaneous mourning of the president by millions of people" in "a manner impossible until recently." But this process was dependent upon more traditional forms of communication, such as church services, gun salutes, the peals of bells, or respectful silences in communities across Britain timed "to coincide precisely with Garfield's funeral." The growth of mass-circulation newspapers in cheap form also fueled the thirst for distant knowledge derived from the new, speedier communications. Changes in technology had "dramatically influenced" how such "gestures" of Anglo-Saxon solidarity were "staged and received." The "spread of telegraphic reporting" along with the newspaper platforms that fed upon it created "an audience" for commemorative events "far beyond those present" (Sewell 1991, 672–673). Technology encouraged a sense of shared experience in English-speaking nations whose news could be communicated and understood, unobstructed by translation, and often extracted directly from each other's daily press.

Because cable coverage was far from complete in the late nineteenth century, the spotty global range produced frustration at the failure of technology to realize the benefits of connectedness. The American experience of formal imperialism that emerged from the 1898 war with Spain emphasizes this point. Communication between Washington and Manila, the seat of the government of the new American colony of the Philippine Islands, for example, seemed in the expectations of users to take an eternity (Giddings 1900, 25; Winkler 2007, 6; 10–11). That was because there was no cable across the Pacific. During the Spanish-American War, US military cables had to be sent via Europe, and retransmitted fourteen times at cable stations controlled by a variety of national jurisdictions, in order to reach their final destination in Hong Kong or Manila. A record American message sent in 1896 to East Asia and back took 47 minutes, but that could not circle the globe. For military strategists, this was not adequate in speed, or, equally important, in safety from hostile powers or the mistakes of innocently mistranslated messages (*Railroad Telegrapher* 1896; *Los Angeles Herald* 1903).

The result of military, strategic, and political imperatives was not to despair of the new connectivity, but to spur intensification of these networks, and to make the networks align with political divisions. Cables that went through third-party nations in time of war were especially vulnerable to disruption. It was such considerations that led Britain to complete the "all-red" cable route across the Pacific by October 1902, and that pushed the United States to have similar access through a dedicated American link. So important was this concern over cable security in 1899 that the United States immediately began, through licensing of the Commercial Pacific Cable Co., construction of an all-American cable service to Manila from San Francisco via Honolulu and Guam, which opened in 1903. The new cable service carried the first message ever to travel completely around the globe from a US president, a feat achieved in just 12 minutes. This compared with a French time for a commercial telegraph transaction of six hours and 20 minutes via the recently completed all-British route across the Pacific, and the 47-minute delay of 1896 to East Asia noted above (*Los Angeles Herald* 1903, 1, 2).

Jonathan Winkler (2007) dates serious American government interest in controlling international cable as the product of World War I, and early efforts as merely "flirtation" with the technology, but this argument misses the cultural, commercial, and indeed imperial significance of earlier developments. The turn-of-the-century initiatives were of broad consequence for the United States. The self-congratulation that followed President Theodore Roosevelt's triumphal missive of 1903 indicated the cultural importance. Governor-General William Howard Taft and others hailed the new link as evidence of American greatness and of tighter ties with the Philippines in the interests of that colony's "progress" toward modernity. The new communications fostered a more global and imperially oriented outlook as much as they evoked national pride. Just as the American states were "enmeshed" in wires, Giddings (1900, 17) noted that "nations," too, were entering the same set of networks by "means of communication which knows neither time nor space."

Despite the whoopla, what the Pacific cable demonstrated was not an independent American global cable presence, but US communications connected to a global system in which British telecommunications interests were dominant. This, like dependence upon British shipping and maritime insurance, fits arguments for the importance of the British World or "Anglosphere" to American imperialism (Sexton 2014, 401–402). Though the Pacific Commercial Cable Company was registered in the United States, it was financed with British capital and worked in informal partnership with British telegraph interests. Only with the coming of World War I would the effort to divorce American communications from the British be seriously undertaken (Winkler 2007). This does not reduce the importance of US global connectivity, but highlights thinking in the Theodore Roosevelt administration about the United States not as separate from "the world" but as an ascendant force within an Anglo-Saxon coalition leading the world (Tyrrell 2015b).

This connectivity was to receive a further acceleration with the arrival of the radiotelephone – and the work of the English-based Italian Guglielmo Marconi. Before World War I the radiotelephone was of limited military significance, but its cultural potential was highlighted in the *Titanic* sinking of 1912. Equipped with a Marconi radiotelegraphy device, the *Titanic* was in radio communications with other vessels, of which there were dozens in the same iceberg-prone zone of the North Atlantic. Radio communication between those vessels was credited with saving many passengers after the iceberg struck. But there was also a negative side to the story, and one that prompted the first regulation of the fledgling radio industry. The *Titanic's* radio operator was either unable or unwilling to break off the receipt of personal messages coming via the wireless station at Cape Race, Newfoundland to take seriously the urgent warning of the *SS Californian* on the presence of icebergs. This breakdown in communications contributed to the disaster and led directly to regulation under the Radio Act of 1912, thus showing how international communications affected national legislation (Sidak 1997, 23). To be sure, the radio medium did not become widespread and democratically available until the 1920s, and radio use in World War I was militarily based. Yet the rush of wealthy passengers to use the radiotelegraphy facilities of the *Titanic* as soon as it was in range of the Newfoundland relay station in 1912 gave a glimpse of the future. It confirms a pattern already illustrated by Seward, showing how highly valued was the ability to communicate at will—and quickly—within a transnational space, for those who could afford it.

Cultural Implications of the New Technologies

These cultural implications of speed in steamship travel require similar attention from historians. The trans-Pacific crossing was made easier by the regular steamship routes operating with government postal subsidies to Yokohama from 1867 (later with services to China). This was the route that Seward took in 1870. In 1898 six steamship lines covered the route to East Asia, and were "crowded with passengers" and cargo due to growing trans-Pacific trade (Denby 1898, 32–33). The San Francisco–Yokohama trip took 22 days in 1886, but less than 12 by 1898. For the Atlantic, of course, the connections were more intense and speedier. By 1890, a journalist reported on the North Atlantic passenger trade that there were "twelve steamship lines who have regular sailing days each week, and some have sailings twice and three times a week." Servicing these lines were "eighty-four steamships which carry saloon and passengers" (*Transatlantic Steamship Routes* 1893).

Once again it was the emotional and cultural response that impresses, especially the obsession with quick passage, just as the annihilation of distance was a source of the telegraph cable's cultural importance. In both cases speed records were at the center of publicity over the new technology. The speed with which steamships crossed the Atlantic produced great popular interest, with huge crowds turning out in New York to greet ships such as the Cunard Line's *Lusitania.* Later sunk by the Germans during World War I, the *Lusitania* reduced the record time for a transatlantic crossing to 4 days, 19 hours and 53 minutes in October 1907, before losing the record once more to another British steamer, the *Mauretania.* That a ship like the *Lusitania* could be a culturally prominent example of modernist technology and emblematic of the shrinking of space and time puts into a new light its sinking in 1915 as an assault, not only on US passengers, but also on the reigning system of global and peaceful communications that most Americans had come to value. President Woodrow Wilson apparently felt this way, as the role of untrammeled commerce upon the high seas was a key concern leading to the US declaration of war in 1917.

Steamships were not only important as an item of technological change, but also as transnational spaces in themselves. The ships were microcosms of the changing world, where global communications were strengthening transcultural exchanges and economic integration. Passenger steamships carried truly transnational cargoes. Seward reported his trans-Pacific journey to China via Yokohama on the Pacific Mail Steamship Line to show a cultural microcosm of the blossoming world of Pacific commerce. Among the passengers were "General Vlangally, the Russian Minister returning from St. Petersburg to Peking" via New York, Washington, and San Francisco, "and half a dozen English civil officers coming from 'home' to their posts in Japan and China." Along with fifteen American missionaries with their wives and children bound for service in China and Japan there sailed US naval officers, "on their way to join the Asiatic squadron" (Seward 1873, 29, 30; Tolley 1971). Also on board were "four English and as many American youths just emerged from college on an Eastern tour; a United States Treasury agent, going to inspect the Oriental consulates; and one American office-seeker, at least, proceeding to lay his claims before the Emperor of China at Peking." A Japanese juggler kept the passengers amused when they were not doing exercises, resting, eating, or reading. In steerage were five hundred Chinese "returning home." The freight consisted partly of Mexican silver dollars sent to pay Chinese merchants for produce imported to the United States, but also "agricultural machines, carriages, furniture, flour, butter, fruits, drugs, and patent medicines." In exchange Americans would take home "teas, silks, rice, and Chinese emigrants" (Seward 1873, 30).

The transport of people and goods has significance for economic, cultural, and intellectual exchange. The groups stimulated by the rise of this industrial-era communication and technology to engage in foreign activities were, apart from government officials, mostly missionaries, travelers, and businessmen, figures prominently noted in Seward's scrutiny of the passengers on the *SS China.* But among the beneficiaries of the new communications were also journalists, scientists, and reformers. The remainder of this chapter focuses on these diverse human cargoes and argues that American "expansion" in 1898 and after was a product of prior engagement on a global, not just a European level, by such groups. While an imperial American state grew after 1898, international contacts were broader and more diverse than such later developments would suggest. The Gilded Age becomes in this interpretation a period of US engagement with the wider world without the need to compromise or distort the variety and complexity of those exchanges through the lens of formal imperialism. This is not to deny a prior empire in the post-1865 United States. A commercial approach to "empire" as informal economic dominance lay at the heart of globetrotter William Henry Seward's foreign policy. The advances in communications and free trade that he celebrated in his account of his round-the-world trip would, he believed, cement American commercial hegemony, and produce a peaceful global order. Military coercion would not be needed for this purpose (Sexton 2014, 410–411; Immerman 2010). Of course, military coercion and occupation did occur in nineteenth-century American "expansion," but overwhelmingly within what became the continental United States. The continental empire underpinned by indigenous dispossession provides one reason why Gilded Age expansion did not need to be formally "imperialistic" abroad in this way prior to 1898.

The historiography of this topic is mostly in the traditional fields of diplomatic history and international relations. But, influenced by theories and methods of transnational and comparative history, newer studies are approaching this question from fresh angles. For political and social reform, the outstanding work of Daniel Rodgers, *Atlantic Crossings,* must be noted. Rodgers's account is conceptualized as Atlantic history. The problem is not that he excludes the Pacific. Rodgers is well aware of the need to include key British dominions overseas, such as Australia and New Zealand. He discusses the US irrigation expert Elwood

Mead's time in Australia and its influence on American land-settlement proposals after 1913 in California and nationally, rightly pointing out differences of application on either side of the Pacific (Rodgers 1998, 55–56; 245–251). But he sees these places in the American imagination as "outposts" of the British Empire and the Atlantic world. This misses the way Americans who came to Australia framed the antipodes not as an outpost to the Atlantic main game, but as a new world, with its own distinctive innovation centered in the case of Australia and New Zealand on the widely held notion that these places were, albeit only until World War I, considered international "social laboratories" (Lake 2014). It also misses the way that Progressive thought viewed the United States as part of a settler colonial culture (Teisch 2005, 2011). Moreover, the visits of reformers to Australia and New Zealand came as part of a wider purview of the Asia-Pacific, that nebulous intellectual space but attractive world, as a new field for American commerce, and as the site of the nation's colonial adventure in the Philippines.

The work of Victor Selden Clark, a young economist with a doctorate from Columbia University, illustrates this theme of a new global outlook in American Progressivism. In 1906 he published *The Labour Movement in Australasia*, a book giving strong expression to Progressive Era comparative interpretation of labor relations, arbitration of labor conflict, and other class questions, but it is almost entirely neglected (Clark 1906; Durand 1946). The context is important. Rather than a straight Australian–American comparison, Clark's investigations in Australia came as part of a US Department of Commerce tour of East Asia. He was required to study the Australian sugar-cane industry "with a view to furnishing the United States authorities with some points that might be useful to them in developing the Philippine Islands, of which they had then recently become possessed" (*Queensland Times* 1905). He had been sent across the Pacific to examine tropical labor conditions and wrote a substantial report on the Philippine labor situation. Clark received this assignment because he served as a colonial official in Puerto Rico from 1899 to 1902, and had reported on skill and remuneration differentials in Cuban wage practices (Davis 1900, 179–180; Clark 1903, 1905a, b; Angulo 2012, 36–39). His field of investigation was colonial and imperial rather than transatlantic (or Australian).

Granted, a good deal of American interactions with the wider world concerned the North Atlantic, the Caribbean, or Latin America. But the late nineteenth century saw an expansion of American activity in the Pacific, focused at first on missionaries and commerce, then on the exertion of naval power and the establishment of bases. Though the Spanish–American War began over Cuba, immediately the US fleet seized Manila. Assistant Secretary of the Navy Theodore Roosevelt had positioned the fleet in the area prior to the commencement of hostilities in anticipation of taking control of that potentially important port. Desire for a stronger strategic and commercial presence in the Pacific was an objective of the belligerent American policy in 1897–1898. The new interest in the Pacific as a field of American geopolitical interest received theatrical if not effective strategic manifestation in the global circulation of Roosevelt's Great White Fleet in 1907–1908, a publicity maneuver meant to reassure American audiences as much as convince Japan that it would not be allowed to dominate the Pacific. The point is not to pit the Atlantic against the Pacific as discrete theatres of interests, but to stress their interconnection as strategists began to think more commonly within a global framework. The acquisition of the Panama Zone in 1903 was central to that commercial vision of global trade and investment networks in which the Pacific would be increasingly important (Missal 2008; Greene 2009; Herring 2008, 356–357).

Labor reformer and social critic Henry Demarest Lloyd remarked in 1903 that "modern steamships" were "converting the Pacific into a mere Mediterranean, but a Mediterranean of a new civilization, a sea to connect, not to divide, the awakening East and the advancing West" (Lloyd 1903, 5). As part of this new global vision, and as illustrated in Victor Clark's work, Americans began to take a greater interest in the social democracies emerging in Australia and New Zealand. Yet the Australasian contributions to the history of the Gilded Age and Progressive Era thinking is the subject of little detailed research, apart from Peter J. Coleman's *Progressivism and the World of Reform*. Coleman argued for the existence of a global Progressive movement, responding to a worldwide crisis in capitalism, based on the interest that US reformers took in New Zealand (Coleman 1982, 1987). This interest in New Zealand models was closely associated with the work of Lloyd, after he boarded the Oceanic Steamship Line service in San Francisco bound for Auckland in 1899. His *Newest England* urged adoption of New Zealand-style arbitration of labor disputes (Lloyd 1900, 1903; John Wilson 2010). In a similar vein, the irrigation reform advocate and socialist William Ellsworth Smythe called for the "New Zealandization" of the United States around social policies of fairness and democracy (Lee 1973; Coleman 1982). Acutely aware of the "world's markets in sharp competition with the people of all other countries," Lloyd argued that Australasian social innovations and advocacy of government-controlled transport had origins in the new global commerce encroaching on Antipodean isolation. Reforms tinged with socialism were the "natural recourse of a new people coming into existence in the midst of the modern complex industrial system" (Lloyd 1903, 335).

Progressivism and Transatlantic Reform

Progressivism itself is a much-disputed concept, but the impetus to address the problems of urban and industrial society after the 1890s had strong international linkages.

American historians have long recognized that Progressivism could be compared with European social democracy and liberal reform. Since the 1990s, a number of explicitly comparative rather than transnational histories have been published, including *Struggles for Justice: Social Responsibility and the Liberal State* (Dawley 1991). As in Dawley's case, Germany has been the site for much of the comparison because, like the United States, it was rapidly developing into a leading industrial power (with all of its problems of modernity and class). In *American Progressives and German Social Reform*, Axel Schäfer stresses German–American connections and influences upon Progressive thought in developing a regulatory state, not as an authoritarian German one, but one of public participation, thus modifying the German model in America (Schäfer 2000). Adaptation within a common experience of modernity and its contradictions is also central to Thomas Welskopp and Alan Lessoff's *Fractured Modernity: America Confronts Modern Times, 1890s to 1940s.* Carefully distinguishing transnational from comparative analysis, they portray "an incoherent, ruptured modernity" with "diverse and often contentious reactions" to industrialization, immigration and racial strife (Welskopp and Lessoff 2013; Lessoff 2013). Special topics such as nature conservation are rarely seen in a comparative perspective, due to the historiographical emphasis on the American origins of conservation policy, and the tendency for Progressive historiography to concentrate on social, political, and intellectual history rather than environmental. But Welskopp and Lessoff includes Frank Uekoetter's study of environmental modernism and conservation, comparing American Progressivism with Germany (Uekoetter 2009, 2013).

These comparative studies recognize cross-fertilization, as Rodgers's seminal work in transnational history does. Rodgers analyzes not only legal and social scientific experts, but also "transatlantic social Protestantism" through the settlement house movement influenced by Toynbee Hall in London, England. Rodgers is alert to inevitable differences across the Atlantic brought about by different institutional conditions. The settlement house movement's women's college networks in the United States led by Jane Addams meant that the movement there became "much more quickly and deeply feminized than its English model" (Rodgers 1998, 64). The circulation of ideas and people via the new communications networks aided this process of exchange immensely. Declining travel prices and speedier passages encouraged reformers to crisscross the Atlantic for conferences and speaking engagements. Transatlantic vessels themselves became sites for religious proselytizing and moral improvement, as speakers offered the travelers on board short courses on moral improvement and internationalism. One such American lecturer who plied the Atlantic on those steamships, the Rev. Wilbur Crafts of the International Reform Bureau, remarked in 1908: "international travel and international commerce—and I might add, international reading—are developing an increasing group of international men" (quoted in Tyrrell 2010, 25). More tourists and college students also visited Europe. Young doctoral candidates studied there in the 1880s and 1890s, as historian Charles Beard did in Britain. These students and those that they taught back in the United States were particularly important as conduits for European ideas of social reorganization because the US version of social democracy came to rely highly on university expertise (Rodgers 1998, 79, 86–89, 132). Less has been written about British–American comparisons than these continental European ones, but the connection was strong. The importance of British interest in Gilded Age Reform and Progressivism emerges from Robert P. Frankel's examination of British travelers to the United States. These comparisons qualify the widely perceived exceptionalism of the American social science literature of the Gilded Age. Lawrence Goldman (1998) has shown strong parallels and linkages in the transition to social science from social reform among the late nineteenth- century Anglo-American intellectual elite.

Because women were denied political equality within the American nation-state (and most other places), international action became prominent among women's groups. Suffragist Katharine Anthony claimed that gender discrimination had bred "an unconscious internationalism" among women that was in the process of becoming a formal internationalism (Anthony 1915, 3–4). Certainly women used international contacts to gain leverage back home, and their exclusion from national institutions also encouraged a more genuinely international outlook among an elite able to travel. This response took the shape of leadership in the International Council of Women (1888) and the International Woman Suffrage Association (1904). Some of women's political work was based on Anglo-American cooperation in reforms such as temperance and Woman suffrage. Ellen DuBois's biography of Harriot Stanton Blatch documents Anglo-American exchanges of women's suffrage tactics and strategies in the 1880s and 1890s (DuBois 1997). Radical suffrage agitation in Britain became a particular focus of American interest. Alice Paul's experience of militant suffragette demonstrations in Britain in 1908–1909 spurred her introduction of similar tactics in the United States, founding the Congressional Union in 1914 with her colleague, friend, and fellow-traveler in Britain, Lucy Burns (Tyrrell, 2008).

Faced with the constitutional division of powers and the weaker American party system, moderate suffragists doubted the applicability of Paul's English experience. They rejected her attempts to punish the Democratic Party for failure to pass Woman suffrage by opposing party candidates in the congressional elections of 1914. Significantly, however, Paul's opponents in this debate, the suffragists led by Carrie Chapman Catt, also had extensive international experience in the women's movement. They, too, visited Britain or networked with internationally oriented suffrage activists, but for tactical reasons adapted rather than adopted the innovative British militant tactics to persuade the US Congress to act on Woman suffrage (Tyrrell 2008; Zahniser and Fry 2014; Lunardini 2012).

As in other areas of social and political action, women's agitation followed global rather than purely North Atlantic circuits. Women responded to the opportunities for the global spread of information and followed the example of women's missionaries into globally oriented work. Women as well as men had benefited from cheaper and more reliable communications, and became deeply involved in international movements for peace and social reform. The Woman's Christian Temperance Union (WCTU), the most extensive and active of the women's international organizations during the Gilded Age, adopted a specifically global focus and championed such causes as international arbitration as well as temperance, Woman suffrage, and prohibition. Its self-styled "missionaries" went around the world, and from this women's temperance movement came leading moderate suffragists such as Carrie Chapman Catt and Anna Howard Shaw. Catt had extensive international experience as a president of the International Woman's Suffrage Association. She followed the example of the WCTU missionaries when she went on a round-the-world tour in 1911–1912 on behalf of Woman suffrage, and acclaimed on her return "The Awakening of Women around the World" (Tyrrell 1991; Van Voris 1987; Franzen 2014). This sense of internationalism was challenged by World War I, but pacifists from the United States were prominent in the creation of the Women's International League for Peace and Freedom (1919) that grew out of the Woman's Peace Party, founded in 1915 (Marchand 1972; Schott 1997).

Progressive Experts Abroad

If the import of reform ideas and institutions from abroad flourished as part of the communications revolution, another phenomenon—less noticed in historiography because of the Atlantic focus of existing research (Rodgers 2002)—was the outflow of American expertise. Inspiring this trend was the global vision concerning the new opportunities for personal advancement and instruction. Due to the greater ease of international travel, various groups of American experts moved out in the 1880s and 1890s to influence international economic and social development. Again, this movement was not limited to Europe. German colonial rulers in Togoland solicited technical advice on the growth of cotton from Tuskegee, Alabama experts, where coerced African American labor seemed useful as a model for colonial development. But this case was unusual, as the teachers were African Americans (Zimmerman 2010). Mostly the expansion of professional expertise came from white Americans. American engineers were prominent within the British Empire and Latin America; their practical qualifications were highly regarded, and they contributed to agriculture as well as the mining industry. Because of their extensive technical training in the United States, there were by 1900 over one thousand American engineers in the British Empire "occupying top positions" (Hoover 1952, 131; Blainey 1963, 53–70). The Exploration Company of London "served as an import–export agency for capital and expertise." Introducing American "mining securities into the British market," it secured "British financing for mines in Mexico, Venezuela, Alaska, and South Africa." Working in partnerships with international companies it supplied engineers as a labor-contract hire company (Teisch 2011, 99; Wilkins 1970).

But it was more than technical advice that engineers provided. They tried, with mixed success, to change the cultures of work and production and the wider political economy that they encountered abroad. Especially was this so for the future president Herbert Hoover, who from 1897 to 1914 moved from the Western Australian gold fields to mining operations in China. Although an engineer, Hoover's major accomplishment was to rationalize production in the interests of business efficiency, thus extracting larger profits for mines. Reorganizing labor relations to cut wages and increase productivity was at the heart of his work, and he was richly rewarded in both a financial and organizational sense within this business. But he was also disliked among his Australian employees as a "hard-driving, self-driven Yankee." Hoover used the vast improvements in shipping, rail, and telegraph to build this international business, and to travel around the world seven times between 1895 and 1908 (Nash 1983, 84; Hoover 1952, 33). But he was not alone as a travelling international expert. John Hays Hammond, the American engineer, who first came to public attention as a supporter of the 1895 Jameson Raid in the Boer state of Transvaal, is similarly illustrative of the nexus between globetrotting engineers and business. His *Autobiography* (Hammond 1974) reveals political traction coming from knowledge of world affairs in his role as a Republican Party advisor back home in the United States during the Progressive Era (Israel 1971, 83, 84).

Led by Gifford Pinchot, Theodore Roosevelt's chief advocate of conservation, foresters also travelled widely during the Progressive Era, studying in Germany and France and examining the forests of the Philippines and South America (Miller, 2001; Barton, 2002). But best covered in scholarly work are the irrigation experts. The latter went to many places, including South Africa, Palestine, Australia, Egypt, and Hawaii. Their contribution abroad has been analyzed by Jessica Teisch (2011). Elwood Mead was one such figure. Serving as River and Water Supply Commissioner in Victoria, Australia, from 1907 to 1915, he travelled frequently back to the United States and maintained contacts there, eventually becoming the Commissioner for Reclamation in Washington, DC in 1924. In a long career, he also served on commissions in Haiti and Cuba and was a water policy adviser in Mexico, the Dutch East Indies,

Canada, and South Africa (Teisch 2011; Mead 1920; Rook 2000; Tyrrell 1999; Rodgers, 1998). Ideas for conservation were widely shared internationally, particularly across the settler societies of the British Empire, a circumstance that made South Africans, Australians, Canadians, and New Zealanders interested in American conservation policy. The latter seemed especially useful for its blend of efficient use of resources and protection of "nature" through national parks (Tyrrell 2015b; cf. Dunlap 1999).

Alongside this international aspect of irrigation the Progressive Era brought greater intrusion of the federal government into irrigation policy. From the time of the National Reclamation Act of 1902, irrigation policy became a major initiative of Theodore Roosevelt's presidency, and was closely tied to greater state regulation of the economy, and a nation-focused approach to strengthen the US agricultural and industrial resource base in the growing inter-imperial competition. But historians have done little to tie these internal developments to external ones in this way. An exception is Donald Worster's *Rivers of Empire*, a condemnation of dams as a policy that sold an agrarian dream but furthered the industrialization of the West's farm production, creating a kind of hydraulic "empire" that undermined natural systems. Worster was one of the first to recognize the global context of agrarian reform at the hands of experts as the United States rose to world power (Worster 1985). On the other hand, Donald Pisani examines the role of the US Bureau of Reclamation, and sees the rise of irrigation as resulting from local factors and the peculiarities of the American federal system. Pisani's intricate focus on federalism and the complexities of American politics at the local and state levels sets up a possible comparison of national policies with Australia and Canada, but this work has yet to be done (Pisani 2002; Rowley 1996).

Globetrotting experts in irrigation, forestry, geology, mining engineering, and other fields gained professional opportunities, and forged a stronger global outlook on their work. They became parts of international networks exchanging technological and scientific information (Tyrrell 2015b). Yet their experiences did not necessarily produce a cosmopolitan outlook, perhaps because these peripatetic professionals did not typically set down roots in foreign cultures. In 1912 Hoover claimed "the American is always an alien abroad. He can never assimilate." Historian John Milton Cooper asserts of Hoover: "The longer he was away, the more American he became" (Cooper 2003, 41). Apparently not influenced by foreign cultures, Hoover learned only a smattering of Mandarin during his years in China, though his wife studied the language more intensively (*Chicago Tribune* 2012; Nash 1983, 115). Yet Hoover's well-known and robust American chauvinism abroad was tempered by the fact that he moved easily between countries and cultures as an engineer in the years before World War I, when London was his base. While his heart was in the United States, he observed that "there is less and less of a niche for him (the American) when he returns" (Pursell 2010, 111). The expatriate American was almost a "foreigner" within his own home country, a transnational figure, one might be tempted to say.

Missionaries, Humanitarianism and American Cultural Expansion

Though similarly inspired by the improvements in communications to export American culture, missionaries settling among foreign populations differed from the traveling engineers. American missionaries had gone abroad before the 1880s in fairly small numbers, but an exponential rise occurred from 1886 to 1914. As the North American Young Men's Christian Association (YMCA) official Sherwood Eddy pointed out, missionaries rejoiced at the "students of Christendom awaking, with steam and electricity to carry us to the ends of the earth in a month, with typewriter and telegraph for our epistles, [and] bicycle and railways to speed the gospel" (Eddy 1896). Evangelist Arthur T. Pierson, whose *Crisis of Missions* was a major stimulus to the missionary outpouring, seized upon this same point, arguing that technological change and European commercial penetration made South and Southeast Asia ripe for religious conquest: "The telegraphic circuit embraces her (Asia) and binds her to the Christian world" (Pierson 1886, 76–77). Long before this, Protestant evangelicalism forged expansive ambitions based on biblical injunctions, and these Christian impulses and experiences, rather than new technology, provided key motive for missionaries. Dramatic communication changes allowed these dreams to be realized more fully by the 1880s and 1890s. Prominent studies focused on missionaries deal especially with the role of women (Hunter 1984; Sklar, Reeves-Ellington, and Shemo 2010). The study of the target audiences for missionaries abroad is in its infancy despite important work by Ussama Makdisi on American missionaries in the Ottoman Empire, but the reciprocal missionary impacts on the United States in this period were profound (Makdisi 2007; Bays and Wacker 2003; Tyrrell 2010).

A major theme within this literature is the extent of cultural imperialism. While missionaries were quite Eurocentric, they did have the capacity to adapt to foreign cultures as a result of experience, though the degree and the type of adaptation varied. The debate over cultural imperialism sometimes falsely degenerates into an either/or proposition, and does not take sufficient account of change over time, or the possibility that both internationalist and imperialist dispositions existed in the same people. Prominent missionaries who returned from Japan or China, for example, became ambassadors for goodwill between the United States and Asian countries, and were critics of the extreme US racial exclusion policies erected between 1882 and 1908, governing initially Chinese people, but from 1907–1908 the Japanese as well. Yet few missionaries were as prominent as the Rev. Sidney Gulick, a major supporter of Japanese–American friendship, who wrote extensively in support of tolerant attitudes toward Japanese immigrants and for cooperation between the two countries. Gulick affirmed the importance of technological changes for his work, and for cultural understanding. He found that modern communications "annulled the ancient barriers which so long separated the nations." He predicted the inevitable triumph of a new moral order of international understanding and progress (Gulick 1908, 8; Taylor 1984; Snow 2003). This Panglossian statement was written in 1908. The coming of World War I jarred such thinking but did not eliminate it. While the war reinforced the theme of exceptionalism in American efforts to export moralism abroad, both Christian ecumenism that began to flourish in the interwar years and the rise of a religious cosmopolitanism among liberal Protestants was influenced by the missionary movements and the encounter with non-Christian cultures. Syncretic ideas, such as theosophy, and events such as the World's Parliament of Religions, held in Chicago in 1893 in conjunction with the World's Fair and Columbian Exposition, spoke to the diversity of American Protestant Christianity's encounter with the Other that resulted from both an economic expansion of the west and diverse missionary experiences. Though confined to a minority, Eastern religions such as Buddhism and Hindu sects became more widely discussed and understood.

Missionaries took a range of Western cultural practices with them overseas, including sport and recreation. Increasing attention is being given to the role of sport and related activities at home in the United States, such as Muscular Christianity. But few works broach the exertion of masculinity abroad except in the service of imperialism. Here Kristin Hoganson (1998) has made a pioneering contribution to the framing of American imperialism in gender terms. Muscular Christianity thrived in the late nineteenth century, and the missionary movements of the Student Volunteer Movement (founded 1886) and the YMCA carried these Christian ideals and cultural assumptions into their mission work. Missionaries and the YMCA tried to spread American sports in the Philippines, China, India, and Japan (Tyrrell 2010; Garrett 1970).

Americans also began to take a much greater interest in overseas giving and humanitarian relief in the Gilded Age in ways that complemented but then moved beyond purely religious enthusiasms. During World War I and just after, Americans provided food relief first to Belgium, and then throughout Europe under the auspices of the American Relief Committee. The work of future president Herbert Hoover in this philanthropy is well known (Burner 1979; Nash, 1988, 1989). But humanitarian relief was not new. International humanitarianism flourished in the Euro-American world in the Gilded Age, and Americans played an important role, often in partnership with Europeans in the dispensing of food and other material aid. The pioneering overview, Merle Curti's *American Philanthropy Abroad* (1963), remains the standard work on US humanitarian participation in the nineteenth century. In addition to material aid, Americans took part in "rescue" work concerning political refugees in eastern Europe (Wilson 2010). Though American humanitarian efforts pre-dated the Gilded Age, the entire impulse to "save" the world expanded in the 1880s and 1890s. In some cases humanitarians had strong philanthropic support in the United States, but much of the funding came in small donations, and relied on the new communications networks for raising money, and for making Americans speedily aware of crises of a humanitarian kind abroad. These emergencies energized Americans in the 1890s (Bloodworth 2011). The Russian famine; the Armenian crisis of 1894–1896 in the Ottoman Empire; the Indian famine of 1896–1897; and the Cuban crisis of 1897–1898 concerning displaced refugees and atrocities against the civilian population by the Spanish colonial rulers all produced greater humanitarian effort as unprecedented levels of information became available, including photographs of the victims of atrocities and mass starvation. The Red Cross rose to prominence as the chief agent of the nation's humanitarian action during the Spanish–American War, but the churches had contributed substantially to the earlier relief of the Armenian persecution and the Indian famine problems. These humanitarian efforts were not merely American moral outpourings but rather were networked within the British Empire. This cooperative stance was a shift from the 1870s, when Americans showed relatively little awareness of the Indian famines of 1876–1878, despite the deaths of millions and an organized British famine relief campaign. Something had changed for Americans by the 1890s. That change seems to have stemmed from enhanced knowledge of foreign distress brought to the attention of home audiences by improved communications and technology, and through the services of the expanding battalions of Christian missionaries who moved to and fro between European colonies and metropoles in the wake of improvements to shipping and railroad transport (Bloodworth 2011; Wilson 2009; Curtis 2012; Digby 1878).

This tradition of humanitarianism continued after 1900, but became more professionalized, as Julia Irwin (2013) has shown in her study of the international activities of the American Red Cross. During World War I, closer relationships between humanitarians and the state also linked these philanthropic and moral causes to the projection of American power abroad (Burner 1979; Nash 1988, 1989; Rothbard 1979). This development corresponded with, but was by no means subordinate to, Wilsonian diplomacy. Studies of Woodrow Wilson have long acknowledged his Christian and moralistic outlook as much as his capacity for *Realpolitik*, but his association with the nongovernmental sector, including philanthropy and missionaries, was used to develop his agenda of a new internationalism based on free exchange of commerce and liberal freedoms (Tyrrell 2010, 198–208; Mayer 1961, 372; Rossini, 2008, 2; Manela 2007, 101).

Business and Cultural Expansion

It is important to realize that this project of American cultural influence abroad in the late nineteenth and early twentieth centuries was not cohesive. Especially, there was antagonism between missionaries and businessmen over the extra-territoriality treaties that allowed American law to take precedence over the conduct of citizens abroad in many non-Western countries. In the treaty ports of China and Japan, where US extra-territorial law applied, missionaries found businessmen to be as unsatisfactory and poor in moral conduct as some of the consuls who served them, and called for the reform of the consular service, implemented from 1906 to 1924 (Scully 2001). But the antagonism with missionaries comes out most clearly in a study of late nineteenth-century Japan. Missionaries were more solicitous for the welfare of their potential converts than businessmen were of their customers. Businessmen did not want to alter their privileged treaty port status, while the missionaries were willing to do so, provided treaty revision gave fresh proselytizing access to the interior of Japan. The special business advantage and tariff privileges of the businessmen would be lost under this circumstance (Murphy 2004). American missionaries also criticized European imperialism and, at times, US imperialism, though in the latter case they tended, after the formal empire was established in 1898, to focus on trying to reform American colonial government. By making US rule in the colonies in the Philippine Islands and Puerto Rico more moral, moral reformers and missionaries helped to reinforce ideas of American exceptionalism and cemented a modified colonial rule (Tyrrell 2009, 2010).

Alongside missionaries were the much publicized efforts of the purveyors of popular culture, such as Albert G. Spalding's baseball exhibition tour. The quasi-missionary motives of these baseball tourists in spreading American culture stood out, and Spalding himself used this "missionary" terminology. Well documented by Thomas Zeiler and others, the tour of 1888–1889 was not particularly successful in spreading baseball, however (Zeiler 2006; Lamster 2006). Individual missionaries and businessmen and (for Cuba, Panama, and Puerto Rico) military and US colonial officials did that. But Spalding's venture did enhance the importance of baseball back home and revealed the importance of English-speaking nations as a market for US entrepreneurs. The two teams of players proceeded from the west coast, and then sailed around the world, visiting Hawaii and Australia, Sri Lanka, Egypt, and Europe. They followed the comfortable and available steamship routes opened up in the 1870s and 1880s to the South Pacific and then on through the Suez Canal to Europe via Britain's Pacific and Orient Steamship Company. Spalding's trip was intended to boost the sport of baseball back home via the newspaper reports sent by steamship, railroads, and the telegraph wires, but it also served to proclaim the superiority of American business methods (for example in sporting goods manufacture) and rejoiced in the new opportunities that the communications revolution created in the British Empire for expanded economic opportunities.

Rob Kroes and Robert Rydell's *Buffalo Bill in Bologna* is the most systematic analytical work on such American cultural influence abroad in the Gilded Age and Progressive Era. It wisely cautions over the idea that US culture simply rolled over the cultures that it "invaded." The case of Buffalo Bill's Wild West show abroad reveals the European fascination for the exploits of the American frontier, especially the idea of a wild and savage nature being tamed in North America. But it also shows how Europeans adapted these entertainments in ways that assimilated them to a more general concern, by combining American cultural references with exotic ones on a global scale, rather than perpetuate a specific American exceptionalism. Kroes and Rydell thereby provide a sophisticated assessment of US cultural penetration abroad for the 1890s and early twentieth century, even though their work is limited to impacts on Europe (Kroes and Rydell 2005).

Much of this US cultural influence did flow east across the Atlantic, and was the subject of European anxiety over an American commercial and entertainment invasion (McKenzie 1902; Stead 1972), but the Pacific, too, was a zone of enhanced cultural circulation. The Spalding tour was only the tip of an iceberg regarding US Pacific cultural exchange (Wittmann 2010). Many outbound travelers went not just to the American West, but further. They embraced international travel through what David Wrobel calls a "Global West," in which the frontiers of the United States were figuratively extended, but also were viewed in comparative perspective. Some of this travel concerned the Pacific, as in the case of Jack London's ramblings to Hawaii and the South Sea Islands. Other travelers emphasized the global experience and the speed of communications. Peripatetic lecturers such as Mark Twain went south from San Francisco to New Zealand and across to Australia as part of their own circumnavigations, taking advantage not only of improved communications but English-language commonalities (Wrobel, 2013). Most spectacularly, Nellie Bly wrote *Around the World in 72 Days*, and recorded for the *New York World* her whirlwind visit to Japan and China in 1890. US contacts with these and other countries on the Pacific Rim were growing due to the communications links in the emergence of a global civil society exemplified in Bly's newsworthy stunt to circumnavigate the world (Tyrrell, 2015a).

Business and cultural expansion often went together. American businessmen traveled to Asia on the new steamship routes and contributed to the dissemination of American popular culture. In *The Diplomacy of Involvement*, David Pletcher painstakingly documents the uneven but growing extent of American economic engagement with East Asia between 1865 and 1900, an involvement that laid foundations for the emergence of American Pacific trade interests (Pletcher 2001). These businessmen often resided in port cities in China and Japan and the Philippines, among other places, engaging in the import and export trade with the United States. Along with naval personnel and missionaries, businessmen encouraged the spread of baseball (Guthrie-Shimizu 2012).

American economic interests in the Caribbean, and in Central and South America, flourished in the Gilded Age and Progressive Era, and have been extensively studied. The development of the United Fruit Company's (UFC) vertically integrated monopoly after 1900 showed how Central America became part of US international consumerism's commodity chains. In the UFC case, this involved tropical fruit for consumers delivered by a speedy and near-military shipping timetable, possible only through the spread of cable services, and aided by US government mail subsidies for its private fleet. But American entrepreneurs also sought oil and copper in Mexico, and coffee in Brazil and Colombia (Tucker 2000; Colby 2011; Hart 2002). In Cuba, American sugar interests were so extensive that they drew the United States into serious conflict with the Spanish government during the latter's repression of the Cuban independence rebellion during 1895 to 1898. But these economic interests were not enough to produce war with Spain. It was the moral and humanitarian outcry against Spain's actions in that guerrilla war that most raised the stakes. The heightened, missionary-stimulated humanitarianism of the 1890s did not cause the war either but, together with the immediacy of increased press coverage of events on the island, made a war with Spain more likely. This issue concerns formal American diplomacy and foreign policy, but American action was greatly influenced by the web of transnational nongovernmental activity—commercial, humanitarian and media communications—documented in this chapter (Pratt 1936; Hofstadter 1965, 145–187; McCartney 2006).

Future Research

These pathways to formal and informal empire have rightly been extensively studied, but the wider global connections must be further investigated. They provided the context and framework of growing American participation in economics and politics abroad. The pattern of information flows and cultural activity under the new communications regime of the 1880s and 1890s shows that the focus on US–East Asian links and Latin American and Caribbean penetration has overshadowed too much the importance of the British Empire to US cultural expansion. Outreach to settler societies of British origin was common—both as a conduit for American global circulations, and a key target for ideas, due to presumed political, linguistic and cultural affinities. The importance of the Australian goldmines to Herbert Hoover's pre-World War I mining activities is a case in point from the economic realm. Hoover advanced his own and American capitalist interests under the umbrella of British financial organization. The same pattern was true of missionaries in many instances.

Further research on this area would dovetail with, and benefit from, scholarship on the "British World." That idea recognizes the importance of an "Anglosphere" in the late nineteenth century centered on ideas of "white" settlement, Anglo-Saxonism, racial destiny, parliamentary institutions, and the rule of law. The United States was implicated in and contributory to such ideas, even as the underlying concepts of an Anglo-Saxon race and culture were "mythic" and ultimately unrealistic, especially in view of the multicultural and multi-ethnic immigration to the United States by 1900. Closely linked is the research derived from theories of settler colonialism, for which there is an expanding comparative literature that American historians could utilize (Belich 2009; Magee and Thompson 2010; Mead 2007; Detweiler 1938; Veracini 2010; Hixson 2013; Lake and Reynolds 2008).

Common themes of settler societies, including the United States as one such society, offer rich prospects for scholarship, even as it is necessary to understand profound differences in the history and social composition of all of these societies, including the United States. Sentiments concerning these places as sharing a common tradition, experience, and prospects emerged at that time, when the modernization of the world, the growth of industrialization, and the communications revolutions brought English-speaking peoples closer in effective proximity and in commercial and cultural interaction during the Gilded Age.

References

Adler, Jacob 1960. "The Oceanic Steamship Company: A Link in Claus Spreckels' Hawaiian Sugar Empire." *Pacific Historical Review* 29: 257–269.

Angulo, A.J. 2012. *Empire and Education: A History of Greed and Goodwill from the War of 1898 to the War on Terror*. New York: Palgrave Macmillan.

Anthony, Katharine. 1915. *Feminism in Germany and Scandinavia*. New York: Henry Holt.

Baldwin, Simeon E. 1907. "The International Congresses and Conferences of the Last Century as Forces Working toward the Solidarity of the World." *American Journal of International Law* 1: 565–578.

Ballantyne, Tony and Antoinette Burton. 2012. "Empires and the Reach of the Global." In *A World Connecting 1870–1945*, ed. Emily S. Rosenberg, 285–431. Cambridge, MA: Belknap Press of Harvard University Press.

Bartky, Ian R. 2000. *Selling the True Time: Nineteenth-century Timekeeping in America*. Stanford, CA: Stanford University Press.

Barton, Gregory A. 2002. *Empire Forestry and the Origins of Environmentalism*. New York: Cambridge University Press.

Bays, Daniel and Grant Wacker, ed. 2003. *The Foreign Missionary Enterprise at Home: Explorations in North American Cultural History*. Tuscaloosa: University of Alabama Press.

Beard, Charles and Mary Beard. 1927. *The Rise of American Civilization*. New York: Macmillan.

Belich, James. 2009. *Replenishing the Earth: The Settler Revolution and the Rise of the Anglo-World, 1783–1939*. Oxford: Oxford University Press.

Blainey, Geoffrey. 1963. "Herbert Hoover's Forgotten Years." *Business Archives and History* 3, 1: 53–70.

Bloodworth, Jeff. 2011. "A Complicated Kindness: The Iowa Famine Relief Movement and the Myth of Midwestern and American Isolationism." *The Historian* 73: 480–502.

Burner, David. 1979. *Herbert Hoover: A Public Life*. New York: Knopf.

Chicago Tribune. "Republican Hopeful would not be First Chinese-Speaking President". January 10, 2012.

Clark, Victor S. 1903. "Industrial Conditions in America. Interview with Mr Victor S. Clarke [*sic*]. American Workmen and Trades Unionism." *Daily Telegraph*, September 9, 1903: 6.

—. 1905a. "Labor Conditions in Java." *Bulletin of the Bureau of Labor* 58: 906–954. Washington, DC: US Department of Commerce and Labor.

—. 1905b. "Labor Conditions in the Philippines." *Bulletin of the Bureau of Labor* 58: 721–905. Washington, DC: US Department of Commerce and Labor.

—. 1906. *The Labour Movement in Australasia: A Study in Social Democracy*. New York: Henry Holt.

—. Colby, Jason M. 2011. *The Business of Empire: United Fruit, Race, and U.S. Expansion in Central America*. Ithaca, NY: Cornell University Press.

Coleman, Peter J. 1982. "New Zealand Liberalism and the Origins of the American Welfare State." *Journal of American History* 69: 372–391.

—. 1987. *Progressivism and the World of Reform: New Zealand and the Origins of the American Welfare State*. Lawrence: University Press of Kansas.

Cooper, John Milton. 2003. "Not So Innocent Abroad: The Hoovers' Early Years." In *Uncommon Americans: The Lives and Legacies of Herbert and Lou Henry Hoover*, ed. Timothy Walch, 39–47. Westport, CT: Praeger.

Curti, Merle. 1963. *American Philanthropy Abroad: A History*. New Brunswick, NJ: Rutgers University Press.

Curtis, Heather D. 2012. "Depicting Distant Suffering: Evangelicals and the Politics of Pictorial Humanitarianism in the Age of American Empire." *Material Religion: The Journal of Objects, Art and Belief* 8: 154–183.

Davis, George W. 1900. *Report on Civil Affairs of Porto Rico, 1899*. Washington, DC: Government Printing Office.

Dawley, Alan. 1991. *Struggles for Justice: Social Responsibility and the Liberal State*. Cambridge, MA: Harvard University Press.

Denby, Charles, Jr. 1898. "America's Opportunity in Asia." *North American Review* 166: 32–33.

DeSantis, Vincent P. 1988. "The Gilded Age in American History." *Hayes Historical Journal: A Journal of the Gilded Age* 7, winter. http://www.rbhayes.org/hayes/content/files/Hayes_Historical_Journal/gildedageamericanhist.html/accessed July 18, 2016.

Detweiler, Frederick G. 1938. "The Anglo-Saxon Myth in the United States." *American Sociological Review* 3: 183–189.

Digby, William. 1878. *The Famine Campaigns in Southern India (Madras and Bombay Presidencies and Province of Mysore) 1876–1878*. London: Longmans, Green.

DuBois, Ellen C. 1987. *Harriot Stanton Blatch and the Winning of Woman Suffrage*. New Haven, CT: Yale University Press.

Dunlap, Thomas R. 1999. *Nature and the English Diaspora: Environment and History in the United States, Canada, Australia, and New Zealand*. Cambridge: Cambridge University Press.

Durand, E. Dana. 1946. "Dr. Victor Selden Clark." *Journal of the American Statistical Association* 41: 390–392.

Eddy, Sherwood, 1896. Letter No. 1, Nov. 15, 1896, in India, Eddy, G. Sherwood, Report Letters, 1896–1903, National Committee, 1891–1926, Y-57-1, Kautz Family YMCA Archives, University of Minnesota.

Edwards, Rebecca. 2009. "Politics, Social Movements, and the Periodization of American History." *Journal of the Gilded Age and the Progressive Era* 8: 463–473.

Fernandes, Felipe Tâmega. 2009. "Telegraphs, Shrinking Economic Distances? A Preliminary Enquiry (1870s–1912)." Unpublished paper, http://people.hbs.edu/ffernandes/TELEGRAPHS.pdf/accessed July 18, 2016.

Flanagan, Maureen A. 2007. *America Reformed: Progressives and Progressivisms, 1890s–1920s*. New York: Oxford University Press.

Franzen, Trisha. 2014. *Anna Howard Shaw: The Work of Woman Suffrage*. Urbana: University of Illinois Press.

Garrett, Shirley S. 1970. *Social Reformers in Urban China: The Chinese Y.M.C.A., 1895–1926*. Cambridge, MA: Harvard University Press.

Giddings, Howard A. 1900. *Exploits of the Signal Corps in the War with Spain*. Kansas City: Hudson-Kimberley.

Goldman, Lawrence. 1998. "Exceptionalism and Internationalism: The Origins of American Social Science Reconsidered." *Journal of Historical Sociology* 11, March: 1–36.

Greene, Julie. 2009. *The Canal Builders: Making America's Empire at the Panama Canal*. New York: Penguin.

Gulick, Sidney. 1908. "Internationalism: The Characteristic of the 20th Century." *Twentieth Century Quarterly* 8: 8.

Guthrie-Shimizu, Sayuri. 2012. *Transpacific Field of Dreams: How Baseball Linked the United States and Japan in Peace and War*. Chapel Hill: University of North Carolina Press.

Gutiérrez, David G. 1995. *Walls and Mirrors: Mexican Americans, Mexican Immigrants, and the Politics of Ethnicity*. Berkeley: University of California Press.

Hammond, John Hays. 1974 (1935). *The Autobiography of John Hays Hammond*. Reprint. Vols 1–2. New York: Arno Press.

Hart, John Mason. 2002. *Empire and Revolution: The Americans in Mexico since the Civil War*. Berkeley: University of California Press.

Hartfield, John. 1896. *New Leviathan Cable Code*. New York: Hartfield Telegraphic Code Publishing.

Headrick, Daniel C. 1981. *The Tools of Empire: Technology and European Imperialism in the Nineteenth Century*. New York: Oxford University Press.

Herring, George C. 2008. *From Colony to Superpower: U.S. Foreign Relations since 1776*. New York: Oxford University Press.

Hixson, Walter. 2013. *Settler Colonialism: A History*. New York: Palgrave Macmillan.

Hochfelder, David. 2012. *The Telegraph in America, 1832–1920*. Baltimore, MD: Johns Hopkins University Press.

Hofstadter, Richard. 1965. *The Paranoid Style in American Politics and Other Essays*. New York: Knopf.

Hoganson, Kristin, 1998. *Fighting for American Manhood: How Gender Politics Provoked the Spanish-American and Philippine-American Wars.* New Haven, CT: Yale University Press.

Hoover, Herbert. 1952. *The Memoirs of Herbert Hoover, Volume 1: Years of Adventure, 1874–1920.* New York: Macmillan.

Howe, Daniel Walker. 2007. *What Hath God Wrought: The Transformation of America, 1815–1848.* New York: Oxford University Press.

Hughes, J. T. R. 1987. *American Economic History.* 2nd edn. Glenview, IL: Scott Foresman.

Hunter, Jane. 1984. *The Gospel of Gentility: American Women Missionaries in Turn of the Century China.* New Haven, CT: Yale University Press.

Immerman, Richard H. 2010. *Empire for Liberty: A History of American Imperialism from Benjamin Franklin to Paul Wolfowitz.* Princeton, NJ: Princeton University Press.

Irwin, Julia. 2013. *Making the World Safe: The American Red Cross and a Nation's Humanitarian Awakening.* New York: Oxford University Press.

Israel, Jerry. 1971. *Progressivism and the Open Door: America and China, 1905–1921.* Pittsburgh, PA: University of Pittsburgh Press.

John, Richard. 2010. *Network Nation: Inventing American Telecommunications.* Cambridge, MA: Belknap Press of Harvard University Press.

Josephson, Matthew. 1938. *The Politicos, 1865–1896.* New York: Harcourt, Brace.

Kern, Stephen. 2003. *The Culture of Time and Space, 1880–1918: With a New Preface.* Cambridge, MA: Harvard University Press.

Kemble, John H. "A Hundred Years of the Pacific Mail." *American Neptune* X April 1950: 123–143.

Knoblock, Glenn A. 2014. *The American Clipper Ship, 1845–1920: A Comprehensive History, with a Listing of Builders and Their Ships.* Jefferson, OH: McFarland.

Kroes, Rob and Robert Rydell. 2005. *Buffalo Bill in Bologna: The Americanization of the World, 1869–1922.* Chicago, IL: University of Chicago Press.

Kuehl, Warren. 1969. *Seeking World Order: The United States and International Organization to 1920.* Nashville, TN: Vanderbilt University Press.

Lake, Marilyn. 2014. "Challenging the 'Slave-Driving Employers': Understanding Victoria's 1896 Minimum Wage through a World-History Approach." *Australian Historical Studies* 45, 1: 87–102. doi: 10.1080/1031461X.2013.877501.

— and Henry Reynolds. 2008. *Drawing the Global Colour Line: White Men's Countries and the International Challenge of Racial Equality.* Melbourne: Melbourne University Press.

Lamster, Mark. 2006. *Spalding's World Tour: The Epic Adventure that Took Baseball Around the Globe—And Made It America's Game.* New York: Public Affairs.

Lee, Lawrence B. 1973. "William E. Smythe and San Diego, 1901–1908." *Journal of San Diego History* 14: 10–24.

Lessoff, Alan. 2013. "American Progressivism: Transnational, Modernization, and American Perspectives." In *Fractured Modernity: America Confronts Modern Times, 1890s to 1940s*, ed. Thomas Welskopp and Alan Lessoff, 61–80. Munich: Oldenbourg.

Licht, Walter. 1983. *Working for The Railroad: The Organization of Work in the Nineteenth Century.* Princeton, NJ: Princeton University Press.

Lloyd, Henry Demarest. 1900. *A Country without Strikes: A Visit to the Compulsory Arbitration Court of New Zealand.* New York: Doubleday, Page.

—. 1903. *Newest England: Notes of a Democratic Traveller in New Zealand.* New York: Doubleday, Page.

Los Angeles Herald. July 5, 1903.

Lunardini, Christine. 2012. *Alice Paul: Equality for Women.* Boulder, CO: Westview.

Magee, Gary B. and Andrew S. Thompson, 2010. *Empire and Globalisation: Networks of People, Goods, and Capital in the British World, c.1850–1914.* Cambridge: Cambridge University Press.

Makdisi, Ussama. 2007. *Artillery of Heaven: American Missionaries and the Failed Conversion of the Middle East.* Ithaca, NY: Cornell University Press.

Malone, Michael P. 1996. *James J. Hill: Empire Builder of the Northwest.* Norman: University of Oklahoma Press.

Manela, Erez, 2007. *The Wilsonian Moment: Self-Determination and the International Origins of Anticolonial Nationalism.* New York: Oxford University Press.

Marchand, C. Roland. 1972. *The American Peace Movement and Social Reform, 1898–1918.* Princeton, NJ: Princeton University Press.

Matthews, Frederick C. 1987. *American Merchant Ships, 1850–1900.* Vol 1. Mineola, NY: Dover.

Mayer, Arno J. 1961. *Political Origins of the New Diplomacy, 1917–1918.* New Haven, CT: Yale University Press.

McCartney, Paul T. 2006. *Power and Progress: American National Identity, the War of 1898, and the Rise of American Imperialism.* Baton Rouge: Louisiana State University Press.

McDowell, Carl E., and Gibbs, Helen M. 1954. *Ocean Transportation.* New York: McGraw-Hill.

McKenzie, Frederick A. 1902. *The American Invaders.* London: G. Richards.

McLean, Gavin. 1990. *The Southern Octopus: The Rise of a Shipping Empire.* Wellington: New Zealand Ship & Marine Society and the Wellington Harbour Board, Maritime Museum.

Mead, Elwood. 1920. *Helping Men Own Farms.* New York: Macmillan.

Mead, Walter Russell. 2007. *God and Gold: Britain, America, and the Making of the Modern World.* New York: Knopf.

Miller, Char. 2001. *Gifford Pinchot and the Making of Modern Environmentalism.* Washington, DC: Shearwater Press.

Missal, Alexander. 2008. *Seaway to the Future: American Social Visions and the Construction of the Panama Canal.* Madison: University of Wisconsin Press.

Murphy, Kevin C. 2004. *The American Merchant Experience in Nineteenth-Century Japan.* New York: Routledge.

Nash, George H. 1983. *The Life of Herbert Hoover, Volume 1: The Engineer, 1874–1914.* New York: W.W. Norton.

—. 1988. *The Life of Herbert Hoover, Volume 2: The Humanitarian, 1914–1917.* New York: W.W. Norton.

—. 1989. "'An American Epic': Herbert Hoover and Belgian Relief in World War I." *Prologue* 21, 1: 75–86.

Nickles, David Paull. 2003. *Under the Wire: How the Telegraph Changed Diplomacy.* Cambridge, MA: Harvard University Press.

Ninkovich, Frank. 2014. *The Global Republic: America's Inadvertent Rise to World Power.* Chicago, IL: University of Chicago Press.

Nugent, Walter. 2013. "Preface to the Second Edition." In *The Tolerant Populists.* Chicago, IL: University of Chicago Press.

Ogle, Vanessa. 2013. "Whose Time is It? The Pluralization of Time and the Global Condition, 1870s to 1940s." *American Historical Review* 120, 5: 1376–1402.

Paolini, Ernest. 1973. *The Foundations of the American Empire: William Henry Seward and U.S. Foreign Policy*. Ithaca, NY: Cornell University Press.

Parrington, Vernon Louis. 1930. *The Beginnings of Critical Realism in America, 1860–1920*. New York: Harcourt, Brace.

Pierson, Arthur Tappan. 1886. *The Crisis of Missions: Or, the Voice Out of the Cloud*. New York: Robert Carter.

Pisani, Donald. 2002. *Water and American Government: The Reclamation Bureau, National Water Policy, and the West, 1902–1935*. Berkeley: University of California Press.

Pletcher, David M. 2001. *The Diplomacy of Involvement: American Economic Expansion across the Pacific, 1784–1900*. Columbia: University of Missouri Press.

Plowman, Peter. 2010. *Across the Pacific: Liners from ANZ to North America*. Dural, NSW: Rosenberg.

Postel, Charles. 2007. *The Populist Vision*. New York: Oxford University Press.

Pratt, Julius. 1936. *Expansionists of 1898: The Acquisition of Hawaii and the Spanish Islands*. Baltimore, MD: Johns Hopkins University Press.

Pursell, Carroll. 2010. "Herbert Hoover and the Transnational Lives of Engineers." In *Transnational Lives: Biographies of Global Modernity*, ed. Desley Deacon, Penny Russell, and Angela Woollacott, 109–20. Basingstoke: Palgrave Macmillan.

Queensland Times Ipswich Herald and General Advertiser. June 3, 1905: 4.

Railroad Telegrapher. July 1, 1896.

Reinsch, Paul S. 1907. "International Unions and Their Administration." *American Journal of International Law* 1, July: 579–623.

Rodgers, Daniel. 1998. *Atlantic Crossings: Social Politics in a Progressive Age* Cambridge, MA: Harvard University Press.

—. 2002. "An Age of Social Politics." In *Rethinking American History in a Global Age*, ed. Thomas Bender, 250–73. Berkeley: University of California Press.

Rook, Robert E. 2000. "An American in Palestine: Elwood Mead and Zionist Water Resource Planning, 1923–1936." *Arab Studies Quarterly* 22, winter: 71–89.

Rosenberg, Emily S. 2012. "Transnational Currents in a Shrinking World." In *A World Connecting 1870–1945*, ed. Emily Rosenberg, 815–996. Cambridge, MA: Belknap Press of Harvard University Press.

Rossini, Daniela. 2008. *Woodrow Wilson and the American Myth in Italy: Culture, Diplomacy, and War Propaganda*. Cambridge, MA: Harvard University Press.

Rothbard, Murray. 1979. "Hoover's 1919 Food Diplomacy in Retrospect." In *Herbert Hoover: The Great War and Its Aftermath, 1914–1923*, ed. L. Gelfand, 89–110. Iowa City: University of Iowa Press.

Rowley, William D. 1996. *Reclaiming the Arid West: The Career of Francis G. Newlands*. Bloomington: Indiana University Press.

Sanders, Elizabeth. 1999. *Roots of Reform: Farmers, Workers, and the American State, 1877–1917*. Chicago, IL: University of Chicago Press.

Schäfer, Axel. 2000. *American Progressives and German Social Reform, 1875–1920: Social Ethics, Moral Control, and the Regulatory State in a Transatlantic Context*. Stuttgart: Steiner.

—. 2001. "W.E.B. Du Bois, German Social Thought, and the Racial Divide in American Progressivism, 1892–1909." *Journal of American History* 88: 925–949.

Schott, Linda. 1997. *Reconstructing Women's Thoughts: The Women's International League for Peace and Freedom before World War II*. Stanford, CA: Stanford University Press.

Scully, Eileen. 2001. *Bargaining with the State from Afar: American Citizenship in Treaty Port China, 1844–1942*. New York: Columbia University Press.

Seward, William H. 1873. *William H. Seward's Travels Around the World. Ed. by Olive Risley Seward … With two hundred illustrations*. New York: D. Appleton.

Sewell, Mike. 1991. "'All the English-Speaking Race is in Mourning': The Assassination of President Garfield and Anglo-American Relations." *Historical Journal* 34: 665–86.

Sexton, Jay. 2014. "William H. Seward in the World." *Journal of the Civil War Era* 4, December: 404–405.

Sidak, J. Gregory. 1997. *Foreign Investment in American Telecommunications*. Chicago, IL: University of Chicago Press.

Sinn, Elizabeth. 2014. "Pacific Ocean: Highway to Gold Mountain, 1850–1900." *Pacific Historical Review*, Special Issue: Conversations on Transpacific History 83, 2: 220–37.

Sklar, Kathryn, Barbara Reeves-Ellington, and Connie Shemo, eds. 2010. *Competing Kingdoms: Women, Mission, Nation, and Empire*. Durham, NC: Duke University Press.

Snow, Jennifer C. 2003. "A Border Made of Righteousness: Protestant Missionaries, Asian Immigration, and Ideologies of Race, 1850–1924." PhD diss., Columbia University.

Stahr, Walter. 2012. *A Thread across the Atlantic; Seward: Lincoln's Indispensable Man*. New York: Simon & Schuster.

Stead, W. T. 1972 (1901). *The Americanization of the World, or, The Trend of the Twentieth Century*. Reprint. New York: Garland.

Steel, Frances. 2013. "Lines Across the Sea: Trans-Pacific Passenger Shipping in the Age of Steam." In *The Routledge History of Western Empires*, ed. Robert Aldrich and Kirsten McKenzie, 315–329. New York: Routledge.

Stewart, Watt, 1946. *Henry Meiggs: Yankee Pizarro*. Durham, NC: Duke University Press.

Tate, E. Mowbray. 1986. *Transpacific Steam: The Story of Steam Navigation from the Pacific Coast of North America to the Far East and the Antipodes, 1867–1941*. New York: Cornwall Books.

Taylor, Sandra C. 1984. *Advocate of Understanding: Sidney Gulick and the Search for Peace with Japan*. Kent, OH: Kent State University Press.

Teisch, Jessica. 2005. "'Home Is Not So Very Far Away': Californian Engineers in South Africa, 1868–1915." *Australian Economic History Review* 45, July: 139–60.

—. 2010. "Sweetening the Urban Marketplace: California's Hawaiian Outpost." In *Cities and Nature in the American West*, ed. Char Miller, 17–33. Reno: University of Nevada Press.

—. 2011. *Engineering Nature: Water, Development, and the Global Spread of American Environmental Expertise*. Chapel Hill: University of North Carolina Press.

Tolley, Kemp. 1971. *Yangtze Patrol: The U.S. Navy in China*. Annapolis, MD: Naval Institute.

Transatlantic Steamship Routes: Supplement to the Pilot Chart of the North Atlantic Ocean, January, 1893. http://texashistory.unt.edu/ark:/67531/metapth190428/m1/1/zoom/accessed July 18, 2016.

Truett, Samuel. 2006. *Fugitive Landscapes: The Forgotten History of the U.S.-Mexico Borderlands.* New Haven, CT: Yale University Press.

Tucker, Richard P. 2000. *Insatiable Appetite: The United States and the Ecological Degradation of the Tropical World.* Berkeley: University of California Press.

Tyrrell, Ian. 1991. *Woman's World/Woman's Empire: The Woman's Christian Temperance Union in International Perspective, 1880–1930.* Chapel Hill: University of North Carolina Press.

—. 1999. *True Gardens of the Gods: Californian-Australian Environmental Reform, 1860–1930.* Berkeley: University of California Press.

—. 2007. "Looking Eastward: Pacific and Global Perspectives on American History in the Nineteenth and Early Twentieth Centuries." *Japanese Journal of American Studies* 18: 41–57.

—. 2008. "Transatlantic Progressivism in Women's Temperance and Suffrage." In *Britain and Transnational Progressivism*, ed. David Gutzke, 133–148. New York: Palgrave Macmillan.

—. 2009. "Empire in American History." In *Colonial Crucible: Empire in the Making of the Modern American State*, ed. Alfred W. McCoy and Francisco A. Scarano, 541–556. Madison: University of Wisconsin Press.

—. 2010. *Reforming the World: The Creation of America's Moral Empire.* Princeton, NJ: Princeton University Press.

—. 2015a. *Transnational Nation: United States History in Global Perspective since 1789.* 2nd edn. Basingstoke: Palgrave Macmillan.

—. 2015b. *Crisis of the Wasteful Nation: Empire and Conservation in Theodore Roosevelt's America.* Chicago, IL: University of Chicago Press.

Uekoetter, Frank. 2009. *The Age of Smoke, Environmental Policy in Germany and the United States, 1880–1970.* Pittsburgh, PA: University of Pittsburgh Press.

—. 2013. "Conservation: America's Environmental Modernism." In *Fractured Modernity: America Confronts Modern Times, 1890s to 1940s*, ed. Thomas Welskopp and Alan Lessoff, 81–96. Munich: Oldenbourg.

Van Voris, Jacqueline. 1987. *Carrie Chapman Catt: A Public Life.* New York: Feminist Press.

Veracini, Lorenzo. 2010. *Settler Colonialism: A Theoretical Overview.* Basingstoke: Palgrave Macmillan.

Welskopp, Thomas and Alan Lessoff, ed. 2013. *Fractured Modernity: America Confronts Modern Times, 1890s to 1940s.* Munich: Oldenbourg.

White, Richard. 2011. *Railroaded: The Transcontinentals and the Making of Modern America.* New York: W.W. Norton.

Wilkins, Mira, 1970. *The Emergence of Multinational Enterprise: American Business Abroad from the Colonial Era to 1914.* Cambridge, MA: Harvard University Press.

Wilson, Ann-Marie. 2009. "In the Name of God, Civilization, and Humanity: The United States and the Armenian Massacres of the 1890s." *Le Mouvement Social* 227: 27–44.

—. 2010. "Taking Liberties Abroad: Americans and the International Humanitarian Advocacy, 1821–1914." PhD diss., Harvard University.

Wilson, John, 2010. "The Democratic Traveller: Henry Demarest Lloyd's Visit to New Zealand, 1899." *Studies in Travel Writing* 14: 365–82.

Winchester, Simon, 2014. "The Eruption Plunged Europe into Winter and America into its First Economic Crisis." *Wall Street Journal*, April 25.

Winkler, Jonathan Reed. 2007. *Nexus: Strategic Communications and American Security in World War I.* Cambridge, MA: Harvard University Press.

Wittmann, Matthew. 2010. "Empire of Culture: U.S. Entertainers and the Making of the Pacific Circuit, 1850–1890." PhD diss., University of Michigan.

Worster, Donald. 1985. *Rivers of Empire.* New York: Pantheon.

Wrobel, David M. 2013. *Global West, American Frontier: Travel, Empire, and Exceptionalism from Manifest Destiny to the Great Depression.* Albuquerque: University of New Mexico Press.

Zahniser, J.D. and Amelia R. Fry, 2014. *Alice Paul: Claiming Power.* New York: Oxford University Press.

Zeiler, Thomas 2006. *Ambassadors in Pinstripes: The Spalding World Baseball Tour and the Birth of the American Empire.* Lanham, MD: Rowman & Littlefield.

Zimmerman, Andrew. 2010. *Alabama in Africa: Booker T. Washington, the German Empire, and the Globalization of the New South.* Princeton, NJ: Princeton University Press.

Chapter Thirty

Empire, Expansion, and Its Consequences

Allan E. S. Lumba

Introduction

The Gilded Age and Progressive Era is inextricable from the history of US empire. It is during this crucial period—from the late nineteenth century through the early twentieth century—that the United States emerged diplomatically, militarily, and economically as a truly global power. It is this formation of the so-called "American Century" that has led myriad historians of the last five decades to constantly and consistently return to this period. Moreover, scholars of this era have access to an immense number of archives that capture the manner in which multitudes of historical agents debated, invested in, killed for, and resisted empire.

This chapter explores the crucial significance of the Gilded Age and Progressive Era for the historical analysis of US empire and expansion. The first section gives a brief historical context of US imperial expansion beginning at the end of the nineteenth century and ending in the early twentieth century. It specifically lays out the historic pivot and shift from the United States' focus on settler colonialism and the Atlantic world and toward overseas colonialism and the Pacific. The second and third sections introduce the two major scholarly streams that have critically engaged with the concept of US imperialism during the Gilded Age and Progressive Era: the Wisconsin School of diplomatic history and the multidisciplinary assemblage of Global American Studies. Both of these streams critically address the grammar of American exceptionalism. The fourth section highlights more contemporary scholarship. These works examine the histories of the turn of the twentieth century, shedding light on contemporary imperial conditions of securitization over bodies and capitalism. At the same time, these works also attempt to recover global histories of anti-imperial resistance, articulating archives traditionally estranged from the discipline of history. The final section argues to reorient studies of US empire and the grammar of exceptionalism away from contradiction and instead toward paradox.

Imperial Conditions and Imperial Futures

US empire in the long Gilded Age and Progressive Era was profoundly conditioned by the eighteenth and nineteenth centuries' histories of settler colonialism and slavery (Blackhawk 2006; Johnson 2013; Lowe 2015; Ostler 2004; Robinson 1983). The settlement of the North American continent, the mass displacement and forced resettlement of native peoples, and the debates over "free" territories enabled the proliferation of frontier capitalism during the middle decades of the nineteenth century. The securitization of the frontier and the acceleration of industry and the expansion of markets beyond the northeast United States led to greater cohesion and uniformity of intercontinental currency, banking, and financial systems. In turn, previous foreign interventions of the century, for example the Mexican–American War, Perry's naval aggression in Japan, and the United States' role in the Opium Wars, went hand in hand with desires for expansion, slaveholding cartels, and visions of empire in Latin America, and Ulysses Grant's schemes for the Dominican Republic. The desire for expansion and global political influence were reinvigorated by fantasies of novel frontiers, such as Asia, the Pacific, and the entire western hemisphere. By the 1880s these fantasies had given birth to a comprehensive foreign policy that would ensure that independent nation-states throughout Latin America and the Caribbean would serve US geopolitical and economic interests.

At the same time, during the Gilded Age and Progressive Era imperial expansion was conditioned by economic crises and imperial rivalries. Inundated by decades of panic, recession, and depression, the last three decades of the nineteenth

A Companion to the Gilded Age and Progressive Era, First Edition. Edited by Christopher McKnight Nichols and Nancy C. Unger.
© 2017 John Wiley & Sons, Inc. Published 2017 by John Wiley & Sons, Inc.

century illuminate the paradoxical manner in which the immense growth of American industrial capitalism was propelled by chronically unstable finance capital. Anxieties over the overproduction of manufactured commodities combined with underinvestment of capital drove the desire for new markets beyond the continental United States. This economic desire dovetailed with the increasing instability of Spanish imperial hegemony in its remaining Asian and Caribbean colonies (due to nationalist and indigenous revolutions and rebellions), as well as the overthrow of the Hawaiian monarchy by white American planters. The seeming political insecurity of this moment, due to faltering imperial powers and the fear of other imperial rivals occupying any power vacuum in the Pacific or the Caribbean, led to the increased public and business pressure for foreign and military intervention. The combination of economic insecurities and imperial fantasies led to greater US military aggression. In some instances military aggression led to the "peaceful" overthrow of native rule, for example the forced submission of Lili'uokalani (Marry 2000). In other instances US aggression would lead to all-out war, such as the Spanish–American War and Philippine–American War (McCoy and Scarano 2009). By the end of the nineteenth century, the United States had taken possession of Hawai'i, the Philippines, Guam, Samoa, Puerto Rico, and Cuba.

The end of the Spanish–American War radically opened up a new global horizon for American geopolitical ambitions. The first decade of the twentieth century witnessed American desires for increased political and economic security within and around its new possessions. Under the Roosevelt regime, the United States pursued constant interventions in Venezuela, Argentina, Columbia, and Panama, grounded in a new military promise to police the western hemisphere. This foreign policy, called the Roosevelt Corollary (to the Monroe Doctrine), was dedicated to—either by force, coercion, or collaboration—maintaining political and economic orders that were friendly to US interests in nominally independent Latin American nation-states. Later the Taft regime would expand this policy by encouraging American cartels and corporations to establish asymmetrical economic relations of trade, finance, banking, and currency to be regulated and policed by collaborative local elites. This collaborative and coercive form of imperial governance across the region would be called "dollar diplomacy."

A complex of ideologies that is best described as exceptionalism undergirded US imperial expansion during this period (Ricard 1994; Rodgers 1998). Indeed, progressive commitments to reform and development were an extremely powerful dimension of American exceptionalism. Myriad powerful discourses of benevolent assimilation, racial uplift, and civilizational development emerged in both colonial and metropole settings. The prevalence and reach of these discourses resulted in exceptionalism becoming a common grammar regularly utilized by a diverse assortment of voices and perspectives. In this way, many colonized nationalists (both collaborationists and radicals) and anti-imperialists oftentimes were forced to use the same exceptionalist grammar as the most fervent pro-imperialists. Indeed, exceptionalism allowed US empire to be defined not by what it limited or controlled, but rather by what it enabled. Exceptionalism was thus not dissimulation of reality, but rather produced reality. The pursuit to transform the political, economic, and social life of non-Americans, with the United States as the primary gauge and model, consequently led to deeply invasive and extensive changes throughout multiple realms, such as education, health, labor, and government. The result was a global proliferation of imperfect doppelgangers that consistently generated unintended and uncanny kinds of socialities and subjectivities, challenging and troubling the very foundations of US empire. Nevertheless, the grammar of exceptionalism crucially set the terms for what would be considered the American Century. At the same time, this grammar did not go unchallenged by scholars. The next section examines one of the strongest and foundational critiques of American empire and exceptionalist grammar: the Wisconsin School.

Against Exceptionalism

The Wisconsin School approach to US empire gained its name from the foundational works of University of Wisconsin's William Appleman Williams, and scholars who studied in Madison during his tenure, most famously Walter LaFeber and Thomas McCormick. The Wisconsin School, influenced by Progressive historians, sought to challenge orthodox Cold War diplomatic histories that touted the global spread of American political and economic ideals. Combining the economic analysis of Charles Beard and the safety-valve theory of Frederick Jackson Turner, Wisconsin School scholars looked upon the late nineteenth-century overseas empire as a logical consequence of the end of the continental empire and the displacement of internal economic antagonisms and industrial crisis (Buhle and Rice-Maximin 1995; Morgan 2014). Unlike the more non-academic "New Left" movement, which leaned toward Marxian analyses, the Wisconsin School could be defined as an anti-authoritarian critique, suspicious of forms of illegitimate authority (by way of force) or capitalist power. The Wisconsin School, therefore, was a response to a kind of increasing authoritarianism that had occurred across the country in the early Cold War. Its adherents were skeptical of what US geopolitical/military interventions and unbridled capitalism would do to what they believed to be core American values. Moreover, the Wisconsin School's analysis proved amazingly timely as US military intervention and investment increased within Southeast Asia, most publically in the Vietnam War.

The work of William Appleman Williams, undoubtedly, represents, though does not completely exhaust, the basic core arguments and interventions of the Wisconsin School.

According to Williams, there were three primary ways orthodox historians had rationalized US overseas empire and simultaneously continued the narrative of American exceptionalism. The first considered empire as a burden or necessary evil thrust upon the United States in order to bring freedom and democracy to oppressed societies. The second posited the United States as inherently anti-imperialist and saw its expansion abroad as a brief and rapidly dispelled aberration from the nation's essential values. The final approach argued that its national culture of economic, intellectual, and technological genius obligated America to build a better world through peace and progress, which was later misconceived as empire. In contrast to what he believed were alibis of previous historians, Williams argued for a view of imperialism that did not strictly adhere to European forms of colonialism. Instead, Williams argued that the United States practiced "informal empire" in which the strategies and impulses were guided less by the control of colonial territories, but rather by the desire for economic hegemony. According to Williams, certain histories of formal colonialism, like the military occupation of the Philippines, had less to do with Philippine resources and the prestige of holding sovereignty over a substantial population of natives, and more to do with the Philippines' strategic proximity to the coveted China market (Williams 1972).

The crucial foundation of "informal empire" was what Williams called the pursuit of "Open Door" policies. Guided by a particularly American *Weltanschauung*, a coalition of capitalists, intellectuals, experts, and politicians successfully pushed through Open Door policies at the turn of the twentieth century. This worldview consisted of a desire to open up new foreign markets in reaction to the increased social and political tensions brought about by industrialization and capitalist overproduction in the United States. Williams asserted, however, because of America's increasing presence as the world's economic leader, the Open Door, in actuality, planned to dominate foreign markets without getting into the dirty business of political and territorial imperialism. For Williams, this construction of empire as Open Door had two dire and simultaneous consequences. First, the Open Door neglected domestic issues, tensions, and developments in favor of foreign opportunities. Second, the Open Door's externalization allowed foreign policy to act akin to a phantasmagoria, projecting blame onto foreign societies and bodies. The displacement of domestic tensions and contradictions onto foreign spaces and peoples meant not only the potential for large-scale violence abroad, but also the potential explosion of crisis and violence at home (Williams 1972).

More historical studies branched off of Williams's foundational concepts of informal empire and Open Door thesis. Different tracks of informal imperialism emphasized different dimensions and impulses for informal imperialism. Some found the impulse for overseas empire in settler-colonial anxieties, like agrarian uprisings and populist politics (Crapol 1973; Crapol and Schonberger 1972; Williams 1970). Others emphasized the collaboration between industrialists, statesmen, and policymakers, most notable in McKinley supporters and the author of the Open Door policies, Secretary of State John Hay (LaFeber 1963; McCormick 1967). Still others detailed the role of finance, currency, and credit in the making of empire, such as the overseas advocacy of money experts Charles Conant and Jeremiah Jenks under the Taft administration's strategy of "dollar diplomacy" (Parrini 1993; Parrini and Sklar 1983; Rosenberg 1999). All scholarship, however, was grounded in the belief that US imperialism was mainly guided by the desire to control foreign markets and, more generally, for the stable and secure growth of an American-led capitalist world system.

Despite adding more complexity and nuance to the analysis of US empire, scholars of the Wisconsin School did not exist in a vacuum. It had a simultaneously generative and fraught relation with the so-called American New Left; a heterogeneous mix of radical intellectuals and activists who worked both within and without academia. The Wisconsin School also found fellow travelers and collaborators with critics of global capitalism, such as scholars of dependency theory and world-systems theory. Indeed, the Wisconsin School's historical analysis of martial violence and diplomatic maneuvers necessary in securing and ensuring that foreign markets remain open to the free flow of US commodities and capital provided new dimensions to the more structural economic arguments of dependency and world-systems scholarship (Weinstein 1968; Kolko 1969).

The most innovative advancement of informal empire thesis, by way of including its ideological underpinnings, was Emily Rosenberg's *Spreading the American Dream*. Through the concept of what she called "liberal-developmentalism," Rosenberg illuminated the ways that ideological goals and fantasies of historical actors shaped political and economic apparatuses of formally and informally colonized peoples and places. In addition Rosenberg revealed the deep contradictions within liberalism itself. On one hand, there is the economic form of liberalism, which sought free-market capitalism—the opening of foreign economies to US exports, cash, and credit. On the other hand, free markets also meant the influx of new connections with foreign peoples, races that were, according to a majority of powerful and influential Americans at the time, at different civilizational and economic developmental stages. Free markets thus exposed the problem of political liberalism, which espoused that any rational and able-bodied individual was endowed with inalienable liberties and freedoms. This meant the necessity of changing political and social conditions within spaces outside of the United States as well, in order to cultivate an environment that was not only friendly to US notions of liberalism, but also perhaps modeled on it (Rosenberg 1982). At the same time, Rosenberg's text inadvertently revealed two glaring blind spots within the Wisconsin School approach. First, there was the assumption that imperial transformation only went one way, unilaterally following political or economic lines. Second, informal imperialism supposedly governed without force or violence. However, as the next section reveals, US empire and expansion produced immeasurable effects, not only violently generating transformations outside the United States, but within it as well.

The Optics of Difference

Despite the exciting new ways that it challenged previous Gilded Age and Progressive Era historians who consistently disavowed or downplayed US empire, the Wisconsin School nevertheless could not account for the myriad aspects of imperial formation that were not purely political or economic. In other words, the Wisconsin School had difficulty analyzing the histories of imperial institutions, knowledge, and apparatuses propelled not by capitalist accumulation or political ideologies, but by the violent pursuit and maintenance of racial, gender, and sexual hierarchical orders. Moreover, the Wisconsin School tended to elide the activities and experiences of vast swathes of non-Americans, creating a narrative of a passive colonial world of natives acted upon by American imperialists.

In some ways a direct response to the Wisconsin School, the second major stream to take on the question of US empire, especially during the Gilded Age and Progressive Era, could be categorized as Global American Studies. An assemblage of multiple disciplinary works, Global American Studies was catalyzed by the irruption of the highly publicized and media-centric overseas American military conflict, the first Gulf War of the early 1990s. As a result, the Gulf War saturated the public with images and videos of US military power, destruction, and violence. The Gulf War—especially the spectacular fashion in which it played out—subsequently sparked considerable critical dialogue about the role of US cultures of imperialism in what was then touted as a truly globalized post-Cold War capitalist system. This "imperial turn" in American studies coincided with other parallel changes in academic scholarship, specifically the "intersectional turn" in history and the "American turn" in postcolonial studies.

The foundational piece that formally and institutionally set out to challenge the dominant kinds of American studies and cultural historical scholarship was *Cultures of United States Imperialism*, coedited by Amy Kaplan and Donald Pease. Inaugurating a distinctly American form of cultural studies, this book sought to reorient the place of cultural production and subjectivity in the production and reproduction of US empire. Pease and Kaplan demanded more analysis of imperialism in American cultural studies as well as more cultural studies methods in the analysis of US empire (Kaplan and Pease 1993). In her chapter "Left Alone with America," Kaplan provocatively combined the thinking of William Appleman Williams with Toni Morrison in order to jolt scholars of the mutual development of the "domestic" and "foreign" in US history (Kaplan 1993).

This rethinking of the cultural effects of empire—both domestically and abroad—was followed up in Kaplan's monograph *The Anarchy of Empire*. Drawing from such diverse sources as Mark Twain's nostalgic longing for the lost native world of Hawaii in the 1860s and the violent spectacle of Theodore Roosevelt's battle of San Juan Hill, Kaplan revealed the white masculine anxieties that drove these imperial images and narratives of foreign places and people. Moreover, through these sources, Kaplan illuminated the ways US empire abroad offered a mode through which to domesticate the anarchic incoherence and violent contradictions of racial and gendered orders at home (Kaplan 2002). Although Kaplan's methodologies, which primarily looked at cultural texts and artifacts, were grounded in literary analysis, the theoretical provocations provided strong research possibilities for historians of the long disavowed era of turn-of-the-century colonialism, particularly the troubling of geopolitical and status quo borders between foreign and domestic (Hoganson 2007; Tyrrell 2010; Stoler 2006).

In this way, by looking at the shaping of "domestic" history by foreign relations and occupations, Global American Studies became intimately intertwined with the latest phase of the cultural turn in history: intersectionality. Pushing beyond the class analysis and stories of non-elites of social history and older forms of cultural history which relied upon European social theory and philosophy, intersectionality emphasized categories of difference—most notably race, gender, and sexuality—as interlocking analytical frameworks. Emerging from black radical feminist thinking of the 1960s and 1970s, intersectionality forced historians to think how multiple, interconnecting, and entangled systems of oppression and norms changed and were changed over time (Combahee River Collective 1986; Crenshaw 1989; Lorde 2007). Although many historians of gender had been successfully applying intersectional analysis to domestic US history, the method did not seem to resonate in academic analysis of US foreign relations. As the so-called American Century drew to a close, however, a critical mass of US historians began to ask probing questions about the intersecting roles of gender, race, and sexuality in laying the historical groundwork of the United States as *the* lone global superpower. Moreover, these works—at the time mainly categorized under the umbrella of gender history—daringly illustrated that diplomatic, military, and economic relations were shot through by social relations such as gender, race, and sexuality. Although these monographs may not have been solely dedicated to the history of empire during the Gilded Age and Progressive Era, they nevertheless ushered in novel approaches to an imperial history long dominated by orthodox exceptionalist narratives of empire or an unwavering economic analysis of geopolitics.

One significant text to apply intersectional methods is Kristin Hoganson's *Fighting for American Manhood.* Tackling the crucial periods of US overseas empire—the Spanish–American War and the Philippine–American War—Hoganson argued that anxieties over the loss of American manhood drove overseas aggression and martial desires in the Caribbean and the Philippines. As the war in the Philippines dragged on, American authorities became vexed by disruptions to heterosexual orders within military ranks. Progressive reformers were especially fearful of the ways prostitution, venereal diseases, and non-heteronormative relations challenged American notions of whiteness (Hoganson 1998). Control over sexuality—especially the productive and reproductive capacity of native female bodies—was also of central concern for US empire in the Caribbean. As Laura Briggs illuminates in *Reproducing Empire*, anxieties over Puerto Rican overpopulation and non-normative households in the post-industrial era had roots in prostitution laws and policies of the early American colonial period. The figure of Puerto Rican prostitutes became a key site for battles over Puerto Rican masculine nationalism and white women progressive reformers, violently silencing the voices and perspectives of Puerto Rican women in the process. Briggs, therefore, underlined the complex levels through which imperialism operated, subjugating not only the bodies of poor native women, but also the historical agency of the most vulnerable (Briggs 2002).

In addition to gender and sexuality, race has perhaps been the most prevalent and generative framework when thinking about US empire. Race's endurance as a generative frame for the Gilded Age and Progressive Era is easily visible in the ways historical actors at the time obsessed over racial difference. Moreover, racial discourse was not only dictated by civilizational and cultural differences between colony and metropole, but also how American whiteness itself mutated and was debated throughout different imperial spaces. For example, as Mary Renda's *Taking Haiti* illustrates, the notion of American whiteness as a more virtuous paternal figure in comparison to French white civilization propelled US imperial rule over black Haitians. American white paternalism, however, was not limited to one monolithic concept. Indeed as Renda shows, white masculinity was heterogeneous and unstable, forged through multiple levels of decision-making, from Woodrow Wilson in Washington to a white soldier's first encounter with a black Haitian. Renda thus gestures to the reality that empire was never a static thing, but was necessarily dynamic, contingent, and often contained the germs to its own disorder (Renda 2001).

The analytic of race can reveal not only the complexity of whiteness, but also the heterogeneity of non-whites in the colony. Moreover, the ambiguities and disagreements over the shape of colonial racial orders were deeply entangled with local and imperial politics. One of the more striking examples of how race and empire were inextricably linked can be found in Paul Kramer's *Blood of Government.* Although on a general level, Kramer focused on political institutions in the American colonial Philippines, he also illustrated how stratified, diverse, and complicated racial politics were in the colony. While US historians tended to homogenize Filipinos (often lumping all "natives" into one kind of voice and perspective), Kramer shed light upon different and competing voices within the political realm. These voices, moreover, were delineated and sharpened by complex histories of ethnicity, religion, ideology, geography, and language (Kramer 2006). Although committed to the genre of diplomatic history, Kramer nevertheless sharpened focus on US empire's long overshadowed, though radically necessary, other: the colony.

For certain, deep knowledge of colonies and colonialism has long been the domain of area studies specialists and historians of the non-west. But even area studies itself had long been undergoing a transformation, especially pushed by postcolonial theory. After the Gulf War, postcolonial scholarship began to move past the dichotomy of nation versus empire, branching out toward questions of rival and collaborative empires and the complex and heterogeneous (and non-national) subjectivities proliferating in the colony (B. Anderson 2006; Chakrabarty 2000; Chatterjee 1993; Mehta 1999; Said 1979; Siegel 1999; Spivak 1988). At the same time, however, these changes in postcolonial studies, long dominated by scholars of British colonial India and Dutch colonial Indonesia, had often ignored US empire before the Cold War. Much like the global turn in American Studies, therefore, postcolonial studies developed its own "American" turn. Grounded in Area Studies, a cascade of works deliberately drew attention to the United States' "formal" colonial history throughout Asia, Pacific, and the Caribbean during the late nineteenth century and the twentieth century. Vicente Rafael's book *White Love*, for instance, boldly applied poststructural, postcolonial, and intersectional theory to a wide-ranging set of colonial apparatuses and practices during the Philippine–American War. Seemingly apolitical objects, such as the census, or the ostensibly mundane practice of homemaking and cooking in the new American frontier, were constantly haunted by potential conflict and dangerously threatened by disorder. These anxieties over the potential breakdown of colonial rule by sheer intimacy between imperial agents and colonial subjects, moreover, led to ever more imperial policies that could accommodate institutions in both the colony and the metropole (Rafael 2000).

Later works would explore the creation of specific imperial institutions and policies, challenging older schools of thought that relied on "export" models of analysis. Indeed, scholars like Alfred McCoy (historian), Warwick Anderson (historian of medicine) and Julian Go (sociologist) have recast the transnational movement and mutations of imperial policies, apparatuses, and institutions of the Philippine–American War and the first decade of colonial state-building in new light, prompting new lines of comparative study. Indeed, according to these area studies specialists, the colonization of the Philippines was not only influenced by trans-imperial thinking and correspondences, but the very forms of governing—for example policing, surveillance, and hygiene in the Philippines or electoral politics and processes in Puerto Rico—were highly mobile, moving not just between US colony and metropole but to colonies and metropolitan centers of other empires (W. Anderson 2006; Go 2008; McCoy 2009).

The return to deep analysis of colonial institutions and policies also challenged the fuzzy demarcation between "formal" and "informal" empire. By looking at the high mobility and fungibility of colonial policies and institutions on a global scale, these works illuminate and gesture to how US empire can quickly move between recognizably state-backed forms of power, private or corporate interests, and the power of social and cultural normative orders (Go and Foster 2003; McCoy and Scarano 2009). At the same time, the following section explores how contemporary conditions would again inspire novel forms of engaging the histories of Gilded Age and Progressive Era empire. These newer kinds of approaches, moreover, would have to address the emergence of a novel kind of exceptionalism, one that no longer disavows empire but rather expresses nostalgia for empire.

After the "American Century"

The 2001 invasion of Iraq and Afghanistan signaled the beginning of what would define both domestic and foreign policy for most of the twenty-first century: the United States' global war on terror. Much like the Vietnam War and the Gulf War pushed historians to scrutinize military occupation, formal colonialisms, and informal empire in the Pacific, Caribbean, and Latin America during the Gilded Age and Progressive Era, scholars since 2000 have found novel resonances of the imperial past in the present. However, unlike previous debates, pundits and orthodox scholars could no longer deny that the United States was an empire. Instead, the debate became whether a US empire was not only justified, but also absolutely necessary for the contemporary international political and economic order to remain stable. The specter of American exceptionalism—particularly the discourse of benevolent global power—so prevalent throughout the twentieth century continued to haunt the twenty-first (Ferguson 2005; Hoffman 2013; Suri 2012). This section highlights the ways that the two major traditions—the Wisconsin School and Global American Studies—shaped these newer studies of empire and at the same time reveal how newer studies exposed the limits of previous traditional approaches.

Like the field of American studies in general, Global American Studies has rapidly gained new dimensions through its embrace of the provocative questions of race and migration posed by ethnic studies. Since the advent of the Global War on Terror, ethnic studies has increasingly moved beyond crafting exceptional histories of the United States—particularly by narrowly focusing on an "immigrant" narrative or decontextualized community studies—to combine borderlands studies (Chicano, Latino, and Native American) with transnational movement of bodies, commodities, and ideas (African diaspora and Asian and Pacific diaspora). In these studies the concept of security has consistently become the focus. By exploring the transnational forceful policing and surveillance of racialized, gendered, and sexualized bodies and populations in the Americas and the transpacific especially, these studies have provocatively posited the history of imperial security (and military intervention in the name of domestic national security) to challenge the exceptionalist narrative of the United States as an unconditionally hospitable "nation of immigrants" or "beacon of freedom."

Matthew Frye Jacobson's *Barbarian Virtues*, although on the whole speculative, provocatively brought together the post-Reconstruction history of military occupation and intervention overseas with the histories of domestic security apparatuses that emerged in response to large-scale global migrations (Jacobson 2001). Others, such as Erika Lee's *At America's Gates* and Catherine Choy's *Empire of Care* have built off of these more "global" approaches to immigrant history during the Gilded Age and Progressive Era to build useful, if tangential readings of various and complicated subjectivities of migrants circulating throughout US imperial space (Choy 2003; Lee 2003). Some more recent works such as Kornel Chang's *Pacific Connections* and Nayan Shah's *Stranger Intimacy* reveal how security was not only a concern of Americans but was constantly an inter-imperial concern between British and American authorities in North America. Moreover, both Chang and Shah, in different and distinct ways, illuminate the manner in which Asian migrants circulated throughout imperial routes, collaborated with other racialized laborers, and resisted and evaded national authorities (Chang 2012; Shah 2011).

If the twenty-first century has reinvigorated questions about the United States' role as an empire which has taken upon itself the task of ensuring political security at home and abroad, then this new era has also sparked concerns over economic security of the international capitalist system. The 2008 financial crisis and the so-called Great Recession shed new light on the effects of capitalist crisis and the precarious position even the United States occupies in an utterly interconnected and interdependent global capitalist system. As a result of current economic conditions there has been a surge, both within the academy and the general public, of what has been called the "New History of U.S. Capitalism" (Schuessler 2013). Although its origins could be traced to the height of "globalization" debates during the end of the twentieth century, the recent international financial crisis has intensified, greatly formalized, and gained public recognition of contemporary historical works on US capitalism. Although most studies tend to privilege North Atlantic capitalist networks, particularly during the long nineteenth century (Baptist 2014; Beckert 2014; Levy 2012), few of these works have paid close attention to the role of imperial orders and force in the proliferation and augmentation of capital accumulation during the Gilded Age and Progressive Era.

The silence from these newer histories of US capitalism regarding spaces other than the transatlantic is perhaps due to the long shadow of the Wisconsin School. Indeed, although the works of Crapol, McCormick, and Parrini are especially relevant for their focus on business and corporate interests in the making of foreign policy, several texts stand out for anticipating the significant and complex relationship between global finance and US imperialism. The Progressive Era foreign policy of "dollar diplomacy" and the control of foreign loans and international credit as a crucial dimension of US empire have served as rich sources for those carrying on the spirit of the Wisconsin School. For example, Emily Rosenberg's *Financial Missionaries to the World* provides an account of how banking and finance—mostly through the operations of international currencies, bonds, and loans in the Philippines, the Caribbean, and Latin America during the first decades of the twentieth century—laid the groundwork for contemporary US empire (Rosenberg 1999). Cyrus Veeser's *A World Safe for Capitalism* illuminates how Wall Street caused the instability of the Dominican Republic through crediting its foreign debt and public infrastructure and institutions such as its national bank and railroad system. The consequential economic crisis enabled the United States to justify intervention and gave birth to Roosevelt's Corollary to the Monroe Doctrine (Veeser 2002). Subsequently other works have tracked the long-term effects of the deep entanglements between private financial entities and US trade policies in the continued underdevelopment of Latin America (Colby 2011; Grandin 2006; Westad 2005).

Building off of the legacies of the Wisconsin School are new histories of capitalism and empire that have bucked the trend of the New History's focus on North Atlantic capitalists, firms, and financiers. Unlike the Wisconsin School, however, revising diplomatic history is not the main concern. Rather, these new histories, deeply affected by Global American Studies, ethnic studies, and intersectional and postcolonial thinking, are deeply committed to illuminating the histories of movement, survival, and resistance of laboring and colonized people within a world of capitalist empires.

These newer works examine capitalism within empire and empire within capitalism by exploring multiple scales, from the scale of production to the scale of currency and finance. Indeed, new histories of labor and empire have been crucially providing new and comparative insight into the different kinds of hidden and subversive histories in such diverse projects as the sugar plantations of Hawaii, the Panama Canal, and the roads of the American colonial Philippines (Baldoz 2014; Bender and Lipman 2015; Greene 2009; Jackson 2014; Poblete 2014). In parallel, new histories of finance have revealed that US economic intervention in places such as the Caribbean and the Philippines were not only dictated by market rationalities or great power politics, but were also propelled by desires to maintain racial hierarchies. Perhaps most significantly, these studies of capitalism differ from the New History by foregrounding imperial violence as not oppositional to capital accumulation, but co-constitutive with the growth of global capitalism (Hudson forthcoming; Lumba forthcoming). Indebted simultaneously to the Wisconsin School and World Systems/Dependency Theory, these new histories of capitalism emphasize the role of the state (imperial, colonial, and postcolonial) in structuring violence throughout civil society and transnational divisions of labor.

At the same time, new historical work elucidates the unintended consequences of empire and capital. These works reveal alternative histories of internationalism, the myriad and oftentimes hidden spaces of resistance built into the structures of an imperial and capitalist world system. Highlighting from the formal and elite to the radical and marginalized sectors of the political world, these studies reveal the proliferation of anti-imperial resistance to American empire and expansion. Multiple studies are exploring the ways many of these anti-imperial movements were not limited to any bounded geography but instead were constantly open to transnational and international alliances and solidarities. Heterogeneous histories conditioned these anti-imperial movements. Some of these histories include: Wilsonian notions of self-determination; transnational anarchism, socialism, and Communism, the growth of anticolonial nationalisms; the intensified militancy of organized labor; and the vast effects of transnational black radicalism across colonies (Ewing 2014; Heatherton forthcoming; Jung forthcoming; Manela 2007; Mukherji forthcoming; Prashad 2007).

The new scholarly critiques of US empire have taken on long-ignored subjects such as migration and immigration as well as engaged older questions of capitalism and resistance. Exciting as these works are, the grammar of exceptionalism, both within the academy and in the broader public realm, remains deeply entrenched. The next and concluding section briefly outlines some possible ways of approaching empire and exceptionalism in future scholarship.

Conclusion: The Paradoxes of Empire

Paul Kramer's 2011 essay, "Power and Connection: Imperial Histories of the United States in the World," importantly highlighted the intellectual unease of US historians and American studies scholars in considering US empire as anything other than contradictory to American foundational republicanism. In other words, according to Kramer, by taking on this line of reasoning, scholars of US empire oftentimes reify the fantasies of nation building, positioning the United States as a republic in its essential core before its historical "corruption" (or historical "responsibility" depending on the scholar) as an empire (Kramer 2011).

To disrupt this line of thinking, future scholarship must challenge prevailing approaches that see US empire as fundamentally in contradiction with American notions of republicanism (the protection of liberties and individual rights). The Progressive Era, for instance, is a highly germane historical site for exploring these supposed contradictions between empire and republicanism. Specifically, the Progressive Era form of liberalism (particularly the ideas of reform and development of the good life for all) was not some sort of instrument, or deception, of empire. Rather, future scholarship could approach the myriad and sometimes dissonant ideologies of Progressivism as an ensemble of the truths greatly shaped by histories of settler colonialism and slavery that guided and structured US imperialism both formally and informally. This consideration of Progressive Era liberalism would reorient understanding of republicanism and imperialism as a paradoxical relationship that resonates deeply in the contemporary moment.

To consider imperialism and republicanism as a paradoxical relation does not necessary mean the acceptance of exceptionalism. Rather, it unsettles the nationalist origin story of a republic that has gone awry, or the reparative desire to recover some essential long-lost core of America. This paradoxical condition, moreover, enables future scholarship of US empire to explore how modern concepts commonly seen as oppositional—for instance freedom and violence or settler colonialism and overseas empire—are fundamentally necessary for each other (Byrd 2011; Goldstein 2014; Reddy 2011). Perhaps further scrutiny of the intended and unintended consequences of US imperialism would illuminate antagonisms within the very foundations of empire. Scholarship of US empire, therefore, must take these concepts and relations to its very limits, pushing the boundaries to seek alternative modes of knowledge and imagine other possible grammars of resistance.

References

Anderson, Benedict. 2006. *Imagined Communities: Reflections on the Origin and Spread of Nationalism.* New York: Verso.

Anderson, Warwick. 2006. *Colonial Pathologies: American Tropical Medicine, Race, and Hygiene in the Philippines.* Durham, NC: Duke University Press.

Baldoz, Rick. 2014. *Third Asiatic Invasion: Migration and Empire in Filipino America, 1898–1946.* New York: New York University Press.

Baptist, Edward. 2014. *The Half Has Never Been Told: Slavery and the Making of American Capitalism.* New York: Perseus Books.

Beckert, Sven. 2014. *Empire of Cotton: A Global History.* New York: Knopf.

Bender, Daniel and Jana Lipman. 2015. *Making the Empire Work: Labor and United States Imperialism.* New York: New York University Press.

Blackhawk, Ned. 2006. *Violence over the Land: Indians and Empires in the Early American West.* Cambridge, MA: Harvard University Press.

Briggs, Laura. 2002. *Reproducing Empire: Race, Sex, Science, and U.S. Imperialism in Puerto Rico.* Berkeley: University of California Press.

Buhle, P. and E. Rice-Maximin. 1995. *William Appleman Williams: The Tragedy of Empire.* New York: Routledge.

Byrd, Jodi. 2011. *The Transit of Empire: Indigenous Critiques of Colonialism.* Minneapolis: University of Minnesota Press.

Chakrabarty, Dipesh. 2000. *Provincializing Europe: Postcolonial Thought and Historical Difference.* Princeton, NJ: Princeton University Press.

Chang, Kornel. 2012. *Pacific Connections: The Making of the U.S.–Canadian Borderlands.* Berkeley: University of California.

Chatterjee, Partha. 1993. *The Nation and Its Fragments: Colonial and Postcolonial Histories.* Princeton, NJ: Princeton University Press.

Choy, Catherine. 2003. *Empire of Care: Nursing and Migration in Filipino American History.* Durham, NC: Duke University Press.

Colby, Jason. 2011. *The Business of Empire: United Fruit, Race, and U.S. Expansion in Central America.* Ithaca, NY: Cornell University Press.

Combahee River Collective. 1986. *The Combahee River Collective Statement.* Albany, NY: Kitchen Table.

Crapol, Edward. 1973. *America for Americans: Economic Nationalism and Anglophobia, 1876–1896.* Madison: University of Wisconsin Press.

— and Howard Schonberger. 1972. "The Shift to Global Empire, 1865–1900." In *From Colony to Empire: Essays in the History of American Foreign Relations*, ed. William Appleman. New York: John Wiley.

Crenshaw, Kimberly. 1989. "Demarginalizing the Intersection of Race and Sex: A Black Feminist Critique of Antidiscrimination Doctrine, Feminist Theory and Antiracist Politics." *Chicago Legal Forum* 140: 139–167.

Ewing, Adam. 2014. *The Age of Garvey: How a Jamaican Activist Created a Mass Movement and Changed Global Black Politics.* Princeton, NJ: Princeton University Press.

Ferguson, Niall. 2005. *Colossus: The Rise and Fall of the American Empire.* New York: Penguin.

Grandin, Greg. 2006. *Empire's Workshop: Latin America, the United States, and the Rise of the New Imperialism.* New York: Owl Books.

Go, Julian. 2008. *American Empire and the Politics of Meaning: Elite Political Cultures in the Philippines and Puerto Rico during U.S. Colonialism.* Durham, NC: Duke University Press.

— and Anne Foster, ed. 2003. *The American Colonial State in the Philippines: Global Perspectives.* Durham, NC: Duke University Press.

Goldstein, Alyosha. 2014. *Formations of United States Colonialism.* Durham, NC: Duke University Press.

Greene, Julie. 2009. *The Canal Builders Making America's Empire at the Panama Canal.* New York: Penguin.

Heatherton, Christina. Forthcoming. *The Color Line and the Class Struggle: The Mexican Revolution, Internationalism, and the American Century.*

Hoffman, Elizabeth. 2013. *American Umpire*. Cambridge, MA: Harvard University Press.

Hoganson, Karen. 1998. *Fighting for American Manhood: How Gender Politics Provoked the Spanish–American and Philippine–American Wars*. New Haven, CT: Yale University Press.

—. 2007. *Consumers' Imperium: The Global Production of American Domesticity, 1865– 920*. Chapel Hill: University of North Carolina Press.

Hudson, Peter. Forthcoming. *Dark Finance: Wall Street and the West Indies, 1873–1933*.

Jacobson, M. 2001. *Barbarian Virtues: The United States Encounters Foreign Peoples at Home and Abroad, 1876–1917*. New York: Hill & Wang.

Jackson, Justin. 2014. "The Work of Empire: The U.S. Army and the Making of American Colonialisms in Cuba and the Philippines, 1898–1913." PhD diss., Columbia University.

Johnson, Walter. 2013. *River of Dark Dreams: Slavery and Empire in the Cotton Kingdom*. Cambridge, MA: Harvard University Press.

Jung, Moon-Ho. Forthcoming. *The Unruly Pacific: Race and the Politics of Empire and Revolution, 1898–1941*.

Kaplan, Amy. 1993. "Left Alone With America." In *Cultures of United States Imperialism*, ed. Amy Kaplan and Donald Pease. Durham, NC: Duke University Press.

—. 2002. *The Anarchy of Empire in the Making of U.S. Culture*. Cambridge, MA: Harvard University Press.

— and Donald Pease, ed. 1993. *Cultures of United States Imperialism*. Durham, NC: Duke University Press.

Kolko, Gabriel. 1969. *The Roots of American Foreign Policy: An Analysis of Power and Purpose*. Boston, MA: Beacon Press.

Kramer, Paul. 2006. *The Blood of Government: Race, Empire, the United States, and the Philippines*. Chapel Hill: University of North Carolina Press.

—. 2011. "Power and Connection: Imperial Histories of the United States in the World." *American Historical Review* 116, 5: 1348–1391.

LaFeber, Walter. 1963. *The New Empire: An Interpretation of American Expansion, 1860–1898*. Ithaca, NY: Cornell University Press.

Lee, Erika. 2003. *At America's Gates: Chinese Immigration during the Exclusion Era, 1882–1943*. Chapel Hill: University of North Carolina Press.

Levy, Jonathan. 2012. *Freaks of Fortune: The Emerging World of Capitalism and Risk in America*. Cambridge, MA: Harvard University Press.

Lorde, Audre. 2007. *Sister Outsider: Essays and Speeches*. New York: Random House.

Lowe, Lisa. 2015. *The Intimacies of Four Continents*. Durham, NC: Duke University Press.

Lumba, Allan. Forthcoming. *Monetary Authorities: Economic Policy and Policing in the American Colonial Philippines*.

Manela, Erez. 2007. *The Wilsonian Moment: Self-Determination and the International Origins of Anticolonial Nationalism*. New York: Oxford University Press.

Marry, Shelley. 2000. *Colonizing Hawai'i: The Cultural Power of Law*. Princeton, NJ: Princeton University Press.

McCormick, Thomas. 1967. *China Market: America's Quest for Informal Empire, 1893–1901*. Chicago, IL: Quadrangle Books.

McCoy, Alfred. 2009. *Policing America's Empire: The United States, the Philippines, and the Rise of the Surveillance State*. Madison: University of Wisconsin Press.

— and Francisco Scarano, ed. 2009. *The Colonial Crucible: Empire in the Making of the Modern American State*. Madison: University of Wisconsin Press.

Mehta, Uday. 1999. *Liberalism and Empire: A Study in Nineteenth-Century British Liberal Thought*. Chicago, IL: University of Chicago Press.

Morgan, James. 2014. *Into New Territory: American Historians and the Concept of US Imperialism*. Madison: University of Wisconsin Press.

Mukherji, S. Ani. Forthcoming. *The Anticolonial Imagination: Race, Empire, and Migrant Radicalism before World War II*.

Ostler, Jeffrey. 2004. *The Plains Sioux and U.S. Colonialism from Lewis and Clark to Wounded Knee*. Cambridge: Cambridge University Press.

Parrini, Carl. 1993. "Charles A. Conant, Economic Crises and Foreign Policy, 1896–1903." In *Behind the Throne: Servants of Power to Imperial Presidents, 1898–1968*, ed. Thomas J. McCormick and Walter LaFeber. Madison: University of Wisconsin Press.

— and Sklar, Martin. 1983. "New Thinking About the Market, 1896–1904: Some Economists on Investment and the Theory of Surplus Capital." *Journal of Economic History* 43: 559–578.

Poblete, Joanna. 2014. *Islanders in the Empire: Filipino and Puerto Rican Laborers in Hawai'i*. Urbana: University of Illinois Press.

Prashad, Vijay. 2000. *White Love: and Other Events in Filipino History*. Durham, NC: Duke University Press.

—. 2007. *The Darker Nations: A People's History of the Third World*. New York: The New Press.

Rafael, Vicente. 2000. *White Love and Other Events in Filipino History*. Durham, NC: Duke University Press.

Reddy, Chandan. 2011. *Freedom With Violence: Race, Sexuality, and the US State*. Durham, NC: Duke University Press.

Renda, Mary. 2001. *Taking Haiti: Military Occupation and the Culture of U.S. Imperialism, 1915–1940*. Chapel Hill: University of North Carolina Press.

Ricard, Serge. 1994. "The Exceptionalist Syndrome in U.S. Continental and Overseas Expansionism." In *Reflections on American Exceptionalism*, ed. David K. Adams and Cornelis A. van Minnen. Keele: Ryburn.

Robinson, Cedric. 1983. *Black Marxism: The Making of the Black Radical Tradition*. Chapel Hill: University of North Carolina Press.

Rodgers, Daniel. 1998. "Exceptionalism." In *Imagined Histories: American Historians Interpret the Past*, ed. Anthony Molho and Gordon S. Wood. Princeton: Princeton University Press.

Rosenberg, Emily. 1982. *Spreading the American Dream: American Economic and Cultural Expansion, 1890–1945*. New York: Hill & Wang.

—. 1999. *Financial Missionaries to the World: the Politics and Culture of Dollar Diplomacy, 1900–1930*. Cambridge, MA: Harvard University Press.

Said, Edward. 1979. *Orientalism*. New York: Vintage.

Shah, Nayan. 2011. *Stranger Intimacy: Contesting Race, Sexuality, and Law in the North American West*. Berkeley: University of California Press.

Schuessler, Jennifer. 2013. "In History Departments, It's Up With Capitalism." *New York Times*, April 6. www.nytimes.com/2013/04/07/education/in-history-departments-its-upwith-capitalism.html/accessed July 19, 2016

Siegel, James. 1999. *Fetish, Recognition, Revolution*. Princeton, NJ: Princeton University Press.

Spivak, Gayatri. 1988. "Can the Subaltern Speak?" In *Marxism and The Interpretation of Culture*, ed. Carey Nelson and Lawrence Grossberg. Urbana: University of Illinois Press.

Stoler, Ann. 2006. *Haunted By Empire: Geographies of Intimacy in North American History*. Durham, NC: Duke University Press.

Suri, Jeremi. 2012. *Liberty's Surest Guardian: Rebuilding Nations After War from the Founders to Obama*. New York: Free Press.

Tyrrell, Ian. 2010. *Reforming the World: The Creation of America's Moral Empire*. Princeton, NJ: Princeton University Press.

Veeser, Carl. 2002. *A World Safe for Capitalism: Dollar Diplomacy and America's Rise to Global Power*. New York: Columbia University Press.

Westad, Odd. 2005. *The Global Cold War: Third World Interventions and the Making of Our Times*. Cambridge: Cambridge University Press.

Weinstein, James. 1968. *The Corporate Ideal in the Liberal State: 1900–1918*. Boston, MA: Beacon Press.

Williams, William. 1970. *The Roots of the Modern American Empire: A Study of the Growth and Shaping of Social Consciousness in a Marketplace Society*. New York: Vintage.

—. 1972. *The Tragedy of American Diplomacy*. New York: W.W. Norton.

Further Reading

Abinales, Patricio. 2003. "Progressive-Machine Conflict in Early-Twentieth-Century U.S. Politics and Colonial-State Building in the Philippines." In *The American Colonial State in the Philippines: Global Perspectives*, ed. Julian Go and Ann Foster, 148–181. Durham, NC: Duke University Press.

Agoncillo, Teodoro. 1960. *Malolos: The Crisis of the Republic*. Quezon City: University of the Philippine Press.

Ambrosius, Lord. 2002. *Wilsonianism: Woodrow Wilson and His Legacy in American Foreign Relations*. New York: Palgrave.

Anderson, Stuart.1981. *Race and Rapprochement: Anglo-Saxonism and Anglo-American Relations, 1895–1904*. Rutherford, NJ: Fairleigh Dickinson University.

Arrighi, Giovanni. 2005. "Hegemony Unraveling 2." *New Left Review* 33: 83–116.

Ayala, César. 1999. *American Sugar Kingdom: The Plantation Economy of the Spanish Caribbean, 1898–1934*. Chapel Hill: University of North Carolina Press.

Bacevich, Andrew. 2002. *American Empire: The Realities and Consequences of U.S. Diplomacy*. Cambridge, MA: Harvard University Press.

Barbusse, Edward. 1966. *The United States in Puerto Rico, 1898–1900*. Chapel Hill: University of North Carolina Press.

Beckert, Sven. 1993. *Monied Metropolis: New York City and the Consolidation of the American Bourgeoisie, 1850–1896*. Cambridge, MA: Harvard University Press.

Bederman, Gail. 1995. *Manliness and Civilization: A Cultural History of Gender and Race in the United States, 1880–1917*. Chicago, IL: University of Chicago Press.

Benjamin, Jules. 1977. *The United States and Cuba: Hegemony and Dependent Development, 1880–1934*. Pittsburgh, PA: University of Pittsburgh Press.

Brody, David. 2010. *Visualizing American Empire: Orientalism and Imperialism in the Philippines*. Chicago, IL: University of Chicago Press.

Caban, Pedro. 1999. *Constructing a Colonial People: Puerto Rico and the United States, 1898–1932*. Boulder, CO: Westview.

Capozzola, Christopher. 2008. *Uncle Sam Wants You: World War I and the Making of the Modern American Citizen*. New York: Oxford University Press.

Cheng, Lucie and Edna Bonacich. 1984. *Labor Immigration Under Capitalism: Asian Workers in the United States Before World War II*. Berkeley: University of California Press.

Cooper, John, Jr. 1983. *The Warrior and the Priest: Woodrow Wilson and Theodore Roosevelt*. Cambridge, MA: Harvard University Press.

Corpuz, Onofre. 1957. *American Colonial Bureaucracy in the Philippines*. Quezon City: University of the Philippines.

Cullinane, Michael. 2003. *Ilustrado Politics: Filipino Elite Responses to American Rule, 1898–1908*. Quezon City: Ateneo de Manila University Press.

Dawley, Alan. 2003. *Changing the World: American Progressives in War and Revolution*. Princeton, NJ: Princeton University Press.

Eichengreen, Barry. 1996. *Golden Fetters: The Gold Standard and the Great Depression, 1919–1939*. New York: Oxford University Press.

Elliot, John. 2006. *Empires of the Atlantic World: Britain and Spain in America 1492–1830*. New Haven, CT: Yale University Press.

Ferrer, Ada. 1999. *Insurgent Cuba: Race, Nation, and Revolution, 1868–1898*. Chapel Hill: University of North Carolina Press.

Foster, Anne. 2010. *Projections of Power: The United States and Europe in Colonial Southeast Asia, 1919–1941*. Durham, NC: Duke University Press

Fry, Joseph. 1996. "From Open Door to World Systems: Economic Interpretations of Late Nineteenth Century." *Pacific Historical Review* 62, 2: 277–303

Fujita-Rony, Dorothy. 2003. *American workers, Colonial Power: Philippine Seattle and the Transpacific West, 1919–1941*. Berkeley: University of California Press.

Gaines, Kevin. 1996. *Uplifting the Race: Black Leadership, Politics, and Culture in the Twentieth Century*. Chapel Hill: University of North Carolina Press.

Gerstle, Gary. 2001. *American Crucible: Race and Nation in the Twentieth Century*. Princeton, NJ: Princeton University Press.

Gindin, Sam and Leo Panitch. 2013 *The Making of Global Capitalism: The Political Economy of American Empire*. New York: Verso.

Go, Julian. 2011. *Patterns of Empire: The British and American Empires, 1688 to the Present*, New York: Cambridge University Press.

Golay, Frank. 1998. *Face of Empire: United States–Philippine Relations, 1898–1946*. Quezon City: Ateneo de Manila University Press.

Guerrero, Milagros. 1977. "Luzon at War: Contradictions in Philippine Society, 1898–1902." Ph.D. Diss., University of Michigan.

Harris, Susan. 2011. *God's Arbiters: Americans and the Philippines, 1898–1902*. New York: Oxford University Press.

Herring, George. 2008. *From Colony to Superpower: U.S. Foreign Relations since 1776*. New York: Oxford University Press.

Israel, Jerry. 1971. *Progressivism and the Open Door: America and China, 1905–1921*. Pittsburgh, PA: University of Pittsburgh Press.

Joseph, Gilbert. 1988. *Revolution from Without: Yucatan, Mexico, and the United States, 1880–1924*. Durham, NC: Duke University Press.

Knock, Thomas. 1992. *To End all Wars: Woodrow Wilson and the Quest for a New World Order*. New York: Oxford University Press.

LaFeber, Walter. 1978. *The Panama Canal: The Crisis in Historical Perspective*. New York: Oxford University Press.

Linn, Brian. 2000. *The Philippine War, 1899–1902*. Lawrence: University Press of Kansas.

Livingston, James. 1986. *Origins of the Federal Reserve System: Money, Class and Corporate Capitalism, 1890–1913*. Ithaca, NY: Cornell University Press.

May, Glenn. 1980. *Social Engineering in the Philippines: The Aims, Execution, and Impact of American Colonial Policy, 1900–1913*. Westport, CT: Greenwood.

Munro, John. 2008. "Empire and Intersectionality: Notes on the Production of Knowledge about US Imperialism" *Globality Studies Journal* 12. https://gsj.stonybrook.edu/article/empire-and-intersectionality-notes-on-the-production-of-knowledge-about-us-imperialism/accessed July 19, 2016.

Ngai, Mae. 2004. *Impossible Subjects: Illegal Aliens and the Making of Modern America*. Princeton, NJ: Princeton University Press.

Nichols, Christopher. 2011. *Promise and Peril: America at the Dawn of a Global Age*. Cambridge, MA: Harvard University Press.

Ninkovich, Frank. 1999. *The Wilsonian Century: U.S. Foreign Policy since 1900*. Chicago, IL: University of Chicago Press.

Pérez, Luis. 1986. *Cuba Under the Platt Amendment, 1902–1934*. Pittsburgh, PA: University of Pittsburgh Press.

Rodgers, Daniel. 1998. *Atlantic Crossings: Social Politics in a Progressive Age*. Cambridge, MA: Harvard University Press.

Rodríguez-Silva, Ileana. 2012. *Silencing Race: Disentangling Blackness, Colonialism, and National Identities in Puerto Rico*. New York: Palgrave Macmillan.

Schoonover, Thomas. 1991. *The United States in Central America 1860–1911: Episodes of Social Imperialism and Imperial Rivalry in the World System*. Durham, NC: Duke University Press.

Seldes, George. 1934. *Iron, Blood and Profits: An Exposure of the World-Wide Munitions Racket*. New York: Harper.

Sklar, Martin. 1988. *Corporate Reconstruction of American Capitalism, 1890–1916: The Market, the Law, and Politics*. Cambridge: Cambridge University Press.

Skowronek, Stephen. 1982. *Building a New American State: The Expansion of National Administrative Capacities, 1877–1920*. Cambridge: Cambridge University Press.

Stanley, Peter. 1974. *A Nation in the Making: the Philippines and the United States, 1899–1921*. Cambridge, MA: Harvard University Press.

Widenor, William. 1980. *Henry Cabot Lodge and the Search for an American Foreign Policy*. Berkeley: University of California Press.

Chapter Thirty-One

The United States in the World during the Gilded Age and Progressive Era

Katherine Unterman

During the spring and summer of 1914, three events reflected the state of American foreign relations. In April, the occupation of Veracruz, Mexico, exemplified the United States' self-proclaimed role as the international policeman of the western hemisphere. In the midst of the Mexican Revolution, Edward House, advisor to President Woodrow Wilson, insisted that the United States was simply "helping [Mexico] adjust her unruly household" (Herring 2008, 393). His assertion echoed the justifications for nearly twenty US interventions in Latin America and the Caribbean between 1898 and 1920. Next, the opening of the Panama Canal in August, after a decade of construction, was widely celebrated as the greatest engineering feat ever accomplished. It also marked a milestone in the history of globalization. Not only did the canal result in the faster movement of goods and people, it was also the product of a massive migration of foreign laborers. Despite the magnitude of the Panama Canal, however, its inauguration was overshadowed by even bigger news: the outbreak of war in Europe. As the guns of August fired, Americans debated the proper international role of the United States.

This chapter reflects on the United States in the world during the Gilded Age and Progressive Era by considering each of these themes: the expansion of international policing, increased global interconnectedness, and the involvement of the United States in World War I. Historians often conceive of power abstractly, but the study of policing provides a specific focal point and a concrete way to explore power relations. Additionally, by looking at the transnational movement of people, goods, capital, culture, and ideas, this moment of accelerated mobility can be better understood. While globalization is frequently construed as a homogenizing force or a rising tide that lifts all boats, in actuality it often accentuated national differences, reinforced inequalities, and led to new forms of coercive state action. Finally, Woodrow Wilson's foreign policy during the Great War has been called a watershed moment in American foreign relations. The legacy of his vision continues to fuel debates over the United States' international responsibilities in the twenty-first century.

Policing: The Hemisphere, the Colonies, and the Borders

In 1904, President Theodore Roosevelt issued the foreign policy position that would come to be known as the Roosevelt Corollary to the Monroe Doctrine. The year before, during the Venezuela Crisis of 1902–1903, Britain, Germany, and Italy had imposed a naval blockade on the South American nation after it defaulted on its debt. Now, it looked like the same thing might happen in the Dominican Republic. In order to ensure foreign creditors were paid and thus prevent European incursions, Roosevelt pledged that the United States would take on an "international police role" in the western hemisphere. He added that "in flagrant cases of … wrongdoing or impotence," the United States would step in to bring stability and order to the internal affairs of the American nations (Message to Congress, December 6, 1904). In practice, however, the Corollary ended up having little to do with European invasions. Instead, it served as a justification for US military invasions into countries including Cuba, Haiti, Nicaragua, and the Dominican Republic.

In his classic work of diplomatic history, *The Latin-American Policy of the United States* (1943), Samuel Flagg Bemis presents American actions in the western hemisphere in predominantly positive terms. Though he concedes that the United States was an empire after 1898, he characterizes it as a short-lived and "comparatively mild imperialism," motivated by the need for hemispheric security (Bemis 1987, 386). Both the Roosevelt Corollary and the subsequent Latin American interventions

A Companion to the Gilded Age and Progressive Era, First Edition. Edited by Christopher McKnight Nichols and Nancy C. Unger.
© 2017 John Wiley & Sons, Inc. Published 2017 by John Wiley & Sons, Inc.

were necessary, Bemis claims, for the protection of the Panama Canal. Later historians would strongly disagree with Bemis's defense of US policy. Walter LaFeber (2013) argues that Roosevelt actually inverted the Monroe Doctrine; while the original doctrine protected Latin American revolutionaries against foreign intervention, the Corollary justified US intervention against Latin American revolutionaries. Moreover, it greatly enhanced presidential powers in foreign affairs.

The Roosevelt administration first applied the Corollary to the Dominican Republic in 1905, an intervention that historians Emily Rosenberg (2003) and Cyrus Veeser (2002) identify as a turning point in American foreign policy. Rather than annexing the nation or holding it as a protectorate (like Cuba and Panama), the United States took a new path: it assumed administration of the Dominican customs houses. In true Progressive Era fashion, the Dominican experiment brought together diplomats, financial advisors, and bankers to employ "scientific" methods to promote stability and modernization. This would eventually evolve into dollar diplomacy, in which the Taft administration pressured, and sometimes forced, a number of foreign nations to accept US supervision of their finances in exchange for loans from US banks. The Dominican Republic served as "a laboratory" for working out new methods to "rehabilitate" struggling economies; similar "dollar diplomacy dependencies" would be established or attempted in Nicaragua, Haiti, and Honduras (Rosenberg 2003, 41). Dollar diplomacy was even applied as far away as Liberia and China.

Another new imperial form was the corporate enclave. The peoples of Central America and the Caribbean did not just experience US power through the American state, but through interactions with private corporations. By the 1910s, the United Fruit Company (UFC) was the most powerful economic force in Central America. Lester Langley and Thomas Schoonover's *The Banana Men* (1995) recounts some of the most colorful American entrepreneurs, such as Sam "The Banana Man" Zemurray and mercenary Lee Christmas, who orchestrated revolutions in Honduras in the name of making a profit. In *The Business of Empire* (2011), Jason Colby bridges foreign relations, business, and labor history to show how foreign peoples experienced US imperial domination through the labor control strategies of the UFC. Methods included the importation of workers and the manipulation of tensions between different ethnic groups. These tactics were similar to those used by the US government in the building of the Panama Canal, as described by Julie Greene in *The Canal Builders* (2009).

Historians have taken an interest in how these occupations affected both the invaded country and the invaders. Michel Gobat (2005), for example, examines how Nicaraguans responded to US political, economic, and cultural forms before and during the occupation of 1912–1933. But policing abroad did not just affect foreigners and foreign states; it also influenced the American state, society, and culture. In *Taking Haiti* (2001), Mary Renda analyzes how the experiences of the US Marines, who occupied the island from 1915 until 1934, caused Americans to think about gender, race, and power in new ways.

American policing extended beyond the western hemisphere to the nation's newly acquired colony, the Philippines. Ironically, a significant consequence of US efforts to oversee the Philippines was the strengthening of state power and policing capabilities at home. In 1898, the relatively weak central government of the United States had virtually no federal policing capacity. The Philippine Constabulary, however, fused the centralized Spanish police system with advanced American information technology. As Alfred McCoy (2009) shows, this unprecedented capacity for mass surveillance percolated into domestic policing. During World War I, the Philippine Constabulary provided both personnel and procedures for the creation of a national security apparatus. The Justice Department drew upon colonial procedures to conduct the world's largest mass surveillance effort, monitoring millions of Americans suspected of subversion.

US colonial officials justified their presence in the newly acquired island territories through the politics of policing the body. For example, Philippine experiments created precedents for the policing and prohibition of drugs. This led to the passage of the Harrison Narcotics Act in 1914—the start of US drug prohibition, and, as Anne L. Foster (2009) points out, the first federal law controlling individual rights over the human body. Other scholars show how colonial officials in Puerto Rico monitored sex and reproduction. Laura Briggs (2002) explains how ideologies of gender, sexuality, and reproduction shaped relations between the island and the mainland, while Eileen J. Suárez Findlay (1999) links race to standards of sexual norms and practices in Puerto Rico. Similarly, Anne Perez Hattori (2004) explores the US Navy's introduction of western medicine and sanitation to the island of Guam, showing how the American healthcare regime helped solidify power and moral authority over the native Chamorro people.

The United States also policed its colonies through law. When the United States took control of these territories, American courts were faced with a new question: Does the Constitution follow the flag? In other words, do full constitutional rights extend to all areas under US control? In 1901, the Supreme Court addressed this matter in a series of decisions known as the *Insular Cases*. Drawing a novel distinction between different types of territories, the Supreme Court ruled that full constitutional rights do not automatically apply in "unincorporated" territories such as Puerto Rico and the Philippines (*Downes v. Bidwell* 1901). Bartholomew Sparrow (2006) provides the fullest account of how the *Insular Cases* were instrumental in the creation of an American empire in which colonized peoples were denied full political rights. However, Christina Duffy Ponsa (previously Burnett, 2005) takes a revisionist interpretation of the *Insular Cases*, arguing that their real significance was in the creation of a new type of territory that could be de-annexed—that is, governed temporarily and then relinquished, rather than becoming a state or part of a permanent empire. Although the *Insular Cases* were steeped in the racism of the justices—at one point, they called territorial inhabitants "alien races" unfamiliar with "Anglo-Saxon principles"—the cases still remain law today (*Downes v. Bidwell* 1901).

The United States took divergent courses with regard to the Philippines and Puerto Rico. In 1916, Congress passed the Jones Act, which promised Philippine independence as soon as the Filipinos could establish a "stable government" (Jones Act, August 29, 1916). It was a vague pledge, but an indication that the United States intended eventually to let go of the Philippines (it would finally do so in 1946). The next year, however, the United States communicated the opposite message with regard to Puerto Rico. The Jones–Shafroth Act of 1917 granted US citizenship to the people of Puerto Rico, a clear signal that the United States planned to maintain political links with the island. Historians have pondered the difference in US policy toward the two insular territories. The Philippines was the "larger and more intractable" territory, while Puerto Rico was smaller and seen as more "loyal" (Cabranes 1978, 396). However, despite the implication of equality that the word citizenship implies, many have argued that Puerto Ricans were second-class citizens, as they were not afforded the same rights under the American system. Others have attacked the Jones–Shafroth Act as conferring an imposed citizenship, pointing out that it paved the way for Puerto Ricans to be conscripted into World War I just a few months later.

The Progressive Era also saw US authorities policing their geographical boundaries with a new urgency. International borders became more pronounced and harder to cross. Although there would not be widespread immigration quotas or a Border Patrol until the 1920s, Americans in the early years of the twentieth century became increasingly wary of foreigners entering the country. New immigration restrictions (such as the Anarchist Exclusion Act, the Gentlemen's Agreement with Japan, the Asiatic Barred Zone, and the literacy test) limited the numbers of people eligible to enter the United States. In 1911, a Congressional committee known as the Dillingham Commission completed a four-year study of recent immigration to the United States, which concluded that immigration from southern and eastern Europe posed a grave threat to American society and should therefore be reduced. The findings of the Dillingham Commission would provide the rationale for the Emergency Quota Act of 1921 and the Immigration Act of 1924. Meanwhile, the turmoil of the Mexican Revolution and then World War I also resulted in new state formations and stricter regulation of border crossings.

Even before the Zimmermann Telegram in 1917, US authorities viewed the open Mexican border as a national security threat. Between July 1910 and July 1920, an estimated 890,000 Mexican refugees legally entered the United States. Many Americans feared that revolutionary violence would spill over the border, and arms smuggling was a persistent problem. In 1915, an ethnic Mexican uprising in Texas known as the Plan de San Diego sparked a bloody counterinsurgency by vigilantes and Texas Rangers (Johnson, 2003). The next year, Pancho Villa killed eighteen Americans in his raid on Columbus, New Mexico. However, Rachel St. John (2011) explains that the desire to shore up the border went in both directions. Responding to US incursions like the occupation of Veracruz and General John Pershing's pursuit of Villa, Mexicans also wanted to make the border harder to cross. During the war years, both nations heightened crossing restrictions, sent soldiers to patrol the line, and built fences between border towns. Additionally, as a result of World War I, passports became necessary as border-crossing documents (Robertson, 2012). This marked the beginning of a new era of border security and surveillance.

An Interconnected World

It has become commonplace to call nearly every period of human history an age of globalization. Nevertheless, in *A World Connecting* (2012), Emily Rosenberg identifies the period between 1870 and 1945 as a new era in global interconnectedness. The world experienced a qualitative shift in the ability of people, commodities, capital, and ideas to cross international borders. Indeed, as Rosenberg points out, "The Great War in Europe became a world war precisely because of the global connections that had been forged in previous decades" (2012, 12). For the United States, the trend of increasing global interconnectedness had been accelerating since the end of the Civil War. By the 1910s, ships crossed the Panama Canal, airplanes traversed the skies, and radios broadcast new ideas to millions. The world felt the outward spread of American influence, and America felt the inward influence of the rest of the world.

Perhaps the most obvious international encounter that Americans experienced was with foreign peoples. Between 1900 and 1914, 12.9 million people immigrated to the United States—an average of almost one million new residents per year. At the same time, US troops and bureaucrats came face to face with foreign peoples in America's far-flung colonies. These two phenomena were intimately connected. In *Barbarian Virtues* (2000), Matthew Frye Jacobson deems immigration and imperialism "two sides of the same coin"—both "generated by the same economic engines of industrialization" (4). Cheap and abundant foreign labor was needed to keep factories running, and foreign markets were needed to absorb the nation's surplus. Americans experienced a double exposure to the foreigner: both as low-wage worker and as colonial subject.

Many immigration historians have concentrated on the experiences of the immigrants themselves and their ongoing ties to their homelands. In so doing, they heed the familiar call of transnational history: to move beyond the confines of the nation-state and to bridge different national historiographies. Madeline Hsu and Catherine Ceniza Choy, for example, link American history to Asian history in their studies of Chinese and Filipino migrants. In *Dreaming of Gold, Dreaming of Home* (2000), Hsu follows Chinese migrants from the county of Taishan, Guangdong Province, to the American West. The money that immigrants sent back to Taishan transformed their home community, and transnational ties endured despite the difficulty of movement during the Chinese Exclusion Era. Choy's *Empire of Care* (2003) connects migration history to US imperial history, tying the movement of Filipino nurses to the United States after World War II to the creation of the labor force of professional nurses during the colonial period. Donna Gabaccia, in *Foreign Relations* (2012), bridges top-down studies of US foreign policy with bottom-up immigration histories. It is no coincidence, she argues, that the high tide of immigration exclusion legislation during the late nineteenth and early twentieth centuries corresponded to the dawning of American empire. Empire caused internal disruptions in other countries that led to migration, and it also generated xenophobic fears about outside threats that resulted in US immigration restrictions.

In addition to people, commercial goods crossed borders. Indeed, by the early twentieth century, the United States was well on its way to becoming a great exporting commercial power. American mass culture circled the globe, as Robert Rydell and Rob Kroes describe in *Buffalo Bill in Bologna* (2005). Yet products and culture did not simply flow in one direction, out from America to the rest of the world. In the years before World War I, American households eagerly consumed foreign imports in an effort to appear more cosmopolitan. Kristin Hoganson, in *Consumers' Imperium* (2007), shows how middle- and upper-class American white women expressed their fascination with other cultures through home décor, fashion, and food, as well as social gatherings like travel clubs. She not only highlights globalization as a two-way process, but also gives women a central role in traditionally male-dominated foreign relations history. In *Blessed among Nations* (2006), Eric Rauchway explains how the United States benefited from globalization in the early twentieth century—and indeed, developed its distinct character from it. Imported resources—from foreign capital invested in the United States to immigrant labor—were crucial to making the United States the world's leading industrial power.

Ideas also crossed international borders. Attacking the notion of American exceptionalism, historians have demonstrated that Progressivism was not a purely domestic phenomenon, and have compared notions of reform in the United States and other countries during the early twentieth century. In *Uncertain Victory* (1986), James Kloppenberg situates American Progressivism within a transatlantic intellectual discourse. Thinkers from France, Germany, Great Britain, and the United States created the theoretical foundations for new programs of social democracy and Progressivism. Daniel Rodgers, in *Atlantic Crossings* (1998), similarly argues that US social policy in the first four decades of the twentieth century was the product of a cosmopolitan, transatlantic internationalism. Reform-minded Americans traveled to Europe, studied there, and consulted with Europeans engaged in sociopolitical experiments. Ideas about reform circulated in both directions across the Atlantic.

Ideas crossed colonial borders as well, yet often ended up transformed in translation. In Puerto Rico and the Philippines, US colonial officials set up American-style public schools, elections, and governmental institutions. The officials aimed their lessons in democratic government at the local political elite. Yet, as sociologist Julian Go (2008) demonstrates, Puerto Rican and Filipino elites often ascribed different meanings to concepts such as liberty, democracy, and self-government. In a study of cultural clash, accommodation, and transformation, Go ultimately finds that Puerto Rican and Filipino elites took divergent paths with respect to US rule. Yet, at times, both manipulated and even subverted the US-established institutions and the cultural ideas behind them.

The global dissemination of ideas resulted in transnational social movements. Leila Rupp, in *Worlds of Women* (1997), explores how women from different countries came together in three transnational women's organizations and attempted to construct an international collective identity. Though they did not always agree, these turn-of-the-century women had a consciously international feminist agenda—what Rupp calls the first wave of an international women's movement. While unsuccessful in their quest to end World War I through mediation, international networks of women made a difference with the League of Nations, where they managed to put feminist concerns such as peace, work, nationality, and women's rights on the agenda. Progressives also tried to change the world. While Alan Dawley's earlier *Struggles for Justice* (1991) dealt with American Progressivism in a domestic context, *Changing the World* (2003) examines foreign-reform initiatives by figures from Theodore Roosevelt to Jane Addams. For American Progressives, especially during the World War I years, foreign reform was inseparable from domestic change. The "dual quest for improvement at home and abroad was at the heart of what it meant to be a progressive" (2).

Ian Tyrrell (2010) also examines how American moral reformers exported their ideas, but he situates their efforts as an important component of US imperialism, both formal and informal. Proselytizing groups sought to remake the world in terms of Protestant cultural values. For example, Young Men's Christian Association (YMCA) leader John R. Mott's pamphlet, *Evangelization of the World in this Generation* (1900), inspired a crusade to promote

American-style Christianity around the globe. From missionaries to the Women's Christian Temperance Union (WCTU), these groups exercised a cultural hegemony abroad, linking morality to the spread of American power.

The United States in World War I

After war broke out in Europe in August 1914, the United States immediately took a position of neutrality in the conflict. President Wilson publicly urged Americans to be "neutral in fact as well as in name … impartial in thought as well as action" (Message to Congress, Aug. 19, 1914). In reality, however, few Americans were truly neutral. Many favored the Allies because of cultural and economic ties to Britain and France. Some immigrant groups supported the Central Powers—Irish Americans out of anti-British sentiment, German Americans out of loyalty to their homeland.

As the immensity of the conflict in Europe became clear, World War I sparked a foreign policy debate about the proper role of the United States in the world. Traditionally, accounts of this debate have pitted the internationalists against the isolationists. Internationalists insisted that the United States must become more involved with the international community and world politics in order to secure global peace and democracy. Isolationists, in contrast, wanted to preserve America's longstanding tradition of noninvolvement in foreign conflicts. Classic accounts of the debates over the merits of internationalism versus isolationism include Ernest R. May's *The World War and American Isolation* (1959) and John Milton Cooper's *The Vanity of Power* (1969).

Yet more recent historians have shown that the internationalist–isolationist dichotomy is overly simplified. In contrast to May and Cooper, they focus not simply on politics and traditional diplomacy, but also on cultural, social, and intellectual phenomena. Thomas Knock, in *To End All Wars* (1992), draws a distinction between two types of internationalism: conservative and Progressive. Conservative internationalists, like William Howard Taft and Elihu Root, sought global stability through international law. Progressive internationalists, such as Jane Addams, believed that peace was essential to ensure advancement of domestic social reforms. Isolationism needs to be complicated as well. Although the United States was still considered isolationist in the years before its entry into World War I, this was hardly a period of detachment or seclusion. In *Promise and Peril* (2011), Christopher McKnight Nichols demonstrates that even so-called isolationists envisioned a significant international role for the United States. The diverse swath of Progressives who wanted the United States to stay out of the war embraced a new and hybrid philosophy, born out of the debates over empire in the 1890s, which included a certain amount of international engagement.

Despite the United States' formal neutrality, Americans were involved in the European conflict long before Congress actually declared war. US bankers extended loans to the Allies. The United States supported Britain's blockade and took a firm stance against German U-boat attacks, and Americans expressed sorrow and outrage at the sinking of the British ship *Lusitania* in May 1915. Nearly 1200 civilians died after the German attack on the passenger liner, including 128 Americans. Later investigations showed that the ship had indeed been carrying munitions to Great Britain, as Germany claimed. In response to the *Lusitania* incident, President Wilson issued three notes to Germany, demanding that Germany pledge to never again attack a commercial ship, affirming the right of Americans to travel on passenger ships, and warning that the United States would consider subsequent attacks on commercial vessels to be "deliberately unfriendly" acts (Wilson, note of July 21, 1915). Yet Wilson refused to send a note to London condemning Britain's blockade, as requested by Secretary of State William Jennings Bryan, who remained committed to strict American neutrality. Concerned that the United States was favoring the Allies, Bryan resigned in protest of the Wilson administration's lack of true neutrality. Bryan's departure removed an important dissenting voice from Wilson's cabinet, paving the way for eventual American entry into the war.

Americans also participated in the war by enthusiastically providing humanitarian assistance to war-torn areas, with the American Red Cross at the forefront of this aid. Julia Irwin (2013), in her study of the American Red Cross, points out that the history of foreign relief is an important, though often overlooked, component of American foreign relations. While less controversial than imperial conquest, religious proselytizing, or capitalist penetration, the actions of the American Red Cross were nonetheless a crucial part of the way that Americans engaged with the world. Humanitarian work was a form of diplomacy, Irwin argues. It helped foster global political and social order, ensured stable trade, and reduced potential US security threats. It also served as a form of propaganda, projecting a positive image of the United States abroad.

When Wilson campaigned for a second term in 1916, he used the slogan "He Kept Us Out of War." Yet America's days of peace were numbered. The steady drumbeat of war was growing louder. In January 1917, Germany decided to resume unrestricted submarine warfare on passenger and merchant ships. Throughout February and March 1917, German submarines targeted and sank several US vessels, resulting in multiple deaths. In March, America learned of the Zimmermann Telegram, in which Germany asked Mexico to ally with the Central Powers in exchange for the land from Texas to California. Wilson, meanwhile, believed the United States must play a key role in making and sustaining the postwar settlement, but would only gain a place at the peace table by entering the conflict. On April 2, 1917, he asked Congress for a declaration of war. Using lofty rhetoric, he declared that this would be the "war to end war," which would make the world "safe for democracy." Four days later, Congress voted for the United States to join Europe's Great War.

Since the US invasion of Iraq in 2003, commentators from both history and political science have likened Wilson's foreign policy to George W. Bush's. David M. Kennedy (2005) has called Bush the natural successor of Wilson, as both presidents took the country to war in the name of promoting democracy and peace. Likewise, Walter Russell Mead (2004) describes Bush's foreign policy as Wilsonianism "on steroids" (89). Many of these comparisons are explicitly condemnatory. Pointing not only to World War I but also to Latin American interventions, Joan Hoff (2008) claims that Wilson set the precedent of making "pacts with the devil" in order "to impose American values and win foreign policy conflicts at any cost" (4). Presidents like Bush, she contends, have followed in Wilson's footsteps in their pursuit of brutal, exploitative, and imperialist policies. Whether praising or damning Wilson's foreign policy, historians have posed several questions: What does Wilsonianism actually stand for? What effects has it had on US foreign policy, in the World War I era and beyond? And was the Wilsonian legacy good or bad?

Much of the attention given to Wilson focuses on his plans for a postwar peace. In 1917, he sketched out a vision of the war's end that would bring a "just and secure peace" and a "peace without victory," not merely a "new balance of power" (speech to Congress, Jan. 22, 1917). On January 8, 1918, he delivered the famous Fourteen Points speech to Congress, outlining his plan for the postwar settlement. Taking domestic Progressive ideals and translating them into foreign policy, Wilson urged free trade, open agreements, and arms limitations. While he did not use the word self-determination, he insisted that the "interests" of colonial populations hold "equal weight" with the imperial powers. He also set forth plans for European territorial settlements. Finally, his fourteenth point, which would eventually form the basis for the League of Nations, called for "a general association of nations … for the purpose of affording mutual guarantees of political independence and territorial integrity to great and small states alike" (Fourteen Points speech, January 8, 1918). Wilson's idealism, especially his desire for future world peace, permeated the Fourteen Points. Yet he also had practical objectives. After the Bolshevik Revolution in October 1917, the Allies feared that Vladimir Lenin would pull Russia out of the war. Wilson hoped to show Russia that it should stand behind his peace plan.

One group of scholars seeks to rediscover what Wilson's actual ideas were, apart from the way his internationalist rhetoric may have been distorted or decontextualized. Knock (1992), for example, emphasizes that Wilson's ideas were dramatically different from Cold War invocations of Wilsonianism, which linked the concept to the national security state. In truth, Knock contends, Wilson stood for the peaceful settlement of international disputes and reducing the danger of massive armaments. Cold War security pacts like NATO (formed in 1949) did not affirm Wilson's international legacy but rather negated it; it was balance-of-power politics all over again. Similarly, Trygve Throntveit (2011) urges historians and policy-makers to look back to Wilson's actual rhetoric, not the misguided perceptions of what he said. Throntveit argues that contemporaries as well as historians misinterpreted Wilson by using the phrase self-determination to describe part of his peace program. Wilson almost never used the phrase self-determination or said that groups bound by common language or ethnicity had a right to political and territorial independence. Instead, Wilson advocated what Throntveit calls self-government, or participation by all constituents of a polity in determining its political affairs. Thus, Throntveit concludes, Wilson never violated his principles by abandoning self-determination, as he never envisioned a postwar order that privileged the ethnic nation-state.

Others find that the popular perception of Wilson's ideas was equally if not more significant than their true content. In *The Wilsonian Moment* (2007), Erez Manela focuses on how colonized peoples in Asia and Africa received Wilson's liberal internationalist rhetoric. He describes a Wilsonian moment in which the American president was briefly the savior of these lands, due to the perception that he was calling for their self-determination and independence. Unintentionally, Wilson sparked nationalist movements that endured long after his fall from grace, when the people he inspired felt betrayed by his refusal to attack colonialism at Versailles. In their disillusion, anticolonial activists turned to more radical approaches and against the West.

Wilson certainly has his defenders. In *The Warrior and the Priest* (1983), John Milton Cooper, Jr. compares the lives and presidencies of Theodore Roosevelt and Woodrow Wilson. He argues that, contrary to the popular perception of Wilson as an idealist, Wilson was actually more pragmatic, less emotional, and more of a realist than Roosevelt—and, as a result, accomplished more as a reformer. Arthur Link, a critic of Wilson in *Wilson the Diplomatist* (1959), revised his views twenty years later in *Woodrow Wilson: Revolution, War, and Peace* (1979). In the later book, Link defends Wilson's leadership and, like Cooper, calls his vision realistic. Although Wilson suffered significant defeats in his foreign policy—he failed both to achieve his vision of peace at Versailles and to convince the Senate to ratify the Versailles Treaty and join the League of Nations—Link sees these less as an inadequacy of leadership, and more as the unfortunate result of Wilson's deteriorating health. Cooper, in *Breaking the Heart of the World* (2001), also views Wilson's fight for the League of Nations sympathetically, arguing that the fundamental problem was not the president's vision or ideology, but his heart condition and massive stroke.

In contrast to the positive assessments of Wilson's ideas, critics express skepticism about whether Wilson's foreign policies and legacy were fundamentally sound. Lloyd Ambrosius's *Wilsonianism* (2002) contends that Wilson failed to provide a realistic vision or legacy for the United States in world affairs. Wilson may have epitomized the liberal tradition—values of democracy and capitalism, freedom and human rights. But, as a realist, Ambrosius analyzes Wilson's ideas not just in theory, but in how they were fulfilled in practice, and finds them severely lacking. Some historians, looking at a wider temporal span of American foreign relations, have treated Wilson's presidency as a disastrous turning point. Walter McDougall (1997) claims that Wilson's liberal internationalism ultimately led to the Vietnam War. Frank Ninkovich also takes a bleak view of Wilsonianism in his sweeping review of twentieth-century foreign policy, *The Wilsonian Century* (1999). According to Ninkovich, Wilson's presidency ushered the shift from a "normal" internationalism, defined by its optimism about transnational cooperation and America's liberal influence, to a "crisis of internationalism" grounded in fear (12).

When Wilson returned from Versailles, he faced eight months of bitter, partisan fighting in the Senate. Republican enemies like Henry Cabot Lodge were determined to defeat Wilson at any cost. Even Progressive internationalists, Wilson's onetime allies, were angry about his suppression of civil liberties and abandonment of the Fourteen Points. Irreconcilables rejected the League of Nations completely, while others accepted it in some form, as long as American obligations were limited. In *The Peace Progressives and American Foreign Relations* (1995), Robert David Johnson points to the Treaty of Versailles and the ensuing debate over US entry into the League of Nations as the key period in the development of a new ideological stance. The Peace Progressives emerged from these arguments as a congressional faction that would challenge American foreign policy until the mid-1930s, providing an alternative to both Wilsonianism and the business internationalism of the 1920s. The group, which included senators Robert La Follette of Wisconsin and William Borah of Idaho, stood for anti-imperialism, disarmament, and self-determination for colonized peoples.

Ultimately, the Senate failed to form the two-thirds majority necessary to ratify the Treaty of Versailles. Above all, Republicans in the Senate objected to Article 10 of the treaty. This provision called for members of the League of Nations to "respect and preserve as against external aggression the territorial integrity and existing political independence of all Members of the League" (Treaty of Versailles, 1919). Opponents feared that this clause would compel the United States to defend a League of Nations member if it were attacked. Not only did this bind the United States to the declining European colonial powers, it also threatened Congress's power to declare war. In an attempt to pressure the Senate into ratifying the treaty, Wilson turned to the American people. He embarked on a cross-country speaking tour in September 1919, but it was cut short when he suffered a severe stroke. When the Senate voted in November 1919 and again in March 1920, the treaty they considered contained reservations by Senator Henry Cabot Lodge, modifications that attempted to remove automatic US commitment to the League. Democrats loyal to Wilson voted against it, as did Republican Irreconcilables.

In the end, there were multiple reasons why the United States failed to ratify the Treaty of Versailles and join the League of Nations. First, Wilson only brought Democrats to the peace conference in France, whereas he might have built bipartisan support by inviting a prominent Republican to accompany him. Second, the president's declining health prevented him from making a strong personal plea on behalf of the treaty. Third, political stubbornness doomed it: staunch isolationists condemned new international attachments, while a headstrong Wilson urged his own party to reject the amended treaty. Finally, ethnic groups in the United States contributed to its defeat. German Americans felt Germany was treated too harshly, Italian Americans believed Italy should have been granted more territory, and Irish Americans faulted the treaty for failing to address the matter of Irish independence.

Without the United States joining the League of Nations, many have argued, the organization was doomed to failure. Yet recently, historians have reevaluated the League of Nations and identified limited achievements. In *The Guardians* (2015), Susan Pedersen argues that the League's Permanent Mandates Commission gave colonial subjects a platform and a voice, and ultimately had profound implications for their movements for independence. Moreover, it is unlikely that US membership could have prevented the horrors of the 1930s and the outbreak of World War II.

Directions for Future Research

With the centennial of World War I, an abundance of works have emerged to commemorate the conflict. Journals such as *Diplomatic History* (September 2014) and the *Journal of American History* (September 2015) have published special issues or forums addressing the role and legacies of the United States in the war. Major new works such as Adam Tooze's *The Deluge* (2014) were released to coincide with the beginning of the Great War. Wilsonianism and idealism, as well as issues of intervention related to World War I, are popular themes at this anniversary moment and will likely continue to produce a wave of scholarship.

While non-state actors and activists have long played a significant role in domestic histories of the Gilded Age and Progressive Era, they are emerging as notable players in the international historiography as well. From nongovernmental organizations (NGOs) like the Red Cross (Irwin) to Christian missionaries (Tyrrell) to colonial medical authorities

(Briggs, Findlay), the line between private and public actions has increasingly blurred. In Katherine Unterman's *Uncle Sam's Policemen* (2015), private Pinkerton detectives often performed international manhunts on behalf of the state. With the creation of the Bureau of Investigation (the precursor to today's FBI) in 1908, the state adopted many of the policing techniques and even the personnel of the private investigation firms. The boundaries between policies administered directly by state agents and those implemented by non-state actors were complex and shifting.

Historians of the Gilded Age and Progressive Era have also begun to bridge what Mary Dudziak (2016) calls the traditional divide between legal and foreign relations history. They have been particularly successful in exploring the relationship between law and the overseas empire of the United States. Benjamin Coates (2016) highlights the importance of lawyers in legitimizing and maintaining American empire in the early twentieth century. Christina Duffy Ponsa (previously Burnett, 2008) and Sam Erman (2008) analyze the legal status of Puerto Ricans in the years before the Jones–Shafroth Act of 1917, which granted US citizenship to residents of the island, while Clara Altman (2014) writes about the development of the Philippine legal system under US rule. Historians have also found it helpful to examine the League of Nations through the framework of international law. Stephen Wertheim (2011, 2012) uncovers the dispute between advocates of a more legalistic body, which would have enforced the judicial settlement of disputes, and the eventual architects of the League, who grounded the organization in politics rather than law.

Histories of capital and capitalism that involve international and transnational actors and exchanges are flourishing and open up new avenues for research related to questions regarding commerce, multinational corporations, flows of goods, currencies, labor, and ideas related to markets. Economic historians of the period also touch upon the international dynamics of capitalism in their larger domestic-centered analyses. Julia C. Ott (2011) tracks the history of Americans' attitudes toward investment in stocks and bonds, and finds that the Liberty Loans, Victory Loans, and War Savings programs of the World War I era were a key moment in the creation of the citizen-investor. David Huyssen (2014) likens Progressive Era reform efforts in New York City to US imperialism in the early twentieth century. In both cases, affluent white Americans empowered by the state inserted themselves into the spaces and lives of largely poor, foreign-born populations.

For more than a decade, there has been a resurgence of interest related to empire and imperialism. In American Studies, this is taking the shape of analysis of settler colonialism and its impacts on literature, the arts, and culture more broadly, as well as state formation and power. Some of these works decenter the US narrative by focusing more fully on "abroad"—the Philippines, Puerto Rico, the Canal Zone, and more. Additionally, histories of place show the inherent connections between the local, national, and international, through the lens of the city, fairgrounds, steamships, or specific commodities.

Another promising trend involves intellectual histories of the US role in the world. In *Promise and Peril*, for instance, Nichols treats isolationism not as a static political viewpoint but as a malleable, evolving set of ideas about America's global role. David Milne's *Worldmaking* (2015) takes a new perspective on the traditional subject of American diplomacy, looking at how public intellectuals influenced US foreign affairs. Other recent intellectual histories have dealt with international relations more broadly, and particularly utilize the concept of the global. Vanessa Ogle, in *The Global Transformation of Time* (2015), examines attempts to standardize clock times and calendars in the late nineteenth and early twentieth centuries, revealing changing ideas about time, space, and distance in an increasingly interconnected world. The essays in *Global Intellectual History* (2013), edited by Samuel Moyn and Andrew Sartori, interrogate the very meaning of the global and offer a number of approaches for understanding the global interconnectedness of ideas.

With the transnational turn over the last two decades, there has been a renewed fascination with the global Gilded Age and Progressive Era. Historians of the United States in the world have conducted research in international and multilingual archives, and interesting insights about the period have emerged from this approach. For example, Manela (2007) draws from archives in China, France, Great Britain, India, and Korea, in addition to well-trodden sources like the Woodrow Wilson Papers in the Library of Congress. In so doing, he brings a new and exciting perspective to debates about the international impact of Wilsonianism. The Gilded Age and Progressive Era was a global moment for the United States, and discoveries continue to reveal just how rich and nuanced were the levels of its global interaction.

References

Altman, Clara. 2014. "Courtroom Colonialism: Philippine Law and U.S. Rule, 1898–1935." PhD diss., Brandeis University.

Ambrosius, Lloyd E. 2002. *Wilsonianism: Woodrow Wilson and His Legacy in American Foreign Relations.* New York: Palgrave Macmillan.

Bemis, Samuel Flagg. 1967. (1943). *The Latin-American Policy of the United States.* Reprint. New York: W.W. Norton.

Briggs, Laura. 2002. *Reproducing Empire: Race, Sex, Science, and U.S. Imperialism in Puerto Rico.* Berkeley: University of California Press.

Burnett, Christina Duffy. 2005. "*Untied* States: American Expansion and Territorial Deannexation." *University of Chicago Law Review* 72: 797–879.

—. 2008. "'They Say I Am Not An American…': The Noncitizen National and the Law of American Empire." *Virginia Journal of International Law* 48: 659–718.

Cabranes, José A. 1978. "Citizenship and the American Empire: Notes on the Legislative History of the United States Citizenship of Puerto Ricans." *University of Pennsylvania Law Review* 127: 391–492.

Choy, Catherine Ceniza. 2003. *Empire of Care: Nursing and Migration in Filipino American History.* Durham, NC: Duke University Press.

Coates, Benjamin. 2016. *Legalist Empire: International Law and American Foreign Relations in the Early Twentieth Century.* New York: Oxford University Press.

Colby, Jason M. 2011. *The Business of Empire: United Fruit, Race, and U.S. Expansion in Central America.* Ithaca, NY: Cornell University Press.

Cooper, John Milton. 1969. *The Vanity of Power: American Isolationism and the First World War, 1914–1917.* Westport, CT: Greenwood.

—. 1983. *The Warrior and the Priest: Woodrow Wilson and Theodore Roosevelt.* Cambridge, MA: Belknap Press of Harvard University Press.

—. 2001. *Breaking the Heart of the World: Woodrow Wilson and the Fight for the League of Nations.* New York: Cambridge University Press.

Dawley, Alan. 1991. *Struggles for Justice: Social Responsibility and the Liberal State.* Cambridge, MA: Belknap Press of Harvard University Press.

—. 2003. *Changing the World: American Progressives in War and Revolution.* Princeton, NJ: Princeton University Press.

Dudziak, Mary L. 2016. "Legal History as Foreign Relations History." In *Explaining the History of American Foreign Relations, Volume 3*, ed. Michael J. Hogan and Thomas G. Paterson. New York: Cambridge University Press.

Erman, Sam. 2008. "Meanings of Citizenship in the U.S. Empire: Puerto Rico, Isabel Gonzalez, and the Supreme Court, 1898 to 1905." *Journal of Ethnic History* 27: 5–33.

Foster, Anne L. 2009. "Prohibiting Opium in the Philippines and the United States: The Creation of an Interventionist State." In *Colonial Crucible: Empire in the Making of the Modern American State*, ed. Alfred W. McCoy and Francisco A. Scarano. Madison: University of Wisconsin Press.

Gabaccia, Donna. 2012. *Foreign Relations: American Immigration in Global Perspective.* Princeton, NJ: Princeton University Press.

Go, Julian. 2008. *American Empire and the Politics of Meaning: Elite Political Cultures in the Philippines and Puerto Rico during U.S. Colonialism.* Durham, NC: Duke University Press.

Gobat, Michel. 2005. *Confronting the American Dream: Nicaragua under U.S. Imperial Rule.* Durham, NC: Duke University Press.

Greene, Julie. 2009. *The Canal Builders: Making America's Empire at the Panama Canal.* New York: Penguin.

Herring, George C. 2008. *From Colony to Superpower: U.S. Foreign Relations since 1776.* New York: Oxford University Press.

Hoff, Joan. 2008. *A Faustian Foreign Policy from Woodrow Wilson to George W. Bush: Dreams of Perfectibility.* New York: Cambridge University Press.

Hoganson, Kristin L. 2007. *Consumers' Imperium: The Global Production of American Domesticity, 1865–1920.* Chapel Hill: University of North Carolina Press.

Hsu, Madeline Y. 2000. *Dreaming of Gold, Dreaming of Home: Transnationalism and Migration between the United States and South China, 1882–1943.* Stanford, CA: Stanford University Press.

Huyssen, David. 2014. *Progressive Inequality: Rich and Poor in New York, 1890–1920.* Cambridge, MA: Harvard University Press.

Irwin, Julia F. 2013. *Making the World Safe: The American Red Cross and a Nation's Humanitarian Awakening.* New York: Oxford University Press.

Jacobson, Matthew Frye. 2000. *Barbarian Virtues: The United States Encounters Foreign Peoples at Home and Abroad, 1876–1917.* New York: Hill & Wang.

Johnson, Benjamin Heber. 2003. *Revolution in Texas: How a Forgotten Rebellion and Its Bloody Suppression Turned Mexicans into Americans.* New Haven, CT: Yale University Press.

Johnson, Robert David. 1995. *The Peace Progressives and American Foreign Relations.* Cambridge, MA: Harvard University Press.

Kennedy, David M. 2005. "What 'W' Owes to 'WW.'" *The Atlantic* 30: 36–40.

Kloppenberg, James T. 1986. *Uncertain Victory: Social Democracy and Progressivism in European and American Thought, 1870–1920.* New York: Oxford University Press.

Knock, Thomas J. 1992. *To End All Wars: Woodrow Wilson and the Quest for a New World Order.* New York: Oxford University Press.

LaFeber, Walter. 2013. *The American Search for Opportunity, 1865–1913.* New York: Cambridge University Press.

Langley, Lester D. and Thomas Schoonover. 1995. *The Banana Men: American Mercenaries and Entrepreneurs in Central America, 1880–1930.* Lexington: University Press of Kentucky.

Link, Arthur S. 1959. *Wilson the Diplomatist: A Look at His Major Foreign Policies.* Baltimore, MD: Johns Hopkins University Press.

—. 1979. *Woodrow Wilson: Revolution, War, and Peace.* Arlington Heights, IL: H. Davidson.

Manela, Erez. 2007. *The Wilsonian Moment: Self-Determination and the International Origins of Anticolonial Nationalism.* New York: Oxford University Press.

May, Ernest R. 1959. *The World War and American Isolation, 1914–1917.* Cambridge, MA: Harvard University Press.

McCoy, Alfred W. 2009. *Policing America's Empire: The United States, the Philippines, and the Rise of the Surveillance State.* Madison: University of Wisconsin Press.

McDougall, Walter A. 1997. *Promised Land, Crusader State: The American Encounter with the World since 1776.* New York: Houghton Mifflin.

Mead, Walter Russell. 2004. *Power, Terror, Peace, and War: America's Grand Strategy in a World at Risk.* New York: Knopf.

Milne, David. 2015. *Worldmaking: The Art and Science of American Diplomacy.* New York: Farrar, Straus, & Giroux.

Moyn, Samuel and Andrew Sartori, eds. 2013. *Global Intellectual History.* New York: Columbia University Press.

Nichols, Christopher McKnight. 2011. *Promise and Peril: America at the Dawn of a Global Age.* Cambridge, MA: Harvard University Press.

Ninkovich, Frank A. 1999. *The Wilsonian Century: U.S. Foreign Policy since 1900.* Chicago, IL: University of Chicago Press.

Ogle, Vanessa. 2015. *The Global Transformation of Time, 1870–1950.* Cambridge, MA: Harvard University Press.

Ott, Julia C. 2011. *When Wall Street Met Main Street: The Quest for an Investors' Democracy.* Cambridge, MA: Harvard University Press.

Pedersen, Susan. 2015. *The Guardians: The League of Nations and the Crisis of Empire.* New York: Oxford University Press.

Perez Hattori, Anne. 2004. *Colonial Dis-Ease: U.S. Navy Health Policies and the Chamorros of Guam, 1898–1941*. Honolulu: University of Hawaii Press.

Rauchway, Eric. 2006. *Blessed among Nations: How the World Made America*. New York: Hill & Wang.

Renda, Mary. 2001. *Taking Haiti: Military Occupation and the Culture of U.S. Imperialism, 1915–1940*. Chapel Hill: University of North Carolina Press.

Robertson, Craig. 2012. *The Passport in America: The History of a Document*. New York: Oxford University Press.

Rodgers, Daniel T. 1998. *Atlantic Crossings: Social Politics in a Progressive Age*. Cambridge, MA: Belknap Press of Harvard University Press.

Rosenberg, Emily S. 2003. *Financial Missionaries to the World: The Politics and Culture of Dollar Diplomacy*. Durham, NC: Duke University Press.

Rosenberg, Emily, ed. 2012. *A World Connecting, 1870–1945*. Cambridge, MA: Belknap Press of Harvard University Press.

Rupp, Leila J. 1997. *Worlds of Women: The Making of an International Women's Movement*. Princeton, NJ: Princeton University Press.

Rydell, Robert W. and Rob Kroes. 2005. *Buffalo Bill in Bologna: The Americanization of the World, 1869–1922*. Chicago, IL: University of Chicago Press.

Sparrow, Bartholomew H. 2006. *The* Insular Cases *and the Emergence of American Empire*. Lawrence: University Press of Kansas.

St. John, Rachel C. 2011. *Line in the Sand: A History of the Western U.S.–Mexico Border*. Princeton, NJ: Princeton University Press.

Suárez Findlay, Eileen J. 1999. *Imposing Decency: The Politics of Sexuality and Race in Puerto Rico, 1870–1920*. Durham, NC: Duke University Press.

Throntveit, Trygve. 2011. "The Fable of the Fourteen Points: Woodrow Wilson and National Self-Determination." *Diplomatic History*35:445–481.doi:10.1111/j.1467-7709.2011.00959.x/accessed July 18, 2016.

Tooze, Adam. 2014. *The Deluge: The Great War, America and the Remaking of the Global Order, 1916–1931*. New York: Viking.

Tyrrell, Ian. 2010. *Reforming the World: The Creation of America's Moral Empire*. Princeton, NJ: Princeton University Press.

Unterman, Katherine. 2015. *Uncle Sam's Policemen: The Pursuit of Fugitives across Borders*. Cambridge, MA: Harvard University Press.

Veeser, Cyrus. 2002. *A World Safe for Capitalism: Dollar Diplomacy and America's Rise to Global Power*. New York: Columbia University Press.

Wertheim, Stephen. 2011. "The League That Wasn't: American Designs for a Legalist-Sanctionist League of Nations and the Intellectual Origins of International Organization, 1914–1920." *Diplomatic History* 35: 797–836. doi:10.1111/j.1467-7709.2011.00986.x/accessed July 18, 2016.

—. 2012. "The League of Nations: A Retreat from International Law?" *Journal of Global History* 7: 210–232. doi:10.1017/S1740022812000046/accessed July 18, 2016.

Further Reading

Cooper, John Milton, Jr. ed. 2008. *Reconsidering Woodrow Wilson: Progressivism, Internationalism, War, and Peace*. Baltimore, MD: Johns Hopkins University Press.

Epstein, Katherine C. 2014. *Torpedo: Inventing the Military-Industrial Complex in the United States and Great Britain*. Cambridge, MA: Harvard University Press.

Gilderhus, Mark T. 1986. *Pan American Visions: Woodrow Wilson and the Western Hemisphere, 1913–1921*. Tucson: University of Arizona Press.

Ikenberry, G. John, Thomas Knock, Anne-Marie Slaughter, and Tony Smith. 2009. *The Crisis of American Foreign Policy: Wilsonianism in the Twenty-First Century*. Princeton, NJ: Princeton University Press.

Iriye, Akira. 2013. *The Globalizing of America, 1913–1945*. New York: Cambridge University Press.

Katz, Friedrich. 1981. *The Secret War in Mexico: Europe, the United States, and the Mexican Revolution*. Chicago, IL: University of Chicago Press.

Kennedy, David M. 1982. *Over Here: The First World War and American Society*. New York: Oxford University Press.

Kennedy, Ross A. 2009. *The Will to Believe: Woodrow Wilson, World War I, and America's Strategy for Peace and Security*. Kent, OH: Kent State University Press.

Langley, Lester D. 1983. *The Banana Wars: An Inner History of American Empire, 1900–1934*. Lexington: University Press of Kentucky.

Rosenberg, Emily S. 1982. *Spreading the American Dream: American Economic and Cultural Expansion, 1890–1945*. New York: Hill & Wang.

Rossini, Daniela. 2008. *Woodrow Wilson and the Making of the American Myth in Italy: Culture, Diplomacy, and War Propaganda*. Cambridge, MA: Harvard University Press.

Smith, Neil. 2003. *American Empire: Roosevelt's Geographer and the Prelude to Globalization*. Berkeley: University of California Press.

Part VIII

Major Works and Contemporary Relevance

Chapter Thirty-Two

Decades of Upheaval and Reform

Maureen A. Flanagan

During the decades of the Gilded Age and Progressive Era, the United States underwent profound and rapid changes in its political, economic, and social life. The conditions produced by these upheavals troubled many Americans. Political democracy, they feared, was being undermined by a government that appeared hopelessly corrupt and unable, or unwilling, to cope with these changes. A "corrupt bargain" between greedy politicians and leading economic figures seemed to be undermining the opportunities supposedly open to all Americans and making a mockery of democratic rule.

The economy of industrial capitalism, for all the benefits that it was bringing to the country, had dramatically changed the nature of work and production, turning workers into unskilled disposable labor, easily replaced by employers who exploited the vast pool of immigrants pouring into the country. The new economy produced enormous wealth for a few while leaving growing numbers of Americans in wretched poverty. The gulf between the haves and the have nots, the growing antagonism between workers and employers, seemed ready to erupt at any moment into open class warfare.

Socially, the waves of immigrants being drawn to the country by the promise of opportunity were changing the nature of the American population and supposedly challenging previously agreed upon cultural norms undergirding democratic ideals. Newcomers from southern and eastern Europe introduced different ethnicities, cultural backgrounds, and religions into a heretofore relatively homogenous population of white, protestant, and northern European background. But homegrown social upheaval was also shaking confidence in the cultural norms. The recent end of legal slavery confronted Americans with the dilemma of how, or whether, to integrate former slaves, who were American citizens by definition, into an overwhelmingly white society that continued to look upon them as inferior beings. The growing Woman suffrage movement attacked the lack of women's citizenship rights in a country that considered itself the most democratic in the world. Women's demands for political rights, legal equality, and economic opportunity endangered the nineteenth-century division between the public and private realms that most men continued to advocate.

The vision of the United States as an agrarian nation, filled with industrious and virtuous farm families, was now being challenged by the specter of rapidly expanding urban, industrial centers. New immigrants flooded into these cities seeking work in factories and industrial plants. Young people were leaving the farms and looking to the city as the promising site of economic opportunity and social excitement. The flood of young women who were coming to the city alone, "adrift" and unmoored from family especially troubled many Americans. Their presence in the city as workers also challenged the separation of the public and the private. By the end of the century, 3.5 million people lived in New York City. Chicago's population reached 1.7 million. No region of the country was untouched by urban expansion, even if not as dramatic as that of major industrial centers. The population of San Francisco was almost 350,000, while New Orleans was closing in on 300,000. By 1920, the census would show that the country was now 50% urban.

Such changing circumstances caused many Americans to reflect on the nature of their society and to rethink many of their underlying assumptions about their country and its promise of democratic equality and opportunity. They began to ask themselves the meanings and appropriate contours of a democratic society and how it should be constituted. What, they pondered, was the meaning of democratic citizenship? Should it promise more than political rights and guarantee more social and economic democracy? Was it

A Companion to the Gilded Age and Progressive Era, First Edition. Edited by Christopher McKnight Nichols and Nancy C. Unger.
© 2017 John Wiley & Sons, Inc. Published 2017 by John Wiley & Sons, Inc.

right to protect individual opportunity at the expense of social and economic equality? Should it be the job of government to regulate economic development and to foster social justice? What was the role of law in protecting and fostering a more just society? What did it mean to be a modern society that looked forward into the urban future and not back to the agrarian past for its identification?

Reflecting on these and other questions, Americans produced a broad array of writings, speeches, even Supreme Court decisions, that were disseminated throughout society and accelerated debate. New technologies and faster communication systems brought these works to the attention of people throughout the country. National communication networks made it impossible to escape the ferment of change and to remain ignorant of conditions throughout the country. Information flowed through new elite publications such as *The Nation*, muckraking magazines such as *McClure's*, and the multitude of daily newspapers. Innovations in publishing produced books and pamphlets at reasonable prices. Americans consumed the popular dime-novels as well as more literary fictional works. Non-fiction investigations exposing conditions across the country were readily available to anyone who cared to read them. The continent-wide railroad system brought speakers across the country to address gatherings from large public ones to smaller, select meetings. The telephone and telegraph allowed Americans to share news more easily than posting letters had done in the past.

Technological developments in photography accompanied those in communication. Dry-plate chemistry, for example, made it easier for the amateur photographer to use a camera. Of even more importance was the innovation of a "flash powder" that made it possible to take photos in the dark. Innovations of this type helped to move photography out of its stylized formal presentation into a dynamic one documenting the realities of daily life for millions of Americans. Those Americans concerned about the problems of society turned to photography to capture scenes of daily life and work and put into pictures what words could not adequately convey. Newspaper use of photography presented graphic representation of current local and national events, the more startling or controversial the better for newspaper sales. Yesterday's tragedy or exposé in New York City could be seen the next day in Chicago and San Francisco.

With such a broad range of information circulating through society, it would be futile to attempt to pinpoint any one most influential work. Appreciating the influence of such a massive amount of information is best approached by identifying how and why these works could be seen as challenging Americans to reconsider conventional thinking and assumptions about the existing political, social, and economic structures. This essay, thus, assesses as influential those works that caused people to think differently about the nature of their society and to advocate for change on the basis of new ideas. It was also discusses those works that produced a negative reaction. Most of the influential works of these decades do not fit neatly into any one category, as they overlap one or more of them. Rather than approach them within a category, this essay discusses how and why these works had multiple effects and influences for Americans.

Defending the Status Quo

In late 1880s, Andrew Carnegie began publishing work extolling the virtues of American industrial capitalism and democracy. While it is doubtful that a vast array of Americans read this work, it struck a chord with those who continued to promote the country as the epitome of human development. In *The Triumph of Democracy*, Carnegie enumerated all the ways in which he believed that the United States had surpassed old Europe in greatness. Carnegie's list of what he reckoned were the vast achievements of the country would have pleased other conservative thinkers. According to Carnegie, for example, not only had the United States risen to international commercial and military prominence, it occupied "a commanding position in nations in intellectual activity." It was superior in "application of science to social and industrial uses" and responsible for "many of the most important practical inventions which have contributed to the progress of the world during the past century" (Carnegie 1886, 9 and 10). *The Triumph of Democracy* contained another Carnegie idea about the American population that, unfortunately, captured another belief held by a segment of American society. Following the ideas of Herbert Spencer about the biological fitness of the Aryan races, Carnegie declared that America's greatness stemmed from its British ethnic foundations.

> We have only to imagine what America would be to-day if she had fallen, in the beginning, into the hands of any other people than the colonizing British to see how vitally important is this question of race.…The special aptitude of this race for colonization, its vigor and enterprise, and its capacity for governing…Fortunately for the American people they are British. (Carnegie 1886, 12; 23)

With such a British foundation, Carnegie assured his readers, the country would be able to absorb all newcomers and assimilate them into the British character. At a time when the country was beginning to experience immigration from non-Aryan lands, Carnegie's ideas could be reassuring, but also provide a basis for discrimination against foreign ideas and cultures.

Carnegie's personal experiences of emigrating from Scotland to the United States as a poor teenager, working as a bobbin boy in a cotton factory, and ultimately becoming one of the richest men in the country also underlay his thinking about the opportunity afforded to anyone who worked hard. In this regard, his ideas meshed with the

"Ragged Dick" stories by clergyman Horatio Alger that had captured a popular imagination from the late 1860s. These stories about life among New York City's shoe shine boys were intended to show that hard work, honesty, thrift, and initiative would bring success even to those in the lowest strata such as Alger's street urchin characters.

Carnegie, in one of his "Gospel of Wealth" essays ("How I Served My Apprenticeship"), turned his experience into a paean to the virtues of poverty for impelling hard work and competition that would lead to success and wealth. According to Carnegie, he had become wealthy in this fashion and now it became his prescription to success. In another essay, titled "The Problem of the Administration of Wealth," he praised the disparities in wealth and poverty resulting from industrial capitalism.

> The contrast between the palace of the millionaire and the cottage of the laborer with us to-day measures the change which has come with civilization. This change, however, is not to be deplored but welcomed as highly beneficial. It is well, nay essential, for the progress of the race that the houses of some should be homes for all that is highest and best in literature and the arts, and for all the refinements of civilization, rather than none should be so. Much better this irregularity than universal squalor. (Carnegie 1901, 2)

The advantages flowing from the law of competition, Carnegie continued, are greater than its costs and "while the law may be sometimes hard for the individual, it is best for the race, because it ensures the survival of the fittest in every department" (Carnegie 1901, 4). Here, too, one can see the influence of social scientific theories about evolution that had been circulating through American society from at least the 1860s with the advent of the writings of Herbert Spencer. According to Spencer, those individuals who adapted to their environment received their just rewards and were the fittest to survive. Spencer's theories had a broad readership among educated men and they were taught at the leading universities. The writing of even a self-educated man such as Carnegie reflected the prominence, and acceptance, of Spencerian theories whether or not he actually read Spencer.

Formulating New Conceptions of Society

While Carnegie defended the status quo on the basis of a deterministic social survival derived from Spencer's readings of Darwin, intellectuals such as historian Henry Adams and Harvard professor of psychology William James sought ways between science and religion to understand society. In one of his most famous essays Adams wavered between seeing the Virgin or the Dynamo, the miracle of religion or the miracle of industrialization. But William James forthrightly challenged the Spencerian determinism while he simultaneously rejected older religious-based explanations of society. For James, who pioneered studying the mind as a means for understanding the validity of ideas, truth could best be established by testing its workability through lived experience. His master work, *The Principles of Psychology* (1890) articulated the idea of such a pragmatic method for arriving at truth. Pragmatism, as a philosophy, advocated evaluating all situations and ideas according to evidence and experience in order to conclude their truth or falseness. Neither Carnegie's nor James's theories would likely have reached far down into society, and James's ideas provoked immediate intellectual controversy. Yet acceptance of the fundamental premise of pragmatism made it a decisive influence in several areas of social importance, especially on ideas about education. In 1892 James abridged his 1890 book "to make it more directly available for classroom use" (James 1892, iii). But his most profound affect may have been on fellow academic John Dewey, who adapted pragmatism to theories about education.

Beginning with The *School and Society: Being Three Lectures* (1899) and culminating in 1916 with *Democracy and Education*, Dewey argued that education must have a practical, social nature. Dewey rejected what he considered the individualistic rote-learning of education. He advocated instead that the experience of students working together to solve problems would create a sense of social organization. "A spirit of free communication, of interchange of ideas, suggestions, results, both successes and failures of previous experiences becomes the dominating note," which he concluded, would produce "the genuine community standard of value" (Dewey 1899, 29–30). Dewey followed his ideas to their logical conclusion in *Democracy and Education: An Introduction to the Philosophy of Education* (1916) in which he attributed the growth of democracy directly to the "development of the experimental method in the sciences, evolutionary ideas in the biological sciences, and the industrial reorganization" (Dewey 1916, v). Education, according to Dewey, had to be instrumental; the teacher had to help students to develop the ability to think in order to confront problems. Confronting the problems of a democratic society could then produce just solutions. Dewey's emphasis on practicality and instrumentalism underlay his founding of the University of Chicago Laboratory School.

Questioning Wealth

The intellectual production of men such as James and Dewey would have a far-reaching impact on the development of intellectual disciplines. But other writers directly confronted the fundamental assumptions about opportunity, the strength of American democracy, and the wealth of American society as espoused by Carnegie and Alger as either misguided or totally inadequate to meet the needs of a modern, industrial society. No one was better at ridiculing such ideas than Mark Twain. His 1873 publication, *The*

Gilded Age: A Tale of Today, satirized the incessant search for wealth among ordinary people. But in this volume Twain also painted a picture of corrupt and vain Senators buying votes and using their office to advance their own fortunes (Twain and Warner 1873). In his short essay "Poor Little Stephen Girard," published in 1879, Twain parodied the Horatio Alger myth of the poor boy who makes good. In that story, little Stephen was mocked and threatened by a wealthy banker for daring to think that he would be rewarded for his initiative.

The spectacle of the widening gulf between wealth and poverty and the potential threat of concentrated wealth troubled a growing number of men who perceived the unequal social structure of wealth and poverty as a threat to democratic ideals. These men also attacked previous ideals about the positive impact of wealth in society. Beginning in the late 1870s, Henry George began publishing editorials, pamphlets, and essays questioning the existence of poverty in a supposedly wealthy country. He set down his theory and his remedy, as he called it, for this problem in *Progress and Poverty: An Inquiry into the Cause of Industrial Depressions and Increase of Want with Increase of Wealth.* George charged that the unequal distribution of wealth, which he labeled "the curse and menace of modern civilization," was produced by the private, non-productive, and unequal ownership of land. The remedy for this menace, he wrote, was to "make land common property" (George 1886, 295), a solution to be arrived at by a tax on the value of land (George 1886, 372). George reasoned that such a tax, first, could replace all other taxes. But more important in his calculation was that a tax on land values could not be passed onto others. Thus, it would become the "single" and most just tax because "by compelling those who hold land on speculation to sell or let for what they can get, a tax on land values tends to increase the competition between owners, and thus to reduce the price of land" (George 1886, 373). On the one hand, George was upholding the sacred capitalist principle of competition that, he believed, monopoly of land was violating. If the value of land was open to competition, he theorized, rents would fall and poorer Americans would benefit. Rents would be lowered because the owners of land would have no incentive to see the value of their land increase through high rental income if it were accompanied by higher taxes. Lower rents would relieve the pressure of poverty. George proposed this solution to the unequal distribution of wealth because he rejected the efficacy of any other solution. He did not believe in 1879 that there was any probable way to secure higher wages for all workers. Thus, with lower rents wages would go further and poverty reduced. On the other hand, he was attacking another sacred principle: the sanctity of private property. Despite raising legitimate questions about the role of wealth in society, George's proposed solution was not likely to receive broad acceptance. The message was sure to be rejected by land owners. But the book was also highly theoretical. Wading through 500 pages of detailed economic theory was not going to appeal to a many Americans. Nevertheless, the work was a harbinger of the entry of professional theory into the discussion of the problems facing American society.

As universities introduced into their curricula new professional disciplines such as economics and sociology, men trained in those disciplines began to consider how to reform American society. In *The Theory of the Leisure Class,* Thorstein Veblen identified the economic role of a leisure class as the conspicuous consumption and non-production responsible for the unequal distribution of wealth.

> The relation of the leisure (that is, propertied, non-industrial) class to the economic process is a pecuniary relation – a relation of acquisition not of production; of exploitation, not of serviceability….Their office is of a parasitic character, and their interest is to divert what substance they may to their own use and to retain whatever is under their hand. (Veblen 1899, 209)

Veblen directly attacked the belief of Carnegie that a wealthy class benefitted society as a whole, arguing that the idea of a leisure class was an antiquated survivor of older predatory cultures whose only purpose was to perpetuate itself (Veblen 1899, 337). In such a case, it could not benefit society as a whole and certainly did not represent the survival of the fittest.

Veblen's work was undoubtedly more accessible to his fellow intellectuals and university professors who were working out new theories of society than it was to either a popular readership or even a class of more serious readers. In this regard, it contributed to theoretical developments in new academic disciplines and professional training. Other works, however, were catching the interest of that broader readership even before Veblen's book. Henry Demarest Lloyd's *Wealth against Commonwealth* was an assault on the greed and power of corporations, written in plain and direct language. Lloyd was particularly incensed by the power of big business to dictate production to benefit itself and to impoverish the rest of society. "They assert the right, for their private profit, to regulate the consumption by people of the necessities of life, and to control production, not by the needs of humanity, but by the desires of the few for dividends" (Lloyd 1894, 1). Selfish individualism through monopoly of production and wealth, and the alliance of government with business fostering this monopoly, Lloyd argued, was destroying liberty. Lloyd called for Americans to develop a new type of cooperative self-interest that would counter the prevailing, pernicious individualistic search for wealth and power. In a phrase, Lloyd believed in the power of the people. He asserted that only industrial liberty for all could guarantee political liberty. Lloyd expressed optimistically his faith that the American people were determined to achieve this industrial independence and reform their society. His book was part diatribe, and part utopian vision. He rejected any half-measures, such as economic regulation, to reform the country; true reform could only be done by a commonwealth of citizens united in conscious cooperation to assure the benefits of liberty for all (Lloyd 1894, 527–528).

Most accessible to a broader range of Americans was Edward Bellamy's utopian novel, *Looking Backward: 2000--1887.* As with Demarest Lloyd, Bellamy sought the construction of a more cooperative society in which everything needed for daily existence would be produced and distributed to benefit everyone. Bellamy did not deal in economic theory, but rather looked to convince his readers that what they lived and believed about wealth and inequality in the nineteenth century would look very peculiar to Americans 100 years later. The novel has been called a socialist utopian vision of society. Its premise, however, that society could be reconstructed along more humane and equitable lines by replacing the competitive economic system of capitalism with a cooperative system of production resonated with many Americans who would not have called themselves socialists. The book spawned the organization of Bellamy Clubs, also called Nationalist Clubs, in which people debated the merits of Bellamy's ideas.

In *Christianity and the Social Crisis*, Walter Rauschenbusch, a professor of church history, added another dimension to the idea of socialism. He attacked industrial capitalism's pursuit of wealth and competitive individualism as antithetical to Christianity and responsible for producing an "antiquated form of social organization." The spirit of Christianity, Rauschenbusch argued, "has more affinity for a social system based on solidarity and human fraternity than one based on selfishness and mutual antagonism" (Rauschenbusch 1907, 397). For Rauschenbusch, socialism and Communism were actually Christian principles for organizing a just society. He claimed that any study of history demonstrates that "Christian thought was in favor of Communism as more in harmony with the genius of Christianity and with the classical precedents of its early social life" (Rauschenbusch 1907, 396; 397).

In a series of lectures collected in *Democracy and Social Ethics*, Jane Addams prescribed a different approach to understanding the problems confronting American society. She argued not for religious or socialistic principles, but for a democracy based on a sense of social morality, something that she believed was currently absent in American society. The individual rights of property, she urged, had to be replaced with recognition of the interdependency of all individuals and acceptance of a responsibility of the individual for the welfare of all. No one's welfare could be ignored, and the social and industrial value of every individual had to be acknowledged (Addams 1902, 85). To achieve this social morality, individual philanthropy, for example, had to give way to social obligation because the individual was bound to focus on himself and his own goodness.

> He makes an exception of himself, and thinks that he is different from the rank and file of his fellows. He forgets that it is necessary to know the lives of our contemporaries, not only in order to believe in their integrity, which is after all but the first beginnings of social morality, but in order to attain to any mental or moral integrity for ourselves or any such hope for society. (Addams 1902, 79).

For Addams, all political and economic systems had to have the welfare of all the people as their guiding principle. Hers was a deeply systemic attack on how the lack of social morality and social obligation in every aspect of American society meant that it was not truly democratic. As a series of open lectures, and then in book form, Addams's voice reached deeply into American society.

Multiple Problems/Multiple Reform Proposals

The general concern, and outrage, about the shape of American society could also be seen in the variety of new organizations and individual reformers who had begun to identify specific social, political, and economic problems and advocate ways to reform society. In a broad sense, what all of them were attacking was their perception that democratic ideals were being undermined by individualism and competitive capitalism. One measure of the influence of such works was how their ideas were incorporated into the political party system.

The Farm Protest

A national agrarian protest movement led to the organization of the Populist, or People's, Party which directly challenged the two prevailing political parties for failing to advance the welfare of "the people." At its founding convention in 1892, the party issued its declaration of principles in the "Omaha Platform." Corrupt government and the law at every level, the concentration of land in the hands of the wealthy, the rights of labor stifled by both business and government, a vast public debt owed to the creation of money to enrich bondholders, had steadily stratified society into the "two great classes – tramps and millionaires" – and brought the country to the brink of "moral, political, and political ruin." In a refrain that would become embedded in the populist movement, the Platform focused on monetary policy, especially the prevailing gold standard of valuation, as the root of much of the evil pervading the country. The Platform called for vast changes in the monetary system that would expand the available money circulating in society; demanded a graduated income tax; and called for land reform that would end the ownership speculation of land for profit. The members and leaders of the populist movement may not have read either Henry George or Thorstein Veblen, but working from their own perspective, they were identifying the same problem. Their solution was different: they advocated that government reclaim all corporate lands not serving actual needs and any alien-owned land and make it available for settlement.

These sentiments were carried forward four years later when the party's presidential candidate William Jennings Bryan gave his fiery "Cross of Gold" speech. And, as the Omaha Platform had alluded to, there was an international dimension to his protest as he challenged Americans to free themselves from dependence on international monetary policy, specifically tied to England. Bryan reminded his listeners that the country had declared independence from England over 100 year previous, and should not now succumb to foreign dictates to remain on the gold standard. "You shall not press down upon the brow of labor this crown of thorns, you shall not crucify mankind upon a cross of gold." The Democratic Party soon absorbed the Populists into its fold, nominating Bryan as its presidential candidate. The agrarian focus and moralistic protestant perspective of populism did not attract sufficient urban labor vote to prevail over the wealth and influence of the Republicans in 1896. Nevertheless, the populists had elevated popular protest into the political process to a greater extent than ever before.

Labor Asserts Its Rights

Terence Powderly's declaration of the "Purposes and Program of the Knights of Labor," issued not long after the great railroad strike of 1877, drew attention to the growing alarm over the devaluing of productive labor that was percolating through the country. The contestation over the creation of wealth, and to whom wealth belonged, was never far beneath the surface of so much protest in the Gilded Age. Powderly declared that wealth belonged to those toilers who actually produced it and not to businessmen who produced nothing. To restore it to those producers, Powderly and the Knights called for a network of cooperative institutions. Here again was the call for cooperation to replace competition, although now from a labor perspective. The Program of the Knights also demanded that government be compelled to effect this cooperative society by enacting new laws to protect workers' wages, to acknowledge their rights to bargain collectively, to reduce hours of labor, and to rein in the power of banks over a national currency.

No matter the source, calls for a cooperative, non-competitive society did little to blunt the power of capital or to reform government. By the early 1890s, labor's response to its position in society was moving distinctly in other directions as business remained intransigent. The violent 1894 railway strike against George Pullman's car works on Chicago's south side followed hard on the massive 1893 economic depression that had swept across the country. The strike was broken with the help of military force. In its aftermath, the socialist labor leader of the American Railway Union Eugene Debs was sentenced to prison for defying the legal injunction that Pullman had secured against the strikers. In a letter he wrote from prison to union members, Debs charged that all the forces of business, government, and law had colluded to crush the union. He called upon the workers to recognize that they had been fight a holy battle in which "this solidified mass of venality, venom, and vengeance constituted the foe against which the American Railway Union fought Labor's greatest battle for humanity" (Debs 1908, 292). If Debs' words were hyperbolic, and intended mainly for his membership, the growth of a socialist labor movement under his and others' leadership was arousing fears that the unfair advantage that wealth and influence held over millions of Americans might provoke class war.

The Rights of Women

Arguments about women's rights in a democratic society, particularly the right to vote, came from a variety of quarters and were disseminated through venue targeted to specific groups and also popular magazines. Elizabeth Cady Stanton, writing in *The Woman's Column* in 1892, argued that Woman suffrage was an extension of the democratic concept of individual citizenship and the ability of women to protect themselves. In 1905, Adela Hunt Logan promoted Woman suffrage in *The Colored American Magazine*, arguing among other reasons, that black women should have the vote because they needed its protection even more than did white women. Jane Addams explained that suffrage was a social good. In a 1910 issue of the *Ladies Home Journal.* Addams urged Woman suffrage as an aspect of democratic self-government, calling it a social responsibility. The Socialist activist and newspaper editor Josephine Kaneko, in the March 1914 issue of *The Coming Nation,* called for Woman suffrage as necessary to good social order. As women bore the burdens of society, she asserted, they should similarly be able to share in its privileges. Publishing even short pieces in such venues made available to a broad range of Americans the various arguments about Woman suffrage, and in this sense, the body of such work helped persuade Americans that Woman suffrage was both a need and a right.

Woman suffrage was not the only cause of the women's rights movement. In several works, Charlotte Perkins Gilman adopted a social evolutionary perspective to describe the debilitating effects of women's subordinate economic position in American society and to undermine the false premises on which this situation was based. In *Women and Economics: A Study of the Economic Relation between Men and Women As a Factor in Social Evolution* she noted that not only were humans "the only animal species in which the female depends upon the male for food," but that they were the only species for which survival was dependent on a sexual relationship (Gilman 1898, 5). In this context, Gilman asserted, women could never reach their fulfillment as individuals and would forever be victims of arrested development. A woman's labor, she argued, did not belong to her for she never received any wages for all the work that she performed in the household. Gilman also labeled absurd the prevailing idea that women received their support in food, clothing, etc., on the basis of motherhood. In this case, she claimed, motherhood became an exchangeable commodity forced upon women in order to be supported. Moreover, women's economic worth was then weighed according to her ability to procreate (Gilman 1898, 15–16).

Discussion of the social dimension of women's position in society produced a document with a different type of argument from Gilman's, but dedicated to having law recognize women as both workers and mothers. Reformers wanted to protect women in both capacities through protective labor laws. The "Brandeis Brief" that the lawyer Louis Brandeis would use to argue the case for protective labor laws for women was compiled by a group of women led by Josephine Goldmark. In what was becoming a hallmark of social scientific investigation into the problems of American society, the women amassed a 113-page report on the dangers to women's health and social organization from long hours of hard work. The women who assembled the brief sought to have law recognize women's multiple roles in society as a way to foster their legal rights, but they also hoped that it could be used as an opening wedge to secure protective labor laws for all workers. The 1905 Supreme Course ruling *Lochner v. New York* had rejected limiting the hours of labor for men as against the constitutional right to contract one's labor. The Brandeis Brief was a chance to surmount that legal obstacle. Brandeis and the women were attempting to argue for a new understanding of law, one predicated on social reality rather than the common law reliance on precedent to determine cases.

Brandeis presented this report to the Supreme Court, in the case *Muller v. Oregon* to argue for the constitutionality of laws to limit the hours of work for women. The Court ruling in favor of Brandeis produced what might be described as one of those episodes that warn you to be careful what you wish for. Goldmark and her coworkers had assembled a document that argued for protecting women's health as a social good. The Supreme Court unanimously upheld the Brandeis but offered its own rationale that would subordinate women's economic and legal rights for decades to come. The *Muller v. Oregon* ruling reasserted women's special position as a mother, unequal under the laws.

> That woman's physical structure and the performance of maternal functions place her at a disadvantage in the struggle for subsistence is obvious. This is especially true when the burdens of motherhood are upon her…as healthy mothers are essential to vigorous offspring, the physical well being of woman becomes an object of public interest and care in order to preserve the strength and vigor of the race.

Women, the ruling continued, are always dependent on men. Moreover, the ruling equated women with children: "As minors, though not to the same extent, she has been looked upon in the courts as needing especial care that her rights may be preserved." And, the ruling continued, even if women were now more educated and practiced in understanding business affairs, "it is still true that, in the struggle for subsistence, she is not an equal competitor with her brother…there is that in her disposition and habits of life which will operate against a full assertion of [her] rights…looking at it from the viewpoint of the effort to maintain an independent position in life, she is not upon an equality" (*Muller v. Oregon* 1908, 421; 422).

Social Realism and Legal Reform

The Brandeis Brief sought to bring about a significant change in American law. That it succeeded mainly in restricting women to a subordinate position vis-à-vis their labor and made it an article of law that women's reproductive capacities were a concern of the state, is not surprising given the strong social, political, and economic biases embedded in American law. But if one were to take a long term view of the Brief and the Supreme Court ruling, one can see how women's control over their bodies became a contested legal issue thereafter.

Racial Justice

The 1896 Supreme Court ruling *Plessy v. Ferguson* that upheld the validity of racial segregation – within the false pretense that separate could ever be equal – legally damaged the equal rights of African Americans. But its injection of the idea that culture should determine law would also affect the nature of democratic society well into the future, for it revealed how groups could be singled out legally. The Court allowed that the 14th amendment had been intended to enforce absolute equality before the law, but the Justices ruled,

> in the nature of things, it could not have been intended to abolish distinctions based upon color, or to enforce social, as distinguished from political, equality, or a commingling of the two races upon terms unsatisfactory to either. Laws permitting, and even requiring, their separation in places where they are liable to be brought into contact do not necessarily imply the inferiority of either race to the other…[the individual state] is at liberty to act with reference to the established usages, customs, and traditions of the people, and with a view to the promotion of their comfort and the preservation of the public peace and good order. Gauged by this standard, we cannot say that a law which authorizes or even requires the separation of the two races in public conveyances is unreasonable… (Plessy v. Ferguson 1896, 544; 550)

Although the ruling was specific to a case brought against the state of Louisiana for segregating public conveyances, from 1896 southern states used its language to justify segregation of a broad range of public facilities right down to public drinking fountains and entrances to private establishments such as hotels.

Plessy v. Ferguson worsened the struggle for equality and justice in which African Americans were already engaged. Between 1892 and 1900, Ida B. Wells published articles decrying the lynching of African Americans. In her pamphlet "Southern Horrors: Lynch Law in All Its Phases" and the 1895 pamphlet, "A Red Record: Tabulated Statistics and Alleged Causes of Lynchings in the United States," Wells struggled to make white Americans aware of the lethal injustices practiced against black Americans. In the latter pamphlet she even broadened her argument that lynching as a practice and any form of mob violence was an injustice to any society that considered itself civilized.

The leading African American intellectual of the early twentieth century was W.E.B. Du Bois. In his master works, *The Philadelphia Negro: A Social Study* and *The Souls of Black Folk*, Du Bois chronicled the pernicious legacy of slavery as a racial system for African Americans struggling to assert their democratic rights. In the former work, which was an extensive survey of the city's African American community, Du Bois directly addressed the question of race prejudice as a powerful social force that determined how the city's black population could live and work and relegated them to lower economic and social status. In the latter work, Du Bois posited his theory of double consciousness: that African Americans always had to see themselves as white Americans saw them. As a result, every black American had two souls: one American, one Negro that negated any true self-consciousness. "The history of the American Negro," according to Du Bois, "is the history of this strife – the longing to obtain self-conscious manhood, to merge his double self into a better and truer self" (Du Bois 1903, 12–13). In the short afterword to the book, Du Bois expressed his hope that through understanding of this problem reason would prevail and remove the obstacles to equality.

In little more than a decade after the publication of *Souls of Black Folk*, however, Marcus Garvey was proclaiming that African Americans could never attain equality in a white society. In a 1921 speech, "If You Believe the Negro Has a Soul," Garvey called African Americans "fellow citizens of Africa," and entreated "every Negro to work for one common object, that of building a nation of his own on the great continent of Africa." Garvey accepted the proposition that there were separate races in the world; that "each race and each nationality is endeavoring to work out its own destiny, to the exclusion of other races and other nationalities." By 1921, such ideas resonated with black Americans who perceived that even their wholehearted participation in World War I, either in the military or on the home front, had result in little progress toward equality. Garvey also disseminate his ideas in his newspaper, *Negro World*, and the book *The Philosophy & Opinions of Marcus Garvey, or Africa for Africans* compiled by his wife Amy Jacques Garvey. When he was convicted of mail fraud and subsequently deported in 1927 to Jamaica, his birthplace, Garvey lost immediate influence and control of the black empire that he had created, but his ideas of panAfricanism continued to resonate with black Americans across the decades.

Outrage, Prescriptions, and the Steady DrumBeat for Reform

Outrage over the conditions of life in the United States entered the consciousness of a broad range of Americans. By the late nineteenth century, new technologies helped produce new venues for publicizing and disseminating information and exposés of these conditions to a willing reading public. A new tradition of investigative journalism, subsequently labeled muckraking by Theodore Roosevelt, arose to seek out and publicize these conditions in newspapers, new magazines, and books. The older literary-style magazines such as *The Nation*, although it still commanded attention among the well-educated, were now joined by mass-market magazines such as *McClure's* (1893–1929) and *Everybody's Magazine* (1899–1929), that became publishing venues for the investigation and exposé of corruption in business and politics. Beginning in 1902, *McClure's* serialized in nineteen installments the investigative findings of Ida Tarbell that detailed the predatory monopoly practices of John D. Rockefeller and Standard Oil. The entire investigation was published as *The History of the Standard Oil Company.* Tarbell's work helped lead to the 1911 break-up of Standard Oil into separate companies. *McClure's* also published the investigations of Lincoln Steffens into urban political corruption. Steffens too compiled his work into a book, *The Shame of the Cities.* This exposé of the greed and corrupt practices of urban politics, especially pointing to the machinations of party leaders and businessmen who enriched themselves at the expense of the people, outraged the public. It also gave the growing number of good government reformers in cities across the country the ammunition they needed to promote reform of both the political party system and politicians.

Probably no exposés of the dark side of American life were more influential than those of Jacob Riis and Upton Sinclair. In *How the Other Half Lives*, newspaper reporter Riis, accompanied by a photographer, utilized the new technology of flash photography to illuminate the dark sides – literally – of poverty in New York City's lower east side. The text was dramatic, but the photos depicting these horrific conditions of the city's poorest residents could hardly be ignored. Photos of these conditions and the people living in them transformed poverty into reality; one did not need to imagine poverty, one could see it. In that case, one had to choose whether to ignore it, or to seek reform. Subsequent analyses of Riis' work have debated whether, or how much, Riis posed his subjects in order to depict the worst possible conditions. In any event, *How the Other Half Lives* pricked the consciences of many Americans. Among them was Theodore Roosevelt, who had accompanied Riis on some of his journeys through the dark side of the city. Roosevelt credited Riis with awakening his sensibilities and ultimately turning him into a progressive reformer.

Upton Sinclair chose a different method for exposing lives of desperate poverty, exploitation, and lack of opportunity. *The Jungle* was a protest novel, set in Chicago's south side stockyards district. Sinclair's immigrants, the Rudkus family, arrived in Chicago determined to work hard and carve out a better life. Instead, they were systematically broken by atrocious working conditions in the city's stockyards, rapacious business men taking advantage of the hopes of immigrants, and a totally uncaring city. Sinclair had hoped that his book would awaken the sensibilities of Americans to the need for socialism to reform the economic and social systems of the country so that people would no longer suffer the fate of the Rudkus family. What resulted instead was a widespread revulsion with the unsafe and unsanitary conditions of production of meat in "Packingtown" as Sinclair described them. There is a story, probably apocryphal, that President Roosevelt read the book while eating his breakfast sausages. Whether true or not, Roosevelt was sufficiently appalled by what Sinclair had written that he immediately ordered an investigation of the meatpacking industry. The focus on food safety rather than the social conditions of workers and immigrants did result in passage of new federal legislation regulating food production, the Meat Inspection and the Pure Food and Drug Acts. Sinclair philosophically noted that he had aimed for the hearts of Americans but hit their stomachs instead.

Along with the muckrakers, other writers were calling upon Americans to wake up to the conditions of the country that were giving lie to the ideals of democracy. After visiting the Columbian Exposition in Chicago in 1893 and exploring the city, the English reformer William Stead shamed the better-off residents for their inattention to their city's deplorable conditions in a book that he titled *If Christ Came to Chicago*. Drawing upon Christian principles to ask Chicagoans what they would say to Christ about their lack of concern, Stead's book and speeches had an immediate impact, the formation of a new reform organization, the Civic Federation, by the city's middle-class reform-minded residents. The Civic Federation was immediately embroiled in the 1894 strike at George Pullman's carworks. The reformers' response to the strike revealed that Christian morality was not sufficient for solving the problems that were pitting individualist businessmen against workers struggling to assert their rights to their labor.

Jane Addams offered a different vision. Recounting her experiences as a settlement house leader in *Twenty Years at Hull-House,* she urged Americans to empathize with each other. Addams emphasized that people needed to learn from each other about other experiences and cultures, as she said she had learned from the people of her neighborhood. Addams was convinced that only by appreciating and accepting difference could a better society be created for everyone. Addams expressed this value of experience in her Preface: "this volume endeavors to trace the experiences through which various conclusions were forced upon me." In this work, Addams reemphasized the need for personal experience of other people's lives rather than impersonal philanthropy. "One of the first lessons we learned at Hull-House," she wrote, "was that private beneficence is totally inadequate to deal with the vast numbers of the city's disinherited" (Addams 1911, chapter 14). Instead, there had to be civic cooperation among all sectors of society.

Stead and Addams sought to awaken individual consciousness of responsibility for resolving social and economic problems. Other writers, including Frederick Howe, focused on how to reform economic and political structures. In *The City, the Hope of Democracy*, Howe moved beyond Lincoln Steffens' attack on urban political corruption to proffer ways for the city to become the best site of democracy through empowered municipal government. "The great problem now before the American people is," he argued, "how can opportunity be kept open." Howe theorized that if a city was "free to determine what activities it will undertake, and what shall be its sources of revenue, then the city will be consciously allied to definite ideals, and the new civilization which is the hope as well as the problem of democracy, will be open to realization" (Howe 1906, 311–313). Howe's solution to urban problems was top down; changing the laws and structures and city leaders would craft a better and more efficient city. If structures were changed, then the city could be organized to bring more opportunity to its residents. Mary Parker Follett advocated a bottom up approach through the implementation of public democracy. In *The New State: Group Organization the Solution of Popular Government* she called for cities to be organized around neighborhood forums, planned and run by people of the neighborhood. Not only would real democracy prevail in the city, she argued, but democracy on the local level would then percolate upwards to result in a truly democratic state. Antithetical to Howe's ideas, Follett asserted that "you cannot establish democratic control by legislation…there is only one way to get democratic control – by people learning how to evolve collective ideas" (Follett 1918, 159). Follett and Addams brought a feminist perspective into the discourse over reform. Unlike Howe, who focused on structures of government of create order and provide opportunity, Follett and Addams emphasized the role of individuals in creating a democratic society. Without suffrage women could not participate in crafting such political solutions. Women's exclusion from the formal mechanisms of politics made it easy for men to ignore women's ideas. Nevertheless, women's organization across the country continued to work to make the welfare of the people the central concern of all individuals.

The West: Final Frontier of Democracy

As the final frontier for westward settlement, the West loomed large in discussions about American democracy. In 1893, for the occasion of the Columbian Exposition, the historian Frederick Jackson Turner gave an address that would influence new considerations about the nature of American society. In "The Significance of the Frontier in American History," Turner declared that once the 1890 census had concluded that the frontier was settled, this marked "the closing of a great historic movement." Westward settlement, according to Turner, was crucial to understanding American development. "This perennial rebirth, this fluidity of American life, this expansion westward with its new opportunities, its continuous touch with the simplicity of primitive society, furnish the forces dominating American character." Published first in the *American Historical Review* and amplified by a series of essays on the West, Turner presented the frontier as the source of America's democratic triumph. Its settlement meant that "the first period of American history" was closed and its consequences for the future of the country were uncertain.

The West always loomed large in the mind of future president Theodore Roosevelt who had spent some time there, including camping under the stars of Yosemite with the environmentalist John Muir in 1903. These experiences left a lasting impression of the West on Roosevelt; as much as the source of democracy, he saw the West as the reserve of the natural resources that helped make the country great. Now that settlement of the area was secured, President Roosevelt turned his attention to conserving those resources. Although most people would not hear his 1907 address to Congress on this issue, his message to that body expressed not just an ideal of conservation, but tied it to the ongoing opportunity and prosperity of the country. Striving for immediate profit had helped settle the West. Now, Roosevelt declared, "the conservation of our natural resources and their proper use constitute the fundamental problem which underlies almost every other problem of our national life." It was time "to substitute a planned and orderly development of our resources." Planning and regulation through scientific management of natural resources by government would bring efficiency to conserving the country's resources in the public interest. With this idea of governing in the public interest, the Roosevelt administration was signaling a shift away from rapacious individualist capitalism, and toward the idea that government had to consider a public interest in all economic decisions.

Roosevelt's conservation policies, thus, accorded well with his other economic policy decisions such as the Meat Inspection Act that moved government into the realm of economic regulation. Many other reformers supported such moves. Herbert Croly, in *The Promise of American Life*, implicitly agreed with Turner that an era had ended, and that in order to preserve the democratic promise of American life, government now had to intercede to ensure that the benefits of democracy were more evenly distributed through society.

Science Will Cure the Problems

In the introduction to *The Principles of Scientific Management*, the mechanical engineer Frederick Winslow Taylor quoted Theodore Roosevelt telling a meeting of Governors at the White House that "the conservation of our natural resources is only preliminary to the larger question of national efficiency." Taylor advocated extending efficiency into the realm of production. In his book he laid out the principles he believed would produce more efficiency, including advocating the scientific study of potential workers to find out which ones could be best managed in the most efficient manner, and how. Careful selection of workmen who could then be properly trained and managed scientifically, he believed, would result in efficient mass production techniques, which was his main objective. For a variety of reasons, some less benign than others, Taylor's scientific management caught the imagination of many Americans. Workers, of course, rejected this idea that would further devalue their labor. Manufacturers, on the other hand, embraced it not just for its ideas of efficiency but also as another means for controlling labor. Ultimately, Taylor's ideas evolved into the "American system of manufacturing" that transformed human craft work into a mechanized, and ultimately automated, system of production.

Taylor's ideas that scientific management would bring efficiency in production resonated with a broad range of Americans who were not industrialists or businessmen but reformers seeking social and economic reforms that would benefit Americans generally. Louis Brandeis argued before the Interstate Commerce Commission that if railroads adopted its methods, they would save money on labor costs, which in turn would mean not having to raise rates and thereby benefit all consumers. Josephine Goldmark argued that efficiency would save laborers from long hours and being overworked. She also believed that efficiency of production would save women from unhealthy work situations. For individuals such as Brandeis and Goldmark, efficiency could be used to foster democracy, because it would lessen burdens. But in adopting it they were rejecting the idea of industrial democracy in which there would be a democratic relationship between workers and employers. As Jane Addams had put it earlier in *Democracy and Social Ethics*, the problem was that employers needed not to be good to workers but to be good with them (Addams 1902, 70). Her ideas, of course, were not a prescription for industrial democracy, but they were decidedly one solution for ending the conflict between workers and employers in which workers would share in the value of their labor.

Bringing Democracy to the World/Defining the American Character

An alternate response to the ending of the frontier provoked anxiety of a different sort in Americans. If all the West were settled, and its frontier experience had been, as Turner claimed, a crucible for American democracy, what would this mean for the American character and democracy going forward? And, if natural resources in the West were to be conserved rather than simply exploited, where were the new resources to fuel the economy? Once Turner had articulated the benefits of the frontier to American character development, there were imperialist projects on the horizon in the late nineteenth century that could satisfy these questions, and Americans ready to justify expansion beyond the country's borders in both cases.

Since the United States had promoted isolationism since the Civil War, it needed to justify any leap into international affairs. Admiral Alfred Thayer Mahan's 1890 publication, *The Influence of Sea Power upon History*, opened the way for such justification when it tied the country's commercial prowess to its overseas trade. Since the United States did not presently have colonies to support its naval power as did European powers, Mahan argued that the United States needed to establish bases around the world where naval ships could refuel and find safe harbor in the effort to protect such trade. By the turn of the century, several influential political leaders, including Theodore Roosevelt, supported a new militant internationalism. As Assistant Secretary of the Navy, Roosevelt had supported war in 1898 and establishing colonies in the Caribbean and Pacific. Serving as Secretary of War under Presidents McKinley and Roosevelt, Elihu Root sought a renewed international engagement that included defending the country's new colonial interests after the 1898 war.

Mission of Civilization/Mission of Manhood

In 1895, Roosevelt and his friend Senator Henry Cabot Lodge wrote a volume celebrating the heroic accomplishments of American men. In it they connected masculinity and militant internationalism. "America will cease to be a great nation," they asserted, "whenever her young men cease to possess energy, daring, and endurance, as well as the wish and the power to fight the nation's foes" (Roosevelt and Lodge 1895, x). Roosevelt continued to propound this theme in public speeches. Addressing the Chicago men's Hamilton Club following the 1898 war, and the invasion of the Philippines that he had promoted, Theodore Roosevelt inextricably entwined the two ideas. Declaring that the United States had to accept new responsibilities toward these conquests, he informed the men of the state that gave the country former presidents Lincoln and Grant, that he did not come before them to preach the life of "ignoble ease," but to preach of the strenuous life of toil and effort, labor and strife:

> If we are to be a really great people, we must strive in good faith to play a great part in the world. We cannot avoid the responsibilities that confront us [in the world]…our country calls not for the life of ease, but for the life of strenuous endeavor…if we shrink from the hard contexts where men must win at hazard of their lives and at the risk of all they hold dear, the bolder and stronger peoples will pass us by, and will win for themselves the domination of the world. (Roosevelt 1901, 21)

Roosevelt's ideas were enthusiastically accepted by other public figures as Americans were confronted with the specter of becoming an imperial power. Senator Albert Beveridge added a different dimension when he told Congress that it was the duty of Americans to bring civilization to the world: "[God] has marked the American people as His chosen nation to finally lead in the regeneration of the world. This is the divine mission of America…We are trustees of the world's progress, guardians of its righteous peace" (Beveridge 1900).

Roosevelt's speech in Chicago did not stop with his call for dominance of the world, or for leading a strenuous life. It specifically injected into discourse his gendered ideas about masculinity that would carry the country through World War I.

> The man must be glad to do a man's work, to dare and endure and to labor; to keep himself and to keep those dependent on him. The woman must be the housewife, the helpmeet of the homemaker, the wise and fearless mother of many healthy children…When men fear work, or fear righteous war, when women fear motherhood, they tremble on the brink of doom; and it is well that they should vanish from earth. (Roosevelt 1901, 5).

With such rhetoric circulating in American society, it is small wonder that women found themselves in such a difficult struggle to achieve political, social, and economic rights, especially when the rhetoric appeared again within the debate over entering World War I. The Woman's Peace Party declared itself to be "the mother half of humanity," registering 40,000 members, and a popular song titled "I Didn't Raise My Boy to Be a Soldier" circulated through the country as an anti-war anthem. The advocates of US entry into the war, connecting pacifism with feminism, went on the attack. Roosevelt declared the proper place for women who opposed the war was "in China – or by preference in a harem – and not in the United States" (Roosevelt 1916, 228).

Women attempted to counter such masculine rhetoric. At a 1915 peace conference, Indiana suffragist Mae Wright Sewall declared the disappointment of women "that, at this stage of its development, the men of the world still continue to use armies as their instruments of rule; still continue to believe that war is a proper method of adjusting their disagreements with other peoples" (Sewall 1915, 16). In *Peace and Bread in Time of War* (1922), Jane Addams advocated a peaceful approach to understanding international needs. International justice, she argued, needed to be sought and could not be achieved by war, but only through understanding and fellowship among nations (Addams 1922, 5). She called for new moral relations among nations as she had called for a social morality in the United States (Addams 1922, 31). She hoped, undoubtedly in vain considering the way in which society was organized, that "as women entered into politics when clean milk and the premature labor of children became factors in political life, so they might be concerned with international affairs when these at least were dealing with such human and poignant matters as food for starving people who could be fed only through international activities" (Addams 1922, 47).

Saving the World

Addams, the Woman's Peace Party, and all women who rejected war as the means to solve the world's problems were held in contempt by many men for questioning male authority. The contempt was often couched in rhetoric about these women not fulfilling their presumptive feminine roles, as newspaper editorials characterized as "foolish virgins," among other pejoratives, and Americans were warned that they had to join the war and fight or they would become "a nation of Jane Addamses" (*New York Herald*, cited in Dawley 2003, 158). So, they not only had to fight against the equation of warfare with masculinity, but they confronted the belief held by many powerful men that Americans were a striving, strenuous people who were bringing civilization to the world. Beveridge had declared, for example, that Filipinos and other racial inferiors were so incapable of governing themselves that the United States had a duty to bring civilization to them and the rest of the world (Beveridge 1900). Militant internationalism morphed into messianic internationalism. President Woodrow Wilson's 1917 war message set the tone for the country's involvement in international affairs for the coming century. In asking Congress to declare war, Wilson said that "our object…is to vindicate the principle of peace and justice in the life of the world as against selfish and autocratic power… the world must be made safe for democracy." Wilson also declared that the United States had no selfish ends in entering the war, but that it was one of the "champions of the rights of mankind." Strong rhetorical support for Wilson's ideas came immediately from several senators. "This country has been specially favored by Providence" declared Democrat Henry Myers from Montana. The country's "historic position as the leader and noble pioneer in the vanguard of progress and human liberty" was praised by Democrat Henry Ashurst from Arizona. But leaders of both parties supported the messianic possibilities of war. For Henry Cabot Lodge war would bring national regeneration also. Entering the war, he declared, would unify the country "into one Nation, and national degeneration and national cowardice will slink back into the darkness from which they should never have emerged" (Myers, et al. 1917, 223; 222; 208).

Conclusion

Choosing which works of the Gilded Age and Progressive Era were most influential is a daunting task. The decades saw such a prolific outpouring of books, pamphlets, speeches on so many issues as Americans confronted the problem of reforming their society for the modern age. The ones chosen for this chapter attempt to present both the breadth and depth of the ideas Americans expressed about what they believed was good and bad about the country and what they wanted it to be for the future. The optimism of the calls for change that would produce a better, more democratic, and more just society resulted in a number of significant reforms. Women finally received the national suffrage. Labor obtained new rights to organize. New legislation mitigated some of the worst excesses of capitalist exploitation of workers and of the country's natural resources and protected consumers from impure food and drugs. Cities undertook reforms to unsanitary living conditions. Investigative journalism brought economic and political corruption and social injustice to light so people could no longer pretend that such problems did not exist.

On the other hand, grave injustices remained. African Americans, for example, were systematically and legally disfranchised and segregated in many states following the Supreme Court ruling of *Plessy v. Ferguson*. As president, Woodrow Wilson segregated the federal government, much to the outrage of Belle Case La Follette, who had been publishing articles in *La Follette's Magazine,* lamenting the continuing discrimination of African Americans. Following Wilson's decree, La Follette wrote a series of scathing articles criticizing the racism of such a policy and that of its supporters in Congress. As a feminist, La Follette also took the opportunity of this outrageous policy to highlight the plight of African American women who worked in the government and yet were treated as second-class citizens by the very government that they served (La Follette 1913).

The suffrage amendment did not automatically confer complete equality on women. States reserved the right to prohibit or impede women from serving on juries. The equal rights amendment proposed by the National Woman's Party in 1923 that said nothing more radical than "Equality of rights under the law shall not be denied or abridged by the United States or by any state on account of sex," lingered as a contentious issue until finally defeated in 1982.

The United States was a country of immigrants, but in the later decades of the Gilded Age and Progressive Era, a backlash against new immigrants led to new exclusionary legislation. On the other hand, the pioneering social work of Grace Abbott, provided many people, especially women's organizations and settlement house workers, with new information for countering anti-immigrant sentiment. Investigating the conditions of immigrant life in Chicago, Abbott sought to depict "concretely how the immigrant and the [larger] community have suffered materially and spiritually by our failure to plan for his protection and or his adjustment to American life" (Abbott 1917, preface). Despite her use of the masculine pronoun, Abbott was especially concerned about immigrant girls. She predicted there would be an influx of female immigrants from Eastern Europe after the war, and warned that the country still did not understand the obstacles that they encountered, especially in finding decent housing and employment. The administration of immigration laws, she lamented, "is so entirely in the hands of men" (Abbott 1917, 78). She pointed out the "double standard of morality in the tests for exclusion and deportation" that were being used to exclude "immoral" young women from entry, but not "immoral" men (Abbott 1917, 76).

The rhetoric of war unleashed during World War I continues to color American perceptions of its role in the world. There is a direct line from Wilson's war message and the rhetoric of war's supporters to the rationalization for incursion into international affairs that has been used across the past 100 years. The articulation of the idea that the United States had only altruistic motives in intervening as a belligerent around the world continues to be heard today. Assuming the righteousness of the country's international motives has justified castigating anyone who objects to that foreign policy. Jane Addams wrote that she was not entirely surprised when attacked vehemently for her anti-war stance. She and others were "apparently striking across and reversing [a] popular conception of patriotism." They were called "traitors and cowards" for advocating "a reasonable and vital alternative to war" (Addams 1922, 64).

Weighed in the balance, the benefits of democracy were extended to more people and more social justice was embedded into society by 1920. The outpouring of writings and speeches forced an increasing number of Americans, willingly or unwillingly, to take stock of their society and its failings and to support change. Change meant accepting new ideas about the nature of a good democratic society and the role that all individuals needed to play in its construction. The age of innocence, of attention to manners and form, about which Edith Wharton wrote, had never really existed for most people. But it had been too easy for those people at the top of society to ignore its problems by being the self-absorbed and self-righteous individuals that she described. After 1920, most Americans could no longer pretend that their society was without defects nor could unfettered and unregulated capitalism any longer be justified.

References

Abbott, Grace. 1917. *The Immigrant and the Community*. New York: Century.

Addams, Jane. 1902 (2002). *Democracy and Social Ethics*. New York: Macmillan. Reprint, Urbana: University of Illinois Press. Citations refer to the University of Illinois edition.

—. 1910. "Why Women Should Vote." *Ladies Home Journal*, 27.

—. 1911. *Twenty Years at Hull-House*. New York: Macmillan.

—. 1922 (2002). *Peace and Bread in Time of War*. New York: Macmillan. Reprint, Urbana: University of Illinois Press. Citations refer to the University of Illinois edition.

Alger, Horatio. 1885. *Ragged Dick, Or Street Life In New York with the Boot-Blacks*. Philadelphia, PA: Henry T. Coates.

Beveridge, Albert. 1900. "In Support of an American Empire." *Congressional Record*, 56th Congress, 1st session.

Brandeis, Louis D. 1908. Brief before the Supreme Court in the case *Muller v. Oregon*. https://louisville.edu/law/library/special-collections/the-louis-d.-brandeis-collection/the-brandeis-brief-in-its-entirety Accessed July 23, 2016.

Bryan, William Jennings. 1896. Speech to the 1896 Populist Party Convention, popularly referred to as the Cross of Gold Speech. http://historymatters.gmu.edu/d/5354/Accessed July 23, 2016.

Carnegie, Andrew. 1886. *Triumphant Democracy: Or, Fifty Years March of the Republic*. New York: Scribners.

—. 1901. *The Gospel of Wealth and Other Timely Essays*. New York: Century.

Croly, Herbert. 1909. *The Promise of American Life*. New York: Macmillan.

Debs, Eugene V. 1908. "Proclamation to American Railway Union" In *Debs: His Life, Writings and Speeches*, ed. Eugene V. Debs, Bruce Rogers, and Stephen Marion Reynolds. Girard, PA: *The Appeal to Reason*.

Dewey, John. 1899. *The School and Society: Being Three Lectures*. Chicago, IL: University of Chicago Press.

—. 1916. *Democracy and Education: An Introduction to the Philosophy of Education*. New York: Macmillan.

Du Bois, W.E.B. 1899. *The Philadelphia Negro: A Social Study*. Philadelphia: University of Pennsylvania.

—. 1903 (2008). *The Souls of Black Folk*, Chicago: A.C. McClurg. Reprint, Rockville, MD: ARC Manor. Citations refer to the Arc Manor edition.

Follett, Mary Parker. 1918. *The New State: Group Organization the Solution of Popular Government*. New York: Longmans, Green.

Garvey, Amy Jacques. 1923. *The Philosophy & Opinions of Marcus Garvey, or Africa for Africans*. London: Universal Publishing House.

Garvey, Marcus. "If You Believe the Negro Has a Soul." http://historymatters.gmu.edu/d/5124/. Accessed July 15, 2016.

George, Henry. 1886. *Progress and Poverty: An Inquiry into the Cause of Industrial Depressions and Increase of Want with Increase of Wealth*. New York: D. Appleton.

Gilman, Charlotte Perkins. 1898. *Women and Economics: A Study of the Economic Relation between Men and Women as a Factor in Social Evolution*. Boston, MD: Small, Maynard.

Howe, Frederic. 1906. *The City: the Hope of Democracy*. New York: Scribners.

James, William. 1890. *Principles of Psychology*. New York: Henry Holt.

—. 1892. *Psychology*. New York: Henry Holt.

Kaneko, Josephine. 1914. *The Coming Nation*. March.

La Follette, Belle Case. 1913. "Segregation in the Civil Service." *La Follette's Magazine* 5, 50: 6.

Lloyd, Henry Demarest. 1894. *Wealth against Commonwealth*. New York: Harper.

Logan, Adella Hunt. 1905. "Woman Suffrage." *The Colored American Magazine*, 9.

Muller v. Oregon. 1908. https://www.law.cornell.edu/supremecourt/text/208/412 Accessed July 23, 2016.

Myers, Henry et al. 1917. *Congressional Record*. 65th Congress, 1st Session.

Plessy v. Ferguson. 1896. https://www.law.cornell.edu/supremecourt/text/163/53 Accessed July 23, 2016.

Populist (People's) Party. 1892. "Omaha Platform."

Powderly, Terrence V. 1889, "The Purposes and Program of the Knights of Labor," from *Thirty Years of Labor*. Columbus, OH: Excelsior.

Rauschenbusch, Walter. 1907. *Christianity and the Social Crisis*. New York: Macmillan.

Riis, Jacob. 1890. *How the Other Half Lives: Studies Among the Tenements of New York*. New York: Scribners.

Roosevelt, Theodore. 1901. *The Works of Theodore Roosevelt: Strenuous Life*. New York: P.F. Collier.

—. 1907. "To the Senate and House of Representatives." In *Congressional Record*, 60th Congress, 1st Session.

—. 1916. *Fear God and Take Your Own Part*. New York: George Doran.

Roosevelt, Theodore and Henry Cabot Lodge. 1895. *Hero Tales from American History*. New York: Century.

Sewall, Mae Wright. 1915. "Women, World War and Permanent Peace," *Proceedings of International Conference of Women Workers to Promote Peace*. San Francisco.

Sinclair, Upton. 1906. *The Jungle*. New York: Jungle.

Stanton, Elizabeth Cady. 1892. *The Woman's Column*. January.

Stead, William T. 1894. *If Christ Came to Chicago*. Chicago: Laird & Lee.

Steffens, Lincoln. 1904. *The Shame of the Cities*. New York: McClure, Phillips.

Tarbell, Ida M. 1904. *The History of the Standard Oil Company*. New York: McClure, Phillips.

Taylor, Frederick Winslow. 1913. *Principles of Scientific Management*. New York: Harper.

Turner, Frederick Jackson. 1894. "The Significance of the Frontier in American History." *American Historical Review*.

Twain, Mark (Samuel Clemens) and Charles Dudley Warner. 1873. *The Gilded Age: A Tale of Today*. New York: American Publishing.

—. 1878. "Poor Little Stephen Girard," *Carleton's Popular Readings*. New York: G.W. Carleton.

Veblen, Thorstein. 1899. *The Theory of the Leisure Class*. New York: Macmillan.

Wells-Barnett, Ida B. 1892. "Southern Horrors: Lynch Law in All Its Phases." *The New York Age*.

—. 1895. "A Red Record: Tabulated Statistics and Alleged Causes of Lynchings in the United States." Chicago, IL: Donohue & Henneberry.

Wharton, Edith. 1920. *The Age of Innocence*. New York: D. Appleton.

Wilson, Woodrow. 1917. *Congressional Record*, 65th Congress, 1st Session.

Chapter Thirty-Three

Influential Works about the Gilded Age and Progressive Era

Robert D. Johnston

The scholarly literature on the Gilded Age and Progressive Era is exciting, vital, rich, complex, challenging, imaginative, and engaging. The works on the period therefore match the vitality of the era itself. The richness of the historiographical tradition of the Gilded Age and Progressive Era extends back more than a hundred years, to the contemporary histories written at the time—not surprising when one considers that the two premier progressive presidents, Theodore Roosevelt and Woodrow Wilson, were also presidents of the American Historical Association. And the most enduring works go back more than three-quarters of a century, continuing to inform an intellectual dialog that is one of the most significant among the community of American historians.

Historians battle over what to call the time period from, roughly, Reconstruction to World War I, but all generally agree that the age was intensely civic. The intensity of the era's public engagement is reflected well in the best scholarly writings, which speak eloquently both about the past, and to the present. Fortunately, the scholarly literature reveals much about American capitalism, radicalism, race, gender, empire, and democracy from these enduring volumes, whether written in 1934 or in the current decade.

The Politics of Synthesis

Frequently, a historian who attempts to bring together an entire era within a work of synthesis comes off writing the worst kind of textbook, cramming fact after fact into a work that pretends to be definitive—but, because there is always too much to "cover," never can be. The syntheses of the Gilded Age and Progressive Era, however, fortunately do not share this problem—and instead do share interpretive power and, often, sheer brilliance. Any consideration of the most influential works of the period must begin with these landmarks.

There remains one landmark among landmarks: Richard Hofstadter's Pulitzer Prize-winning *The Age of Reform: From Bryan to F.D.R.* (1955). Hofstadter, dean of the consensus, or "counter-Progressive" historians, carried a dyspepsia about democracy into his consideration of Populist and Progressive activists, whom he considered to be the defining feature the period. Writing in an age where Joe McCarthy seemed to Hofstadter's community of New York intellectuals like a harbinger of fascism, Hofstadter's purpose was to warn about the dark side of reform, and indeed popular politics as a whole.

An ever-urbane dweller in the ivory tower of Columbia University, Hofstadter placed the Populists at the origin story of modern reform. He recognized the hardships that inspired the late nineteenth-century agrarian movement, but even more he was impatient with the romanticism of left-leaning liberal historians, such as his friend C. Vann Woodward, toward the supposedly hardscrabble tillers of the soil. Populists posed as far-reaching democrats, attacking corporate power and seeking greater accountability from a corrupt government. But deep down, the most hardcore agrarian ultimately sought to be a successful capitalist. Such was the trap of America for all time, Hofstadter rued—all radicalism would ultimately be swallowed up in the maw of the market. But not before, at least in the case of the Populists, spinning out conspiracy theories: against British bankers and absentee landowners … and against Jews. The charge of Populist anti-Semitism was Hofstadter's most controversial, and the least well-sourced and contextualized. It was also his argument that was most subject to critical scrutiny in coming decades from scholars ranging from Woodward (1959) to Walter Nugent (1963) to Robert

A Companion to the Gilded Age and Progressive Era, First Edition. Edited by Christopher McKnight Nichols and Nancy C. Unger.
© 2017 John Wiley & Sons, Inc. Published 2017 by John Wiley & Sons, Inc.

Collins (1989). Still, the problem of pseudo-Populist demagoguery, Hofstadter correctly noted, was an issue that left-leaning historians had swept under the rug—and, unfortunately, they continue to do so (Johnston 2007). Such civic provocation reveals Hofstadter's sloppiness in engaging with complex evidence, but it also demonstrates why *The Age of Reform* continues to have such impressive intellectual power. Few books that old remain on graduate student exam lists, but the questions that Hofstadter raised truly matter.

Hofstadter was not that much kinder to the next reformers up in his docket, the Progressives. Once more, he was not completely out to get them. He understood that their motivations were, generally, to help the downtrodden, and that they produced a number of valuable reforms that used an expanded government to protect the weak and vulnerable. And they were better—more sophisticated, and more tolerant—than the Populists. That said, Hofstadter sought to take the common glow off the Progressives, seeing them not as noble saints uplifting the masses, but rather as middle or upper -middle-class agents of privilege anxious about their status at a time of massive immigration engulfing them from below and grasping Robber Barons threatening them from above. The Progressives' desire to anchor themselves in a rapidly changing society helped to explain their anti-democratic actions (curtailing voting rights), their flirtation with xenophobia (advocating immigration restriction), and their repressive streak (pushing for prohibition).

Hofstadter concluded *The Age of Reform* with a short reflection on the New Deal. Temperamentally and intellectually Hofstadter preferred the New Dealers' more restrained and more pragmatic take on politics. Still, he missed the moralism—even as dangerous as it could be—that the Populists and, especially, the Progressives brought to their civic mission. Ultimately, Hofstadter was using the reformers of the Gilded Age and Progressive Era as ciphers—as ways to grapple with some of the largest issues of the United States as a democratic, and anti-democratic, country. With elegant prose—and, to be sure, with inattention to archives—there is good reason why Alan Brinkley has characterized *The Age of Reform* as "the most influential book ever published on the history of twentieth-century America" (Brinkley 1998, 132).

For decades, the questions flowing from *The Age of Reform* have structured, either directly or indirectly, a huge part of the conversation about the era. Even as the multiplicity of subjects, and the babel of interpretations, have grown like Topsy, scholars keep returning to the enduring themes of democracy capitalism, exclusion and inclusion, and political morality.

By no means did Hofstadter command universal assent; indeed, if anything, his academic stock fell dramatically after his untimely death in 1970, extending through the 1990s (even if Advanced Placement students continued to read him). The first bold general counter-attack against the vision of *The Age of Reform* came in 1967, when Robert Wiebe published *The Search for Order*. Wiebe agreed with Hofstadter that the middle class was at the heart of the era's dramas, particularly Progressivism. Yet he turned Hofstadter on his head, arguing that a confident "new" middle class boldly embraced modern life and sought to shape society in its bureaucratic image. Indeed, Wiebe wrote an entirely different kind of history, one that largely displaced people and put economic and organizational imperatives at the center of the late nineteenth- and early twentieth-century story (see Galambos 1970). Increasingly vanishing like dinosaurs were Victorian "island communities" that, whether in the form of the rural village, the small town, or the urban neighborhood, were relatively isolated and even self-sufficient. Instead, in rushed (above all) corporations, government bureaucracies, labor unions, and civic associations—all with a national vision and a continent-wide set of capacities. Wiebe was, unlike Hofstadter, quite cagey about what this all meant in terms of American democracy (although in his later *Self-Rule* (1995) he was deeply pessimistic). In the end, for Wiebe and many of his fellow-creators of the "organizational synthesis" school of interpretation, impersonal forces were in control. What the People did did not really matter so much—and in this way, the book served as a fine companion to both the all-encompassing systemic nature of contemporary modernization theory and those thinkers and activists in the New Left who railed against the System.

As it turned out, *The Search for Order* represented at least a temporary watershed in thinking of Progressivism as a unified impulse and movement at the center of the era's social and political dramas. No big new work of synthesis would come out for twenty years, until Nell Painter's *Standing at Armageddon* (1987). In the meantime, as the country's cultural and political framework fractured, scholars turned to writing more careful, more complex, but also more cautious tales about specific Gilded Age communities or diverse kinds of progressive reform. Indeed, the most influential syntheses between *The Search for Order* and Painter's book were actually two exquisitely crafted articles that severely called into question any sense of unity to the period.

To be clear, neither Peter Filene nor Daniel Rodgers attempted to tackle the Gilded Age. Their target, though, was the historiographical core of the entire period from 1877 to 1920: "progressivism." For Filene, the assault on Hofstadter—which, among other matters, seemed to show that there were few demographic differences between Progressives and non-Progressives—pointed toward a daring conclusion. Progressive reform was a mirage, and Filene's 1970 obituary for the movement argued that responsible historians interested in the complexity of the era needed to move on from such a comforting myth. In contrast, Rodgers, writing a dozen years later in what would become the most influential historiographical essay ever written about the period, went "In Search of Progressivism" (1982). Perhaps in the age of Reagan not willing to give up the liberal hopes represented by the term, Rodgers took on Filene's challenge by noting that progressivism came in a variety of forms, which in fact often worked at cross-purposes. Rodgers focused on the languages of anti-monopoly, social bonds, and social efficiency. Rodgers's three categories did not in and of themselves deeply influence later scholarship, but on a larger level they pointed toward scholars' increasing willingness to consider multiple progressivisms without killing off progressivism. The plurality of reform officially came of age a quarter-century after Rodgers's intervention with Maureen Flanagan's textbook *American Reformed: Progressives and Progressivisms, 1890s–1920s* (2007).

The tempered renaissance of progressivism that Rodgers cautiously seemed to be both describing and nurturing took on a much more forceful expression in 1987 with Nell Painter's *Standing at Armageddon*. Painter did not say so directly, but it was difficult not to see her implicit invocation of Charles and Mary Beard's framework of the people versus the interests as a protest both against the first Gilded Age and the 1980s version of rule by Wall Street. Painter's neo-Progressivism pitted the forces of hierarchy and order against the forces of democracy and equity. Poverty, economic inequality, and class played central roles in *Standing at Armageddon*, but Painter went beyond that traditional emphasis in progressive historiography to also focus on the highly interrelated matters of race and empire. Still, the heroes were traditional: the Populists and Progressives who fought against the forces of repression, from the first Red Scare of 1877 to the much more devastating Red Scare of 1919–1920. A few years later, Alan Dawley would show how comfortable at least some Reagan-era Marxists had become in celebrating a similar popular front of working-class and middle-class liberals and radicals in his *Struggles for Justice: Social Responsibility and the Liberal State* (1987).

Building on Painter's and Dawley's complex celebration of the Progressives, Robert Johnston called, in a 2002 essay in the inaugural issue of the *Journal of the Gilded Age and Progressive Era*, for an explicit "Re-Democratizing the Progressive Era." Johnston recognized the repressive qualities of the period, and even of many of the period's celebrated reforms, but argued that the era's democratic ideals, activism, and even mainstream politics could serve as inspiring sources of civic hope. He pointed especially to the need to recognize the democratic potential of the middle class—a category, and constellation of people, that most historians continued to place, perhaps somewhat reflexively, at the center of progressivism. The following year Johnston's monograph on petit-bourgeois populism in Portland, Oregon, *The Radical Middle Class*, extended this new vision of the middle class by means of portraits of middling struggles for the single tax, direct democracy, medical freedom, and even rights for Native Americans, and against empire and American involvement in World War I. (For a more recent historiographical survey, see Johnston 2011.)

Not all scholars, however, followed Johnston's invocation to appreciate, if not come to love, the Progressive Era middle class. Michael McGerr's *A Fierce Discontent* (2003) represented an especially fierce return to the terrain of Hofstadter. Unlike Johnston's divided and complex middle class, McGerr's middle class was unified in its culture, politics, and even psychological impulses. Seeking to create a utopian society in its own image, the middle-class Progressives sought to run roughshod over both the capitalist elite and the working class. The result: anti-monopoly economics, for sure, but even more tellingly repressive Americanization efforts, prohibition, and even Jim Crow—the middle class's grand attempt to keep blacks and whites from killing each other. McGerr too wrote out of a strong sense that his tale would speak to the current day. Again like Hofstadter, suspicious of utopian politics of the type supposedly originated by the Progressives, McGerr blamed these reformers for many of the excesses of all of twentieth-century politics—and, in turn, the resultant allergy to politics shared by most Americans who had become so deeply disillusioned by utopianism behaving badly. This was a tale that greatly credited the power of the Progressives, but ultimately with the purpose of confirming the profoundly cynical view of transformative politics (or any politics) nurtured by the birth of the current-day totalizing American national security state.

Although it was difficult to discern the political tradition from which McGerr wrote, the same was not the case for the author of another cynical study of the middle-class Progressives. Shelton Stromquist, in *Re-inventing "The People": The Progressive Movement, the Class Movement, and the Origins of Modern Liberalism* (2006), argued out of a Marxism more orthodox than Alan Dawley's. Stromquist not only placed the reformers in the middle of the social spectrum but contended that their entire social vision flowed out of a desperate, and deluded, desire for class harmony in an age of increasingly violent class conflict. Stromquist's was the latest in a tradition of New Left-inspired books that saw most forms of liberalism as repressive, if not the Enemy.

Jackson Lears, a scholar in turn most deeply influenced by the cultural Marxism of Antonio Gramsci and Raymond Williams, presented a considerably more nuanced treatment of the entire period from 1877 to 1920 in his *Rebirth of a Nation* (2009). Letting his prose flow out of his despair at the debacles of Iraq and Guantánamo Bay, Lears crafted a meditation that was ultimately a *cri de coeur* against the American Empire. Lears saw the main trend in the period as not only depressing, but dangerous, as American elites forged an increasingly powerful, and undemocratic, managerial corporate behemoth at home at the same time that they fashioned a dominating American presence abroad. By

World War I, these elites began to think in terms of hierarchies of class, race, and nation that were eerily similar to fascism. Yet unlike many older New Leftists who used to see fascism everywhere they went, Lears provided hope as well as cynicism, cheerleadingly narrating the many democratic insurgencies of the period, ranging from the Populists to Wobblies and including even many mainstream Progressives. At this moment, Lears's book remains the most impressive recent synthesis of the period.

Lears's cautiously hopeful tale amid race and class conflict and imperialist depredation served as a quite relevant work at the dawn of the age of Obama. Similar leftist political good cheer animated the two most important current textbooks on the period. Both highly interpretive, and thus both scholarly interventions as well as surveys for students, these books effectively put into play both hierarchy and dissent. Rebecca Edwards's *New Spirits*, first published in 2006, placed the many democratic social movements—ranging from labor to sexuality—at the center of her exploration of the supposedly repressive Gilded Age. Even more daringly, Edwards used her book to show what it would mean to abandon the very term "Gilded Age," a censorious label that she actually put in quotation marks in the title of her second edition in 2011. Better to think of the entire period from 1865 to 1917, and perhaps on up to the New Deal, as a "long Progressive Era" in which the continuity of reform movements mattered more than an arbitrary division between Robber Barons and reformers, Populists and Progressives (see also Edwards 2009). In turn Walter Nugent, deeply influenced by Elizabeth Sanders's *Roots of Reform* (1998), also robustly invoked the powerful connections between nineteenth-century agrarian rebels and early twentieth-century urban reformers in his *Progressivism: A Very Short Introduction* (2010). Nugent simultaneously celebrated those Populists who forged populist Progressivism and the arch anti-Populist Theodore Roosevelt, who came to do so much to forge an activist, social democratic state that served as the foundation for modern liberalism.

The Political Economy of the Gilded Age Progressive Era

Much of the power of every single one of these influential syntheses comes from a genuine intellectual and political grappling with the origin, in this period, of modern American capitalism. In turn, the synthetic works have built on a rich literature on the birth of the corporate economy, beginning with Matthew Josephson's 1934 muckraking attack on *The Robber Barons*.

As befits the left-leaning politics of the historical profession, a good portion of this scholarship is critical of capitalism—often deeply so. Gabriel Kolko's *The Triumph of Conservatism* pioneered this tradition in 1963 with his early New Left-inspired reversal of political labels. Kolko presented as trivial the supposed differences in the policies and visions of political economy of Theodore Roosevelt, William Howard Taft, and Woodrow Wilson. All such reforms, from trust busting to banking regulation, ultimately served to rationalize corporate capitalism against a surprisingly powerful and economically viable competitive small-enterprise market economy. Such "liberalism" was, therefore, in the end deeply conservative—and provided the legacy for the deeply anti-democratic "corporate liberalism" that ruled the American political economy throughout the twentieth century. In 1968, James Weinstein, a scholar but also an activist/journalist, extended this portrait of an iron cage when, in *The Corporate Ideal in the Liberal State*, he sought to show that even the supposedly most radical political movements of the period, especially the Socialists (themselves quite enamored of large-scale enterprise), were, at best, ineffective at fighting the corporate beast or, at worst, guilty of colluding in its rise to power.

Martin Sklar coined the term "corporate liberalism" and did more than anyone to spread its usage among both scholars and New Left activists. First writing in 1960, he severely indicted the motivations and the consequences of early twentieth-century liberals. The politics of liberalism could be complex, but the result was simple: liberals above all served corporations and empire. Over the decades that Sklar worked out his theories, however, his corporate liberalism became much more differentiated, contested, and even worthy of democratic consideration. In his 1988 masterwork *The Corporate Reconstruction of American Capitalism, 1890–1916*, he uncovered significant differences between Roosevelt, Taft, and Wilson. Sklar even admiringly upheld what he contended to be their socialist impulses as these presidents and their advisors sought to socialize an economy that Populists and other petit-bourgeois nuisances, often supported by the Supreme Court, sought to keep hyper-individualist and cut-throat competitive.

Sklar tended to tie himself into knots trying to bring all of the politics and economics that he surveyed under one interpretive roof. His efforts to constantly reconsider, and make more multi-faceted, his foundational argument was, however, commendable—especially when other works, such as Richard White's snarky *Railroaded: The Transcontinentals and the Making of Modern America* (2011), more simplistically followed in the Josephson tradition of condemnation over analytical complexity.

By no means, though, did all considerations of the birth of corporate capitalism proceed from a critical stance. An entire other vein of scholarship originated not in New Left collectives but rather in the Harvard Business School. The masterwork of this tradition remains Alfred Chandler's *The Visible Hand: The Managerial Revolution in American Business* (1977). As Chandler's title indicated, the rise of reorganization of American enterprise in the post-Civil War period created a distinctively post-Smithian economics. Managerial control became separated from ownership, and revolutions in transportation, communication, marketing, and mass production led to the creation of the kinds of integrated firms that inspired American dominance in the global economy. Indeed, managerial capitalism turned out to be one of the most profound of American inventions. Chandler was not completely comfortable with this form of capitalism—Richard John (1997) even places him within the camp of "Progressive" historians. Yet most scholars view *The Visible Hand*, which does not substantively take into account either inequality or poverty, as, at the least, a quiet celebration as well as a sprawling explanation of the new corporate economy.

One weakness in both the New Left and the Chandlerian traditions was an almost complete failure to consider workers, despite the dramatic rise of the subfield of labor history during the period in which they were writing (or, perhaps because of the even more dramatic fall of the labor movement itself during the same time period). David Montgomery's *The Fall of the House of Labor* (1987) provided the most important rebuke to this tendency. Montgomery did not, however, just pour iron puddlers and Wobblies into the standard narrative of capitalism and stir. His fundamental argument was that capitalists, and the politicians who were their representatives, were forced at every turn to grapple with both workers on the shop floor pushing their prerogatives and the many different movements—ranging from the American Federation of Labor to the new Communist parties—that represented a genuine threat to the dreams of corporate capital. Taylorism turned out differently because of what workers did on the shop floor. Social welfare turned out differently because of what workers did in the political sphere. Such seemingly simple insights were necessary because so many historians were intent on ignoring the proletariat. Yet Montgomery's analysis was complex, as was his morality tale: although workers won plenty of battles between 1865 to 1925, it was, as promised in the title, ultimately the *fall* of labor in the 1920s that Montgomery sought most to illuminate.

Radicals and Rebels, Peasants and Populists

Montgomery's tales of labor activists took root from a long tradition of studies of the Gilded Age and Progressive Era's rebels, radicals, revolutionaries, and, of course, more ordinary reformers. Arguably the richest literature on such dissidents relates to the Populists. Indeed, well before *The Age of Reform* came forth one of the masterpieces of all historical scholarship: C. Vann Woodward's *Tom Watson: Agrarian Rebel* (1938). Woodward had dabbled with Communism during the 1930s (as had Hofstadter), but eventually spurned Moscow and settled into the more native American radicalism of Populism (before, later, turning close to neoconservatism). *Tom Watson* was not Woodward's most influential book—that would be the book that became the so-called secular Bible of the Civil Rights movement (and that was also fundamentally about the late nineteenth century): *The Strange Career of Jim Crow* (1955). Yet this biography was not only his most sustained monograph; it was also Woodward's most lyrical narrative.

Woodward set himself a significant challenge in coming to grips with this son of the Confederacy. Watson shared many of the racial views of the white planter class, and far from all of his attacks on northern capital and bankers came from altruistic or democratic motivations. Yet for Woodward, Watson became the shining knight of democratic, radical Populism, eventually coming to fight genuinely, and courageously, for the mudsills versus the economic elites of both South and North. Most bravely—indeed, at the risk of his life—Watson defended black Populists and articulated an interracial vision of black–white cooperation at a time when such actions were almost unthinkable among whites. But then … Watson, tortured by the violence and corruption that accompanied the defeat of the People's Party, turned viciously away from these noble ideals, becoming one of the most powerful national voices for anti-black, anti-Catholic, and anti-Jewish bigotry—as Leo Frank would find when Watson poured out his hatred against the Atlanta Jewish factory owner. Woodward found it possible to both admire populism and illuminate its darker currents—just one reason why Lawrence Goodwyn would four decades later remark that the "magnificent biography of the tortured life of Tom Watson is one of the enduring triumphs of American historical literature and, indeed, of American letters" (1978, 342).

Goodwyn actually sang this praise in what itself would become the next great book on Populism after Hofstadter. His massive *Democratic Promise* from 1976 (abridged in 1978 in the even more influential *The Populist Moment*) was both a full-throated hymn to the best in Populism and a full-throated cry of betrayal for those forces—many internal to the world of agrarian reform—that brought Populism down. Goodwyn took his own activist days into the archives, focusing on the movement's process of organizing and collective democratic education and mobilization. Camp meetings were critical to this democracy pedagogy, but even more important were the economic cooperatives that came to blossom under the aegis of the Farmers' Alliance, particularly in Texas. C.W. Macune's theory of a sub-treasury to level the economic playing field provided the national strategy necessary to truly empower small and middling farmers. Yet a "shadow movement" centered in the Midwest then came into rob the democratic vitality from the agrarian rebellion. Politicians who cared more for their own interests than those of the People stole the Populists' thunder, leading in the end to a disastrous fusion with the Democratic Party. And that was the end of democracy in America, for ever since 1896 the country has been locked in the grip of a corporate oligarchy undergirded by a two-party system responsive only to elites.

Just as *The Age of Reform* inspired a host of critics, so did Goodwyn, with various historians characterizing his work as a simplistic, politicized morality tale. Yet no scholar would produce a work of Goodwyn's power and scholarly (if not political) influence until Charles Postel's *The Populist Vision* (2007). Postel sympathized with the Populists, but he was not an overt partisan in the mode of Goodwyn. Instead, he especially wished to move beyond the standard myth of the Populists as a purely agrarian movement. Postel's Populists were from California as well as Georgia, and they were freethinkers as well as traditionalist evangelical Protestants. Most crucially, these Populists were not just small farmers resisting the big changes happening in the American economy. Rather, Populists embraced bigness and centralization in the name of a democratic (not a corporate) modernity. To Postel, these Populists represented a viable alternative path not taken, one that might have, if it had not met political defeat, blossomed into an American version of Scandinavian social democracy.

Postel's remaking, and in certain ways rehabilitation, of the Populists for the current moment of cosmopolitan globalization did not break new chronological ground, but it dramatically contributed to rebuking the idea that the Populists—however noble and virtuous they may have been—simply were too angelic for the new world of the twentieth century. *The Populist Vision* in that way served as companion to political scientist Elizabeth Sanders's *Roots of Reform* (1998). In form a very different book from Postel's (Sanders leaned toward systematic quantification of voting records, while Postel was more likely to qualitatively explore the ideology embedded in newspapers), *Roots of Reform* showed that the Populists actually bequeathed not defeat, but rather success, to the politics of reform. Indeed, the core of what scholars have long considered urban middle-class Progressivism was, according to Sanders, in fact agrarian. Agrarian theorists envisioned all the classic Progressive reforms in political economy——in banking, transportation, antitrust, and land-grant education—that were then passed by a Congress dominated by Democratic representatives from the Populist/Progressive agrarian periphery. With labor unions politically weak, and middle-class intellectuals vastly overrated in terms of their actual power to influence politics, the United States would in fact not have birthed an activist state in the early twentieth century without the continuing power of farmers and their political allies. That said, the expanded activist state advocated by agrarians was not at all the same entity as the modern regulatory state with its unelected bureaucracies having extensive discretionary power; populist Progressives wanted to hem in the new state with transparent democratic safeguards at every turn.

Unfortunately, Sanders unnecessarily dismissed other brands of reform as either politically inert or insufficiently Progressive. Fortunately, other scholars have imaginatively revealed the power and democratic promise of more bourgeois forms of radicalism. Aaron Sachs, for example, asks us as both scholars and inhabitants of the natural world to explore the tradition of a "middle landscape" between city and wilderness, an *Arcadian America* where citizens formed, and actively used as part of their daily lives, cemeteries and parks to create a truly communal—and beautiful—republic. Landscape architects such as Frederick Law Olmsted feature prominently in Sachs's moving blend of historical narrative and memoir, but so too do political radicals such as Ignatius Donnelly and Henry George, who simultaneously developed an environmental ethic of modest cultivation and land stewardship that rivaled the creation of national parks as one of the period's distinctive democratic achievements. And in a study also quite sensitive to the psychology of her subject, Nancy C. Unger admiringly, but not uncritically, illuminates the staunchly democratic convictions and policies of one of the most powerful mainstream bourgeois radicals ever to come out of the Midwest, in *Fighting Bob La Follette* (2000).

The most influential study of an American radical of this period, however (with the possible exception of *Tom Watson*) is of a decidedly non-bourgeois activist, Eugene Victor Debs. Nick Salvatore's Bancroft Prize-winning portrait of Debs is a loving, but also lovingly critical, exploration of both the tender psyche and the public charisma of the most important socialist in American history. Proudly arising from a petit-bourgeois milieu in Terre Haute, Indiana, Debs never gave up on the promise of America. Such an embrace of patriotic republicanism was, according to Salvatore, the source of Debs's intense connection to so much of the American public. Yet that same American culture that Debs celebrated—while of course fighting with all his might against those who held an iron grip over its economy and politics—also severely circumscribed the potential success of socialism. Weighing in gently on a long debate about the failure of socialism in the United States, Salvatore emphasized the entrenched cultural power of an individualism that would forever render collectivist economics too far out of the boundaries of acceptability. Romantic celebration of such leftist dissent was appropriate—but only as long as said celebrant then took a long cold shower in the waters of political realism.

The Rise of Segregation and the Fall of Segregated Histories

Some scholars view biographies such as those of Watson, La Follette, or Debs as hardly "history," because they supposedly leave out far too much of the context that is necessary to explain the evolution of a society. Not only do Woodward, Unger, and Salvatore prove that conceit wrong, writing powerfully about larger social forces, but so too do some of the other great biographies of the Gilded Age and Progressive Era. In particular, Louis Harlan's two-volume study of Booker T. Washington (1972 and 1983) has long been a landmark in the study of black life and thought (although Robert Norrell's 2011 biography decisively challenges Harlan's dismissive attitude toward Washington). And David Levering Lewis explored the larger political culture, and with even more literary flair and psychological insight, in his two volumes on W.E.B. Du Bois (1993 and 2000).

These works have often been placed in a sort of intellectual ghetto, with "the Gilded Age" and "Progressive Era" occurring in textbook chapters separate from "the rise of Jim Crow." Increasingly, however, such segregation has begun to weaken as the study of race and ethnicity has become central to the understanding of the period. Once again, the pioneer in this attempt to bring, especially, African American history into the mainstream was C. Vann Woodward. In 1951, he produced *The Origins of the New South*, a sweeping and magisterial synthesis that, while primarily focusing on white actors, demonstrated that the major transformation in the post-Reconstruction South was the construction of a rock-solid regime of white supremacy. Populists revolted against both the rule of eastern capitalism and the dominance of the Democratic Party. Southern white elites, however, were more than happy to cooperate with the new regime of corporate industrialism while smashing their mixed-race agrarian opposition. Even the most enlightened strain of "new" southern thinking, Progressivism, was "for whites only." Forty years later, Woodward's student Edward Ayers produced his own creative and sweeping account of the same period and region, pointing toward more complexity and democratic cultural openness in *The Promise of the New South* (1992), but Woodward's account remains authoritative for the South in much the same way as Hofstadter's is for the period as a whole.

Ayers and (especially) Woodward—despite their commitment to racial equality—did not place African Americans at the center of southern politics. However, with the maturing of what one might call post-Civil Rights historiography—or perhaps, better, "Long Civil Rights"-oriented historians—blacks became not just integrated into the southern narrative but fundamental to the retelling of the both South and nation in the late nineteenth and early twentieth centuries. Arguably the most fundamental challenge came from Glenda Gilmore, who would go on to hold the Peter V. and C. Vann Woodward Chair of History at Yale. Gilmore's *Gender and Jim Crow: Women and the Politics of White Supremacy in North Carolina, 1896–1920* (1996) told a dazzling set of stories of black women who forged a vital underground politics centering on education, public health, parks, and civic respect but that ultimately built up to formal challenges to segregation and to exclusion from the ballot box. By exploring African American politics from the ground up, Gilmore reflected not some romantic sense of the agency of the oppressed, but the necessity of rewriting the entire story line of southern politics away from mere tragic racial oppression. Terrorism and haunting defeats mark plenty of *Gender and Jim Crow*, but so does a hopeful sense that black North Carolinians—especially women—were able to construct a new kind of Progressivism that ultimately would serve as one of the many streams that would eventually coalesce into the formal civil rights movement of the 1950s and 1960s.

Gilmore's political activists operated with great courage, but also pragmatism, within a relatively fluid North Carolina political system, and they had some hope for interracialism as well as pride in black accomplishments. The African American political actors in Steven Hahn's Pulitzer Prize-winning *A Nation under Our Feet: Black Political Struggles in the Rural South from Slavery to the Great Migration* (2003), however, labored much more outside the formal mechanisms of the American political system, highly wary of the gifts that supposedly egalitarian Populists and Republicans claimed to bring. Instead, black politics for Hahn's protagonists would not culminate in the mainstream civil rights movement, but rather in the separatism and black nationalism of Marcus Garvey. Forged in the fierce struggle for familial communalism under slavery, black politics was, in many ways, a kind of peasant politics, focusing on demands of land and freedom in a manner akin to rural currents throughout the globe rather than forged in an exceptionalist promise of American life.

For much of the twentieth century, the history of race in America continued to have as its central location the South and its fundamental conflict as black and white. Yet with the flowering of multiculturalism, and the powerful intellectual and political challenges to the black–white binary in the final decades of the millennium, a much broader sense of race came to the fore in historical studies as well as throughout the culture.

A major renaissance in explorations of race in American history came especially from the contested, but increasingly accepted, assertion that ethnicity and race are and always have been comparable companion political and cultural constructs of hierarchy and power, exclusion and division. The landmark study of ethnicity in this period did not make that precise claim but would nevertheless come to cast a long shadow over future scholarship that did find inspiration in the race/ethnicity confluence. John Higham's 1955 *Strangers in the Land* focused on, in the words of the subtitle, patterns of American nativism from 1860 to 1925. The choice of the end period indicated where the rivers of nativism ultimately flowed together: toward a strain of virulent anti-immigrant sentiment that concluded with the acts of legal exclusion that served as the central feature of American immigration policy throughout the middle decades of the twentieth century. Emphasizing the deep hostility toward immigrants in American culture, Higham's work—as did that twin tower of 1955, *The Age of Reform*—had as its backdrop the angry irrationality of McCarthyism. Yet Higham also offered some glimmers of hope, some way out of systematic hatred, as he pointed as well toward a vision of cosmopolitan universalism gaining intellectual strength concomitantly with the political strength of nativism.

Although plenty of scholarship in recent decades has provided evidence of a better life for many American immigrant groups in the land of the golden door, the primary strain of scholarship in ethnic studies has continued to emphasize the exclusionary patterns in American culture. Most prominently, a whole school of interdisciplinary "whiteness" studies spoke to how a variety of different groups, from Hebrews to Balts, moved from being their own separate races to becoming ethnic variations of a hegemonic white race. For the Gilded Age and Progressive Era, Matthew Jacobson's *Barbarian Virtues: The United States Encounters Foreign Peoples at Home and Abroad, 1876–1917* (2000) was arguably the most influential synthetic statement of this school while also decisively connecting the country's internal politics of ethnicity to the nation's imperial expansion abroad. The most elegant and innovative study in this realm, though, was Linda Gordon's *The Great Arizona Orphan Abduction* (1999). Gordon told the story of Irish Catholic orphans from New York City sent to Arizona for adoption by Mexican families—only to be forcefully taken from their new families by supposedly more civilized Anglos, with women taking the lead role in this kidnapping—in alternating chapters, with an analysis of such themes as copper mining interwoven with an exploration of the lives of the actors on the ground. Gordon represented a kind of narrative increasingly popular in academe: storytelling that could appeal to the public and that did not always have a direct argumentative/historiographical bent. Yet, again, Gordon's message was clear: white supremacy was in the saddle in the early twentieth century, and hardly just in Georgia. Indeed, the Arizona abduction ultimately received the sanctification of the US Supreme Court.

Cultural matters (inseparable from the political, but still autonomous) came to the fore in this recent literature. Perhaps the most influential book within this cultural turn in the history of race and ethnicity has been Gail Bederman's *Manliness and Civilization: A Cultural History of Gender and Race in the United States, 1880–1917* (1995). A series of case studies of such figures as Jack Johnson, Ida B. Wells, G. Stanley Hall, Charlotte Perkins Gilman, Theodore Roosevelt, and ultimately Edgar Rice Burroughs, Bederman argued that both white women (such as Gilman) and elite men constructed a hegemonic culture of white supremacy through highly gendered discourses of civilization. The increasing power of white supremacist ideology depended on a reconstruction of the archetype of a civilized white man leading the United States at a moment when the darker races represented a global threat. Yet at the same time that Bederman showcased an approach that emphasized culture, her circling back to figures such as Roosevelt demonstrated that the new cultural history had its sights set on re-envisioning all of the period's most powerful figures and ideas.

Feminism: Contemporary and Historiographic

Bederman's book, which received a multitude of plaudits both inside and outside the historical discipline, represented the maturation of studies not just of race, but also of women and gender. Indeed, *Manliness and Civilization* was an argument for the tight connection—the intersectionality—of race and gender, class and gender, and empire and gender. Indeed, women's history would itself ultimately move away from a focus on women's politics to explorations of changing cultural systems of gender—becoming, ultimately, an entirely new field where discourses about men and manhood became just as much the subject as did "women." (For an insightful reflection on these historiographical trends, see Wickberg 2005.)

Yet scholars often do not recognize that historians' connections between women's politics and the construction of a white supremacist racial order go back decades. In this case, the foundational text is Aileen Kraditor's *The Ideas of the Woman Suffrage Movement* (1965). Kraditor, at the time a self-professed radical New Left historian (she would relatively soon turn decisively to the right side of the political spectrum), believed that the Woman suffrage movement dramatically changed from 1890 to 1920 from a politics of justice and equal rights to one of "expediency." Under this new philosophical regime, white women (particularly but not exclusively in the South) could fight for their rights by arguing not that they were equal citizens guaranteed the rights of all Americans, but instead, pragmatically, that they were better cultured and more civilized than black women—and that they would vote more frequently. Kraditor thus offered a bitter critique of bourgeois radicalism, and her arguments would for decades continue to structure much of the debate about Woman suffrage—even if most scholars came to doubt the binary that Kraditor had constructed (see Newman 2015).

The study of formal mainstream political history—dealing with such matters as the presidency and parties—went into relative decline in the years after Kraditor published her book. Yet scholars in women's history both followed and departed from Kraditor in creating a vital subfield of women's political history. The key work marking the inauguration of this area was Paula Baker's 1984 essay "The Domestication of Politics." Baker, who published this pathbreaking article as a graduate student, extended the insights of historians of nineteenth-century women's moral mission in American culture. She argued that such movements as temperance, which was both inspired by and reinforced separate gendered spheres during the Victorian era, increasingly moved into the mainstream as some women gained suffrage and anti-corruption crusades feminized the rough-and-tumble of partisan politics. Increasingly, citizens of both sexes came to value women's politics as more moral, and better, than that of men's, as the public household needed to be cared for. Ironically, at the same time, this rise of women to political power was undercut by the generalized movement of politics away from partisan electoral competition and toward specialized administrative expertise isolated from any part of the electorate.

The polymath social scientist Theda Skocpol put forth the most sustained and wide-ranging exploration of Baker's gendered political culture in her *Protecting Soldiers and Mothers: The Political Origins of Social Policy in the United States* (1992). Skocpol's ambitions were huge: she wished to do no less than revise the origins and status of the American welfare state. Arguing against the common idea that the United States lagged behind—and indeed would and perhaps could never catch up with—European social democracies, Skocpol contended that the United States actually constructed the first mass welfare state—and that women had been key to building the institutions of the welfare state. Well in advance of European mass welfare provisioning, the United States provided pensions for Union veterans of the Civil War. And based on that precedent, women, even though they generally did not yet have the vote, were able to argue through the nineteenth century and especially into the Progressive Era for a "maternalist welfare state" that would protect women and children. Such a welfare state was far from universalist, but so were European models that upheld the ideal of the manly breadwinner. Americans had a different—not a lesser—welfare state. And that meant that the nation's citizens might once again build an innovative, and more inclusive, set of communal institutions.

Important studies such as Kathryn Kish Sklar's biography of Florence Kelley (1995) effectively supplemented the broad vision of Skocpol. At the same time, scholars began to think outside of the formal realm of politics, also placing women's activism in a wider cultural context. The landmark for such studies was Nancy Cott's *The Grounding of Modern Feminism* (1987). Cott compellingly contended that "feminism," as both word and concept, was born in the early twentieth century as radical women sought to seek modes of empowerment that transcended both suffrage and a supposedly more moral female culture. They embraced the heterodox modernism of the early years of the century, and figures such as Crystal Eastman replaced Elizabeth Cady Stanton as the pioneers of a fully egalitarian feminist vision. At the same time, feminism actually frequently gained strength from one of its inherent and unsolvable tensions—a creative discussion about whether or not equality or difference was the most effective and ethical strategy for women's empowerment (although, ultimately, this tension inspired a difficult and often destructive conflict within the feminist movement over the Equal Rights Amendment). Cott's message to the present was clear: feminists should not be seeking to win the argument between equality and difference, but rather generously and resourcefully seeking to play out the best implications of both sets of ideas.

The Grounding of Modern Feminism—and even more, Christine Stansell's eloquent companion study of Eastman and her comrades within the culture of bohemian Greenwich Village, *American Moderns* (2000) eloquently explored issues of sexuality as well as suffrage. The personal became the political within historical scholarship, in the process inspiring an even more far-reaching set of studies of gendered politics outside of formal political institutions. The foremost study in this genre was *Gay New York: Gender, Urban Culture, and the Making of the Gay Male World, 1890–1940* by Cott's Ph.D. advisee George Chauncey. *Gay New York* engrossingly revealed the historical contingencies of sexual experience that were lived far outside of the binary categories of sexuality that proved hegemonic at the time that Chauncey wrote in 1994. His study of fairies and wolves, the Young Men's Christian Association (YMCA) and bathhouses, class differences and police repression, demonstrated that gender differences absolutely could no longer be just about women, as has largely been the case in previous feminist historiography—but about all kinds of men as well. (At the same time, Chauncey's work pointed toward the even more radical destabilization of gender within both the historical profession and the broader culture).

American Imperial Visions

Gender would become a major theme in the new history of American foreign relations—although some old schoolers accepted such ideas only grudgingly. Scholars began to produce powerful first books such as Kristin Hoganson's transparently titled *Fighting for American Manhood: How Gender Provoked the Spanish-American and Philippine-American Wars* (1998). Such work was highly critical of American empire—a tradition that dated back to the most influential work in the field, William Appleman Williams's *The Tragedy of American Diplomacy* (1959). Williams cared not a whit for gender, but like scholars decades later, he saw the fate of American democracy intimately enmeshed with the country's imperial dreams and practices. For Williams, a proud small-town Midwestern radical who had been blacklisted early in his career, American empire was foundationally homegrown, seeded not only in Thomas Jefferson's continental dreams of expansion but in ordinary farmers' desire for a market for their exports. Indeed, for Williams and his influential students such as Walter LaFeber (whose own highly influential 1963 *The New Empire* followed quickly upon *Tragedy*), empire was as much about Open Door economics as about military might and visions of conquest. At its heart, though, for Williams—a stern moralist as well as ambivalent Marxist—empire was an infection of the heart and soul, a corruption of the democratic instincts in American culture.

Williams's highly argumentative—and not always well-sourced—contentions placed him within a set of controversies throughout the subfield of diplomatic history, particularly revolving around the Cold War. Plenty of more liberal, and in various ways more complex, books shined a more generous light on American motivations as well as the consequences of American intervention. One example would be David Kennedy's *Over Here: The First World War and American Society* (1980). Kennedy, an ambivalent liberal, did not approve of the increasing corporatization and repression of dissent in the United States as the result of the war, but he did credit Woodrow Wilson and his intellectual followers with some genuine contributions to a liberal internationalism—even if Wilson himself betrayed much of the promise of that liberalism. Erez Manela's very different *The Wilsonian Moment* (2007) in many ways contains much the same moral, as he reveals the powerful ways that Wilsonian visions of self-determination animated nationalists from Egypt to China to Vietnam—even if Wilson and the United States could not see, much less support, the revolutionary visions that they helped unleash.

As with so much that involves the left-wing tilt of the American historical profession, though, ambivalent liberalism has its occasional moment, but radical critique still maintains hegemony. Within the Williams mode, Emily Rosenberg's *Spreading the American Dream* (1982) explored the ideological and cultural spread of American ideals of capitalism as a fundamental means by which Americans sought to justify empire both abroad and at home. The more common recent critique has not ignored capitalism but has focused much more on racial dominance as the foundation for imperial ideology and its often nakedly brutal practice. Mary Renda's *Taking Haiti* (2001) and Paul Kramer's *The Blood of Government: Race, Empire, the United States, and the Philippines* (2006) both provided powerful and often wrenching case studies of supposedly benevolent racial uplift gone wrong, ultimately providing all-too-real justifications not just for dispossession but torture and genocide.

The Williams tradition fruitfully insisted on tight connections between domestic and imperial politics and practices, and Renda's and Kramer's books also insightfully connect those two realms. However, they share with Williams a tendency to paint the United States in one shade when, in fact, the politics of the period flowered in multicolored hues. One book that effectively brings together the complexity of the domestic civic realm with genuine conflicts over American foreign relations is Christopher McKnight Nichols's *Promise and Peril* (2011). Above all a recovery and redemption of isolationism within American thought, Nichols reveals how politicians ideologically ranging from the conservative Henry Cabot Lodge to the socialist Eugene Debs, from the rugged individualist/libertarian western William Borah to the genteel pacifist Emily Balch, articulated a vision of non-interventionism that powerfully constrained the overreach of early twentieth-century empire (and arguably even beyond). *Promise and Peril* therefore brightly illuminates the complex nature of American democracy during this key moment of American modernization.

Restoring Democracy to a Democratic Age

Strains of monolithic thinking exist in all the subfields surveyed in this chapter, often presenting powerful arguments about the subversion and betrayal of democracy during the Gilded Age and Progressive Era. Leftist critiques in particular have frequently been more jeremiad than supple analysis. They therefore often leave readers without hope, as the destruction of democracy a century ago becomes a reason why Americans cannot discover the inspiration to work on rebuilding genuine rule by the people today (see Johnston 2002).

The major syntheses of the period, from Hofstadter to Lears, are all powerful intellectually in direct relationship to how boldly they speak to the nature of American democracy. Indeed, the progress of Lears's intellectual temperament is in many ways discernible in his move from thundering sermonizing in his beautiful first book, *No Place of Grace* (1981), to the thoughtful complexity amid condemnation in *Rebirth of a Nation* (2009).

Beyond these syntheses, the best political history has of course always served as a reflection on the strengths and weaknesses of the country's democratic traditions. The scholarship on the Gilded Age and Progressive Era has produced, for example, excellent work in presidential biography, from John Blum's *The Republican Roosevelt* and Arthur Link's *Woodrow Wilson and the Progressive Era* (the twin towers of 1954) to John Milton Cooper's 1983 dual biography of those two titans, *The Warrior and The Priest*. Each of these authors wrote from the perspective of a chastened but affirming liberalism that saw Roosevelt and Wilson as admittedly imperfect, but still often heroic, avatars of a generous twentieth-century pluralism and social democracy.

Perhaps ironically, the subfield that is often justifiably viewed as the most elitist may well provide the firmest grounds for thinking about the Gilded Age and (especially) the Progressive Era as some of the most fertile moments for democracy in American history. A series of sparkling books within intellectual history, even if they have very different emphases, provided between 1986 and 1998 an inspiring sense of the possibilities of progressive politics—inspiration that may even continue to animate the current American search for a more perfect democracy.

James Kloppenberg's *Uncertain Victory* (1986), for instance, reveals how Progressives such as Herbert Croly,

Walter Lippman, John Dewey, and William James sought to create a middle way—a robustly liberal and genuinely democratic third path—between radicalism and reaction in a way quite similar to social democratic intellectuals in contemporary Europe. Robert Westbrook, in *John Dewey and American Democracy* (1991), actually lifts Dewey out from that group and places him on the left wing of progressivism, arguing that the famous philosopher and educator actually had a distinctive and deep commitment to the thorough democratic renewal of almost all American institutions. Daniel Rodgers, in *Atlantic Crossings* (1998), follows Kloppenberg in pointing toward the transatlantic orientation of progressive intellectuals as the source of democratic innovation in fields ranging from economics to urban planning. And most grandly, Christopher Lasch passionately preached in *The True and Only Heaven* (1991) on behalf of the centuries-long American tradition that combined theological humility, a cultural and environmental sense of limits, an insistence on civic equality, and demands for petit-bourgeois economic leveling. No era witnessed the flowering of this populist democracy more than the age of the Populists in the late nineteenth century and the syndicalists of the early twentieth.

All four books in the previous paragraph deserve their own paragraph—even their own articles—given their eloquence, intellectual power, and their enduring influence. Yet, in the spirit of Laschian limits, one must stop somewhere. A brief nod to the future, however, might well be in order. Given the recent compelling critiques relating to the conceptualization and periodization of "Gilded Age" and "Progressive Era," it is intriguing to speculate about whether or not the most influential works about the period from 1870 to 1920 from the vantage point of, say, 2047 will care much about those terms. Already, some of the best work in the field comes from scholars who would not first think of joining the Society for the Historians of the Gilded Age and Progressive Era but instead have other primary subdisciplinary commitments. It also seems likely that previously marginalized subfields such as the histories of sexuality and disability will produce a good number of the boldest books of the future. At the same time, the mainstream political issues that the era originally raised show no signs of moving to the margins of civic concern. As long as Americans continue to struggle with each other over corporate capitalism, economic inequality, racial hierarchy, and empire, they will surely return to exploring these fundamental themes in what in many ways was their founding period. (One likely new strain to this future intellectual debate, however, will come from conservative perspectives, previously drowned out in the overwhelmingly left-liberal milieu of scholarly historical writing—see Johnston 2014.)

What, then, ultimately is the moral of this historiographical story? To put it simply: the literature on the Gilded Age and Progressive Era has been and remains a true treasure, at its best open not just to fellow historians but to students and citizens of all stripes. This scholarship reflects—indeed, is a noble part of—America's democratic heritage.

References

Ayers, Edward L. 1992. *The Promise of the New South: Life after Reconstruction*. New York: Oxford University Press.

Baker, Paula. 1984. "The Domestication of Politics: Women and American Political Society, 1780–1920." *American Historical Review* 89: 620–647.

Bederman, Gail. 1995. *Manliness and Civilization: A Cultural History of Gender and Race in the United States, 1880–1917*. Chicago, IL: University of Chicago Press.

Blum, John. 1954. *The Republican Roosevelt*. Cambridge, MA: Harvard University Press.

Brinkley, Alan. 1998. "Hofstadter's *The Age of Reform* Reconsidered," in Brinkley, *Liberalism and its Discontents*. Cambridge, MA: Harvard University Press.

Chandler, Alfred D., Jr. 1977. *The Visible Hand: The Managerial Revolution in American Business*. Cambridge, MA: Harvard University Press.

Chauncey, George. 1994. *Gay New York: Gender, Urban Culture, and the Making of the Gay Male World, 1890–1940*. New York: Basic Books.

Collins, Robert M. 1989. "The Originality Trap: Richard Hofstadter on Populism." *Journal of American History* 76: 150–167.

Cooper, John Milton, Jr. 1983. *The Warrior and the Priest: Woodrow Wilson and Theodore Roosevelt*. Cambridge, MA: Harvard University Press.

Cott, Nancy. 1987. *The Grounding of Modern Feminism*. New Haven, CT: Yale University Press.

Dawley, Alan. 1987. *Struggles for Justice: Social Responsibility and the Liberal State*. Cambridge, MA: Harvard University Press.

Edwards, Rebecca. 2009. (2006) "Politics, Social Movements, and the Periodization of U.S. History." *Journal of the Gilded Age and Progressive Era* 8: 461–473. doi: http://dx.doi.org/ 10.1017/S1537781400001432/accessed July 18, 2016.

—. 2011. *New Spirits: America in the "Gilded Age," 1865–1905*. 2nd edn. New York: Oxford University Press.

Filene, Peter. 1970. "An Obituary for the 'Progressive Movement." *American Quarterly* 22: 20–34.

Flanagan, Maureen. 2007. *America Reformed: Progressives and Progressivisms, 1890s–1920s*. New York: Oxford University Press.

Galambos, Louis. 1970. "The Emerging Organizational Synthesis in Modern American History." *Business History Review* 44: 279–290.

Gilmore, Glenda E. 1996. *Gender and Jim Crow: Gender and the Politics of White Supremacy in North Carolina, 1896–1920*. Chapel Hill: University of North Carolina Press.

Goodwyn, Lawrence. 1976. *Democratic Promise: The Populist Moment in America*. New York: Oxford University Press.

—. 1978. *The Populist Moment: A Short History of the Agrarian Revolt in America*. New York: Oxford University Press.

Gordon, Linda. 1999. *The Great Arizona Orphan Abduction*. Cambridge, MA: Harvard University Press.

Hahn, Steven. 2003. *A Nation under Our Feet: Black Political Struggles in the Rural South from Slavery to the Great Migration*. Cambridge, MA: Harvard University Press.

Harlan, Louis R. 1972. *Booker T. Washington: The Making of a Black Leader, 1856–1901.* New York: Oxford University Press.

—. 1983. *Booker T. Washington: The Wizard of Tuskegee, 1901–1915.* New York: Oxford University Press.

Higham, John. 1955. *Strangers in the Land: Patterns of American Nativism, 1860–1925.* New Brunswick, NJ: Rutgers University Press.

Hofstadter, Richard. 1955. *The Age of Reform: From Bryan to F.D.R.* New York: Knopf.

Hoganson, Kristin. 1998. *Fighting for American Manhood: How Gender Politics Provoked the Spanish-American and Philippine-American Wars.* New Haven, CT: Yale University Press.

Jacobson, Matthew. 2000. *Barbarian Virtues: The United States Encounters Foreign Peoples at Home and Abroad, 1876–1917.* New York: Hill & Wang.

John, Richard R. 1997. "Elaborations, Revisions, Dissents: Alfred D. Chandler, Jr.'s *The Visible Hand* after Twenty Years." *Business Historical Review* 71: 151–206.

Johnston, Robert D. 2002. "Re-Democratizing the Progressive Era: The Politics of Progressive Era Political Historiography." *Journal of the Gilded Age and Progressive Era* 1: 68–92.

—. 2003. *The Radical Middle Class: Populist Democracy and the Question of Capitalism in Progressive Era Portland, Oregon.* Princeton, NJ: Princeton University Press.

—. 2007. "*The Age of Reform*: A Defense of Richard Hofstadter Fifty Years On." *Journal of the Gilded Age and Progressive Era* 6, April: 127–138.

—. 2011. "The Possibilities of Politics: Democracy in America, 1877–917." In *American History Now*, ed. Eric Foner and Lisa McGirr, 96–124. Philadelphia, PA: Temple University Press in cooperation with the American Historical Association.

—. 2014. "Long Live Teddy/Death to Woodrow: The Polarized Politics of The Progressive Era in the 2012 Election." *Journal of the Gilded Age and Progressive Era* 13, July: 411–443.

Josephson, Matthew. 1934. *The Robber Barons: The Great American Capitalists, 1861–1901.* New York: Harcourt, Brace.

Kennedy, David M. 1980. *Over Here: The First World War and American Society.* New York: Oxford University Press.

Kloppenberg, James T. 1986. *Uncertain Victory: Social Democracy and Progressivism in European and American Thought, 1870–1920.* New York: Oxford University Press.

Kolko, Gabriel. 1963. *The Triumph of Conservatism: A Reinterpretation of American History, 1900–1916.* New York: Free Press.

Kraditor, Aileen. 1965. *The Ideas of the Woman Suffrage Movement, 1890–1920.* New York: Columbia University Press.

Kramer, Paul. 2006. *The Blood of Government: Race, Empire, the United States and the Philippines.* Chapel Hill: University of North Carolina Press.

LaFeber, Walter. 1963. *The New Empire: An Interpretation of American Expansion, 1860–1898.* Ithaca, NY: Cornell University Press.

Lasch, Christopher. 1991. *The True and Only Heaven: Progress and its Critics.* New York: Norton.

Lears, Jackson. 1981. *No Place of Grace: Antimodernism and the Transformation of American Culture, 1880–1920.* New York: Pantheon.

—. 2009. *Rebirth of a Nation: The Making of Modern America, 1877–1920.* New York: Harper.

Lewis, David Levering. 1993. *W.E.B. Du Bois: Biography of a Race, 1868–1919.* New York: Henry Holt.

—. 2000. *W.E.B. Du Bois: The Fight for Equality and the American Century, 1919–1963.* New York: Henry Holt.

Link, Arthur S. 1954. *Woodrow Wilson and the Progressive Era, 1910–1917.* New York: Harper & Row.

Manela, Erez. 2007. *The Wilsonian Moment: Self-Determination and the International Origins of Anticolonial Nationalism.* New York: Oxford University Press.

McGerr, Michael E. 2003. *A Fierce Discontent: The Rise and Fall of the Progressive Movement in America, 1870–1920.* New York: The Free Press.

Montgomery, David. 1987. *The Fall of the House of Labor: The Workplace, State, and American Labor Activism, 1865–1925.* New York: Cambridge University Press.

Newman, Louise M. 2015. "Reflections on Aileen Kraditor's Legacy: Fifty Years of Woman Suffrage Historiography, 1965–2014." *Journal of the Gilded Age and Progressive Era* 14: 290–316. doi: http://dx.doi.org/10.1017/S1537781415000055

Nichols, Christopher McKnight. 2011. *Promise and Peril: America at the Dawn of the Global Age.* Cambridge, MA: Harvard University Press.

Norrell, Robert J. 2011 (2009). *Up from History: The Life of Booker T. Washington.* Cambridge, MA: Harvard University Press.

Nugent, Walter T. K. 1963. *The Tolerant Populists: Kansas Populism and Nativism.* Chicago, IL: University of Chicago Press.

—. 2010. *Progressivism: A Very Short Introduction.* New York: Oxford University Press, 2010.

Painter, Nell Irvin. 1987. *Standing at Armageddon: The United States, 1877–1919.* New York: W.W. Norton.

Postel, Charles. 2007. *The Populist Vision.* New York: Oxford University Press.

Renda, Mary A. 2001. *Taking Haiti: Military Occupation and the Culture of U.S. Imperialism.* Chapel Hill: University of North Carolina Press.

Rodgers, Daniel T. 1982. "In Search of Progressivism." *Reviews in American History* 10: 113–132.

—. 1998. *Atlantic Crossings: Social Politics in a Progressive Age.* Cambridge, MA: Harvard University Press.

Rosenberg, Emily. 1982. *Spreading the American Dream: American Economic and Cultural Expansion, 1890–1945.* New York: Hill & Wang.

Sachs, Aaron. 2013. *Arcadian America: The Death and Life of an American Tradition.* New Haven, CT: Yale University Press.

Salvatore, Nick. 1982. *Eugene V. Debs: Citizen and Socialist.* Urbana: University of Illinois Press.

Sanders, Elizabeth. 1999. *Roots of Reform: Farmers, Workers, and the American State, 1877– 1917.* Chicago, IL: University of Chicago Press.

Sklar, Kathryn Kish. 1995. *Florence Kelley and the Nation's Work: The Rise of Women's Political Culture, 1830–1930.* New Haven, CT: Yale University Press.

Sklar, Martin J. 1960. "Woodrow Wilson and the Political-Economy of Modern States Liberalism. *Studies on the Left* 1: 17–47.

—. 1988. *The Corporate Reconstruction of American Capitalism, 1890–1916: The Market, the Law, and Politics.* New York: Cambridge University Press.

Skocpol, Theda. 1992. *Protecting Soldiers and Mothers: The Political Origins of Social Policy in the United States.* Cambridge, MA: Harvard University Press.

Stansell, Christine. 2000. *American Moderns: Bohemian New York and the Creation of a New Century.* Princeton, NJ: Princeton University Press.

Stromquist, Shelton. 2006. *Re-inventing "The People": The Progressive Movement, the Class Problem, and the Origins of Modern Liberalism.* Urbana: University of Illinois Press.

Unger, Nancy C. 2000. *Fighting Bob La Follette: The Righteous Reformer.* Chapel Hill: University of North Carolina Press.

Weinstein, James. 1968. *The Corporate Ideal in the Liberal State, 1900–1918.* Boston, MA: Beacon.

Westbrook, Robert. 1991. *John Dewey and American Democracy.* Ithaca, NY: Cornell University Press.

White, Richard. 2011. *Railroaded: The Transcontinentals and the Making of Modern America.* New York: W.W. Norton.

Wickberg, Daniel. 2005. "Heterosexual White Male: Some Recent Inversions in American Cultural History." *Journal of American History* 92: 136–157.

Wiebe, Robert H. 1967. *The Search for Order, 1877–1920.* New York: Hill & Wang.

—. 1995. *Self-Rule: A Cultural History of Democracy.* Chicago, IL: University of Chicago Press.

Williams, William Appleman. 1959. *The Tragedy of American Diplomacy.* Cleveland, OH: World Publishing.

Woodward, C. Vann. 1938. *Tom Watson: Agrarian Rebel.* New York: Oxford University Press, 1938.

—. 1951. *Origins of the New South, 1877–1913.* Baton Rouge: Louisiana University Press.

—. 1955. *The Strange Career of Jim Crow.* New York: Oxford University Press.

—. 1959. "The Populist Heritage and the Intellectual." *American Scholar* 29: 55–72.

Chapter Thirty-Four

Why the Gilded Age and Progressive Era Still Matter

Michael Kazin

Aside from historians, few Americans give the Gilded Age or the Progressive Era any respect. The ungainly names used for the period (GAPE, for short) are certainly part of the reason: the first comes from a mediocre novel written in 1873 by Mark Twain and a friend of his (Charles Dudley Warner) that hardly anyone still reads; while few people ever see a "gilded" object outside of an art museum or an antique store. To define the second term requires a short lecture. There is no quick way to explain why some dedicated "Progressives" founded the National Association for the Advancement of Colored People (NAACP), while, at the same time, other "Progressives" were erecting the racist Jim Crow order. Capturing the nuances of the era is exceedingly difficult. Try parsing out, in brief, the differences between the 1912 Progressive Party of Theodore Roosevelt, the 1924 Progressive Party of Robert La Follette (who despised TR), and the 1948 Progressive Party of Henry Wallace (a campaign organized mainly by Communists).

Another problem is the GAPE's lack of obvious, recognizable heroes or villains and unambiguously heroic events. Edmund Morris lionized Theodore Roosevelt in a bestselling, three-volume biography (Morris 1979, 2001, 2010). But even Morris, an uncommonly elegant writer, struggled to defend Roosevelt's slaughter of over five hundred wild mammals in East Africa and his equally ardent lust for killing other men in combat. Neither of the two overseas wars the US fought in the period is easy to defend today: one colonized the Filipinos against their will; the other helped defeat imperial Germany but also spurred the rise of both Communism and Fascism rather than creating "a world made safe for democracy," as Woodrow Wilson promised it would.

Popular films and TV shows—fictional and non-fictional—appear regularly about other, shorter periods from the American Revolution to the era of the Civil War, to the Great Depression and World War II, to the 1960s. Often, they become the subject of intense commentary, both political and aesthetic. The 2013 film, *Twelve Years a Slave*, won a slew of awards and touched off a lively conversation, across several media, about the nature of the institution of bondage that has come to be called America's "primal sin." In 2015, an innovative hip-hop musical about Alexander Hamilton became the hottest ticket on Broadway in years and was hailed in *The New York Times* for having "the perfect voice for expressing the thoughts and drives of the diverse immigrants in the American colonies who came together to forge their own contentious, contradictory nation" (*New York Times*, August 6, 2015).

Only the 1997 blockbuster *Titanic* raised global interest in the GAPE. Although the film was almost exclusively valued for its star-crossed romance and dramatic re-creation of the ship's sinking, critics and fans alike recognized the modern messages inherit in its critique of GAPE class and gender norms. At least two additional big-budget productions about the GAPE also gained some attention in recent decades, although considerably less than *Titanic.* Several characters in the fictional HBO series, *Boardwalk Empire* (2010–2014) were affected by GAPE events, particularly US involvement in World War I. But its focus was on the illegal liquor business in the 1920s and early 1930s. Warren Beatty's 1981 film, *Reds*, about the lives of the radical journalist–activists John Reed and Anita Bryant, won three academy awards. Not many Americans, however, remember the 1981 movie *Ragtime*. There is no US version of *Downtown Abbey*, and not many saw the 2011 PBS series *Prohibition*, created by Lynn Novick and Ken Burns—whose 1990 documentary on the Civil War remains the most watched program in the history of public television.

Lack of popular respect does not, however, mean that the GAPE is less significant than other periods of the American past that appeal strongly to people who have no professional interest in history. In fact, what occurred during the forty-odd

A Companion to the Gilded Age and Progressive Era, First Edition. Edited by Christopher McKnight Nichols and Nancy C. Unger.
© 2017 John Wiley & Sons, Inc. Published 2017 by John Wiley & Sons, Inc.

years from the end of Reconstruction in the South to the end of World War I shaped the United States in profound and lasting ways. The GAPE was, in the words of historian Jackson Lears, the "rebirth of a nation" – a second founding whose cultural, economic, political, and technological impact twenty-first-century Americans experience every day, although few may realize it (Lears 2009, 1).

Begin with the material inventions, all of which remain ubiquitous and many of which are still essential to life in a modern, industrial or postindustrial society: the bicycle, the airplane, the automobile, fast transoceanic cargo ships, the instant camera, the telephone, electric lights, the radio, motion pictures, and factories equipped to turn out a seemingly infinite variety of products that consumers want or can be persuaded to desire. Then add such symbiotic institutions as the advertising industry, the sprawling department store, and daily newspapers and magazines read by a majority of Americans in a variety of languages (usually now, online). And do not neglect the emergence of professional baseball, the first team sport that both attracted huge audiences and made it possible for talented young men (nearly all of them white) to make a living playing it.

The temporal order itself was altered during the GAPE as well. Three new federal holidays—Memorial Day, Armistice (now Veterans) Day, and Labor Day—were added to the calendar. In 1883, the major railroad companies, to rationalize their schedules, created the four continental time zones Americans now take for granted.

Just as vital, if less celebrated, features of contemporary American life were the many political innovations made in the GAPE that were intended to create a more democratic and humane state, but also a more bureaucratic one. They included the civil service, party primaries, a strong president who travels around the nation and the world, initiative and referendum and recall, the secret ballot, antitrust laws, workers' compensation, income tax, the Federal Reserve system, the Food and Drug Administration, woman suffrage, a national labor movement, the first environmental movement (then called "conservation"), and a welfare state. During World War I, the largest expansion of the military in US history took place, the military performed the first mass-psychology and IQ tests, and the federal government created and sanctioned the national surveillance state headed by the Bureau of Investigation, soon to be renamed the FBI (Gerstle 2015).

Taken together, this "age of reform," as the historian Richard Hofstadter called it, expanded the size and muscle of the federal government, yet only began to reduce what, under "the police power" individual states could do (Hofstadter 1955). At the dawn of the Gilded Age, the only part of the federal government most Americans routinely encountered was the Post Office. By 1920, the national state sought to regulate the size of businesses; inspected the meats and medicines that Americans digested; forbade the immigration of illiterates, anarchists, the sick, and laborers from China; and enforced a ban on the "traffic" of nearly every type of alcoholic beverage. But individual states could still forbid interracial marriage and ban the sale of any kind of birth-control device.

The driving force behind nearly all these changes was the most significant development in history since human beings began growing crops and domesticating animals: the supremacy of industrial and financial capitalism in the United States and in most other nations in the northern hemisphere. Although these processes began in the eighteenth century, principally in Great Britain, they expanded mightily during the final decades of the next one.

The primary agent and beneficiary of this expansion was the corporation, a legal convenience that took on immense powers to affect daily life, for good and ill. During the 1880s, the Supreme Court ruled that corporations, like individual persons, were entitled to "the equal protection of the laws" under the Fourteenth Amendment—ratified in 1868 primarily to prohibit any state from denying the rights of citizenship to African Americans. In so doing, the Court made it difficult for individual states to regulate how corporations operate in the marketplace, for the federal government to restrict donations by corporate officials to political campaigns, or for prosecutors to punish corporate officials who mistreat their employees, their consumers, or the public at large. Under the doctrine of "corporate personhood," the legal entity can be sued, pay fines, or go bankrupt. But the individuals responsible for such wrongs often lose nothing more than their reputations.

During the GAPE, corporations, with aid from the courts, became the dominant actors in the American economy. In industry after industry, such firms as Standard Oil, Carnegie Steel, Ford Motor, the Armour meatpacking company, and the Southern Pacific Railroad gobbled up market share and made it increasingly difficult for small businesses to compete against them. Politicians aided their growth with tax exemptions and high tariffs on imported goods. When disgruntled workers went on strike against a major corporation, judges often handed down injunctions to stop them, and governments dispatched police and soldiers to enforce the court's rulings. By the 1920s, despite a mass outcry against "monopoly" and the enactment of antitrust laws, public officials had essentially decided to accept the dominance of big businesses, while pursuing ways to regulate some of their activities.

Applying advanced technologies and economies of scale, large corporations were able to produce cheaper goods of more standardized quality – and gave birth to a modern consumer economy, with all its pleasures and anxieties. But by 1920, "private enterprise" had become something of a misnomer. That remains no less true today.

It was also during the GAPE that American corporations became the model for future big businesses around the globe. Beginning with transcontinental railroads, US executives pioneered the vertical integration of every factor of the production process—from the acquisition of raw materials to marketing finished goods to consumers—and initiated such internal departments as advertising and "government relations" (or lobbying) to enhance a company's image. The classical work about the evolution of the structure of American corporations is Alfred D. Chandler, Jr., *The Visible Hand: The Managerial Revolution in American Business* (1977). By the early twentieth century, this corporate structure, aided by the federal government, helped the United States become the world's largest economy, as measured by Gross Domestic Product. It retained that status for over a century, until China, with its thriving manufacturing sector (many of whose products are made for Walmart and other US-owned firms) and huge population surpassed it.

One cultural facet of the rise of the United States to economic power in the GAPE was the making of industrialists like Andrew Carnegie and John D. Rockefeller and financiers like J.P. Morgan into celebrities, widely admired yet also routinely vilified. Their critics called them "robber barons" who fleeced the public, battered their competitors, and "devised schemes by which they thrive on the work others do for them," as the popular author Henry George put it (*New York Times*, October 6, 1886). But they also gave millions of dollars away to charities and museums. And Carnegie and Rockefeller endowed major foundations that still bear their names.

Industrialization also spurred urbanization. America's economic boom during the GAPE attracted to its burgeoning cities immigrants from all over the globe who hoped to find a secure job paying a living wage and, perhaps, start a business in "the land of dollars." Until the 1880s, most newcomers had been western or northern Europeans; except for the Irish, the large majority were Protestants. But during the next four decades, people of all religions and most nations in Europe and the Mideast crowded into big cities and industrial towns. During World War I, African Americans began their own "great migration" from the rural South to the urban North; while Mexicans began to move, in large numbers, to industrial centers like Chicago as well as to such incipient southwestern metropoles as Phoenix and Los Angeles. As a consequence of these transoceanic and transcontinental shifts, the US population became nearly as ethnically heterogeneous as it is today—with the exception of Asians, most of whom were barred from immigrating due to racial fears of "a Yellow peril."

The United States was also fortunate to be an ocean away from World War I—the conflict in which over ten million Europeans died and which touched off three decades of massacres, genocide, and armed conflicts between and within nations that the great historian Eric Hobsbawm has called "The Age of Catastrophe" (Hobsbawm 1994). The United States provided loans and material aid but did not enter the war until 1917, almost three years after it began. American troops engaged in major combat for only a few months, before the rulers of imperial Germany gave up the fight.

The end of World War I left US leaders in a supreme position to shape the world to their desires and the national self-interest, although most Americans had no taste for future military interventions abroad. As Hobsbawm, no admirer of American policies, put it, the United States was "by any standards the success story among twentieth-century states. Its economy became the world's largest, both pace- and pattern-setting, its capacity for technological achievement was unique, its research in both natural and social sciences, even its philosophers became increasingly dominant, and its hegemony of global consumer civilization seemed beyond challenge." The United States also became, he added, "the preferred destination of most human beings who must, or decide to, move to a country other than their own, certainly of those who know some English" (Hobsbawm 2003, 404). In short, it was the GAPE that made the twentieth century an "American century," as publisher Henry Luce exuberantly remarked in *Life* magazine in 1941.

While the United States is no longer so dominant, its politics remains, much as in the era of World War I, a contest between pro-business conservatives who despise the regulatory state and egalitarian liberals who want to expand its purview. Neither side has been able to win an outright victory. Then as now, Americans were a demographically and ideologically heterogeneous lot, whose political leanings were hard to summarize. But most seemed eager to find a middle ground between plutocracy and collectivism, a moral capitalism that would encourage both entrepreneurs and the activists, in and out of government, who seek to curb their influence and tax their profits. Both Presidents Theodore Roosevelt and Woodrow Wilson understood this, and their administrations helped make this kind of progressivism the common sense of the land.

Despite the hazards of drawing historical analogies, the United States may now be on the cusp of a similar transition. The huge gap between the rich and everyone else—and the embattled status of labor unions that seek to narrow it—has led many commentators, especially on the left, to follow Paul Krugman in describing the nation as enduring a "new Gilded Age" (*New York Review of Books*, May 8, 2014). *Capital in the Twenty-First Century* (2014), by French economist Thomas Piketty, underscored interpretations of this age as a second Belle Époque by detailing long-term trends in the transformation of capital and inequality. Most Americans favor a higher minimum wage and, whatever their income, want the government to guarantee that everyone has health insurance. Global corporations enjoy earnings that Andrew Carnegie and Henry Ford could only dream about. But anxiety about climate change has also spawned a global mass movement that could herald a new dawn of environmental controls. If a new Progressive Era has yet to begin, it is more because liberals, who have taken to call themselves "Progressives," aren't able to mobilize public sentiment than because that sentiment is not lumbering their way.

So the political echoes, or perhaps ghosts, of the GAPE are all around in the present age. "Progressive" activists campaign for universal healthcare and against military intervention, while conservative scholars view the "Progressivism" of a century ago as a nefarious "intellectual and political reform movement that aimed to alter the American constitutional system" and whose legacy continues to shackle the freedoms of ordinary citizens (O'Neill 2011). During the 2016 presidential campaign, Bernie Sanders on the left and Donald Trump on the right both railed against entrenched elites in ways that drove many journalists to label them both "populists," although neither adopted a program that resembled that of the farmer-labor insurgents of the 1890s who coined the term. To paraphrase the last line of F. Scott's Fitzgerald's *The Great Gatsby* (a novel written just a few years after the end of World War I), we beat on, often against the current of reality, borne back ceaselessly into our past.

References

Chandler, Alfred D., Jr. 1977. *The Visible Hand: The Managerial Revolution in American Business.* Cambridge, MA: Harvard University Press.

Gerstle, Gary. 2015. *Liberty and Coercion: The Paradox of American Government from the Founding to the Present.* Princeton, NJ: Princeton University Press.

Hobsbawm, Eric. 1994. *The Age of Extremes: The Short Twentieth Century, 1914–1991.* London: Michael Joseph.

—. 2003. *Interesting Times: A Twentieth-Century Life.* New York: Pantheon.

Hofstadter, Richard. 1955. *The Age of Reform: From Bryan to FDR.* New York: Knopf.

Lears, Jackson. 2009. *Rebirth of a Nation: The Making of Modern America, 1877–1920.* New York: HarperCollins.

Morris, Edmund. 1979. *The Rise of Theodore Roosevelt.* New York: Coward, McCann & Geoghegan.

Morris, Edmund. 2001. *Theodore Rex.* New York: Random House.

—. 2010. *Colonel Roosevelt.* New York: Random House.

O'Neill, Jonathan. "The First Conservatives: The Constitutional Challenge to Progressivism," July 5, 2011, First Principles Series Report #39 on Political Thought, Heritage Foundation. http://www.heritage.org/research/reports/2011/06/the-first-conservatives-the-constitutional-challenge-to-progressivism/ accessed July 19, 2016.

Piketty, Thomas. 2014. *Capital in the Twenty-First Century.* Trans. from the French by Arthur Goldhammer. Cambridge, MA: Belknap Press/Harvard University Press.

Further Reading

Bederman, Gail. 1996. *Manliness in Civilization: A Cultural History of Gender and Race in the United States, 1880–1917.* Chicago, IL: University of Chicago Press.

Edwards, Rebecca. 2006. *New Spirits: Americans in the Gilded Age, 1865–1905.* New York: Oxford University Press.

Fraser, Steve. 2015. *The Age of Acquiescence: The Life and Death of American Resistance to Organized Wealth and Power.* Boston: Little, Brown.

Hobsbawm, Eric. 1987. *The Age of Empire, 1875–1914.* New York: Pantheon.

Johnston, Robert. 2014. "'Long Live Teddy/Death to Woodrow': The Polarized Politics of the Progressive Era in the 2012 Election." *Journal of the Gilded Age and Progressive Era* 13, 3: 411–443.

Kazin, Michael. 1987. *Barons of Labor: The San Francisco Building Trades and Union Power in the Progressive Era.* Champaign: University of Illinois Press.

—. 1999. *The Populist Persuasion: An American History.* Revised edn. Ithaca, NY: Cornell University Press.

—. 2006. *A Godly Hero: The Life of William Jennings Bryan.* New York: Knopf.

—. 2017. *War Against War: The American Fight for Peace, 1914–1918.* New York: Simon & Schuster.

Kennedy, David. 1980. *Over Here: The First World War and American Society.* New York: Oxford University Press.

Kraut, Alan M. 1986. *The Huddled Masses: The Immigrant in American Society, 1880–1921.* Arlington Heights, IL: Wiley-Blackwell.

Postel, Charles. 2007. *The Populist Vision.* New York: Oxford University Press.

Sanders, Elizabeth. 1999. *Roots of Reform: Farmers, Workers, and the American State, 1877–1917.* Chicago: University of Chicago Press.

Schmidt, Eric Leigh. 1991. "The Commercialization of the Calendar: American Holidays and the Culture of Consumption, 1870–1930." *Journal of American History* 78, 3: 887–916.

Bibliography

1911. "The American Newspaper." *Collier's Weekly* 2, September: 22–23.

1912. "Let the People Rule." *Nation*. September 26.

Abbott, Carl. 2008. *How Cities Won the West: Four Centuries of Urban Change in Western North America*. Albuquerque: University of New Mexico Press.

Abbott, Grace. 1917. *The Immigrant and the Community*. New York: The Century Company.

Abram, Michael and Joseph Cooper. 1968. "The Rise of Seniority in the House of Representatives." *Polity* 1, 1: 52–85.

Abramowitz, Jack. 1950. "Accommodation and Militancy in Negro Life, 1876–1916." PhD diss., Columbia University.

Adam, Thomas. 2009. *Buying Respectability: Philanthropy and Urban Society in Transnational Perspective, 1840s to 1930s*. Bloomington: Indiana University Press.

Adams, David Wallace. 1995. *Education for Extinction: American Indians and the Boarding School Experience, 1875–1929*. Lawrence: University Press of Kansas.

Adams, Samuel Hopkins. 1906. *The Great American Fraud: Articles on the Nostrum Evil and Quacks, in Two Series, Reprinted from Collier's Weekly*. United States: P. F. Collier and Son.

Adas, Michael. 2006. *Dominance By Design: Technological Imperatives and America's Civilizing Mission*. Cambridge: Belknap Press of Harvard University Press.

Addams, Jane. 1902 (2002). *Democracy and Social Ethics*. New York: The Macmillan Company. Reprint, Urbana: University of Illinois Press. Citations refer to the University of Illinois edition.

—. 1910. "Why Women Should Vote." *Ladies Home Journal*, 27.

—. 1911. *Twenty Years at Hull House*. New York: The Macmillan Company.

—. 1912. *Twenty Years at Hull House with Autobiographical Notes*. New York: The Macmillan Company.

—. 1922 (2002). *Peace and Bread in Time of War*. New York: The Macmillan Company. Reprint, Urbana: University of Illinois Press. Citations refer to the University of Illinois edition.

Adler, Jacob 1960. "The Oceanic Steamship Company: A Link in Claus Spreckels' Hawaiian Sugar Empire." *Pacific Historical Review* 29: 257–69.

Albanese, Catherine L. 2007. *A Republic of Mind & Spirit: A Cultural History of American Metaphysical Religion*. New Haven: Yale University Press.

Aldrich, John H., and David W. Rohde. 2005. "Congressional Committees in a Partisan Era." In *Congress Reconsidered*, ed. Lawrence C. Dodd and Bruce I. Oppenheimer. 8th edition. Washington, DC: Congressional Quarterly Press.

Alexander, De Alva. 1916. *History and Procedure of the House of Representatives*. Boston: Houghton Mifflin.

Alexander, Michelle. 2010. *The New Jim Crow: Mass Incarceration in the Age of Colorblindness*. New York: The New Press.

Alexander, Ruth. 1995. *The Girl Problem: Female Sexual Delinquency in New York, 1900–1930*. Ithaca: Cornell University Press.

Alger, Horatio. 1881. *From Canal Boy to President*. Boston: DeWolfe, Fiske.

—. 1885. *Ragged Dick, Or Street Life In New York with the Boot-Blacks*. Philadelphia: Henry T. Coates and Co.

Ali, Omar H. 2010. *In The Lion's Mouth: Black Populism in the New South, 1886–1900*. Jackson: University Press of Mississippi.

Allen, Judith A. 2009. *The Feminism of Charlotte Perkins Gilman: Sexualities, Histories, Progressivism*. Chicago: University of Chicago Press.

Alter, Stephen G. 2005. *William Dwight Whitney and the Science of Language*. Baltimore: Johns Hopkins University Press.

Altman, Clara. 2014. "Courtroom Colonialism: Philippine Law and U.S. Rule, 1898–1935." PhD diss., Brandeis University.

Ambrosius, Lloyd E. 1987. *Woodrow Wilson and the American Diplomatic Tradition: The Treaty Fight in Perspective*. Cambridge: Cambridge University Press.

—. 2002. *Wilsonianism: Woodrow Wilson and His Legacy in American Foreign Relations*. New York: Palgrave Macmillan.

—. 2007. "Woodrow Wilson and *The Birth of a Nation*: American Democracy and International Relations," *Diplomacy and Statecraft* 18: 689–718.

American Indian Citizenship Act. 1924. 8 U.S. Code 1401 (b).

Ammerman, Nancy Tatom. 1990. *Baptist Battles: Social Change and Religious Conflict in the Southern Baptist Convention*. New Brunswick: Rutgers University Press.

A Companion to the Gilded Age and Progressive Era, First Edition. Edited by Christopher McKnight Nichols and Nancy C. Unger.
© 2017 John Wiley & Sons, Inc. Published 2017 by John Wiley & Sons, Inc.

Anderson, Benedict. 2006. *Imagined Communities: Reflections on the Origin and Spread of Nationalism.* New York and London: Verso.

Anderson, Eric. 1981. *Race and Politics in North Carolina, 1872–1901: The Black Second.* Baton Rouge: Louisiana State University.

—, and Moss, Alfred A. Jr. 1999. *Dangerous Donations: Northern Philanthropy and Southern Black Education, 1902–1930.* Columbia: University of Missouri Press.

Anderson, James. 1988. *The Education of Blacks in the South, 1860–1935.* Chapel Hill: University of North Carolina Press.

Anderson, Jeffrey E. 2005. *Conjure in African American Society.* Baton Rouge: Louisiana State University Press.

Anderson, Robert Mapes. 1979. *Vision of the Disinherited: The Making of American Pentecostalism.* New York: Oxford University Press.

Anderson, Warwick. 2006. *Colonial Pathologies: American Tropical Medicine, Race, and Hygiene in the Philippines.* Durham: Duke University Press.

Andrei, Mary Anne. 2005. "The Accidental Conservationist: William T. Hornaday, the Smithsonian Bison Expeditions and the US National Zoo." *Endeavor* 29, 3: 109–113.

Andrews, Thomas G. 2008. *Killing for Coal: America's Deadliest Labor War.* Cambridge: Harvard University Press.

Angulo, A.J. 2012. *Empire and Education: A History of Greed and Goodwill from the War of 1898 to the War on Terror.* New York: Palgrave Macmillan.

Anonymous. 1892. "California: Its Attractions for the Invalid, Tourist, Capitalist, and Homeseeker." San Francisco: Southern Pacific Rail Road Company.

Anonymous. 1900. "Loma Linda California for Health and Pleasure." Loma Linda: Loma Linda Sanitarium.

Anonymous. 1900. "Secret Nostrums and the Journal." *Journal of the American Medical Association* 34, June 2: 1420.

Anonymous. 1901a. "Doctors Make Raid." *New York Times* February 2, 10.

Anonymous. 1901b. "Vaccine and Antitoxin." *New York Times* December 8, 6.

Anonymous. 1902. "Protection Against Public Nuisances." *Medical News* 80: 463.

Anonymous. 1905. "Doctors Assail Patent Medicine Advertising." *New York Times* October 19, 6.

Anonymous. 1906a. "Miles Loses Suit in Equity." *American Druggist and Pharmaceutical Record* 48, January – June: 177.

Anonymous. 1906b. "Dr. Miles Medical Company vs. the May Drug Company." *Journal of the American Medical Association* 46, May 12: 1459–1460.

Anthony, Katharine. 1915. *Feminism in Germany and Scandinavia.* New York: Henry Holt.

Anthony, Susan Hall. 2005. "Dr. Herbert J. Hall: Originator of Honest Work for Occupational Therapy, 1904–1923." *Occupational Therapy in Health Care: A Journal of Contemporary Practice* 19: 3–32.

Appiah, K. Anthony. 1992. *In My Father's House: Africa in the Philosophy of Culture.* New York: Oxford University Press.

Apple, Rima D. 2006. *Perfect Motherhood: Science and Childbearing in America,* New Brunswick: Rutgers University Press.

Appleby, R. Scott. 1992. *Church and Age Unite: The Modernist Impulse in American Catholicism.* South Bend: University of Notre Dame Press.

Applegate, Edd. 1997. *Journalistic Advocates and Muckrakers: Three Centuries of Crusading Writers.* Jefferson: McFarland.

Argersinger, Peter. 2012. *Representation and Inequality in Late Nineteenth-Century America: The Politics of Apportionment.* Cambridge: Cambridge University Press.

Armitage, Kevin C. 2007. "The Child Is Born a Naturalist: Nature Study, Woodcraft Indians, and the Theory of Recapitulation." *Journal of the Gilded Age and Progressive Era* 6: 43–70.

—. 2009. *The Nature Study Movement: The Forgotten Popularizer of America's Conservation Ethic.* Lawrence: University Press of Kansas.

Arnerson, Eric. 1991. *Waterfront Workers of New Orleans: Race, Class, and Politics, 1863–1923.* New York: Oxford University Press.

Arnold, Andrew B. 2014. *Fueling the Gilded Age: Railroads, Miners, and Disorder in Pennsylvania Coal Country.* New York: New York University Press.

Arnove, Robert F., ed. 1980. *Philanthropy and Cultural Imperialism: The Foundations at Home and Abroad.* Boston: G. K. Hall.

Aron, Cindy S. 1999. *Working at Play: A History of Vacations in the United States.* New York: Oxford University Press.

Arrighi, Giovanni. 2010. *The Long Twentieth Century: Money, Power, and the Origins of Our Times,* 2nd edition. New York: Verso.

Arrington, Leonard. 1954. *Great Basin Kingdom: An Economic History of the Latter-day Saints, 1830–1890.* Cambridge: Harvard University Press.

Arthur, Anthony. 2006. *Radical Innocent: Upton Sinclair.* New York: Random House.

Ascoli, Peter M. 2006. *Julius Rosenwald: The Man Who Built Sears, Roebuck and Advanced the Cause of Black Education in the American South.* Bloomington: Indiana University Press.

Atherton, Lewis. 1954. *Main Street on the Middle Border.* Chicago: Quadrangle Books.

Atkins, Annette. 1988. "Minnesota." In *Heartland,* ed. James J. Madison, 9–31. Bloomington: Indiana University Press.

Attie, Jeanie. 1998. *Patriotic Toil: Northern Women and the American Civil War.* Ithaca: Cornell University Press.

Axson, Stockton. 1993. *"Brother Woodrow": A Memoir of Woodrow Wilson.* Princeton: Princeton University Press.

Ayers, Edward L. 1992. *The Promise of the New South: Life after Reconstruction.* New York: Oxford University Press.

Azuma, Eiichuro. 2005. *Between Two Empires: Race, History, and Transnationalism in Japanese America.* New York: Oxford University Press.

Bailey, Hugh C. 1969. *Liberalism in the New South; Southern Social Reformers and the Progressive Movement.* Coral Gables: University of Miami Press.

Bailey, Thomas A. 1966. *Presidential Greatness: The Image and the Man from George Washington to the Present.* New York: Appleton-Century.

Baker, Jean H. 2011. *Margaret Sanger: A Life of Passion.* New York: Hill & Wang.

Baker, Lee D. 2010. *Anthropology and the Racial Politics of Culture.* Durham: Duke University Press.

Baker, Paula. 1984. "The Domestication of Politics: Women and American Political Society, 1780–1920." *American Historical Review* 89: 620–647.

—. 1991. *The Moral Frameworks of Public Life: Gender, Politics, and the State in Rural New York, 1870–1930.* New York: Oxford University Press.

Baker, Ray Stannard. 1903. "The Right to Work: The Story of the Non-striking Miners." *McClure's Magazine* 20: 323–335.

—. 1908. *Following the Color Line: An Account of Negro Citizenship in the American Democracy.* New York: Doubleday, Page.

—. 1909. "The Spiritual Unrest: The Case Against Trinity Church." *American Magazine* 68: 3–16.

—. 1932. *Woodrow Wilson: Life and Letters.* 8 volumes. London: Heinemann.

Balch, Stephen. 1972. "Party Government in the United States House of Representatives, 1911–1919." PhD diss., University of California at Berkeley.

Bald, Vivek. 2013. *Bengali Harlem and the Lost Histories of South Asian America.* Cambridge: Harvard University Press.

Baldasty, Gerald E. 1992. *The Commercialization of News in the Nineteenth Century.* Madison: University of Wisconsin.

Baldoz, Rick. 2014. *Third Asiatic Invasion: Migration and Empire in Filipino America, 1898–1946.* New York: New York University Press.

Baldwin, Davarian L. 2008. "From the Washtub to the World: Madam C. J. Walker and the 'Re-creation' of Race Womanhood, 1900–1935." In *The Modern Girl Around the World: Consumption, Modernity, and Globalization*, ed. Alice Eve Weinbaum et. al. Durham: Duke University Press.

Baldwin, Peter C. 2012. *In the Watches of the Night: Life in the Nocturnal City, 1820–1930.* Chicago: University of Chicago Press.

—. 1999. *Domesticating the Street: The Reform of Public Space in Hartford, 1850–1930.* Columbus: Ohio State University Press.

Baldwin, Simeon E. 1907. "The International Congresses and Conferences of the Last Century as Forces Working toward the Solidarity of the World." *American Journal of International Law* 1: 565–78.

Ballantyne, Tony, and Antoinette Burton. 2012. "Empires and the Reach of the Global." In *A World Connecting 1870–1945*, ed. Emily S. Rosenberg, 285–431. Cambridge: Belknap Press of Harvard University Press.

Balmer, Randall. 2010. *The Making of Evangelicalism: From Revivalism to Politics and Beyond.* Waco: Baylor University Press.

Balogh, Brian. 2015. *The Associational State: American Governance in the Twentieth Century.* Philadelphia: University of Pennsylvania Press.

—. 2009. *A Government Out of Sight: The Mystery of National Authority in Nineteenth-Century America.* Cambridge: Cambridge University Press.

—. 2002. "Scientific Forestry and the Roots of the American State: Gifford Pinchot's Path to Progressive Reform," *Environmental History* 7:198–225.

Bankoff, Greg. 2009. "First Impressions: Diarists, Scientists, Imperialists and the Management of the Environment in the American Pacific, 1899–1902." *Journal of Pacific History* 44, 3: 261–280.

Banner, Lois. 1983. *American Beauty: A Social History…through Two Centuries…of the American Idea, Ideal and Image of the Beautiful Woman.* New York: Alfred Knopf.

Banner, Stuart. 2007. *How the Indians Lost Their Land: Law and Power on the Frontier.* Cambridge: Belknap Press.

Baptist, Edward E. 2014. *The Half Has Never Been Told: Slavery and the Making of American Capitalism.* New York: Basic Books.

Barbier, Edward. 2011. *Scarcity and Frontiers: How Economies Have Developed through Natural Resource Exploitation.* Cambridge: Cambridge University Press.

Barfield, Claude E. 1965. "The Democratic Party in Congress, 1909–1913." PhD diss., Northwestern University.

—. 1970. "'Our Share of the Booty': The Democratic Party, Cannonism, and the Payne–Aldrich Tariff." *Journal of American History* 57, 2: 308–23.

Barker-Benfeld, Ben. 1976. *The Horrors of the Half-Known Life: Male Attitudes Toward Women and Sexuality in Nineteenth-Century America.* New York: Harper & Row.

Barnes, James A. 1931. *John G. Carlisle: Financial Statesman.* New York: Dodd, Mead.

Barnes, Kenneth C. 2004. *Journey of Hope: The Back-to-Africa Movement in Arkansas in the Late 1800s.* Chapel Hill: University of North Carolina Press.

Baron, Ava, ed. 1991. *Work Engendered: Toward a New History of American Labor.* Ithaca: Cornell University Press.

Barrett, James and David Roediger. 1997. "Inbetween Peoples: Race, Nationality and the 'New Immigrant' Working Class." *Journal of American Ethnic History* 16, Spring: 3–44.

—. 1987. *Work and Community in the Jungle: Chicago's Packinghouse Workers, 1894–1922.* Urbana: University of Illinois Press.

—. 2013. *The Irish Way: Becoming American in the Multiethnic City.* New York: Penguin.

Barreyre, Nicolas. 2015. *Gold and Freedom: The Political Economy of Reconstruction.* Charlottesville: University of Virginia Press.

Barrows, John H. 1893. *The World's Parliament of Religions: An Illustrated and Popular History of the World's Parliament of Religions, Held in Chicago in Connection with the World's Columbian Exposition.* Chicago: Parliament Publishing.

Barrows, Robert G. 2007. "Urbanizing America." In *The Gilded Age: Perspectives on the Origins of Modern America*, 2nd ed., ed. Charles W. Calhoun, 101–118. Lanham: Roman and Littlefield.

Barth, Gunther Paul. 1975. *Instant Cities: Urbanization and the Rise of San Francisco and Denver.* New York: Oxford University Press.

—. 1980. *City People : the Rise of the Modern City Culture in Nineteenth-Century America.* New York: Oxford University Press.

—. 1988. *Instant Cities.* Albuquerque: University of New Mexico Press.

Bartky, Ian R. 2001. *Selling the True Time: Nineteenth-century Timekeeping in America.* Stanford: Stanford University Press.

Barton, Gregory A. 2002. *Empire Forestry and the Origins of Environmentalism.* New York: Cambridge University Press.

Basch, Linda, Nina Glick Schiller, and Cristina Szanton Blanc. 1994. *Nations Unbound: Transnational Projects, Postcolonial Predicaments, and Deterritorialized Nation-States.* Newark: Gordon and Breach.

Bass, Gary J. 2008. *Freedom's Battle: the Origins of Humanitarian Intervention.* New York: Alfred A. Knopf.

Bates, Anna Louise. 1991. "Protective Custody: A Feminist Interpretation of Anthony Comstock's Life and Laws." Ph.D. diss., State University of New York.

Bates, Leonard J. 1957. "Fulfilling American Democracy: The Conservation Movement, 1907 to 1921." *Mississippi Valley Historical Review* 44: 29–57.

Batlan, Felice. 2010. "Notes from the Margins: Florence Kelley and the Making of Sociological Jurisprudence." In *Transformations in American Legal History, II: Essays in Honor of Professor Morton J. Horwitz*, ed. Daniel W. Hamilton and Alfred L. Brophy, 239–53. Cambridge: Harvard University Press.

—. 2015. *Women and Justice for the Poor: A History of Legal Aid, 1863–1945.* Cambridge: Cambridge University Press.

Battan, Jesse F. 1999. "The 'Rights' of Husbands and the 'Duties' of Wives: Power and Desire in the American Bedroom, 1850–1910." *Journal of Family History* April: 165–86.

—. 2004. "'You Cannot Fix the Scarlet Letter on my Breast!': Women Reading, Writing, and Reshaping the Sexual Culture of Victorian America." *Journal of Social History* Spring: 601–624.

Bauer, William. 2012. *We Were All Like Migrant Workers Here: Work, Community, and Memory on California's Round Valley Reservation, 1850–1941.* Chapel Hill: University of North Carolina Press.

Bay, Mia. 2009. *To Tell the Truth Freely: The Life of Ida B. Wells.* New York: Hill and Wang.

Bayly, C. A., et al. 2006. "AHR Conversation: On Transnational History." *The American Historical Review* 111, 5: 1441–1464.

Bays, Daniel H., and Grant Wacker, eds. 2003. *The Foreign Missionary Enterprise at Home: Explorations in North American Cultural History.* Tuscaloosa: University of Alabama Press.

—. 2011. *A New History of Christianity in China.* New York: John Wiley & Sons.

Beale, Howard K. 1956. *Theodore Roosevelt and the Rise of America to World Power.* Baltimore: Johns Hopkins University Press.

Beard, Charles, and Mary Beard. 1927. *The Rise of American Civilization.* New York: Macmillan.

Beard, George M. 1881. *American Nervousness: Its Causes and Consequences.* New York: G. P. Putnam's Sons.

Beatty, Jack. 2007. *Age of Betrayal: The Triumph of Money in America, 1865–1900.* New York: Knopf.

Beaver, R. Pierce. 1966. *Church, State, and the American Indians.* St. Louis: Concordia Publishing House.

Beck, Andrew H. 2004. "The Flexner Report and the Standardization of American Medical Education." *The Journal of the American Medical Association* 291, May: 2139–2140.

Beck, Paul Allen. 1979. "The Electoral Cycle and Patterns of American Politics." *British Journal of Political Science* 9: 129–156.

Becker, Carl. 1932. "Everyman His Own Historian." Annual address of the president of the American Historical Association, Minneapolis, MN. December 29, 1931. *American Historical Review* 37, 2: 221–36.

Beckert, Sven. 2001. *The Monied Metropolis: New York City and the Consolidation of the American Bourgeoisie, 1850–1896.* Cambridge: Cambridge University Press.

—. 2014. *Empire of Cotton: A Global History.* New York: Knopf.

—. and Seth Rockman, ed. 2016. *Slavery's Capitalism: A New History of American Economic Development.* Philadelphia: University of Pennsylvania Press.

Bederman, Gail. 1989. "'The Women Have Had Charge of the Church Work Long Enough': The Men and Religion Forward Movement of 1911–1912 and the Masculinization of Middle-Class Protestantism," *American Quarterly* 41, September: 432–465.

—. 1995. *Manliness & Civilization: a Cultural History of Gender and Race in the United States, 1880–1917.* Chicago: University of Chicago Press.

Beeby, James M. 2008. *Revolt of the Tar Heels: The North Carolina Populist Movement, 1890–1901.* Jackson: University Press of Mississippi.

—, ed. 2012. *Populism in the South Revisited: New Interpretations and New Departures.* Jackson: University Press of Mississippi.

Beede, Benjamin R. 1994. *The War of 1898 and U. S. Interventions, 1898–1934.* New York: Garland.

Behling, Laura L. 2001. *The Masculine Woman in America, 1890–1935.* Chicago: University of Illinois Press.

Beisel, Nicola. 1998. *Imperiled Innocents: Anthony Comstock and Family Reproduction in Victorian America.* Princeton: Princeton University Press.

Beisner, Robert. 1975. *From the Old Diplomacy to the New, 1865–1890.* Arlington Heights: AHM Publishing.

Beito, David T. 2000. *From Mutual Aid to the Welfare State: Fraternal Societies and Social Services, 1890–1967.* Chapel Hill: The University of North Carolina Press.

Belich, James. 2009. *Replenishing the Earth: The Settler Revolution and the Rise of the Anglo-World, 1783–1939.* Oxford: Oxford University Press.

Bellamy, Paul B. 1997. *A History of Workmen's Compensation, 1898–1915: From Courtroom to Boardroom.* New York: Garland Publishing.

Bemis, Samuel Flagg. 1943 (1967). *The Latin-American Policy of the United States.* San Diego: Harcourt, Brace, and Company. Reprint, New York: W. W. Norton. Citations refer to the Norton edition.

Benbow, Mark E. 2010. *Leading Them to the Promised Land: Woodrow Wilson, Covenant Theology, and the Mexican Revolution, 1913–1915.* Kent: Kent State University Press.

Bender, Daniel E. 2003. "'Too Much of Distasteful Masculinity': Historicizing Sexual Harassment in the Garment Sweatshop and Factory." *Journal of Women's History* 15, 4: 91–116

—. 2009. *American Abyss: Savagery and Civilization in the Age of Industry.* Ithaca: Cornell University Press.

—, and Jana Lipman. 2015. *Making the Empire Work: Labor and United States Imperialism.* New York: New York University Press.

Bender, Thomas. 2006. *A Nation among Nations: America's Place in World History.* New York: Hill and Wang.

Benedict, Michael Les. 1978. "Preserving Federalism: Reconstruction and the Waite Court." *Supreme Court Review*: 39–79.

—. 1985. "Laissez-Faire and Liberty: A Re-Evaluation of the Meaning and Origins of Laissez-Faire Constitutionalism." *Law and History Review* 3, 2: 293–331.

Benjamin DeWitt, 1915. *The Progressive Movement: A Non-Partisan, Comprehensive Discussion of Current Tendencies in American Politics.* New York: Macmillan.

Benjamin, Jules. 1977. *The United States and Cuba: Hegemony and Dependent Development, 1880–1934.* Pittsburgh: University of Pittsburgh Press.

Benjamin, Ludy T. Jr., and David B. Baker. 2003. *From Séance to Science: A History of the Profession of Psychology in America.* Belmont: Thomson-Wadsworth.

Bennett, James B. 2005. *Religion and the Rise of Jim Crow in New Orleans.* Princeton: Princeton University Press.

Bennett, Lyn Ellen, and Scott Abbott. 2014. "Barbed and Dangerous: Constructing the Meaning of Barbed Wire in Late Nineteenth-Century America." *Agricultural History* 88, 4: 566–590.

Bensel, Richard Franklin. 1990. *Yankee Leviathan: The Origins of Central State Authority in America, 1859–1877.* Cambridge: Cambridge University Press.

—. 2000. *The Political Economy of American Industrialization: 1877–1900.* Cambridge: Cambridge University Press.

—. 2008. *Passion and Preferences: William Jennings Bryan and the 1896 Democratic Nominating Convention.* Cambridge: Cambridge University Press.

Benson, Susan Porter. 1986. *Counter Cultures: Saleswomen, Managers, and Customers in American Department Stores, 1890–1940.* Urbana: University of Illinois Press.

Berebitsky, Julie. 2012. *Sex and the Office.* New Haven: Yale University Press.

Berg, A. Scott. 2013. *Wilson.* New York: G. P. Putnam's Sons.

Berger, Meyer. 1951. *The Story of the New York Times: The First Hundred Years, 1851–1951.* New York: Simon & Schuster.

Berger, Molly W. 2011. *Hotel Dreams: Luxury, Technology, and Urban Ambition in America, 1829–1929.* Baltimore: Johns Hopkins University Press.

Berk, Gerald. 1994. *Alternative Tracks: The Constitution of American Industrial Order, 1865–1917.* Baltimore: Johns Hopkins University Press.

Berkhofer, Robert F., Jr. 1978. *The White Man's Indian: Images of the American Indian from Columbus to the Present.* New York: Vintage Books.

Berman, Ari. 2015. "Alabama, Birthplace of the Voting Rights Act, Is Once Again Gutting Voting Rights." *The Nation*, October 1. http://www.thenation.com/article/alabama-birthplace-of-voting-rights-act-once-again-gutting-voting-rights/

Bernhard, William, and Brian Sala. 2006. "The Remaking of an American Senate: The 17th Amendment and Ideological Responsiveness." *Journal of Politics* 68, 2: 345–57.

Bernstein, David E. 2011. *Rehabilitating Lochner: Defending Individual Rights against Progressive Reform.* Chicago: The University of Chicago Press.

Berry, Mary Frances. 2005. *My Face is Black is True: Callie House and the Struggle for Ex-Slave Reparations.* New York: Knopf.

Berwanger, Eugene H. 1981. *The West and Reconstruction.* Urbana: University of Illinois.

Beveridge, Albert J. 1900. "In Support of an American Empire." *Congressional Record*, 56th Congress, 1st session.

—. 1999. "Our Philippine Policy." In *The Philippines Reader: A History of Colonialism, Neocolonialism, Dictatorship, and Resistance*, ed. Daniel B. Schirmer and Stephen Rosskamm Shalom. Boston: South End Press.

Bierce, Ambrose. 1970. *Fantastic Fables.* New York: Dover.

Billings, Dwight B. 1979. *Planters and the Makings of a "New South": Class, Politics, and Development in North Carolina, 1865–1900.* Chapel Hill: University of North Carolina Press.

Billington, David P., and David P. Billington, Jr., 2006. *Power, Speed and Form. Engineers and the Making of the Twentieth Century.* Princeton: Princeton University Press.

Biltekoff, Charlotte. 2013. *Eating Right in America: The Cultural Politics of Food and Health*, Durham: Duke University Press.

Birk, Megan. 2015. *Fostering on the Farm: Child Placement in the Rural Midwest.* Urbana: University of Illinois Press.

Bittel, Carla Jean. 2005. "Science, Suffrage, and Experimentation: Mary Putnam Jacobi and the Controversy over Vivisection in Late Nineteenth-Century America." *Bulletin of the History of Medicine* 79, 4: 664–694.

—. 2009. *Mary Putnam Jacobi and the Politics of Medicine in Nineteenth-Century America.* Chapel Hill: University of North Carolina Press.

Bix, Amy Sue. 2014. *Girls Coming to Tech! A History of American Engineering Education for Women.* Cambridge: Massachusetts Institute of Technology Press.

Bjelopera, Jerome P. 2005. *City of Clerks: Office and Sales Workers in Philadelphia, 1870–1920.* Urbana: University of Illinois Press.

Black, Brian. 2006. *Nature and the Environment in 20th Century American Life.* Westport: Greenwood Press.

Black, Edwin. 2003. *War Against the Weak: Eugenics and America's Campaign to Create a Master Race.* Washington, DC: Dialog Press.

Blackhawk, Ned. 2006. *Violence over the Land: Indians and Empires in the Early American West.* Cambridge: Harvard University Press.

Blackmon, Douglas A. 2008. *Slavery by Another Name: The Re-Enslavement of Black Americans from the Civil War to World War II.* New York: Random House.

Blainey, Geoffrey. 1963. "Herbert Hoover's Forgotten Years." *Business Archives and History* 3, 1: 53–70.

Blair, Cynthia M. 2010. *I've Got to Make My Livin': Black Women's Sex Work In Turn-Of-The-Century Chicago.* Chicago: University of Chicago Press.

Blair, Karen J. 1980. *Clubwoman as Feminist True Womanhood Redefined, 1868–1914.* New York: Holmes and Meier.

Blake, Angela M. 2006. *How New York Became American, 1890–1924.* Baltimore: Johns Hopkins University Press.

Blevins, Cameron. 2014. "Space, Nation, and the Triumph of Region: A View of the World from Houston." *Journal of American History* 101: 122–147.

Blight, David W. 2002. *Race and Reunion: The Civil War in American Memory.* Cambridge: Belknap Press.

Bloodworth, Jeff. 2011. "A Complicated Kindness: The Iowa Famine Relief Movement and the Myth of Midwestern and American Isolationism." *The Historian* 73: 480–502.

Bloodworth, Jr., William A. 1977. *Upton Sinclair.* Boston: Twayne.

Bloom, Harold. 2002. *Upton Sinclair's The Jungle.* Philadelphia: Chelsea House.

Bluestone, Daniel. 2011. *Buildings, Landscapes, and Memory: Case Studies in Historic Preservation.* New York: Norton.

Blum, Edward J. 2007. 2009. *Reforging the White Republic: Race, Religion, and American Nationalism, 1865--1898.* Baton Rouge: Louisiana State University Press.

Blum, John Morton. 1954. *The Republican Roosevelt.* Cambridge: Harvard University Press.

—. 1959. "Review of Leech." *New York Review of Books* November 1: 1.

Boag, Peter, 2003. *Same-Sex Affairs: Constructing and Controlling Homosexuality in the Pacific Northwest.* Berkeley: University of California Press.

Bodnar, John. 1977. *Immigrants and Industrialization: Ethnicity in an American Mill Town, 1870–1940.* Pittsburgh: University of Pittsburgh Press.

—. 1985. *The Transplanted: A History of Immigrants in America.* Bloomington: University of Indiana Press.

Bogart, Michele H. 1989. *Public Sculpture and the Civic Ideal in New York City, 1890–1930.* Chicago: University of Chicago Press.

—. 2006. *The Politics of Urban Beauty: New York and Its Art Commission.* Chicago: University of Chicago Press.

Bogue, Allan G. 1955. *Money at Interest; the Farm Mortgage on the Middle Border.* Ithaca: Cornell University Press.

—. 1963. *From Prairie to Corn Belt: Farming on the Illinois and Iowa Prairies in the 19th Century.* Chicago: Quadrangle Books.

Bolles, Blair. 1951. *Tyrant from Illinois: Uncle Joe Cannon's Experiment with Personal Power.* New York: Norton.

Boodry, Kathryn. 2016. "August Belmont and the World the Slaves Made." In *Slavery's Capitalism: A New History of American Economic Development*, ed. Sven Beckert and Seth Rockman, 163–178. Philadelphia: University of Pennsylvania Press.

Boorstin, Daniel. 1973. *The Americans: The Democratic Experience.* New York: Vintage Books.

Bordin, Ruth. 1981. *Women and Temperance: The Quest for Power and Liberty, 1873–1900.* Philadelphia: Temple University Press.

Boris, Eileen. 1994. *Home to Work: Motherhood and the Politics of Industrial Homework in the United States.* Cambridge: Cambridge University Press.

Borus, Daniel H. 2001. "Cultural Hierarchy and Aesthetics Reconsidered." *Intellectual History Newsletter* 23: 61–70.

Bourdieu, Pierre. 1979. *La distinction: critique sociale du jugement.* Paris: Éditions de Minuit.

Bouvier, Virginia Marie. 2001. *Whose America? The War of 1898 and the Battles to Define the Nation.* Westport: Prager.

Bowen, William G. 1994. *The Charitable Nonprofits: An Analysis of Institutional Dynamics and Characteristics.* San Francisco: Jossey-Bass Publishers.

Bowers, Claude G. 1932. *Beveridge and the Progressive Era.* Boston: Houghton Mifflin.

Bowman, Matthew. 2014. *The Urban Pulpit: New York City and the Fate of Liberal Evangelicalism.* New York: Oxford University Press.

Bowser, Eileen. 1994. *The Transformation of Cinema, 1907–1915.* Berkeley: University of California Press.

Boyer, Paul. 1978. *Urban Masses and Moral Order in America, 1820–1920.* Cambridge: Harvard University Press.

—. 2002. *Purity in Print: Book Censorship in America from the Gilded Age to the Computer Age.* Madison: University of Wisconsin Press.

Boyle, Eric W. 2013. *Quack Medicine: A History of Combating Health Fraud in Twentieth-Century America.* Santa Barbara: Praeger.

Brace, Charles Loring. 1872. *The Dangerous Classes of New York and Twenty Years' Work Among Them.* New York: Wynkoop & Hallenbeck.

Brackenridge, R. Douglas. 1999. *The Presbyterian Church (U.S.A.) Foundation: A Bicentennial History.* Louisville: Geneva Press.

Brady, David W. 1972. "Congressional Leadership and Party Voting in the McKinley Era: A Comparison to the Modern House." *Midwest Journal of Politics* 6, 2: 439–59.

—. 1973. *Congressional Voting in a Partisan Era.* Lawrence: University of Kansas Press.

—. and David Epstein. 1997. "Intraparty Preferences, Heterogeneity, and the Origins of the Modern Congress: Progressive Reformers in the House and Senate, 1890–1920." *Journal of Law, Economics, and Organization* 13, 1: 26–49.

—, and Philip Althoff. 1974. "Party Voting in the U.S. House of Representatives, 1890–1910: Elements of a Responsible Party System." *Journal of Politics* 36, 3: 753–75.

—, Richard Brody, and David Epstein. 1989. "Heterogeneous Parties and Political Organization: The U.S. Senate, 1880–1920." *Legislative Studies Quarterly* 14 2: 205–223.

Brady, Kathleen. 1984. *Ida Tarbell: Portrait of a Muckraker.* New York: Seaview/Putnam.

Braeman, John. 1971. *Albert J. Beveridge: American Nationalist.* Chicago: University of Chicago Press.

Brandeis, Louis D. 1908. Brief before the Supreme Court in the case *Muller v. Oregon.*

Brands, Henry W. 1997. *T. R.: The Last Romantic.* New York: Basic Books.

—. 2003. *Woodrow Wilson.* New York: Times Books.

Brandt, Allan. 1985. *No Magic Bullet: A Social History of Venereal Disease in the United States Since 1880.* New York: Oxford University Press.

Braudel, Fernand. 1982. *The Wheels of Commerce.* New York: Harper & Row.

Brecher, Jeremy. 1972. *Strike!* Boston: South End Press.

Brechin, Gray A. 1996. "Conserving the Race: Natural Aristocracies, Eugenics, and the Conservation Movement." *Antipode* 28: 229–245.

—. 1999. *Imperial San Francisco: Urban Power, Earthly Ruin.* Berkeley: University of California Press.

Bremner, Robert. 1988. *American Philanthropy.* 2nd ed. Chicago: The University of Chicago Press.

Brewer, George D. 1910. *The Fighting Editor, or, Warren and the Appeal.* Girard: George D. Brewer.

Bridges, Amy. 1997. *Morning Glories.* Princeton: Princeton University Press.

—. 2008. "Managing the Periphery in the Gilded Age: Writing Constitutions for the Western States." *Studies in American Political Development* 22: 32–58.

Bridges, Lamar W. 1984. "George Kibbe Turner of *McClure's Magazine.*" *Journalism Quarterly* 61: 178–182.

Briggs, Laura. 2002. *Reproducing Empire: Race, Sex, Science, and U.S. Imperialism in Puerto Rico.* Berkeley: University of California Press.

Brinkley, Alan. 1998. "Hofstadter's *The Age of Reform* Reconsidered," in Brinkley, *Liberalism and its Discontents.* Cambridge: Harvard University Press.

Brinkley, Douglas. 2009. *The Wilderness Warrior: Theodore Roosevelt and the Crusade for America.* New York: Harper Collins.

Britten, Thomas A. 1997. *American Indians in World War I: At War and at Home.* Albuquerque: University of New Mexico Press.

Brock, William R. 1984. *Investigation and Responsibility: Public Responsibility in the United States.* Cambridge: Cambridge University Press.

Brodie, Janet Farrell. 1994. *Contraception and Abortion in 19th-Century America.* Ithaca: Cornell University Press.

Brodkin, Karen. 1998. *How Jews Became White Folks and What That Says About Race In America.* New Brunswick: Rutgers University Press.

Brodsky, Alyn. 2000. *Grover Cleveland: A Study in Character.* New York: St. Martin's.

Brooks, Charlotte. 2009. *Alien Neighbors, Foreign Friends: Asian Americans, Housing, and the Transformation of Urban California.* Chicago: University of Chicago Press.

Brooks, Tim. 2004. *Lost Sounds: Blacks and the Birth of the Recording Industry, 1890–1919.* Champaign: University of Illinois Press.

Brophy, Alfred L. 2013. "Did Formalism Never Exist?" Review of *Beyond the Formalist Realist Divide: the Role of Politics in Judging,* by Brian Z. Tamanaha. *University of Texas Law Review* 92, 2: 383–412.

Broun, Haywood, and Margaret Leech. 1927. *Anthony Comstock, Roundsman of the Lord.* New York: The Literary Guild of America.

Brown, David S. 2006. *Richard Hofstadter: An Intellectual Biography*. Chicago: University of Chicago Press.

Brown, Dorothy M., and McKeown, Elizabeth. 1997. *The Poor Belong to Us: Catholic Charities and American Welfare*. Cambridge: Harvard University Press.

Brown, Elspeth H. 2005. *The Corporate Eye: Photography and the Rationalization of American Commercial Culture, 1884–1929*. Baltimore: Johns Hopkins University Press.

Brown, Harry James and Frederick D. Williams. 1967–81. *The Diary of James A. Garfield*. East Lansing: Michigan State University Press.

Brown, Leslie. 2008. *Upbuilding Black Durham: Gender, Class, and Black Community Development in the Jim Crow South*. Chapel Hill: University of North Carolina Press.

Brown, Richard D. 1973. "The Emergence of Voluntary Associations in Massachusetts, 1760–1830." *Journal of Voluntary Action Research* II: 64–73.

Brown, Thomas J. 2006. *Reconstructions: New Perspectives on Postbellum America*. New York: Oxford University Press.

Brown, Victoria Bissell. 2004. *The Education of Jane Addams*. Philadelphia: University of Pennsylvania Press.

Brownell, Blaine A. 1975. *The Urban Ethos in the South, 1920–1930*. Baton Rouge: Louisiana State University Press.

Bruinius, Harry. 2006. *Better For All the World: The Secret History of Forced Sterilization and America's Quest for Racial Purity*. New York: Random House, Inc.

Brundage, W. Fitzhugh. 2011. "Introduction." In *The Folly of Jim Crow: Rethinking the Segregated South*, ed. Stephanie Cole and Natalie J. Ring, 1–16. Arlington: The University of Texas at Arlington.

Bryan, William Jennings. 1996. Speech to the 1896 Populist Party Convention, popularly referred to as the Cross of Gold Speech: http://historymatters.gmu.edu/d/5354/.

Bryce, James. 1891. *The American Commonwealth*. 2 volumes. New York: Macmillan.

Bsumek, Erika. 2008. *Indian Made: Navajo Culture in the Marketplace, 1868–1940*. Lawrence: University Press of Kansas.

Budig, Gene A. 2013. *George Norris, Going Home: Reflections of a Progressive Statesman*. Lincoln: University of Nebraska Press.

Buenker, John D., John C. Burnham, and Robert M. Crunden. 1977. *Progressivism*. Cambridge: Shenkman.

—. 1973. *Urban Liberalism and Progressive Reform*. New York: Scribner.

—. 1978. *Urban Liberalism and Progressive Reform*. New York: W. W. Norton.

—. 1998. *The History of Wisconsin, Volume IV: The Progressive Era, 1893–1914*. Madison: Wisconsin Historical Society.

Buhle, P. and E. Rice-Maximin. 1995. *William Appleman Williams: The Tragedy of Empire*. New York: Routledge.

Bularzik, Mary. 1978. "Sexual Harassment at the Workplace: Historical Notes." *Radical America* 12: 25–43.

Bullough, Vern. 1975. "Sex and the Medical Model." *The Journal of Sex Research* 11, 4: 291–303.

Bulmer, Martin. 1984. *The Chicago School of Sociology: Institutionalization, Diversity, and the Rise of Sociological Research*. Chicago: University of Chicago Press.

Burgess, Ernest W. 1925. "The Growth of the City: An Introduction to a Research Project." In *The City*, ed. Robert E. Park, Ernest W. Burgess, and Roderick D. McKenzie. Chicago: University of Chicago Press.

Burke, Colin B. 1982. *American Collegiate Populations: A Test of the Traditional View*. New York: New York University Press.

—. 2001. "Nonprofit History's New Numbers (and the Need for More)." *Nonprofit and Voluntary Sector Quarterly* 30, 2: 174–203.

Burner, David. 1979. *Herbert Hoover: A Public Life*. New York: Knopf.

Burnett, Christina Duffy, and Burke Marshall, eds. 2001. *Foreign in a Domestic Sense: Puerto Rico, American Expansion, and the Constitution*. Durham: Duke University Press.

—. 2005. "Untied States: American Expansion and Territorial Deannexation." *University of Chicago Law Review* 72: 797–879.

—. 2008. "'They Say I Am Not An American…': The Noncitizen National and the Law of American Empire." *Virginia Journal of International Law* 48: 659–718.

Burnham, John C. 1973. "The Progressive Era Revolution in American Attitudes toward Sex." *The Journal of American History* 59, 4: 885–908.

Burnham, Walter Dean. 1967. "Party Systems and the Political Process." In *The American Party Systems: Stages of Development*, ed. Burnham and William Chambers, 277–307. New York: Oxford University Press.

—. 1970. *Critical Elections and the Mainspring of American Politics*. New York: W. W. Norton and Company.

—. 1974. "Theory and Voting Research: Some Reflections on Converse's 'Change in the American Electorate.'" *The American Political Science Review* 68, 3: 1002–1023.

Burns, Ken. 2014. "The Roosevelts: An Intimate History." PBS Documentary.

Burns, Sarah. 1996. *Inventing the Modern Artist: Art and Culture in Gilded Age America*. New Haven: Yale University Press.

—. 1997. "Modernizing Winslow Homer." *American Quarterly* 49: 615–639.

Burnstein, Daniel Eli. 2006. *Next to Godliness: Confronting Dirt and Despair in Progressive Era New York City*. Urbana: University of Illinois Press.

Burris, John P. 2001. *Exhibiting Religion: Colonialism and Spectacle at International Expositions 1851–1893*. Charlottesville: University Press of Virginia.

Busbey, L. White. 1927. *Uncle Joe Cannon: the Story of a Pioneer American*. New York: H. Holt and Company.

Butler, Anne M. 1985. *Daughters of Joy, Sisters of Misery: Prostitutes in the American West, 1865–1890*. Urbana: University of Illinois Press.

Butler, Jon, Grant Wacker, and Randall Balmer. 2003. *Religion in American Life: A Short History*. New York: Oxford University Press.

Butler, Leslie. 2007. *Critical Americans: Victorian Intellectuals and Transatlantic Liberal Reform*. Chapel Hill: University of North Carolina Press.

Byrd, Jodi. 2011. *The Transit of Empire: Indigenous Critiques of Colonialism*. Minneapolis: University of Minnesota Press.

Byrd, W. Michael and Linda A. Clayton. 2000. *An American Health Dilemma: A Medical History of African Americans and the Problems of Race: Beginnings to 1900*. New York: Routledge.

Cabranes, José A. 1978. "Citizenship and the American Empire: Notes on the Legislative History of the United States Citizenship of Puerto Ricans." *University of Pennsylvania Law Review* 127: 391–492.

Cachan, Manuel. 2002. "Justice Stephen Field and 'Free Soil, Free Labor Constitutionalism': Reconsidering Revisionism." *Law and History Review* 20, 3: 541–76.

Caddoo, Cara. 2014. *Envisioning Freedom: Cinema and the Building of Modern Black Life*. Cambridge: Harvard University Press.

Cahan, Abraham. 1969. *The Education of Abraham Cahan*. Philadelphia: Jewish Publication Society of America.

Cahill, Cathleen D. 2011. *Federal Fathers and Mothers: A Social History of the United States Indian Service, 1869–1933*. Chapel Hill: University of North Carolina Press.

Calder, Lendol. 2001. *Financing the American Dream: A Cultural History of Consumer Credit*. Princeton: Princeton University Press.

Caldwell, Robert Granville. 1931. *James A. Garfield, Party Chieftain*. New York: Dodd, Mead.

Calhoun, Charles W. 1986. "Making History: The Society for Historians of the Gilded Age and Progressive Era: A Retrospective View." *Journal of the Gilded Age and Progressive Era* 1, 1: 12–24.

—. 1988. "Benjamin Harrison, Centennial President: A Review Essay." *Indiana Magazine of History* 84: 134–60.

—, ed., 1996. *The Gilded Age: Essays on the Origins of Modern America*. Wilmington, DE: Scholarly Resources.

—. 1996. "Political Economy in the Gilded Age: The Republican Party's Industrial Policy." *Journal of Policy History* 8, 3: 291–309.

—. 2002. "Reimagining the 'Lost Men' of the Gilded Age: Perspectives on the Late Nineteenth Century." *Journal of the Gilded Age and Progressive Era* 1: 225–57.

—. 2005. *Benjamin Harrison*. New York: Henry Holt.

—. 2007. "The Political Culture: Public Life and the Conduct of Politics." In *The Gilded Age: Perspectives on the Origins of Modern America*, ed. C.W. Calhoun. 2nd edition. Lanham: Rowman & Littlefield.

—. 2010. *From Bloody Shirt to Full Dinner Pail: The Transformation of Politics and Governance in the Gilded Age*. New York: Hill & Wang.

Campbell, Bruce. 1980. *Ancient Wisdom Revived: A History of the Theosophical Movement*. Berkeley: University of California Press.

Campbell, Charles C. 1976. *The Transformation of American Foreign Relations, 1865–1900*. New York: Harper and Row.

Campbell, W. Joseph. 2006. *The Year That Defined American Journalism: 1897 and the Clash of Paradigms*. New York: Routledge.

Canon, David. T. Garrison Nelson, and Charles Stewart III. 2002. *Committees in the U.S. Congress, 1789–1946*. 4 volumes. Washington, DC: Congressional Quarterly Press.

Cantley, A. C. 1898. "Some Facts about Making Patent Medicines." *The Chautauquan: A Weekly Newsmagazine* 27, July: 389.

Capozolla, Christopher. 2008. *Uncle Sam Wants You: World War I and the Meaning of the Modern American Citizen*. New York: Oxford University Press.

Carden, Maren Lockwood. 1969. *Oneida: Utopian Community to Modern Corporation*. Baltimore: Johns Hopkins University Press.

Carey, Patrick W. 1987. *People, Priests, and Prelates: Ecclesiastical Democracy and the Tensions of Trusteeism*. Notre Dame: Notre Dame University Press.

Carlson Allan C. 2009. "Comstockery, Contraception, and the Family: The Remarkable Achievements of an Anti-Vice Crusader." *The Family in America* 23, 1.

Carlton, David L. 1982. *Mill and Town in South Carolina, 1880–1920*. Baton Rouge: Louisiana State University Press.

Carnegie, Andrew. 1886. *Triumphant Democracy: Or, Fifty Years March of the Republic*. New York: Scribner's.

—. 1901. *The Gospel of Wealth and Other Timely Essays*. New York: The Century Company.

Carnes, Mark C., and Clyde Griffen, eds. 1990. *Meanings for Manhood: Constructions of Masculinity in Victorian America*. Chicago: University of Chicago Press.

Caro, Robert. 2002. *The Years of Lyndon Johnson: Master of the Senate*. New York: Knopf.

Caron, Simone M. 2008. *Who Choses? American Reproductive History Since 1830*. Gainesville: University of Florida Press.

Carosso, Vincent P. 1970. *Investment Banking in America, a History*. Cambridge: Harvard University Press.

Carpenter, Daniel P. 2001. *The Forging of Bureaucratic Autonomy: Reputations, Networks, and Policy Innovation in Executive Agencies, 1862–1928*. Princeton: Princeton University Press.

Carpenter, Niles. 1927. *Census Monographs VII: Immigrants and their Children*. Washington, DC: Government Printing Office.

Carson, John. 2007. *The Measure of Merit: Talents, Intelligence, and Inequality in the French and American Republics, 1750–1940*. Princeton: Princeton University Press.

Carson, Mina. 1990. *Settlement Folk: Social Thought and the American Settlement Movement, 1885–1930*. Chicago: University of Chicago Press.

Carter, Heath. 2015. *Union Made: Working People and the Rise of Social Christianity in Chicago*. New York: Oxford University Press.

Carter, Paul L. 1971. *The Spiritual Crisis of the Gilded Age*. DeKalb: Northern Illinois University Press.

Carter, Susan B., and Richard Sutch, eds. 2006. *Historical Statistics of the United States*. Millennial edition. Cambridge: Cambridge University Press.

Casey, Robert. 2008. *The Model T: A Centennial History*. Baltimore: Johns Hopkins University Press.

Cash, W. J. 1941. *The Mind of the South*. New York: A.A. Knopf.

Cashman, Sean. 1993. *America in the Gilded Age*. New York: New York University Press.

Cassedy, James H. 2009. *John Shaw Billings: Science and Medicine in the Gilded Age*. Philadelphia: Xlibris Corporation.

Catt, Carrie Chapman, and Nettie Rogers Schuler. 1926. *Woman Suffrage and Politics: The Inner Story of the Suffrage Movement*. New York: Scribner and Sons.

Cauthen, Kenneth. 1962. *The Impact of American Religious Liberalism*. Washington DC: University Press of America.

Cayton, Andrew R. L., and Peter S. Onuf. 1990. *The Midwest and the Nation*. Bloomington: Indiana University Press.

Ceaser, James. 1979. *Presidential Selection: Theory and Development*. Princeton: Princeton University Press.

Cell, John Whitson. 1982. *The Highest Stage of White Supremacy: The Origins of Segregation in South Africa and the American South*. New York: Cambridge University Press.

Censer, Jane Turner. 2003. *Reconstruction of Southern White Womanhood 1865–1895*. Baton Rouge: Louisiana State University Press.

Cervenak, Sarah Jane. 2014. *Wandering: Philosophical Performances of Racial and Sexual Freedom*. Durham: Duke University Press.

Chakrabarty, Dipesh. 2000. *Provincializing Europe: Postcolonial Thought and Historical Difference*. Princeton: Princeton University Press.

Chalberg, John C. 2008. *Emma Goldman: American Individualist*. New York: Pearson.

Chamberlain, John. 1932. *Farewell to Reform: Being a History of the Rise, Life, and Decay of the Progressive Mind*. New York: Liveright.

—. 1965. *Farewell to Reform: The Rise, Life and Decay of the Progressive Mind in America*. Chicago: Quadrangle Books.

Chandler, Alfred D, Jr. 1956. *Henry Varnum Poor, Business Editor, Analyst, and Reformer*. Cambridge: Harvard University Press.

—. 1977. *The Visible Hand: The Managerial Revolution in American Business*. Cambridge: Belknap Press of Harvard University Press.

—. 1994. *Scale and Scope: The Dynamics of Industrial Capitalism*. Cambridge: Belknap Press.

Chang, Derek. 2010. *Citizens of a Christian Nation: Evangelical Missions and the Problem of Race in the Nineteenth Century*. Philadelphia: University of Pennsylvania Press.

Chang, Kornel S. 2012. *Pacific Connections: The Making of the U.S.-Canadian Borderlands*. Berkeley: University of California Press.

Chatterjee, Partha. 1993. *The Nation and Its Fragments: Colonial and Postcolonial Histories*. Princeton: Princeton University Press.

Chauncey, George. 1994. *Gay New York: Gender, Urban Culture and the Making of the Gay Male World, 1890–1940*. New York: Basic Books.

—. 2004. "'What Gay Studies Taught the Court': The Historians' Amicus Brief in Lawrence v. Texas." *GLQ: A Journal of Lesbian and Gay Studies* 10, 3: 509–538.

Cheape, Charles W. 1980. *Moving the Masses: Urban Public Transit In New York, Boston, and Philadelphia, 1880–1912*. Cambridge: Harvard University Press.

Cherny, Robert W. 1994. *A Righteous Cause: The Life of William Jennings Bryan*. Norman: University of Oklahoma Press.

—. 1997. *American Politics in the Gilded Age, 1868–1900*. Wheeling: Harlan Davidson.

Chesler, Ellen. 1992. *Woman of Valor: Margaret Sanger and the Birth Control Movement in America*. New York: Simon & Schuster.

Chin, Carol C. 2007. "'Uplifting the Barbarian.'" In *A Companion to Theodore Roosevelt*, ed. Serge Ricard. Malden: Wiley-Blackwell.

Choy, Catherine Ceniza. 2003. *Empire of Care: Nursing and Migration in Filipino American History*. Durham: Duke University Press.

Churella, Albert J. 2012. *The Pennsylvania Railroad. Volume 1: Building an Empire, 1846–1917*. Philadelphia: University of Pennsylvania Press.

Clanton, Gene. 1969. *Kansas Populism: Ideas and Men*. Lawrence: University Press of Kansas.

—. 1991. *Populism: The Humane Preference in America, 1890–1901*. Boston: Twayne.

Clapp, Elizabeth. 1999. *Mothers of All Children: Women Reformers and the Rise of Juvenile Courts in Progressive-Era America*. University Park: Penn State University Press.

Clark, Christopher. 2012. "The Agrarian Context of American Capitalist Development." In *Capitalism Takes Command: The Social Transformation of Nineteenth-Century America*, ed. Michael Zakim and Gary J. Kornblith, 39–68. Chicago: University of Chicago Press. DOI: 10.7208/chicago/9780226977997.001.0001

Clark, Daniel A. 2010. *Creating the College Man: American Mass Magazines and Middle-Class Manhood, 1890–1915*. Madison: University of Wisconsin Press.

Clark, Victor S. 1903. "Industrial Conditions in America. Interview with Mr Victor S. Clarke [sic.]. American Workmen and Trades Unionism." *Daily Telegraph*, 9 September 1903: 6.

—. 1905. "Labor Conditions in Java." *Bulletin of the Bureau of Labor* 58: 906–54. Washington, DC: U.S. Department of Commerce and Labor.

—. 1905. "Labor Conditions in the Philippines." *Bulletin of the Bureau of Labor* 58: 721–905. Washington, DC: U.S. Department of Commerce and Labor.

—. 1906. *The Labour Movement in Australasia: A Study in Social Democracy*. New York: H. Holt & Co.

Clarke, Edward H. 1873. *Sex in Education; or, a Fair Chance for Girls*. Boston: J. R. Osgood and Co.

Clarke, Michael Tavel. 2007. *These Days of Large Things: The Culture of Size in America, 1865–1930*. Ann Arbor: University of Michigan Press.

Clemens, Elizabeth. 1997. *The People's Lobby: Organizational Innovation and the Rise of Interest Group Politics in the United States, 1890–1925*. Chicago: University of Chicago Press.

—. 2000. "The Encounter of Civil Society and the States: Legislation, Law, and Association, 1900–1920." Paper presented at the annual meeting of the Social Science History Association, Chicago, Illinois.

Clement, Elizabeth Alice. 2006. *Love for Sale: Courting, Treating, and Prostitution In New York City, 1900–1945*. Chapel Hill: University of North Carolina Press.

Clow, Richmond L. 1987. "The Indian Reorganization Act and the Loss of Tribal Sovereignty: Constitutions on the Rosebud and Pine Ridge Reservations." *Great Plains Quarterly* 7: 125–134.

Clune, Erin Elizabeth. 2010. "From Light Copper to the Blackest and Lowest Type: Daniel Tompkins and the Racial Order of the Global New South." *The Journal of Southern History* 76, 2: 275–314.

Coates, Benjamin. 2016. *Legalist Empire: The United States, Civilization, and International Law in the Early Twentieth Century*. New York: Oxford University Press.

Coates, Peter. 2006. *American Perceptions of Immigrant and Invasive Species: Strangers on the Land*. Berkeley: University of California Press.

Cobb, James C. 1984. *Industrialization and Southern Society, 1877–1984*. Lexington: University Press of Kentucky.

Coben, Stanley. 1976. "Foundation officials and fellowships: Innovation in the patronage of science." *Minerva* 14, 2: 225–240.

Cocks, Catherine. 2006. "Rethinking Sexuality in the Progressive Era." *The Journal of the Gilded Age and Progressive Era* 5, 2: 93–118.

Cohen, Lizabeth. 1990. *Making a New Deal: Industrial Workers in Chicago, 1919–1939*. New York: Cambridge University Press.

Cohen, Michael P. 1984. *The Pathless Way: John Muir and American Wilderness*. Madison: University of Wisconsin Press.

Cohen, Nancy. 2002. *The Reconstruction of American Liberalism, 1865–1914*. Chapel Hill: University of North Carolina Press.

Cohen, Naomi Wiener. 1999. *Jacob H. Schiff: A Study in American Jewish Leadership*. Hanover: University Press of New England for Brandeis University Press.

Cohen, Warren I. 1968. *The American Revisionists: the Lessons of Intervention in World War I*. Chicago: University of Chicago Press.

Cohen-Solal, Annie. 2001. *Painting American: The Rise of American Artists, Paris 1867—New York, 1948.* Translated by Laurie Hurwitz-Attias. New York: Knopf.

Colby, Jason M. 2011. *The Business of Empire: United Fruit, Race, and U.S. Expansion in Central America.* Ithaca: Cornell University Press.

Cole, Peter. 2007. *Wobblies on the Waterfront: Interracial Unionism in Progressive-Era Philadelphia.* Urbana: University of Illinois Press.

Coleman, Peter J. 1982. "New Zealand Liberalism and the Origins of the American Welfare State." *Journal of American History* 69: 372–91.

—. 1987. *Progressivism and the World of Reform: New Zealand and the Origins of the American Welfare State.* Lawrence: University Press of Kansas.

Collin, Richard H. 1985. *Theodore Roosevelt, Culture, Diplomacy, and Expansion: A New View of American Imperialism.* Baton Rouge: Louisiana State University Press.

Collins, Robert M. 1989. "The Originality Trap: Richard Hofstadter on Populism." *Journal of American History* 76: 150–167.

Colwell, Mary Anna Culleton. 1993. *Private Foundations and Public Policy: The Political Role of Philanthropy.* New York: Garland.

The Combahee River Collective. 1986. *The Combahee River Collective Statement.* Albany: Kitchen Table.

Commons, John R., et al. 1918–1935. *History of Labour in the United States.* New York: Macmillan.

—, ed. 1905. *Trade Unionism and Labor Problems.* Boston: Ginn.

Conn, Steven. 2004. *History's Shadow: Native Americans and Historical Consciousness in the Nineteenth Century.* Chicago: University of Chicago Press.

—. 1998. *Museums and American Intellectual Life, 1876–1926.* Chicago: University of Chicago Press.

Connolly, James J. 1998. *The Triumph of Ethnic Progressivism: Urban Political Culture in Boston, 1900–1925.* Boston: Harvard University Press.

—. 2005. "The Public Good and the Problem of Pluralism in Lincoln Steffens's Civic Imagination." *The Journal of the Gilded Age and Progressive Era* 4, 2: 125–147.

Conway, Cecilia. 1995. *African Banjo Echoes in Appalachia: A Study of Folk Traditions.* Knoxville: University of Tennessee Press.

Conzen, Kathleen Neils, et al. 1992. "The Invention of Ethnicity: A Perspective From the United States." *Journal of American Ethnic History* 12, 1: 4–41.

Cooley, Thomas M. 1868. *A Treatise on the Constitutional Limitations Which Rest Upon the Legislative Power of the States of the American Union.* Boston: Little, Brown.

Coolidge, Calvin. 1929. *The Autobiography of Calvin Coolidge.* New York: Cosmopolitan.

Cooper, John Milton, Jr. 1983. *The Warrior and the Priest: Woodrow Wilson and Theodore Roosevelt.* Cambridge: Belknap Press of Harvard University Press.

—. *Woodrow Wilson: A Biography.* New York: Alfred A. Knopf.

—, ed. 2008. *Reconsidering Woodrow Wilson: Progressivism, Internationalism, War, and Peace.* Washington, DC: Woodrow Wilson Center Press.

—. 1969. *The Vanity of Power: American Isolationism and the First World War, 1914–1917.* Westport: Greenwood.

—. 2001. *Breaking the Heart of the World: Woodrow Wilson and the Fight for the League of Nations.* New York: Cambridge University Press.

—. 2003. "Not So Innocent Abroad: The Hoovers' Early Years." In *Uncommon Americans: The Lives and Legacies of Herbert and Lou Henry Hoover,* ed. Timothy Walch, 39–47. Westport: Praeger.

Corey, Lewis. 1935 (1992). *The Crisis of the Middle Class.* New York: Covici-Friede. Reprint, New York: Columbia University Press. Citations refer to the Columbia edition.

Corn, Joseph J. 2011. *User Unfriendly: Consumer Struggles with Personal Technologies, from Clocks and Sewing Machines to Cars and Computers.* Baltimore: Johns Hopkins University Press.

Cornwell, Elmer. 1965. *Presidential Leadership of Public Opinion.* Bloomington: Indiana University Press.

Corwin, Edward Henry Lewinski. 1946. *The American Hospital.* New York: The Commonwealth Fund for the New York Academy of Medicine.

—. 1941. *Constitutional Revolution, Ltd.* Claremont: Claremont Colleges.

Cott, Nancy. 1979. "Passionlessness: An Interpretation of Victorian Sexual Ideology, 1790–1850." In *A Heritage of Her Own: Toward a New Social History of American Women,* ed. Nancy F. Cott and Elizabeth H. Pleck, 162–181. New York: Simon and Schuster.

—. 1987. *The Grounding of Modern Feminism.* New Haven: Yale University Press.

—. 2000. *Public Vows: A History of Marriage and the Nation.* Cambridge: Harvard University Press.

Cottom, Robert Irving, Jr. 1975. "To Be Among the First: The Early Career of James A. Garfield, 1831–1868." PhD diss., Johns Hopkins University.

Couvares, Frances G. 1984. *The Remaking of Pittsburgh: Class and Culture in an Industrializing City, 1877–1919.* Albany: State University of New York Press.

Cowan, Ruth Schwartz. 1983. *More Work for Mother: The Ironies of Household Technology from the Open Hearth to the Microwave.* New York: Basic Books.

Cox, Gary W., and Matthew D. McCubbins. 2002. "Agenda Power in the U.S. House of Representatives, 1877 to 1986." In *Party, Process, and Political Change in Congress,* ed. David W. Brady and Matthew D. McCubbins. Palo Alto: Stanford University Press.

Cox, Karen C. 2003. *Dixie's Daughters: The United Daughters of the Confederacy and the Preservation of Confederate Culture.* Tallahassee: University of Florida Press.

Cox, Robert. 2003. *Body and Soul: A Sympathetic History of American Spiritualism.* Charlottesville: University of Virginia Press.

Cranston, Sylvia. 1993. *HPB: The Extraordinary Life and Influence of Helena Blavatsky.* New York: Tarcher.

Crapol, Edward and Howard Schonberger. 1972. "The Shift to Global Empire, 1865 – 1900." In *From Colony to Empire: Essays in the History of American Foreign Relations,* ed. William Appleman. New York: John Wiley.

—. 1973. *America for Americans: Economic Nationalism and Anglophobia in the Late Nineteenth Century.* Westport: Greenwood.

Cray, William C. 1984. *Miles 1884–1984: A Centennial History.* Englewood Cliffs: Prentice Hall.

Creech, Joe. 2015. "The Tolerant Populists and the Legacy of Walter Nugent." *Journal of the Gilded Age and Progressive Era* 14, 2: 141–159. DOI: 10.1017/S1537781414000760.

Crenshaw, Kimberly. 1989. "Demarginalizing the Intersection of Race and Sex: A Black Feminist Critique of Antidiscrimination Doctrine, Feminist Theory and Antiracist Politics." *Chicago Legal Forum* 140: 139–167.

Crenson, Matthew, and Benjamin Ginsberg. 2007. *Presidential Power: Unchecked and Unbalanced.* New York: Norton.

Critchlow, Donald T. 1986. *Socialism in the Heartland.* Notre Dame: Notre Dame University Press.

Crocker, Ruth. 2000. *Mrs. Russell Sage: Women's Activism and Philanthropy in Gilded Age and Progressive Era America.* Bloomington: Indiana University Press.

Croly, Herbert. 1909. *The Promise of American Life.* New York: The Macmillan Company.

—. 1914. *Progressive Democracy.* New York: MacMillan.

Cronon, William. 1983. *Changes in the Land: Indians, Colonists, and the Ecology of New England.* New York: Hill and Wang.

—. 1991. *Nature's Metropolis: Chicago and the Great West.* New York: W.W. Norton.

—. 1995. "The Trouble with Wilderness; or, Getting Back to the Wrong Nature." In *Uncommon Ground: Toward Reinventing Nature*, ed. William Cronon, 69–90. New York: W.W. Norton.

Crosby, Alfred W. 1973. *The Columbian Exchange: Biological and Cultural Consequences of 1492.* Westport: Greenwood.

—. 2003. *America's Forgotten Pandemic: The Influenza of 1918.* New York: Cambridge University Press.

Crunden, Robert M. 1982. *Ministers of Reform: The Progressives' Achievement in American Civilization, 1889–1920.* New York: Basic Books.

—. 1993. *American Salons: Encounters with European Modernism, 1885–1917.* New York: Oxford University Press.

Cullinane, Michael Patrick. Forthcoming. *Theodore Roosevelt's Ghost: The History of an American Icon.*

Cumings, Bruce. 2009. *Dominion from Sea to Sea: Pacific Ascendancy and American Power.* New Haven: Yale University Press.

Current, Richard N. 1950. *Pine Logs and Politics: A Life of Philetus Sawyer, 1816–1900.* Madison: State Historical Society of Wisconsin.

Curti, Merle, and Roderick Nash. 1965. *Philanthropy in the Shaping of American Higher Education.* New Brunswick: Rutgers University Press.

—. 1958. "American Philanthropy and the National Character." *American Quarterly* 10, Winter: 420–437.

—. 1963. *American Philanthropy Abroad: a History.* New Brunswick: Rutgers University Press.

Curtis, Heather D. 2007. *Faith in the Great Physician: Suffering and Divine Healing in American Culture, 1860–1900.* Baltimore: Johns Hopkins University Press.

—. 2012. "Depicting Distant Suffering: Evangelicals and the Politics of Pictorial Humanitarianism in the Age of American Empire." *Material Religion: The Journal of Objects, Art and Belief* 8: 154–83.

Cushman, Barry. 1998. *Rethinking the New Deal Court: The Structure of a Constitutional Revolution.* Oxford: Oxford University Press.

—. 2000. "Formalism and Realism in Commerce Clause Jurisprudence." *University of Chicago Law Review* 67, 4: 1089–1150.

Cushman, Barry. 2013. "Carolene Products and Constitutional Structure." *Supreme Court Review* 2012, 1: 321–77.

Dagbovie, Pero Gaglo. 2010. *African American History Reconsidered.* Urbana: University of Illinois Press.

Dailey, Jane. 2000. *Before Jim Crow: The Politics of Race in Postemancipation Virginia.* Chapel Hill: The University of North Carolina Press.

Dalton, Kathleen. 1981. "Why America Loved Teddy Roosevelt: Or Charisma is in the Eyes of the Beholders." In *OurSelves/Our Past: Psychological Approaches to American History*, ed. Robert J. Brugger. Baltimore: Johns Hopkins University Press.

—. 1992. "The Bully Prophet: Theodore Roosevelt and American Memory." In *Theodore Roosevelt: Many-Sided American*, ed. Natalie A. Naylor, Douglas Brinkley, and John Allen Gable. Interlaken: Heart of the Lakes Publishing/Hofstra University.

—. 2001. "Between the Diplomacy of Imperialism and the Achievement of World Order by Supranational Mediation: Ethnocentrism and Theodore Roosevelt's Changing Views of World Order." In *Ethnocentrism et diplomatie: l'Amerique et le monde au XXe siècle*, ed. Pierre Melandri and Serge Ricard. Paris: Editions L'Harmattan.

—. 2002. *Theodore Roosevelt: A Strenuous Life.* New York: Alfred A. Knopf.

Dalzell, Robert F. 1987. *Enterprising Elite: The Boston Associates and the World They Made.* Cambridge, MA: Harvard University Press.

Daniels, Doris Groshen. 1989. *Always a Sister: The Feminism of Lillian D. Wald.* New York: Feminist Press at the City University of New York.

Daniels, Roger. 2004. *Guarding the Golden Door: American Immigration Policy and Immigrants Since 1882.* New York: Hill and Wang.

Darby, Robert. 2003. "The Masturbation Taboo and the Rise of Routine Male Circumcision: A Review of the Historiography." *Journal of Social History* 36, 3: 737–57.

Davidson, James West. 2007. *"They Say": Ida B. Wells and the Reconstruction of Race.* New York: Oxford University.

Davies, Richard O. 1998. *Main Street Blues.* Columbus: Ohio University Press.

Davies, Robert Bruce. 1976. *Peacefully Working to Conquer the World: Singer Machines in Foreign Markets, 1854–1920.* New York: Arno Press.

Davis, Allen F. 1964. "The Social Workers and the Progressive Party 1912–1916." *American Historical Review* 69, April: 671–688.

—. 1967. *Spearheads for Reform: The Social Settlements and the Progressive Movement, 1890–1914.* New York: Oxford University Press.

Davis, Clark. 2000. *Company Men: White-Collar Life and Corporate Cultures in Los Angeles, 1892–1941.* Baltimore: Johns Hopkins University Press.

Davis, Cyprian. 1995. *The History of Black Catholics in the United States.* New York: Crossroads.

Davis, Elmer. 1921. *History of the New York Times, 1851–1921.* New York: New York Times.

Davis, George W. 1900. *Report on Civil Affairs of Porto Rico, 1899.* Washington, DC: Government Printing Office.

Davis, Janet. 2002. *The Circus Age: Culture and Society under the American Big Top.* Chapel Hill: University of North Carolina Press.

Davis, Lance. 1958. "Stock Ownership in the Early New England Textile Industry, A Case Study." *Business History Review* 32: 204–222.

—. 1960. "The New England Textile Mills and the Capital Markets: A Study of Industrial Borrowing 1840–1860." *The Journal of Economic History* 20: 1–30.

—. 1966. "The Capital Markets and Industrial Concentration: The U.S. and U.K., a Comparative Study." *Economic History Review* 19: 255–72.

—, and Robert E. Gallman. 2001. *Evolving Financial Markets and International Capital Flows: Britain, the Americas, and Australia, 1865–1914.* Cambridge: Cambridge University Press.

Davison, Kenneth E. 1972. *Presidency of Rutherford B. Hayes.* Westport: Greenwood.

—. 1978. "The Search for the Hayes Administration." *Hayes Historical Journal* 2: 107–18.

Dawley, Alan. 1987. 1991. *Struggles for Justice: Social Responsibility and the Liberal State.* Cambridge: Belknap Press of Harvard University Press.

—. 2003. *Changing the World: American Progressives in War and Revolution.* Princeton: Princeton University Press.

Daynes, Kathryn. 2001. *More Wives than One: The Transformation of the Mormon Marriage System, 1840–1910.* Urbana: University of Illinois Press.

de la Peña, Carolyn Thomas. 2005. *The Body Electric: How Strange Machines Built the Modern American.* Los Angeles: University of California Press.

De Santis, Vincent P. 1959. *Republicans Face the Southern Question: The New Departure Years.* Baltimore: Johns Hopkins Press.

—, Vincent P. 1975. "The Political Life of the Gilded Age: A Review of the Recent Literature." *History Teacher* 9, November: 73–106.

Debo, Angie. 1940. *And Still the Waters Run: The Betrayal of the Five Civilized Tribes.* Princeton: Princeton University Press.

Debs, Eugene V. 1908. "Proclamation to American Railway Union" In *Debs: His Life, Writings and Speeches*, ed. Eugene V. Debs, Bruce Rogers, and Stephen Marion Reynolds. Girard: The Appeal to Reason.

Degler, Carl N. 1974. "What Ought To Be and What Was: Women's Sexuality in the Nineteenth Century." *American Historical Review* 79: 1467–90.

—. 1991. *In Search of Human Nature: The Decline and Revival of Darwinism in American Social Thought.* New York: Oxford University Press.

—. 1997. *Place Over Time: The Continuity of Southern Distinctiveness.* Athens: University of Georgia Press.

DeJong, David. 2009. *Stealing the Gila: The Pima Agricultural Economy and Water Deprivation, 1848–1921.* Tucson: University of Arizona Press.

DeLay, Brian. 2008. *War of a Thousand Deserts: Indian Raids and the U.S.-Mexican War.* New Haven: Yale University Press.

—. 2015. "Indian Polities, Empire, and the History of American Foreign Relations." *Diplomatic History* 39: 927–942.

Delfino, Dusanna and Michele Gillespie, eds. 2008. *Technology, Innovation and Southern Industrialization: From the Antebellum Era to the Computer Age.* Columbia: University of Missouri Press.

Deloria, Philip J. 2004. *Indians in Unexpected Places.* Lawrence: University Press of Kansas.

—. 2015. "American Master Narratives and the Problem of Indian Citizenship in the Gilded Age and Progressive Era." *Journal of the Gilded Age and Progressive Era* 14: 3–12.

Deluzio, Crista. 2007. *Female Adolescence in American Scientific Thought, 1830–1920.* Baltimore: Johns Hopkins University Press.

DeMallie, Raymond. 1985. *The Sixth Grandfather: Black Elk's Teachings as Given to John G. Neihardt.* Lincoln: University of Nebraska Press.

Denby, Charles, Jr, 1898. "America's Opportunity in Asia." *North American Review* 166: 32–33.

Denning, Michael. 1987. *Mechanic Accents: Dime Novels and Working-Class Culture in Nineteenth-Century America.* New York: Verso.

—. 1990. "The End of Mass Culture." *International Labor and Working-Class History* 37: 4–18.

Dennis, James S. 1902. *Centennial Survey of Foreign Missions.* New York: Fleming H. Revell Company.

Department of Homeland Security. 2003. "Yearbook of Immigration Statistics: 2003 Immigrants, Table 2, 'Immigration by Region and Selected Country of Last Residence, 1820–2003'." Accessed August 2. http://www.dhs.gov/publication/yearbook-immigration-statistics-2003–immigrants.

DeRogatis, Amy. 2003. *Moral Geography: Maps, Missionaries, and the American Frontier.* New York: Columbia University Press.

Derthick, Martha and John Dinan. 1999. "Progressivism and Federalism." In *Progressivism and the New Democracy*, ed. Sidney M. Milkis and Jerome M. Mileur. Amherst: University of Massachusetts Press.

Des Jardins, Julie. 2010. *The Madam Curie Complex: The Hidden History of Women in Science.* New York: City University Press.

DeSantis, Vincent P. 1988. "The Gilded Age in American History." *Hayes Historical Journal: A Journal of the Gilded Age* 7, winter. http://www.rbhayes.org/hayes/content/files/Hayes_Historical_Journal/gildedageamericanhist.html.

Detweiler, Frederick G. 1938. "The Anglo-Saxon Myth in the United States." *American Sociological Review* 3: 183–89.

—. 1922. *The Negro Press in the United States.* Chicago: University of Chicago.

Deutsch, Sarah. 2000. *Women and the City: Gender, Space, and Power in Boston, 1870–1940.* Oxford: Oxford University Press.

Deverell, William, and Tom Sitton. 1994. *California Progressivism Revisited.* Berkeley: University of California Press.

DeWeese, Truman A. 1915. *Keeping a Dollar at Work. Fifty "Talks" on Newspaper Advertising Written for the N.Y. Evening Post.* New York: New York Evening Post.

Dewey, John. 1899. *The School and Society: Being Three Lectures.* Chicago: University of Chicago Press.

—. 1916. *Democracy and Education: An Introduction to the Philosophy of Education.* New York: The Macmillan Company.

Diamond, Stephen. 2002. "Efficiency and Benevolence: Philanthropic Tax Exemptions in 19th-Century America." In *Property-Tax Exemption for Charities: Mapping the Battlefield*, ed. Evelyn Brody. Washington, DC: The Urban Institute.

Digby, William. 1878. *The Famine Campaigns in Southern India (Madras and Bombay Presidencies and Province of Mysore) 1876–1878.* London: Longmans, Green, and Co.

DiMaggio, Paul J. 1986. *Nonprofit Enterprise in the Arts: Studies in Mission and Constraint.* New York: Oxford University Press.

Diner, Hasia R. 2000. *Lower East Side Memories: A Jewish Place in America.* Princeton: Princeton University Press.

Diner, Steven J. 1998. *A Very Different Age: Americans of the Progressive Era.* New York: Hill and Wang.

Dinnerstein, Leonard. 1994. *Anti-Semitism in America*. New York: Oxford University Press.

Dinnerstein, Leonard. 2008. *The Leo Frank Case*. Athens: University of Georgia Press.

Dion, Douglas. 1997. *Turning the Legislative Thumbscrew: Minority Rights and Procedural Change in Congress*. Ann Arbor: University of Michigan Press.

Diouf, Sylviane. 2014. *Slavery's Exiles: The Story of the American Maroons*. New York: New York University Press.

Dippie, Brian. 1982. *The Vanishing American: White Attitudes and Indian Policy*. Middletown: Wesleyan University Press.

Dittmer, John. 1977. *Black Georgia in the Progressive Era, 1900–1920*. Urban: University of Illinois Press.

Dix, Morgan. 1895. *Report as to the Sanitary Condition of the Tenements of Trinity Church and Other Documents*. New York: Evening Post Job Printing House.

Doenecke, Justus D. 1981. *The Presidencies of James A. Garfield & Chester A. Arthur*. Lawrence: University Press of Kansas.

Donald, David Herbert. 2001. *Lincoln Reconsidered: Essays on the Civil War Era*. Revised edition. New York: Vintage.

Dorman, Jacob S. 2013. *Chosen People: The Rise of American Black Israelite Religions*. New York: Oxford University Press.

Dorr, Gregory Michael. 2006. "Defective or Disabled? Race, Medicine, and Eugenics in Progressive Era Virginia and Alabama." *Journal of the Gilded Age and Progressive Era* 5, 4: 359–392.

—. 2008. *Segregation's Science: Eugenics and Society in Virginia*. Charlottesville: University of Virginia Press.

Dorrien, Gary. 2003. *The Making of American Liberal Theology: Idealism, Realism and Modernity*. Louisville: Westminster/John Knox Press.

Dorsett, Lyle W. 1968. *The Pendergast Machine*. New York: Oxford University Press.

Douglas, Ann. 1998. *The Feminization of American Culture*. New York: Farrar, Straus and Giroux.

Downey, Kirstin. 2009. *The Woman behind the New Deal: the Life of Frances Perkins, FDR's Secretary of Labor and his Moral Conscience*. New York: Nan A. Talese/Doubleday.

Downs, Gregory and Masure, Kate, eds. 2015. *The World the Civil War Made*. Chapel Hill: University of North Carolina Press.

Doyle, Don Harrison. 1990. *New Men, New Cities, New South: Atlanta, Nashville, Charleston, Mobile, 1860–1910*. Chapel Hill: University of North Carolina Press.

Drachman, Virginia G. 1998. *Sisters in Law: Women Lawyers in Modern American History*. Cambridge: Harvard University Press.

Dru Stanley, Amy. 1992. "Beggars Can't Be Choosers: Compulsion and Contract in Postbellum America." *Journal of American History* 78, 4.

Du Bois, W.E.B. 1907. *Economic Co-Operation Among Negro Americans*. Atlanta: Atlanta University.

—, and Isabel Eaton. 1899. *The Philadelphia Negro: A Social Study*. Philadelphia: University of Pennsylvania.

—. 1903. *The Souls of Black Folk*. Chicago: A.C. McClure.

—. 1935. *Black Reconstruction in America*. New York: Free Press.

Duany, Jorge. 2002. *The Puerto Rican Nation on the Move: Identities on the Island and in the United States*. Chapel Hill: University of North Carolina Press.

Dubber, Markus Dirk. 2005. *The Police Power: Patriarchy and the Foundations of American Government*. New York: Columbia University Press.

DuBois, Ellen Carol and Gordon, Linda. 1983. "Seeking Ecstasy on the Battlefield: Danger and Pleasure in Nineteenth-Century Feminist Sexual Thought." *Feminist Studies*, Spring 9, 1: 7–25.

DuBois, Ellen Carol. 1982. "Beyond the Victorian Syndrome: Feminist Interpretations of the History of Sexuality." *Radical America*. 16, 1/2: 149–153.

—. 1987. *Harriot Stanton Blatch and the Winning of Woman Suffrage*. New Haven: Yale University Press.

Dudden, Faye. 2011. *Fighting Chance: The Struggle over Woman Suffrage and Black Suffrage in Reconstruction America*. New York: Oxford University Press.

Dudziak, Mary L. 2016. "Legal History as Foreign Relations History." In *Explaining the History of American Foreign Relations, Volume 3*, ed. Michael J. Hogan, and Thomas G. Paterson. New York: Cambridge University Press.

Duffin, Jacalyn. 1999. *History of Medicine: A Scandalously Short Introduction*. Toronto: University of Toronto Press.

Duggan, Lisa. 1996. "The Trials of Alice Mitchell: Sensationalism, Sexology, and the Lesbian Subject in the Turn-of-the-Century America." *Signs* 18, 4: 791–814.

Duis, Perry. 1983. *The Saloon: Public Drinking In Chicago and Boston, 1880–1920*. Urbana: University of Illinois Press.

Dunbar, Willis Frederick. 1968. *How It Was in Hartford*. Grand Rapids: Eerdmans.

Dunch, Ryan. 2002. "Beyond Cultural Imperialism: Cultural Theory, Christian Missions, and Global Modernity," *History and Theory* 41, 3: 301–325.

Dunlap, Leslie K. 1999. "The Reform of Rape Law and the Problem of White Men: Age-of-Consent Campaigns in the South, 1885–1910." In *Sex, Love, Race: Crossing Boundaries in North American History*, ed. Martha Hodes, 352–372. New York: New York University Press.

Dunlap, Thomas R. 1999. *Nature and the English Diaspora: Environment and History in the United States, Canada, Australia, and New Zealand*. Cambridge: Cambridge University Press.

Durand, E. Dana. 1946. "Dr. Victor Selden Clark." *Journal of the American Statistical Association* 41: 390–92.

Duxbury, Neil. 1995. *Patterns of American Jurisprudence*. Oxford: Oxford University Press.

Dye, Nancy Schrom. 1980. *As Equals and Sisters: Feminism, the Labor Movement, and the Women's Trade Union League of New York*. Columbia: University of Missouri Press.

Dyer, Thomas G. 1980. *Theodore Roosevelt and the Idea of Race*. Baton Rouge: Louisiana State University Press.

Eddy, Sherwood, 1896. Letter No. 1, 15 Nov. 1896, in India, Eddy, G. Sherwood, Report Letters, 1896–1903, National Committee, 1891–1926, Y-57-1, Kautz Family YMCA Archives, University of Minnesota.

Edwards, Brent Hayes. 2003. *The Practice of Diaspora: Literature, Translation, and the Rise of Black Internationalism*. Cambridge: Harvard University Press.

Edwards, Laura F. 1997. *Gendered Strife and Confusion: The Political Culture of Reconstruction*. Urbana: University of Illinois Press.

Edwards, Rebecca. 1997. *Angels in the Machinery: Gender in American Party Politics from the Civil War to the Progressive Era*. New York: Oxford University Press.

—. 2006. *New Spirits: Americans in the Gilded Age, 1865–1905*. New York: Oxford University Press.

—. 2011. *New Spirits: America in the "Gilded Age," 1865–1905.* 2nd edition. New York: Oxford University Press.

—. 2009. "Politics, Social Movements, and the Periodization of U.S. History." *Journal of the Gilded Age and Progressive Era* 8, 4: 461–473. doi: 10.1017/S1537781400001432

Ehrenreich, Barbara and Deirdre English. 1973. *Complaints and Disorders: The Sexual Politics of Sickness.* New York: The Feminist Press.

Eisenach, Eldon J. 1994. *The Lost Promise of Progressivism.* Lawrence: University Press of Kansas.

Elazar, Daniel J. 1995. *Community and Polity: The Organizational Dynamics of American Jewry.* Revised ed. Philadelphia: Jewish Publication Society of America.

Elias, Megan J. 2010. *Stir it Up: Home Economics and American Culture.* Philadelphia: University of Pennsylvania Press.

Ellenberg, George B. 2007. *Mule South to Tractor South: Mules, Machines, and the Transformation of the Cotton South.* Tuscaloosa: University of Alabama Press.

Eller, Cynthia. 2011. *Gentlemen and Amazons: The Myth of Matriarchal Prehistory, 1861–1900.* Berkeley: University of California Press.

Ellis, Clyde. 2003. *A Dancing People: Powwow Culture on the Southern Plains.* Lawrence: University Press of Kansas.

Ellis, Mark. 2001. *Race, War, and Surveillance: African Americans and the United States Government during World War I.* Bloomington: Indiana University Press.

Ellis, Richard. 2012. *The Development of the American Presidency.* New York: Routledge.

Endersby, Jim. 2013. "Mutant Utopias. Evening Primroses and Imagined Futures in Early America." *ISIS* 104: 471–503.

Engelman, Peter C. 2011. *A History of the Birth Control Movement in America.* Santa Barbara: Praeger Press.

Engs, Ruth Clifford. 2003. *The Progressive Era's Health Reform Movement.* Westport: Praeger Press.

Engstrom, Erik J., and Samuel Kernell. 2005 "Manufactured Responsiveness: The Impact of State Electoral Laws on Unified Party Control of the Presidency and House of Representatives, 1840–1940." *American Journal of Political Science* 49, 3: 531–49.

Enstad, Nan. 1999. *Ladies of Labor, Girls of Adventure: Working Women, Popular Culture, and Labor Politics at the Turn of the Twentieth Century.* New York: Columbia University Press.

Epstein, Barbara. 1983. "Family, Sexual Morality, and Popular Movements in Turn-of-the-Century America." In *Powers of Desire: The Politics of Sexuality,* ed. Ann Snitow, Christine Stansell, and Sharon Thompson, 117–130. New York: Monthly Review Press.

Erenberg, Lewis. 1981. *Steppin' Out: New York Nightlife and the Transformation of American Culture, 1890–1930.* Westport: Greenwood Press.

Erickson, Emily. 2008. "The Press and a New America, 1865–1900." In *The Age of Mass Communication,* ed. David Sloan, 217–234. Northport: Vision Press.

Erman, Sam. 2008. "Meanings of Citizenship in the U.S. Empire: Puerto Rico, Isabel Gonzalez, and the Supreme Court, 1898 to 1905." *Journal of Ethnic History* 27: 5–33.

—. 2014. "Citizens of Empire: Puerto Rico, Status, and Constitutional Change." *California Law Review* 102, 5: 1181–1242.

Ernst, Daniel R. 1993. "The Critical Tradition in the Writing of American Legal History." Review of *Transformation of American Law 1870–1960: Crisis of Legal Orthodoxy,* by Morton J. Horwitz. *The Yale Law Journal* 102, 4: 1019–76.

Ernst, Daniel R. 1995. *Lawyers Against Labor: From Individual Rights to Corporate Liberalism.* Urbana: University of Illinois Press.

—. 1998. "Law and American Political Development, 1877–1938." *Reviews in American History* 26, 1: 205–19.

Eskridge, William, Jr. 2008. *Dishonorable Passions: Sodomy Laws in America, 1861–2003.* New York: Viking.

Essig, Mark. 2003. *Edison and the Electric Chair: A Story of Light and Death.* New York: Walker Publishing Co.

Ettling, John. 1981. *The Germ of Laziness: Rockefeller Philanthropy and Public Health in the New South.* Cambridge: Harvard University Press.

Evans, Christopher. 2004. *The Kingdom is Always but Coming: A Life of Walter Rauschenbusch.* Grand Rapids: Eerdmans.

Evensen, Bruce J. 1989. "The Evangelical Origins of the Muckrakers." *American Journalism* 6: 5–29.

—. 2004. *God's Man for the Gilded Age: D.L. Moody and the Rise of Modern Mass Evangelicalism.* New York: Oxford University Press.

—. 2005. "Progressivism, Muckraking, and Objectivity." In *Fair & Balanced: A History of Journalistic Objectivity,* ed. Steven R. Knowlton and Karen L. Freeman, 136–148. Northport: Vision Press.

—. 2008. "Dwight Lyman Moody." In *Encyclopedia of American Journalism,* ed. Stephen L. Vaughn, Bruce J. Evensen, and James Landers, 304–305. New York: Routledge.

Ewen, Elizabeth and Stuart Ewen. 1982. *Channels of Desire: Mass Images and the Shaping of American Consciousness.* New York: McGraw Hill.

—. 1985. *Immigrant Women and the Land of Dollars: Life and Culture on the Lower East Side, 1890–1925.* New York: Monthly Review Press.

Ewen, Stuart. 1976. *Captains of Consciousness: Advertising and the Social Roots of Consumer Culture.* New York: McGraw Hill.

Ewing, Adam. 2014. *The Age of Garvey: How a Jamaican Activist Created a Mass Movement and Changed Global Black Politics.* Princeton: Princeton University Press.

Faber, Doris. 1996. *Printer's Devil to Publisher: Adolph S. Ochs of the New York Times.* Hensonville: Black Dome.

Faderman, Lillian. 1978. "The Morbidification of Love Between Women by 19th-Century Sexologists." *Journal of Homosexuality* 4: 73–90.

—. 1991. *Odd Girls and Twilight Lovers: A History of Lesbian Life in Twentieth-Century America.* New York: Penguin Books.

Fairchild, Amy L. 2003. *Science at the Borders: Immigrant Medical inspection and the Shaping of the Modern Industrial Labor Force.* Baltimore: Johns Hopkins University Press.

Falk, Candace. 1990. *Love, Anarchy, and Emma Goldman.* New Brunswick: Rutgers University Press.

—, ed. 1995. *Emma Goldman: A Guide to her Life and Documentary Sources.* Cambridge: Chadwyck-Healey.

Faragher, John Mack. 1988. *Sugar Creek.* New Haven: Yale University Press.

Farland, Maria. 2006. "W.E.B. Du Bois, Anthropometric Science, and the Limits of Racial Uplift." *American Quarterly* 58, 4: 1017–1044.

Farmer, Jared. 2013. *Trees in Paradise: A California History.* New York: W.W. Norton.

Faulkner, Harold Underwood. 1931. *The Quest for Social Justice, 1898–1914.* New York: Macmillan.

Feimster, Crystal N. 2009. *Southern Horrors: Women and the Politics of Rape and Lynching.* Cambridge: Harvard University Press.

Fenske, Gail. 2008. *The Skyscraper and the City: the Woolworth Building and the Making of Modern New York.* Chicago: University of Chicago Press.

Ferguson, Charles Wright. 1937. *Fifty Million Brothers; A Panorama of American Lodges and Clubs.* New York: Farrar & Rinehart.

Ferguson, Niall. 2005. *Colossus: The Rise and Fall of the American Empire.* New York: Penguin Books.

Fernandes, Felipe Tâmega. 2009. "Telegraphs, Shrinking Economic Distances? A Preliminary Enquiry (1870s-1912)." Unpublished paper, http://people.hbs.edu/ffernandes/TELEGRAPHS.pdf

Ferris, Marcie Cohen, ed. 2006. *Jewish Roots in Southern Soil: A New History.* Providence: Brandeis University Press.

Fiege, Mark. 2012. *The Republic of Nature: An Environmental History of the United States.* Seattle: University of Washington Press.

Fields, Barbara Jean. 1982. "Ideology and Race in American History." In *Region, Race and Reconstruction: Essays in Honor of C. Vann Woodward,* ed. J. Morgan Kousser and James M. McPherson. New York: Oxford University Press.

—. 1985. "The Advent of Capitalist Agriculture: The New South in a Bourgeois World." In *Essays on the Postbellum Southern Economy,* ed. Thavolia Glymph et al., 73–94. Arlington: The University of Texas at Arlington.

Fields, Jill. 2007. *An Intimate Affair: Women, Lingerie, and Sexuality.* Los Angeles: University of California Press.

Fields, Karen E. and Barbara J. Fields. 2012. *Racecraft: The Soul of Inequality in American Life.* London: Verso.

Filene, Peter G. 1970. "An Obituary for the Progressive Movement." *American Quarterly* 22, 1: 20–34.

—. 1998. *Him/Her/Self: Gender Identities in Modern America.* 3rd ed. Baltimore: Johns Hopkins Press.

Filler, Louis. 1966. *The Unknown Edwin Markham: His Mystery and Significance.* Yellow Springs: Antioch Press.

Findlay, Eileen J. Suarez. 1999. *Imposing Decency: The Politics of Sexuality and Race in Puerto Rico, 1870–1920.* Durham: Duke University Press.

Findlay, Ronald, and Kevin H. O'Rourke. 2007. *Power and Plenty: Trade, War, and the World Economy in the Second Millennium.* Princeton: Princeton University Press.

Fink, Leon. 1991. "'Intellectuals' versus 'Workers': Academic Requirements and the Creation of Labor History." *The American Historical Review* 96, 2: 395–421.

Fink, Leon. 2011. *Sweatshops at Sea: Merchant Seamen in the World's First Globalized Industry, from 1812 to the Present.* Chapel Hill: University of North Carolina Press.

—. 2015. *The Long Gilded Age: American Capitalism and the Lessons of a New World Order.* Philadelphia: University of Pennsylvania Press.

—. 2015. *Major Problems in the Gilded Age and the Progressive Era: Documents and Essays.* 3rd ed. Stamford: Cengage Learning.

Finke, Roger and Rodney Stark. 2005. *The Churching of America 1776–2005: Winners and Losers in our Religious Economy.* New Brunswick: Rutgers University Press.

Finnegan, Margaret. 1999. *Selling Suffrage: Consumer Culture and Votes for Women.* New York: Columbia University Press.

Finocchiaro, Charles J., and David W. Rohde. 2007. "Speaker David Henderson and the Partisan Era of the U.S. House." In *Party, Process, and Political Change in Congress, Volume 2: Further New Perspectives on the History of Congress,* ed. David W. Brady and Matthew D. McCubbins. Palo Alto: Stanford University Press.

Fiorina, Morris P., David W. Rohde, and Peter Wissel. 1975. "Historical Change in House Turnover." In *Congress in Change: Evolution and Reform,* ed. Norman J. Ornstein. New York: Praeger.

Fischer, David Hackett 1989. *Albion's Seed: Four British Folkways in America.* New York: Oxford University Press.

Fisher, C. 2006. "African Americans, Outdoor Recreation, and the 1919 Chicago Race Riot." In *"To Love the Wind and the Rain": African Americans and Environmental History,* ed. Dianne D. Glave and Mark Stoll. Pittsburgh: University of Pittsburgh Press.

Fisher, James. 2008. *Communion of Immigrants: A History of Catholics in America.* New York: Oxford University Press.

Fishman, Robert. 1987. *Bourgeois Utopias: the Rise and Fall of Suburbia.* New York: Basic Books.

Fiss, Owen M. 1993. *Troubled Beginnings of the Modern State 1888–1910.* New York: Macmillan.

Fitzpatrick, Ellen. 1990. *Endless Crusade: Women Social Scientists and Progressive Reform.* New York: Oxford University Press.

—. 2002. *History's Memory: Writing America's Past 1880–1980.* Cambridge: Harvard University Press.

Flake, Kathleen. 2003. *The Politics of American Religious Identity: The Seating of Senator Reed Smoot, Mormon Apostle.* Chapel Hill: University of North Carolina Press.

Flanagan, Maureen A. 2002. *Seeing with Their Hearts: Chicago Women and the Vision of the Good City, 1871–1933.* Princeton: Princeton University Press.

—. 2007. *America Reformed: Progressives and Progressivisms, 1890s-1920s.* New York: Oxford University Press.

Fleissner, Jennifer. 2004. *Women, Compulsion, Modernity: The Moment of American Naturalism.* Chicago: University of Chicago Press.

Flores, Dan. 1991. "Bison Ecology and Bison Diplomacy: The Southern Plains from 1800 to 1850," *Journal of American History* 78, 2 (September 1991), 465–485.

Daniel, Pete. 1986. *Standing at the Crossroads: Southern Life Since 1900.* New York: Hill and Wang.

—. 1986. *Breaking the Land: The Transformation of Cotton, Tobacco, and Rice Cultures since 1880.* Urbana: University of Illinois Press.

—. 2001. *The Natural West.* Norman: University of Oklahoma Press.

Fogelson, Robert M. 2001. *Downtown: Its Rise and Fall, 1880–1950.* New Haven: Yale University Press.

Fogelsong, David S. 1998. *America's Secret War against Bolshevism: U.S. Intervention in the Russian Civil War, 1917–1920.* Chapel Hill: University of North Carolina Press.

Fogg-Meade, Emily. 1901. "The Place of Advertising in Modern Life." *Journal of Political Economy* 5, 2: 218–242.

Foley, Neil. 1998. "Becoming Hispanic: Mexican Americans and the Faustian Pact With Whiteness." In *Relexiones,* ed. Neil

Foley, 53–71. Austin: Center for Mexican American Studies, The University of Texas at Austin.

Foley, Neil. 2014. *Mexicans in the Making of America.* Cambridge: Harvard University Press.

Follett, Mary Parker. 1918. *The New State: Group Organization the Solution of Popular Government.* New York: Longmans, Green & Company.

Foner, Eric and John A. Garraty, eds. 1991. *The Reader's Companion to American History.* Boston: Houghton Mifflin Company.

Foner, Eric. 1988. *Reconstruction: America's Unfinished Revolution, 1863–1977.* New York: Harper & Row.

—, and Lisa McGirr. 2011. *American History Now.* Philadelphia: Temple University Press.

—. 2014. *Reconstruction: America's Unfinished Revolution, 1863–1877.* Updated Edition. New York: Harper Perennial Modern Classics.

Foner, Nancy. 1997. "What is New about Transnationalism: New York Immigrants Today and at the Turn of the Century." *Diaspora: A Journal of Transnational Studies* 6, 3: 355–75.

Foner, Philip Sheldon. 1941. *Business & Slavery: The New York Merchants & the Irrepressible Conflict.* Chapel Hill: The University of North Carolina Press.

Forbath, William E. 1985. "The Ambiguities of Free Labor: Labor and the Law in the Gilded Age." *Wisconsin Law Review* 1985, 4: 767–817.

—. 1991. *Law and the Shaping of the American Labor Movement.* Cambridge: Harvard University Press.

Forgette, Richard G. 1997. "Reed's Rules and the Partisan Theory of Legislative Organization." *Polity* 29, 3: 382–84.

Foster, Anne L. 2009. "Prohibiting Opium in the Philippines and the United States: The Creation of an Interventionist State." In *Colonial Crucible: Empire in the Making of the Modern American State,* ed. Alfred W. McCoy, and Francisco A. Scarano. Madison: University of Wisconsin Press.

—. 2010. *Projections of Power: The United States and Europe in Colonial Southeast Asia, 1919–1941.* Durham: Duke University Press.

Foster, Gaines M. 1982. 1988. *Ghosts of the Confederacy: Defeat, the Lost Cause, and the Emergence of the New South, 1865–1913.* New York: Oxford University Press.

—. 2002. *Moral Reconstruction, Christian Lobbyists and the Federal Legislation of Morality, 1865–1920.* Chapel Hill: University of North Carolina Press.

Foster, Lawrence. 1981. "Free Love and Feminism: John Humphrey Noyes and the Oneida Community." *Journal of the Early Republic* 1, 2: 165–83.

Foucault, Michel. 1994. *The Birth of the Clinic: An Archaeology of Medical Perspective,* trans. A. M. Sheridan Smith. New York: Vintage Books.

Fouche, Rayvon. 2003. *Black Inventors in the Age of Segregation.* Baltimore: Johns Hopkins University Press.

—. 2006. "Say It Loud, I'm Black and I'm Proud: African Americans, American Artifactual Culture, and Black Vernacular Technological Creativity." *American Quarterly* 58, 3: 639–661.

Fox, Cybelle. 2012. *Three Worlds of Relief: Race, Immigration, and the American Welfare State from the Progressive Era to the New Deal.* Princeton: Princeton University Press.

Fox, Daniel M. 1963. *Engines of Culture: Philanthropy and Art Museums.* Madison: State Historical Society of Wisconsin.

—. 2006. "The Significance of the Milbank Memorial Fund for Policy: an Assessment at its Centennial." *Milbank Quarterly* 84, 1: 5–36.

Fox, Richard Wightman. 1999. *Trials of Intimacy: Love and Loss in the Beecher-Tilton Scandal.* Chicago: University of Chicago Press.

Fox, Stephen. 1981. *John Muir and His Legacy: The American Conservation Movement.* Boston: Little, Brown and Co.

Frank, Dana. 1998. "White Working-Class Women and the Race Question." *International Labor and Working-Class History* 54, Fall: 80–102.

Franklin, Kay and Norman Schaeffer, 1983. *Duel for the Dunes: Land Use Conflict on the Shores of Lake Michigan.* Urbana: University of Illinois Press.

Franks, Angela. 2005. *Margaret Sanger's Eugenic Legacy: The Control of Female Fertility.* Jefferson: McFarland & Co.

Franzen, Trisha. 2014. *Anna Howard Shaw: The Work of Woman Suffrage.* Urbana: University of Illinois Press.

Fraser, Steve. 1983. "Dress Rehearsal for the New Deal: Shop Floor Insurgents, Political Elites, and Industrial Democracy in the Amalgamated Clothing Workers." In *Working-Class America: Essays on Labor, Community, and American Society,* ed. Michael Frisch and Daniel Walkowitz. Urbana: University of Illinois Press.

—. 2015. *Age of Acquiescence: The Life and Death of American Resistance to Organized Wealth and Power.* New York: Little, Brown and Company.

Frederickson, George. 1965. *The Inner Civil War.* New York: Harper & Row.

—. 1982. *White Supremacy: A Comparative Study of American and South African History.* New York: Oxford University Press.

—. 1997. *The Comparative Imagination: on the History of Racism, Nationalism, and Social Movements.* Berkeley: University of California Press.

Freedman, Estelle. 2006. "When Historical Interpretation Meets Legal Advocacy: Abortion, Sodomy, and Same-Sex Marriage." In *Feminism, Sexuality & Politics,* ed. Estelle Freedman. Chapel Hill: University of North Carolina Press.

—. 2013. *Redefining Rape: Sexual Violence in the Era of Suffrage and Segregation.* Cambridge: Harvard University Press.

Friday, Chris. 1995. *Organizing Asian American Labor: The Pacific Coast Canned-Salmon Industry, 1870–1942.* Philadelphia: Temple University Press.

Fried, Barbara H. 1998. *The Progressive Assault on Laissez Faire: Robert Hale and the First Law and Economics Movement.* Cambridge: Harvard University Press.

Friedman, Jean E. 1985. *The Enclosed Garden: Women and Community in the Evangelical South, 1830–1900.* Chapel Hill: University of North Carolina Press.

Friedman, Lawrence J. and Mark D. McGarvie, eds. 2003. *Charity, Philanthropy, and Civility in American History.* New York: Cambridge University Press.

Friedman, Milton and Anna Jacobson Schwartz. 1963. *A Monetary History of the United States.* Princeton: Princeton University Press.

—. 1994. *Money Mischief: Episodes in Monetary History.* San Diego: Mariner Books.

Frisken, Amanda. 2004. *Victoria Woodhull's Sexual Revolution: Political Theater and the Popular Press in Nineteenth-Century America.* Philadelphia: University of Pennsylvania Press.

—. 2008. "Obscenity, Free Speech, and 'Sporting News' in 1870s America." *Journal of American Studies* 42, 3: 537–77.

Fronc, Jennifer. 2009. *New York Undercover: Private Surveillance in the Progressive Era.* Chicago: University of Chicago Press.

Fry, Joseph. 1996. "From Open Door to World Systems: Economic Interpretations of Late Nineteenth Century." *Pacific Historical Review* 62, 2: 277–303.

Fujita-Rony, Dorothy. 2002. *American Workers, Colonial Power: Philippines Seattle and the Transpacific West, 1919–1941.* Berkeley: University of California Press.

Furner, Mary. Forthcoming. "The U.S. Laissez Faire Era: From *In re Jacobs* and *E. C. Knight* to *Northern Securities* and *Muller v. Oregon.*"

Gabaccia, Donna R. 1988. *Militants and Migrants: Rural Sicilians Become American Workers.* New Brunswick: Rutgers University Press.

—. 2000. *Italy's Many Diasporas.* Seattle: University of Washington Press.

—. 2012. *Foreign Relations: American Immigration in Global Perspective.* Princeton: Princeton University Press.

Gable, John. 1978. *The Bull Moose Years: Theodore Roosevelt and the Progressive Party.* New York: Kennikat.

—. 1992. "The Historiography of Theodore Roosevelt." In *Theodore Roosevelt: Many-Sided American.* New York: Heart of the Lakes Publishing/Hofstra University.

Gage, Beverly. 2009. *The Day Wall Street Exploded.* New York: Oxford University Press.

Gaines, Kevin. 1996. *Uplifting the Race: Black Leadership, Politics, and Culture, in the Twentieth Century.* Chapel Hill: University of North Carolina Press.

—. 2011. "African American History." In *American History Now*, ed. Eric Foner and Lisa McGirr. Philadelphia: Temple University Press.

Gaither, Gerald H. 1977. *Blacks and the Populist Revolt: Ballots and Bigotry in the 'New South.'* Tuscaloosa: University of Alabama Press.

Galambos, Louis. 1970. "The Emerging Organizational Synthesis in Modern American History." *Business History Review* 44: 279–290.

Gamm, G., & Putnam, Robert D. 2001. "The Growth of Voluntary Associations in American, 1840–1940." In *Patterns of Social Capital: Stability and Change in Historical Perspective*, ed. R.I. Rotberg, 173–219. Cambridge: Massachusetts Institute of Technology Press.

Garb, Margaret. 2005. *City of American Dreams: a History of Home Ownership and Housing Reform in Chicago, 1871–1919.* Chicago: University of Chicago Press.

Garraty, John A. 1953. *Henry Cabot Lodge: A Biography.* New York: Knopf.

Garrett, Shirley S. 1970. *Social Reformers in Urban China: The Chinese Y.M.C.A., 1895–1926.* Cambridge: Harvard University Press.

Garvey, Amy Jacques. 1923. *The Philosophy & Opinions of Marcus Garvey, or Africa for Africans.* London: Universal Publishing House.

Garvey, Ellen Gruber. 1996. *The Adman in the Parlor: Magazines and the Gendering of Consumer Culture, 1880s to 1910s.* New York: Oxford University Press.

—. 2012. *Writing with Scissors: American Scrapbooks from the Civil War to the Harlem Renaissance.* New York: Oxford University Press.

Garvey, Marcus. "If You Believe the Negro Has a Soul." http://historymatters.gmu.edu/d/5124/

Gates, William Bryan. 1951. *Michigan Copper and Boston Dollars; an Economic History of the Michigan Copper Mining Industry.* Cambridge: Harvard University Press.

Geiger, Roger L. 1986. *To Advance Knowledge: The Growth of American Research Universities, 1900–1940.* New York: Oxford University Press.

—, ed. 2000. *The American College in the Nineteenth Century.* Nashville: Vanderbilt University Press.

Gelber, Scott M. 2011. *The University and the People: Envisioning American Higher Education in the Era of Populist Protest.* Madison: University of Wisconsin.

George, Henry. 1886. *Progress and Poverty: An Inquiry into the Cause of Industrial Depressions and Increase of Want with Increase of Wealth.* New York: D. Appleton & Company.

Gerring, John. 1998. *Party Ideologies in America: 1828–1996.* Cambridge: Cambridge University Press.

Gerrish, Frederic Henry. 1889. "The Special Function of the American Academy of Medicine." *Philadelphia Medical Times* 19, April: 465–476.

Gerstle, Gary. 2001. *American Crucible: Race and Nation in the Twentieth Century.* Princeton: Princeton University Press.

—. 2015. *Liberty and Coercion: The Paradox of American Government from the Founding to the Present.* Princeton: Princeton University Press.

Gerteis, Joseph. 2007. *Class and the Color Line: Interracial Class Coalition in the Knights of Labor and the Populist Movement.* Durham: Duke University Press.

Gertner, John. 2012. *The Idea Factory: Bell Labs and the Great Age of American Innovation.* New York: Penguin Press.

Gibson, Campbell J., and Emily Lennon. 1999. "Nativity of the Population and Place of Birth of the Native Population, 1850–1990." *Historical Census Statistics on the Foreign-born Population of the United States: 1850–1990.* http://www.census.gov/population/www/documentation/twps0029/tab01.html.

Giddings, Howard A. 1900. *Exploits of the Signal Corps in the War with Spain.* Kansas City: Hudson-Kimberley Pub. Co.

Giddings, Paula J. 2008. *Ida: A Sword Among Lions: Ida B. Wells and the Campaign Against Lynching.* New York: Harper Collins.

Giesberg, Judith Ann. 2000. *Civil War Sisterhood: The U.S. Sanitary Commission and Women's Politics in Transition.* Boston: Northeastern University Press.

Giesen, James C. 2011. *Boll Weevil Blues: Cotton, Myth, and Power in the American South.* Chicago: University of Chicago Press.

Gifford, Carolyn DeSwarte and Amy R. Slagell, eds. 2007. *Let Something Good Be Said: Speeches and Writings of Frances E. Willard.* Urbana: University of Illinois.

Gilbert, James. 1991. *Perfect Cities: Chicago's Utopias of 1893.* Chicago: University of Chicago Press.

Gilderhus, Mark T. 1986. *Pan American Visions: Woodrow Wilson in the Western Hemisphere, 1913–1921.* Tucson: University of Arizona Press.

Gilfoyle, Timothy. 1992. *City of Eros: New York City, Prostitution, and the Commercialization of Sex, 1790–1920.* New York: W. W. Norton & Co.

Gilkeson, John S. 2010. *Anthropologists and the Rediscovery of America, 1886–1965.* New York: Cambridge University Press.

Gillette, William. 1979. *Retreat from Reconstruction: 1869–1879.* Baton Rouge: Louisiana State University Press.

Gillman, Howard. 1993. *The Constitution Besieged: The Rise and Demise of Lochner Era Police Powers Jurisprudence*. Durham: Duke University Press.

Gilman, Charlotte Perkins. (1898) 1966. *Women and Economics: A Study of the Economic Relation between Men and Women as a Factor in Social Evolution*. Boston: Small, Maynard, and Company. Reprint, New York: Harper Torchbook.

—. 1892 (1973). "The Yellow Wallpaper." *New England Magazine* 11, 5: 647–657. Reprint, New York: The Feminist Press.

—. 1898. *Women and Economics: A Study of the Economic Relation between Men and Woman As a Factor in Social Evolution*. Boston: Small, Maynard and Company.

—. 1916. "The Nervous Breakdown of Women." *Forerunner* 7, August: 202–206.

Gilmore, Glenda Elizabeth, ed. 2002. *Who Were the Progressives?* Boston: Bedford, St. Martin's.

—. 1996. *Gender and Jim Crow: Women and the Politics of White Supremacy in North Carolina, 1896–1920*. Chapel Hill: University of North Carolina Press.

—. 2008. *Defying Dixie: The Radical Roots of Civil Rights, 1919–1950*. New York: W.W. Norton.

Ginger, Ray. 1965. *Age of Excess: The United States from 1877 to 1914*. New York: The Macmillan Company.

Ginzberg, Lori D. 1990. *Women and the Work of Benevolence: Morality, Politics, and Class in the Nineteenth-Century United States*. New Haven: Yale University Press.

Glenn, Susan A. 1991. *Daughters of the Shtetl: Life and Labor in the Immigrant Generation*. Ithaca: Cornell University Press.

— 2000. *Female Spectacle: The Theatrical Roots of Modern Feminism*. Cambridge: Harvard University Press.

Glickman, Lawrence B. 1997. *A Living Wage: American Workers and the Making of a Consumer Society*. Ithaca: Cornell University Press.

—. 2011. "The 'Cultural Turn.'" In *American History Now*, ed. Eric Foner and Lisa McGirr. Philadelphia: Temple University Press.

Glotzer, Paige. 2015. "Exclusion in Arcadia: How Suburban Developers Circulated Ideas about Discrimination, 1890–1950." *Journal of Urban History* 41, 3: 479–494.

Glymph, Thavolia. 2008. *Out of the House of Bondage: The Transformation of the Plantation Household*. New York: Cambridge University Press.

Go, Julian and Anne Foster, eds. 2003. *The American Colonial State in the Philippines: Global Perspectives*. Durham: Duke University Press.

—. 2008. *American Empire and the Politics of Meaning: Elite Political Cultures in the Philippines and Puerto Rico during U.S. Colonialism*. Durham: Duke University Press.

Gobat, Michel. 2005. *Confronting the American Dream: Nicaragua under U.S. Imperial Rule*. Durham: Duke University Press.

Godshalk, David Fort. 2005. *Veiled Visions: The 1906 Atlanta Race Riot and the Reshaping of American Race Relations*. Chapel Hill: The University of North Carolina Press.

Goff, James. 1997. *Plain Folk of the South Revisited*. Baton Rouge: Louisiana State University Press.

Gold, Martin B. 2012. *Forbidden Citizens: Chinese Exclusion and the U.S. Congress: A Legislative History*. Washington, DC: TheCapitolNet.

Goldberg, Michael Lewis. 1997. *An Army of Women: Gender and Politics in Gilded Age Kansas*. Baltimore: Johns Hopkins University Press.

Goldfield, David R. 1982. *Cotton Fields and Skyscrapers: Southern City and Region, 1607–1980*. Baton Rouge: Louisiana State University Press.

Goldman, Emma. 1977. *Living My Life*. New York: New American Library.

Goldman, Eric F. 1952. *Rendezvous with Destiny: A History of Modern American Reform*. New York: Knopf.

—. 1956. *Rendezvous with Destiny: A History of Modern American Reform*. New York: Vintage.

Goldman, Lawrence. 1998. "Exceptionalism and Internationalism: The Origins of American Social Science Reconsidered." *Journal of Historical Sociology* 11, March: 1–36.

Goldman, Marion S. 1981. *Gold Diggers and Silver Miners: Prostitution and Social Life on the Comstock Lode*. Ann Arbor: University of Michigan Press.

Goldstein, Daniel. 2008. "Outposts of Science. The Knowledge Trade and the Expansion of Scientific Community in Post-Civil War America." *ISIS* 99: 518–546.

Goldstein, Alyosha. 2014. *Formations of United States Colonialism*. Durham: Duke University Press.

Goldstone, Lawrence. 2011. *Inherently Unequal: The Betrayal of Equal Rights by the Supreme Court, 1865–1903*. New York: Walker Publishing.

Gollaher, David L. 2000. *Circumcision: A History of the World's Most Controversial Surgery*. New York: Basic Books.

Goodwin, Doris K. 2013. *The Bully Pulpit: Theodore Roosevelt, William Howard Taft, and the Golden Age of Journalism*. New York: Simon and Schuster.

Goodwin, Lorine Swainston. 1999. *The Pure Food, Drink, and Drug Crusaders, 1879–1914*. Jefferson: McFarland.

Goodwyn, Lawrence. 1976. *Democratic Promise: The Populist Moment in America*. New York: Oxford University Press.

—. 1978. *The Populist Moment: A Short History of the Agrarian Revolt in America*. New York: Oxford University Press.

Gordon, Ann D. 2007. "Stanton and the Right to Vote: On Account of Race or Sex." In *Elizabeth Cady Stanton, Feminist as Thinker: A Reader in Documents and Essays*, eds. Ellen Carol DuBois and Richard Cándida Smith, 111–127. New York: New York University Press.

Gordon, Linda. 1986. "Family Violence, Feminism, and Social Control." *Feminist Studies* 12, 3: 452–478.

—. 1988. *Heroes of Their Own Lives: the Politics and History of Family Violence: Boston, 1880–1960*. New York: Viking.

—, ed. 1990. *Woman's Body, Woman's Right: Birth Control in America*. New York: Penguin Books.

—, ed. 1990. *Women, the State, and Welfare*. Madison: University of Wisconsin Press.

—. 1995. *Pitied But Not Entitled: Single Mothers and the History of Welfare, 1890–1935*. Cambridge: Harvard University Press.

—. 1999. *The Great Arizona Orphan Abduction*. Cambridge: Harvard University Press.

Gordon, Lynn D. 1990. 1992. *Gender and Higher Education in the Progressive Era*. New Haven: Yale University Press.

Gordon, Robert. 1983. "Legal Thought and Legal Practice in the Age of American Enterprise." In *Professions and Professional Ideologies in America*. In *Professions and Professional Ideologies in America*, ed. Gerald L. Geison, 70 – 110. Chapel Hill: University of North Carolina Press.

Goren, Arthur. 1970. *New York Jews and the Quest for Community*. New York: Columbia University Press.

Gorn, Elliott. 1986. *The Manly Art: Bare-Knuckle Prize Fighting in America*. Ithaca: Cornell University Press.

Gosling, F.G. 1987. *Before Freud: Neurasthenia and the American Medical Community, 1870–1910*. Urbana: University of Illinois Press.

Gossett, Thomas F. 1965. *Race: The History of an Idea in America*. New York: Schocken Press.

Gottlieb, Robert. 1993. *Forcing the Spring: The Transformation of the American Environmental Movement*. Washington, D.C.: Island Press.

Gould, Lewis L. 1980. *The Presidency of William McKinley*. Lawrence: Regents Press of Kansas.

—. 1991. *The Presidency of Theodore Roosevelt*. Lawrence: The University Press of Kansas.

—. 2008. *Four Hats in the Ring: The 1912 Election and the Birth of American Politics*. Lawrence: University Press of Kansas.

—. 2014. *The Republicans: A History of the Grand Old Party*. Oxford: Oxford University Press.

Gournay, Isabelle, and Marie-Laure Crosnier Leconte. 2013. "American Architecture Students in Belle Epoque Paris: Scholastic Strategies and Achievements at the Ecole des Beaux Arts." *Journal of the Gilded Age and Progressive Era* 12: 154–198.

Graff, Henry F. 2002. *Grover Cleveland*. New York: Times Books.

Grant, Colin. 2008. *Negro with a Hat: The Rise and Fall of Marcus Garvey*. New York: Oxford University Press.

Grandin, Greg. 2006. *Empire's Workshop: Latin America, the United States, and the Rise of the New Imperialism*. New York: Owl Books.

Grant, James. 2011. *Mr. Speaker! The Life and Times of Thomas B. Reed, The Man Who Broke the Filibuster*. New York: Simon and Schuster.

Grant, Madison. 1916. *The Passing of the Great Race; or, The Racial Basis of European History*. New York: Scribner's.

Grant, Susan. 1992. "Whistler's Mother Was Not Alone: French Government Acquisitions of American Paintings, 1871–1900." *Archives of American Art Journal* 32: 2–15.

Grantham, Dewey W. 1981. "The Contours of Southern Progressivism." *American Historical Review* 86, 5: 1035–1059.

—. 1983. *Southern Progressivism: The Reconciliation of Progress and Tradition*. Knoxville: University of Tennessee Press.

Gray, Susan E. 1996. *The Yankee West*. Chapel Hill University of North Carolina Press.

Green, James R. 2006. *Death In the Haymarket: a Story of Chicago, the First Labor Movement and the Bombing That Divided Gilded Age America*. New York: Pantheon Books.

Green, Matthew N. 2002. "Institutional Change, Party Discipline and the House Democratic Caucus, 1911–1919." *Legislative Studies Quarterly* 27, 4: 601–33.

Green, Norma, Stephen Lacy, and Jean Folkerts. 1989. "Chicago Journalists at the Turn of the Century: Bohemians All?" *Journalism Quarterly* 66: 813–821.

Greene, Julie. 2006. *Pure and Simple Politics: The American Federation of Labor and Political Activism, 1885–1917*. Cambridge: Cambridge University Press.

—. 2009. *The Canal Builders: Making America's Empire at the Panama Canal*. New York: Penguin.

—. 2015. "The Wages of Empire: Capitalism, Expansionism, and Working-Class Formation." In *Making the Empire Work: Labor and United States Imperialism*, ed. Daniel E. Bender and Jana Lipman, 35–58. New York: New York University Press.

Greenwald, Richard A. 2005. *The Triangle Fire, the Protocols of Peace, and Industrial Democracy in Progressive Era New York*. Philadelphia: Temple University Press.

Grenier, Judson. 1960. "Muckraking and Muckrakers: An Historical Definition." *Journalism Quarterly* 37: 552–558.

Grese, Robert. 2000. "Jens Jensen: the Landscape Architect as Conservationist." In *Midwestern Landscape Architecture*, ed. William H. Tishler, 117–141. Urbana: University of Illinois Press.

Grey, Thomas. 1983. "Langdell's Orthodoxy." *University of Pittsburgh Law Review* 45, 1: 1–53.

Groneman, Carol. 1994. "Nymphomania: The Historical Construction of Female Sexuality." *Signs* 19: 337–367.

Gros, Raymond. 1910. *T.R. in Cartoon*. New York: Saalfield Pub. Co.

Gross, Kali N. 2006. *Colored Amazons: Crime, Violence, and Black Women In the City of Brotherly Love, 1880–1910*. Durham: Duke University Press.

Grossberg, Michael. 1985. *Governing the Hearth: Law and Family in Nineteenth Century America*. Chapel Hill: University of North Carolina Press.

Grossman, James R. 1989. *Land of Hope: Chicago, Black Southerners, and the Great Migration*. Chicago: University of Chicago Press.

Grossman, Lewis A. 2002. "James Coolidge Carter and Mugwump Jurisprudence." *Law and History Review* 20, 3: 577–629.

Grusin, Richard. 2004. *Culture, Technology, and the Creation of America's National Parks*. New York: Cambridge University Press.

Guarneri, Carl. 2007. *America in the World: United States History in World Context*. New York: McGraw-Hill Companies.

Guelzo, Allen E. 1999. *Abraham Lincoln: Martyred President*. Grand Rapids: Eerdmans.

Guglielmo, Jennifer. 2012. *Living the Revolution: Italian Women's Resistance and Radicalism in New York City, 1880–1945*. Chapel Hill: University of North Carolina Press.

Guglielmo, Thomas. 2003. *White on Arrival: Italians, Race, Color, and Power in Chicago, 1890–1945*. New York: Oxford University Press.

Gulick, Sidney. 1908. "Internationalism: The Characteristic of the 20th Century." *Twentieth Century Quarterly* 8: 8.

Gurda, John. 1999. *The Making of Milwaukee*. Milwaukee: Milwaukee County Historical Society.

Guridy, Frank. 2010. *Forging Diaspora: Afro-Cubans and African Americans in a World of Empire and Jim Crow*. Chapel Hill: University of North Carolina Press.

Gurstein, Rochelle. 1996. *The Repeal of Reticence: A History of America's Legal and Cultural Struggles over Free Speech, Obscenity, Sexual Liberation, and Modern Art*. New York: Hill and Wang.

Gusfield, Joseph R. 1963. *Symbolic Crusade: Status Politics and the American Temperance Movement*. Urbana: University of Illinois Press.

Gustav-Wrathall, John Donald. 1998. *Take the Young Stranger by the Hand: Same-Sex Relations and the YMCA*. Chicago: University of Chicago Press.

Gustin, Lawrence R. 2008. *Billy Durant: Creator of General Motors*. Ann Arbor: University of Michigan Regional Press.

Guthrie-Shimizu, Sayuri. 2012. *Transpacific Field of Dreams: How Baseball Linked the United States and Japan in Peace and War*. Chapel Hill: University of North Carolina Press.

Gutiérrez, David G. 1995. *Walls and Mirrors: Mexican Americans, Mexican Immigrants, and the Politics of Ethnicity.* Berkeley: University of California Press.

Gutman, Herbert. 1976. *The Black Family in Slavery and Freedom.* New York: Pantheon.

—. 1977. *Work, Culture, and Society in Industrializing America.* New York: Vintage.

Gyory, Andrew. 1998. *Closing the Gate: Politics and the Chinese Exclusion Act.* Chapel Hill: University of North Carolina Press.

Ha, Nathan Q. 2011. "The Riddle of Sex: Biological Theories of Sexual difference in the Early Twentieth-Century." *Journal of the History of Biology* 44:505–546.

Hackney, Sheldon. 1972. "'Origins of the New South' in Retrospect." *Journal of Southern History* 38, 2: 191–216.

Hacsi, Timothy A. 1997. *Second Home: Orphan Asylums and Poor Families in America.* Cambridge: Harvard University Press.

Hahn, Barbara. 2011. *Making Tobacco Bright: Creating an American Commodity, 1617–1937.* Baltimore: Johns Hopkins University Press.

Hahn, Steven. 1983. *The Roots of Southern Populism: Yeoman Farmers and the Transformation of the Georgia Upcountry, 1850–1890.* New York: Oxford University Press.

—. 1990. "Class and State in Postemancipation Societies: Southern Planters in Comparative Perspective." *American Historical Review* 95, 1: 85–98.

—. 2003. *A Nation Under Our Feet: Black Political Struggles in the Rural South from Slavery to the Great Migration.* Cambridge: Harvard University Press.

—. 2013. "Slave Emancipation, Indian Peoples, and the Projects of a New American Nation-State." *Journal of the Civil War Era* 3: 307–30.

Hale, Grace Elizabeth. 1998. *Making Whiteness: the Culture of Segregation In the South, 1890–1940.* New York: Pantheon Books.

—. 1999. *Making Whiteness: The Culture of Segregation in the South, 1890–1940.* New York: Vintage.

Haley, Sarah. 2016. *No Mercy Here: Gender, Punishment, and the Making of Jim Crow Modernity.* Chapel Hill: University of North Carolina Press.

Hall, Jacquelyn Dowd. 1983. "'The Mind that Burns in Each Body': Women, Rape, and Racial Violence." In *Powers of Desire: The Politics of Sexuality*, ed. Ann Snitow, Christine Stansell, and Sharon Thompson, 328–349. New York: Monthly Review Press.

—. 2005. "The Long Civil Rights Movement and the Political Uses of the Past." *Journal of American History* 91, 4: 1233–1263.

Hall, Peter Dobkin. 1992. *Inventing the Nonprofit Sector and Other Essays on Philanthropy, Voluntarism, and Nonprofit Organizations.* Baltimore: Johns Hopkins University Press.

Hall, Peter Dobkin. 2006. "Nonprofit, Voluntary, and Religious Entities." In *Historical Statistics of the United States: Millennial Edition*, ed. Carter, S. B., et al. New York: Cambridge University Press.

Hall, Stuart. 1981. "Notes on Deconstructing 'The Popular.'" In *People's History and Socialist Theory*, ed. Raphael Samuel, 227–240. London: Routledge.

Haller, John S. and Robin M. 1977. *The Physician and Sexuality in Victorian America.* New York: W. W. Norton.

Hämäläinen, Pekka. 2008. *The Comanche Empire.* New Haven: Yale University Press.

Hamilton, Andrea. 2004. *A Vision for Girls: Gender, Education, and the Bryn Mawr School.* Baltimore: Johns Hopkins University Press.

Hamlin, Kimberly A. 2004. "Bathing Suits and Backlash: The First Miss America Pageants, 1921–1927." In *"There She Is, Miss America": The Politics of Sex, Gender, and Race in America's Most Famous Pageant*, eds. Elwood Watson and Darcy Martin, 27–52. New York: Palgrave/St. Martin's.

—. 2011. "'The Case of a Bearded Woman': Hypertrichosis and the Construction of Gender in the Age of Darwin." *American Quarterly* 63, December: 955–981.

—. 2014. *From Eve to Evolution: Darwin, Science, and Women's Rights in Gilded Age America.* Chicago: University of Chicago Press.

Hammack, David C. 1998. *Making the Nonprofit Sector in the United States: A Reader.* Bloomington: Indiana University Press.

—. "Growth, Transformation, and Quiet Revolution in the Nonprofit Sector over Two Centuries." *Nonprofit and Voluntary Sector Quarterly* June: 157–173.

—. 2002. "Nonprofit Organizations in American History: Research Opportunities and Sources" *The American Behavioral Scientist* 45, 11: 1638–1674.

—. 2006. "American Debates on the Legitimacy of Foundations." In *The Legitimacy of Philanthropic Foundations: United States and European Perspectives*, ed. Kenneth Prewitt, Mattei Dogan, Steven Heydemann, and Stefan Toepler. New York: Russell Sage Foundation.

—, and Wheeler, Stanton. 1994. *Social Science in the Making: Essays on the Russell Sage Foundation, 1907–1947.* New York: Russell Sage Foundation.

—, and Helmut K. Anheier. 2013. *A Versatile American Institution: The Changing Ideals and Realities of Philanthropic Foundations.* Washington, DC: The Brookings Institution Press.

Hammond, John Hays. 1935 (1974). *The Autobiography of John Hays Hammond.* Reprint. Volumes 1–2. New York: Arno Press.

Hanagan, Michael P. 2004. "An Agenda for Transnational Labor History." *International Review of Social History* 49: 455–74.

Hanchett, Thomas W. 1998. *Sorting Out the New South City: Race, Class, and Urban Development in Charlotte, 1875–1975.* Chapel Hill: University of North Carolina Press.

Handlin, Oscar. 1941. *Boston's Immigrants, 1790–1880.* Cambridge: Harvard University Press.

—. 1948. *Race and Nationality in American Life.* Boston: Little, Brown, and Company.

—. 1951. *The Uprooted: The Epic Story of the Great Migrations that Made the American People.* Boston: Little, Brown.

—, and Mary F. Handlin. 1961. *The Dimensions of Liberty.* Cambridge: Belknap Press of Harvard University Press.

—. 1973. *The Uprooted.* 2nd ed. enl. Boston: Little, Brown.

Haney, Robert W. 1960. *Comstockery in America: Patterns of Censorship and Control.* Boston: Beacon Press.

Haney-Lopez, Ian. 1996. *White By Law: The Legal Construction of Race.* New York: New York University Press.

Hansen, Miriam. 1994. *Babel and Babylon: Spectatorship in American Silent Film.* Cambridge: Harvard University Press.

Harbaugh, William H. 1997. *Power and Responsibility: The Life and Times of Theodore Roosevelt.* Reprint. Newtown: American Political Biography Press.

Hard, William. 1908. "De Kid Wot Works at Night." *Everybody's Magazine* 18: 25–37.

Harlan, Louis R. 1958. *Separate and Unequal; Public School Campaigns and Racism in the Southern Seaboard States, 1901–1915.* New York: Athenaeum.

—. 1972. *Booker T. Washington: The Making of a Black Leader, 1856–1901.* New York: Oxford University Press.

—. 1983. *Booker T. Washington: The Wizard of Tuskegee, 1901–1915.* New York: Oxford University Press.

Harmon, Alexandra. 1998. *Indians in the Making: Ethnic Relations and Indian Identities around Puget Sound.* Berkeley: University of California Press.

—. 2001. "Tribal Enrollment Councils: Lessons on Law and Indian Identity." *Western Historical Quarterly* 32: 175–200.

—. 2003. "American Indians and Land Monopolies in the Gilded Age." *Journal of American History* 90: 106–133.

—. 2010. *Rich Indians: Native People and the Problem of Wealth in American History.* Chapel Hill: University of North Carolina Press.

Harmon, Mark D. 1987. "The New York Times and the Theft of the 1876 Presidential Election." *Journal of American Culture* 10, 2: 35–41.

Harold, Claudrena N. 2007. *The Rise and Fall of the Garvey Movement in the Urban South, 1918–1942.* New York: Routledge.

Harper, Ida Husted. 1898. *Life and Work of Susan B. Anthony.* Volume 2. Indianapolis: The Hollenbeck Press.

Harper, Keith. 2008. *American Denominational History: Perspectives on the Past, Prospects for the Future.* Tuscaloosa: University of Alabama Press.

Harris, Joseph E. 1971. *The African Presence in Asia.* Evanston: Northwestern University Press.

—, ed. 1982. *Global Dimensions of the African Diaspora.* Washington, DC: Howard University Press.

Harris, Leon. 1975. *Upton Sinclair, American Rebel.* New York: Thomas Y. Crowell.

Harris, Neil. 1962. "The Gilded Age Revisited: Boston and the Museum Movement." *American Quarterly* 4: 545–566.

—. 1966. *The Artist in American Society: The Formative Years, 1790–1860.* New York: George Braziller.

Harrison, Robert. 2010. *Congress, Progressive Reform and the New American State.* Cambridge: Cambridge University Press.

Hart, John Mason. 2002. *Empire and Revolution: The Americans in Mexico since the Civil War.* Berkeley: University of California Press.

Hartfield, John. 1896. *New Leviathan Cable Code.* New York: Hartfield Telegraphic Code Publishing Co.

Hartog, Hendrik. 2000. *Man and Wife in America: A History.* Cambridge: Harvard University Press.

Hartz, Louis. 1955. *The Liberal Tradition in America: An Interpretation of American Political Thought since the Revolution.* New York: Harcourt, Brace, and Company.

Harvey, David. 2005. *A Brief History of Neoliberalism.* Oxford: Oxford University Press.

Harvey, Paul. 2007. *Freedom's Coming: Religious Cultures and the Shaping of the South.* Chapel Hill: University of North Carolina Press.

—. 1997. *Redeeming the South: Religious Cultures and Racial Identities among Southern Baptists, 1865–1925.* Chapel Hill: The University of North Carolina Press.

Harwood, Craig S. and Gary B. Fogel. 2012. *Quest for Flight: John J. Montgomery and the Dawn of Aviation in the West.* Norman: University of Oklahoma Press.

Haskell, Thomas. 1977. *The Emergence of Professional Social Science: The American Social Science Association and the Nineteenth-Century Crisis of Authority.* Urbana: The University of Illinois Press.

Hathaway, Jay. 2004. *The Gilded Age Construction of Modern American Homophobia.* New York: Palgrave, MacMillan.

Hattori, Anne Perez. 2004. *Colonial Dis-Ease: U.S. Navy Health Policies and the Chamorros of Guam, 1898–1941.* Honolulu: University of Hawaii Press.

Haw, Richard. 2005. *The Brooklyn Bridge: A Cultural History.* New Brunswick: Rutgers University Press.

Haworth, Paul Leland. 1906. *The Hayes-Tilden Disputed Presidential Election of 1876.* Cleveland: The Burrows Brothers Company.

Hays, Samuel P. 1957. *Response to Industrialism, 1885–1914.* Chicago: University of Chicago Press.

—. 1959. *Conservation and the Gospel of Efficiency.* Cambridge: Harvard University Press.

—. 1964. "The Politics of Reform in Municipal Government in the Progressive Era." *Pacific Northwest Quarterly* 55: 157–169.

Hazard, Wendy. 2004. "Thomas Brackett Reed, Civil Rights, and the Fight for Fair Elections." *Maine History* 42, 1: 1–23.

Headrick, Daniel C. 1981. *The Tools of Empire: Technology and European Imperialism in the Nineteenth Century.* New York: Oxford University Press.

Heap, Chad. 2008. *Slumming: Sexual and Racial Encounters in American Nightlife, 1885–1940.* Chicago: University of Chicago Press.

Heatherton, Christina. Forthcoming. *The Color Line and the Class Struggle: The Mexican Revolution, Internationalism, and the American Century.*

Heaton, John. 2005. *The Shoshone-Bannocks: Culture and Commerce at Fort Hall, 1870–1940.* Lawrence: University of Press of Kansas.

Heckscher, August. 1991. *Woodrow Wilson.* New York: Charles Scribner's Sons.

Heersink, Boris and Jeffery A. Jenkins. 2015. "Southern Delegates and Republican National Convention Politics, 1880–1928." *Studies in American Political Development* 29: 68–88.

Heinrich, Thomas and Bob Batchelor. 2004. *Kotex, Kleenex, and Huggies: Kimberly-Clark and the Consumer Revolution.* Columbus: Ohio State University Press.

Hempton, David. 2001. "A Tale of Preachers and Beggars: Methodism and Money in the Great Age of Transatlantic Expansion, 1780–1830." In *God and Mammon: Protestants, Money, and the Market, 1790–1860*, ed. Mark A. Noll, 123–146. New York: Oxford University Press.

Henderson, George L. 1999. *California and the Fictions of Capital.* New York: Oxford University Press.

Hepp, John Henry. 2003. *The Middle-class City: Transforming Space and Time In Philadelphia, 1876–1926.* Philadelphia: University of Pennsylvania Press.

Herbert, Hilary A., et al., 1890. *Why the Solid South?* Baltimore: R. H. Woodward & Company.

Hermans, Tessa. 1993. "Robert Abbott's *Defender*: The Strongest Weapon." *Media History Digest* 13: 38–42 and 64.

Hernández, Sonia. 2014. *Working Women into the Borderlands.* College Station: Texas A&M University Press.

Herring, George C. 2008. *From Colony to Superpower: U.S. Foreign Relations since 1776.* New York: Oxford University Press.

Herron, John P. 2010. *Science and the Social Good: Nature, Culture, and Community, 1865–1965.* New York: Oxford University Press.

Hersey, Mark D. 2006. "Hints and Suggestions to Farmers: George Washington Carver and Rural Conservation in the South." *Environmental History* 11, April: 239–268.

—. 2011. "'What We Need is a Crop Ecologist': Ecology and Agricultural Science in Progressive-Era America." *Agricultural History* 85, 3: 297–321.

—. *2011. My Work is That of Conservation: An Environmental Biography of George Washington Carver.* Athens: University of Georgia Press.

Hertzberg, Hazel W. 1971. *The Search for an American Indian Identity: Modern Pan-Indian Movements.* Syracuse: Syracuse University Press.

Herzig, Rebecca. 2006. *Suffering for Science: Reason and Sacrifice in Modern America.* New Brunswick: Rutgers University Press.

—. 2015. *Plucked: A History of Hair Removal.* New York: New York University Press.

Hess, Herbert W. 1922. "History and Present Status of the 'Truth-in-Advertising' Movement." *Annals of the American Academy of Political and Social Science* 101 May: 214.

Hickman, Timothy A. 2004. "'Mania Americana': Narcotic Addiction and Modernity in the United States, 1870–1920." *Journal of American History* 90, 4: 1269–1294.

Hicks, Cheryl D. 2010. *Talk with You Like a Woman: African American Women, Justice, and Reform In New York, 1890–1935.* Chapel Hill: University of North Carolina Press.

Hicks, John D. 1931. *The Populist Revolt: A History of the Farmers' Alliance and the People's Party.* Minneapolis: University of Minnesota Press.

Higginbotham, Evelyn Brooks. 1993. *Righteous Discontent: the Women's Movement In the Black Baptist Church, 1880–1920.* Cambridge: Harvard University Press.

High, Jack and Clayton A. Coppin. 1988. "Wiley and the Whiskey Industry: Strategic Behavior in the Passage of the Pure Food Act." *Business History Review* 62, 2: 286–309.

Higham, John, with Leonard Krieger and Felix Gilbert. 1965. *History: Professional Scholarship in America.* New York: Prentice-Hall.

—. 1955. *Strangers in the Land: Patterns of American Nativism, 1860–1925.* New Brunswick: Rutgers University Press.

—. 1955. *Strangers in the Land: Patterns of American Nativism 1860–1925.* New York: Atheneum.

—. 1955. *Strangers in the Land: Patterns of American Nativism.* New York: Harper.

—. 1965. "The Re-Orientation of American Culture in the 1890s" In *The Origins of Modern Consciousness*, ed. John Weiss, 25–48. Detroit: Wayne State University Press.

Hild, Matthew. 2007. *Greenbackers, Knights of Labor, and Populists: Farmer-Labor Insurgency in the Late-Nineteenth Century South.* Athens: University of Georgia Press.

Hilderbrand, Robert C. 1981. *Power and the People: Executive Management of Public Opinion in Foreign Affairs, 1897–1921.* Chapel Hill: University of North Carolina Press.

Hilkey, Judy. 1997. *Character Is Capital: Success Manuals and Manhood in Gilded Age.* Chapel Hill: University of North Carolina Press.

Hill, Patricia. 1985. *The World their Household: The American Women's Foreign Mission Movement and Cultural Transformation, 1870–1920.* Ann Arbor: University of Michigan Press.

Hill, Robert A., ed. 2011. *Marcus Garvey and the Universal Negro Improvement Association Papers.* Durham: Duke University Press.

Hinckley, Barbara. 1971. *The Seniority System in Congress.* Bloomington: Indiana University Press.

Hines, Robert V., and John Mack Faragher. 2000. *The American West.* New Haven: Yale University Press.

Hines, Thomas S. 2009. *Burnham of Chicago: Architect and Planner*, 2nd ed. Chicago: University of Chicago Press.

Hinnershitz, Stephanie. 2015. *Race, Religion, and Civil Rights: Asian Students on the West Coast, 1900–1968.* New Brunswick: Rutgers University Press.

Hirshson, Stanley. 1962. *Farewell to the Bloody Shirt: Northern Republicans and the Southern Negro, 1877–1893.* Bloomington: Indiana University Press.

Hirt, Paul W. 2012. *The Wired Northwest: The History of Electric Power, 1870–1920.* Lawrence: University Press of Kansas.

Historical Statistics of the United States: Colonial Times to 1970. 1975. Bicentennial ed. Washington, DC: U.S. Department of Commerce, Bureau of the Census.

Hixson, Walter. 2013. *Settler Colonialism: A History.* New York: Palgrave Macmillan.

Hoagland, Alison K. 2010. *Mine Towns.* Minneapolis: University of Minnesota Press.

Hobsbawm, Eric J. 1989. *The Age of Empire, 1875–1914.* New York: Vintage.

—. 1994. *The Age of Extremes: The Short Twentieth Century, 1914–1991.* London: Michael Joseph.

—. 2003. *Interesting Times: A Twentieth-Century Life.* New York: Pantheon Books.

Hochfelder, David. 2012. *The Telegraph in America, 1832–1920.* Baltimore: Johns Hopkins University Press.

Hodes, Martha. 1997. *White Woman, Black Men: Illicit Sex in the Nineteenth-Century South.* New Haven: Yale University Press.

Hoff, Joan. 2008. *A Faustian Foreign Policy from Woodrow Wilson to George W. Bush: Dreams of Perfectibility.* New York: Cambridge University Press.

Hoffman, Andrew J. 1995. "Mark Twain and Homosexuality." *Journal of American Literature* 67, 1: 23–49.

Hoffman, Elizabeth. 2013. *American Umpire.* Cambridge: Harvard University Press.

Hofstadter, Richard. 1948. *American Political Tradition and the Men Who Made It.* New York: Alfred A. Knopf.

—. 1948. *The American Political Tradition and the Men Who Made It.* New York: Vintage Books.

—. 1955. *Academic Freedom in the Age of the College.* New York: Columbia University Press.

—. 1955. *Age of Reform: From Bryan to F.D.R.* New York: Vintage.

—. 1955. *The Age of Reform: From Bryan to F.D.R.* New York: Knopf.

—. 1965. *The Paranoid Style in American Politics and Other Essays* New York: Knopf.

—. 1968. *The Progressive Historians: Turner, Beard, Parrington.* New York: Knopf.

Hoganson, Kristin L. 1998. *Fighting for American Manhood: How Gender Politics Provoked the Spanish-American and Philippine-American Wars.* New Haven: Yale University Press.

—. 2007. *Consumers' Imperium: The Global Production of American Domesticity, 1865–1920.* Chapel Hill: University of North Carolina Press.

Hoing, Willard L. 1957. "David B. Henderson: Speaker of the House." *Iowa Journal of History* 55, 1: 1–34.

Holbo, Paul S. 1970. "Economics, Emotion, and Expansion: An Emerging Foreign Policy." In *The Gilded Age: A Reappraisal*, ed. H. Wayne Morgan. Revised edition. Syracuse: Syracuse University Press.

Holbrook, M.L. 1878. *Hygiene of the Brain and Nerves and the Cure of Nervousness. With Twenty-Eight Original Letters From Leading Thinkers and Writers Concerning Their Physical and Intellectual Habits.* New York: M. L. Holbrook.

Holler, Clyde. 1995. *Black Elk's Religion: The Sun Dance and Lakota Catholicism*. Syracuse: Syracuse University Press.

Holley, I. B., Jr. 2008. *The Highway Revolution, 1895–1925: How the United States Got Out of the Mud*. Durham: Carolina Academic Press.

Holli, Melvin. 1999. *American Mayor*. University Park: Pennsylvania University Press.

Holloway, Pippa. 2006. *Sexuality, Politics, and Social Control in Virginia, 1920–1945.* Chapel Hill: University of North Carolina Press.

Holm, Tom. 2005. *The Great Confusion in Indian Affairs: Native Americans and Whites in the Progressive Era*. Austin: University of Texas Press.

Holmes, Oliver Wendell. 1860. "Currents and Counter-Currents in Medical Science: An Address Delivered before the Massachusetts Medical Society and the Annual Meeting, May 30, 1860." Boston: Ticknor and Fields.

Holmes, William F. 1970. *White Chief: James Kimble Vardaman*. Baton Rouge: Louisiana State University Press.

Holt, Michael. 2008. *By One Vote: The Disputed Presidential Election of 1876*. Lawrence: University Press of Kansas.

Holt, Sharon Ann. 2003. *Making Freedom Pay: North Carolina Freedpeople Working for Themselves, 1865–1900*. Athens: University of Georgia Press.

Hood, Clifton. 1993. *722 Miles: the Building of the Subways and How They Transformed New York*. New York: Simon & Schuster.

Hoogenboom, Ari. 1988. *The Presidency of Rutherford B. Hayes*. Lawrence: University Press of Kansas.

—. 1995. *Rutherford B. Hayes: Warrior and President*. Lawrence: University Press of Kansas.

Hoover, Herbert. 1952. *The Memoirs of Herbert Hoover, Volume 1: Years of Adventure, 1874–1920*. New York: Macmillan.

Hopkins, C. Howard, and Ronald White. 1976. *The Social Gospel Movement in America*. New York: Harper and Row.

Hopkins, Mary Alden. 1914. "Some Working People." *Child Labor Bulletin* 3: 47–49.

Hornaday, William Temple. 1914. *Wild Life Conservation in Theory and Practice: Lectures Delivered Before the Forest School of Yale University*. New Haven: Yale University Press.

Horowitz, Helen Lefkowitz. 1976. *Cultural Philanthropy in Chicago*. Chicago: University of Chicago Press.

—. 1984. *Alma Mater: Design and Experience in the Women's Colleges from Their Nineteenth Century Beginnings to the 1930s*. New York: Alfred A. Knopf.

—. 1984. *Alma Mater: Design and Experience in the Women's Colleges from Their Nineteenth-century Beginnings to the 1930s*. Amherst: University of Massachusetts Press.

—. 2002. *Rereading Sex: Battles over Sexual Knowledge and Suppression in Nineteenth-Century America*. New York: Alfred A. Knopf.

Horsman, Reginald. 1981. *Race and Manifest Destiny: The Origins of American Racial Anglo-Saxonism*. Cambridge: Harvard University Press.

Horwitz, Morton J. 1992. *The Transformation of American Law, 1870–1960: The Crisis of Legal Orthodoxy*. Oxford: Oxford University Press.

Hosmer, Brian C. 1999. *American Indians in the Marketplace: Persistence and Innovation among the Menominees and Metlakatlans, 1870–1920*. Lawrence: University Press of Kansas.

Hou, Shen. 2013. *The City Natural: Garden and Forest Magazine and the Rise of American Environmentalism*. Pittsburgh: University of Pittsburgh Press.

House, Albert V. 1934. "The Political Career of Samuel Jackson Randall." PhD diss., University of Wisconsin.

Hovenkamp, Herbert. 1991. *Enterprise and American Law, 1836–1937*. Cambridge: Harvard University Press.

—. 2014. *The Opening of American Law: Neoclassical Legal Thought, 1870–1970*. Oxford: Oxford University Press.

Hovey, Elizabeth Bainum. 1998. "Stamping out Smut: The Enforcement of Obscenity Laws, 1872–1915." Ph.D. diss., Columbia University.

Howard, John R. 1999. *The Shifting Wind: The Supreme Court and Civil Rights from Reconstruction to Brown*. New York: State University of New York Press.

Howe, Daniel Walker. 2007. *What Hath God Wrought: The Transformation of America, 1815–1848*. New York: Oxford University Press.

Howe, Frederic. 1906. *The City: the Hope of Democracy*. New York: Charles Scribner's Sons.

Howe, Irving, and Kenneth Libo. 1976. *World of Our Fathers*. 1st ed. New York: Harcourt Brace Jovanovich.

Howe, Julia Ward, 1900. *Reminiscences, 1819–1899*. Boston: Houghton, Mifflin.

Hoxie, Frederick E. 1979. "From Prison to Homeland." *South Dakota History* 10: 1–24.

—. 1984. *A Final Promise: The Campaign to Assimilate the Indians, 1880–1920*. Lincoln: University of Nebraska.

—. 1989. *Final Promise: The Campaign to Assimilate the Indians, 1880–1920*. New York: Cambridge University Press.

—, ed. 2001. *Talking Back to Civilization: Indian Voices from the Progressive Era*. New York: Bedford/St. Martin's.

—. 2012. *This Indian Country: American Indian Activists and the Place They Made*. New York: Penguin Press.

Hsu, Madeline Y. 2000. *Dreaming of Gold, Dreaming of Home: Transnationalism and Migration between the United States and South China, 1882–1943*. Stanford: Stanford University Press.

Hudson, John C. 1985. *Plains Country Towns*. Minneapolis: University of Minnesota Press.

Hudson, Peter. Forthcoming. *Dark Finance: Wall Street and the West Indies, 1873 – 1933*.

Hughes, J. T. R. 1987. *American Economic History*. 2nd edition. Glenview: Scott Foresman.

Hughes, Robert. 1997. *American Visions: The Epic History of Art in America*. New York: Knopf.

Hunter, Jane. 1984. *The Gospel of Gentility: American Women Missionaries in Turn of the Century China*. New Haven: Yale University Press.

Hunter, Robert. 1904. *Poverty*. New York: Macmillan.

Hunter, Tera W. 1997. *To 'Joy My Freedom: Southern Black Women's Lives and Labors After the Civil War*. Cambridge: Harvard University Press.

Hurt, R. Douglas. 1987. *Indian Agriculture in America: Prehistory to the Present*. Lawrence: University Press of Kansas.

—. 2013. "The Agricultural Power of the Midwest during the Civil War." In *Union Heartland*, ed. Ginette Aley and J.L. Anderson, 68–96. Carbondale: Southern Illinois University Press.

Hurtado, Albert. 1988. *Indian Survival on the California Frontier*. New Haven: Yale University Press.

Hutchison, William. 1976. *The Modernist Impulse in American Protestantism*. Cambridge: Harvard University Press.

—. 1987. *Errand to the World: American Protestant Thought and Foreign Missions*. Chicago: University of Chicago Press.

—. 1989. *Between the Times: The Travail of the Protestant Establishment in America, 1900–1960*. New York: Cambridge University Press.

—. 2004. *Religious Pluralism in America: The Contentious History of a Founding Ideal*. New Haven: Yale University Press.

Huthmacher, J. Joseph. 1962. "Urban Liberalism and the Age of Reform." *Mississippi Valley Historical Review* 44: 231–241.

Huyssen, David. 2014. *Progressive Inequality: Rich and Poor in New York, 1890–1920*. Cambridge: Harvard University Press.

Hyde, Charles K. 2005. *The Dodge Brothers: The Men, the Motor Cars, and the Legacy*. Detroit. Wayne State University Press.

Hylton, Gordon. 1998. "David Josiah Brewer and the Christian Constitution." *Marquette Law Review* 81, 2: 417–26.

Immerman, Richard H. *Empire for Liberty: A History of American Imperialism from Benjamin Franklin to Paul Wolfowitz*. Princeton: Princeton University Press.

"Interchange: The History of Capitalism." 2014. *Journal of American History* 101, 2: 503–536.

Irwin, Julia F. 2013. *Making the World Safe: The American Red Cross and a Nation's Humanitarian Awakening*. New York: Oxford University Press.

Isenberg, Alison. 2004. *Downtown America: a History of the Place and the People Who Made It*. Chicago: University of Chicago Press.

Isenberg, Andrew C. 1999. *The Destruction of the Bison: An Environmental History, 1750–1920*. Cambridge: Cambridge University Press.

Israel, Fred L., ed. 1897. *Sears, Roebuck Catalogue*. Chicago: Sears, Roebuck and Co.

Israel, Jerry. 1971. *Progressivism and the Open Door: America and China, 1905–1921*. Pittsburgh: University of Pittsburgh Press.

Jablonsky, Thomas J. 1994. *Duty, Nature, and Stability*. Brooklyn: Carlson Publishing.

Jackson, Justin. 2014. "The Work of Empire: The U.S. Army and the Making of American Colonialisms in Cuba and the Philippines, 1898 – 1913." PhD diss., Columbia University.

Jackson, Kenneth T. 1985. *Crabgrass Frontier: the Suburbanization of the United States*. New York: Oxford University Press.

Jackson, Richard H. 1995. "Federal Lands in the Mountainous West." In *The Mountainous West*, ed. William Wyckoff and Lary M. Dilsaver, 253–277. Lincoln: University of Nebraska Press.

Jackson, Robert H. 1941. *The Struggle for Judicial Supremacy; a Study of a Crisis in American Power Politics*. New York: A.A. Knopf.

Jacob, Kathryn A. 2009. *King of the Lobby: The Life and Times of Sam Ward, Man About Washington in the Gilded Age*. Baltimore: Johns Hopkins University Press.

Jacobson, Matthew Frye. 2000. *Barbarian Virtues: The United States Encounters Foreign Peoples at Home and Abroad, 1876–1917*. New York: Hill and Wang.

—. 2006. "More 'Trans', Less 'National.'" *Journal of American Ethnic History* 25, 4: 74–84.

Jacoby, Karl. 2001. *Crimes Against Nature: Squatters, Poachers, Thieves, and the Hidden History of American Conservation*. Berkeley: University of California Press.

Jacoby, Susan. *Freethinkers: A History of American Secularism*. 2004. New York: The Free Press.

Jenkins, Philip. 2014. *The Great and Holy War: How World War I Became a Religious Crusade*. New York: Harper Collins.

James, Joy, and T. Denean Sharpley-Whiting, eds. 2000. *The Black Feminist Reader*. Malden: Blackwell Publishers.

James, Scott C. 2000. *Presidents, Parties, and the State: A Party System Perspective on Democratic Regulatory Choice, 1884–1936*. Cambridge: Cambridge University Press.

—. 2007. "Timing and Sequence in Congressional Elections: Interstate Contagion and America's Nineteenth-Century Scheduling Regime." *Studies in American Political Development* 21, 2: 181–202.

—, and Brian L. Lawson. 1999. "The Political Economy of Voting Rights Enforcement in America's Gilded Age: Electoral College Competition, Partisan Commitment, and the Federal Election Law." *American Political Science Review* 93, 1: 115–131.

James, William. 1890. *Principles of Psychology*. New York: Henry Holt.

—. 1892. *Psychology*. New York: Henry Holt.

James, Winston. 1998. 1999. *Holding Aloft the Banner of Ethiopia: Caribbean Radicalism in Early Twentieth-Century America*. London: Verso.

Jameson, Fredric. 1979. "Reification and Utopia in Mass Culture." *Social Text* 1: 130–148.

Janney, Caroline E. 2013. *Remembering the Civil War: Reunion and the Limits of Reconciliation*. Chapel Hill: University of North Carolina Press.

Jeffers, Harry P. 2000. *An Honest President: The Life and Presidencies of Grover Cleveland*. New York: W. Morrow.

Jenkins, Jeffery A. 2004. "Partisanship and Contested Election Cases in the House of Representatives, 1789–2002." *Studies in American Political Development* 18, 1: 113–35.

—. 2007. "The First 'Southern Strategy': The Republican Party and Contested-Election Cases in the Late 19th-Century House." In *Party, Process, and Political Change in Congress. Volume 2: Further New Perspectives on the History of Congress*, ed. David W. Brady and Matthew D. McCubbins. Palo Alto: Stanford University Press.

Jensen, Carl. 2000. *Stories That Changed America: Muckrakers of the 20th Century*. New York: Seven Stories.

Jensen, Richard. 1971. *The Winning of the Midwest: A Social Analysis of Midwestern Politics, 1880–1896*. New York: Oxford University Press.

—. 1971. *The Winning of the Midwest: Social and Political Conflict, 1888–1896*. Chicago: University of Chicago Press.

Jensen, Robin E. 2010. *Dirty Words: The Rhetoric of Public Sex Education, 1870–1924*. Champaign: University of Illinois Press.

Jentz, John B., and Richard Schenirov. 2012. *Chicago in the Age of Capital*. Urbana: University of Illinois Press.

Jewett, Andrew. 2012. *Science, Democracy, and the American University: From the Civil War to the Cold War*. New York: Cambridge University Press.

John, Richard R. 1997. "Elaborations, Revisions, Dissents: Alfred D. Chandler, Jr.'s *The Visible Hand* after Twenty Years." *Business Historical Review* 71: 151–206.

—. 2004. "Farewell to the 'Party Period': Political Economy in Nineteenth-Century America." *Journal of Policy History* 16, 2: 117–25.

—. 2006. "Ruling Passions, Political Economy in Nineteenth-Century America." *Journal of Policy History* 18, 1: 1–20.

—. 2009. "Who Were the Gilders? And Other Seldom-Asked Questions about Business, Technology, and Political Economy in the United States, 1877–1900." *Journal of the Gilded Age and Progressive Era* 8: 474–80.

—. 2010. *Network Nation: Inventing American Telecommunications.* Cambridge: Belknap Press of Harvard University Press.

Johnson, Arthur M., and Barry E. Supple. 1967. *Boston Capitalists and Western Railroads; a Study in the Nineteenth-Century Railroad Investment Process.* Cambridge: Harvard University Press.

Johnson, Benjamin Heber. 2003. *Revolution in Texas: How a Forgotten Rebellion and Its Bloody Suppression Turned Mexicans into Americans.* New Haven: Yale University Press.

—. 2017. *Escaping the Dark, Gray City: Fear and Hope in Progressive Era Conservation.* New Haven: Yale University Press.

Johnson, Gerald W. 1946. *An Honorable Titan: A Biographical Study of Adolph S. Ochs.* New York: Harper & Bros.

Johnson, Richard Christian. 1973. "Anthony Comstock: Reform, Vice, and the American Way." PhD diss., University of Wisconsin.

Johnson, Robert David. 1995. *The Peace Progressives and American Foreign Relations.* Cambridge: Harvard University Press.

Johnson, Sylvester A. 2015. *African American Religions, 1500–2000: Colonialism, Democracy and Freedom.* New York: Cambridge University Press.

Johnson, Val. 2006. "'The Moral Aspects of Complex Problems': New York City Electoral Campaigns against Vice and the Incorporation of Immigrants, 1890–1901." *Journal of American Ethnic History* 25, 2/3: 74–106.

Johnson, Walter. 1947. *Selected Letters of William Allen White, 1899–1943.* New York: Henry Holt.

—. 2013. *River of Dark Dreams: Slavery and Empire in the Cotton Kingdom.* Cambridge: Harvard University Press.

Johnson, William R. 1999. *William and Henry Walters: The Reticent Collectors.* Baltimore: Johns Hopkins University Press.

Johnston, Robert D. 1998. "Beyond 'The West': Regionalism, Liberalism, and the Evasion of Politics in the New Western History," *Rethinking History* 2: 239–277.

—. 2002. "Re-Democratizing the Progressive Era: The Politics of Progressive Era Political Historiography." *Journal of the Gilded Age and Progressive Era* 1: 68–92.

—. 2003. *The Radical Middle Class: Populist Democracy and the Question of Capitalism in Progressive Era Portland, Oregon.* Princeton: Princeton University Press.

—. 2007. "*The Age of Reform*: A Defense of Richard Hofstadter Fifty Years On." *Journal of the Gilded Age and Progressive Era* 6, April: 127–138.

—. 2011. "The Possibilities of Politics: Democracy in America, 1877–1917." In *American History Now*, ed. Eric Foner and Lisa McGirr, 96–124. Philadelphia: Temple University Press in cooperation with the American Historical Association.

—. 2014. "Long Live Teddy/Death to Woodrow: The Polarized Politics of The Progressive Era in the 2012 Election." *Journal of the Gilded Age and Progressive Era* 13, July: 411–443.

Jones, Alan. 1967. "Thomas M. Cooley and 'Laissez-Faire Constitutionalism': A Reconsideration." *Journal of American History* 53, 4: 751–71.

Jones, Charles O. 1968. "Joseph G. Cannon and Howard W. Smith: An Essay on the Limits of Leadership in the House of Representatives." *Journal of Politics* 30, 3: 617–46.

Jones, Jacqueline. 1985. *Labor of Love, Labor of Sorrow: Black Women, Work, and the Family, from Slavery to the Present.* New York: Basic Books.

—. 1985. *Labor of Love, Labor of Sorrow: Black Women, Work and the Family, From Slavery to the Present.* New York: Vintage.

—. 1992. *Soldiers of Light and Love: Northern Teachers and Georgia Blacks, 1865–1873.* Athens: University of Georgia Press.

Jordan, Ben. 2010. "'Conservation of Boyhood': Boy Scouting's Modest Manliness and Natural Conservation, 1910–1930." *Environmental History* 15: 612–642.

Jorgenson, Lloyd P. 1987. *The State and the Non-Public School, 1825–1925.* Columbia: University of Missouri Press.

Joseph, Gilbert. 1988. *Revolution from Without: Yucatan, Mexico, and the United States, 1880 – 1924.* Durham: Duke University Press.

Josephson, Hannah. 1974. *Jeanette Rankin, First Lady in Congress: A Biography.* Indianapolis: Bobbs-Merrill.

Josephson, Matthew. 1934. *The Robber Barons: The Great American Capitalists, 1861–1901.* New York: Harcourt, Brace and Company.

—. 1938. *The Politicos, 1865–1896.* New York: Harcourt, Brace.

Judd, Richard W. 1997. *Common Lands, Common People: The Origins of Conservation in Northern New England.* Cambridge: Harvard University Press.

Jung, Moon-Ho. Forthcoming. *The Unruly Pacific: Race and the Politics of Empire and Revolution, 1898–1941.*

Justesen, Benjamin R. 2001. *George Henry. White: An Even Chance in the Race of Life.* Baton Rouge: Louisiana State University Press.

Juzda, Elisa. 2009. "Skulls, Science, and the Spoils of War: Craniological Studies at the United States Army Medical Museum, 1868–1900." *Studies in History and Philosophy of Biomedical Sciences* 40: 156–167.

Kahan, Michael B. 2012. "'There are Plenty of Women on the Street': The Landscape of Commercial Sex in Progressive-Era Philadelphia, 1910–1918." *Historical Geography* 40: 37–58.

—. 2013. "The Risk of Cholera and the Reform of Urban Space: Philadelphia, 1893." *Geographical Review* 103: 517–536.

Kalisch, P. A., & Kalisch, B. J. 2004. *American Nursing: A History.* 4th ed. Philadelphia: Lippincott, Williams, and Wilkins.

Kalman, Laura. 2005. "The Constitution, the Supreme Court, and the New Deal." *American Historical Review* 110, 4: 1052–80.

Kaneko, Josephine. 1914. *The Coming Nation.* March.

Kantrowitz, Stephen. 2000. *Ben Tillman and the Reconstruction of White Supremacy.* Chapel Hill: University of North Carolina Press.

Kaplan, Amy. 1993. "Left Alone With America." In *Cultures of United States Imperialism*, ed. Amy Kaplan and Donald Pease. Durham: Duke University Press.

—, and Donald Pease, eds. 1993. *Cultures of Imperialism.* Durham: Duke University Press.

Kaplan, Amy. 2002. *The Anarchy of Empire in the Making of U.S. Culture.* Cambridge: Harvard University Press.

Karamanski, Theodore J. 1989. *Deep Woods Frontier.* Detroit: Wayne State University Press.

Karl, Barry D. and Stanley N. Katz. 1981. "The American Private Philanthropic Foundation and the Public Sphere 1890–1930." *Minerva: A Review of Science, Learning and Policy* 19: 236–70.

Karl, Barry.1983. *The Uneasy State: The United States from 1915–1945.* Chicago: University of Chicago Press.

Kasson, John F. 1978. *Amusing the Million: Coney Island at the Turn of the Century.* New York: Hill and Wang.

—. 2001. *Houdini, Tarzan, and the Perfect Man: The White Male Body and the Challenge of Modernity in America.* New York: Hill and Wang.

Kates, James. 1995. "A 'Square Deal' for a 'Primitive Rebel': Alfred E. Roese and the Battle of Cameron Dam, 1904–1910." *Wisconsin Magazine of History* 79: 83–108.

Katz, Daniel. 2013. *All Together Different: Yiddish Socialists, Garment Workers, and the Labor Roots of Multiculturalism.* New York: New York University Press.

Katz, Michael B. 1996. *In the Shadow of the Poorhouse: a Social History of Welfare In America.* 2nd edition. New York: Basic Books.

—, and Mark J Stern. 2006. *One Nation Divisible: What America Was and What it Is Becoming.* New York: Russell Sage Foundation.

Katz, Stanley N., Barry Sullivan, and C. Paul Beach. 1985. "Legal Change and Legal Autonomy: Charitable Trusts in New York, 1777–1893." *Law and History Review* 3: 51–89.

Kazal, Russell A. 2004. *Becoming Old Stock: the Paradox of German-american Identity.* Princeton: Princeton University Press.

Kazin, Michael. 2006. *A Godly Hero: the Life of William Jennings Bryan.* New York: Knopf.

Keating, Ann Durkin. 2005. *Chicagoland: City and Suburbs In the Railroad Age.* Chicago: University of Chicago Press.

Keil, Hartmut and John B. Jentz, eds. 1983. *German Workers in Industrial Chicago, 1850–1910: A Comparative Perspective.* DeKalb: Northern Illinois University Press.

Keiner, Christine. 2009. *The Oyster Question: Scientists, Watermen, and the Maryland Chesapeake Bay since 1880.* Athens: University of Georgia Press.

Keire, Mara. 2010. *For Business and Pleasure: Red-Light Districts and the Regulation of Vice in the United States, 1890–1933.* Baltimore: Johns Hopkins University Press.

Keith, Jeanette. 2004. *Rich Man's War, Poor Man's Fight: Race, Class, and Power in the Rural South during the First World War.* Chapel Hill: University of North Carolina Press.

Keller, Lisa. 2009. *Triumph of Order: Democracy & Public Space In New York and London.* New York: Columbia University Press.

Keller, Morton. 1977. *Affairs of State: Public Life in Late-Nineteenth-Century America.* Cambridge: Belknap Press of Harvard University Press.

—. 1990. *Regulating a New Economy: Public Policy and Economic Change in America, 1900–1933.* Cambridge: Harvard University Press.

—. 2007. *America's Three Regimes: A New Political History.* New York: Oxford University Press.

Keller, Robert H., Jr. 1983. *American Protestantism and United States Indian Policy.* Lincoln: University of Nebraska Press.

Kelley, Blair Murphy. 2010. *Right to Ride: Streetcar Boycotts and African American Citizenship In the Era of Plessy v. Ferguson.* Chapel Hill: University of North Carolina Press.

Kelley, Florence. 1895. "The Sweating System." In *Hull-House Maps and Papers,* by Residents of Hull-House, 27–48. Boston: Thomas Y. Crowell & Co.

Kelley, Robert. 1969. *The Transatlantic Persuasion: The Liberal-Democratic Mind in the Age of Gladstone.* New York: Knopf.

—. 1989. *Battling the Inland Sea.* Berkeley: University of California Press.

Kelley, Robin D. G. 1992. "Notes on Deconstructing 'The Folk.'" *American Historical Review* 97, 5: 1400–1408.

—. 1990. *Hammer and Hoe: Alabama Communities during the Great Depression. Chapel Hill*: University of North Carolina Press.

Kemble, John H. "A Hundred Years of the Pacific Mail." *American Neptune* X April 1950: 123–143.

Kemp, Kathryn W. 2007. "'The Dictograph Hears All': An Example of Surveillance Technology in the Progressive Era." *Journal of the Gilded Age and Progressive Era* 6, 4: 209–230.

Kennedy, David M. 1970. *Birth Control in America: The Career of Margaret Sanger.* New Haven: Yale University Press.

—. 1980. *Over Here: The First World War and American Society.* New York: Oxford University Press.

—. 2005. "What 'W' Owes to 'WW.'" *The Atlantic* 30: 36–40.

Kennedy, Duncan. 1975. *The Rise and Fall of Classical Legal Thought.* Washington, DC: Beard Books.

Kennedy, Ross A.2009. *The Will to Believe: Woodrow Wilson, World War I, and America's Strategy for Peace and Security.* Kent: Kent State University Press.

—, ed. 2013. *A Companion to Woodrow Wilson.* Malden: Wiley-Blackwell.

Kenny, Kevin. 2000. *The American Irish: A History.* New York: Routledge.

—. 1998. *Making Sense of the Molly Maguires.* New York: Oxford University Press.

Kens, Paul. 1997. *Justice Stephen Field: Shaping Liberty from the Gold Rush to the Gilded Age.* Lawrence: University Press of Kansas.

Kerber, Linda K. 1998. *No Constitutional Right to Be Ladies: Women and the Obligations of Citizenship.* New York: Hill and Wang.

Kern, Louis J. 1981. *An Ordered Love: Sex Roles and Sexuality in Victorian Utopias—the Shakers, the Mormons, and the Oneida Community.* Chapel Hill: University of North Carolina Press.

Kern, Stephen. 1983. 2003. *The Culture of Time and Space, 1880–1918.* Cambridge: Harvard University Press.

Kernell, Samuel. 1977. "Toward Understanding Nineteenth Century Congressional Careers: Ambition, Competition, and Rotation." *American Journal of Political Science* 21, 4: 669–93.

Kerr, K. Austin. 1985. *Organized for Prohibition: A New History of the Anti-Saloon League.* New Haven: Yale University Press.

Kessler-Harris, Alice. 1982. 2003. *Out to Work: A History of Wage-Earning Women in the United States.* New York: Oxford University Press.

—. 1995. "The Paradox of Motherhood: Night Work Restrictions in the United States." In *Protecting Women: Labor Legislation in Europe, the United States, and Australia, 1880–1920,* eds. Ulla Wikander et al., 337–357. Chicago: University of Illinois Press.

—. 2001. *In Pursuit of Equity: Women, Men, and the Quest for Economic Citizenship in 20th-Century America.* New York: Oxford University Press.

Kessner, Thomas. 1977. *The Golden Door: Italian and Jewish Immigrant Mobility In New York City 1880–1915.* New York: Oxford University Press.

Kevles, Daniel J. 1977. *The Physicists: The History of a Scientific Community in Modern America*. New York: Vintage Books.

—. 1985. *In the name of Eugenics: Genetics and the Uses of Human Heredity*. Berkeley: University of California Press.

—. 2007. "Patents, Protections, and Privileges: The Establishment of Intellectual Property in Animals and Plants." *ISIS* 98: 323–331.

Key Jr., V. O. 1955. "A Theory of Critical Elections." *Journal of Politics* 17, 1: 3–18.

—. 1984. *Southern Politics in State and Nation*. New edition. Knoxville: University of Tennessee Press.

Killick, John R. 1977. "The Cotton Operations of Alexander Brown and Sons in the Deep South, 1820–1860." *Journal of Southern History* 43: 169–94. DOI:10.2307/2207344.

Killingray, David, et al. 2011. *The Spanish Influenza Pandemic of 1918–1919: New Perspectives*. New York: Routledge.

Kimmelman, Barbara A. 2006. "Mr. Blakeslee Builds His Dream House: Agricultural Institutions, Genetics, and Careers 1900–1915." *Journal of the History of Biology* 39: 241–280.

Kingsland, Sharon E. 2005. *The Evolution of American Ecology, 1890–2000*. Baltimore: Johns Hopkins University Press.

Kirby, Jack Temple. 1972. *Darkness at the Dawning: Race and Reform in the Progressive South*. Philadelphia: Lippincott.

Kitch, Carolyn. 2001. *The Girl on the Magazine Cover: The Origins of Visual Stereotypes in American Mass Media*. Chapel Hill: University of North Carolina Press.

Klein, Maury. 2007. *The Genesis of Industrial America, 1870–1920*. Cambridge: Cambridge University Press.

Kleinberg, S. J. 1989. *The Shadow of the Mills: Working-class Families In Pittsburgh, 1870–1907*. Pittsburgh: University of Pittsburgh Press.

Kline, Ronald R. 2003. *Consumers in the Country: Technology and Social Change in Rural America*. Baltimore: Johns Hopkins University Press.

Kline, Wendy. 2001. *Building a Better Race: Gender, Sexuality, and Eugenics from the Turn of the Century to the Baby Boom*. Berkeley: University of California Press.

Klinghard, Daniel. *The Nationalization of American Political Parties, 1880–1896*. New York: Cambridge University Press.

Klingle, Matthew W. 2007. *Emerald City: An Environmental History of Seattle*. New Haven: Yale University Press.

Kloppenberg, James T. 1986. *Uncertain Victory: Social Democracy and Progressivism in European and American Thought, 1870–1920*. New York: Oxford University Press.

Knight, Louise W. 2005. *Citizen: Jane Addams and the Struggle for Democracy*. Chicago: University of Chicago Press.

Knoblock, Glenn A. 2014. *The American Clipper Ship, 1845–1920: A Comprehensive History, with a Listing of Builders and Their Ships*. Jefferson: McFarland.

Knock, Thomas J. 1992. *To End All Wars: Woodrow Wilson and the Quest for a New World Order*. New York: Oxford University Press.

Knupfer, Anne Meis. 1996. *Toward a Tenderer Humanity and a Nobler Womanhood: African American Women's Clubs in Turn-of-the-Century Chicago*. New York: New York University Press.

Kobrin, Rebecca. 2010. *Jewish Bialystok and Its Diaspora*. Bloomington: Indiana University Press.

Kohler, Robert E. 1991. *Partners in Science: Foundations and Natural Scientists, 1900–1945*. Chicago: University of Chicago Press.

—. 2006. *All Creatures: Naturalists, Collectors, and Biodiversity, 1850–1950*. Princeton: Princeton University Press.

—. 2008. "From Farm and Family to Career Naturalist: The Apprenticeship of Vernon Bailey." *ISIS* 99: 28–56.

Kohlstedt, Sally Gregory. 2005. "Nature, Not Books. Scientists and the Origins of the Nature-Study Movement in the 1890s." *ISIS* 96: 324–352.

—. 2008. "'A Better Crop of Boys and Girls': The School Gardening Movement, 1890–1920." *History of Education Quarterly* 48, 1: 58–93.

—. 2010. *Teaching Children Science. Hands-On Nature Study in North America, 1890–1930*. Chicago: University of Chicago Press.

—. 2011. "Place and Museum Space: The Smithsonian Institution, National Identity, and the American West, 1846–1896." In *Geographies of Nineteenth-Century Science*, ed. David N. Livingstone and Charles W. J. Withers. Chicago: University of Chicago.

—. 2013. "Innovative Niche Scientists: Women's Role in Reframing North American Museums, 1880–1930." *Centaurus* 55: 153–174.

Kolchin, Peter. 2003. *A Sphinx on the American Land: The Nineteenth-Century South in Comparative Perspective*. Baton Rouge: Louisiana State University Press.

Kolko, Gabriel S. 1963. *The Triumph of Conservatism: A Reinterpretation of American History, 1900–1916*. New York: Free Press of Glencoe.

—. 1965. *Railroads and Regulation, 1877–1916*. Princeton: Princeton University Press.

—. 1969. *The Roots of American Foreign Policy: An Analysis of Power and Purpose*. Boston: Beacon Press.

Kornbluh, Mark. 2000. *Why America Stopped Voting: The Decline of Participatory Voting and the Emergence of Modern American Politics*. New York: New York University Press.

Kousser, J. Morgan. 1974. *The Shaping of Southern Politics: Suffrage Restriction and the Establishment of the One-Party South, 1880–1910*. New Haven: Yale University Press.

—. 1980. "Progressivism - for Middle Class Whites Only: North Carolina Education, 1880–1910." *Journal of Southern History* 46, 2: 169–94.

Koven, Seth and Sonya Michel. 1993. *Mothers of a New World: Maternalist Politics and the Origins of Welfare States*. New York: Routledge.

Kraditor, Aileen. 1965. *The Ideas of the Woman Suffrage Movement, 1890–1920*. New York: Columbia University Press.

Kramer, Paul. 2006. *The Blood of Government: Race, Empire, the United States and the Philippines*. Chapel Hill: University of North Carolina Press.

—. 2011. "Power and Connection: Imperial Histories of the United States in the World." *American Historical Review* 116, 5: 1348 - 1391.

—. 2015. "Imperial Openings: Civilization, Exemption, and the Geopolitics of Mobility in the History of Chinese Exclusion, 1868–1910." *Journal of the Gilded Age and Progressive Era* 14: 317–47.

Krehbiel, Keith, and Alan E. Wiseman. 2001. "Joseph G. Cannon: Majoritarian from Illinois." *Legislative Studies Quarterly* 26, 3: 357–89.

—. 2005. "Joe Cannon and the Minority Party: Tyranny or Bipartisanship?" *Legislative Studies Quarterly* 30, 4: 479–505.

Kremer, Richard L. 2011. "Reforming American Physics Pedagogy in the 1880s: Introducing 'Learning By Doing' Via Student Laboratory Exercises." In *Learning By Doing. Experiments and Instruments in the History of Science Teaching*, ed. Peter Heering and Roland Wittje, 243–280. Stuttgart: Franz Steiner Verlag.

Kroeger, Brooke. 1994. *Nellie Bly: Daredevil, Reporter, Feminist.* New York: Times Books.

Kroes, Rob and Robert Rydell. 2005. *Buffalo Bill in Bologna: The Americanization of the World, 1869–1922.* Chicago: University of Chicago Press.

Kuehl, Warren. 1969. *Seeking World Order: The United States and International Organization to 1920.* Nashville: Vanderbilt University Press.

Kunzel, Regina. 2008. *Criminal Intimacy: Prison and the Uneven History of Modern American Sexuality.* Chicago: University of Chicago Press.

Kusmer, Kenneth L. 1978. *A Ghetto Takes Shape.* Urbana: University of Illinois Press.

Kwolek-Folland, Angel. 1994. *Engendering Business: Men and Women in the Corporate Office, 1870–1930.* Baltimore: Johns Hopkins University Press.

La Follette, Belle Case. 1913. "Segregation in the Civil Service." *La Follette's Magazine* 5, 50: 6.

La Follette, Robert. 1913. *La Follette's Autobiography: A Personal Narrative of Political Experiences.* Madison: Robert La Follette Company.

La Forte, Robert S. 1966. "Theodore Roosevelt's Osawatomie Speech." *Kansas Historical Society* 32: 187–200.

Lachman, Charles. 2013. *A Secret Life: The Lies and Scandals of President Grover Cleveland.* New York: Skyhorse Publishing.

Ladd-Taylor, Molly. 1994. *Mother-Work: Women, Child Welfare, and the State, 1890–1930.* Chicago: University of Chicago Press.

LaFeber, Walter. 1963. *The New Empire: An Interpretation of American Expansion, 1860–1898.* Ithaca: Cornell University Press.

—. 1993. *The Cambridge History of American Foreign Relations: Volume II, The American Search for Opportunity, 1865–1913.* Ed. Warren I. Cohen. New York: Cambridge University Press.

—. 2013. *The American Search for Opportunity, 1865–1913.* New York: Cambridge University Press.

Lagemann, Ellen Condliffe. 1983. *Private Power For the Public Good: A History of the Carnegie Foundation for the Advancement of Teaching.* Middletown: Wesleyan University Press.

—. 1989. *The Politics of Knowledge: The Carnegie Corporation, Philanthropy, and Public Policy.* Middletown: Wesleyan University Press.

Laird, Pamela Walker. 1998. *Advertising Progress: American Business and the Rise of Consumer Marketing.* Baltimore: Johns Hopkins University Press.

Lake, Marilyn and Henry Reynolds. 2008. *Drawing the Global Colour Line: White Men's Countries and the International Challenge of Racial Equality.* Melbourne: Melbourne University Press.

—. 2014. "Challenging the 'Slave-Driving Employers': Understanding Victoria's 1896 Minimum Wage through a World-History Approach." *Australian Historical Studies* 45, 1: 87–102. doi: 10.1080/1031461X.2013.877501

Lamphere, Louise. 1987. *From Working Daughters to Working Mothers: Immigrant Women in a New England Industrial Community.* Ithaca: Cornell University Press.

Lamoreaux, Naomi R. 1985. *The Great Merger Movement in American Business, 1895–1904.* Cambridge: Cambridge University Press.

Lamster, Mark. 2006. *Spalding's World Tour: The Epic Adventure that Took Baseball Around the Globe—And Made It America's Game.* New York: Public Affairs.

Lancos, John R. 1992. "Theodore Roosevelt Birthplace: Study in Americanism." In *Theodore Roosevelt: Many-Sided American.* Interlaken: Heart of the Lakes Publishing.

Landau, Emily Epstein. 2013. *Spectacular Wickedness: Sex, Race, and Memory in Storyville, New Orleans.* Baton Rouge: Louisiana State University Press.

Langa, Helen. 2004. "Recent Feminist Art History: An American Sampler." *Feminist Studies* 30: 705–730.

Langley, Lester D. and Thomas Schoonover. 1995. *The Banana Men: American Mercenaries and Entrepreneurs in Central America, 1880–1930.* Lexington: University Press of Kentucky.

Langston, Nancy. 1995. *Forest Dreams, Forest Nightmares: The Paradox of Old Growth in the Inland West.* Seattle: University of Washington Press.

Lankton, Larry. 1999. *Beyond the Boundaries.* New York: Oxford University Press.

Lansing, Michael J. 2009. "'Salvaging the Man Power of America': Conservation, Manhood, and Disabled Veterans during World War I." *Environmental History* 14: 32–57.

LaPier, Rosalyn R., and David R.M. Beck. 2015. *"Determining Our Own Destiny": American Indians in Chicago, 1893–1934."* Lincoln: University of Nebraska Press.

Laqueur, Thomas. 2004. *Solitary Sex: A Cultural History of Masturbation.* New York: Zone Books.

Largent, Mark A. 2008. *Breeding Contempt: The History of Coerced Sterilization in the United States.* New Brunswick: Rutgers University Press.

Larson, Edward J. 1996. *Sex, Race, and Science: Eugenics in the Deep South.* Baltimore: Johns Hopkins University Press.

Larson, Jane. 1997. "'Even a Worm Will Turn at Last': Rape Reform in Late Nineteenth Century America." *Yale Journal of Law and Humanities* 9, 1: 1–71.

Larson, Pier M. 2009. *Ocean of Letters: Language and Creolization in an Indian Ocean Diaspora.* New York: Cambridge University Press.

Lasch, Christopher. 1991. *The True and Only Heaven: Progress and its Critics.* New York: Norton.

Lasch-Quinn, Elisabeth. 1993. *Black Neighbors: Race and the Limits of Reform in the American Settlement House Movement, 1890–1945.* Chapel Hill: University of North Carolina Press.

Laskin, David. 2004. *The Children's Blizzard.* New York: Harper Collins.

Laslett, John H.M. 1986. "Swan Song or New Social Movement?" In *Socialism in the Heartland*, ed. Donald T. Critchlow, 167–214. Notre Dame: Notre Dame University Press.

Lassiter, Matthew D. and Joseph Crespino, eds. 2009. *The Myth of Southern Exceptionalism.* New York: Oxford University Press.

Latham, Angela J. 2000. *Posing a Threat: Flappers, Corus Girls, and Other Brazen Performers of the American 1920s.* Hanover: University Press of New England.

Laurie, Bruce. 1989. *Artisans into Workers: Labor in Nineteenth-Century America.* New York: Hill and Wang.

Le Page du Pratz, Antoine Simon. 1758 (1763). *The History of Louisiana, or the Western Parts of Virginia and Carolina.* Translation, London: T. Becket and P. A. De Hondt.

Leach, William. 1993. *Land of Desire : Merchants, Power, and the Rise of a New American Culture.* New York: Pantheon Books.

Lears, T. J. Jackson. 1981. *No Place of Grace: Antimodernism and the Transformation of American Culture, 1880–1920.* New York: Pantheon.

—. 1985. "The Concept of Cultural Hegemony: Problems and Possibilities." *American Historical Review* 90, 3: 567–593.

—. 1992. "Making Fun of Popular Culture." *American Historical Review* 97, 5: 1417–1426.

—. 1994. *Fables of Abundance: A Cultural History of Advertising in America.* New York: Basic Books.

—. 2009. *Rebirth of a Nation: The Making of Modern America, 1877–1920.* New York: Harper.

LeCain, Timothy J. 2009. *Mass Destruction: The Men and Great Mines That Wired America and Scarred the Planet.* Piscataway: Rutgers University Press.

Lee, Erika. 2003. *At America's Gates: Chinese Immigration During the Exclusion Era, 1882–1943.* Chapel Hill: University of North Carolina Press.

Lee, Lawrence B. 1973. "William E. Smythe and San Diego, 1901–1908." *Journal of San Diego History* 14: 10–24.

Lee, Mordecai. 2008. *Bureaus of Efficiency.* Milwaukee: Marquette University Press.

Leech, Margaret. 1959. *In the Days of McKinley.* New York: Harper & Brothers.

—, and Harry J. Brown 1978. *The Garfield Orbit: The Life of James A. Garfield.* New York: Harper and Row.

LeFlouria, Talitha L. 2015. *Chained in Silence: Black Women and Convict Labor in the New South.* Chapel Hill: University of North Carolina Press.

Lehrer, Susan. 1987. *Origins of Protective Labor Legislation for Women, 1905–1925.* Albany: SUNY Press.

Leidenberger, Georg. 2006. *Chicago's Progressive Alliance: Labor and the Bid for Public Streetcars.* DeKalb: Northern Illinois University Press.

Leloudis, James L. 1999. *Schooling the New South: Pedagogy, Self, and Society in North Carolina, 1880–1920.* Chapel Hill: University of North Carolina Press.

Lemann, Nicholas. 2006. *Redemption: The Last Battle of the Civil War.* New York: Farrar, Straus & Giroux.

Lentz-Smith, Adriane. 2009. *Freedom Struggles: African Americans and World War I.* Cambridge: Harvard University Press.

Lepore, Jill. 2014. *The Secret History of Wonder Woman.* New York: Alfred A. Knopf.

Leroux, Karen. 2009. "'Unpensioned Veterans': Women Teachers and the Politics of Public Service in Late Nineteenth Century United States." *Journal of Women's History* 21: 34–62.

Lessoff, Alan. 2013. "American Progressivism: Transnational, Modernization, and American Perspectives." In *Fractured Modernity: America Confronts Modern Times, 1890s to 1940s,* ed. Thomas Welskopp and Alan Lessoff, 61–80. Munich: Oldenbourg Verlag.

Lester, Connie L. 2006. *Up From the Mudsills of Hell: The Farmers' Alliance, Populism, and Progressive Agriculture in Tennessee, 1870–1915.* Athens: University of Georgia Press.

Leuchtenburg, William E. 1952. "Progressivism and Imperialism: The Progressive Movement and American Foreign Policy, 1898–1916." *Mississippi Valley Historical Review* 39, 3: 483–504.

—. 1986. "The Pertinence of Political History: Reflections on the Significance of the State in America." *Journal of American History* 73, 3: 585–600.

—. 1995. *The Supreme Court Reborn: The Constitutional Revolution in the Age of Roosevelt.* Oxford: Oxford University Press.

Leupp, Francis E. 1910. *The Indian and His Problem.* New York: Charles Scribner & Sons.

Levin, Miriam R. 2005. *Defining Women's Scientific Enterprise: Mount Holyoke Faculty and the Rise of American Science.* Hanover: University Press of New England.

Levin, Phyllis Lee. 2001. *Edith and Woodrow: The Wilson White House.* New York: Scribner.

Levine, Lawrence W. 1977. *Black Culture and Black Consciousness: Afro-American Folk Thought from Slavery to Freedom.* New York: Oxford University Press.

—. 1988. *Highbrow/Lowbrow: The Emergence of Cultural Hierarchy in the United States.* Cambridge: Harvard University Press.

—. 1992. "The Folklore of Industrial Society: Popular Culture and Its Audiences." *American Historical Review* 97, 5: 1369–99.

Levine, Susan. 1984. *Labor's True Woman: Carpet Weavers, Industrialization, and Labor reform in the Gilded Age.* Philadelphia: Temple University Press.

Levy, Jonathan. 2012a. *Freaks of Fortune: The Emerging World of Capitalism and Risk in America.* Cambridge: Harvard University Press.

—. 2012b. "The Mortgage Worked the Hardest: The Fate of Landed Independence in Nineteenth-Century America." In *Capitalism Takes Command: The Social Transformation of Nineteenth-Century America,* ed. Michael Zakim and Gary J. Kornblith, 39–68. Chicago: University of Chicago Press. DOI:10.7208/chicago/9780226977997.003.0003

Lewinnek, Elaine. 2014. *The Working Man's Reward: Chicago's Early Suburbs and the Roots of American Sprawl.* Oxford: Oxford University Press.

Lewis, Arnold. 1997. *An Early Encounter with Tomorrow: Europeans, Chicago's Loop, and the World's Columbian Exposition.* Urbana: University of Illinois Press.

Lewis, David Levering. 1993. 1994. *W.E.B. Du Bois: Biography of a Race, 1868–1919.* New York: Holt.

—. 2000. *W.E.B. Du Bois: The Fight for Equality and the American Century, 1919–1963.* New York: Holt.

Lewis, David Rich. 1991. "Reservation Leadership and the Progressive-Traditional Dichotomy: William Wash and the Northern Utes, 1865–1928." *Ethnohistory* 18: 124–148.

—. 1997. *Neither Wolf nor Dog: American Indians, Environment, and Agrarian Change.* New York: Oxford University Press.

Lewis, Earl. 1990. *In Their Own Interests: Race, Class, and Power In Twentieth-century Norfolk, Virginia.* Berkeley: University of California Press.

Licht, Walter. 1983. *Working for The Railroad: The Organization of Work in the Nineteenth Century.* Princeton: Princeton University Press.

Limerick, Patricia Nelson. 1987. *The Legacy of Conquest.* New York: W.W. Norton.

Lindeman, Eduard C. 1939. *Wealth and Culture.* New York: Harcourt, Brace, & Co.

Lindsay, Vachel. 1925. *Collected Poems.* New York: Macmillan.

Link, Arthur S. 1946. "The Progressive Movement in the South, 1870–1914." *North Carolina Historical Review* 23: 172–95.

—. 1947–1965. *Wilson.* 5 volumes. Princeton: Princeton University Press.

—. 1954. *Woodrow Wilson and the Progressive Era, 1910–1917.* New York: Harper and Row.

—. 1959. *Wilson the Diplomatist: A Look at His Major Foreign Policies.* Baltimore: Johns Hopkins Press.

—. *Woodrow Wilson: Revolution, War, and Peace.* Arlington Heights: H. Davidson.

Link, Arthur and Richard L. McCormick. 1983. *Progressivism.* Arlington Heights: Harlan Davidson, Inc.

Link, William A. 1991. "The Social Context of Southern Progressivism, 1880–1930."In *The Wilson Era: Essays in Honor of Arthur S. Link*, ed. John Milton Cooper, Jr. and Charles Neu, 55–82. Arlington Heights: Harlan Davidson, Inc.

—. 1992. *The Paradox of Southern Progressivism, 1880–1930.* Chapel Hill: University of North Carolina Press.

—. 1998. *Trouble in Mind: Black Southerners in the Age of Jim Crow.* New York: Alfred A. Knopf.

Lipsky, Seth. 2013. *The Rise of Abraham Cahan.* New York: Nextbook/Schocken.

Littlefield, Alice, and Martha C. Knack. 1996. *Native Americans and Wage Labor: Ethnohistorical Perspectives.* Norman: University of Oklahoma Press.

Livingston, James. 1986. *Origins of the Federal Reserve System: Money, Class, and Corporate Capitalism, 1890–1913.* Ithaca: Cornell University Press.

—. 1994. *Pragmatism and the Political Economy of Cultural Revolution, 1850–1940.* Chapel Hill: University of North Carolina Press.

Lloyd, Henry Demarest. 1894. *Wealth against Commonwealth.* New York: Harper & Brothers.

—. 1900. *A Country without Strikes: A Visit to the Compulsory Arbitration Court of New Zealand.* New York: Doubleday, Page and Co.

—. 1903. *Newest England: Notes of a Democratic Traveller in New Zealand.* New York: Doubleday, Page & Co.

—. 1983. *The Life of Herbert Hoover, Volume 1: The Engineer, 1874–1914.* New York: W.W. Norton.

—. 1988. *The Life of Herbert Hoover, Volume 2: The Humanitarian, 1914–1917.* New York: W.W. Norton.

—. 1989. "'An American Epic': Herbert Hoover and Belgian Relief in World War I." *Prologue* 21, 1: 75–86.

Lockwood, Jeffrey A. 2004. *Locust: The Devastating Rise and Mysterious Disappearance of the Insect that Shaped the American Frontier.* New York: Basic Books.

Logan, Adele Hunt. 1905. "Woman Suffrage." *The Colored American Magazine*, 9.

Logan, Rayford W. 1954. *The Negro in American Life and Thought: The Nadir, 1877–1901.* New York: The Dial Press.

Loizides, Georgios P. 2015. *Henry Ford's Project in Human Engineering: The Sociological Department of the Ford Motor Company (1913–1941).* Lewiston: Edwin Mellen.

Lombardo, Paul A. 2008. *Three Generations. No Imbeciles. Eugenics, the Supreme Court, and Buck v. Bell.* Baltimore: Johns Hopkins University Press.

—, ed. 2011. *A Century of Eugenics in America.* Bloomington: University of Indiana Press.

Lorant, Stefan. 1959. *The Life and Times of Theodore Roosevelt.* New York: Doubleday & Co.

Lord, Alexandra M. 2010. *Condom Nation: The U.S. Government's Sex Education from World War I to the Internet.* Baltimore: Johns Hopkins University Press.

Lorde, Audre. 2007. *Sister Outsider: Essays and Speeches.* New York: Random House.

Los Angeles Herald. 5 July, 1903.

Lott, Eric. 1993. *Love and Theft: Blackface Minstrelsy and the American Working Class.* New York: Oxford University Press.

Low, John N. 2011. "Chicago's First Urban Indians – the Potawatomi." Ph.D. diss., University of Michigan.

Lowe, Lisa. 2015. *The Intimacies of Four Continents.* Durham: Duke University Press.

Lower, Richard C. 1993. *A Bloc of One: The Political Career of Hiram W. Johnson.* Palo Alto: Stanford University Press.

Lowery, Malinda Maynor. 2010. *Lumbee Indians in the Jim Crow South: Race, Identity, and the Making of a Nation.* Chapel Hill: University of North Carolina Press.

Lowitt, Richard. 1963. *George W. Norris: The Making of a Progressive.* Syracuse: Syracuse University Press.

—. 1971. *George W. Norris: The Persistence of a Progressive, 1913–1933.* Urbana: University of Illinois Press.

Lucassen, Jan and Leo Lucassen, eds. 1997. *Migration, Migration History, History: Old Paradigms and New Perspectives.* New York: Peter Lang.

Lucier, Paul. 2009. "The Professional and the Scientist in Nineteenth-Century America." *ISIS* 100: 699–732.

—. 2012. "The Origins of Pure and Applied Science in Gilded Age America." *ISIS* 103: 527–536.

Ludmerer, Kenneth M. 1996. *Learning to Heal: The Development of American Medical Education.* Baltimore: Johns Hopkins University Press.

Luebke, Frederick C. 1974. *Bonds of Loyalty: German Americans and World War I.* DeKalb: Northern Illinois University Press.

Lui, Mary Ting Yi. 2005. *The Chinatown Trunk Mystery: Murder, Miscegenation, and Other Dangerous Encounters In Turn-of-the-century New York City.* Princeton: Princeton University Press.

Luker, Kristin. 1984. *Abortion and the Politics of Motherhood.* Berkeley: University of California Press.

Lumba, Allan. Forthcoming. *Monetary Authorities: Economic Policy and Policing in the American Colonial Philippines.*

Lunardini, Christine. 2012. *Alice Paul: Equality for Women.* Boulder: Westview.

Lunbeck, Elizabeth. 1996. *The Psychiatric Persuasion: Knowledge, Gender, and Power in Modern America.* Princeton: Princeton University Press.

Lutz, Jessie Gregory. 1971. *China and the Christian Colleges, 1850–1950.* Ithaca: Cornell University Press.

Lutz, Tom. 1991. *American Nervousness, 1903: An Anecdotal History.* Ithaca: Cornell University Press.

Lyon, Peter. 1963. *Success Story: The Life and Times of S. S. McClure.* New York: Charles Scribner's Sons.

Lystra, Karen. 1989. *Searching the Heart: Women, Men, and Romantic Love in Nineteenth-Century America.* New York: Oxford University Press.

MacFarland, Gerald W. 1975. *Mugwumps, Morals, and Politics, 1884–1920.* Amherst: University of Massachusetts Press.

Mack, Kenneth W. 1999. "Law, Society, Identity, and the Making of the Jim Crow South: Travel and Segregation on Tennessee Railroads, 1875–1905." *Law & Social Inquiry* 24, 2: 377–409.

Mackenzie, Fred. 1902. *The American Invaders.* Grant Richards: London.

MacLean, Nancy. 1991. "The Leo Frank Case Reconsidered: Gender and Sexual Politics in the Making of Reactionary Populism." *Journal of American History* 78, 3: 917–48.

Macmillan, Margaret. 2002. *Paris 1919: Six Months That Changed the World.* New York: Random House.

MacPherson, Myra. 2014. *The Scarlet Sisters: Sex, Suffrage, and Scandal in the Gilded Age.* New York: Hachette Book Group.

Maddox, Lucy. 2005. *Citizen Indians: Native Intellectuals, Race, and Representation.* Ithaca: Cornell University Press.

Madsen-Brooks, Leslie. 2009. "Challenging Science as Usual: Women's Participation in American Natural History Museum Work, 1870–1950." *Journal of Women's History* 21, 2: 11–38.

—. 2013. "A Synthesis of Expertise and Expectations: Women Museum Scientists, Club women and Populist Natural Science in the United States, 1890–1950." *Gender and History* 25, 1: 27–46.

Magee, Gary B. and Andrew S. Thompson, 2010. *Empire and Globalisation: Networks of People, Goods, and Capital in the British World, c. 1850–1914.* Cambridge: Cambridge University Press.

Magee, Malcolm D. 2008. *What the World Should Be: Woodrow Wilson and the Crafting of a Faith-Based Foreign Policy.* Waco: Baylor University Press.

Maggor, Noam. 2016a. *Brahmin Capitalism: Frontiers of Wealth and Populism in America's First Gilded Age.* Cambridge: Harvard University Press.

—. 2016b. "To 'Coddle and Caress These Great Capitalists': Eastern Money and the Politics of Market Integration in the American West." *American Historical Review* 121, 5.

Maher, Neil M. 2010. "Body Counts: Tracking the Human Body Through Environmental History." In *A Companion to American Environmental History*, ed. Douglas Sackman, 163–179. Oxford: Wiley-Blackwell.

Maier, Charles S. 2014. *Leviathan 2.0: Inventing Modern Statehood.* Cambridge: The Belknap Press of Harvard University Press.

Maines, Rachel P. 1999. *The Technology of Orgasm: "Hysteria," the Vibrator, and Women's Sexual Satisfaction.* Baltimore: Johns Hopkins University Press.

Makdisi, Ussama. *Artillery of Heaven: American Missionaries and the Failed Conversion of the Middle East.* 2007. Ithaca: Cornell University Press.

Malone, Michael P. 1996. *James J. Hill: Empire Builder of the Northwest.* Norman: University of Oklahoma Press.

—, and F. Ross Peterson. 1994. "Politics and Protests." In *The Oxford History of the American West*, ed. Clyde A. Milner, Carol O'Connor, and Martha A. Sandweiss, 501–533. New York: Oxford University Press.

Malone, Preston S. C. 1962. "The Political Career of Charles Frederick Crisp." PhD diss., University of Georgia.

Mandell, Daniel R. 2008. *Tribe, Race, History: Native Americans in Southern New England, 1780–1880.* Baltimore: Johns Hopkins University Press.

Mandle, Jay R. 1978. *The Roots of Black Poverty: The Southern Plantation Economy after the Civil War.* Durham: Duke University Press.

Manela, Erez, 2007. *The Wilsonian Moment: Self-Determination and the International Origins of Anticolonial Nationalism.* New York: Oxford University Press.

Marable, Manning. 1983. *How Capitalism Underdeveloped Black America: Problems in Race, Political Economy, and Society.* Cambridge: South End Press.

Marchand, C. Roland. 1972. *The American Peace Movement and Social Reform, 1898–1918.* Princeton: Princeton University Press.

Marcus, Alan I. 2004. "Manufacturing Government: Total Quality Management, the National Performance Review, and the Bridge to the Twenty-First Century." Annual Meeting of the American Historical Association, January 8. Washington, DC.

—. 2007. "Reagan, Bush, and Clinton: The Rise and Fall of American Technology Policy." Annual Meeting of the American Historical Association, January 4. Atlanta.

—, and Amy Sue Bix. 2007. *Science and Technology Policy in America Since 1950.* New York: Prometheus Books.

Margulies, Herbert F. 1976. "Robert M. La Follette Goes to the Senate, 1905." *Wisconsin Magazine of History and Biography* 59, 3: 214–225.

Markham, Edwin, Ben B. Lindsey, and George Creel. 1914. *Children in Bondage: A Complete and Careful Presentation of the Anxious Problem of Child Labor—its Causes, its Crimes, and its Cure.* New York: Hearst's International Library.

—. 1907. "The Hoe-Man in the Making: The Sweat-Shop Inferno." *Cosmopolitan* 41: 327–333.

Marks Frederick W., III. 1979. *Velvet on Iron: The Diplomacy of Theodore Roosevelt.* Lincoln: University of Nebraska Press.

Marry, Shelley. 2000. *Colonizing Hawai'i: The Cultural Power of Law.* Princeton: Princeton University Press.

Marschall, Rick. 2011. *Bully! The Life and Times of Theodore Roosevelt Illustrated with More Than 250 Vintage Political Cartoons.* New York: Regnery History.

Marsden, George. 2008. *Fundamentalism and American Culture.* Revised ed. New York: Oxford University Press.

Marti, Donald B. 1991. *Women of the Grange: Mutuality and Sisterhood in Rural America, 1866–1920.* New York: Greenwood Press.

Martin, Albro S. 1971. *Enterprise Denied: Origins of the Decline of American Railroads, 1897–1917.* New York: Columbia University Press.

Martin, Justin. 2012. *Genius of Place: The Life of Frederick Law Olmsted.* Cambridge: Da Capo Press.

Martin, S. Walter. 1954. "Charles F. Crisp: Speaker of the House." *Georgia Review* 8, 2: 164–77.

Marx, Karl. 1963. *The Eighteenth Brumaire of Louis Bonaparte.* New York: International Publishers.

Mashaw, Jerry L. 2010. "Federal Administration and Administrative Law in the Gilded Age." *Yale Law Journal* 119, 7: 1362–1472.

Massey, Douglas S., and Nancy A. Denton. 1993. *American Apartheid: Segregation and the Making of the Underclass.* Cambridge: Harvard University Press.

Masur, Kate. 2010. *An Example for all the Land: Emancipation and the Struggle over Equality in Washington, D.C.* Chapel Hill: University of North Carolina Press.

Mather, Cotton. 1722. *An Account of the Method and Success of Inoculating the Small-Pox, in Boston in New-England.* London: J. Pells.

Matthews, Frederick C. 1987. *American Merchant Ships, 1850–1900.* Volume 1. Mineola: Dover.

Mattson, Kevin. 2006. *Upton Sinclair and the Other American Century*. Hoboken: John Wiley & Sons.

May, Elaine Tyler. 1980. *Great Expectations: Marriage and Divorce in Post-Victorian America*. Chicago: University of Chicago Press.

May, Ernest R. 1959. *The World War and American Isolation, 1914–1917*. Cambridge: Harvard University Press.

Mayer, Arno J. 1961. *Political Origins of the New Diplomacy, 1917–1918*. New Haven: Yale University Press.

Mayhew, David R. 2002. *Electoral Realignments: A Critique of an American Genre*. New Haven: Yale University Press.

McAfee, Ward. 1998. *Religion, Race, and Reconstruction: The Public School in the Politics of the 1870s*. Albany: State University of New York Press.

McCann, Carole R. 1994. *Birth Control Politics in the United States, 1916–1945*. Ithaca: Cornell University Press.

McCarthy, Kathleen D. 1982. *Noblesse Oblige: Charity & Cultural Philanthropy in Chicago, 1849–1929*. Chicago: University of Chicago Press.

—. 1990. *Lady Bountiful Revisited: Women, Philanthropy, and Power*. New Brunswick: Rutgers University Press.

—. 1991. *Women's Culture: American Philanthropy and Art, 1830–1930*. Chicago: University of Chicago Press.

—. 2003. *American Creed: Philanthropy and the Rise of Civil Society, 1700–1865*. Chicago: University of Chicago Press.

McCartney, Paul T. 2006. *Power and Progress: American National Identity, the War of 1898, and the Rise of American Imperialism*. Baton Rouge: Louisiana State University Press.

McCloskey, Robert G. 1960. *The American Supreme Court*. Chicago: University of Chicago Press.

McCormick, Thomas. 1967. *China Market: America's Quest for Informal Empire, 1893 – 1901*. Chicago: Quadrangle Book.

McCormick, Richard L. 1981. "The Discovery that Business Corrupts: A Reappraisal of the Origins of Progressivism." *American Historical Review* 86: 247–274.

—. 1986. 1989. *The Party Period and Public Policy: American Politics from the Age of Jackson to the Progressive Era*. New York: Oxford University Press.

McCoy, Alfred and Francisco Scarano, eds. 2009. *The Colonial Crucible: Empire in the Making of the Modern American State*. Madison: University of Wisconsin Press.

McCoy, Alfred W. 2009. *Policing America's Empire: The United States, the Philippines, and the Rise of the Surveillance State*. Madison: University of Wisconsin Press.

McCullough, David. 1981. *Mornings on Horseback*. New York: Simon and Schuster.

—. 1989. "Issues and Constituencies in the Progressive Era: House Roll Call Voting on the Nineteenth Amendment, 1913–1919." *Journal of Politics* 51, 1: 119–36.

McCurdy, Charles W. 1975. "Justice Field and the Jurisprudence of Government-Business Relations: Some Parameters of Laissez-Faire Constitutionalism, 1863–1897." *Journal of American History* 61, 4: 970–1005.

—. 1979. "The Knight Sugar Decision of 1895 and the Modernization of American Corporation Law, 1869–1903." *Business History Review* 53, 3: 304–42.

—. 1984. "Roots of Liberty of Contract Reconsidered: Major Premises in the Law of Employment, 1867–1937." In *Yearbook of the Supreme Court Historical Society*. Washington, DC: Supreme Court Historical Society.

—. 1998. "The 'Liberty of Contract' Regime in American Law." In *The State and Freedom of Contract*, ed. Harry N. Scheiber, 161–197. Stanford: Stanford University Press.

McCutcheon, John T. 1910. *T.R. in Cartoons*. Chicago: A. C. McClurg & Co.

McDonagh, Eileen L. 1993. "Constituency Influence on House Roll-Call Votes in the Progressive Era, 1913–1915." *Legislative Studies Quarterly* 18, 2: 185–210.

McDonald, Forrest, Leslie E. Decker, and Thomas P. Govan. 1972. *The Last Best Hope: A History of the United States*. Reading: Addison-Wesley.

McDonald, Michael. "National VEP Turnout Rates, 1789–Present." United States Elections Project. Last modified June 11, 2014. http://www.electproject.org/home/voter-turnout/voter-turnout-data.

McDonald, Terrence J. 1986. *The Parameters of Urban Fiscal Policy: Socio-economic Change and Political Culture in San Francisco, 1860–1906*. Berkeley: University of California Press.

McDougall, Walter A. 1997. *Promised Land, Crusader State: The American Encounter with the World since 1776*. New York: Houghton Mifflin.

McDowell, Carl E., and Gibbs, Helen M. 1954. *Ocean Transportation*. New York: McGraw-Hill.

McDowell, John Patrick. 1982. *The Social Gospel in the South: The Women's Home Mission Movement in the Episcopal Church, South, 1886–1939*. Baton Rouge: Louisiana State University Press.

McElroy, Robert. 1923. *Grover Cleveland, the Man and the Statesman*. New York: Harper and Brothers.

McGarry, Molly. 2008. *Ghosts of Futures Past: Spiritualism and the Cultural Politics of Nineteenth-Century America*. Berkeley: University of California Press.

McGerr, Michael E. 1986. *The Decline of Popular Politics: the American North, 1865–1928*. New York: Oxford University Press.

—. 2003. *A Fierce Discontent: The Rise and Fall of the Progressive Movement in America, 1870–1920*. New York: The Free Press.

McGreevy, John. 2004. *Catholicism and American Freedom: A History*. New York: W.W. Norton.

McKenna, Marion C. 1961. *Borah*. Ann Arbor: University of Michigan Press.

McKenzie, Frederick A. 1902. *The American Invaders*. London: G. Richards.

McKeown, Thomas. 1979. *The Role of Medicine: Dream, Mirage, or Nemesis*. Princeton: Princeton University Press.

McKillen, Elizabeth. 2013. *Making the World Safe for Workers: Labor, the Left, and Wilsonian Internationalism*. Urbana: University of Illinois Press.

McKinley, William. "First Inaugural Address." March 4, 1897.

McLaren, Angus. 2002. *Sexual Blackmail: A Modern History*. Cambridge: Harvard University Press.

McLean, Gavin. 1990. *The Southern Octopus: The Rise of a Shipping Empire*. Wellington: New Zealand Ship & Marine Society and the Wellington Harbour Board, Maritime Museum.

McLoughlin, William. 1955. *Modern Revivalism: From Charles Grandison Finney to Billy Graham*. New York: The Ronald Press.

McPherson, James M. 1988. *Battle Cry of Freedom: The Civil War Era*. New York: Oxford University Press.

—. 1975. 1995. *The Abolitionist Legacy: From Reconstruction to the NAACP*. Princeton: Princeton University Press.

McShane, Clay. 1994. *Down the Asphalt Path: The Automobile and the American City*. New York: Columbia University Press.

—, and Joel A. Tarr. 2007. *The Horse In the City: Living Machines In the Nineteenth Century*. Baltimore: Johns Hopkins University Press.

Mead, Elwood. 1920. *Helping Men Own Farms*. New York: Macmillan.

Mead, Walter Russell. 2004. *Power, Terror, Peace, and War: America's Grand Strategy in a World at Risk*. New York: Knopf.

—. 2007. *God and Gold: Britain, America, and the Making of the Modern World*. New York: Alfred A. Knopf.

Mehta, Uday. 1999. *Liberalism and Empire: A Study in Nineteenth-Century British Liberal Thought*. Chicago: University of Chicago Press.

Mehrotra, Ajay K. 2013. *Making the Modern American Fiscal State: Law, Politics, and the Rise of Progressive Taxation, 1877–1929*. New York: Cambridge University Press.

Meis-Knupfer, Anne. 2001. *Reform and Resistance: Gender Delinquency and America's First Juvenile Court*. New York: Routledge.

Meinig, D. W. 2000. *The Shaping of America: A Geographical Perspective on 500 Years of History, Volume 3: Transcontinental America, 1850–1915*. New Haven: Yale University Press.

Melosi, Martin V. 1981. *Garbage in the Cities: Refuse, Reform, and the Environment: 1880–1980*. College Station: Texas A & M Press.

—. 2011. *Precious Commodity: Providing Water for America's Cities*. Pittsburgh: University of Pittsburgh Press.

Menand, Louis. 2001. 2002. *The Metaphysical Club: A Story of Ideas in America*. New York: Farrar, Straus and Giroux.

Mencken, H.L. 1920 (1967) "Roosevelt I." Reprinted in *Theodore Roosevelt: A Profile*, ed. Morton Keller. New York: Hill and Wang. Citations refer to the Hill edition.

Merchant, Carolyn. 1982. *The Death of Nature: Women, Ecology, and the Scientific Revolution*. San Francisco: Harper.

—. 1984. "Women of the Progressive Conservation Movement, 1900–1916." *Environmental Review* 8: 55–85.

—. 1989. *Ecological Revolutions: Nature, Gender, and Science in New England*. Chapel Hill: University of North Carolina Press.

—. 2010. "George Bird Grinnell's Audubon Society: Bridging the Gender Divide in Conservation." *Environmental History* 15: 3–30.

Merrill, Horace S. 1957. *Bourbon Leader Grover Cleveland and the Democratic Party*. Boston: Little, Brown.

Mettler, Suzanne. 2011. *The Submerged State: How Invisible Government Policies Undermine American Democracy*. Chicago: University of Chicago Press.

Meyer, Carrie A. 2007. *Days on the Family Farm*. Minneapolis: University of Minnesota Press.

Meyer, Melissa L, and Kerwin Lee Kline. 1999. "Native American Studies and the End of Ethnohistory." In *Studying Native America: Problems and Prospects*, ed. Russell Thornton, 182–216. Madison: University of Wisconsin Press.

—. 1999. *The White Earth Tragedy: Ethnicity and Dispossession at a Minnesota Anishinaabe Reservation, 1880–1920*. Lincoln: University of Nebraska Press.

Meyerowitz, Joanne J. 1988. *Women Adrift: Independent Wage Earners In Chicago, 1880–1930*. Chicago: University of Chicago Press.

Meyer, David R. 1989. "Midwestern Industrialization and the American Manufacturing Belt in the Nineteenth Century." *Journal of Economic History* 49: 921–37. DOI: 10.1017/S0022050700009505.

—. 2001. "The National Integration of Regional Economies, 1860–1920." In *North America: The Historical Geography of a Changing Continent*, 2nd edition, ed. Thomas F. McIlwraith and Edward K. Muller, 307–332. Lanham, Md: Rowman & Littlefield Publishers.

Meyers, Robert C.V. 1902. *Theodore Roosevelt: Patriot and Statesman, The True Story of an Ideal American*. Chicago: P.W. Ziegler & Co.

Mezzano, Michael. 2005. "The Progressive Origins of Eugenics Critics: Raymond Pearl, Herbert J. Jennings, and the Defense of Scientific Inquiry." *Journal of the Gilded Age and Progressive Era* 4, 1: 83–97.

Michele, Mitchell. "'Lower Orders,' Racial Hierarchies, and Rights Rhetoric: Evolutionary Echoes in Elizabeth Cady Stanton's Thought during the Late 1860s." In *Elizabeth Cady Stanton, Feminist as Thinker: A Reader in Documents and Essays*, ed. Ellen Carol DuBois and Richard Cándida Smith, 128–151. New York: New York University.

Mickulas, Peter. 2007. *Britton's Botanical Empire: The New York Botanical Garden and American Botany, 1888–1929*. Bronx: New York Botanical Garden Press.

Middleton, William D. and William D. Middleton III. 2009. *Frank Julian Sprague: Electrical Inventor and Engineer*. Bloomington: Indiana University Press.

Mihesuah, Devon A. 1998. *Natives and Academics: Researching and Writing about American Indians*. Lincoln: University of Nebraska Press.

Miles, Tiya. 2005. *Ties That Bind: The Story of an Afro-Cherokee Family in Slavery and Freedom*. Berkeley: University of California Press.

Milkis, Sidney M. 2009. *Theodore Roosevelt, the Progressive Party, and the Transformation of American Democracy*. Lawrence: University Press of Kansas.

Millard, Candice. 2005. *The River of Doubt: Theodore Roosevelt's Darkest Journey*. New York: Doubleday.

—. 2011. *Destiny of the Republic: A Tale of Madness, Medicine and the Murder of a President*. New York: Doubleday.

Miller, Char. 2001. *Gifford Pinchot and the Making of Modern Environmentalism*. Washington, D.C.: Island Press.

Miller, Edward A., Jr. 1995. *Gullah Statesman: Robert Smalls from Slavery to Congress, 1839–1915*. Columbia: University of South Carolina.

Miller, George Frederick. 1922. "The Academy System of the State of New York." Ph.D. diss., Columbia University.

Miller, George Hall. *Railroads and the Granger Laws*. Madison: University of Wisconsin Press, 1971.

Miller, Karl Hagstrom. 2010. *Segregating Sound: Inventing Folk and Pop Music in the Age of Jim Crow*. Durham: Duke University Press.

Miller, Kerby A. 1988. *Emigrants and Exiles: Ireland and the Irish Exodus to North America*. Revised ed. New York: Oxford University Press.

Miller, Zane. 1968. *Boss Cox*. Columbus: Ohio State University Press.

Milne, David. 2015. *Worldmaking: The Art and Science of American Diplomacy*. New York: Farrar, Straus, and Giroux.

Minnix, Kathleen. 1993. *Laughter in the Amen Corner: The Life of Evangelist Sam Jones.* Athens: University of Georgia Press.

Miraldi, Robert. 2000. *The Muckrakers: Evangelical Crusaders.* Westport: Praeger.

—. 2003. *The Pen Is Mightier: The Muckraking Life of Charles Edward Russell.* New York: Palgrave Macmillan.

Miranti, Paul J. 1986. "Associationalism, Statism and Professional Regulation: Public Accountants and the Reform of Financial Markets, 1896–1940." *Business History Review* 60, 3: 438–68.

Mirel, Jeffrey E. 2010. *Patriotic Pluralism: Americanization Education and European Immigrants.* Cambridge: Harvard University Press.

Missal, Alexander. 2008. *Seaway to Future: American Social Visions and the Construction of the Panama Canal.* Madison: University of Wisconsin Press.

Mitchell, Michele. 2004. *Righteous Propagation: African Americans and the Politics of Racial Destiny after Reconstruction.* Chapel Hill: University of North Carolina Pres.

Mitchell, S. Weir. 1869. "Wear and Tear." *Lippincott's Magazine of Literature, Science and Education* 4: 493–502.

—. 1888. *Doctor and Patient.* Philadelphia: J. B. Lippincott.

Mitman, Greg. 2003. "Hay Fever Holiday: Health, Leisure, and Place in Gilded-Age America." *Bulletin of the History of Medicine* 77, 3: 600–635.

Mitman, Greg. 2008. *Breathing Space: How Allergies Shape Our Lives and Landscapes.* New Haven: Yale University Press.

Moehring, Eugene P. 2004. *Urbanism and Empire in the Far West.* Reno: University of Nevada Press.

Mohr, James C. 1978. *Abortion in America: The Origins and Evolution of National Policy, 1800–1900.* New York: Oxford University Press.

Montgomery, David. 1967. *Beyond Equality: Labor and the Radical Republicans, 1862–1872.* Urbana: University of Illinois Press.

—. 1974. "The 'New Unionism' and the Transformation of Workers' Consciousness in America, 1909–1922." *Journal of Social History* 7, 4: 509–529.

—. 1987. *The Fall of the House of Labor: The Workplace, the State, and American Labor Activism, 1865–1925.* New York: Cambridge University Press.

—. 1993. *Citizen Worker: The Experience of Workers in the United States with Democracy and the Free Market During the Nineteenth Century.* Cambridge: Cambridge University Press.

Montgomery, William E. 1993. 1994. *Under Their Own Vine and Fig Tree: The African-American Church in the South, 1865–1900.* Baton Rouge: Louisiana State University Press.

Moore, R. Laurence. 1977. *In Search of White Crows: Spiritualism, Parapsychology, and American Culture.* New York: Oxford University Press.

Moore, Sarah J. 2013. *Empire on Display: San Francisco's Panama-Pacific International Exposition of 1915.* Norman: University of Oklahoma Press.

Moran, Jeffrey. 2000. *Teaching Sex: The Shaping of Adolescence in the 20th Century.* Cambridge: Harvard University Press.

Morantz-Sanchez. 2000. *Sympathy & Science: Women Physicians in American Medicine.* Chapel Hill: University of North Carolina Press.

—. 1985. *Sympathy & Science: Women Physicians in American Medicine.* New York: Oxford University Press.

—, and Regina Markell. 1999. *Conduct Unbecoming a Woman: Medicine on Trial in Turn-of-the-Century Brooklyn.* New York: Oxford University Press.

—, and Regina Markell. 2000. "Negotiating Power at the Bedside: Historical Perspectives on Nineteenth-Century Patients and their Gynecologists." *Feminist Studies* 26, Summer: 287–309.

Morgan, David. 1998. *Visual Piety: A History and Theory of Popular Religious Images* Berkeley: University of California Press.

Morgan, James. 2014. *Into New Territory: American Historians and the Concept of US Imperialism.* Madison: University of Wisconsin Press.

Morgan, H. Wayne, ed. 1963. *The Gilded Age: A Reappraisal.* Syracuse: Syracuse University Press.

—, ed. 1986. *An American Art Student in Paris: The Letters of Kenyon Cox, 1877–1882.* Kent: Kent State University Press.

—, ed. 1989. *Keepers of Culture: The Art-Thought of Kenyon Cox, Royal Cortissoz, and Frank Jewett Mather, Jr.* Kent: Kent State University Press.

—. 1963. *William McKinley and His America.* Syracuse: Syracuse University Press.

—. 1966. "McKinley as Political Leader." *Review of Politics* 28: 417–32.

—. 1969. *From Hayes to McKinley: National Party Politics, 1877–1896.* Syracuse: Syracuse University Press.

Morin, Karen M. 2011. *Civic Discipline: Geography in America, 1860–1890.* Burlington: Ashgate Press.

Morison, Elting E., John Morton Blum, and Alfred Chandler, eds. 1951–54. *The Letters of Theodore Roosevelt.* Cambridge: Harvard University Press.

Mormino, Gary R. and George E. Pozzetta. 1987. *The Immigrant World of Ybor City: Italians and their Latin Neighbors in Tampa, 1885–1985.* Gainesville: University Press of Florida.

Morrello, John A. 2001. *Selling the President: Albert D. Lakser, Advertising, and the Election of Warren G. Harding.* Westport: Praeger.

Morris Jr., Roy. 2003. *Fraud of the Century: Rutherford B. Hayes, Samuel Tilden, and the Stolen Election of 1876.* New York: Simon and Shuster.

Morris, Edmund. 1979. *The Rise of Theodore Roosevelt.* New York: Coward, McCann and Geohagan.

—. 2001. *Theodore Rex.* New York: Random House.

—. 2010. *Colonel Roosevelt.* New York: Random House.

Morse John T. 1920. "Memoir of Henry Lee Higginson." *Proceedings of the Massachusetts Historical Society,* 53: 105–127.

Morton, David L., Jr. 2004. *Sound Recording: The Life Story of a Technology.* Baltimore: Johns Hopkins University Press.

Moses, L.G. 1999. *Wild West Shows and the Images of American Indians, 1882–1933.* Albuquerque: University of New Mexico Press.

Moss, Lemuel. 1868. *Annals of the United States Christian Commission.* Philadelphia: J. B. Lippincott & Company.

Motomura, Hiroshi. 2007. *Americans in Waiting: The Story of Immigration and Citizenship in the United States.* New York: Oxford University Press.

Mowry, George E. 1946. *Theodore Roosevelt and the Progressive Movement.* New York: Hill and Wang.

—. 1946. *Theodore Roosevelt and the Progressive Movement.* Madison: University of Wisconsin Press.

—. 1958. *Era of Theodore Roosevelt and the Birth of Modern America 1900–1912.* New York: Harper Torchbooks.

—. 1971. "The Election of 1912." In *History of American Presidential Elections, 1789–1968*. 4 volumes. New York: Chelsea.

Moyn, Samuel, and Andrew Sartori, eds. 2013. *Global Intellectual History*. New York: Columbia University Press.

Muhammad, Khalil Gibran. 2011. *The Condemnation of Blackness: Race, Crime, and the Making of Modern Urban America*. 1st ed. Cambridge: Harvard University Press.

Muir, John. 1912. *The Yosemite*. New York: The Century.

Mukherji, S. Ani. Forthcoming. *The Anticolonial Imagination: Race, Empire, and Migrant Radicalism before World War II*.

Muller v. Oregon. 1908.

Mumford, Kevin J. 1997. *Interzones: Black/white Sex Districts In Chicago and New York In the Early Twentieth Century*. New York: Columbia University Press.

Mumford, Lewis. 1982. *Sketches from Life: The Autobiography of Lewis Mumford*. New York: Dial Press.

—. 1955. *Sticks and Stones: A Study of American Architecture and Civilization*, 2nd ed. New York: Dover.

Muncy, Raymond Lee. 1973. *Sex and Marriage in Utopian Communities*. Bloomington: Indiana University Press.

Muncy, Robin. 1997. "Trustbusting and White Manhood in America, 1898–1914." *American Studies* 38: 21–42.

—. 1991. *Creating a Female Dominion in American Reform*. New York: Oxford University Press.

—. 1994. *Creating a Female Dominion in American Reform, 1890–1935*. New York: Oxford University Press.

—. 1999. "The Ambiguous Legacies of Women's Progressivism." *OAH Magazine of History* 13, 3: 15–19.

Murolo, Priscilla. 1997. *Common Ground of Womanhood: Class, Gender, and Working-Girls' Clubs, 1884–1928*. Urbana: University of Illinois Press.

Murphy, Kevin C. 2004. *The American Merchant Experience in Nineteenth-Century Japan*. New York: Routledge.

—. 2008. *Political Manhood: Red Bloods, Mollycoddles, and the Politics of Progressive Era Reform*. New York: Columbia University Press.

Musto, David F. 1999. *The American Disease: Origins of Narcotic Control*. 3rd ed. New York: Oxford University Press.

Muzzey, David S. 1934. *James G. Blaine: A Political Idol of Other Days*. New York: Dodd, Mead.

Myers, et al. 1917. *Congressional Record*. 65th Congress, 1st Session.

Napolitano, Andrew P. 2012. *Theodore and Woodrow: How Two American Presidents Destroyed Constitutional Freedom*. Nashville: Thomas Nelson.

Nasaw, David. 1985. *Children of the City: At Work and At Play*. Garden City: Anchor Press/Doubleday.

Nash, Linda. 2006. *Inescapable Ecologies: A History of Environment, Disease, and Knowledge*. Berkeley: University of California Press.

Nelson, Bruce C. 1998. *Beyond the Martyrs: A Social History of Chicago's Anarchists, 1870–1900*. New Brunswick: Rutgers University Press.

Nelson, Daniel. 1995. *Farm and Factory*. Bloomington: Indiana University Press.

Nelson, Paul David. 1974. "Experiment in Interracial Education at Berea College, 1858–1908." *Journal of Negro History* 59, 1: 13–27.

Nelson, Scott. 1999. *Iron Confederacies: Southern Railways, Klan Violence, and Reconstruction*. Chapel Hill: University of North Carolina Press.

Nelson, William E. 1974. "The Impact of the Antislavery Movement upon Styles of Judicial Reasoning in Nineteenth Century America." *Harvard Law Review* 87, 3: 513 - 566.

—. 1988. *The Fourteenth Amendment: From Political Principle to Judicial Doctrine*. Cambridge: Harvard University Press.

Neu, Charles E. 2015. *Colonel House: A Biography of Woodrow Wilson's Silent Partner*. New York: Oxford University Press.

Neuman, R. P. 1976. "Masturbation, Madness and the Modern Concept of Childhood and Adolescence." *Journal of Social History* 9: 1–27.

Neverdon-Morton, Cynthia. 1989. *Afro-American Women of the South and the Advancement of the Race, 1895–1925*. Knoxville: University of Tennessee Press.

Nevins, Allan, ed. 1933. *Letters of Grover Cleveland, 1850–1908*. Boston: Houghton Mifflin.

—. 1933. *Grover Cleveland: A Study in Courage*. New York: Dodd, Mead.

Newman, Louise M. 2015. "Reflections on Aileen Kraditor's Legacy: Fifty Years of Woman Suffrage Historiography, 1965–2014." *Journal of the Gilded Age and Progressive Era* 14: 290–316. doi: http://dx.doi.org/ 10.1017/S1537781415000055

—. 1999. *White Women's Rights: The Racial Origins of Feminism in the United States*. New York: Oxford University Press.

Ngai, Mae, and Jon Gjerde. 2013. *Major Problems in American Immigration History*. 2nd ed. Boston: Wadsworth, Cengage Learning.

—. 2014. *Impossible Subjects: Illegal Aliens and the Making of Modern America*. Princeton: Princeton University Press, updated edition.

Nicholosi, Anne Marie. 2007. "'The Most Beautiful Suffragette:' Inez Milholland and the Political Currency of Beauty." *Journal of the Gilded Age and Progressive Era* 3, July: 287–309.

Nichols, Christopher McKnight. 2011. *Promise and Peril: America at the Dawn of the Global Age*. Cambridge: Harvard University Press.

Nickles, David Paull. 2003. *Under the Wire: How the Telegraph Changed Diplomacy*. Cambridge: Harvard University Press.

Nicolaides, Becky M. 2002. *My Blue Heaven*. Chicago: University of Chicago Press.

Nightingale, Carl Husemoller. 2012. *Segregation: a Global History of Divided Cities*. Chicago: University of Chicago Press.

Ninkovich, Frank. 1986. "Theodore Roosevelt: Civilization as Ideology." *Diplomatic History*, 10, 3: 221–245.

—. 1994. *Modernity and Power: a History of the Domino Theory in the Twentieth Century*. Chicago: University of Chicago Press.

—. 1999. *The Wilsonian Century: U.S. Foreign Policy since 1900*. Chicago: University of Chicago Press.

—. 2006. "The United States and Imperialism." In *A Companion to American Foreign Relations*, ed. Robert D. Schulzinger. Malden: Wiley-Blackwell.

—. 2014. *The Global Republic: America's Inadvertent Rise to World Power*. Chicago: University of Chicago Press.

Noll, Mark A. 2001. *God and Mammon: Protestants, Money, and the Market, 1790–1860: Protestants, Money, and the Market, 1790–1860*. New York: Oxford University Press.

Noll, Richard. 2011. *American Madness: The Rise and Fall of Dementia Praecox*. Cambridge: Harvard University Press.

Nord, David Paul. 1984. "The Business Values of American Newspapers: The 19th Century Watershed in Chicago." *Journalism Quarterly* 61: 265–273.

—. 2004. *Faith in Reading: Religious Publishing and the Birth of Mass Media in America*. New York: Oxford University Press.

Nordstrom, Justin. 2006. *Danger on the Doorstep: Anti-Catholicism and American Print Culture in the Progressive Era*. South Bend: University of Notre Dame Press.

Norrell, Robert J. 2009. *Up from History: The Life of Booker T. Washington*. Cambridge: Harvard University Press.

Norris, George W. 1945. *Fighting Liberal*. New York: Macmillan.

North, Douglass. 1961. *The Economic Growth of the United States, 1790–1860*. Englewood Cliffs: Prentice-Hall.

Novak, Barbara. 1979. *American Painting of the Nineteenth Century: Realism, Idealism, and the American Experience*. 2nd ed. New York: Harper & Row.

Novak, William J. 1996. *The People's Welfare: Law and Regulation in Nineteenth-Century America*. Chapel Hill: University of North Carolina Press.

—. 2008. "The Myth of the 'Weak' American State." *The American Historical Review* 113, 3: 752–72. Oxford: Oxford University Press.

—. 2010. "Law and the Social Control of American Capitalism. *Emory Law Journal* 60: 377–405.

—. 2015. "Beyond Max Weber: The Need for a Democratic (not Aristocratic) Theory of the Modern State." *Tocqueville Review/ La Revue Tocqueville* 36: 43–91.

Nugent, Walter T. K. 1963. *The Tolerant Populists: Kansas Populism and Nativism*. Chicago: University of Chicago Press.

—. 1963, 2013. *The Tolerant Populists: Kansas Populism and Nativism*. Chicago: University of Chicago Press.

—. 2010. *Progressivism: A Very Short Introduction*. New York: Oxford University Press.

—. 2013. "Preface to the Second Edition." In *The Tolerant Populists*. Chicago: University of Chicago Press.

Nye, David E. and Mick Gidley, eds. 1994. *American Photographs in Europe*. Amsterdam: VU Press.

O'Brien, Michael. 1973. "C. Vann Woodward and the Burden of Southern Liberalism." *American Historical Review* 78, 3: 589–604.

O'Connor, Thomas H. 1968. *Lords of the Loom, the Cotton Whigs and the Coming of the Civil War*. New York: Scribner.

O'Donnell, Edward. 2015. *Henry George and the Crisis of Inequality: Progress and Poverty in the Gilded Age*. New York: Columbia University.

O'Neill, Jonathan. "The First Conservatives: The Constitutional Challenge to Progressivism," July 5, 2011, First Principles Series Report #39 on Political Thought, Heritage Foundation. Accessed March 5, 2016, http://www.heritage.org/research/reports/2011/06/the-first-conservatives-the-constitutional-challenge-to-progressivism

O'Neill, Karen M. 2006. *Rivers by Design: State Power and the Origins of U.S. Flood Control*. Durham: Duke University Press.

O'Sullivan, Mary. 2007. "The Expansion of the U.S. Stock Market, 1885–1930: Historical Facts and Theoretical Fashions." *Enterprise & Society* 8: 489–542. DOI: 10.1093/es/khm075

—. 2010. "Finance Capital in Chandlerian Capitalism." *Industrial and Corporate Change* 19: 549–589. DOI: 10.1093/icc/dtq016.

Oates, Mary J. 1995. *The Catholic Philanthropic Tradition in America*. Bloomington: University of Indiana Press.

Odem, Mary E. 1995. *Delinquent Daughters: Protecting and Policing Adolescent Female Sexuality in the United States, 1885–1920*. Chapel Hill: University of North Carolina Press.

Ogle, Vanessa. 2013. "Whose Time is It? The Pluralization of Time and the Global Condition, 1870s to 1940s." *American Historical Review* 120, 5: 1376–1402.

—. 2015. *The Global Transformation of Time, 1870–1950*. Cambridge: Harvard University Press.

Ohmann, Richard. 1996. *Selling Culture: Magazines, Markets, and the Class at the Turn of the Century*. New York: Verso.

Olasky, Marvin. 1992. *The Tragedy of American Compassion*. Washington, DC: Regnery Publishing, Inc.

Olcott, Charles S. 1916. *The Life of William McKinley*. 2 volumes. Boston: Houghton Mifflin.

Oleson, Alexandra, and John Voss. 1979. *The Organization of Knowledge in Modern America, 1860–1920*. Baltimore: Johns Hopkins University Press.

Oliver, M. 2007. "George Eastman's Modern Stone-Age Family: Snapshot Photography and the Brownie." *Technology and Culture* 48, 1: 1–19.

Olmstead, Alan L. and Paul W. Rhode. 2008. *Creating Abundance: Biological Innovation and American Agricultural Development*. New York: Cambridge University Press.

Opie, Frederick Douglass. 2009. *Black Labor Migration in Caribbean Guatemala, 1882–1923*. Gainesville: University Press of Florida.

Oriard, Michael. 1993. *Reading Football: How the Popular Press Created an American Spectacle*. Chapel Hill: University of North Carolina Press.

Orleck, Annelise. 1995. *Common Sense and a Little Fire: Women and Working-Class Politics in the United States, 1900–1965*. Chapel Hill: University of North Carolina Press.

Orren, Karen. and Stephen Skowronek. 2004. *The Search for American Political Development*. New York: Cambridge University Press.

Orsi, Jared. 2004. *Hazardous Metropolis: Flooding and Urban Ecology in Los Angeles*. Berkeley: University of California Press.

Orsi, Richard J. 2005. *The Southern Pacific Railroad and the Development of the American West, 1850–1930*. Berkeley: University of California Press.

Orsi, Robert A. 1985. *The Madonna of 115th Street: Faith and Community in Italian Harlem*. New Haven: Yale University Press.

—. 1999. "Introduction: Crossing the City Line." In *Gods of the City: Religion and the American Urban Landscape*, ed. Robert A. Orsi. Indianapolis: Indiana University Press.

—. 2010. *The Madonna of 115th Street: Faith and Community in Italian Harlem, 1880–1950*. 3rd ed. New Haven: Yale University Press.

Ortiz, Paul. 2005. *Emancipation Betrayed: The Hidden History of Black Organizing and White Violence in Florida from Reconstruction to the Bloody Election of 1920*. Berkeley: University of California Press.

Oshinsky, David. M. 1996. *"Worse Than Slavery": Parchman Farm and the Ordeal of Jim Crow Justice*. New York: Simon and Schuster.

Osterhammel, Jürgen. 2014. *The Transformation of the World: A Global History of the Nineteenth Century*. Princeton: Princeton University Press.

Osterud, Nancy Grey. *Bonds of Community: The Lives of Farm Women in Nineteenth-Century New York*. Ithaca: Cornell University Press.

Ostler, Jeffrey. 2001. "The Last Buffalo Hunt and Beyond: Plains Sioux Economic Strategies in the Early Reservation Period." *Great Plains Quarterly* 21: 115–130.

—. 2004. *The Plains Sioux and U.S. Colonialism from Lewis and Clark to Wounded Knee*. Cambridge: Cambridge University Press.

Ott, John. 2010. "The Manufactured Patron: Staging Bourgeois Identity through Art Consumption in Postbellum America." In *The American Bourgeoisie: Distinction and Identity in the Nineteenth Century*, ed. Sven Beckert and Julia B. Rosenbaum, 257–276. New York: Palgrave MacMillan.

Ott, Julia C. 2011. *When Wall Street Met Main Street: The Quest for an Investors' Democracy*. Cambridge: Harvard University Press.

Ottley, Roi. 1955. *The Lonely Warrior: The Life and Times of Robert S. Abbott*. Chicago: Henry Regnery.

Pafford, John M. 2013. *The Forgotten Conservative: Rediscovering Grover Cleveland*. New York: Regnery.

Page, Brian, and Richard A. Walker. 1991. "From Settlement to Fordism : The Agro-Industrial Revolution in the American Midwest." *Economic Geography* 67: 281–315.

Painter, Nell Irvin. 1977. *Exodusters: Black Migration to Kansas After Reconstruction*. New York: W.W. Norton.

—. 1987. *Standing at Armageddon: The United States, 1877–1919*. New York: Norton.

—. 1996. *Sojourner Truth: A Life, A Symbol*. New York: W.W. Norton.

Pak, Susie J. 2013. *Gentlemen Bankers: The World of J.P. Morgan*. Cambridge: Harvard University Press.

Palmer, Bruce. 1980. *"Man Over Money": The Southern Populist Critique of American Capitalism*. Chapel Hill: University of North Carolina Press.

Paolini, Ernest. 1973. *The Foundations of the American Empire: William Henry Seward and U.S. Foreign Policy*. Ithaca: Cornell University Press.

Parezo, Nancy J. and Don D. Fowler. 2007. *Anthropology Goes to the Fair: The 1904 Louisiana Purchase Exposition*. Lincoln: University of Nebraska Press.

Paris, Leslie. 2008. *Children's Nature: The Rise of the American Summer Camp*. New York: New York University Press.

Parker, Alison M. 1997. *Purifying America: Women, Cultural Reform, and Pro-Censorship Activism, 1873–1933*. Urbana: University of Illinois Press.

Parrillo, Nicholas R. 2014. *Against the Profit Motive: The Salary Revolution in American Government, 1780–1940*. New Haven: Yale University Press.

Parrington, Vernon Louis. 1930. *The Beginnings of Critical Realism in America, 1860–1920*. New York: Harcourt, Brace and Co.

—. 1963. "The Progressive Era: A Liberal Renaissance." Reprinted in *The Progressive Era: Liberal Renaissance or Liberal Failure?*, ed. Arthur Mann. New York: Holt, Rinehart and Winston.

Parrini, Carl, and Sklar, Martin. 1983. "New Thinking About the Market, 1896 – 1904: Some Economists on Investment and the Theory of Surplus Capital." *Journal of Economic History* 43: 559 – 578.

—. 1993. "Charles A. Conant, Economic Crises and Foreign Policy, 1896 – 1903." In *Behind the Throne: Servants of Power to Imperial Presidents, 1898–1968*, ed. Thomas J. McCormick and Walter LaFeber. Madison: The University of Wisconsin Press.

Parsons, Gail Pat, 1977. "Equal Treatment for All: American Medical Remedies for Male Sexual Problems: 1850–1900." *Journal of the History of Medicine* 32, 1: 55–71.

Pascoe, Peggy. 1990. *Relations of Rescue: The Search for Female Moral Authority in the American West, 1874–1939*. New York: Oxford University Press.

—. 2009. *What Comes Naturally: Miscegenation Law and the Making of Race in America*. New York: Oxford University Press.

Passet, Joanne. 2003. *Sex Radicals and the Quest for Women's Equality*. Chicago: University of Illinois Press.

Patterson, Andrea. 2009. "Germs and Jim Crow: The Impact of Microbiology on Public Health Policies in Progressive Era American South." *Journal of the History of Biology* 42: 529–559.

Patterson, James T. 1994. *America's Struggle against Poverty, 1900–1994*. Cambridge: Harvard University Press.

Paul, Arnold M. 1960. *Conservative Crisis and the Rule of Law: Attitudes of Bar and Bench, 1887–1895*. Ithaca: Cornell University Press.

Pauly, Philip J. 2008. *Fruits and Plains: The Horticultural Transformation of America*. Cambridge: Harvard University Press.

Payne, Elizabeth. 1988. *Reform, Labor, and Feminism: Margaret Dreier Robins and the Women's Trade Union League*. Chicago: University of Illinois Press.

Pearson, Chad. 2015. *Reform or Repression: Organizing America's Anti-Union Movement*. Philadelphia: University of Pennsylvania Press.

Peck, Gunther. 2006. "The Nature of Labor: Fault Lines and Common Ground in Environmental and Labor History." *Environmental History* 11, 2: 212–238.

Pedersen, Susan. 2015. *The Guardians: The League of Nations and the Crisis of Empire*. New York: Oxford University Press.

Peirce, Neil R. 1973. *The Great Plains States of America*. New York: W.W. Norton Press.

Peiss, Kathy Lee. 1986. *Cheap Amusements: Working Women and Leisure In Turn-of-the-century New York*. Philadelphia: Temple University Press.

Peiss, Kathy. 1998. *Hope in a Jar: The Making of America's Beauty Culture*. New York: Metropolitan Books.

Perez, Louis A. Jr. 1998. *The War of 1898: The United States and Cuba in History and Historiography*. Chapel Hill: University of North Carolina Press.

Perlman, Selig. 1928. *A Theory of the Labor Movement*. New York: Macmillan.

Perlmann, Joel 1988. *Ethnic Differences: Schooling and Social Structure Among the Irish, Italians, Jews, & Blacks in an American City, 1880–1935*. New York: Cambridge University Press.

Pernick, Martin S. 1996. *The Black Stork: Eugenics and the Death of "Defective" Babies in American Medicine and Motion Pictures since 1915*. New York: Oxford University Press.

Perry, Elisabeth Israels. 2002. "Men are From the Gilded Age, Women Are from the Progressive Era." *Journal of the Gilded Age and Progressive Era* 1: 25–48.

Perry, Jeffrey B. 2009. *Hubert Harrison: The Voice of Harlem Radicalism, 1883–1918*. New York: Columbia University Press.

Peskin, Allan. 1973. "Was There a Compromise of 1877?" *Journal of American History* 60, 1: 63–75.

—. 1978. *Garfield*. Kent: Kent State University Press.

—. 1980. "President Garfield Reconsidered." *Hayes Historical Journal* 3: 35–40.

Pestritto, Ronald J. 2005. *Woodrow Wilson and the Roots of Modern Liberalism*. Lanham: Rowman & Littlefield.

Peters, Ronald M., Jr. 1997. *The American Speakership: The Office in Historical Perspective*, 2nd edition. Baltimore: Johns Hopkins University Press.

Peterson, Jon A. 2003. *The Birth of City Planning in the United States, 1840–1917*. Baltimore: Johns Hopkins University Press.

Petit, Jeanne D. 2010. *The Men and Women We Want: Gender, Race, and the Progressive Era Literacy Test Debate*. Rochester: University of Rochester Press.

Pettit, Michael. 2013. *The Science of Deception: Psychology and Commerce in America*. Chicago: University of Chicago Press.

Pfaelzer, Jean. 2007. *Driven Out: the Forgotten War Against Chinese Americans*. New York: Random House.

"Philadelphia Settlement Report." 1894. In *Fourth Annual Report of the College Settlements Association*. Philadelphia: Avil Printing and Lithographing Co.

Phillips, David G. 1964. *The Treason of the Senate*. Chicago: Quadrangle Books.

Phillips, Kate. 2003. *Helen Hunt Jackson: A Literary Life*. Berkeley: University of California Press.

Phillips, Kevin 2003. *William McKinley*. New York: Times Books.

Phillips, Ulrich B. 1928. "The Central Theme of Southern History." *American Historical Review* 34, 1: 30–43.

Philpott, Thomas Lee. 1978. *The Slum and the Ghetto: Neighborhood Deterioration and Middle-class Reform, Chicago, 1880–1930*. New York: Oxford University Press.

Picard, Alyssa. 2002. "'To Popularize the Nude in Art': Comstockery Reconsidered." *Journal of the Gilded Age and Progressive Era* 1, 3: 195–224.

Pickens, Donald. 1968. *Eugenics and the Progressives*. Nashville: Vanderbilt University Press.

Pierson, Arthur Tappan. 1886. *The Crisis of Missions: Or, the Voice Out of the Cloud*. New York: Robert Carter and Brothers.

Piketty, Thomas. 2014. *Capital in the Twenty-First Century*. Cambridge: Belknap Press of Harvard University Press.

Pisani, Donald. 2002. *Water and American Government: The Reclamation Bureau, National Water Policy, and the West, 1902–1935*. Berkeley: University of California Press.

Pitti, Stephen J. 2004. *The Devil in Silicon Valley: Northern California, Race, and Mexican Americans*. Princeton: Princeton University Press.

Pivar, David. 1973. *Purity Crusade: Sexual Morality and Social Control, 1868–1900*. Westport: Greenwood Press.

Platt, Harold L. 2005. *Shock Cities: the Environmental Transformation and Reform of Manchester and Chicago*. Chicago: The University of Chicago Press.

Pleck, Elizabeth. 1983. "Feminist Responses to 'Crimes against Women.'" Signs 8, 3: 451–70.

—. 1987. *Domestic Tyranny: The Making of American Social Policy against Family Violence from Colonial Times to the Present*. New York: Oxford University Press.

Plessy v. Ferguson. 1896.

Plesur, Milton 1971. *America's Outward Thrust: Approaches to Foreign Affairs, 1865–1890*. De Kalb: Northern Illinois University Press.

Pletcher, David M. 1962. *The Awkward Years: American Foreign Relations under Garfield and Arthur*. Columbia: University of Missouri Press.

—. 2001. *The Diplomacy of Involvement: American Economic Expansion across the Pacific, 1784–1900*. Columbia: University of Missouri Press.

Pliley, Jessica. 2013. "The Petticoat Inspectors: Women Boarding Inspectors and the Gendered Exercise of Federal Authority." *Journal of the Gilded Age and Progressive Era* 12: 95–125.

Plotnick, Rachel. 2012. "At the Interface: The Case of the Electric Push Button, 1880–1923." *Technology and Culture* 53, 4: 815–845.

Plowman, Peter. 2010. *Across the Pacific: Liners from ANZ to North America*. Dural: Rosenberg.

Plunz, Richard. 1990. *A History of Housing in New York City*. New York: Columbia University Press.

Poblete, Joanna. 2014. *Islanders in the Empire: Filipino and Puerto Rican Laborers in Hawai'i*. Urbana: University of Illinois Press.

Pokagon, Simon. 1893. *The Red Man's Rebuke*. Hartford, Michigan: C.H. Engle.

Pollack, Norman. 1962. *The Populist Response to Industrial America*. Cambridge: Harvard University Press.

Polsby, Nelson W. 1968. "The Institutionalization of the U.S. House of Representatives." *American Political Science Review* 62, 1: 144–68.

—, Miriam Gallaher, and Barry S. Rundquist. 1969. "The Growth of the Seniority System in the U.S. House of Representatives." *American Political Science Review* 63, 3: 787–807.

Pope, Thomas E. 2002. *The Weary Boys: Colonel J. Warren Keifer and the 110th Ohio Volunteer Infantry*. Kent: Kent State University Press.

Populist (People's) Party. 1892. "Omaha Platform."

Porter, Glenn, and Harold C. Livesay. 1971. *Merchants and Manufacturers; Studies in the Changing Structure of Nineteenth-Century Marketing*. Baltimore: Johns Hopkins Press.

Posadas, Barbara. 1999. *The Filipino Americans*. Westport: Greenwood Press.

Postel, Charles. 2007. *The Populist Vision*. New York: Oxford University Press.

Potter, David M. 1954. *People of Plenty: Economic Abundance and the American Character*. Chicago: University of Chicago Press.

Powderly, Terrence V. 1889, "The Purposes and Program of the Knights of Labor," from *Thirty Years of Labor*. Columbus: Excelsior Publishing Company.

Powers, Madelon. 1998. *Faces Along the Bar: Lore and Order In the Workingman's Saloon, 1870–1920*. Chicago: University of Chicago Press.

Prashad, Vijay. 2000. *White Love: and Other Events in Filipino History*. Durham: Duke University Press.

—. 2007. *The Darker Nations: A People's History of the Third World*. New York: The New Press.

Pratt, John Webb. 1967. *Religion, Politics, and Diversity: The Church-State Theme in New York History*. Ithaca: Cornell University Press.

Pratt, Julius. 1936. *Expansionists of 1898: The Acquisition of Hawaii and the Spanish Islands*. Baltimore: Johns Hopkins University Press.

Prescott, Lawrence F. 1896. *1896: The Great Campaign or Political Struggles of Parties, Leaders and Issues*. Peoria: Loyal Publishing Company.

Price, Jennifer. 1999. *Flight Maps: Adventures with Nature In Modern America*. New York: Basic Books.

Prieto, Laura R. 2001. *At Home and in the Studio: The Professionalization of Women Artists in America*. Cambridge: Harvard University Press, 2001.

—. 2013. "A Delicate Subject: Clemencia Lopez, Civilized Womanhood, and the Politics of Anti-Imperialism." *Journal of the Gilded Age and Progressive Era* 12: 199–233.

Primm, James Neal. 2013. *Lion of the Valley*. St. Louis: Missouri Historical Society Press.

Prince, K. Stephen. 2014. *Stories of the South: Race and the Reconstruction of Southern Identity, 1865–1915*. Chapel Hill: The University of North Carolina Press.

Pringle, Henry F. 1931. *Theodore Roosevelt: A Biography*. New York: Harcourt Brace.

Proceedings of the First National Convention of the Progressive Party. 1912. August 5–7. Progressive Party Archives, Theodore Roosevelt Collection, Houghton Library, Harvard University.

Progressive Party. 1912. Platform, August 7. http://teachingamericanhistory.org/library/document/progressive-platform-of-1912/

Prothero, Stephen. 1996. *The White Buddhist: The Asian Odyssey of Henry Steel Olcott*. Indianapolis: Indiana University Press.

Prucha, Francis Paul. 1984.1995. *The Great Father: The United States Government and the American Indian*. Lincoln: University of Nebraska Press.

Punke, Michael. 2007. *Last Stand: George Bird Grinnell, the Battle to Save the Buffalo, and the Birth of the New West*. Washington, DC: Smithsonian Books.

Pursell, Carroll. 2010. "Herbert Hoover and the Transnational Lives of Engineers." In *Transnational Lives: Biographies of Global Modernity*, ed. Desley Deacon, Penny Russell, and Angela Woollacott, 109–20. Basingstoke: Palgrave Macmillan.

Putnam, James Jackson. 1895. "Remarks on the Psychical Treatment of Neurasthenia." *Boston Medical and Surgical Journal* 132, May: 505–508.

Putnam, John C. 2008. *Class and Gender Politics in Progressive-Era Seattle*. Reno: University of Nevada Press.

Putnam, Lara. 2013. *Radical Moves: Caribbean Migrants and the Politics of Race in the Jazz Age*. Chapel Hill: University of North Carolina Press.

Putney, Clifford. 2001. *Muscular Christianity: Manhood and Sports in Protestant America, 1880–1920*. Cambridge: Harvard University Press.

Pyne, Stephen J. 1982. *Fire in America: A Cultural History of Wildland and Rural Fire*. Princeton: Princeton University Press, 1982.

Quarles, Benjamin. 1988. *Black Mosaic: Essays in Afro-America History and Historiography*. Amherst: University of Massachusetts Press.

Queensland Times Ipswich Herald and General Advertiser. 3 June, 1905: 4.

Rabban, David M. 2013. *Law's History: American Legal Thought and the Transatlantic Turn to History*. Cambridge: Cambridge University Press.

Rabinovitch-Fox, Einav. 2015. "[Re]fashioning the New Woman: Women's Dress, the Oriental Style, and the Construction of American Feminist Imagery in the 1910s." *Journal of Women's History* 12, 2: 14–36.

Rabinovitz, Lauren. 1998. *For the Love of Pleasure: Women, Movies, and Culture in Turn-of-the-Century Chicago*. New Brunswick: Rutgers University Press.

Rabinowitz, Howard N. 1978. *Race Relations in the Urban South, 1865–1890*. New York: Oxford University Press.

—. 1988. "More than the Woodward Thesis: Assessing the Strange Career of Jim Crow." *Journal of American History* 75, 3: 842–56.

Rafael, Vicente. 2000. *White Love and Other Events in Filipino History*. Durham: Duke University Press.

Rafferty, Edward C. 2003. *Apostle of Human Progress. Lester Frank Ward and American Political Thought, 1841–1913*. New York: Rowan and Littlefield.

Raibmon, Paige. 2005. *Authentic Indians: Episodes of Encounter from the Late Nineteenth Century Northwest Coast*. Durham: Duke University Press.

The Railroad Telegrapher. 1896. 1 July.

Ransom, Roger L. and Richard Sutch. 1977. *One Kind of Freedom: The Economic Consequences of Emancipation*. Cambridge: Cambridge University Press.

Rast, Raymond. 2007. "The Cultural Politics of Tourism in Chinatown, 1882–1917." *Pacific Historical Review* 76:29–60.

Rauchway, Eric. 2003. *Murdering McKinley: The Making of Theodore Roosevelt's America*. New York: Hill and Wang.

—. 2005. "William McKinley and Us." *Journal of the Gilded Age and Progressive Era* 2: 235–53.

—. 2006. *Blessed among Nations: How the World Made America*. New York: Hill and Wang.

Rauschenbusch, Walter. 1907. *Christianity and the Social Crisis*. New York: The Macmillan Company.

Rawson, Michael. 2010. *Eden on the Charles: The Making of Boston*. Cambridge: Harvard University Press.

Reagan, Leslie J. 1997. *When Abortion was a Crime: Women, Medicine, and Law in the United States, 1867–1973*. Berkeley: University of California Press.

Recchiuti, John Louis. 2007. *Civic Engagement: Social Science and Progressive-Era Reform in New York City*. Philadelphia: University of Pennsylvania Press.

Redlich, Fritz. 1951. *The Molding of American Banking: Men and Ideas*. New York: Hafner.

Reed, James. 2011. *From Private Vice to Public Virtue: The Birth Control Movement and American Society Since 1830*. Princeton: Princeton University Press.

Reddy, Chandan. 2011. *Freedom With Violence: Race, Sexuality, and the US State*. Durham: Duke University Press.

Reed, Thomas B. 1889a. "Rules of the House of Representatives." *Century Magazine* 37: 792–95.

—. 1889b. "Obstruction in the National House." *North American Review* 149: 431–28.

Rees, Jonathan. 2013. *Refrigeration Nation: A History of Ice, Appliances, and Enterprise in America*. Baltimore: Johns Hopkins University Press.

Reeve, W. Paul. 2015. *Religion of a Different Color: Race and the Mormon Struggle for Whiteness*. New York: Oxford University Press.

Regal, Brian. 2002. *Henry Fairfield Osborn: Race and the Search for the Origins of Man*. Burlington: Ashgate.

Regier, Cornelius C. 1932. *The Era of the Muckrakers*. Chapel Hill: University of North Carolina.

Rehnquist, William. 2004. *Centennial Crisis: The Disputed Election of 1876*. New York: Alfred A. Knopf.

Reid, Joshua L. 2015. *The Sea Is My Country: The Maritime World of the Makahs*. New Haven: Yale University Press.

Reinsch, Paul S. 1907. "International Unions and Their Administration." *American Journal of International Law* 1, July: 579–623.

Reiss, Elizabeth. 2012. *Bodies in Doubt: An American History of Intersex*. Baltimore: Johns Hopkins University Press.

Rembis, Michael A. 2011. *Defining Deviance: Sex, Science, and Delinquent Girls, 1890–1960*. Urbana: University of Illinois Press.

Remillard, Arthur. 2011. *Southern Civil Religions: Imagining the Good Society In the Post Reconstruction era*. Athens: University of Georgia Press.

Renda, Mary A. 2001. *Taking Haiti: Military Occupation and the Culture of U.S. Imperialism*. Chapel Hill: University of North Carolina Press.

"Report of the Commissioner of Labor on Hawaii." 1903. *Bulletin of the United States Bureau of Labor* 8, 47.

"Republican Hopeful would not be First Chinese-Speaking President." 2012. *Chicago Tribune*. 10 January.

Reynolds, David S. 1995. *Walt Whitman's America: A Cultural Biography*. New York: Alfred A. Knopf.

Ricard, Serge. 1994. "The Exceptionalist Syndrome in U.S. Continental and Overseas Expansionism." In *Reflections on American Exceptionalism*, ed. David K. Adams and Cornelis A. van Minnen. Staffordshire: Ryburn.

—. 2014. "The State of Theodore Roosevelt Studies." *H-Diplo*. October 24. http://tiny.cc/E116.

Rice, Myiti Sengstacke. 2012. *Chicago Defender*. Charleston: Arcadia Publishing.

Richard Ely, et. al. 1917. *The Foundations of National Prosperity: Studies in the Conservation of Permanent National Resources*. New York: MacMillan.

Richardson, Heather Cox. 1997. *Greatest Nation of the Earth: Republican Economic Policies During the Civil War*. Cambridge: Harvard University Press.

—. 2001. *The Death of Reconstruction: Race, Labor, and Politics in the Post-Civil War North, 1965–1901*. Cambridge: Harvard University Press.

—. 2007. *West From Appomattox: The Reconstruction of America After the Civil War*. New Haven: Yale University Press.

Riegel, Robert E. 1968. "Changing American Attitudes Toward Prostitution (1800–1920)." *Journal of the History of Ideas* 29, 3: 437–452.

Riis, Jacob A. 1890. *How the Other Half Lives: Studies Among the Tenements of New York*. New York: Charles Scribner's Sons.

—. 1904. *Theodore Roosevelt, the Citizen*. New York: The Outlook Co.

Rimby, Susan. 2005. "'Better Housekeeping Out of Doors': Myra Lloyd Dock, The State Federation of Pennsylvania Women, and Progressive Era Conservation." *Journal of Women's History* 17: 9–34.

—. 2012. *Mira Lloyd Dock and the Progressive Era Conservation Movement*. University Park: Pennsylvania State University Press.

Ring, Natalie J. 2012. *The Problem South: Region, Empire, and the New Liberal State, 1880–1930*. Athens: University of Georgia Press.

Rischin, Moses. 1962. *The Promised City: New York Jews, 1870–1914*. Cambridge: Harvard University.

—. 1985. *Grandma Never Lived in America: The New Journalism of Abraham Cahan*. Bloomington: Indiana University.

Ristaino, Jean Beagle, ed. 2008. *Pioneering Women in Plant Pathology*. St. Paul: APS Press.

Ritchie, Donald A. 1992. *Press Gallery: Congress and the Washington Correspondents*. Cambridge: Harvard University Press.

Rittenhouse, Mignon. 1956. *The Amazing Nellie Bly*. New York: Dutton.

Ritterhouse, Jennifer. 2006. *Growing Up Jim Crow: How Black and White Southern Children Learned Race*. Chapel Hill: University of North Carolina Press.

Robbins, William G. 1982. *Lumberjacks and Legislators: Political Economy of the U.S. Lumber Industry, 1890–1941*. College Station: Texas A & M University Press.

—. 1994. *Colony and Empire*. Lawrence: University Press of Kansas.

Roberts, B.H. 1899. "The Church of Jesus Christ of Latter-day Saints at the Parliament of Religions: Preliminary Agitation." *Improvement Era* 2, 9: 671–677.

Rusling, James. 1903. "Interview With President William McKinley." *Christian Advocate* 22, January.

Roberts, Dorothy. 2011. *Fatal Invention: How Science, Politics, and Big Business Re-Create Race in the Twenty-First Century*. New York: New Press.

Roberts, Samuel K. 2009. *Infectious Fear: Politics, Disease, and the Health Effects of Segregation*. Chapel Hill: University of North Carolina Press.

Robertson, Craig. 2012. *The Passport in America: The History of a Document*. New York: Oxford University Press.

Robertson, Stephen. 2002. "Age of Consent Law and the Making of Modern Childhood in New York City, 1886–1921." *Journal of Social History* 35, 4: 781–98.

—. 2006. "Sexual Violence and Marriage in New York City, 1886–1955." *Law and History Review* 24, 2: 331–73.

—. 2010. "Shifting the Scene of the Crime: Sodomy and the American History of Violence." *Journal of the History of Sexuality* 19, 2: 223–42.

Robinson, Cedric. 1983. *Black Marxism: The Making of the Black Radical Tradition*. Chapel Hill: University of North Carolina Press.

Robinson, William A. 1930. *Thomas B. Reed: Parliamentarian*. New York: Dodd and Mead.

Rodgers, Daniel T. 1978. *The Work Ethic in Industrial America, 1850–1920*. Chicago: University of Chicago Press.

Rodgers, Daniel T. 1982. "In Search of Progressivism." *Reviews in American History* 10: 113–132.

—. 1998a. *Atlantic Crossings: Social Politics In a Progressive Age*. Cambridge: Belknap Press of Harvard University Press.

—. 1998b. "Exceptionalism." In *Imagined Histories: American Historians Interpret the Past*, ed. Anthony Molho and Gordon S. Wood. Princeton: Princeton University Press.

—. 2002. "An Age of Social Politics." In *Rethinking American History in a Global Age*, ed. Thomas Bender, 250–73. Berkeley: University of California Press.

Rodriguez, Sarah W. 2014. *Female Circumcision and Clitoridectomy in the United States*. New York: University of Rochester Press.

Roediger, David R. 1991. *Wages of Whiteness: Race and the Making of the American Working Class*. London: Verso.

—. 1999. *The Wages of Whiteness: Race and the Making of the American Working Class*. Revised ed. London: Verso Books.

—. 2005. *Working Toward Whiteness: How America's Immigrants Became White. The Strange Journey from Ellis Island to the Suburbs*. New York: Basic Books.

Roger, Scott W. 1998. "Uncle Joe Cannon: The Brakeman of the House of Representatives, 1903–1911." In *Masters of the House: Congressional Leadership over Two Centuries*, ed. Raymond W. Smock and Susan W. Hammond. Boulder: Westview Press.

Rome, Adam. 2006. "'Political Hermaphrodites': Gender and Environmental Reform in Progressive America." *Environmental History* 11: 440–463.

Rook, Robert E. 2000. "An American in Palestine: Elwood Mead and Zionist Water Resource Planning, 1923–1936." *Arab Studies Quarterly* 22, winter: 71–89.

Roosevelt, Theodore, and Lodge, Henry Cabot. 1895. *Hero Tales from American History*. New York: The Century Company.

—. 1901a. "Reform Through Social Work: Some Forces That Tell for Decency in New York City." *McClure's Magazine* 16: 448–454.

—. 1901b. *The Works of Theodore Roosevelt: Strenuous Life*. New York: P.F. Collier and Son, Publishers.

—. 1907. "To the Senate and House of Representatives." In *Congressional Record*, 60th Congress, 1st Session.

—. 1910a, 1926. *Roosevelt: The Works of Theodore Roosevelt*. Volumes 17 and 20. New York: Scribner's.

—. 1910b. *Presidential Addresses and State Papers*. Vol. 5. New York: Review of Reviews.

—. 1912b. "A Charter for Democracy." Address before the Ohio Constitutional Convention at Columbus, Ohio. February 21. Roosevelt Collection, Houghton Library, Harvard University.

—. 1912c. "Confession of Faith." In *Roosevelt: The Works of Theodore Roosevelt*, volume 17, 219. New York: Scribner's.

—. 1916. *Fear God and Take Your Own Part*. New York: George Doran & Co.

—. 1919–1926. *The Works of Theodore Roosevelt*. Memorial Edition. New York: Charles Scribner's Sons.

Rose, Anne C. 2012. "An American Science of Feeling: Harvard's Psychology of Emotion During the World War I Era." *Journal of the History of Ideas* 73, 3: 485–506.

Rosen, Christine. 2004. *Preaching Eugenics: Religious Leaders and the American Eugenics Movement*. New York: Oxford University Press.

Rosen, F. Bruce. 1977. "The Influence of the Peabody Fund on Education in Reconstruction Florida." *The Florida Historical Quarterly* 55, 3: 310–320.

Rosen, George. 1985. "The First Neighborhood Health Center Movement: Its Rise and Fall." In *Sickness & Health in America: Readings in the History of Medicine and Public Health*, ed. Judith Walzer Leavitt and Ronald Numbers, 475–489. Madison: University of Wisconsin Press.

Rosen, Hannah. 2009. *Terror in the Heart of Freedom: Citizenship, Sexual Violence, and the Meaning of Race in the Postemancipation South*. Chapel Hill: University of North Carolina Press.

Rosen, Robyn L. 2003. *Reproductive Rights: Reformers and the Politics of Maternal Welfare, 1917–1940*. Columbus: The Ohio State University Press.

Rosen, Ruth. 1982. *The Lost Sisterhood: Prostitution in America, 1900–1918*. Baltimore: Johns Hopkins University Press.

—. 1999. *Financial Missionaries to the World: the Politics and Culture of Dollar Diplomacy, 1900–1930*. Cambridge: Harvard University Press.

Rosenberg, Charles E. 1985. "Social Class and Medical Care in 19th-Century America: The Rise and Fall of the Dispensary." In *Sickness & Health in America: Readings in the History of Medicine and Public Health*, ed. Judith Walzer Leavitt and Ronald Numbers, 273–286. Madison: University of Wisconsin Press.

Rosenberg, Emily S. 1982. *Spreading the American Dream: American Economic and Cultural Expansion, 1890–1945*. New York: Hill and Wang.

—. 2003. *Financial Missionaries to the World: The Politics and Culture of Dollar Diplomacy*. Durham: Duke University Press.

—. 2012a. "Transnational Currents in a Shrinking World." In *A World Connecting 1870–1945*, ed. Emily Rosenberg, 815–996. Cambridge: Belknap Press of Harvard University Press.

—, ed. 2012b. *A World Connecting, 1870–1945*. Cambridge: Belknap Press of Harvard University Press.

Rosenberg, Rosalind. 1982. *Beyond Separate Spheres: Intellectual Roots of Modern Feminism*. New Haven: Yale University Press.

—. 2004. *Changing the Subject: How the Women of Columbia Shaped the Way We Think About Sex and Politics*. New York: Columbia University Press.

Rosenstone, Steven J., Roy L. Behr, and Edward H. Lazarus. 1996. *Third Parties in America: Citizen Response to Major Party Failure*. Princeton: Princeton University Press.

Rosenzweig, Roy. 1983. *Eight Hours for What We Will: Workers and Leisure In an Industrial City, 1870–1920*. Cambridge: Cambridge University Press.

Rosier, Paul C. 2015. "Crossing New Boundaries: American Indians and Twentieth Century U.S. Foreign Policy." *Diplomatic History* 39: 955–966.

Rosner, David. 1982. *A Once Charitable Enterprise: Hospitals and Health Care in Brooklyn and New York, 1885–1915*. Princeton: Princeton University Press; selection in Hammack, *Making the Nonprofit Sector*, 1998.

Ross, Andrew. 1989. *No Respect: Intellectuals and Popular Culture*. London: Routledge.

Ross, Brian. 1989. "The New Philanthropy: The Reorganization of Charity in Turn of the Century Cleveland." Ph.D. diss., Case Western Reserve University.

Ross, Steven J. 1998. *Working-Class Hollywood: Silent Film and the Shaping of Class in America*. Princeton: Princeton University Press.

Ross, Thomas R. 1958. *Jonathan Prentiss Dolliver: A Study in Political Integrity and Independence*. Iowa City: State Historical Society of Iowa.

Rossini, Daniela. 2008. *Woodrow Wilson and the American Myth in Italy: Culture, Diplomacy, and War Propaganda*. Cambridge: Harvard University Press.

Rossiter, Margaret. 1984. *Women Scientists in America: Struggles and Strategies to 1940*. Baltimore: Johns Hopkins University Press.

Rostow, Walt Whitman. 1960. *The Stages of Economic Growth: A Non-Communist Manifesto*. New York: Cambridge University Press.

Rothbard, Murray. 1979. "Hoover's 1919 Food Diplomacy in Retrospect." In *Herbert Hoover: The Great War and Its Aftermath, 1914–1923*, ed. L. Gelfand, 89–110. Iowa City: University of Iowa Press.

Rothman, Adam. 2005. "The "Slave Power" in the United States, 1783–1865." In *Ruling America: A History of Wealth and Power in a Democracy*, ed. Steve Fraser and Gary Gerstle, 64–91. Cambridge: Harvard University Press.

Rothman, David J. 1966. *Politics and Power: The United States Senate, 1869–1901*. Cambridge: Harvard University Press.

Rothman, Ellen K. 1987. *Hands and Hearts: A History of Courtship in America*. Cambridge: Harvard University Press.

Rotundo, E. Anthony. 1989. "Romantic Friendship: Male Intimacy and Middle-Class Youth in the Northern United States, 1800–1900." *Journal of Social History* 23, 1: 1–25.

—. 1993. *American Manhood: Transformations in Masculinity from the Revolution to the Modern Era*. New York: Basic Books.

Rovinsky, Alexander. 1901. "The Physician as a Social Factor." *Medical News* 79, November: 692.

Rowley, William D. 1996. *Reclaiming the Arid West: The Career of Francis G. Newlands*. Bloomington: Indiana University Press.

Roy, William G. 1997. *Socializing Capital: The Rise of the Large Industrial Corporation in America*. Princeton: Princeton University Press.

Rudolph, Frederick. 1962. *The American College and University: A History*. New York: Alfred A. Knopf.

Rudwick, Elliott. 1982. *Race Riot in East St. Louis*. Urbana: University of Illinois Press.

Runstedtler, Theresa. 2012. *Jack Johnson, Rebel Sojourner: Boxing in the Shadow of the Global Color Line*. Berkeley: University of California Press.

Runte, Alfred. 1979. *National Parks: The American Experience*. Lincoln: University of Nebraska Press.

Ruotsila, Markku. 2006. *John Spargo and American Socialism*. New York: Macmillan.

Rupp, Leila J. 1997. *Worlds of Women: The Making of an International Women's Movement*. Princeton: Princeton University Press.

—. 1999. *A Desired Past: A Short History of Same-Sex Love in America*. Chicago: University of Chicago Press.

Rusk, Jerrold G. 1970. "The Effect of the Australian Ballot Reform on Split Ticket Voting: 1876–1908." *American Political Science Review* 64, 4: 1220–1238.

Russell, Charles E. 1931. *Blaine of Maine*. New York: Cosmopolitan Book Corporation.

Russell, Edmund. 2001. *War and Nature: Fighting Humans and Insects with Chemicals from World War I to Silent Spring*. Cambridge: Cambridge University Press.

Russett, Cynthia Eagle. 1989. *Sexual Science: The Victorian Construction of Womanhood*. Cambridge: Harvard University Press.

Rutenbeck, Jeffrey B. 1995. "Newspaper Trends in the 1870s: Proliferation, Popularization, and Political Independence." *Journalism & Mass Communication Quarterly* 72: 361–375.

Ruthkow, Ira. 2006. *James A. Garfield*. New York: Times Books.

Rydell, Robert W. 1987. *All the World's a Fair: Visions of Empire at American International Expositions*. Chicago: University of Chicago Press.

—, and Rob Kroes. 2005. *Buffalo Bill in Bologna: The Americanization of the World, 1869–1922*. Chicago: University of Chicago Press.

Sachs, Aaron. 2013. *Arcadian America: The Death and Life of an Environmental Tradition*. New Haven: Yale University Press.

Sacks, Marcy S. 2006. *Before Harlem: the Black Experience In New York City Before World War I*. Philadelphia: University of Pennsylvania Press.

Sage, Leland. 1956. *William Boyd Allison: A Study in Practical Politics*. Iowa City: State Historical Society of Iowa.

Said, Edward. 1979. *Orientalism*. New York: Vintage Books.

Salamon, Lester. 1999. *America's Nonprofit Sector: A Primer*. 2nd ed. New York: The Foundation Center.

Saldin, Robert F. 2011. *War, the American State, and Politics Since 1898*. New York: Cambridge University Press.

Salem, Dorothy. 1990. *To Better Our World: Black Women in Organized Reform, 1890–1920*. Brooklyn: Carlson.

Salvatore, Nick. 1982. *Eugene V. Debs: Citizen and Socialist*. Urbana: University of Illinois Press.

Salyer, Lucy E. 1995. *Laws Harsh as Tigers: Chinese Immigrants and the Shaping of Modern Immigration Law*. Chapel Hill: University of North Carolina Press.

Sampsell-Willman, Kate. 2009. *Lewis Hine as Social Critic*. Jackson: University Press of Mississippi.

Sampson, Robert J. 2011. *Great American City: Chicago and the Enduring Neighborhood Effect*. Chicago: University of Chicago Press.

Sanchez Korrol, Virginia E. 1994. *From Colonia to Community: The History of Puerto Ricans in New York City*. Berkeley: University of California Press.

Sanchez, George J. 1995. *Becoming Mexican American: Ethnicity, Culture, and Identity in Chicano Los Angeles, 1900–1945*. New York: Oxford University Press.

—. 1999. "Race, Nation, and Culture in Recent Immigration Studies." *Journal of American Ethnic History* 18, 4: 66–84.

Sandeen, Ernest. 1970. *The Roots of Fundamentalism: British and American Millennarianism, 1800–1930*. Chicago: University of Chicago Press.

Sander, Kathleen Waters. 2008. *Mary Elizabeth Garrett: Society and Philanthropy in the Gilded Age*. Baltimore: Johns Hopkins University Press.

Sanders, Elizabeth. 1999. *Roots of Reform: Farmers, Workers, and the American State, 1877–1917*. Chicago: University of Chicago Press.

Sanders, Haywood T. 1980. "Paying for the 'Bloody Shirt': the Politics of Civil War Pensions." In *Political Benefits*, ed. Barry S. Rundquist. Lexington: D.C. Heath and Co.

Sanders, James. 1977. *The Education of an Urban Minority: Catholics in Chicago, 1833–1965* New York: Oxford University Press.

Sanders, Ronald. 1969. *The Downtown Jews: Portrait of an Immigrant Generation*. New York: Harper & Row.

—. 1987. *The Lower East Side Jews: An Immigrant Generation*. Mineola: Dover.

Sando, Joe S. 1982. *Nee Hemish: A History of Jemez Pueblo*. Albuquerque: University of New Mexico Press.

Sandoz, Mari. 2005. *Old Jules*. Lincoln: University of Nebraska Press.

Sarasohn, David. 1989. *The Party of Reform: Democrats in the Progressive Era*. Jackson: University Press of Mississippi.

Sarna, Jonathan. 2004. *American Judaism: A History*. New Haven: Yale University Press.

Satter, Beryl. 2001. *Each Mind a Kingdom: American Women, Sexual Purity, and the New Thought Movement, 1875–1920*. Berkeley: University of California Press.

Savage, Kirk. 1997. *Standing Soldiers, Kneeling Slaves: Race, War, and Monument in Nineteenth-Century America*. Princeton: Princeton University Press.

Sawyer, Laura Phillips. 2013. "Contested Meanings of Freedom: Workingmen's Wages, the Company Store System, and the Godcharles v. Wigeman Decision." *Journal of the Gilded Age and Progressive Era* 12, 3: 285–319.

Sawyer, Logan E. 2012. "Creating Hammer v. Dagenhart." *William & Mary Bill of Rights Journal* 21, 1: 62–127

Sawyers, June Skinner. 1991. *Chicago Portraits*. Chicago: Loyola University Press.

Saxton, Alexander. 1990. *The Rise and Fall of the White Republic: Class Politics and Mass Culture in Nineteenth Century America*. London: Verso.

Scanlon, Jennifer. 1995. *Inarticulate Longings: The Ladies' Home Journal, Gender and the Promise of Consumer Culture*. New York: Routledge.

Schäfer, Axel. 2000. *American Progressives and German Social Reform, 1875–1920: Social Ethics, Moral Control, and the Regulatory State in a Transatlantic Context*. Stuttgart: Steiner.

—. 2001. "W.E.B. Du Bois, German Social Thought, and the Racial Divide in American Progressivism, 1892–1909." *Journal of American History* 88: 925–49.

Schechter, Patricia A. 2001. *Ida B. Wells-Barnett and American Reform, 1880–1930*. Chapel Hill: University of North Carolina Press.

Schulman, Bruce. 2005. "Governing Nature, Nurturing Government: - Resource Management and the Development of the American State, 1900–1912," *Journal of Policy History* 17, 4: 375–403.

Schuessler, Jennifer. 2013. "In History Departments, It's Up With Capitalism." *New York Times*, April 6.

Schiller, Dan. 1981. *Objectivity and the News: The Public and the Rise of Commercial Journalism*. Philadelphia: University of Pennsylvania.

Schiller, Reuel E. 1997. "Regulation's Hidden History." Review of *The People's Welfare: Law and Regulation in Nineteenth-Century America*, by William Novak. *Reviews in American History* 25, 3: 416–21.

Schiller, Wendy J. 2006. "Building Careers and Courting Constituents: U.S. Senate Representation 1889–1924." *Studies in American Political Development* 20, 2: 185–197.

Schlesinger, Arthur M. 1944. "Biography of a Nation of Joiners." *American Historical Review*: 1–25.

—, and Charles Stewart III. 2014. *Electing the Senate: Indirect Democracy before the Seventeenth Amendment*. Princeton: Princeton University Press.

Schmidt, Leigh Eric. 2005. *Restless Souls: the Making of American Spirituality*. Berkeley: University of California Press.

Schneirov, Richard. 1998. *Labor and Urban Politics: Class Conflict and the Origins of Modern Liberalism in Chicago, 1864–97*. Urbana: University of Illinois Press.

—. 2006. "Thoughts on Periodizing the Gilded Age: Capital Accumulation, Society, and Politics, 1873–1898." *Journal of the Gilded Age and the Progressive Era* 5, 3: 189–224.

Schomburg Center for Research in Black Culture, The New York Public Library. 2011. "The African Diaspora in the Indian Ocean World." Accessed January 31. http://exhibitions.nypl.org/africansindianocean/index2.php

Schoonover, Thomas. 1991. *The United States in Central America 1860 - 1911: Episodes of Social Imperialism and Imperial Rivalry in the World System*. Durham: Duke University Press.

—. 2003. *Uncle Sam's War of 1898 and the Origins of Globalization*. Lexington: University Press of Kentucky.

Schott, Linda. 1997. *Reconstructing Women's Thoughts: The Women's International League for Peace and Freedom before World War II*. Stanford: Stanford University Press.

Schrag, Peter. 2011. *Not Fit for Our Society: Immigration and Nativism in America*. Berkeley: University of California Press.

Schrepfer, Susan R. 1983. *The Fight to Save the Redwoods: A History of Environmental Reform, 1917–1978*. Madison: University of Wisconsin Press.

Schudson, Michael. 1978. *Discovering the News: A Social History of American Newspapers*. New York: Basic Books.

Schulte Nordholdt, Jan Willem. 1991. *Woodrow Wilson: A Life for World Peace*. Berkeley: University of California Press.

Schultz, Mark Roman. 2006. *The Rural Face of White Supremacy: Beyond Jim Crow*. Urbana: University of Illinois Press.

Schultz, Stanley K. 1965. "The Morality of Politics: The Muckrakers' Vision of Democracy." *Journal of American History* 52: 527–547.

Schuster, David G. 2011. *Neurasthenic Nation: America's Search for Health, Happiness, and Comfort, 1869–1920*. New Brunswick: Rutgers University Press.

Schwabe, Klaus. 1985. *Woodrow Wilson, Revolutionary Germany, and Peacemaking, 1918–1919: Missionary Diplomacy and the Realities of Power*. Chapel Hill: University of North Carolina Press.

Schweiger, Beth Barton and Donald G. Mathews. 2004. *Religion in the American South: Protestants and Others in History and Culture*. Chapel Hill: University of North Carolina Press.

Schweiger, Beth Barton. 2000. *The Gospel Working Up: Progress and the Pulpit in Nineteenth-Century Virginia*. New York: Oxford University Press.

Scott, Ann Firor. 1970. *The Southern Lady: From Pedestal to Politics, 1830–1930*. Chicago: University of Chicago Press.

—. 1991. *Natural Allies: Women's Associations in American History*. Chicago: University of Illinois Press.

Scott, James C. 1985. *Weapons of the Weak: Everyday Forms of Peasant Resistance*. New Haven: Yale University Press.

Scott, Joan. 1986. "Gender: A Useful Category of Analysis." *The American Historical Review* 91, 5: 1053–1075.

—. 1999. *Gender and the Politics of History*, revised ed. New York: Columbia University Press.

Scott, William R. 1915. *Scientific Circulation Management for Newspapers*. New York: The Ronald Press Company.

Scully, Eileen. 2001. *Bargaining with the State from Afar: American Citizenship in Treaty Port China, 1844–1942*. New York: Columbia University Press.

Seager, R.H. 1993. *The Dawn of Religious Pluralism: Voices from the World's Parliament of Religions, 1893*. La Salle: Open Court.

Sealander, Judith. 1997. *Private Wealth and Public Life: Foundation Philanthropy and the Reshaping of American Social Policy from the Progressive Era to the New Deal*. Baltimore: Johns Hopkins University Press.

Searle, R. Newall. 1977. *Saving Quetico-Superior: A Land Set Apart*. St. Paul: Minnesota Historical Society Press.

Sears, Hal. 1977. *The Sex Radicals: Free Love in High Victorian America*. Lawrence: Regents Press of Kansas.

Sehat, David. 2008. *Americans All: The Cultural Gifts Movement*. Cambridge: Harvard University Press.

—. 2010. *The Myth of American Religious Freedom*. New York: Oxford University Press.

Selden, Steven. 2005. "Transforming Better Babies into Fitter Families: Archival Resources and the History of the American Eugenics Movement, 1908–1930." *Proceedings of the American Philosophical Society* 149, 2: 199–225.

Selig, Diana. 2008. *Americans All: The Cultural Gifts Movement*. Cambridge: Harvard University Press.

Sellers, Charles. 1991. *The Market Revolution: Jacksonian America, 1815–1846*. New York: Oxford University Press.

Sellers, Christopher. 1997. *Hazards of the Job: From Industrial Disease to Environmental Health Science*. Chapel Hill: University of North Carolina Press.

Senior, Olive. 2014. *Dying to Better Themselves: West Indians and the Building of the Panama Canal.* Jamaica: University of West Indies Press.

Serrin, Judith and William Serrin. 2002. *Muckraking! The Journalism That Changed America.* New York: New Press.

Sewall, Mae Wright. 1915. "Women, World War and Permanent Peace," *Proceedings of International Conference of Women Workers to Promote Peace.* San Francisco.

Seward, William H. 1873. *William H. Seward's Travels Around the World. Ed. by Olive Risley Seward … With two hundred illustrations.* New York: D. Appleton and Co.

Sewell, Mike. 1991. "'All the English-Speaking Race is in Mourning': The Assassination of President Garfield and Anglo-American Relations." *Historical Journal* 34: 665–86

Sexton, Jay. 2014. "William H. Seward in the World." *Journal of the Civil War Era* 4, December: 404–05.

Shah, Courtney Q. 2010. "'Against Their Own Weakness': Policing Sexuality and Women in San Antonio, Texas, during World War I." *Journal of the History of Sexuality* 19, 3: 458–82.

—. 2015. *Sex Ed, Segregated.* New York: University of Rochester Press.

Shah, Nayan. 2001. *Contagious Divides: Epidemics and Race In San Francisco's Chinatown.* Berkeley: University of California Press.

—. 2011. *Stranger Intimacy: Contesting Race, Sexuality, and Law in the North American West.* Berkeley: University of California Press.

Shales, Ezra. 2010. *Made in Newark: Cultivating Industrial Arts and Civic Identity in the Progressive Era.* New Brunswick: Rutgers University Press.

Shaw, Albert. 1910. *A Cartoon History of Roosevelt's Career.* New York: The Review of Reviews Co.

Sheila M. Rothman. 1995. *Living in the Shadow of Death: Tuberculosis and the Social Experience of Illness in American History.* Baltimore: Johns Hopkins University Press.

Shepperson, George. 1966. "The African Diaspora—or the African Abroad." *African Forum: A Quarterly Journal of African Affairs* 1, 2: 76–93.

Shi, David E. 1995. *Facing Facts: Realism in American Thought and Culture, 1850–1920.* New York: Oxford University Press.

Shorter, Edward. 1993. *From Paralysis to Fatigue: A History of Psychosomatic Illness in the Modern Era.* New York: Free Press.

Shpaḳ-Lisaḳ, Rivḳah. 1989. *Pluralism & Progressives: Hull House and the New Immigrants, 1890–1919.* Chicago: University of Chicago Press.

Shulman, Peter A. 2003. "'Science Can Never Demobilize': The United States Navy and Petroleum Geology, 1898–1924." *History and Technology* 19, 4: 365–385.

Shumsky, Neil Larry. 1986. "Tacit Acceptance: Respectable Americans and Segregated Prostitution, 1870–1910." *Journal of Social History* 19, 4: 665–679.

Sidak, J. Gregory. 1997. *Foreign Investment in American Telecommunications.* Chicago: University of Chicago Press.

Siegel, James. 1999. *Fetish, Recognition, Revolution.* Princeton: Princeton University Press.

Siegel, Reva B. 2004. "A Short History of Sexual Harassment." *In Directions in Sexual Harassment Law*, ed. Catharine A. MacKinnon & Reva B. Siegel, 1–39. New Haven: Yale University Press.

Siegel, Stephen A. 1990. "Historism in Late Nineteenth Century Constitutional Thought." *Wisconsin Law Review* 6: 1431–1547.

—. 1995. "Joel Bishop's Orthodoxy." *Law and History Review* 13, 2: 215–59.

—. 2002. "The Revision Thickens." *Law and History Review* 20, 3: 631–37.

—. 2004. "Francis Wharton's Orthodoxy: God, Historical Jurisprudence, and Classical Legal Thought." *American Journal of Legal History* 46, 4: 422–46.

Sievers, Harry J. 1968. *Benjamin Harrison, Hoosier President: Volume 3, The White House and After.* Indianapolis: Bobbs Merrill.

Silber, Nina. 1997. *The Romance of Reunion: Northerners and the South, 1865–1900.* Chapel Hill: The University of North Carolina Press.

Silber, Norman J. 2001. *A Corporate Form of Freedom: The Emergence of the Nonprofit Sector.* Boulder: Westview.

Silverstein, Alan. 1994. *Alternatives to Assimilation: The Response of Reform Judaism to American Culture, 1840–1930.* Hanover: University Press of New England.

Simkins, Francis B. 1944. *Pitchfork Ben Tillman, South Carolinian.* Baton Rouge: Lousiana State University Press.

Simmons, Christina. 2009. *Making Marriage Modern: Women's Sexuality from the Progressive Era to World War II.* New York: Oxford University Press.

Simon, John G. 1987. "The Tax Treatment of Nonprofit Organizations: A Review of Federal and State Policies." In *The Nonprofit Sector: A Research Handbook*, ed. Walter W. Powell, 67–98. New Haven: Yale University Press.

Simon, Linda. 2004. *Dark Light: Electricity and Anxiety from the Telegraph to the X-Ray.* San Diego: Harcourt Brace Jovanovich.

Sims, Anastatia. 1997. *The Power of Femininity in the New South: Women's Organizations and Politics in North Carolina, 1880–1930.* Columbia: University of South Carolina Press.

Sinclair, Upton. 1906a. *The Jungle.* New York: Doubleday, Page.

—. 1906b. *The Jungle.* New York: The Jungle Publishing Company.

—. 1919. *The Brass Check: A Study of American Journalism.* Pasadena: Upton Sinclair.

Sinn, Elizabeth. 2014. "Pacific Ocean: Highway to Gold Mountain, 1850–1900." *Pacific Historical Review,* Special Issue: Conversations on Transpacific History 83, 2: 220–37.

Sitton, Tom. 1992. *John Randolph Haynes.* Palo Alto: Stanford University Press.

Sklansky, Jeffrey. 2002. *The Soul's Economy. Market Society and Selfhood in American Thought, 1820–1920.* Chapel Hill: University of North Carolina Press.

—. 2004. "Progress and Populism." *Reviews in American History* 32, 1.

—. 2014. "Labor, Money, and the Financial Turn in the History of Capitalism." *Labor: Studies in Working-Class Histories of the Americas* 11, 1: 23–46.

—. 2017. *Sovereign of the Market: The Money Question in Early America.* Chicago: University of Chicago Press.

Sklar, Kathryn Kish. 1993. "The Historical Foundations of Women's Power in the Creation of the American Welfare State, 1830–1930." In *Mothers of a New World: Maternalist Politics and the Origins of Welfare States*, ed. Seth Koven and Sonya Michel, 43–93. New York: Routledge.

—. 1995a. *Florence Kelley and the Nation's Work: The Rise of Women's Political Culture, 1830–1900.* New Haven: Yale University Press.

—. 1995b. "Two Political Cultures in the Progressive Era: The National Consumer's League and the American Association for

Labor Legislation." In *U.S. History as Women's History*, eds. Linda Kerber et al., 36–62. Chapel Hill: University of North Carolina Press.

—. 2001. "Florence Kelley." In *Women Building Chicago: A Biographical Dictionary, 1790–1990*, ed. Rima Lunin Schultz and Adele Hast. Bloomington: University of Indiana Press.

—, Barbara Reeves-Ellington, and Connie Shemo, eds. 2010. *Competing Kingdoms: Women, Mission, Nation, and Empire*. Durham: Duke University Press.

Sklar, Martin J. 1960. "Woodrow Wilson and the Political-Economy of Modern States Liberalism. *Studies on the Left* 1: 17–47.

—. 1988. *The Corporate Reconstruction of American Capitalism, 1890–1916: The Market, the Law, and Politics*. New York: Cambridge University Press.

Sklar, Robert. 1975. *Movie-Made America: A Cultural History of American Movies*. New York: Random House.

Skocpol, Theda. 1980. "Political Response to Capitalist Crisis: Neo-Marxist Theories of the State and the Case of the New Deal." *Politics and Society* 10: 155–201. DOI: 10.1177/003232928001000202

—. 1982. *Building a New American State: The Expansion of National Administrative Capacities: 1877–1920*. Cambridge: Cambridge University Press.

—. 1992. *Protecting Soldiers and Mothers: The Political Origins of Social Policy in the United States*. Cambridge: The Belknap Press of Harvard University Press.

—, and Fiorina, Morris P. 1999. *Civic Engagement in American Democracy*. New York: Russell Sage Foundation for Brookings Institution Press.

—, M. Ganz, and Z. Munson. 2000. "A Nation of Organizers: The Institutional Origins of Civic Voluntarism in the United States." *American Political Science Review* 94, 3: 527–546.

Skok, Deborah A. 2008. "The Historiography of Catholic Laywomen and Progressive Era Reform." *U.S. Catholic Historian* 26, 1: 1–22.

Skowronek, Stephen. 1982. *Building a New American State: The Expansion of National Administrative Capacities, 1877–1920*. Cambridge: Cambridge University Press.

Slate, Nico. 2011. *Colored Cosmopolitanism: The Shared Struggle for Freedom in the United States and India*. Cambridge: Harvard University Press.

Slavitsky, Gail, Laurette E. McCarthy, and Charles H. Duncan. 2013. *The New Spirit: American Art in the Armory Show, 1913*. Montclair: Montclair Art Museum.

Sleeper-Smith, et al., eds. 2015. *Why You Can't Teach United States History without American Indians*. Chapel Hill: University of North Carolina Press.

Sloan, Douglas. 1994. *Faith and Knowledge: Mainline Protestantism and American Higher Education*. Louisville: Westminster John Knox Press.

Smalley, Andrea. 2005. "'Our Lady Sportsmen': Gender Class, and Conservation in Sport Hunting Magazines, 1873–1920." *Journal of the Gilded Age and Progressive Era* 4: 355–380.

Smil, Vaclav. 2005. *Creating the Twentieth Century: Technical Innovations of 1867–1914 and Their Lasting Impact*. New York: Oxford University Press.

Smith, Carl. 1995. *Urban Disorder and the Shape of Belief*. Chicago: University of Chicago Press.

Smith, Daniel Scott. 1973. "Family Limitation, Sexual Control, and Domestic Feminism in Victorian America." *Feminist Studies* 1, 3/4: 40–57.

Smith, Douglas J. 2002. *Managing White Supremacy: Race, Politics, and Citizenship in Jim Crow Virginia*. Chapel Hill: University of North Carolina Press.

Smith, Henry Nash. 1950. *Virgin Land*. Cambridge: Harvard University Press.

Smith, Sherry. 2000. *Reimagining Indians: Native Americans through Anglo Eyes, 1880–1940*. New York: Oxford University Press.

—. 2010. "Comments: Native Americans and Indian Policy in the Progressive Era." *Journal of the Gilded Age and Progressive Era* 9: 503–507.

Smith, Stacey L. 2014. *Freedom's Frontier: California and the Struggle Over Unfree Labor, Emancipation, and Reconstruction*. Chapel Hill: University of North Carolina Press.

Smith, Theodore Clarke. 1925. *The Life and Letters of James Abram Garfield*. 2 volumes. New Haven: Yale University Press.

Smith-Rosenberg, Carroll. 1973. "The Female Animal: Medical and Biological Views of Woman and Her Role in Nineteenth-Century America." *Journal of American History* 60, 2: 332–356.

—. 1975. "The Female World of Love and Ritual." *Signs*, 1: 1–29.

—. 1985. *Disorderly Conduct: Visions of Gender in Victorian America*. New York: Alfred A. Knopf.

Smoak, Gregory. 2006. *Ghost Dances and Identity: Prophetic Religion and American Indian Ethnogenesis in the Nineteenth Century*. Berkeley: University of California Press.

Smuts, Alice Boardman. 2006. *Seen and Heard: The Scientific Study of Children. Science in the Service of Children, 1893–1935*. New Haven: Yale University Press.

Smythe, Ted Curtis. 1980. "The Reporter, 1880–1900: Working Conditions and Their Influence on the News." *Journalism History* 7: 1–10.

Snow, Dean R. 1994. *The Iroquois*. Cambridge: Blackwell Publishers.

Snow, Jennifer C. 2003. "A Border Made of Righteousness: Protestant Missionaries, Asian Immigration, and Ideologies of Race, 1850–1924." PhD diss., Columbia University.

Socolofsky, Homer E. and Allan B. Spetter. 1987. *Presidency of Benjamin Harrison*. Lawrence: University Press of Kansas.

Sokal, Michael K. 2010. "Scientific Biography, Cognative Deficits, and Laboratory Practice. James McKeen Cattell and Early American Experimental Psychology, 1880–1904." *ISIS* 101: 531–554.

Solnit, Rebecca. 2003. *River of Shadows. Eadweard Muybridge and the Technological Wild West*. New York: Penguin Press.

Soluri, John. 2006. *Banana Cultures: Agriculture, Consumption, and Environmental Change in Honduras and the United States*. Austin: University of Texas Press.

Sommerville, Diane Miller. 2004. *Rape & Race in the Nineteenth-Century South*. Chapel Hill: University of North Carolina Press.

Sorin, Gerald. 1985. *The Prophetic Minority: American Jewish Immigration Radicals, 1880–1920*. Bloomington: Indiana University.

Sotiropoulos, Karen. 2006. *Staging Race: Black Performers in Turn of the Century America*. Cambridge: Harvard University Press.

Soyer, Daniel. 1997. *Jewish Immigrant Associations and American Identity in New York, 1900–1939*. Cambridge: Harvard University Press.

Spain, Daphne. 2001. *How Women Saved the City*. Minneapolis: University of Minnesota Press.

Spargo, John. 1903. "The Shame of Minneapolis: The Rescue and Redemption of a City That Was Sold Out." *McClure's Magazine* 20: 227–239.

—. 1906. *The Bitter Cry of the Children*. New York: Macmillan.

Sparrow, Bartholomew H. 2006. *The* Insular Cases *and the Emergence of American Empire*. Lawrence: University Press of Kansas.

Spear, Alan. 1967. *Black Chicago*. Chicago: University of Chicago Press.

Spear, Robert J. 2005. *The Great Gypsy Moth War: The History of the First Campaign in Massachusetts to Eradicate the Gypsy Moth, 1890–1901*. Boston: University of Massachusetts Press.

Spence, Mark David. 1999. *Dispossessing the Wilderness: Indian Removal and the Making of the National Parks*. New York: Oxford University Press.

Spetter, Allan. 1993. "Rev. Harry J. Sievers, S.J., the Arthur Jordan Foundation and the Biography of President Benjamin Harrison." *Presidential Studies Quarterly* 23: 555–65.

Spiro, Jonathan Peter. 2009. *Defending the Master Race: Conservation, Eugenics, and the Legacy of Madison Grant*. Burlington: University of Vermont Press.

Spivak, Gayatri. 1988. "Can the Subaltern Speak?" In *Marxism and The Interpretation of Culture*, ed. Carey Nelson and Lawrence Grossberg. Urbana: University of Illinois Press.

Sproat, John G. 1968. *"The Best Men": Liberal Reformers in the Gilded Age*. New York: Oxford University Press.

Spruhan, Paul. 2006. "A Legal History of Blood Quantum in Federal Indian Law to 1935." *South Dakota Law Review* 51: 24–46.

St. John, Rachel C. 2011. *Line in the Sand: A History of the Western U.S.-Mexico Border*. Princeton: Princeton University Press.

Stage, Sarah and Virginia B. Vincenti, eds. 1997. *Rethinking Home Economics: Women and the History of a Profession*. Ithaca: Cornell University Press.

Stahr, Walter. 2012. *A Thread across the Atlantic; Seward: Lincoln's Indispensable Man*. New York: Simon and Schuster.

Stampp, Kenneth. 1965. *The Era of Reconstruction, 1865–1877*. New York: Alfred A. Knopf.

Standing Bear, Luther. (1933) 1978. *Land of the Spotted Eagle*. Boston: Houghton Mifflin. Reprint, Lincoln: University of Nebraska Press. Citations refer to the University of Nebraska edition.

Stanley, Amy Dru. 1998. *From Bondage to Contract: Wage Labor, Marriage, and the Market in the Age of Slave Emancipation*. Cambridge: Cambridge University Press.

Stansell, Christine. 2000a. *American Moderns: Bohemian New York and the Creation of a New Century*. New York: Henry Holt and Co.

—. 2000b. *American Moderns: Bohemian New York and the Creation of a New Century*. Princeton: Princeton University Press.

Stanton, Elizabeth Cady. 1892. *The Woman's Column*. January.

Starr, Paul. 1982. *The Social Transformation of American Medicine*. New York: Basic Books.

Stead, William T. 1894. *If Christ Came to Chicago*. Chicago: Laird & Lee Publishers.

—. 1901 (1972). *The Americanization of the World, or, The Trend of the Twentieth Century*. Reprint. New York: Garland.

Steel, Frances. 2013. "Lines Across the Sea: Trans-Pacific Passenger Shipping in the Age of Steam." In *The Routledge History of Western Empires*, ed. Robert Aldrich and Kirsten McKenzie, 315–29. New York: Routledge.

Steffens, Lincoln. 1904. *The Shame of the Cities*. New York: McClure, Phillips and Co.

—. 1906. *Struggle for Self-Government; being an attempt to trace American political corruption to its sources in six states of the United States, with a dedication to the czar*. New York: McClure, Phillips & Co.

—. 1931. *Autobiography of Lincoln Steffens*. New York: Harcourt, Brace, and Company.

Stephens, Randall. 2008. *The Fire Spreads: Holiness and Pentecostalism in the American South*. Cambridge: Harvard University Press.

Stern, Alexandra. 2005. *Eugenic Nation: Faults and Frontiers of Better Breeding in Modern America*. Berkeley: University of California Press.

Stevens, Rosemary. 1989. *In Sickness and in Wealth: American Hospitals in the Twentieth Century*. New York: Basic Books.

Stewart, Jacqueline Najuma. 2005. *Migrating to the Movies: Cinema and Black Urban Modernity*. Berkeley: University of California Press.

Stewart, Jane Agnes. 1906. *The Frances Willard Book*. Philadelphia: The Current Syndicate.

Stewart, Watt, 1946. *Henry Meiggs: Yankee Pizarro*. Durham: Duke University Press.

Stidger, William L. 1933. *Edwin Markham*. New York: Abingdon Press.

Stiles, T. J. 2003. *Jesse James: Last Rebel of the Civil War*. New York: Vintage.

Stivers, Camilla. 2000. *Bureau Men, Settlement Women: Constructing Public Administration in the Progressive Era*. Lawrence: University Press of Kansas.

Stocking Jr., George W. 1985. *Objects and Others*. Madison: University of Wisconsin Press.

Stolberg, Benjamin. 1926. "The Man behind the Times." *Atlantic Monthly* 138: 721–730.

Stoler, Ann. 2006. *Haunted By Empire: Geographies of Intimacy in North American History*. Durham: Duke University Press.

Stoneley, Peter. 1996. "Rewriting the Gold Rush: Twain, Harte, and Homosociality." *Journal of American Studies* 30, 2: 189–209.

Stowell, Daniel W. 1998. *Rebuilding Zion: The Religious Reconstruction of the South, 1863–1877*. New York: Oxford University Press.

Stowell, David O. 1999. *Streets, Railroads, and the Great Strike of 1877*. Chicago: University of Chicago Press.

Stradling, David. 1999. *Smokestacks and Progressives: Environmentalists, Engineers, and Air Quality in America, 1881—1951*. Baltimore: Johns Hopkins University Press.

Striner, Richard. 2014. *Woodrow Wilson and World War I: A Burden Too Great to Bear*. Lanham: Rowman & Littlefield.

Strom, Claire. 2009. *Making Catfish Bait Out of Government Boys: The Fight against Cattle Ticks and the Transformation of the Yeoman South*. Athens: University of Georgia Press.

Stromquist, Shelton. 2006. *Reinventing 'The People': The Progressive Movement, the Class Problem, and the Origins of Modern Liberalism*. Urbana: University of Illinois Press.

Suggs, Henry Lewis. 1983. *The Black Press in the South, 1865–1979.* Westport: Greenwood Press.

—. 1996. *The Black Press in the Middle West, 1865–1985.* Westport: Greenwood Press.

Suisman, David. 2012. *Selling Sounds: The Commercial Revolution in American Music.* Cambridge: Harvard University Press.

Sumner, Charles. 1870. *The Works of Charles Sumner.* Boston: Lee and Shepard.

Sundquist, James L. 1983. *Dynamics of the Party System: Alignment and Realignment of Political Parties in the United States.* Revised Edition. Washington DC: The Brookings Institution.

Supple, Barry E. 1957. "A Business Elite: German-Jewish Financiers in Nineteenth-Century New York." *Business History Review* 31: 143–78. DOI:10.2307/3111848.

Suri, Jeremi. 2011. *Liberty's Surest Guardian: American Nation-Building from the Founders to Obama.* New York: Free Press/ Simon & Schuster.

Susman, Warren. 1985. *Culture as History: The Transformation of American Society in the Twentieth Century.* New York: Pantheon.

Sutton, Matthew Avery. 2014. *American Apocalypse: A History of Modern American Evangelicalism.* Cambridge: Harvard University Press.

Swinth, Kirsten. 2001. *Painting Professionals: Women Artists and the Development of Modern American Art, 1870–1930.* Chapel Hill: University of North Carolina Press.

Taft, William Howard. 1912. "Acceptance Address." August 1.

Tamanaha, Brian Z. 2010. *Beyond the Formalist-Realist Divide: The Role of Politics in Judging.* Princeton: Princeton University Press.

Tarbell, Ida M. 1904. *The History of the Standard Oil Company.* New York: McClure, Phillips and Co.

—. 1939. *All in the Day's Work.* New York: Macmillan.

Tate, E. Mowbray. 1986. *Transpacific Steam: The Story of Steam Navigation from the Pacific Coast of North America to the Far East and the Antipodes, 1867–1941.* New York: Cornwall Books.

Taves, Ann. 1999. *Fits, Trances and Vision: Experiencing Religion and Explaining Experience from Wesley to James.* Princeton: Princeton University Press.

Taylor III, Joseph E. 1999. *Making Salmon: An Environmental History of the Northwest Fisheries Crisis.* Seattle: University of Washington Press.

Taylor, Frederick Winslow. 1913. *Principles of Scientific Management.* New York: Harper and Brothers.

Taylor, Quintard. 1998. *In Search of the Racial Frontier: African Americans in the American West.* New York: W. W. Norton.

Taylor, Sandra C. 1984. *Advocate of Understanding: Sidney Gulick and the Search for Peace with Japan.* Kent: Kent State University Press.

Teaford, Jon C. 1984. *The Unheralded Triumph, City Government In America, 1870–1900.* Baltimore: Johns Hopkins University Press.

—. 1993. *Cities of the Heartland.* Bloomington: Indiana University Press.

Teisch, Jessica. 2005. "'Home Is Not So Very Far Away': Californian Engineers in South Africa, 1868–1915." *Australian Economic History Review* 45, July: 139–60.

—. 2010. "Sweetening the Urban Marketplace: California's Hawaiian Outpost." In *Cities and Nature in the American West*, ed. Char Miller, 17–33. Reno: University of Nevada Press.

—. 2011. *Engineering Nature: Water, Development, and the Global Spread of American Environmental Expertise.* Chapel Hill: University of North Carolina Press.

Terrill, Tom E. 1973. *The Tariff, Politics, and American Foreign Policy, 1874–1901.* Westport: Greenwood.

Terry, Jennifer. 1999. *An American Obsession: Science, Medicine, and Homosexuality in Modern Society.* Chicago: University of Chicago Press.

Testi, Arnaldo. 1995. "The Gender of Reform Politics: Theodore Roosevelt and the Culture of Masculinity." *Journal of American History* 81, March: 1509–33.

Thelen, David P. 1970. "Social Tensions and the Origins of Progressivism." *Journal of American History* 56: 323–341.

—. 1976. *Robert La Follette and the Insurgent Spirit.* Boston: Little, Brown.

Theriot, Nancy. 1993. "Women's Voices in Nineteenth-Century Medical Discourse: A Step Toward Deconstructing Science." *Signs* 19: 1–31.

Thernstrom, Stephan. 1964. *Poverty and Progress: Social Mobility In a Nineteenth Century City.* Cambridge: Harvard University Press.

Thiesen, William H. *Industrializing American Shipbuilding: The Transformation of Ship Design and Construction, 1820–1920.* Gainesville: University Press of Florida.

Thistlethwaite, Frank. 1964. "Migration from Europe Overseas in the Nineteenth and Twentieth Century." In *Population Movements in Modern European History*, ed. Herbert Moller. New York: Macmillan.

Thompson, E.P. 1963. *The Making of the English Working Class.* London: Victor Gollancz Ltd.

Thompson, John A. 2002. *Woodrow Wilson.* London: Longman.

Thompson, Margaret S. 1985. *The "Spider Web": Congress and Lobbying in the Age of Grant.* Ithaca: Cornell University Press.

Throntveit, Trygve. 2011. "The Fable of the Fourteen Points: Woodrow Wilson and National Self-Determination." *Diplomatic History* 35: 445–481. doi:10.1111/j.1467-7709.2011.00959.x.

Thurtle, Phillip. 2007. *The Emergence of Genetic Rationality.* Seattle: University of Washington Press.

Tichenor, I. T. 1901. "The Home Mission Board of the Southern Baptist Convention, in Albert Henry Newman." *A Century of Baptist Achievement.* Philadelphia: American Baptist Publication Society.

Tifft, Susan E. and Alex S. Jones. 1999. *The Trust: The Private and Powerful Family behind the New York Times.* Boston: Little, Brown.

Tilchin, William N. 1997. *Theodore Roosevelt and the British Empire: A Study in Presidential Statecraft.* New York: St. Martin's Press.

—. 2014. "Then and Since: The Remarkable and Enduring Foreign Policy of Theodore Roosevelt." *Theodore Roosevelt Association Journal* Winter-Spring: 45–51.

Tocqueville, Alexis de. 2000. *Democracy in America.* Ed. Harvey C. Mansfield and Delba Winthrop. Chicago: University of Chicago Press.

Tolley, Kemp. *Yangtze Patrol: The U.S. Navy in China.* Annapolis: Naval Institute, 1971.

Tomchuk, Travis. 2015. *Transnational Radicals: Italian Anarchists in Canada and the U.S., 1915–1940.* Winnipeg: University of Manitoba Press.

Tomes, Nancy. 1999. *The Gospel of Germs: Men, Women, and the Microbe in American Life.* Cambridge: Harvard University Press.

—. 2005. "The Great Medicine Show Revisited." *Bulletin of the History of Medicine* 79, Winter: 627–663.

Tomkins, Mary E. 1974. *Ida M. Tarbell.* New York: Twayne.

Tomlins, Christopher L. 1985. *The State and the Unions: Labor Relations, Law, and the Organized Labor Movement in America, 1880–1960.* Cambridge: Cambridge University Press.

—. 1993. *Law, Labor, and Ideology in the Early American Republic.* New York: Cambridge University Press.

—. 2008. "Necessities of State: Police, Sovereignty, and the Constitution." *Journal of Policy History* 20, 1: 47–63.

Tone, Andrea. 1996. *Devices & Desires: A History of Contraceptives in America.* New York: Hill and Wang.

Tooze, Adam. 2014. *The Deluge: The Great War, America and the Remaking of the Global Order, 1916–1931.* New York: Viking.

Trachtenberg, Alan. 1979. *Brooklyn Bridge: Fact and Symbol.* 2nd ed. Chicago: University of Chicago Press.

—. 1982. *The Incorporation of America: Culture and Society in the Gilded Age.* New York: Hill and Wang.

Tracy, Sarah W. 2005. *Alcoholism in America: From Reconstruction to Prohibition.* Baltimore: Johns Hopkins University Press.

Transatlantic Steamship Routes: Supplement to the Pilot Chart of the North Atlantic Ocean, January, 1893. http://texashistory.unt.edu/ark:/67531/metapth190428/m1/1/zoom/

Trask, David F. 1981. *The War with Spain in 1898.* New York: Macmillan.

Trask, Jeffrey. 2012. *Things American: Art Museums and Civic Culture in the Progressive Era.* Philadelphia: University of Pennsylvania Press.

Trattner, Walter I. 1974. *From Poor Law to Welfare State: A History of Social Welfare in America.* New York: The Free Press.

Trefousse, Hans L. 2002. *Rutherford B. Hayes.* New York: Times Books.

Trilling, Lionel. 1972. *Sincerity and Authenticity.* Cambridge: Harvard University Press.

Trimberger, Ellen Kay. 1983. "Feminism, Men, and Modern Love: Greenwich Village, 1900–1925." In *Powers of Desire: The Politics of Sexuality,* ed. Ann Snitow, Christine Stansell, and Sharon Thompson, 131–152. New York: Monthly Review Press.

Tripp, C. A. 1997. *The Intimate World of Abraham Lincoln.* New York: Free Press.

Tripp, Steven Elliott. 1997. *Yankee Town, Southern City: Race and Class Relations in Civil War Lynchburg.* New York: New York University Press.

Trotter, Joe William. 2006. *Black Milwaukee.* Urbana: University of Illinois Press.

Troy, Gil. 1997. "Money and Politics: The Oldest Connection." *The Wilson Quarterly* 21, 3: 14–32.

Truett, Samuel. 2006. *Fugitive Landscapes: The Forgotten History of the U.S.-Mexico Borderlands.* New Haven: Yale University Press.

Tucker, Richard P. 2000. *Insatiable Appetite: The United States and the Ecological Degradation of the Tropical World.* Berkeley: University of California Press.

—. 2007. *Woodrow Wilson and the Great War: Reconsidering America's Neutrality, 1914–1917.* Charlottesville: University of Virginia Press.

Tulis, Jeffrey. 1987. *The Rhetorical Presidency.* Princeton: Princeton University Press.

Turner, Elizabeth Hayes. 1997. *Women, Culture and Community: Religion and Reform in Galveston 1880–1920.* New York: Oxford University Press.

Turner, Frederick Jackson. 1894. "The Significance of the Frontier in American History." *American Historical Review.*

—. 1920. *The Frontier in American History.* Reprint. New York: Holt, Rinehart, and Winston.

Turner, George Kibbe. 1907. "The City of Chicago: A Study of the Great Immoralities." *McClure's Magazine* 28: 575–592.

—. 1909. "Tammany's Control of New York by Professional Criminals: A Study of a New Period of Decadence in the Popular Government of Great Cities." *McClure's Magazine* 33: 117–134.

Turner, Steven. 2011. "Changing Images of the Inclined Plane, 1880–1920: A Case Study of a Revolution in American Scientific Education." In *Learning By Doing. Experiments and Instruments in the History of Science Teaching,* ed. Peter Heering and Roland Wittje, 207–242. Stuttgart: Franz Steiner Verlag.

Tuttle, William M. 1970. *Race Riot: Chicago in the Red Summer of 1919.* 1st ed. New York: Atheneum.

—. 1996. *Race Riot.* Urbana: University of Illinois Press.

Twain, Mark (Samuel Clemens) and Charles Dudley Warner. 1873. *The Gilded Age: A Tale of Today.* New York: American Publishing Company.

—. 1878. "Poor Little Stephen Girard," *Carleton's Popular Readings.* New York: G.W. Carleton and Company.

Tweed, Thomas A. 2000. *The American Encounter with Buddhism, 1844–1912.* Chapel Hill: University of North Carolina Press.

Twiss, Benjamin R. 1942. *Lawyers and the Constitution; How Laissez Faire Came to the Supreme Court.* London: H. Milford, Oxford University Press.

Tyrrell, Ian. 1991. *Woman's World/Woman's Empire: The Woman's Christian Temperance Union in International Perspective, 1880–1930.* Chapel Hill: University of North Carolina Press.

—. 1999. *True Gardens of the Gods: Californian-Australian Environmental Reform, 1860–1930.* Berkeley: University of California Press.

—. 2007a. "Looking Eastward: Pacific and Global Perspectives on American History in the Nineteenth and Early Twentieth Centuries." *Japanese Journal of American Studies* 18: 41–57.

—. 2007b. *Transnational Nation: United States History in Global Perspective since 1789.* New York: Palgrave Macmillan.

—. 2008. "Transatlantic Progressivism in Women's Temperance and Suffrage." In *Britain and Transnational Progressivism,* ed. David Gutzke, 133–48. New York: Palgrave Macmillan.

—. 2009. "Empire in American History." In *Colonial Crucible: Empire in the Making of the Modern American State,* ed. Alfred W. McCoy and Francisco A. Scarano, 541–56. Madison: University of Wisconsin Press.

—. 2010. *Reforming the World: The Creation of America's Moral Empire.* Princeton: Princeton University Press.

—. 2015a. *Crisis of the Wasteful Nation: Empire and Conservation in Theodore Roosevelt's America.* Chicago: University of Chicago Press.

—. 2015b. *Transnational Nation: United States History in Global Perspective since 1789.* 2nd edition. Basingstoke: Palgrave Macmillan.

Uekoetter, Frank. 2009. *The Age of Smoke, Environmental Policy in Germany and the United States, 1880–1970.* Pittsburgh: University of Pittsburgh Press.

—. 2013. "Conservation: America's Environmental Modernism." In *Fractured Modernity: America Confronts Modern Times, 1890s to 1940s,* ed. Thomas Welskopp and Alan Lessoff, 81–96. Munich: Oldenbourg Verlag.

Ullman, Sharon R. 1997. *Sex Seen: The Emergence of Modern Sexuality in America.* Berkeley: University of California Press.

Underhill, Lois Beachy. 1996. *The Woman Who Ran for President: The Many Lives of Victoria Woodhull.* New York: Penguin.

Unger, Nancy C. 2000. *Fighting Bob La Follette: The Righteous Reformer.* Chapel Hill: University of North Carolina Press.

—. 2008. *Fighting Bob La Follette: The Righteous Reformer.* Second edition. Madison: Wisconsin Historical Society Press.

—. 2012. *Beyond Nature's Housekeepers: American Women in Environmental History.* New York: Oxford University Press.

—. 2016. *Belle La Follette: Progressive Era Reformer.* New York: Routledge.

United States Bureau of the Census. 1929. *Census of Religious Bodies: 1926: Lutherans. Statistics, History, Doctrine and Organization.* Consolidated Report. Washington, DC: United States Government Printing Office.

United States Office of Education. 1914. *Annual Report of the Commissioner of Education*, vol. 1. Washington, DC: United States Government Printing Office.

Unterman, Katherine. 2015. *Uncle Sam's Policemen: The Pursuit of Fugitives across Borders.* Cambridge: Harvard University Press.

Upchurch, Thomas A. 2004. *Legislating Racism: The Billion Dollar Congress and the Birth of Jim Crow.* Lexington: University Press of Kentucky.

Urban, Andrew T. 2015. "The Advantages of Empire: Chinese Servants and Conflicts over Settler Domesticity in the 'White Pacific,' 1870–1900." In *Making the Empire Work: Labor and United States Imperialism* ed. Daniel E. Bender and Jana Lipman, 185–207. New York: New York University Press.

Urofsky, Melvin I. 1985. "State Courts and Protective Legislation During the Progressive Era: A Reevaluation." *Journal of American History* 72, 1: 63–91.

Usselman, Steven W., and Richard R. John. 2006. "Patent Politics: Intellectual Property, the Railroad Industry, and the Problem of Monopoly." *Journal of Policy History* 18, 1: 96–125.

Valaik, J. David. 1993. *Theodore Roosevelt, an American Hero in Caricature.* Buffalo: Western New York Heritage Institute of Canisius College.

Vale, Thomas R. 1995. "Mountains and Moisture in the West." In *The Mountainous West*, ed. William Wyckoff and Lary M. Dilsaver, 141–165. Lincoln: University of Nebraska Press.

Valelly, Richard. M. 2009. "The Reed Rules and Republican Party Building: A New Look." *Studies in American Political Development* 23, 2: 115–42.

Van Campen, Cretien. 2008. *The Hidden Sense. Synesthesia in Art and Science.* Cambridge: Massachusetts Institute of Technology Press.

Van Hook, Bailey. 1996. *Angels of Art: Women and Art in American Society, 1876–1914.* University Park: Pennsylvania State University Press.

—. 2003. *The Virgin and the Dynamo: Public Murals in American Architecture.* Athens: Ohio University Press.

Van Slyck, Abigail A. 1995. *Free to All: Carnegie Libraries & American Culture, 1890–1920.* Chicago: University of Chicago Press.

Van Voris, Jacqueline. 1987. *Carrie Chapman Catt: A Public Life.* New York: Feminist Press.

Van Vorst, Bessie McGinnis, and Marie Van Vorst. 1903. *The Woman Who Toils: Being the Experiences of Two Ladies as Factory Girls.* New York: Doubleday, Page.

—. 1908. *The Cry of the Children: A Study of Child-Labor.* New York: Moffat, Yard.

Vapnek, Lara. 2009. *Breadwinners: Working Women and Economic Independence, 1865–1920.* Chicago: University of Illinois Press.

Veblen, Thorstein. 1899. *The Theory of the Leisure Class.* New York: The Macmillan Company.

Veeser, Cyrus. 2002. *A World Safe for Capitalism: Dollar Diplomacy and America's Rise to Global Power.* New York: Columbia University Press.

Veracini, Lorenzo. 2010. *Settler Colonialism: A Theoretical Overview.* Basingstoke: Palgrave Macmillan.

Vertinsky, Patricia Anne. 1994. *The Eternally Wounded Woman: Women, Doctors, and Exercise in the Late Nineteenth Century.* Urbana: University of Illinois Press.

Vetter, Jeremy. 2008. "Field Science in the Railroad Era: The Tools of Knowledge Empire in the American West, 1869–1916." *Historia, Ciencias, Saude-Manguinhos* 15, 3: 597–613.

—. 2012. "Labs in the Field? Rocky Mountain Biological Stations in the Early Twentieth Century." *Journal of the History of Biology* 45: 587–611.

Veysey, Laurence R. 1965. *The Emergence of the American University.* Chicago: University of Chicago Press.

Vickers, Jason. 2013. "'That Deep Kind of Discipline of Spirit': Freedom, Power, Family, Marriage, and Sexuality in the Story of John Humphrey Noyes and the Oneida Community." *American Nineteenth Century History* 14, 1: 1–26.

Volwiler, Albert T. 1940. *The Correspondence between Benjamin Harrison and James G. Blaine.* Philadelphia: American Philosophical Society.

Wacker, Grant. 2002. *Heaven Below: Early Pentecostals and American Culture.* Cambridge: Harvard University Press.

Wallace, Anthony F.C. 1956. "Revitalization Movements." *American Anthropologist* 58: 264–281.

Wallenstein, Peter. 2011. "Identity, Marriage, and Schools: Life Along the Color Lines in the Era of Plessy v. Ferguson." In *The Folly of Jim Crow: Rethinking the Segregated South*, ed. Stephanie Cole and Natalie J. Ring, 17–53. Arlington: The University of Texas at Arlington.

Walters, Ronald. 1974. *Primers for Prudery: Sexual Advice to Victorian America.* Englewood Cliffs: Prentice-Hall.

Walters, Ryan S. 2012. *The Last Jeffersonian: Grover Cleveland and the Path to Restoring the Republic.* Nashville: Westbow.

Wander, W. Thomas. 1972. "Patterns of Change in the Congressional Budget Process, 1865–1974." *Congress and the Presidency* 9, 4: 501–27.

Ware, Caroline F. 1931. *The Early New England Cotton Manufacture: A Study in Industrial Beginnings.* Boston: Houghton Mifflin.

Ware, Alan. 2006. *The Democratic Party Heads North: 1877–1962.* Cambridge: Cambridge University Press.

Warner, Amos Griswold. 1908. *American Charities: A Study in Philanthropy and Economics.* Revised by Mary R. Coolidge. New York: Thomas Y. Crowell & Co.

Warner, Charles Dudley and Mark Twain. 1923. *The Gilded Age: A Tale of Today.* Chicago: American Publishing Company.

Warner, H.H. 1891. *Warner's Safe Cure Almanac 1892.* Rochester: H. H. Warner.

Warner, John Harley. 2003. *Against the Spirit of System: The French Impulse in Nineteenth-Century American Medicine.* Baltimore: Johns Hopkins University Press.

Warner, Sam Bass. 1962. *Streetcar Suburbs: the Process of Growth In Boston, 1870–1900.* Cambridge: Harvard University Press.

Warren, Charles. 1913. "The Progressiveness of the United States Supreme Court." *Columbia Law Review* 13, 4: 294–313.

Warren, Louis S. 1997. *The Hunter's Game: Poachers and Conservationists in Twentieth-Century America.* New Haven: Yale University Press.

—. 2015. "Wage Work in the Sacred Circle: The Ghost Dance as Modern Religion." *Western Historical Quarterly* 46: 141–68.

Wasik, John F. 2006. *The Merchant of Power. Sam Insull, Thomas Edison, and the Creation of the Modern Metropolis.* New York: Palgrave Macmillan.

Watts, Sarah Lyons. 2003. *Rough Rider in the White House: Theodore Roosevelt and the Politics of Desire.* Chicago: University of Chicago Press.

Waugh, Joan. 1997. *Unsentimental Reformer: The Life of Josephine Shaw Lowell.* Cambridge: Harvard University Press.

Weatherson, Michael A. 1995. *Hiram Johnson: Political Revivalist.* Lanham: University Press of America.

Webb, Walter Prescott. 1931. *The Great Plains.* Boston: Ginn and Company.

Weber, Adna Ferrin. 1899. *The Growth of Cities in the Nineteenth Century: a Study In Statistics.* New York: Published for Columbia University by the Macmillan Co.

Weber, Max. 1930. *The Protestant Ethic and the Spirit of Capitalism,* trans. Talcott Parsons. London: G. Allen and Unwin.

Webster, Sally. 2004. *Eve's Daughter/Modern Woman: A Mural by Mary Cassatt.* Urbana: University of Illinois Press.

Weinberg, H. Barbara, Doreen Bolger, and David Park Curry. 1994. *American Impressionism and Realism: The Painting of Modern Life, 1885–1915.* New York: Metropolitan Museum of Art.

Weiner, Lynn Y. 1985. *From Working Girl to Working Mother: The Female Labor Force in the United States, 1820–1980.* Chapel Hill: University of North Carolina Press.

Weinstein, James. 1968. *The Corporate Ideal in the Liberal State, 1900–1918.* Boston: Beacon.

Weir, Robert. 2000. *Knights Unhorsed: Internal Conflict in a Gilded Age Social Movement.* Detroit, MI: Wayne State University Press.

—. 2010. *Beyond Labor's Veil: the Culture of the Knights of Labor.* University Park: Penn State University Press.

Weisberger, Bernard A. 1994. *The La Follettes of Wisconsin: Love and Politics in Progressive America.* Madison: University of Wisconsin Press.

Welch, Richard E., Jr. 1988. *The Presidencies of Grover Cleveland.* Lawrence: University Press of Kansas.

Welke, Barbara Young. 2001. *Recasting American Liberty: Gender, Race, Law, and the Railroad Revolution, 1865–1920.* New York: Cambridge University Press.

—. 2010. *Law and the Borders of Belonging in the Long Nineteenth Century United States.* New York: Cambridge University Press.

Wells, Ida. B. 1892. *Southern Horrors: Lynch Laws in All Its Phases.* New York: New York Age.

—. 1895. *Tabulated Statistics and Alleged Causes of Lynchings in the United States, 1892–1893–1894.* Chicago: Donohue & Henneberry.

—, and Alfreda M. Duster. 1970. *Crusade for Justice: The Autobiography of Ida B. Wells.* Chicago: University of Chicago.

Welskopp, Thomas and Alan Lessoff, eds. 2013. *Fractured Modernity: America Confronts Modern Times, 1890s to 1940s.* Munich: Oldenbourg Verlag.

Welter, Barbara, 1966. "The Cult of True Womanhood: 1820–1860." *American Quarterly* 18, 2: 151–74.

Wertheim, Stephen. 2011. "The League That Wasn't: American Designs for a Legalist-Sanctionist League of Nations and the Intellectual Origins of International Organization, 1914–1920." *Diplomatic History* 35: 797–836. doi:10.1111/ j.1467-7709.2011.00986.x.

—. 2012. "The League of Nations: A Retreat from International Law?" *Journal of Global History* 7: 210–232. doi:10.1017/ S1740022812000046.

West, Elliott, 2009. *The Last Indian War: The Nez Perce Story.* New York: Oxford University Press.

—. 1998. *The Contested Plains: Indians, Goldseekers, and the Rush to Colorado.* Lawrence: University of Kansas Press.

Westad, Odd. 2005. *The Global Cold War: Third World Interventions and the Making of Our Times.* Cambridge: Cambridge University Press.

Westbrook, Robert. 1991. *John Dewey and American Democracy.* Ithaca: Cornell University Press.

Westhoff, Laura M. 2007. *A Fatal Drifting Apart: Democratic Social Knowledge and Chicago Reform.* Columbus: Ohio State University Press.

Whalen, Carmen Teresa. 2005. "Colonialism, Citizenship, and the Making of the Puerto Rican Diaspora: An Introduction." In *The Puerto Rican Diaspora: Historical Perspectives,* ed. Carmen Theresa Whalen and Victor Vazquez-Hernandez. Philadelphia: Temple University Press.

Wharton, Edith. 1920. *The Age of Innocence.* New York: D. Appleton.

Wheatley, Steven. 1988. *The Politics of Philanthropy: Abraham Flexner and Medical Education.* Madison: The University of Wisconsin Press.

Wheeler, Leigh Ann. 2004. *Against Obscenity: Reform and the Politics of Womanhood in America, 1873–1935.* Baltimore: Johns Hopkins University Press.

White, Deborah Grey. 1999. *Too Heavy a Load: Black Women in Defense of Themselves, 1894–1994.* New York: W. W. Norton.

White, G. Edward. 1980. *Tort Law in America: An Intellectual History.* Oxford: Oxford University Press.

—. 1993. "Transforming History in the Postmodern Era." Review of *Transformation of American Law: The Crisis of Legal Orthodoxy,* by Morton Horwitz. *Michigan Law Review* 91, 6: 1315–1352.

—. 2000. *The Constitution and the New Deal.* Cambridge: Harvard University Press.

White, Leonard D. 1958. *The Republican Era, 1869–1901: A Study in Administrative History.* New York: Macmillan.

White, Richard. 1978. "The Winning of the West: The Expansion of the Western Sioux in the Eighteenth and Nineteenth Centuries." *Journal of American History* 65: 319–343.

—. 1985. "American Environmental History: The Development of a New Historical Field." *Pacific Historical Review* 54: 297–335.

—. 2011. *Railroaded: The Transcontinentals and the Making of Modern America.* New York, W.W. Norton.

—. 1991. *It's Your Misfortune and None of My Own: A New History of the American West.* Norman: University of Oklahoma Press.

—. 1995. *The Organic Machine: The Remaking of the Columbia River.* New York: Hill & Wang.

—. 2011. *Railroaded: The Transcontinentals and the Making of Modern America.* New York: W. W. Norton.

White, Shane, and Graham White. 1998. *Stylin': African American Expressive Culture from Its Beginnings to the Zoot Suit.* Ithaca: Cornell University Press.

White, William Allen. 1925. *Some Cycles of Cathay.* Chapel Hill: University of North Carolina.

Whorton, James C. 2002. *Nature Cures: A History of Alternative Medicine in America.* New York: Oxford University Press.

Wickberg, Daniel. 2005. "Heterosexual White Male: Some Recent Inversions in American Cultural History." *Journal of American History* 92: 136–157.

Widenor, William C. 1980. *Henry Cabot Lodge and the Search for an American Foreign Policy.* Berkeley: University of California Press.

Wiebe, Robert H. 1961. "The Anthracite Strike of 1902: A Record of Confusion." *Mississippi Valley Historical Review* 48.

—. 1962. *Businessmen and Reform: A Study of the Progressive Movement.* Cambridge: Harvard University.

—. 1967. *The Search for Order, 1877 – 1920.* New York: Hill and Wang.

—. 1995. *Self-Rule: A Cultural History of Democracy.* Chicago: University of Chicago Press.

Wiecek, William M. 1998. *The Lost World of Classical Legal Thought: Law and Ideology in America, 1886–1937.* Oxford: Oxford University Press.

Wiener, Jonathan M. 1978. *Social Origins of the New South: Alabama, 1860—1885.* Baton Rouge: Louisiana State University Press.

Wiener, Gary. 2008. *Workers Rights in Upon Sinclair's The Jungle.* Detroit: Greenhaven Press/Gale.

Wild, Mark. 2005. *Street Meeting: Multiethnic Neighborhoods In Early Twentieth-century Los Angeles.* Berkeley: University of California Press.

Wilder, Gordon M. 2012. *The American Reaper: Harvesting Networks and Technology, 1830–1910.* Burlington: Ashgate.

Wilkerson, Isabel. 2011. *The Warmth of Other Suns: The Epic Story of America's Great Migration.* New York: Vintage.

Wilkins, Mira, 1970. *The Emergence of Multinational Enterprise: American Business Abroad from the Colonial Era to 1914.* Cambridge: Harvard University Press.

—. 1989. *The History of Foreign Investment in the United States to 1914.* Cambridge: Harvard University Press.

Wilkinson, Charles F. 1987. *American Indians, Time, and the Law.* New Haven: Yale University Press.

Willard, Frances. 1889. *Glimpses of Fifty Years: The Autobiography of an American Woman.* Chicago: H. J. Smith.

Williams, George Washington. 1882. *History of the Negro Race in America from 1619 to 1880.* New York: G. P. Putnam's Sons.

Williams, Jr., Vernon J. 2006. *The Social Sciences and Theories of Race.* Urbana: University of Illinois Press.

Williams, R. Hal. 1972. *The Democratic Party and California Politics, 1880–1896.* Stanford: Stanford University Press.

Williams, R. Hal. 2010. *Realigning America: McKinley, Bryan, and the Remarkable Election of 1896.* Lawrence: University of Kansas Press.

Williams, Raymond. 1989. "Culture is Ordinary." In *Resources of Hope: Culture, Democracy, Socialism,* 3–14. London: Verso.

Williams, William Appleman. 1959. *The Tragedy of American Diplomacy.* Cleveland: World Publishing.

—. 1962. *The Tragedy of American Diplomacy.* New York: Dell Publishing Co.

—. 1970. *The Roots of the Modern American Empire: A Study of the Growth and Shaping of Social Consciousness in a Marketplace Society.* New York: Vintage.

—. 1972. *The Tragedy of American Diplomacy.* New York: W.W. Norton & Company.

Williamson, Joel. 1968. *The Origins of Segregation.* Boston: D.C. Heath.

—. 1984. *The Crucible of Race: Black/white Relations in the American South since Emancipation.* New York: Oxford University Press.

Willis, Carol. 1995. *Form Follows Finance: Skyscrapers and Skylines In New York and Chicago.* New York: Princeton Architectural Press.

Willrich, Michael. 2003. *City of Courts: Socializing Justice in Progressive Era Chicago.* Cambridge: Cambridge University Press.

—. 2011. *Pox: An American History.* New York: Penguin Press.

Wilson, Ann-Marie. 2009. "In the Name of God, Civilization, and Humanity: The United States and the Armenian Massacres of the 1890s." *Le Mouvement Social* 227: 27–44.

—. 2010. "Taking Liberties Abroad: Americans and the International Humanitarian Advocacy, 1821–1914." PhD diss., Harvard University.

Wilson, Charles Reagan. 2009. *Baptized in Blood: The Religion of the Lost Cause.* Revised ed. Athens: University of Georgia Press.

Wilson, Francille Rusan. 2006. *The Segregated Scholars: Black Social Scientists and the Creation of Black Labor Studies, 1890–1950.* Charlottesville: University of Virginia Press.

Wilson, John, 2010. "The Democratic Traveller: Henry Demarest Lloyd's Visit to New Zealand, 1899." *Studies in Travel Writing* 14: 365–82.

Wilson, Mark R. 2010. *The Business of Civil War: Military Mobilization and the State, 1861–1865.* Baltimore: Johns Hopkins University Press.

Wilson, Raymond. 1983. *Ohiyesa: Charles Eastman, Santee Sioux.* Urbana: University of Illinois Press.

Wilson, Rick K. 1986. "What Was It Worth to Be on a Committee in the U.S. House, 1889 to 1913?" *Legislative Studies Quarterly* 11, 1: 47–63.

Wilson, William H. 1989. *The City Beautiful Movement.* Baltimore: Johns Hopkins University Press.

Wilson, Woodrow. 1885. *Congressional Government: A Study in American Politics.* Boston: Houghton Mifflin Company.

—. 1889. *The State: Elements of Historical and Practical Politics.* Boston: D. C. Heath & Co., Publishers.

—. 1900 *Congressional Government: A Study in American Politics.* Boston: Houghton Mifflin.

—. 1913. "Wilson to Alexander Mitchell Palmer, February 5." In *The Papers of Woodrow Wilson,* ed. Arthur S. Link. 69 volumes. Princeton: Princeton University Press.

—. 1917. *Congressional Record,* 65th Congress, 1st Session.

—. 1966–1994. *The Papers of Woodrow Wilson.* Ed. Arthur S. Link. Princeton: Princeton University Press.

Winchester, Simon, 2014. "The Eruption Plunged Europe into Winter and America into its First Economic Crisis." *Wall Street Journal.* 25 April.

Winkler, Jonathan Reed. 2007. *Nexus: Strategic Communications and American Security in World War I.* Cambridge: Harvard University Press.

Winn, Kenneth H. 1993. "The Mormon Region." In *Encyclopedia of American Social History*, ed. Mary K. Cayton and Elliot J. Gorn, 1089–1098. New York: Charles Scribner's Sons.

Winter, Ella and Granville Hicks, eds. 1938. *The Letters of Lincoln Steffens*. Vol. 2. New York: Harcourt, Brace.

Wisner, Elizabeth. 1970. *Social Welfare in the South from Colonial Times to World War I*. Baton Rouge: Louisiana State University Press.

Witt, John Fabian. 2004. *The Accidental Republic: Crippled Workingmen, Destitute Widows, and the Remaking of American Law*. Cambridge: Harvard University Press.

—. 2010. "Law and War in American History." Review of *Myth of the "Weak" American State*, by William J. Novak. *American Historical Review* 115, 3: 768 -778.

Wittmann, Matthew. 2010. "Empire of Culture: U.S. Entertainers and the Making of the Pacific Circuit, 1850–1890." PhD diss., University of Michigan.

Wolcott, Virginia W. 1997. "'Bible, Bath, and Broom': Nannie Helen Burroughs's National Training School and African-American Racial Uplift." *Journal of Women's History* 9: 88–110.

Wolfe, Thomas. 1935. *From Death to Morning*. New York: C. Scribner's Sons.

Wolloch, Nancy. 1996. *Muller v. Oregon: A Brief History with Documents*. Boston: Bedford Books of St. Martin's Press.

—. 2011. *Women and the American Experience*, 5th ed. New York: McGraw Hill.

—. 2015. *A Class by Herself: Protective Laws for Women Workers, 1890s-1990s*. Princeton: Princeton University Press.

Wolseley, Roland E. 1971. *The Black Press, U. S. A.* Ames: Iowa State University.

Wood, Amy Louise. 2009. *Lynching and Spectacle: Witnessing Racial Violence in America, 1890–1940*. Chapel Hill: University Of North Carolina Press.

Wood, Ann Douglas. 1973. "'The Fashionable Diseases': Women's Complaints and Their Treatment in Nineteenth-Century America." *Journal of Interdisciplinary History* 4: 36–44.

Wood, Donna J. 1985. "The Strategic Use of Public Policy: Business Support for the 1906 Food and Drug Act." *Business History Review* 59, 3: 403–32.

Wood, Gordon S. 2009. *Empire of Liberty: A History of the Early Republic, 1789–1815*. New York: Oxford University Press.

Wood, Sharon E. 2005. *The Freedom of the Streets: Work, Citizenship, and Sexuality in a Gilded Age City*. Chapel Hill: University of North Carolina Press.

Woodman, Harold D. 1987. "Economic Reconstruction and the Rise of the New South." In *Interpreting Southern History: Historiographical Essays in Honor of Sanford W. Higginbotham*, ed. John Boles and Evelyn Thomas Nolen, 254–307. Baton Rouge: Louisiana State University Press.

—. 1997. "Class, Race, Politics and the Modernization of the Postbellum South." *Journal of Southern History* 63, 1: 3–22.

—. 2001. "The Political Economy of the New South: Retrospects and Prospects." *Journal of Southern History* 67, 4: 789–810.

Woods, Mary N. 1999. *From Craft to Profession: The Practice of Architecture in Nineteenth- Century America*. Berkeley: University of California Press.

Woodward, C. Vann. 1938a. *Tom Watson, Agrarian Rebel*. New York: Macmillan.

—. 1938b. *Tom Watson: Agrarian Rebel*. New York: Oxford University Press.

—. 1951. *Origins of the New South, 1877–1913*. Baton Rouge: Louisiana State University Press.

—. 1951. *Reunion and Reaction: The Compromise of 1877 and the End of Reconstruction*. Boston: Oxford University Press.

—. 1955. *The Strange Career of Jim Crow*. New York: Oxford University Press.

—. 1959. "The Populist Heritage and the Intellectual." *American Scholar* 29: 55–72.

—. 1960. *The Burden of Southern History*. Baton Rouge: Louisiana State University Press.

—. 1974. *The Strange Career of Jim Crow*. 3rd edition. Oxford: Oxford University Press.

—. 1988. "Strange Career Critics: Long May They Persevere." *The Journal of American History*, 75, 3: 857–868.

Worster, Donald. 1978. *Dust Bowl: The Southern Plains in the 1930s*. New York: Oxford University Press.

—. 1985. *Rivers of Empire*. New York: Pantheon Books.

—. 2008. 2010. *A Passion for Nature: The Life of John Muir*. New York: Oxford University Press.

Wosh, Peter J. 1994. *Spreading the Word: The Bible Business in Nineteenth-Century America*. Ithaca: Cornell University Press.

Wright, Carroll Davidson. 1889. *Working Women in Large Cities*. Washington: Government Publishing Office.

Wright, Gavin. 1986. *Old South, New South: Revolutions in the Southern Economy since the Civil War*. New York: Basic Books.

Wrobel, David M. 2013. *Global West, American Frontier: Travel, Empire, and Exceptionalism from Manifest Destiny to the Great Depression*. Albuquerque: University of New Mexico Press.

Wynes, Charles E. 1961. *Race Relations in Virginia, 1870–1902*. Charlottesville: University of Virginia Press.

Yenne, Bill. 2006. *Indian Wars*. Yardley: Westholme Publishing.

Yoder, Jon A. 1975. *Upton Sinclair*. New York: Frederick Ungar.

Yohn, Susan Mitchell. 1995. *Contest of Faiths: Missionary Women and Pluralism in the American Southwest*. Ithaca: Cornell University Press.

Young, Cristobal. 2009. "The Emergence of Sociology From Political Economy in the United States: 1890–to 1940." *Journal of the History of the Behavioral Sciences* 45, 2: 91–116.

Young, James Harvey. 1961. *The Toadstool Millionaires: A Social History of Patent Medicines in America before Federal Regulation*. Princeton: Princeton University Press.

—. 1974. *American Self-Dosage Medicines: An Historical Perspective*. Lawrence: Coronado Press.

Young, Terence. 2004. *Building San Francisco's Parks, 1850–1930*. Baltimore: Johns Hopkins University Press.

Youngdahl, Jay. 2011. *Working on the Railroad, Walking in Beauty: Navajos, Hozho, and Track Work*. Logan: Utah State University Press.

Zahniser, J.D. and Amelia R. Fry. 2014. *Alice Paul: Claiming Power*. New York: Oxford University Press.

Zeiger, Susan. 2010. *Entangling Alliances: Foreign War Brides and American Soldiers in the Twentieth Century*. New York: New York University Press.

Zeiler, Thomas 2010. *Ambassadors in Pinstripes: The Spalding World Baseball Tour and the Birth of the American Empire*. Lanham: Rowman and Littlefield.

Zesch, Scott. 2012. *The Chinatown War*. New York: Oxford University Press.

Ziegler, Edith M. 2012. "The Burdens and the Narrow Life of Farm Women." *Agricultural History.* 86, 3: 77–103.

Zimmer, Kenyon. 2015. *Immigrants against the State: Yiddish and Italian Anarchism.* Urbana: University of Illinois Press.

Zimmerman, Andrew. 2010. *Alabama in Africa: Booker T. Washington, the German Empire, and the Globalization of the New South.* Princeton: Princeton University Press.

Zimmerman, Jonathan. 2015. *Too Hot to Handle: A Global History of Sex Education.* Princeton: Princeton University Press.

Zink, Clifford W. 2011. *The Roebling Legacy.* Princeton: Landmark Publications.

Zissu, Erik M. 1995. "Conscription, Sovereignty, and Land: American Indian Resistance during World War I." *Pacific Historical Review* 64: 537–66.

Zitkala-Sa [Gertrude Simmons Bonnin]. 1902. "Why I Am a Pagan." *The Online Archive of Nineteenth-Century U.S. Women's Writings*, ed. Glynis Carr. Posted: Winter 1999, http://www.facstaff.bucknell.edu/gcarr/19cUSWW/ZS/WIAP.h.

—. 1921. *American Indian Stories.* Washington, DC: Hayworth Publishing House.

Zolberg, Aristide. 2006. *A Nation by Design: Immigration Policy in the Fashioning of America.* New York: Russell Sage Foundation and Cambridge: Harvard University Press.

Zunz, Olivier. 1982. *The Changing Face of Inequality: Urbanization, Industrial Development, and Immigrants in Detroit, 1880–1920.* Chicago: University of Chicago Press.

—. 2012. *Philanthropy in America: A History.* Princeton: Princeton University Press, 2012.

Zurier, Rebecca, Robert W. Snyder, and Virginia M. Mecklenburg. 1995. *Metropolitan Lives: The Ashcan Artists and Their New York.* New York: Norton.

Zweig, Stefan. 1925 (1944). "The Monotonization of the World." In *The Weimar Republic Sourcebook*, ed. Anton Kaes, Martin Jay, and Edward Dimendberg, 397–400. Berlin: Berliner Borsen-Courier. Translated in, Berkeley: University of California Press. Citations refer to the University of California edition.

Index

A Companion to the Gilded Age and Progressive Era, First Edition. Edited by Christopher McKnight Nichols and Nancy C. Unger.
© 2017 John Wiley & Sons, Inc. Published 2017 by John Wiley & Sons, Inc.